M000248821

How to use your Connected Casebook

Step 1: Go to **www.CasebookConnect.com** and redeem your access code to get started.

Access Code:  STXT92352977471

Step 2: Go to your **BOOKSHELF** and select your Connected Casebook to start reading, highlighting, and taking notes in the margins of your e-book.

Step 3: Select the **STUDY** tab in your toolbar to access a variety of practice materials designed to help you master the course material. These materials may include explanations, videos, multiple-choice questions, flashcards, short answer, essays, and issue spotting.

Step 4: Select the **OUTLINE** tab in your toolbar to access chapter outlines that automatically incorporate your highlights and annotations from the e-book. Use the My Notes area for copying, pasting, and editing your book notes or creating new notes.

Step 5: If your professor has enrolled your class, you can select the **CLASS INSIGHTS** tab and compare your own study center results against the average of your classmates.

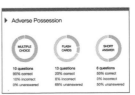

Cases and Materials on
Business Entities

ASPEN CASEBOOK SERIES

Cases and Materials on
Business Entities

Fourth Edition

Eric A. Chiappinelli

Frank McDonald Endowed Professor of Law
Texas Tech University School of Law

Wolters Kluwer

Published by Wolters Kluwer in New York.

Wolters Kluwer Legal & Regulatory U.S. serves customers worldwide with CCH, Aspen Publishers, and Kluwer Law International products. (www.WKLegaledu.com)

To contact Customer Service, e-mail customer.service@wolterskluwer.com, call 1-800-234-1660, fax 1-800-901-9075, or mail correspondence to:

    Wolters Kluwer
    Attn: Order Department
    PO Box 990
    Frederick, MD 21705

Printed in the United States of America.

1 2 3 4 5 6 7 8 9 0

ISBN 978-1-4548-9349-3

Library of Congress Cataloging-in-Publication Data

Names: Chiappinelli, Eric A., 1953- author.
Title: Cases and materials on business entities / Eric A. Chiappinelli, Frank
    McDonald Endowed Professor of Law, Texas Tech University School of Law.
Description: Fourth edition. | New York : Wolters Kluwer, [2018] | Series:
    Aspen casebook series | Includes bibliographical references and index.
Identifiers: LCCN 2018000455 | ISBN 9781454893493
Subjects: LCSH: Corporation law—United States. | Business enterprises—Law
    and legislation—United States. | LCGFT: Casebooks
Classification: LCC KF1414 .C478 2018 | DDC 346.73/066—dc23
LC record available at https://lccn.loc.gov/2018000455

About Wolters Kluwer Legal & Regulatory U.S.

Wolters Kluwer Legal & Regulatory U.S. delivers expert content and solutions in the areas of law, corporate compliance, health compliance, reimbursement, and legal education. Its practical solutions help customers successfully navigate the demands of a changing environment to drive their daily activities, enhance decision quality and inspire confident outcomes.

Serving customers worldwide, its legal and regulatory portfolio includes products under the Aspen Publishers, CCH Incorporated, Kluwer Law International, ftwilliam.com and MediRegs names. They are regarded as exceptional and trusted resources for general legal and practice-specific knowledge, compliance and risk management, dynamic workflow solutions, and expert commentary.

Dedication

I've always thought that dedicating a book to family is more than a little propitiatory. While some books might actually atone to the author's loved ones for the time spent away from them, certainly few casebooks fall into that category. I have no illusions that this book is any compensation to my son, Peter, for the hours and hours I spent writing it. I have thanked him, and do so again here, for his willingness to put up with all the time I spent away from him while I was writing. But, in fact, although he was largely cheerful about all of this, he really had no choice. I was the one who decided to write this book and I was the one who decided how much time to spend on it. So this dedication is more in the way of apology than propitiation. I hope it will remind all parents that sometimes the professional choices they make for themselves affect their children in ways that can be rationalized but can't really be remedied.

This book is dedicated to my son, Peter, who is the most wonderful person and who was the most wonderful child. I am sorry that I spent so much time away from you to write it. Thank you, Peter, for sharing so much of your life with me and for letting me be your father. I am grateful to you for far more than you can ever imagine. I love you any time, every time, all the time.

Summary of Contents

Contents

B. The Corporation and Its Finances

F. Change of Control

Preface

You have already encountered business entities, even if you are just beginning your second year of law school. Some entities, such as corporations, were parties in cases you read (or were supposed to have read). In other instances the litigants may have been employed by, or dealt with, a business entity, though the entity was not a party. This course is different from the other courses in which you've encountered business entities because it deals with the internal working of business entities. Among other topics, we will look at the ways in which business entities are formed, how they get money from owners and lenders, and how they are governed.

A. HOW TO APPROACH THE COURSE

Your professor will doubtless suggest to you the way in which he or she wants you to think about the course. However, it may be useful to give you my own view as well, in part because I suspect most professors share most of my views in this regard, and in part because sharing my view may help you to understand this casebook better. If there is one big idea that runs through the law of business entities it is *capital formation*. That is, the process of collecting money from more than one person for the purpose of engaging in an enterprise.

The process of capital formation leads, in turn, to three key legal questions. First, what are the economic rights between the money providers? That is, how do the providers share profits? Equally? Proportionally to their investment? Do some providers (e.g., lenders) get paid before others (e.g., owners)? Second, what are the management rights between the money providers? Does each provider have an equal say? Do some providers have no say at all? Finally, what are the rights of outsiders against the business entity and its owners? Obviously contract and tort law provide the answer in many instances. But business entities law also provides answers in many settings. Are the owners liable with the entity? Are the owners liable only after the entity's assets are exhausted? Are the owners not liable at all, even if the entity's assets are gone?

I also want to give you two suggestions for approaching business entities as a law student. First, as you read the cases you should spend the necessary time to understand the transactions and the underlying motivations. Some students find a temptation to ignore those elements (especially if they're not initially interested in the subject) and they resolve to learn only the legal rules. This is a mistake for both high-road and low-road reasons. On the high road, the legal rules are not immutable laws of physics. They're developed in response to business transactions and the motivations behind them. So you can't come to any informed judgment about the propriety of business entities law until you understand the milieu that generates that law. Second, on the low road, it's pretty nearly impossible to succeed in a business entities class simply by trying to learn only the legal rules. There are just too many rules of law in this course and you probably haven't got enough memory to learn them all without knowing the business context that generated those rules. So understanding the transactions will be a way for you to remember and understand more rules and how they relate to one another.

My second suggestion is to pay attention to the *text* of the statutes. For many law students, business entities is their first exposure to an area of law in which the rules are primarily statutory rather than judge-made. You will be repaid many times over for the time you put into reading the statutes.

B. THE PLAN OF THIS CASEBOOK

This casebook is organized into five parts. Part I is about practicing business law. Chapter 1 describes the various practice settings in which business lawyers work. Chapter 2 talks about business itself, and does so largely apart from the question of business entities. Chapter 3 talks about a few of the most central economic concepts that business entities face and also explores the rudiments of accounting. Every lawyer, and especially every business lawyer, needs an exposure to some economic ideas. This exposure is necessary if for no other reasons than that your clients will have this knowledge and you need to be conversant with the basics, at least.

Part II consists of a single chapter. Chapter 4 deals with the law of agency. Agency is not an entity but rather it is a system of relationships and consequences that exist when one person acts for another. Agency problems pervade business entities and other private law areas, as well.

Part III takes up the majority of the book. It deals with the law of corporations, which is the principal business entity. Chapter 5 deals with creating corporations and the difficulties that can be encountered in doing so. Chapters 6, 7, and 8 focus on the "dough-ray-mi," that is, the financial aspects of corporate law. Chapter 6 is about getting money from investors into the corporation; Chapter 7 is about getting it out to them. Chapter 8 is concerned with the ability of creditors to get paid when the entity does not have enough money.

Chapter 9 is about the power of the board of directors to govern a corporation. Chapters 10 through 13 talk about constraints on the board's power to govern. As you intuit, those constraints constitute a significant part of the law of business entities. Chapter 10 looks at external constraints on the board's power. Chapters 11 and 12 are concerned with the directors' duties of loyalty and care, called their fiduciary duties and the standards by which courts will decide whether those duties have been breached. Finally, Chapter 13 assesses whether the constraints are effective.

Chapters 14 and 15 explore shareholder rights. Chapter 14 mostly concerns publicly held corporations, and Chapter 15 is more focused on privately held companies. Chapter 16 is about changing control of corporations. That subject is typically a separate course in most law schools, so this chapter is primarily an introduction.

Part IV comprises two chapters, and its focus is on business entities other than corporations. They are much briefer than the discussion of corporate law, not because they are less important, but because much of corporate law carries over to these other entities. Chapter 17 looks at partnerships, including limited partnerships. This is an important business entity in large part because it is the default entity. That is, when more than one person owns a business, those owners are usually partners of a partnership unless they've taken specific action to form another entity instead. Chapter 18 involves limited liability companies (LLCs). This is perhaps the most frequently selected business entity for new businesses. From a legal standpoint, LLCs are essentially a blend of corporate law and partnership law. Thus, if you've paid attention from Chapter 5 through Chapter 17, Chapter 18 will be quite easy.

Finally, Part V, Chapter 19, is a look at the way in which lawyers and their clients go about choosing the appropriate entity for a particular business. The placement of this chapter at the end of the book may seem paradoxical, because choosing the appropriate entity is one of the first decisions planners usually make. However, as a student you won't be able to make real sense of Chapter 19 unless you have a detailed knowledge of the business entities from which to select. Hence its placement at the end.

C. HOW EACH CHAPTER IS ORGANIZED

It might help you, when reading the materials for the first time and when reviewing, to know how each chapter is organized. I have deliberately been relatively consistent in the way the material is presented. Most of the chapters have sections entitled "Background and Context" and "The Current Setting." Background and Context material is designed to put the law into some social or historical milieu. These sections provide a richer understanding of the material, but some professors may omit all of them and most professors will omit at least some of them. I've set these sections out separately to make it easier for professors to assign the material and to make the divisions within the material clearer to you. "The Current Setting" is meant to signal to you, and your professor, that the material is not background and context. That is, it focuses mainly on legal, rather than historical or social, ideas and primarily on the law as it exists in the United States currently.

A problem with many casebooks, especially those that go through several editions, is that the editors leave in old cases when they should take them out. I have been guided by Justice Holmes's observation that the reported cases, "in the course of a generation take up pretty much the whole body of the law, and restate it from the present point of view. We could reconstruct the corpus from them if all that went before were burned"[1] I have eliminated from each edition cases reported more than 20 years before. I either have included a newer case discussing the same issue, written new text discussing that issue in lieu of adding a new case, or eliminated any mention of the issue. I believe this approach has several advantages. First, and most important, if I have been unable to find a suitable newer case to replace an old one, that strongly suggests that the issue is no longer of real importance. Thus, a brief discussion or perhaps even elision of the issue is best for students.

Second, if the issue is still important enough to be litigated, a fresher case is likely to present more nuance than the older one. Perhaps it will bring in legal or social developments occurring since the original case. In any event, the newer case is likely to be written in a more modern style that makes the issue and discussion more easily understood. All of these are advantages to law students, in my view.

Nonetheless, I have made two exceptions to the twenty-year rule. The first is two of the federal insider trading cases. Those cases are still bedrock law, always cited by the courts, and are in an area that many professors (including me) omit from the basic business entities course. The other exception is that I proudly feature *Meinhard v. Salmon* in the partnership chapter, even though it was decided in 1928. I could make up reasons for including it, but the real explanation is that I like the facts, I like the language of Chief Judge Cardozo's majority opinion (and Judge Andrews' dissent, for that matter), and I very much like teaching it to law students. In my defense, I must fall back on Emerson's aphorism that "a foolish consistency is the hobgoblin of little minds."

One of the most useful features of this casebook is the way in which the "Notes and Questions" sections are organized. I have divided the notes and questions into five types, labeled each, and set them out in the same order throughout the book. Not every "Notes and Questions" section will have each type. The first type is called, believe it or not, *Notes*. This has factual information, usually about the preceding case, the kind of transaction, or the applicable law. The second type is called *Reality Check*. These questions are designed to make sure you understand the transaction, the dispute, and the resolution. They should be of particular value before class and at the end of the course, when you're preparing for the final exam. The third type is called *Suppose*. These questions ask you to be a bit flexible in your thinking. They ask you to imagine that the facts or the law were slightly different from the actual case. One of a lawyer's most frequent tasks is to analogize or distinguish one set of facts from another. The *Suppose* questions give you practice in doing that. The fourth type is *What Do You Think?* These are policy and theory questions. They ask you for your view of the case's result on the parties, the social effect of the rule in the case, or a more general theoretical question. These may seem a bit divorced from reality at first, but I think law students tend to underestimate the power of theory on the world in which they live.

Finally, some of the "Notes and Questions" sections end with a *You Draft It* exercise. These are, as you see by the name, opportunities to hone your drafting skills. My pedagogical view is that drafting exercises that are simply made up by the professor are not nearly as valuable as those drawn from actual legal practice. Moreover, many drafting assignments that law students undertake require them to

---

1. Oliver Wendell Holmes, *The Path of the Law*, 10 Harv. L. Rev. 457, 458 (1897).

draft whole documents or at least extended sections of documents. These are, of course, valuable skills. However, I believe that an underappreciated writing skill is the talent to draft small, very focused, pieces. These pieces are often absolutely critical to the success or failure of a transaction. So, based on those two premises, I have created the *You Draft It* sections. In every instance, the assignment is based on actual language that was important in the case just discussed. Frequently I will ask you to redraft language that was at the center of the case so that first one party and then the other would clearly prevail. Sometimes the drafting involves a statute. In any event, your professors might not assign these exercises (and certainly won't assign all of them to be turned in and evaluated!) but they are quite useful nonetheless. You might find it particularly useful to swap your draft with that of another student in the course to critique one another's work. Another approach is to have the members of a study group take turns so that only one student's draft is critiqued. This approach, incidentally, would replicate a frequent practice setting. That is, a legal issue has arisen, sometimes without warning, and one member of a legal team is given the task of drafting language that solves the problem. The other members then critique that draft as a group.

Periodically in almost every chapter I have inserted problems called *Putting it to Work*. These are more extended problems that either pull together several issues or that examine an issue in more depth than in the Notes and Questions. My hope is that these problems will give you a taste of what it is like to be a practicing corporate lawyer. I've tried to make the *Putting it to Work* problems replicate the kinds of issues a new lawyer in a firm might be asked to handle. Of course, these problems are necessarily truncated to make them manageable in light of the time available to both students and professors. Nonetheless, I am hopeful they will make you practice sensitive. That is, that by working through them you will come away with a better understanding of the skills you will need in practice.

There's another element of this casebook that I think sets it apart from other books and that, I'm hoping, will make it more useful to students and their professors. At the end of each chapter is a list of *Terms of Art in This Chapter*. Each term of art is one that is first discussed more than tangentially in the chapter. The term of art is also italicized at its first principal appearance. You might want to preview the chapter by looking at the list before you read the chapter. I think that becoming aware of important terms and then finding the definitions within the chapter context is vital to learning. For that reason I have not placed the definitions with the terms of art at each chapter's end. However, I have assembled them in a glossary at the back along with definitions. So, if you need a quick refresher on a particular term, you can look in the glossary for help.

Let me say a word about the footnote conventions in this casebook. Footnotes in my own text are sequentially numbered in each chapter. Footnotes in cases and in other extracts retain their original numbers. Footnotes that I have inserted in a case or extract are indicated both by an asterisk and by *ED.* at the end of the footnote.

I hope you enjoy using this casebook. It seems to me that students often don't reflect on the book they're using unless it's so problematic that it's a hindrance to their learning. I sincerely hope that this book helps you rather than hinders you as you learn the law of business entities. I also hope you like it.

Eric A. Chiappinelli

February 2018

Acknowledgments

This book would not exist if Lynn Churchill, acquisitions editor at Aspen, hadn't asked me to write it. She first suggested that I might enjoy, and be good at, writing a casebook on business entities. She also shepherded me through the process of submitting a book proposal. As she suspected, I have very much enjoyed writing this book. Thank you, Lynn.

My development editor was Susan Boulanger. Actually, Susan and I have only communicated by e-mail. It is entirely possible that "Susan Boulanger" is someone's *nom de crayon bleu* or that she is a collective person, like Carolyn Keene. Nonetheless, I believe she exists. I had no idea what a development editor was until Susan introduced herself. It turns out that a development editor is sort of a personal coach. She gave me tips for dividing the writing into manageable parts. She also tried to keep me on deadlines that I, myself, had blithely agreed to meet. Nonetheless, I missed (often by a significant margin) every single deadline. She took my drafts and sent them to anonymous reviewers, collected their comments, synthesized them, and helped me to accept and understand them. More than anything else, though, Susan provided enormous support to me during the long writing and rewriting process. That support has been of incalculable help. I am deeply thankful for your help, Susan.

This casebook has been improved a great deal by the anonymous reviewers. I was astonished at the care with which they read the manuscript. They had insights and perspectives that I never would have considered. Thank you, for engaging so thoroughly with me. Lauren Arnest copyedited the manuscript and improved its readability significantly. Thanks, Lauren. The unforgettable Laurel Ibey was the manuscript editor. She answered many of my questions (and posed many more) and ensured that the book sailed through the production process. I appreciate all you've done, Laurel.

A number of my colleagues have helped in this effort. John B. "Jack" Kirkwood used drafts of this book in several of his classes and provided me with much valuable feedback. He also provided a fair bit of help with the economics portions of the text. He was very generous with his time, as well, amounting to hours of conversation on topics large and small. Thank you,

Jack. Russell Powell also used this casebook in two of his classes and also gave me his reaction to it. I know the book is much better than it would have been without their help. Annette Clark helped to convince me to accept Lynn Churchill's suggestion that I write this casebook and also provided support during the periods when I was particularly discouraged. My friend and former student Professor Danshera Cords was terrifically supportive and helpful in both the initial writing of this book and in subsequent revisions. My deans, Rudy Hasl and Kellye Testy, provided financial support during the summers, when much of the manuscript was written and edited. I appreciate their support. Finally, my secretary, Laurie Sleeper, coordinated endless details, answered questions from students and colleagues, and obtained all the permissions. Thank you very much, Laurie.

Probably a dozen or more classes of business entities used all or portions of this book. I appreciate their patience with me and with the development of the manuscript. I told them they were beta testing it, but they were really alpha testing it. Many of them provided helpful comments and I appreciate their taking the time to do so.

I was blessed with having a number of absolutely terrific research assistants for the first edition. Laura Weber, Carli West, Cabrelle Able, Sarah Massey, Chris Wyant, David Petteys, Hallie Eads, Erin Warren, Samia Staehle, Diana Chamberlain, and Jason Knight all did work above and beyond what was necessary. They were literally indispensable to me in writing this book. A very large thank you to each of you.

In preparing the second edition of this book, my editors at Aspen were Kathy Yoon Langone and Darren Kelly. I was assisted by two incredible student assistants. Patrice D. Ott and Samuel J. Skorepa were fantastically talented and dedicated. I was truly astonished by the quality and quantity of the work they did.

Darren Kelly and Kenny Chumbley were my Wolters Kluwer editors for the third edition and I am grateful for their help and their patience with my revisions. I had two fantastic Texas Tech University research assistants for the third edition, Sara Norman and Evan Johnston. I am thankful to both of them beyond words.

For the fourth edition of this book Darren Kelly, now of the Froebe Group, was once again the editor. As with the second and third editions, Darren's wisdom, patience, and deft hand very much helped me get the revisions done. I think the revisions for the fourth edition were the least late of any work I have ever done on this book. Darren is completely to thank for that. He is truly a casebook whisperer, as any number of other casebook authors can attest. Kate Foley did incredible research assistance on the fourth edition, often on very short notice. Thank you so much, Kate.

I'm also quite thankful to Caffè Ladro in Seattle, Washington and to the Starbucks stores in Seattle, Omaha, and Lubbock. The vast majority of the text was written and revised in their fine establishments and I highly recommend them to other authors and coffee drinkers.

Throughout the entire process of producing this tome one person has been uppermost in my thoughts as the person whose intellect and cast of mind most resemble my own. He is the Reverend Edward Casaubon. I do not blush to say that I have followed his example in the way of pigeonholes. If my small book bears even the faintest resemblance to his book,[1] then I shall have acquitted myself well, indeed.

Finally, I would like to thank the authors, publishers, and copyright holders for their permission to reproduce materials from their publications.

Allen, William T. *Our Schizophrenic Conception of the Business Corporation*, 14 Cardozo Law Review 261 (1992). Copyright © 1992 Cardozo Law Review. Reprinted with permission of the author and Cardozo Law Review.

Alsop, Ronald. *Right and Wrong*. The Wall Street Journal, September 17, 2003, at R9. Reprinted with permission of Dow Jones & Company, Inc.; permission conveyed through Copyright Clearance Center, Inc.

Arnold, M. Thomas. *Shareholder Duties Under State Law*, 28 Tulsa Law Journal 213, 242-257 (1992).

Badaracco, Joseph L., Jr. *The Discipline of Building Character*, 76 Harvard Business Review 115 (1998). Reprinted by permission of the Harvard Business School Publishing Corporation.

Bainbridge, Stephen M. *The Board of Directors as Nexus of Contracts*, 88 Iowa Law Review 1, 5-6, 9-11 (2002). Reprinted with permission of the Iowa Law Review; permission conveyed through Copyright Clearance Center, Inc.

Bart, Peter. *The Studios' Plethora of Presidents*, by Peter Bart, Variety, March 2, 2003. Copyright © 2014 Variety Media, LLC. Reprinted with permission of Penske Media Corporation.

Berle, Adolf A., Jr., and Gardiner C. Means. *The Modern Corporation and Private Property*, 333-338, 343, 353-356 (1933). Reprinted with permission of Transaction Publishers; permission conveyed through Copyright Clearance Center, Inc.

Blair, Margaret M. *Locking in Capital: What Corporate Law Achieved for Business Organizers in the Nineteenth Century*, 51 U.C.L.A. Law Review 387, 389-394, 442-447 (2003). Reprinted with permission of the author.

Booth, Richard. *Form and Function in Business Organizations*. 58 Business Lawyer 1433 (2003). Reprinted with permission of the author.

Branson, Douglas M. *The Very Uncertain Prospect of "Global" Convergence in Corporate Governance*, 34 Cornell International Law Journal, 321, 323-327 (2001).

Browning, E. S. *Burst Bubbles Often Expose Cooked Books And Trigger SEC Probes, Bankruptcy Filings*, The Wall Street Journal, February 11, 2002, at C1. Reprinted with permission of Dow Jones & Company, Inc.; permission conveyed through Copyright Clearance Center, Inc.

---

1. Edward Casaubon, *The Key to All Mythologies* (forthcoming).

Chandler, Alfred D. *The Visible Hand: The Managerial Revolution in American Business,* pp. 9-10, 28, 36-37, 50-51, 76-78, 82-86, 87, 195-196, 207, 209, 240-241, 285-289, 491-494, 497-498 (1977). Reprinted by permission of The Belknap Press of Harvard University Press.

DeBaise, Colleen. *Corporate-Governance Law Is the Rage,* The Wall Street Journal, September 1, 2004, at B7. Reprinted with permission of Dow Jones & Company, Inc.; permission conveyed through Copyright Clearance Center, Inc.

Fitting In: In Bow to Retailers' New Clout, Levi Strauss Makes Alterations, The Wall Street Journal, June 17, 2004, at A1. Reprinted with permission of Dow Jones & Company, Inc.; permission conveyed through Copyright Clearance Center, Inc.

Floum, Jessica, *Portland to stop corporate investing despite Mayor Ted Wheeler's opposition,* Oregonlive.com, Apr. 6, 2017. Copyright © 2017 Oregon Live LLC. Reprinted with permission of Oregon Live LLC; permission conveyed through Copyright Clearance Center, Inc.

Gilson, Ronald J. *Globalizing Corporate Governance: Convergence of Form or Function,* 49 American Journal of Comparative Law 329, 329-34 (2001).

Hamill, Susan Pace. *The Origins Behind the Limited Liability Company,* 59 Ohio State Law Journal 1459 (1998). Reprinted with permission of Ohio State Law Journal.

Haynsworth, Harry J., *The Unified Business Organizations Code: The Next Generation,* 29 Delaware Journal of Corporate Law 83 (2004).

Kapner, Suzanne, and Joshua Jamerson, *Coach Goes Younger In Nabbing Kate Spade,* Wall St. J. (May 9, 2017). Reprinted with permission of Dow Jones & Company, Inc.; permission conveyed through Copyright Clearance Center, Inc.

Kirk, William E., III. *A Case Study in Legislative Opportunism: How Delaware Used the Federal-State System to Attain Corporate Pre-Eminence,* 10 Journal of Corporation Law 233, 244-259 (1984).

Klein, Alec. *Borrowers Find System Open to Conflicts, Manipulation,* Washington Post, November 22, 2004, at A01. Reprinted with permission of the Washington Post Writers Group; permission conveyed through Copyright Clearance Center, Inc.

Koniak, Susan P. *Who Gave Lawyers a Pass,* Forbes, August 12, 2002 at 58. Copyright © 2010. Reprinted by Permission of Forbes Media LLC.

Murdock, Charles W., *The Evolution of Effective Remedies for Minority Shareholders and its Impact Upon Valuation of Minority Shares,* 65 Notre Dame Law Review 425, 452-470 (1990). Reprinted with permission. Copyright © 1990 by Notre Dame Law Review, University of Notre Dame.

Tversky, Amos, and Daniel Kahneman. *Judgment Under Uncertainty: Heuristics and Biases*, from 185 Science 1124-1131 (1974). Reprinted with permission from AAAS. Permission conveyed through Copyright Clearance Center, Inc.

Weil, Jonathan. *Missing Numbers-Behind Wave of Corporate Fraud: A Change in How Auditors Work*, The Wall Street Journal, March 25, 2004, at A1. Reprinted with permission of Dow Jones & Company, Inc.; permission conveyed through Copyright Clearance Center, Inc.

Wells, C.A. Harwell. *The Cycles of Corporate Social Responsibility: An Historical Retrospective for the Twenty-First Century*, 51 University of Kansas Law Review 77 (2002). Reprinted with permission of the Kansas Law Review.

Wells, Harwell. The Life (and Death?) of Corporate Waste, 74 Wash. & Lee L. Rev. 1239 (2017). Reprinted with permission of the author.

Cases and Materials on
Business Entities

Part I.
THE PRACTICE OF BUSINESS LAW

1

Practicing Corporate Law[1]

The subject of this casebook is sometimes loosely called "corporate law." It follows that lawyers who specialize in this subject are "corporate lawyers." We'll start out by defining the term *corporate lawyer*. Then, we'll spend the rest of this chapter exploring three other questions. First, what do corporate lawyers do? Second, where do corporate lawyers work? Third, what substantive legal knowledge do corporate lawyers need?

In the broadest sense, the term *corporate lawyer* means a lawyer whose clients are for-profit or nonprofit entities rather than individuals. The legal work performed by such a corporate lawyer could be in any substantive area, including representing business entities in litigation.

Sometimes the phrase *corporate lawyer* is used to mean a lawyer who is employed by a corporation. When used in this sense, the phrase distinguishes such lawyers from those who are self-employed or who work in law firms, government, or academia.

Corporate lawyer, in its most typical usage within the legal community, denotes a lawyer whose practice is devoted to legal questions that arise under the substantive laws governing business entities. This is the definition we will use throughout this book. Such a lawyer does not litigate, nor does he or she deal primarily with other substantive areas such as taxation, labor and employment, intellectual property, or bankruptcy. A corporate lawyer in this sense could be employed in one of several settings and, while he or she probably represents business entities, might represent the government, an interest group, or a charity instead.[2]

---

1. Greg Duff and Alison Ivey, two corporate lawyers who have practiced in a variety of settings, gave me valuable advice about this chapter. My thanks to them.

2. In some ways it might be more accurate to refer to "corporate lawyers" as "transaction lawyers" to better distinguish them from litigators and to reflect the fact that they may represent entities other than corporations. However, the term *corporate lawyer* is so ingrained in legal culture that we're going to use that term throughout this book.

A. WHAT DO CORPORATE LAWYERS DO?

1. A Different Paradigm from Litigators

In the first year of law school, the paradigm lawyer is the litigator. Two fundamental assumptions underlie the lawyer-as-litigator idea. First, the lawyer's task is to be the client's champion. The lawyer should vindicate the client either by redressing a harm suffered by the client or by defeating a claim that the client has harmed another. Second, in litigation the lawyer is truly the principal actor. The client, though not passive, assists the lawyer in preparing for the conflict. The client rarely decides the legal theory of the case and rarely makes litigational decisions such as whether to move for summary judgment or what discovery to seek.

Corporate lawyers differ from this paradigm in three important ways. As you read about the ways in which corporate lawyers differ from litigators, ask yourself whether your own temperament and preferences might make you better suited to be a corporate lawyer rather than a litigator.

First, corporate lawyers generally deal with prospective matters rather than retrospective ones. The litigator focuses primarily on what happened, not on what will happen. The litigator helps the client pick up the pieces but is not directly concerned with advising the client about the future.[3] The corporate lawyer, by contrast, is looking ahead. The corporate lawyer is enmeshed in effecting future actions on behalf of the business client. This difference in temporal focus may seem small, but it results in an immense difference in the personalities between litigators and corporate lawyers.

The second main difference is that the corporate lawyer's goal is more variegated than vindication. Litigation, in its most abstract, is a zero-sum proposition. Certainly most lawsuits are compromised before trial, and such a settlement is seldom a win-lose result. Furthermore, many lawsuits involve multiple claims or parties and your client may win even though opposing parties do not entirely lose. Nonetheless, the basic mindset of the litigator is that doing a good job for the client means defeating someone else.

Corporate lawyers, by contrast, deal with other parties and their lawyers at arm's length, but not adversarially. They recognize that their client will have different interests from the other parties, but they also recognize that the ultimate goal of all parties is to effect a particular transaction or business structure. Thus your client does not gain unless others gain as well. Nonetheless, because the parties do have differing interests and a lawyer typically does not represent all parties in a transaction, a corporate lawyer must deal with others at arm's length. This requires the corporate lawyer to work with other parties honestly and candidly, but at the same time understand that the client's interests are paramount. Many lawyers find this approach more challenging and more rewarding than the litigation approach.

Finally, whereas the litigator is in charge of the litigation, the corporate lawyer's client is in charge of the business proposal. Hence, much of the corporate lawyer's

---

3. Obviously the results of litigation over past matters may have an important effect on the client's future, but the litigator's concern is mostly with the past.

professional time is spent talking *with* clients[4] instead of talking *at* them. The corporate lawyer's advice is seldom categorical ("You must do X." "You can't do Y.")[5] but is instead a reflection of the lawyer's own judgment both about the law and, as the lawyer becomes more seasoned, about business and negotiating. This is frequently more nuanced and often more frustrating than controlling litigation. The interpersonal skills required to be an effective corporate lawyer are considerable. One must be able to engage with a wide variety of nonlawyers, to assess their needs and wants, and to communicate one's own views clearly. One frustrating element of a corporate lawyer's life is that clients don't always agree with their corporate lawyer's judgment and advice. One inevitable fact is that the corporate lawyer's views don't always prevail and the client moves in a direction the lawyer believes is not the optimal one.

2. The Typical Roles of the Corporate Lawyer

The corporate lawyer serves in four recurring roles in professional life. First, as you no doubt intuited from the discussion above, is the *corporate lawyer as counselor*. The lawyer's job here is to give advice to the client. The context of the advice might involve transactions with others, such as when the client is buying or selling another entity or when the client is entering into a business venture in concert with others. But the context of the lawyer's advice might not involve a business deal. That is, the corporate lawyer may be giving advice about such things as the law surrounding corporate elections or compliance with a regulatory agency's rules.

A second recurring role is the *corporate lawyer as conciliator*. Here the corporate lawyer is called upon to help resolve a conflict between the client and another, often regarding a potential transaction. The corporate lawyer uses analytical powers to assess the source of the conflict, the parties' interests, and the potential solutions. The corporate lawyer typically does not represent more than one party in such a setting and so any proposed solution must be consonant with the lawyer's client's best interests. Nonetheless, the client is often best served when the lawyer is able to find a solution to a conflict that threatens to derail an otherwise viable business opportunity.

A corporate lawyer might also facilitate a transaction between the client and another party. The *corporate lawyer as facilitator* role might comprise three different skills. The corporate lawyer may negotiate the substantive elements of a transaction such as price, quantity, and other essential points. Some clients prefer to do all negotiating themselves; others prefer the lawyer to do much of that work. One consideration in choosing who will be the primary negotiator is the message sent by having the lawyer or the client negotiate. It sometimes happens that the client

---

4. We're using *client* in this context to mean the actual human or humans who manage the business entity that is the lawyer's true client.

5.   A lawyer shall not counsel a client to engage, or assist a client, in conduct that the lawyer knows is criminal or fraudulent, but a lawyer may discuss the legal consequences of any proposed course of conduct with a client and may counsel or assist a client to make a good faith effort to determine the validity, scope, meaning or application of the law.

Utah R. of Prof. Conduct 1.2(d) (2005). The Utah Rules of Professional Conduct are substantially identical to the ABA's Model Rules of Professional Conduct (MRPC).

believes that another party will not react well if the client's lawyer negotiates. Thus the client himself or herself will negotiate even though the client's abstract preference might be for the lawyer to do so.

Whether or not the corporate lawyer negotiates the deal points, the lawyer may facilitate the transaction by ensuring that the transaction complies with applicable regulations. Common examples are Securities and Exchange Commission (SEC) regulations on issuing stock, Federal Trade Commission or Department of Justice antitrust regulations, and Internal Revenue Service regulations on the tax treatment of the proposed transaction. Regulations might also be imposed at the state or local levels. While the corporate lawyer may well call upon lawyers with special expertise in these areas, he or she will doubtless carry the laboring oar in identifying and ensuring compliance with these regulations.

The third essential skill for the corporate lawyer as facilitator is that of drafter. Obviously, few corporate transactions will be effected orally. A transaction must be reduced to writings that both accurately capture the agreed-upon terms and legally effect the anticipated transaction. Frequently, the lawyer must draft documents in addition to the primary, deal-effecting document. Side agreements with other parties are often called for as are documents such as director resolutions and shareholder consents.

Many of these drafting tasks are assigned to more junior lawyers so you might be exposed to this facet of corporate lawyer as facilitator relatively quickly and deeply. Good drafting is a difficult skill in the best of circumstances. In the real world of corporate law, good drafting, especially by junior lawyers, is made more difficult by two common phenomena: the lawyer is relatively inexperienced and the lawyer is frequently not given all the information necessary to make the final documents accurate and advantageous to the client. In this casebook you will find many cases that turn on the drafting of a particular document. Ask yourself how the document likely came to be and how you might have acted differently, which may include more than simply using different words, to avoid the litigation that developed.

A final role, and the most controversial, is the *corporate lawyer as guardian*. Corporate lawyers may be called upon to protect the client and the public against some contemplated actions by persons acting on the client's behalf. This role is sometimes called a "gatekeeper" function, the idea being that the corporate lawyer has the power to deny the corporate client access to the lawyer's skills and reputation. Under the Rules of Professional Conduct (RPC) of most states, a corporate lawyer is required to accept and help implement decisions made by the appropriate corporate managers on behalf of the corporation. *See, e.g.*, Utah R. of Prof. Conduct 1.13.[6] A corporate lawyer is also ordinarily required to keep

---

6.   When constituents of the organization make decisions for it, the decisions ordinarily must be accepted by the lawyer even if their utility or prudence is doubtful. Decisions concerning policy and operations, including ones entailing serious risk, are not as such in the lawyer's province. [H]owever, . . . when the lawyer knows that the organization is likely to be substantially injured by action of an officer or other constituent that violates a legal obligation to the organization or is in violation of law that might be imputed to the organization, the lawyer must proceed as is reasonably necessary in the best interest of the organization. [K]nowledge can be inferred from circumstances, and a lawyer cannot ignore the obvious.

Utah R. of Prof. Conduct 1.13, cmt. 3.

confidential any client information. *See, e.g.*, Utah R. of Prof. Conduct 1.6. In some situations, though, these norms are superseded by a corporate lawyer's ability and, sometimes, obligation to take other action.

More precisely, the RPC require a corporate lawyer to object when

> [A]n officer, employee or other person associated with the organization is engaged in action, intends to act or refuses to act in a matter related to the representation that is a violation of a legal obligation to the organization, or a violation of law that reasonably might be imputed to the organization, and that is likely to result in substantial injury to the organization. . . .

Utah R. of Prof. Conduct 1.13(b)

The RPC require the lawyer ordinarily to challenge such an action up to the highest corporate authority, typically the board of directors. *See, e.g.*, Utah R. of Prof. Conduct 1.13(b). This is sometimes called the lawyer's obligation to report "up the ladder." The Comment to Utah Rules of Professional Conduct 1.13 fleshes out a lawyer's role:

> [T]he lawyer should give due consideration to the seriousness of the violation and its consequences, the responsibility in the organization and the apparent motivation of the person involved, the policies of the organization concerning such matters, and any other relevant considerations. Ordinarily, referral to a higher authority would be necessary. In some circumstances, however, it may be appropriate for the lawyer to ask the constituent to reconsider the matter; for example, if the circumstances involve a constituent's innocent misunderstanding of law and subsequent acceptance of the lawyer's advice, the lawyer may reasonably conclude that the best interest of the organization does not require that the matter be referred to higher authority. If a constituent persists in conduct contrary to the lawyer's advice, it will be necessary for the lawyer to take steps to have the matter reviewed by a higher authority in the organization. If the matter is of sufficient seriousness and importance or urgency to the organization, referral to higher authority in the organization may be necessary even if the lawyer has not communicated with the constituent. Any measures taken should, to the extent practicable, minimize the risk of revealing information relating to the representation to persons outside the organization. Even in circumstances where a lawyer is not obligated by Rule 1.13 to proceed, a lawyer may bring to the attention of an organizational client, including its highest authority, matters that the lawyer reasonably believes to be of sufficient importance to warrant doing so in the best interest of the organization.

Utah R. of Prof. Conduct 1.13, cmt. 4

The RPC allow a corporate lawyer to disclose client information to people outside the business in at least two settings. First,

> [I]f
>
> (1) despite the lawyer's efforts [in reporting up the ladder] . . . the highest authority that can act on behalf of the organization insists upon or fails to address in a timely and appropriate manner an action or a refusal to act, that is clearly a violation of law, and
> (2) the lawyer reasonably believes that the violation is reasonably certain to result in substantial injury to the organization, then the lawyer may reveal information relating to the representation whether or not Rule 1.6 permits such disclosure, but only if and to the extent the lawyer reasonably believes necessary to prevent substantial injury to the organization.

Utah R. of Prof. Conduct 1.13(c)

Second, a lawyer may

> (b) [R]eveal information relating to the representation of a client to the extent the lawyer reasonably believes necessary:
>> (1) to prevent reasonably certain death or substantial bodily harm;

(2) to prevent the client from committing a crime or fraud that is reasonably certain to result in substantial injury to the financial interests or property of another and in furtherance of which the client has used or is using the lawyer's services;

(3) to prevent, mitigate or rectify substantial injury to the financial interests or property of another that is reasonably certain to result or has resulted from the client's commission of a crime or fraud in furtherance of which the client has used the lawyer's services;

Utah R. of Prof. Conduct 1.6(b)

Congress and the SEC have imposed requirements on corporate lawyers in addition to those of the RPC. *See* D. Federal Securities Regulation, below.

Notes and Questions

1. Notes

a. In England, the essential difference between litigators and corporate lawyers was captured and institutionalized in the distinction between *barristers* and *solicitors*. Barristers had the exclusive right to appear in court on behalf of clients and derive their title from having been admitted to the bar.[7] Solicitors were not admitted to the bar and could not be heard in court. They undertook all other legal work, however, including what we would today call corporate work. Paradoxically, although barristers were considered to be more elite and more prestigious than solicitors, they were, at least in theory, under the control of solicitors. A barrister could not communicate with a client except with the solicitor's consent, and it was the solicitor who crafted the legal argument that the barrister presented in court. In legal parlance, the solicitor *briefed* the barrister.

b. The RPC *require* a corporate lawyer to disclose client information outside the corporation, "when disclosure is necessary to avoid assisting a criminal or fraudulent act by a client, unless disclosure is prohibited by Rule 1.6." Utah R. of Prof. Conduct 4.1(b).

> Model Rule 4.1(b)'s disclosure mandate only applies to lawyer conduct "in the course of representing a client" — i.e. before representation has ceased. Thus, Comment [3] to Model Rule 4.1(b) points out that "[o]rdinarily, a lawyer can avoid assisting a client's crime or fraud" — and thus avoid the Rule's disclosure obligation — "by withdrawing from the representation." Model Rules Rule 4.1 cmt. 3 (2002).
>
> Lawrence A. Hamermesh, *The ABA Task Force on Corporate Responsibility and the 2003 Changes to the Model Rules of Professional Conduct*, 17 Geo. J. Legal Ethics 35, 54 n.92 (2003)

2. Reality Check

a. How does the mindset of a trial lawyer — a litigator — differ from that of a corporate lawyer?

b. What roles do corporate lawyers routinely fill?

c. If the authorized decision makers of a corporation disagree with a corporate lawyer's advice, how may the lawyer respond?

---

7. Note that baristas, too, derive their title from their connection with a bar.

d. When may a lawyer present a legal issue to a corporate authority higher than the authority he or she is presently dealing with? Must a lawyer ever do so?

e. When may a lawyer disclose client information to people outside the client without client consent? Must a lawyer ever do so?

3. Suppose

a. Suppose a corporate lawyer in a law firm discovered that a corporate client had overstated its earnings in recently published financial statements. How should the corporate lawyer identify the course(s) of action he or she has available? What additional information, if any, would the corporate lawyer need?

b. Assume that the lawyer in question *a* was an in-house lawyer rather than a lawyer in a law firm. Would your analysis of question *a* be different?

c. Suppose that the corporation in questions *a* and *b* intends to publish, next month, financial statements that overstate its earnings. Would your analysis of questions *a* or *b* be different? Suppose publication were scheduled for next week or were scheduled for tomorrow. Would those facts change your analysis?

4. What Do You Think?

a. Do you think the similarities between litigators and corporate lawyers are more important than the differences between them?

b. Are in-house corporate lawyers or law firm corporate lawyers more likely to face hard ethical choices under the RPC?

c. Do you think the RPC's disclosure rules are in tension with the corporate lawyer's other roles? If so, how should that tension be resolved? The current version of MRPC 1.6(b) was adopted by the ABA House of Delegates by a vote of 218 to 201. The principal objections were that the rule would be unlikely to prevent corporate wrongdoing, that the rule would distort the attorney-client relationship, and that the rule would increase the potential liability of lawyers who could disclose client information but who chose not to do so. *See* Lawrence A. Hamermesh, *The ABA Task Force on Corporate Responsibility and the 2003 Changes to the Model Rules of Professional Conduct*, 17 Geo. J. Legal Ethics 35, 48-53 (2003).

5. You Draft It

a. Draft disclosure rules that provide the optimum balance between the corporate lawyer's obligations to the client and to society. The text of Utah Rules of Professional Conduct 1.6 and 4.1 follow.

> (a) A lawyer shall not reveal information relating to the representation of a client unless the client gives informed consent, the disclosure is impliedly authorized in order to carry out the representation or the disclosure is permitted by paragraph (b).
>
> (b) A lawyer may reveal information relating to the representation of a client to the extent the lawyer reasonably believes necessary:
>
> > (1) to prevent reasonably certain death or substantial bodily harm;
> >
> > (2) to prevent the client from committing a crime or fraud that is reasonably certain to result in substantial injury to the financial interests or property of another and in furtherance of which the client has used or is using the lawyer's services;
> >
> > (3) to prevent, mitigate or rectify substantial injury to the financial interests or property of another that is reasonably certain to result or has resulted from the client's

commission of a crime or fraud in furtherance of which the client has used the lawyer's services;

(4) to secure legal advice about the lawyer's compliance with these Rules;

(5) to establish a claim or defense on behalf of the lawyer in a controversy between the lawyer and the client, to establish a defense to a criminal charge or civil claim against the lawyer based upon conduct in which the client was involved, or to respond to allegations in any proceeding concerning the lawyer's representation of the client; or

(6) to comply with other law or a court order.

Utah R. of Prof. Conduct 1.6

In the course of representing a client a lawyer shall not knowingly:

(a) make a false statement of material fact or law to a third person; or

(b) fail to disclose a material fact when disclosure is necessary to avoid assisting a criminal or fraudulent act by a client, unless disclosure is prohibited by Rule 1.6.

Utah R. of Prof. Conduct 4.1

B. WHERE DO CORPORATE LAWYERS WORK?

1. Private Practice

The vast majority of corporate lawyers work in private practice, which means they practice as part of an entity — a law firm — that provides legal services to others. A few corporate lawyers are sole practitioners, but the nature of corporate representation[8] is such that few corporate lawyers are able or inclined to have such a practice. The corporate lawyer in a small firm, say fewer than ten lawyers, probably finds that he or she is called upon to render advice in a wide variety of substantive legal areas. Typically, small firms rely heavily on litigation for much of their revenue. Indeed, nonlitigators in small firms are often thought of as "the business lawyer" and may be called upon to render legal advice in any legal area that isn't connected with litigation.

This kind of practice can be quite fulfilling in at least two respects. First, many lawyers chafe at the idea of becoming too specialized in their practice. Thus they embrace the chance to have a practice that constantly presents new legal areas in which to work but in which they don't have to litigate. Second, the clients of such firms tend to be smaller businesses, which means that the lawyer has the opportunity to make a genuine difference for an entire business.

On the other hand, some lawyers do not like a practice that requires knowledge of a broad array of substantive areas. Further, the legal issues that arise with clients of small firms are often quite routine, which may lead to professional disaffection. Finally, some corporate lawyers in small firms feel isolated because they have no other corporate lawyer colleagues.

Corporate lawyers in medium-sized firms, between 10 and 100 lawyers, still have the opportunity to make an important difference for their corporate clients.

---

8. Corporate law practice usually entails a range of legal issues such that the client needs the advice of lawyers in more than one legal specialty. A law firm that can provide such a range of lawyers in one place is typically more attractive to corporate clients than the alternative of seeking out lawyers in separate sole practices for each of their legal needs.

They also are able to focus their practice more narrowly on "corporate law" rather than on "nonlitigation" areas, because other lawyers in the firm are likely to specialize in tax, labor and employment, environmental, or intellectual property law. Thus a corporate lawyer is likely to be *in* the corporate department rather than to *be* the corporate department. The firm's larger size means that it can provide legal services in a range of substantive areas, and so more established business entities are likely to be attracted to such a firm. In turn, these larger and more established business entities are likely to generate more sophisticated, and hence more interesting, legal problems for the corporate lawyer.

Corporate lawyers in medium-sized firms face professional frustration, however. A medium-sized firm is in constant need of new clients, because as clients get bigger, they may migrate to larger law firms. Much of the medium-sized firm lawyer's time is taken up with developing new clients. At the same time, the corporate lawyer is trying to prevent current clients from being snatched away by larger, often more prestigious, law firms that may be perceived as offering more or better services for the client. Even when clients are retained, the corporate lawyer may find himself or herself shunted aside when a large transaction comes along; the client may retain additional counsel from a larger firm to provide particular expertise. These lawyers may squeeze out the lawyer at the mid-sized firm.

Finally, lawyers in large firms, over 100 lawyers, frequently find themselves grappling with extremely sophisticated and complex corporate law issues, often on behalf of the largest corporations in the world. These lawyers are supported by an astonishing array of resources, from support staff to IT equipment, to information services (that's the library to you and me). A corporate lawyer in a large firm will probably find that the corporate department comprises several more focused practice areas and the lawyer will probably practice in only one or two of those focused areas. For instance, a typical large firm's corporate department comprises practice areas devoted to mergers and acquisitions;[9] securities (often called public financing or corporate finance);[10] and venture capital or private equity[11] in addition to a general corporate law practice.

Big firm corporate lawyers may find themselves frustrated by the narrowness of their practice's focus. They may feel that they are simply legal machines rather than productive lawyers. Corporate lawyers in big firms may also feel distanced from clients because they deal with in-house lawyers and corporate managers who are not senior policymakers. Finally, many or most of the corporate lawyer's projects may be very small pieces of very big deals, which may lead to the feeling that the lawyer's efforts are rather superfluous or fruitless.

---

9. The subject of Chapter 16 and, doubtless, a separate course in law school.

10. *Securities* means the application of the federal securities laws to proposed issuances of stock. This area is certainly a separate course, or courses, in your law school. In this casebook, securities regulation is a separate section at the end of each chapter in which there are significant securities law issues. *See*, most directly, the Federal Securities Regulation portions of Chapters 6, 7, and 14.

11. *See* in particular Chapter 6.

2. Corporations (In-House Lawyers)

Probably the most typical alternative to practicing corporate law in a law firm is to work directly for a corporation. Here the corporate lawyer works as an employee *of* the client rather than working in a law firm that is hired *by* the client. Obviously, the smaller the business, the more the in-house lawyer is expected to be a general practitioner and possibly a savvy businessperson as well. At the other extreme, a large, well-established, publicly held corporation may have a legal department that resembles a medium-sized firm in terms of both the number of lawyers employed and the division of those lawyers into practice groups.

The differences between practicing corporate law in a firm and in a corporation can be striking. Having a single client can allow the corporate lawyer to develop a deep knowledge not only of the client but of the whole industry of which the company is a part. This knowledge can allow the corporate lawyer to render advice that is more informed and to apply judgment that is better suited to the client than can a lawyer who practices in a law firm. The in-house lawyer, or at any rate the in-house legal department as a whole, can often have a more direct influence on the corporate client, because the lawyers are permanently connected to the client, than can a law firm that has been retained to provide advice. Furthermore, many times the in-house lawyer will deal with nascent legal issues that are too inchoate or too sensitive to refer to an outside firm. This quality again allows the in-house corporate lawyer to be more effective than a lawyer in private practice might be.

On the other hand, the in-house lawyer runs a risk of being psychologically "captured" by the company. In other words, the in-house corporate lawyer may come to believe that, in effect, the company is always right and the lawyer's advice may come to be less valuable than more dispassionate advice rendered by lawyers in private practice. Also, nonlawyers in the corporation may be required by company policy to deal with in-house lawyers on certain matters. The upshot is that nonlawyers may view in-house lawyers as impediments rather than allies. Furthermore, nonlawyers may discount in-house lawyers' opinions on the ground that "if they're working for the company, how good can they be?" and may give more credence to advice from outside law firms because "if we're paying lots of money to outsiders, they must know what they're doing."

Moreover, an in-house lawyer might find himself or herself subjected to increased ratcheting (*see* Chapter 4) in two ways. First, because the in-house lawyer is paid a salary rather than an hourly rate, there is a temptation to increase the lawyer's workload because the increased cost is minimal. Second, the in-house lawyer might be consulted by senior executives for advice on the executive's stock portfolio, retirement plan, or employment agreement. These issues may not only be outside the scope of the lawyer's employment but may frequently raise delicate conflict of interest issues if the in-house lawyer could also be considered to have established an attorney-client relationship with the executive.

In terms of the difference in substantive law focus, an in-house lawyer may spend much, or even all, of his or her time supervising legal matters that have been sent to outside law firms rather than spending time working on those legal matters directly. Some lawyers prefer this sort of once-removed contact with corporate law, especially as it often involves working primarily with other lawyers (in the firms to which the legal work has been sent) who are knowledgeable about the subjects. Other corporate lawyers may find such indirect practice frustrating. In-house lawyers usually have the opportunity to undertake three kinds of corporate law work more regularly than lawyers in a law firm. First, if the corporation is publicly held, the in-house lawyer may be involved in ensuring compliance with the periodic reporting requirements of the SEC and stock exchanges. Relatedly, if the corporation does business in a regulated industry such as banking or communications, the in-house lawyer may participate in the corporation's compliance obligations. Finally, the in-house lawyer may be more continuously involved in the corporation's legal and corporate governance compliance and auditing efforts than a lawyer practicing in a law firm.

3. Other Practice Settings

Private practice and in-house employment are by far the most common practice settings for corporate lawyers. Nonetheless, there are other settings for corporate lawyers that may be of interest to you. These practice settings may be thought of as niche practices because, though important, they do not afford employment opportunities for significant numbers of lawyers. First, some corporate lawyers work in not-for-profit organizations devoted in whole or in part to issues of corporate law. These organizations often focus on issues of corporate governance or corporate social responsibility.[12]

Another niche corporate law practice setting is in the government. Intuitively you might think that there are lots of employment opportunities for lawyers in various levels of government. True, but very few of them involve corporate law. The SEC employs many corporate lawyers who focus on the federal securities laws. To some extent these lawyers also deal with state corporate law issues, but such work is essentially ancillary to their focus on the federal securities laws.[13]

Some law students seek judicial clerkships after graduation. Although there's no official "corporation court," much of the most important and sophisticated corporate law cases arise in Delaware.[14] The Delaware Court of Chancery has five jurists, and the Delaware Supreme Court has five justices. Each of these judges has law clerks selected annually. Your school's career services office can provide you with more information.

Finally, a wonderful niche is in academia. The person teaching this course is a corporate lawyer. It is common knowledge that corporate law scholars occupy the

---

12. Corporate governance involves issues of the allocation of the power to manage a corporation among various constituencies such as large shareholders, directors, and senior managers. *See* in particular Chapters 9-13. Other important constituencies include suppliers, customers, and employees. Corporate social responsibility generally refers to the relation between business entities (usually large corporations) and the communities (large or small) in which they do business. Often the emphasis is on the obligations corporations have to the societies in which they operate and the abilities and propriety of governments to enforce those obligations. *See* in particular Chapters 2 and 10.

13. Every state government also has a securities department. Lawyers in those departments focus on the state's securities laws rather than corporate law, more broadly understood.

14. As you will discover, many of the cases in this casebook are from the Delaware courts and certainly more cases in this book are from Delaware than from any other state. *See* in particular Chapters 2 and 5 on the importance of Delaware to corporate law.

highest level in the legal academic hierarchy — followed, in order, by tax scholars, other law professors, and finally constitutional law profs.

4. Who Practices Corporate Law?

This section shifts to a consideration of the demographics of corporate lawyers. Given that the definition of "corporate lawyer" is imprecise, the statistics that follow are also imprecise. Nonetheless, I suspect they reflect a roughly accurate presentation of the demographics of those who practice corporate law. The numbers focus on lawyers in law firms and in-house lawyers and do not include corporate lawyers working in other practice settings.

The total number of lawyers in the United States is probably around 1.3 million, of whom around 75 percent are in private practice. According to the American Bar Association, there are around 5,200 law firms in the country with 11 or more lawyers. These law firms doubtless employ the great majority of all corporate lawyers in private practice. In total, these firms employ about 312,000 lawyers. If, speaking quite generally, about one-third of medium-to-large firm lawyers are primarily engaged in corporate work, then there are roughly 102,000 corporate lawyers (about 7.8 percent of all U.S. lawyers) in private practice.

The number of in-house lawyers is probably around 117,000. Not all these lawyers practice corporate law, however. In-house lawyers as a whole spend roughly 20 percent of their time on essentially corporate matters. Recognizing, of course, that some in-house lawyers spend all their time on corporate law matters and others spend none, a reasonable estimate might be that 15 percent of in-house lawyers are primarily corporate lawyers. So maybe 15,000 to 20,000 corporate lawyers work in-house. All in all, there are probably around 120,000 corporate lawyers, either in private practice or in-house.

Let's look at the demographics of corporate lawyers.

First, 66 percent of lawyers working in law firms are male and 34 percent are female. By comparison, among all lawyers the ratio of men to women is 65 percent to 35 percent. Looking to the race or ethnicity of law firm lawyers, we find the following breakdown (percentages of all lawyers are in parentheses):

White[15]	85.0%	(87.6%)
Asian	7.0%	(2.0%)
African American	2.9%	(4.1%)
Hispanic	3.3%	(3.9%)

Further dividing these figures into partners and associates, the demographics of law firms looks like this: Among partners, 78 percent are men and 22 percent are women; 92 percent are white and 8 percent are people of color. Among associates,

---

15. In these statistics, white means those lawyers who have not identified themselves as African American, Hispanic, Asian, Native American, or multiracial.

55 percent are men and 45 percent are women; 77 percent are white and 23 percent are people of color.

According to NALP, the number of openly lesbian, gay, bisexual, and transgender lawyers in law firms is about 2.5 percent. This suggests that about 2,600 corporate lawyers are openly LGBT.

Notes and Questions

1. What Do You Think?

a. Do you think that law firm corporate lawyers and in-house corporate lawyers encounter roughly comparable ethical issues? If you believe there are differences, what are they?

C. WHAT DO CORPORATE LAWYERS NEED TO KNOW?

This section touches on the substantive areas in which corporate lawyers need to be particularly competent. This discussion certainly isn't meant to suggest that other substantive areas and lawyer skills are unimportant. Rather, the point is to give you a sense of the areas in which corporate lawyers find themselves working on a daily basis so that you can assess whether a career in corporate law is one in which you might be particularly interested.

1. Core Areas of Knowledge

Corporate lawyers need to have a deep knowledge of, and keep current in, five substantive legal areas. Most obviously, they need to know the law of business entities. What a good idea it was to take this course and buy this book! Business entities law comprises the law governing corporations, partnerships, and limited liability companies (LLCs). This book covers the law surrounding each of these entities in depth. You will need to know the corporations law of both the state in which you will practice and of Delaware as well.[16] Partnerships are governed by the Uniform Partnership Act, which has been widely adopted. Finally, LLCs are governed by statutes that vary from state to state. As with corporations, you will need to be familiar with the LLC law in your own state and probably that of Delaware, too.

The second substantive area is the law of agency. Again, this casebook will provide you with an introduction to agency law. Unlike business entities law, agency law is almost entirely common law. The American Law Institute has issued the

---

16. *See* Chapter 5 for an explanation of why Delaware law is important to all business entities lawyers.

Restatement (Third) of Agency, which provides an excellent exposition of the workings of agency law. Agency is not itself a business entity, but it pervades business life because business entities can act only through humans, and those actions usually invoke agency law.[17]

The third main area of corporate lawyers' concern is, for reasons I hope are obvious even at this point in the course, contracts. You've already had that.[18] The fourth area is tax, because many of the actions that business entities take have tax consequences. Your client will probably have an accountant or tax lawyer to do the heavy lifting on tax matters. Nonetheless, you must understand enough tax to be able to converse intelligently with the accountants and tax lawyers, who, after all, are working for the same client, and on the same matter, as you. For many law students, the introductory course in tax will suffice. Many students find it profitable, though, to take at least one additional tax course, usually called Corporate Tax.

Finally, every corporate lawyer needs to have a fairly high degree of comfort with securities regulation. As you'll see, business entities spend a fair bit of time scrounging dough from investors in exchange for various claims on the entity's future earnings.[19] From a legal standpoint, these exchanges frequently trigger the elaborate registration and compliance obligations of the federal securities acts and, to a lesser extent, state securities laws. However, nearly all these exchanges can be exempt from these obligations with basic planning. Corporate lawyers also need to be conscious of the federal securities laws' antifraud provisions. If you're contemplating a career in corporate law, you should strongly consider taking a course in securities regulation.

2. Secondary Areas of Knowledge

Corporate lawyers encounter other substantive areas with some frequency and so need to be cognizant of the basic principles of those areas even if they're not well versed in them.

A first ancillary area is employment and labor law. Business entities frequently take actions that affect employees, and you should be aware of at least the general outlines of the legal principles that shape the employee-employer relationship. Furthermore, the workforce at many business entities is represented by unions, so you may wish to have a basic knowledge of collective bargaining law.

Second, you should take at least one course that covers secured transactions[20] under the Uniform Commercial Code (UCC). Corporate lawyers need to know how to obtain and perfect security interests regardless of whether their client is a borrower or a lender. Third, you should have some exposure to the law governing

---

17. *See* Chapter 4 for a detailed explanation of how agency law is suffused throughout the remainder of this course.

18. Yes, you did. It was the one about "more than a peppercorn," "what is a chicken," and "two ships called the *Peerless*."

19. *See* in particular Chapter 6.

20. Make sure to keep separate the ideas of "security interests," which are liens on property, and "securities," which are property interests in a business entity. Security interests are covered in UCC and bankruptcy courses (and perhaps a bit in contracts); securities are covered in this casebook and in much more detail in the securities regulation courses.

intellectual property. Nearly every business entity owns something under this rubric, and you need to know how to protect your client's rights. Indeed, some business entities' primary asset consists of intellectual property.

Finally, you need a smattering (and I mean a smattering) of three nonlegal areas: business, economics, and accounting. The next two chapters will give you pretty much everything you need to know in all three of these areas to get you through this course.

Notes and Questions

1. Notes

a. Another corporate lawyer requisite is a skill rather than knowledge of a particular subject matter. Every corporate lawyer must be highly skilled at working with statutory language. As you know by this stage in your legal career, the first-year curriculum is mostly (though not entirely) focused on case-reading skills. For many of you, this course is your first sustained experience in a "statutory course." You'll need to be able to find the applicable statutory section, home in on the words (often, one word) upon which the legal problem turns, understand the range of possible meanings of those words, and understand the process of selecting one of those meanings over others. This selection will frequently turn on (a) one meaning being seen as the most typical or natural, (b) one meaning being more consonant with the functioning of the remainder of the section and other sections of the statute, (c) the section's and statute's purpose (as expressed by the drafters or legislature), and (d) prior cases interpreting the words, section, or statute.

D. FEDERAL SECURITIES REGULATION

In 2002 Congress passed the Sarbanes-Oxley Act in response to the Enron and WorldCom corporate governance scandals. Among the most controversial provisions was §307, which required the SEC to include "a rule — (1) requiring an attorney to report evidence of a material violation of securities law or breach of fiduciary duty or similar violation by the company or any agent thereof, to the chief legal counsel or the chief executive officer of the company; and (2) if the counsel or officer does not [adopt], as necessary, appropriate remedial measures or sanctions with respect to the violation, requiring the attorney to report the evidence to the audit committee of the board of directors of the issuer or to another committee of the board of directors comprised solely of directors not employed directly or indirectly by the issuer, or to the board of directors." In corporate lawyer parlance, Sarbanes-Oxley implemented "up-the-ladder reporting." The SEC rules implementing §307 flesh out these requirements in often problematic ways. The intricacies of these rules are beyond an introductory course in business entities. You should be aware that neither the statute nor the SEC rules requires a lawyer to report misdeeds outside the corporation nor to withdraw from representing the client.

E. TERMS OF ART IN THIS CHAPTER

Barristers
Corporate lawyer as
   conciliator

Corporate lawyer as
   counselor
Corporate lawyer as
   facilitator

Corporate lawyer as
   guardian
In-house lawyer
Solicitors

Business and Businesses

In this chapter we look at commerce, which we'll call *business*.[1] You can't really understand the rest of the course, and you certainly can't have an informed judgment on the propriety of business entities laws, unless you know something about business as it's conducted by business entities.

We start with the idea of *a business*. That is, how do you define a business enterprise, and why are some large and others small? Then we will look at the rise of big business in America and the management patterns of large American corporations. Third, we take up the question of how a business may be owned by more than one human. This is where we first discover the "entities" part of business entities. Within this examination we'll also see why Delaware has become so important to American corporate law and take a look at the question of corporate law in a global setting.

A. WHAT IS A "BUSINESS"?

For our purposes, a *business* or *firm* engages in sustained profit-seeking efforts. Profit seeking means that the intent is to undertake activities that generate more wealth than they use. For a manufacturer, it means selling products for more than it costs to make them. For a trader, it means selling things for more than it costs to buy them. For an investor, it means allowing others to use the investor's assets, often money, in return for more than the cost of those assets. Examples are rent, interest, or dividends. For a worker, that means working for wages greater than the worker's job-related costs such as the costs of clothes, tools, or transportation.

---

1. We could continue to call it *commerce*, but a law school course called Commerce Entities sounds odd and Commercial Entities is probably too easily confused with Commercial Law (i.e., UCC).

1. Why Businesses Vary in Size

Every business must obtain the ingredients necessary to operate, which requires labor; raw materials, which may be natural resources or manufactured component parts; and capital goods, like machines used to produce the goods the business sells.[2] The business then has to perform the operations necessary to prepare the goods for sale. A restaurant must cook the food, for example; a greeting card retailer must keep the cards safe and create an inventory. Finally, the business has to sell the goods to customers, who may themselves be businesses. That is, a business may manufacture components for sale to other manufacturers.

Conceptually, each business firm might perform only one kind of operation at only one location. Take the potato chip business as an example. Potatoes are grown and processed, and the chips are sold to customers. Each of those three activities could be undertaken by a separate business. Each of these firms would be replicated by other firms in other locations, ultimately providing the whole economy with potato chips.

We can change this example along two dimensions. We could imagine that each of these three firms was national in scope, with multiple business locations. We'll call this the *horizontal dimension*. Or, we could imagine that a single business undertook all three activities in a single locale. This is the *vertical dimension*. If we combined these dimensions, we'd have a single firm performing every potato chip-related function from growing potatoes to retailing bags of chips throughout the country.

The potato chip example is more than a little artificial, but if we substitute coffee for potato chips, these two models become surprisingly realistic. On one hand, many business firms specialize in doing only one of the following operations: growing coffee, importing raw beans, roasting beans, distributing beans to retailers, retailing beans, or retailing coffee drinks latte by latte. Each of these firms tends to be relatively localized in its operations. On the other hand, Starbucks undertakes every one of these operations except growing the beans, and it certainly could purchase coffee-growing firms if it chose to do so. Furthermore, Starbucks has retail operations throughout the United States and much of the world.

What determines the boundary between a business, its suppliers, and its customers? Relatedly, what determines how large a business is? In economics language, why are some businesses very *integrated*, vertically, horizontally, or both, while others are not? This may seem a tad esoteric, but the answer has important implications. The answer to the integration question suggests whether your business client is likely to increase in size, either horizontally or vertically, or whether your client itself may be acquired. In any case, your understanding of these business dynamics will help you understand the kinds of transactions in which your client is involved (e.g., negotiating a contract with a supplier versus negotiating to buy the supplier's firm) and the business choices the client is likely to face.

The economists' answer to the question of horizontal integration has to do, at the core, with the idea of economies of scale. Take the fully integrated potato chip firm we imagined above. If that firm produced just one bag of chips per day, its costs

---

2. Economists would say each business must obtain inputs, which are the factors of production.

would quickly overrun its revenues, and bankruptcy would ensue. Intuitively, the more bags of chips the firm produces, the lower its costs per bag will be. Assuming that the retail price of potato chips is relatively fixed, the lower the per-bag cost, the higher the firm's profits.

These cost reductions have limits, for reasons we won't explore, so there is a theoretical optimum size for every production process. The optimum size for some operations is large, which tends to produce an industry in which most of the firms are large. Conversely, the optimum size for other operations is small, so that each operating unit in the industry is small. Note, though, that in the latter setting one firm might own a great number of these small units. The coffee beverage industry is one example. The optimum size of an espresso machine is small; some coffee drink retailers are single-unit businesses, and others are like Starbucks.

Turning to vertical integration, the most accepted answer to the question of how integrated a business should be has to do with the transaction costs of obtaining raw materials and selling goods. These transaction costs include finding sources of raw materials, finding customers, and negotiating price and terms of supply contracts. When, overall, the transaction costs of contracting between businesses is less than the transaction costs of administering the allocation of assets within a business, the business will not integrate. Thus firms will tend not to integrate with their suppliers (upstream integration) if supplying firms are plentiful, if the products they supply are plentiful, and if the supplied products are relatively fungible. There seems to be little economic need for a firm that owns a chain of home improvement stores to integrate upstream with its supplier of light bulbs or hammers.

a. Background and Context — Two Examples

We will see more concrete examples of the drive to integrate vertically or horizontally in the next section when we see the rise of big business in America. For now, though, in case you think that the consequences of horizontal or vertical integration are only of theoretical or historical interest, consider the following news stories.

Fitting In: In Bow to Retailers' New Clout, Levi Strauss Makes Alterations

Wall St. J. (June 17, 2004) A1

When Levi Strauss & Co. was preparing for its biggest new jeans launch in decades, it hired as a sales executive someone it considered the perfect choice: a vice president from motor-oil maker Pennzoil Co. The main reason he won the job last year, executives say, was that he knew how to sell to Wal-Mart.

The unorthodox bet reflects a fundamental power shift. For much of Levi's 151-year history, it was a powerful supplier. It produced an iconic brand that millions wore, or aspired to wear. It could choose its own styles and sell them where it pleased. Shoppers wanted Levi's and didn't care where they got them.

But in today's world, Levi finds itself the supplicant, and it's retailers who call the shots. Not just in apparel but in a broad swath of product categories, power is swinging to the companies that deliver goods: retailers and other distributors who literally get products into the hands of the consumer. The suppliers are being forced to adapt.

With the tables turned, once-mighty brands such as Levi must undergo transformations to put retailers' wishes ahead of their own. When Levi began to sell to Wal-Mart Stores Inc. last year, it overhauled its entire operation, from design to production, pricing to distribution. The process was wrenching and full of setbacks, and it is only now showing signs of paying off. "We had to change people and practices," [Levi Chief Executive Officer Philip Marineau] says.

Many forces underpin the power shift. Retailers have consolidated. Wal-Mart's vast growth gives it a hugely dominant role, accounting for 9% of all non-auto-related consumer sales in the U.S.

In addition, computer systems now let retailers track sales in real time. While grocers used to rely on a Procter & Gamble Co. to tell them how many tubes of Crest toothpaste to stock, today big retailers know what is selling at each of their stores every day by the hour. So they don't have to rely on suppliers to tell them how much to stock.

As stores have improved inventory controls, they have also been better able to cut costs and lower prices. The lower prices, in turn, helped spur Americans to keep shopping through the recent recession. And to the extent they shop on price, brand clout is weakened and more power flows to the company that comes in direct contact with the consumer.

Retailers' increasing strength has led some to upgrade stores and introduce private-label and exclusive products, such as those bearing famous names like Isaac Mizrahi and Martha Stewart, sold at Target and Kmart respectively. Some of these marketing changes have enticed consumers to buy across traditional demographic lines, so that a shopper who frequents a high-end store like Neiman Marcus may now be willing to shop Target as well, maybe even for part of the same outfit.

The story of Levi Strauss's capitulation to the new power of retail began in 1999. The company was struggling to boost declining sales and to reduce debt, which had ballooned in a buyout that had consolidated ownership in the hands of a few descendants of the founder. To turn itself around, the company hired as chief executive Mr. Marineau, then running PepsiCo Inc.'s North American beverage business.

Mr. Marineau had no apparel or fashion experience and appealed to Levi for marketing reasons. He had been schooled in PepsiCo's direct-to-store delivery system of bringing soda and snacks to stores in its own trucks — bypassing the warehouses and outside trucking companies used by most packaged-goods makers.

Within days of his appointment, Wal-Mart called him to broach the idea of selling Levi's at its stores. It believed the famous Levi brand would add star power to its burgeoning apparel offerings and attract even more shoppers.

The new CEO initially rejected the overture. He says he felt Levi couldn't meet Wal-Mart's strict production demands. Levi had a history of making late and incomplete deliveries. Wal-Mart needed it to be fast and accurate.

In addition, some senior-level executives were dubious about selling a Levi brand to mass retailers. Some managers worried that doing so would damage the brand's cachet and further undermine Levi's shrinking business of selling jeans at regular prices. For a brand that cherishes a classy image, there is always concern that selling at a discounter or mass merchant could downgrade it.

Indeed, Levi already had a retail problem. It had alienated some of its traditional department-store customers by expanding to lower-end chains like J.C. Penney Co. and Sears, Roebuck & Co. over the years. The company also was losing ground to Gap Inc., which stopped selling Levi in 1991 when it went exclusively with its own brand.

But Mr. Marineau believed that Wal-Mart offered an opportunity too great to ignore. Mass merchants such as Wal-Mart were selling a third of all jeans in the U.S., and their share of apparel sales was growing. Selling to Wal-Mart would be the fastest way to boost sales of Levi jeans, which had suffered from declining sales in department stores and specialty chains for years.

Wal-Mart agreed to wait while Mr. Marineau prepared the jeans company to meet its demands. Levi opened an office in Wal-Mart's hometown of Bentonville, Ark., and, between October 2002 and July 2003, built an entirely new distribution system for Wal-Mart.

Historically, Levi jeans arrived from factories at company-owned distribution centers, where they were labeled with store tags. After a short wait, they were packed back up and sent to retailers' distribution centers or stores. Under the new system, Levi goods would arrive from independent factories with store tags already attached. After a short stay at one of two "pool points," Wal-Mart's own trucks would pick them up and deliver them to Wal-Mart's distribution centers, from where they would be sent to individual stores.

The speed, combined with feedback from Wal-Mart, would let Levi reduce guesswork about the number of pairs needed. The goal was to greatly reduce excess stock and markdowns.

Some big Levi customers such as J.C. Penney and Kohl's worried they might lose shoppers who could buy Levi jeans at Wal-Mart or Target for as much as 25% less. Mr. Marineau contended they would actually benefit from the decision to sell to Wal-Mart. "By learning to do business with Wal-Mart, you improve your supply chain and logistics in general," he says. He recalls telling skeptical department-store retailers, "Our service to you will only get better as we service Wal-Mart."

To persuade the different types of retailers — department stores, specialty chains, upscale boutiques and mass merchants — to all carry Levi-brand products, Mr. Marineau proposed a segmentation strategy: He would sell different versions of jeans for different prices, from Levi Strauss Signature jeans to $150 upscale vintage designs.

The idea included positioning Levi Strauss Signature as a "premium" mass brand. To differentiate Levi Strauss Signature, the company developed new labeling and styles. They'd have no distinctive "red tab" peeking out from the back pocket, no trademark Levi pocket stitching and no famous two-horse logo. Instead, they would bear the Levi name in a cursive scrawl. They also got less-expensive fabric. Levi Strauss Signature jeans were expected to sell at about $23 — higher than other mass brands of jeans but below Levi's regular brand, which often sold for about $29.

Last July 15, Levi Strauss Signature jeans went on sale at all 2,800 Wal-Mart stores in the U.S. The launch didn't go as well as planned. After a few weeks, Wal-Mart complained that some styles were selling more slowly than its other denim brands, which were priced at \$15 to \$18. "Inventory turns," the rate at which a product sells out and has to be replenished, were slower than planned. Three months later, Wal-Mart slashed the cost of a basic pair of men's Levi Strauss Signature jeans to \$19 from \$23, hurting Levi's profit margins.

Meanwhile, important parts of Levi's core business began to deteriorate as executives focused on Wal-Mart. Some department stores reduced orders. Sales of regular Levi's, which had begun to show signs of stabilizing before the launch of Levi Strauss Signature, resumed their decline. Fashion experiments, such as a new high-fashion line called Type 1 jeans, flopped. An explosion of new varieties flowing from Mr. Marineau's segmentation strategy didn't do enough to boost volume.

In a sign of how poorly its jeans were doing, last year Levi began selling its regular-price Levi styles to Costco Wholesale Corp., the big warehouse-club chain. Previously, Levi had refused to sell its traditional jeans line in Costco, thinking the warehouse retailer, with its steep discounts, would tarnish its brand image. Levi sold Costco more than \$150 million of jeans in 2003, according to industry sources, and Costco now is among Levi's 10 biggest customers, according to filings with the Securities and Exchange Commission.

But things began getting better early this year. After Wal-Mart had cut prices on Levi Strauss Signature, the line's rate of turnover improved, says Mr. LaPorta, the new brand's president.

Levi began to tweak Signature to inject more style into the line, in a move executives hope will help it command higher prices. Mr. LaPorta says sales are rising for \$22.95-to-\$23.95 jeans that offer more fashion details, such as embroidered tabs tucked into back pockets, pants with cargo pockets and cropped hems, and women's corduroy pants with wider waistbands and button details. With several months of selling to the mass customer under its belt, Levi has adjusted its pricing and product design strategy so that it is giving discount shoppers more fashion at a good price.

Wal-Mart appears satisfied. It says the introduction of Levi's has attracted a new apparel customer to the chain. Instead of existing customers trading up to the Levi Strauss Signature brand, some customers who normally shopped only for necessities have begun to sample clothes, the company's treasurer said at a March meeting with industry analysts.

In its first quarter this year, Levi narrowed its losses and reported a 10% jump in sales, thanks in large part to Signature, which contributed about \$105 million in sales. Levi's revamping of its distribution and production to serve Wal-Mart helped the jeans company improve its overall record of timely deliveries. Producing a season of new jeans styles used to take Levi 12 to 15 months, from conception to store shelves. Today, it's just 10 months for Levi Strauss Signature, and for regular Levi's, the time is now down to 7½ months.

Levi's expansion into Wal-Mart is part of a turnaround plan aimed at improving style and fit and at making the brand available to a broader range of consumers. Recently, Levi began selling to some higher-end stores that hadn't carried its brand for years, including Bloomingdale's and Barneys New York. Both retailers report strong sales of Levi's higher-priced "premium" line, which is more cutting-edge and uses better quality fabrics than the Levi's sold at Wal-Mart.

Notes and Questions

1. Notes

a. Levi Strauss & Co. was owned by members of the two founding families from the nineteenth century until 1971, when it became a publicly owned company. In 1985 the descendants of the founding families bought out the public shareholders for $1.45 billion, making the company privately owned. The families borrowed much of that purchase price, using the company's shares as security for repayment. In 1996 the company refinanced that debt, but the interest and principal payments remained challenging for the company to meet.

2. Reality Check

a. Why are some businesses large and others small?

b. Why are some industries conducive to large businesses and others are not?

c. What is the difference between integrating horizontally and vertically?

d. What problems was Levi Strauss facing in 1999? How did the company try to solve them?

e. Why did negotiating power shift in the apparel industry between manufacturers and retailers?

3. Suppose

a. Suppose no retail company sold a significant percentage of the jeans sold in the United States. Would Levi Strauss have changed its business?

4. What Do You Think?

a. Do you think Levi Strauss would have benefited from increased integration? If so, how? Why didn't Levi Strauss integrate its business?

b. Do you think Wal-Mart would have benefited from increased integration? If so, how? Why didn't Wal-Mart integrate its business?

c. Do you think consumers of jeans were economically better off in 1999 or 2004?

d. Do you think the United States benefited from the changes in the jeans industry that took place between 1999 and 2004?

e. Do you think the changes in jeans retailing will have an economic effect on the companies that supply manufacturers such as Levi Strauss? If so, what is that effect likely to be?

The relation between Levi Strauss and Wal-Mart is an example of the possibility of vertical integration. The following article shows an example of a company that integrated horizontally.

≡ **Suzanne Kapner and Joshua Jamerson, *Coach Goes
≡ Younger in Nabbing Kate Spade***
≡ Wall St. J. (May 9, 2017)

Coach Inc. agreed to acquire rival Kate Spade & Co. for $2.4 billion, as the handbag and accessories maker seeks to tap younger consumers amid slower growth in the handbag market.

Sales of handbags are lagging as women have traded down to smaller, less expensive purses and aggressive discounting both in stores and online has pressured profits. The proposed merger would combine two big U.S. players, creating a company with $5.9 billion in annual sales and 1,300 retail stores and outlets around the world.

On Monday, Coach Chief Executive Victor Luis said there is little overlap between customers of the two brands, especially since Coach has tried to move upscale in recent years. The attraction of Kate Spade was its appeal to younger shoppers, Mr. Luis said, adding that only 10% of consumers say they buy both brands.

"Millennials offer a market that is substantial in terms of size and allows us to recruit younger customers" [Mr. Luis said]. According to Jefferies analyst Randal Konik, millennials account for about two-thirds of Kate Spade's shoppers.

"I've been buying Kate Spade since I got my first job," said Bianca Damionne, a 22-year-old who works in New York City.

"I hope Coach doesn't change things, because I like Kate Spade now," she said on Monday while shopping in a Kate Spade shop on Fifth Avenue. "The style, the colors, everything."

The North American handbag market has slowed to about 2% annual growth from as much as 15% growth six years ago, said Craig Johnson, an analyst at Customer Growth Partners. Coach has responded by targeting a slightly older and wealthier client with higher-priced bags, creating a gap for younger 20-something shoppers that it can fill with Kate Spade, Mr. Johnson said.

The industry could see more consolidation, said Neil Saunders, managing director of the research firm GlobalData Retail. "If you want growth in North America, you will have to make an acquisition, because the market is saturated."

Mr. Luis said he still has confidence handbags and leather goods are better positioned than other corners of retail.

"Consumers continue to shift dollars away from apparel to handbags, accessories and footwear," he said.

Coach will pay Kate Spade shareholders $18.50 a share in cash. That represents a 28% premium to Kate's closing price as of Dec. 27, the last trading day before a Wall Street Journal report that Kate was exploring a sale of the company after coming under pressure from an activist shareholder. The company confirmed it was reviewing such options in February.

Kate Spade shares rose 8.3% to $18.38 on Monday, while Coach shares climbed 4.8% to $44.71.

The companies, both based in New York, have battled a retail environment that has been challenging, especially for designers with significant exposure to department stores, where traffic has declined. U.S.-based luxury brands are also hurt by a strong U.S. dollar.

Sales at Coach started to grow again in recent quarters as it pulled back from department stores, closed a third of its full-priced stores in North America and cut back on promotions.

The company said it plans to reduce online flash sales as well as distribution in off-price chains like T.J. Maxx for Kate Spade after the deal closes, which is expected to occur in the third quarter.

Mr. Luis said 35% of Coach stores overlap with Kate Spade stores in North America but he doesn't foresee widespread closures following the combination. However, analysts said there are still too many stores given sluggish traffic at malls.

"Anybody who's been to Woodbury Common outlets and seen two Coach (women and men) and two Kate Spade stores (accessories and apparel) all within 30 yards of each other doesn't need a rocket science degree to know that the combined company doesn't need all that space," Mr. Johnson said, referring to an outlet center outside of New York City.

Coach does plan to expand Kate Spade outside the U.S., particularly in China and Europe, where the brand has a few dozen stores and outlets.

The two brands will be kept separate and there are no plans to cross-sell products at each other's stores, executives said. Mr. Luis said Craig Leavitt will continue to serve as chief executive of the Kate Spade brand.

Coach has been on the hunt for acquisitions as Mr. Luis seeks to build a collection of brands and respond to the rapid rise of Michael Kors Holdings Ltd. Coach approached Burberry Group PLC about a takeover last year but was rebuffed, according to people familiar with the situation, and it was seen by analysts as a potential suitor for Jimmy Choo, which put itself up for sale last month.

But Choo, which is valued at over $1 billion by some estimates, would likely be too big for Coach to swallow in the wake of its Kate Spade deal. Mr. Luis said the company could make additional acquisitions in the near term, but they would likely be of a size similar to Stuart Weitzman Holdings LLC, a shoe maker it bought in 2015 for about $574 million.

Notes and Questions

1. Notes

a. The paradigm example of horizontal integration is where one company acquires another that is engaged in exactly the same business in a different geographic location. But as the Coach-Kate Spade example shows, a company can also integrate horizontally by acquiring a company that is engaged in a similar business in the same geographic location, but which has a different customer base. Both companies are nationwide retailers of leather handbags and accessories but only 10 percent of their customers overlap.

b. Even though Coach said it had no plans to combine Coach stores with Kate Spade stores, it estimated that it would save money by eliminating central expenses, such as general administrative costs. It also said that it could save money because both Coach and Kate Spade used some of the same leather manufacturers and the combined company could negotiate for lower prices from those suppliers.

c. Two months after Coach announced that it was buying Kate Spade, Coach's principal rival, Michael Kors Holdings Ltd., announced that it was buying Jimmy Choo.

B. THE DEVELOPMENT OF BIG BUSINESS IN AMERICA

How did big businesses such as Levi Strauss and Wal-Mart develop in America? Much of the character and size of American business can be attributed to the increasing availability of information and the decreasing cost of transportation. These changes affected the optimal firm size in many industries. Alfred D. Chandler, the foremost historian of American business, describes a widely accepted view of how American business came to take its current form. As you read this excerpt, look for the way in which optimal size changed, which affected the degree of firm integration. You should also keep in mind Chandler's distinction between production activity (making things), distribution activity (moving things), and communication.

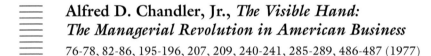

Alfred D. Chandler, Jr., *The Visible Hand:*
The Managerial Revolution in American Business
76-78, 82-86, 195-196, 207, 209, 240-241, 285-289, 486-487 (1977)

Of all the technological constraints [in the 1830s], the lack of coal was probably the most significant in holding back the spread of the factory in the United States. As long as . . . production remained powered by humans, animals, wind, and water, the volume of output was rarely large enough to require the creation of sub-units . . . or to call for the services of a salaried manager to coordinate and monitor the work. . . . The opening of the anthracite coal fields in eastern Pennsylvania lifted this constraint. Anthracite first became available in quantity for industrial purposes in the 1830s.

In the decade and a half before the Civil War, as the availability of coal and the introduction of coal-using technologies brought fundamental changes in the processes of production, the railroad and the telegraph were . . . beginning to transform the processes of distribution. They made it possible for middlemen to receive and distribute goods in a far greater volume than ever before. These basic changes in production and distribution reinforced one another. The factory could only maintain high levels of production if materials flowed steadily in and out of the factory site in volume and on schedule. And the new factories provided the goods that railroads carried in unprecedented volume to be distributed by jobbers and other marketers. The almost simultaneous availability of an abundant new form of energy and revolutionary new means of transportation and communication led to the rise of modern business enterprise in American commerce and industry.

During the 1840s the technology of railroad transportation was rapidly perfected. As technology improved, railroads became the favored means of overland transportation. The reason for the swift commercial success of the railroads over canals and other inland waterways is obvious enough. The railroad provided more direct communication than did the river, lake, or coastal routes. They were, of course, faster. The railroad's fundamental advantage, however, was not in the speed it carried passengers and mail but its ability to provide a shipper with dependable, precisely scheduled, all-weather transportation of goods. Railroads were far less affected by droughts, freshets, and floods than were waterways. Most important of all, they remained open during the winter months.

A communication revolution accompanied the revolution in transportation. The railroad permitted a rapid increase in the speed and decrease in the cost of long-distance, written communication; while the invention of the telegraph created an even greater transformation by making possible almost instantaneous communication at great distances. The railroad and the telegraph marched across the continent in unison. [T]he telegraph companies used the railroad for their rights-of-way, and the railroad used the services of the telegraph to coordinate the flow of trains and traffic. In fact, many of the first telegraph companies were subsidiaries of railroads, formed to carry out this essential operating service. The second basic innovation in communication technology, the telephone, . . . was administered through a national enterprise similar to that operating the telegraph. The initial growth of railroads [also] had a powerful impact on the United States postal system. The drop in rates and the speed and certainty of transportation greatly facilitated long-distance business communication. It also encouraged a much greater use of the mails for personal correspondence as well as business correspondence.

The revolution in . . . distribution and production rested in large part on the new transportation and communication infrastructure. Modern mass production and mass distribution depend on the speed, volume, and regularity in the movement of goods and messages made possible by the coming of the railroad, telegraph, and steamship. As the basic infrastructure came into being between the 1850s and 1880s, modern methods of mass production and distribution and the modern business enterprises that managed them made their appearance.

Transformation in the size and activities of business enterprises came most swiftly in distribution. In the 1840s the traditional mercantile firm, operating much as it had for half a millennium, still marketed and distributed the nation's goods. Within a generation it was replaced . . . by . . . the modern commodity dealer, who purchased directly from the farmer and sold directly to the processor. . . . In the same years the full-line, full-service wholesaler began to market most standardized consumer goods. Then in the 1870s and 1880s the modern mass retailer — the department store, the mail-order house, and the chain store — started to make inroads on the wholesaler's markets.

[T]hese mass marketing enterprises, . . . by using the railroads, the telegraph, the steamship, and improved postal services, coordinated the flow of agricultural crops and finished goods from a great number of individual producers to an even larger number of individual consumers. By means of such administrative coordination, the new mass marketers reduced the number of transactions involved in the flow of goods, increased the speed and regularity of that flow, and so lowered cost and improved productivity of the American distribution system.

The revolution in production came more slowly than did the revolution in distribution, for it required further technological as well as organizational innovation. The new methods of transportation and communication, by permitting a large and steady flow of raw materials into and finished products out of a factory, made possible unprecedented levels of production. The realization of this potential required, however, the invention of new machinery and processes. Once these were developed, manufacturers were able to place within a single establishment (that is, to internalize) several processes of production.

Where the underlying technology of production permitted, increased throughput from technological innovations, improved organizational design, and perfected human skills led to a sharp decrease in the number of workers required to produce a specific unit of output. The ratio of capital to labor . . . became higher. Such high-volume industries soon became capital-intensive, energy-intensive, and manager-intensive.

The modern industrial enterprise — the archetype of today's giant corporation — resulted from the integration of . . . mass production with . . . mass distribution within a single business firm. Almost nonexistent at the end of the 1870s, these integrated enterprises came to dominate many of the nation's most vital industries within less than three decades.

By integrating mass production with mass distribution, a single enterprise carried out the many transactions and processes involved in making and selling a line of products. The visible hand of managerial direction had replaced the invisible hand of market forces in coordinating the flow of goods from the suppliers of raw and semifinished materials to the retailer and ultimate consumer. The internalizing of these activities and the transactions between them reduced transaction and information costs. More important, a firm was able to coordinate supply more closely with demand, to use its working force and capital equipment more intensively, and thus to lower its unit costs.

The modern industrial enterprise followed two different paths to size. Some . . . firms moved directly into building their own national and global marketing networks and extensive purchasing organizations and obtaining their own sources of raw materials and transportation facilities. For others, mergers came first. By 1917 the integrated industrial enterprise had become the most powerful institution in American business and, indeed, in the entire American economy. By then, too, leading American industries and the economy as a whole had taken on their modern form.

As the twentieth century opened, the new integrated multifunctional, often multinational, enterprise was becoming the most influential institution in the American economy. It surpassed the railroad in size and in complexity and diversity of operations. The decisions of its managers affected more businessmen, workers, consumers, and other Americans than did those of railroad executives. It soon replaced the railroad as the focus for political and ideological controversy. In fact, in the first decade of the twentieth century the control of the new industrial corporations became the central domestic political issue of the day.

In all these new enterprises — the railroads, the telegraph, the mass marketers, and the mass producers — a managerial hierarchy had to be created to supervise several operating units and to coordinate and monitor their activities.

Once such a hierarchy had successfully taken over the function of coordinating flows, the desire of the managers to assure the success of their enterprise as a profit-making institution created strong pressures for its continuing growth. Such growth normally resulted from two quite different strategies of expansion. One was defensive or negative and stemmed from a desire for security. Its purpose was to prevent sources of supplies or outlets for goods and services from being cut off or to limit entry of new competitors into the trade. The other strategy was more positive. Its aim was to add new units, permitting by means of administrative coordination a more intensive use of existing facilities and personnel. Such positive growth might be considered as productive expansion and negative or defensive growth as nonproductive expansion. One increased productivity by lowering unit costs, the other rarely did.

Notes and Questions

1. Reality Check

a. Why was the availability of large amounts of coal so important to the development of big businesses?

b. How did the production of goods change after 1830?

c. How did the transportation of goods change after 1840?

d. How did communication change after 1840?

e. How did changes in communication and in producing and transporting goods result in large business enterprises?

2. What Do You Think?

a. Do you think important changes have occurred in communication or in producing or transporting goods since Chandler wrote in the late 1970s? If so, what are they? If so, what effects have these changes had?

1. Management Patterns in Large Corporations

In the last excerpt, Chandler pointed out that large business enterprises need a hierarchy of managers to run them. This hierarchy was not necessary and did not exist until the growth of large railroad companies in the late nineteenth century. In fact, Chandler sees the rise of big business as important mainly for fostering a new type of worker: the middle manager who supervised managers below and reported to managers above.[3] In its most basic form, the middle manager supervised the factory shop floor foreman and reported to the owner. These workers conceived of their career as being managers — neither laborers nor owners. The development of middle managers creates a theoretical and philosophical problem that concerns us as lawyers.

---

3. The importance of middle management is underscored in the very title of Chandler's book: *The Visible Hand: The Managerial Revolution in American Business.*

As a matter of property law, the presence of middle managers with increasing knowledge of, and therefore power over, a business means that the owners have correspondingly reduced power. Isn't that a big change in the definition of property when the owner has, as a practical reality, attenuated power to make decisions about the property?

As a matter of corporate law, this change has another effect. When businesses are held by a large number of widely scattered owners, as in a publicly held corporation, power over the business resides entirely with the managers. The problem for corporate law is that traditionally the owners — the shareholders — have been endued with ultimate power over the enterprise. How should corporate law respond to this shift of control from owners to managers?

In the next excerpt, Chandler describes how control of large corporations shifted to corporate managers.

Alfred D. Chandler, Jr., *The Visible Hand: The Managerial Revolution in American Business*
9-10, 491-494, 497-498 (1977)

The rise of modern business enterprise brought a new definition of the relationship between ownership and management and therefore a new type of capitalism to the American economy. Before the appearance of the multiunit firm, owners managed and managers owned. The traditional capitalist firm can, therefore, be properly termed a personal enterprise.

From its very beginning, however, modern business enterprise required more managers than a family or its associates could provide. In some firms the entrepreneur and his close associates (and their families) who built the enterprise continued to hold the majority of stock. They maintained a close personal relationship with their managers, and they retained a major say in top management decisions. [A]n economy or sectors of an economy dominated by such firms may be considered a system of entrepreneurial or family capitalism.

Where the creation and growth of an enterprise required large sums of outside capital, the relationship between ownership and management differed. The financial institutions providing the funds normally placed part-time representatives on the firm's board. In such enterprises, salaried managers had to share top management decisions, particularly those involving the raising and spending of large sums of capital, with representatives of banks and other financial institutions. An economy or sector controlled by such firms has often been termed one of financial capitalism.

In many modern business enterprises neither bankers nor families were in control. Ownership became widely scattered. The stockholders did not have the influence, knowledge, experience, or commitment to take part in the high command. Salaried managers determined long-term policy as well as managing short-term operating activities. They dominated top as well as lower and middle management. Such an enterprise controlled by its managers can properly be identified as managerial, and a system dominated by such firms is called managerial capitalism.

As family- and financier-controlled enterprises grew in size and increased in age, they became managerial. Unless the owners or representatives of financial houses became full-time career managers within the enterprise itself, they did not have the information, the time, or the experience to play a dominant role in top-level decisions. Of necessity, they left current operations and future plans to the career administrators. In many industries and sectors of the American economy, managerial capitalism soon replaced family or financial capitalism.

[B]y 1917 representatives of an entrepreneurial family or a banking house almost never took part in middle management decisions on prices, output, deliveries, wages, and employment. . . . Even in top management decisions concerning the allocation of resources, their power remained essentially negative. They could say no, but unless they themselves were trained managers with long experience in the same industry and even the same company, they had neither the information nor the experience to propose positive alternative courses of action.

[M]embers of the entrepreneurial family rarely became active in top management. . . . Since the profits of the family enterprise usually assured them of a large personal income, they had little financial incentive to spend years working up the managerial ladder. Therefore, in only a few of the large American business enterprises did family members continue to participate for more than two generations in the management of the companies they owned.

The descendants of the founders of and early investors in such industrial enterprises continued to reap the profits of successful administrative coordination. Indeed, the majority of American fortunes came from the building and operation of modern business enterprises. These families remain the primary beneficiaries of managerial capitalism, but they are no longer involved in the operation of its central institution.

The financiers who provided or arranged to obtain funds . . . remained on the boards of consolidated industrial enterprises. They rarely, however, had a strong influence on the boards of directors of industrial enterprises. . . . Their influence was significant only when the enterprise decided to go to the money markets to supplement retained earnings. With a few notable exceptions, such as United States Steel, managers soon came to command those enterprises where financiers were originally influential. Financial capitalism in the United States was a narrowly located, short-lived phenomenon.

As the influence of the families and the financiers grew even weaker in the management of modern business enterprise, that of the workers through representatives of their union increased. Union influence, however, directly affected only one set of management decisions — those made by middle managers relating to wages, hiring, firing, and conditions of work. Such decisions had only an indirect impact on the central ones that coordinated current flows and allocated resources for the future.

The actions of government officials, particularly those of the federal government, have had an increasingly greater impact on managerial decisions than have those of the representatives of workers, owners, or financiers. By and large, however, their impact has been indirect. They have helped to shape the environment in which management makes its decisions, but, except in time of war, these officials have only occasionally participated in the making of the decisions themselves. And since the market has always been the prime factor in management decisions, the government's most significant role has been in shaping markets for the goods and services of modern business enterprise.

In the United States, neither the labor unions nor the government has taken part in carrying out the basic functions of modern business enterprise. . . . Such decisions remain market-oriented. They continued to reflect the managers' perceptions of how to use technology and capital to meet their estimates of market demand.

The appearance of managerial capitalism has been, therefore, an economic phenomenon. It has had little political support among the American electorate. At least until the 1940s, modern business enterprise grew in spite of public and government opposition. Many Americans — probably a majority — looked on large-scale enterprise with suspicion. The concentrated economic power such enterprises wielded violated basic democratic values. Their existence dampened entrepreneurial opportunity in many sectors of the economy. Their managers were not required to explain or be accountable for their uses of power.

For these reasons the coming of modern business enterprise in its several different forms brought strong political reaction and legislative action. The control and regulation of the railroads, of the three types of mass retailers — department stores, mail-order houses, and the chains — and of the large industrial enterprise became major political issues. In the first decade of the twentieth century, the control of the large corporation was in fact the paramount political question of the day. The protest against the new type of business enterprise was led by merchants, small manufacturers, and other businessmen, including commercial farmers, who felt their economic interests threatened by the new institution. By basing their arguments on traditional ideology and traditional economic beliefs, they won widespread support for their views. Yet in the end, the protests, the political campaigns, and the resulting legislation did little to retard the continuing growth of the new institution and the new class that managed it.

Modern business enterprise has appeared in all technologically advanced market economies. Comparable protests, even stronger ideological and political opposition, has not prevented its emergence and spread in western Europe and Japan. In recent years the same type of multiunit enterprises, using comparable administrative procedures and organizational structures, have come to dominate much the same type of industries as in the United States. In these industries a new managerial class has become responsible for coordinating current flows of goods and services and allocating resources for future production and distribution.

Notes and Questions

1. Notes

a. Managerial capitalism has most famously been described in the 1932 book *The Modern Corporation and Private Property* by law professor Adolf A. Berle[4] and economics professor Gardner C. Means. In corporate law scholarship, the paradigm of the large, publicly held corporation that is run by senior managers, is often called the *Berle and Means type of corporation*. Although many who have not read the book assume that Berle and Means were supportive of the separation of ownership from

---

4. Pronounced "burly."

control, in fact, they were quite critical of it. The premise they started from was the traditional property idea that an owner had (nearly) absolute power over the thing owned. Far from being the forward-looking analysis many assume it to be, *The Modern Corporation and Private Property* is a reactionary work that decries the loss of property owners' powers.

Much current corporate law scholarship challenges the normative suggestions of the traditional interpretation of Berle and Means. We will explore the traditional interpretation and its critiques in some detail in Chapter 10.

2. Reality Check

a. What are the three categories of capitalism Chandler describes?

b. Why and how did managerial capitalism become dominant?

c. Why did labor unions not develop more control over the management of large businesses?

d. Why has the federal government not asserted more control over the management of large businesses?

3. What Do You Think?

a. Why did managerial capitalism become so dominant when large businesses were generally looked upon with suspicion by more Americans?

b. Is managerial capitalism a good thing? Is it better than family capitalism or financial capitalism?

c. Should organized labor or the federal government exert more control over the management of large corporations? If so, how would that control be effected?

C. FORM FOLLOWS FUNCTION — ENTITIES FOR BUSINESSES

1. The Current Setting — From Partnerships to Corporations

A concomitant to the growth of businesses was the development of appropriate legal entities, or forms, to own those businesses. Chandler and Margaret Blair sketch the shift from the partnership to the corporation as the dominant legal entity for businesses.

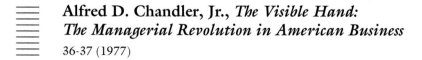

Alfred D. Chandler, Jr., *The Visible Hand:*
The Managerial Revolution in American Business
36-37 (1977)

Until well after 1840 the partnership remained the standard legal form of the commercial enterprise. . . . The partnership, normally a family affair, consisted of two or three close associates. It was a contractual arrangement that was changed when a partner retired, died, or decided to go into another business or join another associate. A partnership was often set up for a single voyage or venture. And one man could be involved in several partnerships. The partnership was used by all types of business, from the small country storekeepers to the great merchant bankers who dominated the Anglo-American trade.

The most powerful business enterprises of the day were international interlocking partnerships. Thus, the Brown family was represented by Brown, Shipley & Company in Liverpool; Brown Brothers & Company in New York; Browns and Bowen in Philadelphia; and Alexander Brown & Sons in Baltimore. The name and makeup of all these interlocking partnerships changed constantly over time. Except in forming enterprises . . . requiring the pooling of [large amounts of] capital (namely banks, insurance, turnpike, and canal companies), American merchants did not yet feel the need for a legal form that could give an enterprise limited liability, the possibility of eternal life, or the ability to issue securities.

Use of the corporate form instead of the partnership was beneficial not only because large amounts of capital needed to be pooled, Margaret Blair details another aspect of the shift from partnerships to corporations.

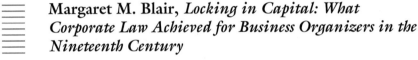

Margaret M. Blair, *Locking in Capital: What Corporate Law Achieved for Business Organizers in the Nineteenth Century*

51 UCLA L. Rev. 387, 389-394 (2003)

Why did the corporate form become the preferred way to organize large-scale business when it did? And what did the adoption of a corporate form accomplish for the organizers of business that could not have been accomplished through other nineteenth century legal forms? Business historians have hypothesized three possible explanations: the ability to amass large amounts of capital, limited liability, and the centralization of control. While these abilities were important in many situations, it was a fourth factor that turned out to be the critical advantage of the corporate form: the ability to commit capital, once amassed, for extended periods of time — for decades and even centuries. How exactly does organizing a business through a corporation facilitate these things, and why were they important?

The first way was that incorporation gave the enterprise "entity" status under the law, and the second was that incorporation required governance rules that legally separated business decisionmaking from contributions of financial capital.

Entity status for incorporated businesses meant that a chartered corporation was recognized as a distinct legal entity, separate from any of its investors or managers, for purposes of buying, selling, or holding property, of making contracts, and of suing and being sued. [T]he creation of a separate legal entity allows business organizers to partition the assets used in the business. Partitioning has two aspects: Individual participants in the business are not held personally responsible for the debts or liabilities of the business (this aspect is commonly referred to as "limited liability" in the context of business corporations), and participants and third parties are assured that the pool of assets used in the business will be available to meet the needs of the business first (such as, to pay the claims of the business's creditors) before these assets can be distributed to shareholders.

Perhaps as important as protecting the assets of the enterprise from participants' creditors, however, was the role that incorporation played in establishing a pool of assets that was not subject to being liquidated or dissolved by any of the individual participants who might want to recover their investment. This role extends also to the heirs of these participants, who might prefer to see the assets of the business liquidated rather than accept a pro rata claim on potential distributions from the business in the settlement of the estate of the deceased corporate participant. Such a protected pool of assets could therefore be committed more credibly to the enterprise for a substantial amount of time.

Which brings us to the second critical contribution of corporate law, as it evolved in the nineteenth century. Incorporating a firm created a governance mechanism which separated the role of contributing financial capital from the role of operating the business and making regular decisions about the use of assets in the business. [I]nitial investors . . . yield control over the business assets and activities to a board of directors that is legally independent of both shareholders and managers. [S]uch a yielding of legal control rights . . . became increasingly important in bringing together teams of managers who specialized in running the business, as well as in establishing long-term stable relationships with suppliers and customers.

By themselves, entity status and separate governance do not ensure the success of a business. But once the initial capital had been contributed by equity investors, entity status and separate governance helped keep that capital in the enterprise, and thereby helped the firm draw in other valuable resources. If the resources were successfully used, the firm could accumulate both organizational and reputational assets, as well as additional specialized physical assets. These tangible and intangible assets, in turn, further increased the pool of bonding assets in the firm, facilitating the continued use of specialized assets.

Notes and Questions

1. Notes

a. We will look at partnership law in much more detail in Chapter 17.

b. You may have noticed that we have not considered the limited liability company in any detail here. LLCs did not develop into important legal entities until the mid-1990s and so are omitted from this discussion. Chapter 18 explores the legal aspects of LLCs, and their origin and development, in more depth.

2. Reality Check

a. What benefits did incorporation provide that partnerships did not?

3. What Do You Think?

a. Which aspects of incorporation do you think were the most important to the business's owners? Which were most important to the business's creditors?

b. Do you think the United States was best served by permitting the separation of ownership from control and the limited liability of owners found in corporations?

c. Is either of these qualities (separation of ownership from control and limited liability of owners) necessary to facilitate the pooling of large amounts of capital?

2. Background and Context — A Vignette

This discussion of the advantages of incorporation has been quite abstract up until now. Blair provides an example of the consequences of incorporation in the following excerpt, the facts of which are drawn from Ruth Brandon, *A Capitalist Romance: Singer and the Sewing Machine* (1977).

≡ **Margaret M. Blair,** *Locking in Capital: What*
≡ *Corporate Law Achieved for Business Organizers in the*
≡ *Nineteenth Century*
51 UCLA L. Rev. 387, 442-447 (2003)

[T]he story of the rise of the Singer Sewing Machine Company provides an example in which the corporate form was used . . . to lock in existing capital, to provide a mechanism for settling any subsequent disputes among the leading participants in the firm, and ultimately to support the development of a massive marketing organization. The I.M. Singer & Company began in 1851, when Isaac Merritt Singer got his first patent on a machine that would make a continuous series of stitches.

Singer . . . took on [a] partner, . . . one who was his equal in shrewdness, and who could stand up to his bullying behavior. Edward Clark was a lawyer, and was granted a one-third share in the business in exchange for supplying legal services, especially in the ongoing patent battles. Clark and Singer became the only partners in I.M. Singer & Company.

During the next ten years, the market for sewing machines grew, slowly at first. Building a market for sewing machines was difficult because the machines represented a very substantial investment relative to typical levels of household wealth and income. Moreover the product was at first seen as something that had no purpose other than to save time for women, women were viewed as unlikely to be able to operate such a mechanical device, and in any case, "respectable" women would probably not choose to use a complex mechanical device. Moreover, the legal feuding among holders of various sewing machine patents became increasingly intense, costing I.M. Singer & Company most of their profits, and virtually all of Clark's time and energies during the years from 1851 to 1856. In the fall of that year, . . . [w]ith the patent wars settled, . . . Singer and Clark were rapidly becoming wealthy, and though still organized as a conventional partnership, were beginning to build a substantial manufacturing, distribution, and sales organization. Singer and Clark, though they didn't particularly like or trust each other, had managed to establish a reasonably successful working relationship.

[H]owever, Singer was thoroughly enjoying his new wealth, and was living an unusually flamboyant life. In 1860, a series of incidents brought public attention to the fact that Singer had domestic relationships with, and numerous children by, four different women, only one of whom he was legally married to. To escape the wrath of the woman with whom he had been living the longest and the most openly, who called herself Mrs. Isaac Singer, and with whom he had fathered eight children,

Singer fled to England. There he promptly became involved with a fifth woman, whom he eventually did marry once his divorce from his first wife was finalized.

Apart from the unseemliness and notoriety of this lifestyle (which might have had a negative impact on the ability of the firm to market Singer machines to "respectable" households) why did this matter to Clark? The problem, Clark could easily foresee, was that if the firm were still organized as a partnership at the point at which Singer died, the valuable business that the two of them had built over the previous years would be destroyed in the legal battles over claims to Singer's estate. Singer's heirs, however many of them there might be, would all have some legal claim to some share of the business, and it would probably require years of court battles to establish who was to get what. Clark feared that without liquidating much of the firm, he would not be able to come up with enough cash to prevent catastrophe by buying out . . . the heirs.

Clark realized that the solution to this problem was to incorporate the business and to ease Singer out of active management. [O]nce incorporated, the business assets would no longer be the joint property of Clark and Singer, but would belong to the corporation. Equity shares would be issued to Clark and Singer . . . [b]ut any . . . distribution would be at the discretion of a board of directors of the company, and could not be compelled by either former partner, nor by the executor of the estate, nor would it likely be compelled by any court of law handling the proceedings. Heirs could be given equity shares in the business out of Singer's estate without disturbing or breaking up the assets and governance structure of the business.

By this time, the company had no need to raise additional capital, as it was generating cash faster than it could reinvest it. Nor were there any particular concerns about limiting the liability of shareholders: The firm had little or no debt (except perhaps small amounts of trade credit from materials suppliers), and class action lawsuits for fingers injured by sewing machine thread guides and presser feet had not yet been invented. The only function that incorporation served was to ensure that the substantial organizational capital that had been accumulated by the firm could not be torn apart, nor could its reputation be easily destroyed, as a result of the messy personal affairs of one of the partners.

According to Singer's biographer, it took three more years for Clark to get Singer to agree to incorporation of the business, but in August of 1863, I.M. Singer & Company was dissolved, and the business was reorganized as the Singer Manufacturing Company. Within four years after incorporation, it had established manufacturing and sales operations overseas, becoming the first American firm to produce and market extensively in Europe. According to Chandler, Singer was also the first manufacturing company to establish a sales force of its own salaried employees, rather than relying on sales agents. The Singer organization that developed in the 1860s and 1870s included retail branch offices in virtually every community in the United States of at least 5,000 in population (as well as in many communities in Europe and South America).

Notes and Questions

1. Reality Check

a. What benefit of incorporation was most important to Mr. Clark? Why were the other benefits less important?

3. Which State's Law? — The Rise of Delaware

The fact that a business incorporates says nothing about the state in which it incorporates. Chapter 5, on the incorporation process, explains that a business can incorporate in any state, even one in which it has no other connection. By doing so, the business's internal governance matters will be regulated by the law of the state of incorporation, regardless of where the corporation does business. Most small corporations choose to be incorporated in the state in which they will do business, but many businesses choose other states. As the following excerpt shows, there has often been an active competition among the states to attract new incorporations.

William E. Kirk, III, *A Case Study in Legislative Opportunism: How Delaware Used the Federal-State System to Attain Corporate Pre-Eminence*
10 J. Corp. L. 233, 247-258 (1984)

[In the 1870s] New Jersey experienced increasing financial difficulties, due in large part to the tax-exempt status of much property held by her railroads. By 1884, . . . a franchise tax was levied upon all the corporations chartered in the state, a tax which had the sole aim of generating revenue.

Soon after the imposition of the new taxes a young New York corporation lawyer named James B. Dill came to New Jersey with a plan. His plan had been rejected in New York, possibly because that state's financial straits were not as dire as her neighbor's. Dill proposed that the state "liberalize" its general corporation laws (i.e., make them attractive to management), and form a corporation to advertise this fact in the business community. When corporations were attracted by the friendly climate, the resulting increase in franchise tax revenues would alleviate the state's financial difficulties.

Dill's plan received the backing of the Democratic governor and legislature. In 1894, New Jersey elected a Republican governor and legislature for the first time in thirty years. Partisan politics notwithstanding, the new administration gave its blessing to Dill's plan. A commission was appointed to further liberalize the laws, and the resulting corporation act of 1896 (largely Dill's work) was a landmark among corporate statutes.

The success of Dill's plan may . . . be seen by examining the numbers of corporations obtaining charters in New Jersey. In 1889, . . . the year after the first of the revolutionary Dill acts . . . New Jersey passed Ohio as the nation's leading incorporating state. In 1899, New Jersey gave charters to 2,186 corporations, including at least 61 with capitalization in excess of $10 million. These 61 corporations compared with only 60 of equal size in all other states together.

New Jersey had set out quite consciously to attract capital investment, and had done so by permitting management flexibility, coupled with light taxation. By 1894, it had been noted that New Jersey "now runs the state government very largely on revenues derived from New York enterprises."

In 1892, New York granted a special charter to General Electric Company, which included many of the most favorable provisions of the New Jersey general act. According to New York's Governor Flowers, the charter was granted because it "will keep within the state a corporation which, . . . without the concessions allowed by its proposed charter, would be incorporated under the laws of New Jersey."

Still other states joined New York in its belated strategy of imitation. One state, however, was successful in its imitation. [A] group was formed to implement a plan similar to Dill's, under which a liberal incorporation law would be drafted, and a corporation formed to solicit charters for the state [of Delaware]. An act was drafted, and it was piloted through the 1899 session of the General Assembly without a dissenting vote.

Even after the heavy borrowing from New Jersey law, Delaware had little competitive edge over her sister; that edge was supplied by Delaware's tax rates. Delaware's annual franchise taxes were set at half of New Jersey's, up to an authorized capital of $5 million; above that amount, Delaware's franchise taxes were set at sixty per cent of her neighbor's.

The results of Delaware's policy were not as immediate or spectacular as New Jersey's. Delaware's position improved steadily, however. In 1913, Delaware passed New Jersey, with 1,613 charters granted to 1,445. The benefits to Delaware were enormous. In 1899, filing fees and franchise taxes had provided the state with $36,000 of the total state revenues of $511,000. By 1916, $314,000 out of $945,000 had been derived from corporations, and by 1919, the figures were $1.2 million out of $3.5 million.

Part of the explanation for Delaware's early success lies in the willingness of its legislature to adopt new devices as they were thought of by counsel for management. For the rest of the explanation, the historian must look back to New Jersey. In New Jersey's gubernatorial election of 1910, [Woodrow] Wilson had raised the issue of antitrust, but he exercised little leadership in the field. . . . When he revived the issue as a candidate for President in 1912, . . . [President Theodore] Roosevelt pointed out that Wilson had done nothing as governor to reform New Jersey's notorious corporation laws. Wilson was elected, but his bitterness over this rebuke made him determined to pass an antitrust law while still governor; he did not become President until March, 1913.

Accordingly, he had legislation drafted, though he himself was uninterested in the details. The "Seven Sisters," as the bills were called, . . . passed in February 1913 with little serious opposition.

The effects were swift and drastic. Between 1912 and 1914, the number of annual incorporations fell from 1,900 to 1,280. The number of new corporations with over $1 million in authorized capital stock fell from 46 in 1912 to 10 in 1914. The total authorized capital stock of corporations chartered in 1912 was $428 million, and by 1914 the figure had fallen to $95 million.

By 1917, sentiment in the state ran against the acts, and in that year a special commission recommended their repeal. The repeal came too late, however. New Jersey had lost her competitive advantage, and Delaware remained the leader in the field.

Notes and Questions

1. Notes

a. Delaware currently receives about 20 percent of its total revenues from incorporation and franchise fees and taxes.

b. Delaware remains the leader in attracting out of state incorporations so-called *pseudo-domestic* incorporations. Nearly 90 percent of corporations that do not incorporate in their headquarters state incorporate in Delaware. Nevada is second in pseudo-domestic incorporations with about 8 percent.

2. Reality Check

a. Why would a state want firms to incorporate under its laws if the firm will conduct little or no actual business there?

b. Why were the states able to compete for business incorporations?

c. How did New Jersey become successful at attracting incorporations? Why did that success end?

d. How did Delaware become the most successful state in attracting incorporations?

3. What Do You Think?

a. Should states be able to compete for incorporations? If not, how should that competition be prevented?

4. Which Nation's Law? — Globalization and Corporation Law

The question of where a business will incorporate, and hence which jurisdiction's laws will govern its management, arises in the international setting as well as within the United States. Will the increasingly global and interconnected qualities of big business affect corporation law among or within countries? Below are two different views of the question.

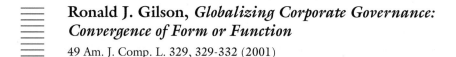

Ronald J. Gilson, *Globalizing Corporate Governance: Convergence of Form or Function*
49 Am. J. Comp. L. 329, 329-332 (2001)

Globalization has led to a remarkable resurgence in the study of comparative corporate governance. Some corporate governance systems, notably those of the United States and other Anglo-Saxon countries, are built on the foundation of a stock market-centered capital market. Other systems, like those of Germany and Japan, rest on a bank-centered capital market. Some systems are characterized by large groupings of related corporations, like the Japanese *keiretsu*, Korean *chaebol*, or European holding company structures. Still others are notable for concentrated family control of large businesses, including Canada, Italy and, notably, Germany. Management styles also differ across national systems. In the United States and France, managerial power is concentrated, by practice in the U.S. and with statutory support in France, in an imperial-style American chief executive officer or French *présidente directeur générale*.

The explosive decompression of trade barriers that gave rise to global competition also had an impact on academics. [C]omparative scholars began to treat institutional differences as having competitive consequences. Competition was not just between products, but also between governance systems. Michael Porter argued that the bank centered capital markets of Germany and Japan allowed executives to manage in the long run while U.S. managers invested myopically out of fear that, unless catered to by a sharp focus on quarter to quarter earnings growth, the stock market's fickleness would be enforced by the market for corporate control. At the same time, other commentators extolled the American system because its openness to external monitoring through a stock market-centered capital market allowed it to respond quickly to changes in the economic environment. Whichever side of the issue one took, the corporate governance debate came to turn on arguments about the link between particular national governance institutions and competitiveness: Is this institution efficient?

From this point, it was no great leap to predictions of convergence: The force of competition would lead national systems to adopt a single efficient form. To be sure, the form on which systems would converge differed depending on which national system appeared most successful at the time of the prediction. Before the bursting of the Japanese "bubble economy," the main bank system represented the future; this array of complementary governance institutions was necessary to support lean manufacturing, the emerging standard of efficient production. Not long thereafter, the Japanese bubble burst and the American economy boomed . . . due to its rapid response to global competition, stock market-centered capital market, and the external monitoring to which stock markets are complementary. The American system then became the apparent end point of corporate governance evolution, a consensus that appears clearly from the IMF and the World Bank's response to the 1997-1998 East Asian financial crisis. In addition to these agencies' traditional emphasis on macroeconomic matters . . . , countries accepting financial assistance also had to commit to fundamental reform of their corporate governance system, in the direction of the American model.

These predictions of governance convergence had a more serious problem than the conflict in their prophecies. National governance systems turned out to be more adaptive . . . , and therefore more persistent . . . , than the prophets of convergence expected. For example, it was thought that Japanese lean production, supported both by employees rendered cooperative and inventive by lifetime employment, and by close, long-term ties to suppliers, could not be matched without dramatic changes in U.S. governance institutions. In fact, American manufacturers adopted lean production, but adapted lean production to fit their governance institutions, rather than adapting their institutions to lean production. The American system's functional adaptivity proved to be greater than expected, leaving institutional form largely intact. Thus, the debate over convergence is not quite joined. Are we expecting a formal convergence of legal rules, . . . or merely functional convergence . . . ?

≡ **Douglas M. Branson,** *The Very Uncertain Prospect of*
≡ *"Global" Convergence in Corporate Governance*
≡ 34 Cornell Intl. L.J. 321, 323-326 (2001)

Today the academy has become much enamored with the notion of "global" convergence in corporate governance. That is to say, in the opinion of a number of the élites in the United States corporate law academy, the governance structure and practices of larger corporations all over the world soon will take on a resemblance one to another. The telecommunications revolution, the ease of international jet travel, and pressure from law makers, stock exchanges, pension funds, and others, combine to motivate and enable those who control larger corporations to become conversant with corporate governance structures and practices. Those who control large corporations feel considerable pressure to adopt the best of such practices and structures gleaned from a global inventory.

Assuming that such a convergence is taking place, the further question is toward what point are those global corporate governance vectors converging? According to United States scholars writing on the subject, with little dissent, the agreement is that the convergence will be on a set of governance parameters that will replicate the American model of corporate governance. Increasingly, corporate directors are familiar with governance developments in other nations. But it is a limited phenomenon. There is no massive "global" convergence in corporate governance. At best the evidence is of some incomplete transatlantic convergence with an outlier here and there.

In other cultures and economies great resentment exists toward United States economic imperialism and Americanocentric notions of the United States as the universal nation that, as unstated premises, underlie much of the global convergence scholarship.

Convergence advocates posit convergence based upon their study of capitalism in the United States, the United Kingdom, Germany and perhaps Japan. They ignore most of the world's remaining 6 billion people, the largest nations on earth (the People's Republic of China, India, Indonesia), and the culture beneath law and economic systems that is as or more important than law or capitalism itself. Cultural diversity militates against convergence.

A rich literature, ignored by the global convergence advocates, exists on capitalism in contrasting cultures. While most (but not all) nation states may now be said to have a capitalistic economic system, comparisons to United States and U.K. style capitalism are inapt. Worldwide the prevailing form of capitalism is said to be an "embedded capitalism" that serves and is integrated into the social order rather than the stand alone, highly individualistic Reagan-Thatcher style of capitalism that, for convergence advocates, constitutes the platonic form for capitalism everywhere. There are many cultures and many kinds of capitalism — family capitalism, managed capitalism, bamboo capitalism, crony capitalism, even the gangster capitalism of modern day Russia — and most of them may be ill-suited for United States style corporate governance.

Another worldwide phenomenon is backlash. . . . From France to Indonesia and from South Africa to Sweden there is a backlash against passing off United States culture, including its economic and legal culture, as universal ("one size fits all") culture that presents the obvious solution to national and regional problems. These powerful emerging forces of backlash militate against anything that could be said to be "global" convergence in corporate governance.

Perhaps the best argument against global convergence in corporate governance is its irrelevancy if, indeed, some convergence is taking place. The recent growth of huge multinationals is the most striking worldwide economic development of the late 1990s and the early 21st century. United States style and traditional forms of corporate governance simply are not responsive to the problems the growth of large multinationals portend. Worker exploitation, degradation of the environment, economic imperialism, regulatory arbitrage, and plantation production efforts by the growing stable of gargantuan multinationals, whose power exceeds that of most nation states, is far higher on the global agenda than is convergence in governance.

Notes and Questions

1. Notes

a. Many of the largest corporations in the world are incorporated in the United States. According to the FT Global 500 list, around 37 percent of the 500 largest corporations are American. Another 25 percent are incorporated in Europe, and 17 percent are incorporated in Asia.

2. Reality Check

a. What is corporate "convergence"?

3. What Do You Think?

a. Do you believe that the law that governs a corporation's management has an effect on the economics of the corporation? In other words, does a corporation's governance structure affect the places where the corporation does business?

b. Do you think corporate governance principles are likely to converge around a common model? If so, what will be the features of that model?

D. TERMS OF ART IN THIS CHAPTER

A business	Family capitalism	Middle manager
Berle and Means type of corporation	Financial capitalism	Pseudo-domestic corporation
Convergence	Horizontal integration	Vertical integration
	Managerial capitalism	

3

Economics

In this chapter you will get an explanation of the economic concepts necessary to be a corporate lawyer. We will treat these concepts under four headings. First, we'll explore the idea of "risk." Then we will look at the question of how one places a value on an economic opportunity. Valuation is probably the most central economic concept in a corporate lawyer's professional life. Third, we will take apart the basic economic assumption that humans, and the business entities they control, make business decisions in an objectively rational way. The final section in this chapter looks at the conventional way in which the financial performance of a business is reported. That is to say, the final section deals with accounting.

A. RISK

Four statements form the core of this discussion:

What you expect to happen might not happen.

There may be many possible alternatives and consequences to what you expect to happen.

The range of consequences among the alternatives may be large or small.

The number of alternatives and the range of their consequences can sometimes be changed by present actions.

Future events are uncertain, but to paraphrase George Orwell, some events are more uncertain than others. This quality of uncertainty is a synonym for *risk*.[1] More specifically, some future events are nearly certain to occur, while others are nearly certain not to occur.

Many people associate the word *risk* with the possibility of a worse-than-expected outcome. But, in most instances uncertainty also includes the possibility of

---

1. Some economists distinguish "risk" from "uncertainty." Risk, in this view, means that the likelihood of the possible uncertainties can be quantified, while uncertainty means it cannot. This distinction is not universal among economists.

a better-than-expected outcome. If you bet on number 12 at the roulette table, the risk — chance of getting something different — of the ball landing on a different number is quite high. In that case, of course, you lose your money. But the ball might, indeed, land on number 12, giving you a better-than-expected result.[2] In reality, risk means the chance that something *different* than expected will happen. **What you expect to happen might not happen.**

Furthermore, some future events have one alternative possibility while others have lots of alternative possibilities. For instance, on the next spin of a roulette wheel the ball could end up in any one of 38 pockets. But the consequence of 37 of those outcomes is the same: you lose. These 38 alternatives really represent only two possible consequences. The consequences of most alternatives, though, are more varied. Suppose your cousin hits you up for a $2,000 loan to buy a new car. The two of you agree on the interest ($100) and repayment date (one year). Your cousin might repay you:

> In full and on time
> In full and late
> In full and early
> Less than agreed upon and on time
> More than agreed upon[3] and on time
> Less than agreed upon and late
> Less than agreed upon and early
> More than agreed upon and late
> More than agreed upon and early

And, of course, your cousin might not repay you at all, ever. Unlike the roulette table, each of these alternatives has a different economic, and possibly social, consequence. **There may be many possible alternatives and consequences to what you expect to happen.**

Three points are worth exploring here. First and most important, measuring how much the outcomes deviate from our *agreement* may be different from measuring how much the outcomes deviate from our *expectation*. As in the roulette bet, our hope may be different from our realistic expectation. We certainly want to know how much the outcome is likely to vary from our agreement for purposes of ethics and possibly for purposes of litigation. Economically, it is far more important to know how much the outcome is likely to vary from our realistic expectation.

If you were being thoroughly honest, you might assess the loan to your cousin like this: "This cousin is pretty much a deadbeat, but because the loan is from me, a family member, the likelihood of getting no payment ever is pretty slim. I'll almost certainly get paid late and quite probably less than I'm owed. There's an outside chance I'll get paid in full and on time. The possibility of getting paid early or getting paid more than we agreed is minuscule."

---

2. Note the tension between "hope" and "expectation." When you bet on a particular number in roulette, you *hope* it comes up; you *expect* that it won't.

3. Your relative might pay you more than agreed upon for at least two reasons. First, the extra money might be a way to say thank you, possibly but not necessarily with the idea that you could be induced to make more loans in the future. Also, extra payment might be recompense for paying late; a spontaneous "late fee."

Economists say you should quantify the likelihood of each outcome (i.e., each outcome's probability), which will total 100 percent, then multiply each probability by its economic result and add the products together. This is your *expected return* and is the point from which you really want to measure the possible alternatives and consequences. The analysis of the loan example might look like this:

Table 3-1

Outcome	Probability	x	Economic Result	=	Value
In full and on time	5%	×	$2,100	=	$105
In full and late	10%	×	$2,100[4]	=	$210
In full and early	1%	×	$2,100	=	$21
Less than agreed upon and on time	15%	×	$1,500	=	$225
More than agreed upon and on time	1%	×	$2,500	=	$25
Less than agreed upon and late	60%	×	$1,500	=	$900
Less than agreed upon and early	5%	×	$1,500	=	$75
More than agreed upon and late	1%	×	$2,500	=	$25
More than agreed upon and early	1%	×	$2,500	=	$25
Nothing ever	1%	×	$0	=	$0
Expected Return					**$1,611**

An economist would say your expected return is $1,611.[5]

A second point is that it isn't clear how much harm each possible outcome causes us. *In full and late* might not be any real harm to you if "late" means one day late or if the loan amount is inconsequential. On the other hand, a day late and a dollar short (to coin a phrase) might be disastrous if you need all the money back on time because, for example, you have a tuition bill due. Third, an alternative's likelihood and its potential harm (i.e., the degree to which the actual result was different from the expected result) are not related. **The range of consequences among the alternatives may be large or small.**

Let's look at the last of the assertions: that it may be possible to affect the number of alternative outcomes or the range of consequences among alternatives. If we reduce the number of possible alternatives or reduce the range of consequences among alternatives (or both), then the outcome we expect is more likely to happen

4. As we will see shortly, the value today of $2,100 to be received later will depend on how much later it is received. Money is more valuable the sooner it is received. For simplicity's sake, however, we'll treat the value today of $2,100 to be received either earlier or later than agreed upon as being $2,100 even though an earlier payment will be worth more and a later payment will be worth less.

5. Notice that you're being asked to shell out $2,000 now and your expected return is $1,611. This isn't a profitable transaction for you economically but, as we all know, it may be a transaction you'll enter into anyway. Don't say I didn't warn you.

or the consequence of something different happening is less likely to be different from the consequence of the expected outcome. That is, there's more certainty and, hence, less risk.

Let's try to detail some of the more common risks involved with investments such as loans or stock. The first, most obvious, risk is that the other side will not perform, either because of unwillingness or inability. This risk is sometimes called a *default* or *counterparty* risk. Another risk is *inflation* (or, less frequently, deflation) in which the buying-power of money received in the future is less.

The *tax laws* may change so the money received in the future may, after taxes, be different from what was anticipated. More generally, a *regulatory risk* may make an investment more uncertain. A government might impose unanticipated regulations, such as environmental regulations.

If the investment involves investing assets in another country, that country might change its rules regarding foreign investment. Thus, a country may change the terms under which foreign investors can withdraw money from the country. This is called a *foreign investment risk*. Furthermore, if the investment involves more than one currency, there is a *currency risk* that exchange rates may change, resulting in more or less home currency than was anticipated.

We can reduce the potential consequences of some risks by contracting for certain minimum returns. An investor might also take a security interest, sometimes called a lien or mortgage, to help ensure repayment. You might take a lien on your cousin's car that permits you to seize the car and sell it if your cousin doesn't repay you on time. We can also reduce risk by contracting for particular actions rather than for specific results. For example, you might require your cousin to deposit money in a savings account each month so that repayment in a year is more certain.

But these contracts are problematic in two ways. First, many investments are simply too complicated to permit meaningful contracting for particular actions. Conversely, they may be too simple to warrant such agreements.

Second, where the contract requires actions, the investor has to monitor whether the actions are, in fact, being performed. Effective monitoring may be difficult or impossible and is always an additional expense.

We can also contractually reduce uncertainty by allocating the consequences of differing outcomes among the parties. A lender, for example, would ordinarily bear the risk that inflation will be greater than anticipated. The parties could agree, however, that the interest will increase if inflation increases more than anticipated. This agreement does not eliminate the possibility that inflation will be greater than expected, but it changes the consequence of that event by moving the disadvantage from one party to the other.

Why would both parties agree to such a clause? First, one party may have deeper pockets, and thus the harm may be less for that party, making that party more willing to take on inflation risk. Another reason is that the parties have differing beliefs about the uncertainty. If one party believes that high inflation is very likely while the other believes the possibility of high inflation is quite remote, then the other party may put the risk of high inflation on the party who thinks such occurrence is remote.

Third, a party may take on a particular risk because the other party provides a sufficiently large inducement to do so. Finally, and relatedly, the parties may allocate risk simply because one party has more bargaining power or is a better negotiator. In such cases a party will take on risk in return for little or no compensation simply because the deal hinges upon such an allocation.

One final method to reduce the consequences of risk assumes the possibility of making more than one investment.[6] This method requires no separate contracting, no changing of the terms of any investment. It can also eliminate the consequences of uncertainties that can't be otherwise eliminated. All this method requires is the ability to make multiple investments.

Where an investor makes multiple investments (e.g., buys stock in more than one company) the expected return in toto is simply the proportionate amount of the expected return of each stock. By contrast, the investor's total risk (i.e., the likely range of variation from the expected return) may be significantly reduced (i.e., the range is narrowed) if each investment responds differently to a particular risk. The classic example is a company that makes air conditioners and another that makes room heaters. The economic success of each company is, to a large extent, dependent upon the weather. Hot years are good for the air conditioner company but bad for the room heater company; cold years have the opposite effect. An investor can eliminate the consequence of the uncertainty of hot and cold years by investing in both companies. This method, *diversification*, is the ultimate goal for many investors.

The trick is to make sure the investments truly react differently to the same uncertainty. An investor who invests in both the air conditioner company and a swimsuit company has not reduced the consequences of uncertainty in the weather; in fact, the consequences of that uncertainty have increased. So, the more ways in which investments differ, the more uncertainties become of less consequence.

An investor who invests in a dozen or so companies engaged in completely different businesses has eliminated the consequences of nearly every uncertainty except one: If all the companies are publicly traded in the United States, the investor still bears the consequences of the fact that the prices of publicly traded companies tend to move in the same direction. Thus, the investor still bears the risk of a larger-than-anticipated price movement of the market as a whole. The consequences of that uncertainty can be eliminated by diversifying among different kinds of investments — for example, stock of publicly traded companies, real estate, or collectibles.

To bring this discussion back to the business entities setting, your clients may often focus upon negotiating contract terms that are specifically directed to reducing the consequences of certain risks and to allocating other risks. For example, a contract may require one party or the other to obtain insurance coverage for certain events. Another contract may provide a sinking fund. Yet another may provide for splitting gains. They may also seek to invest in a variety of different businesses so that diversification leaves your client exposed to the consequences of fewer risks. **The number of alternatives and the range of their consequences can sometimes be changed by present actions.**

---

6. Not all investors are capable of making multiple investments. People who work, for example, are often not able to invest (i.e., work) for a large number of employers. Full-time employees might be able to moonlight one other job while those who work part-time (e.g., cleaning houses) may indeed be able to make multiple investments (i.e., work for several employers).

Notes and Questions

1. Notes

a. At least one other risk concerns investors. Some investments, such as publicly traded stock, can be more easily sold than others, such as a house. Stock in public companies is usually sold quite easily. By contrast, stock in a privately held company may not be readily transferred at all. This relative ease of transfer, called *liquidity*, is valuable in and of itself. The rise of eBay has increased the value of many objects simply by increasing their liquidity. However, an investment's liquidity may change in an unanticipated way, thus creating a *liquidity risk*.

b. In general, the expected return among investments varies according to their relative riskiness. That is, riskier investments usually have higher expected returns than less risky investments, other things being equal.

2. Reality Check

a. What is risk?
b. Can risk be categorized?
c. How can risk be reduced?

B. VALUATION

We've been talking about making investments but haven't said anything about the price or the value of an investment. Let's start by understanding that *price* means the actual consideration for a particular investment. Price may be determined by active negotiation between the parties or it may be determined by reference to a market. If an asset is sold, then the parties have agreed upon a price. If there's no agreement on price, there's no transaction.

Value, by contrast, is the economic worth of an investment to an owner. Value means, then, the wealth an asset will likely produce for its owner. Furthermore, because value is dependent upon an asset's use, the same asset might have different values to different owners. For example, a small business located on property it owns in the middle of a block might have one value to someone who wants to run that sort of a business. It might, though, have a different, much higher, value to the business that owns the rest of the real estate on the block and that would very much like to redevelop the entire block.

Generally speaking, throughout this book we will encounter four uses, and hence four values, for assets. First is simply running the asset as a discrete business, as the current small business owner does above. This is sometimes called the asset's *going concern value*. Second is operating the asset in conjunction with other assets the investor already owns. As you saw in Chapter 2, this conjoined operation might produce more profits than operating the assets separately. We can value the asset, then, for its *synergy value*.

Third is a business comprising assets that would be worth more if operated separately. The asset's value in that case would be called a *break-up value*. Finally, assets have a value even when they're not operating. Typically this value is derived from the value of the components, which may be simply the value of the metal out of which the asset is made. This value is called the *salvage* or *scrap value*.

Different potential owners may place different values on the same asset depending upon such things as the use to which they intend to put the asset, the information each person has about the asset, and each person's assessment of that information.

1. Value as Discounted Cash Flow

If economic value is the amount of wealth an asset likely will create for its owner, how can we measure that? An asset generates wealth in two ways. It can produce something that can be sold for more than the total costs of production. This *net cash flow* is one form of wealth to the owner. Second, an asset might generate wealth if it appreciates in price.

One dynamic should be clear: We need to value the wealth to be generated over the entire time the owner intends to own the asset. So first we need to determine for each time period (probably year by year, but it could be any period) how much net cash the asset is likely to generate. Note that while revenues are likely to be relatively smooth, costs may be more variable. This variability arises because many assets require periodic large infusions of cash. So there will likely be periods in which the net cash drops significantly and then rebounds. An automotive analogy is apt. A car requires periodic maintenance, much of which is of modest cost. On occasion, however, a car requires quite expensive periodic maintenance.[7]

A second datum will be the length of time the asset will be owned. At the end of the ownership period, the asset will be disposed of for a price. Another datum is the likely sales price[8] of the asset at the end of the holding period.[9] This price is sometimes called the *terminal price*. Again a good example is an automobile. Some owners intend to own their cars for only a couple of years while others intend to own them for ten years or more. Relatedly, at the end of the holding period, we find that some cars actually get more valuable over the years, but most lose value either slowly or quickly.

So up to now we've determined[10] three things: net cash flows throughout the holding period, the holding period, and the terminal price. We're on the verge of calculating the asset's total wealth, and hence its value, but we need to take a detour.

a. "I'll Gladly Pay You Tuesday for a Hamburger Today" — The Time Value of Money

Why does Wimpy want to pay next Tuesday for a hamburger he receives today? Because he has no intention of paying at all; he's stealing the hamburger. For the hamburger seller, Wimpy is the classic embodiment of counterparty risk. If Wimpy

---

7. Note that this expense is different from unanticipated major expenses.

8. Note that we're concerned with the price we can get at the end of the holding period, not the asset's economic value. That is, we want to know what someone else is likely to pay us for the asset at the end of the holding period.

9. The highest price might simply be salvage value — indeed, we may have to pay to get rid of the asset — a negative price!

10. That is to say, guessed at.

is honorable, though, and economically rational, he still would prefer to pay next Tuesday for a hamburger he receives today. Here's why. He has three options:

1. Pay next Tuesday for a hamburger today
2. Pay today for a hamburger today
3. Pay next Tuesday for a hamburger next Tuesday

Wimpy will prefer to enjoy the hamburger today instead of next Tuesday because people generally prefer to consume in the present rather than in the future. This preference is in part a reflection of human nature, in part a reflection of the uncertainty as to whether one will be able to enjoy a hamburger next Tuesday, and in part a reflection of the expectation that one will be wealthier in the future so that a unit of consumption (e.g., the hamburger) will have less additional value in the future than it does now. So Wimpy will prefer either 1 or 2 to 3.

This pervasive human preference for current consumption means that those who want to borrow money need to offer an interest rate sufficiently high that people with money will lend it rather than spend it on their own current consumption. This inducement to postpone consumption means that each unit of money in the present is more valuable to its owner than the same unit of money in the future. Thus each unit of money in the present is worth the same unit *and interest* in the future. This phenomenon is known as the *time value of money.*

Wimpy can lend the hamburger's purchase price today to some third party, collect the loan and interest next Tuesday, pay his hamburger bill next Tuesday, and wallow in the left-over money (i.e., the interest) he has. To make the example concrete, suppose Wimpy buys a $10.00 hamburger today with payment due in one week and loans $10.00 to another person for one week. If interest rates for one-week loans are, say, 0.2 percent (which is around 10% per year), Wimpy will have $10.02 next Tuesday, leaving him $0.02 better off than if he had paid for his hamburger last Tuesday.

While one week's interest on the price of a hamburger is minimal, imagine that Wimpy purchased a house today with payment due in a year. Assume that Wimpy has $200,000. If Wimpy buys a house for $200,000 with payment due in one year and loans $200,000 to a third party for one year at 10 percent interest, he will pay for the house in one year and have an extra $20,000. So, Wimpy would prefer alternative 1 over alternative 2. That is, he'd gladly pay you Tuesday for a hamburger today. Note that one requirement in this setting is that the price of the hamburger or house not increase during the time between sale and payment. If the house seller sells to Wimpy today in return for payment next year at next year's house price, Wimpy may find that he owes more than $200,000 next year.

Wimpy may go even one step further. Wimpy can loan less than $200,000 today and be owed exactly $200,000 in one year. The trick is to figure out exactly how much less than $200,000 he needs to loan today to get $200,000 in one year. This turns out not to be much of a trick at all. Any spreadsheet can do the math. To have $200,000 in one year Wimpy must lend only $181,818.18 today at 10 percent. Wimpy will have the $200,000 he needs in one year to pay for his house and he still has $18,181.82 to use today.

Economically, of course, it is to Wimpy's benefit to take this second approach, because the extra money can be consumed now or used in a chain of transactions. For instance, if Wimpy buys a house, he can also buy a new car for $20,000 due in one year, loan $18,181.82 today at 10 percent for one year, and have a house *and a car*, fully paid for, in one year. Wimpy could get a hamburger *and fries*.

b. Discounting to Present Value

This process of figuring out how much money one needs to loan today to receive a given amount at a certain time in the future is called *discounting to present value*. To return to the question of how to value the wealth likely to be generated by an asset, the answer is that we have to take the likely net cash flows for each period between now and the end of the holding period and the likely sales price of the asset at the end of that period and discount each amount to present value. Then we can add those amounts together to arrive at the total wealth the asset seems likely to generate during the period we intend to own it. If we subtract the cost of the asset from its present value, we get the *net present value*.

If an asset's net present value is negative, it doesn't make economic sense to purchase it. Just because the net present value is positive, though, doesn't mean we should buy it. You and your clients need to make two further assessments. Each of these consumes a large part of client (and often lawyer) time, so you should understand that you will discuss these things fairly often with clients. First is the question of whether the price can be lowered through negotiating. If so, the net present value will become greater. Second, an investment decision is actually comparative. Your client needs to compare one investment to others currently available. Using the net present value technique, investments in very different kinds of businesses can be readily compared.

We've seen that determining the net cash flows, holding period, and sales price at the end of the holding period are all subject to significant conjecture. The amounts become more conjectural the further out in time the projections go. Here's one more element of conjecture: the interest rate, which we'll call the *discount rate* because we're computing backward in time. We've talked about one component of the interest rate, the preference for current consumption over future consumption. Here are two more. First, interest is, in part, simply a function of the supply and demand for money. Second, remember that "what you expect to happen might not happen." Another component of interest is compensation for lenders assuming the uncertainty of repayment.

How on earth are you or your client supposed to take these components and come up with a discount rate? Fortunately, this is one case in which the market works relatively well. The worldwide market for money provides a ready-made set of interest rates we can adapt. The Web shows interest rates for a variety of standardized loans. These loans differ from one another in three important ways: amount (larger loans usually incur higher interest because of the difficulty in putting together such a large sum and because the lender is more exposed to the risk of default), maturity (interest rates usually increase with maturity), and type of borrower (government, corporation, individual).

As a first approximation, you determine a discount rate by looking at comparable loans. Then you adjust the rate in light of the degree to which the contemplated investment presents, in your view, more or less overall uncertainty than the comparable loan. It's partly a matter of reasoning and largely a matter of judgment.

c. An Example

Let's now use an example of these elements and look at a possible acquisition by your client of an apartment house.[11] We know we need to make assumptions about three aspects of this asset. First, your client has told you that he or she intends to retain the building for ten years. Second, your client, based upon representations by the seller, believes the following:

> The building has 100 apartments.
> It is nearly always fully rented.
> The apartments average $1,000 per month in rent.
> The annual maintenance costs are $100,000.[12]
> Insurance is $75,000 per year.
> Property taxes are $25,000 per year.

Based on these assumptions, you and your client conclude that the apartment building currently generates $1,000,000 per year in net cash. To simplify this example, let's assume that you and your client believe that these numbers are not likely to change over the course of the next ten years except for inflation, which you expect to be 3 percent per year. The expected net cash flow each year from the present until the end of the anticipated holding period is as follows:

Table 3-2

	Expected Net Cash
This Year	$1,000,000.00
Year 2	$1,030,000.00
Year 3	$1,060,900.00
Year 4	$1,092,727.00
Year 5	$1,125,508.81
Year 6	$1,159,274.07
Year 7	$1,194,052.30
Year 8	$1,229,873.87
Year 9	$1,266,770.08
Year 10	$1,304,773.18

---

11. This apartment house opportunity will recur throughout this chapter, so you might as well pay attention.

12. These costs include utilities; a free apartment for the building manager; lost rent while vacant apartments are prepared for new tenants; frequently incurred maintenance, such as vacuuming the common areas and minor repairs to the apartments; and infrequently incurred maintenance, such as a new roof every ten years and exterior painting every three years. Note that the costs of large but infrequent maintenance items are taken into consideration each year by putting a portion of those expenses aside each year. This makes such funds available when needed and smoothes out the anticipated cash flow.

Next, you and your client need to determine a discount rate. You look up the interest rates for ten-year mortgages[13] and see that the rates run around 7 percent. Your client believes that the operation of the apartment house is subject to more risks than a home mortgage to an individual would be. Thus you and your client come to the conclusion that an appropriate discount rate is 12 percent per year.

With expected net cash flows and a discount rate you can now discount each cash flow to its present value. Another way to think about this process is to ask: What amount do I need to invest at 12 percent today to get $1,000,000 this year, $1,030,000 next year, and $1,060,900 the year after that . . . ? The answers are given in Table 3-3:

Table 3-3

	Present Value
This Year	$1,000,000.00
Year 2	$919,642.86
Year 3	$845,742.98
Year 4	$777,781.49
Year 5	$715,281.20
Year 6	$657,803.24
Year 7	$604,944.06
Year 8	$556,332.48
Year 9	$511,627.19
Year 10	$470,514.29
Total	**$7,059,669.79**

Adding the discounted cash flows together, we get $7,059,669.79 as the present value of the expected net rental payments for the next ten years.

Now we need to estimate the likely price of the apartment building when we sell it in ten years and discount that price to present value. Guessing that the building will continue to produce the same net cash flows after we sell it, we estimate that the economic value of the building ten years from now will be about $10.8 million.[14] We'll also assume that $10.8 million will be the sales price. Discounting $10.8 million to present value gives $3,477,310.96. Finally, we add the discounted cash flows and the discounted value of the price when we dispose of the building in ten years and get $10,536,980.75 as the present value of the apartment building.

Then you and your client will need to decide what price the seller would likely accept; subtract that price and transaction costs, such as your professional fee, from the present value; and arrive at the net present value. Finally, your client will need to decide whether this investment represents the best investment for him or her in light of each other possible alternative investment. Then you two can break for lunch.

---

13. Which seems a more appropriate analogue than an investment in government debt or corporate debt because mortgages on houses involve at least some of the same risks as a loan on an apartment building.

14. The question to ask is: What amount of money will I need to invest at 12 percent interest to generate $1,304,773.18 per year? The answer is $10,873,109.83.

Notes and Questions

1. Notes

a. You can use a discounted cash flow analysis to find the present value of anything that will generate cash over time. For example, you could figure out the present value of your legal career.

b. We need to think about value more broadly for just a moment. We've implied that an asset's desirability (i.e., its allure to a potential owner) is a function of its economic value. What we're leaving out is that some assets may be desirable to some owners because of additional, noneconomic qualities. For example, it is not uncommon to see a very rich person purchase a major sports team. Quite often the price distinctly exceeds the value, yet often there is no lack of interested buyers.

The reason is that ownership of such an asset generates more than economic value. The owner benefits (in a subjective if not objective sense) by becoming a local celebrity, from socializing with the players, and in other ways. Economists refer to the complete benefits an asset provides to its owner as the asset's *utility*. The noneconomic aspects of an asset's utility are often central to the decision to buy or sell and to other decisions regarding the asset's operation.

2. Reality Check

a. What are the four kinds of uses to which capital assets can be put?

b. When is market price likely to approximate economic value?

c. Why do people prefer to consume things now? How does this propensity affect the process of valuing assets?

d. What is the time value of money?

e. How do you determine the value today of future money?

f. What is net present value, and how is it different from discounted cash flow?

3. Suppose

a. Suppose your school were selling its law school. How would you determine its value?

2. A Practical Illustration

Discounted cash flow (DCF) is the standard approach to valuing a capital asset, but it is not the only approach in frequent use. The Delaware Court of Chancery details other valuation methods.

> The following valuation approaches have been routinely utilized by this court . . . : (1) the DCF approach; (2) the comparable company approach; and (3) the comparable transactions approach. The DCF approach "involves projecting operating cash flows for a determined period, setting a terminal value at the end of the projected period, and then discounting those values at a set rate to determine the net present value of a company's shares." "The comparable compan[y] method of valuation determines the equity value of the company by: (1) identifying comparable publicly traded companies; (2) deriving appropriate valuation multiples [i.e. ratios] from the comparable companies; (3) adjusting those multiples to account for the differences from the company being valued and the comparables; and (4) applying those multiples to the revenues, earnings, or other values for the company being

valued." The comparable transactions approach involves finding similar transactions, quantifying those transactions through financial metrics, and applying those metrics to the company at issue in order to arrive at a value.

Despite the prevalence of the DCF approach . . . , the Delaware Supreme Court has clearly stated that "the ultimate selection of a valuation framework is within the Court of Chancery's discretion." "As this court has recognized, methods of valuation, including a discounted cash flow analysis, are only as good as the inputs to the model."

Dobler v. Montgomery Cellular Holding Co., Inc., 2004 WL 2271592 (Del. Ch.) (Lamb, V.C.) (citations omitted)

Where the asset is a publicly traded company, much of its value can be measured by its *market cap,* or *float,* which is the price per share multiplied by the number of shares outstanding. That measure does not capture the entire value of the public company, though. An additional component is the value of the right to control the company. A purchaser of an entire public company would pay the market cap and a *control premium* for the right to run the enterprise. Conversely, the market price per share is said to include a *minority discount* from the full value (i.e., float plus control premium) of the corporation.

The following case shows the practical problems that arise in valuing corporations. It also involves a control premium/minority discount aspect. At one point Vice Chancellor Lamb discusses something called EBITDA (pronounced with a long "e" and short "i"). That's an acronym for earnings before interest, taxes, depreciation, and amortization. It is a popular way to measure a company's profitability and is similar, but not identical, to the company's cash flow.

Doft & Co. v. Travelocity.com Inc.

2004 WL 1152338 (Del. Ch.)

LAMB, V.C.

[Sabre Holdings Corp. ("Sabre") owned 70% of the shares of Travelocity.com Inc., a Delaware corporation ("Travelocity"). In April 2002 Sabre paid $28 per share in cash for each of the Travelocity shares it did not already own.[*] In such a forced sale, corporate law gives shareholders the right to have their shares valued by the court and to receive "fair value" *instead of* the buyer's price. The court may find that "fair value" is higher or lower than the buyer's price and shareholders who have elected "fair value" are bound by the court's valuation. Sabre set its price with the assistance of Salomon Smith Barney ("Salomon"), an investment bank that prepared an analysis for Sabre of Travelocity's value. Doft & Co. is a Travelocity shareholder that has sued to obtain "fair value." The only issue is the value of Travelocity at the time Sabre bought out the other shareholders.]

Travelocity is in the business of providing online travel services. When Travelocity went public in 2000, the online travel industry was in nascent form and the future of the online travel industry was uncertain. By early 2001, the online travel

---

[*] Sabre was able to purchase those shares, even over the objections of the shareholders who owned them, through a merger. Mergers are explained in more detail in Chapter 16. For now, simply understand that the majority shareholder, Sabre, can force out the minority shareholders, though it must pay "fair value." *ED.*

industry was beginning to show profitability. By that time, Travelocity was the leading online travel agency.

The events of September 11, 2001, however, created great uncertainty in the online travel business. Even though the industry slowed in the period after September 11, analysts predicted that the negative effect would be temporary. Travelocity, however, also faced strong competition in the market at this time. Expedia, Travelocity's main competitor, surpassed Travelocity as the industry leader in early 2002. . . .

Additionally, airlines began reducing the traditional commissions paid to travel agencies for airline tickets in the mid-1990s. The airlines specifically targeted online travel agents in mid-2000 and began actively cutting commissions for online travel agents. In June 2001, in a further effort to reduce the commissions paid to online travel agencies, five major airlines created Orbitz to sell discounted airfares directly to online consumers. Orbitz had exclusive access to the discounted web fares offered by its owners and online travel agents were forced to renegotiate their relationships with major airlines in order to have access to web fares.

Even though Travelocity was facing tough competition from Expedia in the fourth quarter of 2001, analysts expressed the belief that the gap in performance was temporary and that Travelocity would continue to be competitive. In fact, Travelocity's performance in early 2002 was ahead of the management forecast.

The petitioners' trial expert was William H. Purcell. Purcell has a B.A. in Economics from Princeton University and an M.B.A. from New York University. He has been an investment banker for more than 35 years, 24 years of which are with Dillon, Read & Co. Inc. Over the span of his career, Purcell has worked on approximately 100 merger and acquisition related projects. He has performed numerous financial valuations of private and public companies in various industries. He also served as advisor to special committees of boards of directors in connection with corporate transactions. Purcell has testified many times as an expert regarding a wide range of investment banking matters, including a number of valuation issues. He has also testified as an expert before various regulatory agencies, including the Securities and Exchange Commission.

Travelocity's trial expert was Professor Paul A. Gompers of the Harvard Business School. Gompers has an A.B. in Biology from Harvard College, an M.Sc. in Economics from Oxford, and a Ph.D in Business Economics from Harvard University. He was an assistant professor of Finance and Business Policy at the Graduate School of Business at the University of Chicago for two years before joining the Harvard Business School faculty. He is also the Director of Research at the Harvard Business School and his research focuses on financial issues, valuation financing, and the markets related to young, growing technology companies. Although Gompers had never before testified as a trial expert, he had been retained 15 times as an expert in the area of finance and valuation of emerging technology companies in other legal matters.

Both experts used essentially the same methods to value Travelocity's stock; i.e., a discounted cash flow analysis ("DCF") and a comparable company analysis. Despite the similar approaches taken, the results arrived at by Gompers and Purcell vary widely. Gompers opines that, on a DCF basis, Travelocity common stock was worth between $11.38 and $21.29 per share. Using the same methodology, but using different inputs, Purcell opines that a share of Travelocity common stock was worth between $33.70 and $59.95 as of the Merger Date. The two experts' comparable company analyses also yield significantly divergent results because they disagree about the appropriate discount to apply to reflect Travelocity's competitive disadvantages.

DCF involves projecting operating cash flows for a determined period, setting a terminal value at the end of the projected period, and then discounting those values at a set rate to determine the net present value of a company's shares. It is an exercise in appraising the present value at a set date of the expected future cash flows earned by the company. A DCF analysis is a useful tool for valuing shares and is frequently relied on by this court in appraisal actions.

The utility of a DCF analysis, however, depends on the validity and reasonableness of the data relied upon. The problem in this case is that the most fundamental input used by the experts — the projections of future revenues, expenses and cash flows — were not shown to be reasonably reliable.

Delaware law clearly prefers valuations based on contemporaneously prepared management projections because management ordinarily has the best first-hand knowledge of a company's operations. Here, management prepared . . . 5-year projections for the period 2002-2005 and gave them to Sabre for use in its routine planning processes. In this case, however, the court is persuaded from a review of all the evidence that the Travelocity 5-year plan does not provide a reliable basis for forecasting future cash flows.

To begin with, Travelocity's management held the strong view that these projections should not be relied upon because the industry was so new and volatile that reliable projections were impossible. Punwani [Travelocity's CFO] . . . testified that because of the limited financial history of Travelocity, together with a rapidly evolving marketplace, it was difficult "to forecast the next quarter, let alone five years out." He also confirmed that the events of September 11 led to more doubt about the future of the industry and Travelocity's positioning in the market.

Although it was aware of the 5-year forecasts, Salomon did not conduct a DCF analysis of Travelocity as part of its work in connection with the merger. Purcell's DCF relies more or less uncritically on the Travelocity 5-year plan. Despite the normal preference for management projections, the court concludes that the petitioners failed to prove that Purcell's reliance on these projections was justified. Thus, the court must disregard Purcell's DCF analysis.

Gompers takes a different approach, after concluding that the 5-year projections were "merely meant as a rough plan and were considered to be optimistic targets" and not a reliable basis for a DCF analysis. Instead of eschewing a DCF analysis, however, Gompers sets about to create a new set of projections, covering periods of 10 and 15 years into the future, based on his expert analysis of Travelocity and post-merger discussions with certain members of its management. Gompers's exercise is strikingly at odds with the views of Travelocity management and Salomon that no one could reliably predict Travelocity's future cash flows.

The reliability of Gompers's projections is further undermined by the fact that he selectively picks and chooses variables from management's 5-year forecast that conveniently fit into his exercise in creating less "optimistic" projections. Although Gompers's valuation is facially more credible than Purcell's, in that he provides both the numerical calculations and the academic theories for his assumptions, his selective reliance on aspects of management's projections is suspect.

The only reasonable conclusion the court can draw from the record evidence is that no one, including Professor Gompers, is able to produce a reliable set of long-range projections for Travelocity, as of the Merger Date. This conclusion is substantially reinforced by the observation that Gompers's DCF produced values ranging from $11.38 to $21.29 relative to a . . . merger in which Travelocity's 70% parent agreed to pay $28 per share to acquire the minority interest.

For these reasons, the court reluctantly concludes that it cannot properly rely on either party's DCF valuation. The goal of the DCF method of valuation is to value future cash flows. Here, the record clearly shows that, in the absence of reasonably reliable contemporaneous projections, the degree of speculation and uncertainty characterizing the future prospects of Travelocity and the industry in which it operates make a DCF analysis of marginal utility as a valuation technique in this case. If no other method of analysis were available, the court would, reluctantly, undertake a DCF analysis and subject the outcome to an appropriately high level of skepticism. The court, however, now turns to the other method of valuation offered by the parties.

The comparable company approach entails the review of publicly traded competitors in the same industry, then the generation of relevant multiples* from public pricing data of the comparable companies and finally the application of those multiples to the subject company to arrive at a value. Both experts and Salomon use Expedia as the single comparable company in their analyses, but disagree on the appropriate discount to be applied to the multiples derived from their analyses of Expedia. The court agrees that Expedia is clearly comparable to Travelocity.

Gompers states that the discount to Expedia should be at least 40% and concludes that Travelocity's valuation as of the merger date is $22.08. Purcell states that a 10% discount to Expedia is appropriate and concludes that the value should be no less than $35 a share. Salomon applies a 20%-30% discount range to Expedia and concludes that the appropriate value is between $24 and $32 a share. The independent valuation performed by Salomon provides the court with a neutral framework from which to analyze Purcell and Gompers's divergent values. With all of these factors in mind, the court concludes that it should apply a 35% discount to the valuation multiples derived from the analysis of Expedia, to reflect the competitive obstacles Travelocity confronted as of the Merger Date. This decision reflects the court's view that Gompers is substantially correct, albeit unduly pessimistic, in his critical comparison of Travelocity to Expedia. Instead of relying on Gompers's assessment that a discount of at least 40% is warranted, the court adopts, instead, the mid-point of Gompers's 40% and the high end of Salomon's 20%-30% range.

Gompers and Purcell agree that [the ratio of] firm value to EBITDA is the most important valuation metric. Based on the expert reports . . . , the court isolates the 2002 [firm-value-to-]EBITDA multiple and the price-to-earnings multiple as the most important multiples in calculating Travelocity's firm value.

Discounting Expedia's [firm-value-to-]EBITDA multiple (34.8) by 35% produces an EBITDA multiple of 22.62 [for Travelocity]. Applying this multiple to

_____

* I.e., ratios. *ED.*

Travelocity's expected 2002 EBITDA of $47.80 million yields a value of $1,081,236,000. Discounting Expedia's [price-to-earnings] multiple (50.77) by 35% produces [a price-to-earnings] multiple of 33.00 [for Travelocity]. Applying this multiple to Travelocity's expected 2002 net earnings of $39.45 million yields a value of $1,301,850,000. The court gives ⅔ weight to the EBITDA calculation and ⅓ weight to the [price-to-earnings] calculation, yielding an enterprise value of $1,154,774,000. To determine the equity value, Gompers adds back the cash of $114 million and subtracts out the debt of $4.03 million. This leads to an equity valuation of $1,264,744,000, or $25.20 per share.

Delaware law recognizes that there is an inherent minority trading discount in a comparable company analysis because "the [valuation] method depends on . . . trading information for minority blocks of the comparable companies." Therefore, the court, in appraising the fair value of the equity, "must correct this minority trading discount by adding back a premium designed to correct it." Relying on recent precedents, the court will adjust the $25.20 per share value by adding a 30% control premium. This results in a per share value of $32.76.

Notes and Questions

1. Note

a. Vice Chancellor Lamb's finding that the fair value of Travelocity was $32.76 per share means that the fair value of the entire corporation in April 2002 was about $1.644 billion. Over the years, Travelocity did not compete well against Expedia and Orbitz, the other two large online travel sites. In January 2015, Sabre sold Travelocity to Expedia for $280 million, a decline of over 80 percent in Travelocity's value from the 2002 value. In February 2015, Expedia bought Orbitz for $1.34 billion.

2. Reality Check

a. Which valuation method did the court use? Why did it use that method?
b. How did the court arrive at a price of $32.76 per share?
c. How did Purcell and Gompers differ in their approach to valuing Travelocity? How were their approaches alike?
d. Did Vice Chancellor Lamb find one expert more credible than the other?
e. Which elements of a DCF analysis did Vice Chancellor Lamb find most problematic when applied to Travelocity? Do you agree?

3. What Do You Think?

a. Do you think the different values proposed by Purcell and Gompers were the result of genuinely held views of Travelocity's worth?
b. Which expert did you find more reliable? Why?
c. Do you think the parties could have generated better projections of Travelocity's future? If so, how?
d. Do you think the DCF approach is valid in the real world? If not, what alternative would you propose?

3. Background and Context: Options and How to Value Them

Children learn very early on that parents or caregivers can force them to do very few things. The alternatives to not doing something may be so unattractive that the child, in the end, chooses to comply with the parent's or caregiver's request, but the child almost always has a choice. This knowledge is reflected in young children's delight in saying "no."

So it is in the business world. Business people, especially if they have had formal business education, learn that many business settings can be described as a choice, hence they have the power to say "no." This insight turns out to be quite central to much of the planning that businesses undertake.

A latent example of this power is a business that has taken out a loan. The business has the power to default — to say "no" to repayment. The consequences of doing so may be unacceptably high to the business, but sometimes may not be. Another example is the contract principle of efficient breach. A business might, for economically rational reasons, repudiate or breach a contract. Economists and business people refer to these choices as *options*. Businesses use options in three main ways. First, they can be part of a business's plan to obtain money from investors: the corporation may grant options to invest in the company in the future in return for a current payment. These options are briefly described in Chapter 6.

Second, firms often obtain or grant options with third parties to reduce risk in their business. A prime example is a business that uses a commodity such as chocolate or coffee beans as a raw ingredient. One serious risk such businesses face is fluctuation in the supply and the price of that raw ingredient. To reduce this risk many businesses enter into option agreements with suppliers to provide fixed quantities of the needed commodity at fixed prices in the future. The business pays money to the supplier as consideration for the option, which increases the business's costs. However, that cost is more than offset by the reduction in risk; the business is more certain to be able to obtain the commodities it needs at prices it can predict. Options that are used to reduce business risk in this way are sometimes called *hedges*.

Third, a business might characterize relationships with others as options. These options are sometimes called *real options* to distinguish them from financial options and hedges. Two reasons to characterize relationships as options are to understand more clearly the choices the firm has and to quantify the value of those choices. Options are valuable because it's worth more to have a choice than not to have a choice, and modern finance theory gives methods to quantify and compare that value.

We will focus on real options. Real options can be categorized on several dimensions, but for our purposes it is sufficient to divide them into those that permit the business to do something (a *call option*) and those that permit the business to cease doing something (a *put option*).

Perhaps the most common, and certainly the most readily apprehended, real option is the option to invest now or later. Suppose the decision to purchase the apartment building does not need to be made now. The offeree, your client, has the power to invest now or to wait and see. Intuitively, that power is valuable, but how do you analyze it? This option to decide later is a call option. That is, the option, if exercised, gives your client the power to do something — own and operate the apartment building. Another example of a commonly encountered real option is the option to cease a particular business activity. For example, many large retail companies entered the Internet retail business in the late 1990s, usually to their regret. After they did so, each firm had the option to cease retailing on the Internet.[15] The choice to cease their Internet retailing business is a put option.

Many other business opportunities can be conceived of as options, but the next issue we need to explore is how to value an option. Ah, you may say, we've just finished learning how business folks value things: by looking at the present value of anticipated future cash flows. That must be what happens here.

No, it isn't. The reason why is that an option's value depends upon the value of the thing optioned (in option-talk called the *underlying*). In the apartment house example, our client's call option is the right to invest at a fixed price at any time between now and the option's expiration. But the apartment house's DCF is likely to vary during the option period. As events unfold, the underlying might become more or less valuable. Thus, our option to make the investment at a fixed price might become more or less valuable. Because an option's value is a function of the underlying's constantly changing value we can't use the DCF method to value options.

There are methods to value options, though. These methods are among the most esoteric topics in corporation finance, so we won't even begin to work through the theory. Here's what you need to know about option valuation. First, the further the option price is from the underlying's initial value, the higher the option's value because the chance of getting a good price is increased. So, the more the purchase price is below the apartment house's economic value, the more valuable the option is. Second, the more the underlying's value is likely to change (up or down or both) during the option period, the higher the option's value. This is because the more volatile the underlying's value, the more likely the option holder is to get a great deal at the time of exercise. Thus an option on the apartment house is less valuable than an option on a new restaurant, for example, because the apartment house is less likely to change in value than a new restaurant is. Third, an option is more valuable the longer its duration.

These considerations are the core of any option valuation technique. Two economists, Fisher Black and Myron Scholes, derived the first successful method of valuing financial options, and several other methods are now in use as well. Your business-savvy clients will frequently refer to the Black-Scholes formula when talking about options. You should nod knowingly and reply that although Black-Scholes is great, it can't be used on all real options, so the value needs to be approximated by a binomial method. They will then nod knowingly, and the two of you can get on with the rest of your day.

C. MAKING ECONOMIC DECISIONS

Understanding risk and valuation techniques is essential to assessing an economic decision. But those insights do not, by themselves, dictate the decision. We now

---

15. They also, of course, had the option to cease retailing in traditional fashion and continue to retail goods only through the Internet.

look at how economic decisions get made. This is of quite practical importance to corporate lawyers, because they are constantly involved in economic decisions either as participants or as observers. We start with the long-standing paradigm of economic rationality and then look at how that paradigm has changed.

1. Rational Self-Interest: The Classical Paradigm

The same basic assumptions about behavior are used in all applications of economic analysis. . . . The two key assumptions are rationality and self-interest. People are assumed to want to get as much for themselves as possible, and are assumed to be quite clever in figuring out how best to accomplish this aim.

The most prominent defense of the rational model was offered by Milton Friedman. He uses the analogy of an expert billiards player who doesn't know either physics or geometry, but makes shots as if he could make use of this knowledge. Basically, Friedman's position is that it doesn't matter if the assumptions [that people are self-interested and rational] are wrong if the theory still makes good predictions.

A defense in the same spirit as Friedman's is to admit that of course people . . . [are not always self-interested or rational], but the mistakes are not a problem in explaining aggregate behavior as long as they tend to cancel out. Unfortunately, this line of defense is . . . weak because many of the departures from rational choice that have been observed are systematic — the errors tend to be in the same direction. If most individuals tend to err in the same direction, then a theory which assumes that they are rational also makes mistakes in predicting their behavior.

Richard H. Thaler, *The Winner's Curse: Paradoxes and Anomalies of Economic Life* 2-3 (1992)*

2. The Myth of Rational Self-Interest: How Humans Actually Make Economic Decisions

Obviously, rational self-interest is a model that does not cover every economic decision. We now look at how real humans make real decisions. We look at self-interest first and then the idea of rationality.

a. Self-Interest

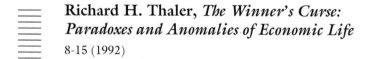

Richard H. Thaler, *The Winner's Curse: Paradoxes and Anomalies of Economic Life*
8-15 (1992)

A public good is one which has the following two properties: (1) once it is provided to one person, it is costless to provide to everyone else; (2) it is difficult to prevent someone who doesn't pay for the good from using it. The traditional example of a public good is national defense. Another example is public radio and television. [E]conomic theory [of rational self-interest] predicts that when confronted with public goods, people will "free ride." That is, even if they enjoy listening to public radio, they will not make a contribution because there is no (selfish) reason to do so.

The predictions derived from this assumption of rational selfishness are, however, violated in many familiar contexts. Public television in fact successfully raises enough money from viewers to continue to broadcast. The United Way and other charities receive contributions from many if not most citizens. Even when dining at a restaurant away from home in a place never likely to be visited again, most patrons tip the server. And people vote in presidential elections where the chance that a single vote will alter the outcome is vanishingly small.

One currently popular explanation of why we observe so much cooperation . . . invokes reciprocal altruism as the mechanism. This explanation . . . is based on the observation that people tend to reciprocate — kindness with kindness, cooperation with cooperation, hostility with hostility, and defection with defection. Thus, being a free rider may actually be a less fruitful strategy when the chooser takes account of the probable future response of others to his or her cooperation or defection. A cooperative act itself — or a reputation for being a cooperative person — may with high probability be reciprocated with cooperation, to the ultimate benefit of the cooperator.

There are other explanations of why people cooperate. . . . One is that people are motivated by "taking pleasure in others' pleasure." Termed pure altruism . . . , this motive has been eloquently stated by Adam Smith, in the *Theory of Moral Sentiments* (1759): "how selfish soever man may be supposed to be, there are evidently some principles in his nature, which interest him in the fate of others, and render their happiness necessary to him, though he derive nothing from it, except the pleasure of seeing it." While the pleasure involved in seeing it may be considered "selfish" (following the sophomoric argument that altruism is by definition impossible, because people do what they "want" to do), the passage captures the idea that people are motivated by positive payoffs for others as well as for themselves. Consequently, they may be motivated to produce such results through a cooperative act.

Another type of altruism that has been postulated to explain cooperation is that involved in the act of cooperating itself, as opposed to its results. "Doing the right (good, honorable, . . .) thing" is clearly a motive for many people. Sometimes termed impure altruism, it generally is described as satisfaction of conscience, or of noninstrumental ethical mandates.

Notes and Questions

1. Reality Check

a. What are the two assumptions underlying classic economic decision making?

b. Why does it make sense to use those assumptions if they're widely acknowledged to be, at best, artificial?

c. What are the varieties of altruism, and how do they differ?

2. Suppose

a. Imagine if your client were contemplating purchasing the apartment building, as discussed above. How would classical economics suggest that the actual purchase decision would be made? Would your client make the purchase?

3. What Do You Think?

a. Why are people altruistic?

b. Is altruism incompatible with economic well-being? If so, how should the tension between the two be resolved?

b. The Limits of Rationality

Economic rationality, in its classical understanding, posits that unlimited time is available for gathering information, that all information can be gathered, and that all information can be correctly assessed, which includes correctly calculating the probabilities of future events. These are assumptions that, of course, never obtain in the real world. Nonetheless, for reasons pointed out above, they have been used to define economic rationality and to measure whether a decision is economically rational. Beginning in the 1950s, a coherent theory of rationality emerged that does not require the artificial assumptions of the classic model. That theory is described here:

> [Herbert] Simon's vision of bounded rationality has two interlocking components: the limitations of the human mind, and the structure of the environments in which the mind operates. Because of the mind's limitations, humans "must use approximate methods to handle most tasks." These methods include recognition processes that largely obviate the need for further information . . . , heuristics that guide search and determine when it should end, and simple decision rules that make use of the information found.
>
> One form of bounded rationality is Simon's concept of satisficing— . . . a method for making a choice from . . . alternatives encountered sequentially when one does not know much about the possibilities ahead. . . . In such situations there may be no optimal solution for when to stop searching for further alternatives. . . . Satisficing takes the shortcut of setting an adjustable aspiration level and ending the search for alternatives as soon as one is encountered that exceeds the aspiration level. Satisficing . . . respects the limitations of human time and knowledge: it does not require finding out or guessing about all the options and consequences the future may hold. . . .

Gerd Gigerenzer, et al., *Simple Heuristics That Make Us Smart* 12-14 (1999)

i. Heuristics.   Heuristics are shortcuts, rules of thumb as it were, that people routinely employ in deciding how much information to get, how to analyze information, and how to decide. Heuristics are a fact of life, but whether they are good or bad in economic settings is subject to some debate. Gigerenzer, et al., see heuristics as fundamentally beneficial. Tversky and Kahneman take a different view.

> The term "heuristic" is of Greek origin, meaning "serving to find out or discover." [U]p until about 1970, "heuristic" referred to useful, even indispensable cognitive processes for solving problems that *cannot* be handled by logic and probability theory. After 1970, a second meaning emerged . . . : overused, mostly dispensable cognitive processes that people often misapply to situations where logic and probability theory *should* be applied instead.
>
> [W]e see heuristics as the way the human mind can take advantage of the structure of information in the environment to arrive at reasonable decisions, and so we focus on the ways and settings in which simple heuristics lead to accurate and useful inferences.

Gerd Gigerenzer, et al., *Simple Heuristics That Make Us Smart* 25-28 (1999)

Amos Tversky & Daniel Kahneman, *Judgment Under Uncertainty: Heuristics and Biases*
185 Science 1124-1131 (1974)[*]

[P]eople rely on a limited number of heuristic principles. In general these heuristics are quite useful, but sometimes they lead to severe and systematic errors. This article describes three heuristics [in bold face all capitals type]. . . . Biases [i.e. systematic errors] to which these heuristics lead are enumerated [in bold face uppercase and lowercase type]. . . .

REPRESENTATIVENESS

Many of the . . . questions with which people are concerned belong to one of the following types: What is the probability that object A belongs to class B? What is the probability that event A originates from process B? What is the probability that process B will generate event A? In answering such questions, people typically rely on the *representativeness* heuristic, . . . that is, by the degree to which A resembles B.

[C]onsider an individual who has been described by a former neighbor as follows: "Steve is very shy and withdrawn, invariably helpful, but with little interest in people, or in the world of reality. A meek and tidy soul, he has a need for order and structure, and a passion for detail." How do people assess the probability that Steve is engaged in a particular occupation from a list of possibilities (for example, farmer, salesman, airline pilot, librarian, or physician)? In the representativeness heuristic, the probability that Steve is a librarian, for example, is assessed by the degree to which he is representative of, or similar to, the stereotype of a librarian. This approach . . . leads to serious errors, because similarity, or representativeness, is not influenced by several factors that should affect judgments of probability.

Insensitivity to Prior Probability of Outcomes

[T]he fact that there are many more farmers than librarians in the population should enter into any reasonable estimate of the probability that Steve is a librarian rather than a farmer. [But if] people evaluate probability by representativeness . . . prior probabilities will be neglected.

Insensitivity to Sample Size

Consider the following question:

For a period of 1 year, each [of two] hospitals recorded the days on which more than 60 percent of the babies born were boys. Which hospital to you think recorded more such days?

The larger hospital
The smaller hospital
About the same

Most of the subjects judged the probability . . . to be the same in the small and in the large hospital. . . . [Statistically,] the expected number of days on which more than 60 percent of the babies are boys is much greater in the small hospital than in the large one, because a large sample is less likely [than a small sample] to stray from 50 percent.

Misconceptions of Chance

After observing a long run of red on the roulette wheel, for example, most people erroneously believe that black is now due, presumably because the occurrence of black will result in a more representative sequence than the occurrence of an additional red. Chance is commonly viewed as a self-correcting process in which a deviation in one direction induces a deviation in the opposite direction to restore the equilibrium. In fact, deviations are not "corrected" as a chance process unfolds, they are merely diluted.

The Illusion of Validity

[P]eople often predict . . . the outcome that is most representative. . . . The confidence they have in their prediction depends primarily on the degree of representativeness (that is, on the quality of the match between [item A and class B]). . . . The unwarranted confidence which is produced by a good fit . . . may be called the *illusion of validity*.

AVAILABILITY

There are situations in which people assess the frequency . . . or the probability of an event by the ease with which instances or occurrences can be brought to mind. For example, one may [predict] the risk of heart attack among middle-aged people by recalling such occurrences among one's acquaintances. This judgmental heuristic is called *availability*. Availability is a useful clue for assessing frequency or probability. . . . However, availability is affected by factors other than frequency and probability. Consequently, the reliance on availability leads to predictable biases. . . .

Biases Due to the Retrievability of Instances

[S]ubjects heard a list of well-known personalities of both sexes and were subsequently asked to judge whether the list contained more names of men than of women. Different lists were presented to different groups of subjects. In some of the lists the men were relatively more famous than the women, and in others the women were relatively more famous than the men. In each of the lists, the subjects erroneously judged that the class (sex) that had the more famous personalities was the more numerous.

In addition to familiarity, there are other factors, such as salience, which affect the retrievability of instances. For example, the impact of seeing a house burning . . . is probably greater than the impact of reading about a fire. . . . Furthermore, recent occurrences are likely to be relatively more available than earlier occurrences.

ADJUSTMENT AND ANCHORING

In many situations, people make estimates by starting from an initial value that is adjusted to yield the final answer. The initial value, or starting point, may be suggested by the formulation of the problem, or it may be the result of a partial computation. In either case, adjustments are typically insufficient. That is, different starting points yield different estimates, which are biased toward the initial values. We call this phenomenon *anchoring*.

Biases in the Evaluation of Conjunctive and Disjunctive Events

[P]eople tend to overestimate the probability of conjunctive events and to underestimate the probability of disjunctive events. These biases are readily explained as effects of anchoring. The stated probability of the [first] event . . . provides a natural starting point. . . . Since adjustment from the starting point is typically insufficient, the final estimates remain too close to the probabilities of the [first] events. . . .

The successful completion of an undertaking, such as the development of a new product, typically has a conjunctive character: for the undertaking to succeed, each of a series of events must occur. Even when each of these events is very likely, the overall probability of success can be quite low if the number of events is large. The general tendency to overestimate the probability of conjunctive events leads to unwarranted optimism in the evaluation of the likelihood that a plan will succeed or that a project will be completed on time.

Conversely, disjunctive structures are typically encountered in the evaluation of risks. A complex system, such as a nuclear reactor or a human body, will malfunction if any of its essential components fails. Even when the likelihood of failure in each component is slight, the probability of an overall failure can be high if many components are involved. Because of anchoring, people will tend to underestimate the probabilities of failure in complex systems. Thus the direction of the anchoring bias can sometimes be inferred from the structure of the event. The chain-like structure of conjunctions leads to overestimation, the funnel-like structure of disjunctions leads to underestimation.

Notes and Questions

1. Reality Check

a. What is bounded rationality, and how is it different from rationality as traditionally understood in economics?

b. What is satisficing?

c. What are heuristics? What are the three principal heuristics?

d. What are the benefits and potential pitfalls of each heuristic?

2. Suppose

a. Suppose your client, who is presented with the opportunity to buy the apartment house, will satisfice. How will he or she make the decision whether to buy the apartment house?

b. Suppose the same client will use heuristics to help in the decision-making process. How might heuristics affect the decision?

3. What Do You Think?

a. Do you think Simon's concept of bounded rationality is consistent with the way people make decisions?

b. Do you believe heuristics are useful decision-making tools that should be explicitly used? Or do you believe that heuristics are generally unhelpful in making decisions and should be consciously avoided?

c. Are heuristics rational?

c. The Affective Component of Economic Decision Making

Another component of making decisions is affective or emotional. We often think of our emotions as being discrete from, or even antithetical to, the intellectual or rational aspects of our selves. But we can segregate the facets of our personality only so far; at some point emotions combine with our rationality whether we want them to or not. Even further, a rather strong case can be made that we ought to welcome the emotional aspects of our selves when we make decisions.

> [I] wish to stress that avoidance or suppression of one's feelings is likely to impoverish one's ability to cope and solve problems. [M]ost interpersonal situations or chronic social transactions are best dealt with by being aware of our feelings. When we are aware of our emotions, we can seek support . . . or use our feelings as cues to help make a difficult decision vis-à-vis a relationship. Certainly . . . awareness of how we feel generally facilitates effective problem solving. I think intrinsic to acknowledging how we feel and seeing it as part of a complex interaction of ourselves with others means that we are using our feelings as valid cues to a problem to be solved. As a result, we have more complete information for use in generating solutions to problems.

Carolyn Saarni, *The Development of Emotional Competence* 96 (1999)

The subject of emotions is both broad and deep. For our purposes, the main point is that often economic decision making produces anxiety and stress. By assessing our possible actions in light of the emotions generated we can both shape our emotions and use them to make better decisions. Thus emotion and cognition are inextricably linked. The value of this link is heightened when you reflect that work-related, economic, and business decisions are often stress-producing, which frequently means that we are unable to cabin our emotions when resolving these decisions.

People who are good at integrating their emotional and cognitive sides when making decisions are said to be *emotionally competent*. Carolyn Saarni describes emotional competence in the next excerpt.

> Emotional competence entails resilience and self-efficacy (and self-efficacy includes acting in accord with one's sense of moral character). When we speak of resilience, we are talking about the capacity to recover after experiencing adversity. . . . Emotional self-efficacy means that . . . we are living in accord with our personal theory of emotion. . . .
>
> Perhaps this is the key issue for emotional self-efficacy: feeling relatively in control of our emotional experience from the standpoint of mastery, positive self-regard, and acknowledgment of our moral commitments. Such individuals do not feel overwhelmed by the enormity, intensity, or complexity of emotional experience nor do they react to emotional experience by inhibiting, distrusting, or "damping down and numbing it out." The capacity for self-efficacy probably entails some understanding of how one's personality interfaces with one's emotional experience.

Carolyn Saarni, *The Development of Emotional Competence* 2, 8, 218-219, 224, 226, 247-248, 278-279 (1999)

Being a businessperson or being a lawyer who advises businesspeople involves *coping* with a significant amount of stress. Noted psychologist Richard Lazarus describes coping, and Carolyn Saarni writes about coping effectively.

> Coping . . . consists of . . . efforts to manage specific external or internal demands (and conflicts between then) that are appraised as taxing or exceeding the resources of the person. Coping affects the emotion process in two ways:
>
> 1. Some coping processes change the actual relationship, as when an attack or aggressive display wards off or demolishes an enemy.
> 2. Other coping processes change only the way in which the relationship is *attended to* (e.g. a threat that one avoids perceiving or thinking about) or *interpreted* (e.g. a threat that is dealt with by denial or psychological distancing). Even though they do not change the actual relationship, they change its meaning, and therefore the emotional reaction. For example, if we successfully avoid thinking about a threat, the anxiety associated with it is postponed. And if we successfully deny that anything is wrong, there is no reason to experience the emotion appropriate to the particular threat or harm — say, anxiety, anger, guilt, shame, envy, or whatever.

Richard S. Lazarus, *Emotion and Adaptation* 112-113 (1991)

> How do we know when we have coped effectively and adaptively with some upsetting situation that faces us? The answer to this simple question is more complicated than we might at first assume. We have to look at least at three perspectives . . . : (1) whether the resolution that is worked out is mature and functional; (2) whether we can acknowledge our feelings to ourselves, even if they remain unexpressed or otherwise "managed"; and (3) whether we come away with a sense of mastery and resilience, even if the situation itself is not especially under our direct control. [I]t is likely that if our efforts at coping include acting as though our self is not involved, or that our feelings are irrelevant, or that the situation is utterly futile, then our coping attempts will be ineffective. In short, to discount any of these three aspects of coping will probably cause further problems at a later time.
>
> [A] flexible repertoire of coping strategies [includes] . . . active problem solving, . . . recruitment of social support (including gaining social approval), and . . . the capacity to tolerate intensity of aversive emotion. . . . Avoidance, denial, and dissociation appear to be less adaptive coping strategies [because they] short-circuit opportunities for learning or problem solving; they *restrict* one's options rather than expanding them.

Carolyn Saarni, *The Development of Emotional Competence* 2, 8, 218-219, 224, 226, 247-248, 278-279 (1999)

Notes and Questions

1. Reality Check

a. How do we experience and process emotions?
b. What is emotional competence, and why is it important?
c. What is coping, and what important function does it serve?

2. Suppose

a. If your client had the opportunity to purchase the apartment house, how would the ideas of emotion, emotional competence, and coping affect the decision-making process? How would those ideas affect your participation in the decision?

3. What Do You Think?

a. Are emotions antithetical to rationality?

b. Should decision makers strive to include or exclude emotion in making economic decisions?

d. *The Ethical Component of Economic Decision Making*

The final component of economic decision making is the ethical one. The following excerpt is from one of the most frequently cited articles on ethics in economic decision. It presents a very concrete explanation of an approach to making ethical economic decisions.

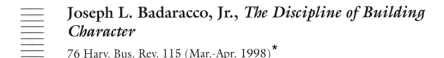

Joseph L. Badaracco, Jr., *The Discipline of Building Character*

76 Harv. Bus. Rev. 115 (Mar.-Apr. 1998)[*]

We have all experienced, at one time or another, situations in which our professional responsibilities unexpectedly come into conflict with our deepest values. A budget crisis forces us to dismiss a loyal, hardworking employee. Our daughter has a piano recital on the same afternoon that our biggest client is scheduled to visit our office. At these times, we are caught in a conflict between right and right. And no matter which option we choose, we feel like we've come up short. [T]hese decisions taken cumulatively over many years form the very basis of an individual's character. For that reason, I call them *defining moments.*

Such challenges rarely have a "correct" response. Rather, they are situations created by circumstance that ask us to step forward and, in the words of the American philosopher John Dewey, "form, reveal, and test" ourselves. We form our character in defining moments because we commit to irreversible courses of action that shape our personal and professional identities. We reveal something new about us to ourselves and others because defining moments uncover something that had been hidden or crystallize something that had been only partially known. And we test ourselves because we discover whether we will live up to our personal ideals or only pay them lip service.

As I have interviewed and studied business leaders, I have found that the ones who are most satisfied with the way they resolve their defining moments possess skills that are left off most job descriptions. Specifically, they are able to take time out from the chain of managerial tasks that consumes their time and undertake a process of probing self-inquiry — a process that is more often carried out on the run rather than in quiet seclusion. They are able to dig below the busy surface of their daily lives and refocus on their core values and principles. Once uncovered, those values and principles renew their sense of purpose at work and act as a springboard for shrewd, pragmatic, politically astute action. By repeating this process again and again throughout their work lives, these executives are able to craft an authentic and strong identity based on their own, rather than on someone else's, understanding of what is right. And in this way, they begin to make the transition from being a manager to becoming a leader.

DEFINING MOMENTS FOR INDIVIDUALS

The most basic type of defining moment demands that managers resolve an urgent issue of personal identity that has serious implications for their careers. Two "rights" present themselves, each one representing a plausible and usually attractive life choice. When caught in this bind, managers can begin by taking a step back and looking at the conflict not as a problem but as a natural tension between two valid perspectives. To flesh out this tension, we can ask, *What feelings and intuitions are coming into conflict in this situation?* As Aristotle discussed in his classic work *Ethics*, people's feelings can actually help them make sense of an issue, understand its basic dimensions, and indicate what the stakes really are. In other words, our feelings and intuitions are both a form of intelligence and a source of insight.

By framing defining moments in terms of our feelings and intuitions, we can remove the conflict from its business context and bring it to a more personal, and manageable, level. Then we can consider a second question to help resolve the conflict: *Which of the responsibilities and values that are in conflict are most deeply rooted in my life and in the communities I care about?* Tracing the roots of our values means understanding their origins and evolution over time. It involves an effort to understand which values and commitments really mean the most to us.

We have all seen managers who unthinkingly throw themselves into a deeply felt personal cause and suffer serious personal and career setbacks. As the Renaissance philosopher Niccolò Machiavelli and other ethical pragmatists remind us, idealism untempered by realism often does little to improve the world. Hence the next critical question becomes, *What combination of shrewdness and expediency, coupled with imagination and boldness, will help me implement my personal understanding of what is right?* This is, of course, a different question altogether from What should I do? It acknowledges that the business world is a bottom-line, rough-and-tumble arena where introspection alone won't get the job done. The process of looking inward must culminate in concrete action characterized by tenacity, persuasiveness, shrewdness, and self-confidence.

DEFINING MOMENTS FOR WORK GROUPS

As managers move up in an organization, defining moments become more difficult to resolve. [M]anagers must add another dimension: the values of their work group and their responsibilities to the people they manage. How, for example, should a manager respond to an employee who repeatedly shows up for work with the smell of alcohol on his breath? How should a manager respond to one employee who has made sexually suggestive remarks to another? In this type of defining moment, the problem and its resolution unfold not only as a personal drama within one's self but also as a drama among a group of people who work together. The issue becomes public and is important enough to define a group's future and shape its values.

Many managers suffer from a kind of ethical myopia, believing that their entire group views a situation through the same lens that they do. This way of thinking rarely succeeds in bringing people together to accomplish common goals. Differences in upbringing, religion, ethnicity, and education make it difficult for any two people to view a situation similarly — let alone an entire group of people. The ethical challenge for a manager is not to impose his or her understanding of what is right on the group but to understand how other members view the dilemma. The manager must ask, *What are the other strong, persuasive interpretations of the ethics of this situation?*

Identifying competing interpretations, of course, is only part of the battle. Managers also need to take a hard look at the organization in which they work and make a realistic assessment of whose interpretation will win out in the end. A number of factors can determine which interpretation will prevail: corporate goals and company policy, and the inevitable political jockeying and battling inside organizations. Therefore, managers need to ask themselves, *What point of view is most likely to win the contest of interpretations and influence the thinking and behavior of other people?*

Planning ahead is at the heart of managerial work. One needs to learn to spot problems before they blow up into crises. The same is true for defining moments in groups. They should be seen as part of a larger process that, like any other, needs to be managed. Effective managers put into place the conditions for the successful resolution of defining moments long before those moments actually present themselves. For in the words of William James, "The truth of an idea is not a stagnant property inherent in it. Truth happens to an idea. It becomes true, is made true by events. Its verity is in fact an event, a process." Managers can start creating the conditions for a particular interpretation to prevail by asking, *Have I orchestrated a process that can make my interpretation win in my group?*

One of the hallmarks of a defining moment is that there is a lot at stake for all the players in the drama. In this type of business setting, neither the most well-meaning intentions nor the best-designed process will get the job done. Managers must be ready to roll up their sleeves and dive into the organizational fray, putting to use appropriate and effective tactics that will make their vision a reality. They need to reflect on the question, *Am I just playing along or am I playing to win?*

DEFINING MOMENTS FOR EXECUTIVES

[T]he men and women charged with running entire companies sometimes face an even more complex type of defining moment. They are asked to make manifest their understanding of what is right on a large stage — one that can include labor unions, the media, shareholders, and many other company stakeholders. Consider the complexity of the dilemma faced by a CEO who has just received a report of package tampering in one of the company's over-the-counter medications. Or consider the position of an executive who needs to formulate a response to reports in the media that women and children are being treated unfairly in the company's foreign plant. These types of decisions force top-level managers to commit not just themselves or their work groups but their entire company to an irreversible course of action.

From a position of strength, leaders can bring forth their vision of what is right in a situation; from a position of weakness, leaders' actions are hollow and desperate. Also, before CEOs can step forth onto society's broad stage with a personal vision, they must make sure that their actions will not jeopardize the well-being of their companies, the jobs of employees, and the net income of shareholders. That means asking, *Have I done all I can to secure my position and the strength and stability of my organization?*

What makes this third type of defining moment so difficult is that executives are asked to form, reveal, and test not only themselves and their work groups but also their entire company and its role in society. That requires forging a plan of action that functions at three levels: the individual, the work group, and society at large. In which areas do we want to lead? In which areas do we want to follow? How should we interact with the government? With shareholders? Leaders must ask themselves, *Have I thought creatively, boldly, and imaginatively about my organization's role in society and its relationship to its stakeholders?*

To make their ethical visions a reality, top-level executives must assess their opponents and allies very carefully. What allies do I have inside and outside my company? Which parties will resist or fight my efforts? Have I underestimated their power and tactical skill or overestimated their ethical commitment? Whom will I alienate with my decision? Which parties will retaliate and how? These tactical concerns can be summed up in the question, *What combination of shrewdness, creativity, and tenacity will make my vision a reality?* Machiavelli put it more succinctly: "Should I play the lion or the fox?"

Notes and Questions

1. Reality Check

a. What are the three settings in which Badaracco sets his discussion?

b. How are the ethical considerations different in each of the three settings? How are they the same?

2. Suppose

a. Suppose you and your client were presented with the opportunity to purchase the apartment house. Would Badaracco's ethical approach affect the process or result of your decision making?

3. What Do You Think?

a. Do you think the ethical norms Badaracco describes are rooted in the ordinary notion of ethics? If not, where are they rooted? If so, are there competing notions of ethics that Badaracco does not consider?

b. Do you agree with William James that "The truth of an idea is not a stagnant property inherent in it. Truth happens to an idea. It becomes true, is made true by events. Its verity is in fact an event, a process"?

c. Is ethics the same as morals? If not, how are they different? If morals are different from ethics, is there a place for morality in economic decision making?

D. ACCOUNTING

Accounting is intellectually engaging because it requires both meticulous attention to detail and frequent exercise of judgment on theoretical matters. It can also be quite difficult. The practice of accountancy can be rewarding but also frustrating, because the profession typically does not have the social standing, influence, and cachet of other professions. We are going to ignore everything that is difficult about accounting and focus on accounting in a functional way almost exclusively.

The point of accounting is to provide information about the financial performance of a firm (or individual) over a period of time. Every firm needs to know how it has performed and many firms have accountants as full-time employees to provide that information. Many others outside the business, such as investors, potential investors, taxing authorities, and other regulatory agencies, use the recent financial performance of a firm to make important judgments, such as deciding to invest in or loan money to the firm, determining how much tax is owed, and determining whether the public is sufficiently protected from the possibility of the firm's bankruptcy. Because of the importance of accurate financial statements, many accountants work in accounting firms that provide accounting services to other businesses. Because they are independent and because they have demonstrated the requisite degree of skill (i.e., they are certified public accountants), these outside accountants are important actors in the business world. Their certification of a firm's financial position is relied upon both by the firm itself and by other constituencies with which the firm deals.

Independent accountants review the accounting records of their clients and prepare standardized reports, *accounting statements*, based on that review. The accounting firm certifies that the accounting statements fairly represent the financial position of the client business as of the date of the statements. We will not concern ourselves with the methods of reviewing a business's accounting records. Those methods are contained in the *Generally Accepted Auditing Standards* (GAAS).[16] Nor will we concern ourselves with the rules that tell accountants how to present the results of an audit. These are contained in *Generally Accepted Accounting Principles* (GAAP). Our focus is on interpreting those accounting statements. That is, assuming that the accounting statements have been competently and honestly prepared,[17] what can they tell us about a firm that might aid us professionally?

Incidentally, many law students assume that being able to interpret accounting statements is a skill only big firm lawyers need. In fact, this skill is actually one that new lawyers in a large law firm probably don't need. This is because clients of a big law firm will have staff accountants and so won't be relying on the law firm to provide any interpretation of its accounting statements. Furthermore, to the extent the client needs to discuss accounting matters with the law firm, the client is unlikely to consult junior lawyers. So new lawyers in big law firms probably do not need to understand accounting statements when they first enter practice.

---

16. Yes, it's pronounced "gas."

17. As you will see in Chapter 13, negligently or fraudulently prepared accounting statements can induce actions that can cause large-scale financial harm. There are sometimes ways to identify such accounting statements, but you can't learn them easily, so we won't even begin to discuss them here. You should be aware that some accountants, called *forensic accountants*, make a living investigating such accounting problems.

Other lawyers, by contrast, will be called upon to interpret accounting statements with considerable frequency. Obviously, if you're a corporate lawyer and not working in a big law firm, you will continually encounter financial statements. Clients and other lawyers in the firm will want you to interpret the statements to plan tax and investment strategies and to assess potential litigation. Even if you're not going to be a corporate lawyer, you'll need to know how to read financial statements. For example, in litigation involving a business, the financial statements can disclose much about past actions and about the business's likely ability to respond in damages. Estate-planning lawyers need to know how to interpret accounting statements so they can understand what their clients own. Lawyers engaged in family law frequently interpret financial statements to understand the financial position of a marital community.

Because we're looking at how accounting can tell us something about the economics of a firm, let's start by asking how one might describe the economic state of an economic entity — you, for example. You might describe your financial position in at least three different ways. These ways aren't meant to be mutually exclusive; after all they're describing the same underlying economic being. Rather, there are different ways of describing the economic state of an entity because the descriptions are useful for different purposes. Let's be more concrete.

One very palpable way to describe the financial you is to show someone around your home. You could point to *all the things you own* including the intangibles, such as a bank account or mutual fund. In fairness, of course, you'd have to point to all the things you *owe*, like a mortgage, car loan, and student loan. You'd also point to the pile of bills waiting to be paid — for things like cable TV and utilities. If you were extra scrupulous, you'd point out that similar bills for other things haven't come in yet this month, and so aren't in the pile of bills you're pointing to, but will certainly arrive soon. This is certainly an accurate way to describe your financial state. But it isn't the only way.

Another, perhaps more common, way to describe your financial state is to look at your *bank account*. More precisely, look not only at the balance today, which is something you pointed to when you were showing everything you owned, but at the balance over time, say the last year. If you looked only at the balance to see how it moved up and down,[18] you could certainly draw some conclusions about how much cash you got and how much you spent over the last year. But you could get more information by looking at what you spent money on. How much of what you spent went for ordinary living expenses like rent and utilities? How much went to pay obligations (both interest and principal) you incurred earlier, like the car payment and student loan payment? How much went for discretionary things like movies and trips to Vegas? Honestly, would your parents be proud?

When you spend money from your bank account by using a debit card or by writing a check, your bank records the person or business to whom you paid money. But you doubtless also withdraw cash from your checking account via an ATM to pay for many small things in cash. These withdrawals show up in your bank account only as a cash withdrawal. You might also buy things by credit card, which is reflected in your bank account only by the monthly payment to the credit card

---

18. Okay, mostly down.

company.[19] If we really want to know *how* you're spending your money, rather than simply *how much* you're spending, we'll keep track of what you buy for cash and look at those credit card purchases, as well as what you use your debit card and write checks for.

Just as we might care about what you spend your cash on, in addition to how much you spend, we might care about where you get your cash from in addition to how much you get. You may get cash from working. If you own a business, you may get cash as profit. You might get cash as a dividend from stock you own. If you're not economically independent, you get periodic cash from someone else such as parents, spouses, or other family members. You might get cash as a gift or as a lottery prize, an ad hoc windfall. You might also get cash by selling something you owned either because you no longer wanted the thing or because you were short on cash. Maybe you've borrowed cash from a bank or a credit card company (i.e., gotten a "cash advance" from the ATM).[20]

Under the bank account method, if you've borrowed something but that something isn't cash, we're not counting it, because it doesn't show up as a deposit in your bank account. So, the car you borrow from your in-laws to use while you're in law school isn't reflected in this method of describing the financial you. Likewise, if you swap something you own for something else, such as when you trade your kegerator to someone else in exchange for a desk, that transaction is not reflected in this method of describing the financial you. We're concerned here only with the do-re-mi.

This bank account method of describing the financial position of you is probably one you use quite frequently, even though you may intuit the information it provides rather than explicitly examine your bank account and credit card statements. Although it doesn't describe your financial state entirely, it has the virtue (vice?) of being pretty explicit. When you were showing people around your home, you could borrow a neighbor's Renoir for the evening or shove some bills in a drawer to make your position look better.[21] By contrast, although it's not impossible to falsify or obscure the cash you get and spend, it's harder and, moreover, it's easier to find out if you've been truthful simply by consulting your bank account and credit card statements.

There's yet one more typical way to describe the financial position of you, one you probably use once a year. You could figure out how much your wealth increased over the last year. In fact, you have to figure out your "income" every year because you have to pay tax on it. By this point in your life, you certainly know how this is

---

19. If you pay interest on your credit card balance, though, that's a separate expense by itself.

20. We could, of course, analyze your position by percentages as well as absolute dollar amounts. That is, we could describe how you spent your cash, and where you got your cash, in terms of the percent spent on necessities versus the percent spent on discretionary things.

21. In effect, this is what Enron did. It undertook a significant amount of potential liability but was able to omit that debt on its own balance sheet because the debts were incurred by legally separate entities. Under GAAP, those entities' financial performance could not properly be combined, *consolidated*, with Enron's as long as Enron owned no more than 97 percent of the company and did not exert control. While Enron followed these rules for some of these separate entities, it did not do so for all of them. For a while the company simply lied on its financial statements with the complicity of its independent auditor, Arthur Andersen. When the facts came to light, Enron's trading partners refused to do business with the company and it quickly declared bankruptcy.

done. If you've repressed the memory, just go online to *www.irs.gov* and look at *Form 1040.*

Think for a moment about how this description is different from the other two we've seen. It is unlike the things you own method because it isn't concerned with the value of what you have but with how much the value of what you have has changed. The "income" method also differs from the bank account method in a couple of ways. Not all the cash you receive counts as "income." Gifts, for example, or loan proceeds you receive don't count as "income." On the other hand, many things that aren't cash do count in describing yourself by the "income" method. You might be entitled to the moving expenses deduction, which is certainly not cash you received but certainly is a good thing and certainly figures into the calculation of your "income."

So what, more exactly, is this "income" method trying to describe? It's meant to tally some, but not all, wealth changes and to adjust that tally by rewarding you for some actions you took and penalizing you for others. For example, if you are furthering your education according to certain criteria, you're rewarded by being able to claim the Lifetime Learning Credit. If you give to charity, you're rewarded by being able to deduct that donated wealth from the increase in wealth you'd otherwise report. If the value of an investment (like stock) appreciates but you don't sell, you're rewarded by not having to include the increase in your wealth-change calculation. Because of the selective way in which this method calculates the change in your wealth, we're using the ironic quotation marks and calling it the "income" method.[22]

Each of these three ways of describing an economic entity has an analogous financial statement. Now that you have a sense of what these methods entail, let's go through each statement. As we do this, be aware that GAAP makes two principal changes from the way in which we've been thinking about economic description. First, when it measures "income," it typically records money moving in and out according to the date when the obligation to pay or be paid was made, not when the moola actually changed hands.[23]

Second, GAAP distinguishes between *operating* expenses and *capital* expenses. Most of the things you buy will be used up soon, say within the next year. These are operating expenses. But some things, like a new refrigerator, will last longer than that. These are capital expenses. To capture the notion that capital expenses buy things that will be used over several time periods, GAAP requires the buyer to spread out capital expenses over the life of the purchase. For example, the cost of the refrigerator would be spread out over the refrigerator's life, say ten years, with only one-tenth of the cost listed as an expense each year. This reflects a smaller decrease in wealth, and hence in "income," over those years than if the whole expense were

---

22. A separable aspect of this "income" method of description is that a tax (i.e., a percentage of your wealth change, as defined by the method) is levied on you. Both the selection of which wealth changes to count and the selection of which actions to reward and penalize reflect Congress's value judgments as to how individuals should be taxed. This taxation aspect explains why rewards for actions you took are reflected by a decrease in your wealth change so that you pay less in tax. Ultimately that reward leaves you with more wealth left over because the tax you paid is less than it would be without the reward.

23. This is because, in the normal course of commerce, there ought to be one date per transaction rather than two. So, the date one business agreed to sell something to another entity is the date that counts. If we looked at when money changed hands, we'd probably find that the buying party wrote a check on one day but the selling party didn't receive it for several days.

lumped only in the first year. By contrast, all operating expenses are considered in calculating each year's "income."[24]

With this introduction let's (finally!) look at some financial statements. The things you own method is analogous to the **balance sheet**. This statement divides things you own into assets and liabilities. It further divides both assets and liabilities into those that are liquid and those that are illiquid. It might well make a difference to someone considering loaning you money, for example, whether the things you own are cash or cashlike, and hence easily transferable to pay the debt, or whether they are not very liquid, possibly leaving you wealthy but strapped for cash. Within each of these categories, assets and liabilities are further grouped. On a business's balance sheet you'll see, for example, inventory—i.e., raw materials, partly finished goods, and goods ready for sale—as a separate entry.

GAAP requires that assets on a balance sheet be listed at their cost when they were acquired. This requirement is primarily a recognition that historic cost is a relatively certain number, while an asset's current fair value may be quite subjective. Be aware, then, that when you look at a business's balance sheet, the assets may be worth considerably more (or less) than the value listed. As we noted above, GAAP distinguishes between operating and capital expenses. The goods purchased with capital expenses are, by definition, long-lived. GAAP requires that a long-lived good's historic price on the balance sheet be reduced by a certain amount each year to reflect the fact that a portion of the good's value has been used up. This reduction is called *depreciation* and is broken out separately and subtracted from the cost of long-lived goods.

You'll also see entries for things that seem both unintuitive and frankly rather hair-splitting. Back to the balance sheet for you as a person for a moment. If you subscribe to a magazine, you probably paid the subscription price up front and will receive the magazine for some time in the future. GAAP says that the right to receive something in the future for which you've already paid is an "asset," so you'll see a line item labeled *prepaid expenses*. This concept seems odd for individuals but it may make quite a bit of sense for a business that may have paid for things like insurance or rent in advance. The right to enjoy those things without paying more is an asset. Likewise, suppose your phone company bills you at the end of each month for all the calls, texts, and data you used during that month. It really isn't accurate to say that, on the 27th of the month, you have no liability to your phone company; really, you owe nearly all the month's charge. To reflect this impending liability, GAAP includes a line item labeled *accrued liabilities*. A second line item, embodying the same concept, is *accrued income taxes*.

You could, of course, subtract the value of all the things you owe from the value of all the things you own. The resulting number, your net worth, wouldn't be terribly significant in the normal course of things. For example, you might have a high net worth, but if your wealth is not very liquid you might have trouble even getting enough cash from the ATM to buy lattes for the next week.

24. In effect, this is how WorldCom got in trouble. The company paid significant amounts each year to other telecommunications companies in exchange for the right to use those other companies' infrastructure. Under GAAP these expenses were operating expenses, which should have been listed in full on each year's income statement. Instead, WorldCom reported most of those expenses as capital expenses, which means that only a portion of those expenses was reported on each income statement. This had the effect of overstating the firm's operating profit and hence its net profit (ironically, it also increased WorldCom's income taxes). When the facts were made public, WorldCom declared bankruptcy.

In the business setting, a firm's net worth goes by a variety of other names such as *partners'* or *shareholders' equity*. Because a business is often owned by several people, GAAP requires that a firm's net worth be described in more detail to show what kind of ownership interests there are. Part of the line item shows how the ownership is divided, for example, the number of shares outstanding is listed. Shareholders' equity also shows how much money was originally paid into the firm by stockholders and how much is earnings from the firm's business (*retained earnings*). Below is an example of the way a business's balance sheet might be presented.

Assets

Current Assets:
- Cash and cash equivalents
- Receivables
- Inventories
- Prepaid expenses

Total Current Assets

Property, Plant and Equipment, at Cost:
- Land
- Buildings and improvements
- Fixtures and equipment
- Transportation equipment
- Less accumulated depreciation
- Property, plant and equipment, net

Other Assets and Deferred Charges:
- Goodwill
- Other assets and deferred charges

Total Assets

Liabilities and Shareholders' Equity

Current Liabilities:
- Accounts payable
- Accrued liabilities
- Accrued income taxes
- Long-term debt due within one year

Total Current Liabilities

- Long-term debt
- Deferred income taxes and other

Shareholders' Equity:
- Common stock (100,000 shares outstanding)
- Retained earnings

Total Shareholders' Equity

Total Liabilities and Shareholders' Equity

The financial statement analogous to the bank account is the ***statement of cash flows***. If we were to analyze your bank account we might want to triage by source the cash you received. For example, if $100,000 were deposited in your bank account it might make a big difference whether the source of that cash was

Wages from your day job, suggesting you're well paid

The sale of your My Little Pony collection, suggesting either that you're changing one form of wealth into a more useful one or that you're so desperate for cash that you're selling important, possibly vital, things

A loan from a bank, suggesting that you need a lot more cash than you have, which might be good, if you have a great idea, or bad if you've simply spent more than you can afford.

Judging a business requires making the same sort of distinctions. GAAP divides all business cash flows into three kinds. First is *cash flow from operations*, a business's "day job." As a convention to tie the financial statements to one another, the cash flow from operations begins with the net "income" figure. The next entries in the statement of cash flows undo all the noncash adjustments to "income." For example, the deduction for depreciation isn't a real expenditure of cash, so depreciation is added back. After these adjustments are made we can see the net cash; that is, the sum of all the bank account deposits and withdrawals from the business's operations.

The second category of cash flows is, somewhat misleadingly, called *cash flows from investing activities*. Investing in this sense means buying new land and equipment and selling off old equipment. The personal analogue would be a category in which you listed purchases of long-term assets like a refrigerator or car and sales of the old ones. This number is nearly always negative, because businesses usually spend more cash buying new equipment than they receive selling off the old equipment. The third category of cash flows is *cash from financing activities*. The personal analogue would be cash from loans you obtained and principal and interest you repaid. Businesses also undertake these activities but, in addition, they might sell or repurchase shares of their own stock. Cash from those activities is reflected in this category as well.

At the end of the statement of cash flows is both a net number (i.e., all cash received minus all cash spent) and a comparison of the year-end cash on hand to the cash on hand one year ago (i.e., your bank balance on December 31st compared to your bank balance a year ago). A typical statement of cash flows looks like this:

Cash flows from operations
        Income from continuing operations
        Adjustments to reconcile net income to net cash provided by operating
            activities:
            Depreciation and amortization
            Decrease/(increase) in accounts receivable
            Increase in inventories
            Increase in accounts payable
            Increase in accrued liabilities
        Deferred income taxes
Net cash provided by operating activities

Cash flows from investing activities
        Payments for property, plant, and equipment
        Proceeds from the disposal of fixed assets
Net cash used in investing activities

Cash flows from financing activities
        Increase/(decrease) in commercial paper
        Proceeds from issuance of long-term debt
        Purchase of company stock
        Dividends paid
        Payment of long-term debt
Net cash used in financing activities

Net increase in cash and cash equivalents

Cash and cash equivalents at beginning of year
Cash and cash equivalents at end of year

The final financial statement is the ***statement of income***. Just like a Form 1040 the statement begins with *revenues*—money the business received. The line item *net sales* or *net revenues* is probably a bit deceptive because it does not mean sales revenues minus costs. Rather, it means sales that are net of returned goods; it means sales that are final. It also means sales net of the depreciation charge that GAAP says must be allocated to the current period. Then, all the business's *costs* during the period are listed. GAAP requires the business to separate costs that are directly attributable to the goods produced (costs of sales) from indirect costs, often called *overhead* (operating, selling, general and administrative expenses). GAAP also requires that a business set out separately expenses that are not intended to yield immediate economic benefit but that are intended to yield profit in the future. These expenses are known as *research and development* (R&D). The costs are subtracted from revenues to yield *operating profit*. This is the business's core profit.

Many businesses earn money from activities other than their core businesses. If these revenues or losses are substantial, GAAP requires that they be separately stated below the company's operating profit. The rubric is *other revenues and expenses*. The firm's operating profit is added to these other profits and the sum is *income before income taxes*.

Income taxes are both important in themselves and analytically separate from the actual business costs, so GAAP requires them to be set out separately after the company's profit is computed. Another reason to set out income taxes separately is that, given the vagaries of the tax code, a firm's income taxes are often only loosely related to its actual performance. Finally, taxes are subtracted to yield *net income*. Here is a typical layout for a business's statement of income:

Operating Revenues:
    Net sales

Operating Costs and Expenses:
    Cost of sales
    Operating, selling, general and administrative expenses
    Research and development

Operating Profit

Other Revenues and Expenses:
    Interest:
        Paid
        Received
    Investments, net

Income Before Income Taxes

Provision for Income Taxes:

Net Income

If you are somewhat keen-eyed you will have noticed that the examples of financial statements above have no dollar amounts connected with them. The reason for this is that if you can understand the ideas behind the statements and the categories within each statement, then the numbers on any particular set of financial statements are simply detail. Nonetheless, you will probably want to look at the real financial statements for a real business. Those are easy to come by. Every public corporation has to file financial statements with the SEC and these are online at www.sec.gov under the link for EDGAR, the SEC's database.

How can you use financial statements to help advise your client? Well, there are three paradigm settings for corporate lawyers. First, your client might be contemplating extending unsecured credit to another firm. If your client will be exposed to a small amount of credit risk, it may well not be worthwhile to analyze the borrower's financial statements. That's the situation where, for example, a cable company is contemplating installing a cable outlet in a small business such as a bar. The total amount of money the cable company could lose in such a transaction is relatively small.[25]

But suppose your client is a seafood supplier and is contemplating extending credit to a restaurant. Then it may well be worthwhile for your client to obtain and analyze the restaurant's financial statements. What can those statements tell you and your client about the restaurant? The statements can suggest to you whether the restaurant will be able to pay the estimated monthly bill. They won't tell you whether the restaurant managers will be motivated to do so, nor will they show whether the restaurant has a good or a bad track record of paying its bills.[26] But in terms of simple ability to pay, the statements will help.

The question to ask is, "if this debtor were motivated to pay my client's bill every month, would it be able to find the money to do so?" Because this kind of debt is recurring, we probably wouldn't expect the restaurant to sell off assets to pay the bill. So, the balance sheet's listing of assets is of little value to us, although the "current assets" might give some clue of how liquid the restaurant's finances are. Because our client is looking to get paid every month, the statement to focus on is the statement of cash flows. We might look at the monthly statements going back a couple of years or so to see whether the restaurant's operations are generating sufficient cash that the restaurant will be able to pay your client's bill, too. If your client is replacing a prior seafood supplier, you'll need to adjust the statement of cash flow to subtract cash paid to the old supplier.

Suppose your client is contemplating lending a large amount of money to another firm with repayment stretched out over ten years. Say your client is a prosperous local businessperson who has been approached about a loan to a business located on the same block. You would want to know the same information as you did before, whether the borrower is likely to be able and willing to make

---

25. E.g., a month or so of unpaid cable charges — until the company cuts off the cable — and possibly some or all of the installation charges.

26. There are other ways to assess these risks. A credit report or check of court filings can reveal whether the restaurant has been in trouble in the past with prior creditors. Also, an analysis of the local business environment for restaurants will help assess the restaurant's motivation to pay. If there are many seafood suppliers and if seafood represents a small proportion of the restaurant's food, then the restaurant may be less attentive to your client's bills. On the other hand, if there are few seafood suppliers and if the restaurant specializes in seafood, then paying your client's monthly bills might be of critical importance to the restaurant.

timely repayment, so a similar examination of the borrower's statement of cash flow would be helpful. But, because this loan is large and for a long term, your client will want to know whether the business has assets that can secure the loan. Now the balance sheet will disclose the amount of other long-term debt (at least as of the balance sheet date) and the statement of cash flows will show how much cash the borrower pays in interest on other loans. Also, because this is serious money, your client might indeed expect the borrower to sell off at least some assets if it were having difficulty paying this loan. So, the balance sheet will disclose something about the assets that might be sold if necessary.

Let's return one more time to the possible purchase of the apartment house. What information relevant to the purchase of the apartment house can the financial statements provide? The balance sheet will show, for example, whether the land is owned by someone else. Other assets, such as lobby furniture or tools, will also show up on the balance sheet. The balance sheet will also, of course, show whether the apartment house is mortgaged or otherwise obligated to pay money over time. The apartment house may, for instance, have a contract with a maintenance company and any accrued obligation will show up on the balance sheet.

The statement of cash flows will show not only whether the apartment house is generating more cash than it consumes but whether that cash comes from rent or other sources such as loans. The income statement will show whether the apartment house is profitable, at least in an accounting sense.

To tie the chapter together, you and your client should list the various kinds of risk to which the apartment house may be subject and compare them to the financial statements to see whether, for example, the counterparty to a transaction has defaulted. The financial statements will also show, if you look at past years, whether the apartment building's economics have been relatively stable or relatively volatile. As you'll remember, the more volatile the results, the more likely it is that any particular year's results will be far from the expected return. This possibility may or may not be significant for your client.

Next, the financial statements can be used to see how much cash the apartment building has generated over time. This data can then be used to project the likely future cash flows. Obviously this is central to a DCF analysis and determining a net present value. The net present value, in turn, leads to you and your client formulating a purchase price offer.

Finally, the financial statements can be used to focus the decision-making process. Rational self-interest and the other considerations in decision making will come into play here. In the end, the financial statements are quite useful tools. They really are not mysterious but are functional instead. Once you understand their function, actual financial statements with real numbers shouldn't disturb you.

Notes and Questions

1. Reality Check

a. How can we measure an economic entity's past financial performance?

b. Why would we want to do so?

c. What are the three kinds of financial statements, and what does each disclose?

2. Suppose

a. Suppose you and your client were considering purchasing the apartment house. How would the apartment house's financial statements affect the decision whether to purchase?

E. TERMS OF ART IN THIS CHAPTER

Accounting statements
Adjustment and anchoring
Availability
Balance sheet
Break-up value
Call option
Capital expenses
Coping
Counterparty risk
Currency risk
DCF
Default
Discount rate
Discounted cash flow
Discounting to present
  value
Diversification
Expected return
Foreign investment
  risk
GAAP
Going concern value
Heuristics
Inflation risk
Liquidity
Net cash flow
Net present value
Operating expenses
Options
Price
Put option
Rational self-interest
Real options
Regulatory risk
Representativeness
Risk
Salvage value
Scrap value
Statement of cash flows
Statement of income
Synergy value
Terminal price
Time value of money
Utility
Value

Part II.
AGENCY

4

Agency

A. BACKGROUND AND CONTEXT

1. The Economic Concept of "Agency" and the Problem of Agency Costs

Economists usually define an agency relationship as one in which an agent and principal agree that the agent will use some degree of judgment to perform a service for the principal's benefit. This relationship is often reciprocal, such as when two people undertake a project as a team. In that setting, each team member is both a principal and an agent. As we will see, this definition of *agency* is broader than the legal definition. The idea of agency and the economic problems that agency relationships generate have spawned a rich literature in economics. In the taxonomy of economics, agency is a concern of microeconomics and is a particular form of the problems raised by information asymmetries between parties. Reduced to the core, the problem is predicting the future: the principal wants to ensure that the agent will perform well. Although neither the principal nor the agent can predict the future with perfect accuracy, the agent tends to know much more than the principal about two central matters: whether the agent is *capable* of performing well (i.e., has the necessary skills) and whether the agent is *motivated* to perform well.

Before the agency agreement is made, potential principals are looking for suitable agents, and potential agents are looking for suitable principals. Almost certainly one or more of these potential parties are objectively less suitable than others. Principals may mistakenly choose agents (and agents may mistakenly choose principals) who are less than optimal. This is called the problem of *adverse selection* and is said by economists to be a problem *ex ante*. As you may intuit, the problem is one of information; potential principals and potential agents can never be entirely sure that they are entering into an agency relationship with the most suitable person. Although the problem of adverse selection is an important economic one, it is not one that concerns the law of agency, because no agency relationship exists until the parties agree.

Principals and agents may use *signaling* to help convince others that they will perform well. Both principals and agents may provide references from others with whom they have worked. They may also provide evidence from third parties such as degrees from universities or law schools that attest to the skills and training they possess. The parties may locate one another through a clearinghouse that acts as a signal to each side. For example, parents (principals) may use a nanny agency (a clearinghouse) to locate an appropriate nanny (agent). The reputation of the nanny agency may be a signal to each side that both the nanny and the parents have been screened and found suitable for one another. Finally, of course, noneconomic qualities may play an important role. A person's general reputation (apart from specific references) may suggest that he or she will act appropriately. Additionally, the parties may frequently look for evidence of another's general sense of ethics when deciding whether to form an agency relationship.

After the agency agreement is made (*ex post*) the parties face the problem of *moral hazard*, a concept you may remember from your contracts course. In general, a moral hazard is the risk that a party with discretion to act will choose an action that decreases the expected value of the transaction to the other party in a way that the other party cannot effectively prohibit. On occasion, human nature being what it is, agents and principals may take exactly such actions out of malevolence toward the other party, or even out of an initial intent to deceive the other party, but economics treats these settings as aberrational. Economically, every agency relationship contains the seeds of moral hazard because the goals of the principal and agent are always different. The principal wants the task performed at the lowest cost; the agent wants the highest remuneration with the least effort. It is important to understand that this tension runs through every agency relationship and can never be completely eliminated.

From the agent's point of view, the main moral hazard is sometimes known as *ratcheting*. Although some tasks that are to be performed by an agent are well defined and self-contained, most are at least somewhat open-ended. This is especially the case where the task is really a continuing series of tasks, as in the case of employment. The danger for the agent is that the principal will increase the task without increasing the agent's recompense. The agent, of course, always has the ability to quit, but may as a practical matter be unable to do so. The agent who agrees to be the principal's secretary may be subject to ratcheting. It is not unusual in such settings for principals to add such tasks as serving as the office receptionist during the lunch hour or performing administrative duties like ordering office supplies without any additional reward. Even where the agency agreement includes (as it often does) "other duties as assigned," the addition of such tasks as a routine part of the agent's job is ratcheting. Measured strictly from the principal's economic best interest, principals have an incentive to ratchet because they get the desired task performed at a lower cost.

Principals face two forms of moral hazards from agents. First is *shirking*, in which the agent chooses to perform less well than the parties anticipated. Shirking may take the form of using suboptimal skill (a shoddy repair job, for example) or using optimal skills on fewer than optimal projects (such as an assembly-line worker who makes each item skillfully, but who makes fewer items per shift than he or she could). Ratcheting and shirking can sometimes be two sides of the same coin. Where a homeowner (principal) and housepainter (agent) disagree about the quality of the job done by the housepainter, is the homeowner trying to ratchet or is the housepainter trying to shirk?

The second moral hazard that principals face is the risk that the agent will use his or her discretion opportunistically to obtain *private benefits* for which the agent will bear only part (or even none) of the cost. Imagine that Mary owns a business in which she is the only worker and that has revenues in excess of costs of $100,000 per year.[1] If the business requires her to travel by air, Mary can choose to travel in first class rather than coach. If she chooses to travel first class, the additional cost (say $10,000 per year) is simply a reduction in her overall remuneration (i.e., the business would have revenues in excess of costs of only $90,000).

Now assume that Mary owns just 50 percent of the business, and that Michael, who does not work in the business, owns the other 50 percent. Mary is now the agent for Michael. They agree that Mary should receive a fair market wage (say $50,000) for her work in the business and that Mary and Michael should split equally any profits. If Mary flies in coach, she will receive $50,000 in salary and she and Michael will each receive $25,000 in profit.

But Mary now has an economic incentive to choose to fly first class. She will receive the same fair salary ($50,000) but the first-class air travel that cost her $10,000 when she was the sole owner would now cost her only $5,000. The business will have $90,000 of revenues in excess of its costs (before paying Mary). Mary will receive $50,000 in salary and she and Michael will each receive only $20,000 in profit. This situation gives Mary private benefits of $5,000. That is, she gets $80,000 in economic benefit ($70,000 in money and $10,000 in first-class air travel), which is $5,000 more than she would get if she did not choose to fly first class. Michael receives $20,000 in benefit, which is $5,000 less than he would if Mary flew coach. Michael is thus a victim of Mary's opportunistic behavior. The economic incentive to obtain private benefits is exacerbated if Michael owns the entire business and Mary is simply an employee at $50,000 per year. In that setting, her choice to fly first class rather than coach is costless to her (i.e., she has $10,000 in private benefits); Michael bears the full $10,000 cost.

Note that private benefits can take nonmonetary forms, as well. In the business setting, managers may make decisions that result in private benefits that may make their job more secure. This will happen when the manager has specialized skills and has the discretion to choose between a project in which such skills are essential and one in which they are not. Obviously the manager has an incentive to choose the project in which his or her skills are absolutely necessary in order to obtain an increased measure of job security. Another private benefit that is not explicitly monetary is the manager who uses discretion to increase the size of the business unit he or she manages. This form of empire building may satisfy the manager's professional ego and may also have the economic consequence of making the manager more highly sought after by other firms or becoming entitled to a higher salary within his or her current firm.

In addition to the moral hazard, there usually exists another economic impetus for agents to choose actions that are not in their principal's best economic interest.

---

1. It does not matter (ignoring tax consequences) whether Mary calls the $100,000 "profit" or "salary" or some combination of both.

An agent who chooses an alternative that turns out well does not receive the gain from that choice but simply receives the agreed-upon remuneration. Even if the principal and agent share the gains, the agent never receives the entire gain from the venture's success. On the other hand, an agent who chooses an alternative that turns out extraordinarily badly does not share in that loss but also may find that the principal is now unable to pay the agreed-upon remuneration. This disparity in consequence tends to make agents more *risk averse* than their principals and hence more likely to take different actions than their principals would like them to take. This tendency is frequently compounded by the fact that riskier actions are often harder to undertake successfully than less risky ones. Thus agents who make less risky choices also typically need to expend less effort to be successful, which increases the ratio of reward-to-effort and makes the agency more profitable for the agent.

These risks to both the principal and the agent make an agency relationship more costly than if the principal undertook to perform the task alone. There are techniques that can ameliorate, but never entirely eliminate, these costs. The parties can agree that the agent's compensation will depend in whole or in part on the degree to which the agent acts in the principal's best interest. Profit sharing or *incentive compensation* plans are common examples. These plans obviously reduce the principal's gain from the transaction because they must be shared with the agent. Another technique is for the principal to *monitor* the agent. Monitoring activities can take many forms, such as simply watching the agent work or measuring the agent's efforts where they are amenable to quantification. Other monitoring techniques include contractual limitations on the agent's discretion such as budget or other operational limitations.

Agents may also expend resources to assure principals they will not shirk or behave opportunistically. This assurance may come in the form of *bonding* actions such as obtaining an insurance policy or agreeing to a financial penalty clause in the agency agreement. Principals, too, may take bonding actions to assure agents that they will not ratchet, but most bonding is done by agents.

Basic economics rules suggest that principals and agents will undertake monitoring and bonding activities and agree on incentive compensation arrangements to reduce the costs of the agency relationship only up to the point at which the cost of further amelioration equals the likely loss from moral hazards. Economists use the term *agency costs* to mean the total of the expenditures made in ameliorating the moral hazard plus the residual loss resulting from moral hazard and risk differences between agent and principal.

2. Where Do Agency Questions Arise?

Questions of agency arise in a wide range of commercial settings. In its starkest, most salient, setting an agency relationship exists between the sole shareholder of a corporation and the corporation's sole employee. In the example of Mary and Michael, Michael was a principal because he co-owned the business. Mary was both a principal and an agent, a not infrequent occurrence. Employees with supervisory powers are both agents (of the managers to whom they report) and principals (to the employees who report to them). In a general partnership (or, more generally, in any economic endeavor in which multiple actors are required and in which the results are not easily attributable to the efforts of particular actors — called a *team production* model) each partner is both an owner and an agent.

Looking at the business entity itself as a unit, agency relationships exist between the entity and its suppliers and the entity and its customers. In the entity-supplier setting, the entity is more like the principal because the supplier usually has more power to act opportunistically; the entity primarily pays money, making it more like the principal. The reverse characterizes the entity-customer relationship because the customer mostly pays money, while the entity provides the good or service.

The dealings between an entity and its lenders present particularly sharp agency problems. Ex ante, lenders (principals) face a distinct adverse selection problem. Once the principal lends money, the agent (entity) has several typical incentives to act in a way that conflicts with the lender's best interest. Most pervasively, the entity, which is required to be managed in the best economic interest of its equity owners, has an incentive to undertake riskier projects than it would if the entity were financed strictly with equity. This is so because any gain from the project is allocated entirely to the equity, while the loss is shared between the lender and equity owners. As the entity approaches insolvency that incentive increases. Businesses on the verge of bankruptcy have a great incentive to undertake hugely risky projects, because the success of such projects is often seen as the only realistic way to remain viable, while the failure of such projects does not place the entity in any worse position than it already is in.

A final word about a paradigmatic relationship: that between a corporation and its board of directors. To the extent that directors are also managers, they fit into the principal-agent matrix we have seen; they are people given discretion to act in another's best interest and so agency problems and agency costs exist. The question arises whether the board is an agent of the corporation or its shareholders under legal concepts, such as those embodied in the *Restatement (Third) of Agency*. As we will see, the consequences of labeling someone an "agent" are considerable. The definition of a legal agent is someone who has agreed to act on someone else's behalf and subject to that person's control (*Restatement (Third) of Agency* §1.01). Note that this is narrower than the economic definition, which simply requires only that the agent have discretion to act in the principal's interest. Because all corporate power is vested in the board of directors (under corporation law), the board is not subject to the corporation's control. Thus it does not meet the legal definition of agent and is not generally held to be subject to the rights and obligations of agents under common law. Individual directors are also not generally considered to be legal agents for an additional reason. Under corporate law, the board's power is collective, such that no individual director has the power to act alone and therefore is not an agent. *See Restatement (Third) of Agency* §1.01 cmt. f(2).

The common law of agency predates the economic definition and understanding of agency problems. One consequence is that the law of agency has not been influenced to any great extent by economic thought. Furthermore, much of the law of agency has been informed by fiduciary notions, which are antithetical to the classic economic assumption that people act in their own economic best interest. As you read about agency relationships in the rest of this chapter, ask yourself how each agency relation would be analyzed by an economist, whether a tension exists between the economic and legal understanding of agency in a particular setting, and what the appropriate resolution of such a tension should be as a matter of social policy.

Notes and Questions

1. Note

a. This description of the economic analysis of agency relationships is based on traditional notions of economically rational behavior. *See* Chapter 3 for the suggestion that economic rationality need not be assumed.

2. What Do You Think?

a. Should the social value of agency law be measured by whether it reflects economists' understanding of agency relationships? What if economic thinking about agency changes radically?

B. THE CURRENT SETTING

1. Definition of the Agency Relationship

Agency rules are among the most important sets of rules that concern business entities. This importance stems from the simple fact that corporations, partnerships, and LLCs cannot take actions except through humans who act for them. The common law has long had rules, most of which can be varied by agreement, covering the settings in which one person or entity, the *agent,* acts on behalf of another, the *principal.* These rules have became relatively standard across the country. Although a few states such as California enacted these rules in statutes, agency law is, in most states, common law. The American Law Institute adopted a *Restatement (Third) of Agency* (hereinafter the *Restatement (Third)*) in 2006.

One quality of agency law is worth emphasizing at the beginning. Because agency relationships are formed consensually but not necessarily contractually, they arise in a wide variety of settings. The person who, as a favor, agrees to drive a friend to the airport may be an agent. Furthermore, because a valid contract is not necessary to create an agency relationship, children can sometimes be principals or agents. The focus of this casebook is on business entities rather than on agency relationships generally. For that reason, the remainder of this chapter will deal primarily with agency relationships in which the principal or agent is a business entity.

The *Restatement (Third)* defines an agency relationship:

> §1.01 Agency Defined
> Agency is the fiduciary relationship that arises when one person (a "principal") manifests assent to another person (an "agent") that the agent shall act on the principal's behalf and subject to the principal's control, and the agent manifests assent or otherwise consents so to act.

The definition does not require that the parties intend to form an agency relationship, and courts will find that an agency relationship exists even though the parties specifically disclaim any intention to create such a relationship as long as the parties

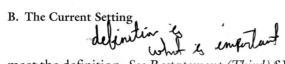

meet the definition. *See Restatement (Third)* §1.02. The agent is a fiduciary as to the principal, which means that the agent has higher duties than the implied duties of good faith and fair dealing ordinarily found in a contractual setting. *See Restatement (Third)* §8.01.

Employees of a business entity are agents, but the entity may have agents who are not employees such as accountants who are retained to audit the entity. Corporate officers such as the president or assistant secretary are agents (and probably employees). Directors of a corporation are not agents, partly because they cannot act alone, but can only act as a board, and partly because the directors govern the corporation and thus are not subject to the corporation's control. By analogy, it is unlikely that managers of a manager-managed LLC would be found to be agents. In both the director and the manager setting, though, the business entity could enter into an agency relationship with a director or manager who would then be an agent *in addition to* being a director or manager.

General partners in a general or limited partnership are agents even though, like corporate directors, they must act as a body and are not subject to the partnership's control. This result is determined by partnership law rather than agency rules. *See* Uniform Partnership Act §301 and Uniform Limited Partnership Act §403.

2. Creation of the Agency Relationship

Basile v. H & R Block, Inc.

761 A.2d 1115 (Pa. 2000)

CASTILLE, J.

H & R Block, Inc., provides tax preparation services nationwide through a network of retail offices. . . . As part of its service, Block offers a program known as "Rapid Refund," which involves electronic filing of tax returns with the Internal Revenue Service (IRS), resulting in quicker refunds than a taxpayer filing a paper return would receive. Block also arranged for Mellon Bank . . . to provide a refund anticipation loan (RAL) program to Block's qualified Rapid Refund customers. Under the RAL program, Mellon Bank advanced to the customer the amount of the customer's anticipated tax refund, less a financing charge, within days of Block's filing of the return. Appellee Sandra Basile applied for, and received, such a loan in 1993.

Basile and Laura Clavin filed this class action against Block and Mellon Bank . . . alleging that Mellon Bank . . . participated with Block in practices designed to deceive consumers as to the true nature of the loans. The trial judge . . . granted Block's motion for summary judgment finding that Block was not appellees' agent. . . .

The parties do not dispute the facts material to the issue of whether an agency relationship existed. In 1990, Block began offering its Rapid Refund program whereby its taxpayer customers could receive speedier refunds using one of three services: (1) electronic filing of the tax return for a fee; (2) electronic filing for a fee with direct deposit of the taxpayer's refund by the IRS to the taxpayer's bank account; or (3) electronic filing for a fee with an RAL arranged by Block with a lender such as Mellon Bank. The third option involving the RALs is the service at issue.

Block offered its RAL program through Mellon Bank to Block's Pennsylvania customers. Between 1990 and 1993, more than 600,000 Pennsylvania residents participated in the RAL program. Specifically, Block customers who filed their returns electronically and met the lender's eligibility requirements were informed of the availability of loans in the amount of their anticipated refunds from Mellon Bank. If the customer was interested in the loan, Block would simultaneously transmit the taxpayer's income tax return information to the IRS and Mellon Bank. Within a few days of the transmittal, the taxpayer, if approved, would receive a check in the amount of the loan minus a bank transaction fee. The taxpayer could also elect to have Block's tax preparation and electronic filing fees withheld by the lender from the RAL check so that the taxpayer would not have to advance any money. When the taxpayer's actual tax refund was ready, usually within a matter of weeks, the IRS would deposit the refund check into an account with Mellon Bank to repay the loan. In exchange for the RAL, the taxpayer paid to Mellon Bank a flat rate finance charge of $29.00 or $35.00, which Block employees presented to the taxpayer as a flat dollar amount rather than as a percentage interest rate on the short term loan.[8] Since the RAL is secured by the tax refund, and the tax refund is paid directly into a proprietary account at Mellon Bank, the lender bank takes on few risks with the program. Block did not disclose to its RAL customers that it received a payment from Mellon Bank for each loan, shared in the profits of the RALs in other ways, or that the taxpayer's endorsement on the back of the loan proceeds check constituted a signature on a loan agreement printed on the reverse of the check.

The law is clear in Pennsylvania that the three basic elements of agency are: "'the manifestation by the principal that the agent shall act for him, the agent's acceptance of the undertaking and the understanding of the parties that the principal is to be in control of the undertaking.'" *Scott v. Purcell*, 415 A.2d 56, 60 (Pa. 1980). . . . "[A]gency results only if there is an agreement for the creation of a fiduciary relationship with control by the beneficiary." *Smalich v. Westfall*, 269 A.2d 476, 480 (Pa. 1971). The burden of establishing an agency relationship rests with the party asserting the relationship. "An agency relationship is a fiduciary one, and the agent is subject to a duty of loyalty to act only for the principal's benefit." *Sutliff v. Sutliff*, 528 A.2d 1318, 1323 (1987). Thus, in all matters affecting the subject of the agency, the agent must act with the utmost good faith in furthering and advancing the principal's interests, including a duty to disclose to the principal all relevant information.

The pleadings here do not establish an agency relationship. With specific respect to the RALs, there is no showing that appellees intended Block to act on their behalf in securing the RALs. To the contrary, Block offered appellees the opportunity to file their tax returns electronically with the *three* options set forth above, only one of which involved RALs. Appellees were not required to apply for an RAL in order to have their returns prepared by Block or filed electronically through Block. It was appellees alone who decided to take advantage of that particular option. Block was

---

8. Due to the short-term nature of these loans (approximately two weeks), the finance charges translate to interest rates as high as 151 percent, depending on the amount of the loan. Appellee Basile's actual interest rate was 77.3 percent.

neither authorized to, nor did it in fact, act on its customers' behalf in this regard. If a customer elected to apply for an RAL, Block simply facilitated the loan process by presenting appellees to Mellon Bank as viable loan candidates. Block neither applied for the loan on behalf of appellees nor determined that appellees should apply; appellees undertook that procedure themselves. The RAL program was merely another distinct and separate service offered by Block to its customers. Furthermore, it was a distinct service that Block's customers were fully aware came at a higher price, just as one would expect for an advance of money. Simply introducing appellees to a lender willing to provide a loan is not sufficient to create an agency relationship. Therefore, we hold that, as a matter of law, Block was not acting as appellees' agent in the RAL transactions, such that they were subject to a heightened, fiduciary duty.

[handwritten margin note: just another service] not sufficient]

We are aware that here Block could be said to have played an "integral part" in arranging the RALs. In our view, however, "integral" or not, Block's mere facilitation of its customers' desire to pursue the loans, as one of the multiple services offered by Block, is not sufficient to establish an agency relationship under Pennsylvania law. The special relationship arising from an agency agreement, with its concomitant heightened duty, cannot arise from any and all actions, no matter how trivial, arguably undertaken on another's behalf. Rather, the action must be a matter of consequence or trust, such as the ability to actually bind the principal or alter the principal's legal relations. Indeed, implicit in the long-standing Pennsylvania requirement that the principal manifest an intention that the agent act on the principal's behalf is the notion that the agent has authority to alter the principal's relationships with third parties, such as binding the principal to a contract.

[handwritten margin note: the element that was missing]

Such power decidedly did not exist here with regard to facilitating the RALs, nor even to preparing and filing the tax returns. Block had no more authority to alter the legal relationship between its customers and the IRS than it had to bind those customers to a loan agreement with Mellon Bank. Block could not file a tax return without the customer's authorization and signature, nor could Block obligate the customer to pay any amount of income tax to the IRS without authorization and consent in the form of the customer's signature on the return. Therefore, no agency relationship existed between Block and its customers.

Our conclusion that there is no agency relationship here carries no judgment regarding Block's business practices. If Block's method of doing business is worthy of the condemnation that appellees suggest, presumably the marketplace will react to correct it. It is not our place to imbue the relationship between Block and appellees with heightened legal qualities that the parties did not agree upon.

NIGRO, J., dissenting:

I respectfully dissent, as I believe that an agency relationship existed between H & R Block and Appellees. [D]irect evidence of specific authority is unnecessary. Rather, the relationship can be inferred from the circumstances of the case by looking at factors such as the relation of the parties and their conduct. *— [handwritten: implied is good enough]*

I believe that Appellees met their burden of establishing that an agency relationship existed. Here, the Superior Court found that Appellees "established that they visited the Block offices in response to media promotions of the Rapid Refund Program to engage Block to achieve two results: (1) to complete and file their tax returns, and (2) to obtain a refund of any overpayment of taxes they had made to the Internal Revenue Service ["IRS"]." Appellees remained at the office while H & R Block employees completed the tax forms. After completion, the H & R Block employees requested that Appellees sign the tax returns before H & R Block sent the returns to the IRS and the state Department of Revenue. These facts indicate that: (1) Appellees manifested that H & R Block, through its employees, compute their taxes and complete and send their tax forms, thereby "rendering service but retaining control of the manner of doing it"; (2) H & R Block, through its employees, accepted the undertaking of completing and sending Appellees' tax forms; and (3) Appellees remained in control, that is, they had to sign their own forms and the H & R Block employees completed the forms pursuant to information given to them by Appellees. For these reasons, I believe that an agency relationship existed between Appellees and H & R Block with respect to the computation of their taxes and the completion and submission of their tax returns to the taxing authority. What remains is to determine whether agency extended to the Rapid Refund portion of the transaction. I believe it does.

H & R Block essentially contends that its relationship with the taxpayer is concluded once the tax return is filed, and that once the tax preparer offers her the application for the Rapid Refund, the taxpayer's relationship is a creditor/debtor one with Mellon Bank. I disagree as I believe that H & R Block's role in facilitating the Rapid Refund for the taxpayer is as the taxpayer's agent as all three elements of agency exist. Here, (1) the taxpayer manifested her consent to the tax preparer that she wished to participate or take advantage of H & R Block's Rapid Refund program when it was offered; (2) the preparer facilitated the process of obtaining a Rapid Refund by offering an application; and (3) the preparer consented to act on the taxpayer's need by matching the taxpayer to a source for the early refund, here, Mellon Bank. Accordingly, I also believe an agency relationship existed between Appellees and H & R Block for purposes of the Rapid Refund Program.

As H & R Block was the agent through which the Rapid Refund was facilitated, it had a duty to disclose the nature of its relationship with Mellon Bank in respect to the Rapid Refund Program. As the majority noted, "Block did not disclose to its [refund application loan] customers that it received a payment from Mellon Bank for each loan, shared in the profits of the [refund application loans] in other ways, or that the taxpayer's endorsement on the back of the loan proceeds check constituted a signature on a loan agreement printed on the reverse of the check." I believe that this is a gross violation of H & R Block's fiduciary duty to Appellees. Since I believe that the evidence creates the inference that an agency relationship existed between H & R Block and Appellees for the entire tax return "package" offered and further, that H & R Block violated the fiduciary duty it owed to Appellees, I respectfully dissent.

SAYLOR, J., dissenting:

I agree with the majority that, to the extent that refund anticipated loans ("RALs") are viewed as discrete transactions, no agency relationship between Block and its customers would be discernible. Like the majority, I would not be inclined to conclude, extrinsic of an existing, underlying agency relationship, that a separate agency role is necessarily undertaken by one who merely facilitates a lending transaction. Nevertheless, I join that portion of Mr. Justice Nigro's analysis which concludes . . . that an agency relationship existed between Block and Appellees for the purposes of preparing Appellees' tax returns, filing them with the IRS, and obtaining refunds. Indeed, I note that H & R Block conceded as much, at least for purposes of Maryland law, in *Green v. H & R Block, Inc.*, 735 A.2d 1039, 1049 (Md. 1999). I also believe that the fiduciary duties associated with such relationship may be viewed as sufficiently broad to compel disclosure of aspects of self-interest in a related loan transaction. Thus, I would [remand] "for disposition of questions of fact concerning the extent to which Block's failure to disclose the nature of the Rapid Refund program and its participation in the profits generated by the RALs constituted a violation of Block's duty as an agent." *Basile v. H & R Block, Inc.*, 729 A.2d 574, 582 (Pa. Super. 1999).

Notes and Questions

1. Note

a. H & R Block operated the refund anticipation loan program nationwide and customers in several other states brought suits similar to *Basile*. Courts have reached different results on the question whether an agency relationship existed between Block and its customers. Compare *Green v. H & R Block, Inc.*, 735 A.2d 1039 (Md. 1999) (agency relationship found), with *Beckett v. H & R Block, Inc.*, 714 N.E.2d 1033 (Ill. App.Ct. 1999), and *Peterson v. H & R Block Tax Services, Inc.*, 971 F. Supp. 1204 (N.D. Ill. 1997) (no agency relationship found).

b. By 2012, RALs had largely disappeared because the federal Office of the Comptroller of the Currency adopted regulations that made such loans unfavorable for banks. But with the increased popularity of low-cost or no-cost online filing, the three major tax preparation firms saw both declining revenues and increased competition among themselves for the remaining customers. In response, each of the three firms began offering refund loans. These loan programs differ from RALs because the tax preparation firm pays all bank fees. Further, the tax preparation firms guarantee that they will repay any loans the bank makes to customers whose refund turns out to be smaller than the refund loan. The firms will not seek to collect that money from their customers.

2. Reality Check

a. What element or elements of the *Restatement (Third)* §1.01 definition of agency are missing from the relationship between Block and Ms. Basile, according to Justice Castille?

b. Does Justice Nigro disagree with the rules Justice Castille uses or with the application of the rules? Or do the two judges disagree about both the rules and their application?

c. How does Justice Saylor differ from Justices Nigro and Castille?

d. Why does it matter whether Block is the plaintiffs' agent? *See Restatement (Third)* §§8.01, 8.02, and 8.11.

3. Suppose

a. What if the RAL had not been a separate optional service but instead were included along with Block's tax preparation? Would these facts make a difference to Justice Castille or Justice Nigro?

b. Suppose a CPA had a sole practice in which he or she prepared tax returns for individuals. If one tax client asked the CPA to contact a bank to arrange a loan to the client secured by the client's anticipated tax refund, and if the CPA agreed to do so, would an agency relationship exist between the CPA and client? If so, how is that setting different from *Basile*?

c. If Block rather than Mellon Bank had made the RALs, would an agency relationship exist between Block and its customers as to the RALs?

4. What Do You Think?

a. If an agency relationship exists, the agent's actions may bind the principal. Does an agency relationship exist between Block and Mellon Bank? If so, which is the principal and which the agent? If so, do you think that Block or Mellon Bank or both should be liable to plaintiffs?

b. Is one implication of *Basile* that professionals can seldom if ever be agents for their clients because the nature of professional services is such that clients will retain insufficient control over the professional's work?

c. If plaintiffs were misled about the RALs, should their recovery be based upon agency law or upon other sources such as commercial law or consumer protection?

Putting It to Work

Problem 4-1

Nick, a real estate agent with his own business, negotiates the buying and selling of homes for individuals and has been doing so for over 10 years. Nick has just negotiated a contract for the sale of a vacation house for a longtime client, which will close in 45 days. The client has asked Nick to arrange a loan from the local bank to be repaid from the proceeds of his upcoming vacation home sale. Seeing a great idea and excellent business growth opportunity, Nick decides to include this "fast cash" option with all his clients' real estate sales. The bank agrees to pay Nick a modest finder's fee for each loan it makes to Nick's clients.

a. Does an agency relationship exist between Nick and his clients? If so, what is the scope? Do Nick and the bank have an agency relationship? If so, who is the principal and who the agent? If an agency relationship exists, has Nick violated his duties to either his clients or the bank?

b. What if Nick personally loans his clients "fast cash" instead of going through a bank? Is there now an agency relationship between Nick and his clients? Has the scope of that relationship changed? Has Nick violated his duties to his clients?

3. Relation of the Principal to Third Parties

A principal can become liable to a third party (i.e., to a natural person or an entity that is not the agent) for the actions of the agent under five theories, which are not mutually exclusive. In most instances liability is predicated on *actual authority* or *apparent authority*. When neither of those two theories results in liability, courts turn to the remaining three theories.

a. Actual Authority

The simplest theory of liability is actual authority. A principal is bound to third parties by anything the agent does that is in accordance with the principal's "manifestation" to the agent. The principal's manifestation is determined by the agent's reasonable interpretation in light of all the circumstances. *Restatement (Third)* §§2.02 and 3.01.

This manifestation can be express—for example, "You are authorized to sell my car for any price in excess of $2000." The manifestation might also be implied rather than express. The agent has actual authority to do collateral acts that are incidental, that usually accompany or are usually done in the business, or that are reasonably necessary to accomplish the acts that the principal has expressly authorized. In the example just given, the agent would doubtless have actual authority to advertise the car. *See Restatement (Third)* §2.02(1).

b. Apparent Authority

Actual authority arises from the manifestations of the principal to the agent. Apparent authority stems from a third party's belief, traceable to the principal's manifestation, that the agent (or even a nonagent) is authorized to act for the principal. *Restatement (Third)* §§2.03, 3.03. As we have seen, a principal is bound by an agent's actions within the scope of the agent's actual authority. But a principal is also bound by an agent's actions within the scope of the agent's apparent authority. Where the manifestations the principal makes to the agent are identical to those the principal makes to a third party, the agent's actual authority and apparent authority are coextensive. What happens when the manifestations made to the agent and to the third party are different?

Udall v. T.D. Escrow Services, Inc.

154 P.3d 882 (Wash. 2007)

FAIRHURST, J.

William Udall purchased real property in a nonjudicial foreclosure sale. The auctioneer gave Udall a receipt, but not the deed of trust for the property. When trustee T.D. Escrow Services, Inc. (hereinafter T.D.) discovered that the auctioneer had opened the bidding $100,000 lower than T.D. had authorized, T.D. refused to deliver the deed to Udall. We reverse the Court of Appeals and reinstate the trial court's summary judgment ruling quieting title in Udall.

FACTUAL AND PROCEDURAL HISTORY

The material facts are undisputed. After the borrowers defaulted on their home mortgage payments, lender U.S. Bancorp directed T.D. to commence nonjudicial foreclosure proceedings on the property. T.D. properly recorded a notice of trustee's sale announcing that it would "sell [the property] at public auction to the highest and best bidder" "as provided by statute" to satisfy the "obligation secured by the Deed of Trust."

T.D. employs ABC Legal Services (hereinafter ABC) to conduct Washington-based nonjudicial foreclosure sales. On the morning of April 16, 2004, T.D. communicated to ABC by telephone the opening bids for that day's sales, identifying the opening bid for the property as $159,421.20. At the auction, ABC auctioneer Donna Hayes distributed to attendees an information sheet listing properties being sold that day and opening bids. The opening bid listed for the property was $59,421.20.

Hayes read the standardized nonjudicial foreclosure sale script and announced the opening bid of $59,421.20. Udall bid one dollar more. There being no other bidders, Hayes closed the sale. Udall tendered full payment and Hayes gave Udall a receipt for the property. Consistent with T.D.'s policy, the deed of trust for the property was not issued to Udall at the sale.[1]

T.D. discovered the discrepancy in the opening bid when Udall's funds were transmitted to its main office. In a letter dated April 21, 2004, T.D. returned to Udall a check for the amount he had paid for the property and explained that ABC had not been authorized to open bidding at $59,421.20. Udall rejected the refund. T.D. refused to issue the deed of trust to Udall.

Udall brought an action to quiet title, naming T.D. and lender U.S. Bancorp as defendants. The trial court granted summary judgment quieting title in Udall. The Court of Appeals Division Two reversed the ruling and entered summary judgment in favor of T.D.

ANALYSIS

The Court of Appeals held that T.D. did not have a duty to deliver the deed to Udall because "ABC lacked actual or apparent authority to sell the property for $59,422.20 [and] to accept a bid for this amount." We disagree with the conclusion that ABC did not have apparent authority to sell the property to Udall.

An agent has apparent authority when a third party reasonably believes the agent has authority to act on behalf of the principal and that belief is traceable to the principal's manifestations. RESTATEMENT (THIRD) OF AGENCY §2.03, at 113 (2006). Apparent authority may exist in agents who act beyond the scope of their actual authority.[5]

The court's focus on ABC's needing apparent authority "to sell the property *at the mistakenly low opening price*," or any particular price, is misplaced. The appropriate analysis focuses on whether Udall believed, based on T.D.'s manifestations, that ABC had "authority to act for" T.D. to sell the property on T.D.'s behalf, and whether that belief was "objectively reasonable." A principal may "make a manifestation by . . . placing an agent in charge of a transaction or situation." RESTATEMENT, *supra*, §3.03 cmt. b at 174. T.D., by issuing the notice of trustee's sale, made just

---

1. It is T.D.'s policy before issuing a deed of trust to verify the validity of a bid and receipt of funds, as well as to check for intervening bankruptcies and other potential problems that might affect the sale.

5. It is undisputed that T.D. directed ABC to open bidding on the property at $159,421.20. As a result, ABC lacked actual authority to open bidding on the property at $59,421.20.

such a manifestation.[6] Based on T.D.'s representation, Udall could reasonably believe that T.D. or its authorized agent would conduct the sale. When ABC auctioneer Hayes in fact conducted the sale, Udall was reasonable in believing that she did so as T.D.'s authorized agent.

T.D. employed ABC to conduct its nonjudicial foreclosure sales in Washington. At this sale, Hayes read the standard script and announced the opening bid as $59,421.20. It is undisputed that the opening bid was erroneous, but the error did not create a duty in Udall, an arm's length third party, to question whether the announced bid was the amount authorized by T.D.

Not the third party's to guess

T.D.'s manifestations provided Udall with an objectively reasonable basis to conclude that ABC, through Hayes, had authority to act for T.D. in conducting the property sale. Hayes thus acted with apparent authority when she accepted Udall's high bid and closed the sale. Principal T.D. was bound by that acceptance. T.D. must deliver the deed of trust to Udall.

Grossly inadequate purchase price together with circumstances indicating some additional unfairness may provide sufficient equitable grounds to set aside a nonjudicial foreclosure sale.

In this case, T.D. made no showing that unfairness prejudiced the borrower, and the price, more than 35 percent of the intended opening bid, cannot be deemed grossly inadequate. We decline to invalidate this nonjudicial foreclosure sale where no grounds for equitable intervention are present.

CONCLUSION

We reverse the Court of Appeals and reinstate the trial court's award of summary judgment quieting title in Udall.

Notes and Questions

1. Notes

a. The Washington Court of Appeals found the following additional facts:

> Nor does the record show that ABC had apparent authority to sell the property at the mistakenly low opening price that Udall bid and ABC "accepted." The only arguable communication between Udall and TD was indirect, through TD's September 19, 2003 Notice of Trustee's Sale; this Notice stated that the property owner owed the lender $148,031.24, and the property would be priced higher than $148,000 in order to satisfy the existing debt. This Notice of Trustee's Sale did not establish that auctioneer ABC had apparent authority to open bidding at $59,421.20 or any other price lower than that necessary to satisfy seller Brown's [the homeowner] debt on the property.
>
> The record contains no other arguable communication between TD and Udall, direct or indirect. Thus, Udall cannot satisfy the requirement that, to establish "apparent authority," the principal (TD) must have manifested to the third party (Udall) that the agent (ABC) had *apparent* authority to act on its behalf. Here, there was no such communication that Udall could have reasonably and objectively interpreted as creating such apparent authority in ABC.[5]

Udall v. T.D. Escrow Services, Inc., 130 P.3d 908, 913 (Wash. App. 2006)

6. The notice announced "NOTICE IS HEREBY GIVEN THAT the undersigned Trustee, [T.D.], will . . . sell at public auction to the highest and best bidder, payable at the time of the sale, the [property]."

5. Further detracting from Udall's claim of apparent authority was his vast experience as a sophisticated, foreclosure-sale purchaser who has purchased 100 foreclosed properties since 1995. Such an experienced

2. Reality Check

a. What was Ms. Hayes' actual authority? What was her apparent authority?
b. In what way did T.D. create apparent authority in Ms. Hayes?

3. Suppose

a. Suppose Ms. Hayes had opened the bidding at $15,942.12. If Mr. Udall had bid one dollar more, would the court have reached the same result?
b. Suppose Ms. Hayes had opened the bidding at $1,594.21. If Mr. Udall had bid one dollar more, would the court have reached the same result?

4. What Do You Think?

a. If agency is a consensual relationship, how can the principal be held to an action by its agent to which it did not consent?
b. Do you think the Supreme Court was correct or was the Court of Appeals correct? Why?
c. Should Mr. Udall have to show some reliance on Ms. Hayes' action or some potential harm from allowing T.D. to reject his bid in order to prevail? Could Mr. Udall have made such a showing?

The scope of apparent authority is determined in analogous fashion to the scope of actual authority. The test is the third party's reasonable interpretation of the principal's manifestations in light of all the circumstances. As with actual authority, an agent has apparent authority to do collateral acts that are incidental, that usually accompany or are usually done in the business, or that are reasonably necessary to accomplish the acts that the agent is apparently authorized to do. *See Restatement (Third)* §2.03 cmt. b & d.

In the business entities context, a concept sometimes called the "power of position" is frequently important. When a principal that is an entity appoints an individual to a particular position, such as Vice President of Purchasing, that appointment may carry with it a great deal of implied actual authority even where the corporation is vague about the actual authority expressly given to that person. Remember that the scope of actual authority is measured by what the agent reasonably believes. So, the question becomes what a reasonable person would believe when the corporation appointed him or her to be Vice President of Purchasing. *See Restatement (Third)* §1.03 cmt. c.

More important such an appointment may carry much implied apparent authority as well. Even if the Vice President of Purchasing has been expressly limited in the actions he or she can take, and therefore has a very narrow scope of actual authority, the corporation, as principal, is bound by the agent's actions if they are within the scope of what a third party reasonably believed a Vice President of Purchasing was authorized to do. The extent of this implied apparent authority varies not only within the context of any particular transaction, but also with the title of the position. The Vice President of Purchasing presumably has a great deal of discretion to act for

---

foreclosure-sale purchaser should have had actual knowledge of ABC's lack of actual or apparent authority to sell the property at the auctioneer's opening bid price because this bid was $90,000 lower than the known amount the foreclosure sale had to yield to satisfy the property owner's debt.

the corporation within the realm of purchasing items for corporate use. The corporation's president obviously has a wide range of powers to act on behalf of the corporation. Ironically, a more generic title such as "vice president" may well carry with it almost no implied powers because the title is so amorphous. *See Restatement (Third)* §303 cmt e.

One particular setting is worth noting as a trap for the unwary corporate planner. Virtually every state's corporation statute requires the corporation to have one person whose duties include keeping corporate records and certifying the actions of the corporation's board and its shareholders. *See, e.g.,* DGCL §142(a) and MBCA §§1.40 and 8.40(c). That person is often called the "Secretary" in the statutes, and case law binds the corporation to any representations about corporation board or shareholder actions given by that person (and to a lesser extent any "Assistant Secretary" or "Vice Secretary"). The upshot is that a negligent or, worse, malfeasing corporate secretary can expose the corporation to significant liability by falsely certifying that an action has been approved or that a particular person has actual authority to act for the entity. *See Restatement (Third)* §3.03 cmt. e(5) & reporter's notes e(5).

If you or your client is dealing with a business entity, that entity must obviously act through humans. How will you or your client know whether those humans are authorized to act on behalf of the entity? If those people act outside their actual authority, can you hold the entity liable under the theory of apparent authority on the basis of the agent's own assertions? Does apparent authority arise from the entity providing the agent a business card with his or her name and title? Does it arise from providing the agent an email account? The next case deals with this very common situation.

CSX Transp., Inc. v. Recovery Express, Inc.

415 F. Supp. 2d 6 (D. Mass. 2006)

Young, District Judge.

I. INTRODUCTION

This is a breach of contract and related equitable action brought by the plaintiff, CSX Transportation, Inc. ("CSX"), against the defendants, Recovery Express, Inc. ("Recovery") and Interstate Demolition and Environmental Corp. ("IDEC"). The case against Recovery turns on the application of that doctrine within the law of agency known as "apparent authority"; specifically, how large a cloak of such authority is provided by access to an e-mail address with a defendant's domain name.

A. Undisputed Facts

CSX is in the business of selling out-of-service railcars and parts. It is a Virginia corporation with its principal place of business in Florida. Recovery is a Massachusetts corporation with its principal place of business in Boston. IDEC was a Delaware corporation with its principal place of business at the same address in Boston. It is now defunct. At all relevant times, IDEC and Recovery shared offices in Boston.

On August 22, 2003, Albert Arillotta ("Arillotta"), a "partner" at IDEC, sent an e-mail to Len Whitehead, Jr. ("Whitehead") of CSX expressing interest in buying "rail cars as scrap" ("the E-mail"). Arillotta represented himself to be "from interstate demolition and recovery express." The e-mail address from which Arillotta sent this inquiry was "albert@recoveryexpress.com." The entire e-mail — horrendous grammar and all — is reproduced here:

> From: Albert Arillotta [albert@recoveryexpress.com]
> Sent: Friday, August 22, 2003 4:57 PM
> To: Whitehead, Len Jr.
> Subject: purchase of out service railcars
>
> lynn this is albert arillotta from interstate demolition and recovery express we are interested in buying rail cars for scrap paying you a percentage of what the amm maket indicator is there are several locations i suggest to work at the exsisting location of the rail cars. we will send you a brochure and financials per your request our address is the following:
> interstate demolition/recoveryexpress
> 180 canal street 5th floor boston mass 02114
> phone number 617-523-7740
> fax number 617-367-3627
> email address albert @recoveryexpress.com
>
> thank you for your time

There apparently were subsequent phone calls between Whitehead and Arillotta, but the substance of the calls is not recounted. CSX alleges that it prepared and forwarded sales order forms which "confirm[ed] the agreed[-]upon terms [of the sale] to IDEC." Neither CSX nor Recovery has provided copies of these forms. Apparently, Arillotta and Whitehead proceeded with this proposed deal.

The railcars were "delivered . . . to the location specified by Arillotta. . . ." Recovery claims that this location was, in fact, CSX's own railyard, to which Arillotta went himself, disassembled the cars, and transported them away. There is no direct evidence on point, but the original e-mail from Arillotta supports Recovery's assertion. ("[I] suggest work at the existing location of the rail cars.") There is no evidence proffered as to the current disposition of the scrap railcars (i.e., where they are) or their proceeds.

After delivery, CSX sent invoices for the scrap railcars totaling $115,757.36 addressed to IDEC at its Boston office (shared with Recovery). Nancy E. Marto ("Marto"), officer and registered agent of Recovery and "partner" in IDEC, states that, upon receipt of the invoices, she attempted several times to contact Whitehead to inquire about them. She says that Whitehead never returned her calls. This was apparently because Arillotta had told him not to speak to her.[1] Not until a check from Arillotta to CSX purporting to pay the invoices bounced did Whitehead call Marto.

Because Recovery and IDEC refused to pay CSX, CSX brought this action alleging (1) breach of contract, (2) account stated, (3) unjust enrichment, and (4) quantum meruit.

---

1. Interestingly, the reason IDEC has ceased to exist is because of fraud by Arillotta. It is unclear if the fraud is related to this case.

Whitehead states that "[a]t all times during [his] dealing with Mr. Arillotta, [he] believed [Arillotta] was representing, and authorized to act on behalf of, Recovery Express and Interstate Demolition." Whitehead apparently based this belief on the E-mail's domain name — recoveryexpress.com[2] and the representations of Arillotta to him both in the E-mail and in subsequent telephone conversations. All invoices were addressed to IDEC, though Whitehead states that Arillotta represented that he was "acting on behalf of Recovery Express." "At no time prior to CSX's delivery of the rail cars . . . did anyone inform [Whitehead] that Mr. Arillotta was not authorized to represent or transact business on behalf of either Recovery Express or Interstate Demolition."

Recovery claims that Arillotta never worked for it. How Arillotta acquired a Recovery e-mail address is explained thus: Marto and Thomas R. Trafton ("Trafton"), Recovery's President and Treasurer, became involved in another venture along with Arillotta and Dominic Ignagni — IDEC. Because of Marto's and Trafton's "personal interest in IDEC," the "fledgling" company was allowed to share the offices and some resources of Recovery, including telephones and facsimile machines — and, apparently, e-mail services. Other than physical resources, there is no evidence that Recovery ever shared anything with IDEC — assets, funds, books of business, bank accounts, or insurance coverage.

B. Procedural Posture

CSX filed its Complaint in October of 2004 alleging breach of contract by Recovery and IDEC and related equitable claims. IDEC is now defunct, and has made no appearance in this litigation. Recovery has moved for summary judgment.

II. DISCUSSION

A. Contract (Legal) Claims

At base, what this case is about is CSX's attempt, having been duped by a fraudulent agent of Recovery, to shift the consequences of its own gullibility to someone else. The primary legal vehicle by which it seeks to do this is the contract doctrine of "apparent authority." "Apparent authority is the power held by an agent or other actor to affect a principal's legal relations with third parties when a third party reasonably believes the actor has authority to act on behalf of the principal and that belief is traceable to the principal's manifestations." RESTATEMENT (THIRD) OF AGENCY at §2.03. It "is not established by the putative agent's words or conduct, but by those of the principal." *Rubel v. Hayden, Harding & Buchanan, Inc.*, 444 N.E.2d 1306 (Ma. App. 1983).

In what looks to be an issue of first impression, the facts of this case set up the question whether an e-mail domain name, by itself, cloaks a purported agent with authority sufficient as matter of law to be called "apparent." Because apparent authority depends on that knowledge held by Whitehead and CSX of Arillotta's authority, which knowledge was derived from actions of Recovery, the only relevant

---

2. With regard to e-mail addresses, the domain name is anything after the "@" symbol. It is a more user-friendly way of identifying the Internet protocol (IP) address needed by the computer network to deliver correctly the e-mail message. *See* Christopher G. Clark, *The Truth in Domain Names Act of 2003 and a Preventative Measure to Combat Typosquatting*, 89 CORNELL L. REV. 1476, 1483 & n. 40 (2004).

conduct by Recovery is that it issued Arillotta an e-mail address with its domain name. Such associations as Recovery having the same offices, mailing address, phone number, or fax number are red herrings; these facts — if Whitehead even possessed them prior to entering the contract — emanated from Arillotta by way of his e-mail signature or telephone representations. There is no evidence of the manifestation of those facts by Recovery to Whitehead and CSX (i.e., by way of its website, as CSX asserted at oral argument) until after the contract was entered and collection efforts had begun.[4]

The only act taken by Recovery known to Whitehead and CSX prior to entering the contract and upon which Whitehead could rely, was its issuance to Arillotta of an e-mail address sporting Recovery's domain name (@recoveryexpress.com). The Court holds that Whitehead and CSX were unreasonable, as matter of law, in their reliance solely on an e-mail domain name. Such a manifestation by Recovery cannot be sufficient to sustain a claim of apparent authority. Granting an e-mail domain name, by itself, does not cloak the recipient with carte blanche authority to act on behalf of the grantee. Were this so, every subordinate employee with a company e-mail address — down to the night watchman — could bind a company to the same contracts as the president. This is not the law.

Though e-mail communication may be relatively new to staid legal institutions, the results in analogous low-tech situations confirm this conclusion. The Court could find no cases where, for example, giving someone a business card with the company name or logo, access to a company car, or company stationery, *by themselves,* created sufficient indicia of apparent authority. *See Muscletech Research & Dev., Inc. v. East Coast Ingredients, LLC,* No. 00-CV-0753A(F), 2004 WL 941815, at *32 (W.D.N.Y. Mar. 25, 2004) (holding that issuance of a company credit card, business cards with company logo, possession of company paraphernalia, and appearing in company advertisements was insufficient to create apparent authority); *Asplund v. Selected Investments in Financial Equities, Inc.,* 103 Cal. Rptr. 2d 34, 48-49 (2000) (issuance of a business card and display of a plaque insufficient to create apparent authority); *Raclaw v. Fay, Conmy and Co.,* 668 N.E.2d 114, 117 (1996) (permitting the occupation of offices, the use of telephones and receptionist, the receipt of mail at company offices, and access to stationery insufficient to create apparent authority); *McFarland v. Entergy Mississippi, Inc.,* 919 So. 2d 894, 902, 2005 WL 2458870, at *6 (Miss. 2005) (holding that putting a purported agent in electric company vehicle, when plaintiff knew that volunteers were assisting crews, was insufficient to create apparent authority); *Alexander v. Tom Chandler, ABS Global, Inc.,* 179 S.W.3d 385, 389-390 (Mo. App. 2005) (holding that providing nitrogen tanks with company logo, billing for services with invoices bearing company logo, sending postcards claiming to be a company representative, distributing business cards indicating representative status, and giving out calendars with

---

4. The same can be said for the authority conveyed by Arillotta's title at IDEC. Whatever authority a title may convey to a third party, nothing in the record indicates that Whitehead and CSX even knew what Arillotta's title was. *See* the E-mail (stating that Arillotta was "from" Recovery and IDEC); Whitehead Decl. ¶2 ("Mr. Arillotta told me that he was acting *on behalf of* Recovery Express. . . ." (emphasis added)). "If the third party . . . is unaware of the agent's position . . . , the principal is not accountable for the third party's belief in the agent's authority. . . . The third party may . . . lack a basis reasonably to believe that the agent is authorized to bind the organization. Such a basis would be lacking, for instance, if the third party is unaware of the agent's position within the organization." Restatement at §3.03, cmt. c.

company logo to be insufficient to create apparent authority); *Cowburn v. Leventis,* 619 S.E.2d 437, 448 (S.C. 2005) (holding that supplying forms and business cards were the only actions of defendant and were not sufficient to create apparent authority); *cf. Thesenga Land Co. v. Cirrus Warehouse, Inc.,* No. C5-03-370, 2003 WL 22889499, at *1-2 (Minn. App. Dec. 9, 2003) (finding support for apparent authority when agent used business card designating him as vice president and when agent met with representatives of plaintiff and directed and negotiated contract terms); *Dorna USA, LLC v. Lighthouse Superscreens, Inc.,* No. 02 Civ. 8973(RLC), 2004 WL 2721239, at *2 (S.D.N.Y. Nov. 29, 2004) (holding that sharing website and e-mail addresses, using identical business cards, and "collectively behav[ing] 'as a single production and sales team,'" as well as other facts "too numerous to detail" supported the existence of apparent authority).

An e-mail domain name is sufficiently analogous to business cards, company vehicles, and letterhead for these cases to be persuasive. Those indicia of apparent authority all convey some degree of association between the purported principal and agent. By themselves, however, no reasonable person could conclude that apparent authority was present. The same is true with e-mail domain names.

In the end, CSX and Whitehead should have been more suspicious of an unsolicited, poorly written e-mail that arrived late one Friday afternoon. There are means by which CSX could have protected itself (e.g., requiring a purchase order form from IDEC or Recovery). Before delivering goods worth over $115,000 to a stranger, one reasonably should be expected to inquire as to the authority of that person to have made such a deal. Given the anonymity of the Internet, this case illustrates the potential consequences of operating—even in today's fast-paced business world—as did CSX.

III. CONCLUSION

Because there is no genuine issue of material fact as to whether Arillotta possessed the apparent authority of Recovery to enter into a contract with CSX—he did not possess such authority—and because there is no evidence that Recovery had the benefit of CSX's railcars, Recovery's Motion for Summary Judgment is ALLOWED and judgment will enter for it.

Notes and Questions

1. Reality Check

a. Why did the court hold that Mr. Arillotta did not have apparent authority?

b. Did Recovery do anything that might reasonably lead CSX to believe that Arillotta was authorized to enter into the railcar transaction?

2. Suppose

a. Suppose CSX had contacted Recovery, trying to reach Mr. Arillotta, and Recovery put the two in touch with one another. Would that create apparent authority in Mr. Arillotta?

b. In one scenario, an employer gave business cards to an employee with the employee's title printed on them. In a second scenario, the employee, without the

You must anticipate that employee will tell third parties of title

employer's knowledge, had business cards printed with the employee's title. If the employer were sued by a third party on a contract entered into by the employee that was beyond the scope of the employee's actual authority, would the result or analysis be different depending upon the method by which the employee obtained business cards?

3. What Do You Think?

a. Is the court correct in its holding? Why shouldn't providing an agent with business cards create at least some apparent authority? Shouldn't providing an email account be treated the same way?

4. You Draft It

a. The medium makes a difference. Redraft the email so that it would be appropriate for a business letter. Then redraft it so that it would be appropriate for a business email. Then redraft it so that it would be appropriate for a business IM. The text of the email follows:

> From: Albert Arillotta [albert@recoveryexpress.com]
> Sent: Friday, August 22, 2003 4:57 PM
> To: Whitehead, Len Jr.
> Subject: purchase of out service railcars
>
> lynn this is albert arillotta from interstate demolition and recovery express we are interested in buying rail cars for scrap paying you a percentage of what the amm maket indicator is there are several locations i suggest to work at the exsisting location of the rail cars. we will send you a brochure and financials per your request our address is the following:
> interstate demolition/recoveryexpress
> 180 canal street 5th floor boston mass 02114
> phone number 617-523-7740
> fax number 617-367-3627
> email address albert @recoveryexpress.com]
>
> thank you for your time

c. Principal's Liability to Third Parties for Actions Actually or Apparently Authorized

Under the *Restatement (Third)*, a principal is liable in contract if the agent acted either with actual authority or apparent authority. *See Restatement (Third)* §6.01(1). This is true even where the third party knows only that the agent is acting on behalf of a principal but does not know the principal's identity (called an *unidentified principal*). *See Restatement (Third)* §6.02(1). Furthermore, the principal is liable for an agent's actually authorized actions even where the third party had no knowledge that the agent was acting on behalf of any principal (called an *undisclosed principal*). *See Restatement (Third)* §6.03(1). The rationale is that the principal initiated the agent's actions and has a right to control them and so should in fairness be bound under the contract made by the agent. This rule typically gives a windfall to third parties who, as we will see below, can either hold the agent, with whom they believed they were contracting, liable and therefore receive their expectation interest, or hold the principal, of whom they had no knowledge, liable. As you think about these settings, be aware that in the undisclosed principal setting the agent cannot be acting with apparent authority because the principal has manifested nothing to the third party. You should be aware that the *Restatement (Second) of Agency*, and hence many courts and commentators, used the term *partially disclosed principal* rather than *unidentified principal*.

d. Estoppel

A principal who has neither authorized nor apparently authorized an agent's action is nevertheless liable to third parties who have changed their position in reliance upon their belief that the action was authorized if the principal caused (intentionally or carelessly) the belief or, if the principal, knowing of the belief, did nothing to notify the third parties of the facts. *See Restatement (Third)* §2.05. Although estoppel has wide application elsewhere in the law, it has a very narrow place in agency law. First, remember that estoppel comes into play only where the agent's action was not actually authorized. Second, apparent authority covers many settings in which estoppel might otherwise apply. In those situations, the plaintiff can prevail against the principal simply by showing that the principal manifested to the plaintiff that the agent had the authority to act.

e. Ratification

The fourth theory of liability (in addition to actual and apparent authority and estoppel) is *ratification*. If *A* took action purportedly on behalf of or for the benefit of *B* (regardless of whether *A* was *B*'s agent) but such action did not bind *B*, *B* may nonetheless *ratify* that action. If *B* ratifies the action, *B* is treated as though *A* originally had actual authority to take the action. *See Restatement (Third)* §§4.02 and 4.03. *B* ratifies by manifesting assent, which is a manifestation of *B*'s election to treat the action as authorized. The manifestation can be express but need not be communicated to *A* or any third party to be effective. *See Restatement (Third)* §4.01 cmt. d. Ratification can also be manifested through conduct that is only principal explicable on the ground that the principal intends to ratify the agent's action. *See Restatement (Third)* §4.01(2)(b).

Putting It to Work

Problem 4-2

PanAmerican is an oil and gas exploration and drilling company. To negotiate and enter into mineral leases from land owners, PanAmerican hires landmen, as does virtually every other oil and gas exploration and drilling company. In March, PanAmerican hired[Robert with the title landman-in-training.] PanAmerican told Robert that if his performance were satisfactory for six months, he would become a permanent landman. PanAmerican also told Robert that during his six-month probationary period he could negotiate leases, but could not accept them, on behalf of PanAmerican.

In May, Robert called William, the attorney responsible for negotiating leases for Maud, a major landowner in an area rich in oil and gas deposits. Robert identified himself as a representative of PanAmerican. Robert informed William that Pan-American was interested in leasing minerals owned by Maud, and the two began negotiating. After agreeing on terms, William asked Robert to send him an offer in writing. Robert responded by sending an email to which he attached a form lease. The email, sent from the address "robert@panam.com" and dated May 28, read:

> Here is the lease form and our offer includes $150.00 per net mineral acre for a 3 year primary term, 1/5th royalty and a 2 yr option at $200.00 per net mineral acre. If you would fill in the lessor's address and make sure i put the correct name on there and if not change it to the capacity they would neet [sic] to sign the lease in.
> Thank you robert 806–555–8576

During the next four days, William and Robert exchanged several emails in which they discussed the lease's format and its contents. Believing the lease had been drafted to both parties' satisfaction, William sent Robert an email on June 2, accepting the offer and asking for the lease bonus on Maud's behalf. When the lease bonus was not paid promptly, William began a two-month campaign to secure its payment. Despite exchanging more emails with Robert, providing Robert with a copy of the signed lease, and mailing the original lease to Robert at PanAmerican's office, William failed to obtain the lease bonus for Maud.

1. Is PanAmerican liable to Maud on the lease under Agency law?
2. Would any of the following additional facts make a difference in your analysis?
   a. PanAmerican provided Robert with his email address, a phone number, and a cubical at PanAmerican's offices.
   b. PanAmerican told Robert he must identify himself to potential lessors as a landman-in-training and must state that he could negotiate leases for Pan-American but could not accept them.
   c. William never attempted to contact anyone at PanAmerican other than Robert.
   d. When Robert received the executed lease from William he sent it to PanAmerican's general counsel, unbeknownst to William. The general counsel did not respond to either Robert or William.

f. Restitution

The final theory is *restitution*. The principal is liable to make restitution to third parties where the principal is unjustly enriched by the agent's actions that are not within the agent's actual or apparent authority. *See Restatement (Third)* §2.07.

g. Principal's Liability for Agent's Torts

The previous theories have essentially involved liability for the agent's agreements made on the principal's behalf. The *Restatement (Third)* also holds a principal liable for an agent's torts in certain instances. Where the principal authorizes the agent to engage in conduct that is tortious, the principal is liable even though the principal may not have intended the conduct to be tortious. The typical setting would be where the agent is authorized to commit intentional torts that do not involve physical injury to people or property. *See Restatement (Thir[...]* is also liable for torts committed by an agent acting with a[...] ability to commit the tort is sufficiently related to the agenc[...] are misrepresentation, defamation, or conversion. *See Rest[...]*

What about torts that cause physical injury to persons o[...] rarely has actual authority to commit such actions and t[...] makes it clear that such injuries are usually too remote fr[...] authority to render the principal liable. *See Restatemen[...]* Nonetheless, principals may be liable for their agents' torts that result in physical injury in certain circumstances. The next three cases explore this theory of *vicarious liability*.

Jefferson v. Missouri Baptist Medical Center

447 S.W.3d 701 (Mo. App. E.D. 2014). *definition of employee*

LISA S. VAN AMBURG, Presiding Judge.

INTRODUCTION

Plaintiffs Collin and Courtney Jefferson, by and through their natural father and next friend, Eric Jefferson, ("the Jeffersons") appeal the Circuit Court of St. Louis County's grant of summary judgment in favor of defendant Missouri Baptist Medical Center ("MBMC"). On appeal, the Jeffersons argue that the trial court erred by granting summary judgment in favor of MBMC on the basis of section 538.210.2(3), R.S. Mo. (Cum. Supp. 2007). Specifically, they argue that the trial court incorrectly defined the term "employee" within the meaning of that section. We agree. We reverse the trial court's grant of summary judgment and remand for further proceedings consistent with this opinion.

FACTS

Viewed in a light most favorable to the Jeffersons, the following facts led to the instant suit. Decedent Crystal Jefferson delivered her first child at age 31 on October 27, 2005, via caesarian section at MBMC. During her time in the hospital, she experienced abdominal pain and underwent a CT scan of the abdomen and pelvis. The CT scan showed a soft tissue mass in the abdomen as well as fluid collection in the pelvis. The attending radiologist recommended a follow-up study.

Ms. Jefferson underwent a follow-up CT scan at MBMC on December 9, 2005. This second scan also showed a soft tissue mass in the abdomen and fluid collection in the pelvis. Again, the attending radiologist recommended a follow-up study to address both the tissue mass and the fluid.

On January 19, 2006, Ms. Jefferson underwent a third CT scan at MBMC. Dr. Mosher, a radiologist, read and interpreted the results of the study and posted remarks to Ms. Jefferson's medical chart. Dr. Mosher informed Ms. Jefferson that the fluid collection had resolved, but failed to mention in her post-study report or to Ms. Jefferson that the soft tissue mass was still present. Accordingly, Ms. Jefferson believed her medical problem had been resolved.

the spring of 2008, however, Ms. Jefferson began to notice an abnormal ssure in her abdomen. Testing soon revealed that the soft tissue mass was not only still present, but was in fact stage-IV colon cancer. By this point, the tissue mass was inoperable. As a result, Ms. Jefferson died of cancer in 2011.

The Jeffersons filed the instant suit on December 15, 2011, alleging that Ms. Jefferson's cancer would have been treated two years earlier if Dr. Mosher had not negligently overlooked the soft tissue mass during the 2006 CT scan.[1] In response, MBMC filed a motion for summary judgment citing section 538.210.2(3), which bars the Jeffersons from recovering against MBMC for the tortious actions of Dr. Mosher if Dr. Mosher is not MBMC's "employee." MBMC asserted that Dr. Mosher was actually an employee of Midwest Radiological Associates,[2] which directly contracted with and paid Dr. Mosher, rather than its own employee. After a hearing, the trial court granted summary judgment in favor of MBMC. This appeal follows.

DISCUSSION

Section 538.210.2(3) bars the Jeffersons from recovering against MBMC for the tortious actions of Dr. Mosher, if Dr. Mosher is not MBMC's "employee."

Because the legislature provided no definition of the term "employee" for the purposes of section 538.210.2(3), we must define that term here. We first address why the Jeffersons are correct that the term "employee" should be defined according to common-law principles of agency and discuss how those principles are applied. Second, we address MBMC's misapprehension that the legislature's use of the term "employee" precludes reference to the law of agency.

It is a familiar rule of construction that "[w]here a statute uses words that have a definite and well-known meaning at common law, it will be presumed that the terms are used in the sense in which they were understood at common law. . . ." *State ex rel. Auto Owners Ins. Co. v. Messina*, 331 S.W.3d 662, 665 (Mo. banc 2011) (quoting *Belcher v. State*, 299 S.W.3d 294, 296 (Mo. banc 2009)). The Restatement (Third) of Agency defines the term "employee" as "an agent whose principal *controls or has the right to control* the manner and means of the agent's performance of work." Restatement (Third) of Agency section 7.07(3)(a) (emphasis added) (referencing respondeat superior).

This focus on the principal's right to control is consistent with other areas of Missouri law where a test for the presence of an employment relationship is germane. Regarding employment security for instance, the legislature provided in section 288.034(5), R.S. Mo. (Cum. Supp. 2011), that the question of whether an individual is an employee, as opposed to a non-employee independent contractor, should be determined according to "the common law of agency right to control." Likewise, in the context of common-law tort liability, Missouri courts have continually used the extent of the principal's control over the agent's work performance as a measure of whether an employment relationship exists. *See Sakabu v. Regency*

1. The Jeffersons also named as defendants Midwest Radiological Associates and Dr. Mosher herself. These claims were resolved separately from the claim against MBMC now on appeal.
2. Midwest Radiological Associates is a partnership of doctors affiliated with MBMC. According to the Jeffersons' reply to MBMC's motion for summary judgment, a radiologist is not permitted to practice at MBMC unless she is also a member of Midwest Radiological Associates.

Constr. Co., 392 S.W.3d 494, 498 (Mo. App. E.D. 2012) ("Employees and independent contractors are distinguished primarily on the basis of the amount of control the alleged employer has over them."); *Bargfrede v. Am. Income Life Ins. Co.*, 21 S.W.3d 157, 162 (Mo. App. W.D. 2000) (distinguishing independent contractor from employee based on the employer's "right or power to control and direct the physical conduct of the [employee or agent] in the performance of the act").

Both the Restatement and Missouri case law provide guidelines for determining whether a sufficient degree of control exists for the establishment of an employment relationship. The Restatement (Third) of Agency counsels that numerous "factual indicia" are relevant to determining whether an agent who does work at the behest of a principal is an "employee," including:

> [1] the extent of control that the agent and the principal have agreed the principal may exercise over details of the work [and the extent of control exercised in practice]; [2] whether the agent is engaged in a distinct occupation or business; [3] whether the type of work done by the agent is customarily done under a principal's direction or without supervision; [4] the skill required in the agent's occupation; [5] whether the agent or the principal supplies the tools and other instrumentalities required for the work and the place in which to perform it; [6] the length of time during which the agent is engaged by a principal; [7] whether the agent is paid by the job or by the time worked; [8] whether the agent's work is part of the principal's regular business; [9] whether the principal and the agent believe that they are creating an employment relationship; [10] and whether the principal is or is not in business.

Restatement (Third) of Agency section 7.07 cmt. f; *cf.* Restatement (Third) of Agency section 7.07 rep. n. f ("[Some s]tatutes . . . explicitly adopt the common-law test articulated in this section to determine whether a person should be characterized as an employee for purposes of the statute. . . . Many cases apply the specific criteria mentioned in the Comment. . . .").

In applying the foregoing Restatement factors, the central rule is that the more control the principal may exercise over the agent, the more likely the agent is an employee. However, it is not a matter of "whether [the principal] actually exercised control over the work . . . [but a matter of] whether [the principal] had the right to exercise that control." *Bargfrede*, 21 S.W.3d at 162.

As to each of the individual Restatement factors, we observe that the following facts would indicate that an employment relationship does exist:

> [1] an agreement for close supervision or de facto close supervision of the [agent's] work; [2] work which does not require the services of one highly educated or skilled; [3] the supplying of tools by the [principal]; [4] payment by hour or month; [5] [working] over a considerable period of time with regular hours; [6] full time [work for one principal]; [7] [work] in a specific area or over a fixed route; [8] the fact that the work is part of the regular business of the [principal]; [9] the fact that the community regards those doing such work as [employees]; [10] the belief by the parties that there is a [employer] and [employee] relation; [11] an agreement that the work cannot be delegated.

Restatement (Second) of Agency section 220 cmt. h. (1958).

Furthermore, an employer's right to control may be attenuated, and an employee may have a significant degree of discretion in her work.[11] Restatement

---

11. The Restatement (Third) of Agency provides the following example of an attenuated employment relationship:

> A, the CEO of P Corporation, exercises general managerial authority over its operations. P Corporation's directors, concerned that A's impaired vision makes it unsafe for A to drive, direct A to use a driver and car

(Third) of Agency section 7.07 cmt. f. Importantly here, "Missouri courts have long recognized that physicians must be free to exercise independent medical judgment." *Scott v. SSM Healthcare St. Louis*, 70 S.W.3d 560, 568 (Mo. App. E.D. 2002). "The mere fact that a physician retains such independent judgment will not preclude a court, in an otherwise proper case, from finding the existence of an employer-employee . . . relationship between a hospital and physician." *Id.* A physician should not be deemed a non-employee agent "merely because the hospital does not have the right to stand over the [physician's] shoulder and dictate to him or her how to diagnose and treat patients." *Id.*

Despite the foregoing authority, MBMC contends that we may not reference "the common law of agency," because the terms "agent" and "employee" are not synonymous. While it is true that these terms are not synonymous, MBMC misapprehends the import of this fact.

An employee is a subset of agent distinguished by the principal's right to control the details of the employee's work performance. *See* Restatement (Third) of Agency section 7.07 cmt. f. (2006) (An "agent [is] . . . not [an] employee[ ] [if she] retain[s] the right to control how [she] perform[s her] work."). In particular, this distinction gains significance in light of the different theories of principal-agent liability, e.g., direct or vicarious, applicable to non-employee agents and employee agents respectively. *See* Restatement (Third) of Agency section 7.03, 7.03 cmt. b. (2006) (noting generally that "direct liability [for, inter alia, a non-employee agent's conduct] requires fault on the part of the principal whereas vicarious liability [for, inter alia, an employee agent's conduct] does not require that the principal be at fault"). Therefore, as MBMC suggests, it is reasonable to conclude that when the legislature used the term "employee" in section 538.210.2(3), it did not mean to include all individuals who might be classified as "agents" in the broadest sense of that term.

Contrary to MBMC's contention, however, the legislature's failure to use the terms "agent" or "agency" in section 538.210.2(3) does not indicate that it intended to ban all reference to "the common law of agency" in determining whether an employment relationship exists. Missouri courts have long referred to the Restatement of Agency when asked to determine whether an employment relationship exists. In fact, they often use the words "agent" and "employee" interchangeably in that context. Thus, the technical distinction between an "agent" and an "employee" is of relatively minor significance here, and the question of whether Dr. Mosher is MBMC's "employee" within the meaning of section 538.210.2(3) should be determined by reference to common-law principles of agency.

CONCLUSION

The trial court erred as a matter of law when it determined section 538.210.2(3) barred the Jeffersons' claim. . . . We reverse the trial court's grant of summary judgment. We remand to the trial court with instructions to apply, in further

---

to be furnished by P Corporation when A travels by car on business. P Corporation's directors have the right so to direct A. A is an employee of P Corporation for this purpose.

Restatement (Third) of Agency §7.07 cmt. f., illus. 15 (2006).

proceedings, the definition of the term "employee" in section 538.210.2(3) in a manner consistent with this opinion.

PATRICIA L. COHEN and PHILIP M. HESS, JJ., concur.

Notes and Questions

1. Notes

a. The *Restatement (Second) of Agency* and many courts and commentators used the terms *master* and *servant* in place of *employer* and *employee*. The *Restatement (Third)*, as you see, uses the more modern terms.

b. The court speaks of *independent contractors*, a status the *Restatement (Third)* does not recognize. The *Restatement (Second)* and some, but not all, commentators found the term useful. The *Restatement (Second)* defined an independent contractor as "a person who contracts with another to do something for him but who is not controlled by the other nor subject to the other's right to control with respect to his physical conduct in the performance of the undertaking. He may or may not be an agent." Analytically, an employee cannot be an independent contractor. Agents who are not employees are independent contractors. However, independent contractors may or may not be agents. Got it? The *Restatement (Third)* abandoned the term independent contractor because it is equivocal and confusing (does it mean agents? Non-agents? Yes.).

c. As the court points out, the agency law definition of employee is used in many other legal settings.

d. Physicians frequently join with other physicians practicing the same specialty through practice groups, which may be partnerships, professional corporations, or LLCs. Many physicians want to treat some or all of their patients in a hospital and to do so, each physician must obtain hospital privileges. Each hospital sets its own standards for education, experience, and competence for granting privileges and a physician's privileges can be revoked for such things as misconduct, incompetence, state disciplinary issues, or lack of insurance. Typically, the grant of privileges to each physician is reviewed periodically. According to the Jeffersons' brief, MBMC contracted with Midwest Radiological Associates to provide radiological services to patients. Midwest was the exclusive provider of radiologists to MBMC. MBMC paid Midwest which, in turn, paid the physicians who owned or worked for it, including Dr. Mosher. MBMC employed all nurses and technicians supporting the radiologists. MBMC also owned all the hospital's radiology office space and radiology equipment, which was selected and purchased by MBMC.

2. Reality Check

a. Why is it important to determine whether Dr. Mosher was an employee? *See Restatement (Third)* §§2.04 and 7.07(1).

b. What is the definition of "employee?" What facts bear on whether a person is an employee?

c. Are "agent" and "employee" mutually exclusive?

d. If Dr. Mosher were an employee, who was her principal/employer? Could she have more than one? *See* footnote 1.

3. Suppose

a. Suppose Dr. Mosher had two principals. Could she be a non-employee agent of one principal and an employee of the other? If so, how?

4. What Do You Think?

a. Do you think Dr. Mosher was an employee of MBMC? Why? Consider the additional facts in Note d above.

b. Why should MBMC's liability depend upon such facts as whether it supplies Dr. Mosher's tools and workspace?

c. Recall that the Jeffersons settled with Dr. Mosher and with her practice group. Why shouldn't the Jeffersons be limited those settlements? After all, Dr. Mosher was the allegedly negligent tortfeasor. MBMC is not alleged to have committed any tort.

d. More generally, do you think a principal should ever be liable for an agent's unauthorized tort? If so, in what situations should liability attach to the principal? Do you think a principal should always be liable for an agent's unauthorized tort? Remember that in all these situations, the agent is personally liable to the plaintiff. Does your answer depend on your view of the purposes of agency law or does it depend on your view of the purposes of tort law?

A careful reading of the *Restatement (Third)* reveals that finding that a tortfeasor is an employee is only half the battle in terms of holding the employer liable under *respondeat superior*. The next case focuses on the second requirement.

Solberg v. Borden Light Marina, Inc.

2014 WL 4245987 (D. Mass. Aug. 25, 2014).

CASPER, District Judge.

MEMORANDUM AND ORDER

Introduction

Plaintiffs Richard Solberg ("Solberg") and Dorine Solberg (collectively, the "Solbergs") have filed this lawsuit against Defendants Borden Light Marina ("BLM"), Michel Lund ("Lund") and Kevin Munro ("Munro"). Solberg alleges general maritime law negligence while Dorine Solberg alleges loss of consortium. BLM has moved for summary judgment. For the reasons stated below, the Court DENIES BLM's motion.

Factual Background and Procedural History

The following facts are drawn from BLM's statement of material facts and are not disputed by the Solbergs. Solberg is a musician who leads a musical group (the "Band"). Lund is the President of BLM. The Tipsy Seagull is a restaurant and bar owned by Barge, LLC, an entity distinct from BLM. Solberg and the Band performed at The Tipsy Seagull on the evening of May 27, 2011 and were scheduled to perform again the following evening.

Before the Band's second performance, Lund took Solberg and others on a boat ride on the Taunton River. With Lund at the helm, the boat struck a submerged rock resulting in injury to Solberg.

The Solbergs also allege that Lund is a manager of Barge, LLC, the alleged owner of The Tipsy Seagull. While not involved in the day to day operations, he supervises The Tipsy Seagull's managers and oversees the hiring of musicians. Prior to May, 2011, the Band had played at The Tipsy Seagull on at least two occasions. For each of the Band's performances, Lund dealt with Solberg to hire the Band and Lund paid the Band's fee.

The Tipsy Seagull is located on BLM premises. The Tipsy Seagull is a floating bar accessed only by a gangway from a float that houses the BLM fuel dock which is owned and maintained by BLM. BLM encouraged its customers to visit The Tipsy Seagull, rewarding them with points they can use to reduce their bills. BLM advertises The Tipsy Seagull on its logo, its website and in its newsletters. BLM also advertises that it is the home of The Tipsy Seagull while the Tipsy Seagull advertises that it is part of the BLM family.

Discussion

The doctrine of *respondeat superior* provides that an employer is subject to liability for the torts of its employees committed while acting within the scope of their employment. Restatement (Third) of Agency §2.04 (2006). An employee is acting within the scope of his employment if (1) his conduct is of the kind he is employed to perform; (2) it occurs substantially within the authorized time and space limits; and (3) it is motivated, at least in part, by a purpose to serve the employer. *Wang Labs., Inc. v. Bus. Incentives, Inc.*, 398 Mass. 854, 859, 501 N.E.2d 1163 (1986) (internal citations omitted); *see Roggio v. City of Gardner*, No. 10-40076-FDS, 2011 U.S. Dist. LEXIS 34731 at *16, 2011 WL 1303141 (D. Mass. Mar. 30, 2011); *Lev v. Beverly Enters.-Mass., Inc.*, 457 Mass. 234, 238, 929 N.E.2d 303 (2010); Restatement (Third) of Agency §7.07 (2006).

BLM argues that it is entitled to summary judgment because the evidence does not demonstrate that BLM was responsible for Lund's actions. According to BLM, Lund was not on duty as president of BLM when the accident occurred, the boat was not owned by BLM and no business was transacted or discussed during the excursion. BLM notes that the boat ride was not part of the any contract between Solberg (or the Band) and any other party. BLM points to Solberg's deposition testimony that he did not expect a boat ride as part of his compensation for performing at The Tipsy Seagull. BLM also relies on Lund's deposition testimony to support its contention that Lund hosted Solberg on the boat purely as a friend and not in his role as president of BLM. The accident occurred on a boat owned by Munro and not by BLM. BLM contends that the unrebutted evidence shows that the boat ride was not authorized or endorsed by BLM and that the boat ride was not part of Solberg's compensation for his performances at The Tipsy Seagull.

The Solbergs respond that there is a genuine issue of material fact as to whether Lund was acting within the scope of his employment with BLM at the time of the accident. They argue that a jury could reasonably conclude that the boat ride was the type of task Lund was employed to perform at BLM, especially given the scope of Lund's responsibilities, and that the boat ride occurred within the time and space limits authorized by BLM where Lund's position requires him to deal with all facets of BLM's daily operations without regard to location or schedule. Moreover, the Solbergs assert that that a jury could reasonably conclude that Lund's motivation for the boat ride was at least in part to serve BLM's interests by providing a business-related "perk" to the Band "as part of the deal" for performing at The Tipsy Seagull.

factors for scope of employment

The Court agrees with the Solbergs that there is a genuine issue of material fact as to whether Lund was acting as a BLM employee when he hosted Solberg on the boat ride. Lund had responsibilities at both The Tipsy Seagull and BLM, and the Court cannot conclude, on the present record, that Lund was not acting on behalf of BLM at the time of the accident, particularly where Lund completed BLM-related tasks immediately prior to the boat ride, he was responsible for organizing social events for BLM customers, and Lund hired Solberg and paid him in cash. Moreover, when Solberg performed at The Tipsy Seagull, Solberg would sleep on boats docked at BLM, and he testified that boat rides, food and lodging were perks he commonly received as a performer. BLM encouraged BLM customers to patronize The Tipsy Seagull and its advertising and communications included The Tipsy Seagull. A jury could reasonably conclude that it was within the purview of Lund's authority at BLM to host a performer on a boat ride.

A jury could also conclude that the boat ride occurred within authorized time and space limits given that the boat left from BLM, the premises containing the performance venue, and occurred on a day on which Lund worked at BLM. Finally, a jury could reasonably conclude that Lund was motivated at least in part to serve BLM. The boat ride could be viewed as a perk to performers hired to entertain BLM customers. Lund's desire to promote BLM and organize events for BLM's customers could have influenced his offer to host Solberg on the boat ride.

The Court need not address BLM's argument that there was no apparent authority bestowed on Lund by BLM. "Apparent authority is the power held by an agent or other actor to affect a principal's legal relations with third parties when a third party reasonably believes the actor has authority to act on behalf of the principal and that belief is traceable to the principal's manifestations." *CSX Transp., Inc. v. Recovery Express, Inc.*, 415 F. Supp. 2d 6, 10 (D. Mass. 2006) (quoting Restatement (Third) of Agency §2.03). Apparent authority depends on the words or conduct of the principal, not the agent, and exists only when the third party's belief that the putative agent is authorized to act on behalf of the principal is reasonable. BLM argues that its conduct did not suggest apparent authority and that nothing in the record indicates Solberg's detrimental reliance. The Solbergs, however, do not assert that there was apparent authority. The parties agree that Lund was an employee of BLM. Once an employer-employee relationship is established, the only remaining inquiry is whether the alleged tort occurred within the scope of employment, . . . a matter that, as discussed above, the Court cannot now resolve in BLM's favor.

Conclusion

For the foregoing reasons, the Court DENIES BLM's motion for summary judgment.

Notes and Questions

1. Notes

a. The oral argument on the motion that resulted in this opinion is at http://www.uscourts.gov/cameras-courts/richard-solberg-et-al-v-borden-light-marina-inc-et-al.

b. The three-part definition of "scope of employment," cited by the court with Massachusetts case law authority, is from the *Restatement (Second) of Agency*. The most significant difference between that definition and §7.07(2) of the *Restatement (Third)* is that §7.07(2) does not consider the time and space limits. Comment b to that section explains that this limitation "does not naturally encompass the working circumstances of many managerial and professional employees and others whose work is not so readily cabined by temporal or spatial limitations. Many employees in contemporary workforces interact on an employer's behalf with third parties although the employee is neither situated on the employer's premises nor continuously or exclusively engaged in performing assigned work." The case law in many states still uses the older formulation of the definition.

c. *Restatement (Third)* §7.07(2) contains a positive and a negative definition of the scope of employment. The two definitions are meant to be reciprocal so that "work assigned by the employer" and "course of conduct subject to the employer's control" are the opposite of "independent course of conduct not intended by the employee to serve any purpose of the employer." Courts often use the phrase "frolic and detour" to describe the conclusion that the agent's action was not within the scope of employment. Originally, the two terms had different meanings. If the employee's actions were not within the scope of employment, the agent was said to be on a "frolic." If the agent's actions were within the scope of employment, the agent was said to be on a "detour."

2. Reality Check

a. Why does the undisputed fact that Lund was an employee of BLM not automatically result in BLM's liability?

b. Does the court decide whether Lund was acting within the scope of employment?

c. What purpose of BLM was Lund trying to serve when he took Solberg out on the boat?

3. Suppose

a. Suppose the court applied *Restatement (Third)* §7.07(2). Would the analysis or the result have been different?

b. Suppose the Solbergs had sued Barge, LLC, the owner of The Tipsy Seagull, instead of BLM. Would 7.07 impose liability on Barge, LLC based on Lund's actions? Was Lund an agent of Barge, LLC? Was he an employee of Barge, LLC? If so, was he acting within the scope of his employment by Barge, LLC?

c. Suppose the Solbergs had sued both Barge, LLC and BLM? Would both entities be liable under *respondeat superior*?

4. What Do You Think?

a. Do you think Lund was acting within the scope of his employment by BLM? Was he trying to help BLM when he took Solberg out on the boat? Was he trying to help Barge, LLC? Neither? Both?

b. Do you think BLM ought to be vicariously liable for Lund's actions? Does it make a difference to you that Solberg and the Band performed at The Tipsy Seagull, owned by different entity?

The final case in this section involves a principal's direct, as well as vicarious, liability to a third party for an agent's torts.

Valentine v. Hodnett

2015 WL 12942069 (S.D. Tex. Sept. 16, 2015)

Diana Song Quiroga, United States Magistrate Judge

REPORT AND RECOMMENDATION

This case arises from a motor vehicle accident between Justin Hodnett ("Hodnett") and Jimmy Martin Valentine ("Valentine"). Valentine died at the scene of the accident, and his wife and children (collectively, "Plaintiffs") brought suit, in relevant part, against Hodnett and his employer LouTex Contractors, Inc. ("LouTex"). The District Court referred LouTex's Motion for Summary Judgment . . . to the undersigned Magistrate Judge. Having considered the parties' arguments and the applicable law, the undersigned . . . recommends that the Motion for Summary Judgment be granted.

BACKGROUND

Hodnett began working for LouTex on Monday, June 11, 2012—four days before the fatal accident. He was employed by the company as a driving assistant; and his main duties included helping LouTex's drivers with directions, guiding its trucks, and flagging traffic when necessary. Hodnett's duties also involved some physical labor including helping to lift heavy equipment. He was not hired for the purpose of driving, and he did not drive a LouTex-owned vehicle during his short tenure with the company. Nor did he drive his personal vehicle for any work-related purpose. Instead, he used his truck for his private purposes—such as running errands. (Hodnett: "[T]he only time I used my vehicle was to go get my own breakfast and my own lunch.").

Because LouTex operated several remote worksites, it provided portable buildings for its employees to rent if they wished to avoid long commutes to work. Hodnett stayed in one of these trailers while working for LouTex and paid the company approximately $150.00 per week in rent. Each morning Hodnett reported to the nearby office area—which was within walking distance of the portable trailer homes—to be transported by another LouTex employee to that day's jobsite. Hodnett testified that he was paid from the moment he was picked up in the morning until the moment he was dropped off in the evening. Consequently, he was not compensated for any time spent living in the portable trailer provided by LouTex, and he was not on-call after his shift was over.

On the evening of June 14, 2012, Hodnett finished his ten-hour shift with LouTex at approximately 5:00 p.m. After work, he went to Doctor's Hospital in Laredo, Texas, to obtain treatment for lower back pain. Hodnett received a shot of narcotics while at the hospital and returned to his portable trailer to sleep.

On the morning of June 15, 2012, Hodnett drove his personal vehicle from his portable trailer to a nearby gas station. According to his undisputed deposition testimony, he was going to the gas station for the purpose of buying breakfast and lunch. After picking up his food, he planned to return to LouTex's office area to be picked up for his next shift. However, Hodnett never made it to work on June 15, 2012, because at approximately 6:25 a.m. he veered into oncoming traffic and collided with the vehicle driven by Valentine while driving to the gas station. Valentine died at the scene, and Hodnett was transported to the hospital. While investigating the scene of the accident, police officers found a bottle of Hydrocodone that was prescribed to Hodnett inside his vehicle. Hodnett was not subjected to a blood test following the accident.

As a [new] employee of LouTex, Hodnett was required to take a drug test before beginning work. Hodnett's drug test was negative for any illicit drugs, however, he admitted to regularly taking prescription Hydrocodone to relieve his back pain both before and during his employment with LouTex. Hodnett testified that his back pain arose from a preexisting back injury that anteceded his employment with LouTex. Hodnett stated that he informed LouTex of his Hydrocodone usage on his first day of work on Monday, June 11th, and that, in response, LouTex's safety inspector told him to "take it properly and not overdo it." He also stated that he had not taken any Hydrocodone on the morning of the accident.

LouTex argues that Hodnett was off-duty at the time of the accident and was acting exclusively for his personal benefit. Consequently, LouTex asserts that, as a matter of law, it cannot be held vicariously liable for the tort of an off-duty employee who was not acting within the scope of his employment and was not furthering LouTex's business purposes.

Plaintiffs [argue] that LouTex is vicariously liable to Valentine for Hodnett's negligence, gross negligence and negligence per se and directly liable for its own negligence and gross negligence. The Court discerns four claims Plaintiffs raise . . . : (1) liability can be imputed to LouTex because Hodnett was acting within the scope of his employment when the accident occurred; . . . and (4) LouTex is directly liable because it negligently hired and supervised Hodnett.

SUMMARY JUDGMENT

LouTex's Duties to Valentine

To establish tort liability, a plaintiff must prove the existence of a duty owed to him by the defendant and a subsequent breach of that duty. *See Otis Eng'g Corp. v. Clark*, 668 S.W.2d 307, 309 (Tex. 1983) (citing *Abalos v. Oil Development Co. of Texas*, 544 S.W.2d 627, 631 (Tex. 1976)). "Liability is grounded in the public policy behind the law of negligence which dictates every person is responsible for injuries which are the reasonably foreseeable consequence of his act or omission."

Nabors Drilling, Inc. v. Escoto, 288 S.W.3d 401, 403 (Tex. 2009) (citing *El Chico Corp. v. Poole*, 732 S.W.2d 306, 315 (Tex. 1987)). "[The] factors which should be considered in determining whether the law should impose a duty are the risk, foreseeability, and likelihood of injury weighed against the social utility of the actor's conduct, the magnitude of the burden of guarding against the injury and the consequences of placing that burden on the employer." *Otis*, 668 S.W.2d at 309 (citing *Robertson v. LeMaster*, 301 S.E.2d 563 (W. Va. 1983)).

Generally, there is no duty to control the conduct of another person even if the practical ability to exercise such control exists. *See Otis*, 668 S.W.2d at 309. However, common law does impose a duty to control the conduct of another when a special relationship—such as parent-child or employer-employee—exists between the individual and the tortfeasor. Here, the relevant relationship is that of employer and employee.

Historically, an employer has possessed a duty to control his employee and prevent harm to others in two limited situations. First, an employer will be held liable for the tortious conduct of its on-duty employee if the employee is acting within the scope of her employment when the harm occurs. Restatement (Third) Agency §2.04 (2006) ("An employer is subject to liability for torts committed by employees while acting within the scope of their employment."). Second, it is generally accepted that an employer will be held liable for the off-duty torts of its employee if the employee committed the tort while on the employer's premises or while using the employer's chattel and the employer had the ability to control the employee and knew of the necessity of exercising such control. *See Otis*, 668 S.W.2d at 309.

In addition to these two well established duties, Texas courts have . . . recognized a duty when an employer knows or should have known its employee is unfit or incompetent to perform her job and the employer is aware of the unreasonable risk of harm presented by the unfit employee.

The primary basis for imposing these narrow duties upon an employer based on its relationship with its employee is that the employer, in certain situations, possesses knowledge of foreseeable danger to others and has the authority to control the acts of its employee to prevent the harm. *See* Restatement (Third) Agency §7.05. Therefore, knowledge and control are essential elements in determining whether LouTex owed any of these narrow duties to Valentine.

i. Vicarious Liability.   Because LouTex employed Hodnett at the time of the accident, Plaintiffs seek to impute Hodnett's alleged negligence, gross negligence and negligence per se to LouTex. One of the most common claims injured parties utilize to hold an employer responsible for the tortious acts of its employee is respondeat superior.[8] For the purpose of resolving this motion, the Court will

---

8. Comment (b) to the Third Restatement of Agency, §2.04, discusses the history and purpose behind the doctrine of respondeat superior:

> The doctrine [of respondeat superior] establishes a principle of employer liability for the costs that work-related torts impose on third parties. Its scope is limited to the employment relationship and to conduct falling within the scope of that relationship *because an employer has the right to control how work is done*. . . . Most often the doctrine applies to acts that have not been specifically directed by an employer but that are the consequence of inattentiveness or poor judgment on the part of an employee acting within the job description.

(Emphasis added.)

assume that Hodnett was, in fact, negligent in causing the accident and will turn to the question of whether his liability can be imputed to his employer, LouTex.

Generally, an employee is not within the scope of the employer's business when driving his own vehicle for his own purposes before or after work. *See, e.g., Ginther v. Domino's Pizza, Inc.*, 93 S.W.3d 300, 303-04 (Tex. App. 2002) (holding that Domino's Pizza was not liable when its off-duty employee caused the death of a third party while driving his friends around in the personal vehicle he also used to deliver pizzas); *see also J & C Drilling Co. v. Salaiz*, 866 S.W.2d 632, 636 (Tex. App. San Antonio 1993) (citing *Am. Gen. Ins. Co. v. Coleman*, 303 S.W.2d 370, 374 (Tex. 1957)) ("It is the general rule that use of public streets or highways in going to or returning from one's place of employment is not within the scope of one's employment."). Moreover, when an employee engages in a personal errand, the employee is not acting within the course and scope of his employment. *See, e.g., J & C Drilling Co.*, 866 S.W.2d at 636 (holding that an employer is not liable under the doctrine of respondeat superior for injuries caused by an employee, who fell asleep while on call for a twenty-four hour period and driving a company-owned car, because the employee was on the way to purchase dinner at a local restaurant); *Diamond M Onshore v. Gutierrez*, 1998 Tex. App. LEXIS 5598 (Tex. App. San Antonio Aug. 31, 1998) (holding an on call employee who injured a third party while driving to a local restaurant was not within the scope of his employment); *Goodyear Tire & Rubber Co. v. Mayes*, 236 S.W.3d 754 (Tex. 2007) (holding that Goodyear was not liable for an accident caused by its employee who drove a company truck to a convenience store to purchase cigarettes). The doctrine of respondeat superior does not impose liability on employers for accidents that occur during their employee's personal time, because the employer has no authority to control, direct or alter the employee's conduct before or after the employee's shift. *See* Restatement (Third) Agency §§7.05, 7.07.

Plaintiffs assert that, "[a]t the time of the accident Justin Hodnett was acting as the agent and employee of LouTex Contractors, Inc . . . and he was acting within the course and scope of his authority and employment and in the furtherance of his employer's business . . . and any negligence of Justin Hodnett is imputed to LouTex Contractors, Inc." However, they concede that at the time of the accident "Hodnett was not 'on the clock' "and that "he was driving his pickup truck to a nearby gas station in order to buy the day's breakfast and lunch."

The summary judgment evidence shows that Hodnett finished his shift on the evening of June 14, 2012, visited the hospital to receive an injection of narcotics to ease his back pain, returned to his portable trailer to sleep and, on the morning of June 15, 2012, woke up and drove his personal vehicle to a local gas station to buy breakfast and lunch. On his way to the gas station, he was involved in a motor vehicle accident that claimed the life of Valentine. At the time of the accident, Hodnett's shift had not begun and he was not on-call. Plaintiffs offer no evidence that Hodnett was acting within the scope of his employment or furthering LouTex's business purposes on the early morning of June 15th. Rather, all of the evidence shows that Hodnett was running a personal errand before the workday began and that LouTex did not control, direct or alter his conduct in any way. Because the Plaintiffs have produced no evidence supporting the essential elements of a respondeat superior claim, they cannot impute Hodnett's alleged negligence, gross negligence, and negligence per se to LouTex.

Having concluded that Plaintiffs' vicarious liability claims are unsupported by law and fact, the Court must now consider whether Plaintiffs' independent negligence claims against LouTex can survive summary judgment.

ii. Direct Liability. Plaintiffs also seek to hold LouTex directly liable as Hodnett's employer for its own negligence and gross negligence with respect to Valentine. Texas employers generally owe no independent duty of care to third parties for the off-duty tortious acts of their employees. Texas courts have recognized three narrow exceptions to this general rule when: . . . (3) an employer hired and retained an employee despite knowing the employee was unfit or incompetent to perform the job.

"Under the common-law doctrine regarding negligent hiring and supervision of employees, an employer's negligent performance of those duties may impose liability on an employer if the complainant's injuries result from the employer's failure to take reasonable precautions to protect the complainant from the misconduct of its employees." 33 Tex. Jur. 3d Employer and Employee §361 (2015); *see also Waffle House, Inc. v. Williams*, 314 S.W.3d 1, 10 (Tex. App. Fort Worth 2007) (citing *Mackey v. U.P. Enterprises, Inc.*, 935 S.W.2d 446, 459 (Tex. App. Tyler 1996)). The duty arises when the employer hires or retains an incompetent employee who the employer knew or, in the exercise of ordinary care, should have known was incompetent or unfit, thereby creating an unreasonable risk of harm to others. In other words, the basis of liability is the employer's own negligence in hiring or retaining an unfit employee. While liability may be imposed on an employer even when its employee's wrongful act falls outside the scope of his employment, the theories of negligent hiring and supervision do require that the harm result from the employment . . . If the law did not require such a connection, "an employer would essentially be an insurer of the safety of every person who happens to come into contact with his employee simply because of his status as an employee." *Dieter v. Baker Services Tools*, 739 S.W.2d 405, 408 (Tex. App. Corpus Christi 1987).

To prevail on a negligent hiring or retention claim, a plaintiff must demonstrate that the employer's negligence in hiring or retaining the employee was the proximate cause of the plaintiff's injury. "Proximate cause has two elements: cause in fact and foreseeability." *W. Invs., Inc. v. Urena*, 162 S.W.3d 547, 551 (Tex. 2005). Texas courts have required some nexus between the plaintiff's injury and the employee's work duties before imposing liability under a theory of negligent hiring or retention. This nexus between the harm and the employee's job is the crux of determining cause-in-fact. *See Najera v. Recana Solutions*, LLC, 2015 Tex. App. LEXIS 8748, *13 (Tex. App. Houston 14th Dist. Aug. 20, 2015) (citing *Wise v. Complete Staffing Servs., Inc.*, 56 S.W.3d 900, 901 (Tex. App. Texarkana 2001)) ("[T]he general negligent hiring rule [ ] is not aimed at avoiding a general propensity for bad acts, but rather at protecting against workers who are unsafe or dangerous on the job—*i.e.*, their incompetency must be somehow job-related.") If the injury causing conduct is wholly unrelated to the employee's job, then the employer's negligence in hiring, retaining, or supervising the employee cannot be the cause-in-fact of the injury.

Foreseeability, the second component of proximate cause, "requires that a person of ordinary intelligence should have anticipated the danger created by a negligent act or omission." *Doe v. Boys Clubs of Greater Dallas, Inc.*, 907 S.W.2d 472, 478 (Tex. 1995). A danger of injury is foreseeable if its "general character . . . might reasonably have been anticipated." *Id.* (internal quotation marks omitted) (quoting *Nixon v. Mr. Property Mgmt. Co.*, 690 S.W.2d 546, 551 (Tex. 1985)). Therefore, an employer is directly liable to third parties only when it places an incompetent employee in a situation that creates a foreseeable risk of harm to others because of that employee's particular duties. An employer is not liable when there is nothing in the employee's background that would lead a reasonable employer not to hire or retain the employee.

Plaintiffs contend that LouTex is liable for negligent hiring and retention because it knew Hodnett was incompetent to perform manual labor because of his preexisting back-injury. They assert that LouTex also knew Hodnett used Hydrocodone to overcome his back pain while conducting manual labor. Therefore, by hiring Hodnett—knowing his unfitness for manual labor—LouTex endorsed and contributed to his use of Hydrocodone which, according to Plaintiffs, proximately caused the death of Valentine.

Plaintiffs' contentions, however, lack factual support in the record. Construing the evidence in the record in the light most favorable to the Plaintiffs, LouTex knew or should have known that Hodnett had a preexisting back injury and was prescribed Hydrocodone. However, Hodnett's injury and use of prescription medication, in and of itself, did not render him incompetent or unfit for the job for which he was hired. According to the uncontested evidence, Hodnett was hired by LouTex to assist with the process of moving heavy equipment from one job-site to another. He was not hired to drive any of LouTex's company-owned vehicles or equipment; but rather was a laborer who assisted other employees with loading the heavy equipment onto flat-bed trailers and then served as a spotter (in the passenger-seat) for the tractor-trailer driver. Thus, because Hodnett was not hired to drive and was never asked to drive for LouTex, his employement with LouTex could not have been the cause-in-fact of the accident.

Additionally, based on the facts in the record, there is nothing in Hodnett's background that would have caused a reasonable employer not to hire him. Hodnett had no record of DWIs, and there is no probative summary judgment evidence of previous workplace misconduct or incapacitation. If courts began imposing liability on employers simply because they knew their employees took prescription medication at the time they were hired, it would set a sweeping precedent that would render vast segments of the population unemployable.

Even indulging in several assumptions that are most favorable to Plaintiffs—including that Hodnett was incompetent to perform heavy manual labor, his work with LouTex caused his back pain and he was intoxicated on the morning of the accident—LouTex could not have reasonably foreseen or prevented Hodnett's tortious conduct and Hodnett's employment with LouTex was not the cause-in-fact of Valentine's death. In this case, there is no nexus between Hodnett's employment with LouTex and the accident. At the time of the accident Hodnett was off-duty and was driving his personal vehicle to purchase his own meals. Because Hodnett left his portable trailer home almost twelve hours after his shift with

LouTex had ended, there was no link between his injury-causing conduct and his job. There was also no opportunity for LouTex to reasonably control Hodnett's conduct or take precautions to prevent injury to others. Because Valentine's injury was not the foreseeable result of Hodnett's employment, LouTex is not liable for an injury to a third party under a negligent hiring theory. Accordingly, the undersigned concludes that, on this record, summary judgment should be granted because no facts support a claim for negligent hiring or retention.

CONCLUSION

For the reasons set forth above, the undersigned . . . recommends that Lou-Tex's Motion for Summary Judgment be granted.

Notes and Questions

1. Notes

a. A large number of cases asserting liability under *respondeat superior* involve motor vehicle accidents. Most courts that have considered the question hold that an employee who is commuting to or from work from the employee's residence is not acting within the scope of employment, although courts' rationales vary. Some courts find that commuting is not fairly characterized as work assigned by the employer. Other courts, like *Valentine*, deny liability on the ground that the employer does not have sufficient control over the employee during the commute. Still other courts hold that the commute itself is not intended by the employee to serve any purpose of the employer. More difficult cases arise when the employee is driving a vehicle during work hours but doing so at least in part to serve his or her own ends.

2. Reality Check

a. What are Valentine's two theories of liability against LouTex? How are they different?

b. Section 7.05(1) of the *Restatement (Third)* imposes direct liability on principals for negligence in selecting, training, or retaining agents. Compare that section to the standard in *Valentine*. Are the rules identical? Are they compatible?

3. Suppose

a. Suppose the court had used *Restatement (Third)* §7.05(1). Would the analysis or the result have been different? Would using the *Restatement (Third)* made LouTex's direct liability more certain or less?

Putting It to Work

Problem 4-3

Jimmynos is a national chain of fast-food restaurants. Most of Jimmynos' business is provided to customers who order online or by phone and have their order delivered. Jimmynos's success is dependent upon its delivery drivers' ability to deliver orders quickly and accurately. Jimmynos advertises that every order will be delivered in 40 minutes. Orders delivered later than 40 minutes are free to the customer. Jimmynos is well known in the public mind for its "40 or Free" policy. All Jimmynos drivers are told to deliver orders as quickly as possible while obeying all laws and driving no faster than the posted speed limit (and slower than that if driving at the speed limit would be unsafe).

Kyle is a high school senior who works part time for Jimmynos as a delivery driver. Kyle is paid the minimum wage by Jimmynos, and customer tips constitute a fairly large percentage of his total remuneration from working at Jimmynos. He delivers orders in his own car. Jimmynos supplies Kyle, and all its drivers, with company polo shirts and an advertising sign to be affixed on the top of the delivery car. Kyle had been a licensed driver for less than six months when he was hired by Jimmynos. At the time he was hired, he had already gotten three parking tickets, which he disclosed to Jimmynos. Like all Jimmynos' delivery people, Kyle watched a 15-minute video on safe driving techniques. The video is online so Kyle was able to watch it on his phone during a lunch break at school. Unbeknownst to Jimmynos, Kyle received a speeding ticket one month before the accident. The ticket was issued while Kyle was driving to school one morning when he was running late for class.

Kyle was dispatched to deliver an order to a customer who lived in a large apartment complex, the residents of which were frequent Jimmynos customers. The complex was at the far end of the delivery area and deliveries often took more than 40 minutes if weather were bad or traffic were heavy. To make the delivery in 40 minutes, Kyle turned off the highway cut and through the parking lot of a shopping mall. Kyle reasonably believed that doing so was the only hope of making the delivery within 40 minutes.

While driving through the parking lot, Kyle struck and seriously injured a pedestrian who was walking from the mall to her car.

Is Jimmynos liable to the pedestrian under Agency law?

b. Liability of the Third Party to the Principal

The contract liability of a third party and a principal is essentially reciprocal. If a principal is liable on a contract to a third party under agency law, the principal can likewise enforce the contract against the third party as though the contract had been made directly by the principal. *Restatement (Third)* §§6.01, 6.02, and 6.03. An exception is where the agent has falsely represented that he or she is not acting for the specific principal and the agent or principal knows that the third party would not have dealt with the principal. Where the agent knows the third party will not deal with the principal, the agent's failure to disclose the principal (without any misrepresentation) may be sufficient to make the contract voidable by the third party. Note that unless the agent or principal knows that the third party will not deal with the principal, the misrepresentation of, or failure to disclose, the principal will not affect the validity of the transaction. For example, an agent for a wealthy principal negotiates to purchase land. The agent knows that the landowner is likely to raise the purchase price if the principal's identity were known to the landowner. The agent may misrepresent the principal's identity or may deny that the agent is acting for a principal without jeopardizing the principal's ability to enforce the contract. A misrepresentation in this regard allows the third party to rescind only where the agent or principal knows the third party will not deal with the principal. *See Restatement (Third)* §6.11(4).

4. Relation of the Agent to Third Parties

a. Agent's Liability on Contract

An agent who contracts on behalf of a disclosed principal is not thereby liable to the third person with whom the contract was made. *See Restatement (Third)* §6.01(2). Conversely, an agent who contracts on behalf of an undisclosed principal ordinarily is liable to the third person with whom the contract was made. *See Restatement (Third)* §6.03(2). In between disclosed and undisclosed principals is the unidentified principal. The distinction between these three is important for determining whether the agent is liable to the third party. Under the *Restatement (Third)* §6.02(2), the agent is liable to third parties when acting for an unidentified principal. A principal is unidentified when "the third party has notice that the agent is acting for a principal but does not have notice of the principal's identity." *See Restatement (Third)* §1.04(2)(c).

Where the principal is an entity rather than an individual, a further issue is presented. That question is the quantum of information about the principal that the third party must have to constitute the principal's "identity." The *Restatement* observes the following:

> When an agent acts on behalf of an organization or a firm . . . the third party may be aware that the agent represents an organization or firm but lack notice of its salient characteristics. Chief among these is whether the firm is a limited-liability entity.

> *Restatement (Third) of Agency* (2006), §6.02, cmt. d

The *Restatement* preserves the longstanding rule that if the third party does not know whether the entity is a limited liability one, then the principal is unidentified and the agent is ordinarily liable on the contract. The *Restatement* creates a presumption that

> facts that form a basis for further sleuthing by a third party, such as searches in public records, do not constitute reasonably sufficient notice of a principal's identity. In particular, an agent's use of a trade name, which may be traced to its registered user through a search of public filings, is not sufficient to disclose a principal's identity.

> *Id.*

Note that

> Ordinarily it is the agent who provides notice of the principal's identity. However, the source of the third party's enlightenment is irrelevant to the legal relations among the parties.

> *Id.*

Does this rule make sense given that the third party knows a principal is involved and has agreed to deal with the principal? Would not a better rule be that such an agent is personally liable to the third party on a contract with an unidentified principal only if the agent and third party explicitly agree to such liability?

b. Other Sources of Agent's Liability to Third Party

Two other theories can render an agent liable to a third party with whom the agent deals. First, every agent who purports to contract on behalf of a principal impliedly warrants that he or she is authorized to do so. If the agent is not so authorized, the agent may be liable on the contract and, if the agent has affirmatively misrepresented his or her authority, the agent may be liable to the third party in tort as well. *See Restatement (Third) §6.10.* Second, simply acting as an agent does not, by itself, confer any immunity from tort liability. So an agent acting on behalf of a principal may be liable in tort to a third party. *See Restatement (Third) §§7.01 and 7.02.*

5. Relation of the Principal to the Agent

a. Duties of the Agent

One of the core elements of the agency relationship is that the agent owes fiduciary duties to the principal, but the principal does not owe such duties to the agent. Because the agent typically has many more actions to perform than the principal does, the *Restatement (Third)* focuses much more on the agent's obligations than on the principal's.

All Duties
8.01
-.15

An agent has a fiduciary duty to act loyally for the principal's benefit and several sections of the *Restatement (Third)* flesh out that duty. The agent may not gain any material benefit from the agency relationship, such as receiving a tip or other gratuity from a third party. The agent may not compete with, nor act adversely to, the principal. Finally, the agent must use the principal's property only for agency purposes and cannot communicate confidential information to others. *See Restatement (Third) §§8.01-8.05 and 8.12.*

The agent also owes other, nonfiduciary, obligations to the principal. The agent has a duty to act only within the scope of actual authority, to comply with all reasonable instructions from the principal, and to comply with any contractual obligations between the agent and principal. *See Restatement (Third) §§8.07 and 8.09.* The agent must use reasonable care and act reasonably so as not to damage the principal's enterprise. *See Restatement (Third) §§8.08 and 8.10.* Finally, the agent must render information to the principal that the agent believes the principal would want to know. *See Restatement (Third) §8.11.*

b. Duties of the Principal

Because the agent undertakes actions for the principal, and not the other way around, the principal has fewer duties toward the agent. Most important, the principal is not a fiduciary and so is generally free to act in his or her own best interest rather than in the agent's best interest. The principal must deal fairly and in good faith with the agent and must honor any contract duties between the two of them. Furthermore, the principal must indemnify the agent for out-of-pocket costs in performing agency duties and whenever else indemnification would be fair. *See Restatement (Third) §§8.13, 8.14, and 8.15.*

6. Termination of the Agency Relationship

a. Termination of Actual and Apparent Authority

The termination of an agent's apparent authority is straightforward and intuitive. Because apparent authority is rooted in the third party's belief, apparent authority ends when it is no longer reasonable for the third party to believe that the agent has actual authority. Note that simply because an agent's actual authority has ended does not mean that the agent's apparent authority has ended. *See Restatement (Third)* §3.11.

Terminating actual authority is trickier. The parties may, of course, agree to end their agency relationship. Furthermore, because agency is based in personal relationships, either party may, with a small exception, unilaterally end the agency relationship. In this setting the agent is said to *renounce* and the principal to *revoke* the agency. Renunciation or revocation is effective only when the other party has notice of it. While renunciation is always possible and effective, revocation is not effective if the power given to the agent has been made irrevocable in certain ways. Historically, because the agency relationship was a personal one, either party could unilaterally end the relationship at any time and a promise not to revoke or renounce was unenforceable, even when supported by consideration. Over time, though, some agents had a heightened interest in the continuation of the agency relationship and such agencies were deemed to be irrevocable so long as the agent retained the additional interest. These were agency powers *coupled with an interest.* That phrase has generated innumerable cases and commentaries. The *Restatement (Third)* uses the phrase *power given as security* to embrace a somewhat broader concept. For business entities purposes, an agency that can be made irrevocable is a proxy. A proxy is simply an agency relationship in which the agent has actual authority to vote the principal's shares of stock either as directed by the principal, a limited proxy, or as the agent thinks best in the principal's interest, a general proxy. *See Restatement (Third)* §§3.09, 3.10, 3.12, and 3.13.

Another consequence of the personal nature of an agency relationship is that death or incapacity may terminate the agency. The agent's death, without more, terminates actual authority. A principal's death terminates an agent's actual authority when the agent receives notice of it. Where a principal loses capacity to act, the agent is likewise prohibited from performing that act. *See Restatement (Third)* §§3.07 and 3.08.

C. TERMS OF ART IN THIS CHAPTER

Actual authority
Adverse selection
Agency costs
Agent
Apparent authority
Bonding
Coupled with an interest
Disclosed principal
Employee

Estoppel
Monitor
Moral hazard
Principal
Private benefits
Ratcheting
Ratification
Renounce
Respondeat superior

Restitution
Revoke
Scope of employment
Shirking
Signaling
Team production
Undisclosed principal
Unidentified principal
Vicarious liability

Part III.

CORPORATIONS

A. Creation

5

The Incorporation Process

This chapter focuses on issues that arise during the process of creating a corporation. It begins with a consideration of the circumstances in which the persons who are organizing the corporation (called the *promoters*) will be personally liable for actions they take to begin doing business in the corporate form. A related question is whether the creation of the corporation affects the promoters' liability. This chapter next looks at the consequences of selecting a state in which the corporation is to be incorporated. As we will see, corporate planners have a large degree of control over the law that will be applied to the corporation's internal governance. A third focus of this chapter is on the steps that must be followed to draft the corporation's basic documents, to ensure the filing of the requisite documents with the state, and to complete the initial organization of the corporation. Although that process is not a difficult one conceptually or legally, in a surprising number of instances a problem develops that delays the formation of the corporation beyond the anticipated incorporation date. A fourth topic for this chapter is the consequences of a defect in the incorporation process. More specifically, we look at the circumstances in which the promoters may be shielded from individual liability even though the corporation is not properly formed. Finally, this chapter considers the ethical considerations that become especially prominent when a lawyer represents multiple individuals engaged in a common enterprise (as often occurs when promoters form a corporation) and when a lawyer represents an entity.

A. PROMOTER LIABILITY

Quest Engineering Solutions, Inc. v. Wilbur
2011 WL 2224953 (Mass. App. June 9, 2011)

By the Court (Kantrowitz, Trainor & Grainger, JJ.)

MEMORANDUM AND ORDER PURSUANT TO RULE 1:28

Quest Engineering Solutions, Inc. (Quest), commenced this action against Eric Wilbur, seeking to hold him personally liable for breach of a sales and services agreement (agreement or preincorporation contract) that contained a noncompetition provision (noncompete).[1] Ruling on the parties' cross motions for summary judgment, a judge sent the issue whether Wilbur signed the agreement in an individual and personal capacity only, or as a promoter, on for trial. After a bench trial in February 2009, a different judge found and ruled that Wilbur had entered into the agreement as a promoter of CMG and that he was personally liable in the amount of $165,215 for various breaches of the noncompete. Although we affirm the liability finding, we conclude that certain components of the damage award were faulty.

Liability. Under the common law rule, a promoter may be personally liable for breach of a preincorporation contract made on behalf of the nonexistent corporation "unless the circumstances demonstrate that the other party looked only to the corporation for performance." *Productora e Importadora de Papel, S.A. de C.V. v. Fleming,* 376 Mass. 826, 836 (1978) (*Productora*). The question of Wilbur's personal liability ultimately turned on the intent of Quest at the time it entered into the agreement. Here, the issues of original intent and novation were improperly conflated. A remand, however, is not required. The only reasonable inference on this record was that Quest did not look exclusively to CMG for performance.[2]

Even after the formation of CMG, its adoption of the preincorporation contract, and its assumption of contractual obligations, Wilbur's liability as a promoter continued until there was a novation or other agreement to release him from liability. "Without the agreement of the parties to an extinguishment of the prior contract and to a substitution of the new contract, there can be no novation." *Pagounis v. Pendleton,* 52 Mass. App. Ct. 270, 273 (2001). An intent to discharge a pre-existing obligation may not be found absent a clear and definite indication of such intent. The existence of a novation was a factual question on which Wilbur had the burden of proof.

Here, the judge was warranted in finding that Wilbur had failed to meet his burden of demonstrating a clear intent to release him from his obligations under the agreement. As the trial judge noted, although the "interim" agreement between Quest and Wilbur was terminable by either party on short notice, a replacement agreement reflecting the creation of CMG was not executed for over two years. Moreover, Wilbur admittedly failed to obtain a release from liability. The judge's finding that no novation occurred was supported by the evidence.

---

1. Effective January 8, 2002, the agreement between Quest and Wilbur stated that it was "intended as an interim agreement." Asked why he did not sign the agreement on behalf of the soon to be formed Compliance Management Group Corporation (CMG), the name he had selected for his business, Wilbur called himself a "naive businessman." Although the exact date of the execution of the agreement was never established, it was undisputed that execution occurred prior to CMG's legal formation. The agreement ended on April 5, 2004.

2. Nothing within the four corners of the agreement would have permitted a contrary inference. Wilbur did not sign the agreement in a representative capacity or on behalf of a corporation. CMG was not even mentioned in the document. Moreover, although the agreement provided that "it [wa]s anticipated that the representative [Wilbur] will form a corporation to undertake its obligations," the agreement contained no language (1) indicating that performance was solely the responsibility of the future corporation or (2) discharging Wilbur from liability as a promoter upon the incorporation of CMG. Herman Held, who signed the agreement on behalf of Quest in his capacity as the company president, testified that at all relevant times, even after the formation of CMG, he looked to Wilbur—and not solely to CMG—for performance of the agreement.

While we agree with Wilbur that *Productora* governed this case, the applicable portion of *Productora* supports the result reached by the judge. See *Productora*, 376 Mass. at 837 (because of his preincorporation involvement, promoter who executed contract as president of a nonexistent corporation may be personally liable for the corporation's breach).

[The Court's discussion of the measure of damages is omitted.]

We do not disturb the ruling that Wilbur is personally liable to Quest. The judgment awarding damages to Quest in the amount of $165,215 is vacated. A new judgment shall enter awarding damages to Quest in the amount of $39,765. This amount represents the $67,775 awarded by the judge, less the $1,500 erroneously included in that amount, i.e., $66,275 (see note 8, *supra*), reduced by forty percent.

Notes and Questions

1. Notes

a. The briefs reveal that Wilbur signed the articles of incorporation for CMG on January 10, 2002 and that the articles were filed by the secretary of state on February 2, 2002.

b. As mentioned in footnote 2 of the court's opinion, the contract stated in section 1.1, "It is anticipated that [Wilbur] will form a corporation to undertake its obligations. . . ."

c. The signature block on the agreement read:

COMPANY   REPRESENTATIVE:
Quest Engineering Solutions, Inc.

/s/ Herman Held   /s/ Eric Wilbur
Herman Held, President   Eric Wilbur

d. According to the briefs, the replacement agreement referred to by the court was executed in April 2004 between Quest and CMG. It provided that it "re-place[d] the January 2002 agreement between Quest and Eric Wilbur."

2. Reality Check

a. What would be the point of the language in section 1.1 if it were not intended to substitute CMG for Wilbur?

b. What theory does the court use to hold Wilbur liable?

c. Could Wilbur have avoided personal liability? If so, how?

d. Why is CMG liable?

3. Suppose

a. Suppose the lease had been executed only in the name of CMG and both Wilbur and Quest knew that the corporation had not yet been incorporated. Would Wilbur still be personally liable?

b. Suppose the lease had been executed, "Representative: Eric Wilbur, as agent for Compliance Management Group Corporation, a corporation to be formed." Would that have made it more likely or less likely that Wilbur was personally liable?

4. What Do You Think?

a. Cases such as this arise with considerable frequency. What do you think the root cause of such cases is?

b. Does the parties' entering into the 2004 agreement work in favor of Wilbur or Quest?

5. You Draft It

a. Redraft section 1.1 and the signature block of the 2002 agreement to make it clear that Wilbur is not personally liable. Then, redraft section 1.1 and the signature block to make it clear that Wilbur is personally liable.

b. Redraft the language in the April 2004 agreement to make it clear that Wilbur is not liable on the 2002 agreement. Then, redraft it to make it clear that Wilbur remains liable on the 2002 agreement.

Putting It to Work

Problem 5-1

Lauren can't wait to start her new juice bar, JuiceJams, and get the business booming before cashing out. Juicing is the way of the nutritional future, she believes, and she is sure it is going to be a raging success. To buy produce and industrial juicers, Lauren obtains a $50,000 line of credit in her name from the bank where she has her personal bank accounts. She tells the bank's business loan officer of her plans for JuiceJams and that she intends to run the business as a corporation. Lauren borrows the entire $50,000 and uses the money to get JuiceJams started.

Six months after starting the business and obtaining the line of credit, Lauren gets around to incorporating JuiceJams and informs the bank of that fact. Once JuiceJams is incorporated, all payments on the line of credit are made from JuiceJams's corporate bank account. A year later, Lauren sells JuiceJams for a nice profit.

a. If JuiceJams's new owners fail to pay the line of credit, will Lauren have to pay?

b. What should Lauren do to ensure she will not be liable for the line of credit payments?

B. CHOICE OF JURISDICTION

1. Why the Corporation's Jurisdiction Matters — The Internal Affairs Doctrine

a. The Current Setting

Usually a business that will operate in only one state will choose to incorporate in that state. Nonetheless, a corporation may be incorporated in any state even though it will have no other connection to that state. If the corporation is to be incorporated in another jurisdiction, the attorney often retains a so-called service corporation to handle the mechanics. These service corporations assist lawyers by preparing the appropriate incorporation papers and shepherding them through the administrative process. For an additional fee, these service corporations will provide the new corporation's registered office and act as its agent for service of process within the state of incorporation.

Now that you understand that you can form a corporation in any state, even one with which it will have no connection, the obvious question is, "why would you want to?" The choice of the state of incorporation has no effect on the corporation in many settings. For example, XYZ, Inc., a corporation that does business only in California, is certainly subject to personal jurisdiction in California even if it is incorporated in New York. California can also impose taxes on XYZ, Inc., and can enforce its consumer protection, employee safety, and environmental laws provided it does not discriminate between corporations incorporated in California (called *domestic* corporations) and those incorporated in other U.S. states (called, somewhat misleadingly, *foreign* corporations).

New York (the state of incorporation) could also exercise personal jurisdiction over XYZ, Inc. Can New York apply its own contract law to XYZ, Inc., even though the corporation operates only in California? What about applying New York's consumer protection, employee safety, and environmental laws to XYZ, Inc.? What happens if the law of the state of incorporation conflicts with the law of a state in which the corporation operates? The American Law Institute's *Restatement (Second) of Conflict of Laws* describes the doctrines that resolve these questions, at least in some instances.

> [C]orporations and individuals alike make contracts, commit torts and receive and transfer assets. Issues involving acts such as these when done by a corporation are determined by the same choice-of-law principles as are applicable to non-corporate parties.

Restatement (Second) of Conflict of Laws §301, cmt. b

The *Restatement (Second) of Conflict of Laws* provides that corporate actions that could *not* be done by an individual will (with a possible exception noted in the Background and Context section below) be governed by the law of the state of incorporation. *Restatement (Second) of Conflict of Laws* §302. That section's comment explains further.

> **Comment:**
>   **Scope of section.** Many of the matters that fall within the scope of the rule of this Section involve the "*internal affairs*" of a corporation — that is the relations inter se of the corporation, its shareholders, directors, officers or agents. . . . Other such matters affect the interests of the corporation's creditors.
>   Matters falling within the scope of the rule of this Section and which involve primarily a corporation's relationship to its shareholders include steps taken in the course of the original incorporation, the election or appointment of directors and officers, the adoption of bylaws, the issuance of corporate shares, preemptive rights, the holding of directors' and shareholders' meetings, methods of voting including any requirement for cumulative voting, shareholders' rights to examine corporate records, charter and bylaw amendments, mergers, consolidations and reorganizations and the reclassification of shares. Matters which may also affect the interests of the corporation's creditors include the issuance of bonds, the declaration and payment of dividends, loans by the corporation to directors, officers and shareholders, and the purchase and redemption by the corporation of outstanding shares of its own stock.

Rationale. Uniform treatment of directors, officers and shareholders is an important objective which can only be attained by having the rights and liabilities of those persons with respect to the corporation governed by a single law. To the extent that they think about the matter, these persons would usually expect that their rights and duties with respect to the corporation would be determined by the [law] of the state of incorporation. This state is also easy to identify, and thus the value of ease of application is attained when the [law] of this state is applied.

[I]t would be impractical to have matters . . . which involve a corporation's organic structure or internal administration, governed by different laws. It would be impractical, for example, if an election of directors, an issuance of shares, a payment of dividends, a charter amendment, or a consolidation or reorganization were to be held valid in one state and invalid in another.

Which legal issues are governed by the state of incorporation and which issues are not is not always clear. The Comment to §302 above lists several legal questions within the internal affairs doctrine. Other sections list these additional issues as being within the internal affairs of a corporation: who the shareholders are (§303); shareholder voting and dividend rights (although not shareholder inspection rights, *see* Comment d and *Sadler v. NCR Corp.*, 928 F.2d 48 (2d Cir. 1991)) (§304); the voting rights of a trustee of a voting trust (but not the rights of the trust's beneficiaries, *see* Comment b) (§305); the fiduciary duty (if any) of a majority shareholder (§306); and director and officer liability (§309). Section 307 includes shareholder liability for the purchase price of shares, but not shareholder liability under piercing the veil principles. The few state courts that have considered the question of choice of law in the piercing the veil context have tended to assume, without significant discussion, that the law of the state of incorporation should apply. *See Kalb, Voorhis & Co. v. American Financial Corp.*, 8 F.3d 130 (2d Cir. 1993) (erroneously interpreting *Restatement (Second) of Conflict of Laws* §307 as applying to piercing issues).

b. Background and Context

The *Restatement (Second) of Conflict of Laws* §302 provides that the internal affairs doctrine will not be applied "in the unusual case where . . . some other state has a more significant relationship to the occurrence and the parties. . . ." The comment and reporter's note to §302 elaborate on this exception:

> **When [law] of state of incorporation will not be applied**. [I]t is in situations where the corporation has little contact with the state of its incorporation that the [law] of some other state is most likely to be applied when (1) the relevant rules of the other state embody an important policy of that state and (2) the matter involved does not affect the corporation's organic structure or internal administration and therefore does not fall within the category of issues which . . . cannot practicably be determined differently in different states.

> **Reporter's Note**
> The great majority of cases have applied the [law] of the state of incorporation to determine issues involving matters peculiar to corporations. [However], [i]n *Western Airlines, Inc. v. Sobieski*, 12 Cal. Rptr. 719 (Cal. App. 1961), a California statute was applied to prevent a Delaware corporation from eliminating cumulative voting. The corporation did no business in Delaware. On the other hand, it had been originally incorporated in California, did substantial business in that state and a substantial number of its shareholders were domiciled there. The opinion of the court does not indicate whether cumulative voting was

required by the [law] of the other States where the corporation did business and where some of its shareholders were domiciled.

The *Restatement (Second) of Conflict of Laws* was adopted before the U.S. Supreme Court decided *CTS Corp. v. Dynamics Corp. of America*, 481 U.S. 69 (1987). That case may, as a practical matter, require the internal affairs doctrine to be applied under the Commerce Clause of the U.S. Constitution. If so, then states no longer have the option to apply their own law to the internal affairs of foreign corporations. Thus the validity of §302(2)'s "more significant relationship" test and the validity of the *Western Airlines* case are in substantial doubt. On the other hand, a few states have statutes that purport to impose their corporations code (or parts of it) on certain foreign corporations. *See, e.g.,* Cal. Corp. Code §2115 and Washington RCW 23B.19.020(19)(b) (purporting to apply Washington's antitakeover act to foreign corporations with specified significant contacts in Washington State).

> The internal affairs doctrine is not, however, only a conflicts of law principle. Pursuant to the Fourteenth Amendment Due Process Clause, directors and officers of corporations "have a significant right . . . to know what law will be applied to their actions"[15] and "[s]tockholders . . . have a right to know by what standards of accountability they may hold those managing the corporation's business and affairs."[16] Under the Commerce Clause, a state "has no interest in regulating the internal affairs of foreign corporations."[17] Therefore, this Court has held that an "application of the internal affairs doctrine is mandated by constitutional principles, except in the 'rarest situations,'"[18] *e.g.,* when "the law of the state of incorporation is inconsistent with a national policy on foreign or interstate commerce."[19]

Vantage Point Venture Partners 1996 v. Examen, Inc., 871 A.2d 1108, 1113 (Del. 1987) (Holland, J.)

Notes and Questions

1. Reality Check

a. When a foreign corporation is sued, what choice of law rule will the court adopt?

b. What are the possible sources of the choice of law rules a court will follow?

2. What Do You Think?

a. Do you think corporations and their advisors should, in effect, be able to choose the internal governance rules that will apply? Are those rules any different from tort rules or employee rules such as maximum hours rules that are imposed by the state in which the business operates, regardless of where it is incorporated?

b. If only one state's law is to be applied to internal governance matters, why should that state be the state of incorporation rather than, for example, the state in which the corporation has its headquarters or has the majority of its assets? Would such a rule be constitutional? If it is constitutional, is it workable?

---

15. *McDermott Inc. v. Lewis,* 531 A.2d 206, 216 (Del. 1987).
16. *Id.* at 217.
17. *Id.* (quoting *Edgar v. MITE Corp.,* 457 U.S. 624, 645-46 (1982)).
18. *Id.* (quoting *CTS Corp. v. Dynamics Corp. of Am.,* 481 U.S. 69, 90 (1987)).
19. *Id.*

2. The Special Role of Delaware

By choosing the state of incorporation one chooses the corporate governance rules that will apply to a new corporation. At first blush this may seem to open up a wide variety of choices for the lawyer and client because there are 50 states and the District of Columbia. But this choice is deceptive for two reasons. First, the substantive rule on many issues is identical in many states. Thus there are not 51 completely different sets of rules. Second, the vast majority of provisions in every statute can be varied in the articles or bylaws. No matter in which state a corporation is incorporated, its governance rules can be tailored considerably. Only rarely will a state's statute contain an unmodifiable provision that is important to the planners.

So why should the choice ever be any state other than the one in which the corporation intends to do business? More specifically, why Delaware? Delaware is certainly the most popular choice for publicly traded companies. More than half of the publicly traded companies in the United States, and over 300 of the 500 largest U.S. companies, are incorporated in Delaware. Furthermore, 90 percent of all companies going public are incorporated in Delaware. Finally, over 80 percent of companies that are not incorporated in their home state are incorporated in Delaware. Nevada is second with 6 percent. Delaware has over 6 percent of the nation's 4.7 million corporations, about 20 times more than its share of the total population (Delaware has 0.3% of the country's population).

What explains this popularity? Delaware's general corporation act is both advantageous to management and quite flexible, so that planners can vary almost any provision. But those qualities do not distinguish Delaware from most other states. The answer is threefold. First, and least important, Delaware corporate law is familiar to most corporate lawyers in the United States. It is their natural suggestion for an alternative to the home state. Second, a large body of case law interpreting the statute provides a measure of predictability, and hence comfort, for corporations. Third, Delaware has a specialized court, the Court of Chancery, that handles corporate matters. The chancellor and four vice chancellors handle cases with the speed often required in important business matters. Appeals go directly to the Delaware Supreme Court (Delaware has no intermediate court of appeals), which can also act with dispatch when necessary.

C. INCORPORATION MECHANICS

Incorporating a new corporation is a quintessential lawyer task. The lawyer must be familiar with the minutiae of the requirements in the state in which he or she practices and, usually, in Delaware as well. The process entails assembling the requisite information from the client; reserving the new corporation's name; preparing the incorporation documents; arranging for payment of the filing fees (for example, states vary considerably as to whether they will accept credit cards, personal checks, or certified checks); transmitting the documents and fees to the appropriate government office (states also vary as to whether they will accept transmittals via private overnight services, whether papers will be accepted at more than one location, and whether incorporation can be effected electronically); ensuring that the incorporation papers are filed and that the corporation has come into existence; organizing the corporation (i.e., electing directors, appointing officers, adopting bylaws, issuing stock, and beginning to engage in business); and filing any post-incorporation forms that may be required.

A misstep in any of these undertakings is often professionally embarrassing, at the least. Sometimes a lawyer's mistake will have more important consequences. For example, suppose the lawyer neglects to determine whether the desired name of the proposed corporation is available. The client may have purchased stationery and signage featuring the desired name and may have to incur additional expenses to reorder such items with a new name if the original name cannot be secured. Even more deleterious is the setting in which a lawyer's mistake delays the formation of a corporation that is to undertake a particular venture. In such instances a valuable business opportunity may be jeopardized because the new corporation cannot enter into agreements because it has not yet been formed. The alternatives are to wait until incorporation is accomplished or to have the promoters bind themselves personally. Neither of these options is particularly appealing to clients, and each has its perils. Business opportunities have an evanescent nature, and delay in accepting a proposal may result in the opportunity being lost. On the other hand, if the promoters accept the proposal personally, they are (as you know from the material above) exposed to expanded liability. Hardly the result anticipated when retaining a lawyer!

The next sections outline the tasks a lawyer must undertake to incorporate a new venture.

1. Reserving the Name

State statutes typically provide that a corporate name may be reserved, usually for 120 days, with the payment of a small fee. *See* DGCL §102(e), MBCA §4.02. Reserving the name allows clients to prepare to do business immediately following incorporation and ensures that the incorporation will not be delayed because an unavailable name has been selected. Under both Delaware and the MBCA the name must be distinguishable from the name of every other corporation on file with the secretary of state. *See* DGCL §102(a)(1), MBCA §4.01(b). In some states this requirement is a narrow one; a corporate name is acceptable if it is different in any way. In other states, including most MBCA states, a name is not distinguishable if it is different in such minor ways as punctuation, capitalization, or use of a definite article or a plural in the name.

Under the law of most states a corporate name must contain some evidence that the entity is a corporation and must not contain words falsely suggesting that the new corporation will engage in certain businesses, usually those involving banking or other financial services. In Delaware, for example, the corporate name must contain the word or abbreviation for *association, company, corporation, club, foundation, fund, incorporated, institute, society, union, syndicate,* or *limited,* or similar words or abbreviations in other languages, and cannot include the words *bank* or *trust* unless the corporation is licensed to engage in banking. *See* DGCL

§102(a)(1).[1] The MBCA requires the word or abbreviation for *corporation, incorporated, company,* or *limited,* and the name may not state or imply that the corporation's purpose is other than that permitted by §3.01 and the articles of incorporation. *See* MBCA §4.01(a).

2. The Incorporation Documents

The document that creates and governs the corporation is called the Certificate of Incorporation in Delaware and the Articles of Incorporation under the MBCA. This book will usually use the term *Articles of Incorporation* or *Articles* unless referring to Delaware alone. In many, if not most, states the statute authorizes a government official, usually the secretary of state, to promulgate a standard form that may or must be used to incorporate. In virtually every state the information required in the Articles is relatively minimal. *See* Del. §102(a), MBCA §2.02(a). The Articles must contain the corporation's name and the name and address of each person who is incorporating the new entity. Often the lawyer or a member of his or her staff acts as the incorporator. The Articles must also name a person, or other corporation, who will act as the corporation's agent upon whom service of process may be made and must identify an address within the state where the registered agent may be served. These requirements exist so that personal jurisdiction may be properly asserted over the corporation. The registered office need not be a place where the corporation does business, nor the registered agent need have any other connection to the corporation. Typically, when a corporation has incorporated in a foreign jurisdiction, it will engage a corporation service company to act as its registered agent and to provide the registered office.

The Articles must also state the maximum number of shares the corporation may issue (the actual number issued may be far fewer than the maximum stated in the Articles) and, if the shares are to have different management or economic rights, a statement as to how the shares will differ from one another. Finally, many states require the Articles to state the purpose for which the corporation is being formed. This requirement has become largely a dead letter, because in every state the Articles may simply state that the corporation may engage in any lawful business. *See* DGCL §102(a)(3). Indeed, at least one state *requires* the Articles to contain such a provision! *See* Cal. Corp. Code §202(b). The MBCA does not require the Articles to state the corporation's purpose. The number of directors, or a process for determining the number of directors, must be stated in the Articles or bylaws. *See* DGCL §141(b), MBCA §8.03(a).

States also permit the Articles to contain certain optional provisions. Perhaps the most practically important of these is the ability to name the initial directors in the Articles. *See* Del. Code §102(a)(6), MBCA §2.02(b)(1). Many persons who agree to act as incorporator intend to have no further power over the new corporation once it is formed. They are often simply the attorney or service corporation employee who is in charge of making sure the new entity is created. By naming the

---

1. These restrictions do not apply to corporations with more than $10 million in total assets, presumably because nearly all entities of such size are corporations.

initial directors in the Articles, the incorporator will be automatically relieved of any authority over, and also relieved of any liability for, the new corporation once it is created. Delaware Code §102(b) provides a list of optional provisions for the Certificate of Incorporation. Official Comments 4 and 5 to the Model Act have extremely useful checklists of the governance provisions that may be modified in the Articles or bylaws.

3. Filing

Filing is the action by which the state accepts the Articles. Filing is of great importance because it is through filing that the corporation comes into existence. *See* DGCL §106, MBCA §2.03(a). The statutes contain surprisingly detailed requirements for filing. The secretary of state (the official usually in charge of corporations) may promulgate additional requirements. A lawyer who fails to follow both the statutory and administrative requirements for incorporating a new venture will find that the Articles are rejected for filing, which will, at best, cause a delay and, at worst, present a large obstacle to the success of the new business venture.

Delaware provides that anyone may form a corporation by delivering a Certificate of Incorporation to the secretary of state. *See* DGCL §§101(a), 103(c)(1). The Certificate must be executed by an incorporator whose signature is "acknowledged" either by the signature alone or by being notarized. *See* DGCL §§103(a)(1), 103(b). When the executed and acknowledged Certificate, along with any required taxes and fees, are delivered to the secretary of state, the Certificate is stamped "filed" and becomes effective at that moment. *See* DGCL §§103(c), 103(d).

The MBCA has a similar process. Anyone may form a corporation by delivering the Articles of Incorporation to the secretary of state. *See* MBCA §2.01. Among other requirements, the Articles must be executed by an incorporator. The Articles (and one copy of them if the incorporator is filing paper documents rather than filing electronically), and the required fees and taxes must be delivered to the secretary of state, who will file them if they are in order by recording them as filed and returning a copy of the Articles to the corporation. *See* MBCA §§1.20, 1.25. The corporation comes into existence as of the date and time of filing. *See* MBCA §1.23.

4. Organizing the New Corporation

Once the corporation has been formed, the lawyer must ensure that it is properly organized. Even if the initial directors were named in the Articles, the corporation has no officers or bylaws, nor has it taken any action. It does not, as yet, even have any owners. The organizational meeting is designed to complete these tasks. In most states, the minimum actions to be accomplished are electing directors (if they are not named in the Articles), adopting bylaws, and appointing officers. Under most statutes, an actual meeting is unnecessary if the incorporators (or initial directors) act by unanimous consent. Acting by consent is the typical method of effecting these tasks, because it is usually easier than convening an actual meeting. *See* DGCL §108(c), MBCA §2.05. Note that the statutes do *not* require the corporation to issue stock at the organizational meeting. Nevertheless, case law in most jurisdictions provides that a corporation cannot engage in business until it has received valid consideration in exchange for shares.

Putting It to Work

Problem 5-2

You work as an attorney for your clients, Rick and Daryl, who want to open a new business for vampire and zombie fanatics. The store will be filled with vampire and zombie memorabilia and a lounge area. Your clients want to incorporate and are mulling over some names for the corporation:

Blood Bank NO
Zombie & Sons
The Fright Club
Aberzombie & Fitch, Co. D M
R&D, Inc.

a. Which of these are permissible under the DGCL?
b. Which of these are permissible under the MBCA?
c. Could any of the impermissible names be permissible if altered slightly?
d. What other steps should you take to ensure that Rick and Daryl can use the name they have chosen?

D. DEFECTIVE INCORPORATION

None of the prerequisites for forming a corporation is particularly challenging. Still, promoters frequently enter into obligations before the corporation is actually formed. In *Quest Engineering Solutions*, the plaintiff claimed to have intended to contract with Eric Wilbur, the promoter, in his personal capacity. But where the intention of the parties is definitely to contract solely with the promoter's corporation, yet the corporation does not exist when the contract is made, may the third party nonetheless hold the promoter personally liable? This issue and its resolution are known as the problem of *defective incorporation*. The background and context section shows that the problem was more acute in an earlier day and also shows the origins of the modern approaches to defective incorporation. Note that most of these also apply to LLCs.

1. Background and Context

Until after World War II, states varied in defining the point in the incorporation process when a corporation actually came into existence. Many states also imposed requirements after incorporation, such as filing the Articles in the county where the corporation's headquarters were to be located, or having received a certain amount of money (often $1,000). These requirements were sometimes conditions subsequent, meaning that the corporation would cease to exist if those subsequent actions were not taken. These variations and uncertainties resulted in many lawsuits in which a promoter was sued personally for obligations ostensibly made in the name of a nascent corporation. The widespread adoption of the original Model Business Corporations Act of 1950 brought a fair degree of clarity to these issues. But by then the common law had developed a number of equitable doctrines that relieved promoters from personal liability in defective incorporation settings. The excerpt from a distinguished prewar treatise describes how these doctrines operated in the days in which defective incorporation was a frequent occurrence.

Robert S. Stevens, *Handbook on the Law of Private Corporations*[*]
101-104, 122-160 (1936)

[W]hen, in the effort to incorporate, there has been an irregular or incomplete compliance with the statutory requirements, questions arise as to the effect to be attributed to the neglect or noncompliance. Are all of the requirements of equal importance so that full compliance with each of them is a necessary condition precedent to incorporation? The statutes are not always specific. The medley of requirements is too frequently jumbled without distinction. A search has to be made for the legislative intention. [I]s it not probable that the Legislature intended some of its requirements to be complied with before incorporation and some of them after incorporation? May it not have attached different degrees of importance to the several requirements? These are the considerations which lead the courts to the discovery of a legislative intention to distinguish between conditions precedent and conditions subsequent and between mandatory and directory provisions.

As a result of this discriminating whittling by the courts, the conclusion is reached that there will be a corporation *de jure*, that is, one unassailable by the state in a direct proceeding, if there has been a substantial compliance with all mandatory provisions which are intended to be conditions precedent to incorporation. [A] failure to comply with directory provisions will not be fatal to valid incorporation. Whether a particular provision is mandatory or merely directory must be determined by ascertaining the intention of the Legislature. As statutory schemes differ somewhat, legislative intentions may differ, and, accordingly, courts of one state reach the conclusion that a certain requirement is only directory, whereas the courts of another state find that its Legislature intended the same type of requirement to be mandatory.

When incorporation is defective to the extent that it is subject to successful attack by the state and yet not open to collateral attack in private litigation, . . . then it is said that there is a *de facto* corporation. The de facto doctrine effects a compromise between conflicting public interests — the one opposed to an unauthorized assumption of corporateness; the other in favor of doing justice to the parties and of establishing a general assurance of security in business dealings with corporations. Is there a statute under which a corporation of this type might have

---

[*] Reprinted with permission of Thomson West.

been validly formed? Has there been a real, though insufficient, attempt to comply with the provisions of this statute? Has there been a user or exercise of corporate privileges? If these questions are answered in the affirmative, it is said that the "elements" of the de facto doctrine are present. Then, granting that these mitigating circumstances are present, a second inquiry is pursued as to the nature of the cause of action and whether the facts out of which it grew are such as to warrant the permission or denial of collateral attack.

While the formula of the de facto doctrine embraces the requirement of a bona fide or colorable attempt to comply with the statute, there is no agreement as to what constitutes a bona fide or colorable compliance. Collateral attack has been permitted where the articles of incorporation were not signed until four months after contracting with the plaintiffs, where a contract was entered into after the articles had been signed but before they had been filed in the county clerk's office and published as required, and where they have been executed and recorded but not filed. On the other hand, collateral attack has been denied where articles have been signed but not filed until after a tort has been committed or a contract entered into by the corporation. [U]ntil comparatively recently it was contended by some that, with one or two exceptions, the de facto doctrine did not prevent collateral attack except in cases where there had been a mutual assumption of corporateness.

The expression "estoppel" has . . . been applied in those cases where the third party, who has contracted with the supposed corporation, is prevented from collaterally attacking the validity of the incorporation. This principle that parties who deal with each other upon a mutual assumption of the existence of a certain fact are prevented from disputing that fact is frequently referred to as "estoppel." The associates have reason to believe that they were validly incorporated, and therefore protected against unlimited liability. The third party contracted for corporate liability and to permit him to hold the associates individually would be to impose upon them an unexpected liability and to confer upon him a more extensive right than was contracted for. According to the decisions in some jurisdictions, there can be no estoppel against an attack on the validity of the corporation unless the elements of the de facto doctrine are present; but, according to what seems to be the majority view, an estoppel will be permitted even when the elements of the de facto doctrine are lacking.

The establishment of the de facto doctrine has not been without protest. The objection has been advanced that, since incorporation is a prerogative of the Legislature, it is not for the courts to create corporations. When the Legislature has prescribed the method of incorporating, it is assumed that the Legislature intended that the associates should not, under any circumstances, be treated as incorporated unless the attempt to incorporate was in all respects complete and regular. If, in the face of this intention, the courts find corporateness, it is said that they are proclaiming themselves de facto legislatures in order to create de facto corporations.

When there is no de jure corporation, and when collateral attack may not be denied upon the basis either of the de facto doctrine or the principles of estoppel, should it follow that all the associates have incurred individual and unlimited responsibility because transactions have been entered into on behalf of the company? It seems surprising that the authorities should be conflicting upon so plain a proposition. Two reasons are advanced for relieving the associates from liability as partners: First, it is emphasized that they have not agreed among themselves to be partners. They have entered the association upon the understanding that liability was to be limited, and they have not conferred upon the board of managers authority to bind them individually as partners. Secondly, it is pointed out that the associates have held themselves out as a corporation and not as a partnership, and the party who has contracted with them has assumed that they were incorporated and contracted for limited liability only.

A rule which would impose partnership liability upon associates who are not entitled to the benefits of the de facto doctrine, . . . would frequently impose great injustice and hardship on innocent shareholders. When, however, the associates cannot claim the benefits of innocence, when they have fraudulently represented that they were incorporated, knowing full well that they had not complied with the statutory provisions, a reason for shielding them from partnership liability vanishes. Similarly, another reason for insulating them from partnership liability is eliminated when it is found that the creditor did not contract with them as a corporation, but, on the contrary, understood that they were a partnership. Justice would be accomplished if all the associates were held at least to the full extent of the liability which they contemplated; that is, the liability that would have been theirs if incorporation had been perfect.

> Over time, the doctrine of de facto corporations has been "roundly criticized." *Robertson v. Levy*, 197 A.2d 443, 445 (D.C. App. 1964). [T]he [Old] Model Business Corporation Act ("MBCA (1950)") . . . strove to . . . provide some clarity and bright-line tests to previously clouded areas. MBCA (1950) sections 56 and 146 contain an express intent to abolish the concept of de facto corporations.* The comment to section 56 states:
>
>> Under the [MBCA (1950)], de jure incorporation is complete upon the issuance of the certificate of incorporation. . . . [A]ny steps short of securing a certificate of incorporation would not constitute apparent compliance. Therefore a de facto corporation cannot exist under the [MBCA (1950)].
>
> Model Business Corporation Act (1950) Ann., §56 cmt., at 205. Similarly, the comment to section 146 states:
>
>> [S]ection [146] is designed to prohibit the application of any theory of de facto incorporation. The only authority to act as a corporation under the [MBCA (1950)] arises from completion of the [statutory] procedures. . . . The consequences of those procedures are specified in section 56 as being the creation of a corporation. No other means being authorized, the effect of section 146 is to negate the possibility of a de facto corporation.
>>
>> Abolition of the concept of de facto incorporation, which at best was fuzzy, is a sound result. No reason exists for its continuance under general corporate laws, where the process of acquiring de jure incorporation is both simple and clear. The vestigial appendage should be removed.
>
> *Id.* §146 cmt., at 908-09.

---

* Section 56 provided: Upon the issuance of the certificate of incorporation, the corporate existence shall begin, and such certificate of incorporation shall be conclusive evidence that all conditions precedent required to be performed by the incorporators have been complied with and that the corporation has been incorporated under this Act, except as against the State in a proceeding to cancel or revoke the certificate of incorporation or for involuntary dissolution of the corporation.

Section 146 provided: All persons who assume to act as a corporation without authority so to do shall be jointly and severally liable for all debts and liabilities incurred or arising as a result thereof. *ED.*

American Vending Services, Inc. v. Morse, 881 P.2d 917 (Ut. App. 1994) (Greenwood, J.). Note that the MBCA (1950) did not purport to affect the doctrine of corporation by estoppel.

2. The Current Setting

Even though complying with the statutory requirements for incorporation is easy, promoters regularly contract on behalf of as-yet unincorporated corporations. This section explores whether promoters can be held personally liable in such settings.

a. *Corporations by Estoppel*

We start with an equitable doctrine in defective incorporation settings. You should be aware that the corporation by estoppel doctrine is often used as a defense to individual liability although neither of the two cases below arises in that setting.

Brown v. W.P. Media, Inc.
17 So. 3d 1167 (Ala. 2009)

SMITH, JUSTICE:

The plaintiffs below, Alabama MBA, Inc., and Hugh W. Brown, Jr., appeal from a summary judgment in favor of the defendant, W.P. Media, Inc., in this action seeking damages for breach of contract. We reverse and remand.

Facts and Procedural History

In 2001, W.P. Media and Alabama MBA executed a contract (hereinafter "the operating agreement") whereby the parties agreed to operate a joint venture named Alabaster Wireless MBA, LLC, a company intended to provide wireless Internet services to consumers. In the operating agreement, W.P. Media agreed to create a wireless network to be used by Alabaster Wireless and to provide certain technical support once the wireless network was created. Under the operating agreement, Alabama MBA was to contribute capital in the amount of $79,300 and W.P. Media was to contribute "proprietary technology" equal to the same amount. Brown signed the operating agreement on Alabama MBA's behalf as its chairman of the board.

In May 2005, Brown and Alabama MBA filed a complaint in the Jefferson Circuit Court alleging that, among other things, W.P. Media had breached the operating agreement by failing to construct a wireless network. In January 2007, W.P. Media moved for a summary judgment on the remaining claim that it had breached the operating agreement. Specifically, W.P. Media maintained that articles of incorporation for Alabama MBA were not filed until 2002, after the operating agreement had been executed. Thus, W.P. Media contended, the operating agreement was void because Alabama MBA lacked capacity to enter into the contract. Additionally, W.P. Media contended that Alabama MBA, as an allegedly improperly incorporated entity, was not a real party in interest and was thus due to be dismissed from the case.

The trial court . . . entered a summary judgment for W.P. Media on the breach-of-contract claim. . . . Brown and Alabama MBA appeal.

Discussion

The issue in this case is whether Alabama MBA was properly incorporated both at the time the operating agreement was executed and at the time Alabama MBA and Brown filed the underlying action.

It is undisputed that, at the time the operating agreement was executed, the articles of incorporation for Alabama MBA had not been filed. However, Brown filed articles of incorporation for Alabama MBA . . . in October 2002, and the secretary of state's records indicate that Alabama MBA was incorporated at that time. The record reveals that Alabama MBA did not hold an organizational meeting, pay taxes, issue stock, or adopt bylaws until early 2007. Further, before then Alabama MBA had no bank accounts or employees; all Alabama MBA's expenses were paid by Brown personally.

In its summary-judgment motion, W.P. Media argued that because Alabama MBA was not incorporated at the time the operating agreement was executed, it lacked capacity to contract. Thus, W.P. Media maintained, the contract was "void ab initio" and no action for its breach could be maintained.

Corporate existence begins when articles of incorporation are filed, unless a later effective date is specified in the articles. [MBCA §2.03]

Although Alabama MBA [did not exist] as either a de jure corporation or a de facto corporation, Alabama MBA contends that W.P. Media is nevertheless estopped from denying Alabama MBA's corporate existence. We agree.

> Corporate action may also be established under principles of estoppel, whether or not an entity or organization qualifies as a de facto corporation. The doctrine is based on conduct by a party which recognizes an organization as a corporation or an express or implied representation by a corporation that it is a corporation. In the first instance, estoppel cannot apply to one who has not dealt with the organization or in any way recognized it as having corporate existence, or who has participated in holding it out as a corporation. In the second instance, where a party has contracted or otherwise dealt with an organization, believing it to be a corporation, there may have been no holding out of corporate status by the organization. In either instance, estoppel arises from the contract or course of dealing by the parties and is applicable in a suit by the party dealing with the organization, as well as in a suit by the organization.

Richard A. Thigpen, *Alabama Corporation Law* §3:59 (3d ed. 2003) (footnotes omitted).

Alabama MBA . . . argues that because W.P. Media treated Alabama MBA as a corporation, W.P. Media is now estopped from denying Alabama MBA's corporate existence.

W.P. Media entered into a contractual relationship with Alabama MBA to operate Alabaster Wireless. The operating agreement identified Alabama MBA as a corporation, was executed in Alabama MBA's corporate name, and was signed by Brown as Alabama MBA's "chairman of the board." W.P. Media further concedes in its brief that Alabama MBA and Brown had essentially "represented" that Alabama

MBA was "a viable, legal corporation" and that W.P. Media had "no reason to doubt" those representations. The record reveals that at no time during the venture did W.P. Media challenge the validity of the operating agreement until after it was sued for breaching the operating agreement. Under the facts of this case, we hold that W.P. Media's actions of entering into a contract with Alabama MBA and participating with Alabama MBA in the joint venture before and after Alabama MBA's articles of incorporation were filed estop W.P. Media from denying Alabama MBA's corporate existence for purposes of challenging the validity of the operating agreement.

WP Media also contends that Alabama MBA was not properly incorporated at the time it filed the instant action; thus, it argues, Alabama MBA was not a "real party in interest" under Rule 17, Ala. R. Civ. P., and cannot maintain this action. In support of its contention that Alabama MBA was not incorporated when the underlying action was filed, W.P. Media argues that Brown "chose not to form the corporation and [instead] treat[ed] everything personal" and that, in addition to filing articles of incorporation, Alabama MBA was *also* required to meet the prerequisites of [MBCA § 2.05(a)(1)].

W.P. Media asserts, and the record supports its assertion, that Alabama MBA held no "organizational meeting" until after it and Brown filed the underlying action. W.P. Media also asserts that Alabama MBA failed to meet the record-keeping requirements of [MBCA § 16.01]. W.P. Media argues that Alabama MBA was improperly incorporated because it failed to comply with these two Code sections after it had filed its articles of incorporation.

As started above, the plain language of [MBCA §2.03] explicitly states that the . . . filing of the articles of incorporation is "*conclusive proof* that the incorporators satisfied all conditions precedent to incorporation." (Emphasis added.) Although [MBCA § 2.05] sets forth procedures to "complete the *organization* of the corporation" (emphasis added), that Code section explicitly states that this occurs "[a]fter incorporation." Moreover, nothing in the language of [MBCA §16.01] requires records to be kept as a prerequisite of proper incorporation—in fact, [MBCA § 16.01] only prescribes duties of existent corporations.

As stated above, it is undisputed that Brown complied with [MBCA §2.03] and that articles of incorporation for Alabama MBA were filed in 2002, years before the underlying action was initiated. Therefore, there is no merit in W.P. Media's argument that Alabama MBA was not properly incorporated at the time this action was filed and thus cannot be a real party in interest in this case.

Conclusion

Alabama MBA has demonstrated that W.P. Media is estopped from denying Alabama MBA's corporate existence. Therefore, the summary judgment is reversed, and the case is remanded for further proceedings.

REVERSED AND REMANDED.

Notes and Questions

1. Notes

a. We will see in Chapter 8 that failure to hold the organization meeting or to take other steps after incorporation may lead a court to disregard a de jure corporation and hold the shareholders personally liable for some corporate debts.

2. Reality Check

a. According to the defendant, what should be the two consequences of the fact that Alabama MBA was not a de jure corporation?

b. What are the elements of a corporation by estoppel? How does that doctrine differ from the de facto corporation doctrine? How are the doctrines alike?

c. Under the doctrine of corporation by estoppel, which party is estopped and why?

d. Could the de facto corporation doctrine apply on these facts?

e. When, if ever, did Alabama MBA become a de jure corporation?

3. Suppose

a. What if Mr. Brown had incorporated Alabama MBA before the contract was signed in 2001 but had not held an organizational meeting until 2007. Would the court's analysis or the result have been different?

4. What Do You Think?

a. Some courts hold that the corporation by estoppel doctrine is not available where the promoter knows or should know that the corporation has not yet been incorporated. Do you agree with that rule? If the focus of the doctrine is on the non-promoter's intent, why should the doctrine turn on the promoter's knowledge, at least in the absence of fraud?

b. Given the ease with which corporations can be formed, should the corporation by estoppel doctrine exist at all?

Payer v. The SGL Carbon, LLC

2006 WL 2714190 (W.D.N.Y.)

Elfvin, Senior District Judge:

INTRODUCTION

This action was originally commenced by plaintiffs Edward L. Payer and Transition Metals Technology, Inc. on May 14, 2004. This case concerns a contract for the purchase of a parcel of industrial property owned by defendant SGL Carbon, LLC ("SGL") in Niagara Falls, New York. Pending before the court [is] SGL's motion for partial summary judgment seeking dismissal of those portions of plaintiffs' claims which seek the remedy of specific performance.

BACKGROUND

Unless otherwise noted, the following facts are not in dispute. In December 2002, the plaintiffs and SGL executed a Purchase and Sale Agreement for the sale of an approximately twenty-two acre parcel of industrial real property, together with improvements, owned by SGL and located at 6200 Niagara Falls Boulevard, Niagara Falls, N.Y. The Agreement was negotiated with, and executed by, Payer as "CEO" of the purported buyer corporation, Transition Metals, for a purchase price of two million dollars, to be satisfied by a promissory note in the amount of 1.5 million dollars with the balance to be paid at closing. Although initial negotiations for the sale of the property were with Payer individually, at some point prior to the contract execution, SGL was advised that the buyer of the property was to be listed on the contract as "Transition Metals Technology, Inc., a New Jersey corporation." On May 20, 2003 Payer signed an amendment to this contract as "President" of Transition Metals. On June 30, 2003 Payer signed a promissory note as "CEO" of Transition Metals. During this time, however, Transition Metals was not yet incorporated. Plaintiffs claim that SGL knew this. SGL claims that it did not. Transition Metals was not incorporated until or about June 15, 2004, approximately 18 months after the initial execution of the contract and over a month after this action was first filed.

The contract contained numerous contingencies which had to be satisfied by all parties prior to closing. SGL claims it satisfied all of its contingency obligations under the contract and repeatedly attempted to close on the purchase and that plaintiffs repeatedly failed to show up on numerous properly scheduled closing dates. Plaintiffs claim that SGL was in breach of contract and, as such, each of the closing dates it attempted to schedule was not proper. Eventually, SGL informed plaintiffs that it had cancelled the agreement and found another buyer. SGL was set to close on the new purchase in June 2004 but the Notices of Pendency filed with the instant suit effectively prevented the closing.

Plaintiffs brought the instant action against SGL for breach of contract, misappropriation of confidential information and tortious interference with contract. Within its first two causes of action, plaintiffs seek specific performance from SGL in the form of the transfer of the real property.

DISCUSSION

SGL seeks summary judgment dismissing those portions of plaintiffs' claims seeking specific performance and removing the Notices of Pendency, and has also moved for sanctions against plaintiffs. The gravamen of both of these motions relates to various allegations and representations plaintiffs made prior to and during the course of this litigation which SGL claims were knowingly false and misleading regarding key elements of the case-to wit, the status of incorporation of Transition Metals.

In its motion for summary judgment, SGL claims that the remedy of specific performance fails as a matter of law in this case because at the time the contract was signed, Transition Metals was not incorporated, hence no contract from which specific performance is sought was formed.

It is undisputed that Transition Metals was not incorporated at any time when Payer signed the Purchase and Sale Agreement, the amendment thereto or the promissory note as "CEO" and "President", respectively. Clearly, Transition Metals was not a *de jure* corporation when it entered into the contract and SGL argues that neither is it entitled to *de facto* corporate status or corporation by estoppel. [The court held that New Jersey does not recognize the de facto corporation doctrine.] The Court will consider whether corporation by estoppel status is warranted.

Citing a line of cases which it found to be persuasive, and with which this Court agrees, the [Court in *Pharmaceutical Sales and Consulting Corp. v. J.W.S. Delavau Co., Inc.*, 59 F. Supp. 2d 398 (D.N.J. 1999) (*Delavau I*)] reasoned that

> [T]he weight of authority holds that in this context, where a defendant seeks to avoid potential liability to a would-be corporate plaintiff by contending that the plaintiff was or is not a lawful corporate entity, the doctrine of corporation by estoppel applies such that plaintiff may pursue the contract claim against the defendant despite plaintiff's noncorporate status. The rationale underlying this approach in this factual circumstance is premised upon the courts' desire to effectuate the parties' intent in entering into the contractual arrangement at issue. ("If the defendant thought it was dealing with a corporation, and later discovered it was in fact dealing with a defective corporation, absent prejudice to the defendant, there is no reason to let the defendant escape liability" based upon a technicality such as defective incorporation). In essence, these cases recognize that permitting the defendant (person or entity) to deny the fact of plaintiff's corporate existence so as to escape potential liability under a contractual arrangement would result in a windfall to defendant beyond that which was expected at the time of the execution of the contract.

Delavau I, 59 F. Supp. 2d at 406, 407 (some internal citations omitted).

The *Delavau I* Court therefore applied corporation by estoppel status to plaintiff company and denied the defendant's summary judgment motion. In analyzing the doctrine, however, the Court, . . . in *Delavau I* . . . , noted that the application of the doctrine to a particular case is fact and context driven. The Court herein is therefore mindful of this when analyzing the doctrine and its applicability to the present case.

The Court will consider three key questions (as discussed in *Delavau I*) in determining whether or not to apply the doctrine of corporation by estoppel herein. First, would permitting defendant to avoid liability under the contract based upon a technicality such as plaintiff's corporate status be contrary to general principles of New Jersey law? This is a global question that has been answered in the affirmative by the District Court in New Jersey, with which this Court agrees.

Second, would accepting defendant's argument be contrary to the parties' intent at the time of the agreement or result in a windfall to defendant? After review of the voluminous evidence submitted by the parties, the Court finds that, although there appears to be no windfall to the defendant, accepting its argument would be contrary to the parties' intent at the time the contract was formed. SGL has submitted no credible proof that the corporate status of Transition Metals was in any way an important factor in the negotiation or execution of the contract. The proof is undisputed that the contract negotiations began with Payer, individually, as the purchaser, and that it was Payer who decided that Transition Metals would be the purchaser. In fact, SGL's President stated that, other than clarifying for legal documentation, he would have done nothing differently in negotiating and forming the contract had either Transition Metals, as a corporation, or Payer, as an individual, been the intended purchaser.[10]

Third, has the defendant relied on plaintiff's alleged misrepresentations regarding its corporate status to its detriment? SGL has provided no credible evidence that Payer purposefully misrepresented Transition Metal's corporate status, or that SGL relied on such alleged corporate status to its detriment. Further, there is no evidence submitted that the contract failed in any way because Transition Metals was not incorporated. It is clear from the evidence before the Court that this was a negotiation driven by, and a contract formed as a result of, negotiations between Payer and SGL. Hence, execution and performance had little to do with Transition Metal's corporate status and SGL did not rely thereon to its detriment.

Based on the above, the Court apples corporation by estoppel status to Transition Metals.

SO ORDERED.

Notes and Questions

1. Reality Check

a. How does the court in this case describe the test for corporation by estoppel? Is it the same test as the court in *Brown*?

2. Suppose

a. What if the facts in *Brown* had been decided by the *Payer* court. Would the court's analysis or the result have been different?

b. What if the facts in *Payer* had been decided by the *Brown* court. Would the court's analysis or the result have been different?

3. What Do You Think?

a. Do you think the *Payer* court's interpretation or the *Brown* court's interpretation is better?

b. If the defense of de facto incorporation or corporation by estoppel is unsuccessful, what should the remedy be? Should the promoters be considered to be parties to any contracts made in the corporation's name? Should the promoters have unlimited personal liability? Should their liability be limited, for example, to the amount they intended to invest in the corporation? If there is more than one promoter, should they be jointly and severally liable or should liability be apportioned based on such factors as the relative amounts they intended to invest or whether some promoters were active and others passive?

---

10. The Court is not as concerned about whether or not SGL knew Transition Metals had incorporated by the time the contract was executed as the parties seem to be. The evidence submitted suggests that the purported lack of knowledge of Transition Metals' corporate status was more a matter of inattentiveness than intentional deceit. This inattentiveness further indicates that this was not a material fact in the negotiations between the parties for the sale of this property. The transfer clause in the contract is also evidence that the ultimate purchaser of the property was not a subject of import to SGL.

b. De Facto Corporations

The two cases on the de facto corporation doctrine actually involve limited liability companies (LLCs), but the courts find that the doctrine is applicable to LLCs as well as to corporations. As you read the cases, try to distinguish the de facto doctrine from promoter liability and corporation by estoppel. You should be aware that an LLC's owners, the equivalent of a corporation's stockholders, are called *members*.

Duray Development, LLC v. Perrin

792 N.W.2d 749 (Mich. App. 2010)

Before: TALBOT, P.J., and WHITBECK and OWENS, JJ.

Per Curiam.

In this breach of contract action, defendant Carl Perrin appeals as of right the August 21, 2008 judgment following a bench trial in which the trial court found that Perrin was in breach of contract and owed damages to plaintiff, Duray Development, LLC, in the amount of $96,637.68. The judgment did not find defendants Perrin Excavating, LLC, or Outlaw Excavating, LLC, in breach of contract, so neither of those defendants are parties to this appeal.

I. BASIC FACTS AND PROCEDURAL HISTORY

Duray Development is a residential development company whose sole member is Robert Munger. Munger's responsibilities were to locate and purchase property, and then work with engineering companies and municipalities to have the property zoned and fully developed for residential living. In 2004, Duray Development purchased 40 acres of undeveloped property called "Copper Corners," located at the intersection of 76th Street and Craft Avenue in Caledonia Township, Michigan.

On September 30, 2004, Duray Development entered into a contract with Perrin, Perrin Excavating, and KDM Excavating for excavating at Copper Corners. In that contract, Munger signed on Duray Development's behalf, Perrin signed on behalf of himself and Perrin Excavating, and Dan Vining signed on behalf of KDM Excavating.

On October 27, 2004, Duray Development and Perrin entered into a new contract, intended to supersede the September 30, 2004 contract. The new contract contained the same language and provisions as the earlier contract. However, the new contract was between Duray Development and Outlaw only. . . . Outlaw was an excavation company that Perrin and Vining had recently formed. Perrin and Vining signed the new contract on behalf of Outlaw, and both held themselves out to Duray Development as the owners and persons in charge of the company. Although the parties did not execute the second contract until October 27, 2004, it was drafted on September 30, 2004, the same day the parties signed the first contract. Once signed, all parties proceeded under the contract as if Outlaw were the contractor for the Copper Corners development.

Two contracts were drafted because Perrin had not yet formed Outlaw at the time of the first contract. However, Duray Development did not want to wait for Perrin to finish forming the company before starting the excavation of Copper

Corners. Therefore, the parties entered into the first contract on September 30, 2004, and then entered into the second contract once the parties thought Outlaw was a valid limited liability company.

Defendants began excavation and grading work pursuant to the contracts, but did not perform satisfactorily or on time. Duray Development then sued defendants for breach of contract. Defendants answered and filed a counterclaim against Duray Development, alleging that they performed the work according to the terms of the contracts and that Duray Development owed defendants approximately $35,000. Duray Development later learned through discovery that Outlaw did not obtain a "filed" status as a limited liability company until November 29, 2004, and therefore Outlaw was not a valid limited liability company at the time the parties executed the second contract.[1]

After trial, the trial court ruled in favor of Duray Development, finding that Perrin was in breach of contract and owed $96,367.68 in damages to Duray Development.

In a posttrial memorandum, Perrin argued that he was not personally liable for Duray Development's damages. He asserted that, although Outlaw was not a valid limited liability company at the time of the execution of the second contract, Outlaw was nevertheless liable to Duray Development under the doctrine of de facto corporation. The trial court opined that if Outlaw were a corporation, then the de facto corporation doctrine most likely would have applied. However, the trial court concluded that the Limited Liability Company Act "clearly and specifically provides for the time that a limited liability company comes into existence and has powers to contract" and therefore superseded the de facto corporation doctrine and made it inapplicable to limited liability companies altogether. Perrin now appeals.

II. PERRIN'S PERSONAL LIABILITY

The Limited Liability Company Act

The Limited Liability Company Act provides precisely when a limited liability company comes into existence. MCL 450.4202(2) provides that "[t]he existence of the limited liability company begins on the effective date of the articles of organization as provided in [MCL 450.4104]." MCL 450.4104(1) requires that the articles of organization be delivered to the administrator of the Michigan Department of Energy, Labor and Economic Growth (DELEG). Under MCL 450.4104(2), after delivery of the articles of organization, "the administrator shall endorse upon it the word 'filed' with his or her official title and the date of receipt and of filing[.]" And under MCL 450.4104(6), "[a] document filed under [MCL 450.4104(2)] is effective at the time it is endorsed[.]"

Once a limited liability company comes into existence, limited liability applies, and a member or manager is not liable for the acts, debts, or obligations of the company. In contrast, a person who signs a contract on behalf of a company that is not yet in existence generally becomes personally liable on that contract. However, a company can become liable if, (1) after the company comes into existence, it either

---

1. According to the Limited Liability Company Act, a limited liability company does not exist until the state administrator endorses the articles of organization with the word "filed."

ratifies or adopts that contract, (2) a court determines that a de facto corporation existed at the time of the contract, or (3) a court orders that corporation by estoppel prevented the opposing party from arguing against the existence of a corporation.

In this case, Perrin signed the articles of organization for Outlaw on the same day as the second contract, October 27, 2004. Perrin then signed the October 27, 2004 contract on behalf of Outlaw. However, the DELEG administrator did not endorse the articles of organization until November 29, 2004. Therefore, pursuant to the Limited Liability Company Act, Outlaw was not in existence on October 27, 2004. Therefore, Perrin became personally liable for Outlaw's obligations *unless* a de facto limited liability company existed or limited liability company by estoppel applied.

De Facto Corporation and Corporation by Estoppel

De facto corporation and corporation by estoppel are separate and distinct doctrines that warrant individual treatment. The de facto corporation doctrine provides that a defectively formed corporation—that is, one that fails to meet the technical requirements for forming a de jure corporation—may attain the legal status of a de facto corporation if certain requirements are met, as discussed later in this opinion. The most important aspect of a de facto corporation is that courts perceive and treat it in all respects as if it were a properly formed de jure corporation. For example, it can sue and be sued. Often, as in this case, the status of the company is crucial to determine whether the parties forming the corporation are individually liable.

Corporation by estoppel, on the other hand, is an equitable remedy and does not concern legal status. The general rule is: "Where a body assumes to be a corporation and acts under a particular name, a third party dealing with it under such assumed name is estopped to deny its corporate existence."[20] Like the de facto corporation doctrine, corporation by estoppel often arises in the context of assessing individual versus corporate liability. The purpose of the doctrine is so "that one who contracts with an association as a corporation is estopped to deny its corporate existence . . . so as to prevent one from maintaining an action on the contract against the associates, or against the officers making the contract, as individuals or partners."[21]

In sum, the de facto corporation doctrine allows a defectively formed corporation to attain the legal status of a corporation. The corporation by estoppel doctrine prevents a party who dealt with an association as though it were a corporation from denying its existence. Stated another way, the de facto corporation doctrine establishes the legal existence of the corporation. By contrast, the corporation by estoppel doctrine merely prevents one from arguing against it, and does nothing to establish its actual existence in the eyes of the rest of the world.

Despite their differences, the two doctrines are often discussed in tandem and the Supreme Court tends to collapse discussion of the two into a single blended analysis. One reason that the two doctrines are often blended together is because a common fact pattern continually emerges in the caselaw: a party conducts business

---

20. Estey Mfg. Co. v. Runnells, 20 N.W. 823 (Mich. 1884).

21. 6 Michigan Civil Jurisprudence, §47, p. 140, citing *Lockwood v. Wynkoop*, 178 Mich. 388, 144 N.W. 846 (1914).

with an association that it believes to be a de jure corporation, but which was defective in some way and never truly incorporated. In that situation, both corporation by estoppel and de facto corporation naturally become relevant.

With that said, we, however, will consider each doctrine separately and deliberately. Each concept involves a separate set of factors, and caselaw suggests that one can exist without the other.

The De Facto Corporation Doctrine

The Michigan Supreme Court established the four elements for a de facto corporation long ago:

> When incorporators have [1] proceeded in good faith, [2] under a valid statute, [3] for an authorized purpose, and [4] have executed and acknowledged articles of association pursuant to that purpose, a corporation *de facto* instantly comes into being. A *de facto* corporation is an actual corporation. As to all the world, except the State, it enjoys the status and powers of a *de jure* corporation.[25]

Here, there is no question that elements (2), (3), and (4) were satisfied. First, the Limited Liability Company Act is a valid statute that allows for limited liability companies in Michigan. Second, Perrin and Vining presumably formed Outlaw for the purpose of starting a new excavation company, which is an authorized purpose. Third, Perrin executed the articles of organization on October 27, 2004, the same day the parties executed the second contract.

It is less obvious whether the first element of the doctrine—good faith—was satisfied. There is little guidance in Michigan caselaw for a definition, or application, of this specific element. But in *Newcomb-Endicott Co. v. Fee*,[26] the Michigan Supreme Court, although applying a different set of elements,[27] did state that in the absence of a claim or evidence of fraud or false representation on the part of the incorporators, and in light of a bona fide attempt to incorporate, there was no reason to deny a company the status of a de facto corporation.

Here, Duray Development does not allege that Perrin set up the corporation through fraud or false representations; that is, Duray Development does not allege that Perrin set up the corporation as a sham, for fraudulent purposes, or as a mere instrumentality under a theory of piercing the corporate veil. Rather, as the record indicates, Duray Development did not learn until after filing the complaint in this case that Outlaw was not a valid limited liability company on October 27, 2004. Duray Development at all times dealt with Outlaw as a valid corporation with which it contracted. Duray Development's sole member, Munger, testified that once the second contract took effect, Duray Development no longer considered Perrin or Perrin Excavating as parties to the contract, but instead considered Outlaw to be the new "contractor." There is no evidence whatsoever to suggest that Perrin formed Outlaw in anything other than good faith. Accordingly, the trial court was correct to conclude that, had Outlaw been formed as a corporation instead of a limited liability company, it would have been a de facto corporation for purposes of liability on the

---

25. *Tisch Auto Supply Co. v. Nelson*, 192 N.W. 600 (Mich. 1923).
26. *Newcomb-Endicott Co.*, 133 N.W. 540 (Mich. 1911).
27. [(1) a charter or statute under which a corporation with the powers assumed might have been organized; (2) a bona fide attempt to organize a corporation under such charter or statute; and (3) an actual use of the corporate powers.]

October 27, 2004 contract. Thus, all elements of a de facto corporation were present in this case.

The trial court, however, concluded that the de facto *corporation* doctrine does not apply to *limited liability companies* and therefore did not apply to Outlaw. It reasoned that the plain reading of the Limited Liability Company Act "clearly and specifically provides for the time that a limited liability company comes into existence and has powers to contract." Thus, the trial court concluded that the Legislature had "clearly spoken on this subject" and did not extend the de facto corporation doctrine to limited liability companies.

Neither this Court nor the Supreme Court has addressed whether the de facto corporation doctrine can be extended or applied to a limited liability company. That is not to say, however, that the doctrine *cannot* be applied to a limited liability company. The 1911 case of *Newcomb-Endicott Co.* is similar to the facts here and suggests that the plain language of the Limited Liability Company Act and the Business Corporation Act should not supplant the de facto corporation doctrine.

In *Newcomb-Endicott Co.*, the defendants formed a corporation by filing the articles of association with the Secretary of State on June 15, 1908, and with the county clerk in March 1909. At the time, the relevant incorporating statute provided that a corporation did not exist until the articles of association were filed with both offices. Therefore, the defendants' corporation did not technically exist until March 1909. However, the defendants' corporation contracted with the plaintiff in July 1908, and accumulated an unpaid debt for which the plaintiff sued. At trial, the circuit court ruled that, although the corporation did not exist at the time of the contract and when the debts were incurred, it was a de facto corporation and, as such, the corporation, not the individual defendants, was liable. The plaintiff appealed and argued, in part, that the de facto corporation doctrine contradicted the plain language of the applicable statute, which clearly stated how and when a corporation was formed. The Supreme Court ruled otherwise, reasoning that, although the plain language of the statute "contemplates the complete organization of the association," including how the articles of association were to be filed, it did not preclude the application of the de facto corporation doctrine.

The Supreme Court's conclusion in *Newcomb-Endicott Co.*, that statutes contemplating complete organization of an association do not preclude application of the de facto corporation doctrine, contradicts the idea that the de facto corporation doctrine perished on enactment of the Business Corporation Act and the Limited Liability Company Act. Although *Newcomb-Endicott Co.* dealt with a corporation rather than a limited liability company, it would be arbitrary to conclude, without any precedent to the contrary, that the de facto corporation doctrine applies to corporations but not to limited liability companies.

Indeed, the similarities between the Business Corporation Act and the Limited Liability Company Act support the conclusion that the de facto corporation doctrine applies to both. The purposes for forming a limited liability company and a corporation are similar. Further, both the Limited Liability Company Act and the Business Corporation Act contemplate the moment in time when a limited liability company or corporation comes into existence. Because the Business Corporation Act and the Limited Liability Company Act relate to the common purpose of forming a business and because both statutes contemplate the moment of existence for each, they should be interpreted in a consistent manner.

Accordingly, we conclude that the de facto corporation doctrine applies to Outlaw, a limited liability company. As a result, Outlaw, and not Perrin, individually, is liable for the breach of the October 27, 2004 contract.

Corporation by Estoppel

As stated previously, generally, a person who signs a contract on behalf of a company that is not yet in existence becomes personally liable on that contract. However, a court can order that the company is instead liable if it finds that corporation by estoppel prevented the opposing party from arguing against the existence of a corporation. The Supreme Court in *Estey Mfg. Co.* summarized the principle of corporation by estoppel as follows: "Where a body assumes to be a corporation and acts under a particular name, a third party dealing with it under such assumed name is estopped to deny its corporate existence."

As with the doctrine of de facto corporation, this Court has not addressed whether corporation by estoppel can be applied to limited liability companies. However, corporation by estoppel is an equitable remedy, and its purpose is to prevent one who contracts with a corporation from later denying its existence in order to hold the individual officers or partners liable. The doctrine has come up on numerous occasions in conjunction with de facto corporations.

With this in mind, and in light of the purpose of corporation by estoppel, the corporate structure has little impact on the equitable principles at stake. In other words, there is no reason or purpose to draw a distinction on the basis of corporate form. Furthermore, like de facto corporation, because corporation by estoppel coexists with the Business Corporation Act, so too can it coexist with the Limited Liability Company Act.

However, we cannot find plain error requiring reversal on the doctrine of limited liability company by estoppel. Perrin did not raise the issue in the trial court, and the trial court did not err by not raising it for him. [W]e reverse the judgment of the trial court that the de facto corporation doctrine cannot apply to limited liability companies. . . . Accordingly, we remand for further proceedings in accordance with this opinion.

Notes and Questions

1. Note

a. The court describes the statutory requirements for forming a corporation in the early twentieth century. Note that valid formation in Michigan required a filing with the secretary of state and with a county clerk. That system of dual filing was quite common before the mid-century. Until the widespread revision of state corporation statutes in the 1950s, the states varied considerably in the requirements for valid formation. A state might provide that a corporation came into existence only after filing with the secretary of state or, as in Michigan, filing with both the secretary of state and a county clerk. In other states, the acts that signified the beginning of the corporation's existence (and hence the end of the promoters' liability) were the issuance of a certificate by the secretary of state; payment of the initial franchise fees; or issuance of a certain amount of stock. Now, virtually every state provides that an entity, whether corporation or LLC, comes into existence when the appropriate state officer files the initial articles.

2. Reality Check

a. How does the court describe the difference between the de facto corporation doctrine and corporation by estoppel? Are those doctrines different in purpose or in approach?

b. What are the elements for finding a de facto corporation? Is there more than one test? If so, is there a substantive difference or simply a difference in wording?

c. Why did the court hold that the corporation by estoppel defense was unavailable?

d. Why did Perrin's actions meet the test for a de facto corporation? Do you agree?

3. Suppose

a. Suppose Perrin had properly raised the estoppel defense. How would the court have ruled?

b. Suppose the court concluded that Perrin was individually liable to Duray Development. Would Vining have been individually liable, as well? If so, how?

4. What Do You Think?

a. Why do you think that Perrin did not form Outlaw before executing the second contract?

b. Do you think Duray could have held Perrin liable under the promoter liability theory?

c. Did Perrin know that Outlaw had not been formed when he executed the second contract? Do you think his personal liability should turn on whether or not he knew?

d. Was Duray Development misled in any way about Outlaw's status? If so, do you think Perrin or Vining intended to mislead? Should individual liability turn on whether Duray Development knew about Outlaw's status?

e. How could this situation have been avoided? What advice would you have given to Perrin, Vining, or Duray Development?

In the Matter of the Estate of Hausman
921 N.E.2d 191 (N.Y. 2009)

CIPARICK, J.

In this probate proceeding, we are asked to decide whether decedent's children formed a de facto limited liability company (LLC) capable of receiving title to real property that was the subject of a deed executed by decedent shortly before her death. Because no "colorable attempt" was made to file the articles of organization with the Department of State prior to the date of the alleged transfer, we conclude that there was no de facto entity in existence capable of receiving title to the property and the conveyance is thus void.

The facts are mainly undisputed. On October 16, 2000, decedent Lena Hausman's will was executed. She divided her residuary estate into four equal shares: 25% to her son, George (the executor of her estate); 25% to her daughter, Susan; 25% to the children of her predeceased son, Gerald; and 25% to the children of her predeceased son, Gilbert. Decedent's will empowered her executor, George, to create an LLC and to transfer ownership of her real estate located at 1373 56th Street, in Brooklyn, which generated rental income, to the LLC for the benefit of her heirs. In the event that the LLC was formed and her real property conveyed to it, the will required that the executor "distribute the membership interests in accordance with the directions set forth above."

On October 4, 2001, George and Susan alone executed articles of organization to own, operate and manage the LLC. They also drafted an operating agreement, providing that they would be the sole members of the company and that it would come into existence upon the filing of the articles of organization with the New York Department of State. This would have the effect of depriving the other heirs, decedent's grandchildren, from receiving any benefit from the rental property. Significantly, the articles of organization were not filed with the Department of State until November 16, 2001. On November 2, 2001—two weeks prior to the filing of the articles of organization—decedent, then 90 years old and residing in a nursing home, executed a deed transferring ownership of the property to the LLC. The deed was recorded on December 3, 2001.

Upon decedent's death in June 2002, her will was admitted to probate. A dispute arose over whether decedent's grandchildren had rights to the real property. They argued that the property was not conveyed to a valid LLC, and that it should be part of the estate subject to their distributive interests, as stated in the will. The executor maintained that the conveyance of the property to the LLC was valid and does not constitute part of the estate. He filed the instant petition to ascertain the validity of the conveyance of the property to the LLC. Surrogate's Court granted the petition, concluding that the LLC operated as a valid de facto company prior to the filing of the articles of organization. The Appellate Division reversed the order, denied the petition and deemed the deed invalid. We granted leave to appeal and now affirm.

Here, no attempt to file articles of organization was made before the conveyance of the property. The executor seeks application of the de facto doctrine and a determination that the transfer of the property to the LLC was valid. The parties do not dispute, and both courts below concluded, that the de facto corporation doctrine is applicable to limited liability companies. We agree. The statutory schemes of the Business Corporation Law and the Limited Liability Company Law are very similar, and we see no principled reason why the de facto corporation doctrine should not apply to both corporations and limited liability companies.

Under very limited circumstances, courts may invoke the de facto corporation doctrine where there exists (1) a law under which the corporation might be organized, (2) an attempt to organize the corporation and (3) an exercise of corporate powers thereafter. There is no question that the first prong has been satisfied, as the Limited Liability Company Law provides for the method of incorporation. With respect to the second prong, however, the formation of a de facto company requires a "colorable attempt to comply with the statutes governing incorporation" prior to the exercise of corporate powers, including the filing requirement (*Kiamesha Dev. Corp. v. Guild Props.*, 151 N.E.2d 214 (N.Y. 1958)). "[W]here there has been an attempt in good faith to comply with the requirements of the law with respect to filing a certificate of incorporation and a certificate has been filed . . . and there has been use of the corporate name, the corporation will be deemed a corporation *de facto*" (*Stevens v. Episcopal Church History Co.*, 125 N.Y.S. 573 (N.Y. App. 1910)). However, "the mere execution of a paper which is not filed and does not become a public record is insufficient" *Id.*

Here, it is undisputed that there was no bona fide attempt to comply with the ministerial, yet essential, requirement of filing the articles of organization prior to the attempted conveyance. Although challenged by defendant and the dissenting opinion, merely executing articles of organization along with an operating agreement and nothing more is insufficient to meet the long-standing requirements of a de facto entity. Because an entity that is neither de facto nor de jure cannot take title to real property, there was no entity in existence capable of receiving title to the real property and the purported conveyance is therefore void.

Accordingly, the Appellate Division's order should be affirmed. . . .

PIGOTT, J. (dissenting).

Because the majority, in my view, takes the holding in *Kiamesha Dev. Corp.* too far—to the point of practically eliminating the legal concept of a de facto corporation—I respectfully dissent.

It is conceded that at the time the property was conveyed from the decedent to the LLC, the articles of organization for the LLC had not yet been filed. But the sequence of events preceding the filing is important. The articles of organization and operating agreement for the LLC were executed on October 4, 2001. The decedent conveyed the property to the LLC on November 2. The articles of organization were filed on November 16 and the deed was filed on December 3, 2001. The delay in filing is about the only misstep, if a misstep at all, in an otherwise fairly normal series of events in the creation of the LLC. Five years later, only after counsel for disinherited legatees in litigation in Surrogate's Court discovered that the filing of the articles of organization followed the execution of the deed, rather than vice versa, did the timing of the filing come into question.

The majority focuses on the "colorable attempt to comply with the statutory requirement" language found in *Kiamesha Dev. Corp.* to state definitively that there can be no de facto corporation here because there was no "colorable attempt." In my view, that case, interesting in its facts, should be limited to them.

In New York, it is clear that if there is no attempt to formally organize, there will be no de facto corporation. Here, however, the organization of the LLC was complete. The record shows that the incorporators prepared and executed the articles of organization as required under Limited Liability Company Law §203. They also executed and adopted the required operating agreement for the LLC pursuant to Limited Liability Company Law §417(a). Those documents reveal that the LLC was organized "solely to own, operate or manage real property and to do any and all things necessary, convenient, or incidental to that purpose." Pursuant to that purpose, the LLC took title as grantee to the real property in the name of the LLC. And it was the decedent as grantor who executed the deed naming the LLC the grantee. Two weeks after the deed was executed—a reasonable period—the articles of organization were filed with the Secretary of State. The related ancillary papers, including a New York City real property transfer tax return as well as city and state transfer tax returns, which named the LLC as grantee, were executed and filed as required.

Under the circumstances of this case, I would find that the incorporators acted with sufficient alacrity to comply with the statutes, and would therefore find the conveyance to the de facto entity that existed at that time valid.

Therefore, I would reverse the order of the Appellate Division.

Chief Judge LIPPMAN and Judges GRAFFEO, READ, SMITH and JONES concur with Judge CIPARICK. Judge PIGOTT dissents and votes to reverse in a separate opinion.

Notes and Questions

1. Reality Check

a. What is the consequence of finding that the de facto corporation doctrine applies (or doesn't apply)? How is that consequence different from *Duray Development*?

b. What test does the court use for the de facto corporation doctrine? Is the test the same or different from *Duray Development*?

c. Why does the court hold that no de facto LLC was created here?

d. Why does Judge Pigott disagree? Does he disagree with the majority's legal standard, its application, or both?

2. Suppose

a. Suppose *Hausman* had been decided by the *Duray Development* court. Would the analysis or result be different?

b. Suppose *Duray Development* had been decided by the *Hausman* court. Would the analysis or result be different?

3. What Do You Think?

a. Given the ease with which entities can be formed, do you think the de facto corporation and corporation by estoppel doctrines should exist?

b. What other actions by George and Susan would have been sufficient to invoke the de facto corporation defense?

c. What other actions by George and Susan would have been sufficient to create a de jure (i.e., completely formed) LLC?

d. Why do you think George and Susan did not form the LLC before the real estate was transferred to it?

e. Do you think that the de facto corporation doctrine should be applied here?

c. The Effect of Modern Corporation Statutes

Both the de facto corporation and the corporation by estoppel doctrines were well established by 1950, when the ABA promulgated the original Model Business Corporation Act ("MBCA (1950)"). The drafters of the MBCA (1950) believed that incorporating was so easy that not even a good faith, but unsuccessful, effort to incorporate should immunize the promoters from personal liability for pre-incorporation actions. In other words, the drafters of the MBCA (1950) believed that the de facto corporation doctrine should be eliminated. They embodied this belief in section 146, which read,

> All persons who assume to act as a corporation without authority to do so shall be jointly and severally liable for all debt and liabilities incurred or arising as a result thereof.

The Official Comments asserted that this language eliminated the de facto corporation doctrine. By the 1980s, about 60% of the states had statutes equivalent to MBCA (1950) §146.

But there were at least two problems with this approach. First, some courts held that the de facto doctrine survived the enactment of §146, either because the language did not expressly eliminate the doctrine or because the statute infringed on the court's inherent power to do equity. Second, some courts held that §146 also eliminated the doctrine of corporation by estoppel, although neither the language of the statute nor the Official Comment supported that result. The drafters of the current MBCA modified old §146 in current §2.04, which reads (with emphasis added),

> All persons purporting to act as or on behalf of a corporation, *knowing there was no incorporation under this Act*, are jointly and severally liable for all liabilities while so acting.

With that change, the MBCA opened the door to a revival of the de facto corporation doctrine in states that had adopted the prior version of the MBCA.

The states are somewhat fractured, as a result, in their approach to these doctrines and in their statutory provisions. A handful still retain the substance of MBCA (1950) §146. Presumably, in those jurisdictions the de facto incorporation doctrine is unavailable, although the corporation by estoppel doctrine might be possible. Just over half of the states have adopted MBCA §2.04 either verbatim or in substance. In those states, the de facto incorporation doctrine and the corporation by estoppel doctrine may be available, although in both settings only if the promoter did not know the corporation had not been incorporated.

Note that, strictly, MBCA §2.04 does not speak to the setting where a promoter acts on behalf of a corporation and did not know the corporation had not been formed. Some courts have read that section as impliedly immunizing such promoters from personal liability, however. In the remaining 40% or so of the states, no statute bears on the question. In those jurisdictions the doctrines of de facto corporation and corporation by estoppel, if they exist under common law, remain.

The next case arose in Tennessee, which has adopted MBCA §2.04. As you read it, ask whether §2.04 is determinative of the liability of all the defendants.

Christmas Lumber Co., Inc. v. Valiga

99 S.W.3d 585 (Tenn. Ct. App. 2002)

D. MICHAEL SWINEY, J.:

After experiencing significant problems with the construction of a house he was having built, Robert E. Valiga ("Valiga") sued Robert H. Waddell ("Waddell") and John Graves ("Graves") (collectively referred to as "Defendants") seeking damages for the poor construction. Although the construction contract was between Valiga and R.H. Waddell Construction, Inc., no corporate charter had been filed when the contract was signed. The Trial Court . . . entered judgment against them individually for $80,045.79. Graves and Waddell appeal, challenging the Trial Court's conclusion that they were . . . subject to individual liability. . . . We affirm.

Background

On January 10, 1990, Christmas Lumber Company, Inc. ("Christmas Lumber") filed a complaint against Valiga, Waddell, and others seeking to enforce a materialmen's lien for building materials purchased by Waddell to be used on the house being built for Valiga.

On December 2, 1992, Valiga filed a separate lawsuit against Waddell and Graves. Valiga claimed he entered into a contract on September 12, 1988, with "what was known as" R.H. Waddell Construction, Inc., for the construction of a house. Valiga claimed he started experiencing problems with the quality of the construction almost immediately after construction began. Valiga complained about the problems, and was assured the house would be constructed according to applicable laws and building codes, etc. Valiga, therefore, allowed construction to continue. The quality of construction did not improve, and Waddell terminated the contract on February 14, 1989, well before construction was completed. Valiga then had the construction work inspected and claims numerous structural defects were found.

Valiga sued Waddell and Graves personally because, according to the complaint, there was no corporation chartered by the State named R.H. Waddell Construction, Inc. when the contract was entered into on September 12, 1988. The corporate charter was issued after Valiga had entered into the construction contract . . . Valiga sought compensatory and punitive damages from Defendants.

The two lawsuits were consolidated. Christmas Lumber . . . was granted summary judgment against Waddell personally for $17,083 . . . . [N]o appeal was taken by Waddell.

On May 8, 2000, Graves filed a motion to dismiss, claiming that neither was he a party to the contract between Valiga and R.H. Waddell Construction Company, Inc., nor was Valiga a third party beneficiary of any agreement between Graves and Waddell. Valiga responded, claiming Waddell and Graves were joint venturers and Graves could be held vicariously liable on that basis. Valiga attached a Joint Venture Agreement entered into between Graves and Waddell dated November 11, 1988. The stated intent of the Joint Venture Agreement was "to enter into an agreement for the purpose of the construction of a residence located on a lot owned by Robert E. Valiga. . . ." The Joint Venture Agreement went on to provide:

1. *PURPOSE*

That this Agreement is entered into in order to assure continuity regarding this particular project in the event of the death or disability of Robert Waddell and/or John Graves. Further, that a significant purpose is to assure shared liability in the event of a lawsuit or other legal action against either Robert H. Waddell or John Graves.

* * *

15. *PROFITS AND LOSSES*

The profits and/or losses as well as expenses are to be divided equally between the parties.

At trial, Waddell testified he is a land surveyor and has a degree in architecture from the University of Tennessee. In 1988, he decided to "go into the contracting business" and entered into a contract with Valiga. Valiga's house was the first and only house Waddell's construction company ever built. When he entered into the contract with Valiga, Waddell signed the contract on behalf of R.H. Waddell Construction, Inc. When asked if the corporate charter had been recorded at the time the contract was entered into with Valiga, Waddell stated he had "no knowledge of that." Waddell was unsure who prepared the charter, although he did not do it himself. Waddell signed this document as the "incorporator" on the stated date of August 19, 1988, although it was not filed with the Secretary of State's office until December 9, 1988. . . .

At trial, Waddell identified a letter he received from Valiga dated November 9, 1988, discussing "requests" being made by Valiga addressing the construction of the house. Valiga terminated Waddell's services the next day by letter dated November 10, 1988. Apparently sensing potential litigation, Waddell and Graves on November 11, 1988, entered into the Joint Venture Agreement ("Agreement"). The only parties to the Agreement were Waddell and Graves. R.H. Waddell Construction, Inc., was not a party to the Agreement. After Waddell "patched things back up" with Valiga, he returned to work on the project from November until February of the next year. On February 11, 1989, Waddell received a letter from Valiga wherein Valiga expressed his shock regarding the cost of the construction job. Three days later, Waddell quit as Valiga's contractor.

Waddell testified [that] Graves was a co-partner in a joint venture agreement for the purpose of constructing the house for Valiga. He also indicated Graves had "arranged the contract with Valiga." During a pretrial deposition, when asked why he and Graves had entered into the Agreement, Waddell stated "since John and I were in partnership—were in a partnership for this project, you know, we both kind of felt that we needed some type of an agreement about our status on the job." Waddell later testified it was his intent to operate as a corporation and not as a partnership or an individual. Waddell admitted he and Graves split the $11,500 contractor's fee received from the Valiga project. He and Graves also equally paid Christmas Lumber's judgment against Waddell. Waddell stated that after the corporation was established, no one paid anything to the corporation for stock and no one contributed any capital. He is unaware of any corporate officers or directors being elected.

Graves testified he does "tax preparation" for a living. Graves acknowledged signing the Joint Venture Agreement which provided he was to receive 50% of the contractor's fee. Graves claimed he made no decisions concerning the construction of the Valiga house. Graves stated he was on the job six to eight hours a day for a majority of the time the house was being constructed. Graves never was a shareholder in R.H. Waddell Construction, Inc. Graves agreed to work on the project because it was not a busy time for his tax preparation business.

Valiga testified he works at Oak Ridge National Laboratory and has a masters degree in nuclear engineering. The house was not completed at the time of trial. Valiga and his wife rented an apartment or house while work continued on the house. Valiga testified as follows with regard to his understanding of the roles of Graves and Waddell during the construction of his house:

> [Graves] knew a number of folks from the Riversound project that was being built at the time. He did a lot of negotiations and hired a lot of the subcontractors. He seemed to be a person that was quite knowledge[able] about the business end of building. . . .
>
> Mr. Waddell was a surveyor [and had an architect degree]. Mr. Waddell was going to help do some of the design changes to the prints. He was going to—I believe he had a contractor's license. He was going to be a—I guess the official contractor's license on [the] job in that sense.

In its memorandum opinion, the Trial Court observed that while the September 12, 1988, contract purportedly was between R.H. Waddell Construction, Inc., and Valiga, [R.H. Waddell Construction, Inc.], did not file its charter with the Secretary of State until December 9, 1988. . . . The construction problems existed before the charter was filed. The Trial Court also noted while the charter was dated August 19, 1988, there was no explanation for the delay in the filing. According to the Trial Court, Waddell and Graves entered into a "Joint Venture Agreement" which "memorializes their partnership status and their partnership obligations." The Trial Court emphasized Waddell testified at his deposition that since he and Mr. Graves were in a "partnership," they felt they needed an agreement concerning their status on the job, and that they divided the contractor fees.

On February 2, 2001, the Trial Court entered judgment for Valiga for $80,045.79, plus prejudgment interest from December 2, 1992. All of the parties filed motions to alter or amend the judgment. As pertinent to this appeal, Graves contended his only contact with this situation was to share in the proceeds and he did not participate in the actual building which took place.

Waddell and Graves appeal. Both Defendants argue [that] the Trial Court erred by imposing personal liability.

Discussion

Defendants . . . argue the Trial Court erred when it concluded they were partners and subject to individual liability. On this issue, Defendants make separate arguments. Waddell relies on [MBCA §2.04].

Waddell argues he signed the necessary paperwork to have his business incorporated and was unaware of the delay in filing the charter with the Secretary of State's office. He claims, therefore, he did not "know" there was no incorporation. Graves argues he had no responsibility on the construction project and there were insufficient facts to conclude he was in a partnership or joint venture with Waddell.

Pursuant to [MBCA §2.03], absent a delayed effective date, the "corporate existence begins when the charter is filed." The issues of whether Waddell "knew" there was no corporate existence and whether Waddell and Graves intended to create a partnership or joint venture are primarily factual issues. In resolving the factual issues presented for appeal, we must keep in mind the Trial Court heard the conflicting testimony from the witnesses. The trial court's determinations regarding credibility, as to those witnesses who testified live, are accorded considerable deference by this Court.

Waddell apparently signed the charter on August 19, 1988. On September 12, 1988, the contract was signed between Valiga and R.H. Waddell Construction, Inc. Two months later, on November 11, 1988, Waddell and Graves entered into the Joint Venture Agreement. On December 9, 1988, the charter was filed with the Secretary of State's office. Waddell's claim he did not "know" the corporate charter had not been filed with the Secretary of State is belied by the fact he and Graves essentially memorialized their relationship in writing with the Joint Venture Agreement which was signed after Waddell claims he "thought" there was a corporation and before the corporation actually was formed. Waddell's assertion is made further suspect by his deposition testimony that he and Graves were "partners."

[T]his Court discussed what constitutes a partnership, stating:

> A partnership is defined in T.C.A. §61-1-105(a) (Supp. 1999) as "an association of two (2) or more persons to carry on as coowners a business for profit. . . ." A partnership can only be created pursuant to a contract of partnership, though such an agreement may be either express or implied. To determine whether a partnership exists, courts must ascertain the intention of the parties. The parties need only intend to do the things which constitute a partnership. A partnership results if the parties place their money, assets, labor, or skill in commerce with the understanding that profits will be shared between them. It is not necessary that the parties intend to actually form a partnership or even that they know the legal result of their actions is to create a partnership. Accordingly, the terminology used by the parties to describe their business relationship is of little import.

Messer Griesheim Indus., Inc. v. Cryotech of Kingsport, Inc., 45 S.W.3d 588, 605-06 (Tenn. Ct. App. 2001) [internal citations omitted].

Based on the roles occupied by Waddell and Graves during the construction of Valiga's house, coupled with: 1) the terms of Joint Venture Agreement; 2) Waddell's deposition testimony he and Graves were "partners"; 3) Graves' testimony that he spent a significant amount of time at the work site; and 4) Waddell and Graves dividing the contractor's fee, we conclude the evidence does not preponderate against the Trial Court's findings leading to its conclusion that Waddell and Graves were partners. We affirm the Trial Court's holding that both Defendants are personally liable.

Conclusion

The judgment of the Trial Court is affirmed.

Notes and Questions

1. Notes

a. Note that under the Tennessee version of the MBCA the Articles of Incorporation are called the charter.

2. Reality Check

a. How does one act "on behalf of" a corporation? In the corporate setting, a signature such as

Acme, Inc.
by [signature],
President

should be sufficient to demonstrate that the agent (i.e., the corporation's president) is causing the principal (the corporation) to act. This distinction is important because under agency rules an agent for a fully disclosed principal is not liable on a contract. Consider whether the following signatures bind the corporation, the signer, both, or neither:

Acme, Inc.
by [signature]

Acme, Inc.
[signature]

[signature],
President of Acme, Inc.

Acme, Inc.
by [signature],
Vice President

Acme, Inc.
by [signature],
Vice President of Advertising

b. Did Mr. Waddell act on behalf of the corporation? Did Mr. Graves do so?

c. Did Mr. Waddell "know" there was no corporation at the time the contract with Mr. Valiga was signed?

d. Did Mr. Graves "know" there was no corporation at the time the contract with Mr. Valiga was signed?

e. Are Mr. Waddell and Mr. Graves individually liable under the same theory? If not, how are the theories different?

3. Suppose

a. Suppose Tennessee had not adopted MBCA §2.04. Would the court's analysis or the result have been different? If so, would it have been different as to both defendants?

b. What if the charter (articles of incorporation) had been executed but never filed at all? Would the analysis or result be the same?

c. Would the analysis or result be different if Mr. Valiga, Mr. Waddell, and Mr. Graves all honestly believed that the corporation had been formed before September 12?

d. Would the analysis or result be different if some of the parties honestly believed that the corporation had been formed before September 12? If so, which party's belief matters?

e. Would the analysis or result be different if Mr. Waddell had signed the charter before September 12 but honestly did not know whether or not the charter had been filed?

4. What Do You Think?

a. Do you think that MBCA §2.04 does or should cover passive promoters such as Mr. Graves?

b. Could Mr. Graves have been individually liable under MBCA §2.04?

c. Could either, or both, of the defendants been liable under a theory of promoter liability or corporation by estoppel?

d. Could either, or both of the defendants been liable under Agency law?

e. Suppose R.H. Waddell Construction, Inc. had sufficient assets to pay a judgment to Mr. Valiga. Would the corporation have been liable?

Putting It to Work

Problem 5-3

Jordan and Cory, best friends and law students, notice they spend more time partying than they do studying but want to start preparing for the bar exam. The ingenious idea of Koozie Quizzes was born. They develop a line of koozies, coolers, and red plastic cups that list common bar exam questions and reveal the answer when they get cold. No longer worried about passing the bar, on April 7 they order 10,000 koozies with bar questions and answers on them after trying out prototypes on their friends. The order was submitted in the name of Party Hearty Bar Prep Incorporated, the name Jordan and Cory selected for their business. Jordan filled out the online order and signed it "Party Hearty Bar Prep Incorporated, by Jordan, President and Chief of Bar Prep." The vendor agreed to accept half the payment upon submitting the order and half when the merchandise shipped. Jordan gave his personal credit card number to the vendor.

The next morning, April 8, Jordan located the forms for forming a corporation on the secretary of state's website. These forms were the articles of incorporation and a cover sheet with contact and payment information. He filled them out properly, listing the corporate name as Party Hearty Bar Prep Incorporated, listing himself as the sole incorporator, stating that he preferred to be contacted by email, and giving his personal credit card number to pay for the filing fees. He then faxed the documents to the secretary of state at 8:45 a.m., to take advantage of the secretary of state's "In by 9, out by 5" filing service.

Later that morning, Jordan placed an online order for 15,000 red plastic cups with bar questions and answers on them. The order was submitted in the name of Party Hearty Bar Prep Incorporated. Again, Jordan filled out the online order and signed it "Party Hearty Bar Prep Incorporated, by Jordan, President and Chief of

Bar Prep." The cup vendor agreed to accept half the payment upon submitting the order and half when the merchandise shipped. Jordan gave his personal credit card number to the vendor. Shortly thereafter, Jordan received an email from the secretary of state informing him that the articles of incorporation had been rejected because Jordan's credit card was declined (he was over his credit limit, thanks to the processing of the koozie and cup orders).

On April 9, Jordan asked Cory to order 5,000 coolers with bar questions and answers on them. Jordan told Cory that he had ordered the koozies and red plastic cups but neglected to mention that he was asking Cory to order the coolers because his credit card was full. Cory, who up until this point had been involved only in writing more questions and answers, located a supplier and placed the order for coolers. The order was submitted in the name of Party Hearty Bar Prep Incorporated. Cory filled out the online order and signed it "Party Hearty Bar Prep Incorporated, by Cory, Vice President and Wing Man." The cooler vendor agreed to accept half the payment upon submitting the order and half when the merchandise shipped. Cory gave his personal credit card number to the vendor.

By the next day, April 10, Jordan had transferred enough money from his checking account to his credit card account so that he could pay the secretary of state's filing fees. He resubmitted the forms to form Party Hearty Bar Prep Incorporated and received an email from the secretary of state that afternoon informing him that the corporation had been incorporated and attaching a copy of the filed articles of incorporation.

The vendors of the koozies, red plastic cups, and coolers all shipped their products to the corporation later that month. However, the business has been an abject failure, and the corporation has no assets. Furthermore, Jordan and Cory have spent so much money holding parties at which they have tried to convince their classmates to buy their koozies, cups, and coolers that their credit cards are full and the vendors' charges are declined.

a. Is Jordan personally liable on any of the contracts if the events take place in a state that has adopted the MBCA? Would your analysis or answer be different if the events took place in a state that has not adopted the MBCA?

b. Is Cory personally liable on any of the contracts if the events take place in a state that has adopted the MBCA? Would your analysis or answer be different if the events took place in a state that has not adopted the MBCA?

c. Would your analysis or answer be different if, on April 9, Jordan told Cory "Yes, the corporation was incorporated yesterday"? Would your analysis or answer be different if, on April 9, Jordan told Cory, "No, I tried but failed to incorporate the corporation yesterday"?

E. LAWYER'S PROFESSIONAL RESPONSIBILITY TO MULTIPLE CLIENTS AND ENTITY CLIENTS

The final section of this chapter explores some ethical problems facing lawyers who create corporations on behalf of individual clients. Perhaps the most salient ethical problem is whether the lawyer can represent more than one participant. As you read the next case, think about how many possible "clients" are involved.

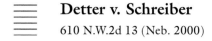

Detter v. Schreiber

610 N.W.2d 13 (Neb. 2000)

WRIGHT, J.

In 1991, Schreiber and Detter commenced a business known as Miracle Hills Animal Hospital, P.C. (the corporation). In connection with the formation of the corporation, on February 27, 1992, Schreiber executed two promissory notes in the total principal sum of $19,000 which was payable to Detter. The articles of incorporation provided that Schreiber and Detter would each own 50 percent of the shares of the corporation and would be the only members of the board of directors. In 1996, Schreiber retained the services of Thomas J. Young to draft a shareholder agreement. These services were paid for by the corporation.

Detter commenced an action against Schreiber on the two promissory notes. Detter alleged that . . . Schreiber had paid $11,000 . . . and that there was then due and owing the sum of $10,430.45 plus interest.

Schreiber's answer and counterclaim denied that there was any balance due on the notes. Schreiber's counterclaim alleged that since the inception and commencement of the business, he had performed all the management duties of the corporation and that pursuant to an oral contract made in March 1998, Schreiber was entitled to ongoing management fees in the amount of $773.33 per month commencing April 1998.

Prior to trial, Detter moved the trial court for an order directing that Young remove himself as attorney of record for Schreiber. The motion alleged that the law firm of Young & LaPuzza had acted as attorneys for the corporation and that Young had acted as the attorney for the corporation with respect to the negotiation of the corporation's lease with Dial Enterprises and a shareholder agreement between Detter and Schreiber.

Detter's affidavit alleged that he was a 50-percent owner of the corporation and was currently serving as its president. Detter claimed that he and Schreiber were the only shareholders of the corporation and that beginning in 1995, the corporation used the services of the law firm of Young & LaPuzza. Detter stated that in 1996, the corporation used the services of Young & LaPuzza to draft a shareholder agreement. Detter claimed that during his discussions with Schreiber and Young, it was his understanding that Young represented the corporation, Detter, and Schreiber with respect to the proposed shareholder agreement. Detter also stated that during his discussions with Young regarding the shareholder agreement, he discussed his thoughts and feelings with respect to the shareholder agreement and that as a result, Young had a great deal of information regarding facts and circumstances surrounding the present litigation and had information regarding Detter's financial plans and needs. The affidavit further claimed that Schreiber had specifically advised Detter that Young was representing Detter's interests, that Detter could ask Young any questions he might have, and that Young & LaPuzza's bill would be paid from the corporate account. Detter also claimed that Young never advised him that Young was not representing his interests.

Schreiber and Young also submitted affidavits which denied that Young was Detter's attorney or that Young had received any confidential information from Detter. Schreiber's affidavit specifically alleged that James T. Blazek was the registered agent of the corporation and its corporate attorney and that Blazek, who had always acted as the attorney for the corporation, continued to do so to date. Schreiber claimed that Detter had specifically refused to allow Young or the Young & LaPuzza law firm to act as the corporate attorneys for the corporation. Schreiber further stated that he had initiated efforts to have a proposed shareholder agreement, which was never executed, signed by Detter and himself and that he had contacted Young to prepare the initial draft of the agreement. Schreiber claimed that Young met with both Detter and Schreiber regarding the proposed shareholder agreement but that at no time during the conversations or discussions was any information relative to Detter's personal financial situation discussed or revealed. Schreiber asserted that he was not privy to Detter's personal financial situation except with regard to the operation, income, and expenses of the corporation.

In addition, Schreiber acknowledged that Detter was free to contact Young or any other attorney regarding the shareholder agreement. Schreiber stated that Young had been his personal attorney since 1990 but that he did not consult Young with regard to the corporation or the various agreements or promissory notes which were executed at the time the corporation was formed.

On November 23, 1998, the trial court found that Young had a conflict of interest and sustained Detter's motion to remove him. Schreiber appeals from the order which sustained Detter's motion to remove Young.

ANALYSIS

An attorney-client relationship is created when a person seeks advice or assistance from an attorney, the advice or assistance sought pertains to matters within the attorney's professional competence, and the attorney expressly or impliedly agrees to give or actually gives the desired advice or assistance.

We have never specifically examined an attorney-client relationship in a closely held corporation setting such as the one presented in the case at bar. There is no dispute that Young was called upon to do some legal work for the corporation regarding a lease and a shareholder agreement. The only evidence of contact between Young and Detter was a conference on June 27, 1996, which concerned the proposed shareholder agreement and which lasted 1½ hours. The remaining contact between Young and the corporation was through Schreiber.

[I]t is Schreiber's position that an attorney-client relationship was never formed between Young and Detter and that all correspondence between Young and the corporation was directed to Schreiber and the corporation only. Schreiber claims that the corporation was billed and paid for Young's legal services and that even though Young may have met with Detter in June 1996 regarding a proposed shareholder agreement, there is no competent evidence that would establish what information, if any, was provided by Detter to Young or what advice or opinions Young allegedly provided Detter.

Schreiber contends that Young's affidavit is sufficient to support his position that the trial court erred in sustaining Detter's motion to remove Young. In his affidavit, Young stated:

> I am aware of absolutely no confidential or privileged information which relates to Dr. Detter that would affect or impact the issues involved in this litigation. Dr. Detter has never revealed to me any financial plans or needs except a discussion with regard to the amount of life insurance and disability insurance which he and Dr. Schreiber carry.
>
> I know of no matters of which I have personal knowledge which would cause me to be a witness at any trial of this matter.

Schreiber argues that there is no evidence that Detter personally sought advice from Young or that Young gave any advice to Detter and that, therefore, no attorney-client relationship exists between Young and Detter. Schreiber claims that it was error for the trial court to conclude that Young had a conflict of interest with Detter. Schreiber asserts that even assuming Young provided legal services to Detter or that an attorney-client relationship existed relative to the office lease or the proposed shareholder agreement, those two instances did not provide a sufficient factual basis to remove Young as Schreiber's counsel.

It is Detter's position that when Young was requested to assist the corporation with the commercial lease and to draft a shareholder agreement, Young was acting on behalf of the corporation and both of the shareholders.

The shareholder agreement appears to be an agreement to govern and restrict the disposition of the shares of the corporation. It sets forth procedures for the annual evaluation of the corporation, restrictions on buying and selling shares, and the manner in which the stock would be purchased upon the death or disability of a shareholder. Preparation of this type of agreement would require Young to work with both Detter and Schreiber and to ascertain their financial and personal interests in order to determine what each wanted in the agreement. Thus, it could reasonably be inferred that Young had knowledge of the two promissory notes executed by the parties and of the management duties which are the subject of the counterclaim. Furthermore, although the evidence establishes that Young and Detter may have met only one time, Detter believed that Young was representing him at that time. Based on the facts of this case, the trial court found that Young had a conflict of interest and should be removed as Schreiber's attorney.

In disqualifying Young as counsel for Schreiber, the trial court had to factually determine that his representation constituted a conflict of interest. We find no clear error in this determination, and we conclude that the trial court correctly determined that Young should be disqualified as Schreiber's attorney.

AFFIRMED.

Notes and Questions

1. Note

a. The Model Rules of Professional Conduct, promulgated by the ABA, do not deal with the question of when the attorney-client relationship is created. The *Restatement (Third) of the Law Governing Lawyers* does deal with the issue.

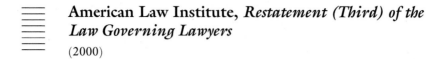

American Law Institute, *Restatement (Third) of the Law Governing Lawyers*

(2000)

§14. FORMATION OF A CLIENT-LAWYER RELATIONSHIP

A relationship of client and lawyer arises when:

(1) a person manifests to a lawyer the person's intent that the lawyer provide legal services for the person; and either

    (a) the lawyer manifests to the person consent to do so; or

    (b) the lawyer fails to manifest lack of consent to do so, and the lawyer knows or reasonably should know that the person reasonably relies on the lawyer to provide the services. . . .

COMMENT

f. Organizational, fiduciary, and class-action clients. Whether the lawyer is to represent the organization, a person or entity associated with it, or more than one such persons and entities is a question of fact to be determined based on reasonable expectations in the circumstances. Where appropriate, due consideration should be given to the unreasonableness of a claimed expectation of entering into a co-client status when a significant and readily apparent conflict of interest exists between the organization or other client and the associated person or entity claimed to be a co-client.

Under Subsection (1)(b), a lawyer's failure to clarify whom the lawyer represents in circumstances calling for such a result might lead a lawyer to have entered into client-lawyer representations not intended by the lawyer. Hence, the lawyer must clarify whom the lawyer intends to represent when the lawyer knows or reasonably should know that, contrary to the lawyer's own intention, a person, individually, or agents of an entity, on behalf of the entity, reasonably rely on the lawyer to provide legal services to that person or entity. Such clarification may be required, for example, with respect to an officer of an entity client such as a corporation. . . . An implication that such a relationship exists is more likely to be found when the lawyer performs personal legal services for an individual as well or where the organization is small and characterized by extensive common ownership and management. But the lawyer does not enter into a client-lawyer relationship with a person associated with an organizational client solely because the person communicates with the lawyer on matters relevant to the organization that are also relevant to the personal situation of the person. In all events, the question is one of fact based on the reasonable and apparent expectations of the person or entity whose status as client is in question.

2. Reality Check

a. What was the basis for the court's finding? What provisions of the Model Rules of Professional Conduct seem applicable?

b. Should Dr. Detter's understanding be given so much weight? Why does the court accept Dr. Detter's understanding over that of Mr. Young?

3. Suppose

a. What if Mr. Young's services had been paid for entirely by Dr. Schreiber rather than by the corporation? Would the analysis or result differ?

b. Would the analysis or result differ if Mr. Young had been engaged to review the shareholder agreement on behalf of Dr. Schreiber, rather than draft it?

c. What if Dr. Detter had retained Mr. Young's services in the suit against Dr. Schreiber? Would Dr. Schreiber have a better or worse case for disqualifying Mr. Young?

4. What Do You Think?

a. Situations frequently arise in the close corporation setting in which the attorney who represented the promoters also represents the corporation. Do you think the Rules of Professional Conduct or the *Restatement (Third) of the Law Governing Lawyers* give sufficient guidance to lawyers and promoters? What changes in the Rules would you make?

Even though the RPC explicitly do not cover the creation of the attorney-client relationship, several Rules deal specifically with the obligations of lawyers to organizational clients.

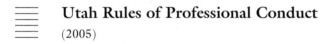

Utah Rules of Professional Conduct

(2005)

RULE 1.13 ORGANIZATION AS CLIENT

(a) A lawyer employed or retained by an organization represents the organization acting through its duly authorized constituents.

(f) In dealing with an organization's directors, officers, employees, members, shareholders or other constituents, a lawyer shall explain the identity of the client when the lawyer knows or reasonably should know that the organization's interests are adverse to those of the constituents with whom the lawyer is dealing.

(g) A lawyer representing an organization may also represent any of its directors, officers, employees, members, shareholders or other constituents, subject to the provisions of Rule 1.7. If the organization's consent to the dual representation is required by Rule 1.7, the consent shall be given by an appropriate official of the organization other than the individual who is to be represented, or by the shareholders.

COMMENT

[1] An organizational client is a legal entity, but it cannot act except through its officers, directors, employees, shareholders and other constituents. Officers, directors, employees and shareholders are the constituents of the corporate organizational client. The duties defined in this Comment apply equally to unincorporated associations. "Other constituents" as used in this Comment means the positions equivalent to officers, directors, employees and shareholders held by persons acting for organizational clients that are not corporations.

[2] When one of the constituents of an organizational client communicates with the organization's lawyer in that person's organizational capacity, the communication is protected by Rule 1.6. Thus, by way of example, if an organizational client requests its lawyer to investigate allegations of wrongdoing, interviews made in the course of that investigation between the lawyer and the client's employees or other constituents are covered by Rule 1.6. This does not mean, however, that constituents of an organizational client are the clients of the lawyer. The lawyer may not disclose to such constituents information relating to the representation except for disclosures explicitly or impliedly authorized by the organizational client in order to carry out the representation or as otherwise permitted by Rule 1.6.

[10] There are times when the organization's interest may be or become adverse to those of one or more of its constituents. In such circumstances the lawyer should advise any constituent, whose interest the lawyer finds adverse to that of the organization of the conflict or potential conflict of interest, that the lawyer cannot represent such constituent, and that such person may wish to obtain independent representation. Care must be taken to assure that the individual understands that, when there is such adversity of interest, the lawyer for the organization cannot provide legal representation for that constituent individual, and that discussions between the lawyer for the organization and the individual may not be privileged.

[11] Whether such a warning should be given by the lawyer for the organization to any constituent individual may turn on the facts of each case.

[12] Paragraph (g) recognizes that a lawyer for an organization may also represent a principal officer or major shareholder.

RULE 1.6 CONFIDENTIALITY OF INFORMATION

(a) A lawyer shall not reveal information relating to the representation of a client unless the client gives informed consent, the disclosure is impliedly authorized in order to carry out the representation or the disclosure is permitted by paragraph (b).

(b) A lawyer may reveal information relating to the representation of a client to the extent the lawyer reasonably believes necessary:

(1) to prevent reasonably certain death or substantial bodily harm;

(2) to prevent the client from committing a crime or fraud that is reasonably certain to result in substantial injury to the financial interests or property of another and in furtherance of which the client has used or is using the lawyer's services;

(3) to prevent, mitigate or rectify substantial injury to the financial interests or property of another that is reasonably certain to result or has resulted from the client's commission of a crime or fraud in furtherance of which the client has used the lawyer's services;

(4) to secure legal advice about the lawyer's compliance with these Rules;

(5) to establish a claim or defense on behalf of the lawyer in a controversy between the lawyer and the client, to establish a defense to a criminal charge or civil claim against the lawyer based upon conduct in which the client was

involved, or to respond to allegations in any proceeding concerning the lawyer's representation of the client; or

(6) to comply with other law or a court order.

RULE 1.7 CONFLICT OF INTEREST: CURRENT CLIENTS

(a) Except as provided in paragraph (b), a lawyer shall not represent a client if the representation involves a concurrent conflict of interest. A concurrent conflict of interest exists if:

(1) the representation of one client will be directly adverse to another client; or

(2) there is a significant risk that the representation of one or more clients will be materially limited by the lawyer's responsibilities to another client, a former client or a third person or by a personal interest of the lawyer.

(b) Notwithstanding the existence of a concurrent conflict of interest under paragraph (a), a lawyer may represent a client if:

(1) the lawyer reasonably believes that the lawyer will be able to provide competent and diligent representation to each affected client;

(2) the representation is not prohibited by law;

(3) the representation does not involve the assertion of a claim by one client against another client represented by the lawyer in the same litigation or other proceeding before a tribunal; and

(4) each affected client gives informed consent, confirmed in writing.

COMMENT

[6] Loyalty to a current client prohibits undertaking representation directly adverse to that client without that client's informed consent. Thus, absent consent, a lawyer may not act as an advocate in one matter against a person the lawyer represents in some other matter, even when the matters are wholly unrelated. The client as to whom the representation is directly adverse is likely to feel betrayed, and the resulting damage to the client-lawyer relationship is likely to impair the lawyer's ability to represent the client effectively. In addition, the client on whose behalf the adverse representation is undertaken reasonably may fear that the lawyer will pursue that client's case less effectively out of deference to the other client, i.e., that the representation may be materially limited by the lawyer's interest in retaining the current client. Similarly, a directly adverse conflict may arise when a lawyer is required to cross-examine a client who appears as a witness in a lawsuit involving another client, as when the testimony will be damaging to the client who is represented in the lawsuit. On the other hand, simultaneous representation in unrelated matters of clients whose interests are only economically adverse, such as representation of competing economic enterprises in unrelated litigation, does not ordinarily constitute a conflict of interest and thus may not require consent of the respective clients.

[7] Directly adverse conflicts can also arise in transactional matters. For example, if a lawyer is asked to represent the seller of a business in negotiations with a buyer represented by the lawyer, not in the same transaction but in

another, unrelated matter, the lawyer could not undertake the representation without the informed consent of each client.

[8] Even where there is no direct adverseness, a conflict of interest exists if there is a significant risk that a lawyer's ability to consider, recommend or carry out an appropriate course of action for the client will be materially limited as a result of the lawyer's other responsibilities or interests. For example, a lawyer asked to represent several individuals seeking to form a joint venture is likely to be materially limited in the lawyer's ability to recommend or advocate all possible positions that each might take because of the lawyer's duty of loyalty to the others. The conflict in effect forecloses alternatives that would otherwise be available to the client. The mere possibility of subsequent harm does not itself require disclosure and consent. The critical questions are the likelihood that a difference in interests will eventuate and, if it does, whether it will materially interfere with the lawyer's independent professional judgment in considering alternatives or foreclose courses of action that reasonably should be pursued on behalf of the client.

[13] A lawyer may be paid from a source other than the client, including a co-client, if the client is informed of that fact and consents and the arrangement does not compromise the lawyer's duty of loyalty or independent judgment to the client. If acceptance of the payment from any other source presents a significant risk that the lawyer's representation of the client will be materially limited by the lawyer's own interest in accommodating the person paying the lawyer's fee or by the lawyer's responsibilities to a payer who is also a co-client, then the lawyer must comply with the requirements of paragraph (b) before accepting the representation, including determining whether the conflict is consentable and, if so, that the client has adequate information about the material risks of the representation.

[28] Whether a conflict is consentable depends on the circumstances. For example, a lawyer may not represent multiple parties to a negotiation whose interests are fundamentally antagonistic to each other, but common representation is permissible where the clients are generally aligned in interest even though there is some difference in interest among them. Thus, a lawyer may seek to establish or adjust a relationship between clients on an amicable and mutually advantageous basis; for example, in helping to organize a business in which two or more clients are entrepreneurs, working out the financial reorganization of an enterprise in which two or more clients have an interest or arranging a property distribution in settlement of an estate. The lawyer seeks to resolve potentially adverse interests by developing the parties' mutual interests. Otherwise, each party might have to obtain separate representation, with the possibility of incurring additional cost, complication or even litigation. Given these and other relevant factors, the clients may prefer that the lawyer act for all of them.

[31] As to the duty of confidentiality, continued common representation will almost certainly be inadequate if one client asks the lawyer not to disclose to the other client information relevant to the common representation. This is so because the lawyer has an equal duty of loyalty to each client, and each client has the right to be informed of anything bearing on the representation that might affect that client's interests and the right to expect that the lawyer will use that

information to that client's benefit. *See* Rule 1.4. The lawyer should, at the outset of the common representation and as part of the process of obtaining each client's informed consent, advise each client that information will be shared and that the lawyer will have to withdraw if one client decides that some matter material to the representation should be kept from the other. In limited circumstances, it may be appropriate for the lawyer to proceed with the representation when the clients have agreed, after being properly informed, that the lawyer will keep certain information confidential. For example, the lawyer may reasonably conclude that failure to disclose one client's trade secrets to another client will not adversely affect representation involving a joint venture between the clients and agree to keep that information confidential with the informed consent of both clients.

[32] When seeking to establish or adjust a relationship between clients, the lawyer should make clear that the lawyer's role is not that of partisanship normally expected in other circumstances and, thus, that the clients may be required to assume greater responsibility for decisions than when each client is separately represented. Any limitations on the scope of the representation made necessary as a result of the common representation should be fully explained to the clients at the outset of the representation. *See* Rule 1.2(c).

[33] Subject to the above limitations, each client in the common representation has the right to loyal and diligent representation and the protection of Rule 1.9 concerning the obligations to a former client. The client also has the right to discharge the lawyer as stated in Rule 1.16.

[34] A lawyer who represents a corporation or other organization does not, by virtue of that representation, necessarily represent any constituent or affiliated organization, such as a parent or subsidiary. *See* Rule 1.13(a). Thus, the lawyer for an organization is not barred from accepting representation adverse to an affiliate in an unrelated matter, unless the circumstances are such that the affiliate should also be considered a client of the lawyer, there is an understanding between the lawyer and the organizational client that the lawyer will avoid representation adverse to the client's affiliates, or the lawyer's obligations to either the organizational client or the new client are likely to limit materially the lawyer's representation of the other client.

[35] A lawyer for a corporation or other organization who is also a member of its board of directors should determine whether the responsibilities of the two roles may conflict. The lawyer may be called on to advise the corporation in matters involving actions of the directors. Consideration should be given to the frequency with which such situations may arise, the potential intensity of the conflict, the effect of the lawyer's resignation from the board and the possibility of the corporation's obtaining legal advice from another lawyer in such situations. If there is material risk that the dual role will compromise the lawyer's independence of professional judgment, the lawyer should not serve as a director or should cease to act as the corporation's lawyer when conflicts of interest arise. The lawyer should advise the other members of the board that in some circumstances matters discussed at board meetings while the lawyer is present in the capacity of director might not be protected by the attorney-client privilege and that conflict of interest considerations might require the lawyer's

recusal as a director or might require the lawyer and the lawyer's firm to decline representation of the corporation in a matter.

Putting It to Work

Problem 5-4

Assume that, instead of rushing to order koozies, red plastic cups, and coolers, Jordan and Cory (from the prior problem) come to you for legal advice on how to set up their proposed business. You were Jordan's attorney before he went to law school when he wanted to set up a venture that would print typical LSAT questions on plastic water bottles that revealed the answer when they got cold. That venture failed miserably. Jordan recently contacted you about a business idea he and his law school friend Cory have, but Jordan provided no other details. You agree to meet with both Jordan and Cory.

At your meeting with Jordan and Cory, they tell you the details for their plan for Koozie Quizzes and that they would like to incorporate under the name Party Hearty Bar Prep Incorporated. It is apparent that Jordan is the "idea person" and also has contacts with potential vendors. Cory is the "money person" who will supply the bulk of the capital and will also write most of the questions and answers. Jordan and Cory want equal ownership and control. You agree to get the business incorporated and to prepare the organizational documents.

a. Is Jordan, Cory, or Party Hearty Bar Prep Incorporated your client? What are the ethical consequences for you of having one, two, or all three as your client?

b. Suppose, after the meeting, Cory calls you and asks for details about Jordan's LSAT water bottle venture, suggesting that Jordan had told Corey it had been a big success. What must you tell Cory? What can you tell him? What are you prohibited from telling him?

c. Suppose, after the meeting, Jordan calls you and tells you to draft the documents so that Jordan purchases 51% of the shares to Cory's 49% and that you should tell Cory that this structure is your idea and is simply to prevent deadlock. Jordan tells you that the real reason for this structure is that Jordan intends to run the business with no input from Cory other than Cory's money and that Jordan will try to buy out Cory's minority interest cheaply once the business is successful. Jordan tells you that this information is confidential. Can you do as Jordan requests? Must you do as Jordan requests? Can you tell Cory about the conversation? Must you do so?

F. TERMS OF ART IN THIS CHAPTER

Corporation by estoppel	Defective incorporation	Internal affairs
De facto	Domestic corporation	Promoters
De jure	Foreign corporation	

6

Capital Formation

This chapter explores a central concern for any corporation or other business entity: how does the corporation get money in? More formally, this topic is known as *capital formation*. The answer is that the corporation gets money in exchange for contractual (and, as we'll see in Chapter 11, fiduciary) rights. The chapter starts by placing the capital formation question in its economic context. Then we describe the kinds of rights that a corporation can grant in exchange for money. These rights have become relatively standardized and the standard bundles of these rights are known as *securities*. "Common stock" and "debentures" are well-known examples of securities. After a description of the standard corporate securities, we address one of the quintessential tasks for a transaction lawyer: choosing the set of securities that a new corporation will issue. That set of securities is called the corporation's *capital structure*. In selecting a capital structure the monetary needs of the new entity must be balanced with the needs of each of the potential investors. The investors' needs include both economic and managerial components. In this connection we also take a brief look at the venture capital and going public processes.

Our attention then shifts to the corporate law mechanics involved in the actual creation of corporate securities and the process by which those securities are issued by the corporation in exchange for consideration. Finally, we glimpse the federal securities regulations that affect the issuance of corporate securities.

A. FINANCING: GETTING MONEY INTO THE BUSINESS

1. Background and Context

Any business has to decide three things. First, what goods and services will it provide? Second, what assets does it need to provide those goods and services? The assets can be tangible, such as factories, machines, or office furniture; and intangible, such as proprietary knowledge, patents, trademarks, and copyrights. Assets also include the services of employees and cash needed to run the business on a day-to-day basis (frequently called *working capital*).

Our concern here is with the third question any business faces, which is how the needed assets will be paid for. When the business is just being formed, its owners have two sources of money. They can contribute the money themselves, or they can borrow it. After the business starts selling goods and services, the business's owners have a third source for money: extra cash generated by the business itself. We'll look at each source separately.

Perhaps the most intuitive source of money for a new business is the owners themselves. They contribute money, and may contribute assets in-kind, in return for their ownership interest. Usually, the owners' interest will be proportional to the value of each owner's contribution. What happens if the business needs more money later on? If the owners agree to contribute in proportion to their past contributions, they can preserve their relative ownership interests. But suppose that the owners are unable or unwilling to contribute proportionately? Will the owners who contribute more money receive a greater proportion of the ownership or will the original division of interests be preserved? A variation of this question, which may arise when the business is first being formed as well as later in the business's existence, is whether the owners will seek additional owners. One of the most classic tensions in the operation of any business is the possibility that the people who had the original Big Idea may see their ownership interest reduced (*diluted*, in the terminology of finance) by later investors.

If the owners do not want to share their ownership with others, they can borrow needed money. In fact, borrowing may be a solution to the problem of the business that needs additional money. Rather than making proportionate additional contributions or facing the prospect of a shift in the owners' relative interests, the owners can borrow the needed money, thus preserving their relative power. The owners do not necessarily need to find a willing lender if they themselves are willing to lend money to the business. Thus an owner might also be a creditor.

Raising money by borrowing poses different questions for a business than does raising money through the sale of ownership interests. An ownership interest is a permanent investment, in contrast to a loan, which must at some point be repaid. One question for a business, then, is how long a term should its loan be? Another question is the rate of interest the business is willing to pay. The interest is, in effect, the price of the money and in that sense is cognate to the question of how much an owner will pay for his or her ownership. Deciding upon an interest rate, though, is more complex because the rate will depend on several factors such as the length of the loan and whether the lender's rights are secured.

The final source of new money for a business is the business itself. Many businesses generate more cash than they need to meet their operating expenses. These operating expenses include buying needed assets, maintaining the business's physical assets, paying employees, paying taxes and interest on loans, and perhaps keeping some assets available for ready use. New businesses and businesses that are growing in size rarely have extra money, but many mature businesses do generate extra money. If the owners of the business decide that the business requires additional money, they may decide to use the business's extra cash rather than to borrow or sell more ownership interests. The primary alternatives to reinvesting this money in the business are to pay it to the owners in the form of dividends or to reduce the business's debts. Which of these choices is best for the business is a subject about which much has been written and about which your clients will spend much time debating.

2. The Current Setting

Corporations get money in three basic ways. They can sell ownership interests (sometimes called *equity*), they can borrow, or they can use money generated by the business itself. When the corporation sells equity or borrows, the person supplying the money receives certain rights in exchange. Those rights delineate whether the supplier is entitled to a return of the money supplied and whether the supplier is entitled to a portion of the business's earnings in addition to or instead of the return of the money supplied. The supplier of money may also receive the right to have some say in the corporation's management. At one level these rights could be infinitely variable depending only upon the inventiveness of the parties and their counsel and the minuteness with which they wish to contract. At a practical level, though, the answers to these basic questions (i.e., "Is my investment permanent or temporary?" "Will my claim on the business's earnings be a fixed *amount* or a fixed *percentage* and will it be paid before, after, or at the same time as other claimants?" and "How much power, if any, over the corporation's management will I have?") have fallen into categories so that corporations and their advisors do not have to start from scratch in devising solutions to these questions.

a. Corporate Securities

One of the great advantages of the corporate form is that the categories of financing solutions have been embodied in traditional forms called *securities*. In this sense, a security is simply a set of rights that, over the years, has proven useful to corporations and those who supply money. Think of the contrast as between couture and ready-to-wear. Sometimes the parties have the resources and the motivation to bargain over, and document, a set of relationships that is unique to the parties and the business. Sometimes they do not have the resources or the motivation and they simply pull something off the rack that, in the end, is serviceable enough and frequently quite good. Often, though, they start with ready-to-wear (i.e., the standard securities terms) and work around the margins to produce a solution that is targeted to the particular parties and setting but not completely built from scratch.

The next four sections describe these standard solutions — these securities — after which we will examine some of the more exotic securities. Throughout the remainder of this section on financing you should pay close attention to the nomenclature. The terms not only have relatively precise meanings that you, as a lawyer, will be expected to use correctly (even though clients have a maddening tendency to misuse the names), but they are a handy shorthand to describe complex bundles of rights.

i. (Common) Stock. Without question, the paradigm corporate security is *stock*. It is a kind of *equity*, meaning that it represents an ownership interest in the business rather than a loan to the business. Originally, the term *stock* referred to a business's assets, as in the phrase "stock in trade." Where the business had more than one owner, each was said to own an undivided percentage, or *share*, of the stock. With the development of the modern corporate form in the nineteenth century, the term *stock* came to mean the collective ownership interests in the corporation rather than the corporation's assets. Shareholder and stockholder both referred to someone who owned shares of stock. In common corporate parlance today, *shares, shares of stock*, and *stock* are essentially interchangeable. As a matter of precision, the MBCA uses the term *shares* and refers to owners as *shareholders*. It does not use the term *stock* at all. The Delaware General Corporation Law does not use the term *shares* alone. Rather, it uses the terms *shares of stock* or *stock*. The DGCL refers to owners as *stockholders*.

The early case-law rule, embodied in MBCA §6.01(a) and DGCL §151(f), is that all shares are identical in the absence of an explicit differentiation in the Articles of Incorporation. If no such differentiation is made, each share of stock has: (1) one vote on every matter submitted to the shareholders (MBCA §7.21(a), DGCL §212(a)); (2) the right to its proportionate amount of any dividend (MBCA §6.40, DGCL §170(a)); and (3) the right to its proportionate amount of the corporation's assets, if any, upon dissolution (MBCA §14.05(a)(4), DGCL §281(a)(4)).

Shares that have all three of these characteristics are sometimes called *common stock* although neither the MBCA nor the DGCL uses that term.[1] Where only one kind of stock exists, which is the norm in most corporations, the term *common stock* is simply a synonym for *stock* or *shares*. The term *preferred stock*, as you will see, has a precise meaning and implies that a corporation has at least two kinds of stock. The term *common stock* is often used to distinguish preferred stock from other stock. It can happen, though, that stock is not preferred AND does not possess all three of the attributes typically ascribed to common stock. In that setting, it may be misleading to refer to it as common stock. Nonetheless, the term is frequently used.

ii. Preferred Stock. Sometimes the various suppliers of money to a corporation will not want to be rewarded proportionately to their investment. Some investors may be more equal than others. Typically this occurs when a particular investor or group of investors is supplying so much money that the success or failure of the business depends upon their investment. For whatever reasons, the investor and the corporation's managers agree that the investor should receive a different reward, which means, economically, either a greater-than-proportionate return, a priority in receiving a return, or both. The investor may also be able to negotiate for heightened management power as well. Again, standard solutions to these problems have been embodied in securities known as *preferred stock*. Precisely, preferred stock is stock that has a priority or preference over other stock (common stock) in either the payment of dividends or the distribution of assets on dissolution or both.[2]

---

1. The DGCL uses the term *common stock* in only one section, §251(f).
2. The only thing one can say for certain about preferred stock is that it is in some measure entitled to something more than other stock in either dividends or assets on dissolution. Clients often seem to have the notion that preferred stock must have other characteristics, such as no voting power. While such attributes may be frequent, they are not required. You should be wary of making assumptions about the attributes of preferred stock without reading for yourself the statement in the Articles of Incorporation that sets out the differences between the preferred stock and the other stock.

Again, speaking precisely and categorically, preferred stock is a *class* of stock, as is common, or nonpreferred, stock. It sometimes happens that different investors negotiate for different preferences such that the corporation issues more than one kind of preferred stock. Such a corporation has two classes of stock (common and preferred) and has two *series* of preferred stock. A series is simply a subset of a class of shares. As noted above, a corporation could have stock that does not have all three characteristics of common stock, for example, stock that has no voting power but is not preferred as to dividends or assets on dissolution. In that case the corporation would have two series of stock. While the distinction between class and series was once of some import, as a practical matter today the terms are essentially interchangeable. You may wish to keep the distinction in mind, however, because many cases and texts you will use in your practice will refer to both series and classes.

The most frequent and most important preference is in the payment of dividends. A typical preference is to grant the preferred stock a fixed amount of money per year as a dividend to be paid before the other stock receives any dividend. This is nearly identical to the payment of interest on debt. The only difference is that interest on a debt is contractually required to be paid. Dividends are always subject to certain statutory restrictions and on the discretion of the board.

Several other concepts apply to preferred stock. First, suppose the preferred stock is entitled to $1 per share per year, but the corporation's board of directors does not declare a dividend in a particular year. If the corporation is prepared to declare dividends in the next year, does the preferred stock receive $1 before the common shares or $2? The answer depends upon whether the preferred stock dividends are *cumulative*. If so, the preferred stock gets $2 per share before the common stock gets any dividend. If the preferred stock is noncumulative, it only gets $1 per share even though it received no dividends the year before. While cumulative dividends protect the preferred stock to some extent, they can have a perverse effect on the corporation as a whole. During any protracted economic downturn (such as the Great Depression) many companies may be unable to pay dividends, and in companies with cumulative preferred stock the accrued but unpaid dividends may grow quite large. The corporation may need additional infusions of capital to continue its business either to weather the bad times or to revamp as the economy turns around. Unfortunately, the corporation will be hampered in its ability to raise new money because of the continuing, and continually increasing, obligation created by the cumulative dividends.

Now suppose a slightly different scenario. A corporation has declared and paid dividends to its preferred stock and finds it has additional money that may safely be paid out in dividends. Does the common stock receive all the additional dividend, or does the preferred stock receive a portion as well? If the preferred stock is *participating*, it receives dividends along with the common stock even though it has already received its preferential dividend. If the preferred stock is nonparticipating, it does not. If the preferred stock is participating, it can do so either *pari passu* (i.e., equal dividends per share) with the common stock or at a multiple or fraction of the amount paid to each share of common stock.

Preferred stock is typically given preferences on dissolution that are similar to those granted for dividends. That is, preferred stock typically gets a fixed amount at dissolution before the common stock gets any money. Because dissolution only occurs once, preferred stock cannot be cumulative as to assets at dissolution. The preferred stock may or may not participate in dissolution after payment of its preference. In the real world these rights are of little consequence because most businesses, if solvent, continue as going concerns and do not liquidate. If the business is insolvent, there is little or no money left after paying creditors, so any preferences are really illusory.

A final word on preferred stock: Remember that the longstanding rule is that "stock is stock." Therefore, preferred stock has all the attributes of common shares unless stated otherwise. In other words, each share of preferred stock is treated identically to every share of common stock, has one vote per share, and is entitled to equal dividends as declared by the board. In other words, preferred stock is noncumulative and participating unless stated otherwise. On preferred stock generally, *see* MBCA §6.01(c), DGCL §151(a), (c), and (d).

iii. Other Relative Rights. Two other aspects of stock need to be discussed. These provisions can attach to stock regardless of whether the stock is preferred. One area is voting rights. The other is the right to have the corporation repurchase shares or convert shares into different securities.

First, a word about voting. A frequent trade-off for granting certain shareholders economic preferences is that they do not receive the right to vote. Sometimes the right to vote is contingent upon the corporation's failure to pay dividends on the preferred stock for a particular period, often one year. In such cases, the preferred stock sometimes gains enough votes to control the management of the corporation either because more shares of preferred stock are outstanding than shares of common stock, or because the preferred stock is entitled to multiple votes per share. Remember that stock could have differing voting rights and yet not be preferred stock. *See* MBCA §6.01(c)(1), DGCL §151(a).

Next we consider the situation in which the corporation has the right to purchase shares, some shareholders have the right to sell shares to the corporation, or some shareholders have the right to change their shares into other securities. Sometimes shareholders bargain for the right to require the corporation to repurchase their shares. In the absence of a public market for the corporation's shares, this right can be quite valuable, because otherwise shareholders would have no ready market for their shares. Hence, repurchase by the corporation may be the only realistic method of ending the investment. This right is called *redemption*.

A variation of redeemable stock is stock that is *convertible*. When stock is convertible, the holder has the option of exchanging the shares for a fixed amount of another security of the corporation. Most typically conversion is available from more senior shares to junior shares (i.e., from preferred stock to common stock or from debt to preferred or common stock) but the statutes permit any sort of conversion agreed to by the corporation and shareholders. The privilege of conversion may have benefits for both the corporation and the investors. The corporation may prefer a conversion provision to a redemption provision because it will not have to return money to its investor; it simply changes the rights among its shareholders. Shareholders may also prefer conversion because it provides a ready-made power to get a different security. In effect, the shareholder has an option to exchange one set of rights for another. Unlike the corporation, however, the shareholder would prefer stock to be both convertible and redeemable, while the corporation would usually prefer convertibility to redemption. Note that shareholders of different classes or series may have different reactions to convertibility. Shareholders of a class or series *into* which another class or series is convertible may be unhappy because they perceive the convertibility ratio to be unfavorable to them. In rare instances, conversion may be at the option of the corporation rather than the shareholder. *See* MBCA §6.01(c)(2), DGCL §151(e).

Conversely, a corporation may negotiate for the power to require the shareholder to return the shares to the corporation in return for a predetermined price. This protects the corporation from having stock outstanding in perpetuity that has provisions such as heightened voting power or large dividends that may become particularly onerous over time. Stock with this kind of provision is *callable*, although both the MBCA and the DGCL use the term *redeemable* to mean stock that must be repurchased at the option of either the shareholder or the corporation. *See* MBCA §6.01(c)(2), DGCL §151(b).

Any variation from the default version of stock must be carefully documented. The following case shows some problems that can arise when sophisticated counsel try to anticipate future events.

Greenmont Capital Partners I, LP v. Mary's Gone Crackers, Inc.

2012 WL 4479999 (Del. Ch. Sept. 28, 2012)

MEMORANDUM OPINION

PARSONS, Vice Chancellor.

This case presents a question about the interpretation of a Delaware corporation's certificate of incorporation. The corporation had authorized and issued common stock and two series of preferred stock, series A and series B. The plaintiff, an investor, purchased series B preferred stock. Series B stockholders have special rights under the certificate of incorporation. Among other things, the series B preferred have the right to a majority vote to validate any action that would "alter or change" the series B preferred stockholder's rights under the certificate. The certificate also grants series B preferred stockholders the right to a majority vote on any amendment to the certificate of incorporation. One action permitted by the certificate is an automatic conversion of the preferred stock into common stock upon a majority vote of the preferred shares. This certificate provision requires a majority vote of the series A and series B preferred voting together and does not afford the series B any special rights.

The corporation decided to seek an automatic conversion. Holders of a majority of the preferred shares, but not a majority of the preferred series B, voted in favor of the automatic conversion. After the purported conversion, the corporation's board voted to amend its certificate to eliminate reference to preferred stock. The plaintiff disputes the validity of the conversion and the subsequent certificate amendment. It maintains that a majority vote from the series B was required to validate the conversion because the conversion of the preferred stock into common stock effectively would deprive the series B preferred of the special rights they enjoyed under the certificate. According to the plaintiff, this action, therefore, would "alter or change" its rights and the certificate requires a majority series B vote to validate such an action. Hence, the question before the Court is whether, under the terms of the certificate and Delaware law, the corporation had the power to implement the automatic conversion and the certificate amendment without the consent of the series B preferred.

Having considered the parties' arguments, Delaware case law on preferred shareholders' rights, and the language of the certificate of incorporation, I find that the execution of the challenged action, which was allowed under the certificate, did not alter or change the rights of a shareholder whose rights are defined by the certificate. For this reason, I rule in favor of the corporation and hold as a matter of law that the challenged conversion of preferred stock into common stock was a valid corporate action. I further conclude that the subsequent certificate amendment was valid because it occurred when no preferred shares remained outstanding and, thus, its validity was not contingent on a majority vote of the outstanding shares of series B preferred.

I. BACKGROUND

A. Parties

Plaintiff, Greenmont Capital Partners I, LP ("Greenmont"), is a Colorado limited partnership. Greenmont invests in companies in the natural products industry. One of Greenmont's investments is in Series B Preferred shares in Mary's Gone Crackers ("MGC" or the "Company").

Defendant, MGC, is a Delaware corporation. MGC produces and distributes organic and gluten-free baked goods. MGC was formed as a California limited liability company in 2004. In 2007, MGC converted to a Delaware corporation upon filing a certificate of incorporation (the "Charter") with the Delaware Secretary of State. The Charter authorizes two classes of stock, Common and Preferred, and two series of the Preferred class, Series A and Series B. MGC authorized 65,000,000 shares: 37,522,485 Common; 15,028,444 Series A Preferred; and 12,449,071 Series B Preferred. The Common stock represents 58% of the total number of authorized shares and the Preferred represents 42%. Of the Preferred, Series A accounts for 55% and Series B accounts for 45%.

B. Facts

At the time of the transactions in question here, Greenmont owned 7,430,503 shares of the Series B Preferred. The Series B Preferred holders enjoy unique rights under the Charter. Article IV, Section D.2(b) lists twelve actions that must be approved by a majority of the Series B Preferred to have effect or to be valid. This Section, entitled Separate Vote of Series B Preferred (the "Voting Provision"), begins as follows:

> For so long as any shares of a series of Series B Preferred remain outstanding, in addition to any other vote or consent required herein or by law, the vote or written consent of the holders of at least a majority of the outstanding shares of the Series B Preferred shall be necessary for effecting or validating the following actions (whether by merger, recapitalization or otherwise): . . . .

Two of the twelve enumerated actions are important to this litigation:

> (i) Any amendment, alteration, repeal or waiver of any provision of the Certificate of Incorporation or the Bylaws of the Company (including any filing of a Certificate of Designation);
> (ii) Any agreement or action that alters or changes the voting or other powers, preferences, or other special rights, privileges or restrictions of the Series B Preferred (including by way of a merger or consolidation);. . . .

The second Charter provision at issue in this dispute is Section D.5, entitled Conversion Rights. Subsection (*l*) to Section D.5 outlines procedures for an "Automatic Conversion." This subsection states:

> Each share of Series Preferred shall automatically be converted into shares of Common Stock, based on the then-effective applicable Series Preferred Conversion Price, (A) at any time upon the affirmative election of the holders of at least fifty-one percent (51%) of the then-outstanding shares of Series Preferred. . . .

On February 8, 2012, MGC solicited certain holders of Preferred to elect an automatic conversion of the Preferred into Common Stock under Section D.5. The Company limited its solicitation to holders of Preferred who indicated that they would support an automatic conversion; it did not solicit Greenmont. On February 17, 2012, MGC received written consent from at least 51% of the Preferred to convert Preferred into Common Stock. Later that same day, the MGC board voted to amend the Charter and filed an amended and restated Charter with the Delaware Secretary of State. The amended and restated Charter eliminates the provisions related to the Preferred.

C. Procedural History

Greenmont filed this action on February 20, 2012 seeking a declaratory judgment that the automatic conversion and the related Charter amendment are unlawful, void, and prohibited. Both parties assert that the Charter is plain and unambiguous and that there are no material facts in dispute. They ask the Court to declare as a matter of law whether the automatic conversion and subsequent Charter amendment violate the Charter or Delaware law.

II. ANALYSIS

In interpreting a corporate charter, the Court applies general principles of contract construction. A certificate should be construed in its entirety and the court "must give effect to all terms of the instrument, must read the instrument as a whole, and, if possible, must reconcile all provisions in the instrument."[8] The existence and extent of special stock rights are contractual in nature and are determined by the issuer's certificate of incorporation. The certificate must expressly and clearly state any rights, preferences, and limitations of the preferred stock that distinguish preferred stock from common stock. This principle equally applies to construing the relative rights of holders of different series of preferred stock. In interpreting an unambiguous certificate of incorporation, the court should determine the document's meaning solely in reference to its language without resorting to extrinsic evidence. Contract language is not ambiguous in a legal sense merely because the

---

8. *Alta Berkeley VI C.V. v. Omneon, Inc.*, 41 A.3d 381, 386 (Del. 2012).

parties dispute what it means. To be ambiguous, a disputed contract term must be fairly or reasonably susceptible to more than one meaning.

A. Series B Preferred Shareholders' Right to Vote on the Conversion

For the reasons outlined below, I find that the Charter is unambiguous and that its language does not entitle the Series B Preferred holders to a series vote on the conversion of Preferred Stock into Common Stock. Under the Voting Provision, two elements must be present for Series B Preferred holders to have rights to a majority vote on a matter: (1) Series B Preferred must be outstanding; and (2) an enumerated action must be at issue. After the execution of the automatic conversion, I conclude that no enumerated action was at issue.

I start by considering the Charter language. The first clause of Section D.2(b) states: "For so long as any shares of a series of Series B Preferred remain outstanding." The parties do not dispute that when the Series Preferred were solicited to vote in favor of an automatic conversion, Series B Preferred was outstanding. Section D.2(b), therefore, is implicated. The second clause reads: "in addition to any other vote or consent required herein or by law." This language indicates that the provision grants Series B Preferred holders rights beyond any voting rights either found in the agreement or required by law. The next clause indicates what additional rights Series B Preferred holders have beyond their voting rights arising under the agreement or required by law. This clause provides that a majority vote of the outstanding Series B Preferred shares "shall be necessary for effecting or validating the following actions (whether by merger, recapitalization or otherwise)." Read together, these clauses compel the conclusion that what starts out broadly ("in addition to *any* other vote") finishes narrowly ("for effecting or validating the following actions"). Only the actions specified in the list of twelve enumerated actions require a majority vote of Series B Preferred in order to be valid.

Greenmont asserts that Section D.2(b)(ii) provides the enumerated action that grants it voting rights as to the automatic conversion. Section D.2(b)(ii) incorporates the following action into the Voting Provision: "Any agreement or action that alters or changes the voting or other powers, preferences, or other special rights, privileges or restrictions of the Series B Preferred (including by way of a merger or consolidation)." Notably, the drafters of the Charter included for a second time a reference incorporating action by merger. This presumably is in response to the Delaware Supreme Court's decision in *Elliott Associates, L.P. v. Avatex Corp.*[16] In *Avatex,* the Court provided a "path for future drafters."[17] The Court held that language granting the right to vote on an "amendment, alteration, or repeal" is not enough to provide preferred stockholders with the right to a class vote on a merger that leads to an amendment, alteration, or repeal of the certificate. A drafter must additionally indicate that the class vote applies when a merger *results in* an amendment, alteration, or repeal. One way to satisfy this requirement is by including the words "whether by merger, consolidation, or otherwise" in the appropriate provision in the certificate.[18]

---

16. 715 A.2d 843 (Del. 1998).
17. *Id*. at 855.
18. *Id*.

Here, the drafters appear to have attempted to take advantage of the safe harbor offered by *Avatex*.[19] They included language in the introductory provision to incorporate actions by "merger, recapitalization or otherwise" and additionally in Section D.2(b)(ii) to include an alteration or change "by way of a merger or consolidation." While this language signals the intent to include the circumstance where a merger results in one of the enumerated actions, it does not touch on the disputed action here.

As noted, Section D.2(b)(ii) applies to "[a]ny agreement or action that alters or changes" the Series B Preferred's "voting or other powers, preferences, or other special rights, privileges or restrictions." The issue, therefore, is whether the automatic conversion of Series B Preferred into Common Stock "alter[ed] or change[d]" the Series B Preferred's powers, preferences, rights, privileges, or restrictions. This issue, in turn, requires a determination of what constitutes the Series B Preferred's "voting or other powers, preferences, or other special rights, privileges or restrictions." To answer this question, we look again to the language of the Charter. One group of rights provided for in the Charter is found in Section D.5 entitled Conversion Rights.

This Section contains subsection (*l*) which allows for an automatic conversion. The plain language of the Charter compels the conclusion that this automatic conversion is one of the "special rights, privileges or restrictions" created by the Charter. When contract language is plain and clear on its face, the Court will determine its meaning based on the writing alone. Because the Automatic Conversion provision exists on equal footing with the Voting Provision, an action taken under the Automatic Conversion provision cannot be seen to "alter or change" any of the Series B Preferred's "voting or other powers, preferences, or other special rights, privileges or restrictions." Rather than "alter or change" a right, the execution of an automatic conversion effectuates an existing right.

Greenmont asserts that this interpretation undermines the rights it bargained for in the Voting Provision. Notably, the Series A shareholders appear to account for a majority of the Preferred shareholders. Further, the Series A enjoy few benefits under the Charter and, therefore, could be expected to be more likely than the holders of Series B to vote for an automatic conversion of Preferred Stock into Common Stock under Section D.5(*l*). The Series B's rights under the Charter, therefore, are somewhat dependent on the Series A's desire to remain holders of Preferred stock. Greenmont avers that it would not have bargained for such contingent rights and that an interpretation along those lines would be wrong. While Greenmont's interpretation makes sense, "its interpretation is not *reasonable* in light of the indisputably clear language of the contract."[24] Instead, the plain language of the Charter indicates that the exercise of an automatic conversion would

---

19. *See Benchmark Capital P'rs IV, L.P. v. Vague*, 2002 WL 1732423, at *10 n. 44 (Del. Ch. 2002) ("As a general matter, drafting guidance, such as that provided in *Avatex*, may be read as creating a 'safe harbor' or as a prudential suggestion and is not typically to be read as the exclusive means of achieving the desired goal.").

24. *Seidensticker v. Gasparilla Inn, Inc.*, 2007 WL 4054473, at *3 (Del. Ch. Nov. 8, 2007) ("Defendants' interpretation makes rational sense (in that it is rational to think that the drafters may not have wanted to allow these shares to get away from the Sharp family), but its interpretation is not *reasonable* in light of the indisputably clear language of the contract.").

not alter or change the Series B Preferred's rights as those rights are defined in the Charter.

Greenmont further argues that this interpretation cannot be correct because an act that extinguishes the powers of the Series B Preferred cannot be interpreted as a "right" of that series. But, Greenmont cites no authority in support of its position. MGC counters that a conversion provision is indeed a "right" of preferred stock. Delaware corporate law recognizes that the ability of holders of preferred stock to convert their shares into shares of common stock is a "right" of the preferred shareholders. Nothing in the language of the Charter indicates that the Preferred shareholders' ability to convert their shares of Preferred Stock into shares of Common Stock under the Automatic Conversion provision is not a "right" of the Preferred shareholders. Indeed, the Automatic Conversion provision is contained in Section D.5 entitled "Conversion Rights."

This conclusion is consistent with the principle of Delaware corporation law that any rights or preferences of preferred stock must be expressed clearly. This conclusion is further supported by the fact that the drafters of the MGC Charter explicitly included one action identified elsewhere in the Charter as an enumerated action requiring a majority Series B Preferred vote under the Voting Provision. Specifically, Section B of Article IV states that the number of authorized shares of Common Stock may be increased or decreased only after a vote of a majority of the stock of the Company. The Voting Provision includes a requirement for a majority Series B Preferred vote in Section D.2(b)(iii) as to: "Any increase or decrease in the authorized number of shares of Common Stock or Preferred Stock." Had the drafters intended for the Automatic Conversion provision to be subject to an additional vote of a majority of the Series B Preferred, they could have listed it expressly in the Voting Provision as they did with the provision regarding an increase or decrease in authorized Common Stock. By expressly including Section B as an enumerated action under the Voting Provision, but not including Section D.5, the drafters implicitly excluded Section D.5.

Greenmont correctly emphasizes that the addition of the words "automatic conversion" to one of the twelve enumerated actions in Section D.2(b) is merely one way the drafters could have granted the Series B Preferred the right to a majority vote on any proposed automatic conversion. If the intent of the drafters was to include automatic conversion as an act requiring a majority Series B Preferred vote, however, then it was incumbent upon the drafters to make the Charter language precise in that regard and to indicate such an intent clearly. As drafted, the Voting Provision does not grant this right. The dispositive question is not whether as a *result* of the vote in favor of automatic conversion the Series B Preferred's rights were altered or changed, but whether the *act* of the vote altered or changed their rights. The Automatic Conversion provision was included in the Series B Preferred's bundle of rights, privileges, and restrictions under the Charter and, thus, the act of at least 51% of the then-outstanding shares of Preferred in voting under Section D.5 to effect an automatic conversion did not alter or change those rights, privileges, and restrictions.

B. Series B Preferred Shareholders' Right to Vote on the Charter Amendment

1. UNDER THE CHARTER

I next must determine whether any Series B Preferred Stock remained outstanding at the time of the purported Charter amendment. If it did, then the Series B holders would have had the right to a majority vote on any Charter amendment under Section D.2(b)(i). If it did not, then the Series B holders would have no such right because the Voting Provision only applies "[f]or so long as any shares of a series of Series B Preferred remain outstanding." For the reasons stated below, I concur with MGC's interpretation of the Charter in this regard. At the time MGC amended the Charter, there were no Series B Preferred shares outstanding and, therefore, that series was not entitled to a separate series vote to validate the amendment.

Under the language of the Charter, a vote by a majority of the Preferred will automatically convert the Preferred into Common Stock. Section D.5(*l*)(ii) states: "Upon the occurrence of either of the events specified in Section D.5[(*l*)](i) above, the outstanding shares of Series Preferred shall be converted automatically without any further action by the holders of such shares. . . ." In contrast, Section D.5(d) sets forth the "Mechanics of Conversion" in the context of an optional conversion of Preferred into Common Stock. The latter provision requires a Preferred holder to surrender its certificate in order for the conversion of its shares into Common Stock to be deemed to have been made. Notably, an optional conversion will be deemed to have been made at the close of business on the date the certificate is surrendered and "the person entitled to receive the shares of Common Stock issuable upon such conversion shall be treated for all purposes as the record holder of such shares of Common Stock *on such date.*"[38] Because the automatic conversion provision states that the Series Preferred Stock shall be converted automatically, "whether or not the certificates representing such shares are surrendered to the Company," it follows that the automatic conversion also will be deemed to have been made on the date on which the holders of 51% of the Preferred voted to convert their shares into shares of Common Stock. In this case, the holders of at least 51% of the Preferred executed written consents to convert the then-outstanding Preferred Stock into Common Stock on February 17, 2012. Under the Charter, therefore, the class of Preferred was no longer outstanding as of that date.

The automatic conversion occurred on February 17, 2012. MGC voted to amend the Charter later that same day. Therefore, as previously noted, the shareholder vote to amend the Charter took place when Common Stock was the only class of MGC stock outstanding. Because the Voting Provision only applies "[f]or so long as any shares of a series of Series B Preferred remain outstanding," that provision did not apply to the Charter amendment.

Greenmont contends that this result is inconsistent with its subjective intent in purchasing its Series B Preferred stock. Indeed, Greenmont argues that the conversion and the amendment to the Charter are inextricably linked and that the conversion and amendment must be interpreted together, such that they collectively would be subject to the Voting Provision. Greenmont, however, cites no authority to support this proposition. To the contrary, Delaware case law generally requires that corporate acts be evaluated or considered independently as they occur. [I]

---

38. Charter art. IV, §D.5(d) (emphasis added).

consider the conversion and the Charter amendment here to have been separate and independent occurrences.

The language of the MGC Charter relevant to this dispute is unambiguous. Therefore, I must interpret that language as it was drafted and consistent with its plain and ordinary meaning. Such an interpretation compels the conclusion that at the time of the challenged amendment, the automatic conversion of Preferred Stock into Common Stock had occurred and thus no Preferred Stock remained outstanding and no Series B Preferred holders had any right to vote on the Charter amendment.

2. UNDER THE DGCL

Plaintiff also asserts that Section 242(b)(2) of the [DGCL] requires a series vote on the Charter amendment because that amendment decreased the number of authorized shares of the Preferred class. For the reasons stated above, I conclude that no Preferred shares were outstanding at the time of the amendment. Because Section 242(b)(2) only applies to the "holders of outstanding shares," it does not apply to the Charter amendment challenged in this case.

III. CONCLUSION

For the foregoing reasons, I deny Plaintiff's Motion for Judgment on the Pleadings and I grant Defendant's Motion for Judgment on the Pleadings.
IT IS SO ORDERED.

Notes and Questions

1. Reality Check

a. What is was the capital structure of the corporation? What classes and series of stock were authorized and how many shares of each were authorized?

b. What transactions did the corporation take that Greenmont objected to?

c. How are the transactions related to each other?

d. What source(s) of law did Vice Chancellor Parsons look to?

2. What Do You Think?

a. Why were the authorized shares of each class and series such odd numbers?

b. Do you think the result reflected the corporation's intent when it created the Series B Preferred?

c. Vice Chancellor Parsons held that the Charter language was plain and unambiguous. Do you agree? If it were plain and unambiguous, why did this litigation result?

3. You Draft It

a. The key language in dispute reads,

For so long as any shares of a series of Series B Preferred remain outstanding, in addition to any other vote or consent required herein or by law, the vote or written consent of the holders of at least a majority of the outstanding shares of the Series B Preferred shall be necessary for effecting or validating the following actions (whether by merger, recapitalization or otherwise): . . .

   (i) Any amendment, alteration, repeal or waiver of any provision of the Certificate of Incorporation or the Bylaws of the Company (including any filing of a Certificate of Designation);

   (ii) Any agreement or action that alters or changes the voting or other powers, preferences, or other special rights, privileges or restrictions of the Series B Preferred (including by way of a merger or consolidation); . . .

Article IV, Section D.2(b).

Each share of Series Preferred shall automatically be converted into shares of Common Stock, based on the then-effective applicable Series Preferred Conversion Price, (A) at any time upon the affirmative election of the holders of at least fifty-one percent (51%) of the then-outstanding shares of Series Preferred. . . .

Article IV, Section D.5(*l*)

Redraft this language so that it clearly supports Greenmont's position.

* * *

iv. Debt.   The difference between *debt* and traditional common stock is clear. A loan is temporary; investment in common stock is permanent. A lender is entitled to periodic interest payments, determined at the time the loan is made. A holder of common stock is entitled to dividends only when and if declared by the board of directors (and subject to other statutory restrictions). If the corporation dissolves, a loan is entitled to be paid in full, but the common stockholders are entitled to all the remaining assets. A lender has no right to participate in the corporation's management; common stock has full voting rights.

   But once debt is compared to other stock, the differences nearly disappear. Stock can be made redeemable or callable, making an investment temporary just like a loan. Both debt and stock can be made convertible into other securities. Preferred stock can have a right to periodic dividends, determined at the time the investment is made, which is similar to the right to receive interest.[3] If the corporation dissolves, preferred stock may have a fixed preference to some of the assets, just as a loan does. Finally, debt can be given voting rights just like typical stock, and stock may have no voting rights just like typical debt.

   What difference does it make whether we characterize a security as debt or equity? It matters in two contexts. First, and most important, a corporation receives a tax benefit by issuing debt rather than equity. Speaking broadly, the Internal Revenue Code provides that corporations may deduct interest payments from their income; dividend payments are not deductible. But note that shareholders that are themselves corporations (i.e., Corporation A owns stock in Corporation B, a frequent occurrence) can, subject to restrictions, exclude 70 percent of the dividends paid to them from their own income. By contrast, a corporation that lends money to another corporation must include all the interest it receives in its own income. Thus corporations seeking additional investors may find that the most suitable investors are corporations that desire preferred stock instead of debt.

   Second, when a corporation enters bankruptcy or voluntarily dissolves, the debt holders have priority over the equity holders. So, an investor whose investment is

---

3. One difference remains, though. If the corporation fails to make an interest payment the lender may sue to compel the payment. If the corporation fails to pay a preferred dividend, the shareholder cannot bring suit to compel the dividend. Nonetheless, the agreement to issue preferred stock may contain other *in terrorem* provisions that give the corporation added incentive to declare the dividend and give the shareholder additional remedies such as voting rights.

characterized as debt may have a more senior, thus more secure, claim on the corporation's assets than an investor whose investment is characterized as stock. Now let's discuss the ways in which corporations and other business entities use debt.

(A) Short-Term Debt. Imagine a small corporation, Fashion Forward! that owns a trendy, retail clothing boutique. After several years of trying, Fashion Forward! has finally gotten a very popular high-end designer of mohair coats, Coats From Goats, to sell to it. Fashion Forward! will be the only store in the area allowed to sell Coats From Goats coats. This sounds like a golden opportunity for Fashion Forward!, and it is, but, as ever in the business world, there are complications.

Because Coats From Goats coats are in such high demand, Fashion Forward! has next to no bargaining power; Coats From Goats will set the terms of the transaction. Coats From Goats will ship a minimum of 100 coats per order because shipping fewer is not efficient. Also, Coats From Goats will not extend credit to Fashion Forward!, because there are plenty of other shops willing to pay cash. Each Coats From Goats coat will cost Fashion Forward! $300, or $30,000 for a minimum order. Coats From Goats coats retail for $750 and Fashion Forward! is certain it can sell the coats quickly and reap a profit of $45,000 on the first order (i.e., $450 profit per coat times 100 coats). Coats From Goats will ship the coats as soon as it receives payment and Fashion Forward! believes the coats will sell out within six weeks.

But Fashion Forward! is a small establishment and does not have $30,000 in ready cash. Fashion Forward! could sell more equity, but its current owners do not want to share their ownership with others. More important, it doesn't make sense to seek a permanent infusion of money (and permanently give up some management rights) when Fashion Forward!'s need for cash is a brief one. Nonetheless, it must find a source for $30,000 for approximately six weeks at reasonable terms.

Fashion Forward!'s solution is to seek a loan from a bank payable in six weeks. This is a relatively safe loan because the amount is small (for a bank, anyway), and the maturity is short (the longer a loan is outstanding, the more things can go wrong and the greater the risk of nonpayment) so the interest rate (which compensates the bank for risking its money) should be low. The bank will probably make its loan even more safe by taking a security interest in the coats. This means that if Fashion Forward! does not repay the loan, the bank can seize the remaining coats and sell them off itself to recoup its loan.

So far, we have been describing this problem and solution in business rather than legal terms. What do business lawyers have to do with this? Several things. First, they may negotiate some or all of the terms between Fashion Forward! and the bank. Second, they will document the transaction to ensure that the parties' intentions are accurately reflected in legally binding agreements. As a matter of corporate law, the statutes explicitly grant corporations the power to borrow money. *See* MBCA §3.02(g), DGCL §122(13). The loan will probably be documented in a loan agreement, a promissory note, and possibly a UCC-1.[4]

Lots of businesses face the same kind of problem on a recurring basis. That is, in the normal course of business they face a gap between the time they must spend

---

4. A UCC-1 is a form that lists the collateral for a loan. Filing the form perfects the creditor's security interest in the collateral.

money and the time they receive the revenues associated with that expense. A vivid example is a toy manufacturer. The vast majority of toys are sold, and hence the vast majority of revenue is received, between November 15th and January 15th. But nearly all those toys have to be manufactured and shipped during the preceding summer and fall. That means toy manufacturers need large amounts of cash for only a few months each year for raw materials, expanded payrolls, and large shipping costs. Such companies may have standing credit arrangements with a bank that will provide a revolving line of credit. This means that the bank is committed to lend money up to a certain amount and, if the toy company has met the repayment requirements, the company has the right to reborrow that money. This works much like the consumer credit card you may carry. Some corporations are such good credit risks and need to borrow such large amounts of money on a regular cycle that their debt is eagerly sought after by investors looking to loan their money for short periods. These loans make up what is called the *commercial paper market* and is an important source of short-term money.

(B) *Long-Term Debt.* Now imagine a corporation, Printing Pros, that operates a local commercial print shop. Advances in printing technology have meant that Printing Pros's current press is rapidly becoming obsolete. Newer presses can do more kinds of printing and do them more cheaply than Printing Pros's press. If Printing Pros wants to remain in business it must purchase a new press, which will last as long as 20 years. Such presses cost $1 million, far more money than Printing Pros has on hand. Because the money will be needed for a long time, it may make sense for Printing Pros to consider selling $1 million in equity to purchase the new press. However, it may not be able to find enough investors willing to put up a total of $1 million, and Printing Pros's current owners will certainly not be happy to see their ownership interests diluted by new equity owners. If Printing Pros decides not to sell more equity, it, like Fashion Forward! may seek a bank loan. Here, though, Printing Pros will want a loan for years rather than weeks. This increases the bank's risk and so it will charge a higher interest rate. Also, a $1 million loan is a much larger percentage of the bank's assets, and so a default will cause more harm than if Fashion Forward! defaults on its $30,000 loan. The bank will also certainly seek to reduce its risk by taking a security interest in the new press. The documentation for this transaction will be similar to the Fashion Forward! loan: a loan agreement, promissory note, and a UCC-1.

As the amount of money a corporation needs increases and as the length of time it needs that money increases, a number of changes in the typical Printing Pros scenario take place. The loan principal (i.e., the amount borrowed) may grow too large for one bank to supply. Several banks, possibly located in several different countries, may get together in a *syndicate* to make the loan. Alternatively, the loan may be divided into very small pieces (usually $1,000) and sold to the public. These loan pieces are usually called *bonds* or *debentures*. Bonds are typically secured by the corporation's assets, while debentures are typically unsecured. This may sound odd, but it is a typical way for large corporations to borrow large amounts of money. In this setting an investment bank serves as an intermediary between the borrowing corporation and the many ultimate lenders. The intermediary will find the investors and may facilitate an active market for lenders who want to sell their bonds or debentures. These bonds and debentures are as readily transferable as stock. In fact, the market for corporate bonds dwarfs the market for corporate stock. The terms of the loan are set out in a document executed by the borrowing company and the investment bank, acting as trustee for the ultimate lenders, called an *indenture*. Indentures are much more detailed and standardized than typical loan agreements between commercial borrowers and lenders.

As the amount and maturity of the loan increase, the loan agreements contain additional, elaborate, provisions that decrease the lenders' risk. Many large corporations have a complex capital structure with common stock, several series of preferred stock, and short-term and long-term debt. When such a corporation issues new debt, the existing lenders may agree that some debt has priority (i.e., is senior) to other debt. The new debt may, then, by its terms be *subordinated* to some or all of the corporation's other debt. The parties may also agree that the interest rate will vary, or *float*, over the life of the loan, possibly with a minimum or maximum rate (or both, called a *collar*) so that changing conditions will not render the loan unfair for either the borrower or lenders. The debt may also be *convertible*, which gives the lenders the option to change the debt into certain other securities.

Often the borrowing corporation agrees to do or refrain from doing certain things that would make the loan more risky. *Affirmative covenants* include such things as maintaining certain financial ratios (e.g., agreeing to keep the ratio of current assets to current liabilities at a particular level) or agreeing to make all scheduled payments of *other* loans in timely fashion. *Negative covenants* prohibit the corporation from increasing its debt beyond an agreed-upon level or prohibit the corporation from paying more dividends that it currently does. A significant or sustained violation of these covenants will constitute an *event of default* and will permit the indenture trustee, on behalf of the ultimate lenders, to declare the entire loan due and payable. In other words, the loan becomes redeemable at the trustee's option.

The borrowing corporation may be required to put aside a certain amount of money each calendar quarter (or even each month) to ensure that it can make its loan payments when due. This money is called a *sinking fund* and can be used to pay the principal as well as the interest. Finally, if it is economically advantageous to the borrower to terminate the loan (e.g., if interest rates have declined so that the corporation could borrow the same amount of money more cheaply) but the loan is not callable, the corporation may put sufficient assets in a trust so that each time an interest or principal payment is due the money comes from the trust. Although the corporation is still legally obligated to repay the loan, as an economic matter the loan has already been prepaid. In this instance, the debt is said to have been *defeased*.

v. More Exotic Securities.   Stock, preferred stock, and the varieties of debt discussed above represent the most frequently used corporate securities. Nonetheless, you should at least be aware of other, slightly more exotic or esoteric, securities available to corporations and their planners. Sometimes a corporation will sell (or give) an option to purchase its securities. Holders of these options are not shareholders and so are not entitled to dividends or a share of the assets upon dissolution, and they do not vote. The nomenclature for these options is more connotative than denotative, so it is important to understand exactly which sort of option is being considered when discussing this question with clients, bankers, accountants, and other lawyers.

A *right* usually means an option granted to an existing security holder. Rights are usually short-term (because the corporation needs money soon) and are often used when the corporation believes its current security holders are a likely source of new capital. For example, when the corporation's prospects are relatively bleak, existing shareholders may be more likely than new investors to put up more money because they hope to salvage their existing investment. Another setting in which rights are used is when the current shareholders care enough about their voting power that they will be likely to invest more money rather than see their interest diluted. Rights are usually, although not always, transferable so that shareholders who do not choose to exercise their rights can realize some gain by selling them.

A *warrant* is usually a long-term (i.e., longer than one year) option to purchase securities. Warrants are usually sold to the general public rather than only to existing security holders. Frequently a corporation will sell both stock and warrants as a package (sometimes called *units*), and purchasers then become security holders and have an option to purchase other securities in the future. Warrants are nearly always transferable and, because of their long life, an active market frequently develops.

In corporate law and finance parlance, an *option* can have one of three meanings. At the broadest level, it has its ordinary meaning: the power but not the obligation to do something. In this sense, rights and warrants are both options. Second, an option can connote a power granted by the corporation to a particular person (often a key employee) to purchase securities. Options in this sense are usually granted for services rendered or to be rendered by the employee and are not transferable. Because this sort of option is typically intended to be an incentive to the employee to work diligently, the option may not be exercisable (i.e., may not *vest*) until several years have passed. Finally, *option* may connote a standardized right sold by someone (the option *writer*) *other than* the corporation to *purchase* securities of the corporation *from* the writer (a *call option*) or *sell* securities of the corporation *to* the writer (a *put option*). These options are a form of speculation and can be used by sophisticated traders to modify their financial risks. There is a very active market in these kinds of financial options. It is important to understand that the corporation is not a party to these kinds of options; they are strictly agreements between other parties.[5] For the statutory grants of power to issue rights, warrants, and options, see MBCA §6.24, DGCL §157.

b. Planning the Corporate Capital Structure

When a new business corporation is being launched, deciding which securities to issue and in what proportions is a quintessential lawyer task. It is, of course, undertaken at the same time that the planners choose and create the legal form the business will take. *See* Chapters 5 and 19. Even if another form is deemed more suitable than a corporation, the owners and their lawyers must still decide the appropriate securities that will be issued. It is simply that the documentation of those interests is a bit more convoluted in other forms than it is in corporations. You should also understand that deciding upon a capital structure may be a continuing process.

---

5. Options in this last sense are a kind of *derivative*, so called because their value is a function of — derives from — the value of the security on which the option is granted. Another kind of derivative is a *future* that, like put and call options, is usually created by and traded among persons other than the corporation. A future is a standardized contract for delivery of stock at a certain future date at a fixed price. You may remember such agreements from your contracts class when they were called forward contracts. The difference between a forward contract and a future is that a future has standard terms to facilitate active trading, while a forward contract connotes a particular agreement that is probably not transferable. A future is different from an option because it *requires* (rather than permits) the purchase or sale of the securities at expiration.

Many established businesses need additional capital and some have a rather constant need for new investment. Thus you may be called upon to render legal (and business) advice in the context of trying to assimilate new interests into an ongoing business.

One challenge, which many lawyers see as simply a complication, is that clients often have ideas about the appropriate capital structure that may differ substantially from your own professional judgment. When the clients are sophisticated business people, your task is, pretty clearly, to embody their desires in documents that will be legally effective. When the clients are not as sophisticated as they believe they are, their desires can be frustrating at best and clearly deleterious to the new business at worst. Although you have a professional obligation to explain your conclusions to your clients, in the end you can, and should, effect their desires — provided, of course, that their preference for one capital structure over another is not illegal (a remote possibility) and that you have explained (typically by letter to the clients) exactly why you disagree and the potential problems you foresee with the structure insisted upon by your clients. In any setting, you must be sensitive to the ethical considerations triggered by entity formation (*see* Chapter 5).

When deciding upon a corporate capital structure, what is your ultimate goal, in addition to satisfying your clients' wishes? One goal is to select a structure that maximizes the value of the entire business. Maximization in this setting means choosing the structure that has the best chance of yielding the most value over time. Is the social value of a new enterprise maximized when the economic value is highest? Nearly all economists recognize that markets fail from time to time and therefore they do not believe that maximizing a business's profits necessarily maximizes social welfare. For example, a business's profits may decline because compliance with environmental regulations has increased its costs. Economists understand that the social benefits from those regulations outweigh the costs of compliance *if* businesses strive to maximize profits while complying with the regulations and *if* those regulations correct for the market failure caused by pollution in a way that is neither too lax nor too strict.

A more nuanced statement of the question is whether businesses should seek to maximize profits even when they believe that government regulations are too lax. Some economists would say that businesses should take actions that those businesses believe increase the overall social welfare even though the business's costs are increased and its profits reduced. This position can be supported by at least two arguments. First, businesses that must comply with regulations are often in the best position to evaluate whether those regulations are socially optimal. Second, businesses are moral actors in society, just as individuals are, and so have the same ethical obligations to act in the manner they perceive will be best for society.

Other economists would say that private businesses should strive to maximize their profits despite their belief that current regulations are inadequate. This view may be supported by the argument that businesses and their managers cannot accurately judge whether regulations are socially optimal. Furthermore, even if they could make such accurate judgments they may be seen as arrogating to private organizations judgments that should only be made by public bodies.[6]

---

6. This discussion of the goals of a corporate capital structure was largely informed by my colleague John B. Kirkwood. Thanks, Jack!

If one measures the success of a corporate capital structure largely by its macro and microeconomic effects, then the goal of a capital structure is to maximize the entire business and effect a division of management and economic rights among the investors that optimizes their relative preferences.

i. The Consequences of Debt — Leverage. We discussed the tax implications of debt and equity briefly above. Now we will expand our examination and look at the tax differences to understand how they affect the choice of a new corporation's capital structure. As you recall, interest payments are deductible by the corporation but dividends are not. A profitable corporation may increase the value of the enterprise by taking on debt.

An example may make this clear. Assume a corporation owns an apartment house and that it had net revenues before interest and income tax of $1,000,000. The corporation wants to distribute as much of its earnings as possible to its investors. In one scenario, the corporation has no debt; its investors own only equity. In the other scenario, the investors own both equity and debt and the interest payments on the debt total $800,000.

Table 6-1

	Equity Only	Equity and Debt
Net Revenue:	$1,000,000	$1,000,000
Interest Paid:	$0	$800,000
Taxable Income:	$1,000,000	$200,000
Tax (35%):	$350,000	$70,000
Dividends (Taxable Income – Tax):	$650,000	$130,000
Total Paid to Investors (i.e., Dividends + Interest):	$650,000	$930,000

Remember, the only difference is that in one setting the corporation obtained its money by selling equity, while in the other the corporation obtained its money by selling equity and incurring debt. Yet by taking on debt, the corporation was able to return over 40 percent ($280,000) more to its investors. As we saw in Chapter 3, the value (and hence the major determinant of price) of an economic asset is a function of the expected return and the uncertainty (riskiness) of that return. Applying that insight here, the expected return is much greater where the corporation is financed in part with debt if the riskiness of the corporation is identical in both settings. The consequence is that economically rational investors should be willing to pay more to invest in the corporation with debt. The corporation is, as an economic matter, more valuable when its capital structure includes debt.[7]

---

7. This example assumes that the investors in both scenarios are identical. That is, that the investors are choosing whether to invest their money in return for equity only or for a mix of equity and debt. While this is frequently accurate, you should understand that the dynamics of the investment decision will change if the lenders will not own equity at all. An example is the typical situation in which the apartment house's equity owners will have gotten a loan from a bank for the bulk of the purchase price. While the total returns will be as set out in Table 6-1, the investors' choice will be between paying the full purchase price and receiving $650,000 in return (the equity-only choice) or paying only a portion of the purchase price (a down payment), getting a bank loan for the rest, and receiving $130,000 in return (with the bank receiving all the $800,000 in interest).

Assume a few more facts about the apartment building. It has 100 apartments that rent for an average of $1,000 per month for a theoretical maximum gross revenue (i.e., assuming every apartment were rented every day of the year) of $1.2 million per year. The costs of the building total $200,000 per year and consist of things such as property taxes, insurance, and maintenance costs.[8] So the net revenue from the apartment building is $1 million per year.

Using the discounted cash flow analysis from Chapter 3, the assumptions above suggest a present value of about $10 million. The table below assumes that the owners purchased the building for $10 million and financed that purchase in one of three possible ways. First, the owners put 20 percent down (i.e., $2 million) and borrowed 80 percent (i.e., $8 million). Second, the owners put only 10 percent down and borrowed 90 percent; third, the owners put a mere 5 percent down and borrowed 95 percent. For simplicity's sake, assume the loans were at 10 percent interest and that no principal was due for 20 years.

Table 6-2

	20/80	10/90	5/95
Net Revenue:	$1,000,000	$1,000,000	$1,000,000
Interest Payments:	$800,000	$900,000	$950,000
Dividends:[9]	$130,000	$65,000	$32,500

Consider, as well, another aspect. If the corporation flourishes, the debt holder does not share in that good news beyond the decreased risk of default implied by the borrower's financial success.[10] Equity holders receive the entire gain. For example, what if the neighborhood in which the apartment house is located suddenly becomes the trendiest part of town in which to live? Or, suppose the owners refurbish the entire building, thus making the apartments more desirable and, hence, more expensive? As a result, the net income rises 30 percent, from $1 million per year to $1.3 million. Regardless of the level of debt, all that additional income goes to the equity owners. Compare Table 6-2 to the next table:

Table 6-3

	20/80	10/90	5/95
Net Revenue:	$1,300,000	$1,300,000	$1,300,000
Interest Payments:	$800,000	$900,000	$950,000
Dividends:	$325,000	$260,000	$227,500
Percent Increase in Dividends:	150%	300%	600%

8. Maintenance costs include such things as periodic repainting and recarpeting of the apartments. The building's manager lives rent free in one of the apartments, so the maintenance cost includes $12,000 of rent that the owners don't receive. Furthermore, when tenants move, it often takes the better part of a month before the apartment can be readied for the next tenant, meaning that the owners receive nothing for those months.

9. The "Dividend" number represents the after-tax money available: 65 percent of (Net Revenue−Interest Payments). That is, it takes the tax benefits of debt into account.

10. That increased assurance of repayment may, to the debt holder, be very valuable indeed, especially if repayment were problematic when the borrower lent. The increased certainty of repayment should mean that the value (though not the principal) of the debt has increased. Still, the debt holder does not share in the increase in the corporation's value.

But, equally important this increase in net revenue, if sustainable in the long run, should mean that the apartment house itself is more valuable. Again, using the discounted cash flow analysis from Chapter 3, the net revenue of $1.3 million suggests a present value of about $13.4 million, an increase of $3.4 million over the $10 million purchase price. If the owners sold the building for $13.4 million, here's how the proceeds would be divided:

Table 6-4

	20/80	10/90	5/95
Sale Proceeds:	$13,400,000	$13,400,000	$13,400,000
Loan Repayment:	$8,000,000	$9,000,000	$9,500,000
Net Proceeds to Equity Owners:	$5,400,000	$4,400,000	$3,900,000
Down Payment:	$2,000,000	$1,000,000	$500,000
Net Gain (Loss):	$3,400,000	$3,400,000	$3,400,000
Net Gain as a Percentage of Down Payment:	170%	340%	680%

In other words, *all* the increase in value goes to the equity holders. As you see in both Table 6-3 and Table 6-4, the more highly leveraged an investment is, the greater the percentage gains.

ii. The Economic Risks of Excessive Debt.   The discussion so far is a tad deceptive because it suggests that planners should choose a capital structure with a very high proportion of debt to equity. But implementing a capital structure that has too much debt in relation to the equity poses both economic and legal risks. This section enlarges upon this idea and its consequences for planning a capital structure.

As the amount of debt increases, the margin for error in predicting future cash falls, which increases the enterprise's risk. The increase in risk should result in a lower value of the enterprise if all other facts remain the same. When the debt level is small or moderate, this increased risk is outweighed by the tax benefits. But when the debt becomes a large percentage of the enterprise's capital, the increased risk makes the enterprise less valuable as a whole.

Lenders are as keenly aware of the deleterious effects of leverage as equity owners are aware of leverage's benefits. As the percentage of debt increases, lenders will seek a higher price (i.e., charge a higher interest rate) for lending their money. Of course, as the interest rate increases the debt service increases, thus increasing a venture's risk even more. To make the apartment house example a bit more realistic, assume that the buyers' financing choices are: (1) 20 percent down (i.e., $2 million) and borrow 80 percent at 10 percent per year; (2) 10 percent down and borrow 90 percent at 11 percent per year; or (3) 5 percent down and borrow 95 percent at 13 percent per year.

Table 6-5

	20/80 (10%)	10/90 (11%)	5/95 (13%)
Net Revenue:	$1,000,000	$1,000,000	$1,000,000
Interest Payments:	$800,000	$990,000	$1,235,000
Dividends:	$130,000	$6,500	($235,000)

In the last example, the interest exceeds the net revenues, and therefore the borrowers must either have another source of income to make up anticipated shortfall or must have a plan for increasing the apartment house's net revenues, and quickly! As a practical matter, the last option is not likely to be available to any but the most sophisticated borrowers and then only if the lender is convinced that the borrowers' plan for meeting the interest payments is economically sound.

Let's return to the apartment house example. Perhaps the primary risk is that the owner will be unable to rent the apartments at sufficient rent to cover the costs of running the building *including the interest on the debt*. If the amount of debt is low, the risk that the rents will not cover the debt service is low. But, if the buyer financed the purchase with a high percentage of debt, even one empty apartment may mean insufficient revenue to cover the debt service.

Think about what happens if the net revenue drops. This could happen in a number of ways, such as an increase in property taxes or insurance premiums. Most likely, though, the net revenue would drop when fewer apartments are occupied. Perhaps the neighborhood has become unfashionable. Perhaps it has become more crime-ridden. Perhaps the apartment house's owners or managers cut back on maintenance and the apartment house itself is now a less desirable place to live. Whatever the cause(s), look at the consequences of having only one apartment unrented for a year.[11] The net revenue will decline by $12,000 ($1,000 × 12) — only 1.2 percent.[12] Again, assume the more realistic scenario in which the interest rate rises with the proportion of debt.

Table 6-6

	20/80 (10%)	10/90 (11%)	5/95 (13%)
Net Revenue:	$988,000	$988,000	$988,000
Interest Payments:	$800,000	$990,000	$1,235,000
Dividends:	$122,200	($2,000)	($247,000)

In the first setting, where the debt is only 80 percent, the owners' gain fell by 6 percent ($7,800) compared to the dividends in Table 6-2. In the second setting, the gain turned into a small loss. Where the owners put up only 5 percent of the purchase price, they must now find $247,000 somewhere to pay the interest. If they don't, the lender presumably will foreclose on the mortgage and sell the building.

---

11. Of course, this needn't mean the same apartment. It simply means some combination of vacancies that totals one fewer apartment over the course of the year.

12. In reality, the maintenance costs will also have gone down a bit, which will offset the loss of revenue, but probably those costs will not have decreased very much as many of the largest costs, such as property taxes and insurance, are the same regardless of how many apartments are rented.

If the dip in net revenue is temporary, the owners may be able to survive, but if the decline is long-term, the value of the apartment house should decline as well. A discounted cash flow approach suggests that if the net revenue falls by 10 percent ($100,000) per year to $900,000 the present value is about $9.25 million. If the owners foresee no likelihood that they can increase that revenue, and they sell the building, the next table shows the consequences. Compare this to Table 6-4.

Table 6-7

	20/80	10/90	5/95
Sale Proceeds:	$9,250,000	$9,250,000	$9,250,000
Loan Repayment:	$8,000,000	$9,000,000	$9,500,000
Net Proceeds to Equity Owners:	$1,250,000	$250,000	$0 or ($250,000)[13]
Down Payment:	$2,000,000	$1,000,000	$500,000
Net Gain (Loss):	($750,000)	($750,000)	($500,000) or ($750,000)

iii. Other Costs of Debt.   Consider these additional facts. First, payment of interest is mandatory, while payment of dividends is in the discretion of the board. This means that a corporation that is in financial difficulty can cut back on, or eliminate entirely, any dividends so that those funds can be used to alleviate the financial problems. By contrast, a corporation's managers have no such discretion as to interest payments. They must be paid even though the corporation's financial state will worsen.

Second, debt, no matter how long-term, must be paid back. When this happens, the investor who held debt is no longer an investor in the corporation. By contrast, the investor who owns stock remains an investor, assuming he or she has not sold the stock. Depending upon the corporation's prospects at the time the debt is repaid, the investor who held debt may regret that he or she is no longer an investor. Obviously the investor and corporation can agree to continue the investment, but such an agreement cannot be assured and, the greater the corporation's prospects the harder the bargain it may drive with the investor. Economists call this danger a *reinvestment risk*. Thus one incentive for equity financing is the assurance to investors (and to the corporation) that the investment is permanent.

Adding debt also has agency costs. Remember from Chapter 4 that from an economic perspective, equity owners are agents of the lenders. This creates the potential for opportunistic behavior, a form of moral hazard that increases the agency costs of the venture. *See* Chapter 4 for a description of those hazards. Devices designed to ameliorate those costs have, themselves, costs that are irreducible.

Finally, there are costs associated when a venture prepares for, and enters, bankruptcy. These costs include lost management time spent trying to stave off the

---

13. In this scenario, the borrowers' entire interest has been wiped out. If the loan was "with recourse" the borrowers remain liable to the bank for the $250,000 shortfall. If the loan was "without recourse," the borrowers are not liable and the bank must absorb the loss. As you may intuit, loans with recourse are typically at lower interest rates than those made without recourse. Likewise, when calculating the borrowers' Net Gain (Loss), the two possibilities represent the setting in which the loan was without recourse ($500,000 loss) or with recourse ($750,000 loss).

bankruptcy and the management time involved with the proceedings. Obviously there are transaction costs such as lawyer fees and administrative fees, as well.

iv. A Real-World Example of the Dangers of Excessive Debt. The apartment building example may seem a bit artificial and abstract to you. What follows is a description of a real-life, concrete example of a business that had too much debt. As a bonus, this example involves a large retail corporation whose name is well-known to almost everyone.

Toys "R" Us, Inc. (Toys) grew out of a discount baby furniture store in Washington, D.C. In 1957, the company became Toys "R" Us and began expansion. It sold stock to the public in 1978 and was a highly successful retailer of toys. It was an example of what was called "category killer" retailers, companies with large stores devoted to a single product line. These category killers competed favorably with traditional department stores, which were the primary nation-wide retailers. In 2005, the public shareholders of Toys were bought out by three well-known private equity firms in a highly leveraged transaction. That is, the private equity firms made a comparatively small investment in Toys. The bulk of the purchase price was borrowed, secured by Toys' assets. The private equity firms put up about $1.3 billion and the company ended up with about $5.3 billion in debt.

Toys' new owners anticipated increasing Toys' revenues by upgrading the company's 1,600 stores and improving its website and its online sales experience. But two dynamics thwarted Toys' plans. First, so-called "big box" retailers, such as Target and Wal-Mart, increased the store space devoted to toys. Second, Amazon.com also increased its emphasis on selling toys and that emphasis made online sales by Toys more difficult because online shoppers preferred the ease of Amazon's website and the fact that Amazon sold a wide variety of goods.

By 2013, the company was in disarray. Gross revenues declined by 7 percent over 2012, which the company attributed to "a series of organizational and operational changes, including senior leadership turnover, undisciplined promotional activity resulting in selling product too cheap, [and] poor inventory management resulting in overstock." The private equity owners replaced virtually all Toys' senior managers in an attempt to get Toys back on course.

The competition continued. As the company's CEO said,

> [I]n light of shifting consumer demand toward online marketplaces and competition from one-stop retailers such as Walmart and Target, [Toys' gross] revenue has trended downwards [since 2012], decreasing profits and increasing leverage.
>
> Practically speaking, this competition [from big box retailers and Amazon.com] manifests itself in price wars; during the 2016 holiday season, big box retailers slashed prices on toys and flooded marketing channels, knowing that if they can get consumers in the door to purchase attractively-priced toys, they can make up for decreased toy revenue with other in-store purchases. Further, online retailers such as Amazon are not concerned with making a profit at this juncture, rendering their pricing model impossible to compete with for a company such as Toys "R" Us. To compete, Toys "R" Us would have needed to slash prices on the same toys to keep traffic coming into its stores, decreasing its [gross] revenue and cash flows in an unrelenting race to the bottom.[1]

---

1. Declaration of David A. Branson, Chairman of the Board and Chief Executive Officer of Toys "R" Us, Inc., in Support of Chapter 11 Petitions and First Day Motions, 24, 37 (Sept. 19, 2017).

However, Toys' costs of operating its stores remained relatively constant and, by 2015, the company believed it had cut the costs of operating its stores as much as possible while still remaining competitive. Thus, Toys' net revenues declined as well as its gross revenues. These competitive pressures thwarted Toys' plans. Because it had less net revenue it could not invest significantly in remodeling its stores or upgrading its online presence. And because it already had so much debt, it could not borrow more money to remodel and upgrade its IT.

As Toys' debt became due, it refinanced its borrowing because it did not have enough money to pay the debts in full. This strategy resulted in no reduction in the amount of Toys' debt or in the amount of debt service (i.e., payments of principal and interest) it paid each year. Toys continued to pay an average of $400 million each year in debt service, just as it did in 2005, and its total debt remained around $5.3 billion. As we saw in the apartment house example, when net revenue declines and debt service remains constant, the debtor has less discretionary revenue with which to expand the business, reduce debt, or pay dividends.

In September 2016, as the company was increasing its inventory for the holiday season (when it traditionally made 40 percent of its yearly sales), CNBC reported that Toys had hired a noted bankruptcy law firm to advise it about the possibility of declaring bankruptcy. That story, in the words of Toys' CEO,

> started a dangerous game of dominos: within a week of its publication, nearly 40 percent of [Toys'] product vendors refused to ship product without cash on delivery, cash in advance, or, in some cases, payment of all outstanding obligations. . . . Given [Toys'] historic average of 60-day trade terms, payment of cash on delivery would require [Toys] to immediately obtain a significant amount — over $1.0 billion — of new liquidity.[2]

Less than two weeks after the story appeared, Toys "R" Us declared bankruptcy. After the 2005 buy-out by the private equity firms, Toys was unable to expand its business or reduce its debt. It paid no dividends to the private equity firms, although they did get annual "management fees" that were relatively modest compared to their $1.3 billion 2005 investment. With Toys "R" Us's bankruptcy, those private equity firms lost their entire investment.

v. The Legal Dangers of Excessive Debt. You should be aware of three particular legal risks associated with the choice of a capital structure that relies too heavily on debt. The first risk has to do with the deductibility of interest on debt. Remember that this deductibility increases the value of the enterprise more than the increase in risk caused by modest levels of debt. However, conceptually, an enterprise cannot be 100 percent debt; someone must have an ownership stake. Because the deduction for interest paid is money that would otherwise be taxed, the Internal Revenue Service is rather suspicious of corporations that deduct large amounts of interest from their income. The consequence of a recharacterization of interest as dividends is that the entity is denied the deduction it took, may have to amend prior tax returns, and must pay tax on the amounts paid out and possibly additional sums as penalties and interest on delayed taxes, as well.

The IRS and the courts have two kinds of inquiries to determine whether the "debt" upon which interest is paid (and hence deductible) is genuine debt or is really equity disguised so that payments are characterized as interest rather than dividends.

---

2. *Id.*, at 5.

The first inquiry looks to whether the obligation has the traditional indicia of debt: for example, an unconditional obligation to pay a sum certain, a fixed maturity date, and interest payable regardless of the debtor's income. When the debt is owed to equity holders, the IRS and courts give greater scrutiny than where the debt is owed to outsiders. For example, where the debt is owed to equity holders, the absence of a written agreement might lead a court to conclude that the debt is not genuine and, hence, to disallow an interest deduction.

The other inquiry for recharacterizing debt is sometimes called the *economic realities* test. This is essentially an objective inquiry to ask whether an unrelated third party would have been willing to make a loan of similar size on similar terms to the corporation. If not, the IRS or court may conclude that the debt is really a contribution to equity. Although it is clear that the loan need not be on terms as stringent as a completely disinterested third party would offer, the further away from such terms (i.e., the more favorable the terms to the borrowing corporation), the more likely it is to be found to be a contribution to equity rather than a loan.

One important element in this inquiry is a comparison of the corporation's debt to its equity. It is quite common for corporations to have debt several times the size of their equity. Whether a particular debt/equity ratio is "excessive," sometimes described as a "top heavy" capital structure or a "thin" capitalization, is really a question of comparing the particular corporation's capital structure to that of similar companies in the same industry. Industries vary widely in their reliance on debt, and it is impossible in the absence of such comparison to opine whether a particular corporation has excessive debt. Another important consideration in this inquiry is to compare the percentage of total equity held by each shareholder to the percentage of total debt that shareholder owns. If each shareholder's percentage of the debt is identical to his or her percentage of the equity, the debt is said to be held proportionally, and this may suggest that at least some of the debt is actually equity in disguise. By contrast, where the percentage of debt is different from the percentage of equity, this militates toward a finding that the debt is genuine.

The second kind of legal risk for a corporation with significant debt is *equitable subordination* in bankruptcy. When an entity declares bankruptcy, the bankruptcy code provides that the entity's assets shall be applied to satisfy the claimants in a fixed order. Debt holders are paid before equity holders. As we have seen, it is frequently the case that equity holders also, and legitimately, hold debt as well. If a bankruptcy judge believes that the equity holder's intention in taking debt was to raise up a portion of his or her investment in the bankruptcy priority system, the judge may reduce the priority of (i.e., subordinate) some or all of that debt. In effect, the judge declares that, for reasons of equity, repayment of debt owned by equity holders should be delayed until debt to nonequity holders, such as trade creditors or bank lenders, has been paid first. This result is particularly likely when equity holders advance new money, in the form of loans, on the eve of bankruptcy or when their investment, which was all equity, is recast as part equity and part debt close to bankruptcy. Equitable subordination is also called the Deep Rock doctrine, after the bankrupt subsidiary in *Taylor v. Standard Gas & Electric Co.,* 306 U.S. 307 (1939).

The third danger of a capital structure with a large proportion of debt is piercing the corporate veil. If the corporation incurs a liability that it cannot satisfy, especially if that liability is incurred near the corporation's formation, a court may disregard the corporate entity and hold its owners personally liable. This doctrine is explored in more detail in Chapter 8, but you should be aware that one factor that may weigh heavily on a court's decision is whether the entity had a significant part of its capital in the form of debt held by the equity holders. If so, the possibility of piercing is heightened.

vi. Other Factors That Make Equity Attractive. For our purposes, an even greater insight into crafting a capital structure comes from understanding that the owner does not have to sell or declare a dividend when the asset appreciates in value. In an economic sense, when the value of the apartment house increases from $10 million to $13.4 million, the owners of the apartment are $3.4 million richer even though they do not convert that wealth to cash by selling. Similarly, if the corporation generated an extra $300,000 in net income in one year, the equity holders do not have to distribute that money as dividends. If that money simply sits in the corporation's bank account, the value of the corporation has, presumably, increased by $300,000 and the owners are thus $300,000 richer even though they have no additional cash in their own hands. As a more general description, an equity holder's total return from his or her investment must be measured by the dividends *and* the increase in the value of the corporation.

Under the Internal Revenue Code, an equity holder receives two advantages from this increase in wealth that is unaccompanied by a sale or dividend. First, the gain is not taxed at all until it is realized. In other words, regardless of how much the value of the equity holder's stock increases, the equity holder will not pay tax on that gain until he or she sells the equity. Only the dividends, if any, will be taxed. This gives the equity holder control over when to realize the gain. The second advantage is that, when gain is recognized, it will result in a lower tax for two reasons. First, as you remember from Chapter 3, a dollar in the future is worth less than a dollar today. So, a tax dollar paid in the future, when the equity holder realizes gain, is less than the same dollar paid today. Second, when the equity holder does sell equity, any gain will be considered a *capital gain* and may be taxed at a lower rate than ordinary income such as wages, dividend, or interest income.

In most startup companies there is yet another factor that attenuates the value of debt over equity. Some or all of the investors will be providing services to the corporation as employees. Most of these people will desire or need periodic payments to cover their own living expenses. Although in theory the corporation could have debt that requires monthly (or weekly or even daily) interest payments and could declare and pay dividends with equal frequency, such solutions are a bit cumbersome. The usual solution is for the investors to become employees of the corporation they own. In return, they receive salaries. As long as the salaries are reasonable and necessary, they can be deducted from the corporation's income, just as interest payments are deducted. Furthermore, the vast majority of new businesses cannot realistically expect profits in the short term. In light of this, the investor/employees are probably expecting the great bulk of their reward to come via salaries rather than either interest or dividends, so at least some of the investors will be fairly neutral as between debt and equity. This reality is yet another attenuation of the need to capitalize the corporation with debt rather than equity.

A further reason why every corporation should not be entirely financed with debt has to do with the nature of the investors. Especially in the startup corporation, the planners will be concerned with a relatively small number of real investors. Assuming our professional obligation runs to each investor equally, which may not necessarily be true, our goal is to maximize the value of the entire business *in the hands of this set of investors.* In the paradigm setting, all investors are individuals. Under the Internal Revenue Code, interest paid to individuals and dividends paid to individuals are treated as *ordinary income* on which the investor will pay income tax. That means that his or her after-tax return from the corporation will be the same, regardless of whether the investor receives a return as interest or dividend. So far, this does not change our conclusion that a corporation is more valuable with debt than without and even that it ought to be financed entirely with debt.

However, the same amount of interest or dividend may have different tax consequences for different investors. Some individual investors may have lower marginal tax rates than others.[14] A typical example is a new corporation that will operate a restaurant. Some investors will be rich individuals with marginal tax rates at the maximum, say 35 percent, while other investors — perhaps the chef or other key, but relatively impecunious, participants — will have marginal tax rates at the minimum, perhaps 15 percent.[15] Investors with lower marginal rates may prefer to invest in debt because capital gains treatment is less valuable to them and because, with lower income, they may prefer the greater certainly of debt to the increased risk of equity. Furthermore, in some situations a corporation unaffiliated with the new corporation may be an investor. Recall that such corporation/investor can exclude 70 percent of dividends from its income. This is a strong incentive for such investors to take equity rather than debt, because each $10 of interest received is only $6.50 after taxes (with a 35% corporate income tax rate) while each $10 of dividends is worth $8.95 (35% of $3.00 = $1.05 paid in tax).

Finally, investors have an incentive to choose equity over debt because equity carries with it management power while debt does not.[16] This is not such a strong incentive as it first appears. If each investor is to have equal voting rights regardless of the size of his or her investment (or if each is making an investment of equal value), each can be issued an equal amount of stock for nominal consideration. If they are to have voting power in proportion to their investments, which are unequal (a common occurrence), the investors could still have differing proportions of debt and equity through using different series or classes of stock that vary from one another only as to voting rights. In a stark example, assume a startup corporation with two investors who are to have equal voting power, one who wants debt and one who wants equity. One solution is to sell debt to one investor, nonvoting stock to the other, and a small amount of voting stock (i.e., common stock) to each. The investor who wants debt has, essentially, a certain and senior claim on the income and assets of the corporation, while the investor who wants equity has a junior claim but will enjoy all the gain in the corporation's value. The small amount of common stock

---

14. The *marginal* tax rate is the percent of the next dollar of income that will be taxed. You must be careful to distinguish this from the *effective* tax rate, which is the ratio of all tax paid to all income. Because marginal rates increase as income increases, the effective rate for most taxpayers is lower than their marginal rate.

15. Congress tinkers with the tax rates rather frequently. In recent decades, however, the minimum individual rate has been around 10 percent to 15 percent, while the top rates have been in the mid-30 percents. Tax rates for corporations are typically around 35 percent.

16. In Delaware, however, debt with voting power can be created. *See* DGCL §221.

each owns will be economically inconsequential in comparison to the size of the other securities yet give each investor equal voting power.

vii. Choosing a Capital Structure for the Startup Corporation. How does one actually plan a new corporation's capital structure, at least when the solution is not dictated to you by the investors? One way to approach this is to examine separately the following areas: (1) the investors' relative claims on the business's income (and assets on dissolution); (2) the investors' relative management power; and (3) the dangers that concern capital structures with excessive debt. In considering the relative management power and economic claims of the investors you should bear in mind that much of the ultimate solution will depend on the bargaining leverage each investor brings. Even in a setting in which your professional obligation runs to each investor equally, some investors' contributions (either knowledge, money, unique assets, or other virtues such as an investor's prestige within the business or other important community) will be more central than others. Those investors have the ability to control the outcome of the management and economic divisions.

In finding the appropriate capital structure as a financial matter, the investors and you, their advisor, should seek the mix of debt and equity that maximizes the value of the entire enterprise in the hands of the anticipated owners. This means sufficient equity that that the risks of excessive debt are sufficiently dampened while maximizing the tax benefits obtainable from debt. Once an appropriate mix of debt and equity has been decided, the planner can turn his or her attention to the problem of dividing up the management power among the participants.

It is worth emphasizing a point that is probably intuitive. The considerations that are set out here as discrete questions considered in a particular order are, in the real world, compounded, conflated, and simultaneous. Nonetheless, they are dissected here so that you can have a better appreciation of the way in which these aspects need to be approached if a thoughtful and appropriate solution for your clients is to be crafted.

Turning to the division of management power, in the simplest dynamic, each investor will want management control commensurate with his or her economic contribution. In that case, the solution is relatively simple: each investor gets stock in proportion to his or her investment. Often, this means the new corporation will only issue common stock. When this is not the parties' desire, the situation can become more complex very quickly. For our purposes, understand that two frequent arrangements are that certain investors are to have, in essence, veto rights either over every decision or at least over certain important decisions. Also, some investors may have no (or no important) management power unless the business falters, in which instance those investors are to have heightened management powers.

The solution to the first setting is to give the investors with veto power either a separate class of shares that votes on important matters or to have a supermajority requirement as to some issues so that the veto can be exercised in appropriate circumstances. The solution to the second setting is to provide for nonvoting stock that has voting rights in certain settings such as when the corporation's financial position deteriorates. The key to these kinds of problems and solutions is to recognize that there are no predetermined answers but simply time-tested approaches that have proved useful. After studying this chapter you should be able to abstract the concerns of the parties and develop a range of solutions to those concerns.

Notes and Questions

1. Suppose

a. Suppose the IRS or Congress had adopted a bright-line test for determining whether an investment would be considered debt or equity. Would that be better than the current system? What bright-line test would you adopt?

2. What Do You Think?

a. When corporations borrow money, the value of the enterprise increases more than if it had issued equity only because the corporation can deduct the interest it pays on the debt. A corporation that has $1,000 in income can pay only $650 in dividends (because it must pay $350 in income tax) but can pay the entire $1,000 as interest. In other words, investors get $350 more only because the U.S. Treasury gets $350 less. Do you think this is fair? Why did Congress choose to reward investment via debt in a way that does not equally reward investment via equity?

b. Should Congress look at the goods and services produced by an enterprise rather than looking at whether the enterprise is financed by debt or equity? Instead of rewarding lenders over shareholders, should Congress focus on rewarding investment (debt or equity) in corporations that undertake ends or use means that Congress considers particularly valuable to society? Which ends or means should Congress reward?

c. Is it ethical (both as a matter of a lawyer's professional responsibility and more broadly) for lawyers to propose and implement capital structures that minimize their clients' tax liability? Why shouldn't they be required to create structures that maximize that liability?

Putting It to Work

Problem 6-1[17]

Sara and Evan have developed a revolutionary new bingo dauber that has an ergonomic shape and uses ecofriendly ink. They believe their new dauber will be commercially successful but they need capital to obtain intellectual property protection (e.g., patents and trademarks) and the resources to satisfy the anticipated demand (e.g., source the component parts and chemicals, hire the employees required to manufacture and market the daubers, and establish a manufacturing facility and corporate offices). They believe they will need at least $2 million dollars to make their company viable. Sara and Evan believe that their sources of capital are realistically limited to the following:

> Sara and Evan will contribute the proprietary information about the design and manufacture of the new bingo dauber. They also have $100,000 in cash

---

17. My thanks to Professor Danshera Cords, who was the author of the exercise on which this problem is based.

from their savings. They are completely committed to the success of their bingo dauber project.

Sara's in-laws are relatively well-off retirees who successfully started several businesses in years past. They have $4 million they could invest. They have natural familial affinity for Sara but are also rational investors.

A local commercial bank has expressed a willingness to invest. The bank's loan policy is to invest no more than $5 million in any single venture.

Conduct a negotiation exercise with other students in which you represent the different parties and attempt to reach agreement on a total investment of at least $2 million and an agreed upon capital structure. Your professor will give you more information about Sara and Evan, the in-laws, and the bank.

viii. Background and Context: A Note on Financing by Going Public and by Venture Capital.

The paradigm we have been considering has been the startup corporation and, primarily, we have been working on an implicit assumption that the equity holders were a small group of individuals or perhaps even a single person. These qualities hold true for the vast majority of corporations. They are generically referred to as *close corporations* or *closely held corporations* because the number of owners is not large. But many corporations do not meet these criteria. They have thousands of shareholders, very few of whom are involved in the corporation's management. Conversely, the managers' total equity investment is a miniscule percentage of the corporation's total equity. How did these large corporations evolve from small ones?

At one level the answer is simply that they were successful in industries that were particularly hospitable, economically speaking, to large firms. For purposes of this chapter, the answer is that those companies typically underwent a fundamental change in their capital structure. That is, at some point in their existence, these corporations obtained significant financing by selling securities (equity, usually, but also debt) to the public. When a corporation sells securities to the general public for the first time, the company is said to *go public* and its sale is called an *initial public offering*, or *IPO*.

One reason to go public is to raise more money than can be raised conveniently from a smaller group of investors, even though those investors might have very deep pockets. An additional reason to go public is that typically the securities sold to the public will thereafter be actively traded among individuals. This is sometimes called the *secondary trading market*. It's the market you and I think of when we think of the stock market. The New York Stock Exchange and NASDAQ[18] are the best-known secondary markets. Shares of IBM or Microsoft may rise or fall every day, but none of the money changing hands in those sales goes to the company. Rather, those sales are simply private transactions between sellers who no longer desire to remain security holders and buyers who wish to become security holders.

Still this secondary market indirectly benefits the corporations that issue the securities. Why? Because buyers of securities from corporations will pay more for securities that can be easily disposed of. In a close corporation, shareholders can

---

18. NASDAQ is an acronym for the National Association of Securities Dealers Automated Quotation system of trading.

often find someone willing to buy their shares only with great difficulty. A shareholder of Microsoft, by contrast, can simply contact a stockbroker and the shares can be sold nearly instantly. This characteristic, called *liquidity*, makes initial buyers more confident in their investment because they can more readily end their investment and so they are willing to pay more. So an additional reason for a company to go public is that it can charge a higher price for its securities than if it sold them to a smaller number of investors who would have more difficulty trading them.

We should mention, though, that not every large corporation has gone public. Some companies are content to meet their financing needs privately rather than go through the elaborate process of offering securities to the public and the continuing strictures of remaining a public company.[19] Furthermore, the management of some companies believes that it will lose control of the business if significant amounts of stock are sold to the public. Some of the best-known names in corporate America, such as Mars Candy and Hallmark Cards, are not publicly held. The Ford Motor Company was formed in 1903 and remained privately held, primarily by the Ford family, until 1956, even though the corporation was quite large by 1920 and had constant needs for large amounts of capital.

The process of going public consists of the corporation selecting an investment bank to be its lead *underwriter*. That investment bank puts together a syndicate of other such investment banks to share the risks and rewards of the offering. The investment bank also canvasses the market and advises the corporation on the kind of security (debt or equity) it should issue and likely price it should charge. Finally, the underwriting syndicate purchases the securities at a discount, which is, in effect, their fee, from the corporation and immediately resells them to the public at the announced price. Sometimes current shareholders of the corporation sell some of their shares to the underwriters as well, allowing them to cash in on the corporation's success. Usually the underwriters also agree to support a secondary market in the security, offering to buy and sell until the market for that security becomes well established. The process is highly regulated by the Securities and Exchange Commission, and a brief outline of the legal implications of going public is found in Section B.

Most companies that end up going public do so as the culmination of a process of involvement with *venture capital* firms. Venture capital is a description of money supplied to nonpublic corporations by entities unconnected with the corporation. Although some of this venture capital is supplied by rich individuals (sometimes called *angels*) most of it is supplied by venture capital firms usually structured as limited partnerships. Startup companies seeking venture capital make presentations to venture capital firms. The venture capital firms see hundreds of presentations every year and make very few investments. Ultimately, about one in ten of those investments is a complete loss and eight of the ten will be very modest successes. The one in ten that is a great success provides the venture capital firm with more than enough profits to cover the costs of the other nine investments.

---

19. These involve compliance with detailed and pervasive federal regulations, which are summarized in Section B. The process of going public is subject to considerable federal regulation and, once a company has securities in the hands of the public, it is required to make detailed periodic reports of its financial and operating results. For some companies, these strictures are simply not worth the benefits to be gained from going public.

The venture capital firm analyzes the new business's plan and identifies a series of important operational and financial milestones leading to a public offering. The venture capital firm also estimates the amount of money the business will need at each stage of its development. The venture capitalists invest just enough money to carry the business through to the next milestone with no guarantee from the venture capital firm of additional funds. Furthermore, as a condition of the venture capital firm's involvement, the key entrepreneurs in the business will be required to invest essentially all their wealth in the business. This means that any savings or home equity is invested in the business, ensuring that the managers are highly motivated to be successful.

At each stage the venture capital firm provides advice on the business's development and watches that development with keen interest. As the stages progress, other venture capital firms may participate in financing as well. Near the end stages, when the business is ready to go public, the venture capital firm will usually identify and help recruit seasoned executives to replace many of the key employees. This replacement may seem harsh but it adds to the likelihood that the business will succeed. It is not unusual for such key employees as the chief operating officer, the general counsel, the chief financial officer, and even the chief executive officer, who is probably the person who had the initial vision for the business, to be replaced at this point. Sometimes the replaced employees remain in a lesser or advisory capacity. Other times they move on to other pursuits. In either event, they have usually been compensated with stock in the business that, if the public offering is successful, will make them quite rich and that goes far in assuaging any damage to their self esteem.

The nearly universal practice is for venture capital firms to invest only in entities that are Delaware corporations. This does not rule out other forms of businesses, but simply means that they must convert to Delaware corporations, which is a relatively simple task. The venture capital firms tend to receive preferred stock for their investment, which gives them priority over the firm's assets. The preferred stock provisions also typically give the venture capitalists the power to select half the board members. This is accomplished by having only the preferred stock vote for half the board and only the common stock (owned by the entrepreneurs) vote for the other half of the board. The preferred stock usually has veto power over extraordinary actions such as incurring large debt, issuing new stock, dissolving, or merging. Perhaps most importantly, the preferred stock typically gets increased voting power in the event the corporation fails to meet its operational and financial milestones. In such event the venture capitalists essentially take over the corporation and may restructure the enterprise by replacing the founders, renegotiating the terms of their investment, or dissolving the corporation.

The following is a description of the various investments in one company, Trados Incorporated, by three venture capital firms.

> Defendant Jochen Hummel and Iko Knyphausen founded Trados in 1984. Hummel became Chief Technology Officer and served on the Board. Knyphausen left the Company and did not play a significant role. . . .
>
> Trados developed proprietary desktop software for translating documents.
>
> At the turn of the third millennium of the Common Era, Trados sought VC funding to spur its growth and help position itself for an IPO. At the time, Trados differed significantly from the stereotypical dot-com startup. Trados had been around for sixteen years and sold a successful desktop product. In 1999, the Company generated $11.3 million in revenue and

. . . [i]n 2000, Trados generated revenue of $13.9 million, representing year-over-year growth of approximately 23%.

In early 2000, Trados came to the attention of . . . Wachovia Capital Partners, LLC ("Wachovia"). Around March 2000, after conducting due diligence, Wachovia invested $5 million. In return, Wachovia received 1,801,303 shares of Series A Participating Preferred Stock ("Series A") and 1,838,697 shares of Series B Non-Voting Convertible Preferred Stock ("Series B"), which were convertible on a 1-for-1 basis into Series A. Wachovia later converted, bringing its total Series A shares to 3,640,000.

Each Series A share had an initial liquidation preference equal to its purchase price of $1.374. The stock paid a cumulative dividend at a rate of 8% per annum with unpaid dividends increasing the liquidation preference. As participating preferred, the Series A shared in any remaining distribution available for the common stock, subject to a cap. . . . At its option, Wachovia could convert the Series A into common stock pursuant to a formula in the Company's certificate of incorporation. The Series A had the right to veto any attempt by Trados to (i) amend its certificate of incorporation, (ii) authorize, issue, or reclassify shares, (iii) make, authorize, or approve dividends or distributions, (iv) redeem, repurchase, or acquire stock, (v) change the number of directors, or (vi) effect any change of control. The Series A also had the right to vote with the common stock on an as-converted basis.

As part of the investment, Wachovia obtained the right to designate a director [on the seven-person board]. Wachovia designated David Scanlan, a Wachovia partner.

Around the same time, Trados came to the attention of . . . Hg Capital LLP ("Hg"). In April 2000, Hg invested $10.25 million in exchange for 5,333,330 shares of Series C Preferred Stock ("Series C"). Each Series C share had an initial liquidation preference equal to its purchase price of $1.922. Its other rights paralleled and participated *pari passu* with the Series A, except that the Series C was not participating preferred.

In August 2000, Hg invested an additional $2 million in exchange for 862,976 shares of Series D Preferred Stock ("Series D"). Each Series D share had an initial liquidation preference equal to its purchase price of $2.3176. Its other rights paralleled and participated *pari passu* with the Series C, including the cumulative dividend and veto rights. In September 2000, Hg bought 1,379,039 shares of common stock for approximately $2.3 million.

Like Wachovia, Hg obtained the right to designate a director. [Hg designated] Lisa Stone, a partner at Hg who joined the Board in mid-2002.

In September 2001, Wachovia and Hg made follow-on investments in Series BB Preferred Stock ("Series BB"). Wachovia paid $1.0 million for 1,007,151 shares. Hg paid $2.0 million for 2,014,302 shares. Each Series BB share had an initial liquidation preference equal to its purchase price of $0.9929. Otherwise the rights of the Series BB paralleled and participated *pari passu* with the Series A, including its status as participating preferred.

In August 2002, Trados raised $2 million from Invision AG, a Swiss private equity firm. Invision received 2,350,174 shares of Series F Preferred Stock ("Series F"). Each share of Series F carried an initial liquidation preference equal to its purchase price of $0.8510. Its other terms paralleled and participated *pari passu* with the Series C.

Invision received the ability to designate a director and named . . . Klaus-Dieter Laidig in December 2002. Unlike Scanlan [and] Stone, . . . Laidig was not [a partner in the investment firm]. Laidig was a technology consultant who previously worked as an executive at Hewlett-Packard for over thirty years. Laidig had a part-time consulting relationship with Invision that paid him a nominal amount for handling various projects. Laidig served on the boards of two other Invision portfolio companies and advised one of Invision's funds.

In August 2003, Invision invested another $2 million and received 2,428,513 shares of Series FF Preferred Stock ("Series FF"). Each Series FF share carried an initial liquidation preference of $0.8235, equal to its purchase price. Its other terms paralleled and participated *pari passu* with the Series C.

In re Trados Incorporated S'holder Litig., 73 A.3d 17, 21-24 (Del. Ch. 2013).

Vice Chancellor Laster describes the business arc of Trados:

> [Trados] obtained venture capital in 2000 to support a growth strategy that could lead to an initial public offering. The VC firms received preferred stock and placed representatives on the Trados board of directors (the "Board"). Afterwards, Trados increased revenue year-over-year but failed to satisfy its VC backers. In 2004, the VC directors began looking to exit. As part of that process, the Board adopted a management incentive plan (the "MIP") that compensated management for achieving a sale even if the transaction yielded nothing for the common stock.
>
> In July 2005, SDL plc acquired Trados for $60 million in cash and stock (the "Merger"). Under Trados's certificate of incorporation, the Merger constituted a liquidation that entitled the preferred stockholders to a liquidation preference of $57.9 million. Without the MIP, the common stockholders [primarily the founders] would have received $2.1 million. The MIP took the first $7.8 million of the Merger consideration. The preferred stockholders received $52.2 million. The common stockholders received nothing.
>
> The plaintiff contended that instead of selling to SDL, the Board had a fiduciary duty to continue operating Trados independently in an effort to generate value for the common stock. Despite the directors' failure to follow a fair process and their creation of a trial record replete with contradictions and less-than-credible testimony, the defendants carried their burden of proof on this issue. Under Trados's business plan, the common stock had no economic value before the Merger, making it fair for its holders to receive in the Merger the substantial equivalent of what they had before. The appraised value of the common stock is likewise zero.

Id., at 19-20.

Although both the venture capitalists and the business's entrepreneurs want to see the corporation succeed, their interests are not identical, as the *Trados* excerpt reveals. The next case shows the kinds of conflicts that can arise. The lessons from this case are applicable beyond the venture capital-versus-entrepreneur setting. They apply any time both passive and active investors hold different kinds of investments in the same entity.

Telcom-SNI Investors, L.L.C. v. Sorrento Networks, Inc.

2001 WL 1117505 (Del. Ch. Sept. 7, 2001)

NOBLE, V.C.

I. FACTUAL BACKGROUND

A. The Parties

Plaintiffs, . . . who have been characterized by the Defendants as "venture capitalists," hold approximately 7.5 million shares of Sorrento's Series A Preferred Stock which, at one time, constituted approximately 84% of the Series A Preferred Stock issued by Sorrento. The only preferred stock issued by Sorrento is the Series A Preferred.

Sorrento designs, manufactures and markets optical network equipment. [Osicom], . . . owns . . . all of the common stock in Sorrento.

Sorrento Networks, Inc. ("[Sorrento]") was incorporated in California on January 21, 2000. [Sorrento], as a startup corporation with no immediate prospects of profitability, required constant and significant cash infusions to sustain it until an initial public offering ("IPO") could be accomplished. On March 3, 2000, [Sorrento], Osicom, and a group of investors, including Plaintiffs, entered into an agreement for the private placement of 8,880,734 million shares of Sorrento's Series A Preferred Stock at a price of $5.45 per share, thereby generating approximately $48.4 million.

The investors (together with [Sorrento] and Osicom) anticipated that the IPO would occur shortly after the investment. They were wrong, and the collapse of this fundamental premise upon which the investors made their investment decision has resulted, perhaps inevitably, in this litigation.

On August 3, 2000, Sorrento was [re-]incorporated as a Delaware corporation. . . .[6] The provisions in Sorrento's Certificate were identical in all material respects to those of [Sorrento]'s charter.

When Plaintiffs agreed . . . to invest in [Sorrento] . . . , they negotiated several "protective provisions" to secure the integrity of their investment. The protective provisions appear both in the Certificate and in the separate Investors' Rights Agreement.

1. Sorrento's Certificate provides in part at Article V.D(6):

> (a) [S]o long as any shares of Series A Preferred Stock are outstanding, the Corporation shall not without first obtaining the approval . . . of the holders of at least a majority of the then outstanding shares of Series A Preferred Stock:
>
>> (i) alter, change or amend the rights, preferences or privileges of the Series A Preferred Stock;
>> (ii) authorize or issue, or obligate itself to issue, any other equity security, including any other security convertible into or exercisable for any equity security having a preference over, or being on a parity with, the Series A Preferred Stock with respect to voting, dividends or upon liquidation . . . ,

2. The Investors' Rights Agreement conferred upon Plaintiffs significant additional rights. Among those rights are the following:

> b. If the IPO was not completed by March 1, 2001, by the written request of the holders of at least 50% of the outstanding Series A Preferred Stock redemption of their shares could be obtained at a price equal to the original purchase price . . . in cash (§2.4(b));
> d. The Series A Preferred Stock holders were granted a "right of first offer" which assured each investor the opportunity to purchase sufficient shares to maintain its proportionate interest in the equity structure of [Sorrento] each time the company offered equity interests (§2.4).

While Sorrento did not go public and did not become profitable, its capacity to consume cash continued. It borrowed more than $36 million from Osicom. Sorrento's indebtedness in at least that amount has continued to the present.

Between mid-April 2001 and early May 2001, Plaintiffs exercised their rights under the Investors' Rights Agreement to redeem their shares. Sorrento rebuffed these efforts with the explanation that it lacked sufficient legally available funds to meet its redemption obligations.

Less than two weeks after receiving the first redemption request, Sorrento, as authorized by an April 26, 2001 board resolution, filed with Delaware's Secretary of

---

6. Re-incorporation in Delaware appears to have been part of a failed IPO effort.

State a certificate of amendment, which purported to authorize an additional 15 million shares of Series A Preferred Stock. No prior approval from the holders of Series A Preferred Stock had been sought or obtained.

Sorrento's board, at the April 26th meeting, approved the sale of 899,437 additional shares of Series A Preferred Stock to Osicom at a price of $5.45 per share. The number of shares issued to Osicom was sufficient, at that time, to reduce the percentage of the Series A shares for which redemption had been sought to slightly below the 50% threshold for redemption. No approval of the Series A holders was sought and no right of first offer was extended until more than two weeks after the sale had closed. No holder of the Series A Preferred Stock exercised its right of first offer.

[P]laintiffs obtained a copy of Osicom's SEC Form 8-K, which indicated that Osicom would acquire more than 6.6 million shares of Sorrento's Series A Preferred Stock to extinguish Sorrento's indebtedness to it. If implemented, that transaction would have reduced Plaintiffs' interests in the Series A Preferred Stock to below 50%.

Plaintiffs promptly, on August 6, 2001, filed this action seeking, *inter alia,* a temporary restraining order prohibiting the issuance of additional Series A Preferred Stock. This Court heard that application on August 7, 2001. However, on August 6, 2001, apparently after it had received notice of the pendency of the temporary restraining order application, Sorrento issued 2.7 million shares of Series A Preferred Stock to Osicom for which Osicom paid $5.45 per share in cash. Sorrento, at the hearing before this Court on August 7, 2001, did not disclose to the Court or to Plaintiffs' counsel that these additional Series A shares had been issued.[13] Evidently, Plaintiffs first learned of the issuance of the additional shares of Series A Preferred Stock on receipt of discovery on or about August 15, 2001.

At the close of the August 7th hearing, the Court issued a temporary restraining order precluding Sorrento from issuing additional shares of Series A Preferred Stock.

II. ANALYSIS

Issuance of additional Series A Preferred Stock has not been supported by the holders of a majority of the outstanding shares of the Series A Preferred Stock. Thus, by the clear language of the Certificate, Sorrento cannot issue additional shares of Series A Preferred Stock if those shares constitute "any other equity security." Plaintiffs and Sorrento part ways, however, on whether additional shares of Series A Preferred Stock are included within the meaning of the phrase "any other equity security."

I start with the plain meaning of the words chosen by sophisticated parties advised by experienced counsel. The phrase "equity security" is defined as "[a] security representing an ownership interest in a corporation, such as a share of stock."[18] The word "other" means "more, additional."[19] Thus, a fair reading of

---

13. Sorrento had not informed its Delaware counsel that it had issued the 2.7 million shares and, accordingly, the failure to disclose this significant development was not the fault of Delaware counsel. Sorrento's counsel in California attended the temporary restraining order hearing on August 7, 2001, by teleconference, but chose not to be forthcoming.

18. *Black's Law Dictionary* 1359 (7th ed. 1999).

"any other equity security" equates to "any additional share." Because the additional shares of Series A Preferred Stock that Sorrento has issued and will issue, if not enjoined, constitute "additional shares" of Series A Preferred Stock, issuance of the additional shares is proscribed by the words chosen by the drafters of Article V.D.6(a)(ii) when those words are given their commonly accepted meaning.

The words employed by contract (or certificate of incorporation) drafters must be evaluated in light of the apparent purposes of the drafters. The language at issue is critical to the protective provisions which clearly were designed to benefit the holders of the Series A Preferred Stock by assuring them that their interests would not be diluted without prior majority approval. Many rights of those holders may be waived upon approval by the holders of more than 50% of the Series A Preferred Stock. The apparent intent of the protective provisions is to protect against the issuance of more equity, without the consent of the holders of a majority of the Series A Preferred Stock, that could result in a reduction of their rights through a restructuring of Sorrento's equity. If Sorrento could avoid the protective provisions drafted for the benefit of the holders of the Series A Preferred Stock simply by issuing more Series A Preferred Stock, then the provision would not serve its apparent purpose. Thus, the plain meaning of the phrase at issue as construed above is consistent with the intent of the drafters as manifested in the Certificate's protective provisions.

Sorrento vigorously contests any interpretation of the phrase "any other equity security" that would restrict its ability to issue more Series A Preferred Stock. First, Sorrento argues that the "other equity security" is any equity security that is not subject to approval by the holders of Series A Preferred Stock. Sorrento reads the provision to restrict the issuance of any equity security other than Series A Preferred Stock or, more specifically, as "any other series or class of equity security." Sorrento's "other than" or "different from" logic does not plainly show that the antecedent of "other" for these purposes is Series A Preferred Stock and not those outstanding shares of Series A Preferred Stock.[21] If the antecedent of "other" is the outstanding shares, then all new shares would be "other than" the issued shares. Thus, Sorrento has not demonstrated that the plain and express language supports its proposed construction of the phrase "any other equity security."

Second, Sorrento contends that the phrase "any other equity security" is ambiguous and must be construed against Plaintiffs. Sorrento correctly argues that the rights and preferences of holders of preferred stock must be clearly stated, are strictly construed, and are subject to the interpretative standard that any ambiguity must be resolved against them. Sorrento devotes so much attention to its unavailing plain meaning argument that it has not developed in detail its argument that the critical language in the certificate is ambiguous. Presumably, Sorrento would have the Court focus on the question of "other than what" equity security, i.e., what is the antecedent of "other"? The Court, at least at this stage, has accepted Plaintiffs' argument that "equity security" refers to a "share" or "unit of ownership" (as

19. *Webster's Third New International Dictionary* 1598 (3d ed. 1993).

21. The Certificate at Art. V.C. provides that the first series of Preferred Stock will consist of 10,000,000 shares of Series A Preferred Stock. The Plaintiffs would be hard pressed to (and do not seriously) argue that issuance in April and August, 2001 of enough additional shares to reach the 10,000,000 share level was wrongful since they entered into their investment with the understanding that Series A Preferred Stock would eventually consist of 10,000,000 shares.

opposed to a series or class of stock). If "equity security" in that context refers to shares (and not to a series) of preferred stock, then it refers back to the "outstanding shares." Thus, while the construction of the phrase is not a simple task and while the language may have been drafted more crisply, it is not ambiguous. That good lawyers can conjure up challenging arguments about multiple meanings of a word or a phrase does not necessarily make the word or phrase ambiguous.

Third, Sorrento asserts that Plaintiffs' suggested construction fails to give meaning to the word "other," thus violating the canon of construction that consideration should be given to every word. In Sorrento's view, Plaintiffs' construction of "any other equity security" is the functional equivalent of "any equity security," since no approval could be required for those shares previously issued. One answer is that "other" when construed to mean "additional" makes apparent that the protective provision applies only to those shares of Series A Preferred Stock that are beyond those already issuable under the Certificate.

Although Sorrento seeks to employ the interpretive guideline to give meaning to all portions of the Certificate, application of that precept actually supports Plaintiffs' reading of the Certificate. For example, under . . . the Certificate, the dividends for Series A Preferred Stock, the liquidation rights and the conversion rights are all determined with reference to the $5.45 per share price for the initial Series A Preferred Stock private placement. Osicom (or anyone else for that matter) is not required by any of the transactional documents to pay $5.45 per share for additional (newly issued) Series A Preferred Stock. Sorrento would have the Court construe the carefully negotiated Certificate as allowing, without approval by the holders of a majority of the outstanding shares, the sale of additional Series A Preferred Stock (with significant rights based on a per share price of $5.45) at some other, and presumably lower, price. It is unlikely that a reasonable drafter would have intended such a result, but Sorrento's interpretation would permit it.

Moreover, Sorrento's interpretation of Article V.D.6(a)(ii) may be viewed as rendering that provision meaningless. Given the purposes of the protective provisions, apparent from the Certificate itself, Sorrento's interpretation defeats Plaintiffs' ability to safeguard their investment. If Sorrento is indeed free to issue up to 25,000,000 shares of Series A Preferred Stock without the approval of the holders of Series A Preferred Stock, then it would be empowered either to eliminate the efficacy of the protective provisions or, if one considers the right of first offer contained in the Investors' Rights Agreement, to compel the Series A holders to contribute significant additional funds to Sorrento in order to preserve the rights which they had already bargained for, paid for, and, presumably, acquired. Sorrento defends its position by suggesting that "[t]he holders of the Series A Preferred Stock continue to have a series vote on the issuance of any senior or parity equity that does not have the precise terms of the Series A Preferred Stock." [S]orrento's interpretation, even when viewed charitably, requires the Court to divine a wide breach in the protective provisions so carefully negotiated. While the Court cannot find or create rights for a preferred stockholder where the certificate does not grant them, it, nevertheless, is not required to struggle to reduce carefully drafted language into insignificance. In short, the precept that the entire document should be construed harmoniously, if possible, favors Plaintiffs' construction of Sorrento's Certificate.

Fourth, Sorrento contends that anti-dilution concerns and other problems such as the potential for issuing Series A Preferred Stock at a price less than $5.45 per share are resolved by the right of first offer in the Investors' Rights Agreement. Under the right of first offer, the holders of Series A Preferred Stock are entitled to purchase shares, when issued, in proportion to their holdings in order to avoid any consequence that might arise from a diminution of their proportionate holdings.

The right to purchase on a pro rata basis any newly issued shares does provide a rational means for addressing anti-dilution concerns. However, because a holder may have the right to purchase new shares does not necessarily lead to the conclusion that the protective provisions of the Certificate do not also serve an anti-dilution function. If nothing else, the right of first offer provides an option to the holder who opposes the issuance of additional shares of Series A Preferred Stock even if the holders of a majority of the outstanding shares approve the issuance of additional shares.

In short, given the numerous rights of the holders of Series A Preferred Stock that depend upon collective ownership of a certain percentage of the issued shares, the Court is not willing, at least at this stage, to interpret either the Certificate or any of the other transactional documents to require the Plaintiffs (and other holders of Series A Preferred Stock) to confront the choice of contributing additional funds to what was to have been a short-term investment or accepting the risk of dilution of equity ownership and the potentially adverse consequences that might accompany such dilution.

In sum, Plaintiffs were induced to invest in Sorrento through a certificate of incorporation (and related transactional documents) that afforded significant protection to their investment by . . . imposing restrictions on Sorrento's ability to issue additional equity, including shares of Series A Preferred Stock. [I]n the absence of injunctive relief, Sorrento is likely to continue to issue additional shares of Series A Preferred Stock with the foreseeable (and from Sorrento's perspective, welcomed) consequence of diluting Plaintiffs' equity interests. Plaintiffs have demonstrated a reasonable likelihood of success on the merits. . . . They have also demonstrated the risk of imminent and irreparable harm. . . . The balancing of equities and hardships decidedly tilts in favor of Plaintiffs, who are being denied the benefits of their bargain and the reasonable expectation of effective and continuing protective provisions. Sorrento's ability to raise additional funds without the consent of the holders of a majority of the Series A Preferred Stock may well be limited, but that is the result of the bargain that it made, and, more significantly, the likelihood of exhausting its cash reserves pending final determination seems unlikely, at least on the present record. Accordingly, after balancing all of these considerations, the Court concludes that a preliminary injunction is warranted to preserve the rights of Plaintiffs established by the protective provisions of the Certificate.

III. CONCLUSION

For the foregoing reasons, the Court is entering an Order . . . preliminarily enjoining Sorrento and those acting in concert with it from . . . issuing additional shares of Series A Preferred Stock, without the prior approval of the holders of a majority of the Series A Preferred Stock. . . .

Notes and Questions

1. Notes

a. Osicom was a publicly held corporation that undertook several startup businesses of which Sorrento's was the most successful.

b. The plaintiffs, who were venture capitalists, also negotiated for restrictions on Sorrento's ability to incur debt without the approval of the Series A stockholders.

2. Reality Check

a. What is the basic business dispute that lead to the legal dispute?

b. Describe each party's definition of the phrase, "any other equity security." Why does it matter which interpretation is correct?

c. How does Vice Chancellor Noble choose between those interpretations?

d. Why does it matter whether the venture capitalists own over 50 percent of the outstanding preferred stock?

e. Could Sorrento have legally issued any more Series A Preferred Stock?

f. Why doesn't the "right of first offer" sufficiently protect the venture capitalists' interests?

3. Suppose

a. Suppose Sorrento's Certificate of Incorporation had originally authorized 25 million of Series A Preferred Stock. Would that have affected the result? *See* footnote 21.

4. What Do You Think?

a. Do you believe the venture capitalists acted improperly by not agreeing to invest more money in Sorrento or, alternatively, by not, in effect, allowing Osicom to find additional sources of financing?

b. Vice Chancellor Noble implies that Osicom acted improperly on August 6th when it caused Sorrento to issue 2.7 million shares of Series A Preferred Stock for about $14.7 million. Do you agree?

5. You Draft It

a. The most central language at issue was found in Sorrento's Certificate of Incorporation:

(a) [S]o long as any shares of Series A Preferred Stock are outstanding, the Corporation shall not without first obtaining the approval . . . of the holders of at least a majority of the then outstanding shares of Series A Preferred Stock:

(ii) authorize or issue, or obligate itself to issue, any other equity security, including any other security convertible into or exercisable for any equity security having a preference over, or being on a parity with, the Series A Preferred Stock with respect to voting, dividends or upon liquidation . . . ,

Redraft this provision so it clearly effects the plaintiffs' best interests. Then redraft it so it clearly effects the defendant's best interests.

*statutorily
authorized*

issued

outstanding

c. The Mechanics of Issuing Stock

In this section we consider the corporate law mechanics involved in the actual issuance of stock. We explore the three principal concepts involved in validly issuing stock: *statutorily authorized*, *issued* (including the kind and amount of valid consideration), and *outstanding*. As you will see, each of these terms has a specialized meaning and lawyers must be aware of those meanings as they advise their corporate clients. We then turn to a further legal implication of issuing stock, preemptive rights.

i. Statutory Authorization.   Chapter 5 explained that the Articles of Incorporation must contain a statement of the number and kinds of shares that the corporation may — is *authorized* to — issue. *See* MBCA §§1.40, 2.02(a)(2), and 6.01(a), and DGCL §102(a)(4). The number of shares is essentially arbitrary although, as Chapter 5 detailed, the corporate planner must decide whether more shares are to be authorized than are currently anticipated to be issued to investors. If a corporation desires to issue more shares than its Articles of Incorporation authorize, it must amend the Articles, a process that is time-consuming and somewhat cumbersome because the amendment must usually be approved at a shareholder meeting. *See* Chapter 14 for a discussion of amending the Articles of Incorporation. A corporation that purports to issue more shares than it has authorized has acted illegally, and the newly issued shares, called an *overissue*, were void at common law although both the DGCL and the MBCA now provide a path to validate some overissues. *See* MBCA §§1.45-1.52 and DGCL §§204 and 205.

We have seen that a corporation may want to issue stock with different attributes than the default qualities provided in the statute. The attributes of such stock, and the ways in which that stock differs from other stock the company may issue, must be set forth in the Articles of Incorporation so that shareholders are protected by knowing exactly what rights they have as stockholders and how those rights compare to the rights of holders of other kinds of stock. Each separate type of stock must also be given a separate name such as "$1 Cumulative Preferred Shares" or "Class B Common Shares." *See* MBCA §6.01(a) and DGCL §102(a)(4).

But it frequently happens that the terms of stock to be issued are subject to considerable negotiation between the corporation and the potential investors and that time is of the essence for all. Because it would jeopardize so many potential issuances of noncommon stock for the corporation to have to seek shareholder approval of an amendment to the Articles of Incorporation and would likewise be impossible to predict the precise terms of noncommon stock in advance so that those terms can be included in the Articles from the initial incorporation, the statutes provide that the Articles may include a provision authorizing more than one class (i.e., preferred as well as common) and more than one series of stock with such attributes as the board decides. The maximum number of noncommon shares must still be stated in the Articles, but the terms of those shares can be decided later, as the corporation is prepared to sell them to an investor. Once the terms of the new stock have been agreed upon, the corporation's board of directors adopts a resolution setting out the terms and files that resolution with the Secretary of State. That resolution becomes a part of the Articles of Incorporation and thus a public record.

A provision allowing this procedure is said to be a *blank check* provision that authorizes *blank stock*. *See* MBCA §6.02 and DGCL §§102(a)(4) and 151(g).

ii. Issuance of Stock.   Simply because shares of stock have been authorized in the Articles of Incorporation does not mean that anyone owns them. The process of putting statutorily authorized shares in the hands of investors is called *issuance*.[19] Issuance comprises two other concepts: the board must approve (authorize) the issuance of the shares and the corporation must receive appropriate consideration. When this happens, the shares are said to have been *validly issued* and *fully paid* and are therefore *nonassessable*.[20]

(A) Board Authorization.   The requirement that stock must be authorized means not only that the appropriate number of shares must be permitted by the Articles of Incorporation. It also means that the corporation, acting through its board of directors, has approved a particular transaction in which statutorily authorized shares will be exchanged for consideration. *See* MBCA §6.21(b) and DGCL §161. Although the mechanics of board authorization are no different in this setting from in any other (and therefore are covered in detail in Chapter 9) and are easily met, the board's failure to observe the statutory requirements can throw significant doubt on the corporation's and the board's power. In the real world, such failures happen with some regularity.

> This action . . . depends, in large part, on whether the corporations' past directors followed the formal requirements of the Delaware General Corporation Law (the "DGCL") when issuing stock.
>
> Plaintiffs John Boris ("John") and Ann Boris ("Ann") filed this action . . . against Defendant Mary Schaheen ("Mary") and Nominal Defendants Numoda Technologies, Inc. ("Numoda Tech.") and Numoda Corporation ("Numoda Corp."). On November 9, 2012, John and Ann acted by written consent . . . as purported majority stockholders to remove Mary from, and elect themselves to, the [board of directors] of Numoda Corp. . . . With this lawsuit, John and Ann have requested the Court to confirm these acts were valid.
>
> John, Ann, and Mary are siblings. Numoda Corp. was their family business: Ann, considered the founder, contributed several patents and invested the proceeds from the sale of personal assets; John invested money earned from his law practice; and Mary brought her business and management expertise. Over the years, they have held various positions at Numoda Corp.: John has been Secretary and General Counsel; Ann has been Secretary and Chief Operating Officer; and Mary has been Chief Executive Officer ("CEO") and President.
>
> As of June 2000, the siblings were all Numoda Corp. stockholders: John held 1,266,667 shares; Ann held 5,100,000 shares; and Mary held 3,333,333 shares. The current amount of Numoda Corp. stock owned by John, Ann, and Mary is in dispute.

---

19. You should be careful to note the term *issue* rather than *sale*. When the corporation exchanges authorized shares for consideration, the corporation issues them. When a shareholder exchanges shares for consideration, the shareholder sells them. This distinction may seem unimportant, and in the vast majority of settings it is, but sometimes the statutes and cases use the terms precisely and it is important to understand that the terms are not always synonymous. We will see this applied in Chapter 7 in connection with treasury shares.

20. *See* MBCA §6.21(d) and DGCL §152. Through the early twentieth century it was common for corporations to issue stock that had not been completely paid for. Such stock was subject to assessment for the remainder of the purchase price. This requirement became problematic when the original shareholder had transferred his or her shares. Because stock certificates are negotiable instruments, a transferee for value who had no notice of the remaining purchase price liability took the shares free from that obligation. So it became important for corporations and their creditors to ensure that transferees were on notice that the shares were subject to assessment by putting a legend on the certificate that the shares had not been fully paid for. This concern continues today, in the formulaic language on stock certificates that says that the shares represented by the certificate are "fully paid and nonassessable."

1. *The Corporate Governance System* Numoda Corp., not unlike some family-operated companies, had an informal corporate governance system. The directors gave no proper board meeting notice, held no proper board meetings, and recorded no proper board minutes.[15] The directors took no proper votes, and their votes were typically not reflected in any written instruments. Although the directors acted informally, the corporation's governing documents contemplated a formal corporate governance system. More specifically, Numoda Corp.'s Secretary was charged with responsibility for giving notice for board and stockholder meetings and for recording the meetings of the directors "in a book to be kept for that purpose." But, John could not remember if he ever gave notice about a board meeting as Secretary, and he testified that he did not record the minutes of any Numoda Corp. board meetings.

One of John's other responsibilities as Numoda Corp.'s Secretary was to manage the company's stock book (the "NC Stock Book"). The NC Stock Book contains the corporation's governing and other important documents. Included in this collection is Numoda Corp.'s original, official stock ledger (the "NC Stock Ledger") that lists, in John's handwriting, the stock issued by holder, date of issue, stock certificate number, and number of shares.

2. *Initial Stockholders of Numoda Corp.* Numoda Corp.'s initial certificate of incorporation authorized twenty million shares of common stock and four million shares of preferred stock. As of June 2000, the NC Stock Ledger reflected six stockholders:

- Certificate 1: Philip Gerbino ("Gerbino"), 2,500 shares.
- Certificate 2: Barry Unger ("Unger"), 2,500 shares.
- Certificate 3: Ann, 5,100, 000 shares.
- Certificate 4: Mary, 3,333,333 shares.
- Certificate 5: John, 1,266,667 shares.
- Certificate 6: Meyer Rothbart ("Rothbart"), 300,000 shares.

But, the NC Stock Ledger is, as John and Ann conceded, inaccurate and incomplete, although the parties disagree on the extent. The initial stock issued to John, Ann, and Mary was validly issued. The parties believe Gerbino, Unger, and Rothbart are not stockholders[25] and that PIDC Penn Venture Fund ("PIDC") is a current voting stockholder. PIDC was allegedly issued 1,016,950 shares of voting stock in November 2008 as reflected by Certificate 23. Because John and Ann would hold a majority of the stock listed on the NC Stock Ledger regardless of whether any combination of Gerbino, Unger, Rothbart, and PIDC was issued valid stock, the Court need not resolve those questions. Whether the NC Stock Ledger is otherwise inaccurate and incomplete, as Mary argues, is a question the Court must answer.

3. *The Informal System for Issuing Stock* The Numoda Corp. board sought to issue stock within its informal process for making decisions. The directors would informally meet and informally vote on the stock to be issued "in terms of percentage ownership." That is, they would agree on who should own what percent of the company, leaving it "up to Ann and John to do the calculations that translated that percentage ownership into the amount of shares issued." This process was employed to issue stock in 2004 and 2006, but the NC Stock Ledger contains no subsequent entries that might reflect an additional stock issue. Instead, according to Mary, Numoda Corp. would document these purported stock issues "on the

---

15. The parties dispute why minutes were not taken. John claimed that Mary, as CEO, "requested that there be no minutes." Mary denied this charge, although she did not dispute that the board normally did not keep meeting minutes.

25. The Gerbino and Unger stock certificates were never sent out and now include a handwritten notation of "VOID" on their face, both of which are facts that, in John's opinion, mean that these certificates and the underlying shares are void. John also claims that the stock issued to Rothbart was redeemed, as evidenced by that certificate's placement in the NC Stock Book. He claimed it was unnecessary to document these developments on the NC Stock Ledger because, since the certificates were kept in the NC Stock Book, this conclusion would have been clear.

Mary largely agreed, believing the stock for Gerbino and Unger was subsequently voided. At trial, Mary did not testify about the Rothbart certificate; at her deposition, she could not recall when it may have been redeemed.

Excel stock ledger that John was tasked with updating as issuances were approved" (the "NC Spreadsheets"). Then, the board would review and approve the NC Spreadsheets.

Of the few documents in the NC Stock Book, none is a written instrument—namely, a board resolution or a unanimous written consent—evidencing board approval of a Numoda Corp. stock issue.

Boris v. Schaheen, 2013 WL 6331287 (Del. Ch. Dec. 2, 2013)

* * *

(1) Subscription Agreements. Subscription agreements are contracts to purchase shares. If the corporation has been formed and is already doing business, a subscription agreement is simply an ordinary contract and thus does not present any legal issues particularly germane to business entities law. *See* MBCA §6.21(e). Before a new corporation has been formed, investors may contract among themselves and with the new corporation's promoters to purchase shares after incorporation. These preincorporation subscription agreements pose a basic agency problem of seeking to bind a nonexistent entity. Furthermore, because the investors often have agreed to invest only on the assumption that others will do so, there is a heightened concern with enforceability of such preincorporation subscription agreements. Niceties of contract law may suggest that a preincorporation subscription agreement may be only a revocable offer or may only bind certain of the concerned parties. To increase the certainty of such agreements and to broaden their reach, both the MBCA and the DGCL provide that a preincorporation subscription agreement is enforceable for six months unless another period is expressly agreed to. *See* MBCA §6.20(a) and DGCL §165.

(B) Consideration. The provisions dealing with consideration under both the MBCA and the DGCL are meant to deal with four basic problems. First, because each share is equivalent to every other share, investors contemporaneously purchasing shares from the corporation must pay the same amount per share. A second concern is that the corporation actually receive the agreed-upon consideration. This problem is acute where the consideration is to be received in the future. A third problem, related to each of the others, is the possibility that a corporation will issue shares to new investors at a price per share that is less than fair. The final problem is the possibility that the corporation's management will overvalue noncash consideration. These problems are addressed by statutory provisions and longstanding common law precepts.

(1) The Problem of Ensuring Equal Payment by Contemporaneous Purchasers (Par Value). The common law solution to this first problem was the idea of *par value.* When a corporation is being organized, the number of shares to be issued and the price per share are completely arbitrary. The only economic constraint is that the corporation receive enough assets to enable it to begin its business. So, in the simplest setting of a new corporation with one shareholder who will contribute, say, $100,000, it does not matter whether the corporation issues one share for $100,000 or 100,000 shares for $1 each, or any other such combination. In that sense the shares cannot be underpriced or overpriced.

This observation remains true, with a caveat, when more than one investor is making the initial investment. It still does not matter whether the corporation issues a few shares at a high price per share or lots of shares at a low price as long as the aggregate consideration is sufficient. But where more than one investor is purchasing from the corporation at the same time, each is concerned that no other contemporaneous purchaser is getting a better deal per share. Par value was a judicial presumption that shareholders had agreed that they would pay an equal amount per share (a par, or equal, value) when purchasing at the same time. This presumed agreement could be enforced by shareholders who purchased for more consideration than others who purchased at the same time. It could also be enforced by a corporation's creditors, if the corporation were insolvent and it were discovered that some shareholders had paid less than other contemporaneous purchasers. Statutes required corporations to state the par value of their shares explicitly in their Articles of Incorporation.

Two developments undercut the effectiveness of the par value system. First, case law determined that, although shares could not be issued for less than par value, they could be issued for more. *See* DGCL §153(a). Second, corporations that fell on hard times found that they could not raise more money, because no rational investor would pay par value and the shares could not legally be issued for less. These developments created a strong incentive for corporations to set very low par value, as low at $0.01 per share, and to issue shares for consideration substantially greater than par value. This virtually ensured that the corporation could raise money in the future because it was unlikely that the value of the corporation's shares would drop below par.

But this low par value technique eviscerated any protection investors derived from the knowledge that other investors were paying par value. The only thing they knew was that each other investor was paying *at least* par value but that par value was a very small percentage of the total consideration. From the 1920s states began to make par value optional and no–par value stock became more frequent. Although the common law rule required (and still requires) that contemporaneous purchasers pay the same price per share, par value is no longer a method of ensuring compliance with this rule.

Why should you care about par value if it is not required by statutes and does not really serve to protect either creditors or shareholders? First, a significant percentage of corporations have par value even though it is no longer required. Thus if you are called upon to advise such a corporation or to deal with such a corporation on behalf of a client, you need to understand how par value works. Furthermore, although Delaware permits the use of no–par value stock, its franchise tax rates penalize corporations that make that choice. Instead, it is advantageous in Delaware to issue low–par value stock. Par value also is important because it bears upon whether the corporation can pay dividends and, if so, how much it can pay.

The MBCA recognizes that the par value system does not provide protection either for shareholders or corporate creditors and is simply a trap for unwary corporate lawyers and their clients. Accordingly, shares under the MBCA do not have par value, although such shares can be issued if desired by placing a par value on shares in the Articles of Incorporation. *See* MBCA §2.02(b)(2)(iv). How are contemporaneous shareholders protected from the original danger that others are paying less per share than they? Simply through case law that provides relief (either by making the other shareholders pay more per share or allowing the aggrieved shareholders to recover the excess they paid) upon a showing of disparate share price.

(2) The Problem of Ensuring That the Corporation Receives the Consideration.   A second concern is with consideration that is to be received in the future. Such consideration presents the danger that it will not be received. This situation, of course, harms shareholders who have actually paid for their shares and creditors of the corporation. Classically, this danger led to the rule that promissory notes and contracts for future services were invalid consideration for shares even though, as an economic matter, such consideration may well have been of sufficient value. Over time, this blanket prohibition on future consideration was deemed too harsh. Today, any kind of property is valid consideration. *See* DGCL §152 and MBCA §6.21(b).

Corporations may take further precautions to ensure they receive the agreed-upon consideration for shares. First, shares that are issued for future consideration may be placed in escrow until all the consideration is received. This prevents their transfer to a bona fide purchaser for value without notice that the shares are not fully paid for. Because stock certificates are negotiable instruments, such a purchaser would own the shares free from the obligation to pay the remaining consideration, although the transferor would remain liable. *See* MBCA §6.21(e). Second, corporations may issue shares that are explicitly partially paid for. The remainder of the consideration must be paid on the corporation's demand or as provided in the agreement between the corporation and the investor. *See* MBCA §6.21 and DGCL §156.

(3) The Problem of Later Issuance at an Inadequate Price.   Where a corporation is just being organized, the only problems regarding consideration are ensuring that the investors will pay the same price per share, ensuring that the corporation actually receives the consideration, and ensuring that the total consideration will be sufficient for the corporation to begin its business. Once the corporation has commenced doing business, though, further share issuances raise another problem: ensuring that the shares are issued at a price at least equal to the value of the currently outstanding shares.[21]

New shares issued at too low a price dilute the value of the existing shares. This danger theoretically leaves the corporation and the new investors liable to lawsuits by existing shareholders to challenge the consideration at which the new shares were issued. Where the corporation's stock is publicly traded, the market price is, presumably, the price at which new stock should be issued. In privately held corporations, though, there is no reliable objective reference to determine the value of currently outstanding shares. At common law, directors were liable to lawsuits by existing shareholders claiming that a subsequent stock issuance was at too low a price. To cut off this latent liability, modern statutes provide that the board of directors' judgment that the consideration for newly issued shares is adequate is conclusive. *See* MBCA §6.21(c) and DGCL §152 (directors' judgment conclusive in the absence of actual fraud).

(4) The Problem of Noncash Consideration.   When the consideration for shares is something other than cash, there is a danger that the consideration may be overvalued by the board. This danger is heightened when the shares are to be issued to investors connected in some way with the corporation's management, because

---

21. The new investors themselves are also, of course, concerned that they not pay a price *greater than* fair, but that is not, economically, a concern of the corporation or its existing shareholders.

the management obviously then has a concrete incentive to overvalue the consideration. In the late nineteenth century, this problem was thought to be particularly endemic and acquired the name *watered stock*. This name alludes to the deceptive practice of some cattle drivers who, at the end of the drive, would feed the cattle excessive amounts of salt to increase their thirst. The cattle would then drink copious amounts of water, which increased their weight. This added to the cattle driver's profits because the cattle were sold on the hoof with the price based on the cattle's weight. The problem of noncash consideration is a specialized instance of the problem of assuring that shares are issued at an adequate price.

Today, valuing noncash consideration has a renewed importance. This is so because so many of the most vital assets in businesses today are intangible "intellectual property." This property often is unique, which makes valuation comparisons to similar property difficult or impossible. Furthermore, such property frequently had no other, secondary, use, unlike physical property, which usually has some other value even if only for sale as scrap. Therefore, its value is a function of the success of the business's plan; if the plan fails, the property is worthless. For example, computer code (intellectual property) that coordinates online purchases of groceries and facilitates those groceries' delivery to the customer's home may be worth billions of dollars *if* customers will shop for groceries online. If they won't, the code may have next to no value.

These characteristics of intangible property make valuation particularly problematic. For our purposes, owners of such property who wish to contribute property in return for securities, other investors in the same enterprise who will contribute cash rather than property, creditors of the enterprise, and the board of directors of the enterprise are all keenly concerned that the property be fairly valued. Each constituency probably has a different view of the value of that property. Where the intellectual property's owner is also represented on the board of directors (a frequent occurrence in a startup company) the conflict of interest is clear and obviously increases the complexity of fairly valuing the property. At the core, the solution is the same as it always has been: the board's decision is conclusive, at least in the absence of fraud. Whether courts will take a harder look at valuations of intellectual property remains to be seen.

iii. The Meaning of *Outstanding*.   Shares are said to be *outstanding* when they have been statutorily authorized, validly issued, and remain in the hands of someone or some entity other than the corporation itself. The shareholder need not be the original shareholder; shares are still outstanding in the hands of a transferee as long as the transferee is not the issuing corporation. *See* MBCA §6.03(a). The concept of outstanding shares (sometimes referred to in the somewhat redundant phrase, "authorized, issued, and outstanding shares") has importance in two settings: Only outstanding shares are entitled to vote and only outstanding shares may receive dividends. *See* MBCA §§7.21(a) and 6.40 and DGCL §§160(c) and 170. Chapter 7 looks at the legal problems of a corporation acquiring its own shares.

iv. Preemptive Rights: The Economic Component.   Even if validly issued, a subsequent issuance of shares can harm current shareholders. First, the price at which the new shares are issued, although legally unassailable by current shareholders, may not, in reality, be the highest price available. Thus the value of the currently outstanding shares will be diluted by the issuance of other shares. Furthermore, current shareholders will have to share all future increases in value and future dividends with the new shareholders and would not have had to do so if the corporation had taken on debt rather than sold equity.

To protect current shareholders from these economic impairments, the courts of equity devised the doctrine of *preemptive rights*. This was the right of each current shareholder to maintain his or her proportionate interest by purchasing the same percentage of to-be-issued shares on the same terms and conditions as proposed by the board of directors. Preemptive rights were never absolute and were traditionally subject to several categories of exceptions. We will revisit the doctrine of preemptive rights when we discuss shareholder voting because, obviously, shareholders can be hurt in their management rights as well as in their economic rights by a new issuance of shares.

Under both the MBCA and the DGCL, preemptive rights do not exist unless granted by the Articles of Incorporation. *See* MBCA §6.30(a) and DGCL §102(b)(3). This represents a decision by the drafters of those acts that shareholders' economic and management rights are better protected by imposing duties on the board of directors than by granting shareholders preemptive rights. Speaking broadly, there are three settings in which the issuance of new shares does not trigger preemptive rights. The first is where the consideration for the new shares is something other than cash. The theory is that such noncash consideration is likely unique (such as intellectual property or a particular person's services) and therefore an existing shareholder's cash, even though nominally equivalent in value, is not a genuine substitute for the proposed consideration and so preemptive rights should not apply.

The second setting is where the newly issued shares are issued pursuant to the corporation's initial plan of financing. A corporation's initial plan probably anticipates several investors; delay in issuing shares to some of these investors is frequent. Denying preemptive rights to existing shareholders when the shares are to be issued pursuant to the original financing plan simply prevents opportunistic behavior among the initial participants. The final scenario in which preemptive rights are frequently unavailable is where the corporation has, or is to have, more than one class or series of shares. If the shares proposed to be issued are significantly different in management or economic rights than the existing shares, courts will frequently deny preemptive rights on the ground that the existing shareholders' rights are not being substantially affected by the newly issued shares.

Putting It to Work

Problem 6-2

Assume that you are the outside lawyer (congratulations) to PetroFab, Inc., a Delaware corporation specializing in producing chemicals used for natural gas drilling. Assume further that PetroFab's certificate of incorporation authorizes 100 shares of no par common stock. The corporation currently has 60 shares issued and outstanding, which are equally owned by A, B, and C.

The following events transpire in the following order:

1. The board issued 10 shares each to D, E, and F. The 10 shares issued to F were issued in exchange for the riparian rights on a nearby river, which the company believes is an auspicious drilling site. The shares issued to D and E were issued for cash. D and E paid the same price per share. A, B, and C were first approached about purchasing additional shares, but each declined to do so.
2. One month later, the board issued 10 additional shares to C. C paid cash in an amount per share that was 80% of the price paid by D and E the month before.
3. Six months later, the board issued 10 additional shares to A, B, D, E, and F. Each person paid cash for the shares in an amount that the board determined was the fair market value of the shares.

Assume that all board actions were taken at meetings at which all directors were in attendance and voted in favor of all actions.

a. What problems to you see with any of the board actions described above? Can any of the problems be rectified? If so, how?

b. How would your answers be different if PetroFab, Inc. were incorporated under the MBCA?

B. FEDERAL SECURITIES REGULATION

Nearly every "corporate" or "transactional" lawyer has some familiarity with federal securities regulation. The most frequent questions that arise for the corporate lawyer are whether a client's issuance of stock or debt is exempt from federal registration and whether a client is the perpetrator or victim of a fraud in which securities changed hands. Other areas of federal securities regulation that affect a corporate lawyer's professional life, although less frequent, tend to involve publicly held companies. These areas include compliance with periodic filing obligations, the regulation of proxies, and securities transactions by corporate insiders. More esoteric securities questions focus on the regulation of mutual funds, the regulation of stock brokers and stock exchanges, and the federal regulation of takeovers. Some lawyers specialize in securities regulation or in some aspect of that work. Focusing on securities work has many rewards. It is intellectually challenging, involves many important issues of national economic importance, and typically involves working with other lawyers who are equally knowledgeable.

Despite the many advantages, there are frustrations as well. The federal securities laws and regulations entail a welter of restrictions. Quite often these regulations provide counterintuitive rules of conduct. Furthermore, it often seems as if every word in every statute and rule is a term of art defined by significant cases. Although the treatment of securities regulation in this book is no substitute for a basic course in the subject, I hope you will pick up enough substance to identify points at which securities regulation may be germane.

First, a word about the hierarchy of federal securities regulation. The highest authority are acts of Congress, of which two merit our attention here. First is the Securities Act of 1933 (15 USC §77a) which is often called the *Securities Act* or the *'33 Act*. The second main act is the Securities Exchange Act of 1934 (15 USC §78a) which is often called the *Exchange Act* or the *'34 Act*. No one ever uses the official USC section numbers. Instead, the provisions are referred to by their original section numbers in the acts themselves.

Congress established the Securities and Exchange Commission (SEC) to oversee and enforce the securities laws. The SEC is an independent regulatory agency comprising five commissioners appointed by the president and confirmed by the Senate. Each commissioner serves for a five-year term and the president has the power to designate one commissioner as chair. The SEC has the power to promulgate regulations under the acts and it has done so in considerable detail. These are embodied in rules that are officially found in the Code of Federal Regulations, but, as with the acts, they are routinely cited by their SEC rule number rather than their CFR designation. Rules under the '33 Act are three digits; rules under the '34 Act are keyed to the '34 Act section under which they are adopted. Thus, perhaps the most famous SEC rule, Rule 10b-5, is a rule adopted under the '34 Act. It is the fifth rule adopted pursuant to Exchange Act Section 10(b). You should be aware that although Congress seldom amends the acts in significant ways, the SEC is constantly changing its regulations in ways large and small.

With this background, we discuss two aspects of federal securities regulation that affect the financing of corporations. First, we look at the definition of *security*, because the federal regulations do not apply at all unless a security is involved. Second, we examine the requirement that issuances of securities be registered with the SEC. In the vast majority of instances, registration is not required, but it is vital for a corporation's attorney to know which transactions are exempt from registration and why, as the penalties for failing to register when required are severe. In this connection, we also look at the process of registering stock so that it may be sold to the public.

1. Definition of a Security

You would think that a fundamental concept such as the definition of a security would be uncontroversial. It isn't. Both the Securities Act and the Exchange Act have nearly identical definitions that consist primarily of a list of investments that are thereby defined as being securities. *See* '33 Act §2(a)(1) and '34 Act §3(a)(10).[22] For our purposes, we need to focus on two more subtle notions. One excludes things that intuitively should be included (such as some stock and debt); the other includes things that intuitively should be excluded (such as ownership of a row of orange trees).

---

22. Section 2(a)(1) of the '33 Act provides: "The term 'security' means any note, stock, treasury stock, security future, bond, debenture, evidence of indebtedness, certificate of interest or participation in any profit-sharing

First, both acts state that their lists of items are defined as securities "unless the context otherwise requires." The Supreme Court has excluded stock in a nonprofit housing corporation because it did not have the traditional indicia of stock. That is, it did not have the right to receive dividends, could not effectively be borrowed against, could not be sold for a profit, and did not have voting power proportional to the number of shares held. *See United Housing Foundation v. Forman*, 421 U.S. 837 (1975). It seems unlikely that shares issued by a for-profit corporation would lack sufficient indicia of "stock" to be considered outside the definition of security.

More problematic is certain debt, such as a bank certificate of deposit or a promissory note, that might or might not be considered a security. The Supreme Court has, not terribly helpfully, adopted a "family resemblance" test for debt.[23] Some kinds of debt, such as a home mortgage, are excluded from the definition of a security. Other kinds of debt, corporate debentures sold to the public, certainly are securities. The task is to determine whether a particular instrument resembles a category that is included or excluded. The factors to be taken into account are (1) whether the motivations of the buyer and seller are akin to those who finance businesses; (2) whether the instrument could be amenable to common trading; (3) whether the investors would reasonably expect the federal securities laws to apply; and (4) whether the investment's risk is significantly reduced (thereby diminishing the need for the securities laws to provide protection) by another regulatory scheme such as federal bank regulation. *See Reves v. Ernst & Young*, 494 U.S. 56 (1990).

On the other hand, a seemingly innocuous instrument listed in the acts is the source for including any number of relationships that would not ordinarily be thought of as securities. In this regard, a lawyer must be careful to consider whether a particular undertaking might fall into this category. The term by which these investments are brought under the aegis of the federal securities laws is *investment contract*. In an early case the Supreme Court defined an investment contract as (1) an *investment of money* (nearly always easy to meet); (2) in a *common enterprise*, which means that the investor's financial success is bound up with that of others; (3) in which the investor has an *expectation of profit* (rather than some other return such as a place to live or fresh orange juice from the trees one has bought); (4) to come *solely from the efforts of others*, which means primarily from the efforts of others. *See SEC v. W.J. Howey Co.*, 328 U.S. 293 (1946). The *Howey* test is the catch-all of the securities laws. It is applied to determine whether partnership interest and LLC interests are securities (they may be or they may not be!) and has brought such things as cosmetics retailing arrangements under the federal securities laws. Any time you are counseling a client involved in an undertaking you should pause, however briefly, and run the *Howey* checklist through your mind.

---

agreement, collateral-trust certificate, preorganization certificate or subscription, transferable share, investment contract, voting-trust certificate, certificate of deposit for a security, fractional undivided interest in oil, gas, or other mineral rights, any put, call, straddle, option, or privilege on any security, certificate of deposit, or group or index of securities (including any interest therein or based on the value thereof), or any put, call, straddle, option, or privilege entered into on a national securities exchange relating to foreign currency, or, in general, any interest or instrument commonly known as a 'security', or any certificate of interest or participation in, temporary or interim certificate for, receipt for, guarantee of, or warrant or right to subscribe to or purchase, any of the foregoing."

23. Unfortunately, DNA testing does not help in this context.

2. Registration

a. Registration Requirements and Exemptions

The registration requirements are contained in the '33 Act and rules. Under the literal terms of the Securities Act, it is illegal to use a means of interstate commerce (such as a telephone, the mails, or the Internet) to *offer* a security unless a *registration statement* (which is a very elaborate document) has been filed with the SEC, and it is illegal to sell a security unless the registration statement has been reviewed by the SEC and declared effective. To compound the problem, the term *offer* has been quite broadly defined to include any attempt to arouse interest in the issuing company or its securities. Such an attempt might easily be construed to include favorable publicity about a company at a time when it intends to issue shares. On the face of it, this includes issuing stock in a startup corporation, a situation that occurs hundreds of times each day! The costs of registering stock are considerable, and the process takes months to accomplish. For those reasons, most planners structure transactions to avoid the registration requirements. We'll look at the process of complying with these registration requirements in the next section. Here the focus will be on identifying exemptions from these registration requirements. They fall into three principal categories.

First, the statute excludes certain kinds of securities, such as those issued by governments or by charitable corporations, from the registration requirements. These exemptions are largely unavailable for ordinary, for-profit corporations. Second, §3(a)(11) of the '33 Act excludes securities that are issued only to residents of the state in which the issuing corporation is incorporated and doing business. This is the so-called *intrastate exemption*. Rule 147 elaborates on the requirements for this exemption, which allows a small amount (20%) of the corporation's business to be done out of state. One trap for planners is that they must ensure that the purchasers are bona fide residents of the state and, more problematic, that they do not intend to transfer their shares to someone out of state. A single share issued or transferred to an out-of-state person renders the exemption unavailable. This restriction on transfer applies for (roughly speaking) nine months from the date that the last share was issued by the corporation. Many corporations issue shares in reliance upon the intrastate exemption.

The third principal kind of exemptions are the so-called *private placement* exemptions. These transactions are exempt from the registration requirements on several theories. The §4(a)(2) exemption is based on the belief that some investors have the sophistication and information to protect their own interests. Rule 506 is primarily justified on the ground that investors in such offerings will be either sophisticated investors, insiders of the issuer, or wealthy people, who presumably are either financially sophisticated or can at any rate afford the loss of their investment. The §4(a)(6) crowdfunding exemption is premised on protecting less sophisticated and less wealthy investors by limiting the amount they can invest. Finally, the §3(b) exemption is justified by the limited scope of the offering.

Section 4(a)(2) exempts securities sold by the corporation in transactions *not involving any public offering*. This is one of the key counterintuitive phrases in all of securities regulation. The Supreme Court has held that a public offering is one in which the offerees (regardless of how few) need the protection of the Securities Act, which is primarily designed to provide corporate information to investors. If all offerees can fend for themselves, there is no public offering and the transaction is exempt from registration. *See SEC v. Ralston Purina Co.*, 346 U.S. 119 (1953). Whether offerees can fend for themselves involves the interplay of two concepts: their investment sophistication and their access to corporate information of the kind that would be contained in a registration statement. Sophisticated investors who are given sufficient information (or realistic access to such information) can clearly fend for themselves. But investors, no matter how sophisticated, cannot fend for themselves if they are not given (or given access to) sufficient information. So, sophisticated offerees alone are not sufficient to make the transaction exempt. Although some courts of appeals would hold that providing sufficient information to an unsophisticated investor is enough to make the transaction exempt (on the theory that this setting replicates the protection provided by a registered public offering) other courts would hold that information alone is insufficient; some showing of sophistication is required.

SEC Rule 506 is a safe harbor (i.e., a nonexclusive method of compliance) for §4(a)(2). Under Rule 506, which is part of *Regulation D*, companies can offer an unlimited amount of securities to so-called *accredited investors*, generally institutional investors such as banks, officers and directors of the issuer, or individuals with either a net worth (excluding their home) of $1 million or an income of $200,000 ($300,000 if married) per year. Under this exemption, there is no requirement that the investor be sophisticated and no required disclosure (although any disclosure made must, of course, not be misleading or fraudulent). Rule 506 is, by far, the most frequently used exemption. Under Rule 506(c), an issuer can raise money from an unlimited number of accredited investors provided, in general, the issuer takes steps to ensure that the purchaser intends to keep the shares for investment and to prevent the resale of those shares to non-accredited investors.

Under Rule 506(b), an issuer can raise money from an unlimited number of accredited investors and up to 35 non-accredited investors. As with Rule 506(c), an issuer relying on Rule 506(b) must take steps to ensure that the purchaser intends to keep the shares for investment and to prevent the resale of those shares to non-accredited investors. However, an issuer using Rule 506(b) must also provide detailed information to any non-accredited investors and cannot offer the shares by any general solicitation or general advertising. These additional restrictions make Rule 506(c) preferable to Rule 506(b) for issuers. In practice, however, many issuers, especially small or nascent companies, cannot raise money solely from accredited investors and must resort to funding from non-accredited investors as well.

An exemption for *crowdfunding* is found in §4(a)(6) of the '33 Act. Crowdfunding is a method of raising capital by collecting small amounts of money from a large number of investors, typically through solicitation on a social media platform. Under §4(a)(6), companies can raise up to $1 million every twelve months, with limits on the amount that can be raised from any single investor based upon each investor's income and net worth. This exemption also regulates the electronic platforms, called funding portals, through which investors must invest.

The final private placement exemption, Section 3(b) of the Securities Act, allows the SEC to exempt certain transactions from the registration requirements either because they involve issuing securities for less than $50 million or because of the limited nature of the offering. The SEC has responded by adopting Rules 504 and 505 (which are included in Regulation D), which allow corporations to raise up to $1 million or $5 million, respectively. Under Rule 504, there are few restrictions (except, of course, a prohibition on fraud!) but Rule 505 requires that there be no general advertising and that the purchasers be either accredited investors, of whom there is no limit, or not more than 35 nonaccredited investors.

b. The Process of Registration — "Going Public"

While the vast majority of stock issuances are exempt from registration, and designed to be so, sometimes a corporation wants to go through the registration process. The goal in doing so is to allow the corporation to offer and sell its stock to anyone in the United States and, at least as important, to allow those persons to resell that stock without restriction on stock exchanges such as the New York Stock Exchange or the NASDAQ. The process of registration begins when the corporation negotiates with an investment banker to serve as the lead *underwriter* for the offering. The lead underwriter will form a syndicate of other investment bankers to buy the securities from the issuer, resell them to a broad cross-section of the investing public, and usually agrees to make a market (i.e., offer to buy and sell) in the security at least until a market for the stock has become established. The underwriters make a profit by purchasing the stock from the corporation at a discount from the public offering price.

As this negotiation proceeds, the company's lawyers, and lawyers for the underwriter, collaborate on drafting a registration statement on *Form S-1*. This is not a fill-in-the-blank kind of form but rather is a long (sometimes 200 pages) document that addresses precise topics prescribed by the SEC. In general, the registration statement details the corporation's business (and includes audited financial statements), the legal characteristics of the securities to be issued, and the issuer's intentions for the money to be raised.

From the time the company begins to negotiate with potential underwriters until the time the registration statement is filed with the SEC, a period of several weeks, the company may not "offer" its securities. Remember, this term has an extremely broad meaning and it is easy to violate this restriction. Once the registration statement is on file, the securities may be offered, but many restrictions on the kinds of written offers that may be made are still in effect. The SEC staff will review the registration statement and respond to the company with comments that, in theory, are supposed to be concerned only with the form of the company's disclosure but that, in fact, often go to the substance of the company's operational or financial performance. This comment period typically takes between three and six weeks. In the interim, the underwriters have lined up potential buyers. When the SEC is satisfied with the registration statement it declares the statement effective and the securities are sold to the underwriters and, in turn, to the public. Afterward, trading in the stock does not involve the corporation at all. Once the shares are sold to the underwriters, the company has received all the consideration it will ever receive for those shares. Subsequent price increases or decreases serve to provide profit or loss for the shareholders, not the company.

C. TERMS OF ART IN THIS CHAPTER

Accredited investors
Affirmative covenants
Angels
Blank stock (or blank
  check provision)
Bonds
Call option
Callable
Capital formation
Capital gain
Capital structure
Class of stock
Close (or closely held)
  corporations
Collar
Commercial paper market
Common stock
Convertible
Crowdfunding
Cumulative
Debentures
Debt
Defeased
Diluted
Economic realities test
Equitable subordination
Equity

Event of default
Exchange Act (or the '34
  Act)
Floating interest rate
Form S-1
Go public
Indenture
Initial public offering
  (IPO)
Intrastate exemption
Investment contract
Issued
Liquidity
Negative covenants
Option
Option writer
Ordinary income
Outstanding
Overissue
Par value
Participating
Preemptive rights
Preferred stock
Private placement
  exemption
Put option
Redemption

Registration statement
Regulation D
Reinvestment risk
Secondary trading
  market
Securities
Securities Act (or the
  '33 Act)
Securities and Exchange
  Commission (SEC)
Series of stock
Share
Shareholder
Sinking fund
Stock
Stock right
Stockholder
Subordinated
Subscription
  agreements
Syndicate
Underwriter
Units
Venture capital
Vest
Warrant
Working capital

7

Cashing Out: Distributing Money to Shareholders

In the last chapter we covered the basics of capital formation. In other words, we managed to get money into a corporation. Now we turn our attention to a related topic: how to get money out of the business. After all, a primary reason for putting money into a firm is the expectation (or at least the hope) of getting something monetary in return. This chapter focuses on getting money from the corporation into the hands of its shareholders. How do shareholders realize a profit on their investment? The next chapter analyzes the ability of creditors to compel payment to them when the corporation has insufficient assets.

In an economic sense, shareholders gain whenever the value of the business increases. Conversely, they lose when the value of the business decreases. But even if the value of their business increases, shareholders are unable to translate that increase into something else. They can't spend that increase unless it is somehow converted into money. Shareholders have two ways to convert the increase in the corporation's value into money.[1] First, the corporation can distribute the increased value (or part of it) to the shareholders. This is called a *dividend*. Second, a shareholder can sell some or all of his or her shares for (one hopes) more than he or she paid for them. Like most other property, shares of stock are presumed to be freely alienable.

Section A explores the corporate law contours of dividends. We look at the discretion placed in the board of directors to decide when dividends will be paid. We also cover the statutory restrictions on dividends. Finally, we examine stock splits and reverse stock splits. Section B deals with restrictions on a shareholder's power to transfer his or her stock. That section also covers the setting in which the shares are sold to the corporation that issued them.

---

1. All right, there's a third way, which is for the shareholder to borrow money using the shares as collateral. Analytically, though, this is really just anticipating a dividend or sale because the loan will have to be repaid either by future dividends or the proceeds of a future sale by the shareholder.

A. MAKING A PROFIT PART I: DIVIDENDS

1. The Current Setting

a. Board Discretion

Modern corporations statutes are straightforward, on the surface, in permitting corporations to pay dividends. Both the MBCA and the DGCL provide that a corporation's board "may" authorize the corporation to pay dividends, subject to certain restrictions we'll see shortly. *See* MBCA §6.40(a) and DGCL §170(a). This means that under the statutes, a corporation cannot pay dividends unless its board of directors approves. When the board authorizes the dividends, they are said to have been *declared*. Because dividends put wealth in the hands of the corporation's owners, why would a board *not* declare dividends when it could legally do so?

One reason would be the board's judgment that the corporation needs to retain the increased wealth to expand the business or to ensure that the corporation can meet future obligations. New businesses almost always need to retain all the wealth they can, so dividends in such corporations are a rarity. Another reason is that the corporation's shareholders may not need dividends to meet their ordinary living expenses. Because shareholders will be taxed on dividends but not on the increased but undistributed value of the corporation, the board may conclude that the shareholders are best served by retaining the increased wealth in the corporation rather than distributing it to the shareholders. This decision is most likely to be made in the closely held corporation where the board knows the economic preferences of its shareholders.

Publicly held corporations will, of course, have shareholders with widely differing economic needs. Typically, established public corporations pay dividends every three months, and an increase in the quarterly dividend is a signal to the investment community that the corporation is continuing to prosper. Conversely, a corporation that cuts or eliminates its dividend sends the opposite message to Wall Street. Thus public companies are usually conservative in their dividend policy because they do not want to increase the dividend unless they are fairly certain it can be maintained in the future for fear of sending the wrong message to investors.

Another reason the board may refuse to declare dividends is strategic. In closely held corporations the board may be controlled by one faction of shareholders that, by virtue of that control, has given its members employment with the corporation. Thus the controlling faction may have no need for dividends because it gets money in the form of corporate salaries. If the controlling group wishes to punish the remaining shareholders, it may refuse to employ them and may refuse to declare dividends. The only recourse for those noncontrolling shareholders to realize gain is to sell their shares. This may be exactly what the control group desires: to eliminate the other shareholders. As you may intuit, there are fiduciary constraints on such actions, but they are not entirely effective. Chapter 15 explores those dynamics in more detail.

If the statutes place dividends in the discretion of the board, and valid reasons not to declare dividends often exist, can shareholders ever compel the board to declare dividends?

More than 75 years ago, the Illinois Supreme Court addressed the issue before us, stating: "There is a difference of opinion among the stockholders as to the reason or desirability of maintaining so large a cash surplus, [one side] believing that . . . it is wise business management to keep a large surplus in reserve . . . , and the [other side] believing that good business judgment and wise economy require the distribution of a large part of the surplus. . . . These are questions of business judgment to be determined by the directors of the corporation in their discretion, which will not be controlled by the court so long as it is exercised in good faith and in honesty of purpose. . . . Each party has sought to avail itself of such advantages as the law gave it, but the record does not show *fraud, oppression, or dishonest conduct.*" (*Hall v. Woods* 156 N.E. 258, 268, (Ill. 1927) italics added.)

Less than 10 years later, the Illinois Appellate Court explained that "[c]ourts will not compel [the declaration of a dividend] on the part of a corporation unless the withholding of the dividend is *oppressive and entirely without merit.* Courts of chancery will not concern themselves with the operations of a private corporation except on the ground of *fraud* or an impairment of the capital structure which would result in complete or very substantial loss. . . .

"[W]e can see no reason for compelling a dividend, particularly in view of the present [economic downturn] and the present attitude of all corporations to conserve as far as possible its working capital for future contingencies. The question of a dividend at this time is one which rests wholly in the business judgment of the board of directors and a court of chancery should not substitute its judgment for that of [the directors] actively engaged in business in the community." (*Hofeller v. General Candy Corp.* 275 Ill. App. 89, 96 (1934) italics added, citation omitted.)

"The decision concerning the declaration of a dividend where a legal dividend fund is available rests within the sole discretion of the board of directors. Courts are reluctant to interfere with the exercise of the directors' business judgment unless the withholding is *fraudulent, oppressive or totally without merit.*" (*Romanik v. Lurie Home Supply Center, Inc.* 435 N.E.2d 712, 723 (Ill. App. 1982) italics added.)

Illinois law is in accord with a leading treatise on corporate decision-making: "The business judgment rule protects a board's decision regarding payment of a dividend or the making of a distribution. A court will not compel a distribution unless withholding the distribution is explicable only on the theory of an *oppressive or fraudulent abuse of discretion.*" (3A Fletcher, *Cyclopedia of the Law of Private Corporations* (2002 rev.) §1041.20, 58, italics added, fn. omitted.)

"The fact that a corporation has earned profits out of which directors might lawfully declare a dividend . . . is insufficient alone to justify judicial intervention compelling a declaration and payment. Because the decision of the board of directors to declare and pay dividends is protected by the business judgment rule, the burden of proof on the shareholder seeking to compel the declaration and payment . . . is particularly stringent." (11 Fletcher, *Cyclopedia of the Law of Private Corporations* (2002 rev.) §5325, 584-586, fns. omitted.)

State Farm Mutual Automobile Ins. Co. v. Superior Court, 8 Cal. Rptr. 3d 56, 70-71 (Cal. App. 2003) (Mallano, J.)

It is settled law in this State that the declaration and payment of a dividend rests in the discretion of the corporation's board of directors in the exercise of its business judgment; that, before the courts will interfere with the judgment of the board of directors in such matter, fraud or gross abuse of discretion must be shown, *Moskowitz v. Bantrell*, 190 A.2d 749 (Del. 1963). There, this Court quoted with approval the time-honored statement of Chancellor Wolcott in *Eshleman v. Keenan*, 194 A. 40, 43 (Del. Ch. 1937) that courts act to compel the declaration of a dividend only upon a demonstration "that the withholding of it is explicable only on the theory of an oppressive or fraudulent abuse of discretion." See also *Baron v. Allied Artists Pictures Corp.*, 337 A.2d 653, 659 (Del. Ch. 1975).

Gabelli & Co., Inc., Profit Sharing Plan v. Liggett Group, Inc., 479 A.2d 276 (Del. 1984) (Herrmann, C.J.)

Although these excerpts, which are representative of the rule in nearly every state, suggest that stockholders could conceivably compel the payment of dividends, the cases show a near uniform refusal to compel dividends in the publicly held corporation setting. In the closely held corporation, courts also generally refuse to compel dividends. The only setting in which courts seem at all willing to entertain the idea of forcing the payment of dividends is as a remedy for shareholder oppression. Chapter 15 deals with oppression and its consequences in more detail.

Notes and Questions

1. What Do You Think?

a. A primary way for shareholders to receive a return on their investment is through dividends. Because dividends are so central to shareholders' investments, do you believe shareholders should have more say over a corporation's dividend policy? If so, what rule would you adopt?

b. Do you think that the shareholders of a public company that has paid quarterly dividends for some length of time should have an enforceable expectation of a quarterly dividend? If so, when should that right accrue? Should the time be measured by the length of time the company has regularly paid dividends? The length of time the plaintiff has held stock in the company? Or a combination of both? Once an enforceable interest attaches, should the corporation have to pay exactly the same amount of dividends as in the past, or should the board have some discretion over the amount?

b. Statutory Restrictions

The board's declaration of dividends, while necessary, is not sufficient. Every state's corporations statutes restrict the ability of a corporation to pay a dividend even when its board wishes to declare one. The public policy behind these restrictions is that shareholders are not the only people interested in getting money from the corporation. That is, creditors, whether employees, suppliers, or lenders, have an expectation that they will be paid by the corporation. If the corporation is financially healthy, of course, these expectations will no doubt be satisfied.

If the corporation is in financial difficulty, though, the corporation's directors (who may also be shareholders) have a distinct incentive to ensure that the shareholders, in whose best interest the directors must act, get as great a return as possible. This means that the board may be tempted to declare large dividends if the corporation's situation seems hopeless. Conversely, the creditors have an incentive to prohibit all dividends so that as much as possible remains for their claims. In some settings creditors have sufficient bargaining power and sophistication to negotiate in advance for contractual restrictions on the board to limit or prohibit dividends. Nonetheless, statutes exist to prevent the payment of dividends in circumstances where creditors may be especially harmed. Unlike nearly every other kind of provision in modern corporate statutes, these restrictions are not waivable and directors are personally liable for knowing breach of these provisions. *See* MBCA §8.32(a) and DGCL §174 (directors liable for wilful *or negligent* violation).

Although every state's corporations statute addresses this problem, the MBCA and older statutes such as the DGCL take quite different approaches. Under the MBCA, a corporation may not pay a dividend if, afterward, "the corporation would not be able to pay its debts as they become due in the usual course of business" or "the corporation's total assets would be less than . . . its total liabilities" plus, the amount necessary to pay the preferred shares (if any) their liquidation preference. *See* MBCA §6.40. While these tests may appear to be mechanical, quantitative, and bright line, the statute specifically permits the directors to make the necessary judgments (i.e., that the corporation will be able to pay its debts as they become due and that the corporation's assets will exceed its liabilities) using any method of valuation that is reasonable under the circumstances. Thus the directors are not bound by the corporation's financial statements or traditional accounting methods if it is reasonable to depart from them. The MBCA approach is sometimes called the *insolvency test* approach.

Delaware and other par value states rely on the so-called *legal capital test* to regulate dividends. Remember that a share's par value is the minimum consideration for which it may be issued (and remember that today par value is typically set very low and that shares are typically issued for many times their par value). The DGCL defines a concept of *capital* that is related to par value. In effect, every corporation, even those that issue only no–par value stock, must have some amount of capital. When the corporation issues shares, the DGCL requires the board to designate how much of the consideration is to be capital. For no-par value stock the board need only designate some portion of the consideration as capital. For par value shares, the minimum amount that can be designated as capital is the par value. If the board does not make the requisite designation, the statute provides that the capital shall be the aggregate par value (for par value shares) and the entire consideration for no–par value shares. *See* DGCL §154.

The DGCL goes on to provide that a corporation's net assets (its total assets minus its total liabilities) less its capital is its *surplus*. *See* DGCL §154. Now, at last, comes the payoff. Dividends can ordinarily be paid only out of a corporation's surplus. *See* DGCL §170(a)(1). Thus in the normal course of a Delaware corporation's existence, you, as the corporation's lawyer, must be able to determine the total assets and total liabilities (for which you may rely on the corporation's financial officers or its outside accountants) and the corporation's capital. Subtract the total liabilities and capital from the total assets and you have the corporation's surplus and, hence, you know the maximum amount that may be paid to shareholders in dividends.

What is the point of requiring "capital"? As you see, this capital does not mean the money that is paid into the company. It is a much more artificial concept than that. For this reason, "capital" in the sense we have been using it in this section, is sometimes called "legal capital" to distinguish it from capital in an economic sense. Although a corporation's capital is a specific dollar amount, related to par value, it is not a separate fund. The capital needn't be kept in cash or kept separate from other corporate assets. It's just a number that has importance in declaring dividends. This fact alone should tell you that the legal capital test does not protect corporate creditors. It is, at bottom, a trap for those lawyers who are insufficiently alert. Nonetheless, because directors face severe personal liability for paying an unlawful dividend, you must understand this system and be able to conclude with some confidence whether a particular corporation can or cannot legally pay a particular dividend.

The DGCL provides another avenue for paying dividends, if a corporation has no surplus, it may nonetheless pay dividends up to the amount of its net profits for the current and preceding fiscal year. *See* DGCL §170(a)(2). Note that this process is available only if the corporation has no surplus. The DGCL does not define "net profits," leaving that concept to the board's good faith judgment.

c. The Mechanics of Paying Dividends

Once the board has passed a resolution declaring a dividend, the shareholders as a group become creditors as to that dividend, assuming the corporation has legally available funds to pay the dividend. Although a corporation could, in theory, issue checks to its shareholders on the date the dividend is declared, there is typically a lag time between declaration and payment. At a minimum, prudence suggests that a corporation wait until the board has officially declared the dividend because unexpected late developments may result in the board failing to make the declaration on the anticipated date. As a result, board resolutions typically fix a future date on which the dividends will be paid.

A further complication is that shares may change hands between the declaration and the payment. In a closely held corporation such a transfer may be unlikely, but in a publicly held corporation shares change hands every day. Who is entitled to the dividend: shareholders on the date the dividend is declared or shareholders on the date the dividend is paid? The default rule is that shareholders on the date of the board's declaration are entitled to the dividend even if they transfer their shares before the payment date. This *record date* is simply a way to fix the list of shareholders entitled to a dividend.

Under every corporations statute, though, the board is given the power to set a different record date between the declaration date and payment date. The reason to provide discretion to set a future record date is to give notice to current (and perhaps to potential) shareholders that an important event — payment of money — will soon occur. Those shareholders who intended to transfer their shares may wish to retain them in light of the dividend to come. Likewise, persons interested in becoming shareholders may have an added incentive to purchase shares before the record date so that they will receive the dividend. A timeline of about six weeks between declaration and payment is typical of a public corporation's dividend process.

The concept of a record date also applies to shareholder meetings — there must be a fixed list of shareholders entitled to notice of a meeting and entitled to vote. Suffice it to say that in the voting context the ability to set a future record date can be used strategically by the board to enhance the possibility of its views' prevailing. Shareholder meetings are covered in detail in Chapters 14 and 15. As to record dates for dividends, see MBCA §6.40(b) and DGCL §213(c).

Putting It to Work
Problem 7-1

Four wealthy entrepreneurial friends want to buy Chimy's, a local student hangout. They negotiate with the current owners and strike a deal to buy the business for $15 million. The four buyers form a Delaware corporation, the certificate of incorporation of which authorizes 5,000 shares of common stock with $0.01 par value per share.

The corporation issues 1,000 shares to each of the four entrepreneurs for $1,000 per share. The corporation then borrows $12 million from a bank and pays Chimy's owners $15 million in cash in return for all the assets and liabilities of Chimy's. The corporation then uses $1 million to refurbish and upgrade Chimy's.

Two years later, Chimy's is a huge success and the four shareholders want to see a return on their investment. They consult you to (a) determine the maximum amount of dividends the corporation can legally pay and (b) advise them how much in dividends the corporation could prudently pay.

Currently (a) the corporation has $300,000 in its bank account, which represents the excess of the company's revenues over its expenses for the past two years; (b) the fair market value of the business (including its bank account) is $20 million; (c) the corporation must make a $100,000 annual payment on its insurance within the next month; (d) the mortgage currently has $11.2 million of principal left to be repaid; and (e) the corporation's other monthly expenses, e.g., supplies, salaries, maintenance, monthly mortgage payments, can easily be paid from the business's monthly revenues.

Would your analysis change if the corporation were incorporated under the MBCA and the stock had no par value?

d. Stock Splits

There is one further concept to explore when considering dividends. You may have heard of a stock split and gotten the impression that such things are good. That's true in part but, as with many things generally pronounced to be good, a large part is illusory. As you remember, when a corporation is first organized, the number of shares to be authorized and issued initially is, in essence, an arbitrary decision. For example, if the new corporation needs $100,000, it probably doesn't matter whether it issues 100,000 shares at $1 each or one share for $100,000. Issuing more shares makes it easier for shareholders to transfer small proportions of their holdings, while issuing fewer shares makes such transfer more difficult. A *stock split* is simply the division of the outstanding shares into more shares. An old analogy is that a stock split simply divides the pie into more slices. Note that the corporation receives nothing in a stock split. Nor do the shareholders change their relative ownership interests. A stock split simply means that those ownership interests are represented by more shares. Nothing is created; no assets are transferred. In that sense a stock split is simply an illusion, although one that fools a great many people. As Yogi said, when asked whether he wanted his pizza cut into four slices or eight, "Four. I don't think I can eat eight."[2]

---

2. Yogi Berra, *The Yogi Book* 80 (1998).

Why does a board of directors want to split the stock? One reason, in the privately held corporation, is to permit transfer of smaller percentages of each shareholder's ownership. In the public company, the received wisdom of Wall Street is that stocks are most popular when they trade somewhere between $10 and $100 per share. This lets an investor buy a *round lot* (i.e., 100 shares, a typical trading unit) for $1,000 to $10,000. If a corporation has successfully increased its value, the price of its stock may, over time, approach or exceed the $100 per share level. At that point the board of directors may effect a split to reduce the price per share.[3]

Few corporations declare a true stock split. Instead, most "splits" are effected through a *stock dividend* of authorized but unissued shares to the existing shareholders. *See* DGCL §173 and MBCA §6.23. Under the MBCA, if the corporation does not have enough authorized but unissued shares, the board can, without shareholder approval, amend the articles of incorporation to increase the number of authorized shares, but only to facilitate a share dividend. *See* MBCA §10.05(d)(2). The DGCL does not contain a comparable provision. Under the DGCL, if the corporation does not have enough authorized but unissued shares, the board must seek stockholder approval to amend the certificate of incorporation. *See* DGCL §242.

If a Delaware corporation is issuing new shares, it must designate at least the aggregate par value of the newly issued shares as capital, which means that the corporation's surplus is reduced by that amount. Because the corporation has already received the capital associated with treasury shares, no capital adjustment is needed when the corporation declares a stock dividend using treasury stock. *See* DGCL §173.

As a matter of nomenclature, stock splits are expressed as a ratio as in a "2-for-1" split or a "3-for-2" split. It is important to realize that a 2-for-1 split means that, after the split is effected, each shareholder will *own* two shares for each share owned before the split. It does *not* mean that each shareholder will *receive* two more shares (i.e., giving the shareholder three shares in total). In a 3-for-2 split, for example, each shareholder will own three shares after the split for every 2 shares he or she owned before the split. This nomenclature is a frequent source of confusion for investors. By contrast, stock dividends are typically described as a percentage of the outstanding predividend shares. Thus a company that has 100 million shares outstanding and is declaring a 1 million share dividend is said to have declared a "1-percent dividend."

In some sense, the illusory nature of a stock split seems harmless enough. However, investors' misunderstanding of the effect of a stock split can lead to serious problems, as the next case illuminates.

---

3. Although in theory a 2-for-1 split should result in a halving of the share price (i.e., each share that was worth $100 is now two shares so each should be worth $50), in practice sophisticated investors believe that a stock split is a signal that the board foresees further increases in the firm's value and so the share price tends to fall by a bit less than half.

Mason v. Mason

904 A.2d 1164 (Vt. 2006)

Skoglund, J.

Wife appeals an order of the family court enforcing the court's final divorce decree by requiring wife to transfer to husband 8,033 shares of stock. We affirm.

The divorce decree in this case was based on and incorporated the parties' stipulation, which sought to divide a single item of marital property: 48,200 shares of Union Bank stock held by wife. Unbeknownst to husband, while the parties were negotiating the stipulation, wife received notice of an impending stock split, although the split did not actually take place until several days after the parties signed the stipulation and the divorce decree was entered. The upshot of this timing was that husband received post-split shares of a drastically reduced value. Thus, it appeared during negotiations that husband would receive shares equivalent to roughly one-third of the total stock value, but he ended up receiving shares that represented only one-fifth of the total stock value. We conclude that, because the entitlement to the stock split vested before the parties signed the stipulation and before the divorce was final, the 16,066 shares awarded to husband in the stipulation carried with them the entitlement to the stock split once it occurred.

I.

Wife and husband negotiated a divorce stipulation that purported to divide the marital property between them. Among the provisions of the stipulation was a paragraph acknowledging that the parties would retain their own investments and property that was in their individual names, with the exception of a certain number of shares of stock in wife's name. With respect to this asset, the stipulation provided that wife was to transfer 16,066[2] shares of stock to husband "immediately." Wife signed the stipulation on August 4, 2003, and husband signed on August 6, 2003. The family court entered its final decree of divorce, which incorporated the stipulation, on August 6, 2003.

Although she did not raise the issue during the parties' negotiations, wife had known since July 31, 2003, that the stock was due to split sometime in the near future. Wife learned of the split from her financial advisor, who received a notice advising of the split and explaining that the benefits of the stock split would go to all shareholders who were shareholders of record as of July 26, 2003.

Thus, wife was aware of the impending stock split during the parties' negotiations, when she signed the stipulation, and when the court entered its order incorporating the stipulation. At no point did wife share this information with husband (or the court, for that matter); neither did husband discover this information on his own. On August [8], 2003, the stock split three-for-two. Wife took steps to initiate the transfer of shares as early as August 6, 2003, but husband did not receive the 16,066 shares until August 14, 2003. By that date, the value of each

---

2. 16,066 shares represents one-third of the 48,200 shares wife held as of December 2002. The fact that the parties were basing the division of property on a number of shares held at a specific time in the past may explain why husband's award was described in terms of a specific number of shares rather than a specific value in or percentage of currently held shares.

individual share of stock had dropped by approximately one-third from its pre-split value. More importantly, rather than receiving one-third of the shares of stock to wife's two-thirds, husband now received only approximately one-fifth of the divided property, while wife retained four-fifths.

Husband filed a motion for relief from judgment which asked the family court to modify the divorce decree to award him the additional shares, emphasizing that wife knew of the impending stock split when she signed the stipulation and alleging that she had fraudulently concealed that information. Husband subsequently withdrew this motion, and instead filed a motion for enforcement, arguing that because the stipulation required wife to transfer the stock to him "immediately," he was entitled to the shares as valued on August 6, 2003 — the day the stipulation was signed and incorporated into the court's order.

II.

The trial court styled its decision as a ruling on the motion for enforcement, although it considered both of husband's arguments as well as other frameworks for assessing wife's conduct in connection with the stock split. Noting that the stock was the only marital asset the parties were dividing, and that the parties had intended a one-third to two-thirds division (although they memorialized it in the agreement as a specific number of shares — an approach recommended by wife's financial advisor with knowledge of the impending stock split), the family court concluded that the transfer of only 16,066 of the newly-devalued shares following the stock split "was not within the range of reasonable expectations" of the parties when they agreed to the stipulation. The family court emphasized that the devaluation in shares did not affect both parties equally, as it would have had the stock price changed over time as the result of normal market fluctuations, but rather husband's loss was wife's gain. The court considered it inequitable both that wife did not transfer the shares to husband "immediately," as required by the stipulation, and that wife permitted this delay despite the fact that she knew the stock split was taking place at the precise time between signing the stipulation and transferring the shares.

The court acknowledged the policy in favor of voluntary agreements between divorcing parties, but noted that even those agreements may be overcome where there is evidence of fraudulent concealment in the formation of the agreement. The court found that all of the elements of fraudulent concealment were present in this case. The court further noted that other states require divorcing parties to fully disclose all information known to them regarding marital property. Accordingly, the family court rejected wife's contention that the situation was husband's own fault for failing to diligently investigate the stock asset, because candor is the expected mode in the dissolution of a marital relationship. Finally, the court referred to the mandate of 15 V.S.A. §751, requiring that marital property be distributed equitably.

III.

There can be no disagreement that the situation engineered by wife and her financial advisor was inequitable and achieved through something less than full candor. The question, however, is whether an equitable result is possible in light of the parties' voluntary agreement, and if so, by what method? While we adopt a different approach from that of the family court, we conclude that result is correct and that there is ample support for that result in the record.

The goal of the stipulation was to divide 48,200 shares of stock between the parties. The parties accomplished the desired division by stipulating that wife would transfer 16,066 shares to husband "immediately"— presumably upon finalizing the stipulation, although the text of the stipulation does not clarify this point.

The right to the benefit of the stock split vested in shareholders of record on July 26, 2003. While husband was not a shareholder of record (and did not receive notice of the split for this reason), the stock was still marital property as of this date, and husband gained an entitlement to the split as part of the marital property. This conclusion is further supported by the mechanism of the stock split, which was for shareholders to "receive one additional share of common stock for every two shares they hold of record on July 26, 2003." Thus, the right to the benefits of the split attached to each individual share (or every two shares) referenced in the stipulation, even though the split had yet to take place.

Stated another way, as of July 26, 2003, every two shares allocated by the stipulation now represented not only those two shares but also the right to the additional share that would be generated at some point in the future by the split. Therefore, in awarding the additional 8,033 shares to husband, the family court did not modify the parties' allocation of the marital property, but simply enforced it. Wife is not entitled to arbitrarily and unilaterally decide that the shares allocated by the stipulation and divorce decree represented the post-split shares . . . , rather than the pre-split shares . . . .

We decline to address a number of wife's other arguments in light of our reasoning above, other than to note them here. Wife argues that husband should have taken into account the possibility of a stock split in negotiating the stipulation because stocks are subject to constant fluctuation on the market. In short, she in essence faults husband for failing to exercise due diligence during their negotiations. This argument is moot in light of our resolution above. Wife also argues that the family court could not rule on the allegation of fraud because husband had withdrawn that motion. This point is moot because our ruling is not based on a finding of fraud. Because the court's ruling is properly considered an order to enforce rather than modify the divorce order, and we affirm it as such, we do not address wife's argument that she was entitled to a broader evidentiary hearing before the trial court could modify the order. Because our decision is not premised on the notion that wife failed to transfer the stock "immediately," we do not address wife's arguments related to this finding by the trial court. Finally, our decision does not require us to conclude that the parties intended for the transfer of stock to husband to have a particular, set value. The only relevant factor supporting enforcement is that the entitlement to the split vested in the shares as of July 26, 2006, when the stock was marital property and the subject of the parties' stipulation.

By enforcing husband's entitlement to his designated portion of the marital property, our result in this case serves equity and our policy in favor of voluntary agreements to divide marital property by supporting the notion that parties should be candid and forthright with one another in negotiating those agreements.

Affirmed.

Notes and Questions

1. Notes

a. The husband's name is Jeffrey and the wife's name is Susan.

b. The corporation's board declared the stock dividend on July 16th with certificates to be issued on August 8th to shareholders of record on July 26th. The corporation issued a press release with this information and filed the press release with the SEC on July 16th and sent a letter with this information to its shareholders on July 30th.

c. In late July 2003, Union Bank stock was trading around $34.50 per share. On August 4 it closed at $33.80. On August 6 it closed at $32.40. On Friday, August 8, 2003, the last trading day before the dividend became effective, it closed at $32.30. The following Monday, August 11, it closed at $21.70 per share.[3] In round numbers, the value of the wife's 48,200 shares pre-dividend was between $1.5 and $1.6 million. The value of the husband's 16,066 pre-dividend shares was about $500,000 to $530,000. Post dividend, the market value of 16,066 shares was just under $350,000.

2. Reality Check

a. Husband voluntarily agreed to accept 16,066 shares of stock. Why is he entitled to an additional 8,033 shares?

b. Is the court punishing Wife for fraud or is it enforcing the terms of the divorce stipulation? If the former, in what way did Wife defraud Husband?

3. Suppose

a. At the same time the corporation split the stock, it declared a dividend of $0.30 per pre-split share, payable on July 30th to shareholders of record on July 26th. Wife, the shareholder of record, received a check for $14,460. If the divorce stipulation were silent, how should the cash dividend be apportioned between the parties?

b. Suppose neither Wife nor Husband nor any of their advisors had been aware of the stock dividend when they entered into the divorce stipulation. Would the court's analysis or the result have been different?

4. What Do You Think?

a. Do you think Wife acted fraudulently? Did either spouse act opportunistically? If so, which spouse?

b. At her pre-stipulation deposition, Wife was not specifically asked whether she knew of an impending stock dividend. Should she have volunteered that information? Should Husband's attorney have specifically inquired about her knowledge?

c. Do you think the spouses or their advisors had an obligation to investigate the capital structure of the corporation to see whether a cash dividend or stock dividend was planned? If so, who had that obligation?

---

3. As noted earlier, stock splits and dividends are generally perceived as positive news by investors, so the stock price per share tends to fall less than the increased number of shares would indicate. A 3-for-2 dividend suggests that price should fall by one-third, thus Union Bank's stock would have been be expected to fall to $21.54 based on the last pre-dividend closing price of $32.30. However, as you see, it fell only to $21.70.

d. Why do you think the parties gave Husband a specific number of shares? How else could the parties have described the division? Would those other descriptions have been better or worse than specifying a particular number? What risks — uncertainties — should the parties have anticipated?

5. You Draft It

a. The language in the divorce stipulation reads:

> Plaintiff shall have all right and title and interest in and to his TIAA CREF retirement account and defendant shall have all right, title and interest in and to the assets of the Susan S. Mason Revocable Trust except that defendant shall immediately transfer 16,066 shares of her Union Bank of Morrisville stock to plaintiff's name.

Redraft the agreement so that it supports Husband's claim. Then redraft it so it supports Wife's claim.

e. Reverse Stock Splits

A board may decide that it is in the best interest of the corporation for fewer, but correspondingly more valuable, shares to be outstanding. This may happen when a public company's stock trades below $10 per share. In fact, stock exchanges may *delist* (refuse to allow trading in) companies whose stock trades below $1 per share. To reduce the number of shares outstanding, the corporation may effect a *reverse stock split*, which is not a split at all but an amalgamation. A 1-for-2 reverse split means that each shareholder will have one share after the split for each two shares he or she owned before. Axiomatically, of course, each remaining share should be twice as valuable as before. Because shares cannot be taken away from shareholders without their consent, a reverse stock split requires an amendment to the articles of incorporation, which must be approved by the board and shareholders. *See* MBCA §10.03 and DGCL §§242(a)(3), 242(b).

Stock splits and reverse stock splits may have ancillary, and sometimes unintended, effects. For example, suppose a shareholder has borrowed money and put up "100 shares of XYZ Corp." stock as collateral. If the corporation declares a 2-for-1 stock split and the shareholder thereafter defaults on the loan, is the lender entitled to seize 100 shares or 200? The next case concerns another area in which this same question arises.

Reiss v. Financial Performance Corporation

715 N.Y.S.2d 29 (N.Y. App. Div. 2000)

FRIEDMAN, J.

Where a warrant to purchase stock is silent as to the effect of a reverse stock split on a warrant holder's right to purchase shares of stock, must the warrant be deemed, after such a split, to reflect a proportional change in both the number of shares that may be purchased and the price of each share? We conclude that, in the absence of any evidence that the parties to a warrant contemplated otherwise, the warrant holder, because of the reverse stock split, is limited to purchasing shares proportionally adjusted as to both number and price.

[In 1993,] the Board of Directors of defendant Financial Performance Corporation (Financial), [issued] a warrant to Rebot Corporation, permitting Rebot to purchase 1,198,904 shares of Financial's common stock at a price of 10 cents per share. The warrant was executed in consideration of a $187,328.79 loan that Financial was unable to repay to Rebot. [F]inancial's Board also gave authorization to issue a warrant to Marvin Reiss (who was, at the time, a member of Financial's Board and apparently Rebot's President), permitting him to purchase 500,000 shares of stock at 10 cents per share. This warrant was issued as an honorarium payment for Reiss' services on Financial's Board. Both the Rebot and Reiss warrants provided that the right to purchase stock would extend for a period of five years. . . .

In . . . 1996, at an annual meeting, Financial's shareholders approved a one-for-five reverse stock split. As a result, each stockholder owned one-fifth the original number of shares, with each share representing that amount of ownership previously represented by five shares of stock.

Thereafter, [in] 1998, plaintiffs sought to partially exercise their warrants. In seeking to do so, plaintiffs asserted that they were entitled to purchase shares of Financial in accordance with the literal language of the warrants without adjustment for the reverse stock split. Financial, on the other hand, asserted that any right to purchase stock under the warrants had to be proportionally adjusted to reflect the reverse stock split.

The line in the sand having been drawn, plaintiffs commenced the instant action seeking a judgment . . . declaring that Rebot and Reiss remained entitled to purchase 1,198,904 and 500,000 shares of stock respectively at 10 cents per share.

Analysis of the issue presented must begin with a detailed examination of *Cofman v. Acton Corp.*, 958 F.2d 494 (1st Cir. 1992), a case bearing striking similarities to the instant case.

[D]efendant corporation executed a reverse stock split that resulted in each stockholder owning one-fifth the original number of shares, with a concomitant increase in value for the new shares. A letter was then sent to the plaintiffs advising them of the reverse stock split and indicating that their [interest] would be deemed modified to reflect the split. The plaintiffs disagreed, contending that their agreement did not provide for any adjustment based upon changes in the structure of the stock.

The court . . . observed that, if plaintiffs' construction of the agreement were accepted, an absurd result would follow. In this regard, if the agreement were read literally, as the plaintiffs urged, the corporation could have eviscerated any possibility of the plaintiffs benefitting from the agreement by simply declaring a stock split, as opposed to a reverse stock split. Stated otherwise, the corporation would be able to dilute the value of its stock to such an extent that the plaintiffs' [interest] was valueless. This being so:

> "It defies common sense" that [plaintiffs] would have agreed that [the corporation] could effectively escape the specified consequences of a rising market price by increasing the number of shares. And if [plaintiffs] would not suffer from any increas[e in the number of shares], it would follow, since a contract must be construed consistently . . . [the corporation] should not suffer from any decreas[e in the number of shares]. *Id.*, at 497.

We find *Cofman* to be dispositive of the issue presented here by force of its logic. . . . In this connection, to accept plaintiffs' interpretation of the contract, namely, that the warrants did not allow for a proportional adjustment to reflect a reverse stock split, would necessarily mean that the warrants also did not allow for a proportional adjustment if there were a stock split. Flowing from that reasoning is the observation that Financial, like the corporation in *Cofman,* could have eviscerated the value of plaintiffs' warrants and escaped its contractual obligations by simply declaring a massive stock split instead of a reverse stock split. Here, as in *Cofman,* it defies all bounds of common sense to believe that plaintiffs could have ever intended such an outcome. We therefore conclude that, just as plaintiffs should not suffer from the possibility of dilution of their warrants resulting from a stock split, so too Financial should not suffer from the consolidation of its shares resulting from a declaration of a reverse stock split (*Cofman v. Acton Corp., supra; cf., Restatement (Second) of Contracts* §204 (1981), comment c [a term can be supplied by logical deduction from the agreed terms and the circumstances of the making of the contract]). Any other conclusion would ignore the plain intent of the parties in issuing and receiving the subject warrants.

Notwithstanding *Cofman,* plaintiffs and the dissent assert that a literalistic approach to the interpretation of the warrants is compelled as a matter of law. We cannot agree. Surely a court is not required to disregard common sense and slavishly bow to the written word where to do so would plainly ignore the true intentions of the parties in the making of a contract. Such formalistic literalism serves no function but to contravene the essence of proper contract interpretation, which, of course, is to enforce a contract in accordance with the true expectations of the parties in light of the circumstances existing at the time of the formation of the contract. We point out that no one makes the claim that there is any other evidence to be offered on the issue of the parties' expectations, other than what has been presented on this appeal. Nor does anyone claim that a trial is necessary to resolve any ambiguity.[4]

In any event, to the extent that the warrants may be viewed as not containing an implicit requirement for the proportional adjustment of Financial's stock upon a split or reverse-split, it means that the parties omitted what is undeniably an essential term of the agreement. Contrary to the dissent's contention, a provision dealing with this eventuality is essential since it fundamentally affects both the number of shares that may be purchased and the price to be paid. In a circumstance where an essential term is omitted, section 204 of the *Restatement (Second) of Contracts* is instructive. That section provides:

> When the parties to a bargain sufficiently defined to be a contract have not agreed with respect to a term which is essential to a determination of their rights and duties, a term which is reasonable in the circumstances is supplied by the court.

Here, following the *Restatement* approach, the only reasonable term would be the one consistent with the self-evident expectations of the parties when the warrants were executed, namely, a term requiring a proportional adjustment of both the number of shares that may be purchased and their price.

---

4. Although certainly not dispositive, plaintiffs themselves seemingly recognized the lack of logic inherent in their position. Thus, at oral argument plaintiffs were forced to concede that, had there been a stock split as opposed to a reverse stock split, they would have asserted a contrary position to that which they presently advocate and would have argued that the parties did not intend that Financial be able to dilute its stock to the point of rendering the warrants valueless.

SULLIVAN, P.J., and WALLACH and RUBIN, JJ., concur with FRIEDMAN, J.

SAXE, J. (dissenting in part):

The law of contracts offers relief from a hard bargain only upon a showing of fraud, duress, mistake, misrepresentation, illegality, impossibility of performance or unconscionability. But, when none of those grounds has been established, and the terms of the agreement under consideration are clearly set forth within the four corners of the document, courts should not alter those terms, even where the alteration achieves a more equitable result. As Judge Cardozo noted:

> A contract is made. Performance is burdensome and perhaps oppressive. If we were to consider only the individual instance, we might be ready to release the promisor. We look beyond the particular to the universal, and shape our judgment in obedience to the fundamental interest of society that contracts shall be fulfilled.
>
> Benjamin N. Cardozo, *The Nature of the Judicial Process*, at 139-140 (1921)

The warrants, by their clear terms, gave plaintiffs an absolute, unconditioned right to purchase the specified number of shares for the price set forth in the warrants, and nothing in the warrants permits their terms to be altered by a reverse stock split.

Defendant believes it to be "axiomatic" that a stock warrant necessarily converts in exactly the same manner as existing common stock converts upon any sort of adjustment to the form of the stock. However, this is an unfounded assumption. If stock warrants were deemed automatically adjusted upon consolidations or reclassifications of corporate stock, so that they maintained their proportionate value, there would be no need for the use of warrant agreements to establish the concept of proportional adjustment of stock warrants.

The majority, employing an analysis grounded in "common sense," reasons that the parties "must have" intended for the stock warrants issued to plaintiffs to be altered in the same proportions as actual shares of stock would be by any stock split occurring during their effective period. However, resort by a court to its subjective view of common sense is not a proper basis for a legal conclusion, particularly when it ignores both plaintiff's assertion of what the parties negotiated and intended, as well as "[t]he cardinal rule of contract interpretation . . . that, where the language of the contract is clear and unambiguous, the parties' intent is to be gleaned from the language of the agreement and whatever may be reasonably implied therefrom" (*see H.K.S. Hunt Club v. Town of Claverack*, 634 N.Y.S.2d 816 (N.Y. App. Div. 1995)).

There is nothing ambiguous about the terms of these stock warrants; they clearly provide that plaintiffs have an absolute right to purchase the named number of shares at the stated price within the defined time frame.

Furthermore, while a new contract provision may be added by a court if the additional term is "essential to a determination" (*see Restatement (Second) of Contracts*, §204), the majority's assertion that "the parties omitted what is undeniably an essential term of the agreement" is simply incorrect, since clearly the agreement can be enforced by reference solely to the terms contained in the document. These terms—amount, price, and time frame—constitute all the essential elements of the agreement. The term the majority believes to have been accidentally omitted amounts to merely a possible condition or limitation.

The majority's insertion of a limitation cannot be accurately characterized as a simple construction of the document's terms. Rather, the majority is actually altering a basic, definite term of the contract, as to the price at which plaintiffs were entitled to purchase stock of the corporation. However, the rules of contract construction do not permit an alteration of a clear contract term, based upon a change in circumstances not provided for by the parties at the time of the contract.

In view of the definitive language of the contract, grafting limitations or conditions onto those warrants amounts to rewriting the contracts, and may not be justified as the application of logic or common sense.

In modifying the parties' rights based upon their presumed intention in the event of future stock splits, the majority adopts the reasoning of the First Circuit Court of Appeals in *Cofman v. Acton Corp.* The crux of *Cofman* is that when the parties gave no thought to the eventuality of a reverse stock split, which thereafter occurred, the omission constituted an ambiguity, and the court could infer the parties' presumed intention on that issue by "reference to all of its language and to its general structure and purpose and in the light of the circumstances under which it was executed" (*id.* at 498 . . .).

Nothing in the language of the stock warrants or their general structure and purpose gives rise to an inference that the parties intended plaintiffs' rights to be automatically altered in the event of a stock split. Moreover, assuming that the purported omission creates an ambiguity, determination of the parties' intent is an issue of fact requiring consideration of the extrinsic evidence submitted by the parties.

Accordingly, at the very least, the finding of an ambiguity by omission creates a disputed issue of fact regarding the parties' intent, which must be resolved at trial. In concluding that the parties "could not have" intended an outcome in which a reverse stock split would have no effect on plaintiffs' rights, the majority weighs the evidence and rejects a factual assertion, neither of which is appropriate in the context of a dismissal or summary judgment motion.

In order to justify inclusion in the agreement of a new term that limits rights set forth in the document, the majority also offers the novel proposition that the court must consider not only the situation at hand, but what the parties' legal positions would be if the reverse situation had occurred. In other words, the majority is making a factual finding that plaintiffs necessarily would not have advanced the same argument had a forward stock split occurred instead,[9] in order to reject the plaintiffs' position in the context of a reverse stock split.

Interesting and, perhaps, commonsensical as this proposition at first appears, it has no foundation in the law of contract construction. The question of what plaintiffs intended when entering into the stock warrant arrangement must be answered based upon what the parties did and said, not upon what the court assumes they would be inclined to argue in a hypothetical situation.

Moreover, had a forward stock split taken place, plaintiffs need not have taken a position contrary to that they take here. Initially, they would have had the option they had all along: to decline to purchase shares whose value was lower than the option price. Additionally, in the event the corporation effectively reduced the value of warrants by arranging for a forward stock split, the warrantholders would be

---

9. The majority buttresses its factual conclusion regarding the plaintiffs' intent by referring to counsel's response to a question at oral argument. Of course, counsel's statements cannot properly be the basis for a finding as to the clients' intent.

entitled to challenge the corporation's conduct as violative of its obligation of good faith and fair dealing; they would not necessarily have to seek an alteration of the terms of the contract.

The concern expressed by defendant, namely, that plaintiffs will unfairly reap a "windfall" if their warrants are not deemed to have been automatically altered by operation of the Corporation's reverse stock split, should not affect the court's analysis of the situation. While an aversion to applying the precise terms of the contract under consideration here is at least facially understandable, the law of contracts offers no relief simply because the contract, as applied, may be unfair. This windfall could have been avoided by inclusion of standard terms and conditions referable to the stock warrants, a precaution which, for whatever reason, the corporation did not take in this instance.

Finally, as a practical matter, it should be recognized that the majority's ruling amounts to a reformation of the contract, in the absence of proper grounds. "Reformation is . . . solely for the purpose of stating correctly a mutual mistake shared by both parties to the contract . . . when it clearly and convincingly appears that the contract, as written, does not embody the true agreement as mutually intended" (*Nash v. Kornblum,* 186 N.E.2d 551 (N.Y. 1962)). Here, there was no mutual mistake in that there was no agreement to any terms other than those in the warrants, the provisions of the warrants were all intended, and no intended provision was accidentally omitted. Nor was there any fraud which resulted in a unilateral mistake on the part of the plaintiffs which would have induced the contract. What the present circumstances amount to is, at best, merely a unilateral mistake, namely, a mistake on the part of the corporation to make provision in the terms of the document for the possibility of an alteration in the character of the stock.

Accordingly, I would reverse. . . .

Reiss v. Financial Performance Corporation
764 N.E.2d 958 (N.Y. 2001)

SMITH, J.

Duly executed stock warrants are contracts entitling the holder to purchase a specified number of shares of stock for a specific price during a designated time period. Here, the warrants are enforceable according to their terms. They have all the material provisions necessary to make them enforceable contracts, including number of shares, price, and expiration date, and were drafted by sophisticated and counseled business persons.

That the warrants do not address the contingency of a reverse stock split does not, of itself, create an ambiguity. Even where a contingency has been omitted, we will not necessarily imply a term since "'courts may not by construction add or excise terms, nor distort the meaning of those used and thereby "make a new contract for the parties under the guise of interpreting the writing"'" (*Schmidt, supra,* quoting *Morlee Sales Corp. v. Manufacturers Trust Co.,* 172 N.E.2d 280 (N.Y. 1961)).

Further, *Cofman v. Acton Corp.*, the decision relied upon by the Appellate Division majority, is inapposite here. The Appellate Division, applying the *Cofman* analysis, reasoned that, in the event of a forward stock split, supplying a term providing for the proportionate adjustment of the number of shares that could be purchased, and the exercise price, would be necessary to save the warrant holders from having the value of their warrants "eviscerated." The Appellate Division then followed *Cofman* in taking a second step, reasoning that "just as plaintiffs should not suffer from the possibility of dilution of their warrants resulting from a stock split, so too Financial should not suffer from the consolidation of its shares resulting from a declaration of a reverse stock split." The second step, however, does not necessarily follow from the first. . . .

It may be that Reiss would be entitled to a remedy if Financial performed a forward stock split, on the theory that he "did not intend to acquire nothing" (*Cofman, supra,* 958 F.2d, at 497). We should not assume that one party intended to be placed at the mercy of the other (*Wood v. Duff-Gordon,* 118 N.E. 214 (N.Y. 1917)). It does not follow, however, that Financial should be given a comparable remedy to save it from the consequences of its own agreements and its own decision to perform a reverse stock split.

Chief Judge KAYE and Judges LEVINE, CIPARICK, WESLEY, ROSENBLATT and GRAFFEO concur.

Notes and Questions

1. Notes

a. A provision that adjusts an option to purchase stock in the event of an increase or decrease in outstanding shares is known as an *antidilution provision.*

b. Amelia Bedelia, the housekeeper with the literal mind, is the protagonist of a series of books by Peggy Parish. In one book, she is told to "dust the furniture" so she sprinkles the furniture with talcum powder. In another story she is hired as a file clerk and told to "file these papers." She takes a nail file and shreds them. Consider whether some of the judges involved in this case have read too many Amelia Bedelia books.

2. Reality Check

a. The question of antidilution adjustments is obviously an old one. How can the Appellate Division rule 4-1 in favor of defendant while the Court of Appeals was 7-0 in favor of plaintiffs?

3. Suppose

a. Suppose Financial Performance Corporation, for reasons unconnected with plaintiffs, effected a 5-for-1 stock split. If plaintiffs sued to adjust the warrants so that it could purchase five times as many shares at one-fifth the price per share, how would the court rule, and why?

4. What Do You Think?

a. Do you think Justice Saxe's view that "if stock warrants were deemed automatically adjusted upon consolidations or reclassifications of corporate stock, so that they maintained their proportionate value, there would be no need for the use of warrant agreements to establish the concept of proportional adjustment of stock warrants" is a bit circular?

b. Why is the default rule that no antidilution provision will be assumed? In what setting would parties ever explicitly agree to such a rule? Was it reasonable for Financial Performance Corporation to believe the warrants automatically adjusted for the reverse stock split?

c. If the court should impose an antidilution term, should such a term be symmetrical? In other words, should the warrants adjust when the outstanding shares are either increased or decreased? Or is justice best served by an asymmetrical antidilution provision?

d. Is the court impermissibly interfering with the parties' agreement?

e. How did this problem arise? Which side do you believe was more responsible for the problem? Should the court consider the answers to those questions in deciding who has the better claim?

5. You Draft It

a. Draft a clause for the warrant that clearly adjusts the number of shares and the purchase price in the event of a stock split or reverse stock split. Draft a clause for the warrant that makes clear that no such adjustments will be made.

Putting It to Work

Problem 7-2

Harry and Harriet Jones, savvy entrepreneurs, founded a Velcro supply company AttachIt! 40 years ago and incorporated it in a state that has adopted the MBCA. Since then, their business and their family grew tremendously. AttachIt!'s articles of incorporation authorize 10,000 shares of common stock. All the shares were validly issued to Harry and Harriet as co-owners.

In an effort to make sure no one could ever keep up with the Joneses, and in an effort to make sure the heirs to the company stayed on the strait and narrow, Harry and Harriet wrote an email to their four grandchildren promising to give each of them, who were then in their late teens, 1,000 shares in the company if all of them would refrain from drinking, using tobacco, swearing, and playing cards or billiards for money until each was 21 years old. Within a few years, each of the four turned 21 and each had met the terms of the promise.

By that time, however, Harry and Harriet had had a change of heart about giving 40% of the company to their grandchildren. Harry and Harriet, as the only two board members, adopted a board resolution effecting a 10:1 stock split. Shortly after adopting that resolution, Harry and Harriet transferred 1,000 of their shares to each grandchild, in fulfillment of their promise. Not long afterwards, the grandchildren found out about the stock split and the grandchildren sued Harry and Harriet demanding that the grandparents transfer additional shares to each grandchild in light of the stock split. Assuming the original promise was enforceable under contract law,

a. Did Harry and Harriet keep their promise or are the grandchildren owed more shares?

b. If the grandchildren can recover, how many additional shares should each grandchild receive?

c. Could the grandchildren have protected themselves from their grandparents' opportunistic behavior?

d. Would the result be different under the DGCL?

Problem 7-3

Assume the facts in Problem 7-2, except that Harry and Harriet did not effect a stock split and did give each grandchild 1,000 shares, retaining the remaining 6,000 shares themselves.

Although each grandchild was generally a good kid, all four started playing a first-person video game and never spent any time doing anything else. In fact, one grandchild, Judy, convinced her brother Jasper to sell 50 of his shares for 10 extra lives on this video game. Harry and Harriet noticed that their grandchildren didn't call or visit and decided that this game was the culprit behind their failing relationship with their grandchildren.

When they found out two of them had traded valuable shares for video game lives, they decided their grandchildren were not mature enough to handle so much responsibility and devised a plan to make it more difficult to transfer small proportions of their wealth. To that end, Harry and Harriet adopted a board resolution effecting a 1:10 reverse stock split.

a. Is the reverse stock split valid under the MBCA? Under the DGCL?

b. If the Jasper wants to transfer 5 shares for 10 video game lives and Judy, the purchaser, wants 50 shares for 10 video game lives because that is what the parties agreed upon, who wins?

2. Background and Context: The Difference Between "Stock Splits" and "Stock Dividends"

A stock split is different from a stock dividend. Suppose a corporation desires to have twice as many shares outstanding as it currently does, the shareholders are to retain their proportionate interests, and the corporation is to receive no new assets. At the most basic level, it makes no difference whether that doubling of outstanding shares is thought of as an issuance of shares (share dividend) or a division of currently outstanding shares in two (share split). But those two approaches do make a difference in at least three ways. First, where the shares have par value, the first approach — share dividend — means the corporation must increase its capital by at least the aggregate par value of the newly issued shares. By contrast, a share split should mean that the corporation's capital remains constant, but that each share of stock has half the par value it did before.

A second way it matters whether a Delaware corporation effects a stock split or a stock dividend is in the mechanics of bringing such an increase about. A share dividend requires only a board of directors resolution if sufficient authorized but unissued shares (or sufficient treasury shares) remain and if the corporation has sufficient surplus to transfer to capital to cover the aggregate par value of the newly issued shares. To split shares in Delaware requires that the Certificate of Incorporation be amended to halve the par value of each currently existing share (and possibly to increase the number of authorized shares if there are not enough to split the stock). This is a much more cumbersome process and in Delaware, unlike under the MBCA, the board alone does not have the power to amend the Certificate.

Finally, in trusts and estates the difference between a split and a dividend is important. Documents frequently provide that dividends are to be allocated to the income and splits to the principal. This distinction may make a very large difference to the recipients of the income and the principal, who may well be different, and antagonistic, groups.

For example, a will may establish a trust with stock as the principal. The testator may require the trust to pay the trust's income every year to his or her spouse and descendants for the rest of their lives. To comply with the Rule Against Perpetuities, the trust must end at some point and the remaining principal must be distributed, often to the testator's then-living heirs. Economically rational income beneficiaries have an incentive to characterize all stock splits and stock dividends as dividends, while the remainder beneficiaries have an incentive to characterize all stock splits and stock dividends as splits. These differing incentives have frequently resulted in acrimonious litigation. Given the highly technical difference between stock splits and stock dividends and the fact that they are economically equivalent, does it make any sense to allocate stock between income and principal on the basis of whether it is technically a stock dividend or a stock split? Does such a division represent the testator's intent in most instances?

The New York Stock Exchange uses another way to distinguish a stock split from a stock dividend. Under this conception, the difference depends upon how many new shares, expressed as a percentage of the currently outstanding shares, are to be outstanding after the increase. If the number of shares is to increase by 25 percent or less (equivalent to a 5-for-4 split) the transaction is considered a stock dividend. If the increase is greater than 25 percent, the transaction is considered a stock split. This method of distinguishing splits from dividends is, obviously, completely unrelated to the traditional corporate law method.

B. MAKING A PROFIT PART II: SALE OF STOCK BY SHAREHOLDERS

Paying dividends is one way shareholders make a profit on their investment. The other way is by selling their stock for more than they paid for it. The norm in the corporate form is that ownership — that is, stock — may be transferred by its owner without any restrictions. While this may seem unremarkable, it actually is one of the key advantages of the corporate form over the partnership model. In a partnership, only a portion of a partner's ownership interest may be transferred. The partner remains connected to the partnership and, equally important, the transferee does not become a partner by virtue of the transfer. He or she simply accedes to some of the transferring partner's rights.

Free alienability of shares is bound up with shareholders' limited liability, although the link is not immediately obvious. Because shareholders are (with notable exceptions described in Chapter 8) liable only for paying in full for their shares, it does not matter to creditors who the shareholders are as long as the shares have been fully paid for. Likewise, as an economic matter it does not matter to the shareholders who the other shareholders are. Because of this indifference to the identity of the shareholder, there is no economic reason to prohibit the transfer of shares. Once a shareholder has sold a share, he or she has no further interest and the buyer becomes a shareholder, exactly as the seller was. Given these economic virtues and the distinction between the corporate and partnership attitudes toward owners' interests, courts have long approached restrictions on transfer with suspicion. The classic judicial incantation is that courts will construe such restrictions narrowly.

In light of this preference for free alienation, why do shareholders want to restrict transfer? There are two main reasons. One is that even though shareholders are indifferent economically about the identity of other shareholders, they may care very much as a matter of management. Particularly where the corporation is closely held, it may be a central expectation of all investors that their coinvestors will remain shareholders for the long term. Second, there may be regulatory reasons to ensure that a corporation's shareholders meet certain criteria. For example, to maintain its status as a Subchapter S corporation, all the shareholders must (with limited exceptions) be individuals. Similarly, to be exempt from federal securities regulations regarding registration, the number of shareholders may be limited or their residence may be restricted to only one state.

It is intuitive to think of *restrictions on transfer* as meaning limitations on a shareholder's power to sell, give, or bequeath shares. This is true, but restrictions on transfer can also mean an obligation to transfer. In other words, sometimes a shareholder may be required to transfer his or her shares even though the shares are not callable and the shareholder does not desire to part with them. Concomitantly, the corporation or other shareholders may be required to purchase a shareholder's shares even though they do not wish to do so.

Shareholders may be compelled to transfer their shares in certain circumstances so that the other shareholders can, in effect, have influence over the management or so that the existing shareholders will have a kind of right of survivorship. Conversely, the corporation or the other shareholders may be compelled to purchase shares to provide the shareholder with cash in some settings. The most frequent triggering of this power is the shareholder's death. Requiring the corporation or other shareholders to buy a deceased shareholder's shares ensures that sufficient money will be available to pay estate taxes and ensures that the shareholder's heirs have a means of exit because they may well not wish to be shareholders of a closely held corporation and would otherwise have little realistic hope of finding a buyer for their shares. Corporate planners typically have the corporation buy life insurance policies on the lives of the shareholders whose shares are subject to repurchase to ensure that the corporation will have sufficient money to pay for that shareholder's shares.

Because restrictions on share transfers are disfavored by courts, every corporations statute explicitly provides that certain restrictions are enforceable. Both the MBCA and the DGCL provide that restrictions are enforceable for any reasonable purpose, including maintaining the corporation's status under tax or securities laws.

See MBCA §6.27(c); DGCL §202(c), (d). Both statutes also permit a prohibition on transfer that either limits transfer to certain classes of transferees (provided those classes are reasonable) or requires prior consent of the corporation or other shareholders. *See* MBCA §6.27(d)(3), (4); DGCL §202(c)(3), (5).

Restrictions on transfer may require transfer or may grant an option to purchase to either the corporation, the other shareholders, or both seriatim. *See* MBCA §6.27(d)(1), (2); DGCL §202(c)(1), (2), (4). Note also that a restriction that requires a transfer is sometimes called a *buy-sell agreement* meaning that both sides are required to effect a transaction. Often lay people, and sometimes even lawyers and courts, loosely refer to any agreement restricting transfer as a buy-sell agreement. Note also that frequently courts and lawyers mistakenly refer to such an option as a "preemptive right." But a preemptive right is the right of existing shareholders to purchase additional shares the *corporation* intends to issue. Here, this option is a right of first refusal to purchase shares from a *shareholder*.

Although restrictions on transfer are sometimes placed in the Articles of Incorporation, they are more frequently found in bylaws or in shareholder contracts that may also be entered into by the corporation itself. Sometimes the restriction is triggered when a shareholder wishes to transfer shares inter vivos, such as when he or she wishes to sell to a third party or give shares to his or her children or other relatives. Other times the restriction is triggered even though the shareholder has no desire to transfer to anyone, such as when the shareholder dies or is divorced. The following cases show common settings and common problems involved in drafting and enforcing restrictions on alienation of shares.

Harrison v. NetCentric Corp.

744 N.E.2d 622 (Mass. 2001)

COWIN, J.

The plaintiff filed a complaint against his former employer, NetCentric Corporation (NetCentric); its chief executive officer, Sean O'Sullivan (O'Sullivan); four of its directors; and two venture capital firms that invested in NetCentric (collectively, the defendants). The plaintiff alleged that the defendants breached their fiduciary duty of utmost good faith and loyalty; breached the implied covenant of good faith and fair dealing; [and] wrongfully terminated his employment. . . . All of the plaintiff's claims stem from his termination as an officer of NetCentric and the company's attempt to repurchase from him certain shares of his stock pursuant to a stock restriction agreement (stock agreement). The defendants asserted a counterclaim for specific enforcement of the purchase option provision of the stock agreement. A Superior Court judge allowed the defendants' motion for summary judgment on all the plaintiff's claims and . . . on their counterclaim. The plaintiff appealed from the grant of summary judgment,[3] and we transferred the case to this court on our own motion. We affirm the judgment of the Superior Court.

Background. In 1994, the plaintiff, O'Sullivan, and his brother, Donal O'Sullivan (Donal) (collectively, the founders) discussed forming a business entity

---

3. The plaintiff did not appeal from the judgment with respect to his wrongful termination claim.

to develop a medium for delivering facsimile transmissions across the world by way of the internet. The founders agreed to a stock ownership arrangement whereby O'Sullivan would receive approximately 4.5 million shares, the plaintiff 2.9 million shares, and Donal 1.5 million shares. They incorporated NetCentric the following year under Delaware law and established offices in Massachusetts.

O'Sullivan was named the chief executive officer and a director. At some point, he became the chairman of the board as well. The plaintiff served initially as the company's president, later as its vice-president of sales and marketing, and as a director.

The plaintiff executed a stock agreement and an employee noncompetition, nondisclosure, and developments agreement (noncompetition agreement). His stock agreement, executed May 16, 1995, provided that he would purchase 2,944,842 shares of stock in NetCentric at $0.001 a share. Forty per cent of the shares (1,177,938) would vest* on May 1, 1996, and an additional five per cent (147,242) would vest each succeeding quarter, until all the shares were vested. According to the agreement, if the plaintiff ceased to be employed by NetCentric "for any reason . . . with or without cause," the company had the right to buy back his unvested shares at the original purchase price.

Both the plaintiff's stock agreement and his noncompetition agreement contained clauses providing that the agreements did not give the plaintiff any right to be retained as an employee of NetCentric and that each agreement represented the entire agreement between the parties and superseded all prior agreements and understandings relating to the same subject matter. In addition, the agreements contained a choice of law provision, providing that they "shall be construed, interpreted and enforced in accordance with the laws of the Commonwealth of Massachusetts."

In June, 1996, Donal's employment was terminated, and the company exercised its right pursuant to Donal's stock agreement to buy back his unvested shares. In September, 1996, the plaintiff's employment was terminated. At that time, forty-five per cent of the plaintiff's shares (1,325,180) had vested; the remaining fifty-five per cent (1,619,662) had not vested. A month later, NetCentric notified the plaintiff in writing that it was exercising its right pursuant to the stock agreement to buy back the plaintiff's unvested shares. The plaintiff has refused to tender the shares to the company.

During and after the time that Donal and the plaintiff were fired, NetCentric was in the process of hiring additional staff. New employees often were offered stock options in the company, issued from the employee stock option pool (pool), as part of their compensation packages. Some employee-shareholders expressed concern that this practice of authorizing new shares from the corporate treasury for issuance to new hires would dilute the value of their shares. Existing shares would not be diluted, however, if NetCentric acquired outstanding shares and offered those to new employees.

After Donal was fired, the number of shares in the pool was increased by the same number that NetCentric had repurchased from him. Within one month after the plaintiff's employment was terminated, NetCentric hired a president and two

---

* "Vest" in this context means the shares were not subject to a contractual obligation to sell. *ED.*

vice-presidents, one of whom replaced the plaintiff as vice-president of sales. All three new employees were granted stock options, totaling 1,812,500 shares.

Breach of fiduciary duty. Initially, we must resolve a choice of law question. As a minority shareholder in a close corporation, the plaintiff maintains that the defendants owed him a duty of good faith and loyalty and that they breached this duty by terminating his employment in order to repurchase his unvested shares. This claim is based on Massachusetts law, which provides that shareholders in a close corporation owe each other the duty of "utmost good faith and loyalty." *Wilkes v. Springside Nursing Home, Inc.,* 353 N.E.2d 657 (Mass. 1976) . . . ; *Donahue v. Rodd Electrotype Co. of New England, Inc.,* 328 N.E.2d 505 (Mass. 1975). . . .

The defendants claim, however, that Massachusetts law is of no avail to the plaintiff, as Massachusetts law is inapplicable to his fiduciary duty claim; NetCentric is a Delaware corporation, Delaware law applies and Delaware law does not impose the heightened fiduciary duty of utmost good faith and loyalty on shareholders in a close corporation. *See Riblet Prods. Corp. v. Nagy,* 683 A.2d 37, 39 (Del. 1996) (noting that Delaware has not adopted duty of utmost good faith and loyalty established in *Wilkes v. Springside Nursing Home, Inc., supra*); *Nixon v. Blackwell,* 626 A.2d 1366, 1380-1381 (Del. 1993) (declining "to fashion a special judicially-created rule for minority investors"). Instead, under Delaware law, minority shareholders can protect themselves by contract (i.e., negotiate for protection in stock agreements or employment contracts) before investing in the corporation. Additionally, founding shareholders can elect to incorporate the company as a statutory close corporation under Delaware law, which provides special relief to shareholders of such corporations.[7]

Traditionally, we have applied the law of the State of incorporation in matters relating to the internal affairs of a corporation (including both closely and widely held corporations), such as the fiduciary duty owed to shareholders.

Today, we adhere to and reaffirm our policy that the State of incorporation dictates the choice of law regarding the internal affairs of a corporation. Our decision accords with that of a majority of the jurisdictions that have addressed this issue. Similarly, our policy is consistent with the *Restatement (Second) of Conflict of Laws* §302 (1971). . . . All three founders, including the plaintiff, deliberately chose to incorporate in Delaware. By so doing, they "determine[d] the body of law that [would] govern the internal affairs of the corporation and the conduct of their directors. . . . The corporation and its shareholders rightfully expect that the laws under which they have chosen to do business will be applied." *Hart v. General Motors Corp.,* 517 N.Y.S.2d 490 (N.Y. App. Div. 1987).

As NetCentric is, and always has been, a Delaware corporation, Delaware law applies to the plaintiff's claim that the defendants breached their fiduciary duty.[10] Because Delaware law does not impose a heightened fiduciary duty on shareholders

---

7. The special protections apply only to a corporation "designated as a 'close corporation' in its certificate of incorporation, and which fulfills other requirements, including a limitation to 30 on the number of stockholders, that all classes of stock have to have at least one restriction on transfer, and that there be no 'public offering.'" *Nixon v. Blackwell,* 626 A.2d 1366, 1380 (Del. 1993), citing [DGCL] 8, §342. There is no claim that NetCentric is a statutory close corporation under Delaware law.

10. That the plaintiff's stock and noncompetition agreements provide that they are governed by Massachusetts law does not mean that the plaintiff's breach of fiduciary duty claim must also be governed by the law of this State. The Restatement distinguishes between the law that governs corporate acts with respect to third persons and the law that governs the corporation's relationship to its shareholders. See *Restatement (Second) of Conflicts of Laws,*

in a close corporation, . . . summary judgment was properly granted to the defendants on this claim.

Breach of implied covenant of good faith and fair dealing. The plaintiff next claims that the defendants violated the implied covenant of good faith and fair dealing implicit in all Massachusetts contracts, including contracts for employment at will. See *Fortune v. National Cash Register Co.,* 364 N.E.2d 1251 (Mass. 1977). The *Fortune* case and its progeny provide that an employer is accountable to a discharged employee for unpaid compensation if the employee were terminated in bad faith and the compensation is clearly connected to work already performed. The plaintiff argues that the defendants terminated his employment in bad faith because they were trying to prevent his remaining shares from vesting; that his unvested shares represent compensation previously earned; and that he was unlawfully deprived of this compensation by the defendants' attempt to repurchase his unvested shares.

In support of his contention, the plaintiff relies on the fact that he accepted a salary substantially lower than he had received in recent years because of the equity he received in NetCentric and because he expected he would be retained at least until his stock had fully vested. He also cites the fact that other employees received only stock options, while the founders received shares up front. . . .

The defendants did not deprive the plaintiff of any income that he reasonably earned or to which he was entitled. His shares vested over time only if he continued to be employed; thus, the unvested shares are not earned compensation for past services, but compensation contingent on his continued employment. The plaintiff's argument to the contrary is belied by the terms of his stock agreement. At the time the plaintiff's employment was terminated, forty-five percent of his shares had vested. He had not yet earned the remaining fifty-five percent. These unvested shares were contingent on the plaintiff providing future services for NetCentric. . . .

The defendants' counterclaim. The defendants filed a counterclaim seeking the return of the plaintiff's unvested shares. Pursuant to the plaintiff's stock agreement, NetCentric has the right to repurchase these shares if the plaintiff ceases working for the company for any reason and the company exercises its right in writing within sixty days after the plaintiff's termination. The plaintiff is then required to tender his unvested shares to NetCentric within ten days. It is undisputed that the plaintiff was fired, that fifty-five percent of his shares were unvested, and that he received a letter from NetCentric exercising its repurchase rights within sixty days of his discharge. The plaintiff has refused to tender his unvested shares to the company. Accordingly, the defendants were entitled to summary judgment on their counterclaim.

We affirm the Superior Court's order allowing the defendants' motion for summary judgment on the plaintiff's claims and the defendants' counterclaim.

So ordered.

---

supra §302 comment e, at 309 ("There is no reason why corporate acts [such as the making of contracts] should not be governed by the local law of different states").

Notes and Questions

1. Notes

a. The provisions of the stock agreement and noncompetition agreement are typical for startup corporations financed with venture capital.

b. Note that NetCentric is defunct. Where a corporation's assets consist primarily of assets that cannot easily be used in other contexts (such as intellectual property that has been shown to be not commercially viable) the corporation may not bother declaring bankruptcy. There simply is no purpose in going through bankruptcy, because there are so few assets available for creditors.

2. Reality Check

a. What are the theories of Harrison's claim that the court discusses?

b. According to Harrison, why did NetCentric terminate his employment?

c. What are the two legal standards for finding a breach of fiduciary duty? How does the court choose between the two?

3. Suppose

a. Suppose the court had applied Massachusetts law of fiduciary duty? Would the analysis or result have been different?

4. What Do You Think?

a. NetCentric, like nearly all venture capital financed entities, is a Delaware corporation. Given the analysis and result in this case, do you think corporate planners should have the power to choose rules of fiduciary duties?

b. Do you think it is fair that Harrison was required to sell his stock back at exactly the same price as he purchased it for?

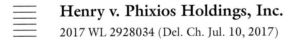

Henry v. Phixios Holdings, Inc.

2017 WL 2928034 (Del. Ch. Jul. 10, 2017)

OPINION

MONTGOMERY-REEVES, Vice Chancellor.

In this action, an alleged stockholder seeks books and records for the purpose of investigating mismanagement of the company, communicating with other stockholders, and valuing his shares. The company has rebuffed all examination efforts because it alleges that the plaintiff is no longer a stockholder. According to the company, its initial three directors adopted bylaws that contain stock transfer restrictions, and all company stock certificates were issued after that time and are subject to those restrictions. Under the restrictions, stock may be revoked by a majority of all voting stockholders if a stockholder is found to be engaging in acts that are damaging to the company. The company contends that after the stock was issued, the stockholder engaged in efforts to compete with the company, and, in response, the company validly rescinded his stock under the bylaws. As such, the company claims he has no right to the documents except to value his shares.

Through this action, the plaintiff stockholder requests that the Court: (1) declare that his stock is not subject to the restrictions and that he is still a stockholder of the company; [and] (2) order the company to grant him access to all documents sought in his demand letter; . . . .

I. BACKGROUND

These are my findings of fact based on the parties' stipulations, documentary evidence, and the testimony of two witnesses during a half-day trial.

A. Parties and Relevant Non-Parties

Plaintiff Jon Henry became a stockholder of Phixios Holdings, Inc. in March 2015. Non-party Rhonda S. Henry is Jon Henry's wife. Non-party RSH Business Consulting Services ("RSH") is a consulting company owned by Rhonda.

Defendant Phixios Holdings, Inc. ("Phixios" or the "Company") is a Delaware corporation formed in July 2013 as a holding company to build product lines, make them successful, and sell them. Non-parties James Walker ("Walker"), Delbert Walker, and Michael Jacobson were the initial directors of Phixios. Walker is the Chief Executive Officer of Phixios. Non-party Jacobson was the Chief Information Officer during all relevant times. Non-party Penni Blake is the Chief Operating Officer of Phixios.

B. Facts

THE DIRECTORS ADOPT BYLAWS THAT CONTAIN STOCK TRANSFER RESTRICTIONS

On July 18, 2013, the board of directors of Phixios, Walker, Delbert, and Jacobson, approved and executed the Phixios Holdings, Inc. Stockholder Agreement (the "Stockholder Agreement").[2] The purpose of the Stockholder Agreement was to "protect the company and everybody in it from somebody who would potentially do something that could be harmful" to the Company. The Stockholder Agreement provides, in relevant part:

> Stock maybe [sic] surrendered only by the registered owner except in the following circumstances:
>
> - A stockholder is found to be engaging in acts, or has previously engaged in acts, that are damaging to Phixios. Examples include but are not limited to:
> - Working for a competitor.
> - Willfully disclosing proprietary information.
> - Other willful acts that are harmful to Phixios as determined by a majority vote of the board of directors and all voting stockholders.

In these circumstances, by a majority vote of all voting stockholders, the ownership of the stock will be revoked and returned to Phixios Treasury and may be

---

2. Walker, Delbert, and Jacobson also were stockholders. Blake testified that she, David Byars, Derek Walker, and Daniel Diaz were also stockholders at the time the Stockholder Agreement was approved. No stock certificates were issued until 2014.

redistributed. . . . Phixios will pay par value of the stock at the time of revocation to the registered stock holder.

The Company did not retain legal counsel but rather Googled how to draft a stockholder agreement. Blake was advised by a "justanswer.com" lawyer "that the majority of the directors had to sign it and that this would be what every shareholder was bound by" so long as Phixios explained the agreement to each potential stockholder before stock in the Company was issued to that stockholder. Blake testified that Phixios had corporate controls in place to ensure every stockholder received an explanation. The Company would e-mail the agreement to every potential stockholder, and Blake would explain each provision to each potential stockholder prior to the issuance of any stock certificate. The Company, however, did not require any written evidence of the potential stockholder's knowledge of or assent to the Stockholder Agreement because the Company "operated on trust."

THE COMPANY HIRES HENRY AND ISSUES STOCK TO HIM

In February 2015, Jacobson contacted Henry to see if he would consider becoming involved with Phixios. On February 27, 2015, Blake e-mailed Henry an employment offer. The offer stated, in relevant part:

> . . . understanding our limited funds right now, I'd like to propose the following:
> 1) We will give you 50,000 shares of Phixios Holdings, Inc. stock immediately.
> 2) Salary of $130,000 per year beginning day you start.
> 3) 30% yearly bonus (based on personal performance, company performance, and customer sat)
> 4) We can only pay you $1,000 per month right now until revenue is high enough to cover your full salary.
> 5) 100% of back pay will be paid as soon as we get to the revenue point to pay your full salary.
> We understand we are asking for a fulltime commitment with a deferred salary. Hence, the 50,000 shares of stock.

Henry accepted the offer and was "officially onboard" as of March 5, 2015.

On March 25, 2015, Walker signed and issued Henry's stock certificate for 50,000 shares of Phixios. The certificate does not contain or note any stock transfer restriction, and there is nothing in writing to show the restrictions were provided to Henry by March 25th. In a March 25, 2015 e-mail exchange titled "Stock Certificates," Blake provided Henry with a tracking number, and Henry responded, ". . .thanks for the discussion today, it made me feel much more comfortable with everything." That e-mail does not attach or reference the Stockholder Agreement. [B]lake stated that the "discussion" referenced in Henry's e-mail was a telephone conversation in which she explained "each and every section of the Stockholder Agreement to Henry." Blake testified at trial that she e-mailed Henry the Stockholder Agreement on the same day she sent the stock certificate. Blake did not provide any credible explanation for why one e-mail exchange from March 25, 2015 could be produced but another exchange from the same day that purportedly attached the Stockholder Agreement could not be produced. She merely stated that the "e-mail has gone missing," presumably because she "switched computers." No explanation was provided as to why "switch[ing] computers" would affect the availability of certain e-mails and not others.

Additionally, Blake's testimony regarding when and how many conversations occurred regarding the Stockholder Agreement changed throughout trial. Initially, there were two conversations between Blake and Henry before February 27, 2015. One conversation was at a "high-level," and the other went through "every single paragraph." Blake testified that she specifically discussed the terms of the Stockholder Agreement, including the stock transfer restrictions, and that Henry said "he was fine, he was happy" and that "it sound[ed] good. He understood." Then Blake testified that there was a conversation on February 27, 2015 and another on March 25, 2015. Later Blake said she had at least three phone calls with Henry. Finally, Blake explained that she didn't "have the dates right in [her] mind," but there were "a bunch" of telephone conversations.

Henry testified that he and Blake did not discuss the Stockholder Agreement before his employment offer. The purpose of their conversation was to address Henry's concern that Phixios had delayed the issuance of shares.

On August 10, 2015, Blake sent an e-mail titled "Stockholder Agreement" to multiple Phixios stockholders attaching the Stockholder Agreement. Blake wrote, "I think everyone already has this, but just sending again as I'm trying to get everything in order with documentation and such to get ready for growth." Henry responded, "Thank you for getting a copy out for my records" and forwarded the email to his wife, Rhonda. Henry testified at trial that he did not look at the Stockholder Agreement when he received it but rather sent it to his wife to print a copy and put it with their "important paperwork." He thought this document was a "set of instructions" that would tell him what day Phixios stockholders had the ability to tender their stock if they wanted to and how to go about tendering if the occasion ever came up.

BUSINESS BEGINS TO SUFFER AND THE COMPANY EXPLORES FURTHER OPPORTUNITIES

By the end of 2015, things at the Company were "slowing down significantly," and there "weren't nearly as many prospects." To deal with these concerns, Walker and Jacobson discussed alternatives to increase the business's lagging revenue. Henry testified that Walker asked Jacobson to explore the Federal Business Opportunities ("FBO") process and to use Henry's services for the "documentation of those processes." On March 10, 2016, Rhonda registered an account for RSH with the FBO Vendor System, and Henry e-mailed Jacobson the information. Henry testified that this registration was necessary in order to obtain an FBO access ID. Henry never attempted to register Phixios through the FBO, and to his knowledge, neither did Jacobson.

After completing the FBO registration process, throughout March and April, RSH began to receive numerous requests for proposals and requests for quotations for various contracts. Henry and Jacobson communicated through their Phixios email accounts, considered many of these solicitations, and worked to document the processes that would be required to pursue these opportunities. Phixios points to several exchanges in particular that it believes evidence RSH's, and thus Henry's, competition with the Company.

Henry testified at trial that he was using RSH to explore potential revenue sources and opportunities for Phixios and reporting his findings back to Jacobson.

Ultimately, because the Company was so overwhelmed in other areas, Phixios did not pursue any of these potential contracts.

HENRY IS FIRED AND THE LITIGATION BEGINS

On May 6, 2016, Walker sent Henry an e-mail stating, in part:

> Jon, I tried to reach you this morning to discuss a layoff. Effective immediately. As a company we can no longer financially support outside contractors. If the company sells or starts making money you will receive what is owed to you.

Henry replied that he had "stopped billing [Phixios] as of April 1st since things had slowed down due to the cut backs in available revenue. This blocked our ability to purchase any parts needed to test, build or deliver anything to sales or the customer base." He also stated that he understood the situation and thanked Walker for the opportunity to work with him for the past year. Henry testified that he went back to being retired after he left Phixios.

In June 2016, Henry, Rhonda, and Jacobson received a cease-and-desist letter from counsel representing Phixios. The letter addressed to Henry alleged that he was "conspiring with Mr. Jacobson to defraud the Company and misappropriate Company assets for [his] own personal gain." On June 8, 2016, Jacobson delivered a Section 220(d) demand to the Company requesting inspection of certain books and records. On June 19, 2016, the Company sent notice to stockholders of a special meeting to be held June 30, 2016. On June 21, 2016, Henry sent a request under Section 219 to examine the list of the Company's stockholders entitled to vote at the special meeting.

On June 23, 2016, Henry and Jacobson delivered a written demand (the "Demand Letter") to the Company requesting that the Company allow Jacobson and Henry "to examine a list of the Company stockholders in connection with a special meeting the [C]ompany has purportedly noticed to take place on June 30, 2016" pursuant to Section 219. The Demand Letter also seeks the inspection of books and records "(i) to communicate with other stockholders concerning the June 30 special meeting; (ii) to value their stock; and (iii) to investigate misman-agement and wrongdoing" pursuant to Section 220(b).

On June 30, 2016, the Company held a special meeting of the stockholders and voted to remove Jacobson as a director. On July 12, 2016, the Company held another special meeting of the stockholders and purported to revoke all of the common stock held by Henry and Jacobson under Section 11 of the Stockholder Agreement. Henry testified that he never received notice of the July 12, 2016 meeting. In a letter dated July 19, 2016, Phixios notified Henry and Jacobson that their common stock had been revoked on July 12, 2016.

II.   ANALYSIS OF THE STOCK TRANSFER RESTRICTIONS

In this case, the Company alleges that the Stockholder Agreement was adopted as part of the bylaws of the Company long before Henry was issued stock in the Company. The Company further maintains that although the restrictions were not noted conspicuously on the stock certificate representing Henry's stock, Henry had actual knowledge both before and after the shares were issued, either of which is adequate under [DGCL] §202(a). Henry concedes that the Stockholder Agreement was in place before Henry's stock was issued. But he contends that the provisions contained in the Stockholder Agreement are not bylaws of the Company. Even accepting as true that the provisions in the Stockholder Agreement are bylaws, Henry argues that he is not bound under Section 202 because he did not have actual knowledge of the restrictions before the stock was issued, and he did not consent to be bound after the stock was issued.

I need not decide whether the provisions in the Stockholder Agreement constituted bylaws because whether the restrictions were adopted through bylaws, through an agreement, or otherwise does not change the analysis. Instead, I must determine whether Henry had actual knowledge by the time the stock was issued. If the answer is no, I must also determine whether under Section 202 Henry may be bound by restrictions that were in place before the securities were issued to him if he gained actual knowledge of the restrictions after the securities were issued to him. If the answer to that question is no, I must determine whether Henry otherwise consented to be bound by a subsequent agreement or vote in favor of the restrictions.

B. Knowledge and Consent Requirements Under Section 202

[A] written restriction on the transfer of a security may be enforceable against a particular stockholder if: (1) it is noted conspicuously on the certificate representing the security in the case of certificated shares; or (2) the person against whom enforcement is sought had actual knowledge of the restriction. [A] stock transfer restriction may be binding on existing securities through one of three ways: (1) by inclusion in the certificate of incorporation; (2) by inclusion in the bylaws of the corporation; or (3) by agreement among stockholders or among stockholders and the corporation. An existing stockholder must affirmatively assent to the restriction in order to be bound either by becoming a party to an agreement or by voting in favor of the restriction. A restriction cannot be retroactively imposed on a current stockholder without his express consent.

"The purpose of §202 is to protect a shareholder's investment from diminishment through post-purchase restrictions placed on the shareholder's shares by the corporation or its other shareholders."[82] "Otherwise, others might circumscribe the stockholder's ability to transfer his or her shares, reducing the investment's liquidity and value."[83] The phrasing in Section 202 was modeled after Section 8-204 of the Uniform Commercial Code, to which the official comments state, "A purchaser who takes delivery of a certificated security is entitled to rely on the terms stated on the certificate."[85] Section 202(a) thus is intended to provide notice such that encumbered securities are easily identified. A stockholder who bargains for a security is entitled to use the certificate's terms as evidence of his economic rights and as proof of the value he bargained for.

Reading the statute holistically to give it its intended purpose, the statute must be read to mean that an existing restriction on the transfer of a security is binding on *subsequent* purchasers of the securities if: (1) it is noted conspicuously on the

---

82. *Di Loreto v. Tiber Hldg. Corp.*, 1999 WL 1261450, at *6 (Del. Ch. Jun. 29, 1999).
83. *Id.*
85. UCC §8-204.

certificate representing the security; (2) the stockholder has actual knowledge of the restriction *at the time he acquires the stock*; or (3) the stockholder consents to be bound by the restriction either through a vote or through a subsequent agreement with the stockholders or with the company. To allow otherwise would "produce the incongruous result of allowing the Board of Directors [or other stockholders] unilaterally to impose stock transfer restrictions, which might be of significant economic consequence, on existing shares without the [knowledge before purchase or] consent [after purchase] of the corporation's stockholders."[88]

Taken to its logical conclusion, the Company's position would allow it to entice an investor into purchasing securities with the expectation that transfer is unrestricted because no restrictions are noted on the certificate representing the securities, while withholding the existence of potentially value-reducing restrictions. "[T]he Legislature could not have intended to produce such onerous results."[89] This absurd result would completely undercut the purpose of Section 202 to protect the stockholder's bargained-for rights.

HENRY DID NOT HAVE ACTUAL KNOWLEDGE OF THE RESTRICTIONS WHEN HE RECEIVED COMPANY STOCK

Phixios argues that Henry had actual knowledge of the restrictions before stock was issued to him because Blake discussed the Stockholder Agreement with Henry before issuing his stock and sent him the Stockholder Agreement on March 25, 2015 (the day she issued the stock). Blake's testimony that she explained each provision to Henry and sent him the Stockholder Agreement prior to the issuance of stock is dubious at best. She claims in her September 7, 2016 affidavit that she discussed the Stockholder Agreement with Henry and sent him the agreement on March 25, 2015. The affidavit does not mention any conversation occurring before March 25, 2015. At trial, however, she contradicted her own sworn affidavit. She stated she had multiple conversations with Henry regarding the Stockholder Agreement. She testified that she could not remember the exact dates of these conversations, but she also testified that she had a phone call about the Stockholder Agreement prior to February 27, 2015, on February 27, 2015, and on March 25, 2015. Her only explanation for why these additional conversations were not included in her affidavit is that she "didn't author this document," but merely "approved" it. Finally, although Blake testified at trial that she e-mailed Henry the Stockholder Agreement on the same day she sent the stock certificate, she did not provide any credible explanation for why the purported e-mail containing the agreement could not be produced when other e-mails from the same day were produced. And she did not produce any documentation showing that she sent the Stockholder Agreement to Henry prior to March 2015. Thus, Phixios offers nothing to rebut Henry's credible testimony that he did not have actual knowledge of the restrictions when he became a stockholder in March 2015.

88. *Joseph E. Seagram & Sons, Inc. v. Conoco, Inc.*, 519 F. Supp. 506, 513 (D. Del. 1981).
89. *Id.* at 514.

HENRY DID NOT ASSENT TO THE STOCK TRANSFER RESTRICTIONS

Both sides acknowledge that the Stockholder Agreement was sent to Henry on August 10, 2015. Even assuming, *arguendo*, that after this date Henry had actual knowledge of the Stockholder Agreement, as discussed above, to impose transfer restrictions on a stockholder who did not have actual knowledge of those restrictions when he became a stockholder and who did not affirmatively assent to the restrictions after he became a stockholder would run afoul of the legislative purpose of Section 202. Thus, the question becomes whether Henry affirmatively assented or became a party to a subsequent agreement containing these restrictions.

"The use of the internet as the vehicle for contract formation 'has not fundamentally changed the principles of contract.'"[100] "The 'threshold issue is the same: did the party who assented online have reasonable notice, either actual or constructive, of the terms of the putative agreement and did that party manifest assent to those terms.'"[101] "A party may assent to an agreement on the internet [or through email] without reading its terms and still be bound by it if she is on notice that she is modifying her legal rights, just as she may with a physical written contract."[102]

On August 10, 2015, Blake sent an e-mail titled "Stockholder Agreement," and wrote "I think everyone already has this, but just sending again as I'm trying to get everything in order with documentation." Henry responded, "Thank you for getting a copy out for my records." The *Newell Rubbermaid Inc. v. Storm*[105] case provides an example of the type of language that gives adequate notice of the modification of legal rights. There, the Court held that a clickwrap agreement modifying an employee's post-employment rights was enforceable because the defendant had to affirmatively click a box next to a bolded, conspicuous sentence stating that she "read and agree[d] to the terms of the" agreement.[106] She also had to affirmatively assent on an additional screen with an "Accept" button that stated in order to complete the agreement, she must "read and accept the terms outlined in the document" and that her "grant acceptance will be final once [she] click[ed] Accept."[107] Although the precise language in *Newell Rubbermaid* is not mandatory to manifest assent, there is no evidence that Henry was on notice that he was modifying his legal rights when he acknowledged receipt of the August 10, 2015 email. To the contrary, Henry credibly testified at trial that he did not open the attachment because he thought it was a set of instructions describing how Phixios stockholders could tender their stock. Phixios does not provide any credible evidence to the contrary. Therefore, Henry did not assent to be bound by the stock transfer restrictions contained in the Stockholder Agreement; his stock was revoked invalidly; and Henry remains a stockholder of Phixios.[109]

---

100. *Newell Rubbermaid v. Storm*, 2014 WL 1266827, at *6 (Del. Ch. Mar. 27, 2014) (quoting *Van Tassell v. United Mktg. Gp., LLC*, 795 F. Supp. 2d. 770, 790 (N.D. Ill. 2011)).

101. *Id.* (quoting *Vernon v. Qwest Commc'ns Int'l, Inc.*, 857 F. Supp. 2d 1135, 1149 (D. Colo. 2012)).

102. *Id.* at *7.

105. *Newell Rubbermaid*, 2014 WL 1266827, at *6-7.

106. *Id.*

107. *Id.*

109. Phixios argues that Henry acquiesced to the terms of the Stockholder Agreement or, in the alternative, is equitably estopped from denying the restrictions contained therein. In support of its arguments, Phixios cites Henry's reply to the August 10, 2015 e-mail attaching the Stockholder Agreement saying "Thank you for getting

[The court's discussion of Henry's books and records claim is omitted.]

CONCLUSION

For the foregoing reasons, I find that Henry is not subject to the stock transfer restrictions contained in the Stockholder Agreement and, therefore, is a stockholder of Phixios. Henry is entitled to inspect the books and records he seeks in this litigation.

Notes and Questions

1. Reality Check

a. Why did Phixios issue shares to Henry?

b. Why would the company make the shares subject to redemption by the corporation?

c. Why is the restriction not binding on Henry?

2. Suppose

a. Suppose Henry had been found to have had actual notice of the transfer restriction. Would the restriction have been valid under the remaining provisions of DGCL §202?

b. Suppose Phixios had retained you as its lawyer. How would you have acted to ensure that the corporation's stock was subject to valid transfer restrictions?

3. What Do You Think?

a. Weren't Henry's shares issued to him as compensation? If so, why are they redeemable?

b. Do you think Phixios's stockholder agreement had all shares redeemable at the corporation's will? If so, would it have been better to describe the redemption power that way rather than the for-cause language used in the shareholder agreement?

c. Does Phixios have a malpractice claim against Justanswer.com? Against Google?

d. Does Phixios have a negligence claim against Blake for her efforts in preparing the shareholder agreement?

e. Do you think Vice Chancellor Montgomery-Reeves's invocation of click-wrap cases is a convincing analogy to the issue of actual notice in this case?

---

a copy out for my records." JX 13. Acquiescence requires that a plaintiff "has full knowledge of his rights and the material facts and (1) remains inactive for a considerable time; *or* (2) freely does what amounts to recognition of the complained act; *or* (3) acts in a manner inconsistent with the subsequent repudiation, which leads the other party to believe the act has been approved." *Klaassen v. Allegro Dev. Corp.*, 2013 WL 5739680, at *20 (Del. Ch. Oct. 11, 2013). Estoppel requires that a "party by his conduct intentionally or unintentionally leads another, in reliance upon that conduct, to change position to his detriment." *Wilson v. Am. Ins. Co.*, 209 A.2d 902, 903-04 (Del. 1965). "To establish an estoppel, it must appear that the party claiming the estoppel lacked knowledge and the means of knowledge of the truth of the facts in question, that he relied on the conduct of the party against whom the estoppel is claimed, and that he suffered a prejudicial change of position in consequence thereof." *Id.* at 904. But Phixios fails to prove that it was misled or changed its position in any way in reliance on Henry's acknowledgement of receipt of the attachment. And Phixios has put forth no other evidence to prove acquiescence or estoppel.

4. You Draft It

a. Redraft the shareholder agreement so that it is clearly enforceable. The pertinent language reads:

> Stock maybe [sic] surrendered only by the registered owner except in the following circumstances:
>
> - A stockholder is found to be engaging in acts, or has previously engaged in acts, that are damaging to Phixios. Examples include but are not limited to:
>   - Working for a competitor.
>   - Willfully disclosing proprietary information.
>   - Other willful acts that are harmful to Phixios as determined by a majority vote of the board of directors and all voting stockholders.
>
> In these circumstances, by a majority vote of all voting stockholders, the ownership of the stock will be revoked and returned to Phixios Treasury and may be redistributed. . . . Phixios will pay par value of the stock at the time of revocation to the registered stock holder.

When drafting a restriction on transfer, the parties must decide upon the price and terms for any required transfers or options. Where the restriction is in the form of a right of first refusal triggered by a shareholder's desire to transfer shares to an outsider, the parties often provide that the option may be exercised only at the price and on the terms agreed to by the shareholder and outside party. In other settings, the most difficult planning and drafting aspect typically is deciding on the price at which the shares will be transferred. There are three basic approaches to this problem. First, the parties may establish a formula for determining the price. This is usually based upon an accounting concept such as book value, earnings, or cash flow at some date near to the restriction's triggering event.

Second, the parties may establish a price in the agreement and may agree that, in the future, they will review or revise the price. In the majority of cases, the parties never review the price once the agreement has been reached. This leaves them, and the courts, with the choice of either transferring the shares at a price the parties may not have intended or guessing what the parties would have agreed to had they revised the price. Third, the parties may provide that one or more neutral appraisers or arbitrators will determine the price based on a standard such as "fair value," "fair market value," or "value as a going concern." This approach may have considerable uncertainty, especially if the corporation's business is unique or difficult to value. It is also expensive and may require significant outlays of money at a time (for example the death of a key shareholder) when prudence would suggest that the corporation conserve its resources.

Note that the parties may not be seeking to find a way to set a price that is "fair" in the sense of representing the price a willing buyer and willing seller would likely agree to. Instead, the parties may deliberately provide a mechanism that undervalues the shares. This may be intended to act as an *in terrorem* inducement to the shareholders to avoid triggering the restrictions or may be to provide as low a value as realistically possible to minimize the value of the shares in the hands of a deceased shareholder's estate and hence minimize estate taxes.

In addition to the question of providing a price, the parties need to consider whether every possible divestment of shares should be subject to the restrictions. A frequent exemption from restriction is a provision allowing a shareholder to leave shares by will to a surviving spouse or direct descendants. Another exemption may be for shares transferred between spouses. Another possible exemption is all or certain gratuitous transfers, which allows shareholders to give shares to direct descendants inter vivos, which may be useful for estate planning purposes. All these issues present questions of ascertaining your client's best interests, ensuring that all parties are in agreement on the solutions, and providing written documents that effect those solutions. This is an area in which many practicing lawyers make serious mistakes, often because they rely on forms for language they simply adopt in their own agreements without ensuring that the language is suitable.

Because restrictions on transfer are strictly construed in favor of alienation, lawyers and their clients must be careful to be explicit in describing the transfers that are prohibited and to understand that those transfers that are not definitely prohibited are likely to be permitted by a court. A relatively frequent issue is involuntary transfers and transfers by operation of law. Shares that are transferred by a court order in a marital dissolution case or shares that pass by intestacy are common examples.

The following case deals with several problematic areas regarding restrictions on transfer.

F.B.I. Farms, Inc. v. Moore
798 N.E.2d 440 (Ind. 2003)

BOEHM, J.

F.B.I. Farms, Inc., was formed in 1976 by Ivan and Thelma Burger, their children, Linda and Freddy, and the children's spouses. Each of the three couples transferred a farm and related machinery to the corporation in exchange for common stock in the corporation. At the time, Birchell Moore ["Birchell"] was married to Linda.

In 1977, the Board of Directors of F.B.I. consisted of [Birchell], Ivan, Freddy and Linda. The minutes of a 1977 meeting of the Board recite that the following restrictions on the transfer of shares were "adopted":

(1) No stock of said corporation shall be transferred, assigned and/or exchanged or divided, unless or until approved by the Directors thereof;

(2) That if any stock be offered for sale, assigned and/or transferred, the corporation should have the first opportunity of purchasing the same at no more than the book value thereof;

(3) Should said corporation be not interested, and could not economically offer to purchase said stock, any stockholder of record should be given the next opportunity to purchase said stock, at a price not to exceed the book value thereof;

(4) That if the corporation was not interested in the stock, and any stockholders were not interested therein, then the same could be sold to any blood member of the family. Should they be desirous of purchasing the same, then at not more than the book value thereof.

Linda's marriage to [Birchell] was dissolved in 1982. As part of the dissolution proceedings, Linda was awarded all of the F.B.I. shares and [Birchell] was awarded a monetary judgment in the amount of $155,889.80, secured by a lien on Linda's shares.

[Birchell]'s judgment against Linda remained unsatisfied, and in April 1998 he sought a writ of execution of his lien. A sheriff's sale went forward and in February 2000 [Birchell] purchased all 2,924 shares owned by Linda at the time for $290,450.67. In December 2000 [Birchell] instituted this suit against F.B.I., its shareholders, and Linda seeking a declaratory judgment that . . . [Birchell] properly retained ownership of the shares, and that the shares were unencumbered by restrictions and were freely transferable.

TRANSFER RESTRICTIONS

A. General Principles

Most of the issues in this case are resolved by the Indiana statute governing share transfer restrictions. Corporate shares are personal property. At common law, any restriction on the power to alienate personal property was impermissible. Despite this doctrine, Indiana, like virtually all jurisdictions, allows corporations and their shareholders to impose restrictions on transfers of shares. The basic theory of these statutes is to permit owners of a corporation to control its ownership and management and prevent outsiders from inserting themselves into the operations of the corporation. Chief Justice Holmes stated the matter succinctly a century ago: "Stock in a corporation is not merely property. It also creates a personal relation analogous otherwise than technically to a partnership. . . . [T]here seems to be no greater objection to retaining the right of choosing one's associates in a corporation than in a firm." *Barrett v. King,* 63 N.E. 934, 935 (Mass. 1902). As applied to a family-owned corporation, this remains valid today.

Transfer restrictions are treated as contracts either between shareholders or between shareholders and the corporation.[1] Apart from any statutory requirements, restrictions on transfer are to be read, like any other contract, to further the manifest intention of the parties. Because they are restrictions on alienation and therefore disfavored, the terms in the restrictions are not to be expanded beyond their plain and ordinary meaning.

For a party to be bound by share transfer restrictions, that party must have notice of the restrictions. [MBCA §6.27](b). Here, the restrictions on transfer of F.B.I. shares were neither "noted conspicuously" on the certificates nor contained in the information statement referred to in [MBCA §6.27](b), but there is no doubt that [Birchell], the buyer at the sheriff's sale, had notice of the restrictions. He was therefore bound by them.

Finally, a closely held corporation is a "corporation in which all of the outstanding stock is held by just a few individuals, or by a small group of persons belonging to a single family." J.R. Kemper, *Validity of "Consent Restraint" on Transfer of Shares*

---

1. The Indiana statute provides that restrictions are valid if included in the articles, the bylaws, an agreement among shareholders or an agreement between the corporation and shareholders. [MBCA §6.27](a). None of these was done here. However, no one challenges the restrictions as defective in their initial adoption. At least as to [Birchell], who approved them as a director and had actual knowledge of them, under these circumstances, the restrictions constitute a contract as to all of those shareholders who approved the adoption of the restrictions.

of Close Corporation, 69 A.L.R.3d 1327, 1328 (1976). In 1977, F.B.I. plainly fell within that description; it was owned by six individuals, all members of a single family. Closely held corporations have a viable interest in remaining the organization they envision at incorporation and transfer restrictions are an appropriate means of maintaining the status quo.

B. Rights of First Refusal

Paragraphs (2) and (3) of the restrictions created rights of first refusal in F.B.I. and its shareholders. A transfer in violation of restrictions is voidable at the insistence of the corporation. F.B.I. and its shareholders argue that [Birchell] should have been obliged to offer the shares to the corporation or a shareholder pursuant to those provisions. [Birchell] responds, and the Court of Appeals agreed, that he was not a shareholder until he purchased the shares at the sheriff's sale. He contends he therefore had no power to offer the shares. This misses the point that before Linda could transfer her shares, she was obliged to offer them to F.B.I. and the other shareholders. [Birchell] was on notice of that requirement. [Birchell], as the buyer, had the right to demand that Linda initiate the process to exercise or waive the right to first refusal.

Thus, if the corporation had insisted on its right of first refusal, Linda would have been obliged to sell to F.B.I. (or its shareholders). And [Birchell], as a buyer on notice of the restrictions, had the right to insist that that process go forward. But the corporation and its shareholders were aware of the sheriff's sale and did nothing to assert the right of first refusal. They cannot sit back and let the sale go forward, await future events, then claim a right to purchase on the same terms as [Birchell]. In sum, F.B.I. and its shareholders had rights of first refusal, but failed to exercise them. As a result, the sale to [Birchell] proceeded as if the shares had been offered and the corporation refused the opportunity. To hold otherwise would be to give F.B.I. and its shareholders a perpetual option to purchase but no obligation to do so. Having failed to demand their right to buy at the time of the sale, the rights of first refusal gave them no ability to upset the sale conducted by the sheriff.

C. Restrictions on Transfer with Board Approval

The restrictions "adopted" in paragraphs (1) and (4) are more problematic. Indiana's statute, reflecting the common law, requires that restrictions on share transfers be reasonable. [MBCA §§6.27](c)(3), (d)(3), and (d)(4). The general common law doctrine surrounding evaluation of the reasonableness of restrictions is well established. A restriction is reasonable if it is designed to serve a legitimate purpose of the party imposing the restraint and the restraint is not an absolute restriction on the recipient's right of alienability. The Indiana statute is somewhat more generous in allowing restrictions on classes of buyers unless "manifestly unreasonable." [MBCA §6.27](d)(4). Several factors are relevant in determining the reasonableness of any transfer restriction, including the size of the corporation, the degree of restraint upon alienation; the time the restriction was to continue in effect, the method to be used in determining the transfer price of shares, the likelihood of the restriction's contributing to the attainment of corporate objectives, the possibility that a hostile stockholder might injure the corporation, and the probability of the restriction's promoting the best interests of the corporation. At one extreme, a restriction that merely prescribes procedures that must be observed before stock may be transferred is not unreasonable. At the other end of the spectrum, restrictions that are fraudulent, oppressive, unconscionable, . . . or the result of a breach of the fiduciary duty that shareholders in a close corporation owe to one another, will not be upheld. The restrictions on F.B.I.'s shares, like most, are somewhere in the middle. They impose substantive limitations on transfer, but are not alleged to be the result of fraud or breach of fiduciary duty.

The trial court, in its order granting partial summary judgment, concluded that the restriction precluding transfer without Board approval was reasonable at the time that it was adopted, but the lengthy and difficult history between the parties had rendered the restriction unreasonable. Under basic contract law principles, the reasonableness of a term of a contract is evaluated at the time of its adoption. The same is true of share transfer restrictions. As a result, evaluating the reasonableness of the restrictions in light of subsequent developments is inappropriate. For that reason, we do not agree that the restriction requiring director approval became unreasonable based upon events and disputes within the family that occurred after the restrictions had been adopted. To be sure, the parties find themselves in a difficult dispute as is sometimes the case in a family business following a dissolution. But when F.B.I. was formed and the family farms were effectively pooled, the shareholders agreed that the Board would be permitted to restrict access to the shares. To the extent that restriction devalues the shares in the hands of any individual shareholder by reason of lack of transferability, it is the result of the bargain they struck. The policy behind enforcement of these restrictions is to encourage entering into formal partnerships by permitting all parties to have confidence they will not involuntarily end up with an undesired co-venturer. Presumably for that reason, the statute permits a restriction that requires a transferee to be approved by the Board of Directors, and to that extent may severely limit transferability.

A "consent restriction" such as this has been considered unreasonable by some courts. However, the General Assembly has allowed precisely this type of restriction in [MBCA §6.27](d)(3). That section provides that transfer restrictions may require the approval of "the corporation, the holders of any class of its shares, or another person" before the shares may be transferred. Board approval is one permissible way of implementing approval by "the Corporation" under this section.

D. Restrictions on Transfer Except to "Blood Members of the Family"

We also find the "blood-member" restriction to be enforceable as protecting a viable interest. These are family farmers in corporate form. It is apparent from the nature of the corporation that the Burger family had an interest in maintaining ownership and operation of F.B.I. in the hands of family members. Although one may quibble with the terminology, and there may be some individuals where status as blood members is debatable, we think it plain enough that all parties to this dispute either are or are not blood members of the Burger family. All are either direct descendants of Ivan or spouses of Ivan or of one of his children.

RESTRICTIONS AS APPLIED TO INVOLUNTARY TRANSFERS

The Court of Appeals held that the restrictions on Linda's shares did not apply by their terms to the sheriff's sale and, as a result, did not bar the sheriff's sale to

[Birchell]. We agree that [Birchell] acquired the shares at the sheriff's sale, but not because the restrictions were inapplicable by their terms.

The Court of Appeals relied on cases stating that involuntary transfers fall within the terms of a restriction only if the language of the restrictions specifically identifies them. This doctrine has been developed largely in cases involving intestate transfers by a decedent, . . . and in marriage dissolution proceedings where a transfer is made to a spouse.

The sheriff's sale where [Birchell] purchased Linda's shares was an involuntary transfer. Transfers ordered incident to marriage dissolutions and transfers under intestate law may also be deemed involuntary. We think the governing principle is not the same for all forms of "involuntary" transfers. The language of the restrictions in this case does not specifically refer to involuntary transfers of any kind. Rather, it seems to contemplate restricting all transfers, voluntary and involuntary, by providing that no stock of the corporation should be "transferred, assigned, exchanged, divided, or sold" without complying with the restrictions. The intent of the parties is thus rather plain: to restrict ownership to the designated group, and to preclude transfer by any means. The question is whether that intent should be permitted to prevail in the face of countervailing policies.

Transfer by intestacy is in some sense involuntary, but it may also be viewed as a voluntary act of the decedent who had the option to leave a will. If a transfer could not be made by gift during lifetime, for example, to an offspring regarded by other shareholders as an undesirable partner, we see no reason to permit it at death by the decedent's choice to die intestate. There are, however, forms of involuntary transfers that a private agreement may not prevent because the agreement would unreasonably interfere with the rights of third parties. In a dissolution, the interests of the spouse require permitting transfer over the stated intent of the parties. Similarly, creditors of the shareholder cannot be stymied by a private agreement that renders foreclosure of a lien impossible. For that reason, we agree with the trial court that the sheriff's sale transferred the shares to [Birchell] despite the restrictions. Transfer restrictions cannot preclude transfer in a foreclosure sale and thereby leave creditors without recourse. This does not turn on a doctrine of construction. Rather we hold that requiring an explicit bar specifically naming transfer by intestacy or by testamentary disposition should not be necessary. If the language purports to bar all transfers, and by its terms would apply to intestacy, devise or any other means of transfer, it should be given effect unless the restriction violates some policy.

Although we agree with [Birchell] that he could purchase the shares at the sale, it is also the case that he purchased the shares with knowledge of the restrictions. We conclude that he could not acquire more property rights than were possessed by Linda as his seller. The shares in Linda's hands were valued with restrictions in place, and therefore it is not unfair to her creditors that a purchaser at a foreclosure sale acquire the disputed shares subject to the same restrictions, and with whatever lessened value that produces. To be sure, the effect of such a restriction may be to make the shares unmarketable to any buyer. But the creditor retains the option to bid at the sale and, if successful, succeed to the shareholders' interest. The creditor then gets the assets the debtor used to secure the underlying obligation. If the creditor wants collateral free of restrictions, the creditor must negotiate for that at the outset of the arrangement.

CONCLUSION

We affirm the trial court's ruling that . . . the transfer restrictions did not prevent the sheriff's sale, and that the transfer restrictions remain applicable to the shares in [Birchell]'s hands. We reverse the trial court's ruling that the two disputed transfer restrictions are unreasonable and therefore unenforceable, and find that the director-approval and blood-member restrictions are reasonable and enforceable. The case is remanded for further proceedings consistent with this opinion.

SHEPARD, C.J., and DICKSON and SULLIVAN, JJ., concur.

RUCKER, J., concurs in result without opinion.

Notes and Questions

1. Notes

a. Indiana's statute governing restrictions on transfer is identical to the MBCA.

b. "Chief Justice Holmes" referred to by Justice Boehm is Oliver Wendell Holmes, Jr. (1841-1935) who left the Harvard Law School faculty in 1882 to become a Justice of Massachusetts's highest court. He became Chief Justice of that court in 1899, and, in 1902, President Theodore Roosevelt appointed him to the Supreme Court of the United States. He retired from the Court in 1932.

2. Reality Check

a. How did Linda acquire the shares?

b. How did Birchell get a lien on the shares?

c. Why did the parties want to restrict transfer?

d. Describe the mechanics of the restrictions.

e. Who contests Birchell's ownership of the shares? Why?

f. Why are some of the restrictions more problematic than others?

g. What should Linda or the company have done when Birchell sought to foreclose?

h. What additional steps should Birchell have taken to ensure that his purchase at the sheriff's sale would be effective?

i. Is Birchell now bound by the restrictions on transfer? Why?

j. If Birchell transfers the shares, is the transferee bound by the restrictions on transfer? In this regard, the Indiana Court of Appeals noted, "We express no opinion as to whether a purchaser of stock at a sheriff's sale without knowledge of the transfer restrictions would be subject to such restrictions in future transfers of the shares." *F.B.I. Farms, Inc. v. Moore*, 769 N.E.2d 688, 693 n.2 (Ind. App. 2002). *See* also MBCA §6.27(b).

3. Suppose

a. Suppose F.B.I. Farms had been incorporated in Delaware. Would the analysis or result have been different? *See* DGCL §202(a).

b. Suppose F.B.I. Farms had prevailed. How would the result and analysis have been different?

c. If the restrictions on transfer had been clearly applicable to the sheriff's sale, would that affect the price a purchaser would be willing to pay for those shares? Why?

d. Imagine that the restrictions on transfer purported to prohibit transfers made voluntarily, involuntarily, or by operation of law. Would the court's analysis or the result have been different?

4. What Do You Think?

a. Do you think each of the restrictions on transfer is equally valid? If not, which restrictions have more claim to legitimacy, and why?

b. Do you think courts should be bound by restrictions on transfer that, by their terms, apply to transfers ordered by a court?

c. Is one of the parties especially culpable? If so, who, and why?

d. In general, what steps should each of the parties and their lawyers have taken to ensure that this conflict did not arise in the first place?

5. You Draft It

a. Redraft the restrictions on transfer so that they are clearly permissible under the MBCA.

b. Redraft the restrictions on transfer so that they clearly apply to transfers ordered to satisfy judgment creditors of the stockholder, to transfers by will or intestacy, and to transfers pursuant to a marital dissolution. Then redraft the restrictions so that they clearly do not apply to such transfers.

1. No stock of said corporation shall be transferred, assigned and/or exchanged or divided, unless or until approved by the Directors thereof;
2. That if any stock be offered for sale, assigned and/or transferred, the corporation should have the first opportunity of purchasing the same at no more than the book value thereof;
3. Should said corporation be not interested, and could not economically offer to purchase said stock, any stockholder of record should be given the next opportunity to purchase said stock, at a price not to exceed the book value thereof;
4. That if the corporation was not interested in the stock, and any stockholders were not interested therein, then the same could be sold to any blood member of the family. Should they be desirous of purchasing the same, then at not more than the book value thereof.

Putting It to Work

Problem 7-4

Carly worked as sales person at Astra Fragrances, a high-end perfumer. As part of her compensation she received 10 shares of stock each month. Carly's employment contract stated that:

> "In the event of employee's termination, Astra may repurchase all shares issued to employee at fair market value within 30 days of the end of employee's employment" and "Shares cannot be sold to any person, other than another current Astra employee, without Astra's approval."

After two years of employment, Carly gave 100 shares to Zach for a birthday present. Zach worked full time as a barista. Zach, shortly thereafter and without Carly's knowledge, sold the shares at half their fair market value to his boss at the coffee shop in order to try to get a promotion from barista to assistant night manager.

After six years with no raise, Carly quit her job with Astra Fragrances one Friday with no prior notice. Over that weekend, knowing she would need money quickly, Carly sold the 620 shares she had (i.e., all the shares she received except the 100 she gave to Zach) on craigslist for about 90% of their fair market value to Sandy, an employee of Astra Fragrances' fiercest competitor. Two days after selling her shares, Carly received a letter from Astra stating that Astra wished to exercise its option to repurchase all 720 shares at fair market value.

    a. Were the restrictions contained in Carly's employment agreement valid?

    b. Can Astra require Carly to sell back to Astra 720 shares of stock?

    c. Are Zach's boss and Sandy valid shareholders of Astra?

    d. If so, are Zach's boss or Sandy bound by any restrictions on transferring the shares?

    e. Should Astra have done anything differently to increase the likelihood that Carly could not validly transfer her shares?

1. When the Purchaser Is the Corporation That Issued the Shares

a. Limitations on a Corporation's Power to Purchase Its Shares

Through the late nineteenth century there was considerable doubt whether a corporation had the power to repurchase its own shares. This doubt centered not only on the propriety of the potential shift in the balance of economic and management power among its shareholders but on the rather metaphysical question of what would happen to such shares. That is, in what meaningful sense could a corporation be a stockholder of itself? Conceptually, this problem is different from the question whether stock can be made redeemable or callable. In those settings, all shares in a particular class or series have the same quality and that quality is embedded in the corporation's Articles of Incorporation. A corporation's purchase of its own shares that it can neither compel to be sold to it nor is under an obligation to purchase is a different matter. This question was of sufficient importance that legislatures specifically provided corporations with the power to purchase their own shares. *See* MBCA §6.31 and DGCL §160(a).

Corporations statutes place two primary limitations on the power of a corporation to repurchase its shares. First, such purchases are subject to the same economic test as dividends. *See* MBCA §6.03(b) and DGCL §160(a). Economically, a repurchase has the same effect as a dividend on a corporation's creditors: fewer corporate assets are available to satisfy the creditors' claims. The second limitation is meant to ensure that at least some shareholder has the power to vote and, in some states, at least some shareholder has the right to the corporate assets on dissolution. Accordingly, the statutes require that at least one such share remain outstanding at all times. *See* MBCA §6.03(c) (at least one outstanding share must have unlimited voting rights and at least one outstanding share must be entitled to the assets on dissolution) and DGCL §151(b) (at least one outstanding share must have full voting powers).

b. Motivations to Repurchase Shares

Given that a corporation *can* buy its own shares, why would it *want* to? One answer is that, as we've seen in the closely held setting, a corporation's managers might wish the corporation to purchase its shares to provide liquidity for a deceased shareholder's estate. The managers might also approve a repurchase where the managers believe it to be in the best interest of a corporation's shareholders to purchase the shares of a living shareholder to terminate that person's interest in the corporation. This is a common solution to the problem of the shareholder who has become chronically at odds with the other shareholders or the corporation's managers. Note that having the corporation purchase those shares allows the economic and voting rights of each remaining shareholder to increase proportionately, which is frequently the desired outcome. Managers and controlling shareholders can use this technique to increase their control at the expense of the minority shareholders, although (as we will see in later chapters) fiduciary duties impose limits on this power. Finally, because repurchasing shares is the functional equivalent of a dividend, a corporation may repurchase shares to provide shareholders a tax advantage because the consideration for the shares purchased is treated as a return of the shareholder's investment (on which no tax is imposed) and then as a capital gain (which may be taxed at a lower rate than ordinary income).[4]

Publicly held corporations, of course, need not repurchase a particular shareholder's shares to provide liquidity because, by definition, shareholders can readily dispose of them on the open market. On occasion, a public corporation will buy back the shares of a large shareholder as a way to ensure that that shareholder's management power is eliminated. The shareholder might prefer to sell to the corporation rather than on the open market in part because of low transaction costs (selling on the open market involves brokerage commissions and may also result in a lower total sale price because the availability of a large number of shares for sale may drive the price down) and in part because the corporation's managers may be willing to pay a premium price (known as *greenmail*) to be rid of the obstreperous shareholder.

Public corporations might also repurchase their shares as part of a change in their capital structure. If the corporation believes it needs a higher ratio of debt to equity, it may borrow money, often by selling debt securities, and use the money to repurchase shares. Not only is the interest on the debt tax deductible to the corporation, unlike dividend payments on the stock, but the mandatory nature of interest payments means that the corporation's senior managers have less discretion over excess cash. For many public corporations, the investment community

---

4. If the corporation repurchases shares from all shareholders pro rata, though, the Internal Revenue Service treats that transaction as a dividend and no tax advantages exist.

perceives this reduction of managerial discretion as a sign that the corporation's excess cash is less likely to be mismanaged (!) and hence the stock price will rise.

Finally, corporate managers may cause the corporation to repurchase its shares as a signal to the investment community that the managers believe the corporation's prospects are good. This seems a bit obtuse at first, somewhat like understanding the signals sent by various bidding conventions in bridge. At its starkest, the idea is that a corporation must decide what to do with cash that it does not need for its current operations. If the corporation wants neither to expand its own business nor purchase other businesses, a dividend would seem to be a likely use for the money. However, by buying back shares instead, the corporation's stock price should rise. This is so because the corporation's value is exactly the same before as after the stock repurchase — remember, the corporation's managers have decided not to use the money in the business — yet there are fewer shares outstanding so the value, hence the price, of each should rise. Sometimes this works. This is especially true where the investment community shares management's belief that the best use for a particular corporation's excess cash is to give it to the shareholders; the only question then is whether to do so via dividends or repurchases. In many settings, though, a decision to repurchase large amounts of shares suggests to investors that corporate managers are bereft of ideas for expanding the current business or for identifying new investment opportunities. In that case, this decline in investors' confidence in management may offset any price increase that should result from fewer outstanding shares. In fact, often a corporation that announces a large buyback sees its stock fall rather precipitously.

c. The Metaphysics of Repurchased Shares

In every state, repurchased shares are not "outstanding," so they cannot be voted, nor do they count as being present for quorum purposes, nor, obviously, may they receive dividends. Repurchased shares also do not count in calculating the proportion (i.e., the denominator) of shares that must be present for a quorum or the shares needed to take action. *See* DGCL §§160(c), 216 (which limits those calculations to "shares entitled to vote"). The MBCA provides that shares that have been authorized and issued are outstanding "until they are reacquired, redeemed, converted, or canceled."[5] *See* MBCA §6.03(a). We have already talked about redeemable and convertible stock. The MBCA provides a default rule that reacquired shares become authorized but unissued. The Articles may provide, though, that reacquired shares may not be reissued. In that case, they simply evaporate and the number of authorized shares is reduced by the number of shares reacquired. *See* MBCA §6.31. In traditional corporate nomenclature, shares treated in either fashion are said to have been *retired*. Although the difference may seem a bit attenuated, the difference between the two approaches makes an immense practical difference. If reacquired shares become authorized but unissued, the board has the power to reissue those shares as it sees fit, which provides the board with the discretion to seek more capital

---

5. "*Canceled*" shares are not reacquired by the corporation but are simply voided. This may happen if the board purported to "issue" shares to third parties but such shares were in excess of number of authorized shares. Cancellation may also happen when two corporations merge and, as frequently happens, the surviving corporation owns some shares of the disappearing corporation. The remaining shareholders of the disappearing corporation receive some consideration for their shares while the shares owned by the surviving corporation are cancelled.

and more shareholders (subject to existing shareholders' preemptive rights) and the board may exercise that power strategically. If the shares evanesce, the shareholders have more control, because if the corporation has exhausted its supply of authorized but unissued shares, the shareholders must approve any amendment to the Articles increasing the number of authorized shares.

In Delaware and many other states, especially those with par value, reacquired shares are not automatically retired. Instead, they remain authorized, issued, but not outstanding. Such shares are traditionally called *treasury stock*. The board of directors clearly has the power to sell (note that the corporation does not reissue them; they remain issued as treasury stock) treasury stock and, because the corporation already received at least the par value of such shares when they were issued, the board is free to sell them for any price it considers adequate. *See* DGCL §§153(c), 160(b). This is sometimes an important power if the stock's par value is higher than an arm's length buyer would reasonably pay. Because stock cannot be issued for less than par value, a corporation could obtain an infusion of cash by selling treasury stock in a setting in which it is, as a practical matter, unable to issue new stock because the price per share will be below par value. Selling treasury shares does not trigger preemptive rights, which may provide the board with another advantage over issuing new shares. *See* DGCL §102(b)(3) (providing that preemptive rights attach to "additional issues of stock"). Treasury stock may be retired by board action and, as under the MBCA, the default rule is that retired stock becomes authorized but unissued, although the Certificate of Incorporation may provide that retired stock cannot be reissued. *See* DGCL §243.

C. FEDERAL SECURITIES REGULATION

You may remember from Chapter 6 that federal securities regulations affect the professional lives of corporate lawyers in two main settings. In this section we consider one of those settings: resales of stock. The '34 Act provides extensive regulation of the stock exchanges and of the stock brokerage companies and their employees. These regulations are highly esoteric but are, in general, designed to protect the investing public by requiring that transactions be public and that the brokerage houses and employees maintain adequate supervision over trading and customer accounts. Our concern here is with federal restrictions on the sale of stock by stockholders — in other words, with restrictions on resale.

1. Restrictions on Resale

a. Section 16(b)

Some restrictions apply only to stockholders in publicly held corporations. Section 16(a) of the '34 Act requires all directors, officers, and holders of 10 percent or more of a public company's stock to file reports that describe their stock holdings in the company. The purpose is to allow the public to know how much stock is held by such key people. Most changes in stockholding must be reported in two business days. The original purpose of §16(a) was to discourage insider trading by making insiders' trades public. A byproduct, however, is the existence of an active group of investors who closely monitor changes in insider holdings. Those investors believe, for obvious reasons, that trends in purchases or sales are good early indicators of near-term stock price changes.

Section 16(b) was originally designed to prevent these insiders from trading on private information. It provides a seemingly bright-line rule that allows the corporation to recover from such insiders any gain made from a purchase and sale (or sale and purchase) of company stock within six months. The statute imposes strict liability on the shareholder without regard to the actor's state of mind.

Because §16(a) covers ownership of *more than* 10 percent of a public company's stock, the Supreme Court has held that the transaction that puts a shareholder above the 10 percent level does not count for §16(b) purposes. On the other hand, the sale that takes a shareholder below 10 percent does count. The Securities and Exchange Commission (SEC) takes the view that all shares are fungible. For example, suppose a shareholder had owned 11 percent of a public company for years. On February 1st the shareholder bought an additional 1 percent and on March 1st the shareholder sold 1 percent. The shareholder has violated §16(b) even though the actual shares sold might have been held for longer than six months. To effect the statute's purpose in deterring insiders from making quick profits, where a shareholder makes multiple sales or purchases within a six-month period, the courts will award the highest damages. That is, the courts will match the shares sold at the highest price with the shares sold at the lowest. Under a strict reading of the statute, a shareholder who loses money on some trades may not offset that loss against gains for §16(b) purposes.

b. Rule 144

You will remember that the vast majority of shares are issued in transactions that are exempt from federal registration. Perfecting such an exemption is only half the battle, because such shares cannot be resold without registration unless the shareholder can use an exemption. Under the intrastate exemption, resale is easy if made to another in-state resident. Shares purchased in reliance on Reg. D are more difficult to resell. At bottom are two dangers. One is that a sale made a short time after the shares were initially issued might suggest that the original purchaser was just a conduit for purposes of claiming an exemption. Hence, there is a danger that a quick resale could be recharacterized as, in effect, the corporation's sale to the new purchaser whose purchase may or may not be in accord with the exemption upon which the issuer is relying.

Second, an unbelievably convoluted series of defined terms in the Securities Act has the effect of rendering unregistered resales by persons who control or are controlled by the issuing corporation illegal when that resale is accomplished with the aid of another person (such as a stockbroker). To avoid the uncertainties of these settings, the SEC has adopted Rule 144, which provides a very detailed safe harbor for such resales. The basic solution is that, with regard to the first danger, a shareholder may resell shares after holding them for one year. As to the second danger, a control person may resell shares if he or she complies with regulations that ensure that the public has sufficient information about the corporation and the resales are done in small enough amounts so as not to disrupt the trading market.

2. Rule 10b-5

This rule, under the '34 Act, is a wide-ranging prohibition against fraud in the purchase or sale of securities. Note that it applies to purchases or sales made through some instrumentality of interstate commerce, such as the telephone, but need not involve stock of publicly traded companies. It also applies to stock that was sold in transactions exempt from the registration requirements. Thus the vast majority of securities transactions, from startup company financing to IPOs to sales of stock in well-established public companies, come within the 10b-5 ambit. The rule prohibits fraudulent trading practices and, most germanely, prohibits misstatements of material fact or half-truths about such facts. The rule provides that

> It shall be unlawful for any person, directly or indirectly, by the use of any means or instrumentality of interstate commerce, or of the mails or of any facility of any national securities exchange,
>   (a) To employ any device, scheme, or artifice to defraud,
>   (b) To make any untrue statement of a material fact or to omit to state a material fact necessary in order to make the statements made, in the light of the circumstances under which they were made, not misleading, or
>   (c) To engage in any act, practice, or course of business which operates or would operate as a fraud or deceit upon any person, in connection with the purchase or sale of any security.
>
> **Rule 10b-5**

The next case shows a typical 10b-5 case and describes the elements of a cause of action.

≡ **Dura Pharmaceuticals, Inc. v. Broudo**
≡ 544 U.S. 336 (2005)

Justice Breyer delivered the opinion of the Court.

I

Respondents are individuals who bought stock in Dura Pharmaceuticals, Inc., on the public securities market between April 15, 1997, and February 24, 1998. They have brought this securities fraud class action against Dura and some of its managers and directors (hereinafter Dura) in federal court. In respect to the question before us, their detailed amended (181 paragraph) complaint makes substantially the following allegations:

(1) Before and during the purchase period, Dura (or its officials) made false statements concerning both Dura's drug profits and future Food and Drug Administration (FDA) approval of a new asthmatic spray device.

([2]) In respect to the asthmatic spray device, Dura falsely claimed that it expected the FDA would soon grant its approval.

([3]) [I]n November 1998, Dura announced that the FDA would not approve Dura's new asthmatic spray device.

([4]) The next day Dura's share price temporarily fell but almost fully recovered within one week.

Most importantly, the complaint says the following (and nothing significantly more than the following) about economic losses attributable to the spray device misstatement: *"In reliance on the integrity of the market, [the plaintiffs] . . . paid artificially inflated prices for Dura securities" and the plaintiffs suffered "damage[s]" thereby* (emphasis added).

In the portion of the court's decision now before us — the portion that concerns the spray device claim — the [Ninth] Circuit held that the complaint adequately alleged "loss causation." The Circuit wrote that "plaintiffs establish loss causation if they have shown that the price *on the date of purchase* was inflated because of the misrepresentation." 339 F.3d, at 938 (emphasis in original; internal quotation marks omitted). It added that "the injury occurs at the time of the transaction." *Ibid.* Since the complaint pleaded "that the price at the time of purchase was overstated," and it sufficiently identified the cause, its allegations were legally sufficient. *Ibid.*

Because the Ninth Circuit's views about loss causation differ from those of other Circuits that have considered this issue, we granted Dura's petition for certiorari. We now reverse.

II

The courts have implied . . . a private damages action [under §10(b) of the 1934 Act and Rule 10b-5], which resembles, but is not identical to, common-law tort actions for deceit and misrepresentation. In cases involving publicly traded securities and purchases or sales in public securities markets, the action's basic elements include:

(1) *a material misrepresentation (or omission)*;
(2) *scienter*, *i.e.*, a wrongful state of mind;
(3) *a connection with the purchase or sale of a security*;
(4) *reliance*, often referred to in cases involving public securities markets . . . as "transaction causation," . . . ;
(5) *economic loss*; and
(6) *"loss causation,"* *i.e.*, a causal connection between the material misrepresentation and the loss.

Dura argues that the complaint's allegations are inadequate in respect to these last two elements.

We begin with the Ninth Circuit's basic reason for finding the complaint adequate, namely, that at the end of the day plaintiffs need only "establish," *i.e.*, prove, that "the price *on the date of purchase* was inflated because of the misrepresentation." 339 F.3d, at 938 (internal quotation marks omitted). In our view, this statement of the law is wrong. Normally, in cases such as this one . . . , an inflated purchase price will not itself constitute or proximately cause the relevant economic loss.

For one thing, as a matter of pure logic, at the moment the transaction takes place, the plaintiff has suffered no loss; the inflated purchase payment is offset by ownership of a share that *at that instant* possesses equivalent value. Moreover, the logical link between the inflated share purchase price and any later economic loss is not invariably strong. Shares are normally purchased with an eye toward a later sale. But if, say, the purchaser sells the shares quickly before the relevant truth begins to leak out, the misrepresentation will not have led to any loss. If the purchaser sells later after the truth makes its way into the market place, an initially inflated purchase price *might* mean a later loss. But that is far from inevitably so. When the purchaser subsequently resells such shares, even at a lower price, that lower price may reflect, not the earlier misrepresentation, but changed economic circumstances, changed investor expectations, new industry-specific or firm-specific facts, conditions, or other events, which taken separately or together account for some or all of that lower price. (The same is true in respect to a claim that a share's higher price is lower than it would otherwise have been—a claim we do not consider here.) Other things being equal, the longer the time between purchase and sale, the more likely that this is so, *i.e.,* the more likely that other factors caused the loss.

Given the tangle of factors affecting price, the most logic alone permits us to say is that the higher purchase price will *sometimes* play a role in bringing about a future loss. It may prove to be a necessary condition of any such loss, and in that sense one might say that the inflated purchase price suggests that the misrepresentation (using language the Ninth Circuit used) "touches upon" a later economic loss. But, even if that is so, it is insufficient. To "touch upon" a loss is not to *cause* a loss, and it is the latter that the law requires.

For another thing, the Ninth Circuit's holding lacks support in precedent. Judicially implied private securities fraud actions resemble in many (but not all) respects common-law deceit and misrepresentation actions. The common law of deceit subjects a person who "fraudulently" makes a "misrepresentation" to liability "for pecuniary loss caused" to one who justifiably relies upon that misrepresentation. *Restatement (Second) of Torts* §525, p. 55 (1977) (hereinafter *Restatement of Torts*). . . . And the common law has long insisted that a plaintiff in such a case show not only that had he known the truth he would not have acted but also that he suffered actual economic loss.

Given the common-law roots of the securities fraud action (and the common-law requirement that a plaintiff show actual damages), it is not surprising that other courts of appeals have rejected the Ninth Circuit's "inflated purchase price" approach to proving causation and loss. Indeed, the *Restatement of Torts,* in setting forth the judicial consensus, says that a person who "misrepresents the financial condition of a corporation in order to sell its stock" becomes liable to a relying purchaser "for the loss" the purchaser sustains "when the facts . . . become generally known" and "as a result" share value "depreciate[s]." §548A, Comment *b,* at 107. Treatise writers, too, have emphasized the need to prove proximate causation. W. Keeton, et al., *Prosser and Keeton on Law of Torts* §110, at 767 (5th ed. 1984) (losses do "not afford any basis for recovery" if "brought about by business conditions or other factors"). We cannot reconcile the Ninth Circuit's "inflated purchase price" approach with these views of other courts. And the uniqueness of its perspective argues against the validity of its approach in a case like this one where we consider the contours of a judicially implied cause of action with roots in the common law.

Finally, the Ninth Circuit's approach overlooks an important securities law objective. The securities statutes seek to maintain public confidence in the marketplace. They do so by deterring fraud, in part, through the availability of private securities fraud actions. But the statutes make these latter actions available, not to provide investors with broad insurance against market losses, but to protect them against those economic losses that misrepresentations actually cause.

The [Private Securities Litigation Reform Act of 1995] insists that securities fraud complaints "specify" each misleading statement; that they set forth the facts "on which [a] belief" that a statement is misleading was "formed"; and that they "state with particularity facts giving rise to a strong inference that the defendant acted with the required state of mind." 15 U.S.C. §§78u-4(b)(1), (2). And the statute expressly imposes on plaintiffs "the burden of proving" that the defendant's misrepresentations "caused the loss for which the plaintiff seeks to recover." §78u-4(b)(4).

The statute thereby makes clear Congress' intent to permit private securities fraud actions for recovery where, but only where, plaintiffs adequately allege and prove the traditional elements of causation and loss. By way of contrast, the Ninth Circuit's approach would allow recovery where a misrepresentation leads to an inflated purchase price but nonetheless does not proximately cause any economic loss. That is to say, it would permit recovery where these two traditional elements in fact are missing.

In sum, we find the Ninth Circuit's approach inconsistent with the law's requirement that a plaintiff prove that the defendant's misrepresentation (or other fraudulent conduct) proximately caused the plaintiff's economic loss.

We reverse the judgment of the Ninth Circuit, and we remand the case for further proceedings consistent with this opinion.

It is so ordered.

Notes and Questions

1. Notes

a. The complaint also included the following allegations:
   (1) In respect to drug profits, Dura falsely claimed that it expected that its drug sales would prove profitable.
   (2) On the last day of the purchase period, February 24, 1998, Dura announced that its earnings would be lower than expected, principally due to slow drug sales.
   (3) The next day Dura's shares lost almost half their value (falling from about $39 per share to about $21).

These allegations are surely sufficient to show that plaintiffs suffered actual loss. Do you think that they sufficiently show loss causation?

2. Reality Check

a. Which elements of a 10b-5 claim did the Supreme Court find missing from the complaint?

b. In what way did the Ninth Circuit approach differ from that of the Supreme Court?

3. Suppose

a. Suppose the price of Dura stayed lower after the company announced that the FDA would not approve Dura's new asthmatic spray device. Would the complaint have stated a claim for relief under Rule 10b-5?

4. What Do You Think?

a. When it is clear that the defendant has made a misstatement of a material fact, why should a shareholder have to show damages and loss causation? Should the burden be on the defendant to show lack of damage or causation?

Dura Pharmaceuticals ticked off six elements for a claim under Rule 10b-5 and discussed two of them. Two of the other elements, the requirement that the fraud be "in connection with" a securities transaction and scienter, are explored in much more detail in the course in securities regulation. Nonetheless, a word or two about each of these requirements is appropriate here. The "in connection with" requirement was broadly defined by the Supreme Court in 1971. It is enough that a fraud touch or concern a securities transaction. The requirement is a frustrating one in that courts, in the end, find the requisite connection whenever the purposes of the securities act (i.e., protecting investors in securities) are met. This open standard generates a fair bit of litigation.

Since the mid-1970s the Supreme Court has held that the words of Section 10(b) proscribe actions that have deception at their core. The Court then held that 10b-5 liability requires that the defendant intend to deceive because deception implies intentional wrongdoing. That is, defendants must have scienter to be liable. Other courts have elaborated on this requirement of scienter. It is clear that the requisite intent to deceive is met where the defendant is aware that the misstatement could mislead. The defendant does not have to intend to bilk the plaintiff. For example, a mining company puts out a press release that falsely states that the company has not had a major ore discovery in a particular area. It does so not to deceive investors, but to give the company's employees time to obtain the mineral rights from other property owners adjacent to the ore discovery. Most courts would hold that the company nonetheless has the requisite scienter to render it liable under 10b-5 because it would have been aware that it was misstating an important fact. Virtually all courts hold that recklessness (that is, an extreme departure from the standards of ordinary care) as to whether a statement is true or false is sufficient to meet the scienter requirement. The Private Securities Litigation Reform Act of 1995 requires plaintiffs in class actions involving publicly traded securities to allege with particularity facts that create a "strong inference" that the defendant acted with scienter. Compare this to FRCP 9(b), which requires only that fraud be stated "with particularity."

The remaining two elements of a 10b-5 claim are that the defendant made a misstatement of a material fact, and that the plaintiff relied on that misstatement in deciding to enter into the transaction. The concept of materiality does much of the heavy lifting in securities regulation. That materiality and the definition of "security" are the two principal concepts that cabin the reach of the securities statutes. Materiality is not only a key component of 10b-5 liability, but much of the securities acts' disclosure requirements (and the related penalties for failing to meet those requirements) are based on the materiality of certain information. Securities lawyers and their clients spend endless hours debating whether a particular fact is material. They spend countless more hours massaging language to be publicly released to ensure that any statement is not misleading as to a material fact.

Materiality, for all its centrality, is nowhere defined in the securities statutes or regulations. Instead, the Supreme Court has adopted the following definition, which incidentally has been adopted verbatim, or nearly so, by many states (including Delaware) in connection with their own corporate laws:

> An omitted fact is material if there is a substantial likelihood that a reasonable shareholder would consider it important in deciding how to [act]. It does not require proof of a substantial likelihood that disclosure of the omitted fact would have caused the reasonable investor to [act]. What the standard does contemplate is a showing of a substantial likelihood that, under all the circumstances, the omitted fact would have assumed actual significance in the deliberations of the reasonable shareholder. Put another way, there must be a substantial likelihood that the disclosure of the omitted fact would have been viewed by the reasonable investor as having significantly altered the "total mix" of information made available.

TSC Industries, Inc. v. Northway, 426 U.S. 438, 449 (1976).

The requirement that the plaintiff rely on the misstatement in deciding to trade is sometimes called *transaction causation*. The next case, *Halliburton*, discusses the reliance requirement in one particularly problematic setting. In face-to-face transactions, the reliance requirement is relatively straightforward. But when the transaction occurs in a publicly traded stock, the defendant, usually the corporation or a director or officer, seldom has any direct contact with the plaintiff. Can the plaintiff rely, in any meaningful sense, on the alleged misstatement?

Halliburton Co. v. Erica P. John Fund, Inc.

134 S. Ct. 2398 (2014)

Chief Justice ROBERTS delivered the opinion of the Court.

Investors can recover damages in a private securities fraud action only if they prove that they relied on the defendant's misrepresentation in deciding to buy or sell a company's stock. In *Basic Inc. v. Levinson*, 485 U.S. 224, 108 S. Ct. 978, 99 L.Ed.2d 194 (1988), we held that investors could satisfy this reliance requirement by invoking a presumption that the price of stock traded in an efficient market reflects all public, material information—including material misstatements. In such a case, we concluded, anyone who buys or sells the stock at the market price may be considered to have relied on those misstatements.

We also held, however, that a defendant could rebut this presumption in a number of ways, including by showing that the alleged misrepresentation did not actually affect the stock's price—that is, that the misrepresentation had no "price impact." The questions presented are whether we should overrule or modify *Basic*'s presumption of reliance and, if not, whether defendants should nonetheless be afforded an opportunity in securities class action cases to rebut the presumption at the class certification stage, by showing a lack of price impact.

I

Respondent Erica P. John Fund, Inc. (EPJ Fund), is the lead plaintiff in a putative class action against Halliburton and one of its executives (collectively Halliburton) alleging violations of section 10(b) of the Securities Exchange Act of 1934, 48 Stat. 891, 15 U.S.C. §78j(b), and Securities and Exchange Commission Rule 10b-5, 17 CFR §240.10b-5 (2013). According to EPJ Fund, between June 3, 1999, and December 7, 2001, Halliburton made a series of misrepresentations regarding its potential liability in asbestos litigation, its expected revenue from certain construction contracts, and the anticipated benefits of its merger with another company—all in an attempt to inflate the price of its stock. Halliburton subsequently made a number of corrective disclosures, which, EPJ Fund contends, caused the company's stock price to drop and investors to lose money.

EPJ Fund moved to certify a class comprising all investors who purchased Halliburton common stock during the class period. [C]ircuit precedent required securities fraud plaintiffs to prove "loss causation"—a causal connection between the defendants' alleged misrepresentations and the plaintiffs' economic losses—in order to invoke *Basic*'s presumption of reliance and obtain class certification. Because EPJ Fund had not demonstrated such a connection for any of Halliburton's alleged misrepresentations, the District Court refused to certify the proposed class. The United States Court of Appeals for the Fifth Circuit affirmed the denial of class certification on the same ground.

We granted certiorari and vacated the judgment, finding nothing in "*Basic* or its logic" to justify the Fifth Circuit's requirement that securities fraud plaintiffs prove loss causation at the class certification stage in order to invoke *Basic*'s presumption of reliance. *Erica P. John Fund, Inc. v. Halliburton Co.*, 563 U.S. ____, ____, 131 S. Ct. 2179, 2185-2186, 180 L.Ed.2d 24 (2011) (*Halliburton I*). "Loss causation," we explained, "addresses a matter different from whether an investor relied on a misrepresentation, presumptively or otherwise, when buying or selling a stock." *Ibid.* We remanded the case for the lower courts to consider "any further arguments against class certification" that Halliburton had preserved. *Id.*, at ____, 131 S. Ct., at 2187.

On remand, Halliburton argued that class certification was inappropriate because the evidence it had earlier introduced to disprove loss causation also showed that none of its alleged misrepresentations had actually affected its stock price. By demonstrating the absence of any "price impact," Halliburton contended, it had rebutted *Basic*'s presumption that the members of the proposed class had relied on its alleged misrepresentations simply by buying or selling its stock at the market price. And without the benefit of the *Basic* presumption, investors would have to prove reliance on an individual basis, meaning that individual issues would predominate over common ones. The District Court declined to consider Halliburton's argument, holding that the *Basic* presumption applied and certifying the class under Rule 23(b)(3).

The Fifth Circuit affirmed. 718 F.3d 423 (2013). The court found that Halliburton had preserved its price impact argument, but to no avail. *Id.,* at 435-436. While acknowledging that "Halliburton's price impact evidence could be used at the trial on the merits to refute the presumption of reliance," *id.,* at 433, the court held that Halliburton could not use such evidence for that purpose at the class certification stage, *id.,* at 435. "[P]rice impact evidence," the court explained, "does not bear on the question of common question predominance [under Rule 23(b)(3)], and is thus appropriately considered only on the merits after the class has been certified." *Ibid.*

We once again granted certiorari, 571 U.S. ____, 134 S. Ct. 636, 187 L.Ed.2d 415 (2013), this time to resolve a conflict among the Circuits over whether securities fraud defendants may attempt to rebut the *Basic* presumption at the class certification stage with evidence of a lack of price impact. We also accepted Halliburton's invitation to reconsider the presumption of reliance for securities fraud claims that we adopted in *Basic.*

II

Halliburton urges us to overrule *Basic*'s presumption of reliance and to instead require every securities fraud plaintiff to prove that he actually relied on the defendant's misrepresentation in deciding to buy or sell a company's stock. Before overturning a long-settled precedent, however, we require "special justification," not just an argument that the precedent was wrongly decided. *Dickerson v. United States,* 530 U.S. 428, 443, 120 S. Ct. 2326, 147 L.Ed.2d 405 (2000) (internal quotation marks omitted). Halliburton has failed to make that showing.

A

Section 10(b) of the Securities Exchange Act of 1934 and the Securities and Exchange Commission's Rule 10b-5 prohibit making any material misstatement or omission in connection with the purchase or sale of any security. To recover damages for violations of section 10(b) and Rule 10b-5, a plaintiff must prove "'(1) a material misrepresentation or omission by the defendant; (2) scienter; (3) a connection between the misrepresentation or omission and the purchase or sale of a security; (4) reliance upon the misrepresentation or omission; (5) economic loss; and (6) loss causation.'" *Amgen Inc. v. Connecticut Retirement Plans and Trust Funds,* 568 U.S. ____, ____, 133 S. Ct. 1184, 1192, 185 L.Ed.2d 308 (2013) (quoting *Matrixx Initiatives, Inc. v. Siracusano,* 563 U.S. ____, ____, 131 S. Ct. 1309, 1317-1318, 179 L.Ed.2d 398 (2011)).

The reliance element "'ensures that there is a proper connection between a defendant's misrepresentation and a plaintiff's injury.'" 568 U.S., at ____, 133 S. Ct., at 1192 (quoting *Halliburton I,* 563 U.S., at ____, 131 S. Ct., at 2184-2185). "The traditional (and most direct) way a plaintiff can demonstrate reliance is by showing that he was aware of a company's statement and engaged in a relevant transaction—*e.g.,* purchasing common stock—based on that specific misrepresentation." *Id.,* at ____, 133 S. Ct., at 1192.

In *Basic,* however, we recognized that requiring such direct proof of reliance "would place an unnecessarily unrealistic evidentiary burden on the Rule 10b-5 plaintiff who has traded on an impersonal market." 485 U.S., at 245, 108 S. Ct. 978.

That is because, even assuming an investor could prove that he was aware of the misrepresentation, he would still have to "show a speculative state of facts, *i.e.,* how he would have acted . . . if the misrepresentation had not been made." *Ibid.*

We also noted that "[r]equiring proof of individualized reliance" from every securities fraud plaintiff "effectively would . . . prevent [ ] [plaintiffs] from proceeding with a class action" in Rule 10b-5 suits. *Id.,* at 242, 108 S. Ct. 978. If every plaintiff had to prove direct reliance on the defendant's misrepresentation, "individual issues then would . . . overwhelm[ ] the common ones," making certification under Rule 23(b)(3) inappropriate. *Ibid.*

To address these concerns, *Basic* held that securities fraud plaintiffs can in certain circumstances satisfy the reliance element of a Rule 10b-5 action by invoking a rebuttable presumption of reliance, rather than proving direct reliance on a misrepresentation. The Court based that presumption on what is known as the "fraud-on-the-market" theory, which holds that "the market price of shares traded on well-developed markets reflects all publicly available information, and, hence, any material misrepresentations." *Id.,* at 246, 108 S. Ct. 978. The Court also noted that, rather than scrutinize every piece of public information about a company for himself, the typical "investor who buys or sells stock at the price set by the market does so in reliance on the integrity of that price"—the belief that it reflects all public, material information. *Id.,* at 247, 108 S. Ct. 978. As a result, whenever the investor buys or sells stock at the market price, his "reliance on any public material misrepresentations . . . may be presumed for purposes of a Rule 10b-5 action." *Ibid.*

Based on this theory, a plaintiff must make the following showings to demonstrate that the presumption of reliance applies in a given case: (1) that the alleged misrepresentations were publicly known, (2) that they were material, (3) that the stock traded in an efficient market, and (4) that the plaintiff traded the stock between the time the misrepresentations were made and when the truth was revealed. See *id.,* at 248, n. 27, 108 S. Ct. 978; *Halliburton I, supra,* at ____, 131 S. Ct., at 2185-2186.

At the same time, *Basic* emphasized that the presumption of reliance was rebuttable rather than conclusive. Specifically, "[a]ny showing that severs the link between the alleged misrepresentation and either the price received (or paid) by the plaintiff, or his decision to trade at a fair market price, will be sufficient to rebut the presumption of reliance." 485 U.S., at 248, 108 S. Ct. 978. So for example, if a defendant could show that the alleged misrepresentation did not, for whatever reason, actually affect the market price, or that a plaintiff would have bought or sold the stock even had he been aware that the stock's price was tainted by fraud, then the presumption of reliance would not apply. *Id.,* at 248-249, 108 S. Ct. 978. In either of those cases, a plaintiff would have to prove that he directly relied on the defendant's misrepresentation in buying or selling the stock.

B

Halliburton contends that securities fraud plaintiffs should *always* have to prove direct reliance and that the *Basic* Court erred in allowing them to invoke a presumption of reliance instead. According to Halliburton, the *Basic* presumption contravenes congressional intent and has been undermined by subsequent developments in economic theory. Neither argument, however, so discredits *Basic* as to constitute "special justification" for overruling the decision.

2

Halliburton's primary argument for overruling *Basic* is that the decision rested on two premises that can no longer withstand scrutiny. The first premise concerns what is known as the "efficient capital markets hypothesis." *Basic* stated that "the market price of shares traded on well-developed markets reflects all publicly available information, and, hence, any material misrepresentations." *Id.,* at 246, 108 S. Ct. 978. From that statement, Halliburton concludes that the *Basic* Court espoused "a robust view of market efficiency" that is no longer tenable, for "'overwhelming empirical evidence' now 'suggests that capital markets are not fundamentally efficient.'" Brief for Petitioners 14-16 (quoting Lev & de Villiers, Stock Price Crashes and 10b-5 Damages: A Legal, Economic, and Policy Analysis, 47 STAN. L. REV 7, 20 (1994)). To support this contention, Halliburton cites studies purporting to show that "public information is often not incorporated immediately (much less rationally) into market prices." Brief for Petitioners 17; see *id.,* at 16-20. See also Brief for Law Professors as *Amici Curiae* 15-18.

Halliburton does not, of course, maintain that capital markets are *always* inefficient. Rather, in its view, *Basic*'s fundamental error was to ignore the fact that "'efficiency is not a binary, yes or no question.' " Brief for Petitioners 20 (quoting Langevoort, *Basic* at Twenty: Rethinking Fraud on the Market, 2009 WIS. L. REV. 151, 167). The markets for some securities are more efficient than the markets for others, and even a single market can process different kinds of information more or less efficiently, depending on how widely the information is disseminated and how easily it is understood. Brief for Petitioners at 20-21. Yet *Basic,* Halliburton asserts, glossed over these nuances, assuming a false dichotomy that renders the presumption of reliance both underinclusive and overinclusive: A misrepresentation can distort a stock's market price even in a generally inefficient market, and a misrepresentation can leave a stock's market price unaffected even in a generally efficient one. Brief for Petitioners at 21.

Halliburton's criticisms fail to take *Basic* on its own terms. Halliburton focuses on the debate among economists about the degree to which the market price of a company's stock reflects public information about the company—and thus the degree to which an investor can earn an abnormal, above-market return by trading on such information. See Brief for Financial Economists as *Amici Curiae* 4-10 (describing the debate). That debate is not new. Indeed, the *Basic* Court acknowledged it and declined to enter the fray, declaring that "[w]e need not determine by adjudication what economists and social scientists have debated through the use of sophisticated statistical analysis and the application of economic theory." 485 U.S., at 246-247, n. 24, 108 S. Ct. 978. To recognize the presumption of reliance, the Court explained, was not "conclusively to adopt any particular theory of how quickly and completely publicly available information is reflected in market price." *Id.,* at 248, n. 28, 108 S. Ct. 978. The Court instead based the presumption on the fairly modest premise that "market professionals generally consider most publicly announced material statements about companies, thereby affecting stock market prices." *Id.,* at 247, n. 24, 108 S. Ct. 978. *Basic*'s presumption of reliance thus does not rest on a "binary" view of market efficiency. Indeed, in making the presumption rebuttable, *Basic* recognized that market efficiency is a matter of degree and accordingly made it a matter of proof.

The academic debates discussed by Halliburton have not refuted the modest premise underlying the presumption of reliance. Even the foremost critics of the efficient-capital-markets hypothesis acknowledge that public information generally affects stock prices. See, *e.g.,* Shiller, We'll Share the Honors, and Agree to Disagree, N.Y. TIMES, Oct. 27, 2013, p. BU6 ("Of course, prices reflect available information"). Halliburton also conceded as much in its reply brief and at oral argument. See Reply Brief 13 ("market prices generally respond to new, material information"); Tr. of Oral Arg. 7. Debates about the precise *degree* to which stock prices accurately reflect public information are thus largely beside the point. "That the . . . price [of a stock] may be inaccurate does not detract from the fact that false statements affect it, and cause loss," which is "all that *Basic* requires." *Schleicher v. Wendt,* 618 F.3d 679, 685 (C.A.7 2010) (EASTERBROOK, C.J.). Even though the efficient capital markets hypothesis may have "garnered substantial criticism since *Basic,*" *post,* at 2420 (THOMAS, J., concurring in judgment), Halliburton has not identified the kind of fundamental shift in economic theory that could justify overruling a precedent on the ground that it misunderstood, or has since been overtaken by, economic realities. Contrast *State Oil Co. v. Khan,* 522 U.S. 3, 118 S. Ct. 275, 139 L.Ed.2d 199 (1997), unanimously overruling *Albrecht v. Herald Co.,* 390 U.S. 145, 88 S. Ct. 869, 19 L.Ed.2d 998 (1968).

Halliburton also contests a second premise underlying the *Basic* presumption: the notion that investors "invest 'in reliance on the integrity of [the market] price.'" Reply Brief 14 (quoting 485 U.S., at 247, 108 S. Ct. 978; alteration in original). Halliburton identifies a number of classes of investors for whom "price integrity" is supposedly "marginal or irrelevant." Reply Brief 14. The primary example is the value investor, who believes that certain stocks are undervalued or overvalued and attempts to "beat the market" by buying the undervalued stocks and selling the overvalued ones. Brief for Petitioners 15-16 (internal quotation marks omitted). See also Brief for Vivendi S.A. as *Amicus Curiae* 3-10 (describing the investment strategies of day traders, volatility arbitragers, and value investors). If many investors "are indifferent to prices," Halliburton contends, then courts should not presume that investors rely on the integrity of those prices and any misrepresentations incorporated into them. Reply Brief 14.

But *Basic* never denied the existence of such investors. As we recently explained, *Basic* concluded only that "it is reasonable to presume that *most* investors—knowing that they have little hope of outperforming the market in the long run based solely on their analysis of publicly available information—will rely on the security's market price as an unbiased assessment of the security's value in light of all public information." *Amgen,* 568 U.S., at ____, 133 S. Ct., at 1192 (emphasis added).

In any event, there is no reason to suppose that even Halliburton's main counterexample—the value investor—is as indifferent to the integrity of market prices as Halliburton suggests. Such an investor implicitly relies on the fact that a stock's market price will eventually reflect material information—how else could the market correction on which his profit depends occur? To be sure, the value investor "does not believe that the market price accurately reflects public information *at the time he transacts.*" *Post*, at 2423. But to indirectly rely on a misstatement in the sense relevant for the *Basic* presumption, he need only trade stock based on the belief that the market price will incorporate public information within a reasonable period. The value investor also presumably tries to estimate *how* undervalued or overvalued a particular stock is, and such estimates can be skewed by a market price tainted by fraud.

C

The principle of *stare decisis* has "'special force'" "in respect to statutory interpretation" because "'Congress remains free to alter what we have done.'" *John R. Sand & Gravel Co. v. United States*, 552 U.S. 130, 139, 128 S. Ct. 750, 169 L.Ed.2d 591 (2008) (quoting *Patterson v. McLean Credit Union*, 491 U.S. 164, 172-173, 109 S. Ct. 2363, 105 L.Ed.2d 132 (1989)). So too with *Basic*'s presumption of reliance. Although the presumption is a judicially created doctrine designed to implement a judicially created cause of action, we have described the presumption as "a substantive doctrine of federal securities-fraud law." *Amgen, supra*, at ____, 133 S. Ct., at 1193. That is because it provides a way of satisfying the reliance element of the Rule 10b-5 cause of action. See, *e.g.*, *Dura Pharmaceuticals, Inc. v. Broudo*, 544 U.S. 336, 341-342, 125 S. Ct. 1627, 161 L.Ed.2d 577 (2005). As with any other element of that cause of action, Congress may overturn or modify any aspect of our interpretations of the reliance requirement, including the *Basic* presumption itself. Given that possibility, we see no reason to exempt the *Basic* presumption from ordinary principles of *stare decisis*.

[The Court held that defendants may attempt to rebut the *Basic* presumption at the class certification state. That discussion is omitted.]

More than 25 years ago, we held that plaintiffs could satisfy the reliance element of the Rule 10b-5 cause of action by invoking a presumption that a public, material misrepresentation will distort the price of stock traded in an efficient market, and that anyone who purchases the stock at the market price may be considered to have done so in reliance on the misrepresentation. We adhere to that decision and decline to modify the prerequisites for invoking the presumption of reliance. But to maintain the consistency of the presumption with the class certification requirements of Federal Rule of Civil Procedure 23, defendants must be afforded an opportunity before class certification to defeat the presumption through evidence that an alleged misrepresentation did not actually affect the market price of the stock.

Because the courts below denied Halliburton that opportunity, we vacate the judgment of the Court of Appeals for the Fifth Circuit and remand the case for further proceedings consistent with this opinion.

It is so ordered.

Notes and Questions

1. Note

a. In *Basic, Inc. v. Levinson*, cited in *Halliburton*, the Court spoke to the dilemma corporations face when asked about information they do not wish to disclose. This is especially sensitive when a corporation is dealing with rumors of a potential merger. Assuming the information about a pending merger is material, the corporation cannot lie in responding to questions. The Court said,

> To be actionable, of course, a statement must also be misleading. Silence, absent a duty to disclose, is not misleading under Rule 10b-5. "No comment" statements are generally the functional equivalent of silence.
>
> It has been suggested that given current market practices, a "no comment" statement is tantamount to an admission that merger discussions are underway. That may well hold true to the extent that issuers adopt a policy of truthfully denying merger rumors when no discussions are underway, and of issuing "no comment" statements when they are in the midst of negotiations. There are, of course, other statement policies firms could adopt; we need not now advise issuers as to what kind of practice to follow, within the range permitted by law.

Basic Inc. v. Levinson, 485 U.S. 224, 239 n.17.

2. Reality Check

a. Is reliance an element of a 10b-5 claim? Why?

b. What is the fraud-on-the-market theory? Why is it important to litigants?

c. What are the arguments the Court cites for and against the fraud-on-the-market theory?

d. Why can't plaintiffs include more precise allegations of reliance in their complaint?

3. What Do You Think?

a. Do you think that the fraud-on-the-market theory makes economic sense? Does it make sense as a matter of securities regulation?

A close reading of 10b-5(b) shows that two things are prohibited. One is a misstatement of a material fact. The other is omitting to state a material fact necessary in order to make the statements made, in the light of the circumstances under which they were made, not misleading. That's a long-winded way of saying that half-truths are prohibited. The corollary of these prohibitions is that corporations (and other potential defendants) have a duty to correct misstatements of material facts and half-truths they have made. A related concept is a duty to update. A statement may be true when made (and not a half-truth), but subsequent events may render the statement untrue. Case law supports an obligation to update the statement if the statement is still likely to be relied upon by the investment community. Seen in this way, the duty to update is really a duty to correct, because the theory is that statements are in some sense continuously "made" until investors stop relying on them. The reality of the securities markets is that publicly made statements have a relatively short half-life. This aspect of the securities markets means that the duty to update is of relatively short duration as to any particular statement.

Notice that 10b-5 does not impose liability for omissions except when a defendant has stated a half-truth. Nonetheless, courts have held that a defendant may be liable for an omission when under a duty to speak, even when no half-truth has been made. A duty to speak can arise in several ways. First, a publicly held company is under a duty to file reports every three months with the SEC. Those reports call for specific disclosure, and surely omitting such disclosure is actionable under 10b-5. Second, state corporate law may impose a fiduciary duty to disclose certain information to shareholders. For example, corporations must disclose all material information to shareholders whenever shareholders are voting. Third, the stock markets, such as the New York Stock Exchange, impose an obligation on listed corporations to release material information quickly, though that standard is applied rather flexibly to permit corporations a fair bit of leeway in deciding when to make disclosures.

a. Insider Trading

A special application of the antifraud provisions of Rule 10b-5 is the prohibition against insider trading. Insider trading is a shorthand phrase meaning a trade made while in possession of material nonpublic information. We have covered the concept of materiality above. You can intuit the contours of issues surrounding whether information has become public. These involve temporal questions — how long must information be available before it's public — and spatial questions — where must the information appear to be considered public? These are developed in the securities regulation course. For our purposes, we'll look at the development of insider trading liability under Rule 10b-5.

We start with the most basic question. Assuming that a high corporate official (e.g., an officer or director, to pick the easy cases) or even the corporation itself buys or sells stock while in possession of material nonpublic information, how does 10b-5 liability attach? Remember, by definition there is no misstatement of a material fact, because there's no statement at all. Likewise, there is no half-truth that must be corrected. In other words, insider trading is a subset of the cases imposing liability for omissions. The first case, which was an SEC administrative proceeding, sets out what is sometimes called the classic theory of insider trading liability.

In the Matter of Cady, Roberts & Co.

40 S.E.C. 907 (1961)

By CARY, Chairman:

On the morning of November 25, the Curtiss-Wright [Corporation] directors . . . approved a dividend for the fourth quarter at the reduced rate of $.375 per share. At approximately 11:00 A.M., the board authorized transmission of information of this action by telegram to the New York Stock Exchange. There was a short delay in the transmission of the telegram because of a typing problem and the telegram, . . . was not delivered to the Exchange until 12:29 P.M. [T]he announcement did not appear on the Dow Jones ticker tape until 11:48 A.M.

Sometime after the dividend decision, there was a recess of the Curtiss-Wright directors' meeting, during which Cowdin [a Board member and a broker at Cady, Roberts & Co.] telephoned . . . and left a message for Gintel [also a Cady, Roberts broker] that the dividend had been cut. Upon receiving this information, Gintel entered two sell orders for execution on the Exchange. . . . These orders were executed at 11:15 and 11:18 A.M. at 40¼ and 40⅜, respectively.

When the dividend announcement appeared on the Dow Jones tape at 11:48 A.M., the Exchange was compelled to suspend trading in Curtiss-Wright because of the large number of sell orders. Trading in Curtiss-Wright stock was resumed at 1:59 P.M. at 36½, ranged during the balance of the day between 34⅛ and 37, and closed at 34⅞.

So many times that citation is unnecessary, we have indicated that the purchase and sale of securities is a field in special need of regulation for the protection of investors. To this end one of the major purposes of the securities acts is the prevention of fraud, manipulation or deception in connection with securities transactions. Consistent with this objective, . . . Section 10(b) of the Exchange Act and Rule 10b-5, issued under that Section, are broad remedial provisions aimed at reaching misleading or deceptive activities, whether or not they are precisely and technically sufficient to sustain a common law action for fraud and deceit.

[They] apply to securities transactions by "any person." Misrepresentations will lie within their ambit, no matter who the speaker may be. An affirmative duty to disclose material information has been traditionally imposed on corporate "insiders," particularly officers, directors, or controlling stockholders. We, and the courts have consistently held that insiders must disclose material facts which are known to them by virtue of their position but which are not known to persons with whom they deal and which, if known, would affect their investment judgment. Failure to make disclosure in these circumstances constitutes a violation of the antifraud provisions. If, on the other hand, disclosure prior to effecting a purchase or sale would be improper or unrealistic under the circumstances, we believe the alternative is to forego the transaction.

These three groups, however, do not exhaust the classes of persons upon whom there is such an obligation. Analytically, the obligation rests on two principal elements; first, the existence of a relationship giving access, directly or indirectly, to information intended to be available only for a corporate purpose and not for the personal benefit of anyone, and second, the inherent unfairness involved where a party takes advantage of such information knowing it is unavailable to those with whom he is dealing. Thus our task here is to identify those persons who are in a special relationship with a company and privy to its internal affairs, and thereby suffer correlative duties in trading in its securities.

Respondents further assert that they made no express representations and did not in any way manipulate the market, and urge that in a transaction on an exchange there is no further duty such as may be required in a "face-to-face" transaction. We reject this suggestion. It would be anomalous indeed if the protection afforded by the antifraud provisions were withdrawn from transactions effected on exchanges, primary markets for securities transactions. If purchasers on an exchange had available material information known by a selling insider, we may assume that their investment judgment would be affected and their decision whether to buy might accordingly be modified. Consequently, any sales by the insider must await disclosure of the information.

Notes and Questions

1. Notes

a. William L. Cary was a longtime corporate and securities law professor at Columbia Law School. He was tapped by President Kennedy to serve as chair of the SEC.

b. The SEC has adopted Rule 10b5-1, which provides a safe harbor for sale of stock by insiders. In brief, the rule provides that insiders may sell shares without violating Rule 10b-5 if they do so pursuant to a preexisting plan of trading. Most top executives of public companies sell their shares pursuant to a plan of this kind.

2. Reality Check

a. Who violated 10b-5? How did they violate the rule?

b. What material fact was omitted?

3. What Do You Think?

a. Should 10b-5 liability for omissions turn on whether a duty runs from the defendant to the plaintiff?

Cady, Roberts predicates its holding on two assertions. "[F]irst, the existence of a relationship giving access, directly or indirectly, to information intended to be available only for a corporate purpose and not for the personal benefit of anyone, and second, the inherent unfairness involved where a party takes advantage of such information knowing it is unavailable to those with whom he is dealing." May liability be imposed when only one of these is met? The next case explores that question.

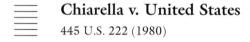

Chiarella v. United States
445 U.S. 222 (1980)

Mr. Justice Powell delivered the opinion of the Court.

I

Petitioner is a printer by trade. In 1975 and 1976, he worked as a "markup man" in the New York composing room of Pandick Press, a financial printer. Among documents that petitioner handled were five announcements of corporate takeover bids. When these documents were delivered to the printer, the identities of the acquiring and target corporations were concealed by blank spaces or false names. The true names were sent to the printer on the night of the final printing.

The petitioner, however, was able to deduce the names of the target companies before the final printing from other information contained in the documents. Without disclosing his knowledge, petitioner purchased stock in the target companies and sold the shares immediately after the takeover attempts were made public. By this method, petitioner realized a gain of slightly more than $30,000 in the course of 14 months.

In January 1978, petitioner was indicted on 17 counts of violating §10(b) of the Securities Exchange Act of 1934 (1934 Act) and SEC Rule 10b-5. After petitioner unsuccessfully moved to dismiss the indictment, he was brought to trial and convicted on all counts.

The Court of Appeals for the Second Circuit affirmed petitioner's conviction. We granted certiorari and we now reverse.

II

This case concerns the legal effect of the petitioner's silence. The District Court's charge permitted the jury to convict the petitioner if it found that he willfully failed to inform sellers of target company securities that he knew of a forthcoming takeover bid that would make their shares more valuable.

Although the starting point of our inquiry is the language of the statute, §10(b) does not state whether silence may constitute a manipulative or deceptive device. Section 10(b) was designed as a catchall clause to prevent fraudulent practices. But neither the legislative history nor the statute itself affords specific guidance for the resolution of this case. When Rule 10b-5 was promulgated in 1942, the SEC did not discuss the possibility that failure to provide information might run afoul of §10(b).

That the relationship between a corporate insider and the stockholders of his corporation gives rise to a disclosure obligation is not a novel twist of the law. At common law, misrepresentation made for the purpose of inducing reliance upon the false statement is fraudulent. But one who fails to disclose material information prior to the consummation of a transaction commits fraud only when he is under a duty to do so. And the duty to disclose arises when one party has information "that the other [party] is entitled to know because of a fiduciary or other similar relation of trust and confidence between them."[9] In its *Cady, Roberts* decision, the Commission recognized a relationship of trust and confidence between the shareholders of a corporation and those insiders who have obtained confidential information by reason of their position with that corporation. This relationship gives rise to a duty to disclose because of the "necessity of preventing a corporate insider from . . . tak[ing] unfair advantage of the uninformed minority stockholders." *Speed v. Transamerica Corp.*, 99 F. Supp. 808, 829 (D. Del. 1951).

The federal courts have found violations of §10(b) where corporate insiders used undisclosed information for their own benefit. The cases also have emphasized, in accordance with the common-law rule, that "[t]he party charged with failing to disclose market information must be under a duty to disclose it." *Frigitemp Corp. v. Financial Dynamics Fund, Inc.*, 524 F.2d 275, 282 (2d Cir. 1975). Accordingly, a purchaser of stock who has no duty to a prospective seller because he is neither an insider nor a fiduciary has been held to have no obligation to reveal material facts.

Thus, administrative and judicial interpretations have established that silence in connection with the purchase or sale of securities may operate as a fraud actionable under §10(b) despite the absence of statutory language or legislative history specifically addressing the legality of nondisclosure. But such liability is premised upon a duty to disclose arising from a relationship of trust and confidence between parties to a transaction. Application of a duty to disclose prior to trading guarantees

---

9. *Restatement (Second) of Torts* §551(a)(2) (1976).

that corporate insiders, who have an obligation to place the shareholder's welfare before their own, will not benefit personally through fraudulent use of material, nonpublic information.

III

In this case, the petitioner was convicted of violating §10(b) although he was not a corporate insider and he received no confidential information from the target company. Moreover, the "market information" upon which he relied did not concern the earning power or operations of the target company, but only the plans of the acquiring company. Petitioner's use of that information was not a fraud under §10(b) unless he was subject to an affirmative duty to disclose it before trading. In this case, the jury instructions failed to specify any such duty. In effect, the trial court instructed the jury that petitioner owed a duty to everyone; to all sellers, indeed, to the market as a whole. The jury simply was told to decide whether petitioner used material, nonpublic information at a time when "he knew other people trading in the securities market did not have access to the same information."

The Court of Appeals affirmed the conviction by holding that "*[a]nyone*— corporate insider or not — who regularly receives material nonpublic information may not use that information to trade in securities without incurring an affirmative duty to disclose." 588 F.2d, at 1365 (emphasis in original). Its decision thus rested solely upon its belief that the federal securities laws have "created a system providing equal access to information necessary for reasoned and intelligent investment decisions." *Id.*, at 1362. The use by anyone of material information not generally available is fraudulent, this theory suggests, because such information gives certain buyers or sellers an unfair advantage over less informed buyers and sellers.

This reasoning suffers from two defects. First not every instance of financial unfairness constitutes fraudulent activity under §10(b). Second, the element required to make silence fraudulent — a duty to disclose — is absent in this case. No duty could arise from petitioner's relationship with the sellers of the target company's securities, for petitioner had no prior dealings with them. He was not their agent, he was not a fiduciary, he was not a person in whom the sellers had placed their trust and confidence. He was, in fact, a complete stranger who dealt with the sellers only through impersonal market transactions.

We cannot affirm petitioner's conviction without recognizing a general duty between all participants in market transactions to forgo actions based on material, nonpublic information. Formulation of such a broad duty, which departs radically from the established doctrine that duty arises from a specific relationship between two parties, . . . should not be undertaken absent some explicit evidence of congressional intent.

As we have seen, no such evidence emerges from the language or legislative history of §10(b). Moreover, neither the Congress nor the Commission ever has adopted a parity-of-information rule.

We see no basis for applying such a new and different theory of liability in this case. As we have emphasized before, the 1934 Act cannot be read "'more broadly than its language and the statutory scheme reasonably permit.'" *Touche Ross & Co. v. Redington*, 442 U.S. 560, 578 (1979), quoting *SEC v. Sloan*, 436 U.S. 103 (1978). Section 10(b) is aptly described as a catchall provision, but what it catches must be fraud. When an allegation of fraud is based upon nondisclosure, there can be no fraud absent a duty to speak. We hold that a duty to disclose under §10(b) does not arise from the mere possession of nonpublic market information. The contrary result is without support in the legislative history of §10(b) and would be inconsistent with the careful plan that Congress has enacted for regulation of the securities markets.

The judgment of the Court of Appeals is *reversed*.

Notes and Questions

1. Reality Check

a. Why was Mr. Chiarella's conviction reversed?

2. Suppose

a. Suppose Mr. Chiarella traded in the stock of a company that had hired his employer to print its annual report to stockholders. Would he be liable under 10b-5? How is that setting different from the facts of *Chiarella*?

3. What Do You Think?

a. Do you agree that a relationship of trust and confidence should be a requirement of insider trading? What about *Cady, Roberts*'s predicate of the unfairness of insider trading? Isn't what Mr. Chiarella did fundamentally unfair?

The result in *Chiarella* turned on the notion that insider trading, in the air, so to speak, will not do. If the defendant breached a duty to someone, but not the plaintiff, is that sufficient to impose liability under 10b-5? The next case resolves that question.

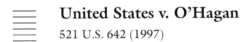

United States v. O'Hagan

521 U.S. 642 (1997)

Justice GINSBURG delivered the opinion of the Court.

Respondent James Herman O'Hagan was a partner in the law firm of Dorsey & Whitney in Minneapolis, Minnesota. In July 1988, Grand Metropolitan PLC (Grand Met), a company based in London, England, retained Dorsey & Whitney as local counsel to represent Grand Met regarding a potential tender offer for the common stock of the Pillsbury Company, headquartered in Minneapolis. Both Grand Met and Dorsey & Whitney took precautions to protect the confidentiality of Grand Met's tender offer plans. O'Hagan did no work on the Grand Met representation. Dorsey & Whitney withdrew from representing Grand Met on September 9, 1988. Less than a month later, on October 4, 1988, Grand Met publicly announced its tender offer for Pillsbury stock.

On August 18, 1988, while Dorsey & Whitney was still representing Grand Met, O'Hagan began purchasing call options for Pillsbury stock. Each option gave him the right to purchase 100 shares of Pillsbury stock by a specified date in September 1988. Later in August and in September, O'Hagan made additional purchases of Pillsbury call options. By the end of September, he owned 2,500 unexpired Pillsbury options, apparently more than any other individual investor. O'Hagan also purchased, in September 1988, some 5,000 shares of Pillsbury common stock, at a price just under $39 per share. When Grand Met announced its tender offer in October, the price of Pillsbury stock rose to nearly $60 per share. O'Hagan then sold his Pillsbury call options and common stock, making a profit of more than $4.3 million.

The Securities and Exchange Commission (SEC or Commission) initiated an investigation into O'Hagan's transactions, culminating in a 57-count indictment. The indictment alleged that O'Hagan defrauded his law firm and its client, Grand Met, by using for his own trading purposes material, nonpublic information regarding Grand Met's planned tender offer. According to the indictment, O'Hagan used the profits he gained through this trading to conceal his previous embezzlement and conversion of unrelated client trust funds. O'Hagan was charged with 20 counts of mail fraud, in violation of 18 U.S.C. §1341; 17 counts of securities fraud, in violation of §10(b) of the Securities Exchange Act of 1934 (Exchange Act) and SEC Rule 10b-5; 17 counts of fraudulent trading in connection with a tender offer, in violation of §14(e) of the Exchange Act and SEC Rule 14e-3(a); and 3 counts of violating federal money laundering statutes, 18 U.S.C. §§1956(a)(1)(B)(i), 1957. A jury convicted O'Hagan on all 57 counts, and he was sentenced to a 41-month term of imprisonment. A divided panel of the Court of Appeals for the Eighth Circuit reversed all of O'Hagan's convictions. Liability under §10(b) and Rule 10b-5, the Eighth Circuit held, may not be grounded on the "misappropriation theory" of securities fraud on which the prosecution relied.

Decisions of the Courts of Appeals are in conflict on the propriety of the misappropriation theory under §10(b) and Rule 10b-5. . . . We granted certiorari and now reverse the Eighth Circuit's judgment.[4]

The "misappropriation theory" holds that a person commits fraud "in connection with" a securities transaction, and thereby violates §10(b) and Rule 10b-5, when he misappropriates confidential information for securities trading purposes, in breach of a duty owed to the source of the information. Under this theory, a fiduciary's undisclosed, self-serving use of a principal's information to purchase or sell securities, in breach of a duty of loyalty and confidentiality, defrauds the principal of the exclusive use of that information. In lieu of premising liability on a fiduciary relationship between company insider and purchaser or seller of the company's stock, the misappropriation theory premises liability on a fiduciary-turned-trader's deception of those who entrusted him with access to confidential information.

The [classical and misappropriation] theories are complementary, each addressing efforts to capitalize on nonpublic information through the purchase or sale of securities. The classical theory targets a corporate insider's breach of duty to shareholders with whom the insider transacts; the misappropriation theory outlaws trading on the basis of nonpublic information by a corporate "outsider" in breach of

---

4. Twice before we have been presented with the question whether criminal liability for violation of §10(b) may be based on a misappropriation theory. In *Chiarella v. United States,* 445 U.S. 222, 235-237 (1980), the jury had received no misappropriation theory instructions, so we declined to address the question. In *Carpenter v. United States,* 484 U.S. 19, 24 (1987), the Court divided evenly on whether, under the circumstances of that case, convictions resting on the misappropriation theory should be affirmed.

a duty owed not to a trading party, but to the source of the information. The misappropriation theory is thus designed to "protec[t] the integrity of the securities markets against abuses by 'outsiders' to a corporation who have access to confidential information that will affect th[e] corporation's security price when revealed, but who owe no fiduciary or other duty to that corporation's shareholders." Brief for United States 14.

In this case, the indictment alleged that O'Hagan, in breach of a duty of trust and confidence he owed to his law firm, Dorsey & Whitney, and to its client, Grand Met, traded on the basis of nonpublic information regarding Grand Met's planned tender offer for Pillsbury common stock. This conduct, the Government charged, constituted a fraudulent device in connection with the purchase and sale of securities.[5]

We agree with the Government that misappropriation, as just defined, satisfies §10(b)'s requirement that chargeable conduct involve a "deceptive device or contrivance" used "in connection with" the purchase or sale of securities. We observe, first, that misappropriators, as the Government describes them, deal in deception. A fiduciary who "[pretends] loyalty to the principal while secretly converting the principal's information for personal gain," Brief for United States 17, "dupes" or defrauds the principal.

Deception through nondisclosure is central to the theory of liability for which the Government seeks recognition. As counsel for the Government stated in explanation of the theory at oral argument: "To satisfy the common law rule that a trustee may not use the property that [has] been entrusted [to] him, there would have to be consent. To satisfy the requirement of the Securities Act that there be no deception, there would only have to be disclosure."

We turn next to the §10(b) requirement that the misappropriator's deceptive use of information be "in connection with the purchase or sale of [a] security." This element is satisfied because the fiduciary's fraud is consummated, not when the fiduciary gains the confidential information, but when, without disclosure to his principal, he uses the information to purchase or sell securities. The securities transaction and the breach of duty thus coincide. This is so even though the person or entity defrauded is not the other party to the trade, but is, instead, the source of the nonpublic information. A misappropriator who trades on the basis of material, nonpublic information, in short, gains his advantageous market position through deception; he deceives the source of the information and simultaneously harms members of the investing public.

The misappropriation theory targets information of a sort that misappropriators ordinarily capitalize upon to gain no-risk profits through the purchase or sale of securities. Should a misappropriator put such information to other use, the statute's prohibition would not be implicated. The theory does not catch all conceivable forms of fraud involving confidential information; rather, it catches fraudulent means of capitalizing on such information through securities transactions.

---

5. The Government could not have prosecuted O'Hagan under the classical theory, for O'Hagan was not an "insider" of Pillsbury, the corporation in whose stock he traded. Although an "outsider" with respect to Pillsbury, O'Hagan had an intimate association with, and was found to have traded on confidential information from, Dorsey & Whitney, counsel to tender offeror Grand Met. Under the misappropriation theory, O'Hagan's securities trading does not escape Exchange Act sanction . . . simply because he was associated with, and gained nonpublic information from, the bidder, rather than the target.

The Government notes another limitation on the forms of fraud §10(b) reaches: "The misappropriation theory would not . . . apply to a case in which a person defrauded a bank into giving him a loan or embezzled cash from another, and then used the proceeds of the misdeed to purchase securities." Brief for United States 24, n.13. In such a case, the Government states, "the proceeds would have value to the malefactor apart from their use in a securities transaction, and the fraud would be complete as soon as the money was obtained." *Ibid.* In other words, money can buy, if not anything, then at least many things; its misappropriation may thus be viewed as sufficiently detached from a subsequent securities transaction that §10(b)'s "in connection with" requirement would not be met. *Ibid.*

The misappropriation theory comports with §10(b)'s language, which requires deception "in connection with the purchase or sale of any security," not deception of an identifiable purchaser or seller. The theory is also well tuned to an animating purpose of the Exchange Act: to insure honest securities markets and thereby promote investor confidence. Although informational disparity is inevitable in the securities markets, investors likely would hesitate to venture their capital in a market where trading based on misappropriated nonpublic information is unchecked by law. An investor's informational disadvantage vis-à-vis a misappropriator with material, nonpublic information stems from contrivance, not luck; it is a disadvantage that cannot be overcome with research or skill.

[C]onsidering the inhibiting impact on market participation of trading on misappropriated information, and the congressional purposes underlying §10(b), it makes scant sense to hold a lawyer like O'Hagan a §10(b) violator if he works for a law firm representing the target of a tender offer, but not if he works for a law firm representing the bidder. The text of the statute requires no such result. The misappropriation at issue here was properly made the subject of a §10(b) charge because it meets the statutory requirement that there be "deceptive" conduct "in connection with" securities transactions.

In sum, the misappropriation theory, as we have examined and explained it in this opinion, is both consistent with the statute and with our precedent. Vital to our decision that criminal liability may be sustained under the misappropriation theory, we emphasize, are two sturdy safeguards Congress has provided regarding scienter. To establish a criminal violation of Rule 10b-5, the Government must prove that a person "willfully" violated the provision. Furthermore, a defendant may not be imprisoned for violating Rule 10b-5 if he proves that he had no knowledge of the Rule. O'Hagan's charge that the misappropriation theory is too indefinite to permit the imposition of criminal liability thus fails not only because the theory is limited to those who breach a recognized duty.

The Eighth Circuit erred in holding that the misappropriation theory is inconsistent with §10(b). The Court of Appeals may address on remand O'Hagan's other challenges to his convictions under §10(b) and Rule 10b-5.

The judgment of the Court of Appeals for the Eighth Circuit is reversed, and the case is remanded for further proceedings consistent with this opinion.

It is so ordered.

Notes and Questions

1. Notes

a. After *O'Hagan,* it is clear that many people who breach a confidence may be liable under 10b-5. A psychiatrist, for example, who uses information gleaned from an executive/patient to trade in company stock may be liable under the misappropriation theory. Similarly, a family member may breach a confidence with another family member. To give some certainty to this area, the SEC adopted Rule 10b5-2. The rule provides that a "duty of trust or confidence" exists

> (1) Whenever a person agrees to maintain information in confidence;
>
> (2) Whenever the person communicating the material nonpublic information and the person to whom it is communicated have a history, pattern, or practice of sharing confidences, such that the recipient of the information knows or reasonably should know that the person communicating the material nonpublic information expects that the recipient will maintain its confidentiality; or
>
> (3) Whenever a person receives or obtains material nonpublic information from his or her spouse, parent, child, or sibling; provided, however, that the person receiving or obtaining the information may demonstrate that no duty of trust or confidence existed with respect to the information, by establishing that he or she neither knew nor reasonably should have known that the person who was the source of the information expected that the person would keep the information confidential, because of the parties' history, pattern, or practice of sharing and maintaining confidences, and because there was no agreement or understanding to maintain the confidentiality of the information.

Rule 10b5-2

2. Reality Check

a. What is the misappropriation theory? How is it different from the classical theory of insider trading?

b. Where is the deception under the misappropriation theory?

c. Is the defendant's misappropriation "in connection with" the purchase or sale of a security?

3. Suppose

a. Suppose the facts of *Chiarella* arose today? Would Mr. Chiarella be held to have violated 10b-5?

b. Suppose Dorsey & Whitney had a policy of permitting its lawyers to trade on nonpublic information, as a way of providing additional compensation. Would Mr. O'Hagan be liable under 10b-5?

c. Suppose Mr. O'Hagan had told Dorsey & Whitney he intended to trade in Pillsbury stock and options. Would Mr. O'Hagan be liable under 10b-5?

4. What Do You Think?

a. Is the misappropriation theory consonant with the classic theory? If not, which should prevail?

b. Does the O'Hagan holding essentially impose liability for insider trading on the ground that such trading is fundamentally and inherently unfair?

Cady, Roberts provides a theoretical structure for traditionally conceived insider trading. *Chiarella* shows the limits of that structure and *O'Hagan* sanctions liability under the misappropriation theory of insider trading. All of those cases involved trading by the insider. Suppose the insider doesn't trade but transmits material nonpublic information to someone else who does trade? Is that trader, called the tippee, automatically liable? What if the original tippee in turn tips others who also trade? The final case describes the legal theory for tippee liability.

Salman v. United States
137 S. Ct. 420 (2016)

OPINION

Justice ALITO delivered the opinion of the Court.

Section 10(b) of the Securities Exchange Act of 1934 and the Securities and Exchange Commission's Rule 10b-5 prohibit undisclosed trading on inside corporate information by individuals who are under a duty of trust and confidence that prohibits them from secretly using such information for their personal advantage. Individuals under this duty may face criminal and civil liability for trading on inside information (unless they make appropriate disclosures ahead of time).

These persons also may not tip inside information to others for trading. The tippee acquires the tipper's duty to disclose or abstain from trading if the tippee knows the information was disclosed in breach of the tipper's duty, and the tippee may commit securities fraud by trading in disregard of that knowledge. In *Dirks v. SEC,* 463 U.S. 646, 103 S. Ct. 3255, 77 L.Ed.2d 911 (1983), this Court explained that a tippee's liability for trading on inside information hinges on whether the tipper breached a fiduciary duty by disclosing the information. A tipper breaches such a fiduciary duty, we held, when the tipper discloses the inside information for a personal benefit. And, we went on to say, a jury can infer a personal benefit—and thus a breach of the tipper's duty—where the tipper receives something of value in exchange for the tip or "makes a gift of confidential information to a trading relative or friend." *Id.,* at 664, 103 S. Ct. 3255.

Petitioner Bassam Salman challenges his convictions for conspiracy and insider trading. Salman received lucrative trading tips from an extended family member, who had received the information from Salman's brother-in-law. Salman then traded on the information. He argues that he cannot be held liable as a tippee because the tipper (his brother-in-law) did not personally receive money or property in exchange for the tips and thus did not personally benefit from them. The Court of Appeals disagreed, holding that *Dirks* allowed the jury to infer that the tipper here breached a duty because he made a " 'gift of confidential information to a trading relative.' " 792 F.3d 1087, 1092 (C.A.9 2015) (quoting *Dirks, supra,* at 664, 103 S. Ct. 3255). Because the Court of Appeals properly applied *Dirks,* we affirm the judgment below.

I

Maher Kara was an investment banker in Citigroup's healthcare investment banking group. He dealt with highly confidential information about mergers and acquisitions involving Citigroup's clients. Maher enjoyed a close relationship with his older brother, Mounir Kara (known as Michael). After Maher started at Citigroup, he began discussing aspects of his job with Michael. At first he relied on Michael's chemistry background to help him grasp scientific concepts relevant to his new job. Then, while their father was battling cancer, the brothers discussed companies that dealt with innovative cancer treatment and pain management techniques. Michael began to trade on the information Maher shared with him. At first, Maher was unaware of his brother's trading activity, but eventually he began to suspect that it was taking place.

Ultimately, Maher began to assist Michael's trading by sharing inside information with his brother about pending mergers and acquisitions. Maher sometimes used code words to communicate corporate information to his brother. Other times, he shared inside information about deals he was not working on in order to avoid detection. Without his younger brother's knowledge, Michael fed the information to others—including Salman, Michael's friend and Maher's brother-in-law. By the time the authorities caught on, Salman had made over $1.5 million in profits that he split with another relative who executed trades via a brokerage account on Salman's behalf.

Salman was indicted on one count of conspiracy to commit securities fraud, and four counts of securities fraud. Facing charges of their own, both Maher and Michael pleaded guilty and testified at Salman's trial.

The evidence at trial established that Maher and Michael enjoyed a "very close relationship." Maher "love[d] [his] brother very much," Michael was like "a second father to Maher," and Michael was the best man at Maher's wedding to Salman's sister. Maher testified that he shared inside information with his brother to benefit him and with the expectation that his brother would trade on it. While Maher explained that he disclosed the information in large part to appease Michael (who pestered him incessantly for it), he also testified that he tipped his brother to "help him" and to "fulfil[l] whatever needs he had." For instance, Michael once called Maher and told him that "he needed a favor." Maher offered his brother money but Michael asked for information instead. Maher then disclosed an upcoming acquisition. Although he instantly regretted the tip and called his brother back to implore him not to trade, Maher expected his brother to do so anyway.

For his part, Michael told the jury that his brother's tips gave him "timely information that the average person does not have access to" and "access to stocks, options, and what have you, that I can capitalize on, that the average person would never have or dream of." Michael testified that he became friends with Salman when Maher was courting Salman's sister and later began sharing Maher's tips with Salman. As he explained at trial, "any time a major deal came in, [Salman] was the first on my phone list." Michael also testified that he told Salman that the information was coming from Maher. (" 'Maher is the source of all this information' ").

After a jury trial in the Northern District of California, Salman was convicted on all counts. He was sentenced to 36 months of imprisonment, three years of supervised release, and over $730,000 in restitution. After his motion for a new trial was denied, Salman appealed to the Ninth Circuit. While his appeal was pending, the Second Circuit issued its opinion in *United States v. Newman,* 773 F.3d 438 (2014), cert. denied, 577 U.S.___, 136 S. Ct. 242, 193 L.Ed.2d 133 (2015). There, the Second Circuit reversed the convictions of two portfolio managers who traded on inside information. The *Newman* defendants were "several steps removed from the corporate insiders" and the court found that "there was no evidence that either was aware of the source of the inside information." The court acknowledged that *Dirks* and Second Circuit case law allow a factfinder to infer a personal benefit to the tipper from a gift of confidential information to a trading relative or friend. But the court concluded that, "[t]o the extent" *Dirks* permits "such an inference," the inference "is impermissible in the absence of proof of a meaningfully close personal relationship that generates an exchange that is objective, consequential, and represents at least a potential gain of a pecuniary or similarly valuable nature."[1]

Pointing to *Newman,* Salman argued that his conviction should be reversed. While the evidence established that Maher made a gift of trading information to Michael and that Salman knew it, there was no evidence that Maher received anything of "a pecuniary or similarly valuable nature" in exchange—or that Salman knew of any such benefit. The Ninth Circuit disagreed and affirmed Salman's conviction. The court reasoned that the case was governed by *Dirks*'s holding that a tipper benefits personally by making a gift of confidential information to a trading relative or friend. Indeed, Maher's disclosures to Michael were "precisely the gift of confidential information to a trading relative that *Dirks* envisioned." 792 F.3d, at 1092 (internal quotation marks omitted). To the extent *Newman* went further and required additional gain to the tipper in cases involving gifts of confidential information to family and friends, the Ninth Circuit "decline[d] to follow it."

We granted certiorari to resolve the tension between the Second Circuit's *Newman* decision and the Ninth Circuit's decision in this case.[2]

II

A

In this case, Salman contends that an insider's "gift of confidential information to a trading relative or friend," *Dirks,* 463 U.S., at 664, 103 S. Ct. 3255 is not enough to establish securities fraud. Instead, Salman argues, a tipper does not personally benefit unless the tipper's goal in disclosing inside information is to obtain money, property, or something of tangible value. He claims that our

---

1. The Second Circuit also reversed the *Newman* defendants' convictions because the Government introduced no evidence that the defendants knew the information they traded on came from insiders or that the insiders received a personal benefit in exchange for the tips. This case does not implicate those issues.

2. *Dirks v. SEC,* 463 U.S. 646, 103 S. Ct. 3255, 77 L.Ed.2d 911 (1983), established the personal-benefit framework in a case brought under the classical theory of insider-trading liability, which applies "when a corporate insider" or his tippee "trades in the securities of [the tipper's] corporation on the basis of material, nonpublic information." In such a case, the defendant breaches a duty to, and takes advantage of, the shareholders of his corporation. By contrast, the misappropriation theory holds that a person commits securities fraud "when he misappropriates confidential information for securities trading purposes, in breach of a duty owed to the source of the information" such as an employer or client. In such a case, the defendant breaches a duty to, and defrauds, the source of the information, as opposed to the shareholders of his corporation. The Court of Appeals observed that this is a misappropriation case, while the Government represents that both theories apply on the facts of this case. We need not resolve the question. The parties do not dispute that *Dirks*'s personal-benefit analysis applies in both classical and misappropriation cases, so we will proceed on the assumption that it does.

insider-trading precedents, and the cases those precedents cite, involve situations in which the insider exploited confidential information for the insider's own "tangible monetary profit." He suggests that his position is reinforced by our criminal-fraud precedents outside of the insider-trading context, because those cases confirm that a fraudster must personally obtain money or property. More broadly, Salman urges that defining a gift as a personal benefit renders the insider-trading offense indeterminate and overbroad: indeterminate, because liability may turn on facts such as the closeness of the relationship between tipper and tippee and the tipper's purpose for disclosure; and overbroad, because the Government may avoid having to prove a concrete personal benefit by simply arguing that the tipper meant to give a gift to the tippee. He also argues that we should interpret *Dirks*'s standard narrowly so as to avoid constitutional concerns. Finally, Salman contends that gift situations create especially troubling problems for remote tippees—that is, tippees who receive inside information from another tippee, rather than the tipper—who may have no knowledge of the relationship between the original tipper and tippee and thus may not know why the tipper made the disclosure.

The Government disagrees and argues that a gift of confidential information to anyone, not just a "trading relative or friend," is enough to prove securities fraud. Under the Government's view, a tipper personally benefits whenever the tipper discloses confidential trading information for a noncorporate purpose. Accordingly, a gift to a friend, a family member, or anyone else would support the inference that the tipper exploited the trading value of inside information for personal purposes and thus personally benefited from the disclosure. The Government claims to find support for this reading in *Dirks* and the precedents on which *Dirks* relied.

The Government also argues that Salman's concerns about unlimited and indeterminate liability for remote tippees are significantly alleviated by other statutory elements that prosecutors must satisfy to convict a tippee for insider trading. The Government observes that, in order to establish a defendant's criminal liability as a tippee, it must prove beyond a reasonable doubt that the tipper expected that the information being disclosed would be used in securities trading. The Government also notes that, to establish a defendant's criminal liability as a tippee, it must prove that the tippee knew that the tipper breached a duty—in other words, that the tippee knew that the tipper disclosed the information for a personal benefit and that the tipper expected trading to ensue.

B

We adhere to *Dirks*, which easily resolves the narrow issue presented here.

In *Dirks*, we explained that a tippee is exposed to liability for trading on inside information only if the tippee participates in a breach of the tipper's fiduciary duty. Whether the tipper breached that duty depends "in large part on the purpose of the disclosure" to the tippee. "[T]he test," we explained, "is whether the insider personally will benefit, directly or indirectly, from his disclosure." Thus, the disclosure of confidential information without personal benefit is not enough. In determining whether a tipper derived a personal benefit, we instructed courts to "focus on objective criteria, *i.e.*, whether the insider receives a direct or indirect personal benefit from the disclosure, such as a pecuniary gain or a reputational benefit that will translate into future earnings." This personal benefit can "often" be inferred "from objective facts and circumstances," we explained, such as "a relationship between the insider and the recipient that suggests a *quid pro quo* from the latter, or an intention to benefit the particular recipient." In particular, we held that "[t]he elements of fiduciary duty and exploitation of nonpublic information also exist *when an insider makes a gift of confidential information to a trading relative or friend.*" (emphasis added). In such cases, "[t]he tip and trade resemble trading by the insider followed by a gift of the profits to the recipient." We then applied this gift-giving principle to resolve *Dirks* itself, finding it dispositive that the tippers "received no monetary or personal benefit" from their tips to Dirks, "*nor was their purpose to make a gift of valuable information to Dirks.*" (emphasis added).

Our discussion of gift giving resolves this case. Maher, the tipper, provided inside information to a close relative, his brother Michael. *Dirks* makes clear that a tipper breaches a fiduciary duty by making a gift of confidential information to "a trading relative," and that rule is sufficient to resolve the case at hand. As Salman's counsel acknowledged at oral argument, Maher would have breached his duty had he personally traded on the information here himself then given the proceeds as a gift to his brother. It is obvious that Maher would personally benefit in that situation. But Maher effectively achieved the same result by disclosing the information to Michael, and allowing him to trade on it. *Dirks* appropriately prohibits that approach, as well. (holding that "insiders [are] forbidden" both "from personally using undisclosed corporate information to their advantage" and from "giv[ing] such information to an outsider for the same improper purpose of exploiting the information for their personal gain"). *Dirks* specifies that when a tipper gives inside information to "a trading relative or friend," the jury can infer that the tipper meant to provide the equivalent of a cash gift. In such situations, the tipper benefits personally because giving a gift of trading information is the same thing as trading by the tipper followed by a gift of the proceeds. Here, by disclosing confidential information as a gift to his brother with the expectation that he would trade on it, Maher breached his duty of trust and confidence to Citigroup and its clients—a duty Salman acquired, and breached himself, by trading on the information with full knowledge that it had been improperly disclosed.

To the extent the Second Circuit held that the tipper must also receive something of a "pecuniary or similarly valuable nature" in exchange for a gift to family or friends, we agree with the Ninth Circuit that this requirement is inconsistent with *Dirks*.

C

Salman points out that many insider-trading cases—including several that *Dirks* cited—involved insiders who personally profited through the misuse of trading information. But this observation does not undermine the test *Dirks* articulated and applied. Salman also cites a sampling of our criminal-fraud decisions construing other federal fraud statutes, suggesting that they stand for the proposition that fraud is not consummated unless the defendant obtains money or property. Assuming that these cases are relevant to our construction of §10(b) (a proposition the Government forcefully disputes), nothing in them undermines the commonsense point we made in *Dirks*. Making a gift of inside information to a relative like Michael is little different from trading on the information, obtaining the profits, and doling them out to the trading relative. The tipper benefits either way. The facts of this case illustrate the point: In one of their tipper-tippee interactions, Michael asked Maher for a favor, declined Maher's offer of money, and instead requested and received lucrative trading information.

III

Salman's jury was properly instructed that a personal benefit includes "the benefit one would obtain from simply making a gift of confidential information to a trading relative." As the Court of Appeals noted, "the Government presented direct evidence that the disclosure was intended as a gift of market-sensitive information." And, as Salman conceded below, this evidence is sufficient to sustain his conviction under our reading of *Dirks*. ("Maher made a gift of confidential information to a trading relative [Michael] . . . and, if [Michael's] testimony is accepted as true (as it must be for purposes of sufficiency review), Salman knew that Maher had made such a gift" (internal quotation marks, brackets, and citation omitted)). Accordingly, the Ninth Circuit's judgment is affirmed.

It is so ordered.

Notes and Questions

1. Reality Check

a. What is tippee liability? What are the two parts of the *Dirks* test?

b. Which part of *Dirks* is at issue in *Salman*?

c. How does the *Dirks* test fit with the classic and misappropriation theories of insider trading?

d. Who is the tipper and who are the tippees?

e. Who owed a duty of trust and confidence? To whom was it owed?

f. Did Salman, Michael, or Maher have to receive a personal benefit in order for Salman to be liable?

g. Did the Court adopt the government's view of liability in its entirety?

h. Why does it matter whether the tippee knows that the tip breaches the tipper's duty?

2. Suppose

a. Suppose Maher, Michael, and Salman were friends but unrelated to each other. Would the Court's analysis or the result have been the same?

b. Suppose Salman did not know the source of Michael's information. Alternatively, suppose Salman guessed, but did not know, that Maher was the source. Would the Court's analysis or the result have been the same?

c. Suppose a corporate insider gave information to a stock analyst hoping the analyst would write more favorably about the corporation. Would the analyst be liable as a tippee?

d. Suppose the conductor of the local symphony orchestra attends a ballet as a guest of the symphony's board chair. During intermission, the conductor overhears the board chair disclosing material nonpublic information to another of the chair's guests. If the conductor trades before that information becomes public is he or she liable as a tippee?

3. What Do You Think?

a. Do you think the government's case against Maher would be based on the classical theory or the misappropriation theory?

b. Do you think it should matter whether the tippee knows the source of the information? Should it matter whether the tippee knows that the source breached a fiduciary duty in tipping?

c. Do you agree that a relationship of trust and confidence should be a requirement of insider trading? What about *Cady, Roberts*'s predicate of the unfairness of insider trading? Isn't what the defendant in all these cases did fundamentally unfair?

D. TERMS OF ART IN THIS CHAPTER

Antidilution provision	Greenmail	Retired
Buy-sell agreement	Insolvency test	Reverse stock split
Capital	Legal capital test	Round lot
Declared	Material	Scienter
Delist	Record date	Stock split
Dividend	Restrictions on transfer	Surplus
		Treasury stock

8

Getting Money to Creditors When the Corporation Can't Pay

Corporations ordinarily pay their creditors in full as their liabilities become due. This is true for suppliers, lenders, and employees and for other claimants on the corporation's funds such as taxing authorities. By and large, it is also true for tort creditors, although much of a corporation's payment may come from insurance that the corporation has purchased, rather than from assets the corporation has on hand. Where the corporation's managers are recalcitrant in paying, which is different from the setting where those managers believe, in good faith, the corporation is not liable, creditors have an array of devices to ensure satisfaction. Litigation is the most obvious of these devices, as well as other dispute resolution mechanisms such as arbitration and mediation. Where a judgment is entered against the corporation, the creditor can seize and sell corporate assets to obtain satisfaction.

Contract creditors frequently bargain in advance for a security interest or mortgage, which permits them to seize specific corporate property in lieu of payment. Ultimately, a corporation's creditors can force an insolvent corporation into bankruptcy, which, although almost guaranteeing that the creditors will not be paid in full, at least ensures an orderly and relatively consistent treatment of creditors' claims.

This chapter deals with situations in which the corporate debtor may have insufficient assets to satisfy its creditors. It explores five areas in which creditors can look to others connected with the corporation for payment. Because the others to whom creditors look are often key people in the planning and management of a corporation, they, and you as their attorney, need to consider these possible avenues of liability. Conversely, because your clients may be owed money by an insolvent corporation, you need to be conversant with these avenues of obtaining redress for your client. Finally, as a matter of social policy, the availability or absence of these avenues of payment directly affects the willingness of third parties to deal with corporations. Where third parties believe that they must look only to the corporation for payment, they will be more likely to demand higher compensation. If they believe they may be able to look beyond the corporation for repayment, at least in some settings, they will be more willing to accept lesser compensation.

The five areas we will consider are: first, liability of individual shareholders by piercing the corporate veil; second, holding related corporations liable through enterprise liability; third, preserving corporate assets for creditors through commercial law and bankruptcy concepts, in particular the doctrine of equitable subordination; fourth, holding successor corporations liable for a predecessor corporation's debts; and finally, holding corporate officers personally liable as direct participants in corporate torts.

A. THE CURRENT SETTING

1. Individual Shareholder Liability by Piercing the Corporate Veil

Corporations statutes typically provide that shareholders are only liable to pay the agreed-upon issuance price for their shares. The statutes also typically go further to make clear that shareholders are not liable for corporate debts. Delaware, for example, provides that unless a provision for personal liability is placed in the Certificate of Incorporation, stockholders "shall not be personally liable for the payment of the corporation's debts except as they may be liable by reason of their own conduct or acts." DGCL §102(b)(6). The MBCA has a similar provision in §6.22(b). The language "by reason of their own conduct or acts" means that a shareholder is not immune from primary liability simply by virtue of being a stockholder. Despite these statutory provisions, courts assume they have the power to hold shareholders liable for corporate debts in appropriate instances. When this power is exercised, the corporation is said to have been disregarded; the corporate veil has been pierced.

The doctrine of *piercing the corporate veil* is a mystery. It is one of the most frequently litigated issues in corporate law but, although the doctrine is quite old, courts are vague and inconsistent in their statement of the legal principles involved. When courts apply the doctrine, their opinions are nearly always simply gestalt results rather than genuinely articulated decisions. Yet, like Daniel Webster's Dartmouth College, there are those who love it. Judge Cardozo called piercing the corporate veil a doctrine "enveloped in the mists of metaphor" while reminding us that "metaphors in the law are to be narrowly watched." *Berkey v. Third Ave. Ry. Co.*, 155 N.E. 58, 61 (N.Y. 1926). Most business entities casebooks devote lots of pages to piercing and law professors seem to devote a fair bit of class time to the subject. Law students, despite forgetting everything else in the course, can always remember "the taxicab case,"[1] in which a New York City taxicab ran down a pedestrian. The pedestrian, Walkovszky, tried to sue the sole shareholder of the corporation that owned the cab. The plaintiff lost.[2]

Piercing the corporate veil is an equitable doctrine that holds a corporation's shareholders liable for the corporation's debts if the corporation is unable to pay. Although it could, in theory, apply in publicly held corporations, in practice it is only

---

1. The taxicab case is *Walkovszky v. Carlton*, 223 N.E.2d 6 (N.Y. 1966).
2. Walkovszky's problem was in the drafting of his complaint. It named Carlton, the individual shareholder, as a defendant, but the facts, as alleged, showed, at most, grounds for holding several other cab companies also owned by Carlton liable. With very broad hints from Judge Fuld, Walkovszky's attorney managed to get the complaint right enough on remand to avoid dismissal and the case ultimately settled before trial.

germane to the closely held corporation. In fact, once the number of shareholders increases above two or three, there is little likelihood that a court will pierce. It is important to know what piercing the corporate veil does *not* do. It does *not* dissolve the corporation and it does *not* make the shareholders liable for all the corporation's debts. If applied, the doctrine renders the shareholders liable only for the plaintiff's claims against the corporation.

What are the elements for piercing the corporate veil? The following excerpt is from a well-written, thoughtful discussion of the standard in one state:

> The principal exception to the limited liability rule is the doctrine of "piercing the corporate veil." This doctrine is equitable in nature and is used by the courts to disregard the distinction between a corporation and its shareholders to prevent fraud or injustice. The general rule which has emerged is that a corporation will be looked upon as a legal entity separate and distinct from its shareholders, officers and directors unless and until sufficient reason to the contrary appears, but when the notion of a legal entity is used to defeat public convenience, justify wrong, protect fraud, or defend crime, then sufficient reason will exist to pierce the corporate veil.
>
> "In deciding whether the corporate veil will be pierced, we recognize that 'each case is *sui generis* and must be decided in accordance with its own underlying facts.'" *Mobridge* [*Community Indus. v. Toure*], 273 N.W.2d [128,] 132 [(S.D. 1978)] (quoting *Brown Brothers Equipment Co. v. State*, 215 N.W.2d 591, 593 (Mich. App. 1974)).
>
> In our past decisions, we have discussed a number of factors[6] that might justify "piercing the corporate veil." After review of those decisions and the factors discussed therein, it is apparent that in making this determination, we have applied a two-part test: (1) was there such unity of interest and ownership that the separate personalities of the corporation and its shareholders, officers or directors are indistinct or non-existent; and (2) would adherence to the fiction of separate corporate existence sanction fraud, promote injustice or inequitable consequences or lead to an evasion of legal obligations?
>
> As to the first part of the test, the "separate corporate identity" prong, we note:
>
> > The "separate corporate identity" prong is meant to determine whether the stockholder and the corporation have maintained separate identities. There are strong public policy reasons for upholding the corporate fiction. Where stockholders follow the technical rules that govern the corporate structure, they are entitled to rely on the protections of limited liability that the corporation affords. In determining whether the personalities and assets of the corporation and the stockholders have been blurred we consider (i) the degree to which the corporate legal formalities have been maintained, and (ii) the degree to which individual and corporate assets and affairs have been commingled.
>
> [*NLRB v.*] *Greater Kansas City Roofing*, 2 F.3d [1047,] 1052 [(10th Cir. 1993)].
>
> Of the six specific factors which we have considered in the past, four are used in determining whether the first prong is met: (1) undercapitalization; (2) failure to observe corporate formalities; (3) absence of corporate records; and (4) payment by the corporation of individual obligations. If these factors are present in sufficient number and/or degree, the first prong is met and the court will then consider the second prong.[9]

---

6. These factors include:

(1) fraudulent misrepresentation by corporation directors;
(2) undercapitalization;
(3) failure to observe corporate formalities;
(4) absence of corporate records;
(5) payment by the corporation of individual obligations; and
(6) use of the corporation to promote fraud, injustice or illegality.

9. We have held that a court should pierce the corporate veil only upon the strongest evidence of these factors.

As to the second part of the test, the "fraud or inequitable consequences" prong, we note:

> Under the fraud, injustice, or evasion of obligations prong of the test we ask whether there is adequate justification to invoke the equitable power of the court. We require an element of unfairness, injustice, fraud, or other inequitable conduct as a prerequisite to piercing the corporate veil.
>
> [T]he showing of inequity necessary to satisfy the second prong must flow from the misuse of the corporate form. The mere fact that a corporation . . . breaches a contract . . . does not mean that the individual shareholders of the corporation should personally be liable. To the contrary, the corporate form of doing business is typically selected precisely so that the individual shareholders will not be liable. It is only when the shareholders disregard the separateness of the corporate identity *and when that act of disregard causes the injustice or inequity or constitutes the fraud* that the corporate veil may be pierced. . . . In most cases the mere fact that a corporation is incapable of paying all of its debts is insufficient for a finding of injustice. . . . That condition will exist in virtually all cases in which there is an attempt to pierce the corporate veil.

Greater Kansas City Roofing, 2 F.3d at 1052-53 (citations omitted) (emphasis original).

The two factors which we have considered in the past to satisfy the second prong include: (1) fraudulent misrepresentation by corporation directors; and (2) use of the corporation to promote fraud, injustice, or illegalities.

If both the "separate corporate identity" prong and the "fraud or inequitable consequence" prong of the test are met and "the court deems it appropriate to pierce the corporate veil, the corporation and its stockholders will be treated identically."

Kansas Gas & Electric Co. v. Ross, 521 N.W.2d 107, 111-113 (S.D. 1994).

This is a comparatively clear statement of the doctrine. Note that the court has used six factors. These turn out to be, on inspection, a two-pronged test. The court will pierce the corporate veil if the three parts of the two-pronged test are met "by the strongest evidence." The first prong is the "no separate corporate identity" prong; the second is the "fraud or inequitable consequence" test and the third is the "court deems it appropriate to pierce" test. Got it?

Professor Stephen M. Bainbridge, in his typically pungent and accurate way, suggests that a necessary but not sufficient predicate for piercing is that the individual shareholder defendant(s) must have control of the corporation, either by owning more than 50 percent of the voting stock or by exercising actual control. Sometimes control is described by courts as using the corporation as the "alter ego" of its shareholders, in which the corporation acts to bring about its shareholders' desires instead of its own. This conception of control is stupid for two reasons. First, anyone with control and ownership of a corporation uses it to effect his or her business ends. Second, at what level of reification (or anthropomorphism) does it make any logical sense at all to say that a corporation has a "personality" or "identity" or "will" of its own?

Control is not enough to pierce the corporate veil. According to Professor Bainbridge, different courts require different additional showings, such as that control was used to bring about some sort of inequity or fraud. Different states vary considerably in both the phrasing of their tests and in the kind and degree of injustice that will suffice to pierce. *See generally* Stephen M. Bainbridge, *Abolishing Veil Piercing,* 26 J. Corp. L. 479 (2001).

Three commonly cited factors are worth focusing on because they are emblematic of the generally unsatisfactory nature of piercing the corporate veil analyses. First, many courts say they look to see whether the corporation has observed the requisite corporate formalities such as holding shareholder and director meetings, appointing officers, and filing annual reports with the secretary of state. Lacking in these discussions is any justification for using this criterion as a reason to hold an individual shareholder personally liable for the corporation's debts. Certainly any causation between the corporate formalities and plaintiff's debt is missing. To the extent courts justify this criterion, they tend to fall back on the argument that because doing business in corporate form is a "privilege," the concomitant limited liability should attach only where the owner of the corporation has had the decency to observe the corporate formalities. Weak at best.

A second criterion, which is sometimes also called observing the corporate formalities, really means evaluating whether the owner has commingled property with the corporation. Where the owner and corporation have a single bank account or where the owner moves funds from corporate to individual accounts or vice versa or, in general, where there is a blurring of the distinction between the individual owner and the corporation, the courts are more likely to pierce. This criterion has at least two valid purposes in a piercing the corporate veil analysis. Often this commingling will be evidence of fraud; the owner is shuffling assets at least in part to create the illusion that the corporation has more assets than it really does. In many instances, as well, the court uses evidence of commingling as a surrogate for a finding that the owner controlled the corporation. But sometimes the commingling has in no way defrauded the plaintiff, and the individual's control is undisputed. In these instances, commingling seems to be simply a makeweight argument.

Finally, many courts use "undercapitalization" as a criterion. Usually this means the court will look to the time when the corporation was first incorporated, which might be some considerable time before the debt in dispute was incurred, to see whether the owner provided enough equity, and insurance, to cover reasonably foreseeable obligations that the corporation might incur. Deliberate undercapitalization can be seen as, in effect, an attempt to defraud (externalize risk might be a better description) others by having the corporation engage in activities as to which there is a likelihood (increasing in probability to a near certainty) of situations in which the corporation will be unable to satisfy its obligations in full. As with the other tests, where this criterion is directly related to the plaintiff's inability to be compensated by the corporation, piercing seems intuitively to be appropriate. However, many courts use these criteria in settings in which they seem to have only the most tenuous connection to the plaintiff's claim.

Although I am tempted to end the discussion of piercing the corporate veil at this point, I'm required, as a business entities law professor, to include at least one full case dealing with the doctrine. Here it is. It is very typical of piercing the corporate veil opinions.

Brevet Int'l, Inc. v. Great Plains Luggage Co.

604 N.W.2d 268 (S.D. 2000)

MILLER, C.J.

During 1994 and 1995, Great Plains Luggage Company was engaged in the business of manufacturing and selling golf bags and golf bag travel covers from its plant located at Tyndall, South Dakota. Its principal officers, directors and shareholders were Christopher D. Crosby, W. Greg Coward, and Alan Krutsch. During that time, Brevet International, Inc., provided management consulting services to businesses, universities, government entities and labor unions.

In early March 1995 Crosby contacted Brevet president Donald MacKintosh about installing a management system in its plant. Great Plains was having difficulty manufacturing its products in a cost-efficient and timely manner so as to ensure prompt delivery to its customers. Because of these difficulties, Great Plains had resolved to close unless a solution could be found for its manufacturing problems. There is no dispute that Crosby informed MacKintosh of Great Plains' precarious financial position in their initial phone conversation.

After speaking with Crosby and visiting the plant, MacKintosh orally agreed to provide management consulting services on behalf of Brevet. This agreement was never reduced to writing. The agreed-upon price for Brevet's services was $35,000. [H]owever, out-of-pocket expenses incurred by Brevet were to be reimbursed by Great Plains as invoiced. In reliance on Brevet's assurances of success, Crosby injected $100,000 of his personal funds into the business, in addition to money he had previously invested.

Over the next three months, Brevet's consultants worked with Great Plains' plant manager installing a management system. Brevet submitted weekly invoices addressed to "Chris Crosby, The Great Plains Luggage Company," for professional fees and expenses incurred. Great Plains reimbursed Brevet for its expenses, but did not pay any of the $35,000 professional fee. Brevet sent Great Plains a final demand letter on November 28, 1995, asking for payment. Great Plains did not respond to the letter.

There is much dispute about the specific terms of the consulting arrangement. First, there is disagreement about the identity of the entity that contracted with Brevet. Brevet maintains that it contracted with the individual defendants, not the corporation. Crosby and the other individual defendants argue, however, that the contract was between Great Plains (the corporation) and Brevet.

Brevet initiated this suit against Great Plains and the individual defendants alleging breach of contract and fraud, for failure to pay the management consulting fee.

On appeal, Brevet raises the following issues:

. . .

2) Whether the trial court properly refused to pierce the corporate veil and hold the individual defendants personally liable.

[I]n discussing whether Brevet had satisfied the test for piercing the corporate veil, the trial judge summarily stated: "The plaintiff has been unable to point to anything arising to the level of fraud, injustice or inequitable consequences."

In granting the defendants' motion for partial summary judgment, the trial court found that although there were some irregularities in the record keeping of the company, Great Plains was a lawfully formed corporation under the laws of the State of South Dakota. Notwithstanding some undisputed problems in formalities, the trial court held the failure to observe corporate rules did not reach the level of the first prong of the test for piercing the corporate veil as found in *Kansas Gas & Electric Co. v. Ross*, 521 N.W.2d 107 (S.D. 1994).

Brevet first contends that the management consulting contract was entered into with the individual defendants, not the corporation. Alternatively, it argues that if Great Plains was a valid corporation, then the corporate veil should be pierced and the individual defendants should be held personally liable.

We only briefly address Brevet's first argument that the contract was entered into with Crosby, Coward and Krutsch individually, rather than with Great Plains as a corporation. This claim is totally contradictory to the evidence in the record. In particular, invoices sent by Brevet were addressed to "Chris Crosby, The Great Plains Luggage Company." Moreover, the invoices were paid by corporate check, not personal checks, without objection by Brevet. An experienced businessman like MacKintosh would surely know that contracting with "Great Plains Luggage Company" is not the same as contracting with Crosby, Coward and Krutsch on an individual basis. Finally, the name "Great Plains Luggage Company" meets the statutory requirements for identification of a corporate entity. If Brevet had any doubt as to the form of the business organization with which he was dealing, he need only have contacted the secretary of state's office for verification of corporate status.

We have long recognized that, as a general rule, a corporation is to be considered a legal entity separate and distinct from its shareholders, officers and directors unless and until there is sufficient reason to the contrary. The concept of limited liability is considered one of the central purposes for choosing the corporate form, because it permits shareholders to limit their personal liability to the extent of their investment. A corporation is looked upon as a distinct entity, but when the notion of a separate legal existence is used to "defeat public convenience, justify wrong, protect fraud, or defend crime, then sufficient reason will exist to pierce the corporate veil." [*Kansas Gas*, 521 N.W.2d at] 112 (citations omitted). Decisions about whether to pierce the corporate veil must be decided in accordance with the unique, underlying facts of each case.

In *Kansas Gas*, we enumerated six factors to consider when determining whether equity demands piercing the corporate veil. Those factors include: (1) undercapitalization; (2) failure to observe corporate formalities; (3) absence of corporate records; (4) payment by the corporation of individual obligations; (5) fraudulent misrepresentation by corporate directors; and (6) use of the corporation to promote fraud, injustice or illegality. The six factors can be grouped into two separate prongs: the "separate corporate identity" prong and the "fraud or inequitable consequences" prong. If the four factors under the "separate corporate identity" prong are present in sufficient number and/or degree, then this Court will consider the two factors under the "fraud or inequitable consequences" prong. "[A] court should pierce the corporate veil only upon the strongest evidence of these factors." *Id.* at 113 n.9.

Kansas Gas controls. Applying those factors to these facts, we conclude the trial court did not err. Brevet has not met its burden of showing why the corporate veil should be pierced.

For all the reasons stated above, we . . . affirm as . . . to the personal liability of the individual defendants.

Notes and Questions

1. Notes

a. This case is from the same jurisdiction, South Dakota, as the excerpt from *Kansas Gas & Electric* above and makes reference to the standard articulated in that case.

2. Reality Check

a. Why did Great Plains hire Brevet?
b. What is the underlying dispute between the parties?

3. What Do You Think?

a. Do you think the court should have pierced the corporate veil here?
b. If you were counsel for Great Plains, what advice would you have given your client to minimize the possibility that Brevet could successfully pierce?

All this is fodder for some amusement, but the potential for piercing raises real problems for corporate planners and their clients. Predictability is a virtue in prospective activities like business planning and the lack of certainty in this area means that you can never assure your clients that they will not be held liable under a piercing the corporate veil theory, at least where there are fewer than half a dozen or so shareholders. Conversely, if you are representing clients who have been harmed by a corporation that seems unlikely to have sufficient assets, the lack of precision for piercing's application may also be undesirable because you and your clients will have to make litigation decisions, often expensive ones, in deciding whether to pursue a piercing claim or not. Greater certainty would help everyone.

One question is whether the piercing doctrine is part of the internal affairs of a corporation. If so, as you'll remember from Chapter 5, then the law of the state of incorporation applies regardless of the state in which the litigation is brought. While there is no definitive answer, and the *Restatement (Second) of Conflict of Laws* is silent, most courts that have addressed the issue have decided that piercing should be subject to the internal affairs doctrine. But while this means that the test that will be applied will probably be that of the state of incorporation (and hence not only predictable but within the planners' choice when they decide on the state in which to incorporate) you should be aware that the actual court applying the test to the facts may be in another state. In practice, such a court may be inclined to use its own sense of equity to decide whether to pierce regardless of the test it believes it is applying.

Treating piercing as part of the internal affairs doctrine makes Delaware law of special importance. Delaware courts are extremely reluctant to pierce, although they do not hesitate to hold individual shareholders of closely held corporations liable for their own actions and, in that regard, are probably a bit more accurate in assigning liability on the ground of direct action than other states are when they impose liability on the same individual actors under a piercing theory. The issue is seldom litigated in the Delaware courts, presumably because the theory simply doesn't succeed. Nonetheless, in recent years the Delaware Court of Chancery has at least left open the possibility of piercing, and a few cases have denied summary judgment on the ground that the possibility of piercing exists. One of the few modern statements of the Delaware rule is:

"Persuading a Delaware court to disregard the corporate entity is a difficult task." In order to state a cognizable claim to pierce the corporate veil . . . plaintiffs must allege facts that, if taken as true, demonstrate . . . complete domination and control. . . . The degree of control required to pierce the veil is "exclusive domination and control . . . to the point that [the corporation] no longer ha[s] legal or independent significance of [its] own."

Piercing the corporate veil under the alter ego theory "requires that the corporate structure cause fraud or similar injustice." Effectively, the corporation must be a sham and exist for no other purpose than as a vehicle for fraud.

Wallace v. Wood, 752 A.2d 1175, 1183-1184 (Del. Ch. 1999) (Steele, V.C. (citations omitted))

One way to decrease the likelihood of piercing when planning a corporation is to use a checklist of things to do and things to avoid. It may be good practice to review this checklist when forming a new entity and counsel your client to avoid as many of them as possible. Recall in *Kansas Gas & Electric* the court ticked off six factors, divided into two prongs, which it used to decide whether to pierce. Many states have such lists in their case law and the lists keep growing. Doubtless lists are passed from law clerk to law clerk at state supreme courts around the country. If you thought South Dakota's list of 6 was impressive, you should be aware that Kansas has 10 factors, Oklahoma has 11, Maine and Massachusetts have 12, and California and West Virginia have 19. A Hawaii case listed the California factors and added others not on the California list. Herewith the factors:

In *Associated Vendors, Inc. v. Oakland Meat Co., Inc.*, 26 Cal. Rptr. 806, 813 (Cal. App. 1962) the California Court of Appeal catalogued factors that many courts have weighed in determining whether a corporate entity is the alter ego of another. These include:

[1] Commingling of funds and other assets, failure to segregate funds of the separate entities, and the unauthorized diversion of corporate funds or assets to other than corporate uses; [2] the treatment by an individual of the assets of the corporation as his own; [3] the failure to obtain authority to issue stock or to subscribe to or issue the same; [4] the holding out by an individual that he is personally liable for the debts of the corporation; [5] the identical equitable ownership in the two entities; [6] the identification of the equitable owners thereof with the domination and control of the two entities; [7] identi[ty] of . . . directors and officers of the two entities in the responsible supervision and management; [8] sole ownership of all of the stock in a corporation by one individual or the members of a family; [9] the use of the same office or business location; [10] the employment of the same employees and/or attorney; [11] the failure to adequately capitalize a corporation; [12] the total absence of corporate assets, and undercapitalization; [13] the use of a corporation as a mere shell, instrumentality or conduit for a single venture or the business of an individual or another corporation; [14] the concealment and misrepresentation of the identity of the responsible ownership, management and financial interest, or concealment of personal business activities; [15] the disregard of legal formalities and the failure to maintain arm's length relationships among related entities; [16] the use of the corporate entity to procure labor, services or merchandise for another person or entity; [17] the diversion stockholder [sic] or other person or entity, to the detriment of creditors, or the manipulation of assets and liabilities between entities so as to concentrate the assets in one and the liabilities in another; [18] the contracting with another with intent to avoid performance by use of a corporate entity as a shield against personal liability, or the use of a corporation as a subterfuge of illegal transactions; and [19] the formation and use of a corporation to transfer to it the existing liability of another person or entity.

This list, however, is not exhaustive. For example, other courts have looked at: (1) incorporation for the purpose of circumventing public policy or statutes; (2) whether the parent finances the subsidiary; (3) whether the subsidiary has no business or assets except those conveyed to it by the parent; (4) whether the parent uses the subsidiary's property as its own; (5) whether the directors of the subsidiary do not act independently in the interest of the corporation but take their orders from and serve the parent; and (6) whether the "fiction of corporate entity . . . has been adopted or used to evade the provisions of a statute." *Kavanaugh v. Ford Motor Co.*, 353 F.2d 710, 717 (7th Cir. 1965). Ultimately, no one factor is dispositive.

Robert's Hawaii School Bus, Inc. v. Laupahoehoe Transportation Company, Inc., 982 P.2d 853, 871 (Haw. 1999)

2. Enterprise Liability

Analytically, piercing the corporate veil theory should be equally applicable regardless of whether the defendant shareholder is an individual or another corporation. But holding a corporate parent liable for its subsidiary's debt is best considered a kind of *enterprise liability*. The difference is that enterprise liability seeks to aggregate corporations into a single enterprise and hold the entire enterprise liable. This aggregation can be *vertical*, where the creditor seeks to hold the debtor corporation's corporate parent, or *horizontal*, where the creditor seeks to aggregate one or more corporations that are under common control.

Conceptually, enterprise liability should be easier to accomplish than piercing the veil to hold individual shareholders liable, because under enterprise liability the ultimate individuals who own the enterprise retain their limited liability. All that happens is that the individuals' attempt to apportion risk among separate corporations is disallowed. As you might imagine, courts have not been any better at articulating a consistent view of enterprise liability than they have in approaching piercing the corporate veil. Because enterprise liability has not been as thoroughly critiqued as other corporate law concepts, you should think particularly carefully about whether the courts are using appropriate standards.

Having said that, though, there seem to be three ways courts think about enterprise liability. Perhaps the most common is simply to treat enterprise liability identically to piercing the corporate veil. The difference between the two being that, as applied, courts are somewhat less reticent to aggregate *affiliated corporations* (that is, corporations under common control whether parent-subsidiary or sibling corporations) than they are to pierce the corporate veil to hold an individual shareholder liable.

The second approach is to impose enterprise liability where, in essence, the court finds that the distinctions between the corporations are sufficiently indistinct that equity is best served by aggregating the corporations. This blurring might be to bring about some sort of fraud, but it might also stem only from sloppiness and inattention to corporate niceties.

Smith v. McLeod Distributing, Inc.

744 N.E.2d 459 (Ind. Ct. App. 2000)

BARNES, J.

CASE SUMMARY

Defendants, Colonial Mat Company, Inc. ("Colonial Mat") and Michael B. Smith, appeal the judgment entered against them for a commercial debt owed to Plaintiff, McLeod Distributing, Inc. ("McLeod"). We affirm in all respects.

FACTS

McLeod was a corporation involved in the wholesale distribution of floor coverings, including carpets. It appears from the evidence that Colonial Mat installed carpets and other floor products in residences and other locations; it was incorporated in 1987. Colonial Industrial Products Company, Inc., ("Colonial Industrial") was incorporated in 1981. At the time Colonial Mat was incorporated, Colonial Industrial was distributing a certain brand of industrial rubber products. A few months after Colonial Mat was incorporated, it applied for a line of credit with McLeod. McLeod initially refused to ship goods to Colonial Mat on credit, but eventually approved a line of credit for Colonial Mat after Smith, the president of both Colonial Mat and Colonial Industrial, signed a personal guarantee for any debt Colonial Mat might incur.

After McLeod and Colonial Mat had been doing business for nearly one-and-a-half years, Smith sent the following letter to McLeod, which we reprint in its entirety:

> March 17, 1989
> To: Carpet Suppliers
> Re: Colonial Carpets
>
> Dear Supplier,
>   In the near future we will be selling our matting products under the name of "Logomatts of America." We are obtaining licensing for custom logo mats from several universities and companies. For marketing reasons we feel a need for a name change.
>   However, we will be registering "Colonial Carpets" to the corporation that we sell floor products under. We presently use "Colonial Carpets" as the name we invoice our carpet jobs.
>   So, as soon as our printing is completed we will be ordering, as well as selling, all floor products except Mats & Matting as "Colonial Carpets" a corporate division of Colonial Industrial Products Co., Inc.
>   If you have any questions, feel free to call me at any time.
>
> Very truly yours,
> Michael B. Smith
> President

On March 27, 1989, Colonial Industrial filed a certificate of assumed name with the Secretary of State, indicating that it would be doing business as Colonial Carpets. After receiving this letter, McLeod changed Colonial Mat's name on its computer billing system to "Colonial Carpets, Inc." It never closed the account originally opened by Colonial Mat, however, and neither Smith nor anyone associated with his businesses did so.

McLeod continued doing business with Colonial Industrial d/b/a Colonial Carpets until February and March of 1990, when several invoices for goods delivered went unpaid. The total unpaid balance accrued to $6,132.65 as of May 11, 1990, when demand for payment was made, and McLeod filed a complaint against Colonial Mat and Smith on September 20, 1990. After this case remained pending for nearly ten years, the trial court conducted a bench trial and entered judgment in favor of McLeod. . . .

ANALYSIS

Colonial Mat argues that it was not a proper party to this suit because it is undisputed that all of the invoices at issue were addressed to "Colonial Carpets, Inc.," which Colonial Mat claims was a distinct corporate entity. It also claims that McLeod had notice before these invoices were issued, via the March 17, 1989, letter, that Colonial Mat and Colonial Industrial d/b/a Colonial Carpets were separate companies. McLeod essentially responds that it would be inequitable not to hold Colonial Mat liable for this debt because Colonial Mat and Colonial Carpets were indistinguishable entities.

Although Indiana courts are reluctant to disregard a corporate entity, they may do so to prevent fraud or unfairness to third parties. That fiction may be disregarded where one corporation is so organized and controlled and its affairs so conducted that it is a mere instrumentality or adjunct of another corporation. "Indiana courts refuse to recognize corporations as separate entities where the facts establish several corporations are acting as the same entity." *General Finance Corp. v. Skinner*, 426 N.E.2d 77, 84 (Ind. Ct. App. 1981).

> [A]n Indiana court considers whether the plaintiff has presented evidence showing: (1) undercapitalization; (2) absence of corporate records; (3) fraudulent representation by corporation shareholders or directors; (4) use of the corporation to promote fraud, injustice or illegal activities; (5) payment by the corporation of individual obligations; (6) commingling of assets and affairs; (7) failure to observe required corporate formalities; or (8) other shareholder acts or conduct ignoring, controlling, or manipulating the corporate form.

Aronson v. Price, 644 N.E.2d 864, 867 (Ind. 1994).

However, *Aronson* specifically concerned piercing the corporate veil in order to hold a shareholder personally liable for a corporate debt; our supreme court was not asked in that case to hold one corporation liable for another closely related corporation's debt. We do not believe the eight *Aronson* factors were intended to be exclusive, particularly when a court is asked to decide whether two or more affiliated corporations should be treated as a single entity. In fact, Indiana courts (in cases cited by *Aronson*) have often evaluated additional factors in such a situation, factors that would not be applicable where one was attempting to pierce the corporate veil to hold a corporation's directors, officers, or shareholders personally liable for a corporate debt. Some of these factors have included whether similar corporate names were used, . . . ; whether there were common principal corporate officers, directors, and employees, . . . ; whether the business purposes of the corporations were similar, . . . ; and whether the corporations were located in the same offices and used the same telephone numbers and business cards. . . . Additionally, we have previously noted that other jurisdictions have disregarded the separateness of affiliated corporations when the corporations are not operated as separate entities but are manipulated or controlled as one enterprise through their interrelationship to cause illegality, fraud, or injustice or to permit one economic entity to escape liability arising out of an operation conducted by one corporation for the benefit of the whole enterprise. Indicia of common "identity," "excessive fragmentation," or "single business enterprise" corporations may include, among other factors, the intermingling of business transactions, functions, property, employees, funds, records, and corporate names in dealing with the public.

McLeod failed to present much evidence relevant to the *Aronson* factors in support of its claim; it presented no evidence of undercapitalization, fraud, absence of corporate records, failure to observe formalities, or shareholder misconduct, for example. Nonetheless, we believe there was sufficient evidence presented from which the trial court might have concluded that Colonial Mat and Colonial Industrial were effectively one and the same corporation, thus justifying a holding that Colonial Industrial was merely an adjunct to or alter ego of Colonial Mat, which is liable for this debt.

First, we note the obvious similarity between the names of the two companies. "Colonial" was apparently used by Smith at the time to identify his businesses generally; the business card that McLeod introduced into evidence had in one corner "Colonial Mat Co., Inc.," and in the opposite corner was simply "Colonial." Second, Colonial Mat and Colonial Industrial d/b/a Colonial Carpets were engaged in virtually identical lines of business. Colonial Industrial's Articles of Incorporation indicated its purpose was "to engage in the sales and distribution of industrial products," while Colonial Mat's purpose was "to engage in the sale, distribution and services related to industrial products including, but not limited to, floor covering products. . . ." The only apparent difference between Colonial Mat and Colonial Industrial d/b/a Colonial Carpets was that Colonial Mat dealt in all floor coverings, while Colonial Industrial dealt in all floor coverings except mats. Third, Smith was president of both Colonial Mat and Colonial Industrial; the only other director for both corporations was the same individual, the treasurer Joe Eller. The two companies also shared the same office manager, Lois Jean Bennett, who testified that she was the only office personnel Smith had at the time. Fourth, the two companies operated at the same address and used an identical phone number. Fifth, while not of major importance, we find it interesting that Colonial Mat's credit application states that it had been in business since 1970. Given that Colonial Mat was incorporated in 1987, it would appear to be reasonable to infer that Smith was referring to 1970 as the date when he, personally, went into business.

Sixth, there is evidence from which a fact finder could have reasonably inferred that Colonial Mat and Colonial Industrial intermingled their assets, or that Colonial Mat paid for obligations of Colonial Industrial, which would satisfy two of the *Aronson* factors. McLeod introduced certain invoices directed to Colonial Mat that were paid by Colonial Mat checks following the March 17, 1989, letter that Colonial Mat and Smith claims gave notice of a change in corporate structure. We understand that a corporation that is going out of business will have a period of "winding up," where it will pay debts incurred before it went out of business. However, included among those invoices, for example, was an order for 500 business cards placed on March 23, 1989, paid for with a Colonial Mat check. It would seem unusual for a company going out of business to order 500 business cards; a reasonable inference would be that this represented some of the "printing" referred to in the March 17, 1989, letter, and that it was paid for out of Colonial Mat's checking account. The record also contains several payroll checks to Smith and Bennett written on Colonial Mat checks in April of 1989, as well as a Colonial Mat check written to McLeod itself in May of 1989. Finally, we address Smith's and Colonial Mat's claim that "[i]t is undisputed that by letter dated March 17, 1989, Michael B. Smith served notice upon McLeod that its carpet business would be affected by a corporate change." Appellant's Brief p. 7. We find this to be far from undisputed; rather, the letter is ambiguous in this regard. First, the letter at no point states that Colonial Mat is going out of business, and in fact makes no mention of Colonial Mat at all. It can be argued that it refers to Colonial Mat inferentially by stating, "we will be registering 'Colonial Carpets' to the corporation that we sell floor products under." That corporation was Colonial Mat, and thus this sentence may have indicated "Colonial Carpets" was going to be "registered" to Colonial Mat, thus lending support to the idea that Colonial Carpets and Colonial Mat were one and the same. The letter also states that the change to Colonial Carpets was a name change made for marketing reasons. Ron McLeod, McLeod's president, testified that this indicated to him that the name change "was a marketing thing that had no bearing on anything else. . . . It didn't change the company, it just had another name. . . . It was just all the same stuff." McLeod also testified that the meaning of the letter to him was "they are adding a name to their Colonial Industrial Products Company, Inc. a company called Colonial Carpets." Thus, far from providing clear and unambiguous notice of a change in corporate structure, the letter appears to have only added to the confusion about the purported corporate separateness of Colonial Mat and Colonial Industrial d/b/a Colonial Carpets.

There is ample indication that, in dealing with the public, Smith treated Colonial Mat and Colonial Industrial d/b/a Colonial Carpets as if they were adjunct corporations, or mere alter egos or instrumentalities of each other that shared a common identity. Therefore, equity requires that Colonial Mat be held liable for the debt at issue here in order to protect an innocent third party, McLeod, from unfairness.

Notes and Questions

1. Notes

a. Smith was the shareholder of both Colonial Mat and Colonial Industrial but plaintiff did not include a cause of action against Smith under a traditional piercing the corporate veil theory.

b. Colonial Mat could not obtain credit from McLeod unless Smith personally guaranteed the indebtedness. This is a typical situation. In this case, although Smith challenged his liability on the guarantee the court had little difficulty holding him liable.

c. Smith described Colonial Carpets as a "corporate division" of Colonial Industrial. The term "division" indicates an aspect of a business that is run relatively separately from other aspects but that is not conducted in a separate corporation.

d. The principal reason why a single business might be conducted by separate but affiliated corporations is because different aspects of the business may have very different risks. By establishing a separate corporation to engage in each separate aspect of the business, only those assets directly connected with a particular risk are liable to be used for liabilities related to that risk. For example, owning and operating a shopping mall might be divided among several corporations. The real estate might be owned by corporation *A*. A second corporation, corporation *B*, might develop the mall (i.e., hire architects and contractors, obtain building permits, etc.). A third corporation, corporation *C*, might own the buildings after the mall is built. This results in the risks of development and operation being contained within corporations *B* and *C*, respectively, without the land, which is owned by corporation *A*, being at risk. Modern finance theory suggests that a corollary to separating the risks is that financing, whether equity or debt, is less expensive to obtain than if the business were operated by a single corporation.

2. Reality Check

a. Which corporation was the debtor corporation?

b. How does McLeod benefit if Colonial Mat is liable for Colonial Industrial's debt?

3. Suppose

a. What if it were clear that McLeod had not confused the two corporations. Would the analysis or result have been different?

b. Suppose Colonial Mat and Colonial Industrial had had very distinct names. Would the court have imposed enterprise liability?

4. What Do You Think?

a. Why would Smith want to form two different corporations?

b. Which of the enterprise liability factors do you think were most important to the court? Do you think the court focused on the right factors?

5. You Draft It

a. Redraft Smith's March 17, 1989 letter to minimize the possibility of piercing the corporate veil and the possibility of aggregating the corporations under the doctrine of enterprise liability. The text read

To: Carpet Suppliers
Re: Colonial Carpets

Dear Supplier,
    In the near future we will be selling our matting products under the name of "Logomatts of America." We are obtaining licensing for custom logo mats from several universities and companies. For marketing reasons we feel a need for a name change.
    However, we will be registering "Colonial Carpets" to the corporation that we sell floor products under. We presently use "Colonial Carpets" as the name we invoice our carpet jobs.
    So, as soon as our printing is completed we will be ordering, as well as selling, all floor products except Mats & Matting as "Colonial Carpets" a corporate division of Colonial Industrial Products Co., Inc.
    If you have any questions, feel free to call me at any time.

Very truly yours,
Michael B. Smith
President

Another very typical setting in which enterprise liability may be applied is where a single business is divided into separate corporations, each of which performs the same (or nearly the same) functions. In other words, one business is fragmented into several entities. This separation is different from the setting in *Smith* in which separate entities might be established because each entity, although part of a larger integrated enterprise, has distinctly different tasks and risks. In the fragmentation setting, all the entities are engaged in the same business with the same risks.

The taxicab industry is a classic business for such fragmentation. Putting each taxicab into a separate entity is a way to limit creditors, especially tort creditors, to only those assets most directly responsible for their claims. A tort plaintiff injured by a taxicab would normally be able to look only to the corporation that owned the taxicab that caused the injury, even though the ultimate owner of that cab might also own an entire fleet of cabs, if each cab is the primary or sole asset of a separate corporation. In general, any business that has multiple locations and anticipates frequent tort claims might be fragmented. In addition to taxicabs, grocery stores, restaurants, and gas stations are obvious examples of industries in which owners of multiple locations might fragment their assets. Courts sometimes disregard the separate corporate forms of sibling corporations to aggregate the assets of each corporation. Where the ultimate owner of the sibling entities has been lax in adhering to the corporate niceties of keeping the corporations separate, enterprise liability is sometimes the result. But even where the ultimate owner has been scrupulous in maintaining the separateness of the entities, a court will sometimes impose enterprise liability (and, perhaps pierce to the ultimate owner, too) on a theory that allowing an owner to cabin liability is simply against public policy. If establishing a single corporation for the express purpose of limiting the ultimate owner's liability is perfectly appropriate, why is establishing multiple such corporations wrong?

Another reason why a business might be fragmented is simply historical. A corporation that acquires a competing business might well do so by purchasing all the competing business's stock with the result that the new, larger enterprise is fragmented into two corporations, each engaging in the same business.

Putting It to Work

Problem 8-1

Christi is the owner/operator of Creamy's Ice Cream, Inc., a business that sends an ice cream truck on demand to the location of the requesting customer. Christi, a mogul in her own right, also wholly owns Fanny's Fun Foods, Corp., the company that produces the ice cream the Creamy's trucks deliver. Both corporations were incorporated in a state that has adopted the MBCA.

After initial success with Creamy's single truck, Christi expanded to a fleet of 20 ice cream trucks and launched a marketing campaign with the tagline "Creamy's: always just a phone call and fifteen minutes away or it's free." Unfortunately, getting *anywhere* in fifteen minutes proved to be difficult and giving away free cones to placate angry customers cut into Christi's profits.

After a few months of operations, Fanny's Fun Foods owed back payments to its milk supplier. The bad news continued for Christi when one of Creamy's drivers hit a pedestrian with her delivery truck in an effort to arrive at a customer's location on time.

a. Could the milk supplier recover from Christi if Fanny's doesn't have enough assets? Could the milk supplier recover from Creamy's?

b. Could the pedestrian recover from Christi if Creamy's doesn't have enough assets? Could the pedestrian recover from Fanny's?

c. Could either the milk supplier or the pedestrian recover from the combined assets of Creamy's and Fanny's to satisfy the judgments? Could either of them recover from Christi personally if Creamy's and Fanny's combined do not have enough assets?

d. Would your analysis or conclusion be different for any of these questions if the corporations were incorporated in Delaware?

When the claim against the subsidiary corporation sounds in tort, can the plaintiff hold the corporate parent directly liable on the ground that the parent's business plan for the subsidiary was a proximate cause of the harm to the plaintiff? The next case takes up this question.

Forsythe v. Clark USA, Inc.
864 N.E.2d 227 (Ill. 2007)

Justice GARMAN delivered the judgment of the court, with opinion:

On March 13, 1995, Michael F. Forsythe and Gary Szabla, mechanics at a refinery owned and operated by Clark Refining and Marketing (Clark Refining), were killed. The estate of each decedent received payment from Clark Refining pursuant to the Workers' Compensation Act. In 1996 and 1997, plaintiffs Marguerite Forsythe and Elizabeth Szabla, as special administrators of the estates of their late husbands, filed suits against Clark Refining and other defendants. Subsequently, plaintiffs added Clark Refining's parent company, Clark USA, as a defendant.

Clark USA is the only defendant involved in this appeal. At the close of discovery, the trial court granted Clark USA's motion for summary judgment. . . . The trial court did not state its reasoning. Plaintiffs appealed, and the appellate court reversed and remanded. Following that decision, defendant petitioned this court for leave to appeal. . . .

We granted defendant's petition to consider . . . whether a parent company can be held liable under a theory of direct participant liability for controlling its subsidiary's budget in a way that led to a workplace accident. . . .

BACKGROUND

Clark Refining operated an oil refinery in Blue Island, Illinois. Defendant is Clark Refining's parent company and sole shareholder. On March 13, 1995, decedents were on their lunch break when a fire broke out at the refinery, killing them both. The fire was apparently caused when other Clark Refining employees attempted to replace a valve on a pipe without ensuring that flammable materials within the pipe had been depressurized. Plaintiffs claim that those employees were not maintenance mechanics and were not trained or qualified to perform the work they were attempting.

Plaintiffs' allegations of liability center around defendant's overall budgetary strategy. Specifically, plaintiffs allege that defendant breached a duty to use reasonable care in imposing its business strategy on Clark Refining by (1) "requiring [Clark Refining] to minimize operating costs including costs for training, maintenance, supervision and safety," (2) "requiring [Clark Refining] to limit capital investments to those which would generate cash for the refinery thereby preventing [Clark Refining] from adequately reinforcing the walls of the lunchroom or relocating the lunchroom to a safe position within the refinery," and (3) "failing to adequately evaluate the safety and training procedures in place at the Blue Island Refinery." Moreover, plaintiffs allege that defendant's strategy of capital cutbacks forced Clark Refining to have unqualified employees act as maintenance mechanics which, in turn, led to the fire that killed the decedents. This, plaintiffs argue, constitutes proximate cause.

In support of its motion for summary judgment, defendant contended that it owed no duty to either decedent by virtue of its status as a mere holding company, which was connected to Clark Refining only as a shareholder. Defendant submitted evidence to prove that Clark Refining owned and operated the refinery while defendant itself had no control over the day-to-day operations. Plaintiffs countered that defendant was directly responsible for creating conditions that precipitated the accident.

In support of their argument, plaintiffs cited evidence that defendant's directors created and approved Clark Refining's budget, striving to "position itself as a low cost refiner and marketer" with the goal of replenishing defendant's cash reserve by "decreas[ing] capital spending * * * to minimum sustainable levels" through the institution of a "survival mode" business plan. Plaintiffs also produced evidence that the boards of directors of Clark Refining and defendant met simultaneously. Moreover, plaintiffs relied upon evidence that the belt-tightening budget created by Clark Refining was overseen by Paul Melnuk, who served as defendant's president as well as chief executive officer of Clark Refining.

ANALYSIS

I. Direct Participant Liability

To state a cause of action for negligence, plaintiffs must show that defendant owed and breached a duty of care, proximately causing the plaintiffs injury. The threshold issue in this case is the existence of a duty, which is a question of law for the court to decide. [T]he touchstone of this court's duty analysis is to ask whether a plaintiff and a defendant stood in such a relationship to one another that the law imposed upon the defendant an obligation of reasonable conduct for the benefit of the plaintiff. Four factors inform this inquiry: (1) the reasonable foreseeability of injury, (2) the likelihood of injury, (3) the magnitude of the burden of guarding against the injury, and (4) the consequences of placing the burden upon the defendant.

Before undertaking our analysis, we note, as did the parties and the appellate court, that the theory of direct participant liability presented here has not previously been addressed in Illinois. It has been addressed in other states and throughout the federal courts, however. We will consider this authority where appropriate in our analysis.

Plaintiffs argue that defendant demanded Clark Refining operate its refinery pursuant to an overall business strategy that it knew would adversely affect safety by forcing reductions in training and maintenance. Indeed, plaintiffs contend that defendant actively and directly mandated unreasonable cuts in Clark Refining's budget in order to carry out its strategy. This strategy was outlined in Clark USA business records calling for a "survival mode" business philosophy accomplished through "reduced capital spending," "reduced working capital investment," and "reduced operating expense level." Plaintiffs allege that this "survival mode" strategy was mandated, despite the fact that defendant knew or should have known that the only feasible budget cuts would come from safety, maintenance, and training expenses. This, plaintiffs conclude, constitutes direct participation by defendant in the harm caused. As such, plaintiffs contend the appellate court correctly found that defendant owed them a duty based on the direct participant theory and not on the legal relationship of defendant to its subsidiary.

Defendant contends that unless the standards for piercing the corporate veil are met, a parent company cannot be held liable for the negligence of its subsidiary. Attendant to that rule is the principle that a parent company does not owe a duty to third parties to supervise or control the conduct of its subsidiary to ensure that the subsidiary acts with reasonable care. Clark Refining owed a nondelegable duty to its employees to provide them with a safe workplace while defendant, as a parent, owed no duty whatsoever to ensure that Clark Refining met its obligations.

Additionally, even if direct liability is a recognized theory of recovery, defendant argues that the simple task of setting financial goals and employing an overall strategy to meet those goals is not improper but, instead, is "consistent with the parent's investor status" and thus "should not give rise to direct liability." *United States v. Bestfoods,* 524 U.S. 51, 69 (1998). Because its conduct was always consistent with its investor status, defendant claims, there is no basis to treat it as a direct participant in the negligence alleged herein.

While the Supreme Court has held that "[i]t is a general principle * * * deeply 'ingrained in our economic and legal systems' that a parent corporation * * * is not liable for the acts of its subsidiaries" (*Bestfoods,* 524 U.S. at 61, quoting W.O. Douglas & C. Shanks, *Insulation from Liability Through Subsidiary Corporations,* 39 Yale L.J. 193 (1929)), a significant body of case law supports the direct participant theory of liability urged by the plaintiffs. Some of that authority relies on the 1929 article quoted above and written, in relevant part, by then-Professor William O. Douglas.

The United States Supreme Court quoted the Douglas & Shanks article approvingly in *Bestfoods,* 524 U.S. at 64-65. The Court noted that the simple fact that directors of a parent corporation serve as directors of its subsidiary does not, standing alone, expose the parent corporation to liability for its subsidiary's acts. *Bestfoods,* 524 U.S. at 69-70. The Court went on to state, however, that "the acts of direct operation that give rise to parental liability must necessarily be distinguished from the interference that stems from the normal relationship between parent and subsidiary," and "[t]he critical question is whether, in degree and detail, actions directed to the facility by an agent of the parent alone are eccentric under accepted norms of parental oversight of a subsidiary's facility." *Bestfoods,* 524 U.S. at 71-72. Plaintiffs also cite other cases approving of direct liability. *Papa v. Katy Industries, Inc.,* 166 F.3d 937, 941 (7th Cir. 1999) . . . ; *Pearson v. Component Technology Corp.,* [247 F.3d 471 (3d Cir. 2001)] . . . ; *Boggs v. Blue Diamond Coal Co.,* 590 F.2d 655, 663 (6th Cir. 1979) . . . ; *Commissioner of Department of Environmental Management v. RLG, Inc.,* 755 N.E.2d 556, 559, 563 (Ind. 2001) . . . ; *Estate of Countryman v. Farmers Cooperative Ass'n,* 679 N.W.2d 598, 605 (Iowa 2004) . . . ; *United States v. TIC Investment Corp.,* 68 F.3d 1082, 1091 n. 9 (8th Cir. 1995) . . . ; *United States v. Kayser-Roth Corp.,* 910 F.2d 24, 27 (1st Cir. 1990) . . . ; and *Dassault Falcon Jet Corp. v. Oberflex, Inc.,* 909 F. Supp. 345, 347, 354 (M.D.N.C. 1995). . . .

In opposition to plaintiffs' theory, defendant contends that a parent corporation owes no duty to supervise its subsidiary's conduct for the benefit of third parties. Defendant cites *Young v. Bryco Arms,* 821 N.E.2d 1078 (Ill. 2004), where this court noted its recognition of the general rule that "one has no duty to control the conduct of another to prevent him from causing harm to a third party, absent a special relationship with either the person causing the harm or the injured party." Building on that point, defendant argues that courts have uniformly rejected the argument that the parent-subsidiary relationship qualifies as the kind of "special relationship" necessary to give rise to a duty to supervise or control the conduct of the subsidiary. Supporting this contention, defendant cites *Joiner v. Ryder System Inc.,* 966 F. Supp. 1478 (C.D. Ill. 1996), where the district court applied Illinois law and concluded that a duty could not be predicated either on the parent's ability to control its subsidiary or on its actual exercise of control.

Additionally, defendant contends that direct participant claims virtually identical to those raised here were rejected by two state appellate decisions, one from Texas and one from California. As defendant points out, *Coastal Corp. v. Torres,* 133 S.W.3d 776 (Tex. App. 2004) and *Waste Management Inc. v. Superior Court of San Diego,* 13 Cal. Rptr. 3d 910 (Cal. App. 2004), stand for the proposition that mere budgetary mismanagement is not enough to support direct participant liability. Additionally, however, the *Coastal Corp.* court noted that "it is apparent that liability is imposed when there is specific control over the activity that caused the accident." *Coastal Corp.,* 133 S.W.3d at 779. Similarly, the *Waste Management* court stated that the plaintiffs' case failed because they could not show that the parent company "directed and authorized the *manner* in which the subsidiary conducted its business." (Emphasis in original). *Waste Management,* 13 Cal. Rptr. 3d at 910. In other words, these courts found that a viable claim of liability under the direct participant theory cannot rest solely upon budgetary mismanagement, but budgetary mismanagement can make up one part of a viable claim, in conjunction with the direction or authorization of the manner in which an activity is undertaken. The *Joiner* decision echoes this sentiment. There, the court granted summary judgment in favor of the parent/defendant, noting significantly that the parent/defendant did "not get involved in the day-to-day activities or management of the subsidiaries." *Joiner,* 966 F. Supp. at 1490. Based upon this analysis, we conclude that budgetary mismanagement, accompanied by the parent's negligent direction or authorization of the manner in which the subsidiary accomplishes that budget, can lead to a valid cause of action under the direct participant theory of liability.

Considering the above, we hold that direct participant liability is a valid theory of recovery under Illinois law. Where there is evidence sufficient to prove that a parent company mandated an overall business and budgetary strategy *and* carried that strategy out by its own specific direction or authorization surpassing the control exercised as a normal incident of ownership in disregard for the interests of the subsidiary, that parent company could face liability. The key elements to the application of direct participant liability, then, are a parent's specific direction or authorization of the manner in which an activity is undertaken and foreseeability. If a parent company specifically directs an activity, where injury is foreseeable, that parent could be held liable. Similarly, if a parent company mandates an overall course of action and then authorizes the manner in which specific activities contributing to that course of action are undertaken, it can be liable for foreseeable injuries. We again stress, though, that allegations of mere budgetary mismanagement alone do not give rise to the application of direct participant liability.

Our finding is supported by the policy-based factors courts use to determine whether a duty exists. Certain heavy industries, like refining, inherently involve a great amount of danger. It is conceivable that severe cutbacks in staffing, safety, maintenance, and training in such industries could lead, with reasonable foreseeability, to the injury of others. The likelihood of injury in those circumstances would not be remote and could be deadly. Additionally, the magnitude of the burden of guarding against such injury would not be great. Parent companies are free to craft overall business and budgetary strategies; such companies simply must not interfere directly in the manner their subsidiaries undertake certain activities such that the subsidiaries are no longer free to utilize their own expertise. Alternatively, if parent companies do interfere directly in the manner their subsidiaries undertake certain activities, they must do so with reasonable care. Finally, it is not an undue burden to require that parent corporations engage in the considered exercise of due care in an already limited role. As we have already acknowledged, parent corporations are generally not liable for the acts of their subsidiaries. *Bestfoods,* 524 U.S. at 61, quoting 39 Yale L.J. 193 (1929). Moreover, the mere fact of a parent-subsidiary relationship, without a great deal more, does not give rise to liability. *Bestfoods,* 524 U.S. at 61, quoting 1 W. Fletcher, Cyclopedia of Law of Private Corporations §33, at 568 (rev. ed. 1990).

Recognizing that a parent company may have a duty based upon direct participant liability does not end the analysis though. Certain facts must still be present to give rise to its application.

II. Direct Participant Liability Applied

Returning to the specific issue in this case, we must resolve whether there exists a question of material fact such that the evidence presented could lead a reasonable observer to believe that defendant's overall business and budgetary strategy involved the negligent direction or authorization of the manner in which Clark Refining conducted its business. If so, the trial court's grant of summary judgment was inappropriate.

Defendant's overall business strategy at the time of the tragic accident involved here mandated increased productivity driven, at least in part, by budgetary cuts. The question remains, though, whether those cuts were negligently directed by or conducted in a manner authorized by defendant at the expense of Clark Refining. Answering this question requires a close look at the role of defendant's president, Paul Melnuk, who also served as chief executive officer of Clark Refining.

In *Bestfoods,* the Supreme Court pointed out that lower courts must "recognize that 'it is entirely appropriate for directors of a parent corporation to serve as directors of its subsidiary, and that fact alone may not serve to expose the parent corporation to liability for its subsidiary's acts.'" *Bestfoods,* 524 U.S. at 69, citing *American Protein Corp. v. AB Volvo,* 844 F.2d 56, 57 (2d Cir.1988). The Court acknowledged the "'well established principle [of corporate law] that directors and officers holding positions with a parent and its subsidiary can and do "change hats" to represent the two corporations separately, despite their common ownership.'" *Bestfoods,* 524 U.S. at 69, citing *Lusk v. Foxmeyer Health Corp.,* 129 F.3d 773, 779 (5th Cir. 1997). Further, the Court noted that it should be presumed that directors are wearing their "subsidiary hats," rather than their "parent hats," when acting for the subsidiary. *Bestfoods,* 524 U.S. at 69.

Accordingly, to establish liability, plaintiffs must establish more than the fact that Paul Melnuk made policy decisions and supervised subsidiary activities. *Bestfoods,* 524 U.S. at 69. Instead, plaintiffs must show that the conduct complained of occurred while Paul Melnuk was acting in his capacity as an officer of Clark USA, rather than as an officer of Clark Refining. *Bestfoods,* 524 U.S. at 69. In attempting to do so, plaintiffs point to additional language from *Bestfoods,* where the Court stated that "the presumption that an act is taken on behalf of the corporation for whom the officer claims to act is strongest when the act is perfectly consistent with the norms of corporate behavior, but wanes as the distance from those accepted norms approaches the point of action by a dual officer plainly contrary to the interests of the subsidiary yet nonetheless advantageous to the parent." *Bestfoods,* 524 U.S. at 70 n. 13.

Seizing upon that language, plaintiffs point to the April 1995 "Memorandum to the Executive Committee," prepared by Paul Melnuk, completed on Clark USA letterhead, and including a document entitled "1995 Economic Imperatives." Moreover, plaintiffs point to another Clark USA business record, the agenda for the February 15, 1995, board of directors meeting, which includes a section entitled "Clark USA Liquidity Overview." That document lays out a "survival mode" business philosophy marked by "reduced capital spending," "reduced working capital investment," and "reduced operating expense level." The document further states that the "goal is to replenish [defendant's] strategic cash reserve to $200 million." Defendant's continued emphasis on this goal is supported by the "1995 Economic Imperatives," one of which was to "[r]eplenish cash balance to 200 million" by reducing capital spending to "minimum sustainable levels." Relying on this, plaintiffs contend that the business and budgetary strategy defendant mandated in this case was carried out for its own benefit at the foreseeable expense of safety and spending at Clark Refining and at the direction of Paul Melnuk. As such, the only benefit of the business and budgetary strategy involved in this case ran to defendant and not Clark Refining. This, plaintiffs argue, proves that Paul Melnuk was acting not on behalf of Clark Refining but, instead, on behalf of Clark USA.

In opposition, defendant cites the testimony of Paul Melnuk himself where he claims that the 1995 Imperatives, though completed on defendant's letterhead, were actually carried out for Clark Refining. Additionally, defendant notes that the 1995 Imperatives include discussion of the continuing need to spend on necessary health and safety as well as ensure that all existing environmental, health, and safety needs are fully supported.

At the very least, there is a genuine issue of material fact as to whose "hat" Melnuk was wearing when he completed the 1995 memorandum. If the fact finder concludes that Melnuk was acting on behalf of defendant and thus wearing his Clark USA "hat," there is some evidence that he was directing or authorizing the manner in which Clark Refining's budget was implemented such that he had a duty, under the direct participant theory of liability, to do so with reasonable care. The additional evidence produced by plaintiffs indicating that Melnuk knew both that the budgetary reductions involved here had to come in large part from controllable costs such as education, training, repairs, and equipment maintenance, and that these reductions were compromising safety at the refinery raises an issue of material fact as to whether or not defendant breached that duty. The trial court's grant of summary judgment was therefore inappropriate.

If Paul Melnuk, acting on behalf of defendant, directed or authorized the manner in which the budget cuts in this case were taken, he had a duty to do so in a nonnegligent way. If Melnuk directed or authorized the manner in which the budget cuts at issues were taken, knowing that safety at the Blue Island refinery would be compromised, and did so superseding the discretion and interest of Clark Refining, direct participant liability could attach. Determining whether this duty applies to the facts of this case, and whether defendant is liable, involves factual inquiry. This inquiry is not suitable for this court on review and not appropriate for disposition at summary judgment, especially considering that this court must interpret the record strictly against the moving party and liberally in favor of the nonmoving party.

CONCLUSION

Drawing no ultimate conclusions on the merits of plaintiffs' case and mindful that summary judgment is an extraordinary remedy, summary judgment was inappropriate in this matter. We recognize the direct participant theory of liability. We note, however, that this theory of liability gives rise to a duty only in limited circumstances. Budgetary oversight alone is insufficient, as is a parent company's commission of acts consistent with its investor status.

If there is sufficient evidence to show that a parent corporation directed or authorized the manner in which an activity is undertaken, however, a duty arises. Specifically, the duty to utilize reasonable care in directing or authorizing the manner in which that activity is undertaken. Accordingly, a parent corporation can be held liable if, for its own benefit, it directs or authorizes the manner in which its subsidiary's budget is implemented, disregarding the discretion and interests of the subsidiary, and thereby creating dangerous conditions.

For these reasons, we affirm the appellate court's reversal of the trial court's grant of summary judgment and its remand of the cause to the circuit court for further proceedings.

Notes and Questions

1. Reality Check

a. What was the plaintiffs' theory of liability? What are its elements?

b. Why did the court accept the plaintiffs' theory? What reservations did the court have?

2. Suppose

a. Suppose it were clear that Mr. Melnuk was acting solely for Clark Refining. Would that make the plaintiffs' case stronger or weaker?

b. Suppose it were clear that Mr. Melnuk was acting solely for Clark USA. Would that make the plaintiffs' case stronger or weaker?

3. What Do You Think?

a. Do you believe that Clark USA was a direct participant in causing the deaths of the workers?

b. Should an owner's business and financial plan for its business render the owner liable for the business's physical torts?

Putting It to Work

Problem 8-2

Patrick had worked as a mechanic for RepairEd, Inc., a wholly-owned subsidiary of Exelon Energy Delivery, Co., for 20 years before he was injured on the job. Although EED has input into general safety rules utilized by RepairEd, it does not control how RepairEd plans specific projects or supervises its own crews. Instead, RepairEd projects are planned, staffed, and implemented solely by RepairEd employees. Similarly, the implementation of safety procedures is performed solely by RepairEd; however, the conduct of RepairEd employees is governed by safety procedures contained within a printed rule book.

In the course of regular repair work to help Rocky, a crew chief employed directly by RepairEd, Patrick left a man lift which did not reach high enough and climbed up a structure to repair a dislodged bolt. Because Patrick believed that the area was de-energized, he did not use protective gloves. Because Patrick was not authorized to work around energized equipment, he stated that he followed the instructions of Rocky. While holding a metal tool in his hand, he reached out to reposition himself and was injured when the metal tool came into contact with an energized bus bar connected to an adjacent capacitor bank.

a. If you were the attorney for Patrick, what would you argue to hold Exelon Corp. liable?

b. If you were the attorney for Exelon Corp., how would you argue that your client is not directly liable for Patrick's injuries?

3. Commercial and Bankruptcy Doctrines

Another line of approach in trying to satisfy a corporate debt from noncorporate sources lies in the areas of commercial and bankruptcy law, both of which are beyond the scope of this book. Commercial law provides the doctrine of *fraudulent conveyances* to protect creditors. Briefly, if a corporate debtor transfers assets for less than fair value at a time when it was insolvent and for the purpose of harming its other creditors, those other creditors can trace the transferred assets into the hands of the transferees.

Similarly, bankruptcy law provides protection through *voidable preferences* and *equitable subordination*. A bankrupt corporation's creditors can recover corporate property transferred to certain corporate insiders within one year of the bankruptcy if the transfer was for an antecedent debt, had the effect of giving the insiders more than they would have received in the bankruptcy, and was made while the corporation was insolvent. Such transfers are considered to be impermissible preferences for insiders.

The concept of *equitable subordination* was discussed in Chapter 6 in connection with planning the corporation's capital structure. The next case is a classic example of equitable subordination in action.

In re Le Café Creme, Ltd., Debtor

244 B.R. 221 (Bankr. S.D.N.Y. 2000)

Tina L. Brozman, Chief Judge.

Introduction

From January 1, 1991 until its business was sold on October 6, 1997 pursuant to an order of this Court, Le Café Creme, Ltd. (the "Debtor") operated a café/restaurant, the last month of that time period under this Court's aegis as a chapter 11 debtor. Xavier and Danielle LeRoux and Denis and Celestine Peron were the Debtor's shareholders, officers and directors from its inception in 1989. Over the years, the LeRouxs and the Perons each loaned over $200,000 to the Debtor. It had no other capitalization. [In] early February, 1994, . . . the LeRouxs sold their stock back to the Debtor, leaving the Perons as the sole owners.

On November 19, 1997, the Debtor commenced an adversary proceeding against the LeRouxs . . . to equitably subordinate the LeRouxs' claim pursuant to section 510(c) of the Bankruptcy Code.

Findings of Fact

On September 9, 1997, the Debtor, a New York corporation incorporated on June 5, 1989, filed a voluntary petition for relief under chapter 11 of the United States Bankruptcy Code. The Debtor operated a café/restaurant from January 1, 1991 to approximately October 6, 1997, when its business was sold pursuant to an order of this Court.

Xavier LeRoux and Danielle LeRoux each owned twenty five (25%) percent of the outstanding stock of the Debtor . . . from [its] inception until February 4, 1994, on which date the LeRouxs and the Debtor entered into the Purchase Agreement. Also parties to the Purchase Agreement were the Perons, and the [Debtor] which repurchased [its] shares of stock from the LeRouxs.

Peron testified that from 1992 through 1996 the Debtor had difficulty meeting its obligations and paying its bills. Checks were returned monthly during these years and 1997 for insufficient funds.

Xavier LeRoux testified that he and his wife advanced $220,000 to the Debtor prior to leaving the Debtor in February, 1994, of which, according to Denis Peron's testimony, approximately $150,000 was advanced in 1989 in connection with the construction and start-up costs of the business. Denis Peron testified that he and his wife advanced $300,000 to the Debtor, of which approximately $140,000 was advanced in 1989 in connection with the construction and start-up costs of the business. The LeRouxs and the Perons stipulated for purposes of this trial that the LeRouxs' pre-February, 1994 advances were loans to the Debtor (collectively, the "Loans"). No interest was paid on the Loans, no promissory note was executed, none of the Debtor's corporate minutes reflected that the LeRouxs had made any loans to the Debtor, and none of the Loans had a stated maturity date. The source of the Loans was second mortgages on two houses the LeRouxs owned and cash.

From August 11, 1989 until March 30, 1993, the LeRouxs were able to sign the Debtor's checks without obtaining the signatures of either Denis or Celestine Peron. After March 30, 1993, all checks required the signatures of either Denis or Celestine Peron and Xavier or Danielle LeRoux.

The Loans were partially repaid in 1991, 1992 and 1993, reducing them to approximately $95,000 from $220,000.

Pursuant to the Purchase Agreement, the Debtor agreed to pay LeRoux $200,000: $105,073.61 (the "Stock Purchase Amount") for the purchase of the LeRouxs' stock (collectively, the "Stock Purchases") and $94,926.36 ("Loan Repayment") as payment of the outstanding balance of the Loans. The parties stipulated that the Debtor paid $135,671.17 to the LeRouxs under the Purchase Agreement, of which $94,926.36 was paid on account of the Loan Repayment and $40,744,81 was paid on account of the Stock Purchases.

In connection with execution of the Purchase Agreement, the Debtor executed a Non-Negotiable Promissory Note dated February 4, 1994 in the amount of $150,000, a Security Agreement granting the LeRouxs a security interest and lien upon the Debtor's equipment, furnishings and fixtures, and a Financing Statement. The LeRouxs also received an assignment of the Debtor's lease upon default under the Purchase Agreement. The LeRouxs perfected their security interest in February, 1994.

The LeRouxs timely filed a secured claim in the chapter 11 case in the amount of $60,836.20 for sums allegedly unpaid by the Debtor pursuant to the Purchase Agreement.

The sources of the Payments, which were made on account of the Stock Purchases and Loan Repayment, were the Debtor's revenue and loans made by the Perons to the Debtor.

Denis Peron testified that the Debtor approached Citibank for a loan in 1990 or 1991, but was informed that the bank would not make loans to restaurants.

Denis Peron testified that in each month from 1991 through 1997, checks made payable by the Debtor to its creditors were returned by the Debtor's bank for insufficient funds, although the number of checks which "bounced" monthly decreased in 1994. Peron testified that in February, 1994, the Debtor had difficulty paying its obligations, had insufficient capital or funds to operate its business on a day-to-day basis, and had personal property, the value of which at the time of its bankruptcy filing (some three and one-half years later), did not exceed $1,600. According to Denis Peron's testimony, the Debtor's fixtures and furnishings were never appraised.

Despite efforts over the years to sell the Debtor's business, no offer was made until one was received from William Byun for $98,000 in August, 1997. The Debtor's business and assets were ultimately sold to Mr. Byun [for $98,000] in October, 1997 by order of this Court.

According to Denis Peron's testimony, Xavier LeRoux's weekly salary prior to 1992 was $1,600 to $1,800, which Mr. Peron believed was reduced to $1,200 a week in 1992 and 1993. Mr. LeRoux testified that he rendered services as a chef and "ran" the Debtor's restaurant six (6) days a week.

Based upon the Debtor's federal tax returns for the years ended 1991 through 1996 and the testimony of Mr. Fishman, the Debtor's expert witness: (i) the Debtor's liabilities exceeded its assets during these years; . . . and (iii) the Debtor's insolvency during the period from 1991 to 1996 deepened.

Discussion

Equitable Subordination Under Section 510(c) of the Bankruptcy Code

The Debtor's . . . claim for relief is to equitably subordinate the LeRouxs' $60,836.20 claim under section 510(c) of the Bankruptcy Code on the grounds that the LeRouxs, as insiders, engaged in conduct that was unfair to creditors.

To determine if conditions exist warranting the equitable subordination of an insider's claim, most courts have followed and applied the criteria articulated by the court in *In re Mobile Steel Co.*, 563 F.2d 692 (5th Cir. 1977). Under the *Mobile Steel* test, a claim is equitably subordinated if there is a showing by a preponderance of the evidence that (i) the claim holder engaged in some type of inequitable conduct, (ii) which injured the creditors of the debtor or conferred an unfair advantage on the claimant, and (iii) equitable subordination of the claim is not inconsistent with the provisions of the Bankruptcy [Code]. *Fabricators, Inc. v. Technical Fabricators, Inc. (In re Fabricators, Inc.)*, 926 F.2d 1458, 1464 (5th Cir. 1991). "A claim arising from the dealings between a debtor and an insider is to be rigorously scrutinized by the courts." *Id.* at 1465 (citations omitted). Nonetheless, "the mere fact of an insider relationship is insufficient to warrant subordination." *Id.* at 1467. Applying the "rigorous scrutiny" standard to review the LeRouxs' conduct, we will now examine whether the LeRouxs engaged in misconduct which injured the Debtor's creditors or conferred an unfair advantage on themselves.

Three categories of misconduct have generally been recognized to constitute inequitable conduct: "(1) fraud, illegality, breach of fiduciary duties; (2) undercapitalization; and (3) claimant's use of the debtor as a mere instrumentality or alter ego." *Fabricators*, 926 F.2d at 1467. Undercapitalization of the debtor alone, absent misconduct by the insider, is insufficient to justify equitable subordination of an insider's debt claim.

The Debtor alleges that the LeRouxs' claim should be equitably subordinated because . . . the LeRouxs, as insiders, engaged in misconduct by repaying their loans first to the detriment of the Debtor's other creditors.

We will now turn to whether the Debtor has sufficiently shown that the LeRouxs engaged in inequitable conduct warranting the subordination of their bifurcated claim.

Conduct engaged in by an insider is subject to rigorous scrutiny. The evidence presented abundantly showed that the LeRouxs, as insiders and having knowledge of the Debtor's financial affairs, repaid themselves on account of their Loans and entered into the Purchase Agreement to convert their equity into debt while the Debtor had insufficient funds to pay its suppliers and routinely paid suppliers with checks which were returned for insufficient funds. Although there is testimony that many of the Debtor's Payments to the LeRouxs actually came from monies loaned by the Perons to the Debtor, the path of these funds does not in any way absolve the LeRouxs of their inequitable conduct because the additional loans from the Perons, who are creditors of the Debtor, only resulted in increasing the amount of their claims and diluting the amount of any potential distribution to the Debtor's other creditors. In effect, the LeRouxs shifted the risk of loss from themselves to the Debtor's creditors, to their obvious detriment. In addition, as part of the LeRouxs' actions to gain an advantage over the position of other creditors, the LeRouxs obtained a security interest in the Debtor's assets. The LeRouxs did not rebut the Debtor's case with any evidence demonstrating their good faith and the fairness of these transactions. Accordingly, I find that the LeRouxs' conduct is inequitable and warrants equitable subordination of their claim.

The next question is to what extent the LeRouxs' claim ought be equitably subordinated. "The general rule is that claims should be subordinated only to the extent necessary to offset the harm which the bankrupt and its creditors suffered as a result of the inequitable conduct." *Fabricators, Inc. v. Technical Fabricators, Inc.* (*In re Fabricators, Inc.*, 926 F.2d 1458, 1470 (5th Cir. 1991) (citation omitted)). I conclude that both the secured and unsecured portions of the LeRouxs' $60,836.20 claim relating to the Payments owed to the LeRouxs warrants equitable subordination below the status of general unsecured creditors. This indebtedness was not incurred on account of monies loaned by the LeRouxs to the Debtor in an attempt to revitalize its business, but to gain an unfair advantage and to siphon money from the Debtor to the injury of its creditors. An examination of the schedules of creditors attached to the Debtor's bankruptcy petition plainly shows a significant increase in the Debtor's liabilities during 1996 and 1997, when the Debtor made the Payments to the LeRouxs on account of the Stock Purchases. The equitable subordination of the remaining indebtedness below the status of general unsecured creditors would offset the harm which the Debtor and its creditors suffered as a result of the inequitable conduct, a result which is fully consistent with the Bankruptcy Code, particularly its policies of preventing prejudice to creditors and ensuring fair distribution.

V. Conclusions of Law.

Both the secured and unsecured portions of the LeRouxs' proof of claim are equitably subordinated below the status of general unsecured creditors.

The Debtor is directed to SETTLE AN ORDER DIRECTING ENTRY OF JUDGMENT in its favor consistent with this decision.

Notes and Questions

1. Reality Check

a. What did the LeRouxs do that was improper?
b. How did the LeRouxs' actions harm the Debtor's other creditors?
c. How are the Debtor's other creditors protected by the court's decision?

2. What Do You Think?

a. What were the LeRouxs trying to accomplish by their actions? Do you think they were deliberately trying to harm the Debtors' other creditors? Were the LeRouxs trying to harm the Perons?
b. Why did the Perons agree to the Purchase Agreement?

4. Successor Liability

The next method by which corporate creditors can seek satisfaction comes into play when control of the corporation has changed in certain ways. Because a corporation is separate from its owners, a change of ownership does not affect a creditor's claim against the corporation. In other words, a corporation does not shed any of its liabilities simply because all its stock has changed hands. Furthermore, as we will see in Chapter 16, when two corporations merge, which is a common way to effect a change of control of one of the corporations, the resulting corporation has the assets *and liabilities* of each of the two merging corporations. *See* MBCA §11.07 and DGCL §259(a).

But what about the liabilities of a corporation that sells its assets?[3] In the clearest setting, a corporation that sells a small amount of its assets does not thereby eliminate any liabilities. Conversely, the purchaser does not acquire any of the selling corporation's liabilities. The purchaser is simply obligated to pay for the assets as it agreed to do. As noted above, where the selling corporation is approaching bankruptcy, an asset sale for less than fair value may render the buyer liable to the seller's creditors. But leaving aside the bankruptcy possibility, and assuming that the sale is to an unrelated third party acting at arm's length, sales of corporate assets should have no effect on the selling corporation's liabilities.

In theory, this rule should apply even where the selling corporation sells a large percentage of its assets; even where it sells all its assets. In fact, where one corporation wants to acquire another, the transaction may be structured as a sale of assets, rather than as a purchase of 100 percent of the seller's stock or as a merger, so

---

3. Of course, corporations sell goods and services all the time. That's how they engage in business and make money (one hopes). The situation posed in this paragraph is meant to focus on the corporation that sells assets in settings that are not in the normal course of its business.

that the purchaser does not become liable for the seller's liabilities. Again, assuming no fraud, the selling corporation's creditors are not harmed. Instead of looking to a corporation that has $X in assets, the creditors are now looking to a corporation that has $X in cash. In some settings, this may make their claims more likely to be satisfied than if the corporation had assets but not much cash. Nonetheless, in some instances creditors of the selling corporation can hold the buying corporation liable for the seller's debts under doctrines that are collectively known as *successor liability*. The following case shows a typical scenario.

DeJesus v. Bertsch, Inc.
898 F. Supp. 2d 353 (D. Mass. 2012)

MEMORANDUM AND ORDER

YOUNG, District Judge.

INTRODUCTION

This is a products liability case brought under a successor liability theory. The main issue presented to this Court is whether the successor corporation, Park Corporation ("Park"), is liable for the torts of its predecessor, Bertsch, Inc. ("Bertsch"), under the *de facto* merger or "mere continuation" exceptions to the usual rules of successor liability.

PROCEDURAL POSTURE

DeJesus and his spouse, Maria L. Cartagena ("Cartagena"), filed an amended complaint in state court against Park as successor to Bertsch, alleging that DeJesus suffered serious personal injuries resulting from the dangerous and defective condition of a "roll-pinch" machine manufactured by Bertsch. Cartagena's claims rest on a loss of consortium theory. Park removed the case to this Court on September 6, 2011. On March 15, 2012, Park filed a motion for summary judgment. On May 16, 2012, after hearing from the parties, the Court took the matter under advisement.

FACTS

DeJesus and Cartagena allege that DeJesus suffered serious personal injuries resulting from the dangerous and defective condition of a "roll-pinch" machine manufactured by Bertsch.

The machine that injured DeJesus was a plate-bending roller, serial number 8826, manufactured by Bertsch and sold to Cambridge Corporation of Lowell, Massachusetts, in 1957.

Bertsch was a family-owned business until 1978, when Deem International, Inc. purchased 80 percent of the shares of Bertsch. The remaining shareholders of Bertsch—James Worl, Robert Wonsetler, Norm Bond, and the Estate of John Worl—were descendants of the Bertsch family, and the three surviving descendants continued to work for Bertsch after the Deem acquisition. [P]ark entered into negotiations to acquire Bertsch. Park and Bertsch agreed to Bertsch's liquidation through a Bankruptcy Protection Plan and then proceed according to the terms of [an] Asset Purchase Agreement. Bertsch ceased operations as of May 3, 1985 [the day the bankruptcy was final. ED]. As part of the Purchase Agreement, Park acquired Bertsch's engineering, engineering drawings, patents, copyrights, licenses, know-how, the trade name "Bertsch," trademarks, customer lists, addresses and contact persons. With respect to liabilities, the Purchase Agreement states that Park is not "undertaking the assumption of any of the liabilities of Seller."

No ownership interests or stock were exchanged in the transaction between Bertsch and Park. None of the directors or officers of Bertsch became directors or officers of Park. Instead, two of three living Bertsch family shareholders at the time of the transaction, James Worl and Norm Bond, were employed by Park post-transaction. The third living Bertsch family shareholder at the time of the transaction was Robert Wonsetler, who left his job as a head of the engineering department after the transaction. Park retained some of the long-time employees who managed the sales, services, and engineering divisions after the transaction.

After the transaction, Park held itself out to customers as Bertsch in its written advertisements, noting that Bertsch now is "a division of Park Corporation." The Bertsch phone number stayed the same and employees continued to answer incoming phone calls with the phrase "Thank you for calling Bertsch." The products offered by Bertsch and the process for creating them also remained the same.

ANALYSIS

Successor Liability

1. *Massachusetts Law Adheres to the Traditional Rules of Successor Liability*

> When one corporation purchases another corporation (or substantially all of another corporation's assets), the doctrine of successor liability determines the distribution of tort liability. Current doctrine often protects the successor corporation from liability for the predecessor's torts, even when the predecessor is unavailable for suit. . . .
>
> . . . .
>
> It would be unreasonable to attach successor liability to each individual asset sold, such that the sale of a single piece of equipment would carry with it some portion of the predecessor's tort liability. But in situations where a successor purchases a significant portion of the predecessor's assets as a going concern, shielding the successor from liability will undermine deterrence by allowing predecessors to evade liability through asset transfers. The traditional version of successor liability allows this evasion to occur.

Note, *Successor Liability, Mass Tort, and Mandatory-Litigation Class Action*, 118 HARV. L. REV. 2357, 2358-59 (2005) (footnotes omitted) (citations omitted).

Under the traditional rule of successor liability, the successor corporation is not liable for the predecessor's torts. Restatement (Third) of Torts: Products Liability §12 (1997). The law, however, seeks to prevent "the owners of the selling corporation [from] avoid[ing] paying creditors without losing control of their business." *National Gypsum Co. v. Cont'l Brands Corp.*, 895 F. Supp. 328, 337-38 (D. Mass.

1995) (GERTNER, J.). To avoid this result, there are four exceptions to the traditional rule:

> (1) when the purchasing corporation expressly or impliedly agreed to assume the selling corporation's liability; (2) when the transaction amounts to a consolidation or merger of the purchaser and seller corporations; (3) when the purchaser corporation is merely a continuation of the seller corporation; or (4) when the transaction is entered into fraudulently to escape liability for such obligations.

Some jurisdictions have adopted two other exceptions, which constitute more expansive models of successor liability; namely, the "product line" and the "continuity of enterprise" approaches.

The "product line" exception has been expressly rejected by the Massachusetts Supreme Judicial Court, *Guzman v. MRM/Elgin*, 409 Mass. 563, 567, 567 N.E.2d 929 (1991)....[3] The "continuity of enterprise" exception constitutes a broader view of the traditional "mere continuation" exception.[4] The main difference between these two exceptions is that the "[c]ontinuity of enterprise analysis does not require that the predecessor and successor corporations have *common shareholders*." *McCarthy v. Litton Indus., Inc.*, 410 Mass. 15, 22, 570 N.E.2d 1008 (1991) (emphasis added) (citations omitted). The Massachusetts Supreme Judicial Court has noted that the "continuity of enterprise" exception remains a minority approach. Similarly, after a detailed analysis of the different approaches to successor liability, Judge Gertner declined to follow the "mere continuation" exception and instead followed Massachusetts law on "the traditional de facto merger or continuation analysis, with its keystones of continuous ownership and inequitable conduct." *National Gypsum Co.*, 895 F. Supp. at 340.

DeJesus and Cartagena do not allege that the Bertsch-Park transaction was fraudulent; therefore, this Court only addresses the other three exceptions. Because the *de facto* merger and "mere continuation" exceptions are so closely related, they will be analyzed together. *National Gypsum Co.*, 895 F. Supp. at 336 ("While these two labels have been enshrined separately in the canonical list of exceptions to the general rule of no successor liability, they appear, in practice to refer to the same concept . . . and courts have often used the two terms interchangeably." (citation omitted)).

---

3. The "product line" exception extends liability to successor corporations when the successor continues manufacturing or marketing the same product line sold by the predecessor. *Ray*, 19 Cal.3d at 34, 136 Cal. Rptr. 574, 560 P.2d 3 ("[A] party which acquires a manufacturing business and continues the output of its line of products . . . assumes strict tort liability for defects in units of the same product line previously manufactured and distributed by the entity from which the business was acquired.").

4. Under "continuity of enterprise," a court will hold the successor liable if the successor is sufficiently similar to the predecessor that it is in essence continuing the predecessor's enterprise. *Turner*, 397 Mich. at 426, 429-30, 244 N.W.2d 873. ("[I]t does not make sense or promote justice to require a merger and a de facto merger to respond to products liability suits, and then to leave a transfer of assets for cash free from suit, when the needs and objectives of both the injured party and the corporation are the same in all three instances." *Id.* at 429-30, 244 N.W.2d 873.). "The continuity of enterprise analysis considers four factors: (1) continuity of management, personnel, physical location, and assets; (2) dissolution of the predecessor; (3) assumption of the ordinary business obligations and liabilities by the successor; and (4) the successor's presentation of itself as the continuation of the predecessor." 15 William Meade Fletcher et al., *Fletcher Cyclopedia of the Law of Private Corporations* §7123.06, at 275 (perm. ed., rev. vol. 1990).

2. The De Facto Merger and "Mere Continuation" Exceptions Under Massachusetts Law

Massachusetts courts consider the following factors in determining whether to characterize a purported sale of assets as a *de facto* merger:

> (1) There is a continuation of the enterprise of the seller corporation, so that there is continuity of management, personnel, physical location, assets, and general business operations.
>
> (2) There is a continuity of shareholders which results from the purchasing corporation paying for the acquired assets with shares of its own stock, this stock ultimately coming to be held by the shareholders of the seller corporation so that they become a constituent part of the purchasing corporation.
>
> (3) The seller corporation ceases its ordinary business operations, liquidates, and dissolves as soon as legally and practically possible.
>
> (4) The purchasing corporation assumes those obligations of the seller ordinarily necessary for the uninterrupted continuation of normal business operations of the seller corporation.

In re Acushnet River & New Bedford Harbor Proceedings re Alleged PCB Pollution, 712 F. Supp. 1010, 1015 (D. Mass. 1989).

Except for the "continuity of shareholders" factor, Park does not dispute the existence of these factors here. Indeed, DeJesus and Cartagena have a very well-developed case as to the other three factors.

The first factor is satisfied. DeJesus and Cartagena produced evidence to support a finding that Park continued Bertsch's enterprise, so that Park retained many employees who managed the sales, services, and engineering divisions after the transaction, including senior employees and two former shareholders. The products offered by Bertsch also remained the same. Park continued using Bertsch's engineering, engineering drawings, the trade name "Bertsch," customer lists, addresses, and contacts persons. The Bertsch phone number stayed the same and employees continued to answer incoming phone calls with the phrase "Thank you for calling Bertsch."

The third factor is also satisfied. DeJesus and Cartagena's evidence also supports that Park assumed all Bertsch operations and liquidated its assets as soon as legally and practically possible through a bankruptcy proceeding.

The fourth factor is also satisfied because Park assumed those obligations of Bertsch ordinarily necessary for the uninterrupted continuation of normal business operations, i.e., Park assumed Bertsch's liabilities under backlogged purchase orders, asked that purchase orders to Bertsch be reissued to Park and that outstanding invoices be resubmitted to Park, and renewed distributor contracts, and Bertsch's terms with vendors like UPS and FedEx were "reset" and assumed by Park.

As to the "continuity of shareholders" factor, Park argues that the *de facto* merger doctrine is inapplicable to the facts of this case because there was no continuity of shareholders or any other indicia of Bertsch shareholders' control after Park purchased the assets. DeJesus and Cartagena respond, arguing that the continuity of shareholders factor is not dispositive, although it is undisputed that Bertsch's shareholders did not retain any type of ownership or control over the business after the asset sale to Park. In other words, DeJesus does not dispute that "[a]ll individuals that held primary control over Bertsch did not possess any such control over the Bertsch Division of Park" or Park itself. The Court agrees with Park that no *de facto* merger occurred.

Under Massachusetts law, a *de facto* merger does not occur absent a showing that there is a continuity of shareholders or other type of transaction that ultimately makes Bertsch's shareholders directly or indirectly constituent owners of Park, the purchasing corporation. This same conclusion is obtained under the "mere continuation" exception.

The successor liability doctrine is an equitable doctrine, and the Court considers whether the shareholders used a disguised mechanism to transfer the legal ownership of the corporation but ultimately retain the same effective control. This is the approach this Court used in *Acushnet*, 712 F. Supp. at 1016-17. In *Acushnet*, this Court held that the failure to show continuity of shareholders is not dispositive when the purchase was achieved through the use of a parent corporation's shares, obtaining virtually the same control. Other courts have arrived at similar conclusions. *See, e.g., Ed Peters Jewelry Co., Inc. v. C & J Jewelry Co., Inc.*, 124 F.3d 252, 273-74 (1st Cir. 1997) (applying Rhode Island law and concluding "that [successor defendant] used the family trust to camouflage his ultimate retention of control over the [purchased company's] manufacturing business which C & J continued to conduct, without interruption"); *National Gypsum*, 895 F. Supp. at 337 ("The intended result in all cases is the same, to permit the owners of the selling corporation to avoid paying creditors *without losing control* of their business." (emphasis added)); *Park v. Townson & Alexander, Inc.*, 287 Ill. App. 3d 772, 775, 223 Ill. Dec. 163, 679 N.E.2d 107 (1997) ("[W]hile the spousal relationship between the owners of the corporations does not in itself establish a continuity of shareholders, it is certainly a factor which can be considered.").

Under the traditional approach to *de facto* merger, the seller must retain some type of ownership or control over the purchasing company; thus, the First Circuit (applying Virginia law) reasoned that the continuation of ownership is a broader concept than mere continuation of shareholders. *Devine & Devine Food Brokers, Inc. v. Wampler Foods, Inc.*, 313 F.3d 616, 619 (1st Cir. 2002) ("While not dispositive, the factor that typically tips the scales in favor of finding a merger is continuity of ownership, usually taking the form of an exchange of stock for assets."); *Ed Peters Jewelry Co., Inc.*, 124 F.3d at 273-74 ("We note that the continuity of shareholders necessary to a finding of mere continuation does not require complete identity between the shareholders of the former and successor corporations." Continuity of shareholders may occur even if there is no complete shareholder identity between the seller and the buyer. *Cargill, Inc. v. Beaver Coal & Oil Co.*, 424 Mass. 356, 361, 676 N.E.2d 815 (1997) (noting that there is "no requirement that there be complete shareholder identity between the seller and a buyer before corporate successor liability will attach" and holding that a 12.5 percent voting interest was sufficient to attach successor liability because the sale left the owner of the predecessor entity with a seat on the successor corporation's board of directors and the largest personal holding of shares of stock).

In the same vein, even when there is continuity of shareholders, the shareholder continuity factor is not dispositive when the transfer of stock does not result in ownership or control. *Devine & Devine*, 313 F.3d at 619 (applying Virginia law and holding that a 10 percent interest composed of voting stock did not suffice to impose successor liability under a *de facto* merger theory because there was neither "wholesale continuity of management or ownership nor a liquidation of the selling corporation"); *American Paper Recycling Corp. v. IHC Corp.,* 707 F. Supp. 2d 114, 121 (D. Mass. 2010) (STEARNS, J.) (holding that under Massachusetts law, acquisition of less than 3.2 percent of buyer corporation's stock in consideration for seller corporation's assets was not sufficient to impose successor liability when seller "has no voting rights, cannot transfer its shares, and holds the shares subject to a right of unilateral redemption," and when none of seller's directors or officers hold a position in buyer's company).

Here, DeJesus and Cartagena have not submitted any evidence that there was a transfer of stock between Bertsch and Park. Instead, DeJesus and Cartagena argue that the "continuation of shareholders" factor is not dispositive, and because Bertsch was insolvent in its bankruptcy petition, Bertsch's stock was worthless.

The question is *not* whether Park continued Bertsch's enterprise as an ongoing business, which could be obtained by working with the assets, intellectual property, and facilities purchased; rather, the question is whether Bertsch's shareholders or parent company sought to remain in control of its business through a merger while avoiding any continued liability. No evidence provided by DeJesus and Cartagena suggest that Bertsch remained in control or ownership of the company after Park's asset buy. Therefore, as matter of law, DeJesus and Cartagena fail to demonstrate that there was a *de facto* merger between Bertsch and Park or that Park merely continued Bertsch's business, so no successor liability attaches.

CONCLUSION

For these reasons, this Court ALLOWS Park's motion for summary judgment, and a judgment of dismissal shall be entered.

SO ORDERED.

Notes and Questions

1. Notes

a. The court, quoting case law, observed that, while de facto merger and mere continuation exceptions "have been enshrined separately in the canonical list of exceptions to the general rule of no successor liability, they appear, in practice to refer to the same concept . . . and courts have often used the two terms interchangeably." Although the court here primarily uses the term "de facto merger," the great majority of courts would have used the term "mere continuation" in discussing the various factors.

b. The complaint alleges that DeJesus was injured on November 5, 2008.

c. According to the briefs, Bertsch's owners originally proposed that Park purchase all Bertsch's stock for $3.6 million. In light of pending product liability claims and creditor lawsuits against Bertsch, Park proposed to purchase only Bertsch's assets, free of all liabilities, for $2 million. In the end, the parties agreed on a sale of substantially all of Bertsch's assets for $1.5 million, which was approved by the Bankruptcy Court.

d. The court considered expanding Park's potential liability beyond the mere continuation/de facto merger exception, under the "continuity of enterprise" and "product line" exceptions, which it discusses in footnotes 3 and 4. Both the continuity of enterprise exception and the product line exception have been rejected by the great majority of courts that have considered them, and the *Restatement (Third) of Torts* has rejected both tests. Nonetheless, because the states in which they have been accepted are quite populous (Michigan has adopted the continuity of enterprise exception; New Jersey, California, and Pennsylvania have adopted the product line exception), the tests remain important. As a matter of choice of law, the few courts that have considered the matter have used the law of the state with the most important contacts to the injury or contract rather than the law of the state of incorporation. Thus planners usually cannot predict with certainty when they are planning a change of control transaction whether expanded notions of successor liability will attach.

2. Reality Check

a. What are the four well-recognized exceptions to the rule that a corporation that obtains all the assets of another corporation is not liable for that corporation's liabilities?

b. What are the elements of the mere continuation/de facto merger exception?

c. How are the continuity of enterprise exception and the product line exception different from the mere continuation exception?

d. Why wasn't DeJesus's claim resolved in the bankruptcy proceeding?

3. Suppose

a. Suppose Park had purchased all of the outstanding stock of Bertsch and that Bertsch did not declare bankruptcy. Would the court's analysis or the result have been different?

4. What Do You Think?

a. Should DeJesus be able to recover against a company that did not manufacture or sell the machine that injured him? Should it make a difference that the machine was manufactured and sold over 50 years before DeJesus was injured?

b. Should Park be able to avoid liability for an injury admittedly caused by a machine manufactured by the company whose assets Park purchased? Should it make a difference that DeJesus cannot sue Bertsch, which no longer exists, and presumably cannot sue under any insurance policy Bertsch might have had? Should it make a difference that the parties structured the transaction specifically to avoid liabilities such as DeJesus's?

c. Do you think that buyer corporations acting at arm's length, should be able to buy only the assets of seller corporations without the associated liabilities?

Putting It to Work

Problem 8-3

Beans Unlimited, Ltd., a Delaware corporation with its principal place of business in Vermont, was devoted to the slow roasting and delivering of flavored organically grown coffee beans. The flavoring process is a tightly guarded proprietary process. Beans Unlimited is wholly owned by Bernard Aranguren, the developer of the flavoring process.

After becoming immensely popular and profitable, Bernard decided to sell the company. Beans Unlimited, Ltd., sold all its assets for cash to Portland's Best Coffee, Inc. a large coffee roasting and retailing company. Portland's Best Coffee kept the Beans Unlimited assets dedicated to making the same flavored coffee by the same methods as before the sale and marketed the beans under the Beans Unlimited brand name. Most of the employees and senior managers of Beans Unlimited, Ltd. stayed on after the sale. The sale was at arm's length. After the sale, Bernard dissolved Beans Unlimited, Ltd., paid off the corporation's creditors, and distributed the rest of the proceeds (several billion dollars) to himself as the sole stockholder. Bernard and the proceeds have moved to another country and locating either Bernard or the proceeds would, effectively, be impossible.

Several years after the sale, many frequent consumers of Beans Unlimited coffees became chronically and seriously ill due to the chemicals used in the flavoring process. A class action has now been brought in Nevada by seriously ill Beans Unlimited coffee consumers against Portland's Best Coffee. All plaintiffs in the class were injured by drinking Beans Unlimited coffee manufactured by Beans Unlimited, Ltd. before the sale to Portland's Best Coffee.

a. If you represented the plaintiffs, what arguments would you make for holding Portland's Best Coffee liable?

b. If you represented Portland's Best Coffee, what arguments against liability would you make?

B. BACKGROUND AND CONTEXT: DIRECT LIABILITY OF CORPORATE OFFICERS

When a corporation enters into a contract, which it can do only through its agent (who may or may not be an officer), the agent is not bound on the contract, assuming the third party knows the identity of the corporation and that the agent is acting on its behalf. *See Restatement (Third) of Agency* §6.01. Of course the parties may agree that the agent will be liable on the contract as well as the corporation. This frequently occurs when a corporation is just beginning business. Creditors are reluctant to contract only with a corporation with few assets and no operating history. The corporation's promoters, who will likely be its officers and directors and possibly its shareholders, too, are required to become personally liable as a condition to entering into the contract at all. None of this is controversial.

But a creditor may also look to a corporate officer (or director or shareholder) who has, subsequent to the contract's formation, guaranteed performance. This is a frequent allegation when a corporation is experiencing financial difficulty and needs help from creditors either in the form of more funds or in forbearing from enforcing contract terms. Corporate insiders may well find themselves personally liable for corporate debts if a court finds that they represented to creditors that they, personally, would in some way guarantee a corporate obligation and the creditor relies to its detriment on that guarantee. You should note that courts will often enforce these representations even when made orally rather than in writing.

A corporation's agent, such as an officer, is liable for his or her own tort that causes personal injury to a third person and the corporation is liable, as well, if the agent is an employee acting within the scope of employment. A corporation's agent is also liable to a third party where his or her actions constitute fraud or conversion on behalf of the corporation, even though the corporation alone benefits and not the agent. *See Restatement (Third) of Agency* §§7.01 and 7.02.

Apart from these settings, the agent is not liable to a third party if the agent's actions constitute only a failure to perform duties owed to the corporation. This is true even where the agent's failure to perform his or her duties is intentional. *See Restatement (Third) of Agency* §7.02, cmt. d.

An officer, who is probably responsible for supervising other agents, may have greater tort exposure than an employee who does not supervise others.

Although courts frequently analyze the liability of corporate officers to third persons under the *Restatement (Third) of Agency*, they also approach the issue through the corporation law doctrine known as the *participation theory of liability*. The following case describes the contours of that doctrine.

Saltiel v. GSI Consultants, Inc.

788 A.2d 268 (N.J. 2002)

STEIN, J.

I

In December 1997, plaintiff Jan Saltiel, doing business as Edgewater Design Associates, filed suit against GSI Consultants, Inc. (GSI), a Pennsylvania corporation, Dr. Henry Indyk, a GSI corporate officer, and Richard Caton, a former GSI corporate officer. The complaint sought damages arising from allegedly defective turfgrass specifications prepared by defendants and used by plaintiff in the reconstruction of a softball field and soccer field located at William Paterson University (WPU) in Wayne, New Jersey. Plaintiff is a landscape architect and GSI is a turfgrass consulting company doing business under the name Turfcon. Plaintiff has since voluntarily dismissed her claims against GSI.

The underlying transaction involved WPU's award to plaintiff in March 1995 of a contract to provide landscaping architectural services for the reconstruction of its athletic fields. Plaintiff in turn requested a proposal from GSI outlining turfgrass specifications for the reconstruction. In February 1995, GSI submitted a proposal, signed by Caton, listing the services that it would perform in connection with the WPU contract. Plaintiff accepted the proposal and engaged GSI to prepare the specifications for the WPU athletic fields.

The soccer field was completed in September 1996. Indyk did not visit the soccer field on a regular basis as had been his practice with respect to the softball field. Almost immediately after its completion, the soccer field developed problems of standing water and inadequate drainage. In response to the problems, WPU installed additional drainage facilities and began core aerification of the soccer field's turf. However, the drainage did not improve and the turfgrass was consistently damp or soggy. The soccer field remained unfit for athletic use.

Plaintiff hired Turf Diagnostics and Design, Inc. (TDD) to determine the cause of the drainage failure. After an investigation, TDD informed plaintiff that, although the soccer field had been constructed in accordance with GSI's field specifications, the field specifications had been negligently prepared because the rootzone designed by GSI formed a nearly impermeable barrier that did not allow for proper water drainage. As required under plaintiff's contract with WPU, she prepared new specifications for the field and hired a contractor to reconstruct it at a cost of $351,000. Plaintiff's contract with GSI did not require GSI to provide a bond or demonstrate evidence of professional liability insurance.

Plaintiff's complaint alleges claims against all defendants for negligent design, negligent misrepresentation, breach of contract, breach of warranty, promissory estoppel, and agency liability. In an unreported opinion the Appellate Division . . . concluded that both Indyk and Caton could be personally liable for negligence under the so-called "participation theory of personal liability."

II

[This case] requires us to consider: (1) the proper application of the participation theory of personal liability for tortious conduct by corporate officers under New Jersey law; and (2) whether the plaintiff's claim against Indyk and Caton sounds in tort or contract.

A.

The Appellate Division's opinion correctly determined that our caselaw has recognized the applicability of the participation theory of personal liability for the tortious conduct of corporate officers. [T]he essence of the participation theory is that a corporate officer can be held personally liable for a tort committed by the corporation when he or she is sufficiently involved in the commission of the tort. A predicate to liability is a finding that the corporation owed a duty of care to the victim, the duty was delegated to the officer and the officer breached the duty of care by his own conduct.

New Jersey cases that have applied the participation theory to hold corporate officers personally responsible for their tortious conduct generally have involved intentional torts. More specifically, the majority of the cases have involved fraud and conversion.

The conduct at issue in this appeal does not implicate intentional tortious conduct, but rather the individual defendants' allegedly negligent conduct in designing the specifications for the soccer field. Indyk and Caton assert that the participation theory is limited to intentional torts by corporate officers. The Appellate Division . . . was unwilling to limit the doctrine to intentionally tortious acts. That court relied on three New Jersey decisions to support its broader application of the participation theory.

[Those decisions] arguably support plaintiff's contention that the participation theory is not limited to intentional torts, and that the theory's application turns only on the question of whether there was actual participation in allegedly tortious conduct rather than on the nature of the tortious conduct. Although the theory may encompass conduct other than intentional torts, that issue has not been settled. Based on the application of the participation theory in other state courts, it may be argued that the theory should be limited to cases involving intentional wrongful conduct by corporate officers, or negligent conduct by such officers that results in personal injuries. . . . Application of the participation theory to negligent conduct by corporate officers in other jurisdictions also has involved personal injury claims.

B.

Whatever may be the appropriate standard for limiting corporate officers' liability under the participation theory, the essential predicate for application of the theory is the commission by the corporation of tortious conduct, participation in that tortious conduct by the corporate officer and resultant injury to the plaintiff. If, however, the breach of the corporation's duty to the plaintiff is determined to be governed by contract rather than tort principles, the participation theory of tort liability is inapplicable. Accordingly, because the plaintiff's relationship with GSI initially was defined by the contract between them, we consider the principles that reliably serve to distinguish contract and tort claims.

III

[B]ecause we are convinced that plaintiff has not pled and supported a cause of action sounding in tort, and has failed to establish that either GSI or defendants Indyk and Caton owed an independent duty to plaintiff outside the scope of the contract, the theory cannot be applied to the facts in this record.

In rejecting the Appellate Division's reliance on the participation theory of liability, we rely on the principles set forth in state and federal cases on whether a cause of action sounds in tort or contract. Plaintiff's complaint alleged causes of action based on negligent design and negligent misrepresentation. Irrespective of the terminology used in the complaint, however, we are persuaded that this case is essentially a basic breach of contract case, and that plaintiff, through her tort allegations, simply is seeking to enhance the benefit of the bargain she contracted for with defendant GSI.

In this case the scope of the parties' obligations was defined by the contract, and the contract imposed responsibilities on defendant GSI only, and not on defendants Indyk and Caton. The expectation was that defendant corporation would design and prepare the requisite specifications for the athletic fields and that plaintiff would compensate the corporation for the work. There appears to have been no expectation that the individual defendants would be personally liable under the contract. Plaintiff's original request for a proposal was directed toward defendant GSI, and the responses received by plaintiff were on a letterhead that specifically included the corporate names "Turfcon" and "GSI, Inc." Clearly, plaintiff was aware throughout the transaction that she was dealing with a corporate entity and that defendants Indyk and Caton were acting on GSI's behalf.

We acknowledge that a different analysis and result could be implicated if a soccer player sustained personal injuries proximately caused by the allegedly deficient design work provided by GSI. In that context, because no contract defined the obligations of the parties, a critical issue would be whether GSI owed an independent duty of care to prospective users of the field and, if so, whether the participation theory would apply. We need not resolve those issues. Here, however, plaintiff alleges damages that do not arise from any duty imposed by law but rather result from GSI's alleged breach of contract, and include the cost of preparing new specifications and of hiring a new contractor to reconstruct the soccer field.

None of the parties dispute the existence of a valid contract between plaintiff and defendant GSI, and GSI's alleged breach of that contract clearly can give rise to contractual liability. However, plaintiff has since voluntarily dismissed her claims against defendant GSI. As noted, that contract did not require GSI to provide a bond or demonstrate evidence of professional liability insurance. Nonetheless, irrespective of the allegations in the complaint that sound in tort, plaintiff cannot convert basic contract claims into negligence claims in order to create a basis for the imposition of personal liability on corporate officers.

IV

Because this appeal essentially involves a breach of contract claim, making the participation theory of individual liability inapplicable, we reverse the Appellate Division's judgment and reinstate summary judgment for defendants Indyk and Caton.

Notes and Questions

1. Notes

a. See also Chapter 10 for a discussion of the potential civil and criminal liability of corporate officers under certain statutes such as CERCLA.

2. Reality Check

a. What element(s) of the direct participation theory did the court find was lacking? Do you agree?

3. Suppose

a. Suppose a soccer player were injured on the field and sued Caton and Indyk individually. How would the court analyze the cause of action?

b. Suppose Saltiel had been injured on the soccer field while inspecting it. If she brought suit against Caton and Indyk individually, would the court's analysis or the result be different?

4. What Do You Think?

a. Why do you think plaintiff voluntarily dismissed her claims against the corporation?

b. Do you think the courts should use agency doctrines or corporate law doctrines to decide the liability of corporate officers to third parties? Why?

You should be aware of two other approaches to finding corporate insiders personally liable. First, think about whether the insider could be considered the *principal* of a principal-agent relationship. If so, you may find liability under the *Restatement (Third) of Agency. See generally* Chapter 4. Second, analyze whether the corporate insider and any other person or entity are carrying on as co-owners a business for profit. If so, they may be liable as partners in a general partnership. *See generally* Chapter 17.

Putting It to Work

Problem 8-4

Sandy had been dreaming of remodeling her kitchen for years, and after extensive saving, she contracted with Austin's Remodels, Inc. (ARI) to complete her dream kitchen for $15,000, which she paid in full after the work was completed. ARI designed and installed the kitchen according to Sandy's preferences. A few weeks after construction was complete, Sandy noticed that all her plates and glasses were continuously slipping off the shelves and breaking on the floor. One night after a particularly plate-shattering dinner party, one of Sandy's guests informed her that her shelves were not level and the angle at which they were installed caused everything to fall out to the floor.

Much to Sandy's surprise, she discovered that although ARI is a licensed contractor, Austin himself is neither an architect, a trained interior designer, nor a licensed contractor, and had never actually used a computer design program before working on Sandy's kitchen remodel.

ARI is equally owned by Austin and Gene. Gene is an architect as well as a trained interior designer and is also an experienced contractor. Austin did all of the work on Sandy's Kitchen. Sandy wants to sue Austin and Gene personally.

a. Discuss whether Austin or Gene could be personally liable to Sandy.

C. TERMS OF ART IN THIS CHAPTER

Affiliated corporations
Continuity of enterprise
   exception
Enterprise liability
Equitable subordination
Fraudulent conveyances

Mere continuation
   exception
Participation theory of
   liability
Piercing the corporate veil
Product line exception

Successor liability
Voidable preferences

9

How Corporations Take Actions

In this chapter we begin to focus on the ways in which corporations are governed and take actions. We start by considering the board of directors. First we examine the conceptual purposes of the board. Next we will explore the way in which directors are selected for the board. Finally we will detail the mechanical aspects of board action—for example, the requirements for meetings. The last part of this chapter deals with the way in which corporate actions are actually performed—that is, the role of officers and other agents. If you have covered Chapter 4 on agency, some of this material may be a review.

A. THE BOARD OF DIRECTORS

1. The Role of the Board of Directors

a. *The Current Setting*

As you may have realized by now, corporations are fictional entities that can only act through humans. You surely know that employees provide the needed labor, that suppliers provide raw materials to, and that customers purchase finished goods or services from, the corporation. Managers supervise the employees (and other managers) and coordinate the corporation's activities. You may also be aware that shareholders (owners) and lenders contribute the money to pay employees and managers and to purchase raw materials.

Conspicuously absent from this list of humans is a group that is nonetheless central to the theory of corporate law and is often central as a practical matter to the functioning of corporations. This group is the *board of directors*. The theoretical place of the board is so vital to corporate law that it warrants highlighting the statutory provisions:

> The business and affairs of every corporation organized under this chapter shall be managed by or under the direction of a board of directors. . . .

DGCL §141(a)

[A]ll corporate powers shall be exercised by or under the authority of . . . , and the business and affairs of the corporation shall be managed by or under the direction, and subject to the oversight, of the board of directors.

MBCA §8.01(b)

The statutes provide that corporations may engage in any lawful business and that they have the same powers an individual has to effect that business. Those provisions mean that the board, in which all those powers reside, is really the center of corporate activity. One concomitant of placing all power in the board is that the shareholders, who are the corporation's owners, do not possess the ultimate management power. In fact, a literal reading of the statutes suggests that the shareholders have absolutely no power. As we will see in Chapters 14 and 15, shareholders do have some powers, notably the power to elect the directors. We will also see that the corporate scheme of power allocation is very different from the partnership paradigm and perhaps from the limited liability company (LLC) paradigm as well. *See* Chapters 17 and 18.

To be strictly accurate, both the DGCL and the MBCA allow a corporate structure that does not have a board of directors. But both statutes anticipate that the person or persons exercising traditional board power will be treated analogously to the board. *See* DGCL §§141(a), 351, and MBCA §§7.32(a)(1), 8.01(a). Analytically, this suggests that the alternative to a board is to place corporate power in the hands of the owners, because if power is placed with nonowners then the corporation is, in effect, governed by a "board of directors" that simply has a different name. In practice, very few corporations are organized without a board, although many corporations provide limitations on the board's power. Where the parties desire to place the entity's management power in the owners, a limited liability company or limited liability partnership would typically be preferable to a corporation without a board. This is because those other forms accommodate such allocations of power better than the corporate form does. *See* Chapters 17, 18, and 19.

As you read the rest of the material on corporate governance, ask yourself how the power allocations are different from other business forms, the reasons for those differences, and whether those differences can be justified.

In the world of corporations, every act must have its genesis in the board of directors. Notice that the statutory words "under the direction of" means that the board itself need not perform, or even approve the performance of, every corporate act. When you buy a latte at Starbucks, the barista is (probably) not a member of the board. Neither does the Starbucks board authorize each latte sale. Nonetheless it should be possible to trace each sale to some action of the board. In the latte example, the board may have authorized the opening of the particular store at which the transaction took place. If not, the board certainly authorized certain senior employees to decide where and when to open new stores. The board doubtless also authorized certain senior employees to decide the menu of drinks the stores will offer and authorized certain senior employees to hire, probably indirectly, baristas. In other words, the senior employees charged with hiring hired other, less senior, employees who, with authorization from those senior employees, hired even less senior employees, so that, eventually, someone with actual authority hired the barista. By contrast, in a small coffee bar the barista might well be a board member, an officer, and a shareholder, too.

Are there limitations on the power of the board to delegate? If so, what is the source of those limits?

Even though a board can delegate power to others within the corporation, the statutory phrase "under the direction of" implies that the board must retain some involvement. The classic statement of the limits of a board's power to delegate is:

> A fundamental precept of Delaware corporation law is that it is the board of directors, and neither shareholders nor managers, that has ultimate responsibility for the management of the enterprise. Of course, given the large, complex organizations through which modern, multi-function business corporations often operate, the law recognizes that corporate boards, comprised as they traditionally have been of persons dedicating less than all of their attention to that role, cannot themselves manage the operations of the firm, but may satisfy their obligations by thoughtfully appointing officers, establishing or approving goals and plans and monitoring performance. Thus Section 141(a) of DGCL expressly permits a board of directors to delegate managerial duties to officers of the corporation, except to the extent that the corporation's certificate of incorporation or bylaws may limit or prohibit such a delegation.
>
> Absent specific restriction in the certificate of incorporation, the board of directors certainly has very broad discretion in fashioning a managerial structure appropriate, in its judgment, to moving the corporation towards the achievement of corporate goals and purposes. In designing and implementing such a structure, the board of course may delegate such powers to the officers of the company as in the board's good faith, informed judgment are appropriate. But this power is not without limit. The board may not either formally or effectively abdicate its statutory power and its fiduciary duty to manage or direct the management of the business and affairs of this corporation. Thus in *Abercrombie v. Davies*, Del.Ch., 123 A.2d 893 (1956) *rev'd on other grounds*, Del.Supr., 130 A.2d 338 (1957), this court voided a shareholders' agreement that purported to bind signatories in their director capacity:
>
>> [b]ecause [the agreemenl] tends to limit in a substantial way the freedom of director decisions on matters of management policy, it violates the duty of each director to exercise his own best judgment on matters coming before the board.
>
> *Id*. at 899 (emphasis added). *See also Chapin v. Benwood Foundation Inc.*, Del.Ch., 402 A.2d 1205 (1979) *aff'd*, Del.Supr., 415 A.2d I 068 (1980).
>
> Thus it is well established that while a board may delegate powers subject to possible review, it may not abdicate them.

Grimes v. Donald, 1995 WL 54441, at *8-*9 (Del.Ch.) (Allen, Ch.).

Boards can also delegate power to a subset of the board—a committee. DGCL §141(c), MBCA §8.25. Where these committees simply investigate or recommend action to the full board, their existence presents no real issue of corporate law. In those settings it is still the full board that is taking action. To the extent that a committee is delegated power to act for the full board, however, the question of delegation versus abdication, described in the excerpt from *Grimes*, comes to the fore. The statutes allow boards to delegate all board powers to committees, with certain exceptions. Both statutes prohibit a board committee from changing the corporation's bylaws and both prohibit a committee from approving fundamental actions, such as mergers, dissolution, or sale of all the corporation's assets that also require shareholder approval. The MBCA further prohibits a board committee from declaring dividends (except pursuant to a board-approved formula) and prohibits a committee from filling board vacancies.

Perhaps the most typical committee is an executive committee that is usually given the power to take any action, subject, of course, to statutory restrictions, necessary between full board meetings. In publicly held corporation other committees include an audit committee, which evaluates the corporation's financial situation and monitors the independent accountants; a compensation committee, which approves general compensation plans and the annual compensation for the corporation's most senior executives; and a nominating committee, which identifies suitable candidates for any board openings that may arise. In the public company setting, the SEC heavily regulates the board committees.

Bound up with the power to delegate is the understanding that the board believes those to whom its powers are delegated are trustworthy. The corporations statutes provide that boards are entitled to rely on information provided by board committees, as well as by (among others) the corporation's officers and employees. DGCL §141(e), MBCA §8.30(f).

Assuming that, in the real world, most boards delegate much of their power to committees, officers, and employees, what does the board itself do? Chancellor Allen, in the *Grimes* case quoted above, said,

> Ordinarily, [the board's] responsibility entails the duty to establish or approve the long-term strategic, financial and organizational goals of the corporation; to approve formal or informal plans for the achievement of these goals; to monitor corporate performance; and to act, when in the good faith, informed judgment of the board it is appropriate to act. While these responsibilities may be satisfied in various ways and with varying degrees of formality, it is essential that the members of the board understand that it is with the board and not with the officers of the corporation that ultimate responsibility lies.

Grimes v. Donald, 1995 WL 54441, at *1 (Del.Ch.) (Allen, Ch.).

The Official Comments to MBCA §8.01 say that boards, at least public company boards, have the responsibility to oversee

> Business performance, plans and strategy;
> Management's assessment of major risks to which the corporation is or may be exposed;
> The performance and compensation of executive officers;
> Policies and practices to foster the corporation's compliance with law and ethical conduct;
> Management's preparation of the corporation's financial statements;
> Management's design and assessment of effectiveness of the corporation's internal controls;
> Plans for the succession of the chief executive officer and other executive officers;
> The composition of the board and of board committees; and
> Whether the corporation has information and reporting systems in place to provide directors with appropriate information in a timely manner.

b. Background and Context

1 Victor Morawetz, *A Treatise on the Law of Private Corporations*

§§510-512, 514, 535-536 (2d ed., 1886)

The active management and direction of the affairs of a business corporation are ordinarily vested in a board of directors or trustees. The board of directors of a corporation have implied authority to do all acts in the management of the company's *regular* business, which the company itself can do without a departure from its chartered powers.

Although the appointment of the directors rests with the majority [of shareholders], it does not follow that the majority can control them or interfere with their management of the business of the company. The authority of the board of directors is derived from the unanimous agreement of the shareholders, expressed in their charter or articles of association; and hence those powers which it is intended shall belong to the directors exclusively cannot be impaired by the majority, or any other agent.

The rule limiting the powers of the majority [of shareholders] to the general supervision of the affairs of the corporation, and the appointment of the regular managing agents, is established for the protection of the individual shareholders, as well as for reasons of practical convenience. It is obvious that a board of directors, selected by the shareholders of a corporation on account of their known business experience and capacity, are far better adapted to carry on the business of the company successfully, than the shareholders themselves assembled at a general meeting.

However, the exclusive powers of the board of directors extend only to the management of the regular business of the corporation. Even an express provision that the powers of the corporation shall be exercised by its board of directors does not deprive the majority [of shareholders] of the power of directing the general policy of the corporation, and of deciding upon the propriety of important changes in the company's business.

A board of directors has no implied authority to make a material and permanent alteration of the business or constitution of a corporation, even though the alteration be within the company's chartered powers. Such an alteration can be effected only by authority of the shareholders at a general meeting.

The board of directors are impliedly authorized to do all acts which are proper to carry out the company's chartered purposes, but they cannot depart from these purposes under any circumstances.

However, the authority of the directors of a corporation to appoint inferior agents with power to represent the company can be implied only where such appointment would be a reasonable measure in carrying on the company's business in the ordinary manner. Those powers of the directors of a corporation which it is intended they should exercise personally, can in no case be delegated.

The general supervision and direction of the affairs of a corporation are especially intrusted by the shareholders to the board of directors; it is upon the personal care and attention of the directors that the shareholders depend for the success of their enterprise. It follows that authority to delegate these general powers of management cannot be implied.

Notes and Questions

1. Notes

a. Victor Morawetz (1859-1938) graduated from the Harvard Law School in 1878. He moved to Chicago to practice corporate law but was unsuccessful, primarily because he was unknown and, due to the prevailing constraints on lawyer advertising, could not ethically make his talents known to potential clients. At 23 he published the first edition of *A Treatise on the Law of Private Corporations*. He revised that book four years later into the two-volume work, which is quoted throughout this chapter. The first edition was immediately recognized as a classic and, even more, the second edition was *the* standard reference work on classical corporation law as late as the 1930s. The success of this book allowed Morawetz to move to New York, where he became a partner in the city's most prominent corporate law firm. He left that position in 1896 (at the age of 37) and served as general counsel for a major railroad corporation for 13 years. In 1909, at the age of 50, he retired. *See* 15 Am. Nat. Bio. 805 (1999).

2. Reality Check

a. How does Morawetz view the power of the board?

b. What control over the board do the shareholders possess, according to Morawetz?

3. What Do You Think?

a. Between the time Morawetz wrote and today, do you think there was a shift in the allocation of corporate power between the board and shareholders? If so, why do you think such a shift occurred? If so, was the shift beneficial?

b. Between the time Morawetz wrote and today, do you think there was a shift in the power of the board of directors to delegate? If so, why do you think such a shift occurred? If so, was the shift beneficial?

c. Given the great increase in the ability of widely dispersed shareholders to communicate via the Internet, do you believe the allocation of power between the shareholders and the board should be reconsidered? If so, what allocation would you suggest?

Putting It to Work

Problem 9-1

You are an associate at a midsized firm charged with handling the affairs of E & E Coffee Co., a boutique coffee shop with a dedicated customer base incorporated in an MBCA state. After opening two other branches and enjoying booming success, the founders, Ernest and Edgar, who are also the only directors, have finally concluded that the business is too big for them to manage directly and have come to you for advice on what boards do. Ernest would like to consider the option of going on a ten-month vacation, since they have employees and store managers and are comfortable delegating to them. However, Edgar would prefer to keep close watch on the branches, since his life's work is wrapped up in the continued success of E & E. Ernest and Edgar each owns one-third of the stock and the remaining one-third is owned by about a dozen of their friends and family, who put up the money needed to get the three locations up and running.

    a. What is your advice to Ernest and Edgar about their proper role and duties as directors?

    b. Would your advice be different if E & E were incorporated in Delaware?

2. Number, Selection, Election, Term, and Removal of Directors

a. Number and Selection of Initial Directors

A board must consist of one or more individuals. See MBCA §8.03(a) and DGCL §141(b). One corporation may own shares in another and may be able to elect directors to the other's board, but it cannot itself serve as a director of the other corporation. How is the number of directors determined? As you may remember from Chapter 5, the number must be stated in either the Articles of Incorporation or the bylaws. Frequently the Articles or bylaws set a minimum and maximum number of directors and grant the board itself the power to determine the exact number of directors. This technique is frequently used in public corporations. This approach allows the board to expand or contract to take advantage of *ad hominem* situations, but it also allows the board to act opportunistically to add friendly members or repel the appointment of hostile members.

    Statutes permit the initial directors to be named in the articles of incorporation. *See* DGCL §102(a)(6), MBCA §2.02(b)(1). If the initial directors are not named in the articles, the incorporator must name the initial directors as part of the organizational meeting process. *See* DGCL §108(a), MBCA §2.05(a)(2), and Chapter 5. The first method is by far preferable to the second because it is immediately certain who the first directors are. This also means that the initial directors are invested with all corporate power at the time of incorporation. Where the directors are instead chosen as part of the organizational meeting process, there is always a time lag during which the incorporator has corporate power. *See* DGCL §107. Of course, where the incorporator will be the sole director, no harm is done, but that is not always the case.

b. Election and Term of Directors

Thereafter, at least one director must be elected at every annual shareholder meeting and the default rule is that all directors are elected annually by all the shareholders. *See* DGCL §211(b), MBCA §8.03(c). This default rule can be varied in two ways. The first way is to create a *classified board*. Under this model, the power to elect at least one director is vested in, or denied to, at least one class or series of stock. The corporation's planners may choose this approach when the shareholders anticipate that they may have strong disagreements in the future. This approach is also useful when the planners desire to give one set of shareholders power disproportionate to their capital contribution. As you doubtless recall, investors purchasing shares contemporaneously must pay the same price per share. By creating a classified board, the different factions of shareholders can receive securities that are identical in all respects except that one faction has the power to select more directors than another faction. When implementing a classified board structure, the practical variations are nearly endless. *See* DGCL §141(d), MBCA §8.04.

The second way to vary the default rule is to divide the directors into two or three classes with each class holding *staggered terms* of two or three years. When this approach is taken, the nearly universal approach is to divide the board into thirds so that each director has a three-year term. *See* DGCL §141(d), MBCA §8.06. Many public Delaware corporations have staggered boards. Note that some courts and commentators use the term *classified board* to refer to a board with staggered terms as well as one that is truly classified.

A close reading of the statutes reveals that the expiration of a director's term does not, by itself, oust the director from office. Rather, a director remains in office until he or she is reelected, another person is elected to fill his or her slot, the board is reduced in number at the end of the director's term, or the slot becomes vacant. *See* DGCL §141(b), MBCA §8.05(e). Although every corporation statute requires an annual meeting of the shareholders to elect directors (DGCL §211(b), MBCA §8.03(c)), that requirement does not translate into fact.[1] Directors who continue in office after the expiration of their term because no election has been held are called *holdover* directors. Holdovers are a surprisingly frequent occurrence.

Sometimes a vacancy occurs either through resignation, death, or removal of an incumbent. Although no statute requires that a vacancy be filled, all corporation statutes provide methods for selecting replacement directors. In Delaware, the default rule is that vacancies can only be filled by the remaining board members. *See* DGCL §223(a)(1). Under the Model Act, the default rule is that vacancies may be filled by either the remaining board members or by the shareholders, whichever constituency acts first. *See* MBCA §8.10(a)(1), (2). As a practical matter, this ordinarily means that the board can fill the vacancy if it chooses to do so because it is usually able to act more quickly than the shareholders.

Putting It to Work

Problem 9-2

E & E Coffee Co. has become a great success. As time passed, Ernest and Edgar decided they needed additional expertise on the board and so, with the consent of the shareholders, amended the articles of incorporation to expand the board to five and to add three additional members. One has financial experience, one has retail

---

1. Glendower
   I can call spirits from the vasty deep.

   Hotspur
   Why, so can I, or so can any man,
   But will they come when you do call for them?

   William Shakespeare, *Henry IV* pt. 1 act 3, sc. 1, ll. 55-57 (Barbara A. Mowat & Paul Werstine, eds., Pocket Books 1994).

coffee experience, and the third has experience with buying coffee beans on the international market.

Tragically, the two coffee experts on the board were killed in an airplane crash coming home from an international coffee conference. Further, the financial expert on the board has resigned because she is unhappy with E & E's recent financial performance and believes that neither Ernest nor Edgar has the financial acumen to run the company successfully. Several critical decisions, including whether to declare a dividend, whether to expand the number of locations, and whether to continue certain important coffee-purchasing relationships, need to be made within the next ten days.

a. Advise Edgar and Ernest on the actions they may take.

c. Removal of Directors

Shareholders have the power, called *amotion*, to remove directors during their term. The default rule under both the DGCL and the MBCA is that directors may be removed with or without cause. *See* DGCL §141(k), MBCA §8.08(a). However, under both statutes directors elected to a classified board may only be removed by the same set of shareholders that elected them. *See* DGCL §141(k), MBCA §8.08(b). Further, if the corporation permits cumulative voting (*see* Chapter 15), under which a minority of shareholders have the power to elect at least some directors, the quantum of votes required to amote must be greater than the quantum required to elect a director. *See* DGCL §141(k)(2), MBCA §8.08(c). Note that the board itself has *no* power to remove a director or to limit the right of a director to obtain corporate information. Note that under MBCA §8.09 and DGCL §225(c), the court has the power to remove a director, though the court's powers in this regard are broader under the MBCA than under the DGCL.

Finally, under the DGCL default rule, directors on a staggered or classified board may be removed only for cause. *See* DGCL §141(k)(1). This provision has become an important element by which incumbent directors of public corporations protect themselves against unwanted takeovers. A common takeover technique for hostile acquiring corporations is to wage a proxy fight seeking to remove the incumbent directors of the target corporation and replace them with more "enlightened" directors. If the target has a staggered board and has not waived the default rule, the raider can amote the target directors only for cause.

This, of course, raises the question of what constitutes "cause." Surprisingly, there is nearly no case law on the question and the statutes are silent. What case law there is deals primarily with the question of process — how corporations must proceed with determining whether cause for removal exists.

In *Superwire.com v. Hampton*, 805 A.2d 904 (Del. Ch. 2002), Superwire.com, Inc. (Superwire) was a large shareholder of Entrata Communications Corporation (Entrata), a Delaware corporation. Dean Hampton was the chair of Entrata's board, its chief executive officer, its president, and its secretary. Superwire had a falling out with Hampton and, on November 8, 2001,

> Superwire joined with other Entrata shareholders to execute an action by written consent of the holders of a majority of Entrata's voting stock purporting to remove Hampton from the board of directors "for cause." The complaint alleges that Superwire delivered the

consents to Entrata and that "Hampton's removal was, therefore, effective on that date." The complaint further alleges that Hampton claims to have received revocations of consents from those stockholders other than Superwire who executed the November 8, 2001 consent and that Hampton and others claim to "have executed a consent of the holders of a majority of Entrata stock to maintain Mr. Hampton as a director."

Defendants move to dismiss because the complaint does not allege facts showing that Hampton was afforded notice of specific charges and an opportunity to be heard. Superwire responds that (a) the consent is valid even if no notice or opportunity to be heard was afforded to Hampton because the certificate of incorporation permitted his removal without cause and, (b) in any case, it is not obligated to allege those facts in order to survive a motion to dismiss.

Superwire misstates the law in contending that the fact that it might have proceeded "without cause" can serve to validate an otherwise invalid attempt to remove Hampton "for cause." Directors of Delaware corporations can be removed "for cause" or, where permitted by the governing documents and the law, "without cause." But there are additional requirements that must be observed when doing so "for cause." A "for cause" removal of a director requires that the individual be given (i) specific charges for his removal, (ii) adequate notice, and (iii) a full opportunity to meet the accusation.[28] The same is true whether the action is taken at a meeting of stockholders or by written consent.[29]

These procedural safeguards are of some importance. In many cases, there are substantial collateral affects of being removed "for cause" that do not attend a removal "without cause." These can include differences in the treatment of rights flowing from contracts or other terms of employment. There are also likely to be significant reputational affects flowing from a "for cause" removal. These consequences alone might justify the conclusion that one choosing to act "for cause" must follow the prescribed procedures.

Moreover, it is a fallacy to suppose that a stockholder who succeeds in obtaining enough consents to remove a director "for cause" without affording the director notice and an opportunity to be heard would necessarily obtain the requisite number of consents if it complies with the law, or even if it seeks to remove the director "without cause." In this case, for example, the complaint reflects a contention that the stockholders who joined with Superwire in executing the November 8 consent promptly executed revocations of those consents, claiming that Superwire misled them into agreeing to remove Hampton. Those revocations may not have been legally effective, since they were expressed after the November 8 consent was delivered to Entrata. But they do serve to illustrate the point that compliance with established legal standards can affect the outcome.

Thus, the validity of the November 8 consent will depend on whether it was solicited in compliance with the procedural safeguards articulated in *Campbell v. Loew's* and specifically applied to actions taken by written consent in *Bossier v. Connell*.

For the purposes of the motion to dismiss, however, the question is whether Superwire was obliged to include in its complaint factual allegations that would support a finding that it gave Hampton notice of the charges against him and an opportunity to be heard. The answer to this question must be "no" because it is sufficient under the general notice pleading standard found in Court of Chancery Rule 8(a) that the complaint "contain . . . a short and plain statement of the claim showing that the pleader is entitled to relief." The allegations found in paragraph 22 of the complaint are sufficient for this purpose because they identify the consent, allege that it was executed by holders of the requisite number of shares, that it was delivered to the corporation and that it was effective on the date of its delivery. These are the elements described in Section 228 of the DGCL. The defense is free to show that the November 8 consent was invalid for whatever reason or reasons may exist. However, there is no requirement that the complaint allege facts sufficient to disprove any of those matters.

Superwire.com, Inc. v. Hampton, 805 A.2d 904 (Del. Ch. 2002) (Lamb, V.C.)

---

28. *Campbell v. Loew's, Inc.*, 134 A.2d 852, 859 (Del. Ch. 1957).
29. *Bossier v. Connell*, 1986 Del. Ch. LEXIS 511, at *15 (Del. Ch.).

[handwritten margin note: "for cause required"]

Notes and Questions

1. What Do You Think?

a. Should directors be allowed to hold over? What would be wrong with a rule that provided that a director ceased to be a director at the expiration of his or her term?

b. Should the shareholders have the power to amove without cause? Why shouldn't directors be entitled to hold office during the term for which they were elected?

c. How would you define "cause" for removal of a director?

d. What process should be used to remove a director for cause? Should there be a presumption that the director has acted properly? Who should decide whether cause is shown? Should an appeal from such a finding be allowed? If so, to whom?

What happens if a corporation fails to hold an annual meeting? *See* DGCL §211(c), MBCA §7.03(a)(1).

Putting It to Work

Problem 9-3

E & E Coffee Co. has amended its articles of incorporation again, this time to provide for a board that varies between two and nine members, the actual number to be determined by board resolution. Ernest and Edgar fixed the number of directors at three and added their cousin Frank to the board. Ernest and Edgar have since rethought their support of Cousin Frank, as he has no skill in the coffee business or business in general. Additionally, Ernest and Edgar have a strong suspicion (but no proof) that Frank is selling blended coffee drink recipes to E & E's largest local competitor.

a. Can Ernest and Edgar get rid of Cousin Frank before he tanks the business? *See* MBCA §§8.05(c), 8.08, 8.09.

b. How would you advise Ernest and Edgar if E & E Coffee Co. were incorporated in Delaware? DGCL §§141(k), 225(c).

d. Background and Context

1 Victor Morawetz, *A Treatise on the Law of Private Corporations*

§§541-543 (2d ed., 1886)

The majority of the board clearly have no power to expel an individual director, or to exclude him from inspecting the company's books and participating in its management, although they may believe him to be hostile to the interests of the association.

Nor have the majority at a shareholders' meeting implied authority to revoke the powers of the directors or managing agents, if their term of office is prescribed by the charter or the articles of association or by-laws of the company. The power of removing the directors of a corporation is sometimes conferred by express provision.

If the charter or articles of a company provide that the shareholders at a general meeting may remove any director "for negligence, misconduct in office, or other reasonable cause," the expression "reasonable cause" does not refer to such a cause as would be deemed reasonable in a court of justice, but only to such a cause as is deemed reasonable by the shareholders, and the discretion of the shareholders in determining what is reasonable cannot be interfered with, in the absence of direct fraud.

Hence, if the removal of the directors is absolutely essential to the protection of the corporation, and the corporation has no means of removing them or of revoking their powers, individual shareholders may apply to the court on behalf of the company, and the courts will grant such redress as justice requires.

It should be observed, that the courts will not remove the directors from office, or restrain them generally from representing the corporation, except in a case of absolute necessity.

Notes and Questions

1. Reality Check

a. How is Morawetz's conception of "cause" different from the modern day conception?

2. What Do You Think?

a. Is Morawetz's idea of "cause" functionally equivalent to removal without cause?

3. The Mechanics of Board Action

a. The Current Setting

Now that you understand the reasons why corporations are governed by boards of directors and how directors are selected by the shareholders, we can turn our attention to the more practical question of how the board takes valid action. One key is to remember that the board is a collective body. A consequence is that each director, individually, has no power and next to no rights. He or she has a right to information about the corporation but cannot act on behalf of the corporation, absent, of course, the creation of an agency relationship between the corporation as principal and the director as agent. *See* DGCL §220(d).

Another important aspect of board action is that many of the rules are not statutory but instead are found only in common law. This may seem surprising given how detailed the corporations statutes are on many matters. This quality of corporate law is not deliberate; it simply happened, possibly because of the insular nature of corporate legal practice. In other words, it may well be that corporate lawyers (who are the primary drafters of corporations statutes) saw no need to write statutes covering many of the most basic workings of boards because such rules were axiomatic among corporate practitioners.

Among the rules governing directors that are not usually found explicitly in the statutes are:

The board has no power to remove a director.
Board meetings may be called in any manner approved in advance by the board.
Each director has one vote on all matters.[2]
Directors may not vote by proxy; each must vote in person.

Boards take action in two ways. First, if they are unanimous in their intention, they may act without a meeting. This action is effected by having each director execute a consent, which, in Delaware and many states, may be electronic. *See* DGCL §§141(f), 232(c) and MBCA §8.21(a). Lawyers who are "inattentive to detail" frequently describe board actions taken by unanimous consent as having been taken at a meeting. These descriptions are likely to appear in correspondence, in certificates prepared for the corporate secretary's certification that certain actions have been authorized, and in other documents. Often such lawyers will even prepare "minutes" purporting to describe a meeting that never occurred and at which a board action was described as having been approved by a vote.

Although the MBCA explicitly permits action by consent to be described as action taken at a meeting, you should avoid doing so. *See* MBCA §8.21(c). In the first place, it is simply inaccurate to describe a board action as having been approved at a meeting when, in fact, it was approved by unanimous consent. Second, the question whether all the directors really had a meeting at a particular place and time may become important, regardless of whether a particular action was approved at such meeting or by consent. Inaccurate minutes will, at best, impede the resolution of the question and, at worst, may cast strong doubts upon your competence and honesty.

The second way in which boards of directors act is at a meeting. Four elements must be met for a board action taken at a meeting to be valid. The meeting must be properly *called*, the corporation must give each director proper *notice*, a *quorum* of directors must be present at the meeting, and the action must be approved by a *sufficient vote*. If any of these elements is lacking, the board's action is subject to attack as being ultra vires. Chapter 10 discusses the ultra vires doctrine in more detail.

i. Call. The *call* of the meeting is simply the decision to hold a meeting at a particular time and place and, often, for a particular reason. *Regular meetings*, which is to say periodic (e.g., monthly, quarterly, or even weekly or annually), may be provided for in the corporation's bylaws. No separate call is necessary for regular meetings, as they are automatically called. In every corporation *special meetings* (i.e., not periodically scheduled) will no doubt be necessary from time to time in addition to the regularly scheduled meetings. Some corporations may not feel the need to provide for periodic board meetings at all. In such instances, the board may call each meeting as the last order of business at the prior meeting or they may act by consent to call a meeting when they feel the need to do so. The bylaws (or, less frequently, the Articles of Incorporation) may also give the power to call board meetings to the

---

2. But note the DGCL permits a certificate of incorporation to endue one or more directors with greater or lesser voting power than other directors, regardless of whether the directors are elected by a particular class of stock. *See* DGCL §141(d).

chair or to other key participants in the corporation's governance. In the absence of such provision, however, the call is a board action that must be made, as every board action is, by unanimous consent or at a meeting. Doubtless in many informally governed corporations key participants convene board meetings even without the explicit power to do so in shocking ignorance or reckless disregard of corporate law niceties. Neither the DGCL nor the MBCA addresses the question of the call of board meetings.

ii. Notice.   The directors must obviously become aware that a meeting has been called. Because the directors are presumed to be knowledgeable about the corporation's business, the notice requirements for board meetings are minimal. The DGCL does not contain explicit provisions for giving notice of board meetings. It relies on common law notions and, thus, gives the board great discretion in establishing procedures for notifying the members so long as each director is given "due notice." The MBCA is more prescriptive. It provides a default rule that no notice need be given for regularly scheduled board meetings. In effect, the fact that the board has a schedule of meetings is notice enough. *See* MBCA §8.22(a). The default rule for special board meetings is that the directors must be given two days' notice of the location and time of the meeting but need not be given notice of the meeting's purpose. *See* MBCA §8.22(b). The Model Act further provides that a director who does not receive proper notice waives any objection by attending the meeting unless the director immediately protests the insufficient notice and does not vote in favor of any measure at that meeting. *See* MBCA §8.23(b).

iii. Quorum.   The third element for a valid board of directors meeting is the presence of a quorum. A *quorum* is simply the minimum amount of voting power that must be present at a meeting for actions to be valid. Because each director has one vote, the quorum for board meetings is defined by the number of directors present. The idea behind a quorum requirement is to prevent a collective body, such as the board or the shareholders, from taking action when so few members are present that the action may be thought to be unrepresentative of the whole body's intent. Under both the Delaware statute and the Model Act, the default rule is that a quorum is a majority of the total number of directors. That number may be raised but may not be lowered below one-third of the total number of directors. *See* DGCL §141(b), MBCA §8.24(a).

Note that the number that constitutes a quorum is measured by the number of authorized director positions, not the number of directors currently in office. For example, suppose a corporation has a board of five directors. The default quorum is three, even when there are fewer than five directors in office. That is, if two vacancies exist (through resignation, removal, or death), *all three* remaining directors must be present to transact business. The presence of two of those three (even though a majority of the directors in office) is not a quorum under the statutory default rule.

What does it mean for a director to be present at a meeting? You yourself may have been physically present in many law school classes yet not "present" in any meaningful sense.[3] Both statutes provide that board meetings may be held by conference call. *See* DGCL §141(i), MBCA §8.20(b). Note that neither statute

---

3. For example, during your Business Entities class, you may be physically located in a classroom yet "present" at *www.craigslist.com*.

specifically permits directors to be considered present when they participate by Internet communication, even though such communication may be in real time, unless the connection is oral rather than written.

iv. Sufficient Vote.   Finally, a board action must be approved by a sufficient vote. Remember that if the board is acting by consent, it must do so unanimously. If the board is acting at a meeting, an action is approved if it receives the assent of a majority of directors present at the meeting. *See* DGCL §141(b), MBCA §8.24(c). Delaware and the Model Act take different views as to a strategic tactic: leaving the meeting before a vote. The idea is to prevent approval of a faction's proposal where that faction has sufficient board votes to approve it. If the directors favoring the proposal are insufficient to constitute a quorum of the board, may the opposing directors thwart the proposal's approval by leaving the meeting? This tactic is called *breaking a quorum*. Under the Model Act, a quorum of directors must be present every time a vote is taken. Hence, if the opposing directors' absence would leave too few directors remaining, those opposed to an action can simply leave the meeting, breaking the quorum, and preventing the remaining directors from taking valid action. *See* MBCA §8.24(c). The wording of the DGCL, by contrast, is a tad ambiguous on the efficacy of breaking a quorum, but caselaw supports the view that directors *cannot* break a quorum. *See Henry v. Delaware Law School of Widener University, Inc.*, 1998 WL 15897 (Del. Ch., Lamb, V.C.).

Suppose the number of directors in office has fallen below a quorum. Is there no remedy except to wait until the next shareholder meeting at which more directors will, one hopes, be elected? Nearly every statute provides that the remaining directors, even though fewer than a quorum, can fill board vacancies. Thus, such directors can add members to bring the number of directors over the number required for a quorum. Indeed, the remaining directors could fill all vacancies at once, if they desire, and the corporation can then continue to function. *See* DGCL §223(a)(1), MBCA §8.10(a)(3).

Notes and Questions

1. Reality Check

a. May a director be considered "present" if he or she is connected to a board meeting by instant messenger?

2. What Do You Think?

a. Would you allow boards to act by majority consent without a meeting?

b. Should directors be able to act unanimously without a meeting?

c. On a nine-person board, a quorum is present if five directors attend a meeting. In such a situation, action is valid if taken by a vote of three to two. Do you think it is fair to allow such a result? If not, what rule would you prefer?

d. Both the DGCL and the MBCA allow for director quorum to be lowered to one-third of the number of director slots. If three directors of a nine-person board attend a meeting, a quorum is present under that rule. In such a setting action would be approved by the affirmative vote of only two directors. Fair?

When the board has divided into factions, each faction may try to impose its views on the corporation by strategically using the governance mechanics. As you read the next case, make sure you understand exactly how the requirements for board meetings were observed. Then ask yourself how you would have advised each side to act had you been retained to represent them. Suffusing your consideration of these issues should be your assessment of when strategic action to effect your (or your client's) ends crosses over to behavior that is impermissible because it is unethical, in either the professional responsibility sense or the more pervasive "reallife" sense.

≡ **Klaassen v. Allegro Development Corp.**
≡ 106 A.3d 1035 (Del. 2014)

JACOBS, J.

INTRODUCTION

Plaintiff-below/appellant Eldon Klaassen ("Klaassen") appeals from a Court of Chancery judgment in this proceeding brought under [DGCL] §225. The judgment determined that Klaassen is not the *de jure* chief executive officer ("CEO") of Allegro Development Corporation ("Allegro"). Klaassen claimed that the remaining Allegro directors (collectively, the "Director Defendants"), in removing him as CEO, violated an equitable notice requirement and also improperly employed deceptive tactics. After a trial and without addressing its merits, the Court of Chancery held that the claim was barred under the equitable doctrines of laches and acquiescence.

We affirm the Court of Chancery judgment. We hold that, to the extent that Klaassen's claim may be cognizable, it is equitable in nature. Therefore, Klaassen's removal as CEO was, at most, voidable and subject to the equitable defenses of laches and acquiescence. We further conclude that the Court of Chancery properly found that Klaassen acquiesced in his removal as CEO, and is therefore barred from challenging that removal.

FACTUAL AND PROCEDURAL BACKGROUND

A.   Facts

Allegro, a Delaware corporation headquartered in Dallas, Texas, is a provider of energy trading and risk management software. From the time that Klaassen founded Allegro in 1984, he has been Allegro's CEO, and until 2007, owned nearly all of Allegro's outstanding shares.

(1) The Series A Investment

In 2007, at which time Allegro was valued at approximately $130 million, Klaassen and Allegro solicited capital infusions from prospective investors. As a result, Allegro entered into transactions with [two venture capital investors] (collectively, the "Series A Investors") in late 2007 and early 2008. In those transactions those investors received Series A Preferred Stock of Allegro in exchange for an

Venture Capital = VC
- will want very significant
control

investment of $40 million. Currently, the Series A Investors own all of Allegro's Series A Preferred Stock, and Klaassen holds the majority of Allegro's Common Stock. As part of that transaction the Series A Investors, together with Klaassen and Allegro, entered into a Stockholders' Agreement (the "Stockholders' Agreement"). In addition, Allegro amended and restated both its certificate of incorporation (the "Charter") and its bylaws (the "Bylaws").

Those three documents created a framework under which Klaassen and the Series A Investors would share control of Allegro's board of directors (the "Board"). Under the Bylaws, Allegro would be governed by a seven member Board. Under the Charter, the holders of Series A Preferred Stock (voting as a separate class) became entitled to elect three directors, and the holders of Common Stock (voting as a separate class) became entitled to elect one director. The remaining three directors would be elected as provided by . . . the Stockholders' Agreement, under which Allegro's CEO would serve as a director, and in his capacity as CEO, would designate two outside directors, subject to the approval of the Series A Investors. The two outside directors would ultimately be elected by the holders of Series A Preferred Stock and Common Stock, voting together as a group.

Although the governing documents provided for a seven member Board, in actuality Klaassen and the Series A Investors settled on a five member Board. From 2010 until November 1, 2012, that Board consisted of Michael Pehl and Robert Forlenza (the "Series A Directors"), George Patrich Simpkins, Jr. and Raymond Hood (the "Outside Directors"), and Klaassen (as the CEO director). During that period, Klaassen, as the majority common stockholder, did not elect a director, nor did the Series A Investors elect a third director.

In negotiating the terms of their investment, the Series A Investors also obtained certain guarantees regarding their eventual exit from Allegro, which was to occur in 2012. At any time after December 20, 2012, the Series A Investors could require Allegro to redeem all outstanding Series A Preferred shares.

(2) Events Leading to Klaassen's Termination

Not long after the Series A Investors became shareholders, Allegro began falling short of its financial performance projections. Although Allegro met its targets for the first three quarters of 2011, the company's fourth quarter performance was a "disaster," and the first quarter of 2012 was similarly disappointing.

Not surprisingly, the Series A Directors, and later the Outside Directors, became discontented with Klaassen's performance as a manager. After the Series A investment transaction, Allegro hired Chris Larsen as chief operating officer to address the Series A Investors' concerns about Klaassen's management. Ten months later, Mr. Larsen resigned, citing difficulty working with Klaassen. While Allegro's financial performance continued to falter, the Series A Directors became particularly frustrated with Klaassen's inability to provide the Board with accurate information. In 2012, only four days before the end of Allegro's best sales quarter to date, Klaassen fired Allegro's senior vice president of sales—disregarding the Board's request to wait until after the quarter's end, and acting without any succession plan in place. Finally, in September 2012, Allegro's chief marketing officer resigned, citing Klaassen's leadership style as the reason.

As frustration with Klaassen mounted, in 2012 the Board began exploring ways to address the Series A Investors' redemption right. At some point before the July 19, 2012 Board meeting, Klaassen proposed that Allegro buy out the Series A Investors' Preferred Stock investment for $60 million. Initially the Series A Investors had demanded $92 million—the approximate value of their initial liquidation preference—but at a July 31, 2012 Board meeting they reduced their demand to $80 million. At that same meeting, Klaassen made a presentation about Allegro's financial performance, apparently hoping to make his $60 million offer to the Series A Investors appear more attractive. Instead, all that Klaassen accomplished was to highlight Allegro's poor performance as compared to its industry peers. As a result, Mr. Forlenza (a Series A Director) concluded that the only viable path for the Series A Investors to achieve a profitable exit was to "grow" the company before exiting.

(3) Klaassen's Termination

In late summer 2012, the Board began seriously to consider replacing Klaassen as CEO. After the July 19 Board meeting, the Outside Directors discussed (with Klaassen), Klaassen's unwillingness to compromise with the Series A Investors. Mr. Hood pointedly told Klaassen that with three director votes, the Board could remove him as CEO.[21] After Klaassen's July 31 Board meeting presentation, Messrs. Pehl and Forlenza (the Series A Directors) became more convinced that Klaassen had to be replaced.[22] In an August 7, 2012 conference call, Messrs. Pehl, Forlenza, Hood, and Simpkins discussed the possibility of replacing Klaassen. Shortly after that call, Mr. Hood asked Baker Botts LLP (legal counsel for the Outside Directors) for advice about the ramifications of replacing Klaassen. On August 17, 2012, the Director Defendants spoke once again.

In mid-September 2012, Messrs. Simpkins and Hood met with Klaassen. Both warned Klaassen that his tenure as CEO was "in jeopardy." At some point, most likely in September, Mr. Pehl asked Mr. Hood whether he (Hood) would consider replacing Klaassen as CEO. Eventually, Hood agreed, and by mid-October, the four Director Defendants (Pehl, Forlenza, Hood, and Simpkins) decided to replace Klaassen at the next regularly scheduled Board meeting on November 1, 2012. Those four directors held two preparatory conference calls—on October 19 and October 26—and asked Baker Botts to prepare a draft resolution removing Klaassen as CEO. The Director Defendants decided not to forewarn Klaassen that they planned to terminate him, because they were concerned about how Klaassen would react while still having access to Allegro's intellectual property, bank accounts, and employees.

On November 1, 2012, before the Board meeting, Mr. Hood emailed Klaassen, asking if Chris Ducanes, Allegro's general counsel, could attend the Board meeting to discuss the Series A redemption issue. Klaassen agreed. Mr. Hood later admitted that that email was "false" because, in fact, Mr. Ducanes' presence was needed to implement Klaassen's termination immediately after Klaassen was informed.[31]

---

21. Klaassen immediately confirmed with Allegro's general counsel that the Board had the power to terminate Klaassen.

22. The Series A Directors had at earlier times considered replacing Klaassen, but after the July 2012 Board meetings, the Series A Directors believed the Outside Directors might also support Klaassen's replacement.

31. The Court of Chancery found that the email had no effect on Klaassen's attendance of the Board meeting.

All five directors attended the November 1, 2012 Board meeting. Also attending were Messrs. Ducanes, and Jarett Janik, Allegro's chief financial officer. Toward the end of the meeting, the Director Defendants asked Messrs. Ducanes, Janik, and Klaassen to leave the room to allow the Director Defendants to meet in executive session. During the executive session, the Director Defendants confirmed their decision to remove and replace Klaassen. They then recalled Messrs. Ducanes and Janik, and informed them that Mr. Hood would be replacing Klaassen as CEO. Thereafter, Klaassen returned to the meeting, at which point Mr. Pehl informed Klaassen that the Board was removing him as CEO. The Board then voted on the resolution (prepared by Baker Botts) that removed Klaassen and appointed Hood as interim CEO, with the Director Defendants voting in favor and Klaassen abstaining.

(4) Post-Termination Events

After his removal as CEO, Klaassen initially offered to help Mr. Hood learn about the industry and Allegro's operations. In early to mid-November 2012, Klaassen also began negotiating the terms of a consulting agreement, under which he would serve as an "Executive Consultant" to Allegro, reporting to Allegro's CEO. The draft consulting agreement expressly precluded Klaassen from holding himself out to third parties as an Allegro employee or agent. In early December 2012, Klaassen communicated to Mr. Simpkins, that he (Klaassen), in his capacity as a director and common shareholder, would hold Hood "accountable" as CEO for Allegro's performance, and that if Allegro's performance did not improve, the "management change should be judged a failure."

In late 2012, Klaassen began expressing displeasure about his termination as CEO. In an email Hood sent in late November 2012, Hood remarked that "Eldon has not accepted his fate." On November 29, 2012, Klaassen emailed ExxonMobil (a major Allegro client), informing Exxon that Allegro was in the midst of a "bitter" shareholder dispute and that the company had become "dysfunctional." Klaassen also began hosting events for Allegro employees, at which he criticized Allegro management and spread rumors of other employee terminations.

On June 5, 2013, Klaassen sent a letter to Messrs. Ducanes, Pehl, and Forlenza, claiming that his (Klaassen's) removal as CEO was invalid. Klaassen also delivered two written consents (in his capacity as majority shareholder) that purported to: (i) remove Messrs. Simpkins and Hood as outside directors; (ii) elect John Brown as the common director; and (iii) elect Dave Stritzinger and Ram Velidi as outside directors.

ANALYSIS

A. The Director Defendants Did Not Violate Any Notice Requirements

No Notice Required for Regular Board Meeting

Klaassen claims that the Board's action to remove him as CEO taken at the November 1 meeting was invalid, because he (Klaassen) received no advance notice that his possible termination would be considered at that meeting. This claim lacks merit. Klaassen was terminated at a regular meeting of Allegro's Board. It is settled Delaware law that corporate directors are not required to be given notice of regular

[handwritten margin note: No Notice required for regular bood meeting]

board meetings.[57] There being no such notice requirement, it follows that there is no default requirement that directors be given advance notice of the specific agenda items to be addressed at a regular board meeting. Nor do any notice provisions of Allegro's Bylaws override that default rule. Therefore, the Director Defendants violated no default rule of Delaware law, or any provision of Allegro's Bylaws, by not giving Klaassen advance notice of their plan to terminate him at the November 1 regular Board meeting.

B. Klaassen's Deception Claim Is Barred by Acquiescence

We turn next to Klaassen's deception-based claim, and uphold the Vice Chancellor's determination that that claim is barred by the equitable doctrine of acquiescence. Klaassen's claim that he was deceived by the Director Defendants during the November 1 Board meeting is equitable in nature. That being the case, any Board action that violated the Board's equitable obligations would be at most voidable and, as such, subject to equitable defenses. Lastly, we conclude that the Court of Chancery correctly found that Klaassen acquiesced in his removal as Allegro's CEO. Because a finding of acquiescence is sufficient to uphold the Court of Chancery's judgment, we do not reach or address the separate issue of whether Klaassen's claim is also barred by laches.

(1) Klaassen's Deception Claim Implicates Board Action That Is Voidable, Not Void

Klaassen claims that the Board action removing him as CEO at the November 1 meeting was invalid, because the Director Defendants employed deceptive tactics—namely, offering false reasons for rescheduling that meeting, and providing a false explanation for Mr. Ducanes' presence at that meeting. Our courts do not approve the use of deception as a means by which to conduct a Delaware corporation's affairs, and nothing in this Opinion should be read to suggest otherwise. Here, however, we need not address the merits of Klaassen's deception claim, because we find, as did the Court of Chancery, that Klaassen acquiesced in his removal as CEO.

Klaassen challenges his removal as a violation of "generally accepted notions of fairness." A claim of that kind is equitable in character. A fundamental principle of our law is that "he who seeks equity must do equity." Consequently, a plaintiff's equitable claim against a defendant may be defeated, in a proper case, by the plaintiff's inequitable conduct towards that defendant. It follows that board action taken in violation of equitable principles is voidable, not void, because "[o]nly voidable acts are susceptible to . . . equitable defenses."[73]

This result is congruent with the well-established distinction between void and voidable corporate actions. As this Court discussed in *Michelson v. Duncan*,[74] "[t]he essential distinction between voidable and void acts is that the former are those which may be found to have been performed in the interest of the corporation but beyond the authority of management, as distinguished from acts which are *ultra vires*, fraudulent or gifts or waste of corporate assets."

---

57. *Lippman v. Kehoe Stenograph Co.*, 95 A.895, 898 (Del. Ch. 1915). . . .
73. *Boris v. Schaheen*, 2013 WL 6331287, at *15 (Del. Ch. Dec. 2, 2013). . . .
74. 407 A.2d 211 (Del. 1979).

(2) Klaassen Acquiesced In His Removal as CEO

Finally, having determined that Klaassen's deception claim is voidable and properly subject to equitable defenses, we address whether the Court of Chancery correctly found that Klaassen's claim was barred by the doctrine of acquiescence. We conclude that the court correctly so found. A claimant is deemed to have acquiesced in a complained-of act where he:

> has full knowledge of his rights and the material facts and (1) remains inactive for a considerable time; or (2) freely does what amounts to recognition of the complained of act; or (3) acts in a manner inconsistent with the subsequent repudiation, which leads the other party to believe the act has been approved. For the defense of acquiescence to apply, conscious intent to approve the act is not required, nor is a change of position or resulting prejudice.[81]

Klaassen does not claim that he lacked full knowledge of either his rights or the material facts. Accordingly, the narrow question is whether Klaassen's conduct amounted, in the eyes of the law, to recognition and acceptance of his removal as Allegro's CEO. We hold that it did. Shortly after his removal, Klaassen (without protest) helped Mr. Hood transition to his new role as CEO. Klaassen also negotiated a consulting agreement (which never came into effect) providing that he would report to Allegro's CEO and that Klaassen would not hold himself out as an Allegro employee or agent. Later, Klaassen proclaimed that he would hold Mr. Hood (as CEO) responsible for Allegro's performance, commented on Hood's employment contract, executed a written consent removing Hood from the audit committee due to Hood's role as CEO, and served as a compensation committee member. Whatever may have been Klaassen's subjective intent, his conduct objectively evidenced that he recognized and accepted the fact that he was no longer Allegro's CEO.

Klaassen points to factual circumstances that (he says) negate the trial court's determination of acquiescence. Klaassen claims that he warned of possible litigation when presenting a proposal to purchase the Series A Preferred shares. But, what he warned of was *shareholder* litigation, and that warning was made within the context of negotiations between Klaassen and the Series A Investors to purchase the Series A Preferred Stock. Indeed, during that very presentation, Klaassen acknowledged that on November 1, 2012, Allegro had hired Hood as its CEO. Klaassen also contends that the negotiation of his consulting agreement (which was never approved) was merely a ploy to remain involved in Allegro while he was negotiating the Series A Preferred share repurchase. But, Klaassen does not substantiate that *ipse dixit* claim, and, moreover, his "conscious intent" is immaterial to an acquiescence finding.

Klaassen also emphasizes Hood's remark, when the negotiations broke down, that Klaassen had not "accepted his fate." Although that vague statement shows that Klaassen was unhappy about his termination, it does not clearly or persuasively evidence that Klaassen was contesting the validity of the removal. Lastly, Klaassen claims that the Director Defendants never relied on Klaassen's written consent appointing him to the audit and compensation committees, from whose meetings the Director Defendants excluded him. Klaassen misapprehends the significance of that written consent. Whether or not Klaassen actively participated in the audit and

81. *Nevins v. Bryan*, 885 A.2d 233, 254 (Del. Ch. 2005), *aff'd*, 884 A.2d 512 (Del. 2005) . . . .

compensation committees' activities, the executed written consent constituted an official, formal acknowledgment that he (Klaassen) was no longer Allegro's CEO and that Hood had succeeded him in that office. The Court of Chancery correctly determined that Klaassen acquiesced in his removal as CEO.

CONCLUSION

For the foregoing reasons, the Court of Chancery judgment is affirmed.

Notes and Questions

1. Notes

a. Section 225 is the typical procedural way to test election procedures. It provides for a summary proceeding in the Court of Chancery. *See also* MBCA §7.49.

2. Reality Check

a. Which elements of a valid board meeting were problematic here according to Justice Jacobs? Do you agree?

b. What is the difference between "void" and "voidable" board actions? Which were involved here and why?

3. Suppose

a. What would have happened if Klaassen had simply left the November 1st meeting?

b. Suppose Allegro were incorporated under the MBCA? Would the analysis or result have been different?

4. What Do You Think?

a. Do you think that the dire financial and operational position of Allegro justifies the board's actions?

4. Curing Defective Board Action

Both the DGCL and MBCA allow a corporation to validate corporate actions that were invalid when taken because of a failure of authorization. DGCL §§204, 205, MBCA §§1.45-1.52. A failure of authorization means that the action was not effected in compliance with the statute (or any requirements in the articles, bylaws, or agreements to which the corporation is a party). Generally speaking, this means either (1) that the board failed to take any action as to a corporate act that required board authorization or (2) that the board's purported authorization was ineffective because of some procedural failure such as lack of call, notice, quorum, or sufficient vote.

The actions eligible to be validated under the statute, and the process by which validation takes place, are substantially the same under each statute. The statutes permit the validation of any corporate action, whether purportedly taken by the incorporator, the board, a board committee, or any officer or agent of the corporation. The only restriction on the actions that can be validated is that the action, when purportedly taken, was one that the corporation could have taken had the action been properly authorized. In addition, the statutes permit validation of an overissue, which you will recall means a purported issuance of stock in excess of the number of shares authorized in the articles of incorporation. Of course, an overissue is not an action that could have been taken by a corporation, even if otherwise properly authorized. *See* DGCL §161 and MBCA §6.03(a). Nonetheless, the statutes permit an overissue to be validated. In contrast to an overissue, putative stock are shares that are statutorily authorized but which are issued by an ineffective board process (or shares as to which it cannot be determined whether effective board authorization ever occurred). Unlike an overissue, putative stock could have been legally issued if the board had followed the appropriate process. The statutes provide that not only can the *issuance* of putative stock be ratified, but the board can declare that the putative stock *itself* is valid and outstanding.

Both statutes provide two paths to validating defective corporate actions. If an action is validated under either path the action is retroactively valid. It is, in common parlance, *nunc pro tunced*. The easier path (sometimes called the self-help path) is for the defective corporate act to be ratified by a board resolution. To effectively ratify an act under the statutes, the board resolution must, among other things, identify the date of the defective act, state why the authorization was defective, and affirmatively declare that the board intends to ratify the act. Where the original act would have required shareholder approval or a filing to become effective, the board must seek shareholder approval and make the required filing, in addition to adopting the requisite ratification resolution. In those instances, the board must affirmatively disclose to the shareholders and in the filing that it is ratifying a defective corporate action. If shareholder approval is not required, the board must give notice to each shareholder that it has ratified a defective corporate action and the notice must state that any action challenging either the original action or the ratification must be filed within 120 days from the ratification. The Official Comments to the MBCA and the Synopsis to the bill that became the DGCL provisions make clear that the statutory provisions are not exclusive and that common law principles of ratification remain open to a corporation that has taken a defective act.

The second path to validating a defective corporate act involves the court. DGCL §205, MBCA §1.52. The corporation itself, any director, any shareholder, or any person claiming to have been substantially and adversely affected by a ratification, can bring suit to challenge a statutory ratification (or to seek a declaratory judgment that such ratification is effective). As noted, such a suit must be brought within 120 days of the ratification. Further, the corporation, a director, or a shareholder can bring suit seeking to have any potentially defective corporate act declared valid. That is, a corporate action can be validated by the court under the statutes even where the board has not taken action to ratify it. This is an explicit grant of rather plenary power to validate or declare valid any action a corporation has purported to take.

Presumably, in the great majority of cases in which a corporation wishes to validate arguably defective corporate action, the board will ratify the action under the first path, without resorting to the courts. Presumably, also, in the great majority of such cases no lawsuit challenging that ratification will be filed. Thus there is likely to be very few cases, and even fewer reported decisions, interpreting the self-help sections of the statutes. Although the lack of litigation is generally a good thing, one side effect is that corporate lawyers advising their clients on how to effectively ratify an arguably defective action will have little guidance beyond the words of the statute itself.

Another notable consequence of the statutes is that counsel or their clients may, in an abundance of caution, seek judicial approval of board ratification (and of the underlying defective action). They may do so in part because of uncertainty (thanks to a lack of reported decisions) as to the self-help provisions, in part because they wish to preempt a potential challenge by a shareholder or third party, and in part for the certainty that a court judgment will provide. Vice Chancellor Laster expressed some frustration with this system in a case filed under DGCL §205 seeking validation of putative stock:

> So my main question is: Why is this my problem and why do you need me? And the reason I ask that is, you know, why isn't this something that just ought to happen through [the self-help provision, DGCL §204]? And I get that, generally speaking, it's nice to have somebody else take responsibility. And so what this does effectively is it transfers it from a 204 decision to a judicial decision, which gets everybody involved in the process a degree of separation. But that degree of separation is achieved by having the decision made by the person in this room who is least informed.
>
> The other thing is, I think of this in terms of an ongoing incentive structure. And I get that there are some things that you have to [submit to the Court pursuant to DGCL §205]. But because I know the informational vacuum in which I usually operate, notwithstanding the fact that you have done a very nice job trying to inform me so that I'm not completely ignorant, I generally think that people ought to do things through 204, unless they really have to use 205, rather than just trying to 205 everything and making us a— not a rubber stamp, but a convenience stamp, a ratifier of convenience, however you want to think of it.
>
> . . . .
>
> I guess, having said that, the one factor is the institutional concern. . . . [I] am leery of inducing a regime where 205 becomes a new rubber-stamp opportunity for people to shift responsibility.
>
> Because what really happens in these settings is the practitioners go in and understand what's going on. They diligence things. They figure out what has to happen. And what [DGCL §204] does is to provide a route whereby really pretty much everything can be cleaned up by parties on their own. I think that is the primary mechanism that people ought to be using to clean these things up, rather than asking for what's usually going to be one-sided, because a lot of these come in as almost ex parte petitions, where there isn't really another side, and the Court really doesn't have a good way of testing the 205 aspects of it. So I'm leery of that.

Steinberg v. Townley, C.A. No. 12539-VCL, transcript at 24-26, 36-40 (Del. Ch. Feb. 27, 2017) (Laster, V.C.).

As Vice Chancellor Laster observed, although the corporation must give all shareholders notice of the filing, the reality is that objectors will seldom appear. Thus the court will be making a decision in essentially a non-adversarial setting. At the

Steinberg v. Townley hearing under DGCL §205, the Vice Chancellor raised the question with counsel in this way:

> I generally have confidence that the people at the table can protect themselves. Is there anybody that wasn't at the table that, when you think about it, would be adversely affected by [a court judgment under DGCL §205]? Regardless of whether or not they have gotten off the couch and sent in an objection or shown up today, is there anybody that is being somewhat shortchanged by this who wasn't in the room when you-all were walking through all these things?
>
> . . . [W]hen you think about things abstractly, I mean, people may miss it, but sometimes when you are actually cutting up a pie or affecting the pie, you can see, even if it's not going to be your slice, you can see that one slice might end up being a little skinnier. But as you think about it, I'm asking you whether you know or you have a feeling that anyone who was not in the room is getting the skinny slice.
>
> *Steinberg v. Townley*, C.A. No. 12539-VCL, transcript at 28-29 (Del. Ch. Feb. 27, 2017) (LASTER, V.C.). (These transcript excerpts are as reported by *The Chancery Daily* (Apr. 25, 2017), which is the indispensable source of information about all corporate litigation in Delaware).

Putting It to Work

Problem 9-4

After the debacle with Cousin Frank, Ernest and Edgar, as the remaining board members, set the size of the board at five and added Adam, Brock, and Carter. Two weeks ago, all of the directors except Carter were in the corporate office and all four agreed that the corporation was doing so well that it should consider declaring its first cash dividend. They all agreed to call a special meeting of the board, for the purpose of considering the declaration of a dividend. The meeting was held yesterday, as agreed by the four directors.

However, on the day of the meeting, Ernest was unable to attend but authorized Edgar to vote for him. Adam could not attend in person, but he communicated by IM during the meeting with the directors who were present. Carter knew nothing about the meeting until he ran into Brock an hour before the meeting began but then rushed to the meeting.

After considerable discussion, a resolution to pay a substantial dividend was moved and seconded. Edgar voted in favor and cast Ernest's proxy in favor, as well. Adam, via IM, voted in favor. Brock and Carter voted against.

a. Was the resolution adopted?

b. Would your answer be different if E & E were incorporated in Delaware?

c. Assume that the corporation pays the dividend and that, in fact, three of the five directors (Ernest, Edgar, and Adam) are in favor of the dividend. If the corporation were incorporated in Delaware, what action, if any, could the corporation take to ensure that the dividend was validly approved? *See* DGCL §§204 and 205, MBCA §§1.45-1.52.

b. Background and Context

1 Victor Morawetz, *A Treatise on the Law of Private Corporations*
§§531-532 (2d ed., 1886)

The general rule is, that the directors of a corporation have no implied authority to act singly; they can act only as a board, unless there be a different custom, or an express delegation of authority to act individually. Either all must be present at a meeting, or the meeting must be called in a regular manner, and all the directors given notice; and in the latter case, if a majority assemble, they may act by a major[ity] vote. A majority of the directors form a quorum, in the absence of a different regulation, and a majority of the quorum determine the action of the board.

It has been held, that, if a quorum of the directors of a corporation meet and unite in any determination, the company is bound thereby, whether the other directors were notified or not. But this view is certainly not correct. The shareholders in a corporation are entitled not only to the votes of the directors, but also to their influence and argument in the discussion which leads to the passage of their resolutions. While it may not be the duty of every director to be present at every meeting of the board, yet it is certainly the intention of the shareholders that every director shall have a right to be present at every meeting, in order to acquire full information concerning the affairs of the corporation, and to give the other directors the benefit of his judgment and advice. If meetings could be held by a bare quorum, without notifying the other directors, the majority might virtually exclude the minority from all participation in the management of the company. If it appears that a meeting of the directors was attended by a quorum, it will be presumed, in the absence of the contrary, that due notice of the meeting was given to all the directors, and that all necessary formalities have been complied with.

B. OFFICERS

1. Officers and Agents

a. Background and Context. Review of Chapter 4 on Agency

H-D Irrigating, Inc. v. Kimble Properties, Inc.
8 P.3d 95 (Mont. 2000)

Justice TERRY N. TRIEWEILER delivered the Opinion of the Court.

The Plaintiffs, H-D Irrigating, Inc. and William H. Lane, Jr., (Buyers), filed this action . . . to recover damages from the Defendants, Kimble Properties, Inc., Hobble Diamond Cattle Co., and Lloyd L. Kimble (Sellers), for misrepresentation and breach of a duty to disclose. The Defendants filed a counterclaim to recover payments due from the Plaintiffs for the property purchased. Following a nonjury trial, the District Court found the Defendants were liable for constructive fraud and that the Plaintiffs were liable for payment pursuant to the promissory note. The Defendants appeal and the Plaintiffs cross-appeal. We affirm in part and reverse in part. . . .

On February 13, 1991, [Buyers] agreed with Hobble Diamond Cattle Co. and Kimble Properties, Inc. to purchase land from Hobble Diamond Cattle Co. for $1,650,000 and irrigation equipment from Kimble Properties, Inc. for $350,000. Lloyd L. Kimble was the president of both companies. Lane was the president of H-D Irrigating, Inc.

On June 16, 1992, the Buyers filed a complaint, in which, among other claims, they alleged misrepresentation and breach of a duty to disclose. The Buyers alleged that Lloyd Kimble falsely represented that the irrigation equipment was in working order; that all pivots could be operated at the same time; that the irrigation system provided sufficient water for the acreage; and that he knew of no irrigation system deficiencies.

Following the trial, the District Court entered findings of fact and conclusions of law. The District Court found:

> 21. Mr. Kimble's failure to disclose the extent and cause of the erosion on pivot three could not be reasonably discovered by Mr. Lane prior to closing and constitutes a material misrepresentation upon which Mr. Lane reasonably relied to his detriment.

The Sellers contend that if anyone, "the entity responsible for constructive fraud . . . was Hobble Diamond Cattle Co., not Kimble Properties or Lloyd 'Monty' Kimble." The Sellers argue "Hobble Diamond Cattle Co. owned and sold the real property to Lane, and Kimble Properties owned and sold only the irrigation equipment." The Buyers respond that Kimble is individually liable for his own conduct regardless of who his principal was at the time. The Buyers argue that a principal and its agent are jointly and severally liable for the agent's wrongful acts.

A principal is liable for wrongs committed by an agent while the agent acts within the scope of his employment. Further, a director or officer is individually liable for his false representations. *Poulsen v. Treasure State Indus., Inc.*, 626 P.2d 822, 829 (Mont. 1981). In *Poulsen,* we said:

> It is clearly established that a director or officer of a corporation is individually liable for fraudulent acts or false representations of his own or in which he participates even though his action in such respect may be in furtherance of the corporation's business. This personal liability attaches regardless of whether liability also attaches to the corporation.

626 P.2d at 829 (citations omitted).

In this case, Lloyd Kimble was the president of Hobble Diamond Cattle Co. and Kimble Properties, Inc., which made him an agent of both companies. Hobble Diamond Cattle Co. sold land to the Buyers and Kimble Properties, Inc. sold irrigation equipment to the Buyers. In assessing liability, neither the District Court's findings of fact and conclusions of law, nor its judgment, make a distinction between Hobble Diamond Cattle Co. and Kimble Properties, Inc.; rather, both documents simply refer to the "Defendants." However, when Lloyd Kimble represented to the Buyers that the irrigation equipment was in working order; that all pivots could be operated at the same time; that the irrigation system provided sufficient water for the acreage; and that he knew of no problems or deficiencies with the irrigation equipment or the irrigation system, he was acting within the scope of his employment as the president of Kimble Properties, Inc., which owned the irrigation equipment. Lloyd Kimble's representations concerned the irrigation equipment, not the land. [A]t the time of the representation Lloyd Kimble was referring to the irrigation equipment and acting as an agent of its owner Kimble Properties, Inc. Hobble Diamond Cattle Co., however, is not liable for Lloyd Kimble's misrepresentations because he was not acting on its behalf when he made representations regarding the irrigation system. Kimble Properties, Inc. and Lloyd Kimble are jointly and severally liable for the Buyers' damages resulting from Lloyd Kimble's constructive fraud, but Hobble Diamond Cattle Co. has no liability. Accordingly we hold the District Court did not err when it assessed damages against Kimble Properties, Inc. and Lloyd Kimble, but the District Court did err when it assessed damages against Hobble Diamond Cattle Co.

Notes and Questions

1. Reality Check

a. For whom was Mr. Kimble acting?
b. Why did plaintiffs not prevail on their claims against all the entities?

2. Suppose

a. Suppose Mr. Kimble had misrepresented the size of the parcel being conveyed. Would that have made a difference in the analysis or result? Should it?
b. Assume that Mr. Kimble and Kimble Properties, Inc. are impecunious and that Hobble Diamond Cattle Co. has large assets. Would that scenario make a difference in the result?
c. Assume that only Mr. Kimble has large assets and that the two corporations have negligible assets. Would that scenario make a difference in the result?

3. What Do You Think?

a. Do you think it is fair to hold only one of the two corporations for which Mr. Kimble was acting liable to plaintiffs? Why?

The rules of agency law are largely common law rules that have been systematized by the American Law Institute in its *Restatement (Third) of Agency* (2006). Nearly every state uses these concepts. This discussion will provide a brief overview of the most important agency concepts as they relate to business entities but is not meant to be a complete synopsis. *See* Chapter 4 for more details.

An agency relationship is a consensual, though not necessarily contractual, relationship in which one person (the agent) agrees to act on behalf of the other person (the principal) and subject to the principal's control. The principal need not have the right to control the physical performance of the agent's task; it is enough that the principal controls the general performance and outcome. An agency relationship, once established, may be ended unilaterally by either the agent or the principal, even if doing so constitutes a breach of contract.

Once an agency relationship is established, the agent may bind the principal in several ways. First, the principal is bound by any acts of the agent within the scope of the agent's actual authority. Actual authority is the agent's reasonable interpretation of the principal's manifestation to the agent. Second, and importantly for corporate purposes, an agent binds the principal for any act done in accordance with apparent authority. Apparent authority is a third party's reasonable interpretation of the principal's manifestation to that third party that the agent is authorized. In many settings actual authority and apparent authority are coterminous. Nonetheless, either is sufficient to bind the principal, and therefore a principal is bound by an agent's actions made in accordance with apparent authority even if done in contravention of actual authority. The principal may also be bound to a third party through estoppel and through ratification of the agent's (originally) unauthorized actions. The agent is not bound to the third party as long as the third party knows that the agent is acting for the principal.

A principal is ordinarily bound by the agent's tortious actions that cause personal injury if (a) the agent is an "employee," a term of art meaning that the principal has the right to control the physical performance of the agent's tasks, and (b) the agent was acting "within the scope of employment," meaning the act giving rise to liability was close in time, space, and manner to those the agent was employed to perform and undertaken at least in part for the principal's benefit. The classic example of such a setting is the delivery person who hits a pedestrian by accident while working. Certainly the agent didn't have actual authority to hit the pedestrian nor did the agent have apparent authority to do so. Liability in this setting is through the concept of "inherent power" a sort of catch-all for unauthorized actions of agents that nonetheless render principals liable essentially on foreseeability and public policy grounds.

b. The Current Setting

Once a corporation's board of directors has authorized an act, someone must actually effect the act for the corporation. That person is the corporation's agent. Of course, all the corporation's employees are agents but the corporation may have other agents who are not employees. For example, the outside accountants and outside lawyers retained by the corporation are agents. Further, the corporation may make use of people to perform services for it but who are not agents; they are nonagent independent contractors. People who supply component parts, for example, are likely to be nonagent independent contractors. Finally, the corporation's directors are *not* agents. This is so because the board must act collectively rather than individually and also because the board is not under the control of the corporation (an agent must be subject to the principal's control). *See Restatement (Third) of Agency* §1.01 cmt. f(2).

Unlike directors, who have their power defined and granted by statute, officers inhabit a much more nebulous world. Strictly speaking, an *officer* is a person who holds an office, which, in turn, is a position to which particular kinds of duties or powers are attached. Thus, by contrast, an agent who is not an officer would have powers and duties defined in a more explicit and ad hoc manner: by board resolution or grant from another agent. The statutes simply provide that a corporation has whatever officers its bylaws or board determines and that those officers have whatever powers are specifically granted to them. *See* DGCL §142(a), MBCA

§8.40(a). Perhaps the best practical definitions of officer are provided by the Securities and Exchange Commission:

> The term *officer* means a president, vice president, secretary, treasurer or principal financial officer, comptroller or principal accounting officer, and any person routinely performing corresponding functions. . . .

> The term *executive officer*, . . . means . . . president, any vice president . . . in charge of a principal business unit, division, or function (such as sales, administration or finance), or an officer who performs a policy making function or any other person who performs similar policy making functions. . . .

Rule 405, 17 C.F.R. §230.405

Notice how the definition of *officer* is narrower than the definition of an *agent*. What difference does it make whether a person who acts on behalf of a corporation does so as an agent or as an officer? It makes a difference in a number of settings. First, officers are explicitly held to fiduciary duties comparable to those of corporate directors, while other agents are held to a less explicit and less stringent standard. Second, officers may be statutorily entitled to indemnity and the corporation may be able to purchase insurance (so-called directors and officers insurance) for officer malfeasance. Agents are sometimes entitled to indemnity, but such protection is more amorphous. Third, officers are sometimes expressly exposed to liability under certain statutes (such as environmental protection laws), whereas ordinary agents are not. Fourth, statutes often provide that service of process on a corporation may be effected by service on any (or certain named) officers; service on an ordinary agent is typically insufficient to bring about personal jurisdiction over the corporation. Fifth, officers (or at least some of them) are usually required to be named in the corporation's annual report filed with the secretary of state, which means that the names and titles held are a matter of public record. Finally, an officer may have certain powers to bind the corporation (called the power of position) that comprise both actual authority and apparent authority. This aspect of being an officer is explored in more depth below.

Given that the corporations statutes seem to be rather unconcerned with what officers the corporation has, and given that being an officer brings with it some heightened obligations, can a corporation protect the people who act on its behalf by having only agents and no officers? A closer reading of the statutes reveals that the corporation must have at least two officers. Under the MBCA, two officers are required to sign share certificates. MBCA §6.25(d). Further, one officer must have "responsibility for preparing minutes of the directors' and shareholders' meetings and for maintaining and authenticating records of the corporation . . . ." That officer could have any title the corporate planners desire but the statute refers to that person as the "secretary" of the corporation. *See* MBCA §1.40 [defining *secretary*].

In Delaware, the question of officers gets a bit more complicated. Section 142(a) provides that "[o]ne of the officers shall have the duty to record the proceedings of the meetings of the stockholders and directors in a book to be kept for that purpose." As with the MBCA, that person is typically referred to as the corporate secretary, although the DGCL, unlike the MBCA, does not explicitly define the office of "secretary." But §142(a) also requires that a corporation must have such officers "as may be necessary to enable it to sign instruments and stock certificates which comply with §§103(a)(2) and 158 of this title." Sections 103(a)(2) and 158 are disappointing in that they simply require that all documents filed after the corporation's initial organization must be signed by "any authorized officer" and that all stock certificates be signed by "any two authorized officers."

The DGCL goes on to provide, as a default rule, that "[a]ny number of offices may be held by the same person," and further provides that the corporation's failure to elect officers shall have no effect on the corporation(!). *See* DGCL §142(a), (d). The MBCA also allows all offices to be held by the same person. *See* MBCA §8.40(d). Within these constraints, however, you and your clients are free to have as many or as few officers as you desire and with whatever titles seem best. For example, an officer of one public corporation holds the title of Vice President and Head of UberEverything. At another large corporation, one of the officers is styled the Vice President of Brewing.[4]

The officers themselves are appointed by the board. The statutes say that the officers are "elected" but in truth they are decided upon in the same fashion that the board makes any other decision. *See* DGCL §142(a), MBCA §8.40(a). Cf. MBCA §8.44(a) ("election or appointment of an officer . . ."). Does being an officer give one a heightened expectation or right to remain in office? Or can an officer be dismissed at will, as an ordinary agent can be dismissed by the principal?

Andrews v. Southwest Wyoming Rehab. Center

974 P.2d 948 (Wyo. 1999)

Lehman, C.J.

[Southwest Wyoming Rehabilitation Center (SWRC)] hired [Phil] Andrews on January 2, 1990, for the position of employee relations coordinator. In May 1991, he was promoted to vice president of SWRC, the position he held when his employment was terminated on June 21, 1995. Andrews' supervisor was Kathy Horn-Dalton, the president of SWRC. According to Andrews, Horn-Dalton fired him because he tried to inform SWRC's board of directors that she was mishandling corporate assets and causing employee morale problems.

On February 5, 1996, Andrews filed suit against SWRC. Andrews alleged that he had a special fiduciary relationship with SWRC and that his termination was wrongfully motivated, and, thus, SWRC breached the duty of good faith and fair dealing.

Wyoming recognizes a limited tort claim for breach of the implied covenant of good faith and fair dealing in employment contracts. Only in those rare and exceptional cases where a special relationship of trust and reliance exists between the employer and employee is a duty created which can give rise to tort liability. A special relationship sufficient to support a cause of action can be found by the existence of separate consideration, rights created by common law or statute, or rights accruing with longevity of service.

---

4. The Vice President and Head of UberEverything is Jason Droege of Uber Technologies Inc. David A. Grinnel is Vice President of Brewing at the Boston Beer Company.

Andrews contends that a special relationship existed between him and SWRC by virtue of [MBCA §8.42]. He argues that, as a corporate officer with a fiduciary duty to the corporation and its members, he was not an "ordinary employee," but occupied a position of trust and reliance. In essence, Andrews' argument is that the "fiduciary relationship" created by the statute amounts to the "special relationship" necessary to support a cause of action for breach of the implied covenant.

We do not agree with Andrews' position. The implied good faith covenant involves a "special element of reliance" by the aggrieved party, the type of trust and dependency that is found, for example, in insurance relationships. Section [8.42] establishes the standard of conduct for corporate officers, imposing on officers a duty of care to their corporations. While an officer may be able to rely on the statute to protect him from personal liability if he has acted in accordance therewith, see [8.42(c)], it goes too far to say that an officer exercising his duty of care under the statute has a right not to be terminated. On the contrary, the Act provides that a board may remove an officer at any time with or without cause. [MBCA §8.43(b)]. Section [8.43(b)] clearly vitiates Andrews' contention that he should be allowed to rely on his employer to maintain his employment until it is determined that he has not acted, or can no longer act, in the corporation's best interest.

In sum, [§8.42] simply does not establish rights on which Andrews was entitled to rely and which would create a special relationship upon which tort liability can rest. Because Andrews did not establish the existence of a special relationship of trust and reliance, the court properly entered summary judgment on Andrews' claim for breach of the implied covenant of good faith and fair dealing.

SWRC was entitled to summary judgment as a matter of law, and the district court's order hereby is affirmed.

Notes and Questions

1. Notes

a. The DGCL is silent on the point raised by this opinion but case law clearly has adopted the same rule. *See also* MBCA §8.44.

b. Morawetz wrote,

> The directors and managing agents of a corporation have undoubted authority to revoke the powers of the inferior agents whom they have appointed. The power is a discretionary one, and the rightfulness of its exercise cannot be investigated by the courts.
>
> But the directors of a corporation have no implied authority to revoke the powers of those agents who are appointed by vote of the shareholders, or whose office is fixed and regulated by the charter. So it would be difficult to imply authority in the board of directors to revoke the powers of any agent, like a president or treasurer, whose term of office is fixed by the charter or articles of association of the company. It does not follow that the directors have authority to remove an agent of this character merely because they appointed him pursuant to the provisions of the charter. There should be an express provision granting the power of removal.
>
> The majority at a shareholders' meeting have no power to revoke the powers of the inferior agents of a corporation because the power of appointing and controlling these agents is delegated to the board of directors exclusively.

1 Victor Morawetz, *A Treatise on the Law of Private Corporations* §§541-542 (2d ed., 1886)

2. Reality Check

a. Mr. Andrews claimed that his status as an officer provided him certain benefits. What were they? Why did the court disagree?

3. Suppose

a. Suppose Mr. Andrews had had a contract for employment to be SWRC's vice president?

4. What Do You Think?

a. Should officers' employment be terminable at will in the absence of an explicit employment contract? Shouldn't corporate officers have some security against capricious board action?

2. Power of Officers

a. The Current Setting

When an outside party deals with a corporation, how does the outsider know whether the humans' acts supposedly on behalf of the corporation actually bind it? As you'll remember, if an agent, including an officer, for a corporation has actual authority, the corporation is bound even if the outsider has no knowledge of the agent's authority. The principal's manifestation to the outsider that the agent has authority creates apparent authority, which also binds the principal, regardless of the agent's actual authority. What if the manifestation to the outsider is simply, "This is our president" (or vice president, or chief global strategist)? Does this create apparent authority? If so, what are the contours of such power? The following case deals with this question. In a larger context, the next case addresses the chronic problem of how a third party may be certain that a corporation is bound by a human's actions where the human purports to be acting for the corporation. Note that the court uses the term *ostensible authority*, which is simply a synonym for *apparent authority. See Restatement (Third) of Agency* §2.03, cmt. b.

Snukal v. Flightways Mfg., Inc.

3 P.3d 286 (Cal. 2000)

GEORGE, C.J.

I

In October 1992, plaintiff Robert Snukal leased a residence he owned in Malibu, California, to defendant Flightways Manufacturing, Inc. (hereafter, Flightways) for a two-year term commencing in November 1992. The residence was to be occupied by Kirt Lyle, who at that time was president, chief financial officer, and secretary of Flightways. On behalf of Flightways, Lyle alone executed the lease agreement, designating his title as president, without indicating that he also was chief financial officer and secretary of the corporation.

Within several months of the commencement of the lease term, Flightways was in arrears in its monthly rent payments, and in September 1993, plaintiff sent Flightways a notice to pay rent or quit. Lyle vacated the premises approximately one year after the inception of the lease term. Plaintiff commenced the present action, seeking recovery of past due rents, payment of future rents according to the terms of the lease, and other relief. In its answer to the complaint, Flightways denied that Lyle was authorized to enter into the lease agreement on its behalf. Flightways filed a cross-complaint alleging that it had not authorized Lyle to enter into the lease agreement on its behalf, and seeking relief in the amount of the monthly rent payments previously made.

The parties stipulated to trial by the court. Plaintiff testified that he personally did not meet with Lyle or Flightways and that the lease transaction was conducted through real estate brokers. Plaintiff was unaware of Lyle's actual interest in Flightways. Plaintiff's secretary received and deposited certain rent checks bearing the name "Lyle Kirtisine" rather than Flightways, but most of the rent checks received were issued on an account bearing the name "Flightways Manufacturing, Inc."

A member of its board of directors testified that Flightways did not authorize Lyle to enter into the lease agreement, and in fact was attempting to reduce its expenses during the period in which Lyle executed the agreement on its behalf. Although Flightway's monthly bank statements clearly reflected the checks (numbered in a sequence distinct from that of most of the checks written on the corporate bank account) written by Lyle on Flightway's bank account to pay the monthly rent for the residence, Lyle's duties also included the preparation (based upon those records) of the monthly corporate financial statements that were examined by the board of directors. At one point, in order to determine the reliability of the financial records, the board of directors employed an accounting firm to review the company's financial statements, but that firm did not detect anything unusual. Lyle told the board members that he was house-sitting for a girlfriend who lived in Malibu.

The municipal court determined that Flightways was bound by the lease agreement, noting that although Flightways had been the apparent victim of fraud on the part of Lyle, in view of the circumstance that a corporation reasonably might lease a residence on behalf of a corporate officer, Flightways was in a better position than plaintiff to detect and prevent the fraud. The municipal court entered a judgment in favor of plaintiff in the amount of $22,300 for past due rent and attorney fees. The parties stipulated to the entry of judgment in favor of plaintiff on Flightway's cross-complaint.

The appellate department [of the superior court] affirmed the judgment of the municipal court, concluding that Corporations Code section 313 was dispositive.

The Court of Appeal reversed the judgment, holding that this statute applies only when the signatures of two corporate officers appear on the document, and therefore was inapplicable in the present case.

II

We now determine whether Corporations Code section 313 is applicable in view of the circumstances that Lyle, holding the corporate offices of president, chief financial officer, and secretary, executed the lease agreement purportedly on behalf of Flightways, but expressly identified himself in the agreement solely as its president.

Corporations Code section 313 provides: "[A]ny . . . instrument in writing . . . executed or entered into between any corporation and any other person, *when signed by the chairman of the board, the president or any vice president and the secretary, any assistant secretary, the chief financial officer or any assistant treasurer of such corporation*, is not invalidated as to the corporation by any lack of authority of the signing officers in the absence of actual knowledge on the part of the other person that the signing officers had no authority to execute the same." (Italics added.)[7]

Corporations Code section 313 . . . may be construed to apply when a single individual who holds a corporate office listed in the first series—the chairman of the board, president, or any vice-president—*as well as* an office listed in the second series—the secretary, assistant secretary, chief financial officer, or assistant treasurer—executes the instrument on behalf of the corporation, regardless whether the individual specifies on the instrument itself all of the designated corporate offices he or she holds.

In the alternative, the provision may be interpreted to apply only when *both* an officer listed in the first series *and* an officer listed in the second series execute the agreement *and* name the corporate offices held on the instrument itself, whether the same individual holds both designated corporate offices or different individuals hold the designated corporate offices.

At common law, a corporate officer may have express authority to enter into an agreement on behalf of the corporation, granted by the board of directors or the corporate bylaws. (*Black v. Harrison Home Co.*, 99 P. 494 (Cal. 1909)). In the alternative, a corporate officer may have ostensible authority to enter into an agreement on behalf of the corporation if he or she "assumed and exercised the power in the past" with the apparent consent and acquiescence of the corporation. (*Black v. Harrison Home Co., supra*, 99 P. 494). In this setting, as is the case generally, ostensible authority requires justifiable reliance by a third party. It must be shown that "the business done by the supposed agent, so far as open to the observation of third parties, is consistent with the existence of an agency, and, as to the transaction in question, the third party was justified in believing that an agency existed. [Citation.]" (*County etc. Bk. v. Coast D. & L. Co.*, 115 P.2d 988 (Cal. App. 1941)).

At common law, the party seeking to enforce a contract with a corporation generally has the burden of establishing the contracting officer's authority to bind the corporation.[8]

For the party seeking to establish the validity of a contract at common law, formerly a corporate seal affixed to an agreement, although "not essential to the validity of such contract," provided presumptive evidence that the officer executing

---

7. The use of the plural . . . "signing officers" in the body of the statute, is not controlling. The General Provisions of the Corporations Code include the following . . . : "The singular number includes the plural, and the plural number includes the singular." (*Id.*, §13.)

8. At common law, when the corporate officer's actual authority to execute the agreement has been established or is not in doubt, the circumstance that he or she does not specify the office held does not invalidate the agreement as to the corporation.

the agreement had the requisite authority to bind the corporation. (*City Street Improvement Co. v. Laird,* 70 P. 916 (Cal. 1902)).

That rule eventually was codified. [H]owever, effective January 1, 1977 . . . former section 833, providing that the corporate seal is prima facie evidence of corporate authority, was repealed. The Legislative Committee comment to Corporations Code section 313 states that the purpose of the statute is "to allow third parties to rely upon the assertive authority of various senior executive officers of the corporation concerning the execution of any instrument on behalf of the corporation." (Legis. Com. com., 23E West's Ann. Corp. Code, *supra,* foll. §313, p. 192.) "Such extra protection for third parties who deal with corporations is warranted since corporations necessarily act through agents." (*Taormina Theosophical Community, Inc. v. Silver,* 140 Cal. App. 3d 964, 971 (1983)).

It is apparent that, if its criteria are met, Corporations Code section 313 precludes the invalidation of an instrument entered into by a corporation, *despite* the presentation of evidence demonstrating that the signing officers lacked authority to execute the instrument on its behalf. Thus, the statute provides a conclusive, rather than a merely rebuttable, evidentiary presumption of authority to enter into the agreement on the part of the specified corporate officers.[10]

In addition, Corporations Code section 313 applies so long as the other party does not have *actual knowledge* that the executing officers lack authority. Because the statute applies even when the other party should have, but does not have, actual knowledge of the officers' lack of authority, that party is relieved of the burden of establishing *justifiable* reliance upon the authority of the executing officers.

At the same time, Corporations Code section 313 leaves intact the other party's ability to assert the validity of an instrument under existing common law doctrines when the signatory or signatories do not hold the corporate offices specified in that statute.

Corporations Code section 313 appears designed to establish a level of formality that, if attained because the requisite number and type of officers have executed the subject instrument, affords the third party protection from subsequent efforts by the corporation to disavow its agents' authority in order to avoid its obligations pursuant to the agreement. The Legislature apparently considered that execution of an instrument on behalf of the corporation by two officers—one officer having general, operational responsibilities (i.e., the chairman of the board, president, or any vice-president) and one officer having recordkeeping or financial responsibilities (i.e., the secretary, assistant secretary, chief financial officer, or treasurer)—sufficed for that purpose. Corporations Code section 313 thus creates a "safe harbor" for persons entering into an agreement with a corporation: pursuant to that section, a corporation may not disclaim its authorization of those persons entering into an agreement on its behalf.

The circumstances of the present case compel us to examine next whether that prerequisite is satisfied when an individual who in fact holds at least one of the

---

10. We stress that when Corporations Code section 313 is applicable and the corporation is prevented from seeking to invalidate the agreement by asserting a lack of authority to enter into it on the part of its signing officers, the corporation is not prevented thereby from asserting the invalidity of the agreement on an alternative theory other than lack of authority (e.g., fraud, mistake, failure of consideration).

designated corporate offices from each category executes an instrument but merely lists thereon *one* of his or her offices.

In determining the legislative intent underlying this enactment, "we consider the statute read as a whole, harmonizing the various elements by considering each clause and section in the context of the overall statutory framework." (*People v. Jenkins*, 893 P.2d 1224 (Cal. 1995)). Corporations Code section 312, also enacted during the 1975 revision of the Corporations Code, provides in part: "(a) A corporation shall have a chairman of the board or a president or both, a secretary, a chief financial officer and such other officers with such titles and duties as shall be stated in the bylaws or determined by the board and as may be necessary to enable it to sign instruments and share certificates. The president, or if there is no president the chairman of the board, is the general manager and chief executive officer of the corporation, unless otherwise provided in the articles or bylaws. Any number of offices may be held by the same person unless the articles or bylaws provide otherwise."

Corporations Code section 313 does not contain any language directing that the signing officers be separate individuals, or that the signing officers specify the office or offices they hold. Accordingly, although Corporations Code section 313 applies only where corporate officers in each of the two designated series or categories execute the instrument, that statute, considered in light of Corporations Code section 312, is satisfied when one individual who in fact holds two of the specified corporate offices executes the instrument.[13]

In view of the statutory purpose, context, and derivation of Corporations Code section 313, we believe that the Legislature did not intend to limit the statute's application only to instances in which two corporate offices are set forth on the face of the instrument. Rather, the signature of one person alone is sufficient to bind a corporation, as long as he or she holds corporate offices in each of the two series or categories described in that statute. In the present case, therefore, because Lyle served both as Flightways' president and as its chief financial officer (and secretary), and because plaintiff did not have actual knowledge of any lack of authority on Lyle's part, the lease agreement was not invalidated by Lyle's lack of authority to enter into such an agreement on behalf of Flightways.

The judgment of the Court of Appeal is reversed, and the matter is remanded to the Court of Appeal with directions to affirm the judgment of the municipal court in favor of plaintiff.

313 Not
On exam

13. Our conclusion that Corporations Code section 313 applies when a corporate officer holding at least one of the designated corporate offices in each series or category of offices executes an instrument on behalf of the corporation, even if he or she omits to record thereon both designated offices, also finds support in Corporations Code section 1502. Subdivision (a) of that statute makes a matter of public record the names and addresses of a corporation's chief executive officer, secretary, and chief financial officer, as part of the information required to be filed biennially with the Secretary of State. Although subdivision (g) of section 1502 expressly forbids construction of that statute "to place any person dealing with the corporation on notice of, or under any duty to inquire about, the existence or content of a statement filed pursuant to this section," nonetheless the statute effectively produces public information as to the actual identities of three primary officeholders of a given corporation, and this information may be relied upon by a third party even if a particular agreement does not list all of the offices held by those signing the agreement.

Notes and Questions

1. Notes

a. Neither the DGCL nor the MBCA has a provision analogous to Cal. Corp. Code §313 but many other states do.

b. Every corporation statute requires a corporation to have one officer whose function is to keep the corporate records and, often, to certify that corporate actions (i.e., shareholder actions and board actions) have been taken. DGCL §142(a), MBCA §8.40(c). That officer is usually referred to as the secretary. MBCA §1.40. A moment's reflection will reveal that a consequence of these provisions is to imbue the secretary with important powers of position. Even the most careful outsider is entitled to rely on a corporate secretary's certificate that a particular transaction has been validly authorized or that particular people are authorized to bind the corporation (at least in the absence of information that makes such reliance unwarranted). An extremely careful (or paranoid) outsider can easily ascertain the corporate secretary's identity by checking with the secretary of state; the secretary is typically one of the officers who must be identified each year in the corporation's annual report. Thus a careless or perfidious corporate secretary can render the corporation liable for large unintended obligations. Hence the selection of the corporate secretary is one that should be made carefully.

2. Reality Check

a. What is the current function of the corporate seal? Has that function changed over time?

b. Did Flightways authorize Mr. Lyle to rent the Malibu residence? If not, why is it liable for the rent?

3. Suppose

a. What if Mr. Lyle had signed the lease but indicated no title at all. Would the analysis or result be different? Would it matter whether Mr. Snukal (or his agent) knew of Mr. Lyle's positions with Flightways?

b. Suppose Mr. Lyle had signed the lease but indicated the wrong offices. Would Flightways be liable?

c. Assume Flightways had a corporate seal and that that seal had been affixed to the lease. What additional signatures, if any, would be necessary to bind Flightways to the lease?

4. What Do You Think?

a. Do you think corporation statutes should be prescriptive about the ways in which agreements must be executed to bind a corporation? If so, should those statutes provide a safe harbor or should they be the exclusive method of binding the corporation in writing?

b. Do you believe that principals (including corporations) should ever be liable for their agents' actions unless those actions were authorized by the principal?

5. You Draft It

a. Redraft Cal. Corp. Code §313 so that it clearly supports plaintiff's claim. Then redraft it so it clearly supports Flightways' claim.

[A]ny . . . instrument in writing . . . executed or entered into between any corporation and any other person, when signed by the chairman of the board, the president or any vice president and the secretary, any assistant secretary, the chief financial officer or any assistant treasurer of such corporation, is not invalidated as to the corporation by any lack of authority of the signing officers in the absence of actual knowledge on the part of the other person that the signing officers had no authority to execute the same.

b. Background and Context

The extent of the powers of agents of a well-defined class, such as presidents, directors, or cashiers, is determined largely by general custom, of which the courts will take judicial notice; and parties dealing with such agents are entitled to assume that they possess all the powers which are usually accorded to agents of the class to which they belong.

1 Victor Morawetz, *A Treatise on the Law of Private Corporations* §509 (2d ed., 1886)

Normally, the president is merely the presiding officer of the board of directors; the secretary is a ministerial officer charged with the duty of preparing and keeping the corporate records and with the custody of the corporate seal, if there be one; the treasurer is a fiscal agent whose duties are to receive, disburse, and account for the corporate moneys. It is not unusual to-day to find that the function of presiding over the board of directors is conferred upon a chairman of the board, while the functions of an executive business manager are conferred upon a president.

Robert S. Stevens, *Handbook on the Law of Private Corporations* §§159-160 (1936)

Notes and Questions

1. Reality Check

a. Have officers been given greater or lesser powers since Morawetz wrote?

2. Suppose

a. Suppose the *Snukal* case had been heard by Morawetz. Would his analysis and result have been the same as Chief Justice George's?

C. FEDERAL SECURITIES REGULATION

Speaking broadly, federal securities laws are designed to protect public company investors primarily by requiring disclosure, rather than by mandating substantive governance rules. Those laws are not intended to displace the traditional role of state corporate law in regulating the internal governance of corporations. Nonetheless, as early as 1934 the SEC was given rather broad powers to regulate the process of obtaining proxies in connection with corporate elections. In the 1970s, and again at the turn of the century, federal regulation of corporate governance, specifically, regulation of boards, increased.

This increase has been effected in two main ways. First, the SEC has used its power to compel disclosure to coerce corporations to adopt desired board structures. For example, the SEC requires public corporations to disclose "whether" the members of the nominating committee are independent of corporate management. Public companies do not wish to say that they do not have structures the SEC deems salutary so, as a practical matter, public companies have only independent directors on their nominating committee. The second device used to impose federal governance ideas on corporations is through the stock exchanges. Although the exchanges, such as the New York Stock Exchange and the National Association of Securities Dealers are private organizations, Congress has placed the SEC in a supervisory role over them. Not only must the SEC approve any rule change, but the SEC can require the exchanges to adopt any rule the SEC believes appropriate. Thus the SEC has used its powers to persuade the stock exchanges to amend their *listing requirements* (i.e., the standards corporations must follow if they want their shares traded on the exchange) to require various corporate governance features. The Sarbanes-Oxley Act of 2002, which was enacted in response to the Enron and WorldCom scandals, gave added impetus to the SEC to impose substantive governance requirements on public companies.

The stock exchanges require that boards have a majority of members who are independent of the company's management and that regular meetings of the nonmanagement directors are held. They also require companies to have audit, compensation, and nominating/corporate governance committees, each of which must be composed only of directors independent of management. The reforms in Sarbanes-Oxley and its aftermath have affected corporate board membership and power principally as they relate to the audit committee.

D. TERMS OF ART IN THIS CHAPTER

Amotion	Holdover	Regular meetings
Board of directors	Notice	Special meetings
Call	Officer	Staggered terms
Classified board	Quorum	

10

Restrictions on the Board's Power

We saw in the last chapter that all corporate power is ultimately in the hands of the board of directors. *See* DGCL §141(a), MBCA §8.01(b). This chapter and the three that follow it now take up the question of the limits of that power. Chapters 11 and 12 focus on what are usually called *director fiduciary duties.* As you may intuit from the number of pages devoted to that subject, fiduciary duties comprise and compose a rather elaborate system that restrains directors' actions. That system is largely immediate and inward looking. It prescribes and evaluates director action primarily by reference to standards that link the director to the corporation and its shareholders. By contrast, the restrictions in this chapter are more mediated and outward looking. They derive from the relationship between the corporation and the state. The restrictions here are most directly ones that limit *corporate* rather than *board* action. The board is indirectly restrained because it cannot legally cause the corporation to take certain actions. The final chapter in this unit, Chapter 13, asks you to assess the efficacy of the restrictions in this chapter and in the fiduciary duties chapters.

This chapter begins by considering legislation that cabins corporate, and by extension, board, actions. We next look briefly at a common law restriction, ultra vires, that has some theoretical but not much practical interest. Finally, we examine restrictions that flow from perhaps the most conceptual aspect of corporate law: Why do corporations exist?

A. LEGISLATION THAT RESTRICTS BOARD POWER

Legal rules typically apply to natural persons as well as artificial entities. The law of contracts, torts, and property, for example, do not typically distinguish between humans and corporations. In some cases, such as taxation, somewhat different rules apply to business entities than apply to natural persons, but on the whole such systems regulate both people and entities alike.

In many instances entities will be more likely to be affected because the regulated activities are undertaken by businesses, most of which are owned by entities rather than by a single individual. Environmental regulations, occupational health and safety (OSHA) requirements, the antitrust laws, and the securities laws are instances of regulatory schemes that primarily restrict business entities rather than individuals. Since business entities can act only via humans, the principles of agency law (Chapter 4) loom large here. Some regulatory schemes, most notably federal environmental regulations (CERCLA) explicitly impose duties and liabilities upon individuals acting on behalf of entities.

All of these restrictions on corporate actions have the obvious effect of restraining board power. We could explore all of them here but that would subsume the entire law school curriculum in this one course; we've got to leave something for you to do in your other courses. We will, though, explore one regulatory area that explicitly, though indirectly, regulates business entities. That area is the Federal Sentencing Guidelines.

When a business entity has committed a federal crime, the Federal Sentencing Guidelines provide a matrix for determining the punishment. Important practical constraints on the entity's response to its discovery that it may have committed a federal crime are imbedded in the Guidelines' matrix. The Guidelines provide that an entity's punishment be, in large part, a function of its "culpability score." That score is adjusted upward or downward by various factors, some of which are entity actions.

The Guidelines include a strong incentive to report possible criminal activity and to cooperate with the government, including providing information about the roles of corporate employees and other agents. The Guidelines provide a reduction in the culpability score,

> If the organization (A) prior to an imminent threat of disclosure or government investigation; and (B) within a reasonably prompt time after becoming aware of the offense, reported the offense to appropriate governmental authorities, fully cooperated in the investigation, and clearly demonstrated recognition and affirmative acceptance of responsibility for its criminal conduct. . . .

U.S. Sentencing Commission, Guidelines Manual §8C2.5(g)(1) (Nov. 2017)

The Application Notes to the Guidelines flesh out the requirements for an entity to obtain a reduction in its culpability score:

> [C]ooperation must be both timely and thorough. To be timely, the cooperation must begin essentially at the same time as the organization is officially notified of a criminal investigation. To be thorough, the cooperation should include the disclosure of all pertinent information known by the organization. A prime test of whether the organization has disclosed all pertinent information is whether the information is sufficient for law enforcement personnel to identify the nature and extent of the offense and the individual(s) responsible for the criminal conduct.

U.S. Sentencing Commission, Guidelines Manual §8C2.5(g)(1) (Application Note 13) (Nov. 2017)

B. ULTRA VIRES AND WASTE

The second restriction on board power is of interest to us primarily because of what it might have been and, perhaps, may be. From the late nineteenth century, corporation statutes required the articles to state the purpose for which the corporation was formed and a common law rule quickly arose that a corporation could be formed for a single purpose only.

Over time, of course, corporate drafters pushed the limits of these restrictions and by the 1930s Articles of Incorporation with purpose clauses running to many pages were quite common. Finally, in the 1950s and 1960s, state legislatures realized that the point of the specific purpose clause had been defeated and amended their corporation statutes to permit all purpose clauses. *See* DGCL §§101(b), 102(a)(3), MBCA §3.01(a). *Compare* MBCA §2.02(b)(2)(i).

During the time when specific purpose clauses were required, the doctrine of *ultra vires* arose and had some potency. The intention of the ultra vires doctrine was to create an avenue to enforce the specific purpose clauses by granting relief when a corporation took actions that were not related to its purposes (i.e., which were beyond—*ultra*—its powers—*vires*). In this way the ultra vires doctrine was a real constraint on board power.

The doctrine was never clear or unified throughout the United States. Its uncertainty was captured by one corporate law commentator,

> In a sense, "ultra vires" was to corporate law what "res gestae" was to the law of hearsay—a concept of uncertain meaning and scope, deplored by academicians and a *bête noire* of law students. Its application was riddled with exceptions and exceptions to exceptions to such an extent that its proper use and impact, if any, was difficult to predict. Nonetheless, during the formative years of corporation law in the 19th and early 20th centuries, the ultra vires doctrine was an oft-recurring theme in litigation seeking to enforce or avoid corporate contractual obligations, leading to much confusion and patently inequitable results.

David A. Drexler, Lewis S. Black, Jr., & A. Gilchrist Sparks, *Delaware Corporation Law and Practice* **§11.05 (2000)**

The main reason for the decline of ultra vires was the demise of the limited purpose clause. Once corporations could be incorporated for any lawful business, nearly nothing could be ultra vires in the precise sense. About the only act that is beyond the power of a corporation (excluding illegal acts, of course) is waste. That is,

> [A]n exchange of corporate assets for consideration so disproportionately small as to lie beyond the range at which any reasonable person might be willing to trade] Most often the claim is associated with a transfer of corporate assets that serves [no corporate purpose] or for which [no consideration at all is received.] Such a transfer is in effect a gift. If, however, there is *any substantial* consideration received by the corporation, and if there is a *good faith judgment* that in the circumstances the transaction is worthwhile, there should be no finding of waste, even if the fact finder would conclude *ex post* that the transaction was unreasonably risky.

[definition of waste]

Lewis v. Vogelstein, **699 A.2d 327, 336 (Del. Ch. 1997) (Allen, Ch.)**

Today, ultra vires is sometimes used to describe corporate actions that are permissible but that have not been properly authorized by the board. This distinction between actions that the corporation cannot take (i.e., pure ultra vires) and those that it could take were they to be properly approved retains some currency in corporate law. Professor Harwell Wells describes the development and function of ultra vires and waste.

Harwell Wells, *The Life (and Death?) of Corporate Waste*

74 Wash. & Lee L. Rev. 1239 (2017)

At first glance, corporate waste makes no sense. The classic definition of waste . . . suggests that waste should never arise, for what corporation would ever enter into a transaction so absurd? Yet waste claims are regularly made. The conventional wisdom is that waste claims never succeed; but empirical studies show that at some stages of litigation they do, and some of the most significant corporate law cases of the last decade have dealt with corporate waste. Respected judges have called for sharply limiting it, referring to it as a "vestige" and deriding it as the mythical "Loch Ness Monster" of corporate law; still, waste survives. It is a remnant of ultra vires, a doctrine proclaimed dead for the last hundred years—but waste is not dead. It confounds our model of managerial responsibility; after decades in which discussion of directors' and officers' duties have focused on the fiduciary duties of care and loyalty, waste still sits outside that framework, for waste until now has not been seen as an aspect of fiduciary duties at all.

Waste has its roots in ultra vires, the doctrine flourishing in the nineteenth century, which held that directors had no power to "perform [] acts outside the corporation's authority" as spelled out in its charter or general law. Ultra vires embodied the nineteenth century's belief that the corporation was a creation of the state, possessing only such powers provided by the state in its charter, and constantly threatening to exceed its bounds. Ultra vires acts were those "not merely irregular in form or done by unauthorized organs, but acts which the corporation could not legally do in any manner without having first changed its constitution." While ultra vires's main justification was in protecting society from corporations' potentially overweening power, it also served to protect shareholders from corporate controllers' departure from the corporation's limited scope. In an era lacking many modern checks on managerial discretion such as mandatory disclosure or efficient capital markets, ultra vires was another means to discipline agents and, together with the fiduciary constraints on negligence, fraud, and self-dealing, was a major guarantor of faithful corporate governance.

Ultra vires was an often-litigated and befuddling topic; according to one authority, there was "perhaps no part of the law concerning corporations in which we meet with so much difficulty, confusion, and conflict of opinion." During the doctrine's heyday, when corporations had narrow and specific purposes, courts frequently found themselves finely parsing charter provisions to determine whether the power to perform a particular act could be discerned in a corporation's enumerated purposes; cases examined whether, for instance, a railroad company could pay for improvements on a resort hotel located on the railroad's line, or whether a company chartered to manufacture musical instruments could guarantee the expenses of a musical festival that would increase the manufacturer's sales. [In both cases the court held the corporate acts ultra vires. ED.]

By early in the twentieth century, however, Americans were becoming more comfortable with corporations, coming to view them not as threatening monoliths wielding special powers but as merely another form in which to conduct business. By the 1920s ultra vires mostly lingered as a dubious mechanism by which some corporations attempted to "evade liability upon an irksome contract, by showing [their] incapacity to make the contract."

By the 1920s, ultra vires had almost completely disappeared, along with rigid corporate codes and narrow corporate purpose provisions in corporate charters. Fiduciary duties still functioned to limit managerial malfeasance, but they were most effective at blocking self-dealing. Other familiar tools for checking managers and protecting shareholders, such as the market for corporate control and robust disclosure requirements, did not yet exist to any great degree. Managerial power and overreach enabled by increasingly dispersed shareholding were, however, becoming public issues. . . . The Great Depression only heightened hostility to corporations and corporate management. Given all this, we should not be surprised that in the 1930s courts were motivated to seek additional tools to police corporate activity, and to find in waste a "fail-safe doctrine[] to enable courts to review director conduct that seem[ed] to satisfy traditional standards used to test director behavior, but where the decision simply [didn't] make sense."

From the 1960s into the 1980s, waste as a doctrine was at a low ebb. It was also at this time that statutory reforms swept away what little was left of ultra vires. In 1950, the Model Business Corporation Act (MBCA) eliminated ultra vires claims except in very limited circumstances, making plain what had already occurred in judicial decisions. In 1967, Delaware followed suit in the revised Delaware General Corporation Law (DGCL), "severely constrict[ing] the categories of claimants who [could] raise the ultra vires defense." These changes illuminate not only the dwindling of ultra vires, but how waste had become detached from its predecessor.

Waste claims had at least one troublesome aspect, though, that made the doctrine difficult to completely ignore: they could be tough to get rid of, at least in Delaware – home of the majority of the nation's giant corporations. At first glance, they should not have been. Waste claims were on their face implausible (a transaction no rational business person would make, at least absent fiduciary duty violations?), and no court after mid-century found a transaction wasteful in a final judgment. But unlike with some fiduciary duty claims, there was no straightforward procedure to eliminate a waste claim – in particular, mere majority ratification by shareholders did not immediately extinguish a waste claim, a rule best explained as a survival of the principle that void acts such as ultra vires could only be ratified by unanimous shareholder vote.

Nor was it always easy for courts to dismiss waste claims in the early stages of litigation. Most notably, waste claims survived summary judgment motions more often than one would expect, in good part due to their fact-specific nature.

[B]y the 1990s Delaware's courts were criticizing the doctrine, perhaps . . . because of the difficulty of harmonizing the waste doctrine with Delaware's fiduciary framework. Whatever the reason, by the mid-1990s Delaware's courts were expressing frustration with waste's persistence and even doubts about its existence.

The capstone to the Delaware courts' increasingly skeptical approach to waste was 1999's *Harbor Finance Partners v. Huizenga*, [751 A.2d 879 (Del. Ch. 1999)] in which stockholder plaintiffs challenged a merger. Then Vice-Chancellor Strine's opinion posed a question, which must have occurred to many thoughtful observers: why could a waste claim not be extinguished by ratification from a majority of informed disinterested shareholders? Shouldn't such ratification by definition signal that this was a transaction on which reasonable businesspersons could differ, and so not meet the test for waste? While the rule not permitting shareholder ratification was a "seemingly sensible doctrine," he wrote, its "actual application has no apparent modern day utility . . . except as an opportunity for Delaware courts to second-guess stockholders." Transactions attacked as waste in Delaware courts were typically "garden variety transactions that may be validly accomplished by a Delaware corporation if supported by sufficient consideration," ranging from stock option plans to corporate mergers. Waste did not, in his account, protect stockholders where there had been ratification. If "fully informed, uncoerced, independent stockholders have approved the transaction, they have, it seems to me, made the decision that the transaction is a 'fair exchange.'" In closing, while the opinion acknowledged that there may be "valid reasons for [waste's] continuation," it called for those reasons to be "articulated and weighed against the costs the vestige imposes on stockholders and the judicial system. Otherwise, inertia alone may perpetuate an outdated rule fashioned in a very different time." Though none of these cases called for waste's complete abolition, each expressed deep doubts about waste as presently constituted. An observer in 1999 would have been entirely justified in assuming the doctrine was about to be further marginalized. That observer would have been wrong.

While waste came under fire in the 1990s, its utility in corporate law had not completely disappeared. . . . The role it would play was summed up in *Sample v. Morgan*, [914 A.2s 647 (Del. Ch. 2007)] a case where shareholders challenged a stock incentive plan that provided three corporate insiders with a significant ownership stake in their firm in exchange for $200. "When pled facts support an inference of waste," the opinion explained, "judicial nostrils smell something fishy and full discovery into the background of the transaction is permitted. In the end, most transactions that actually involve waste are almost found to have been inspired by some form of conflicting self-interest." Waste "allows a plaintiff to pass go at the complaint stage even when the motivations for a transaction are unclear by pointing to economic terms so one-sided as to create an inference that no person acting in good faith pursuit of the corporation's interests could have approved the terms." The opinion then articulated waste's role as a safety valve allowing further scrutiny of transactions that were not on their surface fiduciary duty violations, but were inexplicable otherwise.

* * *

Beginning in the 1930s, state legislatures passed statutes to limit the reach of ultra vires both to curb the perceived abuses and in recognition that the doctrine's ambit was effectively reduced by all purpose clauses. Today, such statutes limit ultra vires to three settings. First, the statutes retain the rule that a shareholder may sue to enjoin executory ultra vires actions. Second, a director, officer, employee, or agent can be held personally liable for causing the corporation to engage in an ultra vires action. Third, and doubtless the most rare setting, permits the state attorney general to sue to enjoin corporations from acting ultra vires. See DGCL §124, MBCA §3.04.

Notes and Questions

1. Notes

a. One of the most chronic ultra vires and waste problems was whether a corporation could make a charitable donation. The theory was that a donation was waste because the corporation received no benefit. Because the donation was waste, it was ultra vires. To the extent the donation could be linked to any long-term corporate benefit, however mild or indirect, courts tended to uphold the action. This linkage was almost always possible for corporations that dealt in any way with the public. Corporations that dealt only with other businesses or that were holding companies (i.e., corporations engaged in the business of owning stock in other companies) had a more difficult conceptual time. Beginning in the 1940s, Delaware and other states passed statutes specifically empowering corporations to make charitable donations. See DGCL §122(9), MBCA §3.02(m).

b. Many corporations statutes, including the DGCL and MBCA, grant specific powers to corporations in addition to a general grant of power. These specific grants are nearly always artifacts of distant case law that prohibited or at least called into question a corporation's power to take certain actions. Look at DGCL §122 and MBCA §3.02 and imagine why a corporation would be denied the powers explicitly granted.

2. Reality Check

a. What are the various ways in which the phrase *ultra vires* is used in corporate law?

b. How is the ultra vires doctrine related to the doctrine of waste?

c. Why did the ultra vires doctrine cease to have practical importance?

3. What Do You Think?

a. Do you think the revival of ultra vires would, as a practical matter, constrain boards? If so, is that a good thing?

b. Do you think corporations should be required to state express, limited purposes in their articles of incorporation?

c. Should a corporation's board of directors be able to change the corporation's line of business without shareholder approval? Does your answer depend upon whether the corporation is closely held or public?

d. Should corporations be able to take any action an individual can lawfully take?

e. As you think about these questions, consider this development:

> Intriguingly, it may be that restrictive purpose clauses are making a comeback in limited liability companies, leading one to wonder whether litigation over LLC purpose can be far behind. See Suren Gomtsian, Contractual Mechanisms of Investor Protection in Non-Listed Limited Liability Companies, 60 VILL. L. REV. 955, 984 (2016) (stating that these company-purpose limitation clauses were used to reduce the discretion of the management); Peter Molk, How Do LLC Owners Contract Around Default Statutory Provisions?, 42 J. CORP. L.

(forthcoming 2017) (discussing how LLCs maneuver around default provisions through operating agreements). My thanks to Professor Mohsen Manesh for this information.

Harwell Wells, *The Life (and Death?) of Corporate Waste*, 74 WASH. & LEE L. REV. 1239, 1249 n.53 (2017).

4. You Draft It

a. Draft a statute that does not permit every corporation to engage in any lawful business but does not unduly inhibit any corporation from engaging in an appropriate variety of businesses.

DGCL §102. CONTENTS OF CERTIFICATE OF INCORPORATION

(a) The certificate of incorporation shall set forth:

. . .

(3) The nature of the business or purposes to be conducted or promoted. It shall be sufficient to state, either alone or with other businesses or purposes, that the purpose of the corporation is to engage in any lawful act or activity for which corporations may be organized under the General Corporation Law of Delaware, and by such statement all lawful acts and activities shall be within the purposes of the corporation, except for express limitations, if any . . .

MBCA §3.01. PURPOSES

(a) Every corporation incorporated under this Act has the purpose of engaging in any lawful business unless a more limited purpose is set forth in the articles of incorporation.

b. Draft a statute that appropriately constrains the common law ultra vires doctrine.

DGCL §124. EFFECT OF LACK OF CORPORATE CAPACITY OR POWER; ULTRA VIRES

No act of a corporation and no conveyance or transfer of real or personal property to or by a corporation shall be invalid by reason of the fact that the corporation was without capacity or power to do such act or to make or receive such conveyance or transfer, but such lack of capacity or power may be asserted:

(1) In a proceeding by a stockholder against the corporation to enjoin the doing of any act or acts or the transfer of real or personal property by or to the corporation. If the unauthorized acts or transfer sought to be enjoined are being, or are to be, performed or made pursuant to any contract to which the corporation is a party, the court may, if all of the parties to the contract are parties to the proceeding and if it deems the same to be equitable, set aside and enjoin the performance of such contract, and in so doing may allow to the corporation or to the other parties to the contract, as the case may be, such compensation as may be equitable for the loss or damage sustained by any of them which may result from the action of the court in setting aside and enjoining the performance of such contract, but anticipated profits to be derived from the performance of the contract shall not be awarded by the court as a loss or damage sustained;

(2) In a proceeding by the corporation, whether acting directly or through a receiver, trustee or other legal representative, or through stockholders in a representative suit, against an incumbent or former officer or director of the corporation, for loss or damage due to such incumbent or former officer's or director's unauthorized act;

(3) In a proceeding by the Attorney General to dissolve the corporation, or to enjoin the corporation from the transaction of unauthorized business.

MBCA §3.04. LACK OF POWER TO ACT

(a) Except as provided in subsection (b), the validity of corporate action may not be challenged on the ground that the corporation lacks or lacked power to act.

(b) A corporation's power to act may be challenged:

(1) in a proceeding by a shareholder against the corporation to enjoin the act;

(2) in a proceeding by the corporation, directly, derivatively, or through a receiver, trustee, or other legal representative, against an incumbent or former director, officer, employee, or agent of the corporation; or

(3) in a proceeding by the attorney general under section 14.30.

(c) In a shareholder's proceeding under subsection (b)(1) to enjoin an unauthorized corporate act, the court may enjoin or set aside the act, if equitable and if all affected persons are parties to the proceeding, and may award damages for loss (other than anticipated profits) suffered by the corporation or another party because of enjoining the unauthorized act.

C. ULTIMATE BENEFICIARIES

Our final constraint on board power is a highly conceptual and philosophical one yet one that is of immense practical importance. Simply put, corporations must be operated for the benefit of some group. Boards of directors and other corporate managers should be prevented from taking actions that deviate from that end. Potentially, identifying the ultimate beneficiaries is a powerful constraint on board actions.

Chancellor Allen describes the philosophical contours of this question.

1. The Current Setting

William T. Allen, *Our Schizophrenic Conception of the Business Corporation*
14 Cardozo L. Rev. 261, 262-277, 279-281 (1992)

I want to discuss this most basic question: What is a corporation?—Two inconsistent conceptions have dominated our thinking about corporations since the evolution of the large integrated business corporation in the late nineteenth century. Each conception could claim dominance for a particular period, or among one group or another, but neither has so commanded agreement as to exclude the other from the discourses of law or the thinking of business people.

At least by the mid-nineteenth century, when the movement to enact general laws of incorporation had become firmly planted, the corporation was seen in this country as an artificial creation of the state designed to enable individuals to associate together for state approved purposes. The emphasis was on the individuals—the shareholders who had been constituted a corporation.

The dominant perception was that the corporation, while an artificial entity, was essentially the stockholders in a special form. This perception colored the way in which the role and power of the board of directors was seen. Directors were seen as agents of stockholders.

Thus, if towards the close of the [nineteenth] century one would have asked to whom directors owe a duty of loyalty, a confident answer could have been expected: The corporation . . . is . . . the property of the shareholders. The directors are elected by shareholders and it is unquestionably on their behalf that the directors are bound to act. This view, with its genesis in the mid-nineteenth century, was plainly expressed in the law and, I suppose, was the view held beyond the legal community as well.

In this conception, [t]he rights of creditors, employees and others are strictly limited to statutory, contractual, and common law rights. Once the directors have satisfied those legal obligations, they have fully satisfied all claims of these "constituencies." This property view of the nature of corporations, and of the duties owed by directors, equates the duty of directors with the duty to maximize profits of the firm for the benefit of shareholders.

This model of the public corporation is highly coherent and offers several alternative arguments to support the legitimacy of corporate power in our democracy. The first argument in favor of the property concept is political and normative. It is premised on the conclusionary notion that shareholders "own" the corporation, and asserts that to admit the propriety of non-profit maximizing behavior is to approve agents spending other people's money in pursuit of their own, perhaps eccentric, views of the public good. This can be seen as morally wrong without more. On a broader level, proponents of this view assert that it is repugnant to our democratic ideals to have corporate oligarchies determining which of many competing claimants for financial support should be awarded that support.

The second rationale for the property model is that the model, and action consistent with it, maximize wealth creation. This rationale asserts that the purpose of business corporations is the creation of wealth, nothing else. It asserts that business corporations are not formed to assist in self-realization through social interaction; they are not formed to create jobs or to provide tax revenues; they are not formed to endow university departments or to pursue knowledge. All of these other things—job creation, tax payments, research, and social interaction—desirable as they may be, are said to be side effects of the pursuit of profit for the residual owners of the firm.

This argument asserts that the creation of more wealth should always be the corporation's objective, regardless of who benefits. The sovereign's taxing and regulatory power can then address questions of social costs and re-distribution of wealth. Thus, profit maximizing behavior is seen as affording the best opportunity to satisfy human wants and is the most appropriate aim of corporation law policy. This second argument for the legitimacy of the corporation as shareholder property is not premised on the conclusion that shareholders do "own" the corporation in any ultimate sense, only on the premise that it can be better for all of us if we act as if they do.

The property conception of the corporation was the conception generally held during the nineteenth century and . . . in the early part of this century as well. But, the last quarter of the nineteenth century saw the emergence of social forces that would oppose the conception of business corporations as simply the property of contracting stockholders. The scale and scope of modern integrated business enterprise that emerged in the late nineteenth century required distinctive professional management skills and huge capital investments that often necessitated risk sharing through dispersed stock ownership. National securities markets emerged and stockholders gradually came to look less like flesh and blood owners and more like investors who could slip in or out of a particular stock almost costlessly. These new giant business corporations came to seem to some people like independent entities, with purposes, duties, and loyalties of their own; purposes that might diverge in some respect from shareholder wealth maximization.

This social entity conception sees the purpose of the corporation as not individual but social. Surely contributors of capital (stockholders and bondholders) must be assured a rate of return sufficient to induce them to contribute their capital to the enterprise. But the corporation has other purposes of perhaps equal dignity: the satisfaction of consumer wants, the provision of meaningful employment opportunities, and the making of a contribution to the public life of its communities. Resolving the often conflicting claims of these various corporate constituencies calls for judgment, indeed calls for wisdom, by the board of directors of the corporation. But in this view no single constituency's interest may significantly exclude others from fair consideration by the board. This view appears to have been the dominant view among business leaders for at least the last fifty years.

One would think that whether the corporation law endorses the property conception or the social entity conception would have important consequences. Our experience in the 1980s demonstrated that it could. But equally as interesting as that 1980s conflict is the fact that for the fifty years preceding that contentious decade, we did not share agreement on the legal nature of the public business corporation and that failure did not seem especially problematic.

The law "papered over" the conflict in our conception of the corporation by invoking a murky distinction between long-term profit maximization and short-term profit maximization. Corporate expenditures which at first blush did not seem to be profit maximizing, could be squared with the property conception of the corporation by recognizing that they might redound to the long-term benefit of the corporation and its shareholders. Thus, without purporting to abandon the idea that directors ultimately owe loyalty only to stockholders and their financial interests, the law was able to approve reasonable corporate expenditures for charitable or social welfare purposes or other actions that did not maximize current profit.

There is a utility in this long-term/short-term device. But corporate directors are also afforded very considerable latitude to deal with all groups or institutions having an interest in, or who are affected by, the corporation.

Thus, while early on much ink was spilled on the question to whom should directors be responsible, in practice the question of the nature of the corporation seemed essentially unproblematic until the emergence of the cash tender offer of the 1980s. The long-term/short-term distinction proved a serviceable, if an intellectually problematic way, for the corporation law to avoid choosing between the alpha of property and the omega of relationships.

[T]he takeover movement [of the 1980s] put so much at stake. The issue was frequently whether all of the shareholders would be permitted to sell their shares;

whether a change in corporate control would occur; and often whether a radical restructuring of the enterprise would go forward, with dramatic effects on creditors, employees, management, suppliers, and communities.

The effects of a takeover were seen by those affected as a form of shareholder exploitation of others who had made contributions of various sorts to the corporation. In the financial setting of the 1980s, dramatically higher stock prices could often be achieved by sharply increasing the debt of the corporation and reducing or eliminating certain operations. But increasing debt substantially made the enterprise riskier and thus reduced the value of the corporation's existing bonds; and restricting operations injured workers and management, who were thrown out of work. The bondholders and employees felt that radical corporate changes made in order to increase share value breached implicit understandings that had been the basis of their participation in the organization, or so one argument went. Thus, the scale of the problems raised by the takeover movement made evasion of the fundamental question of corporate definition difficult.

Courts were not anxious to grapple with this question. To resolve the matter seemed plainly to call for the making of policy in an environment that was warmly contested by powerful interests and in which no widely accepted doctrine offered a clear guide. Nevertheless, ultimately both our courts and, more importantly, our legislatures have, in effect, endorsed the entity view.

The entity conception was . . . clearly endorsed by the law in a remarkable series of legislative acts adopted in some twenty-eight jurisdictions over the course of the last few years of the 1980s. These so-called constituency statutes differ from each other in a number of particulars but they share the same soul. In one way or another each of them authorizes a board of directors to consider the interest of all corporate "stakeholders" when the board exercises corporate power. These statutes seem plainly to be animated by a social entity conception of the corporation.

Thus, under them, a central notion of corporation law as it has developed over the last 150 years—that the law ought to try to align directors' action with shareholder interests by imposition of fiduciary duties—is arguably eviscerated. Surely, stealing is still proscribed and self-dealing transactions still have to be justified as fair to the corporation, but what arguably is eradicated is the command—which while equivocal in practice under the prior regime still demanded respect—that maximizing the financial interests of shareholders through lawful means over some time period is the core duty of a corporate director.

The enactment of the stakeholder statutes . . . came just at the end of the "deal decade," and with those developments the schizophrenia that had long existed in our thinking about corporations was arguably resolved. But was it?

The law, like ourselves, is always in flux, always "becoming." The concept of the corporation is such a structure. [T]he ever-emergent quality of law suggests that the resolution of the conceptual conflict that was reached in the late 1980s by the endorsement of the entity concept, will not be a final answer to the question, what is a corporation.

We cannot of course know the future, but we can see the future stresses that the entity conception of the public corporation will generate. The entity conception inevitably will give rise to claims of inefficiency and illegitimacy; and those are claims that the blunt instruments of stakeholder statutes can neither answer nor suppress.

I suppose that there will be no final move in defining the nature or the purpose of the business corporation. It is perhaps asking too much to expect us, as a people—or our law—to have a single view of the purpose of an institution so large, pervasive, and important as our public corporations. These entities are too important to generate that sort of agreement. Within them exists the tension that a dynamic market system creates between the desire to achieve increases in total wealth and the desire to avoid the losses and injuries—the redistribution—that a dynamic system inevitably engenders.

Thus I conclude that we have been schizophrenic on the nature of the corporation, but as a society we will probably always be so to some extent. The questions "What is a corporation?" and "For whose benefit do directors hold power?" are legal questions only in the sense that legal institutions will be required at certain points to formulate or assume answers to them. But they are not simply technical questions of law capable of resolution through analytical rule manipulation. Even less are they technical questions of finance or economics. Rather in defining what we suppose a public corporation to be, we implicitly express our view of the nature and purpose of our social life. Since we do disagree on that, our law of corporate entities is bound itself to be contentious and controversial. It will be worked out, not deduced. In this process, efficiency concerns, ideology, and interest group politics will commingle with history (including our semi-autonomous corporation law) to produce an answer that will hold for here and now, only to be torn by some future stress and to be reformulated once more. And so on, and so on, evermore.

Notes and Questions

1. Reality Check

a. Why is our conception of the corporation schizophrenic?
b. What are the different conceptions of the corporation?
c. What are the arguments for and against each conception?
d. Why are those conceptions inconsistent?
e. Why does our conception of a corporation matter?

2. What Do You Think?

a. Chancellor Allen says, "It is perhaps asking too much to expect us, as a people—or our law—to have a single view of the purpose of an institution so large, pervasive, and important as our public corporations. These entities are too important to generate that sort of agreement." Do you agree?

b. Is Chancellor Allen's "second rationale for the property model" really a rationale for managing in the shareholders' interest?

c. Which conception of the corporation is more accurate?

Chancellor Allen's description may seem a bit abstract. Chancellor Strine, another Delaware chancellor, makes his point more forcefully.

Leo E. Strine, Jr., *Our Continuing Struggle with the Idea that For-Profit Corporations Seek Profit*

47 Wake Forest L. Rev. 135 (2012)

This Essay addresses an issue that, to be candid, perplexes me. That issue is the continuing dismay evidenced in Western, capitalist nations when public corporations that pursue profit for their stockholders take actions that adversely affect the nation's economic stability, the corporation's employees, or the environment.

When a corporation's ardor for profits leads it to take excessive risks that endanger the firm's solvency, commentators react with shock and dismay. How can corporate managers be so blinded by the immediate prospect of profit that they would ignore what, in hindsight, seem like such obvious risks? Likewise, we rent our garments in anger and chagrin when energy companies take environmental short-cuts in drilling for oil or mining coal, surprised that profit-maximizing firms have been less than optimally protective of the environment and their workers, that they did not go beyond what was simply necessary to ensure that regulators allowed them to operate.

Although I am sympathetic to many of the sentiments and policy concerns that motivate these dismayed reactions, I confess to being weary of the naïveté they manifest. More importantly, the continued failure of our societies to be clear-eyed about the role of the for-profit corporation endangers the public interest. Instead of recognizing that for-profit corporations will seek profit for their stockholders using all legal means available, we imbue these corporations with a personality and assume they are moral beings capable of being "better" in the long-run than the lowest common denominator. We act as if entities in which only capital has a vote will somehow be able to deny the stockholders their desires, when a choice has to be made between profit for those who control the board's reelection prospects and positive outcomes for the employees and communities who do not.

For now, however, the important lesson is simple. For-profit businesses have incentives toward current profit-maximization that make them poorly positioned to evaluate risk and be safe regulators. The environmental wreckage in the Gulf of Mexico and the global human wreckage caused by the financial sector's imprudence should be rather plain evidence of that truth.

Another enduring myth is that there exist "special" for-profit corporations, ones that will behave differently from others over the long-run because they are controlled by visionaries who will place some idea of the public good ahead of profit. In saying this is a myth, I don't mean to imply that there are not very talented entrepreneurs who figure out how to do well by doing good. There are, thankfully, a number of businesses that do pay good wages, provide safe working environments and livable weekly hours, treat the environment with respect, and play the competitive game fairly. Instead, my point is that managers in stockholder-financed corporations are inevitably answerable to the stockholders, whatever the "community values" articulated by the corporation's founders or others, which is why regulations designed to protect against the externality risks inherent in profit-seeking are critical.

Ultimately, any for-profit corporation that sells shares to others has to be accountable to its stockholders for delivering a financial return. This is not a new notion.

The whole design of corporate law in the United States is built around the relationship between corporate managers and stockholders, not relationships with other constituencies. In the corporate republic, only stockholders get to vote and only stockholders get to sue to enforce directors' fiduciary duties. The natural focus of the managers in such a system is therefore supposed to be on advancing the best interests of the stockholders, subject to the legal constraints within which the firm operates. Precisely because it is ultimately the equity market that is the primary accountability system for public firms, efforts to tinker around with the margins of corporate law through initiatives like constituency statutes, the so-called Corporate Social Responsibility movement, and antitakeover provisions have been of very little utility in insulating corporate boards from stockholder and stock market pressures.

The public interest, in the end, depends on protection by the public's elected representatives in the form of law. The well-intentioned efforts of many entrepreneurs and company managers, who have a duty to their investors to deliver a profit, to be responsible employers and corporate citizens is undoubtedly socially valuable. But it is no adequate substitute for a sound legally determined baseline.

By so stating, I do not mean to imply that the corporate law requires directors to maximize short-term profits for stockholders. Rather, I simply indicate that the corporate law requires directors, as a matter of their duty of loyalty, to pursue a good faith strategy to maximize profits for the stockholders. The directors, of course, retain substantial discretion . . . to decide how best to achieve that goal and the appropriate time frame for delivering those returns. But, . . . the market pressures on corporate boards are making it more difficult for boards to resist the pressure to emphasize the delivery of immediate profits over the implementation of longer-term strategies that might yield more durable and more substantial benefits to stockholders, as well as society in general.

To deliver profits, corporations must endure competition from competitors willing to locate jobs in nations without labor or environmental protection. That creates incentives to reduce wage rolls and pay, particularly in the European Union or in nations like Canada and the United States that have responsible regulatory standards, and to take fewer product safety and environmental precautions. When their competitors seem to be making large, short-term profits by suspect means that have substantial long-term risk . . . corporate managers face strong pressure from the capital markets to get in the game, regardless of whether they personally believe the game to be just another form of gambling.

When the pressure to deliver profits becomes, as it has, more intense, the rules of the game become even more important. Human nature, the founders of my nation teach, should be taken into account in designing those rules, and we should not assume that men and women of commerce are somehow better than average.

To ensure that for-profit corporations do not generate excessive externalities, strong boundaries remain critical. To address externality risk and fundamental concerns about appropriate protection of workers and the environment in globalized capital and product markets, the rules of the game must ultimately become global, too. But in the meantime, enlightened societies must resist the temptation to roll back the societal protections that spread the blessings of capitalism more broadly, ended child labor, gave workers safe places to work, protected consumers from harmful products, provided decent wages and humane working hours, and ensured that the pursuit of profit would not pollute the world in which we live. We cannot dispense with the protections provided by the nation-state until we come up with an effective replacement.

The coalition- and consensus-building required to develop an effective global . . . scheme of externality regulation will require enormous leadership and dedication. But it cannot even begin if we delude ourselves into believing that corporations will effectively regulate themselves. That is not what they are built to do and enormous harm will result if we pretend otherwise.

Finally, the question for whose benefit should corporations be managed sometimes results in investors themselves making forceful points.

Jessica Floum, *Portland to Stop Corporate Investing Despite Mayor Ted Wheeler's Opposition*
Oregonlive.com, Apr. 6, 2017

Portland is getting out of corporate investing altogether. The Portland City Council voted unanimously on Wednesday to end the practice following pressure from activists to withdraw from companies that are problematic for the environment, human rights or government.

The city has $539 million invested in corporations this year, City Treasurer Jennifer Cooperman said.

Activists for months have urged the Portland City Council to divest from controversial companies. They pleaded with them in December to withdraw from Wells Fargo due to its investments in the Dakota Access Pipeline and from Caterpillar, a company that makes trucks and bulldozers, some of which they say are used to harm Palestinians in the Israel Palestine conflict.

Instead, commissioners decided not to invest it in any corporations period. In part to avoid the trouble of having to perpetually decide which corporations the city considers bad actors.

As it divests, the city will put its money in federal bonds and other non-corporate options, Cooperman said.

"This is a win," said Hyung Nam, a member of the city's Socially Responsible Investment Committee tasked with looking into companies' environmental, social and government impact scores. "The city is actually willing to lose money to their budget because they want to get out of these big corporate nightmares."

While the vote was unanimous, Mayor Ted Wheeler said his yes vote was solely to support his colleagues.

Cooperman estimated divesting could cost the city a minimum $4.5 million or more this year and even more the following year. The mayor estimated that amounts to more than 200 affordable housing units or more than 600 new shelter beds based on current costs.

Wheeler said he also generally opposes divestment because he sees it as a lost opportunity to influence corporations from the inside. He shared examples of times that he said he successfully changed corporate policy as state treasurer, including a time Oregon's pension fund joined with other Chipotle Mexican Grill shareholders to oppose the bonuses and salaries of top executives.

"Is the right way to simply be out of it or the right way to run towards it and fix it head on?" Wheeler asked.

Commissioner Dan Saltzman told the activists that he based his decision on having limited time that he'd rather spend addressing the city's housing crisis and potholes than regularly evaluating which companies belong on the do-not-buy list.

"I fully respect and appreciate what you're saying, but I think it's the wiser course to get out of the business altogether because I don't want to do this every year," Saltzman said.

The council on Wednesday took testimony from about 40 activists who spoke in favor of socially responsible investing, urging the city to consider creating a municipal bank and to add Wells Fargo, Caterpillar and other companies harmful to the environment and human rights to a do-not-buy list in the meantime.

As a member of the city's Socially Responsible Investment Committee, Katrina Scotts di Carlo researched many companies in the city's investment portfolio. That the city continued to invest in companies that her research found problematic confounded her, she said.

Ted Gleichman, policy advisor for the Oregon chapter of the Sierra Club, said some activists are concerned divesting from all corporations will limit the city's ability to call out particularly bad corporations.

Wednesday's discussion of the city's corporate investing policy attracted an older group of activists than the twenty-somethings rearing black and red, sporting mohawks and bent on creating anarchy more typically seen at council meetings.

People waived paper ribbons. Fingers silently twinkled in support of testimony. A group calling themselves the Raging Grannies and sporting an eclectic variety of hats sang testimony to the mayor.

"I appreciate that we've had a very civil dialogue here today," Commissioner Nick Fish said. "This is the way Portland has hearings and discussions."

2. Background and Context

The shareholder primacy model was first strongly articulated in the early 1930s. What follows is the classic statement of the classic rationale behind the shareholder primacy rule. *The Modern Corporation and Private Property* is an iconic book in corporation law circles. But as the next excerpt makes clear, it makes a much more complex argument than simply a description of shareholder primacy. In fact, the book describes two other models of ultimate beneficiaries. As you identify them, consider how the selection of one set of beneficiaries over others dictates the operational goals of the corporation's managers.

≡ **Adolf A. Berle, Jr. & Gardiner C. Means,** *The Modern*
≡ *Corporation and Private Property*
≡   333-338, 343, 353-356 (1933)

[C]ertain legal, economic, and social questions . . . must now be squarely faced. Of these the greatest is the question in whose interests should the great quasi-public corporations . . . be operated. This problem really asks in a different form the question, who should receive the profits of industry?

The lawyer answers this question in no uncertain terms by applying . . . the traditional logic of property. The common law . . . logically demands the award of the entire profit to the . . . stockholders. According to this logic a corporation should be operated primarily in their interests.

The legal argument is largely historical; but it has been built up through a series of phases which make this conclusion inevitable. From earliest times the owner of property has been entitled to the full use or disposal of his property. . . . Since the use of industrial property consists primarily of an effort to increase its value—to make a profit—the owner of such property, in being entitled to its full use, has been entitled to all accretions to its value—to all the profits which it could be made to earn. The state and the law have sought to protect him in this right.

Yet, . . . are we justified in applying this logic? In the past, the ownership of business enterprise, has always, at least in theory, involved two attributes, first the risking of previously collected wealth . . . ; and, second, the ultimate management of and responsibility for that enterprise. But in the modern corporation [t]he stockholder has surrendered control over his wealth. He has become a supplier of capital, a risk-taker pure and simple, while ultimate responsibility and authority are exercised by directors. . . . Must we not, therefore, recognize that we are no longer dealing with property in the old sense? Does the traditional logic of property still apply? May not this surrender have so essentially changed his relation to his wealth as to have changed the logic applicable to his interest in that wealth? An answer to this question cannot be found in the law itself. It must be sought in the economic and social background of law.

Where is the social advantage in setting aside for the security holder, profits in an amount greater than is sufficient to insure the continued supplying of capital and taking of risk? The prospect of additional profits cannot act as a spur on the security holder to make him *operate* the enterprise with more vigor . . . , since he is no longer in control. Such extra profits if given to the security holders would seem to perform no useful economic function.

Observable throughout the world, and in varying degrees of intensity, is this insistence that power in economic organization shall be subjected to the same tests of public benefit which have been applied in their turn to power otherwise located. In the strictly capitalist countries, and particularly in time of depression, demands are constantly put forward that the men controlling the great economic organisms be made to accept responsibility for the well-being of those who are subject to the organization, whether workers, investors, or consumers. In a sense the difference in all of these demands lies only in degree. [A]s an economic organism grows . . . and its power is concentrated in a few hands, the possessor of power is more easily located, and the demand for responsible power becomes increasingly direct.

In direct opposition to the above doctrine of strict property rights is the view, apparently held by the great corporation lawyers and by certain students of the field, that corporate development has created a new set of relationships, giving to the groups in control powers which are absolute and not limited by any implied obligation with respect to their use. This logic leads to drastic conclusions. For instance, if . . . the men in control of a corporation can operate it in their own interests, and can divert a portion of the . . . income stream to their own uses, such is their privilege. Under this view, since the new powers have been acquired on a quasi-contractual basis, the security holders have agreed in advance to any losses which they may suffer by reason of such use. The result is, briefly, that the existence of the legal and economic relationships giving rise to these powers must be frankly recognized as a modification of the principle of private property.

On the one hand, the owners of passive property, by surrendering control and responsibility over the active property, have surrendered the right that the corporation should be operated in their sole interest. . . . At the same time, the controlling groups, by means of the extension of corporate powers, have in their own interest broken the bars of tradition which require that the corporation be operated solely for the benefit of the owners of passive property. Eliminating the sole interest of the passive owner, however, does not necessarily lay a basis for the alternative claim that the new powers should be used in the interest of the controlling groups. The latter have not presented, in acts or words any acceptable defense of the proposition that these powers should be so used. No tradition supports that proposition. The control groups have, rather, cleared the way for the claims of a group far wider than either the owners or the control. They have placed the community in a position to demand that the modern corporation serve not alone the owners or the control but all society.

This . . . alternative offers a wholly new concept of corporate activity. Neither the claims of ownership nor those of control can stand against the paramount interests of the community. It remains only for the claims of the community to be put forward with clarity and force. When a convincing system of community obligations is worked out and is generally accepted, in that moment the passive property right of today must yield before the larger interests of society. Should the corporate leaders, for example, set forth a program comprising fair wages, security to employees, reasonable service to their public, and stabilization of business, all of which would divert a portion of the profits from the owners of passive property, and should the community generally accept such a scheme as a logical and human solution of industrial difficulties, the interests of passive property owners would have to give way. Courts would almost of necessity be forced to recognize the result, justifying it by whatever of the many legal theories they might choose. It is conceivable,—indeed it seems almost essential if the corporate system is to survive that the "control" of the great corporations should develop into a purely neutral technocracy, balancing a variety of claims by various groups in the community and assigning to each a portion of the income stream on the basis of public policy rather than private cupidity.

Notes and Questions

1. Reality Check

a. What *is* the "traditional logic of property"?

b. What are the two attributes of ownership of a business?

c. How would the traditional logic apply to the modern corporation?

d. Do Berle and Means believe that the traditional logic applies to the modern corporation? If not, for what ultimate beneficiaries *do* corporate managers manage?

e. For what ultimate beneficiaries *should* corporate managers manage?

f. Why shouldn't the traditional logic be applied to the modern corporation?

g. What is Berle's and Means's alternative to the traditional logic of property?

2. What Do You Think?

a. Do you agree that the traditional logic of property should not be applied to large public corporations?

b. Is the alternative suggested by Berle and Means workable? Do you agree with it?

c. Do Berle and Means see the demise of the traditional logic of property as a good development or a bad one? Do you agree with their view?

In the next article Professor Bainbridge sets out a contemporary argument for shareholder primacy.

≡ **Stephen M. Bainbridge,** *The Board of Directors as*
≡ *Nexus of Contracts*
≡ 88 Iowa L. Rev. 1, 5-6, 9-11 (2002)

Traditional variants of shareholder primacy claim that shareholders own the corporation and, accordingly, directors and officers are mere stewards of the shareholders' interests. A more recent variation . . . blends two economic theories —the nexus of contracts theory of the firm and agency cost economics. In contractarian theory, shareholders are merely one of many factors of production bound together in a complex web of explicit and implicit contracts. Influenced by agency cost economics, however, most law and economics scholars continue to treat directors and officers as agents of the shareholders, with fiduciary obligations to maximize shareholder wealth. Shareholders therefore retain a privileged position among the corporation's various constituencies, because their contract with the firm has ownership-like features, including the right to vote and the fiduciary obligations of directors and officers.

The dominant model of the corporation in legal scholarship is the so-called nexus of contracts theory. [M]odern law and economics scholars view the corporation not as an entity but as an aggregate of various inputs acting together to produce goods or services. Employees provide labor. Creditors provide debt capital. Shareholders initially provide equity capital and subsequently bear the risk of losses and monitor the performance of management. Management monitors the performance of employees and coordinates the activities of all the firm's inputs. The firm is the nexus of explicit and implicit contracts establishing rights and obligations among the various inputs making up the firm.

The name "nexus of contracts" is somewhat unfortunate. For lawyers, the term "contracts" carries with it all of the baggage learned in Contracts class during the first year of law school. Among that baggage are two particularly problematic features. First, the word "contract" focuses attention on legal notions such as consideration and mutuality. Second, the word "contract" mainly seems to invoke transactions on spot markets that are thick and relatively untroubled by asymmetric information. Neither has much to do with the internal governance of corporations.

As used by contractarians, however, the term is not limited to relationships constituting legal contracts. Instead, contractarians use the word "contract" to refer generally to long-term relationships characterized by asymmetric information, bilateral monopoly, and opportunism.

Notes and Questions

1. Notes

a. Professor Bainbridge proposes a variation of the nexus of contract model, which he calls the director primacy model:

> In the director primacy model, the corporation is a vehicle by which the board of directors hires various factors of production. Hence, the board of directors is not a mere agent of the shareholders, as standard contractarian theory claims, but rather is a *sui generis* body—a sort of Platonic guardian—serving as the nexus for the various contracts making up the corporation. The board's powers flow from that set of contracts in its totality and not just from shareholders.

Stephen M. Bainbridge, *The Board of Directors as Nexus of Contracts*, 88 Iowa L. Rev. 1, 8 (2002)

2. Reality Check

a. What is the nexus of contracts theory?
b. Where did the nexus of contracts theory come from?
c. Does the nexus of contracts theory depend on shareholder primacy?

3. What Do You Think?

a. Do you think the nexus of contract vision essentially differs from Berle's and Means's vision or is it essentially the same?
b. Is Berle's and Means's approach more accurate than the nexus of contracts approach?
c. Is Professor Bainbridge's variation of the nexus of contracts analysis an improvement?

Chancellor Allen calls the alternative to shareholder primacy the "social entity" or "entity" theory. As you have seen, even Berle and Means did not contend that shareholder primacy was, or should be, the norm. The nexus of contract model does not require shareholder primacy, although many proponents of the nexus of contract model advocate such a position. The more nuanced question is how shall the shareholders' interest in the corporation be balanced against that of other constituencies or of society generally. The final reading places this question in its historical context while emphasizing, as Chancellor Allen does, the timeless nature of this question.

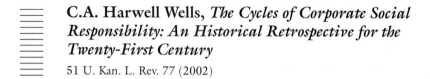

C.A. Harwell Wells, *The Cycles of Corporate Social Responsibility: An Historical Retrospective for the Twenty-First Century*

51 U. Kan. L. Rev. 77 (2002)

Legal debates over corporate social responsibility stretch from the 1930s to the twenty-first century. They have engaged some of the leading legal minds of the century, and advocates and enemies of corporate social responsibility still win publication in the country's most prestigious legal journals. But there is a problem with these debates: they rarely seem to go anywhere. Viewed in historical perspective, it is clear that each new round of debate on corporate social responsibility largely recapitulates the earlier debate in a slightly altered form.

Though separate in time, all these debates shared conceptual foundations. They all were premised on the idea that the American economy was dominated by a relatively small number of enormous, powerful, and stable business corporations that were qualitatively different from their smaller competitors, and the debates all assumed that the solution to pressing social ills was neither to eliminate corporations nor let them alone, but rather to implement legal mechanisms that would lead corporate managers and directors to take into account the needs not only of shareholders but of workers, consumers, and communities when making business decisions.

[From the 1930s], the debate over corporate social responsibility lay dormant for nearly twenty years. Several factors likely contributed to its quiescence. [C]ertainly by 1933 the deepening Depression had thrown into doubt not only the beneficence but even the survival of large corporations. In the New Deal, many of the abuses . . . were solved by legislation such as the Securities Act and the Exchange Act, while the New Deal also offered new vistas for legal reform through new government programs and administrative law, drawing scholars' attention away from issues of corporate social responsibility. World War II and postwar reconstruction provided their own challenges.

Beginning in the mid-1950s, however, attention again turned to corporations' social responsibility. The 1950s legal debate over corporate social responsibility was part of that decade's wider discussion of the corporation's role in American society and politics. . . . Despite its reputation as strait-laced, the 1950s witnessed an outpouring of critical writings on the large corporation. Taken together, . . . these authors agreed that large corporations had been fantastically successful in economic terms, that they had come to wield significant economic, political, and social power, and that their power posed a dilemma for America's democratic society. The implications of such new concentrations of power were unclear; most writers preferred to voice concerns over "corporate power" rather than make specific proposals for reform.

One area where radical proposals did appear was in legal scholarship. Leading the new analysis of corporate social responsibility was a familiar figure: Adolf A.

Berle. The skepticism he displayed about managers in the 1930s was largely gone, replaced by a faith in managers' ability to use their newfound power to benefit all groups involved in the corporation. The legal changes Berle advocated were intended to free managers from their singular duties to shareholders and allow them to direct the corporation's resources for the general welfare.

In [Berle's] *The 20th Century Capitalist Revolution* [1954], . . . the unfettered corporation would produce a kind of utopia, its managers successfully balancing all of society's competing interests. Although Berle was not forthcoming on the details of just how corporate managers would bring about social harmony, he made clear his hopes in the title of the last lecture in his book: Corporate Capitalism and the City of God.

The author he had closest affinity with, . . . and one who would have greater influence on the developing legal debate over corporate social responsibility, was Peter Drucker. Known today chiefly as a pioneering management consultant, in the 1950s Drucker was viewed as a serious analyst of corporate power, having already written two classic works on corporate power. . . . The ideal corporation, Drucker implied, would be run by enlightened managers for the benefit of its shareholders, workers, and the wider community.

Thus Drucker's most dramatic proposal: that managers be freed from their legal subservience to both shareholders and directors. He would transform the board from a governing body to a "maker of policy," with representatives not only of shareholder/investors but from management, labor, and the communities where the enterprise operated. He did not reject the profit motive as a primary guide for this new-model corporation, but he believed it should be sought even as the corporation fulfilled its larger social mission.

Berle and Drucker's chief failing was their inability to clearly address the problems raised by their proposals. How management would reconcile constituents' conflicting demands, or why it would not simply line its own pockets, was left largely unaddressed. They were also not able to articulate precisely what problem they were trying to solve. "Corporate power" was a generalized concern, not a specific issue readily fixed by restructuring the legal duties of director and managers. The vagueness of concerns with the corporation prevented the articulation of a clear reform program. Berle and Drucker's ideas met a chilly reception. For all the popular criticism of corporations, there was little public sentiment to reform them.

The debate over corporate social responsibility was transformed by the events of the 1960s. Genteel discussions over how business statesmen could use their positions to improve society became—under pressure from social unrest, perceptions of environmental degradation, and protests over the Vietnam War—populist campaigns to redirect corporate power to solve looming social and political problems. In the process, the debate over corporate social responsibility underwent a reversal. In the 1950s, advocates of the socially responsible corporation demanded that managers be freed from the shackles of shareholder primacy. By the 1970s, however, reformers were no longer enamored of the "business statesman," and sought to make the corporation more responsible to other constituencies by taking away the manager's autonomy and instituting greater oversight by directors or shareholders.

While in retrospect the Vietnam War appears to be the central event of the 1960s, it was actually domestic concerns that first prodded corporations to be "socially responsible." The riots that broke out in major American cities beginning in 1965 pushed business leaders to implement new programs to help resolve, as they put it, "the urban problem." Large corporations launched a series of programs intended to solve urban ills, as they redirected charitable donations, started new employee training programs, targeted disadvantaged populations, and promised to support a nascent movement for "black capitalism." In part, corporate social activism was a response to public pressure. Whether their programs actually meant the corporation had assumed new legal responsibilities, however, was less clear. Even the most ambitious social investments could be justified as directed to a firm's long-run profits. In short, the majority of corporations that adopted "socially responsible" policies did not thereby acknowledge new legal duties to nonshare-holder constituents.

During the late 1960s and early 1970s, [w]hile many on the left simply disdained business, others with a more reformist bent sought to use existing legal mechanisms, or to invent new ones, to force corporations to take into account constituencies beyond their shareholders when making business decisions.

[T]here was at least one legal mechanism already available: the shareholder proposal. Under S.E.C. Rule 14a-8, a shareholder of a public corporation, who meets certain conditions, can demand that a proposal he or she has prepared be included in the proxy mailed to shareholders before an annual meeting, to be voted on by all shareholders. In the late 1960s, activists seized on the shareholder proposal as a lever to push corporations towards socially responsible actions. [I]n the hands of social activists, shareholder proposals became a way to voice social disapproval of a corporation's actions. Through their proposals, social activists hoped to mobilize shareholders into insisting there were more important things than profits. Despite their opposition to the "corporate system," the activists were surprisingly optimistic, believing that, if asked, shareholders would demand that directors and managers act in a socially responsible manner.

That shareholders ultimately refused to adopt even the most melioristic propos-als highlights the problems that likely limited the success of public-interest share-holder proposals: most shareholders did not want their firms governed in the interests of the wider community. The few public-interest proposals that reached shareholders' hands were overwhelmingly defeated. Yet this immediate record of failure should not obscure the longer-range impact of this movement. [T]hey pioneered a means of bringing shareholder concerns before corporate boards that is still used today.

In the early 1960s, several legal scholars argued that corporate social responsi-bility made little economic sense, promising as it did to distort the price function and so make corporations less efficient, while saddling them with an ill-suited social role. In 1970, this view received its most forceful statement, not in a law review, but in a *New York Times Magazine* article, written by the era's best-known free-market economist, Milton Friedman.

In part, he noted, advocates of corporate social responsibility ultimately believed in replacing market mechanisms with political mechanisms when determining how resources should be used, a process guaranteed to produce economic inefficiency. The funds spent on social projects were . . . in effect "taxed" from the shareholder and then used by the corporate executive as he judged best, "all this guided only by general exhortations from on high. . . ." In Friedman's view, corporate social responsibility was not only inefficient, it was theft.

Although Friedman's was a lonely voice in 1970, over the rest of the decade legal scholars would join the attack on corporate social responsibility, also using economic theory. . . . In 1979 David Engel launched a wide-ranging attack on the decade's social responsibility proposals, arguing that they were not only wrongheaded but incoherent, skipping over major procedural issues, assuming away perhaps intractable problems, and presuming that corporate management would somehow prove better than elected officials at deciding which social goals a firm should pursue.

Public enthusiasm for corporate social responsibility flagged after the mid-1970s. Academic criticism certainly had a role to play in this. At least as important, . . . however, was the changing climate of public opinion concerning government and business. The public trust evinced in business leaders in the early 1960s never returned, but it was not replaced by renewed faith in government. Increasingly, the free market and private ordering were preferred to any legislative or court-ordered economic planning.

From the late 1970s to the mid-1980s, the academic debate over corporate social responsibility dwindled and splintered. As in earlier cycles of scholarly effort, it would take economic and legal developments outside the legal academy to give impetus and form to the next iteration of the debate. This time, the external impetus was the 1980s' boom in corporate takeovers. . . . Producing huge profits for the takeover artists, and significant gains for shareholders of firms bought, the takeovers also resulted in unemployed managers and—at least in public perceptions—shuttered factories and downsized workers. In response, corporations developed anti-takeover defenses and states that feared takeovers and decimation of locally based firms adopted laws aimed at preventing such takeovers. Particularly popular were so-called "corporate constituency statutes."

Corporate constituency statutes explicitly broadened the kinds of constituencies directors could consider when evaluating a takeover bid. . . . Within a decade twenty-nine states had passed similar measures. Even in states where such laws were not passed, notably the corporate-charter capital Delaware, court decisions gave directors greater leeway to weigh a bid's "impact on 'constituencies' other than shareholders." [T]he statutes offered a more capacious view of directors' fiduciary duties, and promised that the needs of a range of "constituencies" could (or must) be taken into account in corporate decision-making. Almost inadvertently, the legal mechanism for corporate social responsibility seemed at last to have been put in place.

Out of the takeover movement, resulting downsizing, and the consequent passage of corporate-constituency statutes came a new round of scholarly work on corporate social responsibility, or as its proponents would rename it, "progressive corporate law." Two other developments also shaped the debate. One was . . . : new concern over the United States' economic competitiveness. Overseas competitors appeared to exceed the productivity of the United States' firms, while also maintaining workplace harmony alien to the American experience. The apparent failure of the giant American corporation opened up new possibilities for legal reform of corporate governance.

A final development . . . was the appearance . . . of the contractarian theory of the firm. This approach conceptualized a corporation as a "nexus of contracts" between the corporation's various constituencies. If . . . the corporation were only a web of contracts, . . . then the corporation as a distinct entity apart from these constituencies was attenuated if not erased. Progressive corporate-law scholars never accepted this vision of the corporation, but the dominance of the nexus-of-contracts approach in the 1990s would force them to spend considerable time grappling with it.

[M]any progressive scholars eagerly seized on corporate-constituency statutes passed in the 1980s. In part, they hoped that the new statutes signaled the end of shareholder primacy. Some scholars simply took the statutes as a sign that shareholder primacy was gone. The statutes encouraged a few scholars to envision further legal steps to insert nonshareholder concerns into board decisions. Ultimately, the enthusiasm for such corporate-constituency statutes faded, as their effects did not meet the expectations of either their supporters or their enemies.

In [1995], a coherent group of scholars . . . set forth a program for their work in the collection *Progressive Corporate Law*. The scholars represented in this volume advanced a new agenda for corporate law, based on their argument that the corporation itself should be viewed as a community (hence the other label, "communitarian") comprised of shareholders, creditors, directors, managers, employees, and maybe even customers. The "social responsibility" they sought to impose on the corporation was, then, responsibility not to society in general, but to those groups that made up the corporation-as-society.

On the surface, the essays proposed several distinct programs for reforming the corporation. Despite their differences, the articles all fit squarely in the line of work on corporate social responsibility stretching back to Berle. . . . First, . . . the articles shared the assumption that there was something distinctive about large corporations that set them qualitatively apart from small firms and made it appropriate to assign them greater responsibilities. Second, the authors all aimed to reform corporate law; none were radical in the sense of believing in either nationalizing or eliminating large corporations. Third, most authors shared the belief that the best way to reform corporate law (and thus corporations) was to make corporate directors and managers legally responsible to a wider range of constituents, including employees, communities, and even the environment, thus abandoning the shareholder primacy norm.

[T]he cycles of legal debates over corporate social responsibility have, since the 1930s, shared deep similarities despite superficial differences. All the separate debates have (1) presupposed that the problems created by business are really problems created by this nation's large publicly held corporations, (2) aimed to reform those corporations, rather than to eliminate them, and (3) seen the imposition of new duties towards nonshareholder constituents on directors and officers as the best way to make corporations answerable not just to shareholders, but to the wider society. To be sure, each debate has also differed from its predecessors and successors, but chiefly in the problems they profess to tackle. [T]he problems change; the solutions remain the same. The result has been an often-stale scholarly critique of corporations as each new cycle of debate recapitulates debates in the past, and as ideas are unwittingly recycled with little awareness of their predecessors, much less why they were rejected thirty (or even seventy years) before.

This is a shame, for the history of corporate social responsibility is of more than historical interest. Corporations remain today, as they were in the 1920s, the most powerful nongovernmental institutions in America. In innumerable ways they shape the nation's politics and culture, and the lives of their employees and consumers. They create great wealth and opportunities, but often deliver them unevenly; they frequently use their power in ways that benefit shareholders and managers, but harm the rest of us. From time to time we are reminded of this, when investors discover their money has disappeared in the collapse of a stock-market bubble, employees wake to find their 401(k) plans are worth nothing, or shareholders discover their firms have been looted by self-serving executives. The task of ameliorating the influence of corporations, and of channeling and limiting their power, should be of concern to all of us.

Notes and Questions

1. Reality Check

a. How has the problem for which social responsibility is the solution changed?

b. What is social responsibility?

c. Why are corporations obligated to be socially responsible?

d. How are the cycles of debate over social responsibility alike? How are they different?

e. What objections to the social responsibility model have been posed?

2. What Do You Think?

a. Has any major commentator seriously argued in favor of the shareholder primacy model?

b. Do you think the debates have pitted shareholder primacy against social responsibility? If not, what have they entailed?

c. Corporate managers were among the most vocal proponents of corporate constituent statutes. Why?

d. Do you agree that, "Corporate social responsibility is not a novel solution to an unchanging problem; quite the contrary, it is an unchanging solution to an ever-new problem"?

e. What will the next debate over the nature of the corporation look like?

f. In whose interest should corporations be managed?

D. FEDERAL SECURITIES REGULATION

1. Foreign Corrupt Practices Act

In the mid-1970s an SEC investigation discovered that over 400 public corporations, including almost a quarter of the 500 largest, had made "questionable or illegal payments," that is to say bribes, to foreign governments, political parties, and politicians. While the SEC investigation focused on whether those corporations had made misleading filings with the SEC about those payments, Congress decided that broader remedial action was necessary. It quickly enacted the Foreign Corrupt Practices Act (FCPA) of 1977, which is most pertinently found as section 30A of the Securities Exchange Act of 1934. Violation is a criminal offense.

The FCPA constrains American corporations that do business in other countries. No public company may pay anything of value to any foreign official or foreign political party for the purpose of influencing a decision, inducing an action, or inducing an official to use his or her influence to obtain or retain business. Corrupt intent is required. Although the basic statement of the FCPA's workings is straightforward, application can be problematic. In brief, two kinds of issues are most frequently faced by public companies. First, it is not unusual for companies doing business in other countries to have relationships with many individuals who act as conduits, finders, or consultants. If those people make payments that would be illegal under the FCPA, when is the corporation liable? Essentially, this becomes an agency problem but the facts of any particular case can often be murky. Second, companies frequently provide gifts of various sorts to suppliers, customers, and others who interact with the business. When such payments are made to a recipient covered under the FCPA, a recurring question is whether such payment is intended to achieve ends the FCPA prohibits.

E. TERMS OF ART IN THIS CHAPTER

All purpose clause
Corporate social
  responsibility
Nexus of contract

Progressive corporate
  law
Shareholder primacy
Special purpose clause

Traditional logic of
  property
Ultra vires
Waste

11

The Fiduciary Duties of Directors (and Officers)

Many corporate law experts would suggest that the topic of the next two chapters is the most important one of all. Even more controversially, some argue that the question of director fiduciary duties is the only corporate law topic worth studying. The basis for these assertions is the recognition that corporation statutes are largely enabling; they provide a set of default rules, nearly all of which are waivable in the Articles of Incorporation, in the bylaws, or by contract. Even more flexibility is provided by the internal affairs doctrine, which allows corporate planners to select the corporation statute of the state they find most beneficial to their legal needs. In this view of corporation law the one legal constraint on a corporation's governance is the fiduciary duties of officers and directors. Hence public policy regarding corporations is, effectively, exclusively concerned with fiduciary duties.

What are these fiduciary duties and where do they come from? One obvious consequence of a person's agreement to serve as a director is the understanding that he or she will strive for the corporation's financial success. Chapter 9 discusses the fact that, broadly speaking, all corporate power is located in the board of directors. Chapter 10 focuses on some of the constraints on the board's exercise of its power arising from the definition of the corporation's ultimate beneficiaries. Further, although directors are not "agents" of the corporation in a legal sense, they are certainly "agents" in an economic sense. Chapter 4, on agency, sets out some of the incentives that keep economic agents from acting solely in their own best economic interest rather than that of their principal.

This chapter and Chapter 12 are concerned with similar issues. "Fiduciary duties" is a shorthand way of describing the legal restrictions on board discretion that are imposed as a consequence of having agreed to act on behalf of a corporation's ultimate beneficiaries. The chapter begins by considering the standard of director allegiance — in what way do directors have to act to meet what is called their *duty of loyalty?* You may remember from Contracts that parties are typically under an obligation of good faith and fair dealing. If you have taken a course involving trust law you know that trustees are under a much more strict obligation to act in the utmost best interest of the trust's beneficiaries. Partners and agents are under a fiduciary duty that includes "not honesty alone, but the punctilio of an honor the most sensitive. . . ." *Meinhard v. Salmon,* 164 N.E. 545, 546 (N.Y. 1928) (Cardozo,

C.J.). What these differing standards and formulations may, in reality, come down to is an obligation to act in accordance with minimal standards of honesty (contracts), maximum other-directed intentions (trusts), or something in between.

Paradigms of problematic director actions have given rise to predictable responses by the courts. In examining these patterns we will understand how the courts' abstract incantations of fiduciary duties are incarnated. More importantly, by seeing the patterns of director behavior we will have a basis upon which to evaluate the fiduciary duty standards of conduct.

This chapter then explores the same sort of issues arising under directors' duty of care. Chapter 12 will turn to issues that may strike you as being better suited to a course in civil procedure or evidence. These are questions of the different standards of review courts use in evaluating claims that directors have breached their fiduciary duties. These standards of review, and their application, inhere in the standards of conduct; one simply cannot understand one without understanding the other. If it is any comfort (and it probably isn't) we will deal with other procedural questions, more discrete from fiduciary duty questions, in Chapter 14 when we take up shareholder litigation. When judges apply a particular standard of review they are, in effect, asking "how do I know whether the plaintiff has proved the requisite elements of his or her claim?" From your first year you are familiar with the standards of "preponderance," "clear and convincing," and "reasonable doubt." If you have taken Evidence you are also comfortable with various evidentiary presumptions. In the procedural courses one policy danger is making the standards too complex for juries to understand and apply. In Delaware, though, that danger does not exist because the Court of Chancery, in which all corporate law cases are heard, is a true court of equity, which means that juries are not used.

Directors' fiduciary duties are traditionally divided into the duty of loyalty and the duty of care. Although those labels are a bit problematic, the case law generally adheres to the traditional division and so it may be useful to continue the separation in the materials below. We begin in this chapter with the duty of loyalty.

A. THE DUTY OF LOYALTY

The MBCA has codified the duty of loyalty in §8.30. Delaware has not codified the duty of loyalty but has adopted a similar statement in its case law. The Delaware Supreme Court has explained,

> This Court has traditionally and consistently defined the duty of loyalty of officers and directors to their corporation and its shareholders in broad and unyielding terms:
>
>> Corporate officers and directors are not permitted to use their position of trust and confidence to further their private interests. . . . A public policy, existing through the years, and derived from a profound knowledge of human characteristics and motives, has established a rule that demands of a corporate officer or director, peremptorily and inexorably, the most scrupulous observance of his [or her] duty, not only affirmatively to protect the interests of the corporation committed to his [or her] charge, but also to refrain from doing anything that would work injury to the corporation, or to deprive it of profit or advantage which his [or her] skill and ability might properly bring to it, or to enable it to make in the reasonable and lawful exercise

of its powers. The rule that requires an undivided and unselfish loyalty to the corporation demands that there be no conflict between duty and self-interest.

Guth [*v. Loft, Inc.*], 5 A.2d [503] at 510 [(Del. 1939)].

. . . Essentially, the duty of loyalty mandates that the best interest of the corporation and its shareholders takes precedence over any interest possessed by a director, officer or controlling shareholder and not shared by the stockholders generally.

Cede & Co. v. Technicolor, Inc., 634 A.2d 345, 361 (Del. 1993) (Horsey, J.).

What sort of actions constitute acting in bad faith or in a manner the director knows is not in the best interest of the corporation? Surely stealing comes within this rubric, and it is clear that directors may not, consistently with their fiduciary duties, steal from the companies they serve. Put less pejoratively and more broadly than the criminal law's definition of "theft," directors may not take things that belong to the corporation. That restriction comfortably covers the easy cases in which a director or officer takes a Van Gogh or Renoir that belongs to the corporate art collection. It also covers situations in which the director or officer takes home a ream of paper for the family computer or a package of sticky notes. Further, this restriction on director or officer action prohibits using corporate assets for noncorporate purposes. For example, a director may not use the nearest company photocopier to make copies of his or her child's progress report from school.[1] Incidentally, you should note that the same restrictions apply to agents, which includes all employees, even those who are not directors or officers.

1. The Corporate Opportunity Doctrine

None of this should really be controversial, but there is a chronic uncertainty in corporate law about a particular kind of "thing" a corporation may "have" that a director may not take. The buzz phrase for this thing is a *corporate opportunity*. We start with corporate opportunity because it is a form of taking and the notion that taking is impermissible is easily apprehended. Here is a description of what a corporate opportunity is and a more formal elaboration of why it is not allowed.

The classic corporate opportunity cases involve instances in which officers or directors use for personal advantage information that comes to them in their corporate capacity, by diverting a profitable transaction from the corporation. Such cases are simply a form of misappropriation, not conceptually dissimilar from general torts of that description. See *Restatement (Second) of Torts* §§222A, 223 (1965).

Since business men and women are not infrequently involved in a number of enterprises (this is especially true of corporate directors and principals in close corporations) the law of misappropriation of corporate opportunities has generated a number of tests to determine whether an opportunity that comes to the attention of such an individual was in equity one that should be regarded as "belonging to" a particular corporation. One question . . . is whether the directors' obligation of loyalty under the corporate opportunity doctrine goes further than the tort of misappropriation would go to restrict business activity. That question is presented because it seems clear from the evidence that Mr. Broz [the defendant] did not

---

1. Most people reading the foregoing paragraph are shocked in one of two ways. One set of people finds it incredible that employees, especially those more senior than they or making more money than they, would take things from the company. The other set of people, intuiting that trying to wrangle the Remington bronze from the corporate headquarters lobby to one's car is wrong, nonetheless is shocked that taking sticky notes or a box of pens or photocopying services is wrong.

misuse proprietary information that came to him in a corporate capacity nor did he otherwise use any power he might have over the governance of the corporation to advance his own interests. Thus if Mr. Broz is guilty of violating the duty of loyalty it must be by reason of a restriction assumed by a corporate director that is greater than the restriction that prevents persons generally from misusing the property or information of another. The corporate law teaches that there is such an obligation voluntarily assumed by every man and woman who agrees to serve as a corporate director. That duty for example prevents a director from personally engaging in material business competition with his corporation without the approval of the corporation.

Cellular Information Systems, Inc. v. Broz, 663 A.2d 1180, 1184-85 (Del. Ch. 1995) (Allen, Ch.)

If a "corporate opportunity" is not coterminous with "property or information of" the corporation, what is it? The question of the definition of corporate opportunity is an important one because corporations, as well as the people who serve them, need a fair degree of predictability in this area. This is especially so, as Chancellor Allen points out, in the close corporation setting because the officers and directors of such enterprises are less likely to be engaged full-time in the corporation's affairs and may be undertaking more than one project at a time.

Brewer v. Insight Technology, Inc.

689 S.E.2d 330 (Ga. App. 2009)

PHIPPS, Judge.

A jury found Darren Brewer, former president of Insight Technology, Inc. ("ITI"), liable to ITI on claims of breach of fiduciary duty and misappropriation of corporate opportunity. The trial court entered a judgment for $395,000 in compensatory damages, $650,000 in punitive damages and $355,000 in attorney fees in favor of ITI. Brewer argues on appeal that the trial court erred: (1) by denying Brewer's motion for directed verdict on the claim for misappropriation of corporate opportunity; (2) by improperly charging the jury on the definition of corporate opportunity; (3) by awarding punitive damages in excess of the $250,000 cap; and (4) by refusing to set off a $1.7 million settlement between ITI and other joint tortfeasors against ITI's jury award. Finding no error, we affirm.

Gary Aliengena formed ITI in 1996 as an internet-based load board business for the trucking industry. Like a traditional trucking load board, the business matched truckers with freight-hauling jobs. Because the business was based on-line, it was able to match truckers with jobs as they became available in real time. At the company's inception, Aliengena hired Brewer as director of marketing. Within months, Brewer became the company's president, overseeing all daily activities, while also working on the technical aspects of the business, including software and website development. In about 1998, ITI expanded its business to include freight factoring, and eventually created a division called FactorLoads. The factoring division, which offered financing to small, independent truckers looking for temporary or one-time jobs, aimed to fill a need within a niche market.

By 2000, Brewer met Pat Hull, who owned a competing load board business, GetLoaded.com, LLC ("GetLoaded"). Hull expressed to Brewer his interest in the factoring business. Brewer attempted to persuade Hull to allow ITI to advertise on GetLoaded's website, but Hull refused.

In 2002, Hull incorporated FreightCheck, LLC, an internet-based factoring business in competition with ITI's FactorLoads. Brewer was made an equal co-owner of FreightCheck with Hull, and they shared responsibility for managing and operating the company. Brewer operated FreightCheck out of the same building as ITI; used the same software for the two businesses; and directed ITI employees to work clandestinely for FreightCheck. Meanwhile, Aliengena was unaware of the formation of FreightCheck and Brewer's daily involvement therein.

By 2003, FactorLoad's revenues had diminished compared with the previous year. Brewer urged Aliengena to sell ITI to GetLoaded, and in 2004 Aliengena agreed. Before the sale was executed, however, an employee of ITI revealed to Aliengena that Brewer was a co-owner and manager of FreightCheck. Aliengena fired Brewer, and ITI filed suit against Brewer, Hull, GetLoaded, and FreightCheck. [The three other] defendants subsequently settled with ITI, and Brewer went to trial.

Brewer contends that the trial court erred when it denied his motion for a directed verdict on ITI's claim for misappropriation of corporate opportunity.

In *Southeast Consultants v. McCrary Engineering Corp.*,[6] the Supreme Court of Georgia stated:

> In order to impose liability for an official's appropriation of a business opportunity, a court must resolve two inquiries. First, a court must determine whether the appropriated opportunity was in fact a business opportunity rightfully belonging to the corporation. If a court finds that the business opportunity was *not* a corporate opportunity, the directors or officers who pursued the opportunity for personal benefit are immune from liability. However, if the court finds that the business opportunity was a bona fide corporate opportunity, the court must determine whether the corporate official violated a fiduciary duty in appropriating that opportunity.

In determining whether the appropriated opportunity was a business opportunity rightfully belonging to the corporation, we have adopted the following test as to current officers:

> [I]f there is presented to a corporate officer or director a business opportunity which the corporation is financially able to undertake, is, from its nature, in the line of the corporation's business and is of practical advantage to it, is one in which the corporation has an interest or a reasonable expectancy, and, by embracing the opportunity, the self-interest of the officer or director will be brought into conflict with that of his corporation, the law will not permit him to seize the opportunity for himself.[8]

The evidence showed that ITI and GetLoaded were both engaged in the business of load boarding. While ITI had an established factoring division, Hull wished to develop a factoring business for GetLoaded or another entity under his control. The evidence further suggested that during 2002 and earlier, ITI was financially able to undertake the new opportunity which ultimately became Freight-Check. Moreover, because the bulk of ITI's business came from factoring, ITI was financially poised to benefit from a merger with another factoring company.

---

6. 246 Ga. 503, 508, 273 S.E.2d 112 (1980).

8. *Parks v. Multimedia Technologies*, 239 Ga. App. 282, 288-289(3)(a), 520 S.E.2d 517 (1999) (citations, punctuation and emphasis omitted).

Aliengena testified that it would have been financially advantageous for ITI to have given up its load board business in a merger with GetLoaded. However, by 2003, after Brewer had been working at FreightCheck for several months to a year, ITI's gross sales had significantly reduced. Brewer, acting as president of ITI, actively explored with Hull the possibility of ITI and GetLoaded combining their marketing efforts, with ITI marketing its services on GetLoaded's website. The jury was thus authorized to find that ITI had an interest or reasonable expectancy in FreightCheck prior to its formation. However, Brewer and Hull created FreightCheck to the exclusion of ITI. The evidence was sufficient to support the verdict on the first part of the *McCrary* test.

The evidence also supported the verdict with respect to the second *McCrary* requirement-showing a breach of fiduciary duty. A corporate officer owes its corporation the duties of utmost good faith and loyalty. A current officer may not engage in direct competition with the corporation's business. The evidence supported the jury's finding that when Brewer became a co-owner of FreightCheck, while remaining an officer of ITI, he engaged in competition, in breach of his fiduciary duties to ITI. The trial court did not err in denying Brewer's motion for directed verdict.

Judgment affirmed.

Grove v. Brown

2013 WL 4041495 (Del. Ch. Aug. 8, 2013)

GLASSCOCK, Vice Chancellor

It requires a certain kind of courage to forgo a salary and strike out on one's own. When individuals launch a small business with little equity beyond their own sweat and dreams, what follows is often a long, hard struggle leading, ultimately, to failure. When that happens, the results should evoke admiration for their efforts and sympathy for their misadventure. This matter involves a rarer bird altogether: here, four individuals launched a small and poorly capitalized business and were, from the outset, wildly successful. Unfortunately, those individuals were unable to cooperate to enjoy the fruits of that success, choosing instead acrimony and, ultimately, this litigation.

I. BACKGROUND

This matter involves a dispute between Plaintiffs Mary Marlene Grove and Larry E. Grove and Defendants Melba E. Brown and Hubert E. Brown, Jr.[1] In 2010, the Groves and the Browns started a successful home health care agency, Heartfelt Home Health, LLC ("Heartfelt"), and they worked together without issue for over a year.

However, in preparing tax returns for their first year in business, and upon discovering that not all four members had made the requisite $10,000 initial capital

---

1. For clarity, I will refer to these individuals by their first names; no disrespect is intended.

contribution, the parties began to dispute the ownership of Heartfelt, and relationships in the workplace started to dissolve. The Groves, meanwhile, established other home health care agencies in Maryland and Delaware without informing the Browns, and the Browns attempted to remove the Groves from Heartfelt by creating another LLC owned solely by the Browns and merging Heartfelt with that company. The Groves sued the Browns for a breach of fiduciary duty arising from the supposed merger. The Browns answered and counterclaimed for breach of fiduciary duty by Larry and Marlene Grove. The matter was tried; this is my post-trial opinion.

A. Background of the Business and Events Leading to the Litigation

Marlene and Melba first met while working at the MBNA America bank. Marlene worked in management, and Melba as a personal banking representative, until both accepted buy-outs from the company in 2005. Several months later, Marlene started working at Home Health Services by TLC ("TLC"), after having been recommended for the job by Melba. As the name suggests, TLC employed aides who delivered health care and assistance to patients in their homes. Melba joined Marlene at TLC a year later, and the two again worked together through 2009. After witnessing many layoffs at TLC and fearing that they would lose their jobs, Melba and Marlene began to discuss opening their own home health care business in late 2009.

In December 2009, Marlene established Heartfelt Home Health, LLC ("Heartfelt"). Heartfelt is a home-care staffing agency that provides assistance to those in need of personal or health care services. Heartfelt offers a range of services, including companion, homemaker, and personal care services. On December 23, 2009, the Browns and the Groves entered into a limited liability company operating agreement (the "Operating Agreement"), which named the Browns and the Groves as the four members of Heartfelt. The Operating Agreement indicated that each of the four members owned an equal portion of Heartfelt and provided that each member was to supply $10,000 as an initial capital contribution.

Heartfelt operations began in early 2010. The company was "very successful" and achieved a "respectable operating profit" during its first year. Marlene served as the Director of Operations, performing various tasks such as hiring, booking, invoicing, and managing the accounts receivable. Melba researched and created various forms needed for Heartfelt. Larry performed assorted maintenance projects, and Hubert maintained a register of payments and managed the technology setup for Heartfelt. In February 2010, Marlene's son, Timothy Grove, began working with Heartfelt as a records specialist. In June 2010, Timothy's wife Michelle joined Heartfelt as a staffing coordinator. Though Melba expressed her concern about working with members of the Grove family at the time, she ultimately agreed to both hires. The Browns, the Groves, Timothy, and Michelle continued to work well together until early 2011.

The unexpected success of Heartfelt led to discussions in January 2011 between Marlene, Melba, and Hubert about possibly expanding into Maryland and southern Delaware. The parties now disagree over the nature and extent of these discussions. The Groves argue that they approached the Browns about opening a new business in Maryland with the Grove family, and that the Browns indicated that they were not interested in joining because they disliked being in business with family and Melba "did not want to travel." Marlene did concede, however, that she never specifically asked the Browns to become members of Heart-N-Home or its Maryland and Delaware successors after these conversations.

For their part, the Browns maintain that though Heartfelt was financially stable enough to expand, they wanted to focus on establishing the existing business in Delaware before opening new offices. The Browns further insist that they never decided *not* to expand to other locations. Melba repeatedly testified that expanding Heartfelt to Maryland, Pennsylvania or Sussex County remained "on the table." The Browns further testified emphatically that they did not grant Marlene or any other Heartfelt employees the right to engage in business competing with Heartfelt.

Though the parties disagree on what was said concerning an expansion of Heartfelt's business, what the parties subsequently *did* is not disputed. While still working at Heartfelt, and without informing the Browns, Marlene formed a new home health agency, a Maryland LLC called Heart-N-Hand Home Care, LLC ("Heart-N-Hand"), on March 10, 2011. Larry Grove, Timothy Grove, and Shawn Grove were named as Directors of Heart-N-Hand, and Marlene was included as an initial member responsible for billing, legal, and compliance matters. Marlene later changed the Name of Heart-N-Hand to No Place Like Home, LLC ("Home MD"). Home MD was located in Elkton, Maryland, less than ten miles from Heartfelt's offices in Newark, Delaware.

Meanwhile, a dispute over the parties' ownership percentages and capital account balances began in April 2011 when Melba, Marlene, and Larry met with an accountant to discuss the preparation of Heartfelt's 2010 tax return. In a meeting on April 5, 2011, Heartfelt's accountant expressed concern over the fact that both Larry and Melba were short on their required initial $10,000 capital contributions as specified by the Operating Agreement and proposed that Marlene and Hubert transfer to their respective spouses an amount sufficient for Larry and Melba to reach the $10,000 mark. Accordingly, Hubert gave Melba $6,500, to bring her cash contribution to $10,000, and Marlene gave Larry $3,657. The Groves argue that the balance of Larry's contribution, $6,343, was satisfied by his donations of furniture and equipment to Heartfelt. The Browns, however, dispute the value of those donations and argue that they did not satisfy Larry's contribution obligation.

From that time, the relationship between the Groves, especially Marlene, and the Browns grew confrontational. Though Hubert testified that he and Marlene never fought, Marlene recalled engaging in arguments with Hubert. Marlene and Larry's son, Timothy, also testified that he had witnessed confrontations between Marlene and Hubert in which Hubert hit Marlene's desk and "talk[ed] down" to her. Marlene began avoiding the Browns at work. On May 10, 2011, Timothy resigned from his position at Heartfelt because of the conflicts. A month later, Marlene "fired" Michelle from her position at Heartfelt, in what an unemployment-insurance-appeals-board referee characterized as a "sham discharge." The parties were ultimately unable to come to an agreement to resolve the tax dispute, and the Browns now assert that they actually own 63% of Heartfelt, and the Groves own 37%, because the Groves' collective cash contribution was $13,657, whereas the Browns' contribution was $23,248.

As the dispute over the parties' capital contributions and ownership intensified, the Groves continued establishing their own competing health care businesses. On

May 3, 2011, Marlene solicited and received via email a licensing agreement for Generation software, the same software package used by Heartfelt, to be used at Home MD. That same day, Marlene also received an application for workers compensation insurance coverage for Home MD, which she completed and submitted on June 21, 2011. Then, after successfully starting Home MD, the Groves expanded their business to Delaware. On July 6, 2011, Anna Keithley, Marlene's sister, signed the Certificate of Formation to create a Delaware LLC, No Place Like Home LLC ("Home DE"), with the help of Marlene. Home DE was headquartered on the same street—in fact, *the same building*—as Heartfelt. Later that month Home DE opened another office in Lewes, Delaware.

The Groves ultimately decided to try to sever ties with the Browns. On May 31, 2011, the Groves sent the Browns a proposal letter suggesting that a purchase price of $941,000 would "be necessary for Mr. and Mrs. Brown to purchase Mr. and Mrs. Grove's interest in [Heartfelt]." The proposal also demanded that the parties "agree that the documents signed by Mr. and Mrs. Grove and their family members that purport to be covenants not to compete are invalid and unenforceable." Additionally, on July 1, 2011 the Groves notified the Browns via email of their intention to file a certificate of dissolution, to liquidate Heartfelt, and to notify the contractor and then-sole client of Heartfelt, Delaware Hospice, of the dissolution of Heartfelt.

The Browns testified that they were surprised to receive this letter. They responded on June 8, 2011, proposing that the parties select an "independent, accredited and reasonably available appraiser with recent, relevant and local experience in the field of closely-held business valuations" to "determine, in a written opinion, the fair market value of Heartfelt on a going-concern basis as of June 30, 2011." The Groves, unwilling to concede that they owned less than 50% of Heartfelt, refused the Brown's offer.

In response to the threatened dissolution, the Browns attempted to use self-help to freeze out the Groves from Heartfelt. On July 5, the Browns purported to merge Heartfelt with Heartfelt Home Health II, LLC ("Heartfelt II"), relying on their alleged 63% ownership of Heartfelt as the basis of their authority to complete the merger. Mrs. Grove first learned of the merger after she was physically barred from entering the Heartfelt office on the morning of July 6, 2011. The Browns also prepared, but never sent, a check for $72,604.99 as payment for the Groves' interest in Heartfelt. The Browns arrived at this value through consulting with a valuation analyst, Mr. Paul Seitz, who calculated the liquidation value of the Groves' interest in Heartfelt. Before the Browns could send the check, the Groves initiated this suit.

B. Nature and Stage of Proceedings

The Groves filed a verified complaint against the Browns on August 18, 2011, seeking monetary damages for an alleged breach of fiduciary duties by the Groves. On October 27, 2011, the Browns filed an answer. The Browns, joined by Heartfelt Home Health II, LLC also filed nine counterclaims against the Plaintiffs. . . . The matter was tried on January 14, 15, and 16, 2013.

II. ANALYSIS

A. The Plaintiffs' Claims

The threshold issue in this case is the percentage of the parties' ownership interests in Heartfelt. If, as the Groves allege, the Browns owned 50% of Heartfelt, then the Browns lacked the legal authority to merge Heartfelt with Heartfelt II. The ownership of Heartfelt is governed by the Operating Agreement, which identifies Hubert Brown, Melba Brown, Larry Grove, and Marlene Grove as the sole members of the LLC. Delaware law gives parties broad latitude as to the structure of an LLC and the duties of its members through the contractual provisions of their LLC agreement.

Here, The Operating Agreement provides that

> [t]he Members initially shall contribute a total of $40,000 to the Company capital. The description and each individual portion of this initial contribution are as follows:

Hubert E. Brown Jr.	$10,000.00	25%
Melba E. Brown	$10,000.00	25%
Larry E. Grove	$10,000.00	25%
Mary Marlene Grove	$10,000.00	25%

The Operating Agreement further provides that profits and losses should be divided among the members "in proportion to each Member [sic] relative capital interest in the company."

I find that these terms are unambiguous and that the Operating Agreement therefore provides that each of the four members was—and is today—an equal 25% owner of Heartfelt. Nothing in the Operating Agreement indicates that the allocation of relative ownership interests was contingent on the Members' actions post-signing. Though the Operating Agreement imposes an obligation on the members to provide capital to Heartfelt, the Operating Agreement does not provide that one member's failure to do so divests that member of his or her share of the company.

The conduct of the parties subsequent to Heartfelt's formation also confirms that both the Groves and the Browns believed that they were equal co-owners of Heartfelt.

Because the Browns were 50% owners of Heartfelt, not 63% owners, I find that the purported merger transaction, in which Heartfelt merged into a company wholly owned by the Browns, was a legal nullity.

Because I find that the merger was a nullity, the Browns and the Groves remain equal members of the original Heartfelt LLC.

B. The Defendants' Counterclaims

I now turn to the Browns' counterclaim that Larry and Marlene Grove breached their fiduciary duties by usurping a corporate opportunity of Heartfelt. . . .

The Groves were managing members of Heartfelt at the time they organized Home DE and Home MD and owed fiduciary duties to the other members.[75] I

---

75. *See Feeley v. NHAOCG, LLC,* 62 A.3d 649, 663 (Del. Ch. 2012) (holding that, absent contrary language in an LLC agreement, managing members of an LLC owe default fiduciary duties to the other members of the

find that the Groves violated those fiduciary duties by wrongfully taking for themselves the corporate opportunities of Heartfelt.

The corporate opportunity doctrine is a consequence of a fiduciary's duty of loyalty, and it exists to prevent officers or directors of a corporation—or, as in this case, a managing member of an LLC—from personally benefiting from opportunities belonging to the corporation. A corporate officer or director may not take a business opportunity as his own if:

> (1) the corporation is financially able to exploit the opportunity; (2) the opportunity is within the corporation's line of business; (3) the corporation has an interest or expectancy in the opportunity; and (4) by taking the opportunity for his own, the corporate fiduciary will thereby be placed in a position inimicable to his duties to the corporation.[76]

Conversely, a director or officer *may* take personal advantage of a corporate opportunity if:

> (1) the opportunity is presented to the director or officer in his individual and not corporate capacity; (2) the opportunity is not essential to the corporation; (3) the corporation holds no interest or expectancy in the opportunity; and (4) the director or officer has not wrongfully employed the resources of the corporation in pursuing or exploiting the opportunity.[77]

Generally, for a corporation to have an expectant interest in any specific property, "there must be some tie between the property and the nature of the corporate business."[78] An opportunity may be said to be in the corporation's line of business where the opportunity embraces "an activity as to which [the corporation] has fundamental knowledge, practical experience and ability to pursue, which, logically and naturally, is adaptable to its business, and . . . consonant with its reasonable needs and aspirations for expansion."[79]

The determination of "[w]hether or not a director has appropriated for himself something that in fairness should belong to the corporation is 'a factual question to be decided by reasonable inference from objective facts.' "[80] The burden is on the fiduciary to show that he or she did not seize a corporate opportunity.[81] As the corporate opportunity doctrine stems from a director's fiduciary duty of loyalty to the corporation, the director bears the burden of demonstrating that there was no breach because either the corporation was presented the opportunity and rejected it, or because the corporation was not in a position to take the opportunity.[82] For example, one way that a director may satisfy this burden is by formally presenting the opportunity to the corporation's board of directors and confirming the board's disinterest.[83]

LLC). Here, neither side disputes that all four members were "managing members," and both sides testified that all four played some role in the day-to-day management of Heartfelt. Both sides also agree that each member owed fiduciary duties to the LLC.

76. *Broz v. Cellular Info. Sys., Inc.,* 673 A.2d 148, 155 (Del. 1996) (citing *Guth v. Loft,* 5 A.2d 503, 509 (Del. 1939)).

77. *Id.*

78. *Johnston v. Greene,* 121 A.2d 919, 924 (Del. 1956).

79. *Guth,* 5 A.2d at 514.

80. *Johnston,* 121 A.2d at 923 (quoting *Guth,* 5 A.2d at 513).

81. *Guth,* 5 A.2d at 512.

82. *See Field v. Allyn,* 457 A.2d 1089, 1099 (Del. Ch. 1996).

83. The Delaware Supreme Court has recognized a "safe harbor" for a director to pursue a corporate opportunity without breach of his fiduciary duty where the officer presents an opportunity to the broad of directors and the corporation decides not to pursue the opportunity. *Broz,* 673 A.2d at 156. However, "[i]t is not the law of

Applying these principles here, I find that Larry and Marlene Grove, as managing members of a Delaware LLC, breached their fiduciary duty of loyalty by usurping the business opportunities of Heartfelt. The business of Home DE and Home MD is the type of business that, absent a waiver from Heartfelt, would qualify as a corporate opportunity. Heartfelt would surely have been financially capable of capitalizing on that opportunity. The business was highly profitable, and, if the experiences of the parties here are indicative, there are few, if any, barriers to entering the market for low-skilled or unskilled home health staffing. Both Home entities are unquestionably engaged in the same market as Heartfelt, thereby infringing on Heartfelt's business interests. Accordingly, the only remaining issue is determining whether Heartfelt disclaimed its interest in expanding to Maryland and other parts of Delaware.

I find that the Groves have not met their burden of demonstrating that Heartfelt disclaimed its right to pursue this corporate opportunity. The only evidence of waiver was self-serving testimony from Marlene Grove. . . . Marlene also asserts that she followed up with Melba two more times, once in February and again in March of 2011. Marlene testified that Melba rebuffed her each time and told her "[n]o, we are not going to go into business in Maryland with you." However, Marlene acknowledged that she did not actually tell the Browns about the existence of any of her family's health care companies before this litigation commenced.

Hubert Brown disagreed with Marlene's characterization of their discussions. He provided testimony—as self-serving as that of Marlene Grove—that neither he nor Melba ever disclaimed the opportunity to expand to Maryland or other parts of Delaware, but rather they wanted to proceed prudently and not expand the company too quickly.

Melba, unsurprisingly, corroborated Hubert's testimony and said that she, Marlene, and Hubert discussed "practically every day" the possibility that Heartfelt would expand to Maryland and southern Delaware. Melba also testified that Marlene had *never* disclosed that she planned to create the Home entities nor invited the Browns to be a part of them. On the contrary, Melba asserted that Heartfelt was actively considering expanding its operations to cover Maryland and Sussex County, Delaware.

Though I find all testimony presented on this issue of questionable credibility, the weight of the evidence favors the Browns' position that there was no express grant of permission for Marlene Grove to open up competing businesses in any location. It is unclear to what extent Marlene's testimony, even if I accepted it as true, supports a finding that Heartfelt waived a corporate opportunity. Marlene did not testify that she presented the opportunity to expand to nearby markets to *Heartfelt*; she avers that she invited the Browns in their personal capacity to join her in creating new, competing entities. Presenting an opportunity to the Browns is not the same as presenting an opportunity to Heartfelt. And even if it were, Marlene's acknowledgment that she never actually told the Browns about the competing entities belies her testimony that the Browns gave her permission to create them. In any event, as mentioned above, the Groves have the burden of proving that they had

---

Delaware that presentation to the board is a necessary prerequisite to a finding that a corporate opportunity has not been usurped." *Id.*

the right to pursue opportunities which would otherwise belong to Heartfelt. I find that they have failed to meet that burden.

C. Remedy

The final question is the appropriate remedy for this breach of the Operating Agreement. Both parties have taken for themselves benefits that should have been shared with the other. The Browns attempted to effectuate a merger contrary to the LLC Act, and Heartfelt has doubtless amassed profits belonging to all four owners thereafter. Likewise, the Groves usurped opportunities that should have belonged to Heartfelt. This Court has "broad latitude to exercise its equitable powers to craft a remedy." I find that the appropriate remedy in this case is to order each side to account to Heartfelt (and thus to one another) for those profits which they have wrongfully kept for themselves. Specifically, the Browns must account for the profits earned by Heartfelt II since the purported merger, and the Groves must account for the profits earned by Heart-N-Hand, Home DE, and Home MD.

Notes and Questions

1. Notes

a. Note that Georgia's definition of corporate opportunity mirrors Delaware's. Other states have different, sometimes very different, definitions. The ALI proposed the following definition, which has been adopted by a few states:

> Definition of a Corporate Opportunity. For purposes of this Section, a corporate opportunity means:
>
> (1) Any opportunity to engage in a business activity of which a director or senior executive becomes aware, either:
>
> (A) In connection with the performance of functions as a director or senior executive, or under circumstances that should reasonably lead the director or senior executive to believe that the person offering the opportunity expects it to be offered to the corporation; or
>
> (B) Through the use of corporate information or property, if the resulting opportunity is one that the director or senior executive should reasonably be expected to believe would be of interest to the corporation; or
>
> (2) Any opportunity to engage in a business activity of which a senior executive becomes aware and knows is closely related to a business in which the corporation is engaged or expects to engage.

AMERICAN LAW INSTITUTE, PRINCIPLES OF CORPORATE GOVERNANCE, §5.05(b) (1994)

b. In contrast to the MBCA, the statutory law in many states is completely silent on the question of corporate opportunities. Is this silence a good idea? Does that silence mean that a corporation may not decline corporate opportunities in advance? Does it mean that a corporation may do so?

c. In many, probably most, corporate opportunity settings, the fiduciary does not intend to compete directly with the corporation.

2. Reality Check

a. If taking a corporate opportunity is a duty of loyalty problem, why is it sometimes permissible?

b. In each of the cases, how did the defendant take a "thing" that "belonged" to the entity?

3. Suppose

a. Suppose the Groves had started health care companies further away from Heartfelt's operations. Would any home health care company be a corporate opportunity no matter how far away?

b. Suppose the Groves had started a company that sold medical supplies to home health care companies. Would that have been corporate opportunity? Do you think any of the definitions of corporate opportunity provide sufficient predictability?

4. What Do You Think?

a. Do you think the ALI definition is preferable to the Delaware definition?

b. Do you think a fiduciary should be held liable for usurping a corporate opportunity if he or she did not intend to compete with the corporation or did not intend to otherwise harm the corporation? Do you think the definitions of corporate opportunity sufficiently reflect the appropriate degree of intent?

As *Brewer* points out, applying the corporate opportunity doctrine requires two distinct inquiries. First, the court must determine whether a transaction into which the fiduciary entered was a corporate opportunity. If it was, the next determination is whether the fiduciary breached a duty by taking it. Most states hold that a fiduciary cannot take a corporate opportunity unless he or she first presented it, with full disclosure, to the corporation and the corporation declined to accept it. Of course, part of the practical problem with the corporate opportunity doctrine is that a fiduciary cannot predict with certainty whether a particular venture will later be determined to have been a corporate opportunity. The rule in many states, and under the ALI formulation, is that a failure to offer a corporate opportunity will not be fatal if the fiduciary believed, in good faith, that the venture was not a corporate opportunity. All of this, as you see, is wildly indeterminate.

The possibility of usurping a corporate opportunity is a real and constant one for business people, who may be involved with more than one business in the same industry. Often someone with particular industry expertise is sought out for business ventures precisely because he or she is an expert. Such people may be reluctant to become officers or directors of entities if doing so would subject them to unpredictable corporate opportunity liability. To lessen the uncertainties, both the DGCL and the MBCA provide that some, or all, corporate opportunities can be disclaimed in advance. The MBCA requires such a provision to be in the articles of incorporation, but Delaware simply provides a grant of power to the board to disclaim corporate opportunities in advance. *See* DGCL §122(17), MBCA §2.02(b)(6). The MBCA goes further and provides a rather elaborate, non-exclusive safe harbor for approval of a "business opportunity." The MBCA does not define business opportunities but the Official Comments make it clear that it is intended to be broader than corporate opportunities.

2. Self-Dealing

Taking a corporate opportunity is one of the paradigms of duty of loyalty problems. Another paradigm is *self-dealing*. Indeed, self-dealing is such a frequent example of duty of loyalty concerns that courts and commentators occasionally use the term *self-dealing* to mean any duty of loyalty question. As the name implies, self-dealing occurs when a director or officer enters into a contract with the corporation, usually to buy something from, or sell something to, the corporation.

A moment's reflection (don't worry, I'm not actually asking you to reflect) will reveal that simply because a director has sold something to the corporation does not mean that he or she has necessarily violated the duty of loyalty. The director might well honestly believe that the contract is in the best interest of the corporation. Viewed entirely objectively, such contracts might indeed be in the corporation's best interest. Certainly such situations frequently arise during the start-up phase of a corporation's existence. One of the promoters will contribute the Big Idea or the unique piece of real estate without which the corporation cannot flourish, in return for stock. Such a transaction is surely in the corporation's best economic interest.

The rub, of course, is whether the corporation is exchanging too much for what it is receiving. This question, which is central to whether a self-dealing transaction violates the duty of loyalty, sometimes raises delicate and difficult questions of valuation. If the asset that is changing hands is untested, it may be difficult to ascertain its value using a discounted cash flow analysis. If the asset is genuinely unique, it may be difficult to find appropriately comparable assets to which to compare its value. Further, the asset's uniqueness may mean that its value to the corporation far outstrips its value in its next-most remunerative use. For example, a delivery truck painted with the company logo might be worth $X to a bakery company but also worth $X (or very nearly so) to another company, which would simply have to repaint the logo. On the other hand, a huge, specially designed machine that only makes My Little Ponies, could be enormously valuable to the company that makes My Little Pony and much less valuable (i.e., scrap value only) to any other company.

As you think about the question of self-dealing, think about the problem of valuation and also think about whether the director's subjective views about the fairness of the transaction to the corporation should be determinative, irrelevant, or somewhere in between. The next case presents an ironic situation regarding whether the corporation received value from the self-dealing transaction.

≡ ### Tomaino v. Concord Oil of Newport, Inc.
≡   709 A.2d 1016 (R.I. 1998)

WEISBERGER, C.J.

In 1976 [Joseph M.] Tomaino became a 25-percent owner of Concord Oil Company (Concord), a closely held Massachusetts corporation. . . . Tomaino, who brought with him seventeen years of experience from his previous employment with Texaco, Inc., became a member of the board of directors and vice president of

Concord. His primary area of responsibility with Concord was the development, maintenance, and enhancement of Concord's retail-gasoline business. The president of Concord was Arthur R. Bethke (Bethke), who . . . owned the rest of the Concord stock [and] ran the company.

Between 1976 and 1978 Concord developed several gasoline retail outlets. Concord would as a general rule either lease its service-station locations [to others] and/or negotiate a supply contract with an existing operator. Regardless of the form of the business, it was routine for Concord to acquire ownership of the underground tanks at each location where it was supplying gasoline. Three witnesses in the business of gasoline retailing . . . testified that during the 1970s it was very common for gasoline distributors to own the underground tanks and related petroleum-marketing equipment (that is, underground fuel lines, underground pump systems, gas pump islands, and the like) at retail locations with which the distributor had a supply or a commission contract. [B]y securing ownership of the gasoline storage tanks, the supplier could "put a lock on [the] business through [the] contractual relationship." In addition, by owning the tanks, the supplier had the power to remove the equipment from the property in the event the onsite vendor was unable or unwilling to meet the supplier's business expectations. According to two of the witnesses this practice did not change until the mid-1980s, upon the advent of greater environmental-testing procedures and the consequent environmental liability, which was never an issue in the 1970s.

Prior to joining Concord, Tomaino had investigated the possibility of purchasing/leasing several retail gasoline businesses . . . owned by Newport Oil Corporation (Newport Oil). In 1978, after joining Concord, Tomaino and Bethke agreed that Tomaino would renew negotiations with Newport Oil in order to pursue jointly these opportunities on behalf of [Tomaino and] Concord. Tomaino negotiated an agreement [to lease from] Newport Oil . . . three properties upon which retail-gasoline businesses were in operation. Specifically the locations were . . . Newport . . . ; One Mile Corner . . . ; and . . . Portsmouth.

Tomaino and Bethke formed a separate corporation, Concord Oil of Newport, Inc. (Concord/Newport) . . . to supply and/or operate the retail-gasoline businesses at each location. Concord owned 68 percent of the stock and Tomaino owned 32 percent. Tomaino served as president of the new entity. . . . Tomaino . . . purchased [the real estate. By separate agreement, he also purchased] all the buildings and improvements constituting the gasoline service stations, including all petroleum-marketing equipment, underground tanks, and ancillary facilities [from Newport Oil] at the price of one dollar.[7]

[Three months later, on] June 12, 1978, [Tomaino] transferred ownership . . . of the underground tanks, pump islands, pump systems, and related lighting at each location to Concord/Newport for $5,000. Tomaino testified that this figure was below market value for the tanks and other improvements. There was additional testimony that this amount was substantially less than Concord/Newport had paid on previous occasions for similar acquisitions.

Tomaino left Concord's employ in February 1993. In May 1993 Concord/Newport notified Tomaino of its intention to quit its tenancy at the One Mile

7. Tomaino testified that such an apparent bargain was justified owing to the value Newport received on the lease itself.

Corner location. Tomaino requested that Concord/Newport remove its underground tanks at that site. After Concord/Newport failed to do so, Tomaino, after notifying Concord/Newport of his intention, removed the tanks at a cost of $18,600.

Frank M. Oliveira . . . , a commercial real estate broker engaged by [Tomaino] to rent the property testified that the presence of the tanks frustrated his efforts because suitable tenants were unwilling to assume the potential liability that the presence of the tanks created. Domino's Pizza . . . eventually agreed to rent the premises on the condition that the tanks be removed. Thereafter Tomaino paid for the removal of the tanks at the One Mile Corner location. When Domino's finally assumed tenancy, the property had been unoccupied for eleven and one-half months. Oliveira's undisputed testimony was that the fair rental value of the One Mile Corner property at that time was $3,000 per month. . . .

On February 3, 1994, plaintiff filed a complaint seeking declaratory relief, injunctive relief, and money damages. In August 1994 Tomaino received further notice from Concord/Newport of its intention to terminate its tenancy at both the Portsmouth and the Newport locations. Concord/Newport removed a portion of the petroleum marketing equipment from each location, but did not remove the underground tanks or the related piping. Tomaino did not, however, remove at his own expense the tanks at either the Newport or the Portsmouth locations. Tomaino was unsuccessful in renting either of these two properties from that time until the time of trial.

A trial was held in Superior Court in June 1995. The jury determined that the tanks were the property of defendant Concord/Newport and awarded plaintiff $88,950 in damages, representing costs incurred in removing two tanks from one location and for lost rental revenue at each additional location. The trial justice denied defendant's motion for a new trial and directed defendant to remove the remaining underground tanks and related equipment. The trial justice conditioned the denial of defendant's motion upon plaintiff's acceptance of a remittitur of $37,650 . . . because . . . Tomaino had failed to mitigate damages by not removing the remaining tanks located at the Newport and the Portsmouth locations and thus render those properties eligible for lease or sale.

The duty of loyalty requires, inter alia, that a director or an officer act in good faith toward the corporation and that transactions or contracts into which he or she enters with the corporation be fair to the corporation. Good faith in this context means full and honest disclosure by the fiduciary of all material facts to allow for a disinterested decision maker to exercise its informed judgment. Fairness to the corporation requires that a transaction or contract benefit the corporation and the stockholders thereof and not confer undue or unjust advantage on the fiduciary.

An interested transaction occurs when a corporate fiduciary (officer, director, or in the case of a close corporation, a shareholder) enters into a contract or transaction with that corporate entity that he or she serves as a fiduciary. Such a transaction is not per se voidable but may be challenged if it was not entered into in good faith and/or was unfair to the corporation.

To be valid, the transaction must have been assented to by the disinterested officers and/or stockholders of the corporation with full knowledge of all the facts. The burden of proving that the challenged transaction both was fair to the corporation and was authorized, approved, or ratified lies with the interested party. Ratification need not, however, be by formal vote but may be implied from a corporation's course of conduct in instances in which the corporation derives a benefit from the challenged contract or transaction and in which the directors had "knowledge of such facts or circumstances as would put a reasonable person on inquiry and [which] would lead to full discovery." *Puritan Medical Center, Inc. v. Cashman*, 596 N.E.2d 1004, 1008 (Mass. 1992). . . .

It is important to appreciate that what lies at the heart of the instant dispute is . . . a significant change in perception, between the time the transaction was effected and the time plaintiff filed suit, about whether an underground gasoline storage tank constitutes an asset or a liability. A reasonable jury could have determined that the sale of the tanks conferred a benefit to the corporation, was not uncommon in the industry or in the usual course of Concord's business, was arguably fair to Concord/Newport at the time of sale, and had the sale been effected by a third party, its validity could not have been doubted.

The defendant argues that even had the sale of the tanks been ratified by Concord/Newport, the deal was not mutually beneficial or fair to the corporation. In support of this assertion it points to the discrepancy between the price [Tomaino] paid for the tanks and equipment and the price Concord/Newport paid for just a portion thereof. Further, defendant insists that the testimony adduced by plaintiff that it was standard practice within the industry for gasoline suppliers to purchase the underground tanks of retail vendors to whom they supplied gasoline is not persuasive on the facts of this case. Concord/Newport, the argument went, had no need to "lock in" Tomaino because Tomaino was in effect Concord/Newport, owning 32 percent of that company's stock. Concord/Newport maintains that it would be ludicrous to conclude that it would seek to lock Tomaino into a gasoline-supply contract.

We find these arguments interesting but ultimately unavailing. The markup on the price of the improvements from [Tomaino] to Concord/Newport is not so shocking in context as the seemingly stark inequity of the increase considered in the abstract. After all, trial testimony established that this amount was below market value and substantially less than what Concord or Concord/Newport had paid for similar acquisitions on previous occasions. Examining the dynamics of all the transactions involved, the jury could reasonably conclude that the difference in price was attributable to business judgment, arm's-length negotiation, or some other justification and did not represent a hidden windfall to Tomaino. Moreover, this $5,000 transaction placed in the context of Concord's and Concord/Newport's financial landscape was slight: testimony at trial revealed that in retail-gasoline business alone, the corporations together supplied gasoline to over thirty service stations throughout New England.

Viewing the evidence and all reasonable inferences therefrom in a light most beneficial to plaintiff, the trial justice properly determined that a jury question existed concerning whether (1) full disclosure of the material facts concerning the tank transaction had been made by plaintiff to Concord/Newport, (2) the sale had been approved, authorized, or ratified by Concord/Newport, and (3) the transaction was fair to Concord/Newport at the time of authorization, approval, or ratification. Accordingly we discern no error in the trial justice's denial of defendant's motion for judgment as a matter of law.

BOURCIER, J., did not participate.

Notes and Questions

1. Reality Check

a. Where is the self-dealing transaction?

b. Which party is trying to nullify the self-dealing transaction? Why?

c. What test does the court use to evaluate self-dealing transactions?

d. Why does the court allow the self-dealing transaction to stand?

2. Suppose

a. Suppose environmental concerns had made underground storage tanks disadvantageous at the time of the sales from Tomaino to Concord/Newport. Would the transaction still be "fair" to Concord/Newport?

3. What Do You Think?

a. Should self-dealing transactions be void per se?

b. Should self-dealing transactions be subjected to any different tests than other board actions?

c. Did Tomaino usurp a corporate opportunity?

Putting It to Work

Problem 11-1

CookR is a discovery website that helps connect people with a love of cooking or food. People create and share collections of recipes (called cookbooks) and pictures of food (called menus). Users can upload menus to their cookbooks, which can then be sorted and shared with others. A commenting system allows other users to rate the menus with * (good of its kind), ** (worth clicking on), or *** (worth going online just to view this menu). CookR was founded three years ago by Alton and Rachael, two foodie friends.

One year ago, Alton and Rachael were at a party and found themselves seated on either side of Mark Parker, founder, controlling shareholder, and a director of FaceMyBook.com, the world's leading social media site. Although CookR had not yet reached a critical number of users to make the site commercially viable, Alton and Rachael were convinced that time and an infusion of money would be all that was needed to make CookR a huge success. Of course, the business model assumed that once CookR was used by a large enough base of people, it would be economically feasible to mine the menus and cookbooks and sell the data. More to the point, after talking with Alton and Rachael, Mark was also convinced that CookR had great potential and needed only time and money.

Within a month of the party, Mark had struck a deal with Alton and Rachael to purchase CookR from them for $1 million, probably its fair market value at the time.

Mark bought CookR personally and paid for it from his own funds. He did not discuss the purchase with any other director or officer of FaceMyBook. Alton and Rachael were required to keep the fact of the sale confidential under the terms of the purchase agreement. No one knew that CookR had changed hands except Mark, Alton, Rachael, and their legal advisors. Mark has kept Alton and Rachael in charge of CookR and has invested an additional $5 million to get the site to a critically large size.

As the parties anticipated, the last year has seen an explosive growth in the popularity of CookR. It is now THE hot website for anyone with any interest in food or cooking. Two weeks ago, Mark announced to the FaceMyBook board that he owns CookR and is willing to sell it to FaceMyBook. Although CookR and FaceMyBook are not equivalent sites (CookR is specialized and FaceMyBook is general), they share many obvious similarities and the chance to own the Next New Thing is terrifically valuable to FaceMyBook, if for no other reason than that it would keep CookR out of the hands of FaceMyBook's major competitors. Mark and the FaceMyBook board reach agreement on the sale of CookR to FaceMyBook for $1 billion, probably 10 percent or so below its fair market value.

a. Does either Mark's purchase of CookR from Alton and Rachael or his sale of CookR to FaceMyBook violate his fiduciary duties?

3. Failure to Monitor and the Duty of Good Faith

Can directors violate their duty of loyalty when they do not "act" at all? That is, are there instances when the board's failure to consider any action may be seen as violating the requirement that "[e]ach member of the board . . . shall act . . . in a manner the director reasonably believes to be in the best interest of the corporation"? The next case explores this possibility.

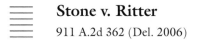 **Stone v. Ritter**
911 A.2d 362 (Del. 2006)

Before STEELE, C.J., HOLLAND, BERGER, JACOBS, and RIDGELY, JJ. (constituting the court *en banc*).

HOLLAND, J.:

This is an appeal from a final judgment of the Court of Chancery dismissing a derivative complaint against fifteen present and former directors of AmSouth Bancorporation ("AmSouth"), a Delaware corporation. The plaintiffs-appellants, William and Sandra Stone, are AmSouth shareholders and filed their derivative complaint without making a pre-suit demand on AmSouth's board of directors (the "Board"). The Court of Chancery held that the plaintiffs had failed to adequately plead that such a demand would have been futile. The Court, therefore, dismissed the derivative complaint under Court of Chancery Rule 23.1.

Facts

In 2004, AmSouth . . . paid $40 million in fines and $10 million in civil penalties to resolve government and regulatory investigations pertaining principally to the failure by bank employees to file "Suspicious Activity Reports" ("SARs"), as required by the federal Bank Secrecy Act ("BSA")[4] and various anti-money-laundering ("AML") regulations. Those investigations were conducted by the United States Attorney's Office for the Southern District of Mississippi ("USAO"), the Federal Reserve, FinCEN and the Alabama Banking Department. No fines or penalties were imposed on AmSouth's directors, and no other regulatory action was taken against them.

The government investigations arose originally from an unlawful "Ponzi" scheme operated by Louis D. Hamric, II and Victor G. Nance. In August 2000, Hamric, then a licensed attorney, and Nance, then a registered investment advisor with Mutual of New York, contacted an AmSouth branch bank in Tennessee to arrange for custodial trust accounts to be created for "investors" in a "business venture." That venture (Hamric and Nance represented) involved the construction of medical clinics overseas. In reality, Nance had convinced more than forty of his clients to invest in promissory notes bearing high rates of return, by misrepresenting the nature and the risk of that investment. Relying on similar misrepresentations by Hamric and Nance, the AmSouth branch employees in Tennessee agreed to provide custodial accounts for the investors and to distribute monthly interest payments to each account upon receipt of a check from Hamric and instructions from Nance.

The Hamric-Nance scheme was discovered in March 2002, when the investors did not receive their monthly interest payments. Thereafter, Hamric and Nance became the subject of several civil actions brought by the defrauded investors in Tennessee and Mississippi (and in which AmSouth also was named as a defendant), and also the subject of a federal grand jury investigation in the Southern District of Mississippi. Hamric and Nance were indicted on federal money-laundering charges, and both pled guilty.

On October 12, 2004, AmSouth and the USAO entered into a Deferred Prosecution Agreement ("DPA") in which AmSouth agreed: first, to the filing by USAO of a one-count Information in the United States District Court for the Southern District of Mississippi, charging AmSouth with failing to file SARs; and second, to pay a $40 million fine. In conjunction with the DPA, the USAO issued a "Statement of Facts," which noted that although in 2000 "at least one" AmSouth employee suspected that Hamric was involved in a possibly illegal scheme, AmSouth failed to file SARs in a timely manner. In neither the Statement of Facts nor anywhere else did the USAO ascribe any blame to the Board or to any individual director.

On October 12, 2004, the Federal Reserve and the Alabama Banking Department concurrently issued a Cease and Desist Order against AmSouth, requiring it,

---

4. 31 U.S.C. §5318 (2006) *et seq.* The Bank Secrecy Act and the regulations promulgated thereunder require banks to file with the Financial Crimes Enforcement Network, a bureau of the U.S. Department of the Treasury known as "FinCEN," a written "Suspicious Activity Report" (known as a "SAR") whenever, *inter alia,* a banking transaction involves at least $5,000 "and the bank knows, suspects, or has reason to suspect" that, among other possibilities, the "transaction involves funds derived from illegal activities or is intended or conducted in order to hide or disguise funds or assets derived from illegal activities." 31 U.S.C. §5318(g) (2006); 31 C.F.R. §103.18(a)(2) (2006).

for the first time, to improve its BSA/AML program. That Cease and Desist Order required AmSouth to (among other things) engage an independent consultant "to conduct a comprehensive review of the Bank's AML Compliance program and make recommendations, as appropriate, for new policies and procedures to be implemented by the Bank." KPMG Forensic Services ("KPMG") performed the role of independent consultant and issued its report on December 10, 2004 (the "KPMG Report").

Also on October 12, 2004, FinCEN and the Federal Reserve jointly assessed a $10 million civil penalty against AmSouth for operating an inadequate anti-money-laundering program and for failing to file SARs. In connection with that assessment, FinCEN issued a written Assessment of Civil Money Penalty (the "Assessment"), which included detailed "determinations" regarding AmSouth's BSA compliance procedures. FinCEN found that "AmSouth violated the suspicious activity reporting requirements of the Bank Secrecy Act," and that "[s]ince April 24, 2002, AmSouth has been in violation of the anti-money-laundering program requirements of the Bank Secrecy Act." Among FinCEN's specific determinations were its conclusions that "AmSouth's [AML compliance] program lacked adequate board and management oversight," and that "reporting to management for the purposes of monitoring and oversight of compliance activities was materially deficient." AmSouth neither admitted nor denied FinCEN's determinations in this or any other forum.

Demand Futility and Director Independence

It is a fundamental principle of the Delaware General Corporation Law that "[t]he business and affairs of every corporation organized under this chapter shall be managed by or under the direction of a board of directors."[6] Thus, by its very nature [a] derivative action impinges on the managerial freedom of directors. Therefore, the right of a stockholder to prosecute a derivative suit is limited to situations where either the stockholder has demanded the directors pursue a corporate claim and the directors have wrongfully refused to do so, or where demand is excused because the directors are incapable of making an impartial decision regarding whether to institute such litigation. Court of Chancery Rule 23.1, accordingly, requires that the complaint in a derivative action "allege with particularity the efforts, if any, made by the plaintiff to obtain the action the plaintiff desires from the directors [or] the reasons for the plaintiff's failure to obtain the action or for not making the effort."[9]

To excuse demand . . . a court must determine whether or not the particularized factual allegations of a derivative stockholder complaint create a reasonable doubt that, as of the time the complaint is filed, the board of directors could have properly exercised its independent and disinterested business judgment in responding to a demand. The plaintiffs attempt to satisfy the . . . test in this proceeding by asserting that the incumbent defendant directors face a substantial likelihood of liability that renders them personally interested in the outcome of the decision on whether to

---

6. [DGCL] §141(a).
9. Ch. Ct. R. 23.1. Allegations of demand futility under Rule 23.1 must comply with stringent requirements of factual particularity that differ substantially from the permissive notice pleadings governed solely by Chancery Rule 8(a).

pursue the claims asserted in the complaint, and are therefore not disinterested or independent.

The standard for assessing a director's potential personal liability for failing to act in good faith in discharging his or her oversight responsibilities has evolved beginning with our decision in *Graham v. Allis-Chalmers Manufacturing Company*,[15] through the Court of Chancery's *Caremark*[*] decision to our most recent decision in *Disney*.[16] A brief discussion of that evolution will help illuminate the standard that we adopt in this case.

Graham *and* Caremark

Graham was a derivative action brought against the directors of Allis-Chalmers for failure to prevent violations of federal anti-trust laws by Allis-Chalmers employees. There was no claim that the Allis-Chalmers directors knew of the employees' conduct that resulted in the corporation's liability. Rather, the plaintiffs claimed that the Allis-Chalmers directors *should have known* of the illegal conduct by the corporation's employees. In *Graham,* this Court held that "*absent cause for suspicion* there is no duty upon the directors to install and operate a corporate system of espionage to ferret out wrongdoing which they have no reason to suspect exists."[17]

In *Caremark,* the Court of Chancery reassessed the applicability of our holding in *Graham* when called upon to approve a settlement of a derivative lawsuit brought against the directors of Caremark International, Inc. The plaintiffs claimed that the Caremark directors should have known that certain officers and employees of Caremark were involved in violations of the federal Anti-Referral Payments Law. That law prohibits health care providers from paying any form of remuneration to induce the referral of Medicare or Medicaid patients. The plaintiffs claimed that the Caremark directors breached their fiduciary duty for having "allowed a situation to develop and continue which exposed the corporation to enormous legal liability and that in so doing they violated a duty to be active monitors of corporate performance."[18]

In evaluating whether to approve the proposed settlement agreement in *Caremark,* the Court of Chancery narrowly construed our holding in *Graham* "as standing for the proposition that, absent grounds to suspect deception, neither corporate boards nor senior officers can be charged with wrongdoing simply for assuming the integrity of employees and the honesty of their dealings on the company's behalf."[19] The *Caremark* Court opined it would be a "mistake" to interpret this Court's decision in *Graham* to mean that:

> corporate boards may satisfy their obligation to be reasonably informed concerning the corporation, without assuring themselves that information and reporting systems exist in the organization that are reasonably designed to provide to senior management and to the board itself timely, accurate information sufficient to allow management and the board, each within

---

15. *Graham v. Allis-Chalmers Mfg. Co.,* 188 A.2d 125 (Del. 1963).
* [*In re Caremark Int'l Litig.,* 698 A.2d 959 (Del. Ch. 1996). *ED.*]
16. *In re Walt Disney Co. Deriv. Litig.,* 906 A.2d 27 (Del. 2006).
17. *Graham v. Allis-Chalmers Mfg. Co.,* 188 A.2d at 130 (emphasis added).
18. *In re Caremark Int'l Inc. Deriv. Litig.,* 698 A.2d 959, 967 (Del. Ch. 1996).
19. *Id.* at 969.

its scope, to reach informed judgments concerning both the corporation's compliance with law and its business performance.[20]

To the contrary, the *Caremark* Court stated, "it is important that the board exercise a good faith judgment that the corporation's information and reporting system is in concept and design adequate to assure the board that appropriate information will come to its attention in a timely manner as a matter of ordinary operations, so that it may satisfy its responsibility."[21] The *Caremark* Court recognized, however, that "the duty to act in good faith to be informed cannot be thought to require directors to possess detailed information about all aspects of the operation of the enterprise."[22] The Court of Chancery then formulated the following standard for assessing the liability of directors where the directors are unaware of employee misconduct that results in the corporation being held liable:

> Generally where a claim of directorial liability for corporate loss is predicated upon ignorance of liability creating activities within the corporation, as in *Graham* or in this case, . . . only a sustained or systematic failure of the board to exercise oversight—such as an utter failure to attempt to assure a reasonable information and reporting system exists—will establish the lack of good faith that is a necessary condition to liability.[23]

Caremark *Standard Approved*

As evidenced by the language quoted above, the *Caremark* standard for so-called "oversight" liability draws heavily upon the concept of director failure to act in good faith. That is consistent with the definition(s) of bad faith recently approved by this Court in its recent *Disney* decision, where we held that a failure to act in good faith requires conduct that is qualitatively different from, and more culpable than, the conduct giving rise to a violation of the fiduciary duty of care (i.e., gross negligence). In *Disney,* we identified the following examples of conduct that would establish a failure to act in good faith:

> A failure to act in good faith may be shown, for instance, where the fiduciary intentionally acts with a purpose other than that of advancing the best interests of the corporation, where the fiduciary acts with the intent to violate applicable positive law, or where the fiduciary intentionally fails to act in the face of a known duty to act, demonstrating a conscious disregard for his duties. There may be other examples of bad faith yet to be proven or alleged, but these three are the most salient.

The third of these examples describes, and is fully consistent with, the lack of good faith conduct that the *Caremark* court held was a "necessary condition" for director oversight liability, i.e., "a sustained or systematic failure of the board to exercise oversight—such as an utter failure to attempt to assure a reasonable information and reporting system exists. . . ."[27] Indeed, our opinion in *Disney* cited *Caremark* with approval for that proposition. Accordingly, the Court of Chancery applied the correct standard in assessing whether demand was excused in this case where failure to exercise oversight was the basis or theory of the plaintiffs' claim for relief.

20. *Id*. at 970.
21. *Id*.
22. *Id*. at 971.
23. *In re Caremark Int'l Inc. Deriv. Litig.*, 698 A.2d at 971.
27. *In re Caremark Int'l Inc. Deriv. Litig.*, 698 A.2d 959, 971 (Del. Ch. 1996).

It is important, in this context, to clarify a doctrinal issue that is critical to understanding fiduciary liability under *Caremark* as we construe that case. The phraseology used in *Caremark* and that we employ here—describing the lack of good faith as a "necessary condition to liability"—is deliberate. The purpose of that formulation is to communicate that a failure to act in good faith is not conduct that results, *ipso facto*, in the direct imposition of fiduciary liability.[29] The failure to act in good faith may result in liability because the requirement to act in good faith "is a subsidiary element[,]" i.e., a condition, "of the fundamental duty of loyalty."[30] It follows that because a showing of bad faith conduct, in the sense described in *Disney* and *Caremark*, is essential to establish director oversight liability, the fiduciary duty violated by that conduct is the duty of loyalty.

This view of a failure to act in good faith results in two additional doctrinal consequences. First, although good faith may be described colloquially as part of a "triad" of fiduciary duties that includes the duties of care and loyalty,[31] the obligation to act in good faith does not establish an independent fiduciary duty that stands on the same footing as the duties of care and loyalty. Only the latter two duties, where violated, may directly result in liability, whereas a failure to act in good faith may do so, but indirectly. The second doctrinal consequence is that the fiduciary duty of loyalty is not limited to cases involving a financial or other cognizable fiduciary conflict of interest. It also encompasses cases where the fiduciary fails to act in good faith. As the Court of Chancery aptly put it in *Guttman*, "[a] director cannot act loyally towards the corporation unless she acts in the good faith belief that her actions are in the corporation's best interest."[32]

We hold that *Caremark* articulates the necessary conditions predicate for director oversight liability: (a) the directors utterly failed to implement any reporting or information system or controls; *or* (b) having implemented such a system or controls, consciously failed to monitor or oversee its operations thus disabling themselves from being informed of risks or problems requiring their attention. In either case, imposition of liability requires a showing that the directors knew that they were not discharging their fiduciary obligations. Where directors fail to act in the face of a known duty to act, thereby demonstrating a conscious disregard for their responsibilities, they breach their duty of loyalty by failing to discharge that fiduciary obligation in good faith.

Chancery Court Decision

The plaintiffs contend that demand is excused under Rule 23.1 because AmSouth's directors breached their oversight duty and, as a result, face a "substantial likelihood of liability" as a result of their "utter failure" to act in good faith to put into place policies and procedures to ensure compliance with BSA and AML obligations. The Court of Chancery found that the plaintiffs did not plead the existence of "red flags" —"facts showing that the board ever was aware that AmSouth's internal controls were inadequate, that these inadequacies would result in illegal activity, and that the

---

29. That issue, whether a violation of the duty to act in good faith is a basis for the direct imposition of liability, was expressly left open in *Disney*. 906 A.2d at 67 n. 112. We address that issue here.

30. *Guttman v. Huang*, 823 A.2d 492, 506 n. 34 (Del. Ch. 2003).

31. *See Cede & Co. v. Technicolor, Inc.*, 634 A.2d 345, 361 (Del. 1993).

32. *Guttman v. Huang*, 823 A.2d 492, 506 n. 34 (Del. Ch. 2003).

board chose to do nothing about problems it allegedly knew existed." In dismissing the derivative complaint in this action, the Court of Chancery concluded:

> This case is not about a board's failure to carefully consider a material corporate decision that was presented to the board. This is a case where information was not reaching the board because of ineffective internal controls. With the benefit of hindsight, it is beyond question that AmSouth's internal controls with respect to the Bank Secrecy Act and anti-money laundering regulations compliance were inadequate. Neither party disputes that the lack of internal controls resulted in a huge fine—$50 million, alleged to be the largest ever of its kind. The fact of those losses, however, is not alone enough for a court to conclude that a majority of the corporation's board of directors is disqualified from considering demand that AmSouth bring suit against those responsible.

This Court reviews *de novo* a Court of Chancery's decision to dismiss a derivative suit under Rule 23.1.

Reasonable Reporting System Existed

The KPMG Report evaluated the various components of AmSouth's longstanding BSA/AML compliance program. The KPMG Report reflects that AmSouth's Board dedicated considerable resources to the BSA/AML compliance program and put into place numerous procedures and systems to attempt to ensure compliance. According to KPMG, the program's various components exhibited between a low and high degree of compliance with applicable laws and regulations.

The KPMG Report reflects that the directors not only discharged their oversight responsibility to establish an information and reporting system, but also proved that the system was designed to permit the directors to periodically monitor AmSouth's compliance with BSA and AML regulations. For example, as KPMG noted in 2004, AmSouth's designated BSA Officer "has made annual high-level presentations to the Board of Directors in each of the last five years." Further, the Board's Audit and Community Responsibility Committee (the "Audit Committee") oversaw Am-South's BSA/AML compliance program on a quarterly basis. The KPMG Report states that "the BSA Officer presents BSA/AML training to the Board of Directors annually," and the "Corporate Security training is also presented to the Board of Directors."

The KPMG Report shows that AmSouth's Board at various times enacted written policies and procedures designed to ensure compliance with the BSA and AML regulations. For example, the Board adopted an amended bank-wide "BSA/AML Policy" on July 17, 2003—four months before AmSouth became aware that it was the target of a government investigation. Among other things, the July 17, 2003, BSA/AML Policy directs all AmSouth employees to immediately report suspicious transactions or activity to the BSA/AML Compliance Department or Corporate Security.

Complaint Properly Dismissed

In this case, the adequacy of the plaintiffs' assertion that demand is excused depends on whether the complaint alleges facts sufficient to show that the defendant *directors* are potentially personally liable for the failure of non-director bank *employees* to file SARs. Delaware courts have recognized that "[m]ost of the decisions that a corporation, acting through its human agents, makes are, of course, not the subject of director attention."[39] Consequently, a claim that directors are subject to personal liability for employee failures is "possibly the most difficult theory in corporation law upon which a plaintiff might hope to win a judgment."[40]

For the plaintiffs' derivative complaint to withstand a motion to dismiss, "only a sustained or systematic failure of the board to exercise oversight—such as an utter failure to attempt to assure a reasonable information and reporting system exists—will establish the lack of good faith that is a necessary condition to liability."[41] As the *Caremark* decision noted:

> Such a test of liability—lack of good faith as evidenced by sustained or systematic failure of a director to exercise reasonable oversight—is quite high. But, a demanding test of liability in the oversight context is probably beneficial to corporate shareholders as a class, as it is in the board decision context, since it makes board service by qualified persons more likely, while continuing to act as a stimulus to *good faith performance of duty* by such directors.[42]

The KPMG Report—which the plaintiffs explicitly incorporated by reference into their derivative complaint—refutes the assertion that the directors "never took the necessary steps . . . to ensure that a reasonable BSA compliance and reporting system existed." KPMG's findings reflect that the Board received and approved relevant policies and procedures, delegated to certain employees and departments the responsibility for filing SARs and monitoring compliance, and exercised oversight by relying on periodic reports from them. Although there ultimately may have been failures by employees to report deficiencies to the Board, there is no basis for an oversight claim seeking to hold the directors personally liable for such failures by the employees.

With the benefit of hindsight, the plaintiffs' complaint seeks to equate a bad outcome with bad faith. The lacuna in the plaintiffs' argument is a failure to recognize that the directors' good faith exercise of oversight responsibility may not invariably prevent employees from violating criminal laws, or from causing the corporation to incur significant financial liability, or both, as occurred in *Graham*, *Caremark* and this very case. In the absence of red flags, good faith in the context of oversight must be measured by the directors' actions to assure a reasonable information and reporting system exists and not by second-guessing after the occurrence of employee conduct that results in an unintended adverse outcome. Accordingly, we hold that the Court of Chancery properly applied *Caremark* and dismissed the plaintiffs' derivative complaint for failure to excuse demand by alleging particularized facts that created reason to doubt whether the directors had acted in good faith in exercising their oversight responsibilities.

Conclusion

The judgment of the Court of Chancery is affirmed.

---

39. *In re Caremark Int'l Inc. Deriv. Litig.*, 698 A.2d at 968.
40. *Id.* at 967.
41. *Id.* at 971.
42. *Id.* (emphasis in original).

Notes and Questions

1. Notes

a. Chancellor Allen decided *Caremark*, and discussed a board's obligation to monitor, strictly as an aspect of the duty of care. That is, part of a board's duty to be informed is to ensure that appropriate monitoring systems are in place. In *Stone*, Justice Holland affirmed what had been generally assumed: *Caremark*, including the standard of review, governs the board's duty to monitor. However, he went on to say that *Caremark* liability "requires a showing that the directors knew that they were not discharging their fiduciary obligations." That's a significant change in *Caremark* jurisprudence.

Stone, without any acknowledgment that it was choosing to redefine a *Caremark* claim from care to loyalty, did exactly that. *Stone* shifted the doctrinal emphasis in considering a duty to monitor from information gathering (duty of care) to the directors' intent (duty of loyalty).

b. Note the distinction between an obligation to follow up on information that comes to a director's attention that suggests the possibility of wrong-doing by the corporation or its agents and an obligation to establish, and monitor the efficacy of, a system of ensuring that sufficient information about the corporation is brought to the directors' attention.

c. The MBCA's duty of care encompasses an obligation to oversee the corporation's actions, which is functionally similar to the obligation imposed in *Caremark*. The MBCA thus retains the original conception of oversight as a component of the duty of care, not the duty of loyalty. *Compare* MBCA §§8.30(b) and 8.31(a), Official Comments.

2. Reality Check

a. What exactly was the court deciding? That is, what is the procedural posture of this case?

b. In what way were the directors of AmSouth alleged to have breached their duty of loyalty?

c. Why did the court find those allegations unconvincing?

d. Did the Supreme Court agree with the Court of Chancery in both reasoning and result?

3. Suppose

a. Suppose the directors knew that SARs were not being filed. Would that change the analysis or result?

b. Suppose the directors knew that SARs were not being filed and made a decision that the bank's likely profit from Hamric and Nance was greater than the bank's likely punishment if it were investigated. Would that change the analysis or result?

4. What Do You Think?

a. If monitoring is so important, and it is absolutely clear that the monitoring by the AmSouth board was inadequate, why is there no liability?

b. Chancellor Allen wrote that the standard for liability under *Caremark*— "sustained or systematic failure of a director to exercise reasonable oversight—is quite high." Is it too high? Why should the standard not be gross negligence or even negligence? On these facts, would the directors be liable if the standard were either gross negligence or negligence?

c. Do you think directors should be able to deflect liability by demonstrating that they relied on others within the corporation? More specifically, should directors be able to avoid liability by demonstrating that they relied on information prepared at their specific request? That they relied on information prepared in the ordinary course of business? That they relied on those corporate officers and other corporate agents to whom the board has delegated authority? In this connection, the MBCA and DGCL provisions on directorial reliance are set out below.

5. You Draft It

a. Draft a statute that appropriately describes a director's ability to rely on the actions of others (including the ability to rely on information provided by others). The MBCA and the DGCL are set out below:

MBCA §8.30

(d) In discharging board or board committee duties, a director who does not have knowledge that makes reliance unwarranted is entitled to rely on the performance by any of the persons specified in subsection (f)(1) or subsection (f)(3) to whom the board may have delegated, formally or informally by course of conduct, the authority or duty to perform one or more of the board's functions that are delegable under applicable law.

(e) In discharging board or board committee duties, a director who does not have knowledge that makes reliance unwarranted is entitled to rely on information, opinions, reports, or statements, including financial statements and other financial data, prepared or presented by any of the persons specified in subsection (f).

(f) A director is entitled to rely, in accordance with subsection (d) or (e), on:

(1) one or more officers or employees of the corporation whom the director reasonably believes to be reliable and competent in the functions performed or the information, opinions, reports or statements provided;

(2) legal counsel, public accountants, or other persons retained by the corporation as to matters involving skills or expertise the director reasonably believes are matters (i) within the particular person's professional or expert competence, or (ii) as to which the particular person merits confidence; or

(3) a board committee of which the director is not a member if the director reasonably believes the committee merits confidence.

DGCL §141(e)

A member of the board of directors, or a member of any committee designated by the board of directors, shall, in the performance of such member's duties, be fully protected in relying in good faith upon the records of the corporation and upon such information, opinions, reports or statements presented to the corporation by any of the corporation's officers or employees, or committees of the board of directors, or by any other person as to matters the member reasonably believes are within such other person's professional or expert competence and who has been selected with reasonable care by or on behalf of the corporation.

Many observers have found *Stone v. Ritter* to be challenging in several ways. First, the case involves a *Caremark*, or duty to monitor, claim, but the court also speaks of a duty of good faith. It has become clear, although it may not be clear simply from reading *Stone*, that a good faith claim can encompass something other than a failure to monitor. The *McPadden* and *ATR-Kim Eng* cases later in the book are illustrations of good faith claims that are not limited to failure to monitor settings.

Second, as we will see in the next chapter, the standard of conduct expected of a fiduciary is different (and higher) than the standard of review a court will apply when a fiduciary's actions are challenged. *Stone*'s discussion of the elements of a good faith or *Caremark* claim seem to conflate the standard of conduct and the standard of review. Third, and perhaps most troubling from the standpoint of fiduciary duty law, *Stone* reiterates the *Disney* opinion that provides three settings for what it calls good faith violations:

> In *Disney*, we identified the following examples of conduct that would establish a failure to act in good faith:
>
>> A failure to act in good faith may be shown, for instance, where the fiduciary intentionally acts with a purpose other than that of advancing the best interests of the corporation, where the fiduciary acts with the intent to violate applicable positive law, or where the fiduciary intentionally fails to act in the face of a known duty to act, demonstrating a conscious disregard for his duties. There may be other examples of bad faith yet to be proven or alleged, but these three are the most salient.

But the first of those settings is simply a general statement of a duty of loyalty violation. That is, the director acts in a manner he or she does not believe to be in the best interest of the corporation. The second is a similar situation, although scholars have long debated whether an intentional violation of the law is a separate wrong or is, by definition, something a fiduciary could not believe is in the best interest of the corporation. It is only the third example, "where the fiduciary intentionally fails to act in the face of a known duty to act, demonstrating a conscious disregard for his duties" that is new and that should fall under the rubric of good faith. If the others are also good faith violations, then aren't "good faith" and "duty of loyalty" essentially synonymous?

4. Trying to Generalize

Can we move from these examples of duty of loyalty problems to a more generalized understanding? The basic statement of the duty of loyalty requires each director to act in good faith and with the genuine belief that his or her actions are in the best interest of the corporation. In other words, the test for whether a director has met his or her duty of loyalty should turn, *entirely*, on whether the director actually believes that the action will be in the corporation's best interest. One way to demonstrate that a director has breached the duty of loyalty is a statement by the director that he or she did not have the requisite belief. This is obviously seldom a reality.

Short of a confession, then, are there objective indications that the director did not act, or may not have acted, with the requisite belief? At bottom, there are two objective indicators, one of which clearly shows the director breached the duty of loyalty. That indicator is where the director takes something from the corporation because the director surely could not believe that the corporation's best interest is served by losing something it had for no recompense. The corporate opportunity doctrine is simply a chronically recurring setting.

The second objective indication that a director may have violated the duty of loyalty is self-dealing. But, the consequence of self-dealing is different from that of taking a corporate opportunity in two ways. First, unlike taking a corporate opportunity, a transaction between a corporation and one of its directors is quite possibly a transaction that the director could reasonably believe is in the corporation's best interest. Finding that a director has engaged in self-dealing does not, then, definitely establish that the director violated his or her fiduciary duty of loyalty.

Second, self-dealing has more shades than does taking a corporate opportunity. Without exploring psychological, epistemological, or literary theories of "self," it is fair to say that the reason a self-dealing transaction may mean a duty of loyalty violation is that directors (like other humans) have an incentive to prefer their own welfare to that of others. Hence a self-dealing transaction raises the possibility that the director believes that the transaction is not in the corporation's best interest, but in the best interest of the director. It is possible, of course, for the director to believe, honestly, that a proposed self-dealing transaction is in the best interest of both the corporation and the director. But in terms of identifying objective suggestions that a director may not have the appropriate belief, the idea of "self" may be larger than simply the director.

Directors care about themselves, of course, but also their families, friends, co-workers, and other businesses with which they may have a relation (e.g., as an employee, director, or owner). A more generalized label for this objective suggestion is *conflict of interest*. It is helpful to remember that *self-dealing* and *conflict of interest* are not synonymous, although many use the terms interchangeably. Self-dealing is a subset of conflict of interest and probably the easiest to grasp. The presence of a director's conflict of interest is in the nature of a warning, a red flag, that the proposed transaction may represent one that the director does not actually believe is in the best interest of the corporation.

In terms of identifying possible breaches of the duty of loyalty, the varieties of conflict of interest are not of equal usefulness. In true self-dealing, as in *Tomaino*, the potential for a directorial breach is clear and strong. But as the connection between the director and benefit becomes more attenuated, the less likely it is that the director violated the duty of loyalty. A good analogy is red nail polish. Really Really Ruby and Code Red are paradigms, but Tickled Pink, Tutu Pink, and Pinkini are included under the rubric of red even though their shades are not close to a pure, deep, red. And we haven't even begun to think about the amalgamations like Champagne, and Limitless Lilac, which could also be considered red nail polish.

Consider *A* Corporation's proposed transaction, to be voted upon by the board of directors, and ask whether a director's conflict of interest should raise a strong presumption, weak presumption, or no presumption at all as to whether a director who votes in favor of the transaction is violating his or her duty of loyalty.

The transaction is between *A* Corporation and the director.
The transaction is between *A* Corporation and *B* Corporation, which is

> Wholly owned by the director.
> Half-owned by the director.
> 1 percent owned by the director.

The transaction is between *A* Corporation and *B* Corporation. The director has
no ownership interest in *B* Corporation but serves on the *B* Corporation
board of directors.

The transaction is between *A* Corporation and the director's

Spouse.
Adult child.
First cousin.
Live-in nanny.

The transaction is between *A* Corporation and *B* Corporation. The director has
no prior connection to *B* Corporation but,

The director will be paid a "finder's fee" by *B* Corporation if the transaction
is approved.

The director will be paid a "finder's fee" by *A* Corporation if the transaction
is approved.

The director will be paid a "finder's fee" by *B* Corporation regardless of
whether the transaction is approved.

The director will be paid a "finder's fee" by *A* Corporation regardless of
whether the transaction is approved.

The director anticipates being asked to become a member of *B* Corporation's
board, a prestigious directorship, if the transaction is approved.

The director anticipates that a close friend of many years' standing who works
for *B* Corporation will get a major promotion if the transaction is approved.

At bottom, the proper inquiry should be whether objective facts suggest (or
show) that the director may not (or does not) believe a corporate action is in the best
interest of the corporation.

Putting It to Work

Problem 11-2

HAL Corp., a computer hardware manufacturer, has nine directors on its board.
Eight of the directors work nearby the corporate headquarters and are always
available for meetings. One director, Bill, is busy with his own technology corporation and almost never attends special meetings due to his own hectic schedule. At
the board's regularly scheduled monthly meeting, at which all the directors were
present, a special meeting was scheduled to take place in two weeks to consider and
vote on the new CEO of HAL. Bill felt that attending the meeting and voting would
not be useful, since he has been unable to learn much about the three CEO finalists
and had missed quite a few board meetings where pertinent information was
exchanged. He decided to skip the meeting and let the other board members make
the decision. At the special meeting, on a vote of four to three, Steve, the current
CEO of Pear Company, a computer software manufacturer, was elected the new
CEO.

Steve turns out to be a horrible CEO with a well-documented history of
mismanagement and bitter tirades at Pear.

a. Has Bill violated any of his fiduciary duties as a board member?

b. Assume that Bill attended the meeting and voted to elect Steve because Bill's daughter, Carly, is a senior executive at Pear who has both borne the brunt of many of Steve's tirades and who also might be well positioned to succeed Steve as Pear's CEO. Has Bill violated any of his fiduciary duties as a board member?

5. Compensation of Directors and Senior Officers

Perhaps the starkest example of director self-dealing is compensation. At common law directors could not award themselves compensation for performing their duties as directors. The theory (often backed up by legal requirements) was that directors were to be shareholders as well and thus would receive their compensation in the form of increased share value or dividends. Once the requirement of share ownership by directors fell away, the statutes were amended to permit boards of directors to provide compensation to themselves. *See* DGCL §141(h) and MBCA §3.02(k). While it is not uncommon for directors of closely held corporations to receive no compensation (they may be compensated either as officers, employees, or shareholders instead), directors of publicly held companies receive remuneration some would consider munificent. Six-figure compensation is not unheard of, and keep in mind that many directors of public companies are not senior executives of that company (such "inside directors" typically do not take additional compensation for serving as directors) and so spend a few hours a month, at most, in return for their compensation.

Compensation of a corporation's senior officers may also be problematic in a duty of loyalty sense. Some senior executives typically serve on the board of directors of public companies. In closely held companies, all the directors may be officers. In theory, of course, a board's approval of executive compensation should not raise a conflict of interest problem directly because directors and officers are separate people. When there is an overlap between the two groups, though, a conflict is presented. Typically a direct conflict is avoided because the inside directors abstain from voting on (and often abstain from participating in the discussion of) their own compensation. Do you think this is a sufficient solution to the conflict of interest problem? If not, what would you propose?

B. THE DUTY OF CARE

We have seen that corporate directors and officers have an obligation to be single-minded in their actions. They must put the best interest of the corporation ahead of all other considerations. What about a director who genuinely intends to act in the best interest of the corporation but who makes absolutely no effort to find out anything about the corporation? Or, who makes no effort to find out anything about a proposed corporate action? If such directors exist (and are not simply phantasms, apparitions, spectres, wraiths, figments of a law professor's underactive imagination) have they met their duty of loyalty? If not, is it meaningful to describe the duty of loyalty's tenor as being solely concerned with directors' intention to benefit the corporation? How else would you describe the duty's requirements? On the other hand, if the duty of loyalty is met by well-intentioned but uninformed directors, is the corporation sufficiently protected from director-inflicted harm? Do we need to impose an additional duty on directors to become informed about the corporation and proposed corporate actions? As you may have guessed, directors and officers are under a duty to be informed and this duty, the *duty of care*, is usually considered to be distinct from the duty of loyalty.

1. The Current Setting

The MBCA's formulation of the duty of care in §8.30(b), was revised in 1998. The case that follows was decided under the prior formulation, which is substantially identical to the North Carolina statute quoted in the opinion.

FDIC v. Rippy
799 F.3d 301 (4th Cir. 2015)

GREGORY, Circuit Judge:

The Federal Deposit Insurance Corporation, as Receiver for Cooperative Bank ("FDIC-R"), brought this civil action against the several officers and directors of a failed North Carolina bank, Cooperative Bank ("Cooperative" or the "Bank"), alleging that the officers and directors were negligent, grossly negligent, and breached their fiduciary duties, resulting in the failure of the Bank. In this summary judgment appeal, the FDIC-R argues that the district court erred in finding that North Carolina's business judgment rule shields the officers and directors from allegations of negligence and breach of fiduciary duty, and that there was insufficient evidence to support claims of gross negligence. For the reasons that follow, we vacate the district court's award of summary judgment to the Bank's officers on the FDIC-R's claims of ordinary negligence and breach of fiduciary duty and remand those claims for further proceedings. We also reverse and remand the district court's order denying as moot the FDIC-R's cross-motion for summary judgment, as well as its order denying as moot the FDIC-R's motion to exclude the declaration of Robert T. Gammill and the attached exhibits. We affirm the district court's judgment with respect to the remaining claims.

I

Cooperative first opened in Wilmington, North Carolina in 1898 as a community bank and operated as a thrift until 1992. As such, it focused on single-family housing loans. In 1992, the Bank converted to a state-chartered savings bank regulated by the FDIC. Cooperative became a state commercial banking institution in 2002, following the board of director's decision to increase the Bank's assets from $443 million to $1 billion by 2005. The Bank's growth strategy focused on commercial real estate lending.

The FDIC and the North Carolina Commission of Banks ("NCCB"), as Cooperative's regulators, performed annual reviews of the Bank.

During July and August of 2006, the FDIC conducted an annual examination of Cooperative as of June 30, 2006. At the conclusion of the examination, the FDIC issued the Bank's 2006 Report of Examination ("2006 FDIC Report"). Cooperative was scored in each of the following categories: Capital, Asset Quality, Management, Earnings, Liquidity, and Sensitivity to Market Risk. The examination categories collectively are commonly referred to by the acronym CAMELS, and are scored on scale from 1-5, with "1" being the best and "5" being the worst. Cooperative received a "2" for each of its CAMELS ratings. The majority of the observations in the 2006 FDIC Report were positive. However, the Report identified deficiencies in credit administration and underwriting, which the FDIC ascribed to oversight weaknesses. Additional problems with audit practices, risk management, and liquidity were also discussed in the Report. Bank management certified that the Report had been reviewed, and the appropriate officials agreed to address the issues.

In September 2007, the NCCB conducted its annual review of Cooperative as of June 30, 2007. At the conclusion of the examination, the NCCB issued its 2007 Report of Examination ("2007 NCCB Report"). Like the 2006 FDIC Report, the 2007 NCCB Report awarded the Bank a rating of "2" for each CAMELS category. Overall, the NCCB concluded that Cooperative was functioning in a satisfactory manner. However, the 2007 NCCB Report also observed that Cooperative's management had been slow to correct deficiencies and weaknesses identified in previous examinations. Such deficiencies included weak credit administration practices, the use of stale financial information in the loan approval process, and problematic audit practices. Again, Bank management promised to address the issues.

Cooperative additionally underwent an external loan review in 2007, which was conducted by Credit Risk Management, L.L.C. ("CRM"). CRM reviewed a sample of the loans originating during or after April 2006. At the conclusion of the review, CRM issued a written report ("2007 CRM Report"). The Report indicated that the reviewed loans had received passing grades. CRM also observed that credit file documentation for the sample loans was generally sufficient, and that the Bank had recently hired additional credit analysts. However, CRM also suggested that credit file documentation should be updated periodically to more accurately reflect the changing status of various construction projects.

CRM conducted a second external loan review in June 2008, which examined new loans made since its 2007 review. CRM issued a written report of its findings ("2008 CRM Report"). The 2008 CRM Report criticized Cooperative for deficiencies relating to loan documentation and monitoring, and for use of stale financial information. The Report reflected the downward trend in grades given to the sample loans. Unlike the 2007 review, many of the loans reviewed in 2008 received failing grades.

In November 2008, the FDIC and the NCCB conducted a joint annual review of Cooperative as of September 30, 2008. At the conclusion of the review, the agencies issued the 2008 Report of Examination ("2008 Joint Report"). Cooperative was given a rating of "5," the lowest possible rating, in all but one of the CAMELS categories. The sole exception was Sensitivity to Market Risk, in which Cooperative was awarded a "4." The 2008 Joint Report was extremely critical, and faulted the Bank for its high commercial real estate loan concentration. The Report also noted that Cooperative's management had ignored or inadequately addressed previously raised concerns about credit administration, underwriting practices, and liquidity. Cooperative's overall condition was traced back to the decision to aggressively pursue commercial real estate lending in its effort to grow the Bank's assets.

On March 12, 2009, the FDIC issued a Cease and Desist Order, to which the Bank, the NCCB, and the FDIC all consented. The Order set forth certain actions that the Bank was required to take, including developing a capital restoration plan. Cooperative was ultimately unable to comply with the terms of the Cease and Desist Order, and on June 19, 2009, the NCCB closed the Bank and named the FDIC-R as the receiver. According to a Material Loss Review conducted by the FDIC Office of Inspector General, the FDIC-R suffered losses of $216.1 million due to the Bank's failure.

The FDIC-R filed a complaint against Cooperative in August 2011, alleging that the named officers and directors were negligent, grossly negligent, and breached their fiduciary duties in their approval of 78 residential lot loans and 8 commercial loans between January 2007 and April 2008. The complaint seeks damages from each named officer and director in amounts ranging from $4.4 million to over $33 million. The Appellees responded with a motion to dismiss arguing, among other things, that North Carolina law does not contemplate negligence claims against officers and directors and, in any event, the North Carolina business judgment rule shielded them from claims of negligence and breach of fiduciary duty. They also argued that the FDIC-R had failed to state facts sufficient to support its claims of gross negligence. The district court denied the motion to dismiss.

The Appellees thereafter filed an answer. Their answer included several affirmative defenses, including that "[t]he FDIC[-R]'s claims are barred in whole or in part by its failure to mitigate damages," and are also barred "in whole or in part by the doctrine of superseding or intervening cause."

After lengthy discovery, the Appellees filed motions for summary judgment on all of the FDIC-R's claims against them. The FDIC-R filed a cross-motion for partial summary judgment on the Appellees' affirmative defenses of failure to mitigate and superseding or intervening cause.

The district court granted summary judgment in favor of the Appellees, and denied the FDIC-R's cross-motion for summary judgment as moot. The court held that the FDIC-R "fail[ed] to reveal any evidence that suggests any defendant has engaged in self-dealing or fraud, or that any defendant was engaged in any other unconscionable conduct that might constitute bad faith," and that their actions were thus protected by the business judgment rule from claims of ordinary negligence and breach of fiduciary duty. *FDIC v. Willetts (Willetts II)*, 48 F. Supp. 3d 844, 850 (E.D.N.C. 2014). The court further found that the FDIC-R had failed to adduce evidence "that any of the defendants approved the challenged loans and made policy decisions knowing that these actions would harm Cooperative and breach their duties to the bank" and thus "[could not] show that any of the defendants engaged in wanton conduct or consciously disregarded Cooperative's well-being." *Id.* at 852.

This appeal followed. The FDIC-R argues that: (1) the district court improperly applied the business judgment rule; (2) it presented evidence sufficient for a reasonable juror to conclude that the directors and officers were grossly negligent; and (3) there are disputed issues of material fact that preclude granting summary judgment to the Appellees on alternative grounds. For the reasons that follow, we affirm the district court in part and reverse in part.

III

As the Supreme Court explained in *Atherton v. FDIC*, "state law sets the standard of conduct" which bank officers and directors must follow "as long as the state standard (such as simple negligence) is stricter than that of the federal statute." 519 U.S. 213, 216 (1997). At issue in *Atherton* was a federal statute, 12 U.S.C. §1821(k). . . . The Supreme Court interpreted §1821(k) as "set[ting] a 'gross negligence' floor, which applies as a substitute for state standards that are more relaxed." *Atherton*, 519 U.S. at 216.

North Carolina, in turn, provides the following standard:

(a) A director shall discharge his duties as a director, including his duties as a member of a committee:

(1) In good faith;
(2) With the care an ordinarily prudent person in a like position would exercise under similar circumstances; and
(3) In a manner he reasonably believes to be in the best interests of the corporation.

N.C.G.S. §55-8-30(a); *see also id.* §55-8-42(a) (providing identical standard for corporate officers). Thus, under North Carolina law, a director or an officer can be held liable for ordinary negligence. In line with *Atherton* and 12 U.S.C. §1821(k), the FDIC-R may sue bank directors and officers for both ordinary negligence and gross negligence.

North Carolina law also allows corporations to protect directors from liability for ordinary negligence by including exculpatory clauses in their articles of incorporation. N.C.G.S. §55-2-02(b)(3) provides:

(b) The articles of incorporation may set forth any provision that under this Chapter is required or permitted to be set forth in the bylaws, and may also set forth:

. . .

(3) A provision limiting or eliminating the personal liability of any director arising out of an action whether by or in the right of the corporation or otherwise for monetary damages for breach of any duty as a director. No such provision shall be effective with respect to (i) acts or omissions that the director at the time of such breach knew or believed were clearly in conflict with the best interests of the corporation. . . .

In other words, a corporation may limit personal liability for a director's breach of a duty of care, so long as the director did not know or believe his or her actions to have been *clearly* contrary to the corporation's best interests. Section 55-2-02(b)(3) does not allow for the limitation of the duty of loyalty or the duty of good faith. *Id.*

With this framework in mind, we turn to the FDIC-R's claims.

A

We consider director liability first. Cooperative's articles of incorporation include an exculpatory provision, as permitted by N.C.G.S. §55-2-02(b)(3).

In accordance with §55-2-02(b)(3), the exculpatory provision in the Bank's articles of incorporation does not eliminate liability for breaches of the duty of loyalty or the duty of good faith. Nor does the provision eliminate liability for gross negligence.

The FDIC-R does not contend that the Director Appellees breached a duty of loyalty. Thus, unless there is a genuine issue of material fact as to whether the Director Appellees breached their duty of good faith, the exculpatory provision will protect them from liability for ordinary negligence.

We find that the FDIC-R has not presented sufficient evidence of a breach of the duty of good faith to raise a genuine issue of material fact.

We therefore affirm the district court's award of summary judgment to the Director Appellees as to the FDIC-R's claims of ordinary negligence and breach of fiduciary duty.

B

We turn next to officer liability. The Bank's exculpatory provision does not cover Bank officers. Thus, we analyze officer liability. . . .

[C]ourts begin with the "initial evidentiary presumption that in making a decision the directors acted with due care (i.e., on an informed basis) and in good faith in the honest belief that their action was in the best interest of the corporation." *ILA Corp.*, 513 S.E.2d at 822. [T]he initial presumption can be rebutted with evidence showing that the Officer Appellees: (1) did not avail themselves of all material and reasonably available information (i.e., they did not act on an informed basis); (2) acted in bad faith, with a conflict of interest, or disloyalty; *or* (3) did not honestly believe that they were acting in the best interest of Cooperative.

The FDIC-R has presented adequate rebuttal evidence. Specifically, its evidence is sufficient to rebut the presumption that the Officers Appellees acted on an informed basis. The FDIC-R presented the expert affidavit and reports of Brian H. Kelley, an independent banking consultant and former "senior bank executive, lender, and attorney at both regional and large commercial banks." His expert report and expert rebuttal report each discuss the general problems with the Appellees' lending and underwriting processes, and also incorporate by reference his loan reports addressing each individual loan.

Kelley stated that, in his opinion, the officers did not act in accordance with generally accepted banking practices. His affidavit states that the Appellees often approved loans over the telephone, without first examining relevant documents. Moreover, they often did not receive the loan documents until after the phone calls, and sometimes not until after the loans had already been funded. Kelley further stated that the review process was inconsistent with practices at other banking institutions, and did not comport with his understanding of officer and director duties. He further noted that the Appellees had failed to address warnings and deficiencies in the Bank's examination reports.

To be sure, the Bank's regulators awarded it "2" ratings on its CAMELS. But, as Kelley observed, the Bank's reports of examination also contained several indications that Cooperative's credit administration and audit processes, among others, needed substantial improvement. He also thought it clear from his review that certain loans should never have been approved.

Kelley's affidavit and reports thus provide a sufficient basis for rebutting the presumption that the Bank's officers acted on an informed basis. Having found that there is evidence to support the notion that the Officer Appellees did not act on an informed basis, we need not address the other two avenues of rebuttal.

[W]e vacate the district court's grant of summary judgment on the FDIC-R's claims of ordinary negligence and breach of fiduciary duty as to the Officer Appellees.

IV

The FDIC-R argues that North Carolina law does not require a showing of intentional wrongdoing in order to sustain a claim of gross negligence. We disagree.

Traditionally, under North Carolina law, the North Carolina Supreme Court "has often used the terms 'willful and wanton conduct' and 'gross negligence' interchangeably to describe conduct that falls somewhere between ordinary negligence and intentional conduct." *Yancey v. Lea,* 354 N.C. 48, 550 S.E.2d 155, 157 (2001). Further, the court has defined " 'gross negligence' as 'wanton conduct done with conscious or reckless disregard for the rights and safety of others.' " *Id.* The court has also noted that " '[a]n act is wanton when it is done of wicked purpose, or when done needlessly, manifesting a reckless indifference to the rights of others.' " *Id.*

[T]he traditional common law definition of gross negligence applies. Accordingly, to survive summary judgment, the FDIC-R must show that there is a genuine issue of material fact as to whether the Appellees' conduct amounted to " 'wanton conduct done with conscious or reckless disregard for the rights and safety of others.' " *Yancey,* 550 S.E.2d at 157 (citation omitted) (" 'An act is wanton when it is done of wicked purpose, or when done needlessly, manifesting a reckless indifference to the rights of others.' " (citation omitted)).

Here, the FDIC-R has failed to present evidence that the Appellees' actions were grossly negligent. To be sure, the Appellees failed to address deficiencies outlined in examination reports issued by the FDIC and the NCCB. But those same reports repeatedly awarded Cooperative ratings of "2" in the CAMELS categories. In the face of this contradiction, we find that there is insufficient evidence that the Appellees acted wantonly or with reckless indifference. We thus affirm the district court's award of summary judgment to all of the Appellees on the issue of gross negligence.

V

The Appellees argue that summary judgment can be entered on alternative grounds. The district court did not address any of these arguments below.

First, the Appellees argue that they "made the challenged loans in reliance on reports, opinions, appraisals, financial data and other information developed and provided by Cooperative's experienced loan officers and credit administrators." Br. of Appellees 54. In advancing their argument, they cite N.C.G.S. §55-8-30(b), which provides:

> In discharging his duties a director is entitled to rely on information, opinions, reports, or statements, including financial statements and other financial data, if prepared or presented by: (1) One or more officers or employees of the corporation whom the director *reasonably believes* to be reliable and competent in the matters presented. . . .

N.C.G.S. §55-8-30(b) (emphasis added); *see also* N.C.G.S. §55-8-42 (providing the same protection to officers of a corporation). Here, there is evidence in the record that Cooperative's regulators, as well as its independent auditor, found its commercial loan administration and underwriting process lacking. The FDIC-R's expert, as detailed above, similarly criticized the loan and credit administration process as contrary to standard banking practices. Accordingly, there is a genuine issue of material fact about whether the Officer Appellees' reliance on the reports of their credit administrators and loan officers was reasonable.

Next, the Appellees argue that the FDIC-R "failed to produce evidence that the defendants, rather than the Great Recession, proximately caused the loan defaults pled." Br. of Appellees 59. Proximate cause is "a cause that produced the result in continuous sequence and without which it would not have occurred, and one from which any man of ordinary prudence could have foreseen that such a result was probable under all the facts as they existed." *Mattingly v. North Carolina R.R. Co.,* 253 N.C. 746, 117 S.E.2d 844, 847 (1961) (citation and internal quotation marks omitted). Foreseeability is necessary for a finding of proximate cause, but "does not require that [the] defendant should have been able to foresee the injury in the precise form in which it actually occurred." *Hairston v. Alexander Tank & Equip. Co.,* 310 N.C. 227, 311 S.E.2d 559, 565 (1984). Rather, a plaintiff need only prove that "in 'the exercise of reasonable care, the defendant might have foreseen that *some injury* would result from his act or omission, *or that consequences of a generally injurious nature might have been expected.*'" *Hart v. Curry,* 238 N.C. 448, 78 S.E.2d 170, 170 (1953) (emphasis added) (citation omitted). Moreover,

> [t]here may be two or more proximate causes of an injury. These may originate from separate and distinct sources or agencies operating independently of each other, yet if they join and concur in producing the result complained of, the author of each cause would be liable for the damages inflicted, and action may be brought against any one or all as joint tort-feasors.

Batts v. Faggart, 260 N.C. 641, 133 S.E.2d 504, 506 (1963) (citation omitted).

Certainly, it is convenient to blame the Great Recession for the failure of Cooperative, and in turn for the losses sustained by the FDIC-R when it took over the Bank. However, there is evidence in the record, as outlined above, that suggests that "in the exercise of reasonable care," the Bank officers could have "foreseen that *some injury* would result from [their] act[s] or omission[s], *or that consequences of a generally injurious nature might have been expected.*" *Hart,* 78 S.E.2d at 170 (emphasis added) (citation omitted). Even before the Recession, exam reports from both of Cooperative's regulators indicated that the Bank was utilizing unsafe practices. And while the Recession undoubtedly contributed to the failure of the Bank, it may have been only one of many contributing factors. This is a genuine issue of material fact, and thus this is a question for a jury. *See Adams v. Mills, 312 N.C. 181, 322 S.E.2d 164, 172 (1984)* ("[P]roximate cause of an injury is ordinarily a question for the jury.").

VI

For the foregoing reasons, the judgment of the district court is
AFFIRMED IN PART, REVERSED IN PART, VACATED IN PART, AND REMANDED.

Notes and Comments

1. Notes

a. The North Carolina statute in this case is based upon a prior version of MBCA §8.30, which remains the law in a handful of states. The current version of the duty of care is MBCA §8.30(b).

b. The North Carolina statute provides that corporations may eliminate director (and in some states, officer) liability for violating the duty of care. *See* DGCL §102(b)(7), MBCA §2.02(b)(4). We will discuss these exculpatory provisions in more detail in the next chapter. For now, understand that the vast majority of public companies, as well as a great many privately held companies, have such provisions. As a result, fiduciary liability for breaching the duty of care is rarely imposed.

c. The DGCL does not contain a statutory statement of directors' duty of care. However, Delaware case law describes the duty of care as,

> The duty of the directors of a company to act on an informed basis, as that term has been defined by this Court numerous times, forms the duty of care. . . .
>
> [W]e have defined a board's duty of care, in a variety of settings. For example, we have stated that a directory's duty of care requires a director to take an active and direct role in the context of a sale of a company from beginning to end. In a merger or sale, we have stated that the director's duty of care requires a director, before voting on a proposed plan of merger or sale, to inform himself [or herself] and his [or her] fellow directors of all material information that is reasonably available to them.

Cede & Co. v. Technicolor, Inc., 634 A.2d 345, 367 (Del. 1993).

d. The court speaks of a presumption that directors met their fiduciary duties and about the evidence necessary to rebut that presumption. As we will see in the next chapter, the standard of review (i.e., what a court must find to impose liability) is different from the standard of conduct (i.e., what a fiduciary must do to meet his or her fiduciary duties). This chapter has been concerned with standards of conduct, but, as this case shows, the standards of conduct and standards of review are intertwined.

2. Reality Check

a. How did the officers' and directors' action result in the bank's failure?

3. Suppose

a. If the court had applied the current version of MBCA §8.30(b), would the analysis or the result have been different?

4. What Do You Think?

a. Should corporations be able to eliminate the duty of care?

b. Do you think fiduciaries should be expected not to be negligent? Grossly negligent?

c. Most courts that have considered the question have held that the duty of care, whether embodied in a statute or in common law, imposes what is called a "unitary standard" of conduct. That is, the standard is a minimum to which all directors will be held, even when a particular director is incapable of meeting that standard. The Official Comment to the MBCA describes these attributes as "common sense, practical wisdom, and informed judgment . . ." *See* MBCA §8.30 Official Comment. But on the other hand, directors who have specialized skills germane to the corporation and its business, will be held to a higher standard of care that reflects what a reasonable director *with those skills* would do. Do you think that this asymmetry makes sense?

d. Do you think that the duty of care for a particular director should depend on whether that director is actively involved in the corporation's business?

e. Do you think that the current version of MBCA §8.30's duty of care is better than the prior version?

f. Notice that one change between the MBCA versions is that the requirement to act as an ordinarily prudent person would act has been deleted. Chancellor Allen discussed the policy reason behind this kind of change:

> It is doubtful that we want business men and women to be encouraged to make decisions as hypothetical persons of *ordinary* judgment and prudence might. The corporate form gets its utility in large part from its ability to allow diversified investors to accept greater investment risk. If those in charge of the corporation are to be adjudged personally liable for losses on the basis of a substantive judgment based upon what an persons [sic] of ordinary or average judgment and average risk assessment talent regard as "prudent" "sensible" or even "rational", such persons will have a strong incentive at the margin to authorize less risky investment projects.

In re Caremark Int'l Inc. Deriv. Litig., 698 A.2d 959, 967 n.16 (Del. Ch. 1996).

5. You Draft It

a. Draft a statute that appropriately describes a director's duty of care. The current and former versions of the MBCA are set out below:

MBCA §8.30(b) current version:

The members of the board of directors . . . , when becoming informed in connection with their decision-making function or devoting attention to their oversight function, shall discharge their duties with the care that a person in a like position would reasonably believe appropriate under similar circumstances.

MBCA pre-1998 version:

A director shall perform his [or her] duties as a director, . . . with such care as an ordinarily prudent person in a like position would use under similar circumstances.

The most intuitive settings for the duty of care are when the board of directors is contemplating a particular action or course of action. Keep in mind that these settings are analytically identical regardless of whether the board's actions are *initiated by* the board or are *in reaction to* developments from inside or outside the corporation. Remember, as well, that a board "acts" for purposes of its fiduciary duties when it decides to take no action.

2. Background and Context

Before we leave the duty of care, there are two further aspects we ought to consider. As you have seen, the basic standard of conduct looks very much like the standard of care each of us is under not to be negligent. There is a temptation, then, to graft other tort concepts onto the duty of care. The first aspect of the duty of care we will examine is whether the analogy to tort law is valid and valuable or, instead, is unwarranted and harmful.

Finally, we ask the question we posed earlier. That is, whether it really makes sense to describe a duty of care that is separate from the duty of loyalty.

a. The Propriety of Analogy to Tort

In Delaware, the plaintiff, at least initially, need not show damage to the corporation or proximate cause. *See Cede & Co. v. Technicolor, Inc.,* 634 A.2d 345, 370-371 (Del. 1994). The rationale of the Delaware rule is that the plaintiff's initial task is simply to overcome a presumption that the board acted properly. Given the difficulty of overcoming that presumption, the Delaware courts believe that adding an additional initial burden would be unfair to plaintiffs. The presumption and other aspects of the standards by which courts evaluate director actions are the subject of the next chapter.

Under the MBCA, by contrast, a shareholder/plaintiff seeking monetary damages from directors has the burden of proving both monetary harm to the corporation and proximate cause between the directors' (in)action and the harm. See MBCA §8.31(b)(1). Yet the drafters of the MBCA share a concern with other commentators, many of whom are distinguished Delaware practitioners.

The concern with analogizing the duty of care to negligence begins with the observation that in the negligence setting it is frequently fair to infer negligence from the fact of harm. For example, a traffic accident seldom occurs unless someone has been negligent. In the business world, however, harm in the sense of a bad outcome is always a possibility. If the duty of care is linked too closely to the idea of negligence, finders of fact may be too prone to impose liability for what is, at bottom, simply a suboptimal business result. Given that the damage to the corporation may easily be quite large and given that the directors are often not the only actors who contributed to the damage, it seems disproportionate to impose liability too quickly.

Notes and Questions

1. What Do You Think?

a. Are there other common situations in which the potential damage is large and the defendants may not be wholly responsible for the loss? If so, how does the law treat those settings? What is the purpose in treating those settings in particular ways? Is it to deter certain conduct? To promote certain conduct? To make plaintiffs whole? To penalize defendants? Do those settings inform your view of the way in which corporate law ought to treat violations of the duty of care?

b. Is There a Duty of Care?

Now that you've read about the duty of care in more detail, think about the question whether the duty of care even exists, or whether it is better to conceive of extreme cases of lapse of care as really involving the duty of loyalty. The following excerpts may help elaborate on the puzzle:

> I start with what I take to be an elementary precept of corporation law: in the absence of facts showing self-dealing or improper motive, a corporate officer or director is not legally responsible to the corporation for losses that may be suffered as a result of a decision that an officer made or that directors authorized in good faith. Thus, to allege that a corporation has suffered a loss as a result of a lawful transaction, within the corporation's powers, authorized by a corporate fiduciary *acting in a good faith pursuit of corporate purposes,* does not state a claim for relief against that fiduciary no matter how foolish the investment may appear in retrospect.
>
> The rule could rationally be no different. Shareholders can diversify the risks of their corporate investments. Shareholders don't want (or shouldn't rationally want) directors to be risk averse. Shareholders' investment interests, across the full range of their diversifiable equity investments, will be maximized if corporate directors and managers honestly assess risk and reward. . . .
>
> But directors will tend to deviate from this rational acceptance of corporate risk *if* in authorizing the corporation to undertake a risky investment, the directors must assume some degree of personal risk relating to *ex post facto* claims of derivative liability for any resulting corporate loss.
>
> Corporate directors of public companies typically have a very small proportionate ownership interest in their corporations and little or no incentive compensation. Thus, they enjoy (as residual owners) only a very small proportion of any "upside" gains earned by the corporation on risky investment projects. If, however, corporate directors were to be found liable for a corporate loss from a risky project on the ground that the investment was too risky (foolishly risky! stupidly risky! egregiously risky!—you supply the adverb), their liability would be joint and several for the whole loss (with I suppose a right of contribution). Given the scale of operation of modern public corporations, this stupefying disjunction between risk and reward for corporate directors threatens undesirable effects. Given this disjunction, only a very small probability of director liability based on "negligence," "inattention," "waste," etc., could induce a board to avoid authorizing risky investment projects to any extent! Obviously, it is in the shareholders' economic interest to offer sufficient protection to directors from liability for negligence, etc., to allow directors to conclude that, as a practical matter, there is no risk that, if they act in good faith and meet minimal proceduralist standards of attention, they can face liability as a result of a business loss.

Gagliardi v. TriFoods Int'l Inc., 683 A.2d 1049, 1051-1052 (Del. Ch. 1996) (Allen, Ch.)

Where a director *in fact exercises a good faith effort to be informed and to exercise appropriate judgment,* he or she should be deemed to satisfy fully the duty of attention. If the shareholders thought themselves entitled to some other quality of judgment than such a director produces in the good faith exercise of the powers of office, then the shareholders should have elected other directors.

In re Caremark Int'l Inc. Derivative Litig., 698 A.2d 959, 969 (Del. Ch. 1996) (Allen, Ch.)

Notes and Questions

1. Reality Check

a. Chancellor Allen wrote both of the squibbed opinions in the same year. Do they represent the same basis for critiquing a separate duty of care?

b. Chancellor Allen's argument envisions investors as being economically rational. How accurate is that vision?

2. What Do You Think?

a. Is there a logical link between the argument that the duty of care should be different from negligence and the argument that a separate duty of care should not exist?

b. In settings in which the directors were *completely* uninformed about a proposed action, their failure to become informed can be seen as evidence (possibly quite strong evidence) that the directors did not believe the proposed action was in the corporation's best interest. That is, they might have *hoped* the action would be beneficial but they had no information upon which to rest that hope. In the more typical setting, the directors will have *some* information about a proposed corporate action but did not (arguably, at least) have all material information reasonably available. Do you think that more typical setting can or should be treated as a duty of loyalty problem?

Putting It to Work

Problem 11-3

Jane is an attorney in the small town in which she went to college. She has a general civil practice. She serves as a director for Chumy's, a popular dive bar. Katie, her former college roommate, is Chumy's general manager. The two have remained close friends. In April, while reviewing the first quarter's expense reports for Chumy's, Jane notices that the expenses for liquor have steadily increased, but that revenues on mixed drinks have not. Knowing that Katie has a habit of drinking at work, Jane assumes Katie has taken a nip here and there while at work. Further, Jane knows that Katie customarily pours free drinks on occasion for regular customers, and, in fact, always gives Jane free drinks on the rare occasions that Jane goes to Chumy's. In July, while reviewing second quarter's expense reports, Jane notices that the expenses for liquor have again gone up considerably while the revenues from mixed drinks have actually decreased. Jane does not mention these facts either at the board meetings or informally to any other director. In late September, the federal Drug Enforcement Agency and the state Liquor Control Board arrest Katie and another Chumy's employee. It turns out that Katie and the other employee had been stealing many cases of Chumy's liquor and selling them on the black market to finance a drug operation, which they ran from the back room at Chumy's. The arrests and resultant publicity have resulted in Chumy's declaring bankruptcy.

a. Has Jane violated her fiduciary duties to Chumy's?

C. FEDERAL SECURITIES REGULATION

Although the federal securities acts operate largely by requiring disclosure of important corporate information, in some respects the laws impose substantive obligations on public companies. In the wake of the Enron and WorldCom scandals (*see* Chapter 14), Congress enacted the Sarbanes-Oxley Act. The SEC implemented Sarbanes-Oxley in part by requiring that public companies "must maintain disclosure controls and procedures and internal control over financial reporting." See SEC Rule 13a-15(a). Further, these controls must be evaluated by the CEO and chief financial officer every calendar quarter.

The disclosure controls and procedures are further defined as those "that are designed to ensure that information required to be disclosed by the issuer in the reports that it files or submits under the [Exchange] Act is recorded, processed, summarized and reported, within the time periods specified in the Commission's rules and forms. Disclosure controls and procedures include, without limitation, controls and procedures designed to ensure that information . . . is accumulated and communicated to the issuer's management, including its principal executive and principal financial officers, . . . as appropriate to allow timely decisions regarding required disclosure." *See* SEC Rule 13a-15(e).

The internal controls over financial reporting, which were the primary focus of Sarbanes-Oxley, are "a process designed . . . to provide reasonable assurance regarding the reliability of financial reporting and the preparation of financial statements . . . and includes those policies and procedures that: 1. Pertain to the maintenance of records that in reasonable detail accurately and fairly reflect the transactions and dispositions of the assets of the issuer; 2. Provide reasonable assurance that transactions are recorded as necessary to permit preparation of financial statements in accordance with generally accepted accounting principles, and that receipts and expenditures of the issuer are being made only in accordance with authorizations of management and directors of the issuer; and 3. Provide reasonable assurance regarding prevention or timely detection of unauthorized acquisition, use or disposition of the issuer's assets that could have a material effect on the financial statements." *See* SEC Rule 13a-15(f).

As you see, these reforms, and the incentives of the Federal Sentencing Guidelines, are entirely consonant with Chancellor Allen's views in *Caremark*.

D. TERMS OF ART IN THIS CHAPTER

| Conflict of interest | Duty of care | Self-dealing |
| Corporate opportunity | Duty of loyalty | |

Standards of Review of Board Actions

In this chapter we turn to the judicial review of board actions that are challenged on the ground that the directors breached their fiduciary duty of loyalty or care. Why do we need this chapter? In the last chapter we covered the directors' (and officers') fiduciary duties of loyalty and care. Doesn't the trial judge (or jury), in this kind of lawsuit, as in ordinary civil litigation, determine whether the plaintiff has shown, by a preponderance of the evidence, each element in the claim for relief?

No. This is different.

The Delaware Supreme Court explains why litigation raising fiduciary duties claims is different from ordinary litigation and describes what the plaintiff must show to prevail:

> Our starting point is the fundamental principle of Delaware law that the business and affairs of a corporation are managed by or under the direction of its board of directors. [DGCL] §141(a). In exercising these powers, directors are charged with an unyielding fiduciary duty to protect the interests of the corporation and to act in the best interests of its shareholders.
>
> The business judgment rule is an extension of these basic principles. The rule operates to preclude a court from imposing itself unreasonably on the business and affairs of a corporation. The rule, though formulated many years ago, was . . . restated by this Court as follows:
>
>> As a rule of evidence, it creates a "presumption that in making a business decision, the directors of a corporation acted on an informed basis [i.e., with due care], in good faith and in the honest belief that the action taken was in the best interest of the company." *Aronson v. Lewis,* 473 A.2d 805, 812 (Del. 1984). The presumption initially attaches to a director-approved transaction within a board's conferred or apparent authority in the absence of any evidence of "fraud, bad faith, or self-dealing in the usual sense of personal profit or betterment." *Grobow v. Perot,* 539 A.2d 180, 187 (Del. 1988).
>
> **Citron v. Fairchild Camera & Instr. Corp., 569 A.2d 53, 64 (Del. 1989)**
>
> The rule posits a powerful presumption in favor of actions taken by the directors in that a decision made by a loyal and informed board will not be overturned by the courts unless it cannot be "attributed to any rational business purpose." *Sinclair Oil Corp. v. Levien,* 280 A.2d 717, 720 (Del. 1971). . . . Thus, a shareholder plaintiff challenging a board decision has the burden at the outset to rebut the rule's presumption. To rebut the rule, a shareholder plaintiff assumes the burden of providing evidence that directors, in reaching their challenged decision, breached any one of . . . their fiduciary dut[ies] — . . . loyalty or due care. If a

shareholder plaintiff fails to meet this evidentiary burden, the business judgment rule attaches to protect corporate officers and directors and the decisions they make, and our courts will not second-guess these business judgments. If the rule is rebutted, the burden shifts to the defendant directors, the proponents of the challenged transaction, to prove to the trier of fact the "entire fairness" of the transaction to the shareholder plaintiff.

Cede & Co. v. Technicolor, Inc., 634 A.2d 345, 360-361 (Del. 1993) (Horsey, J.)

Thus the famous *business judgment rule* is a procedural device that places the initial burden on the plaintiff to show something different than that the director-defendants have breached their fiduciary duties. The nearly universal incantation by the Delaware courts is that the business judgment rule "is a presumption that in making a business decision, the directors of a corporation acted on an informed basis, in good faith and in the honest belief that the action taken was in the best interests of the company" and that the obligation to act on an informed basis means that the directors have "all material information reasonably available to them." *Aronson v. Lewis,* 473 A.2d 805, 812 (Del. 1984).

It is probably more accurate to think of the business judgment rule as an acknowledgment that corporate law recognizes a disconnect between the *stated* fiduciary duties of directors, which we covered in the last chapter, and the *actual conduct* that will result in sanctions. One consequence of this disconnect is that there is a zone of director conduct that does not satisfy the directors' fiduciary duties but that nonetheless will not result in sanctions.

Well, if the plaintiff must show something other than that the directors breached their fiduciary duties, what is it? The Delaware Supreme Court has described the plaintiff's burden this way:

> [D]irectors' decisions will be respected by courts unless the directors are interested or lack independence relative to the decision, do not act in good faith, act in a manner that cannot be attributed to a rational business purpose[,] or reach their decision by a grossly negligent process that includes the failure to consider all material facts reasonably available.

Brehm v. Eisner, 746 A.2d 244, 264 n.66 (Del. 2000) (Veasey, C.J.)

The revisers of the Model Act sidestepped some of this intricacy by expressly stating that they did not intend to codify the business judgment rule. Nonetheless, they admit that their formulation of the standards for director liability "embeds" the business judgment rule's "principal elements." *See* MBCA §8.31, Official Comment. As in Delaware, the MBCA's standards for *liability* (MBCA §8.31) diverge from the standards of director *conduct* (MBCA §8.30). As the Official Comment to MBCA §8.31 puts it, "And while a director whose performance meets the standards of section 8.30 [duties of loyalty and care] should have no liability, the fact that a director's performance fails to reach that level does not automatically establish personal liability for damages that the corporation may have suffered as a consequence."

Notes and Questions

1. Reality Check

a. Parse the Delaware and MBCA requirements into those that apply to duty of loyalty claims and those that apply to duty of care claims. Why are the requirements so jumbled together?

2. What Do You Think?

a. Why is there a divergence between directors' aspirational conduct and their conduct that will render them liable to the corporation? Do you think this divergence is a good idea?

Let us move to a more detailed look at those requirements. Ask yourself two questions: What does the plaintiff need to show to stave off an adverse judgment? And what happens when the plaintiff makes that showing? I suspect you're intuiting that simply because the plaintiff has satisfied the initial showing does not mean he or she is entitled to judgment. You're right. Let's start with the duty of loyalty.

A. THE DUTY OF LOYALTY

Orman v. Cullman
794 A.2d 5 (Del. Ch. 2002)

CHANDLER, CH.

Joseph Orman ("Orman") is and was the owner of General Cigar Class A common stock at all times relevant to this litigation. Orman brings this suit on behalf of himself and the Public Shareholders of General Cigar Class A common stock against General Cigar and its eleven-member board of directors (collectively the "Board").[1]

The defendants moved pursuant to Court of Chancery Rule 12(b)(6) to dismiss the complaint on the grounds that: 1) Orman failed to plead facts sufficient to overcome the presumption of the business judgment rule with respect to the Board's approval of the merger transaction. . . .

II. FACTUAL HISTORY

General Cigar, a Delaware Corporation with its principal executive offices located in New York, New York, is a leading manufacturer and marketer of premium cigars. The Company has exclusive trademark rights to many well-known brands of cigars, including seven of the top ten brands that were previously manufactured in Cuba.

---

1. The individual defendant Board members are: Edgar M. Cullman, Sr. ("Cullman Sr."), Edgar M. Cullman, Jr. ("Cullman Jr."), Susan R. Cullman ("Susan Cullman"), John L. Ernst ("Ernst"), Peter J. Solomon ("Solomon"), Bruce A. Barnet ("Barnet"), John L. Bernbach ("Bernbach"), Thomas C. Israel ("Israel"), Dan W. Lufkin ("Lufkin"), Graham V. Sherren ("Sherren"), and Frances T. Vincent, Jr. ("Vincent"). The first four directors listed are related to one another . . . and are collectively referred to as the "Cullman Group."

The Company went public in an initial public offering ("IPO") . . . Class A stock at $18.00 per share on February 28, 1997. Class A stock was publicly traded and Class B stock was not publicly traded. Class A stock had one vote per share and Class B had ten votes per share. At the time of the proposed merger, the Cullman Group owned approximately . . . 37% of the Company's total outstanding stock. . . . The Cullman Group's equity interest . . . gave it approximately 67% of the voting power in the corporation.

In the early fall of 1999, Swedish Match AB ("Swedish Match") approached certain members of the Cullman Group (the "Cullmans") about purchasing the interest in General Cigar owned by its Public Shareholders. This was seen to be a logical business combination because General Cigar had a strong presence in the United States premium cigar market and Swedish Match had strength in the international cigar and smokeless tobacco markets through its established network of international contacts and resources. At a November 4, 1999 General Cigar board meeting, the Cullmans informed the Board of Swedish Match's interest. The Board then authorized the Cullmans to pursue discussions with Swedish Match assisted by defendant director Solomon's financial advising firm, Peter J. Solomon & Company ("PJSC"). By the end of December 1999 the structure for a proposed transaction had been determined.

Once the negotiations reached agreement . . . , the Board created a special committee (the "Special Committee"), consisting of outside defendant directors Lufkin, Israel, and Vincent, to determine the advisability of entering into the proposed transaction. [T]he Special Committee received copies of the proposed agreements previously reached between the Cullmans and Swedish Match. After a review of these proposals by the Special Committee and its legal and financial advisors, the Special Committee directly negotiated with Swedish Match over the terms of the agreement. On January 19, 2000 the Special Committee unanimously recommended approval of the transaction as modified as a result of their negotiations. That same day, the General Cigar Board unanimously approved the transaction.

Following the merger, [the Cullman Group's] remaining interest would aggregate to approximately 36% of the total outstanding equity interest in the Company. [A]ll publicly owned Class A and Class B shares (those not owned by the Cullman Group) would be purchased for $15.25 per share.

[T]he transaction was structured in such a way that the Cullman Group could not dictate its approval. Despite the fact that the Cullman Group possessed voting control over the Company both before and after the proposed transaction, approval of the merger required that a majority of the Unaffiliated Shareholders of Class A stock, voting separately as a class, vote in favor of the transaction.[28]

III. ANALYSIS

A. Fiduciary Duty Claims

Because a board is presumed to have acted properly, "[t]he burden is on the party challenging the decision to establish facts rebutting the [business judgment

---

28. In order to assure the Unaffiliated Shareholders had the unobstructed right to determine whether or not the merger would close, the Cullman Group "agreed to vote any Class A shares held by them pro rata in accordance with the vote of the Unaffiliated Shareholders."

rule] presumption."[33] Specifically, Orman must allege facts that raise a reasonable doubt as to whether the Board breached either its duty of care or its duty of loyalty to the corporation. In his complaint, Orman alleges that the Board breached its duty of loyalty.

As a general matter, the business judgment rule presumption that a board acted loyally can be rebutted by alleging facts which, if accepted as true, establish that the *board* was either interested in the outcome of the transaction or lacked the independence to consider objectively whether the transaction was in the best interest of its company and all of its shareholders. To establish that a *board* was interested or lacked independence, a plaintiff must allege facts as to the interest and lack of independence of the *individual members* of that board. To rebut successfully business judgment presumptions in this manner, thereby leading to the application of the entire fairness standard, a plaintiff must normally plead facts demonstrating "that a *majority* of the director defendants have a financial interest in the transaction or were dominated or controlled by a materially interested director."[38]

If a plaintiff alleging a duty of loyalty breach is unable to plead facts demonstrating that a majority of a board that approved the transaction in dispute was interested and/or lacked independence, the entire fairness standard of review is not applied and the Court respects the business judgment of the board.

General Cigar had an eleven-member board. In order to rebut the presumptions of the business judgment rule, Orman must allege facts that would support a finding of interest or lack of independence for a majority, or at least six, of the Board members. Orman asserts, and defendants appear to concede, that the four members of the Cullman Group were interested because they received benefits from the transaction that were not shared with the rest of the shareholders. Orman, therefore, would have to plead facts making it reasonable to question the interest or independence of two of the remaining seven Board members to avoid dismissal based on the business judgment rule presumption. With varying levels of confidence, Orman's complaint alleges that each of the seven remaining Board members — Israel, Vincent, Lufkin, Barnet, Sherren, Bernbach, and Solomon — were interested and/or lacked independence.[50]

---

33. *Aronson v. Lewis,* 473 A.2d 805, 812 (Del. 1984).

38. *Crescent/Mach I Partners, L.P. v. Turner,* 2000 WL 1481002 (Del. Ch.) (Steele, V.C., by designation) (emphasis added). . . .

50. Although interest and independence are two separate and distinct issues, these two attributes are sometimes confused by parties. Many plaintiffs allege facts which they assert establish that the defendant "lacked the disinterest and/or independence" necessary to consider the challenged transaction objectively. The plaintiff then asks the Court to select whichever type of disabling attribute is consistent with the facts alleged and that will support the plaintiff's claim. But it is not for the Court to divine the claims being made. A plaintiff must make clear to the Court the bases upon which his claims rest.

As described above, a disabling "interest," as defined by Delaware common law, exists in two instances. The first is when (1) a director personally receives a benefit (or suffers a detriment), (2) as a result of, or from, the challenged transaction, (3) which is not generally shared with (or suffered by) the other shareholders of his corporation, and (4) that benefit (or detriment) is of such subjective material significance to that particular director that it is reasonable to question whether that director objectively considered the advisability of the challenged transaction to the corporation and its shareholders. The second instance is when a director stands on both sides of the challenged transaction. *See* DGCL §144. This latter situation frequently involves the first three elements listed above. As for the fourth element, whenever a director stands on both sides of the challenged transaction he is deemed interested and allegations of materiality have not been required.

"Independence" does not involve a question of whether the challenged director derives a benefit *from the transaction* that is not generally shared with the other shareholders. Rather, it involves an inquiry into whether the director's decision resulted from that director being *controlled* by another. A director can be controlled by another if in fact he is *dominated* by that other party, whether through close personal or familial relationship or through force

1. Directors Israel and Vincent

Perhaps the weakest allegations of interest and/or lack of independence are aimed at directors Israel and Vincent, who were both members of the Special Committee that investigated the advisability of the merger and negotiated with Swedish Match. The complaint states that these two defendants "had longstanding business relations with members of the Cullman Group which impeded and impaired their ability to function independently and outside the influence of the Cullman Group." The only fact pled in support of this assertion is the mere recitation that Israel and Vincent had served as directors of General Cigar since 1989 and 1992, respectively.

To make clear my opinion as to the independence of directors Israel and Vincent, therefore, I conclude that the allegations in the complaint with regard to the lack of independence of these two directors fail as a matter of law. The naked assertion of a previous business relationship is not enough to overcome the presumption of a director's independence. The law in Delaware is well settled on this point. For instance, in *Crescent/Mach I Partners, L.P.* this Court held that allegations of a "long-standing 15-year professional and personal relationship" between a director and the CEO and Chairman of the Board of his company were insufficient to support a finding of control.[54] The Court stated that such allegations, without more, "fail[ed] to raise a reasonable doubt that [the director] could not exercise his independent business judgment in approving the transaction. Therefore, these allegations lack the specific factual predicate" necessary to survive a motion to dismiss. Here too, allegations concerning longstanding business relations fail as a matter of law to place in issue the independence of directors Israel and Vincent.

2. Director Lufkin

Orman asserts that director Lufkin, who was the third member of the Special Committee, lacked independence and was also interested in the merger transaction. With regard to Lufkin's purported lack of independence, Orman makes the same allegations as were directed at Israel and Vincent, namely, Lufkin "had longstanding business relations with members of the Cullman Group which impeded and impaired [his] ability to function independently and outside the influence of the Cullman Group." For the reasons stated above . . . , such bare allegation fails as a matter of law to assert a lack of independence on the part of director Lufkin.

Lufkin's supposedly disabling interest results from the fact that he was "a founder of Donaldson, Lufkin & Jenrette ("DLJ") [and that] DLJ, or a successor or affiliate thereof, was one of two lead underwriters in the Company's IPO and obtained a substantial fee as a result thereof." This bare statement of fact does not suggest, or even lead to a reasonable inference of, a disabling interest on the part of Lufkin as that statement does not show that he " 'will receive a personal financial

---

of will. A director can also be controlled by another if the challenged director is *beholden* to the allegedly controlling entity. A director may be considered beholden to (and thus controlled by) another when the allegedly controlling entity has the unilateral power (whether direct or indirect through control over other decision makers), to decide whether the challenged director continues to receive a benefit, financial or otherwise, upon which the challenged director is so dependent or is of such subjective material importance to him that the threatened loss of that benefit might create a reason to question whether the controlled director is able to consider the corporate merits of the challenged transaction objectively.

54. 2000 WL 1481002 (Del. Ch. Steele, V.C., by designation).

benefit from [the] transaction that is not equally shared by the stockholders.'"[59] Inadequate pleadings in support of separate allegations of interest and lack of independence cannot be combined to create an inference that a director's conduct was improper. Here, the complaint fails, as a matter of law, to set forth facts that would lead this Court to question the presumed objectivity of director Lufkin in making his decision to vote in favor of the merger with Swedish Match.

3. Director Barnet

The *only* fact alleged in support of Orman's allegation of director Barnet's interest is that he "has an interest in the transaction since he will become a director of the surviving company." No case has been cited to me, and I have found none, in which a director was found to have a financial interest *solely* because he will be a director in the surviving corporation. To the contrary, our case law has held that such an interest is not a disqualifying interest. Even if I were to infer that Orman was alleging that the fees Barnet was to receive as a director with the surviving company created a disabling interest, without more, that assertion would also fail. Because Orman alleges no facts in addition to the assertion of continued board membership on the part of Barnett, his assertion of interest fails as a matter of law.

4. Director Bernbach

Orman alleges that director Bernbach was both interested in the merger and lacked the independence to make an impartial decision regarding that transaction because he has "a written agreement with the Company to provide consulting services [and that] [i]n 1998 . . . Bernbach was paid $75,000 for such services . . . and additional funds since that date."

Orman . . . further alleges that the surviving company will be obligated to uphold the contracts of the existing company. Such well-pleaded facts, accepted as true on a motion to dismiss, plainly allege a continuing obligation. Unfortunately for Orman, however, this clearly stated allegation is fatal to his assertion that Bernbach was interested in the transaction. As this Court has stated previously, "a director is considered interested when he will receive a personal financial benefit *from a transaction* that is not equally shared by the stockholders."[66] Accepting Orman's allegations as true reveals that Bernbach does not meet this definition of "interest." Bernbach had a contract with General Cigar. If the merger were consummated, he would have a contract that the surviving company would be obligated to honor. If the merger were not consummated he would still have his contract with the existing General Cigar that it would be obligated to honor. Therefore, director Bernbach would have received no benefit *from the transaction* being challenged that was not shared by the other General Cigar shareholders. As a result of the merger, shareholder Bernbach would be cashed out and receive the same consideration for his General Cigar stock as the rest of the Unaffiliated Shareholders. Since he was to receive the same benefit as the Company's other shareholders, his interest in getting as high a price as possible for the Company's stock from the merger transaction was

59. *In re the Walt Disney Co. Derivative Litig.*, 731 A.2d 342, 354 (Del. Ch. 1998) (quoting *Rales v. Blasband*, 634 A.2d 927, 936 (Del. 1993)).

66. *In re Western Nat'l Corp. Shareholders Litig.*, 2000 WL 710192 (Del. Ch. Chandler, Ch.) (citing *Aronson v. Lewis*, 473 A.2d 805, 812 (Del. 1984)) (emphasis added).

aligned with the Unaffiliated Shareholders. Orman's complaint, therefore, fails to plead adequately that director Bernbach was interested in the merger.

Orman also argues that Bernbach's consulting agreement suggests a lack of independence. At this stage of the litigation, the facts supporting this allegation are sufficient to raise a reasonable inference that director Bernbach was controlled by the Cullman Group because he was beholden to the controlling shareholders for future renewals of his consulting contract. [A]t the time of the challenged transaction, Bernbach's principal occupation was "Chairman and Chief Executive officer of the Bernbach Group, Inc." I believe it is reasonable to question the objectivity of a director who has a consulting contract with his company and will continue to have a consulting contract with the surviving company. This is particularly true when, regardless of whether the merger is approved or not, the challenged director is beholden to the identical group of controlling shareholders favoring the challenged transaction. The Cullman Group would continue to be in a position to determine whether particular contracts are to be renewed as well as the extent to which the company will make use of the consulting services already under contract. Even though there is no bright-line dollar amount at which consulting fees received by a director become material, at the motion to dismiss stage and on the facts before me, I think it is reasonable to infer that $75,000 would be material to director Bernbach and that he is beholden to the Cullman Group for continued receipt of such fees. Although not determinative, the inference of materiality is strengthened when the allegedly disabling fee is paid for the precise services that comprise the principal occupation of the challenged director.

5. Director Solomon

Orman alleges that "Defendant Solomon has an interest in the transaction since his company, PJSC, stands to reap fees of $3.3 million if the transaction is effectuated." The reasonable inference that can be drawn from this contention is that if the merger is consummated PJSC will receive $3.3 million. If the merger is not consummated PJSC will not receive $3.3 million. PJSC, therefore, has an interest in the transaction. Because director Solomon's principal occupation is that of "Chairman of Peter J. Solomon Company Limited and Peter J. Solomon Securities Company Limited," it is reasonable to assume that director Solomon would personally benefit from the $3.3 million *his* company would receive if the challenged transaction closed. I think it would be naïve to say, as a matter of law, that $3.3 million is immaterial. In my opinion, therefore, it is reasonable to infer that director Solomon suffered a disabling interest when considering how to cast his vote in connection with the challenged merger when the Board's decision on that matter could determine whether or not his firm would receive $3.3 million.

Directors Bernbach and Solomon, at this stage, cannot be considered independent and disinterested. Orman has thus pled facts that make it reasonable to question the independence and/or disinterest of a majority of the General Cigar Board — the four Cullman Group directors, plus Bernbach and Solomon, or six out of the eleven directors. Accordingly, I cannot say, as a matter of law, that the General Cigar Board's actions are protected by the business judgment rule presumption. Defendants' motion to dismiss the fiduciary duty claims — based as it is on a conclusion that the challenged transaction was approved by a disinterested and independent board — must be denied.[70]

Notes and Questions

1. Notes

a. The capital structure of General Cigar includes a frequently used psychological technique. When a corporation is to have one class of stock with clear advantages (either economic or voting benefits, or both) over another class, corporate planners often name the more advantageous class "Class B" and the less advantageous class "Class A." This is done, of course, to suggest to potential purchasers of Class A shares that they are getting stock that is somehow "better" than Class B. As long as the differences between the classes of stock are fully disclosed (and remember that the differences must be stated in the Articles), the corporate planners have not committed fraud. Do you think planners should be allowed to engage in this practice?

b. General Cigar appointed a Special Committee of independent and disinterested directors to analyze the proposed transaction. Note also that the transaction was contingent upon approval of a majority of the shares not controlled by the Cullman Group. This technique is called a "majority of the minority" provision. Both Special Committees and majority of the minority provisions are frequently used when a transaction involves a corporation and its controlling interests and are intended to heighten the integrity of the negotiation and approval process.

2. Reality Check

a. Why did Swedish Match want to control General Cigar?

b. Why are the General Cigar shareholders upset at the proposed transaction?

c. What does Mr. Orman have to demonstrate to prevail in his claim? How is that different from the conduct required of directors by their duty of loyalty?

d. Are the terms *independent* and *disinterested* synonymous? Are they mutually exclusive of one another?

e. Why are Messrs. Israel, Vincent, Lufkin, and Barnet differently situated from Messrs. Bernbach and Solomon?

f. Why is Mr. Bernbach disinterested but not independent? Do you agree with Chancellor Chandler's analysis of Mr. Bernbach's situation?

3. Suppose

a. Assume that Mr. Bernbach had not had a consulting contract with General Cigar. What difference would that fact make in analyzing Mr. Orman's claims for relief?

b. Suppose that this case had arisen in an MBCA jurisdiction. What portions of the MBCA would be germane? Would the analysis or result have been different?

4. What Do You Think?

a. Chancellor Chandler cites case law for the proposition that a director's previous business relationship with a controlling shareholder is not enough to defeat

---

70. Since Orman has pled facts from which it is reasonable to question the independence of two of the seven disputed directors, it is unnecessary for me to consider his allegations with regard to director Sherren.

the presumption that the director is independent. Do you think that rule makes sense? If a different rule applied, which directors in this case would be analyzed differently?

   b. Outside directors (i.e., those without full-time jobs with the corporation on whose board they serve) of public companies nearly always have personal, social, or business relationships with someone who has significant input into the selection of candidates for the board. Frequently such directors have multiple relationships with several such influential insiders. Do you think this *structural bias*, as it is called, should render every such director "beholden"?

1. The Entire Fairness Standard

   A consequence of Chancellor Chandler's ruling in *Orman* is that the parties now engage in full discovery. If Orman is successful in establishing his assertions about the General Cigar Board of Directors' lack of disinterest and independence, he has rebutted the business judgment rule and the court will apply the *entire fairness* standard. Why does the court impose this standard?

> [I]t is helpful to examine the underpinnings of applying entire fairness review. Directors control the corporation on behalf of the stockholders. Controlling stockholders also exercise power over the corporation they control, which belongs, in part, to others—the (non-controlling) stockholders. As such, both directors and controllers are fiduciaries for those stockholders and are accordingly constrained to act with fidelity toward them. Most severely constrained are dealings between a corporate fiduciary and the corporation itself, where the fiduciary stands on both sides of the transaction, implicating the fiduciary's duty of loyalty. Early common law prevented corporate directors from transacting business with a corporation for which they served.[38] In the twentieth century, that standard relaxed to permit a fiduciary to transact with the corporation; our Courts clarified that such self-interested transactions are not void, but voidable, such that "where the fairness of such transactions is challenged the burden is upon those who would maintain them to show their entire fairness and where a sale is involved the full adequacy of the consideration."[39] That entire fairness standard—applied in Delaware since at least the 1920s—is premised on the idea that, ordinarily, court review of director decision-making is circumscribed by the deferential business judgment rule, but where a director is interested in the transaction, that presumption cannot apply and the Court must substantively review the interested decision for fairness to the stockholders. Absent fairness, the conflicted transaction can be set aside, or the benefiting fiduciary forced to disgorge any unfair benefits of the transaction.
>
>   The ability of a controlling stockholder to determine the policies of the corporation—often described as control over the "corporate machinery"—is twofold: First, controlling stockholders may exercise an ability to authorize a transaction by stockholder vote, and second, controlling stockholders may exercise the ability to control the composition of the board.
>
> *In re Cornerstone Therapeutics Inc. S'holder Litig.*, 2014 WL 4418169, *6-*7 (Del. Ch. Sept. 10, 2014) *rev'd on other grounds* 115 A.3d 1173 (Del. 2015).

---

   38. *See, e.g., Wardell v. Union Pac. R. Co.*, 103 U.S. 651, 658 (1880) ("It is among the rudiments of the law that the same person cannot act for himself and at the same time, with respect to the same matter, as the agent of another whose interests are conflicting. . . . Directors of corporations, and all persons who stand in a fiduciary relation to other parties, and are clothed with power to act for them, are subject to this rule; they are not permitted to occupy a position which will conflict with the interest of parties they represent and are bound to protect.").
   39. *Geddes v. Anaconda Copper Mining Co.*, 254 U.S. 590, 599 (1921).

The next case shows what is entailed when the entire fairness standard is triggered. Note that Vice Chancellor Strine has held a trial on the merits.

HMG/Courtland Properties, Inc. v. Gray

749 A.2d 94 (Del. Ch. 1999)

STRINE, V.C.

This case involves thirteen year old real estate sales transactions [the Wallingford and NAF transactions ("Transactions") and the Grossman's Portfolio transactions ("Portfolio")] between HMG/Courtland Properties, Inc. as seller and two of HMG's directors, Lee Gray and Norman Fieber as buyers. While Fieber's self-interest in the transactions was properly disclosed, neither he nor Gray informed their fellow directors that Gray — who took the lead in negotiating the sales for HMG — had a buy-side interest. Gray's interest was concealed from HMG for a decade and was only discovered inadvertently by the company in 1996.

A. BREACH OF FIDUCIARY DUTY

Gray and Fieber must demonstrate the fairness of the Wallingford and NAF Transactions.

2. The Entire Fairness Standard

In a recent case, Vice Chancellor Lamb well-summarized the entire fairness standard of review as follows:

> It is a well-settled principle of Delaware law that where directors stand on both sides of a transaction, they have "the burden of establishing its entire fairness, sufficient to pass the test of careful scrutiny by the courts." *Weinberger v. UOP, Inc.*, 457 A.2d 701, 710 (Del. 1983) ("There is no 'safe harbor' for such divided loyalties in Delaware."). Directors will be found to have acted with entire fairness where they "demonstrate their utmost good faith *and* the most scrupulous inherent fairness of the bargain." *Id.*

> * * *

> The concept of entire fairness has two components: fair dealing and fair price. See *Weinberger*, 457 A.2d at 711. Fair dealing "embraces questions of when the transaction was timed, how it was initiated, structured, negotiated, disclosed to the directors, and how the approvals of the directors and the stockholders were obtained." *Id.* Fair price "relates to the economic and financial considerations of the proposed merger, including all relevant factors: assets, market value, earnings, future prospects, and any other elements that affect the intrinsic or inherent value of a company's stock." *Id. In making a determination as to the entire fairness of a transaction, the Court does not focus on one component over the other, but examines all aspects of the issue as a whole. Id.*

Boyer v. Wilmington Materials, Inc., 1999 WL 39549 (Del. Ch.) (Lamb, V.C.) (emphasis added).

i. *FAIR DEALING*

The defendants have failed to convince me that the Wallingford and NAF Transactions were fairly negotiated or ratified. From the beginning of the negotiations, Gray, the primary negotiator for the seller in the Transactions, was interested in taking a position on the buyer's side. As such, Gray lacked the pure seller-side incentive that should have been applied on behalf of HMG—particularly in Transactions in which one director was already on the other side.

Given the intrinsically unique nature of real estate, the bargaining skills and incentives of HMG's negotiator were likely to be more important than if the negotiator was arranging for the sale of a financial asset. As the defendants' own expert conceded, in the context of a real estate sales transaction negotiation skills are "exceedingly important."

Gray took the lead in discussing these Transactions with the Fiebers. His colleagues Wiener and Rothstein relied on his depiction of the bargaining in determining whether to agree to the Fiebers' proposed terms. They did so in ignorance of Gray's conflict. Similarly, HMG's Executive Committee and Board were deprived of information about Gray's conflict.

The process was thus anything but fair. Because neither Gray nor Fieber disclosed Gray's interest, the HMG Board unwittingly ratified Transactions in which a conflicted negotiator was relied upon by the Adviser to negotiate already conflicted Transactions.

ii. FAIR PRICE

The defendants attempt to meet their burden of demonstrating fair price by trying to convince me that the prices used in the Transactions were in a range of fairness, as proven by [independent] 1984 Appraisals.

Once again, I believe the defendants misconceive their burden. On the record before me, I obviously cannot conclude that HMG received a shockingly low price in the Transactions or that the prices paid were not within the low end of the range of possible prices that might have been paid in negotiated arms-length deals. In that narrow sense, the defendants have proven that the price was "fair." But that proof does not necessarily satisfy their burden under the entire fairness standard. As the American Law Institute corporate governance principles point out:

> A contract price might be fair in the sense that it corresponds to market price, and yet the corporation might have refused to make the contract if a given material fact had been disclosed. . . . Furthermore, fairness is often a range, rather than a point, so that a transaction involving a payment by the corporation may be fair even though it is consummated at the high end of the range. *If an undisclosed material fact had been disclosed, however, the corporation might have declined to transact at that high price, or might have bargained the price down lower in the range.*

1 *Principles of Corporate Governance; Analysis and Recommendations*, Part V at 202 (1994) (emphasis added); . . . .

The defendants have failed to persuade me that HMG would not have gotten a materially higher value for Wallingford and the Grossman's Portfolio had Gray and Fieber come clean about Gray's interest. That is, they have not convinced me that their misconduct did not taint the price to HMG's disadvantage. I base this conclusion on several factors.

First, the defendants' own expert on value, James Nolan, testified that his opinion that the prices paid in the Transactions were fair was premised on his assumption that Gray was not the leading negotiator from HMG's side. To the extent that Gray was a principal player in discussing terms with Fieber, Nolan said that his conclusion about the fairness of the price might well be different.

Second, the 1984 Appraisals understated the values of the Wallingford Property and the Portfolio as of early 1986. The Leased Fee Values [$391,000] in the 1984 Appraisals were generated through a discounted cash flow analysis utilizing 1983 actual rents and projected rents for 1984-1986. By 1986, it was clear that the Grossman's stores operating at Portfolio sites were performing better, and thereby generating higher lease payments (because a portion of the lease payments was tied to store sales) than estimated by the appraisers who conducted the 1984 Appraisals. If an update had been done in 1986, it would have produced values well in excess of the 1984 Appraisals.

Third, a skilled and properly motivated negotiator could have done better than Leased Fee Value in price negotiations. As the defendants' expert Nolan testified, the skills of a negotiator are "exceedingly important" in a real estate transaction. Even without an updated appraisal, a properly motivated negotiator could have argued from the actual rents in 1984 and 1985 that the Leased Fee Value understated the value of the Portfolio. Furthermore, a properly motivated negotiator would have focused on the Fee Simple Value [$711,800*] because of the likelihood that many of the Portfolio properties would come off lease from Grossman's. That eventuality—which came true—justified a higher price than the Leased Fee Value. I have no confidence that Gray negotiated with the Fiebers in any vigorous or skillful way. Since he wanted to participate on the buy-side, he had less than a satisfactory incentive to do so. Since the outcome of a real estate negotiation is often heavily influenced by the skills of the negotiators, this factor undercuts the claim that the price was fair to HMG. *See* 1 *Principles of Corporate Governance: Analysis and Recommendations* §5.02 at 220 (1994) (in evaluating the fairness of a transaction, the court should consider the fact that the corporation was not represented by an unconflicted negotiator).

Finally, had Gray disclosed his interest, I believe that HMG would have terminated his involvement in the negotiations and have taken a much more traditional approach to selling the affected properties. To the extent that HMG continued to consider a sales transaction, I believe it would have commissioned new appraisals and would have sought purchasers other than Fieber. This would have been in keeping with the recommendations of Lavin's January 1986 memorandum suggesting rejection of the $300,000 third-party offer for Wallingford. Such an approach would have led to a sales transaction at a level more akin to the Fee Simple Value in the 1984 Appraisals than the Leased Fee Value.

Taken together, these factors lead me to conclude that the defendants have not demonstrated that they paid a fair price in the sense inherent in the entire fairness standard. Therefore, Gray and Fieber have failed to establish to my "satisfaction that the [T]ransaction[s] [were] the product of both fair dealing *and* fair price." *Cinerama*, [*Inc. v. Technicolor, Inc.,*] 663 A.2d 1156, 1179 (Del. 1995) (quotations & citations omitted) (emphasis added).

---

* The Fee Simple Value is the value of the land without the leases. The land was encumbered by leases that generated below-market rents. Thus, the value of the unencumbered land was higher than the value with tenants in place. *ED.*

Notes and Questions

1. Notes

a. The *entire fairness* test is also called the *intrinsic fairness* test.

2. Reality Check

a. What are the elements of the entire fairness test?

b. Wasn't Mr. Fieber's disclosure sufficient to insulate the Transactions from legal attack?

3. What Do You Think?

a. Conceptually, at some point the consideration for a transaction may be so favorable to the corporation that the process by which that consideration was reached becomes irrelevant to the question whether the transaction is entirely fair. Should the courts examine the fair dealing aspect nonetheless? If so, why? If not, doesn't that mean that in the end the courts are indeed concerned only with the substance of a transaction and not the process?

b. Vice Chancellor Strine finds that the prices for the Transactions were, "within the low end of the range of possible prices that might have been paid in negotiated arms-length deals." He goes on to find that defendants failed to meet their burden because they "have failed to persuade me that HMG would not have gotten a materially higher value for Wallingford and the Grossman's Portfolio had Gray and Fieber come clean about Gray's interest. That is, they have not convinced me that their misconduct did not taint the price to HMG's disadvantage." How could defendants make the showing Vice Chancellor Strine requires? How could they have proven, by a preponderance of the evidence, that the company "would not have" gotten a much better price if facts had been different? What sort of evidence would be relevant to this question? Is any such evidence anything other than speculation?

Putting It to Work

Problem 12-1

Prickly Pear Bakery, Co. ("PPB"), a Delaware corporation, is a start-up that became a huge success when it started selling specialty Bundt cakes out of vending machines nationwide. The company is now publicly held. The company bakes the Bundt cakes in its own factories, but the cakes are sold in vending machines owned by other companies and are delivered to those vending machines by independent trucking companies. The seven board members are:

Ina, the founder and Chief Executive Officer of PPB, who owns 8 percent of PPB stock as her separate property;

Terry, the sole owner of TransCorp, a trucking company. Five percent of TransCorp's revenues are derived from distributing PPB Bundt cakes to vending machines and TransCorp delivers 10 percent of PPB's Bundt cakes to vending machines;

Stephanie, a career board member who sits on several public and private corporate boards, including: an airline, a manufacturer of tires used in trucking companies, and a house-cleaning service company. She was a college classmate of Ina and is her long-time friend;

Melanie, the representative of a mutual fund that owns 30 percent of PPB;

Kyle, Vice President of Development of a Silicon Valley tech company that is poised to market a revolutionary new kind of food vending machine;

Undine, the largest stockholder of Spragg Sugar Company, a major sugar producer. Twenty percent of Spragg Sugar Company's revenues are derived from PPB and PPB purchases half of its sugar from Spragg Sugar Company. She was a college classmate of Ina and is her long-time friend; and

Jeffrey, Ina's husband, the dean of an Ivy League business school.

The board agrees that the best way to take the company to the next level is to acquire either a vending machine company or a sugar producer. Either acquisition will allow PPB to cut its costs considerably. After obtaining all material information reasonably available, the board believes that the best companies to acquire are either Duncan & Duncan, a company that owns vending machines nation-wide and has its own fleet of trucks to stock the machines, or Sugr's, Inc., a major sugar producer. Duncan & Duncan could handle all of PPB's distribution and sales, and Sugr's, Inc. could supply all of PPB's sugar needs. If PPB acquired Duncan & Duncan, its costs would go down 15 percent. If PPB acquired Sugr's, Inc., its costs would go down 30 percent. The cost of acquiring either company is comparable.

After considerable debate within the board, the board unanimously votes to acquire Duncan & Duncan. Giada, a PPB stockholder, brings suit in the Delaware Court of Chancery challenging the proposed acquisition on the ground that the directors breached their fiduciary duties. Giada did not make a prior demand on the board, but asserted in her complaint that such demand would be futile.

a. Will the proposed transaction be reviewed under the business judgment rule or entire fairness?

b. Do you think any of the directors have violated their fiduciary duties to PPB? If so, which directors have violated which duties?

2. The Duty of Good Faith

ATR-Kim Eng Financial Corp. v. Araneta
2006 WL 3783520 (Del. Ch. Dec. 21, 2006)

Strine, V.C.

I. INTRODUCTION

Plaintiffs ATR-Kim Eng Financial Corp. ("ATR Financial") and ATR-Kim Eng Capital Partners, Inc. ("ATR Capital") (collectively, "ATR") own 10% of the shares of a holding company — PMHI Holdings Corp. (f/k/a LBC Global Corp.) (the "Delaware Holding Company"). ATR claims that defendant Carlos Araneta, who controlled the remaining 90% of the Delaware Holding Company's equity and served as chairman of its board, caused the corporation to transfer its key assets — its ownership of several businesses worth over $35 million (the "LBC Operating

Companies") — to members of his family in violation of his fiduciary duties. The Delaware Holding Company was formed precisely to enable ATR to share with Araneta in the benefits of owning the LBC Operating Companies. But, after Araneta denuded the Delaware Holding Company of those assets, ATR was left with only a minority stock ownership position in a floundering joint venture that it had undertaken with Araneta, a position that is worth very little. Meanwhile, Araneta and his family were left with sole control of the LBC Operating Companies, which, from the record, appear to be thriving.

Furthermore, ATR claims that the other members of the board of directors of the Delaware Holding Company, defendants Hugo Bonilla and Liza Berenguer, are jointly and severally liable for this harm because they failed to take any steps to monitor Araneta and prevent his self-dealing. Bonilla was the head of Araneta's operations in the United States, and Berenguer served as the Chief Financial Officer of his worldwide enterprise. They essentially admit that they regarded themselves as mere employees of Araneta and failed to take any steps to fulfill their fiduciary duties to the Delaware Holding Company. As directors, they were charged with protecting the interests of their corporation and its stockholders. Yet, Bonilla and Berenguer allowed Araneta to do whatever he wanted, without any examination of whether his conduct benefited the Delaware Holding Company and all of its stockholders, rather than simply Araneta personally.

In this post-trial opinion, I find that Araneta breached his duty of loyalty by impoverishing the Delaware Holding Company for his own personal enrichment. Bonilla and Berenguer also breached their duty of loyalty. Having assumed the important fiduciary duties that come with a directorship in a Delaware corporation, Bonilla and Berenguer acted as — no other word captures it so accurately — stooges for Araneta, seeking to please him and only him, and having no regard for their obligations to act loyally towards the corporation and all of its stockholders. Such behavior is not indicative of a good faith error in judgment; it reflects a conscious decision to approach one's role in a faithless manner by acting as a tool of a particular stockholder rather than an independent and impartial fiduciary honestly seeking to make decisions for the best interests of the corporation. Although it is clearly the case that Araneta is the most culpable of the defendants, Bonilla and Berenguer are accountable for their complicity in his wrongful endeavors.

Bonilla and Berenguer will be held jointly and severally liable for the monetary judgment . . . .

II. FACTUAL BACKGROUND

These are the facts as I find them after trial.

A. Overview of the Key Arrangements Between Araneta and ATR

Before describing the origins of the current dispute between ATR and Araneta in more detail, it is useful to provide a basic overview of the parties and how they came to form the Delaware Holding Company.

Araneta first met ATR's chairman Ramon Arnaiz when they were in kindergarten in the Philippines. During their school days, Araneta and Arnaiz became close friends. After many years of friendship, the two fell out of touch as each embarked on his own career.

Araneta left the Philippines to attend college in the United States. After completing his studies, Araneta returned home to work in his family's business — an empire of companies run from the Philippines that share the initials LBC in their names (collectively, "LBC").[2] Araneta gained prominence by developing LBC Express, Inc. (f/k/a LBC Air Cargo), a Philippine version of Federal Express, into an international money remittance business that facilitates and profits from wire transfers made by Filipino expatriates who have gone abroad to make a living but continue to support their families still living in the Philippines. As a result of his efforts, Araneta came to dominate and control LBC and is the ultimate manager for the thousands of employees working for LBC and the hundreds of locations owned by LBC around the globe.

Meanwhile, Arnaiz went into the financial services field. He gained prominence by spearheading the revitalization of a major financial firm's Hong Kong office. Following that success, Arnaiz ("A"), along with Manuel Tordesillas ("T") and Lorenzo Roxas ("R"), founded ATR, a Philippine corporation licensed to provide investment and financial services. From its creation, ATR has been essentially a capital provider, helping businesses raise capital and investing its own funds (and those of its investors) in various enterprises.

In the late 1990s, Araneta and Arnaiz reunited. At that time, Araneta turned to Arnaiz and ATR for investment banking assistance on behalf of his LBC enterprise. Initially, Araneta engaged ATR to search for capital and to prepare LBC for a public offering. After a while, however, the relationship changed.

In 1999, ATR began investigating an opportunity to purchase a controlling interest in The Professional Group Plans, Inc., a corporation that sold "pre-need" insurance policies designed to cover expenses (such as educational and health costs) that buyers expected to face in the future (the "Pre-Need Company"). Seeing potential synergies in this industry between ATR's financial acumen and LBC's logistical network, which was well-positioned to attract Filipino customers who had traditionally purchased these policies, Arnaiz offered to structure the investment in the Pre-Need Company as a joint enterprise with Araneta. After some negotiation, Araneta agreed to participate in the deal ATR proposed.

Based on this understanding, ATR and Araneta executed two contracts — an "Undertaking Agreement" and a "Joint Venture Agreement" — that set out the terms of their relationship and laid the groundwork for the Delaware Holding Company's incorporation. Through the Joint Venture Agreement, ATR and Araneta bought a controlling interest in the Pre-Need Company, and, as part of this transaction, ATR advanced $3.922 million on Araneta's behalf (the "Advances").[7] In exchange for the Advances, Araneta pledged, in the Undertaking Agreement, to

2. LBC Development Corp., a corporation organized and existing under the laws of the Philippines, was the primary holding company for the Araneta family businesses before the events giving rise to this dispute. Through this entity, the Aranetas owned the non-U.S. LBC Operating Companies that provided courier and money remittance services in the Philippines and to Filipino expatriates working in other nations. The Aranetas also own LBC Holdings USA Corp. (overseen by defendant Bonilla), which serves Filipinos working in the United States.

7. The joint investment in the Pre-Need Company was made through one of ATR's subsidiaries, Professional Mutual Holdings, Inc. ("Professional Holdings") in which both Araneta and ATR had acquired 50% interests at a price of 37.5 million pesos (about $937,500) each. Using its 75 million pesos in contributed capital as well as an additional 239 million pesos nominally contributed on equal terms by ATR and Araneta (119.5 million pesos each),

contribute the LBC Operating Companies along with his newly acquired interest in the Pre-Need Company to a new holding company and to issue to ATR a 10% minority interest in that entity.

Likewise, to safeguard their joint investment in the Pre-Need Company, ATR and Araneta executed a Stockholders Agreement which they attached to their Joint Venture Agreement (the "Stockholders Agreement"). The Stockholders Agreement evenly divided the eight (out of ten) board seats secured by ATR's and Araneta's joint 80% interest in the Pre-Need Company, and unanimously appointed Topax Colayco, the residual 20% shareholder in the Pre-Need Company, to be its President and CEO.

Although the Undertaking Agreement did not require that the holding company it contemplated be a Delaware, or even an American, entity, Araneta perceived the United States as a favorable jurisdiction in which to raise capital and viewed Delaware as a tax haven. In particular, Araneta viewed a Delaware entity as a vehicle that could be used to access the American capital markets through an initial public offering of stock. As a result, in January 2000, Araneta incorporated the Delaware Holding Company and presented ATR with 3,000 of its shares (10%) while personally retaining control over the residual 27,000 shares (90%). Likewise, Araneta appointed and dominated the Delaware Holding Company's board of directors, which consisted of himself, defendant Berenguer (Araneta's niece and the CFO of the LBC group of companies), and defendant Bonilla (the head of LBC's U.S. operations).

B. The Personal Nature of This Dispute

ATR's claims against Araneta boil down to an allegation that he abused his position of control over the Delaware Holding Company. Specifically, ATR claims that Araneta transferred the LBC Operating Companies from the Delaware Holding Company to his children for no consideration without notice to ATR and without following the process required by Delaware law.

Araneta does not dispute that the LBC Operating Companies are now owned by his family or that ATR has no interest in those assets through its minority ownership of the Delaware Holding Company. He merely claims never to have transferred ownership of the LBC Operating Companies to the Delaware Holding Company in the first place. He says that ATR knew that. What he never says is why ATR would have made a nearly $4 million payment to acquire 10% of an entity with no valuable assets. Further, in the event that I conclude that he is lying when he says that the Delaware Holding Company never owned the LBC Operating Companies, Araneta offers only the half-hearted and wholly-illogical defense that he was permitted to reclaim the LBC Operating Companies without payment through an accounting "offset" because he was the one who initially contributed the LBC Operating Companies to the Delaware Holding Company.

To understand how a case as stark as this actually resulted in a trial, rather than a voluntary settlement by Araneta, it is useful to return to Araneta's relationship with his old friend, Ramon Arnaiz. That's right, this case is personal.

Professional Holdings purchased 80% of the Pre-Need Company. In this transaction, ATR advanced Araneta's portion as well as its own. As a result, Araneta owed ATR 157 million pesos (approximately $3.922 million).

But, as a result of their business dealings, Araneta's friendship with Arnaiz has ended. Araneta testified that he considers this case a "personal fight" between himself and Ramon Arnaiz. He stated in his deposition and confirmed at trial that he did not think his co-directors had "anything to do with this tie-up with ATR." And, perhaps most tellingly, he admitted on cross examination that at least "to some extent" this litigation was "over the disintegration of [his] friendship" with Arnaiz.

That disintegration began in November 2002 when ATR sold its 50% interest in Professional Holdings, the corporation that owned 80% of the Pre-Need Company. Having closely aligned himself with Arnaiz and ATR, Araneta felt betrayed by that action. In compliance with the Shareholders Agreement, which secured ATR's right to sell its Professional Holdings shares as long as Araneta was given a right of first refusal, ATR offered its shares to Araneta, but he refused to purchase them. After Araneta declined, ATR sold its interest to Topax Colayco (the "Colayco Sale") giving Colayco co-equal control with Araneta over Professional Holdings and thus over Professional Holdings's 80% control bloc in the Pre-Need Company. But, because Colayco already directly owned the residual 20% of the Pre-Need Company that Professional Holdings did not, Araneta understandably viewed himself as having less leverage than Colayco in this dynamic.

Notwithstanding ATR's contractual right to sell its interest in Professional Holdings and Araneta's own failure to exercise his right of first refusal, Araneta felt victimized by Arnaiz and ATR and blamed them for subjugating him to the role of a minority investor under Colayco's de facto control.

Araneta allowed this hostility to affect his management of the Delaware Holding Company. After the Colayco Sale, Araneta withheld information, effectively closed the lines of communication with ATR, and eventually transferred all of the LBC Operating Companies out of the Delaware Holding Company.

C. The Discovery of Araneta's Misconduct

Araneta began to exact his revenge soon after the Colayco Sale was completed. In the months that followed, ATR repeatedly requested information on the condition of the Delaware Holding Company in which it still had nearly $4 million invested. But Araneta summarily rebuffed those requests. Araneta testified that any request ATR made for information during the entire 2003 calendar year went ignored because he was "no longer talking to them because [he was] upset with Mr. Arnaiz."

Starved for information, ATR filed an action under [DGCL] §220 in this court on October 27, 2003. But still irked by ATR's decision to sell its interest in Professional Holdings, Araneta "deliberately ignored" that lawsuit and instructed Bonilla not to provide the requested information.

Only after being ordered by this court to turn over the records requested by ATR did Araneta do so. On January 14, 2004, Araneta produced a "Compliance" that purported to include all available documents but totaled only nine pages and failed to include many essential corporate papers. The nine pages that Araneta did produce, however, included three documents that caused ATR great concern. Those documents — two balance sheets and a purported resolution of the board of directors — led ATR to believe that Araneta had conducted a de facto (and non-pro rata) liquidation of the Delaware Holding Company's assets and that Araneta was attempting to escape responsibility for that act.

These financial statements indicated that during the last nine months of 2003 Araneta stripped the Delaware Holding Company of the LBC Operating Companies. The only operating asset he left in the Delaware Holding Company was ownership of the de facto minority position in the Pre-Need Company.

D. The Parties' Claims

Based on the balance sheets unearthed in the §220 action, ATR filed this lawsuit on June 3, 2004. ATR claims that it was harmed as a stockholder of the Delaware Holding Company when Araneta effectively made a $36 million liquidation payment to his family without following the required process and without distributing to ATR its pro rata portion thereof. ATR also alleges that the corporation itself was injured by this transaction because it received no substantial consideration for the transfer of substantially all of its assets to the Araneta family.

In response, Araneta mounted three shifting defenses. If his implausible excuses were not expending ATR's and this court's limited resources and impeding ATR's just claim for recompense, Araneta's brazen and abundant falsehoods might be amusing. Because they have these costs, they are appalling.

III. LEGAL ANALYSIS

ATR's allegations against Araneta are clear-cut claims of self-dealing by a controlling shareholder and director of a Delaware corporation. [I] have found as a fact that Araneta removed from the Delaware Holding Company its primary assets — its ownership of the LBC Operating Companies. In its financial statements and tax filings, the Delaware Holding Company had valued this ownership interest at over $36 million. Yet, by the end of 2003, this value had disappeared from the Delaware Holding Company's books. To where did Araneta remove the assets? To his family. What did the Delaware Holding Company receive in exchange? Effectively nothing. Araneta did not even reduce his 90% interest in the Delaware Holding Company when he repossessed the very assets that had secured that interest in the first place. Araneta simply took the LBC Operating Companies back in a fit of pique.

The evidence in this case is clear, and Araneta's attempts to distort that reality only make his conduct less tolerable. Araneta used his majority control and effective dominion over the Delaware Holding Company and its board of directors to engage in a course of unfair dealing that resulted in a de facto liquidation of corporate assets that enriched the Araneta family at the expense of the Delaware Holding Company and ATR.

I now come to a slightly more difficult issue. Namely, to what extent should Araneta's fellow directors, Bonilla and Berenguer, share responsibility for harming the Delaware Holding Company and ATR?

Making this more challenging is that ATR does not allege that either Berenguer or Bonilla participated in, approved of, or directly profited from Araneta's removal of the LBC Operating Companies. Rather, ATR claims that Bonilla and Berenguer consciously breached the important duties articulated in this court's *Caremark*[112]

---

112. *In re Caremark Int'l, Inc. Deriv. Litig.,* 698 A.2d 959 (Del. Ch. 1996).

decision and recently reaffirmed by our Supreme Court in *Stone v. Ritter*.[113] Specifically, ATR alleges that Bonilla and Berenguer failed to monitor Araneta's conduct thereby allowing his self-dealing to continue.

Under Delaware law, it is fundamental that a director cannot act loyally towards the corporation unless she tries—i.e., makes a genuine, good faith effort—to do her job as a director.[114] One cannot accept the important role of director in a Delaware corporation and thereafter consciously avoid any attempt to carry out one's duties.

One of the most important duties of a corporate director is to monitor the potential that others within the organization will violate their duties. Thus, "a director's obligation includes a duty to attempt in good faith to assure that a corporate information and reporting system, which the board considers to be adequate, exists."[115] Obviously, such a reporting system will not remove the possibility of illegal or improper acts, but it is the directors' charge to "exercise a good faith judgment that the corporation's information and reporting system is in concept and design adequate to assure the board that appropriate information will come to its attention in a timely manner as a matter of ordinary questions, so that it may satisfy its responsibility."[116] Thus, as the Supreme Court recently stated:

> *Caremark* articulates the necessary conditions predicate for director oversight liability: (a) the directors utterly failed to implement any reporting or information system or controls; or (b) having implemented such a system or controls, consciously failed to monitor or oversee its operations thus disabling themselves from being informed of risks or problems requiring their attention. In either case, imposition of liability requires a showing that the directors knew that they were not discharging their fiduciary obligations. Where directors fail to act in the face of a known duty to act, thereby demonstrating a conscious disregard for their responsibilities, they breach their duty of loyalty by failing to discharge that fiduciary obligation in good faith.[117]

From the testimony of the directors of the Delaware Holding Company, it is apparent that no reporting system was in place and that no other information systems or controls were ever considered, let alone implemented, by the Delaware Holding Company's board of directors. They did not even have regular board meetings. As a result, the directors were often unaware of corporate activities— despite how easy that would have been given the Delaware Holding Company's modest size. Berenguer testified that although there had been meetings regarding the Delaware Holding Company before the LBC Operating Companies were transferred into the corporation in January 2001, she did not remember any meetings of the board of directors or of the shareholders after that time. Bonilla confirmed this fact, explaining that when the Delaware Holding Company's name was changed from LBC Global, Corp. to PMHI Holdings, Corp., he was never informed about the change, never voted to approve it, and did not even know what the initials PMHI in the new corporate name stood for at the time he signed the

---

113. 911 A.2d 362 (Del. 2006).

114. *See Guttman v. Huang*, 823 A.2d 492, 506 & n. 34 (Del. Ch. 2003).

115. *Caremark*, 698 A.2d at 970.

116. *Id.*

117. *Stone*, 911 A.2d 362.

certificate of amendment as the corporation's authorized agent. Even when corporate activities involved them directly, . . . neither Berenguer nor Bonilla questioned the wisdom of Araneta's actions nor insisted that corporate procedures be followed.

Moreover, both Berenguer and Bonilla testified that they entirely deferred to Araneta in matters relating to the Delaware Holding Company. Berenguer is, as mentioned, Araneta's niece and served as the CFO for the LBC group of companies worldwide. She testified that she would not insert herself into a disagreement between ATR and Araneta about how the Delaware Holding Company should proceed on an issue because such a disagreement would be between those parties and would not affect her as a director of the Delaware Holding Company. Similarly, she stated that she would take Araneta's word as authoritative if he claimed that he had agreed with ATR to take certain actions. Bonilla, the head of Araneta's U.S. operations, was more explicit — explaining that to him Araneta and the Delaware Holding Company were basically one and the same and that he took the word of Araneta as being the word of the company. Moreover, when pressed regarding whether he would undertake an independent inquiry if told to act by Araneta, Bonilla responded, "Why should I ask him all these questions? He's telling me they have already agreed. . . . It's not like I'm going to go out there and check on him, doesn't make sense."

Based on these failures, neither Berenguer nor Bonilla can be said to have upheld their fiduciary obligations. Although it was Araneta who ran amok by emptying the Delaware Holding Company of its major assets, the other directors did nothing to make themselves aware of this blatant misconduct or to stop it.

Put in plain terms, it is no safe harbor to claim that one was a paid stooge for a controlling stockholder. Berenguer and Bonilla voluntarily assumed the fiduciary roles of directors of the Delaware Holding Company. For them to say that they never bothered to check whether the Delaware Holding Company retained its primary assets and never took any steps to recover the LBC Operating Companies once they realized that those assets were gone is not a defense. To the contrary, it is a confession that they consciously abandoned any attempt to perform their duties independently and impartially, as they were required to do by law. Their behavior was not the product of a lapse in attention or judgment; it was the product of a willingness to serve the needs of their employer, Araneta, even when that meant intentionally abandoning the important obligations they had taken on to the Delaware Holding Company and its minority stockholder, ATR.

When required by their office to be loyal to the Delaware Holding Company, Bonilla and Berenguer chose total fealty to Araneta's conflicting interests instead. Consequently, I find them jointly liable for Araneta's fiduciary violations.

IV. CONCLUSION

Based on the foregoing, I find in favor of ATR on each of its claims and award ATR $3,922,000 in damages plus pre-judgment as well as post-judgment interest on this amount.

Notes and Questions

1. Notes

a. Vice Chancellor Strine imposed attorney fees on Mr. Araneta but not Mr. Bonilla or Ms. Berenguer.

b. The pre-judgment interest on the award was over $20,000,000. The final judgment entered jointly and severally was $24,490,422.50, which the Delaware Supreme Court affirmed without a substantive opinion. Four months after Vice Chancellor Strine's opinion was entered, Mr. Bonilla declared personal bankruptcy, seeking to discharge his liability. However, the bankruptcy court held that Mr. Bonilla's debt was non-dischargeable because it was incurred by fraud as a fiduciary. *See ATR-Kim Eng Financial Corp. v. Bonilla*, 2008 WL 4414153 (N.D. Cal. Sept. 25, 2008).

2. Reality Check

a. What is the standard of review for *Caremark* and good faith claims?

b. How is the analysis different for Mr. Araneta, Mr. Bonilla, and Ms. Berenguer?

c. Vice Chancellor Strine wrote, "ATR does not allege that either Berenguer or Bonilla participated in, approved of, or directly profited from Araneta's removal of the LBC Operating Companies." Why, then, are Ms. Berenguer and Mr. Bonilla liable?

d. The court also held, "Under Delaware law, it is fundamental that a director cannot act loyally towards the corporation unless she tries — i.e., makes a genuine, good faith effort — to do her job as a director." Is this the statement of the duty imposed by *Caremark* or by the duty of good faith?

e. Is there causation between the corporation's harm and Mr. Bonilla's and Ms. Berenguer's behavior?

3. What Do You Think?

a. Do you agree with the standard of review for good faith claims? If not, what standard of review would you use?

b. Do you think successful *Caremark* or good faith claims will be frequent?

c. Is this really a *Caremark* claim against Mr. Bonilla and Ms. Berenguer? Isn't it just a duty of loyalty claim? If so, what is the consequence in terms of the standard of review?

d. Do you agree with Vice Chancellor Strine that it would have been "easy" for Mr. Bonilla and Ms. Berenguer to become aware of the corporation's activities? If not, why are they liable?

B. THE DUTY OF CARE

We saw in Chapter 11 that the duty of care is, in Delaware, a duty to be informed. Under the MBCA, becoming informed is certainly an important component of the duty of care. Before you read the next case you should reread the Delaware and MBCA formulations for the standard of conduct in duty of care settings. The next case discusses the standard of review in cases in which the plaintiff asserts that the board violated its duty of care.

In re NCS Healthcare, Inc., Shareholders Litigation
825 A.2d 240 (Del. Ch. 2002)

[The facts are largely drawn from the Delaware Supreme Court's decision in this case.

NCS is a leading independent provider of pharmacy services to long-term care institutions including skilled nursing facilities, assisted living facilities and other institutional healthcare facilities. Jon H. Outcalt is Chairman of the NCS board of directors. Kevin B. Shaw is President, CEO and a director of NCS. Messrs. Outcalt and Shaw collectively owned over 65% of the voting power.

The NCS board has two other members, defendants Boake A. Sells and Richard L. Osborne. Sells is a graduate of the Harvard Business School. He currently sits on the boards of both public and private companies. Osborne is a full-time professor at the Weatherhead School of Management at Case Western Reserve University. He has been at the university for over thirty years. Osborne currently sits on at least seven corporate boards other than NCS.

Genesis is a leading provider of healthcare and support services to the elderly. Omnicare, Inc. is in the institutional pharmacy business.

Beginning in late 1999, NCS began to experience a precipitous decline in the market value of its stock. In the summer of 2001, NCS invited Omnicare to begin discussions regarding a possible transaction. Omnicare responded that it was not interested in any transaction other than purchasing NCS's assets at a sale in bankruptcy. There was no further contact between Omnicare and NCS between November 2001 and January 2002.

In January 2002, Genesis was contacted concerning a possible transaction with NCS. Genesis previously lost a bidding war to Omnicare in a different transaction. This led to bitter feelings between the principals of both companies.

In March 2002, NCS decided to form an independent committee of board members who were neither NCS employees nor major NCS stockholders (the "Independent Committee"). Sells and Osborne were selected as the members of the committee, and given authority to consider and negotiate possible transactions for NCS. The entire four member NCS board, however, retained authority to approve any transaction.

The Independent Committee met for the first time on May 14, 2002. Two days later, Boake Sells met with George Hager, CFO of Genesis, and Michael Walker, who was Genesis's CEO. In June 2002, Genesis proposed a transaction. . . . At the June 26 meeting, Genesis's representatives demanded that, before any further negotiations take place, NCS agree to enter into an exclusivity agreement with it. Genesis wanted the Exclusivity Agreement to be the first step towards a completely locked up transaction that would preclude a higher bid from Omnicare.

By late July 2002, Omnicare came to believe that NCS was negotiating a transaction, possibly with Genesis or another of Omnicare's competitors, that would potentially present a competitive threat to Omnicare. Thus, Omnicare faxed to NCS a letter outlining a proposed acquisition. Late in the afternoon of July 26, 2002, NCS representatives received voicemail messages from Omnicare asking to discuss the letter. The exclusivity agreement prevented NCS from returning those calls.

Despite the exclusivity agreement, the Independent Committee met to consider a response to Omnicare. It concluded that discussions with Omnicare about its July 26 letter presented an unacceptable risk that Genesis would abandon merger discussions. The Independent Committee believed that, given Omnicare's past bankruptcy proposals and unwillingness to consider a merger, the risk of losing the Genesis proposal was too substantial. Nevertheless, the Independent Committee used Omnicare's letter to negotiate for a more favorable transaction with Genesis. On July 27, Genesis proposed substantially improved terms. In return for these concessions, Genesis stipulated that the transaction had to be approved by midnight the next day, July 28, or else Genesis would terminate discussions and withdraw its offer.

The Independent Committee and the NCS board both scheduled meetings for July 28. After concluding that Genesis was sincere in establishing the midnight deadline, the committee voted unanimously to recommend the transaction to the full board. The full board concluded that "balancing the potential loss of the Genesis deal against the uncertainty of Omnicare's letter, results in the conclusion that the only reasonable alternative for the Board of Directors is to approve the Genesis transaction." Under the terms of the merger agreement, NCS would be prohibited from canceling its shareholders' meeting and, because Messrs. Shaw and Outcalt, representing in excess of 50% of the outstanding voting power, would be required by Genesis to enter into stockholder voting agreements, shareholder approval of the merger would be assured even if the NCS Board were to withdraw or change its recommendation. DGCL §251 requires both board and shareholder approval to authorize a merger. These facts would prevent NCS from engaging in any alternative or superior transaction in the future. The board then resolved that the merger agreement and the transactions contemplated thereby were advisable and fair and in the best interests of all the NCS stakeholders. The NCS board further resolved to recommend the transactions to the stockholders for their approval and adoption. A definitive merger agreement between NCS and Genesis and the stockholder voting agreements were executed later that day.

On July 29, 2002, hours after the NCS/Genesis transaction (including the agreement with Messrs. Shaw and Outcalt) was executed, Omnicare faxed a letter to NCS restating its proposal, which offered significantly higher consideration than the Genesis transaction and which Omnicare made irrevocable, and attaching a draft merger agreement. On August 1, 2002, Omnicare expressed a desire to discuss the terms of the offer with NCS. On August 8, 2002, and again on August 19, 2002, the NCS Independent Committee and full board of directors met separately to consider the Omnicare tender offer in light of the Genesis merger agreement. As a result of this offer, on October 21, 2002, the NCS board withdrew its recommendation that the stockholders vote in favor of the NCS/Genesis merger agreement.

The NCS independent committee and the NCS board of directors recognize that (1) the existing contractual obligations to Genesis currently prevent NCS from accepting the Omnicare merger proposal; and (2) the existence of the voting agreements entered into by Messrs. Outcalt and Shaw, whereby Messrs. Outcalt and Shaw agreed to vote their shares of NCS stock in favor of the Genesis merger, ensure

NCS stockholder approval of the Genesis merger. This litigation was commenced by minority shareholders of NCS, to prevent the consummation of the inferior Genesis transaction.]

LAMB, V.C.

In fulfilling their responsibilities to manage the Company's "business and affairs," the Director Defendants certainly owe fiduciary duties to NCS and its stockholders.

The duty of care relates to the process by which a board of directors makes a decision. The applicable standard of conduct when deciding whether directors have properly exercised their duty of care is whether they acted with "gross negligence," and whether they were adequately informed at the time they made their decision.[35] This is the business judgment standard of review. Under the business judgment rule, "[c]ourts do not measure, weigh or quantify directors' judgments," rather they merely look to see if the process employed by the board was reasonable, with "irrationality" functioning as "the outer limit of the business judgment rule."[37] "Where judgment is inescapably required, all that the law may sensibly ask of corporate directors is that they exercise independent, good faith and attentive judgment, both with respect to the quantum of information necessary or appropriate in the circumstances and with respect to the substantive decision to be made."[38]

With this legal backdrop in mind, the plaintiffs make essentially two arguments in attacking the NCS directors' exercise of due care. First, they argue that there was an actionable failure to include Omnicare in negotiations over a possible transaction from as early as May 14, when the Independent Committee first met to consider its options. Second, the NCS stockholders allege it was a breach of the directors' duty of care to fail to contact Omnicare after its July 26 conditional proposal arrived.

With respect to the first argument, the history of relations between Omnicare and NCS demonstrate that NCS made a significant effort to solicit Omnicare's interest in a suitable transaction for more than a year. These attempts failed because Omnicare was only interested in pursuing an asset sale in bankruptcy. In fact, all offers Omnicare made before July 26, 2002, involved a . . . sale in bankruptcy. Such a transaction would have resulted in . . . NCS stockholders receiving nothing for their shares, and NCS's trade and other creditors being left to fight over the remains of the corporation. Such an offer was unacceptable to the NCS directors who felt, at a minimum, they should strive to [obtain] at least . . . some recovery for the NCS stockholders.

In sum, the record does not support an inference that the Independent Committee or the NCS board of directors breached their duty of care by pursuing a transaction with Genesis by a process that did not include additional contact with Omnicare. On the contrary, the record fully supports a conclusion that Omnicare would have continued to press for a bankruptcy transaction in which . . . the NCS stockholders recovered nothing.

The post-May discussions focused on Genesis because (unlike earlier discussions with Omnicare) they quickly moved in a very positive direction. By June 2002,

---

35. *Smith v. Van Gorkom*, 488 A.2d 858, (Del. 1985).
37. *Brehm v. Eisner*, 746 A.2d 244, 264 (Del. 2000).
38. *Equity-Linked Investors, L.P. v. Adams*, 705 A.2d 1040, 1058 (Del. Ch. 1997).

Genesis proposed a transaction outside of bankruptcy . . . and, for the first time since NCS began its search for restructuring alternatives, provided a recovery for NCS stockholders. By July 3, when the exclusivity agreement was signed, Genesis had improved its offer significantly. NCS's stockholders would receive $24 million in Genesis stock. Also, the proposal was structured as a merger and was expected to include a full recovery for NCS trade creditors and other accounts payable. Genesis, however, refused to go any further in negotiations without an exclusive dealing arrangement. It was because this last proposal was so superior to the ones Omnicare had made, . . . that the Independent Committee agreed to a short period of exclusive dealing with Genesis.

At oral argument, the plaintiffs' counsel contended that, by entering into the exclusivity agreement with Genesis, the NCS board breached its duty of care. This argument is unpersuasive. The Independent Committee purposely understood that entering into an exclusivity agreement was the only way to see if a firm deal could be negotiated between NCS and Genesis. And, there was very little reason to believe that, without a competing deal from Genesis, Omnicare would have ever offered a deal other than [an] . . . asset sale in bankruptcy. The record shows that the directors considered these factors and made a rational (and, indeed, reasonable) decision to pursue a transaction with Genesis. Certainly, the record does not reveal any important information that they overlooked in reaching the conclusion they did.

[handwritten margin note: only way]

Viewing the actions of the NCS directors during the period of July 26 (when Omnicare's conditional proposal was received) through July 28 (when NCS executed the merger agreement with Genesis) under the business judgment rule, the court easily concludes that the NCS directors acted with adequate knowledge of all material facts and made a rational judgment as to the risks and rewards of agreeing to the Genesis offer.

The NCS directors realized that the various conditions to the Omnicare proposal, . . . would create real risk if the directors tried to explore that proposal. To begin with, the exclusivity agreement did not permit the NCS directors to discuss or negotiate the July 26 letter with Omnicare. Moreover, Independent Committee member Osborne testified that, even apart from the exclusivity agreement, he would not have considered it wise to risk losing a definitive deal with Genesis for the sake of pursuing Omnicare's "highly conditional expression of interest."[46] According to Osborne, this was a very clear decision. Similarly, in discussing the risk of losing the Genesis bid, director and Independent Committee member Sells noted that, given NCS's past negotiations with Omnicare that had led only to . . . bankruptcy proposals, NCS simply could not assume that Omnicare's conditional proposal would be likely to result in an agreement superior to the Genesis offer.

Although hesitant to approach Omnicare, the Independent Committee members put Omnicare's conditional proposal to good use by [negotiating] with Genesis for better terms. This gambit succeeded in extracting a substantial increase in the consideration offered . . . . This increased offer from Genesis, however, did not come without a cost. Genesis made clear that its new offer was a "take it or leave it" proposition. If the revised proposal was not accepted and the requisite agreements

---

46. The overall quality of testimony given by the NCS directors is among the strongest this court has ever seen. All four NCS directors were deposed, and each deposition makes manifest the care and attention given to this project by every member of the board.

executed by the end of the day on July 28, Genesis would withdraw its offer and terminate negotiations. It is true that in some cases courts have expressed skepticism over threats of this nature. But, the record here is convincing that Genesis would have withdrawn its offer and walked away from the deal if NCS violated the exclusivity agreement or allowed Genesis's deadline to pass.

Given the dynamic existing on July 28, the record before the court does not support even a preliminary finding that the NCS directors failed to fulfill their fiduciary duties when they "shopped" Omnicare's proposal to Genesis, obtained a substantial improvement in the terms of that offer and then approved the transaction without contacting Omnicare. The process they followed was certainly a rational one, given the circumstances they then confronted. After looking for more than two years for a transaction that offered fair value to all NCS stakeholders, the board acted appropriately in approving the Genesis merger proposal, including the "deal protection" devices demanded by Genesis.

Notes and Questions

1. Notes

a. The Delaware Supreme Court, in a deeply divided and highly controversial decision, reversed on the ground that the NCS directors had violated their duty of loyalty by agreeing to provisions that prevented NCS from abandoning the Genesis agreement if a superior transaction presented itself. The court assumed, without deciding, that the NCS board had met its duty of care. *Omnicare, Inc. v. NCS Healthcare, Inc.*, 818 A.2d 914, 929 (Del. 2003).

b. *Smith v. Van Gorkom,* 488 A.2d 858 (Del. 1985), cited by the court, was just as divided and even more controversial than the supreme court's decision in *NCS*. In *Smith*, the directors were held personally liable for violating their duty of care in approving the sale of the entire company. There was no allegation of any duty of loyalty breach. The *Smith* decision presented the first realistic possibility that unquestionably loyal directors could nonetheless be held personally liable for acting with insufficient information. Where the plaintiff can, at some point, show causation between the directors' lack of care and damage to the corporation, a remedy is compensatory. However, where a duty of care violation leads to rescission, then no damage link has been shown; the award is simply to punish the directors. Chancellor Allen describes the case law setting and explores a bit of the theoretical underpinnings:

> Cases holding directors liable for a breach of the duty of attention or care, uncomplicated by self-dealing or conflict of interest are rare. *See, e.g.,* Joseph W. Bishop, Jr., *Sitting Ducks and Decoy Ducks: New Trends in the Indemnification of Corporate Directors and Officers,* 77 Yale L.J. 1078 (1968). One authority identifies only ten modern cases as finding actionable director negligence without a concurrent breach of loyalty or conflict of interest. *See Dennis J. Block, Nancy E. Barton & Stephen A. Radin, The Business Judgment Rule: Fiduciary Duties of Corporate Directors* 72-75 (4th ed. 1993). Of those cases in which liability has been imposed upon directors for failure to act on an informed basis, none has employed a

rescissory damage measure of remedy. Date of transaction or out-of-pocket damages have been the sole remedy afforded.[17]

The lack of authority actually imposing rescissory damages on a corporate director in a negligence case, should not itself be fatal to plaintiff's claim. It does require us to move to the level of principle and policy. That deeper analysis must begin with trust law, which provides a fertile, if sometimes risky, analogy for corporate law.

But before undertaking that analysis, it is important to note the ways in which trust law differs from corporate law. In general, the duties of a trustee to trust beneficiaries (those of loyalty, good faith, and due care), while broadly similar to those of a corporate director to his corporation, are different in significant respects. Corporate directors are responsible for often complex and demanding decisions relating to the operations of business institutions. The nature of business competition insures that these directors will often be required to take risks with the assets they manage. Indeed, an unwillingness to take risks prudently is inconsistent with the role of a diligent director. The trustees role is, classically, quite different. The role of the trustee is prudently to manage assets placed in trust, within the parameters set down in the trust instrument. The classic trusteeship is not essentially a risk taking enterprise, but a caretaking one. Hence, while trustees may be surcharged for negligence, a corporate director is only considered to have breached his duty of care in instances of gross negligence.

The duty of loyalty of a trustee also developed differently than that of a corporate director. Traditionally a trustee could not enter self-dealing transactions, even if the transaction was in all other respects, fair. Modernly at least, corporate directors may negotiate transactions with respect to which they "stand on both sides" if the terms of the deal, and the process by which it was negotiated are entirely fair. This reflects a significant difference in the expectations of the parties to these two relationships. A trusteeship from its inception has been imbued with a moral element; it is considered fundamental that trustees avoid even the appearance of dishonesty or disloyalty to maintain the integrity of this institution. The essence of the director-shareholder relationship while not devoid of moral overtones is more firmly grounded in economics: shareholders expect, and directors are required to avoid only those self-interested actions which come at the expense of the corporation or its shareholders.

The differing nature of the duty of loyalty in these relationships is also reflected in the idea that a trustee's failure to adhere to the requirements set down in the trust instrument is itself a breach of loyalty. A trustee's obligation flows to both the beneficiary, the person for whose benefits the assets are held, as well as the settlor, who often gives specific instructions which constitute an essential aspect of the "trust" placed in the trustee. When a trustee fails to fulfill the dictates of the trust instrument, he has failed in his obligation to the settlor to loyally carry out the settlor's wishes. In corporation law, by contract, such a concept is alien. Typically the certificate of incorporation confers broad minimally constrained authority upon the board to engage the corporation in business in all lawful ways.

These distinctions between trust law and corporate law, while of tone and tenor, are important. They do suggest that, insofar as negligence uncomplicated by a breach of loyalty is concerned, important policies having to do with the nature of the legal institutions of trust and of corporation require that the corporate liability rule should certainly remain less stringent than that of the trust law. To the extent that corporate directors are exposed to liability for negligence under a rescissory damages formula, their ability to fulfill their basic function as prudent risk-takers may be hindered.

Cinerama, Inc. v. Technicolor, Inc., 663 A.2d 1134, 1147-1148 (Del. Ch. 1994) (Allen, Ch.)

---

17. The remaining cases identified by Block, Barton and Radin involved direct losses to the corporation due to negligence, not loss of appreciation which could have accrued to the benefit of the shareholders but for the directors' negligence. In these cases as well, courts did not calculate damages to include the appreciated value of a lost opportunity. *See, e.g., Hoye v. Meek,* 795 F.2d 893 (10th Cir. 1986) (directors liable for the actual losses incurred due to their negligent investing); *Brane v. Roth,* 590 N.E.2d 587 (Ind. Ct. App. 1992) (awarding damages equal to the loss suffered by the corporation attributable to the directors' negligent failure to hedge grain futures); *Francis v. United Jersey Bank,* 432 A.2d 814 (N.J. 1981) (holding a director liable for corporate funds misappropriated by corporate officers).

2. Reality Check

a. Why do plaintiffs claim that the NCS board breached the duty of care?

b. What standard of review does Vice Chancellor Lamb use?

c. How is the standard of review different from the board's standard of conduct?

3. Suppose

a. Suppose this case had arisen in an MBCA jurisdiction. What portions of the MBCA would be relevant? Would the analysis or result have been different?

4. What Do You Think?

a. Do you think the board was grossly negligent in entering into the Genesis transaction?

b. How much did Omnicare's prior actions influence the NCS board? Do you think that influence was warranted?

c. Do you think the standard of review in duty of care cases should be gross negligence? If not, what standard would you propose?

d. Should typical duty of care cases and *Caremark*-type claims have different standards of review?

C. GROSS NEGLIGENCE AND BAD FAITH

Gross negligence is the standard of review, at least in Delaware, for a duty of care claim. Acting in bad faith is a duty of loyalty violation. These relatively amorphous labels may seem to you to be very similar. And, in many instances, they are. But in Delaware jurisprudence they are definitely distinct concepts and can have very different consequences. The next case illustrates the distinctions between gross negligence and bad faith and also shows why the distinction can be crucial.

McPadden v. Sidhu

964 A.2d 1262 (Del. Ch. 2008)

CHANDLER, Ch.

Though what must be shown for bad faith conduct has not yet been completely defined, it is quite clearly established that gross negligence, alone, cannot constitute bad faith.[2] Thus, a board of directors may act "badly" without acting in bad faith. This sometimes fine distinction between a breach of care (through gross negligence) and a breach of loyalty (through bad faith) is one illustrated by the actions of the board in this case.

---

2. *In re Walt Disney Co. Derivative Litig.*, 906 A.2d at 64, 65 (Del. 2006). ("'[W]e address the issue of whether gross negligence (including a failure to inform one's self of available material facts), without more, can constitute bad faith.' The answer is clearly no.").

I. BACKGROUND

In June 2005, the board of directors of i2 Technologies, Inc. ("i2" or the "Company") approved the sale of i2's wholly owned subsidiary, Trade Services Corporation ("TSC"), to a management team led by then-TSC vice president, defendant Anthony Dubreville ("Dubreville") for $3 million. Two years later, after first rejecting an offer of $18.5 million as too low just six months after the sale, Dubreville sold TSC to another company for over $25 million. These transactions engendered this lawsuit and the motions to dismiss presently before me. Plaintiff alleges that the Company's directors caused the Company to sell TSC to Dubreville's team for a price that the directors knew to be a mere fraction of TSC's fair market value.

Plaintiff . . . initiated this action on behalf of i2 to recover the losses it sustained as a result of the alleged bad faith conduct of the board and Dubreville. Plaintiff alleges that demand is excused for futility because the board's approval of the sale was not a proper exercise of business judgment. In his complaint, plaintiff . . . asserts a breach of fiduciary duty claim against the directors who approved the sale of TSC and against Dubreville. All defendants . . . move to dismiss plaintiff's complaint pursuant to Chancery Rule 12(b)(6) for failure to state a claim and Chancery Rule 23.1 for failure to plead particularized facts excusing plaintiff's failure to make a demand upon the board.

i2, a Delaware corporation headquartered in Dallas, Texas, sells supply chain management software and related consulting services. The Company operated a division known as the Content and Data Services Division ("CDSD"), which included both TSC and another subdivision known as CDS. TSC occupied a niche market unrelated to i2's main line of business. Defendants . . . were or still are members of the i2 board of directors. All Director Defendants approved the 2005 sale of TSC. Defendant Dubreville was not a director of i2; he was vice president of CDSD, which, as described above, was a division of i2 that included TSC.

II. FACTS

The gravamen of plaintiff's complaint is that i2's directors caused the Company to sell TSC, its wholly owned subsidiary, to members of TSC's management in bad faith for a price that defendants knew was a fraction of TSC's fair market value.

In early 2001, i2 acquired TSC and a related company for $100 million. By that time, Dubreville was CEO and president of TSC. After i2's acquisition of TSC, Dubreville remained in charge of TSC. By late 2004 or early 2005, i2 decided to sell TSC after determining that TSC was a non-core business that should be divested.

In June 2002, Dubreville caused TSC to sue VisionInfoSoft and its sister company, Material Express.com (together, "VIS/ME"), competitors of TSC, for copyright infringement. In 2002 and 2003, while the copyright litigation was pending, VIS/ME inquired about purchasing TSC, apparently for the purpose of resolving the lawsuit. In January 2003, [VIS/ME] sent a letter to [i2] stating that VIS/ME would be willing to pay up to $25 million for TSC. Later, in June 2004, TSC and VIS/ME settled their copyright infringement dispute with VIS/ME agreeing to pay quarterly licensing fees to TSC.

In December 2004, the i2 board decided to sell TSC. At a board meeting on February 1, 2005, i2's investment banker, Sonenshine Partners ("Sonenshine"), gave a presentation that included various options for the sale of TSC. One of these options was to sell TSC for $4.2 million to TSC employees. At this meeting, the board was also apprised of the plan to let Dubreville conduct the sale process of TSC. By this time, Dubreville was aware that VIS/ME earlier had expressed interest in buying TSC for up to $25 million and Dubreville had already discussed with i2 the possibility of leading a management buyout of TSC. Nevertheless, no business broker or investment banker was hired; the board charged Dubreville with finding a buyer for TSC.

Dubreville did not solicit interest from any of TSC's direct competitors, which were its most likely buyers. In particular, Dubreville did not solicit interest from VIS/ME though he and at least three directors knew VIS/ME had indicated a strong interest in buying TSC and had offered as much as $25 million for TSC in 2003.

While the search for a buyer for TSC was ongoing, on March 9, 2005, the board again discussed Dubreville's proposal to lead a management buyout of TSC. The process Dubreville employed ultimately produced three offers for TSC. First, an electronic parts distributor, HIS, offered $12 million for the entire CDSD division. . . . Because i2 did not want to bundle these two businesses for sale, it rejected IHs's offer. A second offer was from an entity named Sunrise Ventures, the principal of which was Dubreville's former boss at TSC and his partner in a printing company. Sunrise Ventures offered $1.8 million for TSC, which plaintiff alleges was a "lowball" offer designed to make the Dubreville-led group's offer of $3 million appear generous. The third offer was from the Dubreville-led group, Trade Service Holdings, LLC ("TSH"), of which Dubreville was a principal owner. On March 18, 2005, TSH offered to buy TSC for $2 million in cash and $1 million in software licensing agreements. . . .

On April 18, 2005, the board met to discuss the proposed management buyout of TSC and the other two offers for TSC that had been received. [S]onenshine confirmed to the board that its preliminary valuation of TSC was around $3 . . . to $10.8 million. . . . The board then authorized management to move forward with discussions to sell TSC to TSH (the company partially owned by Dubreville), even though the board knew that Dubreville had been responsible for conducting the sale of TSC and that TSC had not been offered to competitors. In addition, plaintiff contends that neither the board nor the special committee negotiated with Dubreville before the letter of intent was signed on April 22, 2005.

In the fall of 2005, TSH offered to sell TSC to VIS/ME. In December 2005, VIS/ME offered $18.5 million. TSH, through Dubreville, rejected this offer as too low and later, in 2007, sold TSC for more than $25 million. Plaintiff contends that no significant changes to TSC's business occurred during that period of time to justify the price difference and instead attributes it to the use of accurate financial statements, which supported a higher valuation of TSC.

III. LEGAL STANDARDS

[I] must first examine whether plaintiff has satisfied the pleading burden imposed by Rule 23.1, which is more onerous than that demanded by Rule 12(b)(6). Rule 23.1 requires that a shareholder first demand that the directors pursue the alleged cause of action or else satisfy "stringent requirements of factual particularity" to demonstrate that such demand would be futile.

[A] stockholder may proceed derivatively on behalf of the corporation without making a presuit demand upon the board if the complaint alleges particularized facts sufficient to create a reasonable doubt that, first, the directors were disinterested or independent or, second, the transaction was otherwise the product of a valid business judgment.[13] Thus, under the second prong of *Aronson,* a plaintiff may proceed with a suit against a disinterested and independent board if the plaintiff pleads particularized facts sufficient to rebut the presumption of the business judgment rule by alleging a breach of fiduciary duty.

Because the standard under Rule 12(b)(6) is less stringent than that under Rule 23.1, a complaint that survives a motion to dismiss pursuant to Rule 23.1 will also survive a 12(b)(6) motion to dismiss, assuming that it otherwise contains sufficient facts to state a cognizable claim. Thus, this Court's analysis properly begins with the second prong of *Aronson.*

IV. ANALYSIS

A. Demand Futility Under the Second Prong of *Aronson*

In his complaint, plaintiff alleges neither interest nor lack of independence and the parties agree that the question of demand futility is properly considered under the second prong of *Aronson.* Plaintiff avers that demand is excused as futile because the board's approval of the sale was not fully informed, not duly considered, and not made in good faith for the best interests of the Company. For the reasons described below, I conclude that, because plaintiff has pleaded a duty of care violation with particularity sufficient to create a reasonable doubt that the transaction at issue was the product of a valid exercise of business judgment, demand is excused as futile.

The challenged transaction at issue — the sale of TSC to Dubreville's group — is analytically a series of discrete board actions. Plaintiff has sufficiently alleged facts to create a reasonable doubt that they, together, cannot be the product of a valid exercise of the board's business judgment. The board's first step in the series of actions culminating in the sale of TSC to Dubreville was also its most egregious: tasking Dubreville with the sale process of TSC when the board knew that Dubreville was interested in purchasing TSC. Certainly Dubreville's interest as a potential purchaser was material to the board's decision in determining to whom to assign the task of soliciting bids and offers for TSC. It would be in Dubreville's own self-interest to obtain low offers for TSC; the more diligent he was about seeking the best offers for TSC, the higher Dubreville himself would have to bid. Had the board not known of Dubreville's interest in the sale, its decision to charge him with finding a buyer for TSC might be less perplexing. Yet, this material information was not merely reasonably available to the board, it was actually known. Dubreville had already discussed with i2 the possibility of leading a management buyout of TSC . . . . Nevertheless, the board decided that Dubreville, whom the board knew was conflicted, would conduct the sale process. From this point forward, the board's actions only exacerbated a misstep that was presumably otherwise correctable or perhaps even unactionable.

Despite having tasked a potential purchaser of TSC with its sale, the board appears to have engaged in little to no oversight of that sale process, providing no

13. *Aronson v. Lewis,* 473 A.2d 805, 813 (Del. 1984).

check on Dubreville's half-hearted (or, worse, intentionally misdirected) efforts in soliciting bids for TSC. Dubreville's limited attempts to find a buyer for TSC did not include contacting the most obvious potential buyers: TSC's direct competitors, particularly a competitor that had previously offered as much as $25 million for TSC in 2003. Perhaps unsurprisingly, Dubreville's group emerged as the highest bidder for TSC from the sale process.

The board, during its consideration of the offers for TSC at the April 18, 2005 meeting, discussed . . . Dubreville's efforts in selectively contacting potential buyers. Thus, the Director Defendants knew that Dubreville did not contact any TSC competitors. Yet the Director Defendants did nothing to remedy the situation they created by tasking an interested purchaser with the sale of an asset of the Company. Instead, they authorized further discussions with TSH and, on April 22, 2005, signed a letter of intent for i2 to sell TSC to Dubreville and his group and, in doing so, missed another opportunity to rectify the situation they had created.

In addition, . . . [t]he Directors Defendants knew that Sonenshine's preliminary valuation of TSC was based on projections provided by management, which were prepared at the direction of Dubreville. Despite this, the board agreed to proceed with an offer of $3 million, which would only ultimately result in a net gain of $2.2 million because of terms in the agreement favorable to Dubreville. The entire offer of $3 million, not even considering its ultimate net value, was at the lowest end of the valuation range of TSC. . . .

The board's actions, to this point, are quite puzzling. In making its decisions, the board had no shortage of information that was both material — because it affected the process and ultimate result of the sale — and reasonably available (or, even, actually known as evidenced by the discussions at the board meetings): Dubreville's interest in leading a management buyout of TSC; Dubreville's limited efforts in soliciting offers for TSC, including his failure to contact TSC competitors, including one he knew had previously expressed concrete interest in purchasing TSC; . . . and that TSH was a group led by Dubreville. That the board would want to consider this information seems, to me, so obvious that it is equally obvious that the Directors Defendants' failure to do so was grossly negligent.

B. Failure to State a Claim

Though plaintiff has demonstrated that it would have been futile to make a demand upon the board, plaintiff fails to state a claim against the Director Defendants, who have the benefit of a section 102(b)(7) exculpatory provision in the i2 certificate, because plaintiff has not adequately alleged that the Director Defendants acted in bad faith.

1. The 102(b)(7) Provision Exculpates the Director Defendants

As authorized by [DGCL §]102(b)(7), i2's certificate of incorporation contains an exculpatory provision, limiting the personal liability of directors for certain conduct. Certain conduct, however, cannot be exculpated, including bad faith actions. Gross negligence, in contrast, is exculpated because such conduct breaches the duty of care. Recently, . . . the Supreme Court has modified Delaware's understanding of the definition of gross negligence in the context of fiduciary duty. In analyzing "three different categories of fiduciary behavior [that] are candidates for the 'bad faith' pejorative label,"[32] the Court made quite clear that gross negligence cannot be such an example of bad faith conduct: "[t]here is no basis in policy, precedent or common sense that would justify dismantling the distinction between gross negligence and bad faith."[33] Instead, the Court concluded that conduct motivated by subjective bad intent and that resulting from gross negligence are at opposite ends of the spectrum. The Court then considered a third category of conduct: the intentional dereliction of duty or the conscious disregard for one's responsibilities. The Court determined that such misconduct must be treated as a non-exculpable, non-indemnifiable violation of the fiduciary duty to act in good faith, a duty that the Court later confirmed was squarely within the duty of loyalty.[37] Thus, from the sphere of actions that was once classified as grossly negligent conduct that gives rise to a violation of the duty of care, the Court has carved out one specific type of conduct — the intentional dereliction of duty or the conscious disregard for one's responsibilities — and redefined it as bad faith conduct, which results in a breach of the duty of loyalty. Therefore, Delaware's current understanding of gross negligence is conduct that constitutes reckless indifference or actions that are without the bounds of reason.

The conduct of the Director Defendants here fits precisely within this revised understanding of gross negligence. In finding that demand is excused as futile, I have already concluded that plaintiff has pleaded with particularity so as to raise a reasonable doubt that the actions of the board were a product of the valid exercise of their business judgment. Thus, for the reasons explained above, the Director Defendants' actions, beginning with placing Dubreville in charge of the sale process of TSC and continuing through their failure to act in any way so as to ensure that the sale process employed was thorough and complete, are properly characterized as either recklessly indifferent or unreasonable. Plaintiff has not, however, sufficiently alleged that the Director Defendants acted in bad faith through a conscious disregard for their duties. Instead, plaintiff has ably pleaded that the Director Defendants quite clearly were not careful enough in the discharge of their duties — that is, they acted with gross negligence or else reckless indifference. Because such conduct breaches the Director Defendants' duty of care, this violation is exculpated by the Section 102(b)(7) provision in the Company's charter and therefore the Director Defendants' motion to dismiss for failure to state a claim must be granted.

2. No Exculpatory Protection for Dubreville

At this point, I pause to note the perhaps unusual circumstances of this case. Here, plaintiff has alleged with particularity that the Director Defendants breached their duties of care so as to rebut the business judgment rule, thereby demonstrating that demand is excused as futile. The Company's certificate, however, contains an exculpatory provision authorized by Section 102(b)(7), shielding the Director

---

32. *In re Walt Disney Co. Derivative Litig.*, 906 A.2d at 64-65.

33. *Id.* at 66. *See also id.* at 64-65 (" '[W]e address the issue of whether gross negligence (including a failure to inform one's self of available material facts), without more, can constitute bad faith.' The answer is clearly no.").

37. *Stone v. Ritter*, 911 A.2d 362 at 369-70 (Del. 2006) (quoting *Guttman v. Huang*, 823 A.2d 492, 506 n. 34 (Del. Ch. 2003)). *See also id.* at 370 ("[T]he fiduciary duty of loyalty is not limited to cases involving a financial or other cognizable fiduciary conflict of interest. It also encompasses cases where the fiduciary fails to act in good faith.").

Defendants from liability for that conduct. Thus, ordinarily, the motion to dismiss would be granted in its entirety. Here, however, Dubreville also moves for dismissal pursuant to Rules 23.1 and 12(b)(6).[39] I have already concluded that demand is excused as futile, meaning that plaintiff has the right to prosecute this litigation on behalf of the Company. As decided above, the case cannot go forward against the Director Defendants because they are exculpated by virtue of the i2 certificate. As against Dubreville, however, the claim for breach of fiduciary duty may, without a doubt, proceed.

Though an officer owes to the corporation identical fiduciary duties of care and loyalty as owed by directors,[40] an officer does not benefit from the protections of a Section 102(b)(7) exculpatory provision, which are only available to directors. Thus, so long as plaintiff has alleged a violation of care or loyalty, the complaint proceeds against Dubreville. Here, plaintiff has more than sufficiently alleged a breach of fiduciary duty and defendants have done nothing to meet their burden of demonstrating with reasonable certainty that, under any set of facts that could be proven to support his claim for breach of fiduciary duty, plaintiff would not be entitled to the relief sought. I have no difficulty in concluding, based on plaintiff's allegations of wrongdoing by Dubreville and defendants' wholly inadequate arguments, which explicitly concede that the complaint states a claim, that the motion to dismiss Count I (breach of fiduciary duty) as to Dubreville must be denied.

V. CONCLUSION

Though this board acted "badly"—with gross negligence—and in doing so provided the basis for my denial of defendants' motion to dismiss pursuant to Rule 23.1, this board did not act in bad faith. Therefore, with the benefit of the protections of the Company's exculpatory provision, the motion to dismiss Count I (breach of fiduciary duty) pursuant to Rule 12(b)(6) is granted as to the Director Defendants. Defendants' Rule 12(b)(6) motion is, however, flatly denied as to Dubreville as to Count I.

Notes and Questions

1. Reality Check

a. What is the definition of gross negligence?

b. How is gross negligence different from bad faith?

c. Why is it important that gross negligence but not bad faith was demonstrated in this case?

---

39. Dubreville is not represented by separate counsel; he and the Director Defendants share counsel, though counsel argues in support of its motion that plaintiff's complaint "amounts to a tale of subterfuge" and fraud committed by Dubreville. If, as [defendants'] counsel contends, "Plaintiff's argument in his brief that the Board consciously disregarded their responsibilities cannot be reconciled with his allegations in the Complaint about how Dubreville allegedly concealed facts concerning the sale," then surely also [defendants'] counsel cannot simultaneously rely on the complaint's assertions that Dubreville defrauded the board or was a thief and also move for dismissal of the counts asserted against Dubreville.

40. *Ryan v. Gifford*, 935 A.2d 258, 269 (Del. Ch. 2007).

2. Suppose

a. Suppose Chancellor Chandler had found evidence of bad faith here. Could he also have found gross negligence?

b. If Chancellor Chandler had found bad faith, would the result or analysis of the case have been different?

3. What Do You Think?

a. Do you believe it makes sense to distinguish between gross negligence and bad faith?

Putting It to Work

Problem 12-2

(Note, this is the same fact pattern as Problem 11-3.)

Jane is an attorney in the small town in which she went to college. She has a general civil practice. She serves as a director for Chumy's, a popular dive bar. Katie, her former college roommate, is Chumy's general manager. The two have remained close friends. In April, while reviewing the first quarter's expense reports for Chumy's, Jane notices that the expenses for liquor have steadily increased, but that revenues on mixed drinks have not. Knowing that Katie has a habit of drinking at work, Jane assumes Katie has taken a nip here and there while at work. Further, Jane knows that Katie customarily pours free drinks on occasion for regular customers, and, in fact, always gives Jane free drinks on the rare occasions that Jane goes to Chumy's. In July, while reviewing the second quarter's expense reports, Jane notices that the expenses for liquor have again gone up considerably while the revenues from mixed drinks have actually decreased. Jane does not mention these facts either at the board meetings or informally to any other director. In late September, the federal Drug Enforcement Agency and the state Liquor Control Board arrest Katie and another Chumy's employee. It turns out that Katie and the other employee had been stealing many cases of Chumy's liquor and selling them on the black market to finance a drug operation, which they ran from the back room at Chumy's. The arrests and resultant publicity have resulted in Chumy's declaring bankruptcy.

a. If a Chumy's shareholder sues the board, what standard of review will the court apply to Jane's actions? To the other directors? Does your answer depend upon whether Chumy's is incorporated in Delaware or under the MBCA?

D. PREVAILING DESPITE THE APPLICATION OF THE BUSINESS JUDGMENT RULE

The Delaware Supreme Court has frequently suggested that a plaintiff who has not overcome the business judgment rule might still succeed if he or she can show that the corporation's action cannot be attributed to any "rational business purpose." *See Sinclair Oil Corp. v. Levien*, 280 A.2d 717, 720 (Del. 1971) (Wolcott, C.J.).

If the Delaware courts mean what they say, is a board decision that has no rational business purpose a violation of the duty of care, the duty of loyalty, a duty of good faith, or a duty to be sane? Chancellor Allen had this to say about this possibility:

> There is a theoretical exception . . . that holds that some decisions may be so "egregious" that liability for losses they cause may follow even in the absence of proof of conflict of interest or improper motivation. The exception, however, has resulted in no awards of money judgments against corporate officers or directors in this jurisdiction and, to my knowledge only the dubious holding in this Court of *Gimbel v. Signal Companies, Inc.*, 316 A.2d 599 (Del. Ch.), *aff'd*, 316 A.2d 619 (Del. 1974), seems to grant equitable relief in the absence of a claimed conflict or improper motivation. Thus, to allege that a corporation has suffered a loss as a result of a lawful transaction, within the corporation's powers, authorized by a corporate fiduciary *acting in a good faith pursuit of corporate purposes,* does not state a claim for relief against that fiduciary no matter how foolish the investment may appear in retrospect.
>
> *Gagliardi v. TriFoods Int'l, Inc.,* 683 A.2d 1049, 1051-1052 (Del. Ch. 1996) (Allen, Ch.)

As a practical matter, how likely is it that a plaintiff who can neither show a duty of loyalty issue nor show that the directors acted without all material information reasonably available can nonetheless show that the board's decision has no rational business purpose? If such a setting seems impossible to you, why do you think the Delaware courts have reiterated this possibility?

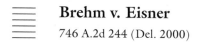

Brehm v. Eisner

746 A.2d 244 (Del. 2000)

Before VEASEY, C.J., WALSH, HOLLAND, HARTNETT and BERGER, JJ., constituting the Court en banc.

VEASEY, C.J.

The claims before us are that: (a) the board of directors of The Walt Disney Company ("Disney") as it was constituted in 1995 (the "Old Board") breached its fiduciary duty in approving an extravagant and wasteful Employment Agreement of Michael S. Ovitz as president of Disney; [and] (b) the Disney board of directors as it was constituted in 1996 (the "New Board") breached its fiduciary duty in agreeing to a "non-fault" termination of the Ovitz Employment Agreement, a decision that was extravagant and wasteful . . . .

The Complaint, consisting of 88 pages and 285 paragraphs, is a pastiche of prolix invective. It is permeated with conclusory allegations of the pleader and quotations from the media, mostly of an editorial nature (even including a cartoon). A pleader may rely on factual statements in the media as some of the "tools at hand" from which the pleader intends to derive the particularized facts necessary to comply with Chancery Rule 11(b)(3) and Chancery Rule 23.1. But many of the quotations from the media in the Complaint simply echo plaintiffs' conclusory allegations. Accordingly, they serve no purpose other than to complicate the work of reviewing courts.

This is potentially a very troubling case on the merits. On the one hand, it appears from the Complaint that: (a) the compensation and termination payout for Ovitz were exceedingly lucrative, if not luxurious, compared to Ovitz' value to the

Company; and (b) the processes of the boards of directors in dealing with the approval and termination of the Ovitz Employment Agreement were casual, if not sloppy and perfunctory. On the other hand, the Complaint is so inartfully drafted that it was properly dismissed under our pleading standards for derivative suits. From what we can ferret out of this deficient pleading, the processes of the Old Board and the New Board were hardly paradigms of good corporate governance practices. Moreover, the sheer size of the payout to Ovitz, as alleged, pushes the envelope of judicial respect for the business judgment of directors in making compensation decisions. Therefore, both as to the processes of the two Boards and the waste test, this is a close case.

But our concerns about lavish executive compensation and our institutional aspirations that boards of directors of Delaware corporations live up to the highest standards of good corporate practices do not translate into a holding that these plaintiffs have set forth particularized facts excusing a pre-suit demand under our law and our pleading requirements.

This appeal presents several important issues, including: . . . the scope of the business judgment rule as it interacts with the relevant pleading requirements. To some extent, the principles enunciated in this opinion restate and clarify our prior jurisprudence.

FACTS

This statement of facts is taken from the Complaint. We have attempted to summarize here the essence of Plaintiffs' factual allegations on the key issues before us, disregarding the many conclusions that are not supported by factual allegations.

A. The 1995 Ovitz Employment Agreement

By an agreement dated October 1, 1995, Disney hired Ovitz as its president. He was a long-time friend of Disney Chairman and CEO Michael Eisner. At the time, Ovitz was an important talent broker in Hollywood. Although he lacked experience managing a diversified public company, other companies with entertainment operations had been interested in hiring him for high-level executive positions. The Employment Agreement was unilaterally negotiated by Eisner and approved by the Old Board. Their judgment was that Ovitz was a valuable person to hire as president of Disney, and they agreed ultimately with Eisner's recommendation in awarding him an extraordinarily lucrative contract.

Ovitz' Employment Agreement had an initial term of five years and required that Ovitz "devote his full time and best efforts exclusively to the Company," with exceptions for volunteer work, service on the board of another company, and managing his passive investments.[5] In return, Disney agreed to give Ovitz a base salary of $1 million per year, a discretionary bonus, and two sets of stock options (the "A" options and the "B" options) that collectively would enable Ovitz to purchase 5 million shares of Disney common stock.

The "A" options were scheduled to vest . . . beginning on September 30, 1998 (i.e., at the end of the third full year of employment) and continuing for the

---

5. The agreement implicitly emphasized the importance of having Disney receive Ovitz' full attention by mentioning, in a section stating the unique nature of Ovitz' services, that the Company would specifically be entitled to equitable relief if Ovitz failed to provide it with "the exclusivity of his services."

following two years . . . . The agreement specifically provided that the "A" options would vest immediately if Disney granted Ovitz a non-fault termination of the Employment Agreement. Although scheduled to vest annually starting in September 2001 (i.e., the year *after* the last "A" option would vest), the "B" options were conditioned on Ovitz and Disney first having agreed to extend his employment beyond the five-year term of the Employment Agreement. Furthermore, Ovitz would forfeit the right to qualify for the "B" options if his initial employment term of five years ended prematurely for any reason, even if from a non-fault termination.

The Employment Agreement provided for three ways by which Ovitz' employment might end. He might serve his five years and Disney might decide against offering him a new contract. If so, Disney would owe Ovitz a $10 million termination payment.[6] Before the end of the initial term, Disney could terminate Ovitz for "good cause" only if Ovitz committed gross negligence or malfeasance, or if Ovitz resigned voluntarily. Disney would owe Ovitz no additional compensation if it terminated him for "good cause." Termination without cause (non-fault termination) would entitle Ovitz to the present value of his remaining salary payments through September 30, 2000, a $10 million severance payment, an additional $7.5 million for each fiscal year remaining under the agreement, and the immediate vesting of the . . . "A" Options.

Plaintiffs allege that the Old Board knew that Disney needed a strong second-in-command. Disney had recently made several acquisitions, and questions lingered about Eisner's health due to major heart surgery. The Complaint further alleges that "Eisner had demonstrated little or no capacity to work with important or well-known subordinate executives who wanted to position themselves to succeed him," citing the departures of Disney executives Jeffrey Katzenberg, Richard Frank, and Stephen Bollenbach as examples. Thus, the Board knew that, to increase the chance for long-term success, it had to take extra care in reviewing a decision to hire Disney's new president.

But Eisner's decision that Disney should hire Ovitz as its president was not entirely well-received. When Eisner told three members of the Old Board in mid-August 1995 that he had decided to hire Ovitz, all three "denounced the decision." Although not entirely clear from the Complaint, the vote of the Old Board approving the Ovitz Employment Agreement two months later appears to have been unanimous. Aside from a conclusory attack that the Old Board followed Eisner's bidding, the Complaint fails to allege any particularized facts that the three directors changed their initial reactions through anything other than the typical process of further discussion and individual contemplation.

The Complaint then alleges that the Old Board failed properly to inform itself about the total costs and incentives of the Ovitz Employment Agreement, especially the severance package. This is the key allegation related to this issue on appeal. Specifically, plaintiffs allege that the Board failed to realize that the contract gave Ovitz an incentive to find a way to exit the Company via a non-fault termination as soon as possible because doing so would permit him to earn more than he could by fulfilling his contract. The Complaint alleges, however, that the Old Board had been advised by a corporate compensation expert, Graef Crystal, in connection with its

---

6. All the "A" options would have vested, but he would not receive the "B" options.

decision to approve the Ovitz Employment Agreement. Two public statements by Crystal form the basis of the allegation that the Old Board failed to consider the incentives and the total cost of the severance provisions, but these statements by Crystal were not made until after Ovitz left Disney in December 1996, approximately 14½ months after being hired.

The first statement, published in a December 23, 1996 article in the web-based magazine *Slate*, quoted Crystal as saying, in part, "Of course, the overall costs of the package would go up sharply in the event of Ovitz's termination (*and I wish now that I'd made a spreadsheet showing just what the deal would total if Ovitz had been fired at any time*)." The second published statement appeared in an article about three weeks later in the January 13, 1997 edition of *California Law Business*. The article appears first to paraphrase Crystal: "With no one expecting failure, the sleeper clauses in Ovitz's contract seemed innocuous, Crystal says, explaining that no one added up the total cost of the severance package." The article then quotes Crystal as saying that the amount of Ovitz' severance was "shocking" and that "*[n]obody quantified this and I wish we had.*" One of the charging paragraphs of the Complaint concludes:

> 57. As has been conceded by Graef Crystal, the executive compensation consultant who advised the Old Board with respect to the Ovitz Employment Agreement, the Old Board *never* considered the costs that would be incurred by Disney in the event Ovitz was terminated from the Company for a reason other than cause prior to the natural expiration of the Ovitz Employment Agreement.

Although repeated in various forms in the Complaint, these quoted admissions by Crystal constitute the extent of the factual support for the allegation that the Old Board failed properly to consider the severance elements of the agreement. This Court, however, must juxtapose these allegations with the legal presumption that the Old Board's conduct was a proper exercise of business judgment. That presumption includes the statutory protection for a board that relies in good faith on an expert advising the Board.[9] We must decide whether plaintiffs' factual allegations, if proven, would rebut that presumption.

B. The New Board's Actions in Approving the Non-Fault Termination

Soon after Ovitz began work, problems surfaced and the situation continued to deteriorate during the first year of his employment. To support this allegation, the plaintiffs cite various media reports detailing internal complaints and providing external examples of alleged business mistakes. The Complaint uses these reports to suggest that the New Board had reason to believe that Ovitz' performance and lack of commitment met the gross negligence or malfeasance standards of the termination-for-cause provisions of the contract.

The deteriorating situation, according to the Complaint, led Ovitz to begin seeking alternative employment and to send Eisner a letter in September 1996 that the Complaint paraphrases as stating his dissatisfaction with his role and expressing his desire to leave the Company. The Complaint also admits that Ovitz would not actually resign before negotiating a non-fault severance agreement because he did

---

9. *See* [DGCL] §141(e). . . .

not want to jeopardize his rights to a lucrative severance in the form of a "non-fault termination" under the terms of the 1995 Employment Agreement.

On December 11, 1996, Eisner and Ovitz agreed to arrange for Ovitz to leave Disney on the non-fault basis provided for in the 1995 Employment Agreement. Eisner then "caused" the New Board[11] "to rubber-stamp his decision (by 'mutual consent')." This decision was implemented by a December 27, 1996 letter to Ovitz from defendant Sanford M. Litvack, an officer and director of Disney.

Although the non-fault termination left Ovitz with what essentially was a very lucrative severance agreement, it is important to note that Ovitz and Disney had negotiated for that severance payment at the time they initially contracted in 1995, and in the end the payout to Ovitz did not exceed the 1995 contractual benefits. Consequently, Ovitz received the $10 million termination payment, $7.5 million for part of the fiscal year remaining under the agreement and the immediate vesting of . . . the "A" options. As a result of his termination Ovitz would not receive the . . . "B" options that he would have been entitled to if he had completed the full term of the Employment Agreement and if his contract were renewed.

The Complaint charges the New Board with waste, computing the value of the severance package agreed to by the Board at over $140 million, consisting of cash payments of about $39 million and the value of the immediately vesting "A" options of over $101 million. The Complaint quotes Crystal, the Old Board's expert, as saying in January 1997 that Ovitz' severance package was a "shocking amount of severance."

The allegation of waste is based on the inference most favorable to plaintiffs that Disney owed Ovitz nothing, either because he had resigned (*de facto*) or because he was unarguably subject to firing for cause. These allegations must be juxtaposed with the presumption that the New Board exercised its business judgment in deciding how to resolve the potentially litigable issues of whether Ovitz had actually resigned or had definitely breached his contract. We must decide whether plaintiffs' factual allegations, if proven, would rebut that presumption.

PRINCIPLES OF CORPORATION LAW COMPARED WITH GOOD CORPORATE GOVERNANCE PRACTICES

This is a case about whether there should be personal liability of the directors of a Delaware corporation to the corporation for lack of due care in the decisionmaking process and for waste of corporate assets. This case is not about the failure of the directors to establish and carry out ideal corporate governance practices.

All good corporate governance practices include compliance with statutory law and case law establishing fiduciary duties. But the law of corporate fiduciary duties and remedies for violation of those duties are distinct from the aspirational goals of ideal corporate governance practices. Aspirational ideals of good corporate governance practices for boards of directors that go beyond the minimal legal requirements of the corporation law are highly desirable, often tend to benefit stockholders, sometimes reduce litigation and can usually help directors avoid liability. But they are not required by the corporation law and do not define standards of liability.

---

11. The composition of the New Board differed slightly from the composition of the Old Board.

The inquiry here is not whether we would disdain the composition, behavior and decisions of Disney's Old Board or New Board as alleged in the Complaint if we were Disney stockholders. In the absence of a legislative mandate, that determination is not for the courts. That decision is for the stockholders to make in voting for directors, urging other stockholders to reform or oust the board, or in making individual buy-sell decisions involving Disney securities. The sole issue that this Court must determine is whether the particularized facts alleged in this Complaint provide a reason to believe that the conduct of the Old Board in 1995 and the New Board in 1996 constituted a violation of their fiduciary duties.

PLAINTIFFS' CONTENTION THAT THE OLD BOARD VIOLATED THE PROCESS DUTY OF CARE IN APPROVING THE OVITZ EMPLOYMENT AGREEMENT

Certainly in this case the economic exposure of the corporation to the payout scenarios of the Ovitz contract was material, particularly given its large size, for purposes of the directors' decisionmaking process.[49] And those dollar exposure numbers were reasonably available because the logical inference from plaintiffs' allegations is that Crystal or the New Board could have calculated the numbers. Thus, the objective tests of reasonable availability and materiality were satisfied by this Complaint. But that is not the end of the inquiry for liability purposes.

Although the Court of Chancery did not expressly predicate its decision on Section 141(e), Crystal is presumed to be an expert on whom the Board was entitled to rely in good faith under Section 141(e) in order to be "fully protected." Plaintiffs must rebut the presumption that the directors properly exercised their business judgment, including their good faith reliance on Crystal's expertise. What Crystal *now* believes *in hindsight* that he and the Board *should have done* in 1995 does not provide that rebuttal. That is not to say, however, that a rebuttal of the presumption of proper reliance on the expert under Section 141(e) cannot be pleaded consistent with Rule 23.1 in a properly framed complaint setting forth particularized facts creating reason to believe that the Old Board's conduct was grossly negligent.

To survive a Rule 23.1 motion to dismiss in a due care case where an expert has advised the board in its decisionmaking process, the complaint must allege particularized facts (not conclusions) that, if proved, would show, for example, that: (a) the directors did not in fact rely on the expert; (b) their reliance was not in good faith; (c) they did not reasonably believe that the expert's advice was within the expert's professional competence; (d) the expert was not selected with reasonable care by or on behalf of the corporation, and the faulty selection process was attributable to the directors; (e) the subject matter (in this case the cost calculation) that was material and reasonably available was so obvious that the board's failure to consider it was grossly negligent regardless of the expert's advice or lack of advice; or (f) that the

---

49. The term "material" is used in this context to mean relevant and of a magnitude to be important to directors in carrying out their fiduciary duty of care in decisionmaking. One must also keep in mind that the size of executive compensation for a large public company in the current environment often involves huge numbers. This is particularly true in the entertainment industry where the enormous revenues from one "hit" movie or enormous losses from a "flop" place in perspective the compensation of executives whose genius or misjudgment, as the case may be, may have contributed substantially to the "hit" or "flop."

decision of the Board was so unconscionable as to constitute waste or fraud.[56] This Complaint includes no particular allegations of this nature, and therefore it was subject to dismissal as drafted.

Plaintiffs also contend that Crystal's latter-day admission is "valid and binding" on the Old Board. This argument is without merit. Crystal was the Board's expert *ex ante* for purposes of advising the directors on the Ovitz Employment Agreement. He was not their agent *ex post* to make binding admissions.

We conclude that, although the language of the Court of Chancery was flawed in formulating the proper legal test to be used and in its reading of the Complaint, that pleading, as drafted, fails to create a reasonable doubt that the Old Board's decision in approving the Ovitz Employment Agreement was protected by the business judgment rule. Plaintiffs will be provided an opportunity to replead on this issue.

PLAINTIFFS' CONTENTION THAT THE OLD BOARD . . . COMMITTED WASTE AB INITIO WITH OVITZ' EMPLOYMENT AGREEMENT

Plaintiffs' principal theory is that the 1995 Ovitz Employment Agreement was a "wasteful transaction for Disney *ab initio*" because it was structured to "incentivize" Ovitz to seek an early non-fault termination. The Court of Chancery correctly dismissed this theory as failing to meet the stringent requirements of the waste test, i.e., "'an exchange that is so one sided that no business person of ordinary, sound judgment could conclude that the corporation has received adequate consideration.'"[58] Moreover, the Court concluded that a board's decision on executive compensation is entitled to great deference. It is the essence of business judgment for a board to determine if "a 'particular individual warrant[s] large amounts of money, whether in the form of current salary or severance provisions.'"[59]

Specifically, the Court of Chancery inferred from a reading of the Complaint that the Board determined it had to offer an expensive compensation package to attract Ovitz and that they determined he would be valuable to the Company. The Court also concluded that the vesting schedule of the options actually was a disincentive for Ovitz to leave Disney. When he did leave pursuant to the non-fault termination, the Court noted that he left 2 million options (the "B" options) "on the table." Although we agree with the conclusion of the Court of Chancery that this particular Complaint is deficient, we do not foreclose the possibility that a properly framed complaint could pass muster.

Plaintiffs' disagreement on appeal with the decision of the Court of Chancery is basically a quarrel with the Old Board's judgment in evaluating Ovitz' worth *vis-à-vis* the lavish payout to him. We agree with the analysis of the Court of

---

56. To be sure, directors have the power, authority and wide discretion to make decisions on executive compensation. *See* [DGCL] §122(5). As the often-cited Court of Chancery decision by Chancellor Seitz in *Saxe v. Brady* warns, there is an outer limit to that discretion, at which point a decision of the directors on executive compensation is so disproportionately large as to be unconscionable and constitute waste. 184 A.2d 602, 610 (Del. Ch. 1962); *see Grimes* [*v. Donald*], 673 A.2d [1207] at 1215 (Del. 1996) (noting that compensation decisions by an independent board are protected by the business judgment rule "unless the facts show that such amounts, compared with the services to be received in exchange, constitute waste or could not otherwise be the product of a valid exercise of business judgment") (citing *Saxe*, 184 A.2d at 610); . . . .

58. *In re The Walt Disney Co. Derivative Litig.*, 731 A.2d at 362 (quoting *Glazer v. Zapata Corp.*, 658 A.2d 176, 183 (Del. Ch. 1993)).

59. *Id.* (quoting *Grimes*, 673 A.2d at 1215).

Chancery that the size and structure of executive compensation are inherently matters of judgment. As former Chancellor Allen stated in *Vogelstein:*

> The judicial standard for determination of corporate waste is well developed. Roughly, a waste entails an exchange of corporate assets for consideration so disproportionately small as to lie beyond the range at which any reasonable person might be willing to trade. Most often the claim is associated with a transfer of corporate assets that serves no corporate purpose; or for which no consideration at all is received. Such a transfer is in effect a gift. If, however, there is *any substantial* consideration received by the corporation, and if there is a *good faith judgment* that in the circumstances the transaction is worthwhile, there should be no finding of waste, even if the fact finder would conclude *ex post* that the transaction was unreasonably risky. Any other rule would deter corporate boards from the optimal rational acceptance of risk, for reasons explained elsewhere. Courts are ill-fitted to attempt to weigh the "adequacy" of consideration under the waste standard or, *ex post,* to judge appropriate degrees of business risk.[63]

To be sure, there are outer limits, but they are confined to unconscionable cases where directors irrationally squander or give away corporate assets. Here, however, we find no error in the decision of the Court of Chancery on the waste test.

Courts do not measure, weigh or quantify directors' judgments. We do not even decide if they are reasonable in this context. Due care in the decisionmaking context is *process* due care only. Irrationality[65] is the outer limit of the business judgment rule. Irrationality may be the functional equivalent of the waste test or it may tend to show that the decision is not made in good faith, which is a key ingredient of the business judgment rule.[66]

PLAINTIFFS' CONTENTION THAT THE NEW BOARD COMMITTED WASTE IN ITS DECISION THAT OVITZ' CONTRACT SHOULD BE TERMINATED ON A "NON-FAULT" BASIS

The plaintiffs contend in this Court that Ovitz resigned or committed acts of gross negligence or malfeasance that constituted grounds to terminate him for cause. In either event, they argue that the Company had no obligation to Ovitz and that the directors wasted the Company's assets by causing it to make an unnecessary and enormous payout of cash and stock options when it permitted Ovitz to terminate his employment on a "non-fault" basis. We have concluded, however, that the Complaint currently before us does not set forth particularized facts that he resigned or unarguably breached his Employment Agreement.

The Complaint does not allege facts that would show that Ovitz had, in fact, resigned before the Board acted on his non-fault termination. Plaintiffs contend, in effect, that the sum total of Ovitz' actions constituted a *de facto* resignation. But the Complaint does not allege that Ovitz had *actually* resigned. It alleges merely that he: (a) was dissatisfied with his role; (b) was underperforming; (c) was seeking and

---

63. [*Lewis v.*] *Vogelstein,* 699 A.2d 327 at 336 (Del. Ch. 1997) (emphasis in original) (citations omitted). . . .

65. Directors' business "decisions will not be disturbed if they can be attributed to any rational business purpose." *Sinclair Oil Corp. v. Levien,* 280 A.2d 717, 720 (Del. 1971).

66. The business judgment rule has been well formulated by *Aronson* and other cases. *See, e.g., Aronson,* 473 A.2d at 812 ("It is a presumption that in making a business decision the directors . . . acted on an informed basis, in good faith and in the honest belief that the action taken was in the best interests of the corporation."). Thus, directors' decisions will be respected by courts unless the directors are interested or lack independence relative to the decision, do not act in good faith, act in a manner that cannot be attributed to a rational business purpose or reach their decision by a grossly negligent process that includes the failure to consider all material facts reasonably available.

entertaining other job offers; and (d) had written to Eisner on September 5, 1996, "express[ing] his desire to quit." These are not particularized allegations that he resigned, either actually or constructively.

Additionally, the Complaint is internally inconsistent with plaintiffs' argument that Ovitz had resigned. The Complaint alleges that Ovitz would not actually resign before he could achieve a lucrative payout under the generous terms of his 1995 Employment Agreement. The clear inference from the Complaint is that he would lose all leverage by resigning.

The Complaint alleges that it was waste for the Board to pay Ovitz essentially the full amount he was due on the non-fault termination basis because he should have been fired for cause. Ovitz' contract provided that he could be fired for cause only if he was grossly negligent or committed acts of malfeasance. Plaintiffs contend that ample grounds existed to fire Ovitz for cause under these terms.

Construed most favorably to plaintiffs, the facts in the Complaint (disregarding conclusory allegations) show that Ovitz' performance as president was disappointing at best, that Eisner admitted it had been a mistake to hire him, that Ovitz lacked commitment to the Company, that he performed services for his old company, and that he negotiated for other jobs (some very lucrative) while being required under the contract to devote his full time and energy to Disney.

All this shows is that the Board had *arguable* grounds to fire Ovitz for cause. But what is alleged is only an *argument* — perhaps a good one — that Ovitz' conduct constituted gross negligence or malfeasance. First, given the facts as alleged, Disney would have had to persuade a trier of fact and law of this argument in any litigated dispute with Ovitz. Second, that process of persuasion could involve expensive litigation, distraction of executive time and company resources, lost opportunity costs, more bad publicity and an outcome that was uncertain at best and, at worst, could have resulted in damages against the Company.

The Complaint, in sum, contends that the Board committed waste by agreeing to the very lucrative payout to Ovitz under the non-fault termination provision because it had no obligation to him, thus taking the Board's decision outside the protection of the business judgment rule. Construed most favorably to plaintiffs, the Complaint contends that, by reason of the New Board's available arguments of resignation and good cause, it had the leverage to negotiate Ovitz down to a more reasonable payout than that guaranteed by his Employment Agreement. But the Complaint fails on its face to meet the waste test because it does not allege with particularity facts tending to show that no reasonable business person would have made the decision that the New Board made under these circumstances.

To rule otherwise would invite courts to become super-directors, measuring matters of degree in business decisionmaking and executive compensation. Such a rule would run counter to the foundation of our jurisprudence.

Nevertheless, plaintiffs will have another opportunity — if they are able to do so consistent with Chancery Rule 11 — to file a short and plain statement alleging particularized facts creating a reasonable doubt that the New Board's decision regarding the Ovitz non-fault termination was protected by the business judgment rule.

CONCLUSION

One can understand why Disney stockholders would be upset with such an extraordinarily lucrative compensation agreement and termination payout awarded a company president who served for only a little over a year and who underperformed to the extent alleged. That said, there is a very large—though not insurmountable—burden on stockholders who believe they should pursue the remedy of a derivative suit instead of selling their stock or seeking to reform or oust these directors from office.

Delaware has pleading rules and an extensive judicial gloss on those rules that must be met in order for a stockholder to pursue the derivative remedy. Sound policy supports these rules, as we have noted. This Complaint, which is a blunderbuss of a mostly conclusory pleading, does not meet that burden, and it was properly dismissed.

Notes and Questions

1. Notes

a. An omitted portion of the opinion affirmed the Chancellor's finding that the boards were disinterested and independent, essentially equivalent to a finding that the boards had met their duty of loyalty. The issue was presented in an odd posture because the plaintiffs did not challenge the Chancellor's findings on appeal; only amici curiae did so. Nonetheless, the Supreme Court affirmed the Chancellor's findings and precluded relitigation of the issue.

b. A subsequent opinion in this litigation is found on pages 522 and 528.

c. The Old Board comprised the following individuals:

Inside or retired inside directors

> Mr. Eisner, chairman of the board and chief executive officer
> Stephen F. Bollenbach, chief financial officer
> Roy E. Disney, vice chair of the board and head of the Animation Department
> Sanford M. Litvak, senior executive vice president and chief of corporate operations
> Richard A. Nunis, chair of Walt Disney Attractions (theme parks and resorts)
> E. Cardon Walker, retired chair of the board, chief executive officer, and president
> Gary L. Wilson, former executive vice president and chief financial officer

Advisors to certain directors
> Irwin E. Russell, Mr. Eisner's personal attorney
> Stanley P. Gold, Mr. Disney's personal attorney

Outside directors
> Reveta F. Bowers, head of school for the Center for Early Education, a private school in Los Angeles that some of Mr. Eisner's children attended
> Ignacio E. Lozano, Jr., owner and publisher of *La Opinion*, the largest Spanish-language newspaper in Los Angeles and former U.S. ambassador to El Salvador
> George J. Mitchell, former U.S. Senator

Sidney Poitier, actor, director, and writer
Robert A.M. Stern, internationally prominent architect
Raymond L. Watson, head of a major Southern California land company.

The New Board was the same as the Old Board except that Mr. Bollenbach resigned and three new members were added:

Thomas S. Murphy, retired head of the American Broadcasting Corporation (ABC), a Walt Disney Company subsidiary
Fr. Leo J. O'Donovan, S.J., President of Georgetown University, which one of Mr. Eisner's children attended
Mr. Ovitz, President.

d. The MBCA has possibly avoided the problem presented by *Brehm* by not expressly stating that directors can be liable for a transaction that violates neither their duty of loyalty nor their duty of care. Does it make any practical difference whether such actions are treated as a violation of the fiduciary duties, the standards of review, or are simply, substantively, impermissible?

2. Reality Check

a. Chief Justice Veasey wrote, "[I]t appears from the Complaint that: (a) the compensation and termination payout for Ovitz were exceedingly lucrative, if not luxurious, compared to Ovitz' value to the Company; and (b) the processes of the boards of directors in dealing with the approval and termination of the Ovitz Employment Agreement were casual, if not sloppy and perfunctory." How can the plaintiffs lose?

b. What were the elements of Mr. Ovitz's compensation?

c. How did the Old Board meet its duty of care?

d. How did the New Board meet its duty of care?

e. What is the standard for waste? When does it apply?

f. Why did the plaintiffs fail to meet their burden as to waste?

g. What is the relation between the duty of care, waste, rational business purpose, and good faith?

3. Suppose

a. Imagine that Mr. Ovitz's compensation upon termination were $1.4 million. Would that affect the court's reasoning or the result? Imagine Mr. Ovitz's compensation upon termination were $1.4 billion. Would that affect the court's reasoning or the result?

4. What Do You Think?

a. Why did Mr. Ovitz's compensation consist of so many different elements? Did these elements serve different functions? If so, what were they? Were they effective?

b. Do you think some of the directors could have their loyalty to the company questioned? If so, which ones?

c. Chief Justice Veasey said that courts do not evaluate the substance of board decisions but only the process by which those decisions were approved. Is he correct? Why does he make this assertion?

5. You Draft It

a. Assume that the New Board decided to terminate Mr. Ovitz for good cause. Draft a letter to Mr. Ovitz that effects that termination, that articulates the board's reasons for termination, and that states the compensation consequences of that termination.

E. AMELIORATION OF LIABILITY FOR VIOLATIONS OF FIDUCIARY DUTIES

This and the previous chapter have set out, in a rather elaborate way, the potential liabilities for officers and directors. Now we turn to several methods by which that liability can be ameliorated. These methods, of course, raise the question whether amelioration should even be permitted. After all, what sense does it make to set up a careful and nuanced system of conduct and liability and then permit directors to circumvent that system?

Before we work through these techniques, though, three other approaches to limiting liability are discussed elsewhere and are simply noted here. First, boards are permitted to rely on reports made to them by board committees and others inside the corporation (and certain advisors not within the corporation), at least in the absence of indications that reliance is unwarranted. *See* DGCL §141(e) and MBCA §8.30(d), (e), (f). In Delaware, to overcome the presumption that reliance is warranted a plaintiff must show that

> (a) the directors did not in fact rely on the expert; (b) their reliance was not in good faith; (c) they did not reasonably believe that the expert's advice was within the expert's professional competence; (d) the expert was not selected with reasonable care by or on behalf of the corporation, and the faulty selection process was attributable to the directors; (e) the subject matter . . . that was material and reasonably available was so obvious that the board's failure to consider it was grossly negligent regardless of the expert's advice or lack of advice; or (f) that the decision of the Board was so unconscionable as to constitute waste or fraud.

Brehm v. Eisner, 746 A.2d 244, 262 (Del. 2000) (Veasey, C.J.)

A second approach, related to the first, is the ability of the board to delegate its powers either to a board committee or, more generally, to others within the corporation. Again, in the absence of an indication that those to whom powers have been delegated are not exercising those powers appropriately, the board is entitled to rely on the assumption that their delegates are acting in the corporation's best interest. *See* DGCL §§141(c) (delegation to board committees) and 142(a) (delegation to corporate officers) and MBCA §8.30(c). Further, DGCL §141(a) has been interpreted to give the board great discretion to delegate by virtue of the requirement that "The business and affairs of every corporation . . . shall be managed by *or under the direction of* a board of directors. . . ."

The third approach is a special case of the power to delegate. When some, but fewer than all, directors are sued for breaching their fiduciary duties, the board frequently constitutes the nondefendant directors as a committee (usually called a *special litigation committee*) to investigate the allegations and recommend whether pursuing those allegations is in the best interest of the corporation. Similar special committees are also frequently appointed when the corporation intends to enter into a transaction that, for some directors, presents a conflict of interest transaction. In that setting the committee is charged with determining whether the transaction is in the best interest of the corporation. Because these transactions are particularly sensitive, the amount of deference, if any, the court should give to these special committees is frequently a hotly contested issue. The use of special committees in these settings is treated separately in Chapter 14 dealing with shareholder litigation and Chapter 16 dealing with change of control situations.

1. Duty of Loyalty: Statutory Safe Harbor for Conflict of Interest Transactions

In Chapter 11 we defined "conflict of interest" as any objective suggestion that a director might not believe that the corporation's action was in the best interest of the corporation. We also saw that conflicts of interest can be laid out on a rough continuum from transactions between the director and the corporation (classic self-dealing) through transactions in which the "conflict" seems quite attenuated. We now revisit that issue in the context of ameliorating the potential for director liability in approving such transactions.

Most states have adopted statutes that affect at least some transactions that raise duty of loyalty problems. The DGCL section is 144(a) and the MBCA provisions are in Subchapter F, §§8.60-8.63. These statutes, which in this chapter we will call *CoI Safe Harbor* statutes, are nonexclusive, which means that parties and courts need not rely upon them. These statutes typically raise three principal issues, which we will examine separately:

1. Which *transactions* are eligible to be affected by the CoI Safe Harbors?
2. What are the procedural or substantive *prerequisites* that eligible transactions must meet to be affected by the CoI Safe Harbors?
3. What is the CoI Safe Harbor's *effect* on transactions that meet those prerequisites?

a. The Current Setting

i. Transactions Eligible to Be Affected.   The following case provides a nice canvass of the kinds of CoI Safe Harbors that have been adopted. Although the focus is on analyzing whether the statute extends to the transactions at issue, you should pay attention to the other two issues listed above, as well.

Shapiro v. Greenfield

764 A.2d 270 (Md. App. 2000)

KENNEY, J.

Charles Shapiro was the operating officer for [College Park Woods, Inc. ("College Park")] during the relevant time period. Other officers and directors included Joan Smith, Charles' sister, and Michael Shapiro, Charles' son. Appellee Marvin Greenfield is Charles Shapiro's cousin [and, along with his wife, Betty, is a minority shareholder of College Park].

In 1961, College Park acquired . . . land in Prince George's County, on which it constructed the . . . Clinton Plaza shopping center. By 1991, Clinton Plaza was only 50% leased and generating insufficient cash flow. It was decided that the best use of the land was not the continuation of Clinton Plaza, but redevelopment of the property into a substantially larger shopping center. Having determined that College Park was not capable of redeveloping Clinton Plaza on its own, the directors explored suitable partnerships or joint ventures, but for some time did not find any.

Charles Shapiro, the operating officer of College Park, subsequently developed a joint venture with . . . an occasional business partner of his with experience developing retail space. The joint venture required the creation of . . . Clinton Crossings Limited Partnership ("Clinton Crossings Partnership"), which was to own the redeveloped Clinton Plaza shopping center . . . [Charles and Michael Shapiro were to own 50% of Clinton Crossings Partnership through certain other entities Charles controlled]. College Park was to transfer its fee simple interest in Clinton Plaza to Clinton Crossings Partnership in exchange for a 50% limited partnership interest in Clinton Crossings Partnership, the owner of the redeveloped center. Clinton Associates was to contribute everything necessary for the shopping center's redevelopment with the exception of the land.

As a limited partner, College Park would have no rights to manage, direct or control the affairs of Clinton Crossings Partnership. Clinton Crossings Partnership and [the Shapiro entities], on the other hand, would assume the risk associated with the redevelopment, while College Park would assume none.

On October 26, 1991, a special meeting of College Park's shareholders was called for the purpose of "considering and approving a resolution authorizing the corporation to enter into a limited partnership agreement with [the Shapiro Entities]." Advance notice of the meeting included documents that described the joint venture in detail [and disclosed the Shapiros' interest].

Appellees, Marvin and Betty Greenfield, did not attend this special meeting. At the meeting, the shareholders present unanimously voted for the proposal. Appellees contend that following the October 26, 1991 meeting, they protested that the votes taken at the meeting were not valid as none of the directors could be considered disinterested directors and thus their votes as shareholders could not be counted.

On April 2, 1992, College Park directors met to ratify actions taken by the corporation at the special meeting and other occasions. Appellees filed this suit on July 15, 1992, against College Park and its directors, Charles S. Shapiro, Michael Shapiro, and Joan Smith, requesting "damages, an accounting, the appointment of a receiver, the imposition of a constructive trust, the dissolution of the corporation, attorneys' fees, costs and other legal and equitable relief."

The matter was tried before the Circuit Court for Montgomery County from May 1 to May 4, 1995. On June 29, 1995, the trial court entered an interlocutory order granting appellees' request for an accounting, and appointed a special master to determine specific factual issues. The special master filed his Report of Factual Findings, Conclusions, and Recommendations ("Report") on October 17, 1997.

On December 2, 1997, appellees filed a motion to appoint a receiver for College Park. On February 23, 1998, the trial court granted appellees' motion, appointing a single receiver for College Park. . . . Appellants filed a notice of appeal.

Concepts related to corporate opportunities and interested director transactions find their genesis in a director's duty of loyalty to the corporation. The longstanding common law rule in Maryland was "that any contract between a corporation and one of its officers or directors as to a matter in which the officer or director had a substantial personal interest was void or voidable." *Sullivan v. Easco Corp.,* 656 F. Supp. 531, 533 (D. Md. 1987) (quoting *Chesapeake Const. Corp. v. Rodman,* 536, 261 A.2d 156 (Md. 1970)). In 1976, Maryland adopted Md. Code §2-419 of the Corporations and Associations Article and rejected the common law rule. Such action recognized that "an interest conflict is not in itself a crime or a tort or necessarily injurious to others" and "in many situations, the corporation and the shareholders may secure major benefits from a transaction despite the presence of a director's conflicting interest." Dennis Block, et al., 1 *The Business Judgment Rule: Fiduciary Duties of Corporate Directors,* 266 (5th ed. 1998) (citing 2 Model Bus. Corp. Act Ann. §§8.60 to.63 Introductory Comment at 8-397 (3d ed. 1996)).

Corporations and Associations §2-419 provides that an interested director transaction is not void or voidable solely because of the conflict of interest and creates a "safe harbor" for certain transactions which satisfy the statute. Under the statute, an interested director could inform the shareholders or directors of his conflicting interests and give the board of directors or shareholders an opportunity to approve or ratify the transaction. Moreover, a nondisclosed interested director transaction may be valid, if it is found to be fair and reasonable to the corporation.

Essentially, appellees complain about the propriety of the transaction, with emphasis on College Park's relinquishment of College Park's fee simple interest in its property, College Park's reduced management role in the redevelopment project, and appellants' personal use of corporate assets. Although Charles Shapiro's involvement in the redevelopment project clearly demonstrates a conflict of interest, this is not a situation where appellants capitalized on an opportunity that should have been presented to the corporation, but was not. Rather, the corporation entered into a business arrangement with other entities in which certain directors had, or potentially had, a direct financial interest. Therefore, we hold that the transaction did not constitute a usurpation of corporate opportunity.

We turn now to the issue of whether the trial court properly conducted the analysis required under CA §2-419 for interested director transactions. In reviewing the Order of February 23, 1998, we note that the order refers to previous rulings on the various transactions, the "Report of the Special Master." . . . Although there is reference to the Report of the Special Master, to which no exceptions were taken, . . . the trial court does not direct the findings of that Report to an interested director analysis and to the determination of whether the Clinton Crossings transaction was fair and reasonable. Thus, we are unable to review the factual underpinnings of the trial court's conclusion that the Clinton Crossings transaction was not fair and reasonable. Under the circumstances, we will remand for reconsideration based on the analysis of an interested director transaction.

Part of that analysis will involve a determination of who are the interested directors. The trial court found that there were no disinterested directors. At oral argument, the parties disputed whether appellant Joan Smith was properly considered an interested director. Because the case is to be remanded to the trial court for reconsideration under CA §2-419, we will discuss Joan Smith's classification as an interested director, based on her family and financial relationship with Charles Shapiro and his financial interest in the transaction.

[T]he Model Business Corporations Act ("MBCA") . . . expressly define[s] interested director.

The MBCA defines "conflicting interest" as

> (1) "Conflicting interest" with respect to a corporation means the interest a director of the corporation has respecting a transaction effected or proposed to be effected by the corporation . . . if:
>
> (i) whether or not the transaction is brought before the board of directors of the corporation for action, the director knows at the time of commitment that he or a related person[10] is a party to the transaction or has a beneficial financial interest in or so closely linked to the transaction and of such financial significance to the director or a related person that the interest would be reasonably expected to exert an influence on the director's judgment if he were called upon to vote on the transaction [or
>
> (ii) the transaction is brought (or is of such character and significance to the corporation that it would in the normal course be brought) before the board of directors of the corporation for action, and the director knows at the time of commitment that any of the following persons is either a party to the transaction or has a beneficial financial interest in or so closely linked to the transaction and of such financial significance to the person that the interest would reasonably be expected to exert an influence on the director's judgment if he were called upon to vote on the transaction: (A) an entity (other than the corporation) of which the director is a director, general partner, agent, or employee; (B) a person that controls one or more of the entities specified in subclause (A) or an entity that is controlled by, or is under common control with, one or more of the entities specified in subclause (A); or (C) an individual who is a general partner, principal, or employer of the director.]

Model Bus. Corp. Act. §8.60 (1999).

Appellants assert that Maryland rejected the MBCA . . . of "interested director" and thereby rejected the concept that a director who may be related to a party with a material financial interest in the transaction would also be classified as an interested party. The history of CA §2-419 suggests that that conclusion is too broad.

The Official Comment to the section provided:

---

10. Related person is defined as "(i) the spouse (or a parent or sibling thereof) of the director, or a child, grandchild, sibling, parent (or spouse thereof) of the director, or an individual having the same home as the director, or a trust or estate of which an individual specified in this clause (i) is a substantial beneficiary; or (ii) a trust, estate, incompetent, conservatee, or minor of which the director is a fiduciary."

Prior to 1976, the Maryland General Corporation Law, unlike most state business corporation laws, contained no provision relating to so called "interested director transactions": that is, transactions between a corporation and any corporation, firm, or other entity in which any of its directors is a director or has a material financial interest.

Chapter 567, Acts of 1976, adds a new §2-419 to the Corporation Law to apply to those transactions. This section — which was modeled after similar provisions in Delaware, New York, California, and other jurisdictions — was added to ensure uniformity of treatment of those transactions in Maryland, as well as to provide clear standards to corporations and directors who engage in such transactions.

Section 2-419 (1977 Cum. Supp.). The Delaware, New York, and California statutes are all quite alike in the treatment of interested director transactions. Similar to Maryland's statute, none define the term "interested director." In New York, case law has defined a director's interest as "either self-interest in the transaction at issue or a loss of independence because a director with no direct interest in a transaction is controlled by a self-interested director." *Park River Owners Corp. v. Bangser Klein Rocca & Blum, LLP*, 703 N.Y.S.2d 465, 466 (App. Div. 2000). All of the cited approaches ultimately focus on a director's ability to exercise independent judgment and the expected influence of a particular relationship on the director. That is the appropriate subject of inquiry in determining whether a director is to be considered an interested director in a particular transaction.

The underlying purpose of the interested director statute is clear. "Directors are required to avoid only those self-interested actions which come at the expense of the [corporation] or its shareholders." *Cinerama, Inc. v. Technicolor, Inc.*, 663 A.2d 1134, 1148 (Del. Ch. 1994), *aff'd*, 663 A.2d 1156 (Del. 1995). An interested director transaction may still be approved by a neutral decision making body. In other words, when a director's loyalty is questioned, courts must seek to ascertain whether the conflict "has deprived stockholders of a 'neutral decision-making body.'" *Technicolor*, 663 A.2d at 1170.

The definitions of the MBCA . . . related to interested directors and conflicting interests reflect this same consideration. When the director is actually involved in the transaction, determination is easy. When the director has no direct interests in the conflicting transaction, neither model creates a per se rule based on a familial or business relationship because a relationship between the parties does not necessarily destroy an individual's independent judgment. The pivotal provision is the second prong of the analysis, whether the relationship "would reasonably be expected to exert an influence on the director's judgment." MBCA. . . . The adoption of a per se rule would effectively undermine the purpose of the statute. If an otherwise uninterested director were to be adjudged an interested director based solely on his relationship, familial or otherwise, to another director interested in the transaction, directors who may well retain independence and their own business judgment will be precluded from considering the transaction. On the other hand, to conclude that directors are automatically disinterested because they are not directly involved in the transaction would also undermine the goal of a neutral decision making body, as some directors, because of their familial, personal, or financial relationship, may well be influenced by those relationships to the detriment of the corporation.

Therefore, when a director does not personally benefit from the transaction but, because of that director's relationship to a party interested in the transaction, it would reasonably be expected that the director's exercise of independent judgment would be compromised, that director will be deemed an interested director within the meaning of the statute.

We are unsure whether the trial court determined Joan Smith to be an interested director simply by virtue of her status as Charles Shapiro's sister. On remand, the trial court should evaluate whether the relationship between Joan Smith and Charles Shapiro, together with their direct or indirect interests in the transaction, would reasonably be expected to influence her decision and compromise her impartiality. If it is then determined that there were no disinterested directors, the trial court should evaluate the Clinton Crossings transaction from the "fair and reasonable" perspective with findings that support the determination.

Notes and Questions

1. Notes

a. Greenfield is the plaintiff and Shapiro is the defendant.

2. Reality Check

a. Which directors have potential conflicts of interest? Will all such directors be treated in the same way?

b. How was the company alleged to have been hurt by the transactions? Who was alleged to gain from those transactions and how did that gain come about?

c. Why was there no usurpation of a corporate opportunity?

3. Suppose

a. Suppose that this transaction arose in a corporation incorporated in a state that has adopted Subchapter F of the MBCA. How should the court analyze the conflicts of interest?

b. Suppose that this transaction arose in a Delaware corporation? How should the court analyze the conflicts of interest?

c. Suppose that this transaction arose in a corporation incorporated in a state that had no CoI Safe Harbor at all? How should the court analyze the conflicts of interest?

4. What Do You Think?

a. Do you think conflict of interest transactions that are not within the statutory definitions are affected at all by the CoI Safe Harbors? Should courts draw any implication about those transactions from the fact that they are not included in the statutory definition?

b. Should CoI Safe Harbors provide a narrow or a broad definition of the kinds of transactions that may be protected?

c. Are CoI Safe Harbors more trouble than they are worth? Why do you think state legislatures adopted them in the first place?

* * *

ii. Prerequisites to Being Affected by the CoI Safe Harbors.   The CoI Safe Harbor statutes typically function as affirmative defenses. That is, the burden is on the defendants to establish both that the challenged transaction comes within the

CoI Safe Harbor and that the requirements for being affected by the CoI Safe Harbor are met.

The CoI Safe Harbor statutes provide three avenues for affecting covered transactions. First, the transaction can be approved by certain directors. Second, the transaction can be approved by certain shareholders. Finally, the transaction can be found to be "fair" to the corporation. These are disjunctive; only one need be met. Further, attempted, but failed, compliance with one avenue does not preclude compliance with another avenue. As a practical matter, corporate managers rely on approval by certain directors rather than approval by certain shareholders, especially in publicly held corporations where a shareholder vote can be particularly expensive. Reliance on a shareholder vote is typically only in situations where the corporation law would require a shareholder vote to effect the particular transaction, even if that transaction did not present a conflict of interest.

Compliance with DGCL §144(a)(1) requires full disclosure to the board and approval by a majority of the *disinterested directors*, a term not defined in the statute, but that, as you might imagine, is defined consistently with the Delaware courts' definition of *disinterested* for duty of loyalty purposes. The MBCA also requires disclosure and approval by a majority (but at least two) of the "qualified directors," which is defined in §1.43.

In similar, but not identical, fashion, compliance with DGCL §144(a)(2) requires full disclosure to the shareholders and approval "in good faith by vote of the stockholders." Compare the MBCA, which, of course, requires disclosure to the shareholders but requires approval of a majority of the "qualified shares" — those shares not controlled by a director with a conflicting interest. *See* MBCA §8.63. Notice that the DGCL does not explicitly disenfranchise shares controlled by conflicted directors. Are such shares implicitly disenfranchised by the requirement that shareholder approval must be "in good faith"?

Finally, and conceptually most troublesome, is the alternative of establishing "fairness." Almost certainly this statutory concept is functionally identical to the entire fairness test we studied above. Theoretically, though, why is fairness a separate *statutory* test? If it were omitted from the statutes, transaction proponents could presumably still fall back on establishing fairness as a justification for the transaction. Further, in at least some states, case law holds that obtaining the requisite director or shareholder approval does not relieve the court of its obligation to do equity, which entails assessing the fairness of the transaction. In those states, a fairness alternative is not really an alternative at all.

iii. The Effect of Compliance with the CoI Safe Harbor. DGCL §144(a) is written in a rather passive fashion. It provides that no covered transaction that has met (1), (2), or (3) "shall be void or voidable solely [because of the conflict of interest], or solely because the director or officer is present at or participates in the meeting of the board or committee which authorizes the contract or transaction, or solely because any such director's or officer's votes are counted for such purpose . . . ." Case law suggests that compliance with §144(a) shifts the burden to the plaintiff to show that the transaction was not entirely fair.

By contrast, the MBCA is much more explicit about the effect of compliance. Section 8.61(b) provides that a complying transaction "may not be the subject of equitable relief, or give rise to an award of damages or other sanctions against a director of the corporation, in a proceeding by a shareholder or by or in the right of the corporation, on the ground that the director has an interest respecting the transaction. . . ."

Both statutes leave a few questions, though. What other reasons may render the transaction vulnerable to shareholder attack, particularly if compliance is achieved through a finding of fairness rather than director or shareholder approval? May or must a court draw any inference from compliance (or noncompliance) with the director or shareholder approval provisions?

Perhaps the most intriguing part of MBCA's Subchapter F is the provision that protects certain transactions that are *not* covered by the CoI Safe Harbor. The *Shapiro* case focused on the policy question of deciding upon which conflict of interest transactions should be eligible for protection. All the CoI Safe Harbor statutes include the core self-dealing situation as the paradigm and then include some other more attenuated transactions. The MBCA goes further and immunizes every transaction not included in the definition of "conflict of interest" from attack on the ground of conflict of interest! *See* MBCA §8.61(a).

Notes and Questions

1. You Draft It

a. Compare DGCL §144(a) and MBCA. Then draft an optimal CoI Safe Harbor statute.

b. Background and Context

i. A Note on Shareholder Ratification.   One of the methods for protecting a conflict of interest transaction is to have the transaction ratified by a fully informed vote of shareholders unaffiliated with the conflicted directors. Shareholder ratification becomes important in several corporate law contexts and Justice Jacobs explains those contexts and the nuances of shareholder ratification under Delaware law.

> Under current Delaware case law, the scope and effect of the common law doctrine of shareholder ratification is unclear, making it difficult to apply that doctrine in a coherent manner. As the Court of Chancery has noted in *In re Wheelabrator Technologies, Inc., Shareholders Litigation*:
>
>> [The doctrine of ratification] might be thought to lack coherence because the decisions addressing the effect of shareholder "ratification" have fragmented that subject into three distinct compartments, . . . In its "classic" . . . form, shareholder ratification describes the situation where shareholders approve board action that, legally speaking, could be accomplished without any shareholder approval. . . . "[C]lassic" ratification involves the voluntary addition of an independent layer of shareholder approval in circumstances where shareholder approval is not legally required. But "shareholder ratification" has also been used to describe the effect of an informed shareholder vote that was statutorily required for the transaction to have legal existence. . . . That [the Delaware courts] have used the same term in such highly diverse sets of factual circumstances, without regard to their possible functional differences, suggests that "shareholder ratification" has now acquired an expanded meaning intended to describe any approval of challenged board action by a fully

informed vote of shareholders, irrespective of whether that shareholder vote is legally required for the transaction to attain legal existence.[52]

To restore coherence and clarity to this area of our law, we hold that the scope of the shareholder ratification doctrine must be limited to its so-called "classic" form; that is, to circumstances where a fully informed shareholder vote approves director action that does *not* legally require shareholder approval in order to become legally effective. Moreover, the only director action or conduct that can be ratified is that which the shareholders are specifically asked to approve. With one exception, the "cleansing" effect of such a ratifying shareholder vote is to subject the challenged director action to business judgment review, as opposed to "extinguishing" the claim altogether (*i.e.,* obviating all judicial review of the challenged action).[54]

To avoid confusion about the doctrinal clarifications set forth in . . . this Opinion, we note that they apply only to the common law doctrine of shareholder ratification. They are not intended to affect or alter our jurisprudence governing the effect of an approving vote of disinterested shareholders under [DGCL] §144.

Gantler v. Stephens, 965 A.2d 695, 713 (Del. 2009) (Jacobs, J.)

Although many other jurisdictions choose to follow Delaware jurisprudence, other jurisdictions take a simpler approach to shareholder ratification. Generally speaking, because the shareholders are the ultimate owners and beneficiaries of the directors' actions, shareholder ratification cuts off all judicial power to redress a finding of breach of fiduciary duty. In virtually every state (including Delaware) the defendant/directors, as proponents of the ratification, have the burden of showing that full disclosure was made to the shareholders, that the shareholders were not coerced, and that approval was given by a majority of shares not controlled by the board.

2. Duty of Care: Limitations Contained in the Articles of Incorporation

DGCL §102(b)(7) permits a corporation to add a provision to its certificate of incorporation capping or eliminating monetary liability of directors for breach of their fiduciary duties. The MBCA and nearly every state have adopted similar statutes, which are sometimes called *charter limitations. See* MBCA §2.02(b)(4). As a matter of corporate law theory these charter limitations are like an advance shareholder ratification because existing corporations must amend their articles, which requires shareholder approval, and new corporations make their articles available to the original shareholders who, in some sense, approve the charter limitation by their purchase. Public companies have commonly taken advantage of

---

52. 663 A.2d 1194, 1202 and n.4 (Del. Ch. 1995) (citations omitted). *See also Solomon v. Armstrong,* 747 A.2d 1098, 1114-15 (Del. Ch. 1999), *aff'd,* 746 A.2d 277 (Table) (Del. 2000) ("The legal effect of shareholder ratification, as it relates to alleged breaches of the duty of loyalty, may be one of the most tortured areas of Delaware law. A different rule exists for every permutation of facts that fall under the broad umbrella of 'duty of loyalty' claims.").

54. To the extent that *Smith v. Van Gorkom* holds otherwise, it is overruled. 488 A.2d 858, 889-90 (Del. 1985). The only species of claim that shareholder ratification can validly extinguish is a claim that the directors lacked the authority to take action that was later ratified. Nothing herein should be read as altering the well-established principle that void acts such as fraud, gift, waste and ultra vires acts cannot be ratified by a less than unanimous shareholder vote. *See . . . also Harbor Fin. Partners v. Huizenga,* 751 A.2d 879, 896 (Del. Ch. 1999) (explaining that ultra vires, fraud, and gift or waste of corporate assets are "void" acts that cannot be ratified by less than unanimous shareholder consent).

these statutes and have adopted limitations in their articles, usually choosing to eliminate, rather than cap, monetary liability.

Does a charter limitation make a great deal of practical difference? The following case shows how Delaware thinking about such provisions has evolved.

In re Cornerstone Therapeutics Inc., S'holder Litig.

115 A.3d 1173 (Del. 2015)

STRINE, Chief Justice:

I. INTRODUCTION

These appeals were scheduled for argument on the same day because they turn on a single legal question: in an action for damages against corporate fiduciaries, where the plaintiff challenges an interested transaction that is presumptively subject to entire fairness review, must the plaintiff plead a non-exculpated claim against the disinterested, independent directors to survive a motion to dismiss by those directors? We answer that question in the affirmative. A plaintiff seeking only monetary damages must plead non-exculpated claims against a director who is protected by an exculpatory charter provision to survive a motion to dismiss, regardless of the underlying standard of review for the board's conduct. . . .

The Court of Chancery in both of these cases denied the defendants' motions to dismiss because it read the precedent of this Court to require doing so, regardless of the exculpatory provision in each company's certificate of incorporation. Under the Court of Chancery's analysis, even if the plaintiffs could not plead a non-exculpated claim against any particular director, as long as the underlying transaction was subject to the entire fairness standard of review, and the plaintiffs were therefore able to state non-exculpated claims against the interested parties and their affiliates, all of the directors were required to remain defendants until the end of litigation. The Court of Chancery was reluctant to embrace that result but felt that it was the reading most faithful to our precedent.

In this decision, we hold that even if a plaintiff has pled facts that, if true, would require the transaction to be subject to the entire fairness standard of review, and the interested parties to face a claim for breach of their duty of loyalty, the independent directors do not automatically have to remain defendants. When the independent directors are protected by an exculpatory charter provision and the plaintiffs are unable to plead a non-exculpated claim against them, those directors are entitled to have the claims against them dismissed, in keeping with this Court's opinion in *Malpiede v. Townson*[4] and cases following that decision.[5] Accordingly, we remand both of these cases to allow the Court of Chancery to determine if the plaintiffs have sufficiently pled non-exculpated claims against the independent directors.

---

4. *See Malpiede v. Townson*, 780 A.2d 1075, 1094 (Del. 2001).
5. *See, e.g., In re Morton's Rest. Grp., Inc. S'holders Litig.*, 74 A.3d 656 (Del. Ch. 2013); *see also DiRienzo v. Lichtenstein*, 2013 WL 5503034 (Del. Ch. Sept. 30, 2013); *In re S. Peru Copper Corp. S'holder Derivative Litig.*, 52 A.3d 761 (Del. Ch. 2011), *aff'd sub nom., Americas Mining Corp. v. Theriault*, 51 A.3d 1213 (Del. 2012).

II. BACKGROUND

These appeals both involve damages actions by stockholder plaintiffs arising out of mergers in which the controlling stockholder, who had representatives on the board of directors, acquired the remainder of the shares that it did not own in a Delaware public corporation. Both mergers were negotiated by special committees of independent directors, were ultimately approved by a majority of the minority stockholders, and were at substantial premiums to the pre-announcement market price. Nonetheless, the plaintiffs filed suit in the Court of Chancery in each case, contending that the directors had breached their fiduciary duty by approving transactions that were unfair to the minority stockholders.

In both appeals, it is undisputed that . . . the entire fairness standard presumptively applied, although the burden of persuasion on that issue might ultimately rest with the plaintiffs. In both cases, the defendant directors were insulated from liability for monetary damages for breaches of the fiduciary duty of care by an exculpatory charter provision adopted in accordance with [DGCL] §102(b)(7). Despite that provision, the plaintiffs in each case not only sued the controlling stockholders and their affiliated directors, but also sued the independent directors who had negotiated and approved the mergers.

In each case, the Court of Chancery did not analyze the plaintiffs' duty of loyalty claims against the independent directors because it determined that it was required to deny their motions to dismiss regardless of whether such claims had been sufficiently pled. But, recognizing the important and uncertain issue of corporate law at stake, the Court of Chancery in each case recommended certification of an interlocutory appeal to this Court to determine whether its reading of precedent was correct.

III. ANALYSIS

In answering the legal question raised by these appeals, we acknowledge that the body of law relevant to these disputes presents a debate between two competing but colorable views of the law. These cases thus exemplify a benefit of careful employment of the interlocutory appeal process: to enable this Court to clarify precedent that could arguably be read in two different ways before litigants incur avoidable costs.

We now resolve the question presented by these cases by determining that plaintiffs must plead a non-exculpated claim for breach of fiduciary duty against an independent director protected by an exculpatory charter provision, or that director will be entitled to be dismissed from the suit. That rule applies regardless of the underlying standard of review for the transaction. When a director is protected by an exculpatory charter provision, a plaintiff can survive a motion to dismiss by that director defendant by pleading facts supporting a rational inference that the director harbored self-interest adverse to the stockholders' interests, acted to advance the self-interest of an interested party from whom they could not be presumed to act independently, or acted in bad faith. But the mere fact that a plaintiff is able to plead facts supporting the application of the entire fairness standard to the transaction, and can thus state a duty of loyalty claim against the interested fiduciaries, does not relieve the plaintiff of the responsibility to plead a non-exculpated claim against each director who moves for dismissal.[27]

No doubt, the invocation of the entire fairness standard has a powerful pro-plaintiff effect against interested parties. When that standard is invoked at the pleading stage, the plaintiffs will be able to survive a motion to dismiss by interested parties regardless of the presence of an exculpatory charter provision because their conflicts of interest support a pleading-stage inference of disloyalty. Indeed, as to the interested party itself, a finding of unfairness after trial will subject it to liability for breach of the duty of loyalty regardless of its subjective bad faith.

The stringency of after-the-fact entire fairness review by the court intentionally puts strong pressure on the interested party and its affiliates to deal fairly before-the-fact when negotiating an interested transaction. To accomplish this, the burden of proving entire fairness in an interested merger falls on the "the controlling or dominating shareholder proponent of the transaction." But applying the entire fairness standard against interested parties does not relieve plaintiffs seeking damages of the obligation to plead non-exculpated claims against each of the defendant directors.

In *Malpiede*, this Court analyzed the effect of a Section 102(b)(7) provision on a due care claim against directors who approved a transaction which the plaintiffs argued should be subject to review under the *Revlon* standard. This Court noted that although "plaintiffs are entitled to all reasonable inferences flowing from their pleadings, . . . if those inferences do not support a valid legal claim, the complaint should be dismissed."[33] Because a director will only be liable for monetary damages if she has breached a non-exculpated duty, a plaintiff who pleads only a due care claim against that director has not set forth any grounds for relief. In such a case, "*as a matter of law* [ ] then Section 102(b)(7) would bar the claim."[34]

Nevertheless, the plaintiffs in each of these cases contend that their exculpated claims against the independent directors cannot be dismissed solely because the transaction at issue is subject to entire fairness review. The plaintiffs argue that they should be entitled to an automatic inference that a director facilitating an interested transaction is disloyal because the possibility of conflicted loyalties is heightened in controller transactions, and the facts that give rise to a duty of loyalty breach may be unknowable at the pleading stage. But there are several problems with such an inference: to require independent directors to remain defendants solely because the plaintiffs stated a non-exculpated claim against the controller and its affiliates would

---

27. *See Malpiede*, 780 A.2d at 1094; *see also Emerald II*, 787 A.2d at 92 (citing *Malpiede* with approval for the proposition that "unless there is a violation of the duty of loyalty or the duty of good faith, a trial on the issue of entire fairness is unnecessary because a Section 102(b)(7) provision will exculpate director defendants from paying monetary damages that are exclusively attributable to a violation of the duty of care"); *Emerald I*, 726 A.2d at 1224 ("Nonetheless, where the factual basis for a claim *solely* implicates a violation of the duty of care, this Court has indicated that the protections of such a [Section 102(b)(7)] charter provision may properly be invoked and applied."); *Arnold v. Soc'y for Sav. Bancorp, Inc.*, 650 A.2d 1270 (Del. 1994); *Wayne Cnty. Employees' Ret. Sys. v. Corti*, 2009 WL 2219260 (Del. Ch. July 24, 2009), *aff'd*, 996 A.2d 795 (Del. 2010) (granting defendants' motion to dismiss when plaintiffs failed to state a non-exculpated claim against the director defendants for breach of fiduciary duty); *In re Lukens Inc. S'holders Litig.*, 757 A.2d 720, 734 (Del. Ch. 1999), *aff'd sub nom.*, *Walker v. Lukens, Inc.*, 757 A.2d 1278 (Del. 2000) (same).

33. *Malpiede*, 780 A.2d 1075, 1094 (Del. 2001).

34. *Id.*; *see also In re Synthes, Inc. S'holder Litig.*, 50 A.3d 1022, 1032 (Del. Ch. 2012) ("Because the directors on the Board are protected by the §102(b)(7) provision exculpating them for personal liability stemming from a breach of the duty of care, the complaint must be dismissed against the directors unless the plaintiffs have successfully pled non-exculpated claims for breach of the duty of loyalty against them.").

be inconsistent with Delaware law and would also increase costs for disinterested directors, corporations, and stockholders, without providing a corresponding benefit.

Adopting the plaintiffs' approach would . . . likely create more harm than benefit for minority stockholders in practice. Our common law of corporations has rightly emphasized the need for independent directors to be willing to say no to interested transactions proposed by controlling stockholders. For that reason, our law has long inquired into the practical negotiating power given to independent directors in conflicted transactions. Although it is wise for our law to focus on whether the independent directors can say no, it does not follow that it is prudent to create an invariable rule that any independent director who says yes to an interested transaction subject to entire fairness review must remain as a defendant until the end of the litigation, regardless of the absence of any evidence suggesting that the director acted for an improper motive.

For more than a generation, our law has recognized that the negotiating efforts of independent directors can help to secure transactions with controlling stockholders that are favorable to the minority. Indeed, respected scholars have found evidence that interested transactions subject to special committee approval are often priced on terms that are attractive to minority stockholders. We decline to adopt an approach that would create incentives for independent directors to avoid serving as special committee members, or to reject transactions solely because their role in negotiating on behalf of the stockholders would cause them to remain as defendants until the end of any litigation challenging the transaction.

As is well understood, the fear that directors who faced personal liability for potentially value-maximizing business decisions might be dissuaded from making such decisions is why Section 102(b)(7) was adopted in the first place. As this Court explained in *Malpiede*, "Section 102(b)(7) was adopted by the Delaware General Assembly in 1986 following a directors and officers insurance liability crisis and the 1985 Delaware Supreme Court decision in *Smith v. Van Gorkom*."[46] Because of that "crisis," the General Assembly feared that directors would not be willing to make decisions that would benefit stockholders if they faced personal liability for making them. The purpose of Section 102(b)(7) was to "free[ ] up directors to take business risks without worrying about negligence lawsuits."[47] Establishing a rule that all directors must remain as parties in litigation involving a transaction with a controlling stockholder would thus reduce the benefits that the General Assembly anticipated in adopting Section 102(b)(7).

Thus, when a complaint pleads facts creating an inference that seemingly independent directors approved a conflicted transaction for improper reasons, and thus, those directors may have breached their duty of loyalty, the pro-plaintiff inferences that must be drawn on a motion to dismiss counsels for resolution of that question of fact only after discovery.[54] By contrast, when the plaintiffs have pled no facts to support an inference that any of the independent directors breached their duty of loyalty, fidelity to the purpose of Section 102(b)(7) requires dismissal of the

---

46. 780 A.2d 1075, 1095 (Del. 2001) (citing *Smith v. Van Gorkom*, 488 A.2d 858 (Del. 1985)).

47. *Id.; see also Prod. Res. Grp., LLC v. NCT Grp., Inc.*, 863 A.2d 772, 777 (Del. Ch. 2004) ("One of the primary purposes of §102(b)(7) is to encourage directors to undertake risky, but potentially value-maximizing, business strategies, so long as they do so in good faith.").

complaint against those directors. Accordingly, we reverse the judgments of the Court of Chancery denying the independent directors' motions to dismiss, and remand each case for the Court of Chancery to determine if the plaintiffs have sufficiently pled facts suggesting that the independent directors committed a non-exculpated breach of their fiduciary duty.

Notes and Questions

1. Reality Check

a. What claims are not eliminated by DGCL §102(b)(7)?

b. Can directors of Delaware corporations always raise an available charter limitation defense immediately?

3. Suppose

a. Suppose *Cornerstone Therapeutics* had been decided under the MBCA. Would the court's analysis or the result have been different?

4. What Do You Think?

2. Earlier we asked whether it made much difference whether a director's action was analyzed under the duty of loyalty, the duty of care, good faith, or waste/no rational business purpose. Now that you've considered the role of charter limitations, would your answer or reasoning change?

5. You Draft It

a. Review DGCL §102(b)(7) and MBCA §2.02(b)(4) and then draft an ideal charter limitation statute.

3. Indemnification by the Corporation

a. The Current Setting

It seems counterintuitive to suggest that the corporation might indemnify a director or officer when such persons are sued by virtue of their service to the corporation but indemnification is a frequent occurrence. The statutory provisions are quite complex and an exhaustive look at indemnification is out of the question. *See* DGCL §145 and MBCA Subchapter E, §§8.50-8.59. Nonetheless, indemnification is one of the most often litigated areas in corporate law and it raises questions of statutory construction and public policy that are worth exploring and, more important, can be presented with (relative) concision.

We'll divide indemnification into three facets. First we'll look at the most important practical issue, advancement of expenses. Then we'll look at when indemnity is required, rather than simply permitted. Third we briefly limn the procedural and substantive predicates to indemnification.

i. Advancement of Expenses. For corporate officers and directors, and only slightly less so for corporations, the question of advancement of expenses looms large. Imagine you are a director who is being sued for some official action you've taken. To make this as pleasant as it can be, imagine further that you are certain to be indemnified should you prevail, and are nearly certain that you will prevail. Even in that setting you face months or years of litigation expenses, especially attorneys' fees, before you are indemnified by the corporation. Where will you get the money to pay those expenses until you are indemnified? Before you read the next case you may find it helpful to read DGCL §145(e) and MBCA §8.53.

Reddy v. Electronic Data Systems Corp.

2002 WL 1358761 (Del. Ch.)

STRINE, V.C.

The origins of this dispute can be traced to the purchase of FACS Incorporated ("FCI") by [Electronic Data Systems Corporation ("EDS")] in 1995. At the time of purchase, FCI was headed by [Michael T.] Reddy.

EDS bought FCI under the terms of a stock purchase agreement calling for an initial payment of $9 million to FCI stockholders, the largest of whom was Reddy. An additional $3 million was escrowed and placed in an account held by FCI's attorney. Two million dollars of these funds could be earned by the former FCI stockholders, subject to FCI's performance during the remainder of 1995. The other $1 million could be earned if certain performance targets were achieved and certain outstanding receivables of FCI were collected.

FCI's post-purchase performance was to occur under the rubric of Global Financial Markets Group ("GFMG"), the new EDS business division created to operate the purchased FCI operations. After the sale, Reddy became division vice-president of the larger EDS strategic business unit of which GFMG was a part. Despite his title, Reddy was not an officer of EDS under its bylaws, but simply an employee. In connection with his new position, Reddy entered into both an employment agreement and an incentive compensation agreement with EDS. Under the incentive compensation agreement, Reddy and other former FCI stock-holders could receive up to $14 million in incentive compensation payments over a three-year period beginning in 1996. These payments were tied to the earnings of GFMG.

In 2001, two actions were filed against Reddy arising out of his conduct as an employee of EDS. The first action . . . is a criminal action brought by the United States Attorney for the Southern District of New York (the "Criminal Action"). The Criminal Action involves charges of conspiracy, mail fraud, and wire fraud. . . .

In sum, the Criminal Action alleges that Reddy purposely manipulated the financial records of EDS to increase the payments he would receive from the escrowed funds and the incentive compensation agreement. In accomplishing his ends, Reddy is alleged to have conspired with the attorney holding the escrowed funds, who helped by falsifying and mislabeling financial entries and payments in order to create the false impression that the pre-requisites for release of those funds to the former FCI stockholders had been met.

The second action was filed against Reddy by EDS itself (the "EDS Action") and is based on the same conduct alleged in the Criminal Action. That is, the EDS Action contends that Reddy manipulated and falsified the financial records of GFMG to inflate improperly the incentive compensation and escrowed funds payments to him and other former FCI stockholders, and to conceal his wrongdoing.

The complaint in the EDS Action avers that this misconduct is actionable as: i) negligence; ii) gross negligence; iii) common law fraud; and iv) breaches of Reddy's employment agreement and the incentive compensation agreement. Among other relief, the complaint seeks tens of millions of dollars in damages to remedy the overpayments supposedly harvested by Reddy and former FCI stockholders, and liabilities incurred by EDS to clients . . . because of Reddy's conduct. . . .

Reddy demanded advancement for both the Criminal and the EDS Action. EDS refused to provide it. Reddy then brought this lawsuit, alleging that he was due advancement under the EDS bylaws.

The only factual dispute raised in the briefs is whether Reddy engaged in the wrongdoing that is alleged in the two actions for which he seeks advancement. That dispute of fact is not a material one, however, in this action for advancement, and does not preclude the entry of a dispositive order.

Reddy contends that he is due advancement under the advancement provision in the EDS bylaws, which he asserts imposes a mandatory obligation on EDS to advance funds to former employees facing charges of official misconduct in their capacities as employees of EDS. By contrast, EDS argues that its bylaws simply give its board the discretion to advance funds to Reddy if they choose to do so, which they do not.

The bylaw provision in question reads:

> *Each person who at any time shall serve or shall have served as a* Director, officer, *employee* or agent *of the Corporation . . . shall be entitled to* (a) indemnification and (b) *the advancement of expenses* incurred by such person *from the Corporation as, and to the fullest extent, permitted by Section 145 of the DGCL* or any successor statutory provision, as from time to time amended.[4]

Although EDS contends otherwise, the plain import of this provision is to require EDS to advance funds to former employees like Reddy if §145 of the DGCL would permit it to do so. By its own scrivening hand, EDS has bound itself to advance funds to Reddy so long as the DGCL allows it to do so.

The pertinent parts of §145 of the DGCL state:

> (e) Expenses (including attorneys' fees) incurred by an officer or director in defending any civil, criminal, administrative or investigative action, suit or proceeding may be paid by the corporation in advance of the final disposition of such action, suit or proceeding upon receipt of an undertaking by or on behalf of such director or officer to repay such amount if it shall ultimately be determined that such person is not entitled to be indemnified by the corporation as authorized in this section. Such expenses (including attorneys' fees) incurred by former directors and officers or other employees and agents may be so paid upon such terms and conditions, if any, as the corporation deems appropriate.
>
> (f) The indemnification and advancement of expenses provided by, or granted pursuant to, the other subsections of this section shall not be deemed exclusive of any other rights to which those seeking indemnification or advancement of expenses may be entitled under any bylaw, agreement . . . or otherwise, both as to action in such person's official capacity and as to action in another capacity while holding such office.[5]

---

4. EDS Bylaws, Art. 6.1 (emphasis added).
5. [DGCL] §145(e), (f).

These capacious provisions of our law clearly provide corporations with the flexibility to advance litigation expenses to former employees like Reddy.

EDS . . . seeks to shift the burden of the company's drafting decisions to Reddy. That argument rests on the absence of any language in the EDS bylaws dealing with the conditions the company may impose on former employees who invoke their right to advancement — in particular, the failure of the bylaws to require former employees to execute an undertaking to repay the advanced funds.

Because directors and officers who seek advancement must — by statute — execute an undertaking,[6] EDS argues that its bylaws cannot reasonably be read as providing mandatory advancement to former employees. Otherwise, former employees would have greater rights than current directors and officers, a result that EDS considers anomalous.

The anomaly to which EDS points, however, is one authorized by §145(e) itself. The General Assembly specifically amended that statutory subsection to give corporations the flexibility to advance funds to employees and agents without an undertaking.[7] In lieu of this required undertaking, corporations may specify by bylaw or contract the terms and conditions upon which employees and agents may receive advancement, which could include an undertaking and more onerous pre-requisites to advancement. Having been accorded the freedom to craft its bylaws as it wished, EDS cannot point to its own drafting failures as a defense to Reddy's advancement claim, however. If it chose, EDS could have conditioned former employees' advancement rights on an undertaking, proof of an ability to repay, or even the posting of a secured bond. But it did not do so.

As a practical matter, moreover, I fail to see the great danger to the corporate republic posed by the lack of a formal undertaking. As the Supreme Court has noted, all contracts for advancement and indemnification are subject to an implied reasonableness term. When that implied term is utilized in concert with the actual language of the EDS bylaw in question, no horrific scenario arises. Rather, by accepting payments expressly termed an "advancement," Reddy necessarily acknowledges that his ultimate right to keep those payments depends on whether his underlying conduct is indemnifiable. If his conduct is not the proper subject of indemnification by EDS, Reddy must repay the funds advanced to him by the corporation.

EDS's next argument is that Reddy is not entitled to any advancement payments because he is a party to neither the Criminal Action nor the EDS Action "by reason of the fact that" he was an "employee" of EDS.[9] The foundation for this argument rests in the proposition that Reddy's motivation for the allegedly wrongful actions he took as an EDS employee was personal — *i.e.*, the desire to increase the amount of escrowed funds and incentive compensation payments he and other former FCI stockholders would receive. As a result of this personal motivation, EDS claims that the conduct for which Reddy is being prosecuted civilly and criminally does not

---

6. *See* [DGCL] §145(e).

7. The evolution of §145(e) suggests that the General Assembly intended to mandate that an undertaking be received only from directors and officers, and not from other possible indemnitees, such as former employees. In 1983, the requirement that employees or agents execute an undertaking was dropped from the statute, leaving corporations free to set the conditions on which advancement to them would take place. *See* 64 Del. Laws. Ch. 112, §7 & commentary (1983).

9. [DGCL] §145(a), (b).

implicate the policy concerns addressed by §145, which broadly empowers corporations to provide advancement and indemnification to corporate employees.

The problem with EDS's argument is that it has no logical stopping point. It is not uncommon for corporate directors, officers, and employees to be sued for breach of the fiduciary duty of loyalty, and to have to defend claims that they took official action for the primary purpose of diverting corporate resources to their own pocketbooks — in the form of contractual compensation benefits (*e.g.,* severance payments or stock options) or an unfair return on a self-dealing transaction. Therefore, it is highly problematic to make the advancement right of such officials dependent on the motivation ascribed to their conduct by the suing parties. To do so would be to largely vitiate the protections afforded by §145 and contractual advancement rights.

Corporate advancement practice has an admittedly maddening aspect. At the time that an advancement dispute ripens, it is often the case that the corporate board has drawn harsh conclusions about the integrity and fidelity of the corporate official seeking advancement. The board may well have a firm basis to believe that the official intentionally injured the corporation. It therefore is reluctant to advance funds for his defense, fearing that the funds will never be paid back and resisting the idea of seeing further depletion of corporate resources at the instance of someone perceived to be a faithless fiduciary.

But, to give effect to this natural human reaction as public policy would be unwise. Imagine what EDS believes to be unthinkable: that the United States government and EDS are in fact wrong about Reddy. What if he in fact did not falsify records? What if he in fact did not do anything that was even grossly negligent? In that circumstance, it would be difficult to conceive of an argument that would properly leave him holding the bag for all of his legal fees and expenses resulting from two cases centering on his conduct as an employee of EDS. That result would make the promise made to Reddy in the EDS bylaws an illusory one.

For these reasons, this court has often been required to uphold the indemnification and advancement rights of corporate officials accused of serious misconduct, because to do otherwise would undermine the salutary public policies served by §145.

EDS's next argument to defeat Reddy's advancement claim involves a bold proposition. Because Reddy seeks advancement to defend accusations that he engaged in serious financial fraud intended to benefit himself at the expense of EDS, EDS contends that the equitable doctrine of unclean hands is implicated. If Reddy in fact purposely harmed EDS, he should be estopped from demanding advancement under EDS's bylaws. To do so would, EDS argues, be to permit a thief to steal twice.

If adopted, EDS's rule would turn every advancement case into a trial on the merits of the underlying claims of official misconduct. Section 145 of the DGCL is an explicit rejection of this approach, because the clear authorization of advancement rights presupposes that the corporation will front expenses before any determination is made of the corporate official's ultimate right to indemnification.

For the foregoing reasons, EDS's motion to dismiss is denied. Reddy's motion for summary judgment is granted and EDS shall advance him his reasonable expenses in the Criminal Action and the EDS Action promptly.

Notes and Questions

1. Notes

a. The provision in the EDS-FCI stock purchase agreement calling for a higher purchase price if FCI met certain financial benchmarks in the near future is a common one. Where the selling company's owners will continue to run the business after the sale, as Reddy did here, they have an economic motivation to shirk because they no longer receive the full benefit of their efforts. The function of an *earn-out* provision is to place the economic consequence of shirking on those best able to avoid shirking: the former owners who now manage.

b. The attorney with whom Mr. Reddy is alleged to have conspired is named John Fasciana. He also filed an action against EDS involving his right to be indemnified. *See Fasciana v. Electronic Data Systems Corp.*, 2003 WL 21538108 (Del. Ch.) (Strine, V.C.)

2. Reality Check

a. What was Mr. Reddy alleged to have done wrong?

b. Why is the issue of whether Mr. Reddy acted wrongfully (or even criminally) irrelevant to this case?

c. Where does the court look to find whether Mr. Reddy is entitled to advancement of his litigation expenses?

d. What are the predicates to EDS's obligation to advance Mr. Reddy's litigation expenses? Do you agree with Vice Chancellor Strine that they are met?

e. What were EDS's arguments against advancing Mr. Reddy's litigation expenses? Why was each rejected?

3. Suppose

a. If EDS were incorporated in a state that had adopted the MBCA (and if EDS's bylaws referenced that statute rather than the DGCL), would the court's analysis or the result be any different?

4. What Do You Think?

a. Do you think that EDS acted wisely in adopting a bylaw that provides for maximum indemnification and advancement?

b. Do you think that EDS acted wisely in adopting a bylaw that explicitly references the DGCL rather than tracking the statute's language? What are the differences between those two approaches?

c. Is DGCL §145(e) wise?

d. Is DGCL §145(k) wise?

e. If you represented EDS would you have made each argument EDS did? If not, how would you select the arguments to present? Which arguments would you press and which would you abandon?

5. You Draft It

a. Redraft EDS's bylaws to make it clear that EDS may, but need not, advance Mr. Reddy's litigation expenses. Then redraft the bylaws to make it clear that EDS must advance those expenses. The bylaw reads,

> Each person who at any time shall serve or shall have served as a Director, officer, employee or agent of the Corporation . . . shall be entitled to (a) indemnification and (b) the advancement of expenses incurred by such person from the Corporation as, and to the fullest extent, permitted by Section 145 of the DGCL or any successor statutory provision, as from time to time amended.

* * *

ii. When Must the Corporation Indemnify?   As the court in *Reddy* pointed out, indemnity questions often arise when the corporation and the potential indemnitee have had a falling out. In such settings the natural tendency is for both sides to take a hard line — the corporation taking the narrowest view of its obligation and the indemnitee taking the broadest. Much litigation is generated between corporations and their former officers or directors about the scope of the indemnity provision.

At the other end of the process, both DGCL §145(c) and MBCA §8.52 require a corporation to indemnify an officer or director who is exonerated "on the merits or otherwise." The courts take these words literally so that an officer or director who successfully raises a statute of limitations defense, for example, or who escapes criminal prosecution after a trial ends in a hung jury and the government elects to dismiss the charges is entitled to full indemnification. Note that this entitlement is statutorily required so that the provisions of any indemnification agreement with the corporation are irrelevant. Courts also read the statutes to require partial indemnification if the defendant is successful as to discrete claims or as to some but not all lawsuits.

Notes and Questions

1. What Do You Think?

a. Should the statutes require indemnification for a defendant who is successful for reasons other than the merits?

b. Should the statutes limit mandatory indemnification to those who were wholly successful? Predominantly successful?

* * *

iii. Procedural and Substantive Prerequisites to Indemnification.   If indemnification is permissive rather than mandatory (or ordered by a court), certain constituencies within the corporation must make certain findings before indemnification may be paid. Under the DGCL, the unconflicted directors or, in the absence of any such directors, the shareholders must make the requisite findings. Under the MBCA authorization may be made by disinterested directors, or disinterested shareholders, or by special legal counsel appointed by the corporation. *See* DGCL §145(d) and MBCA §8.55.

In essence, the appropriate constituency must make a finding that indemnification is permitted by the statute and then a further finding that indemnity is in the best interest of the corporation. In both derivative and nonderivative litigation, there must be an explicit finding by the corporation that the indemnitee has the requisite status to be indemnified (i.e., was a director, officer, or agent who is being sued "by reason of" such status) and had the appropriate state of mind when acting. This state of mind is, at bottom, an intention to aid rather than harm the corporation. The actual statutory requirements are more nuanced than this description so you ought to read the statutes carefully. *See* DGCL §145(a) and (b) and MBCA §8.51. As to the second finding, that indemnity is in the best interest of the corporation, in Delaware and under the MBCA, the corporation may bind itself in advance. That is, the corporation may make a valid decision that it is in the best interest of the corporation to promise to indemnify if possible under the statute. The practical effect of such provisions, which are quite common, is to provide assurance to potential indemnitees that they will be indemnified even if they have a falling out with the corporation. *See* MBCA §8.58(a).

The indemnification statutes draw a distinction between shareholder derivative actions and other litigation. For derivative actions, the corporation may only indemnify for expenses (including attorney's fees) involved in settling the matter. Conceptually this makes sense because otherwise the indemnitee may be held liable to the corporation and then immediately receive indemnification. For nonderivative litigation, the defendant may be indemnified not only for expenses but for settlement amounts and judgments and fines. *See* DGCL §145(a) and (b) and MBCA §8.51.

Despite all these elaborate procedural and substantive requirements, two further methods of indemnification may be available. Under both the DGCL and MBCA a court may determine that indemnification is appropriate even when the statutory provisions are not met. This seems an extraordinary grant of power to the courts, especially in the face of such carefully crafted statutory systems. Undoubtedly this power is not exercised much. *See* DGCL §145(b) and MBCA §8.54.

Second, both statutes permit corporations to provide for indemnification beyond that permitted by the statutes. In Delaware, section 145(f) essentially provides that section 145 is not exclusive. Clearly, however, this section cannot give corporations carte blanche to adopt any indemnification plan they wish because otherwise the rest of section 145 would become superfluous. Some case law suggests that any provision adopted under section 145(f) must at least require a finding that the indemnitee acted in good faith.

The MBCA is a bit murkier in this regard because §8.59 provides that Subchapter E is exclusive as to indemnity provision but 8.51(a)(2), part of Subchapter E, permits corporations to provide broader indemnity than the remainder of Subchapter E would permit. Specifically, §8.51(a)(2) permits corporations to include a provision in their articles (pursuant to MBCA §2.02(b)(5)) that allows or requires indemnification without regard to the limitations or procedures of Subchapter E so long as (speaking broadly) the director does not receive improper benefits or knowingly breaks the law. This certainly allows corporations incorporated in MBCA states greater power to craft indemnity provisions than Delaware corporations enjoy, but, as with Delaware, it is unclear exactly how far a corporation may stray from Subchapter E before a court would find that the indemnification provisions violate a public policy.

4. Insurance

The final technique to ameliorate director and officer liability is tied to indemnification. Virtually every corporations statute permits corporations to purchase insurance covering liability incurred by directors and officers. *See* DGCL §145(g) and MBCA §8.57. The standard *D&O insurance policy* provides two kinds of coverage. First, it reimburses directors and officers for their unindemnified losses in connection with litigation against them by reason of their service as directors or officers. Second, the D&O insurance policy reimburses the corporation itself for indemnity paid to the directors and officers. Note that this policy does not pay the corporation for any loss it suffers by reason of a judgment, fine, or settlement paid to third parties. It only reimburses the company for money it pays to indemnify its own directors and officers.

Nearly every publicly held corporation and many privately held companies have D&O insurance. Statistics suggest that the greater a corporation's assets, the more likely it is to be involved in an indemnification setting and thus to make a D&O insurance claim. Public corporations that report a loss for the first time or those engaged in mergers and acquisitions activity are the most likely to become embroiled in litigation that triggers indemnification and D&O insurance.

Putting It to Work

Problem 12-3

Rex "Sky" King is President and CEO of start-up airline West Tex Air based out of Midland, Texas, and incorporated in Delaware. The airline was created to serve the booming West Texas oil and gas industry with both passenger and commercial cargo service to and from the burgeoning Midland-Odessa metroplex.

The first few years of business were fantastic for West Tex Air. However, even though passenger and cargo flights were full, the company was losing money. It was later discovered that King had made a secret arrangement to purchase all the company's aircraft fuel from his cousin's oil and gas company, Dumas Oil. Where fuel prices averaged $4.85/gallon for the area, King was causing the airline to pay Dumas Oil $7.65/gallon and splitting the extra profits with his cousin. King is now being sued by West Tex Air shareholders and is relying on the company's bylaws as well as DGCL §145 for his demand that West Tex Air advance his attorney expenses during the litigation.

a. Must West Tex Air advance King's expenses?

b. If King is ousted as CEO before the case is resolved, will the company's advancement or indemnification obligations change?

c. What happens if King wins the lawsuit?

F. AN EXERCISE IN SYNTHESIS

The final section is a summation of many of the issues that have arisen in this chapter and the prior chapter. You should reread *Brehm*, p. 520, *supra* because the next case is Chancellor Chandler's statement of the facts in his opinion on remand. After reading the facts you should pause to think about the duties the directors had to meet, the possible claims for relief, and the possible techniques to ameliorate the directors' liability.

In re Walt Disney Co. Deriv. Litig.

825 A.2d 275 (Del. Ch. 2003)

CHANDLER, CH.

I. PROCEDURAL AND FACTUAL BACKGROUND

[T]his case involves an attack on decisions of the Walt Disney Company's board of directors, approving an executive compensation contract for Michael Ovitz, as well as impliedly approving a non-fault termination that resulted in an award to Ovitz (allegedly exceeding $140,000,000) after barely one year of employment. After the Supreme Court's remand regarding plaintiffs' first amended complaint,[4] plaintiffs used the "tools at hand," a request for books and records as authorized under [DGCL] §220, to obtain information about the nature of the Disney Board's involvement in the decision to hire and, eventually, to terminate Ovitz. Using the information gained from that request, plaintiffs drafted and filed the new complaint, which is the subject of the pending motions. The facts, as alleged in the new complaint, portray a markedly different picture of the corporate processes that resulted in the Ovitz employment agreement than that portrayed in the first amended complaint. For that reason, it is necessary to set forth the repleaded facts in some detail. The facts set forth hereafter are taken directly from the new complaint and, for purposes of the present motions, are accepted as true. Of course, I hold no opinion as to the actual truth of any of the allegations set forth in the new complaint; nor do I hold any view as to the likely ultimate outcome on the merits of claims based on these asserted facts.

A. The Decision to Hire Ovitz

Michael Eisner is the chief executive officer ("CEO") of the Walt Disney Company. In 1994, Eisner's second-in-command, Frank Wells, died in a helicopter crash. Two other key executives — Jeffrey Katzenberg and Richard Frank — left Disney shortly thereafter, allegedly because of Eisner's management style. Eisner began looking for a new president for Disney and chose Michael Ovitz. Ovitz was founder and head of CAA, a talent agency; he had never been an executive for a publicly owned entertainment company. He had, however, been Eisner's close friend for over twenty-five years.

Eisner decided unilaterally to hire Ovitz. On August 13, 1995, he informed three Old Board members — Stephen Bollenbach, Sanford Litvack, and Irwin Russell (Eisner's personal attorney) — of that fact. All three protested Eisner's decision to hire Ovitz. Nevertheless, Eisner persisted, sending Ovitz a letter on

---

4. *Brehm v. Eisner*, 746 A.2d 244, 249 (Del. 2000).

August 14, 1995, that set forth certain material terms of his prospective employment. Before this, neither the Old Board nor the compensation committee had ever discussed hiring Ovitz as president of Disney. No discussions or presentations were made to the compensation committee or to the Old Board regarding Ovitz's hiring as president of Walt Disney until September 26, 1995.

Before informing Bollenbach, Litvack, and Russell on August 13, 1995, Eisner collected information on his own, through his position as the Disney CEO, on the potential hiring of Ovitz. In an internal document created around July 7, 1995, concerns were raised about the number of stock options to be granted to Ovitz. The document warned that the number was far beyond the normal standards of both Disney and corporate America and would receive significant public criticism. Additionally, Graef Crystal, an executive compensation expert, informed board member Russell, via a letter dated August 12, 1995, that, generally speaking, a large signing bonus is hazardous because the full cost is borne immediately and completely even if the executive fails to serve the full term of employment.[6] Neither of these documents, however, were submitted to either the compensation committee or the Old Board before hiring Ovitz. Disney prepared a draft employment agreement on September 23, 1995. A copy of the draft was sent to Ovitz's lawyers, but was not provided to members of the compensation committee.

The compensation committee, consisting of defendants Ignacio Lozano, Jr., Sidney Poitier, Russell, and Raymond Watson, met on September 26, 1995, for just under an hour. Three subjects were discussed at the meeting, one of which was Ovitz's employment. According to the minutes, the committee spent the least amount of time during the meeting discussing Ovitz's hiring. In fact, it appears that more time was spent on discussions of paying $250,000 to Russell for his role in securing Ovitz's employment than was actually spent on discussions of Ovitz's employment. The minutes show that several issues were raised and discussed by the committee members concerning Russell's fee. All that occurred during the meeting regarding Ovitz's employment was that Russell reviewed the employment terms with the committee and answered a few questions. Immediately thereafter, the committee adopted a resolution of approval.

No copy of the September 23, 1995 draft employment agreement was actually given to the committee. Instead, the committee members received, at the meeting itself, a rough summary of the agreement. The summary, however, was incomplete. It stated that Ovitz was to receive options to purchase five million shares of stock, but did not state the exercise price. The committee also did not receive any of the materials already produced by Disney regarding Ovitz's possible employment. No spreadsheet or similar type of analytical document showing the potential payout to Ovitz throughout the contract, or the possible cost of his severance package upon a non-fault termination, was created or presented. Nor did the committee request or receive any information as to how the draft agreement compared with similar agreements throughout the entertainment industry, or information regarding other similarly situated executives in the same industry.

---

6. Graef Crystal had been retained to advise Disney on Eisner's employment contract. Although not absolutely clear in the new complaint, it was apparently in this context that Crystal advised Russell of the dangers of a large signing bonus.

The committee also lacked the benefit of an expert to guide them through the process. Graef Crystal, an executive compensation expert, had been hired to provide advice to Disney on Eisner's new employment contract. Even though he had earlier told Russell that large signing bonuses, generally speaking, can be hazardous, neither he nor any other expert had been retained to assist Disney regarding Ovitz's hiring. Thus, no presentations, spreadsheets, written analyses, or opinions were given by any expert for the compensation committee to rely upon in reaching its decision. Although Crystal was not retained as a compensation consultant on the Ovitz contract, he later lamented his failure to intervene and produce a spreadsheet showing the potential costs of the employment agreement.

The compensation committee was informed that further negotiations would occur and that the stock option grant would be delayed until the final contract was worked out. The committee approved the general terms and conditions of the employment agreement, but did not condition their approval on being able to review the final agreement. Instead, the committee granted Eisner the authority to approve the final terms and conditions of the contract as long as they were within the framework of the draft agreement.

Immediately after the compensation committee met on September 26, the Old Board met. Again, no expert was present to advise the board. Nor were any documents produced to the board for it to review before the meeting regarding the Ovitz contract. The board did not ask for additional information to be collected or presented regarding Ovitz's hiring. According to the minutes, the compensation committee did not make any recommendation or report to the board concerning its resolution to hire Ovitz. Nor did Russell, who allegedly secured Ovitz's employment, make a presentation to the board. The minutes of the meeting were fifteen pages long, but only a page and a half covered Ovitz's possible employment. A portion of that page and a half was spent discussing the $250,000 fee paid to Russell for obtaining Ovitz. According to the minutes, the Old Board did not ask any questions about the details of Ovitz's salary, stock options, or possible termination. The Old Board also did not consider the consequences of a termination, or the various payout scenarios that existed. Nevertheless, at that same meeting, the Old Board decided to appoint Ovitz president of Disney. Final negotiation of the employment agreement was left to Eisner, Ovitz's close friend for over twenty-five years.

B. Negotiation of the Employment Agreement

Ovitz was officially hired on October 1, 1995, and began serving as Disney's president, although he did not yet have an executed employment agreement with Disney. On October 16, 1995, the compensation committee was informed, via a brief oral report, that negotiations were ongoing with Ovitz. The committee was not given a draft of the employment agreement either before or during the meeting. A summary similar to the one given on September 26, 1995, was presented. The committee did not seek any further information about the negotiations or about the terms and conditions of Ovitz's agreement, nor was any information proffered regarding the scope of the non-fault termination provision. And, as before, no expert was available to advise the committee as to the employment agreement.

Negotiations continued among Ovitz, Eisner, and their attorneys. The lawyers circulated drafts on October 3, October 10, October 16, October 20, October 23, and December 12, 1995. The employment agreement was physically executed between Michael Ovitz and the Walt Disney Company on December 12, 1995. The employment agreement, however, was backdated to October 1, 1995, the day Ovitz began working as Disney's president. Additionally, the stock option agreement associated with the employment agreement was executed by Eisner (for Disney) on April 2, 1996. Ovitz did not countersign the stock option agreement until November 15, 1996, when he was already discussing his plans to leave Disney's employ. Neither the Old Board nor the compensation committee reviewed or approved the final employment agreement before it was executed and made binding upon Disney.

C. The Final Version of Ovitz's Employment Agreement

The final version of Ovitz's employment agreement differed significantly from the drafts summarized to the compensation committee on September 26, 1995, and October 16, 1995. First, the final version caused Ovitz's stock options to be "in the money"* when granted. The September 23rd draft agreement set the exercise price at the stock price on October 2, 1995, the day after Ovitz began as president. On October 16, 1995, the compensation committee agreed to change the exercise price to the price on that date (October 16, 1995), a price similar to that on October 2nd. The agreement was not signed until December 12, 1995, however, at which point the value of Disney stock had increased by eight percent — from $56.875 per share on October 16th to $61.50 per share on December 12th. The overall stock market, according to the Dow Jones Industrial Average, had also increased by about eight percent at the same time. By waiting to sign the agreement until December, but not changing the date of the exercise price, Ovitz had stock options that instantly were "in the money." This allowed Ovitz to play a "win-win" game at Disney's expense — if the market price of Disney stock had fallen between October 16 and December 12, Ovitz could have demanded a downward adjustment to the option exercise price; if the price had risen (as in fact it had) Ovitz would receive "in the money" options.

Another difference in the final version of Ovitz's employment agreement concerned the circumstances surrounding a non-fault termination. The September 23rd draft agreement stated that non-fault termination benefits would only be provided if Disney wrongfully terminated Ovitz, or Ovitz died or became disabled. The October 16th draft contained a very similar definition. These were the only two drafts of which the compensation committee was made aware. The final version of the agreement, however, offered Ovitz a non-fault termination as long as Ovitz did not act with gross negligence or malfeasance. Therefore, instead of protecting Ovitz

---

* [Stock options such as those granted to Mr. Ovitz in this case are the right (but not the obligation) to purchase a fixed number of shares at a fixed price (called the *exercise price*, usually the market price at the time the options are given to the employee) at any time between the exercise date and the date they expire. If the stock price rises above the exercise price by the time the option is exercisable, the employee benefits because he or she can exercise the option and immediately sell the stock for a profit. Stock options are an incentive to the employee to improve the corporation so that the stock price rises. Employee stock options are said to be *at the money* if the exercise price and the market price are the same. These options are said to be *in the money* if the market price exceeds the exercise price and are said to be *out of the money*, or *under water*, if the market price is below the exercise price. Obviously, an employee will not exercise options that are out of the money. A grant of stock options that are immediately in the money would be unusual because it lessens the employee's incentive as the market price is already above the exercise price. *ED.*]

from a wrongful termination by Disney, Ovitz was able to receive the full benefits of a non-fault termination, even if he acted negligently or was unable to perform his duties, as long as his behavior did not reach the level of gross negligence or malfeasance. Additionally, a non-compete clause was not included within the agreement should Ovitz leave Disney's employ.

The employment agreement had a term of five years. Ovitz was to receive a salary of $1 million per year, a potential bonus each year from $0 to $10 million, and a series of stock options (the "A" options) that enabled Ovitz to purchase three million shares of Disney stock at the October 16, 1995 exercise price. The options were to vest at one million per year for three years beginning September 30, 1998. At the end of the contract term, if Disney entered into a new contract with Ovitz, he was entitled to the "B" options, an additional two million shares. There was no requirement, however, that Disney enter into a new contract with Ovitz.

Should a non-fault termination occur, however, the terms of the final version of the employment agreement appeared to be even more generous. Under a non-fault termination, Ovitz was to receive his salary for the remainder of the contract, discounted at a risk-free rate keyed to Disney's borrowing costs. He was also to receive a $7.5 million bonus for each year remaining on his contract, discounted at the same risk-free rate, even though no set bonus amount was guaranteed in the contract. Additionally, all of his "A" stock options were to vest immediately, instead of waiting for the final three years of his contract for them to vest. The final benefit of the non-fault termination was a lump sum "termination payment" of $10 million. The termination payment was equal to the payment Ovitz would receive should he complete his full five-year term with Disney, but not receive an offer for a new contract. Graef Crystal opined in the January 13, 1997, edition of *California Law/Business* that "the contract was most valuable to Ovitz the sooner he left Disney."

D. Ovitz's Performance as Disney's President

Ovitz began serving as president of Disney on October 1, 1995, and became a Disney director in January 1996. Ovitz's tenure as Disney's president proved unsuccessful. Ovitz was not a good second-in-command, and he and Eisner were both aware of that fact. Eisner told defendant Watson, via memorandum, that he (Eisner) "had made an error in judgment in who I brought into the company." Other company executives were reported in the December 14, 1996 edition of the *New York Times* as saying that Ovitz had an excessively lavish office, an imperious management style, and had started a feud with NBC during his tenure. Even Ovitz admitted, during a September 30, 1996 interview on "Larry King Live," that he knew "about 1% of what I need to know."

Even though admitting that he did not know his job, Ovitz studiously avoided attempts to be educated. Eisner instructed Ovitz to meet weekly with Disney's chief financial officer, defendant Bollenbach. The meetings were scheduled to occur each Monday at 2 P.M., but every week Ovitz cancelled at the last minute. Bollenbach was quoted in a December 1996 issue of *Vanity Fair* as saying that Ovitz failed to meet with him at all, "didn't understand the duties of an executive at a public company[,] and he didn't want to learn."

Instead of working to learn his duties as Disney's president, Ovitz began seeking alternative employment. He consulted Eisner to ensure that no action would be taken against him by Disney if he sought employment elsewhere. Eisner agreed that the best thing for Disney, Eisner, and Ovitz was for Ovitz to gain employment elsewhere. Eisner wrote to the chairman of Sony Japan that Ovitz could negotiate with Sony without any repercussions from Disney. Ovitz and Sony began negotiations for Ovitz to become head of Sony's entertainment business, but the negotiations ultimately failed. With the possibility of having another company absorb the cost of Ovitz's departure now gone, Eisner and Ovitz began in earnest to discuss a non-fault termination.

E. The Non-Fault Termination

Ovitz wanted to leave Disney, but could only terminate his employment if one of three events occurred: (1) he was not elected or retained as president and a director of Disney; (2) he was assigned duties materially inconsistent with his role as president; or (3) Disney reduced his annual salary or failed to grant his stock options, pay him discretionary bonuses, or make any required compensation payment. None of these three events occurred. If Ovitz resigned outright, he might have been liable to Disney for damages and would not have received the benefits of the non-fault termination. He also desired to protect his reputation when exiting from his position with Disney. Eisner agreed to help Ovitz depart Disney without sacrificing any of his benefits. Eisner and Ovitz worked together as close personal friends to have Ovitz receive a non-fault termination. Eisner stated in a letter to Ovitz that: "I agree with you that we must work together to assure a smooth transition and deal with the public relations brilliantly. I am committed to make this a win-win situation, to keep our friendship intact, to be positive, to say and write only glowing things. . . . Nobody ever needs to know anything other than positive things from either of us. This can all work out!"

Eisner, Litvack, and Ovitz met at Eisner's apartment on December 11, 1996, to finalize Ovitz's non-fault termination. The new complaint alleges that the New Board was aware that Eisner was negotiating with Ovitz the terms of his separation. Litvack sent a letter to Ovitz on December 12, 1996, stating that, by "mutual agreement," (1) Ovitz's term of employment would end on January 31, 1997; and (2) "this letter will for all purposes of the Employment Agreement be given the same effect as though there had been a 'Non-Fault Termination,' and the Company will pay you, on or before February 5, 1997, all amounts due you under the Employment Agreement, including those under Section 11(c) thereof. In addition, the stock options granted pursuant to Option A, will vest as of January 31, 1997 and will expire in accordance with their terms on September 30, 2002." On December 12, 1996, Ovitz's departure from Disney became public. Neither the New Board of Directors nor the compensation committee had been consulted or given their approval for a non-fault termination. In addition, no record exists of any action by the New Board once the non-fault termination became public on December 12, 1996.

On December 27, 1996, Litvack sent Ovitz a new letter superseding the December 12th letter. The December 27th letter stated that Ovitz's termination would "be treated as a 'Non-Fault Termination.'" This differed from the December

12th letter, which treated Ovitz's termination "as though there had been a 'Non-Fault Termination.'" It also made the termination of Ovitz's employment and his resignation as a Disney director effective as of the close of business on December 27th, instead of on January 31, 1997, as in the December 12th letter. Additionally, it listed the amount payable to Ovitz as $38,888,230.77, and stated that the "A" options to purchase three million shares of Disney vested on December 27th, instead of January 31, 1997, as in the December 12th letter. Both Eisner and Litvack signed the letter. Again, however, neither the New Board nor the compensation committee reviewed or approved the December 27th letter. No record exists of any New Board action after the December 27th letter became public, nor had any board member raised any questions or concerns since the original December 12th letter became public.

According to the new complaint, Disney's bylaws required board approval for Ovitz's non-fault termination. Eisner and Litvack allegedly did not have the authority to provide for a non-fault termination without board consent. No documents or board minutes currently exist showing an affirmative decision by the New Board or any of its committees to grant Ovitz a non-fault termination. The New Board was already aware that Eisner was granting the non-fault termination as of December 12, 1996, the day it became public. No record of any action by the New Board affirming or questioning that decision by Eisner either before or after that date has been produced. There are also no records showing that alternatives to a non-fault termination were ever evaluated by the New Board or by any of its committees.

Notes and Questions

1. Notes

a. You may wish to review the table of contents for this chapter and the prior chapter as an aide-mémoire.

2. Reality Check

a. How are the facts as alleged in this opinion different from the facts as alleged in *Brehm*? Which set of facts do you find more believable?

3. Suppose

a. Imagine that you are the law clerk to Chancellor Chandler. Make an outline of the possible claims for relief presented by the facts set out above.

b. Suppose the company were incorporated in a state that has adopted the MBCA. Would your outline be different?

4. What Do You Think?

a. Do you believe plaintiffs' counsel violated Rule 11 by filing the complaint in issue here? Did they violate Rule 11 by filing the complaint in *Brehm*? Did they violate Rule 11 by filing both complaints?

b. Did any of the directors violate any of their fiduciary duties?

c. Is any of the directors' conduct actionable under Delaware law? If so, what amelioration of that possible liability may be available?

After a thirty-seven day trial, Chancellor Chandler found for the defendants on all claims. As for Mr. Ovitz's hiring, the Chancellor found that the Compensation Committee had the power to hire without full board approval. Two of the Committee members (Messrs. Russell and Watson) were fully informed and they informed the other two members (Messrs. Lozano and Poitier). The Chancellor found that retaining and relying on Mr. Crystal was appropriate. Thus the full board's action, or inaction, was not at issue.

Under the corporation's certificate of incorporation and bylaws, either the board or the CEO, Mr. Eisner, had the power to terminate senior officers. Mr. Eisner met his fiduciary duties in terminating Mr. Ovitz. The board, then, could not have been liable for terminating Mr. Ovitz regardless of their knowledge, or lack thereof. Finally, the Chancellor found that Mr. Ovitz did not violate his duty of loyalty regarding his termination because he played no part in making the termination decision and did not "improperly inject himself into" nor "manipulate" the process. *See In re Walt Disney Co. Deriv. Litig.*, 907 A.2d 693 (Del. Ch. 2005). The Delaware Supreme Court affirmed Chancellor Chandler's findings and conclusions. *In re Walt Disney Co. Deriv. Litig.*, 906 A.2d 27 (Del. 2006).

G. TERMS OF ART IN THIS CHAPTER

Business judgment rule	Entire fairness	Special litigation committee
Caremark claim	Indemnification	Waste
Charter limitations		

13

Do the Restrictions Work?

We come to the end of our five-chapter consideration of the exercise of, and restriction on, board power over the corporation. Chapter 10 discussed restrictions imposed on the corporation itself. Restrictions on the board are simply a consequence of restrictions on corporate actions. Chapter 11 explored directors' fiduciary duties of loyalty and care. Chapter 12 looked at the standards of review courts use to assess whether liability will be imposed for breach of those fiduciary duties. Now we reflect on whether all these limitations work. That is, are corporate boards genuinely constrained from exercising corporate power in ways deleterious to others? This chapter is divided into three sections. First we will explore the facts surrounding two of the major corporate accounting scandals of the early twenty-first century. Second, and most centrally, we will look at structural constraints that might have been expected to constrain corporations and their boards. Finally, we will take a step back and ask you to decide whether the costs of reforming the current system of constraints are worth the benefits and whether these corporate scandals are exceptions to the norm or represent proof that the system of restraints is fundamentally broken.

Between late 2001 and the end of 2003 a series of corporate financial scandals became public. In response, Congress enacted reforms, the SEC became revivified, and accounting firms, investment bankers, and stock brokerages all reformed their business practices. This section looks at two of the most emblematic of these scandals. We start by describing what happened and what the motivations were. Then we will take a structural approach and ask what institutions were designed to check board power. Third, we will see the responses to these scandals. Finally we will ask whether these scandals were spectacular anomalies or exemplars of systemic problems.

A. TWO TWENTY-FIRST CENTURY EXAMPLES

1. Enron[1]

Enron was one of the largest companies in the world and was considered to be one of the most innovative and successful. *Fortune* magazine ranked Enron as the seventh largest corporation in the world based on its $100 billion in annual revenues. Starting out as a company that had a concentration in natural gas pipelines, it became, by the mid-1990s, a company that depended less on pipelines and transportation and more on energy trading (which was successful) and investing in new technologies and businesses (which was largely unsuccessful).

Enron's expansion during this time made Enron a voracious consumer of cash. Enron's management made it clear to the investment community that it was aware of the issues posed by its expansion and gave assurances that Enron could manage its way through these risks without upsetting investor expectations.

Enron's energy trading segment was by far the most significant of Enron's business segments, accounting for 66 percent of its 1999 income. Enron acted as a principal, buying and selling energy from producers and wholesale users (such as utility companies) and also as a broker between other parties. When it brokered transactions, it also guaranteed performance to each party by the other. In effect, Enron was committed to every trade. To continue the growth of this business, Enron needed to trade with other market participants without being required to post collateral. To do so, Enron needed to keep its credit rating for its unsecured long-term debt at the "investment grade" level. Enron considered its credit ratings critical to its success. Enron's need to maintain its credit rating was known throughout the institution, from its board of directors to its mid-level management.

The continued success of Enron's entire business was dependent upon the continued success of its energy trading segment, which in turn was dependent upon Enron's credit ratings, which depended on achieving certain financial ratios. These ratios were calculated, in large part, by comparing various financial factors to Enron's total debt.

Enron so engineered its reported financial position and results of operations that its financial statements bore little resemblance to its actual financial condition or performance. This financial engineering in many cases violated GAAP and applicable disclosure laws, and resulted in financial statements that did not fairly present Enron's financial condition.

Two key factors drove Enron's management of its financial statements: its need for cash and its need to maintain its investment grade credit rating. Enron was reluctant to issue equity to raise money for fear of an adverse effect on its stock price because the new shares would dilute the existing shares' value. . . . In addition, Enron was reluctant to incur debt to raise money because of the adverse affect on its credit ratings.

---

1. The facts in this discussion are taken, largely verbatim and without further indication, from *In re Enron Corp.*, Second Interim Report of Neal Batson, Court-Appointed Examiner (Jan. 21, 2003).

In the fall of 2001, Enron made a series of financial disclosures that triggered a chain of events culminating in its bankruptcy. In outline, Enron raised the cash it needed by borrowing. To keep that debt from showing up on its financial statements, Enron created many separate legal entities, called *special purpose entities* (SPEs). The SPEs borrowed money that was then used in Enron ventures. Under GAAP, Enron did not have to report the SPEs' debt as its own if Enron owned no more than 97 percent of the SPE and did not manage the SPE. Enron violated both these requirements and thus had to restate its financial statements to reflect that it had significantly more debt than it had disclosed and to reflect that it was losing money on the nonenergy trading segments of its business.

As a result of these disclosures, its trading partners reduced the volume of business they did with Enron, which cut its revenues. Further, Enron's credit rating was reduced severely, which resulted in the acceleration of much of Enron's long-term debt. Unable to service its debt with the assets in hand, Enron declared bankruptcy. Enron stockholders lost $66 billion.

2. WorldCom

WorldCom was a telecom corporation engaged in local, long-distance, and cellular telephone services, as well as Internet services. Through a series of aggressive acquisitions, WorldCom was a leader in all these areas.

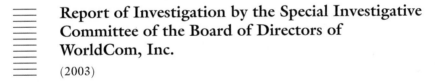

Report of Investigation by the Special Investigative Committee of the Board of Directors of WorldCom, Inc.

(2003)

From 1999 until 2002, WorldCom suffered one of the largest public company accounting frauds in history. As enormous as the fraud was, it was accomplished in a relatively mundane way: more than $9 billion in false or unsupported accounting entries were made in WorldCom's financial systems in order to achieve desired reported financial results. The fraud did not involve WorldCom's network, its technology, or its engineering. Most of WorldCom's people did not know it was occurring. Rather, the fraud occurred as a result of knowing misconduct directed by a few senior executives centered in its Clinton, Mississippi, headquarters, and implemented by personnel in its financial and accounting departments in several locations. The fraud was the consequence of the way WorldCom's Chief Executive Officer, Bernard J. Ebbers, ran the Company. Though much of this Report details the implementation of the fraud by others, he was the source of the culture, as well as much of the pressure, that gave birth to this fraud. That the fraud continued as long as it did was due to a lack of courage to blow the whistle on the part of others in WorldCom's financial and accounting departments; inadequate audits by [independent accounting firm] Arthur Andersen; and a financial system whose controls were sorely deficient. The setting in which it occurred was marked by a serious corporate governance failure.

Line costs are the costs of carrying a voice call or data transmission from its starting point to its ending point. They are WorldCom's largest single expense: from 1999 to 2001, line costs accounted for approximately half of the Company's total expenses. As a result, WorldCom management and outside analysts paid particular attention to line cost levels and trends. One key measure of performance both within WorldCom and in communications with the public was the ratio of line cost expense to revenue (the "line cost E/R ratio").

In 1999 and 2000, WorldCom reduced its reported line costs by approximately $3.3 billion. This was accomplished by improperly releasing "accruals," or amounts set aside on WorldCom's financial statements to pay anticipated bills. These accruals were supposed to reflect estimates of the costs . . . , which WorldCom had not yet paid. "Releasing" an accrual is proper when it turns out that less is needed to pay the bills than had been anticipated. It has the effect of providing an offset against reported line costs in the period when the accrual is released. Thus, it reduces reported expenses and increases reported pre-tax income.

By the end of 2000, WorldCom had essentially exhausted available accruals, at least on the scale needed to continue this manipulation of reported line costs. Thereafter, from the first quarter of 2001 through the first quarter of 2002, WorldCom improperly reduced its reported line costs by $3.8 billion, principally by capitalizing $3.5 billion of line costs — at [CFO Scott] Sullivan's direction — in violation of WorldCom's capitalization policy and well-established accounting standards. The line costs that WorldCom capitalized were ongoing, operating expenses that accounting rules required WorldCom to recognize immediately. Sullivan made comments indicating that he intended ultimately to reduce these inflated asset accounts by including them in a large restructuring charge later in 2002.

By capitalizing operating expenses, WorldCom . . . increased its reported pre-tax income and earnings per share. Had WorldCom not capitalized these expenses, it would have reported a pre-tax loss in three of the five quarters in which the improper capitalization entries occurred. By reducing reported line costs, the capitalization entries also significantly improved WorldCom's line cost E/R ratio. In its public filings, WorldCom consistently emphasized throughout 2001 that its line cost E/R ratio stayed the same — about 42% — quarter after quarter. That representation was false. Had it not capitalized line costs, WorldCom's reported line cost E/R ratio would have been much higher, typically exceeding 50%. This device also made it appear that softening markets were not reducing the Company's profitability, when the opposite was the case. To implement the capitalization strategy, Sullivan needed the acquiescence of a significant number of people within the financial and accounting departments at the Company.

WorldCom marketed itself as a high-growth company, and revenue growth was clearly a critical component of WorldCom's early success. As market conditions throughout the telecommunications industry deteriorated in 2000 and 2001, WorldCom . . . nevertheless continued to post impressive revenue growth numbers, and Ebbers and Sullivan continued to assure Wall Street that WorldCom could sustain that level of growth. In essence, WorldCom claimed it was successfully managing industry trends that were hurting all of its competitors. These promises of double-digit growth translated into pressure within WorldCom to achieve those results. As one officer told us, the emphasis on revenue was "in every brick in every building." Ebbers was intensely focused on revenue performance, receiving and closely examining Monthly Revenue . . . reports from the Revenue Reporting and Accounting group ("Revenue Accounting group").

Beginning in 1999, WorldCom personnel made large revenue accounting entries after the close of many quarters in order to report that it had achieved the high revenue growth targets that Ebbers and Sullivan had established. The questionable revenue entries included in Corporate Unallocated [revenue accounts] often involved large, round-dollar revenue items (in millions or tens of millions of dollars). They generally appeared only in the quarter-ending month, and they were not recorded during the quarter, but instead in the weeks after the quarter had ended. As a result, the total amounts reported in the Corporate Unallocated revenue accounts spiked upward during quarter-ending months, and the largest spikes (ranging from $136 million to $257 million) occurred in those quarters in which WorldCom's operational revenue lagged furthest behind its quarterly revenue targets — the second and third quarters of 2000 and second, third and fourth quarters of 2001.

In the period under investigation, the amounts booked in the Corporate Unallocated revenue accounts were critical to WorldCom's perceived success. Without the revenue booked in those accounts, WorldCom would have failed, in six out of the twelve quarters between the beginning of 1999 and the end of 2001, to achieve the double-digit growth it reported. Our investigation has identified over $958 million in revenue that was improperly recorded by WorldCom between the first quarter of 1999 and the first quarter of 2002. Our accounting advisors have identified $1.107 billion of additional revenue items recorded during this period that they consider questionable, based on the circumstances in which they were recorded and the lack of available or adequate support.

Ebbers, in addition to his full-time job as Chief Executive Officer of WorldCom, was actively involved in buying, building, and running several businesses unrelated to WorldCom. Between 1998 and 2000, Ebbers and the companies he controlled significantly expanded their holdings by purchasing, among other things, the largest working cattle ranch in Canada (approximately 500,000 acres), and approximately 540,000 acres of timberland in four Southern U.S. states. The total scope of Ebbers' non–WorldCom businesses . . . included a Louisiana rice farm, a luxury yacht building company, a lumber mill, a country club, a trucking company, a minor league hockey team, an operating marina, and a building in downtown Chicago.

Nothing we have reviewed indicates that the Compensation Committee [of the Board] or the Board imposed any limits on Ebbers' conduct of non–WorldCom businesses. It does not appear that any Board members seriously pursued, prior to 2002, the question whether Ebbers could devote sufficient attention to managing WorldCom amid his outside business obligations. . . .

The method Ebbers chose to finance many of his acquisitions involved substantial financial risk. Ebbers and companies he controlled took out loans from commercial banks. Many of these commercial loans were margin loans secured by shares of Ebbers' WorldCom stock. Although the terms varied among the various margin loans, each required that the value of Ebbers' stock remain greater than or equal to some multiple of the amount of the loan.

These margin loans totaled hundreds of millions of dollars—perhaps more at various times. This massive indebtedness left Ebbers exposed to declines in the price of WorldCom stock, which began to occur in late 1999. The stock price went from a high of $62.00 a share on June 21, 1999, to $36.52 on Friday, April 14, 2000. The following Monday, Bank of America made a margin call to Ebbers, noting that he was in default and calling for him either to pledge additional collateral or to reduce his outstanding loan amount.

The price of WorldCom stock continued to decline during 2000, and Ebbers continued to face margin calls from his lenders. By September 6, 2000, the day of a scheduled meeting of the Compensation Committee, the stock price was down to $30.27 a share. Shortly before the meeting, Ebbers told . . . the Committee's chairman, about the margin calls he was facing and they discussed the possibility that the Company would give him a loan. There is conflicting evidence whether it was Ebbers who first suggested the loan.

From . . . late September 2000 until Ebbers' forced resignation in April 2002, the Compensation Committee took various steps — including extending . . . loans and guaranties — to enable Ebbers to avoid selling . . . WorldCom stock. Ebbers' personal financial situation became a focus of Compensation Committee attention, particularly in early 2002. From October 18, 2000, until April 1, 2002, the Compensation Committee met and discussed the Company's financial arrangements with Ebbers 26 times, and for 13 of these meetings, Ebbers' financial situation is the only topic specifically identified in the minutes. Unable to persuade Ebbers' lenders to relax their demands or accept other collateral from Ebbers, the Committee proceeded to approve numerous additional loans and guaranties for Ebbers, eventually totaling (including interest) $408 million.

The most serious risk the Committee and the Board overlooked was the risk that Ebbers' personal financial stress posed to his corporate decision making. As a substantial long-term stockholder, Ebbers' interests had been aligned with those of the Company. Beginning in 2000, however, once he was subject to the daily pressure of margin calls and thus in financial jeopardy based on any short-term decline in the price of WorldCom stock, Ebbers' interests were no longer fully aligned with those of the Company. He had strong incentives to pursue whatever short-term action might be necessary to push up the stock price. [T]he fact that Ebbers was so far overextended financially should have prompted much closer Board attention to the way he was running the Company, and he should not have been allowed to use the Company as his personal bank.

Late in the Spring of 2002, the enormous capitalization entries — approximately $3.5 billion — were finally detected and disclosed to the public. They had, of course, been well known for some time in the General Accounting, Property Accounting and Capital Reporting groups. Internal Audit had come across references to the corporate adjustments while doing an audit of Capital Expenditures in late 2001, and first made inquiries at that time. In the Spring of 2002, Internal Audit focused on the adjustments and brought the fraud to the attention of the Board. Simultaneously, others within the Company became aware of these improper adjustments, and some took steps to raise questions about them.

On June 25, 2002, WorldCom announced that it intended to restate its financial statements for 2001 and the first quarter of 2002. It stated that it had determined that certain transfers totaling $3.852 billion during that period from "line cost" expenses (costs of transmitting calls) to asset accounts were not made in accordance with Generally Accepted Accounting Principles ("GAAP"). Less than one month later, WorldCom and substantially all of its active U.S. subsidiaries filed voluntary petitions for reorganization under Chapter 11 of the Bankruptcy Code. WorldCom subsequently announced that it had discovered an additional $3.831 billion in improperly reported earnings before taxes for 1999, 2000, 2001, and first quarter 2002. It has also written off approximately $80 billion of the stated book value of the assets on the Company's balance sheet at the time the fraud was announced.

Notes and Questions

1. Notes

a. As a result of these disclosures, its lenders accelerated much of WorldCom's debt. Unable to service its debt with the assets in hand, WorldCom declared bankruptcy. WorldCom stockholders lost $156 billion.

b. Although the stock of Enron and WorldCom lost nearly all value, you should be aware that the value of all stock in NYSE listed companies was approximately $10 trillion in 2001 and 2002. The stock losses for all companies that experienced accounting fraud in the early twenty-first century aggregated about 3 percent of the value of all companies.

c. Both Enron and WorldCom sponsored retirement plans for their employees. About 60 percent of Enron's retirement plan was invested in Enron stock. That plan lost about $1.3 billion in value when Enron declared bankruptcy. WorldCom's retirement plan has about one-third of its assets invested in company stock; the plan lost about $280 million.

d. WorldCom's $408 million in loans to Mr. Ebbers constituted about 1 percent of WorldCom's annual revenue.

e. Later in the chapter we will look at the workings of credit-rating agencies.

f. Senior managers have several incentives to commit accounting fraud. First, much of their compensation depends upon the company's economic performance. Second, their desire for professional success may motivate them to conceal the company's true economic performance. As you see from the above descriptions, among the immediate pressures to commit accounting fraud are the desire to keep the company's credit rating high, which, in turn, permits the company to borrow more money and to avoid having payment of existing debt accelerated. The executives may also desire to tailor the company's performance to the expectations of securities analysts so that the company's stock price remains high. *See* Joseph T. Wells, *Principles of Fraud Examination* (2005).

g. Accounting frauds fall into a few categories. First, executives may fraudulently increase revenues, either by improperly characterizing certain transactions, by engaging in sham transactions with others, or, as WorldCom did, by simply making up numbers to be included in the company's revenues. Second, executives may fraudulently overstate the value of assets or, more commonly, understate the value of liabilities so that the company appears to have a higher ratio of assets to liabilities than is really the case. This essentially increases the company's borrowing ability.

Enron engaged in this activity by concealing the scope of its debt. Third, managers may fraudulently understate costs, which increases profit. This can be accomplished by ignoring contingent liabilities (like the possibility of customer returns or customer warranty claims), or, as WorldCom did, by improperly designating expenses for current goods and services (which should be reported in full) as expenses for long-term goods and services (which should be reported over time). *See* Joseph T. Wells, *Principles of Fraud Examination* (2005).

2. Reality Check

a. What kinds of accounting fraud did WorldCom commit?
b. Why did WorldCom's managers commit fraud?

B. STRUCTURAL CONSTRAINTS

Statistics strongly suggest that the kinds of financial scandals that most concern us here nearly always involve the top corporate officers. In over 70 percent of financial fraud cases the CEO is complicit and the CFO is involved in over 40 percent of such cases. Either the CEO, the CFO, or both, is a participant in more than 80 percent of reported financial fraud cases. It seems clear, then, that constraining these two senior officers, at the least, is required to stem financial frauds. Four principal institutional constraints work to keep financial frauds from taking place. And yet, financial frauds are perpetrated with some regularity anyway. Because our primary focus in this chapter is on the board of directors, we start with assessments of the Enron and WorldCom boards.

1. Board of Directors

a. Enron

Permanent Subcommittee on Investigations of the Committee on Governmental Affairs United States Senate, *The Role of the Board of Directors in Enron's Collapse*
8-11 (2002)

In 2001, Enron's Board of Directors had 15 members, several of whom had 20 years or more experience on the Board of Enron or its predecessor companies. Many of Enron's Directors served on the boards of other companies as well. At the hearing, John Duncan, former Chairman of the Executive Committee, described his fellow Board members as well educated, "experienced, successful businessmen and women," and "experts in areas of finance and accounting." The Subcommittee interviews found the Directors to have a wealth of sophisticated business and investment experience and considerable expertise in accounting, derivatives, and structured finance.

Enron Board members uniformly described internal Board relations as harmonious. They said that Board votes were generally unanimous and could recall only two instances over the course of many years involving dissenting votes. The Directors also described a good working relationship with Enron management. Several had close personal relationships with Board Chairman and Chief Executive Officer (CEO) Kenneth L. Lay. All indicated they had possessed great respect for senior Enron officers, trusting the integrity and competence of Mr. Lay; President and Chief Operating Officer (and later CEO) Jeffrey K. Skilling; Chief Financial Officer Andrew S. Fastow; Chief Accounting Officer Richard A. Causey; Chief Risk Officer Richard Buy; and the Treasurer Jeffrey McMahon and later Ben Glisan. Mr. Lay served as Chairman of the Board from 1986 until he resigned in 2002. Mr. Skilling was a Board member from 1997 until August 2001, when he resigned from Enron.

The Enron Board was organized into five committees. (1) The **Executive Committee** met on an as needed basis to handle urgent business matters between scheduled Board meetings. (2) The **Finance Committee** was responsible for approving major transactions which, in 2001, met or exceeded $75 million in value. It also reviewed transactions valued between $25 million and $75 million; oversaw Enron's risk management efforts; and provided guidance on the company's financial decisions and policies. (3) The **Audit and Compliance Committee** reviewed Enron's accounting and compliance programs, approved Enron's financial statements and reports, and was the primary liaison with Andersen. (4) The **Compensation Committee** established and monitored Enron's compensation policies and plans for directors, officers and employees. (5) The **Nominating Committee** nominated individuals to serve as Directors.

The Board normally held five regular meetings during the year, with additional special meetings as needed. Board meetings usually lasted two days, with the first day devoted to Committee meetings and a Board dinner and the second day devoted to a meeting of the full Board. Committee meetings generally lasted between one and two hours and were arranged to allow Board members, who typically sat on three Committees, to attend all assigned Committee meetings. Full Board meetings also generally lasted between one and two hours. Special Board meetings, as well as meetings of the Executive Committee, were typically conducted by telephone conference.

Committee chairmen typically spoke with Enron management by telephone prior to Committee meetings to develop the proposed Committee meeting agenda. Board members said that Enron management provided them with these agendas as well as extensive background and briefing materials prior to Board meetings including, in the case of Finance Committee members, numerous deal approval sheets ("DASHs") for approval of major transactions. Board members varied in how much time they spent reading the materials and preparing for Board meetings, with the reported preparation time for each meeting varying between two hours and two days. On some occasions, Enron provided a private plane to transport Board members from various locations to a Board meeting, and Board members discussed company issues during the flight. Enron also organized occasional trips abroad which some Board members attended to view company assets and operations.

During the Committee meetings, Enron management generally provided presentations on company performance, internal controls, new business ventures, specific transactions, or other topics of interest. The Finance Committee generally heard from Mr. Fastow, Mr. Causey, Mr. Buy, Mr. McMahon and, occasionally, Mr. Glisan. The Audit Committee generally heard from Mr. Causey, Mr. Buy, and [Enron's outside auditor, Arthur] Andersen personnel. The Compensation Committee generally heard from the company's top compensation official, Mary Joyce, and from the company's compensation consultant, Towers Perrin. On occasion, the Committees heard from other senior Enron officers as well. At the full Board meetings, Board members typically received presentations from each Committee Chairman summarizing the Committee's work and recommendations, as well as from Enron management and, occasionally, Andersen or the company's chief outside legal counsel, Vinson & Elkins. Mr. Lay and Mr. Skilling usually attended Executive, Finance, and Audit Committee meetings, as well as the full Board meetings. Mr. Lay attended many Compensation Committee meetings as well. The Subcommittee interviews indicated that, altogether, Board members appeared to have routine contact with less than a dozen senior officers at Enron. The Board did not have a practice of meeting without Enron management present.

Regular presentations on Enron's financial statements, accounting practices, and audit results were provided by Andersen to the Audit Committee. The Audit Committee Chairman would then report on the presentation to the full Board. On most occasions, three Andersen senior partners from Andersen's Houston office attended Audit Committee meetings. The Audit Committee offered Andersen personnel an opportunity to present information to them without management present.

Minutes summarizing Committee and Board meetings were kept by the Corporate Secretary, who often took handwritten notes on Committee and Board presentations during the Board's deliberations and afterward developed and circulated draft minutes to Enron management, Board members, and legal counsel. The draft minutes were formally presented to and approved by Committee and Board members at subsequent meetings.

Outside of the formal Committee and Board meetings, the Enron Directors described very little interaction or communication either among Board members or between Board members and Enron or Andersen personnel, until the company began experiencing severe problems in October 2001. From October until the company's bankruptcy on December 2, 2001, the Board held numerous special meetings, at times on almost a daily basis.

Enron Board members were compensated with cash, restricted stock, phantom stock units, and stock options. The total cash and equity compensation of Enron Board members in 2000 was valued by Enron at about $350,000 or more than twice the national average for Board compensation at a U.S. publicly traded corporation.

In re Enron Corp.
Final Report of Neal Batson, Court-Appointed Examiner
119-136 (2003)

The Enron Board could have been the ultimate check in preventing or minimizing the impact of the officers' misconduct. The Board had the authority to stop the misconduct by, for example, terminating the employment of these officers, refusing to approve Enron's financial statements, and other disclosures in its . . . public filings or notifying the SEC of wrongdoing. In practice, however, particularly in circumstances involving complex matters and obfuscation by officers of a company, there are limitations to a board serving as an effective check in the area of oversight. This may help to explain why director liability for breach of the duty of oversight is rare absent egregious facts.

The Enron Board did not serve as an effective check on the officers' misuse of Enron's SPE transactions. There are several factors that might explain this failure. Some of these factors were not within the control of the Enron Board. Other factors, however, were within the control of the Enron Board and, if handled differently, might have resulted in the Board limiting the harm caused to Enron.

The Enron Board generally was not asked to, and did not, approve Enron's SPE transactions. . . . As a result, the Board's role for most of these transactions consisted primarily of providing oversight and being alert for signals or red flags of wrongdoing. The following discusses Enron's policies relating to its transaction approval process and the conduct of the two committees most responsible for monitoring the SPEs: the Finance Committee and the Audit Committee.

ENRON BOARD'S TRANSACTION APPROVAL POLICIES

The Enron Board did not approve most of the SPE transactions. There were several policies established by the Enron Board that were relevant to determining whether a transaction could be consummated without Board approval. These included: (i) Enron's Risk Management Policy; (ii) Enron's Guaranty Policy; and (iii) Enron's asset divestiture policy. Because of the way in which many of the SPE transactions were structured, these policies effectively permitted Enron's officers to incur a virtually unlimited amount of debt through the SPE transactions, without prior approval of the Enron Board.

The Enron Board apparently devoted significant attention to these policies, as evidenced by seven amendments to the Risk Management Policy from December 1998 through May 2000. [T]he Enron Board apparently put significant emphasis on its ability to manage risk under the Risk Management Policy. While these controls may work well in managing true trading activities involving assets that have publicly quoted prices and substantial market liquidity, they did not allow the Board the opportunity to prevent the incurrence of debt through SPE transactions (structured as trading activities).

FINANCE AND AUDIT COMMITTEES

Finance Committee

In the area of SPE transactions and off-balance sheet finance transactions, the Finance Committee failed to serve as an effective check. It should be noted that in the area in which its members had an interest and concern, e.g., the . . . status reports about the trading activities . . . , the Finance Committee appears to have performed well in its oversight function. Perhaps because of this interest and attention on the part of the Finance Committee, this process worked effectively to prevent trading losses at Enron.

The Finance Committee did not do as well in the SPE transactions and the structured finance areas. From at least 1997 until August 2001, the Finance Committee apparently neither requested nor received a schedule of the total amount and maturities of Enron's on- and off-balance sheet obligations.

The Finance Committee Charter required that this committee: review and monitor [the Company's] liquidity, including debt maturities, and its contingent liabilities, including its counter-party and currency risk, exposure under outstanding letters of indemnity, letters of credit and corporate guarantees, and review and approve for recommendation to the Board of Directors, if appropriate, the Company's policies with regard thereto.

Instead of monitoring the amounts and maturities of Enron's obligations, however, the Finance Committee focused on the ratios that guided the credit agency ratings. The problems with relying solely on this system of monitoring Enron's obligations were twofold. First, Enron's use of many of its SPE transactions was designed to have no adverse impact on the ratios. Second, the maturities of these SPE off-balance sheet transactions were not apparent from those ratios. Therefore, the $11 billion of obligations coming due from October 2001 through December 2002 were not disclosed in the ratios.

Management failed to present clearly Enron's SPE transactions and the total amount and maturities of its off-balance sheet debt to the Finance Committee. Similarly, management failed to disclose these transactions adequately in its financial statements. The Finance Committee, however, is subject to criticism for failing to recognize that they were not getting adequate information from management on this increasingly important part of Enron's financial structure. This criticism is not meant to imply that there was not any information being supplied to the Board. In fact, in some circumstances it appears that there was so much information presented that it inhibited any meaningful discussion.

It is not the use of SPE off-balance sheet transactions *per se* that should have concerned the Finance Committee. As the Examiner has observed, their use is acceptable if accounted for and disclosed properly. The question is whether these presentations to the Finance Committee should have caused its members to ask additional questions. A full discussion of questions as simple as the following may have elicited some useful information:

How many transactions?
How much cash was raised?
What are Enron's obligations under these transactions?
When are these obligations due?

How is Enron reporting them?

Why don't these transactions adversely affect Enron's investment grade credit rating ratios?

Audit Committee

The Audit Committee also did not serve as an effective check. It had many items to watch and devoted too little time to watching them. The Audit Committee meetings in February 2000 and 2001 illustrated the shortcomings. In each of these meetings, the committee had three major items to consider. In addition to these three items, it was to consider any other matters brought before it. In February 2000, these other matters included: (i) a report on final New York Stock Exchange and SEC rules regarding audit committees; (ii) a report on the 2000 Internal Audit Plan; (iii) a report on the significant reserves in the financial statements; (iv) a report on market risk including the 1999 profit and loss and value at risk by commodity group; (v) an executive session to consider the appointment of independent auditors for 2000; and (vi) an executive session with Andersen to discuss any problems or disagreements with management. The February 2000 Audit Committee meeting lasted one hour and ten minutes. That amount of time does not appear to be sufficient for meaningful reports, much less full and complete questions and discussion of those matters presented.

Andersen reported that "the Company's sophisticated business practices introduced a high number of accounting models and applications requiring complex interpretations and judgments and that the broadness of the SEC business-related disclosure requirements added to the complexity of the Company's financial reporting." Again, a full discussion of questions as simple as the following may have elicited some helpful information:

What were some of the disclosure issues in the financial statements that are before us and that we are being asked to approve at this meeting?

What are some of the areas on the financial statements that required complex interpretations and accounting judgments so that I can see how much is at stake if others were to reach different judgments than you?

Is there anything we should be doing to make those accounting judgments easier or the disclosures more transparent and complete?

What is the likelihood that these judgments could be incorrect? If so, what are the consequences?

What alternative accounting treatments exist and why did management select and you concur in the treatments used in these financial statements?

There is no record of whether or to what extent any meaningful discussion took place in which Andersen was asked to explain the accounting and disclosure judgments or the magnitude of their impact on Enron's financial statements. In the Audit Committee's defense, however, it did not have the benefit of the concerns that Andersen had expressed internally and it was told that a "clean" opinion would be delivered. Nonetheless, asking questions like those described above may have provoked meaningful discussion of some of these issues.

In February 2001, the Audit Committee meeting lasted one hour and thirty-five minutes plus an additional ten minutes the following morning when the Audit

Committee went into executive session to recommend the approval of Andersen as the company's independent accountants for the following year. In addition to . . . three major items the Audit Committee was to consider and discuss . . . there were six other items: (i) a presentation by Enron's General Counsel, Derrick, on the legal matters in the footnotes to the financial statements; (ii) the required report of the committee to be included in the proxy statement; (iii) the revised Audit and Compliance Committee Charter; (iv) the annual report on executive and director use of company aircraft; (v) a report on the 2001 Internal Control Audit Plan; and (vi) a report on the company's polices and practices for management's communications with analysts.

The minutes of the meeting do not indicate the time spent on individual issues. The length of the meeting, however, raises a question as to whether there could have been meaningful consideration and discussion on any of them. Andersen reminded the Audit Committee, although somewhat obliquely, that "the Company continued to utilize highly structured transactions, such as securitizations and syndications, in which there was significant judgement required in the application of GAAP." Yet again, a full discussion of questions as simple as the following may have elicited some helpful information:

What transactions?
How much money is involved?
Should we consider other products and transactions?
Should we consider alternative accounting treatments or models?
What happens if these judgments are wrong?
Which transactions or judgments are the most risky and what are the primary
    issues?

POSSIBLE EXPLANATIONS FOR THE ENRON BOARD'S FAILURE

Many of Enron's Outside Directors had skills and talents that likely were beneficial to Enron in the operation of its business, and these contributions should not be underestimated. It appears from the evidence, however, that the Outside Directors did not understand important aspects about Enron's use of SPE transactions.

There may be several possible explanations for the Board's failure to understand these transactions. As discussed above, Enron officers often used misleading terms and confusing jargon, and they presented information to the Enron Board and its committees in a manner that obfuscated the substance of the SPE transactions. In addition, the length of Board and committee meetings, given the complexity and the number of agenda items covered, raises questions of whether sufficient time was devoted to allowing the Outside Directors to understand the transactions. Finally, Enron's Board was unusually large, which may have increased the tendency for individual directors not to feel personally responsible for understanding complex matters. Despite the large number of directors, however, the Board did not appear to have sufficient expertise in the kinds of complicated structured financings in which Enron engaged.

Time

In addition to being large and complex, Enron changed its business strategy dramatically during the late 1990s, requiring the Outside Directors to learn and adjust to the company's transition from a "pipeline company" to a "trading company." Board meetings typically lasted a total of about four to five hours, and committee meetings were generally not more than ninety minutes each. With the large number of significant agenda topics presented at each meeting, these circumstances raise questions of whether the Outside Directors had sufficient time to discuss and understand the matters fully. Although none of the Outside Directors admitted in testimony that they felt the Board or committee meetings were too short, several directors provided such criticism in a Board self-assessment they completed in 2001 . . . :

Reliance on Other Board Members

The Enron Board was unusually large. A recent survey of public companies reported an average board size of 9.4 total directors, with an average of 6.9 "independent" or outside directors, less than Enron's 15 to 19 directors. A consequence of the large size can be a tendency for the individual directors not to feel personal responsibility for understanding complex matters. Several of the Outside Directors testified that they might not have understood an area of the company's operations or a particular matter, but they were not concerned because they expected that someone else on the Board did. For example, Chan, who served on both the Audit and Finance Committees, testified that he relied on other Audit Committee members Jaedicke, Gramm and John Duncan to understand whether it was appropriate for Andersen to provide both external and internal audit functions at Enron: "For something like that, I do rely on my colleagues at the audit committee — such as Bob Jaedicke was much more qualified in this regard, and certainly he has, you know, mentioned about — these concepts, and that's how I learned about it."

Lack of Structured Finance Expertise

The Board did not include a large number of Outside Directors who had hands-on experience in the types of sophisticated financings employed by Enron. In the 2001 Board Assessment, the directors acknowledged this lack of depth on the Board.

CONCLUSIONS

For several reasons, the Enron Board did not function as an effective check and balance. This failure may have resulted from (i) a carefully orchestrated strategy of Enron's senior officers, (ii) the failure of Lay and Skilling, in their capacities as executive officers, to assist the Outside Directors, (iii) inadequate assistance from Enron's professionals, (iv) inattention by the Enron Board to its oversight function, or (v) insufficient understanding of how the SPE transactions were being used by Enron's officers.

b. WorldCom

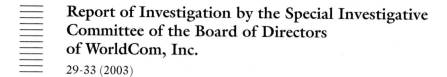

Report of Investigation by the Special Investigative Committee of the Board of Directors of WorldCom, Inc.

29-33 (2003)

WorldCom's collapse reflected not only a financial fraud but also a major failure of corporate governance. The Board of Directors, though apparently unaware of the fraud, played far too small a role in the life, direction and culture of the Company. Although the Board, at least in form, appeared to satisfy many checklists of the time, it did not exhibit the energy, judgment, leadership or courage that WorldCom needed.

We found no evidence that members of the Board of Directors, other than Ebbers and Sullivan, were aware of the improper accounting practices at the time they occurred. We have reviewed materials (including slide presentations) the Board received and have not found information that should reasonably have led it to detect the practices or to believe that further specific inquiry into the accounting practices at issue was necessary.

The Board received regular financial and operational presentations that included a level of detail consistent with what we believe most properly run Boards received during that period. The reduced levels of line costs that resulted from release of accruals and improper capitalization did not appear unusual, in part because the entire purpose of the improper accounting exercise was to hold line costs at a level consistent with earlier periods. It is possible, however, that a Board more closely familiar with what was happening operationally in the Company might have questioned financial trends and comparisons with competitors, including the level of reported capital expenditures: the Board received reports that capital expenditures were declining — as the Board had directed — but in fact capital spending was being slashed much more heavily. There was a disparity between the large cuts that were actually taking place and the reported numbers, which were being pushed back up by the improperly added capitalized line costs.

The Board and its Committees did not function in a way that made it likely that they would notice red flags. The outside Directors had little or no involvement in the Company's business other than through attendance at Board meetings. Nearly all of the Directors were legacies of companies that WorldCom, under Ebbers' leadership, had acquired. They had ceded leadership to Ebbers when their companies were acquired, and in some cases viewed their role as diminished. Ebbers controlled the Board's agenda, its discussions, and its decisions. He created, and the Board permitted, a corporate environment in which the pressure to meet the numbers was high, the departments that served as controls were weak, and the word of senior management was final and not to be challenged.

The Audit Committee in particular needed an understanding of the Company it oversaw in order to be effective. However, the Audit Committee members do not appear to have had a sufficient understanding of the Company's internal financial workings or its culture, and they devoted strikingly little time to their role, meeting as little as three to five hours per year. WorldCom was a complicated Company in a fast-evolving industry. It had expanded quickly, through a series of large acquisitions, and there had been virtually no integration of the acquisitions. WorldCom had accounting-related operations scattered in a variety of locations around the country. These facts raised significant accounting, internal control and systems concerns that required Audit Committee knowledge and attention, and that should also have elicited direct warnings from Andersen. However, the Audit Committee members apparently did not even understand — though the evidence indicates that Andersen disclosed — the nontraditional audit approach Andersen employed. To gain the knowledge necessary to function effectively as an Audit Committee would have required a very substantial amount of energy, expertise by at least some of its members, and a greater commitment of time.

The outside Directors had virtually no interaction with Company operational or financial employees other than during the presentations they heard at meetings. While in this respect the Directors were far from unique among directors of large corporations, this lack of contact meant that they had little sense of the culture within the Company, or awareness of issues other than those brought to them by a few senior managers. They were not themselves visible to employees, and there were no systems in place that could have encouraged employees to contact them with concerns about either the accounting entries or operational matters. In short, the Board was removed and detached from the operations of WorldCom to the extent that its members had little sense of what was really going on within the Company.

Ebbers was autocratic in his dealings with the Board, and the Board permitted it. With limited exceptions, the members of the Board were reluctant to challenge Ebbers even when they disagreed with him. They, like most observers, were impressed with the Company's growth and Ebbers' reputation, although they were in some cases mystified or perplexed by his style. This was Ebbers' company. Several members of the Board were sophisticated, yet the members of the Board were deferential to Ebbers and passive in their oversight until April 2002.

The deference of the Compensation Committee and the Board to Ebbers is illustrated by their decisions beginning in September 2000 to authorize corporate loans and guaranties that grew to over $400 million, so that Ebbers could avoid selling WorldCom stock to meet his personal financial obligations. This was not the first occasion on which Ebbers had overextended himself financially and borrowed from the Company: he had done so in 1994 as well. On neither occasion did anyone on the Board challenge Ebbers with respect to his use of WorldCom stock to extend his personal financial empire to the point that it threatened to cause involuntary liquidation of his stock. The approach of the Board, as one member characterized his own view, was to say nothing to Ebbers because they thought Ebbers was a grownup and could manage his own affairs — even though Ebbers' management of his own affairs involved the use of Company funds, eventually to the tune of hundreds of millions of dollars.

We believe that the extension of these loans and guaranties was a 19-month sequence of terrible decisions — badly conceived, and antithetical to shareholder interests — and a major failure of corporate governance. Indeed, we do not understand how the Compensation Committee or the Board could have concluded that these loans were an acceptable use of more than $400 million of the shareholders' money. These decisions reflected an uncritical solicitude for Ebbers' financial interests, a disregard of the incentives the situation created for Ebbers' management of the Company, and a willingness to subordinate shareholders' interests to Ebbers' financial well-being.

A second example of the Board's deference is its failure to challenge Ebbers on the extent of his substantial outside business interests (and the resulting claim on his time and energies). Those interests included a Louisiana rice farm, a luxury yacht building company, a lumber mill, a country club, a trucking company, a minor league hockey team, an operating marina, and a building in downtown Chicago. We do not believe most properly run Boards of Directors would permit a Chief Executive Officer to pursue an array of interests such as these, certainly not without careful examination of the time and energy commitments they would require. Yet we have seen no evidence of any such challenge.

Notes and Questions

1. Notes

a. Enron is incorporated in Oregon and WorldCom in Georgia. Both are MBCA states.

b. In the wake of Enron, WorldCom, and other corporate scandals, Congress passed the Sarbanes-Oxley Act of 2002 (SOx). Among the requirements applicable to boards of directors, are that audit committees must be directly responsible for retaining the independent accountants and must establish internal corporate procedures for receiving whistle-blowing information. Further, every audit committee must contain at least one "financial expert."[2]

2. Reality Check

a. What sort of activities should the Enron and WorldCom boards have engaged in?

b. How did the directors' conduct fall short?

c. Are there significant differences in the conduct or dynamics of the Enron and WorldCom boards?

In terms of corporate law, it seems clear that the wrongdoers in Enron and WorldCom are liable to the corporation for breach of their fiduciary duties. Even those wrongdoers who were not officers or directors doubtless owe fiduciary duties under agency law. But what about the board members who were not actively involved in the frauds? Presumably they have met their duty of loyalty but may have violated their *Caremark* duties or their duty of care. You may be thinking that Enron and WorldCom shareholders brought actions against those loyal directors, but in fact derivative actions were not pressed. The reason is probably due to the nature of derivative actions, which we will see in more detail in Chapter 14. A breach of

---

2. Actually, SOx only requires companies to state whether the audit committee has at least one financial expert and, if not, why not. As a practical matter, this imposes a requirement that every audit committee have at least one financial expert.

fiduciary duty is a harm to the corporation, not a harm to the shareholders directly. Any recovery goes to the corporation. In the normal course of things, a corporate recovery benefits the shareholders, but when the corporation is bankrupt, as both Enron and WorldCom were, the recovery would benefit the creditors rather than the shareholders. Thus shareholders have little incentive to bring breach of fiduciary duty actions against the loyal directors. Further, given the business judgment rule presumption, how likely is it that a complaint against the loyal directors would survive past the 12(b)(6) stage? As we will see at the end of this chapter, the loyal directors entered into settlements involving significant payments from their personal assets. The theory of that litigation was not state corporate law but federal securities law.

2. Internal Actors Below the Board

All corporate power is located in the board of directors. Obviously, though, the board does not approve every corporate act nor can the board have knowledge of everything that occurs within the corporation. Thus, when we consider whether the constraints explored in Chapters 10-12 are effective, we must also look at the behavior of individuals within the corporation who are not directors. As noted above, nearly every financial accounting fraud, and every such fraud of large size, involves senior officers. These officers report to, and the CEO is typically a member of, the board of directors. The initial descriptions of the Enron and WorldCom scandals detailed the involvement of the senior officers. The following extract speaks to the possible rationalization of Enron and WorldCom officers' conduct. Before you read these excerpts you may wish to review the material on decision making in Chapter 3.

a. Officers

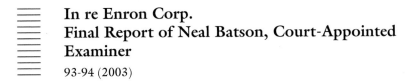

In re Enron Corp.
Final Report of Neal Batson, Court-Appointed
Examiner
93-94 (2003)

The Examiner now focuses on several methods used by these officers to facilitate their use of the [fraudulent] accounting techniques. These methods include:

Justification of Desired Results. In many cases, Enron officers were less concerned about making the correct or best decision, and more concerned with justifying a desired result. Evidence suggests that Enron officers: (i) used accounting rules that did not directly address the accounting question at issue but provided an argument to justify an aggressive position; (ii) searched for reasons to avoid public disclosure; and (iii) obtained professional opinions or advice merely as a necessary procedural step.

Use of Economic Leverage on Third Parties. Evidence suggests that by using Enron's economic power, Enron officers were able to pressure third parties, such as financial institutions and Enron's professionals, to accommodate Enron's financial statement objectives. In many instances, this economic pressure appears responsible for overcoming concerns about reputational risk or other reservations by these third parties.

Lack of Candor. There are many examples of incomplete disclosure by these officers to the Enron Board and the public. In some cases, it appears that officers provided hints or glimpses of facts suggesting possible misuse of SPEs to the Enron Board. In other cases, Enron officers' frequent use of misleading terms and jargon in connection with Enron's SPE transactions appears to have obscured their economic substance. Finally, evidence indicates that when information was presented by the officers to the Enron Board, the information was delivered in a manner not conducive to a full understanding of the SPEs.

Notes and Questions

1. Notes

a. SOx imposed many new obligations on senior officers of public companies. The CEO and CFO must now certify the accuracy of the financial information in each quarterly and annual SEC filing and certify that they have told the independent auditors of any significant deficiencies in internal controls and any fraud of which they are aware. They must also certify that they are responsible for establishing and maintaining internal controls that, in effect, conform to *Caremark* requirements. Further, the corporation's annual report must describe and assess the corporation's internal controls. Corporations must also adopt a code of ethics for their CFOs. Corporations are now prohibited from making loans to senior executives, such as those made to Mr. Ebbers.

2. What Do You Think?

a. Do you think individuals who have careers as senior officers at large public corporations have a greater propensity to commit fraud than other people do? Do you think individuals who have careers as corporate managers have a greater propensity to commit fraud than other people do?

b. In-House Attorneys and Internal Auditors

Within every large corporation (and many small ones, too) are in-house lawyers and other people employed to conduct audits of the corporation's activities. These actors are different from most other employees because their tasks do not lead directly to the production and sale of goods or services. Rather, they are ancillary to the principal activities of the corporation. Nonetheless, they may have important roles to play in constraining corporate actions. You may wish to review the material in Chapter 1 on practicing corporate law.

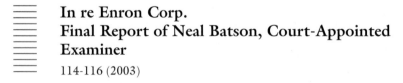

In re Enron Corp.
Final Report of Neal Batson, Court-Appointed Examiner
114-116 (2003)

By analyzing the structure of the SPE transactions and documenting them, and by providing opinions in various transactions, Enron's attorneys also played a vital role in Enron's access to the capital markets. These attorneys could have provided a check and balance against the Enron officers' wrongdoing. Among other things, these attorneys could have apprised [Enron's general counsel] or the Enron Board when they knew of conduct that could result in Enron disseminating materially misleading financial information, or they could have refused to render legal services in connection with SPE transactions when they had concerns about their propriety.

One explanation for the attorneys' failure may be that they lost sight of the fact that the corporation was their client. It appears that some of these attorneys considered the officers to be their clients when, in fact, the attorneys owed duties to Enron. Another explanation may be that some of these attorneys saw their role in very narrow terms, as an implementer, not a counselor. That is, rather than conscientiously raising known issues for further analysis by a more senior officer or the Enron Board or refusing to participate in transactions that raised such issues, these lawyers seemed to focus only on how to address a narrow question or simply to implement a decision (or document a transaction). In other cases, Enron's in-house attorneys knew that the Enron Board did not have all relevant facts before it, but took no action to correct that problem.

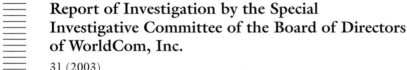

Report of Investigation by the Special Investigative Committee of the Board of Directors of WorldCom, Inc.

31 (2003)

Neither WorldCom's legal department nor Internal Audit was structured to maximize its effectiveness as a control structure upon which the Board could depend. At Ebbers' direction, the Company's lawyers were in fragmented groups, several of which had General Counsels who did not report to WorldCom's General Counsel for portions of the relevant period; they were not located geographically near senior management or involved in its inner workings; and they had inadequate support from senior management. Internal Audit — though eventually successful in revealing the fraud — had been structured in ways that made this accomplishment more difficult: it reported in most respects to Sullivan, and until 2002 its duties generally did not include financial reporting matters.

Notes and Questions

1. Notes

a. The SEC rules adopted in light of SOx impose a duty on lawyers to report misconduct up the corporate hierarchy to the board of directors, if necessary. *See* Chapter 1 for a discussion of this attorney role.

2. What Do You Think?

a. How could these professionals have become so marginalized within the corporations?

b. How can this kind of marginalization be prevented? What do you think are the early warning signs of this kind of dynamic?

3. Reputational Intermediaries

A third, and vital, check on board action comprises independent institutions that vouch for the corporation's actions. You might recall from Chapter 4 that agents and principals often use third parties to signal their quality to one another. Third parties who themselves have a high reputation are able, in effect, to endow others with that reputation. Of course, third parties who vouch for those who turn out to be of low quality will lose their own reputations. Hence they have an incentive to seek out only those for whom they can safely vouch. These third parties are sometimes called *reputational intermediaries*. In the business world, there may be many such reputational intermediaries, but three are of particular importance.

a. Outside Law Firms

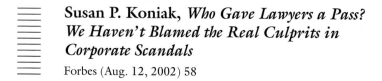

Susan P. Koniak, *Who Gave Lawyers a Pass?*
We Haven't Blamed the Real Culprits in
Corporate Scandals
Forbes (Aug. 12, 2002) 58

We're pointing the finger at everyone but the real culprits in corporate scandals.

We know the usual suspects in the current wave of corporate scandals: accountants, greedy bosses, lackadaisical directors, the projections-for-hire analysts and institutional investors asleep at the switch. But a group's missing: lawyers. The dirty secret of the mess is that without lawyers few scandals would exist, and fewer still would last long enough to cause any real harm. Lawyers need to be regulated. No other legal reform enacted will do any good as long as there are no consequences to lawyers who bless anything a manager wants to do.

Take the Enron case. When Vinson & Elkins, a Texas-based law firm, wasn't approving one of Enron's shady related transactions, another firm was. Chicago's Kirkland & Ellis represented Andrew Fastow's Enron-related partnerships, which engaged in transactions of such doubtful legality that it is difficult to imagine a lawyer not noticing.

Some set of lawyers wrote Arthur Andersen's "document retention" policy, which encourages the destruction of documents even when doing so might be a crime. A lawyer, Nancy Temple, instructed former Andersen partner David Duncan to heed that policy, and he did. A month later, when she told Duncan to preserve everything, he again complied. The testimony given under oath leads me to this conclusion: Had a lawyer explained the law and advised Duncan to follow it from the beginning, Andersen would not have faced obstruction charges.

Is it good that a profession so prone to harming clients and shareholders remain virtually unpoliced? Three avenues of regulation exist: state disciplinary authorities, the Securities & Exchange Commission and private lawsuits against lawyers. None of them now works.

Disciplinary authorities are charged with enforcing state ethics rules, which are law. In all my research, I have come across no state disciplinary authority that has initiated charges against a big law firm for aiding securities fraud. The disciplinary authority would be absurdly outgunned.

Every state's ethics rules prohibit assisting client fraud and demand that a lawyer resign when he "knows" his services are being used for fraud. Lawyers never "know," and thus never have to resign. Other ethics rules allow lawyers to do certain things, like alert the chief executive or board to corporate fraud; some allow lawyers to tell the SEC. But none of that is required.

The law that prohibits aiding and abetting fraud applies to everyone, including lawyers. But prosecutors rarely enforce it against lawyers. Private suits for aiding were allowed until the Supreme Court eliminated those in 1994. Congress worsened matters by limiting the SEC's ability to bring aiding-and-abetting cases.

The SEC scarcely needed any curbing. Twice in its history it had gotten serious about regulating the bar. Both times the bar beat the agency back. In 1981 the SEC in effect conceded defeat, ending efforts to rein in lawyers. And [the] SEC, even post-Enron, has said that policing lawyers is not on its agenda.

Because lawyers are necessary to commit almost any fraud of more than a moment's duration, their firms' survival should be on the line. What's needed is to restore aiding-and-abetting liability, joint-and-several liability and the recklessness standard, at least for lawyers. The Senate passed Senator John Edwards' amendment requiring lawyers to report evidence of fraud up the corporate ladder. . . .

The lawyer problem is systemic: no "few bad apples" here. Neither moral outrage nor proposals for reform have come from the President, our financial wise men like Warren Buffett and Alan Greenspan, or the press. Even companies that suffered greatly from outsize management fraud, all of which should be suing their lawyers for malpractice, aren't and won't — too many skeletons. This is a disgrace.

[Susan Koniak is Professor of Law, Boston University; coauthor, *The Law & Ethics of Lawyering*.]

Notes and Questions

1. Notes

a. SEC rules adopted under SOx requiring lawyers to report misconduct up the ladder to the board, if necessary, also apply to outside counsel.

b. Until the late 1980s virtually every state's laws prohibited lawyers from practicing in entities that provide limited liability. In other words, law firms were general partnerships in which every partner was individually liable for the professional actions of every other partner. Now, virtually every large law firm is either a professional corporation, an LLC, or an LLP. Consider whether there is a link between the rise of limited liability entities for lawyers and the conduct described by Professor Koniak.

b. Independent Accountants

The outside accountants are the quintessential reputational intermediaries. Every public company must be audited each year by an independent accounting firm. Nearly every major public corporation retains one of the Big Four accounting firms.

The following excerpts describe the accounting firm's auditing duties and assess the performance of Arthur Andersen, the auditor for both Enron and WorldCom.

Jonathan Weil, *Missing Numbers—Behind Wave of Corporate Fraud: A Change in How Auditors Work*
Wall St. J. (Mar. 25, 2004) A1

The recent wave of corporate fraud is raising a harsh question about the auditors who review and bless companies' financial results: How could they have missed all the wrongdoing? One little-discussed answer: a big change in the way audits are performed. Consider what happened when James Lamphron and his team of Ernst & Young LLP accountants sat down early last year to plan their audit of Health-South Corp.'s 2002 financial statements. When they asked executives of the Birmingham, Ala., hospital chain if they were aware of any significant instances of fraud, the executives replied no. In their planning papers, the auditors wrote that HealthSouth's system for generating financial data was reliable, the company's executives were ethical, and that HealthSouth's management had "designed an environment for success."

As a result, the auditors performed far fewer tests of the numbers on the company's books than they would have at an audit client where they perceived the risk of accounting fraud to be higher. That's standard practice under the "risk-based audit" approach now used widely throughout the accounting profession. Among the items the Ernst & Young auditors didn't examine at all: additions of less than $5,000 to individual assets on the company's ledger.

Those numbers are where HealthSouth executives hid a big part of a giant fraud. This blind spot in the firm's auditing procedures is a key reason why former HealthSouth executives, 15 of whom have pleaded guilty to fraud charges, were able to overstate profits by $3 billion without anyone from Ernst & Young noticing until March 2003, when federal agents began making arrests.

A look at the risk-based approach also helps explain why investors continue to be socked by accounting scandals, from WorldCom Inc. and Tyco International Ltd. to Parmalat SpA, the Italian dairy company that admitted faking $4.8 billion in cash. Just because an accounting firm says it has audited a company's numbers doesn't mean it actually has checked them.

In a September 2003 speech, Daniel Goelzer, a member of the auditing profession's new regulator, the Public Company Accounting Oversight Board, called the risk-based approach one of the key factors "that seem to have contributed to the erosion of trust in auditing." Faced with difficulty in raising audit fees, Mr. Goelzer said, the major accounting firms during the 1990s began to stress cost controls. And they began to place greater emphasis on planning the scope of their work based on auditors' judgments about which clients are risky and which areas of a company's financial reports are most prone to error or fraud.

Auditors still plow through "high risk" items, such as derivative financial instruments or "related party" business dealings between a company and its executives. But ostensibly "low risk" items—such as cash on the balance sheet or accounts that fluctuate little from year to year — often get no more than a cursory review, for years at a stretch. Instead, auditors rely more heavily on what management tells them and the auditors' assessments of a company's "internal controls."

A 2001 brochure by KPMG LLP, which claims to have pioneered the risk-based audit during the early 1990s, explained the difference between the old and new ways. Under a traditional "bottom up" audit, "the auditor gains assurance by examining all of the component parts of the financial statements, ensuring that the transactions recorded are complete and accurate." By comparison, under the "top down" risk-based audit methodology, auditors focus "less on the details of individual transactions" and use their knowledge of a company's business and organization "to identify risks that could affect the financial statements and to target audit effort in those areas."

In theory, the risk-based approach should work fine, if an auditor is good at identifying the areas where misstatements are most likely to occur. Proponents advocate the shift as a cost-efficient improvement. They also say it forces auditors to pay needed attention to areas that are more subjective or complex.

"The problem is that there's not a lot of evidence that auditors are very good at assessing risk," says Charles Cullinan, an accounting professor at Bryant College in Smithfield, R.I., and co-author of a 2002 study that criticized the re-engineered audit process as ineffective at detecting fraud.

Auditors can't check all of a company's numbers, since that would make audits too expensive, particularly in an age of sprawling multinationals. The tools at auditors' disposal can't ensure the reliability of a company's numbers with absolute certainty. And in many ways, they haven't changed much over the modern industry's 160-year history.

Auditors scan the accounting records for inconsistencies. They ask people questions. That can mean independently contacting a client's customers to make sure they haven't struck undocumented side deals — such as agreeing to buy more products today in exchange for a salesperson's oral promises of future discounts. They search for unrecorded liabilities by tracing cash disbursements to make sure the obligations are recorded properly. They examine invoices and the terms of sales contracts to check if a company is recording revenue prematurely.

Auditors are supposed to avoid becoming predictable. Otherwise, a client's management might figure out how to sneak things by them. It's also important to sample-test tiny accounting entries, even as low as a couple of hundred dollars. An old accounting trick is to fudge lots of tiny entries that appear insignificant individually but materially distort a company's financial statements when taken together.

Facing a crush of shareholder lawsuits over the accounting scandals of the past four years, the Big Four accounting firms say they are pouring tens of millions of dollars into improving their auditing techniques. KPMG's investigative division has doubled to 280 its force of forensic specialists, some hailing from the Federal Bureau of Investigation. PricewaterhouseCoopers LLP auditors attend seminars run by former Central Intelligence Agency operatives on how to spot deceitful managers by scrutinizing body language and verbal cues. Role-playing exercises teach how to stand up to a company's management.

But the firms aren't backing away from the concept of the risk-based audit itself. "It would really be negligent" not to take a risk-based approach, says Greg Weaver, head of Deloitte & Touche LLP's U.S. audit practice. Auditors need to "understand the areas that are likely to be more subject to error," he says. "Some might believe that if you cover those high-risk areas, you could do less work in other areas." But, he adds, "I don't think that's been a problem at Deloitte."

Mr. Lamphron, the Ernst & Young partner, and his firm blame HealthSouth's former executives for deceiving them. Mr. Lamphron declined to comment for this article. Testifying before a congressional subcommittee in November, he said he had looked through his audit papers and "tried to find that one string that, had we yanked it, would have unraveled this fraud. I know we planned and conducted a solid audit. We asked the right questions. We sought out the right documentation. Had we asked for additional documentation here or asked another question there, I think that it would have generated another false document and another lie."

[I]n the U.S., the notion of the auditor as detective never quite took off. The Securities and Exchange Commission in the 1930s made audits mandatory for public companies. The auditing profession faced its first real public test in 1937, when an accounting scandal broke open at McKesson & Robbins: More than 20% of the assets reported by the drug company were fictitious inventory and customer IOUs. The auditors had been fooled by forged documents.

The case triggered some reforms. Auditing standards began requiring that auditors perform more substantive tests, such as contacting third parties to confirm customer IOUs and physically inspecting clients' warehouses to check inventories.

By the 1970s, a new force emerged to erode audit quality: price competition. Bidding wars ensued. The pressures to hold down hours on a job "inadvertently discouraged auditors to look for" fraud, says Toby Bishop, president of the Association of Certified Fraud Examiners, a professional association.

Increasingly, audits became a commodity product. Economic pressures also brought a wave of mergers, winnowing down the number of accounting firms just as the number of publicly traded companies was exploding and corporate financial statements were becoming more complex.

Looking back, the risk-based approach's flaws are on display at a variety of accounting scandals, from WorldCom to Tyco to HealthSouth.

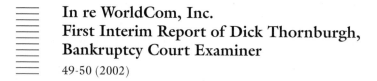

In re WorldCom, Inc.
First Interim Report of Dick Thornburgh,
Bankruptcy Court Examiner
49-50 (2002)

The objective of an audit of a company's financial statements by an independent auditor is the expression of an opinion on the fairness with which the financial statements present, in all material respects, the financial position, results of operations, and cash flows of the company in conformity with GAAP. An independent auditor is required under GAAS to state whether, in its opinion, the financial statements are presented in conformity with GAAP.

[A]n auditor has a responsibility to plan and perform the audit to obtain reasonable, but not absolute, assurance about whether the financial statements are free of material misstatement, whether caused by error or fraud. A proper audit includes examining, on a test basis, evidence supporting the amounts and disclosures in the financial statements, assessing the accounting principles used and significant estimates made by management, and evaluating the overall financial statements presentation. An audit is not intended to provide a guarantee regarding the accuracy of the financial statements. Accordingly, a material misstatement may remain undetected.

Ultimately, a company's financial statements are the responsibility of management. Management is responsible for adopting sound accounting policies and for establishing and maintaining internal controls that will, among other things, record, process, summarize, and report transactions consistently and accurately.

Report of Investigation by the Special Investigative Committee of the Board of Directors of WorldCom, Inc.

25-28 (2003)

WHY WORLDCOM'S AUDITORS DID NOT DISCOVER THE FRAUD

We have found no evidence that WorldCom's independent, external auditors, Arthur Andersen, were aware of the capitalization of line costs or determined that WorldCom's revenues were improperly reported. We had access to only a portion of Andersen's documents, and Andersen personnel refused to speak with us. Therefore, we cannot answer with certainty the question why Andersen failed to detect such a large fraud.

Based on the materials available to us, the blame for Andersen's failure to detect the fraud appears to lie with personnel both at Andersen and at WorldCom. There were apparent flaws in Andersen's audit approach, which limited the likelihood it would detect the accounting irregularities. Moreover, Andersen appears to have missed several opportunities that might have led to the discovery of management's misuse of accruals, the capitalization of line costs, and the improper recognition of revenue items. For their part, certain WorldCom personnel maintained inappropriately tight control over information that Andersen needed, altered documents with the apparent purpose of concealing from Andersen items that might have raised questions, and were not forthcoming in other respects. Andersen, knowing in some instances that it was receiving less than full cooperation on critical aspects of its work, failed to bring this to the attention of WorldCom's Audit Committee.

Andersen employed an approach to its audit that it itself characterized as different from the "traditional audit approach." It focused heavily on identifying risks and assessing whether the Company had adequate controls in place to mitigate those risks, rather than emphasizing the traditional substantive testing of information maintained in accounting records and financial statements. This approach is not unique to Andersen, and it was disclosed to the Audit Committee. But a consequence of this approach was that if Andersen failed to identify a significant risk, or relied on Company controls without adequately determining that they were worthy of reliance, there would be insufficient testing to make detection of fraud likely.

Andersen does not appear to have performed adequate testing to justify reliance on WorldCom's controls. We found hundreds of huge, round-dollar journal entries made by the staff of the General Accounting group without proper support. . . . And where we did find documentary support it was frequently disorganized and maintained haphazardly. These deficiencies made reliance on controls impossible. We do not understand how they escaped Andersen's notice.

Andersen concluded year after year that the risk of fraud was no greater than a moderate risk, and thus it never devised sufficient auditing procedures to address this risk. It did so despite rating WorldCom a "maximum risk" client — an assessment Andersen never disclosed to the Audit Committee — and having given management less than favorable ratings in a few areas (such as accounting and disclosure practices, behavior toward Andersen's work, and policies to prevent or detect fraud) in Andersen internal documents. Andersen relied heavily on senior management and did not conduct tests to corroborate the information it received in many areas. It assumed incorrectly that the absence of variances in the financial statements and schedules — in a highly volatile business environment — indicated there was no cause for heightened scrutiny. As a result, Andersen conducted only very limited audit procedures in many areas where we found accounting irregularities.

WorldCom, for its part, exerted excessive control over Andersen's access to information, and was not candid in at least some of its dealings with Andersen. The WorldCom personnel who dealt most often with Andersen controlled Andersen's access to information in several respects. They denied Andersen's requests to speak with some employees. They "struck" Andersen's requests for detailed information, supporting documentation, or material that they felt was overly burdensome. WorldCom personnel also repeatedly rejected Andersen's requests for access to the computerized General Ledger through which Internal Audit and others discovered the capitalization of line costs. And they fostered an attitude in which questions from Andersen were to be parried, rather than answered openly. Of course, it was Andersen's responsibility to overcome those obstacles to perform an appropriate audit, and to inform the Audit Committee of the difficulties it faced, but it did not do so. Moreover, certain members of WorldCom's management altered significant documents before providing them to Andersen, with the apparent purpose of hampering Andersen's ability to identify problems at the Company.

Notes and Questions

1. Notes

a. Arthur Andersen's involvement with Enron resulted in its indictment and conviction for obstruction of justice. As a consequence, it could no longer act as an accountant for public companies. Arthur Andersen effectively went out of business, reducing the number of major accounting firms to four.

b. Many SOx provisions affect public accounting firms. First, it severely restricts the additional services a company's auditing firm can provide. This is to reduce the accounting firm's incentive to go lightly on the audit in hopes of currying favor with corporate management, who will purchase nonaudit services from the firm. Second, the accounting firm partner (but not the firm itself) in charge of a particular corporation's account must rotate off such assignment every five years. Third, the auditors must report directly to the corporation's audit committee.

2. Reality Check

a. What is the difference between traditional auditing and risk-based auditing?

b. Why has risk-based auditing become so popular?

3. What Do You Think?

a. How do you think Arthur Andersen should have acted differently?

b. If the accountants simply failed to catch fraud that was actively being concealed from them, is it fair to fault them?

c. Credit-Rating Agencies

Both Enron and WorldCom were greatly concerned with the credit rating on their corporate debt. Much of the purpose of the financial fraud at both corporations was to preserve high credit ratings. The following article puts the role of credit-rating agencies in perspective.

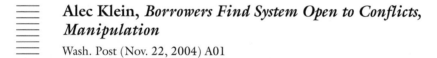

Alec Klein, *Borrowers Find System Open to Conflicts, Manipulation*
Wash. Post (Nov. 22, 2004) A01

In the months leading to the collapse of WorldCom Inc., its shares were in a nose-dive, traders were selling its bonds at junk levels and its chief executive was forced out. But not until investors lost several billion dollars did Congress and others begin to rivet attention to a little-known player in this unfolding drama: the credit raters. WorldCom rose to prominence through voracious acquisitions, including the bold 1998 purchase of MCI, the District-based long-distance telephone company. And it couldn't have done it without the rating companies. WorldCom borrowed money through the sale of bonds, which the rating firms approved by giving them good grades, a signal that they were relatively safe investments.

As it turned out, nothing could have been further from the truth. But the rating firms were among the last to recognize it. It wasn't until weeks before WorldCom disclosed massive fraud and filed the biggest bankruptcy in U.S. history in 2002 that the credit raters finally cut the firm's debt to junk status.

The rating companies say they are not in the business of detecting fraud; rather, they say they give an opinion of the creditworthiness of a company, municipality or nation. But some critics say the WorldCom case highlights a broader problem: that the world's big three credit raters — Moody's Investors Service, Standard & Poor's and Fitch Ratings — have become some of the most important gatekeepers in capitalism without the commensurate oversight or accountability.

From their Manhattan offices, they can, with the stroke of a pen, effectively add or subtract millions from a company's bottom line, rattle a city budget, shock the stock and bond markets and reroute international investment. Without their ratings, in many cases, factories can't expand, schools can't get built, highways can't be paved. Yet there is no formal structure for overseeing the credit raters, no one designated to take complaints about them, and no regulations about employee qualifications.

The big three ostensibly function as a disinterested priesthood. When a company, town or entire nation wants to borrow money by selling bonds, the market almost always requires that the rating companies bless the move by running a kind of credit check. Bonds they deem safe get a good rating. The higher the rating, the lower the interest rate the borrower must pay.

But at the heart of the increasingly profitable business is a conflict: The rating companies get the bulk of their revenue from the fees they charge to the very entities they are rating. Industry insiders say the desire of a rater to hold on to a paying client — or recruit a new one — at times has interfered with the objectivity of a rating.

Those who disagree with a rating have little recourse. Lawsuits generally have been unsuccessful because courts have upheld the rating companies' argument that they are publishers of opinions, like newspapers, and that their views are protected by the First Amendment.

With little public debate about the industry, the rating business has eluded a series of reforms that have been imposed on other parts of the U.S. financial system. For example, while hundreds of companies and institutions, such as the New York Stock Exchange, have eliminated potential conflicts on their boards, Moody's directors continue to serve on the boards of companies that also are Moody's clients. (Moody's officials say that their directors play no role in ratings decisions.)

And even as accounting firms have curtailed offering consulting services to their clients to avoid conflicts, some credit raters have begun to sell their own consulting services, raising concerns that clients may feel pressured to buy them.

For their part, the credit raters say they ably manage potential conflicts. They say they adhere to strict codes of conduct, such as prohibiting any link between the pay and bonuses of their rating analysts and the fees that come in from the companies those analysts rate. The rating companies also say they perform a public service by allowing investors to compare the relative risk of buying bonds from almost any seller.

And the credit raters say their success over time shows the ratings process works, and that their ratings bring stability to the markets, giving companies and countries access to capital.

The rating companies say they do their job without regard to the impact, basing their ratings largely on statistical calculations of a borrower's likelihood of default. Subjective factors sometimes come into play, rating officials say, given that there are some two dozen categories ranging from the best, "AAA," to a low of "C" or "D." That subjectivity can be costly. For a borrower, the difference of a single rating notch could mean millions of extra dollars in interest payments.

The rating companies officially fall under the purview of the Securities and Exchange Commission. But even as the SEC has clamped down on accountants, stock analysts and investment bankers, the regulator has not imposed rules on the rating companies. The SEC, which declined to comment for this article, said it continues to study the issue.

Despite their complaints, the industry has received little public attention largely because its workings are complex and its clients are institutions rather than people. (The creditworthiness of consumers is rated by a different set of companies, which operate under extensive federal and state regulation.) But after the collapse of such companies as WorldCom and Enron Corp., Congress ordered the SEC to consider whether new rules were needed.

The big three credit-rating firms wield power through letter grades they hand out. They explain their ratings approach in pamphlets and on their Web sites. But the process itself has remained a mystery of finance.

Committees of rating analysts, headed by one lead analyst, meet privately to weigh the financial strengths and weaknesses of those who want to sell bonds. Then, they emerge to give the bond a rating, announcing it to the world. The companies don't say who voted or how the vote broke down.

The rating companies say they get their ratings right most of the time, pointing to their own studies showing that the higher the rating, the lower the rate of default. Out of 98 defaults in 2003, S&P said, only three were companies that had in the past 12 months held investment-grade ratings, which are considered relatively safe for investors. Still, since only a tiny fraction of all bond issuers ever default, the odds of being right are very high, some critics point out.

[Vickie A. Tillman, executive vice president of S&P's credit market services] said that because it takes a majority of the committee to approve a rating, no one person can skew the process. Those familiar with the process, however, say the committee usually follows the lead analyst because the others often don't have the time to review the work as closely.

The lead analyst's recommendation is "the basis on which everything is turning" and is upheld about 80 percent of the time, said Hans van den Houten, a former Fitch and Moody's executive who also served as an outside recruiter for S&P until earlier this year.

That can sometimes tempt the lead analyst to let personal feelings influence the review of a client's finances. This happened to a former Moody's analyst rating a company at which one executive was a close friend from a previous job.

"I bent over backward to come up with the best result because I care for this person," said the analyst, who spoke on the condition that neither he nor the company he was rating be identified. Later, after the company's performance sagged, the analyst came to see that he had rated it too high.

If an analyst's feelings go the other way, it can cost a company money. Computer Associates International Inc., which has had recent run-ins with U.S. authorities about its accounting, earned a tough reputation for the way it deals with rating analysts. "They were definitely aggressive and abrasive and engendered a combative response from the rating agency," a former rating analyst said.

Computer Associates, which declined to comment, held a rating last year barely at investment-grade. Based on financials alone, it would likely have been higher, but its combative executives alienated some analysts. The company's rating ended up lower than expected, costing it potentially millions in extra interest payments. "Maybe a full notch is [due to] their personality," the former analyst said.

Analysts say it's reasonable to use their judgment to assess how well a company's executives make business decisions. But reservations about management will not necessarily show up in the rating firm's public report.

"You don't want to say you don't like these guys," another former rating official said. "You have nothing to point to, but it was discussed in the committee."

Moody's president, Raymond W. McDaniel Jr., declined to discuss specific cases. "The ratings process is produced by human beings, and human beings have views and emotions about certain things," he said, adding that Moody's tracks the quality of its ratings.

"We do not deny there are latent or inherent conflicts of interest in our business," McDaniel said. "The important thing is, how do we manage those conflicts?"

Credit raters say that other industries, including newspapers, have to cope with similar conflicts. "Our practice is no different from the *Washington Post* who will run ads from Ford, AT&T, Merrill Lynch or dozens of other companies while at the same time reporting on them every day," Fitch said in a written response to questions.

Some rating companies cited a 2003 study by two economists who work for the Federal Reserve who found "no evidence" that ratings are affected by conflicts of interest, but rather that credit raters "appear to be relatively responsive to reputation concerns and so protect the interests of investors."

Because the major rating companies juggle tens of thousands of debt issues at any given time, many are given cursory attention, according to current and former rating analysts and those they rate. An analyst will cover as many as 55 borrowers at once. And in recent years, the credit raters say analyzing debt has become more complicated, involving more financial provisions.

"You can't monitor all those companies," one former rating analyst said.

So why don't raters hire more analysts? "It would cut into their profitability," he said.

The credit raters say they have a sufficient number of analysts to cover companies throughout the world. Still, at Moody's at least, according to some current officials and former analysts, committee meetings on occasion are hastily arranged, include only two analysts and last minutes, or seconds.

"We had a colloquial term for that," said W. Bruce Jones, a former Moody's official who works for a small competitor, Egan-Jones Ratings Co. "We called it a 'water cooler rating.'"

One meeting that took only minutes involved Omnicare Inc., a supplier of pharmaceutical services to nursing homes, when it announced plans to acquire competitor NCS HealthCare Inc. in 2002, according to another former Moody's analyst.

As soon as the deal, worth more than $400 million, looked imminent, the analyst said he dropped into a supervisor's office and quickly explained that he assumed Omnicare would sell bonds to make the acquisition. As a result, he was going to put its rating on review for a potential downgrade.

He didn't need to explain why: By carrying more debt, the company would become a bigger credit risk. The supervisor promptly gave the analyst approval to proceed.

That was the committee meeting.

Within about a half-hour, the decision flashed to some 5,000 news services around the globe. About six months later, however, Moody's took Omnicare's credit off review. The company planned to use stock, not just loans, to buy its competitor. That meant Omnicare's debt wouldn't be as large as the Moody's analyst had anticipated.

McDaniel of Moody's said his company works diligently to provide well-researched ratings. "We treat the ratings committee process very seriously," he said, but added, "We don't want to waste people's time."

The rating companies said they already have strong internal controls designed to minimize mistakes or conflicts, including codes of conduct at S&P and Moody's.

Moody's, for instance, instructs employees to do nothing that "might, or might appear to, compromise the integrity" of the rating process. The credit raters say they also conduct ethics training in-house.

Still, some lawmakers — Republicans and Democrats — say the system is flawed. In a House hearing last year, Rep. Paul E. Kanjorski (D-Pa.) said the credit raters' failure to identify problems at WorldCom and other major companies "ultimately resulted in the loss of billions of dollars for American investors who little understood the true credit risks."

Notes and Questions

1. Notes

a. SOx required the SEC to investigate whether more stringent regulation of the credit-rating agencies is called for.

2. Reality Check

a. Why are credit rating agencies so important?
b. How can credit rating agencies help to constrain corporate boards?

d. Securities Analysts

The final reputational intermediary is somewhat different from the other three because the relationship between the intermediary and the corporation is not contractual. Rather, it is more symbiotic. Securities analysts work for brokerage houses, many of which are also investment bankers. Securities analysts, much like journalists, are assigned to cover a particular industry, sometimes even a single corporation. They are expected to investigate the industry and its businesses and to write analytical assessments of both the industry and the businesses that compete. These analyses are used by brokerage houses to recommend stock to their clients. They are also used by the investment banks themselves to decide whether to invest for their own account.

Even though there is no direct contractual relationship between securities analysts and the companies they cover there are mutual advantages to be had or withheld. Analysts have an incentive to ferret out important information and so have an incentive to stay within the good graces of corporations so that their informal access to information will not be cut off. Even better, analysts hope that companies will steer important information to them before giving it to others. Securities analysts have another incentive to please the corporations they cover. That is, that the investment banking side of their employer is always looking for new clients and new work. The investment bank whose analyst writes positive reports on a company believes it has a better chance of landing that company's investment banking business.

Corporations, in contrast, have a great incentive to curry favor with the securities analysts, as well. Some analysts are quite well known in the investment community and thus their views are quite influential. A change in a recommendation from such an analyst is likely to have an immediate and often strong effect on the corporation's stock price.

In re WorldCom, Inc.
First Interim Report of Dick Thornburgh,
Bankruptcy Court Examiner
81-99 (2002)

In theory, at least, analysts promote market efficiency by providing investors with a distillation and interpretation of all relevant information about the companies they follow, including public filings, press releases, presentations and conference calls.

In recent months there has been a great deal of discussion and debate about the potential conflicts that arise when securities firms provide analytic, banking and brokerage services. It is generally accepted that, while investment banking generates substantial profits, research, standing alone, is at best a loss leader. Some believe that an analyst can only contribute to a firm's profits if he or she enhances its investment banking business. Some also believe that analysts may be encouraged by their transactional colleagues to publish favorable reports to ingratiate their firms with existing or potential investment banking clients. Indeed, this encouragement may include financial incentives, if an analyst's compensation is tied to the brokerage firm's investment banking revenues. In the view of some regulators, the objectivity of the analyst's research and conclusions may be compromised by these incentives.

In the months following WorldCom's bankruptcy, a great deal of attention has been focused on the Company's relationships with Salomon Smith Barney ("SSB"). Public officials and members of the financial media have strongly suggested that an unhealthy relationship developed between WorldCom and SSB. They have alleged that SSB used the promise of lucrative IPO allocations and flattering analyst reports to entice corporate executives, like Mr. Ebbers, to reward them with highly profitable investment banking assignments. In addition, they have suggested that SSB's chief telecommunications analyst, Jack Grubman, combined forces with corporate executives, like Mr. Sullivan, to project inflated prospects for WorldCom's fortunes, resulting in bloated stock valuations.

Although it would be premature to reach any conclusions on these subjects, the following facts have begun to emerge:

1. In the transactions we have reviewed to date, SSB and its predecessors, Salomon Brothers and Smith Barney, collectively received more engagements from WorldCom than any other investment banking firm during the past five years.

2. SSB and its predecessors also allocated millions of dollars of valuable IPOs to a number of WorldCom directors, including Mr. Ebbers. These directors, in turn, sold their IPO shares for an aggregate profit of more than $18 million.

3. Until April 2002, Mr. Grubman and SSB repeatedly gave WorldCom's stock its highest ratings, enthusiastically urging investors to purchase WorldCom shares, even at times when Mr. Grubman was privately advising WorldCom management on business strategy, acquisitions and investor relations.

4. Until the third quarter of 2000, WorldCom's reported earnings per share consistently met or came close to analyst expectations. In subsequent quarters, WorldCom management publicly attributed its faltering financial performance to a series of allegedly non-recurring causes.

At a minimum, the generous IPO allocations given by SSB to Mr. Ebbers and others created the appearance that valuable corporate business opportunities were being traded for personal gain. Mr. Grubman's behavior also created at least an appearance of impropriety.

WORLDCOM'S GENERAL INTERACTIONS WITH SECURITIES ANALYSTS

As a large and rapidly growing public company, WorldCom had frequent interaction with the many securities analysts who covered its stock. WorldCom executives generally held teleconferences with securities analysts on a quarterly basis. Each call would normally begin with prepared statements from Company executives regarding WorldCom's financial position, financial outlook, and issues of particular importance to the Company. The executives would then answer analysts' questions regarding their prepared statements and other subjects.

WorldCom's management and directors paid very close attention to the views expressed by Wall Street's securities analysts and carefully tracked their stated expectations of the Company. The Company's Investor Relations Department regularly sent memoranda and charts to senior management describing analysts' expectations regarding the Company's quarterly and annual financial performance. Even the materials prepared for Board meetings regularly included transcripts of the most recent teleconference with analysts, a memorandum regarding analysts' expectations, and a summary of their reactions to WorldCom's quarterly financial announcements. Clearly, senior management and the Board recognized the significance of maintaining Wall Street's confidence.

MR. GRUBMAN'S EXTREMELY FAVORABLE ANALYST REPORTS

Prior to their merger in late 1997, Salomon Brothers and Smith Barney expressed substantially different views concerning the future performance of and risks associated with WorldCom stock. In 1997, Smith Barney issued four World-Com reports. . . . These reports reflected a relatively restrained assessment of the stock's prospects.

At the same time, Mr. Grubman, who worked for Salomon, issued a report in which he rated WorldCom a strong buy and declared that "no telecom company of WorldCom's market cap can come close to matching WorldCom's top-line growth, margin expansion potential or strategic position, much less having all of these attributes which is why WorldCom remains our favorite stock." Mr. Grubman's strong buy rating represented an emphatically higher recommendation than Smith Barney's neutral and outperform ratings. Notably, Mr. Grubman said little about the stock's risk factors in his report.

In the wake of the Salomon Smith Barney merger [in 1998], Mr. Grubman emerged as SSB's chief telecommunications analyst and the author of all its WorldCom reports from the time of the merger until March 2002. Consistent with Mr. Grubman's pre-merger view, each and every SSB report during this period included a "buy" recommendation (SSB's highest rating) and a "medium" assessment of risk. Mr. Grubman's reports during this period consistently proclaimed ringing endorsements of WorldCom and its stock.

As WorldCom's stock price steadily rose in 1998 and 1999, Mr. Grubman gave and maintained his highest ratings on WorldCom stock and set target prices that were 17% to 60% (and 100% over a 2 year time frame) higher than the current value of the stock.

Mr. Grubman urged investors to "load up the truck" with WorldCom stock. In fact, he declared that any investor who did not take advantage of current prices to buy every share of WorldCom should seriously think about another vocation.

Mr. Grubman attributed WorldCom's declining stock price during the early part of the year 2000 to the market's ignorance in assessing the realities of the Company's compelling story and to the fact that the market instead was acting on sentiment. Mr. Grubman stated that "investors who are selling WorldCom in the $40s will be buying WorldCom in the $60s in six months."

From the beginning of 2000 through August 2001, when WorldCom's stock fell from $50.06 to $12.44 per share, SSB consistently set target prices that were 90% to 244% higher than the current stock quote.

In June 2000, Mr. Grubman stated categorically that WorldCom was by far the cheapest stock in the world of global telecom and that analysts who continued to worry about WorldCom's failure to excel in the wireless area would be sorely disappointed that they downgraded the stock. As the stock continued to decline, from a high of $49 per share in July to $14 per share in December, Mr. Grubman continued to project a tripling of WorldCom's stock price and labeled the stock "dirt cheap." In November 2000, Mr. Grubman lowered his price target from $87 to $45 a share, but held steadfast to his buy-medium risk ratings.

In 2001, WorldCom revised its earnings estimates downward on several occasions. At the same time, the stock price fell below $20.00 and ultimately to the $12.00 range in September and October 2001. Yet Mr. Grubman maintained his highest rating on WorldCom and announced that WorldCom stock continued to be undervalued. He even claimed that if the Company made its numbers, the stock price could double or triple over the next 12-18 months. In his January 9, 2001 report, Mr. Grubman conceded that WorldCom's line costs would likely be higher, but depreciation would be lower due to intercompany classifications. Mr. Grubman continually advocated that investors take advantage of misguided analysis by aggressively buying WorldCom's shares, noting that there were very few sponsors on "the Street" for the stock.

Mr. Grubman lowered his price target to $35 in July 2001, and subsequently lowered it again in October 2001 to $22 and again in January 2002 to $20. While these downward revisions appear significant on a relative basis, the revised targets still reflected price targets that were 50% to 174% more than contemporaneous stock prices. Moreover, Mr. Grubman maintained his buy-medium risk ratings on the Company.

By the first quarter of 2002, even Mr. Grubman acknowledged that widespread rumors were circulating that: (1) WorldCom was going to be dropped from the S&P 500; (2) the Company's debt rating was being lowered to junk status; (3) the Company's stock was going to be downgraded by a competitor; (4) UUNET's business from AOL was going elsewhere; (5) the Company's accounting and balance sheets were under scrutiny; and (6) Mr. Ebbers was having significant financial problems. Despite all of these significant concerns, Mr. Grubman maintained his buy-medium risk ratings on WorldCom's stock and set a stock price target that was almost 150% of the current price at that time. In fact, Mr. Grubman maintained his buy-medium risk ratings even after the SEC initiated its inquiry into WorldCom's financial reporting, and did not change his risk rating to a buy-*high* risk rating until a week later.

SSB's first downgrade of WorldCom stock came in April 2002. In this report, Mr. Grubman admitted that his previous evaluations of WorldCom were clearly wrong. Mr. Grubman stated that he decided to downgrade the stock even though it "would obviously be easier not to downgrade the stock, and therefore not to suffer the inevitable and justified slings from various parties."

In May 2002, Mr. Grubman further downgraded his risk rating to speculative in response to the deterioration of WorldCom's debt ratings. A final downgrade, to "underperform — speculative," followed on June 21, 2002, a little over a month before WorldCom's filing for bankruptcy.

By then, WorldCom shareholders had lost more than $180 billion in market capitalization since 1999. Conversely, from 1998 until 2001, when he consistently encouraged investors to buy WorldCom's stock, it is alleged that Mr. Grubman reportedly averaged approximately $20 million per year in compensation. When Mr. Grubman resigned from SSB on August 15, 2002, he stated in his resignation letter that "the current climate of criticism has made it impossible to perform my work to the standards I believe the clients of SSB deserve." SSB reportedly agreed to buy out the rest of Grubman's 1998 $32.2 million contract, which included $12 million in stock and options and forgiveness of a $15 million loan, plus about $4 million in interest. Grubman further maintained publicly that he and other analysts were simply "wrong" about the future of telecom.

MR. GRUBMAN'S DEPARTURES FROM THE ROLE OF AN INDEPENDENT SECURITIES ANALYST

Although we are not currently in a position to reach any conclusion on this point, Mr. Grubman's behavior seems to have departed from the role of an independent securities analyst as described above.

Our review of internal WorldCom and SSB documents has revealed a large number of meetings, conferences, e-mail messages and other contacts between Mr. Grubman and WorldCom executives. These include at least four instances in which Mr. Grubman attended WorldCom Board meetings to discuss major transactions, such as the proposed merger between WorldCom and MCI in late 1997 and the proposed merger between WorldCom and Sprint in October 1999. Minutes from these meetings indicate that Mr. Grubman and other SSB representatives were invited to make extensive presentations to the Board analyzing the financial impacts of these mergers on WorldCom's operations as well as other transactions involving the merger parties. These minutes indicate that Mr. Grubman attended the Board's meetings as a "financial advisor" to the Company and performed roles that seem inconsistent with that of an independent securities analyst.

WorldCom employees also consulted with Mr. Grubman from time to time to obtain information about the Company's investors, the opinions and actions of other Wall Street analysts and Mr. Grubman's reactions to negative press reports regarding WorldCom. Moreover, there is evidence that Mr. Grubman consulted with WorldCom's management in advance of analyst conference calls to suggest how they should handle certain topics during those calls. Further, we have seen evidence that Mr. Grubman even suggested a question he might ask during an analyst conference call that might elicit a favorable response.

There is also some evidence to suggest that Mr. Grubman may have played a role in the allocation of valuable IPOs to Mr. Ebbers, since he was copied on internal SSB e-mails regarding those allocations. In March and May 1999, Mr. Grubman received copies of internal SSB e-mails indicating that Mr. Ebbers was on a list of "private wealth clients" who had requested shares. . . .

Randall Smith, et al., *Wall Street Firms to Pay $1.4 Billion to End Inquiry — Record Payment Settles Conflict-of-Interest Charges*

Wall St. J. (Apr. 29, 2003) A1

In a pact that could change the face of Wall Street, 10 of the nation's largest securities firms agreed to pay a record $1.4 billion to settle government charges involving abuse of investors during the stock-market bubble of the late 1990s.

The long-awaited settlement, which followed an intense investigation that brought together three national regulatory bodies and a dozen state securities authorities, centers on civil charges that the Wall Street firms routinely issued overly optimistic stock research to investors in order to curry favor with corporate clients and win their lucrative investment-banking business. The pact also settles charges that at least two big firms, Citigroup Inc.'s Citigroup Global Markets unit, formerly

Salomon Smith Barney, and Credit Suisse Group's Credit Suisse First Boston, improperly doled out coveted shares in initial public offerings to corporate executives in a bid to win banking business from their companies.

Regulators unveiled dozens of previously undisclosed examples of financial analysts tailoring their research reports and stock ratings to win investment-banking business. They added up to a scathing critique that scorched all the firms involved.

The penalties included lifetime bans from the securities business for two former star analysts, Jack Grubman of Salomon and Henry Blodget of Merrill Lynch & Co., who were charged with issuing fraudulent research reports and agreed to pay penalties of $15 million and $4 million, respectively. Both the firms and the individuals consented to the charges without admitting or denying wrongdoing. But the regulators vowed to pursue cases against analysts and their supervisors as far up the chain of command as possible.

Bowing to political pressure from Congress, the regulators, which also included the National Association of Securities Dealers, the New York Stock Exchange and state regulators led by New York's Eliot Spitzer, also won a promise by the firms not to seek insurance repayment or tax deductions for $487.5 million of the settlement payments.

The agreement sets new rules that will force brokerage companies to make structural changes in the way they handle research. Analysts, for instance, will no longer be allowed to accompany investment bankers during sales pitches to clients. The pact also requires securities firms to have separate reporting and supervisory structures for their research and banking operations, and to tie analysts' compensation to the quality and accuracy of their research, rather than how much investment-banking fees they help generate.

Moreover, stock research will be required to carry the equivalent of a "buyer beware" notice. Securities firms, regulators said, must include on the first page of research reports a note making clear that the reports are produced by firms that do investment-banking business with the companies they cover. This, the firms must acknowledge, may affect the objectivity of the firms' research.

Notes and Questions

1. Notes

a. SOx requires the SEC to adopt rules that effectively separate the analysts from the investment bankers within the same firm and requires disclosure of conflicts of interest.

2. Reality Check

a. What do securities analysts do?

b. How can securities analysts constrain corporate behavior?

3. What Do You Think?

a. Who was more culpable, in your view? WorldCom, Mr. Grubman, or SSB?

b. Do you think the reforms are realistic?

4. Intentionality

In the Notes that followed the selections above we adverted to various reforms, chiefly those required by SOx. Here we look at a different approach: reform through people being intentional about reforming themselves, the businesses in which they work, and the system of business. The catalyst for this kind of reform is education.

Evelina Shmukler, *Back to School*
Wall St. J. (Feb. 24, 2003) R6

When Institutional Shareholder Services Inc. put together a formula for rating corporate governance three years ago, the proxy-adviser firm weighed a host of factors — everything from executive compensation to the structure of the board to the level of stock ownership among a company's leaders.

But ISS's special counsel, Patrick McGurn, got an underwhelming reaction when he pressed for another criterion: training for members of the board. Directors, he reasoned, bring diverse business experience to the table, but few have special education in sitting on a corporate board. "People started laughing, saying, 'Oh, you've got to be kidding,'" Mr. McGurn recalls. "'Directors are busy people. They're never going to get continuing education.'"

Then came the scandals at Enron Corp., WorldCom Inc. and a host of other companies. Suddenly, director training is hot on both sides of the Atlantic. Organizations that provide training courses report massive increases in interest and enrollment in their classes, where board members learn everything from how to read a company's books to how to set ethics guidelines for executives.

In the U.K., the Institute of Directors, a business-lobby group, has seen membership triple in its accreditation program for board members. The New York Stock Exchange, meanwhile, is starting its own director-training courses, and its chairman and CEO, Richard Grasso, plans to write the chairmen of all companies listed on the exchange encouraging them to send their directors through one of the courses.

The premise behind training both executive directors — that is, those who work at a company and serve on its board — and nonexecutive, or outside, directors is simple. "Everybody gets trained at companies but directors," says Alexander Keyserlingk, a 30-year veteran of International Finance Corp., the private-sector arm of the World Bank Group, who qualified for the Institute of Directors' "chartered director" accreditation two years ago. "They train the lowest bookkeeper and the lowest truck driver, but they don't spend any time training directors."

"All of the executives have an opinion now on everything we discuss," says [Mike Hall, chief executive of Standard Life Healthcare in the U.K., who qualified as a chartered director last year]. Two years ago, he says, board members would focus on their particular specialty, be it finance, marketing, legal and so on. "Now I see them participating because they know what they're talking about, and they can ask proper, informed questions."

Indeed, the point of many director-training courses is to bring a board member up to speed in an area that isn't his or her specialty. For example, one Institute of

Directors program explains complicated finance-director and accountant terminology, and teaches techniques for evaluating and monitoring the financial health of a company — as well as spotting warning signs of financial trouble.

Other courses are broader, teaching directors the ins and outs of sitting on a board. A course from the Washington-based National Association of Corporate Directors, "Role of the Board in Risk Oversight," offers advice on guidelines that a board can adopt to ensure the integrity of company officers — and what to do if the company finds itself melting down. Another course looks at the duties, roles and legal responsibilities of directors as well as ways to improve board effectiveness.

This education doesn't come cheap. The Institute of Directors' full chartered-director program costs about $12,000. A three-day program at the French business school Insead costs about $8,000. In the U.S., one-day courses at the National Association of Corporate Directors cost almost $800. Who picks up the tab, the corporation or the individual director? Many executives, including Mr. Hall, say the company should foot the bill — he says he looks on the expense as staff development.

In the U.S., ISS has made training for directors part of its "corporate governance quotient," a measure used by ISS's 750 institutional-investor clients. If directors want to boost their companies' governance rating, they can take a training course at one of about 20 programs ISS has accredited. Mr. McGurn says ISS is now "inundated" with calls from education providers, 10 to 20 a week, looking to receive accreditation.

Because of this demand, ISS says it's careful to screen providers for the kind of training it's looking for. "There are a lot of people out there providing education on directors' liability and things like that," Mr. McGurn says. "That's not what we consider to be director education related to governance. We want it to be substantive training — how to look over a financial statement or be a member of an audit committee — or more general programs about improving your governance behavior or how the market views your company."

One group that offers ISS-accredited director education, the National Association of Corporate Directors, has seen demand for programs rise dramatically. Classes are now often sold out, and Mr. McGurn says other programs report similar enrollment gains.

Notes and Questions

1. What Do You Think?

a. Director education programs such as those described above have sometimes been described as "home schooling" for business people. Do you agree?

b. Is there a danger that director education programs will produce director dilettantes rather than directors who are genuinely better educated?

c. What should the components of a director education program be?

Ronald Alsop, *Right and Wrong*

Wall St. J. (Sept. 17, 2003) R9

Harvard Business School boasts that it offered its first course on business ethics — "Social Factors in Business Enterprise" — nearly a century ago, in 1915. But this is no time for Harvard — or any business school, for that matter — to rest on its laurels. Harvard plans to launch a more in-depth, required ethics course called "Leadership, Governance and Accountability" in January. "The new course will expose students to more of the kinds of pressures they are inevitably going to face in business," says Lynn Paine, professor of business administration.

In the post-Enron era, M.B.A. programs — Harvard in particular — have come in for some caustic criticism for producing graduates obsessed with making money regardless of the ethical consequences. To some people, M.B.A. graduates are at the root of all the corporate greed and dishonesty. After all, two infamous Enron executives — former Chief Executive Jeffrey Skilling and former Chief Financial Officer Andrew Fastow — hold M.B.A. degrees from Harvard and Northwestern University's Kellogg School of Management, respectively.

Business schools have gotten the message. They are busy infusing more ethics training than ever before into their curricula, as well as trying to screen applicants for integrity before admitting them. Recently, AACSB International, the major business-school accrediting organization, increased the emphasis on ethics in the standards that business schools must meet to receive accreditation.

Notre Dame, a Roman Catholic university, has a long tradition of ethics research and education, including its Institute for Ethical Business Worldwide and Center for Ethics and Religious Values. Indeed, some recruiters say they are drawn more these days to religious schools like Notre Dame and Brigham Young University.

There's no foolproof method for measuring virtue in M.B.A. students, but many recruiters feel confident they can easily weed out the potential sinners by conducting rigorous interviews, observing students' body language and conversation in social settings, consulting character references, and checking the accuracy of resumes.

Sometimes, though, it just boils down to a gut reaction. More than half of the respondents to [a *Wall St. Journal*] survey said they rely on "a gut feeling or hunch" when interviewing students. But three-quarters said they also depend on responses to interview questions about ethical dilemmas, and about half find students' previous work experience a revealing clue to their character.

M.B.A. students with ties to any of the scandal-tarred companies will encounter resistance from some recruiters. Several respondents to the *Wall Street Journal* survey said they are loath to interview a former employee of Enron or Arthur Andersen, especially with so many other talented graduates to choose from.

The Enron and Andersen cases bring up the issue of whether a student can be taught to behave ethically. When Harvard administrators wondered about the effectiveness of ethics courses, they retained a developmental psychologist for advice. "The psychologist concluded that M.B.A. students in their mid- to late 20s are particularly ripe for discussions about such issues as conflicting responsibilities," says Prof. Paine of Harvard.

Some corporate recruiters are more skeptical. In the *Wall Street Journal*/Harris Interactive survey, nearly a quarter of the respondents said that integrity is inherent in an individual's character and that business schools can't teach ethics. About 60%, however, said they believe schools can provide guidance on making ethical choices.

"I'm not sure you can teach ethics, but you certainly can teach the severe ramifications that come from doing something unethical in business," says Timothy Schuetze, a recruiter for a consumer-products company and graduate of the Yale School of Management.

Academics disagree on the ideal approach to embedding ethics in the curriculum. Should schools require students to take courses focused primarily on ethical responsibilities? Or is it better to sprinkle ethics lessons throughout all of the major courses, including finance, accounting, international business and marketing?

The best answer is probably some of both. That's the strategy at the Columbia University Business School. Its Center for Leadership and Ethics, created with funding from Sanford C. Bernstein & Co., offers elective courses with an ethics theme, and has adopted an ambitious new ethics curriculum that all students must take. It's a unique year-long hybrid of stand-alone lectures plus lessons woven into all of the M.B.A. program's required core courses.

Some corporate recruiters believe schools should go well beyond simply presenting case studies about ethical dilemmas. They favor a community-service requirement, as well. "A one-semester practicum with a nonprofit organization could provide a student with a life-transforming experience," says Marvin Pannell, a project manager at Wells Fargo & Co. "Many students today aren't growing up with religion and aren't replacing religion with their own brand of spirituality."

Besides creating ethics programs, some business schools are working harder to foster a culture of integrity and collegiality on their own campuses. At Ohio State University, the Fisher College of Business created a new honor code that the class of 2003 M.B.A.s were the first to sign. "Honesty and integrity are the foundation from which I will measure my actions," the code states. "I will hold myself accountable to adhere to these standards."

This year, Indiana University's Kelley School of Business has developed a 20-page code of conduct that is modeled closely after the corporate codes that graduates will ultimately have to abide by. Among the areas covered: cheating, fabrication, plagiarism, professional behavior with recruiters, and proper classroom manners ("do not surf on the Internet, avoid eating noisy or odiferous foods, and always close computers during any guest speaker's presentation"). "We especially have to emphasize the code with our international students who may have different ethical standards in their countries," says Idalene Kesner, M.B.A. program chairwoman. "Some cultures don't view plagiarism, for example, in the same serious way that we do."

≡
≡
≡   **Colleen DeBaise,** *Corporate-Governance Law*
≡   *Is the Rage*
≡   Wall St. J. (Sept. 1, 2004) B7

When Tulane University Law School in New Orleans offered a course this spring on "Corporate Governance in a Post-Enron World," the professors expected 20 students to sign up. Instead, 75 students clamored to get in. At Seattle University School of Law, nearly 90 students enrolled in the spring term's corporate-governance course, more than quadruple the 20 students who took it a year earlier.

"Students' interest in the word 'governance' has peaked," said James Cox, a law professor at Duke University, of Durham, N.C., who is teaching a course this fall on "Governance, Responsibility and Crime in the Public Corporation." The class size is limited to 16; more than 30 students are on the waiting list. "It's off the scale this year."

Many law schools say they are adding units to address legal issues raised by corporate misconduct and new regulations encompassed by the Sarbanes-Oxley Act. At Ave Maria School of Law in Ann Arbor, Mich., the new casebooks for the fall term discuss the Enron, Tyco International Ltd., WorldCom Inc. and Martha Stewart cases. Rutgers University School of Law at Camden added a new course, "The Law of Organizational Fraud," to its fall curriculum. Last year, the New Jersey school launched the course "Problems in Corporate Disclosure and Securities Fraud."

At Seattle University School of Law, the response to the newly created Center on Corporations, Law & Society, which hosts debates and conferences on corporate accountability, has been "phenomenally enthusiastic," said Dana Gold, director. Students who might not be interested in traditional "corporate" issues — those studying environmental law, for instance — now understand "that how corporations work is really important," Ms. Gold said. "People are moving a step back and not just dealing with the symptom of whatever the problem is but trying to deal with root causes."

Alexandra Filutowski, a second-year law student at Seattle University, said she decided to study law partly because one of her college classes focused on Enron and other corporate scandals. "Corporations cannot get away with everything that they have in the past," said Ms. Filutowski, a fellow at the center. "Nowadays, we're becoming more and more open to breaking the tradition, and hearing other ideas."

Notes and Questions

1. Reality Check

a. How is MBA ethics education different from business ethics education for JDs?

b. What are the elements common to both programs?

c. Why do some employers and business schools eschew former employees of companies such as Enron or Arthur Andersen?

2. What Do You Think?

a. Is it possible to provide business ethics education to MBA and JD students or are their "moral compasses" already set?

b. Should MBA ethics education be modeled after law school professional responsibility courses?

c. Do law school professional responsibility courses have much relevance for JD business ethics courses?

d. Is the attraction some employers have to religiously affiliated MBA or JD programs justified with regard to ethics programs?

e. Perhaps most important, do you agree with the assertion that surfing the Internet during class violates accepted norms of business conduct?

Intentionality can have its motivation in something other than education. In the excerpt below Professor Stout looks at a vision of internally generated intentionality.

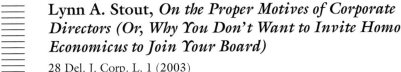

Lynn A. Stout, *On the Proper Motives of Corporate Directors (Or, Why You Don't Want to Invite Homo Economicus to Join Your Board)*
28 Del. J. Corp. L. 1 (2003)

Given directors' apparent lack of external incentives to do a good job — the absence both of good carrots, and of effective sticks — why do we trust directors to manage tens of trillions of dollars of corporate assets? And, why do they seem to mostly live up to our trust? Or at least, live up to it well enough that the U.S. system of corporate governance often is held up as a model for the rest of the world, and board failures of the sort recently observed at Enron and WorldCom can still, one hopes, be viewed as the highly publicized exceptions rather than the rule.

The discussion below . . . explores the hypothesis that the institution of the corporate board works because we do not, in fact, rely on external incentives and pressures, alone, to motivate directors to do a good job. We also rely on internal pressures — including such internal pressures as a director's sense of honor; her feelings of responsibility; her sense of obligation to the firm and its shareholders; and, her desire to "do the right thing."

[I]f we want to understand how boards of directors work, we need to develop a better understanding of the sorts of internal pressures encompassed by terms like "honor," "integrity," "trustworthiness," and "responsibility." Yet how can we gain a firm grasp on such soft and slippery concepts? The neoclassical economic literature offers little guidance. Guidance is available, however, if we expand the search to include the broader social sciences, including psychology, sociology, biology, and anthropology.

There is a large body of literature in the broader social sciences on the phenomenon that will be described below, in general terms, as "other-regarding" behavior. As this label suggests, this literature examines instances in which people behave as if they care about something other than their own payoffs. This "other" might be the welfare of another person, or the fate of an institution like "the firm," or even an abstract principle such as "do the right thing." The point is that the evidence demonstrates that people sometimes behave altruistically — as if they care about others, and not only about themselves.

As an example, let us consider the lessons that can be drawn from studies of human behavior in a kind of experimental game called a social dilemma. In brief, these games are designed to place players in a position where their self-interest conflicts with the interests of other players. This is done by presenting subjects with a choice of strategies: either "cooperate" in a way that benefits the other members of the group, or "defect" and maximize your own personal payoffs. The experiment is structured, however, so that if all the subjects behave self-interestedly and defect, they end up worse off than if all had cooperated. Social dilemma studies . . . do not prove psychological altruism (that people truly care about others' welfare). They do, however, offer compelling evidence of behavioral altruism (people often act as if they care about others).

[P]erhaps we can harness the phenomenon of other-regarding behavior, and encourage directors of public corporations to behave even more altruistically than they already do in looking after the firm's interests.

Let us begin by considering the variable that, perhaps more than any other, seems to influence individuals' decisions about whether or not to cooperate in a social dilemma. This critical variable is something that might be called "social context." Social context can be defined as an amalgam of signals we receive about such matters as what other people expect, what other people need, and what other people are likely to do.

There is a second variable that has proven significant in predicting cooperation rates in social dilemma games that is far more "economic" in flavor. This second variable is the personal cost of altruistic behavior to the actor. It is a common finding in the social dilemma literature that, as the cost of cooperation to the individual player rises, the incidence of cooperative behavior tends to fall. In other words, people are more inclined to behave "nicely" when it does not cost them too much.

What does this result tell us about the behavior of corporate directors? Most important, it tells us that if we want directors to do a good job of looking out for the interests of the firm and its shareholders, it is essential to make sure that "doing a good job" is not too personally costly to the directors. Put differently, if we want directors to do a good job, we do not want to ask them to take on too many tasks. This observation is consistent with the way corporate governance is actually practiced in most large firms. Directors generally do not run the business on a day-to-day basis (this job is delegated to executives and employees), but instead serve an oversight or monitoring role. In effect, directors select senior managers and then step aside, intervening only in times of crisis, or on very large issues such as a merger or major refinancing.

This pattern of relative uninvolvement is sometimes offered as proof of director malfeasance, evidence that directors are not working as hard as they should. Such critiques misunderstand the director's role. Because directors' rewards and punishments are only very loosely tied to their performance, we must inevitably rely on directors' internalized sense of responsibility as their primary if not their sole motive for exercising judgment and care. The empirical evidence suggests that if we place too heavy a burden on such altruistic motivations, they will crumble under the weight. It thus makes sense for large corporations to rely on professional managers for most decisions, and to limit directors' responsibilities primarily to monitoring. Monitoring is not nearly as demanding or as time-consuming as managing. Nevertheless, it can be every bit as important.

A related and very important lesson that can be drawn from the social dilemma evidence on the inverse relationship between cooperation and personal cost is that it is essential that we do not rely too heavily on director altruism in situations where a director has a substantial personal interest adverse to the firm. [I]f we want to rely on outside directors to curb the predictably self-interested behavior of inside directors whose prospects for substantial personal loss or gain may undermine their altruistic motivations, outside directors must be truly independent.

No analysis of the role of other-regarding behavior in promoting good corporate governance would be complete, however, without mentioning a third factor that has proven important in determining cooperation rates in experimental games. This third factor is something a psychologist might call "personality type." Laypersons might call it "character."

Let us return to the general finding that cooperation rates among U.S. subjects playing social dilemma games average 50%. This average cooperation rate, it turns out, reflects a blend of two strategies people tend to adopt in social dilemma games: either they donate all the money they have been given to the common pool, or they donate none of it. Social scientists have investigated whether these patterns of behavior somehow reflect basic personality characteristics. They have concluded that the answer, to some extent, is yes. Although cooperation rates in social dilemmas are highly dependent on social context and considerations of personal cost, people also seem to bring to the experiments a predisposition to either cooperate or defect.

[R]esearchers also found a strong correlation between cooperation rates and the frequency of cooperation and market exchange in the culture studied. This finding suggests that habits of cooperation may be learned: the more frequently members of a particular society cooperate with others in their daily economic lives, the more likely they are to cooperate with strangers in a social dilemma experiment as well.

[T]he evidence also suggests that some people, whether by nature or nurture, are more inclined toward other-regarding behavior than others. These "cooperators" behave altruistically even in situations where the social signals they receive are somewhat mixed, and altruism requires more than a nominal personal sacrifice. In everyday business life, directors often face such situations. Thus, if we want corporate directors to serve an other-regarding role, we should select as directors those individuals who are more inclined toward other-regarding behavior in the first place.

How can we find these directors? There are a number of possibilities, but one of the most obvious is to look at a person's history as evidence of her character. Has she lived up to her commitments, even in situations where she did not have to? Has she undertaken activities that demonstrate that she can care about something other than her own payoffs? Has she given evidence, in the past, of a desire and an ability to do the right thing, even when doing the right thing was not personally advantageous, or particularly popular? If the answers to these questions are "yes," then it is this type of person . . . whom you want to invite to join your board.

Of course, these are lessons that most experienced business people, including most experienced business lawyers, have already learned. Most of us are sophisticated, if not always conscious, observers of human nature. The point here is simply that we should pay attention to what we already know. Personal payoffs count. But so do social context and the quality we call "character."

Notes and Questions

1. What Do You Think?

a. Is intentionality something that can be fostered by education or is it primarily internally generated?

C. BACKGROUND AND CONTEXT

We close this chapter with a look at two broader questions related to whether the current restraints on corporations and boards are effective. First, are the reforms imposed in the wake of Enron and WorldCom effective and worth the costs of compliance? Second, are scandals such as these (1) proof that the current system of constraints is fundamentally ineffective or (2) particularly egregious exceptions in a system that constrains boards and companies appropriately?

1. Are Reforms Working?

Deborah Solomon & Cassell Bryan-Low, *Companies Complain About Cost of Corporate-Governance Rules*
Wall St. J. (Feb. 10, 2004) A1

Some U.S. companies are complaining that new rules aimed at improving corporate accountability will cost them in dollars and in time this year. Most of the rules stem from the 2002 Sarbanes-Oxley Act, which Congress enacted to beef up corporate governance in the aftermath of accounting fraud uncovered at Enron Corp., WorldCom Inc. and elsewhere. Written by the Securities and Exchange Commission, the regulations are aimed at toughening corporate accountability to restore investor confidence and are just now starting to hit bottom lines. Advocates say they will help companies avoid costly problems down the road.

"We can't lose sight of the fact that we came close to an all-out breakdown of investor trust in financial statements and the integrity of the financial-reporting process," says Charles Mulford, an accounting professor at the Georgia Institute of Technology.

While there is agreement that governance rules are needed, some companies cited the increased cost of complying. "The real cost isn't the incremental dollars, it is having people that should be focused on the business focused instead on complying with the details of the rules," said Peter Bible, chief accounting officer at General Motors Corp. "Everybody feels they have to do something to react to the corporate scandals, [but] you really have to scratch your head and say, 'How is this really benefiting our shareholders?'"

The rules are coming into effect at a time when corporations already are battling other increasing costs, including health-care expenses. Even before the most expensive Sarbanes-Oxley rules take effect, companies say their audit costs are increasing by as much as 30% or more this year due to tougher audit and accounting standards, including complex rules to bring more off-balance-sheet items onto the books.

[M]ost companies say they understand the need for tougher standards but complain that some of the rules are duplicative while others force them to devote thousands of staff hours to formalize procedures already in place. The most pointed criticism is aimed at a rule — Section 404 of the act — to improve internal controls over financial reporting. [M]anagement at most large companies must have in place tight internal controls, assess the effectiveness of those controls and then pay for an independent assessment by outside auditors.

A survey of 321 companies to be released today shows that businesses with more than $5 billion in revenue expect to spend an average of $4.7 million each implementing the new 404 rule this year, according to Financial Executives International, which represents top corporate officials. Much of the money is being spent on consultants, lawyers, auditors and new software.

Many costs, such as installing software and designing systems, will decrease after the first year. But other costs are expected to stay constant, including paying an outside auditor to assess the controls every year. Companies with more than $5 billion in revenue expect those fees to be $1.5 million annually, according to the survey.

At World Wrestling Entertainment Inc., management began ramping up internal controls three months ago and is still considering whether to pay $250,000 to hire an outside consultant to oversee the project. The company, which reported revenue of $374 million during fiscal 2003, which ended April 30, already plans to spend about $50,000 on software to help document and track internal-control tests.

It is "a big headache," says Philip Livingston, the company's chief financial officer. "It is a lot of cost to the system without a lot of benefit. It is checking and testing internal controls that are already in place."

Rep. Michael Oxley, the law's co-sponsor, acknowledges that the cost of the internal-controls systems is a burden. "The cost-benefit analysis will always be debated," the Ohio Republican says. But it is "encouraging" that companies already are starting to make disclosures about potential weaknesses, he adds. In the past several months Adecco SA and BearingPoint Inc. disclosed "material weaknesses" in their internal controls.

Douglas Carmichael, the Public Company Accounting Oversight Board's chief auditor, says most companies need to make significant improvements to comply with the rules. "People in the past had a very exaggerated idea of how much time the auditor spent on internal controls," Mr. Carmichael says. "It was viewed by the auditor as strictly an efficiency matter" and auditors "paid little or no attention to internal controls."

One encouraging result of the Financial Executives International survey, according to Mr. Carmichael, is that small companies don't appear to be bearing a disproportionate amount of the cost. Some market observers were worried that increasing costs will dissuade smaller companies from going public. But Mr. Carmichael says small companies may actually benefit from the new requirements, because fraud tends to be more prevalent among small companies, making access to the capital markets harder. The new requirements should reduce uncertainty and therefore improve access, he says.

Notes and Questions

1. What Do You Think?

a. Are the legislative and regulatory reforms enacted in the wake of Enron and WorldCom effective? If not, what reforms would you suggest?

b. Is the value of the reforms worth their costs? What are the elements of those costs?

2. Systemic Problem or Cyclical Anomalies?

Bruce Nussbaum, *Can Trust Be Rebuilt?*

Bloomberg Businessweek Magazine (July 07, 2002)

Are we fools? Have we jeopardized our futures by buying into Corporate America's idea of a market-driven society only to be deceived by corrupt and unethical behavior on an unimaginable scale? As July 4 approaches, millions of Americans, already jittery about possible terrorist attacks, are now worrying about their financial security. With stocks sinking and the dollar swooning, they're wondering what they should do to protect themselves. They want to be safe. What they do in the months ahead will determine not only the course of the economy but also the political direction of the country.

Even President Bush, who has been reluctant to speak on the subject — and only then to blame individual "bad apples" — has broken his silence on corporate corruption. "I am deeply concerned about some of the accounting practices that take place in America," he said at an international meeting in Canada. Bush called revelations about WorldCom's (WCOM) bookkeeping "outrageous" and vowed to "fully investigate and hold people accountable. . . . There is a need for a renewed corporate responsibility in America."

. . .

More reform is on the way. On June 26, Securities & Exchange Commission Chairman Harvey L. Pitt, once the reluctant reformer, filed civil fraud charges against WorldCom. More important, he ordered the CEOs and CFOs of the 1,000 largest U.S. companies to attest personally to the accuracy of financial statements, starting with their most recent annual report. The New York Stock Exchange has also proposed new rules on corporate governance, requiring that a majority of corporate board members be independent and that shareholders get the right to vote on executive compensation (they are the owners, after all). The nonprofit Conference Board may soon propose an "oath" for CEOs to take, requiring them to sign off on a range of issues, from truthful auditing to clean accounting for stock options. The Senate Banking Committee just passed a tough accounting oversight bill that goes a good deal of the way toward reforming the accounting profession — and widespread outrage over the WorldCom fraud makes it much more likely that strong legislation will emerge from Congress. Even a few CEOs, such as Henry Paulson of Goldman Sachs (GS), are beginning to speak out, acknowledging Corporate America's credibility problem and demanding reform.

But will it be enough? The American people appear to be longing for a new Age of Reform, such as the one Teddy Roosevelt advanced at the turn of the century following a similar decline in public trust and confidence in the economic system. People want dramatic action before it is too late. They are shocked by the contrast between the values exhibited by working-class firefighters, police, and soldiers on September 11 and those on parade today by much of the Corporate Elite. They feel that many of the most wealthy, educated, and privileged managers and professionals in society have betrayed their fiduciary trust to the nation.

To most Americans, this goes well beyond being an ethical issue. The high-growth '90s, which generated so many jobs, was based on financial innovation and deregulation. Millions accepted, for the first time in their lives, the conservative argument that they could control their own destinies and prosper by tying their lives to the markets. They were convinced that they could manage the risks through better information and thus garner more of the profits as well.

It worked. From 1995 to 2000, a New Economy delivered enormous prosperity to millions of people. Huge productivity gains were made, pushing up real wages and creating opportunities for mobility. Now, people are discovering that, in the bubble years, starting around 1999 or 2000, some CEOs began to fake this information and corrupt the markets. Checks and balances failed, and professional accountants, lawyers, and analysts became greedy. The truth is that markets can work only if information is honest, rules of the game are clear, and people follow them. Realizing that this isn't the case today has left many Americans doubting their own futures and jeopardizing the future of the economy.

So are we fools? For the sake of the America's future, we had better not be.

E.S. Browning, *Burst Bubbles Often Expose Cooked Books and Trigger SEC Probes, Bankruptcy Filings*

Wall St. J. (Feb. 11, 2002) C1

History confirms what a lot of stock analysts and investors have been discovering to their chagrin lately — that burst bubbles and accounting controversies tend to go hand in hand.

Accounting scandals and bankruptcies, in fact, are one important reason that it can take the stock market years to recover fully from a bubble.

"This is not an isolated event," says Ray Dalio, president of Bridgewater Associates, a money-management firm in Westport, Conn., that oversees $35 billion. "This is something that will spread" as many companies' accounting practices are examined. "Many more stories will come out. The examination will inevitably turn up more cases of aggressive accounting and there will be a penalty for that aggressive accounting."

Consider past experience. Corporate bankruptcies and unraveling frauds were among the hallmarks of the 1930s, following the crash of 1929. One accounting trick of that era was to create elaborate webs of holding companies, each helping hide the others' financial weaknesses, an artifice strangely similar to what Enron did with its partnerships. One of the biggest shocks of the '30s was the collapse of a vast, once-highflying utilities empire called Middle West Utilities, run by an energy magnate and financier named Samuel Insull.

"Our view would be that bubbles create greed on the part of investors but they also create greed on the part of management," says Jeremy Grantham, a co-founder of Boston money-management firm Grantham, Mayo, Van Otterloo. "That was very much the case in 1929 when holding companies put on leverage and bought other holding companies' stock."

As the fallout from the 1929 crash spread, former New York Stock Exchange President Richard Whitney was sucked in and eventually was arrested and jailed for fraud.

A less extensive bubble was inflated in the late 1960s and burst in the early 1970s, when the "Nifty 50" stocks fell apart. Accounting scandals multiplied again. The Securities and Exchange Commission in 1975 censured Peat, Marwick, Mitchell, one of the largest accounting firms of the day, for failing to perform proper audits of five companies that collapsed soon after getting clean opinions.

More trouble followed the crash of 1987, although it was shorter-lived than the problems of the '30s or the '70s. The once-hot junk-bond market unraveled, insider-trading scandals proliferated, the savings-and-loan crisis grabbed the front pages and real-estate investments went bust.

Some market analysts worry that these problems aren't going to go away soon. "It is absolutely what almost invariably happens after every bubble," says investment strategist Barton Biggs at Morgan Stanley, referring to the scandals, bankruptcies and accounting disclosures. "You should expect them, but that doesn't mean that people who haven't been through it before aren't going to be surprised. The bigger the binge, the longer and more severe the hangover."

The root of the accounting problem, say Mr. Dalio and others who have studied the phenomenon, is that stock-market bubbles reward aggressive accounting, since it inflates earnings and helps push up companies' stock prices. As bubbles develop and the continued inflation of stock prices becomes paramount, conservative accountants and executives become discredited, and bending the rules becomes standard.

Phyllis Plitch, *When Market Scandals Erupt,*
Regulation Can Come in a Flood

Wall St. J. (Jan. 15, 2003)

NEW YORK—When two professors exposed trading anomalies in the mid-1990s that raised the specter of collusion among NASDAQ dealers, a top exchange official denounced their work as "unseemly" and sought to have the "unsubstantiated allegations" scrubbed from their paper.

One in-depth investigation later, market regulators were chastened. To settle Securities and Exchange Commission allegations that it failed to investigate signs of possible trading violations, the National Association of Securities Dealers—NASDAQ's parent—pledged $100 million to beef up enforcement and surveillance and restructured itself to strengthen market oversight.

While it may seem like ancient history, NASDAQ's upheaval is reminiscent of what transpired following the fall of Enron Corp.—albeit on a smaller scale.

In the months and years to come, U.S. companies will be operating under new rules. In just about every corner of the capital markets, the perceived evils of once-accepted business practices have become fodder for regulatory changes, many of which will become reality in 2003.

It is what social scientists call a "frame shift," said Dalton Conley, director of New York University's Center for Advanced Social Science Research. "Once something is perceived as wrong, all past history is put through a new lens," he said. "Once it shifts, it's like a flood."

William Christie, one of the two finance professors on the NASDAQ study and now dean of the Owens School of Management at Vanderbilt University, Nashville, Tenn., sees parallels between the events of the 1990s and the past year.

NASDAQ traders' behavior—however suspect in retrospect—had become the norm. Those charged with oversight either failed to see what was going on or looked the other way. Similarly, the scandals of 2002 showed that management and directors failed in their oversight duties to shareholders and employees, he said.

"Human nature sometimes dictates that if you can get away with something on the margins, you have the temptation to do so," said Mr. Christie, who keeps in his scrap book the letter from NASDAQ's then president, Joseph Hardiman, the official who criticized the study. "Someone had to stand up and say the emperor has no clothes."

Regulatory and congressional changes—most notably the sweeping Sarbanes-Oxley Act . . .—contain prescriptive measures that take aim at a wide range of corporate and Wall Street activities, from compensation, accounting and disclosure practices to the way securities analysts recommend stocks and how lawyers do their jobs.

Such frame shifts don't happen often, given the fragmentation of the American political system and anti-big-government feeling, said Rogan Kersh, a professor at Syracuse University's Maxwell School of Citizenship & Public Affairs.

A period of as long as half a century can go by before a cataclysmic event, or series of events, propels significant change, he said.

But it is hard to connect the dots between the recent rush for change to a single root cause, NYU's Mr. Conley said. The change in landscape can't be entirely laid at Enron Corp.'s door, for instance. Several months after the energy company's fall, the drive toward change had actually been losing steam, only to regain momentum after new scandals surfaced, most notably WorldCom Inc.'s outright acknowledgment of accounting fraud in June. The centerpiece of recent accounting measures — Sarbanes-Oxley — might not have become a reality if not for WorldCom.

This shift in thinking can also be seen at the stock exchanges, at times accused by institutional investors of being in "a race to the bottom" to make the regulatory landscape looser to entice new corporate listings. As members of a special New York Stock Exchange corporate governance committee — formed in February — debated what changes to make, scandals continued erupting around them. Concern for restoring market confidence eventually outweighed worries about being at a competitive disadvantage with rival markets, said Leon Panetta, the former White House chief of staff who was co-chairman of the NYSE committee.

"There was no way we could simply tiptoe around, with the scandals taking place," Mr. Panetta said. "We had to deal with them directly."

Academics also invoke "the great man theory," when an influential person suddenly spearheads a new agenda, as in New York Attorney General Eliot Spitzer's relentless effort against Wall Street research and banking conflicts of interest. Mr. Spitzer's crusade culminated in the recent agreement with Wall Street firms.

In terms of the changes of 2002, experts say that without the collapse of the stock market, the stars probably wouldn't have aligned for change. During the frothy bull market days of the late 1990s, before companies like Enron and WorldCom sank under the weight of accounting scandals, naysayers didn't stand much of a chance, anyway.

D. FEDERAL SECURITIES REGULATION

The federal securities laws provide both indirect and direct methods of controlling board power. The indirect methods are of long standing. The direct methods are primarily from the Sarbanes-Oxley Act of 2002 (SOx).

When we looked at a corporation's power to raise capital we adverted to the federal regulations on selling securities to the public. In the next chapter we will see that publicly held companies are required to make public important information concerning their financial and operational aspects. These regulations are couched in the form of mandatory disclosure of facts rather than as substantive restrictions on corporate action. Nonetheless, even the disclosure regulations affect board power in two ways. First, as we've seen, to the extent that the federal regulations require corporations to disclose whether a corporation has certain qualities, such as an independent compensation committee, the regulations effectively require such qualities because companies are loathe to have to disclose that they do not have such beneficial qualities.

Second, the regulations provide for severe penalties, both civil and criminal, for filings that contain false or misleading information. These penalties can be levied both on the corporation and on those officers and directors who sign the filings. Every director signs the most important of such filings and so is exposed to potential liability. One of the most potent penalties is levied on corporations and directors under Section 11 of the Securities Act of 1933. This provision covers filings in connection with selling securities to the public. If a prospectus that is filed with the SEC contains misleading or false information, the corporation is strictly liable and the directors (among other potential defendants) are liable unless they can demonstrate that they exercised due diligence in ascertaining whether the information was true or false. This demonstration is, as a practical matter, quite difficult.

The outside directors of both Enron and WorldCom were sued on the theory that they executed prospectuses that contained false or misleading information. Both sets of directors settled those suits and paid significant amounts of money from their own pockets. Ten of 18 former outside Enron directors settled for $13 million. Twelve former directors of WorldCom settled for over $25 million, each director paying at least 20 percent of his or her net worth.

The more direct methods of controlling board power are contained in SOx, which contains two principal kinds of constraints. First, every public company must have an audit committee of independent directors at least one of whom is a "financial expert." The audit committee must be responsible for retaining and overseeing the corporation's independent accounting firm. Second, the act requires senior officers to certify the corporation's financial statements and to certify that, in effect, the corporation has a *Caremark* system of effective internal controls.

E. TERMS OF ART IN THIS CHAPTER

Credit-rating agencies	Sarbanes-Oxley Act of	Securities analyst
Reputational	2002	
intermediaries		

14

Shareholder Governance Powers: Paradigms and Public Companies

This chapter begins a shift in emphasis from the board's power to govern the corporation (and the restrictions on that power) to the shareholders' power to govern. You may remember that one of the central distinguishing marks of the corporate form is that the ultimate owners, the shareholders, have very little power over the entity. While it is common in closely held corporations for the shareholders to be members of the board and officers or employees as well, and in those capacities to exercise great control over the business, *as shareholders* their powers are quite limited.

We will begin with an examination of the shareholders' power to take actions that affect the corporation. First, we'll look at the areas in which the shareholders can act. These areas are rather limited. Second, we'll describe the mechanics of shareholder meetings, voting of shares (including the use of proxies), and the mechanics of acting without a meeting. If you have already covered Chapter 9, much of the mechanics of this chapter will be familiar. Third, we'll explore the somewhat arcane, yet often vitally important, facets of tabulating votes. This is harder than it sounds.

After looking at the shareholders' power to take action we'll move to another, related, area of shareholder governance, the right to be informed about the corporation. When we've finished that topic, we'll move to a (mercifully) brief overview of shareholder power to redress harms to the corporation. This power is exerted through the shareholder derivative lawsuit. Although many important aspects of derivative suits are, in essence, advanced civil procedure, and thus elided over in this book, some are genuinely corporate law-based and so will be the subject of our examination here.

This chapter contains topics that apply to both privately held corporations and those that are publicly traded. The emphasis, though, is on the public corporation. The next chapter focuses on shareholder governance questions that are mostly encountered in the closely held corporation rather than the public company.

A. SHAREHOLDERS' POWER TO TAKE ACTION

1. Actions That the Shareholders May Take as a Group

In the normal course of a corporation's existence, its shareholders vote on one matter, and one matter only: the people who are to serve as directors. At a minimum, the shareholders should be electing one-third of the board each year and frequently they elect the entire board each year. *See* DGCL §211(b) and MBCA §7.01(a).

The shareholders are also required to approve certain fundamental changes in the corporation before such changes can become effective. Note that the shareholders cannot initiate such changes, which must be proposed by the board (because all corporate power is in the board), but can only vote upon whether to approve such fundamental changes. These fundamental changes are amending the Articles; selling all or substantially all of the corporation's assets; merging with another business entity; and dissolving, or ending, the corporation's power to engage in business.

The board may also choose to present matters to the shareholders for their approval even though not required to do so by the corporation's statutes. These matters are often proposed transactions in which some or all of the directors have a conflict of interest. Although shareholder approval is not required for such transactions, a fully informed vote of shareholders unaffiliated with the conflicted directors may either render the transaction immune from attack on the ground of conflict of interest or may provide the corporate planners with greater comfort that the transaction will be found by a court to be fair if challenged. Relatedly, shareholders may be asked to approve indemnification payments to officers or directors. They are also asked to approve the engagement of the company's independent auditors and to approve management compensation plans.

Shareholders have the power to act in two settings without board concurrence and without the possibility of the board overriding the decision. First, the shareholders have the power, in certain settings, to remove, or *amove*, some or all of the directors and to replace those directors by others. Aside from amoving directors, corporations' statutes permit shareholders, as a group and without board interference, to amend the corporation's bylaws. *See* DGCL §§141(k), 109 and MBCA §§8.08, 10.20.

If the corporation is publicly held, and therefore subject to federal securities regulations, the shareholders vote on additional matters, which are discussed more fully at the end of the chapter.

Under state corporate law, the question of so-called *precatory* motions is murkier. Statutes usually permit a certain quantum of the shareholders (10% under MBCA §7.02(a)(2)) to force the board to call a special shareholders meeting, but those statutes, by themselves, do not expand the power of shareholders to take action beyond what has been described so far. All those statutes do is provide an avenue for obtaining the opportunity for the shareholders to take permitted actions. Note, though, that the DGCL default rule does not permit the shareholders to call a special meeting. *See* DGCL §211(d) and MBCA §7.02(a)(2). Similarly, the fact that the board may call a special shareholder meeting does not give the shareholders the power to effect action. It occasionally happens that a group, sometimes a large group, of shareholders has validly called a special shareholders meeting to vote upon a matter outside of the shareholders' power, which the board opposes. As push comes to shove, the shareholders or the board may go to court to seek a declaratory judgment or equitable relief permitting or prohibiting the meeting and vote. The results of such lawsuits have been mixed. Some courts, especially in an earlier time, have refused to allow shareholder votes on purely precatory matters. Other courts, often in more recent times, have permitted such votes.

Notes and Questions

1. What Do You Think?

a. Shareholders are the ultimate owners of the corporation. Do you think they should be able to vote on any matter that a sufficient percentage of them (say 10 percent, 25 percent, or 33 percent) desires to vote on and to have the result of that vote be binding on the corporation? If, in your view, they shouldn't be allowed to vote on every such matter, are there particular issues on which the shareholders should have this power? If so, which ones?

b. What is the harm in permitting shareholder votes on precatory matters? Should shareholders be permitted to vote on any precatory issue? Every precatory issue? Some precatory issues?

2. How Shareholders Take Action in a Meeting

a. The Current Setting

The paradigm vehicle by which the shareholders act is the shareholder meeting. As with board of director meetings, four elements are required for shareholder action taken at a meeting to be valid. The meeting must be properly *called*, the corporation must give proper *notice*, a *quorum of shares* (*not* shareholders) must be present at the meeting, and the action must be approved by a *sufficient vote*. If any of these elements is lacking, the action is subject to attack as being ultra vires. Chapter 8 discusses the ultra vires doctrine in more detail.

i. Call. The *call* of the meeting is simply the decision to hold a meeting at a particular time and place[1] and, often, for a particular reason. *Annual meetings*, at which the directors are to be elected and at which other valid shareholder actions may be taken, are required by the corporation's statutes. *See* DGCL §211(b) and MBCA §7.01. The bylaws, or less typically the Articles, provide the call for the annual shareholder meeting. Where the board has failed, through oversight or intention, to hold the annual shareholder meeting for a certain length of time, any shareholder may bring suit to compel such a meeting. *See* DGCL §211(c) (earlier of 30 days after the scheduled annual meeting or 13 months after the last annual meeting) and MBCA §7.03(a)(1) (earlier of 6 months after the end of the corporation's fiscal year or 15 months after the last annual meeting).

You may remember that directors hold office until their successors are elected, so that even though their term has expired they remain directors and may

---

1. Under the DGCL a meeting can be held no place. That is, a real-time virtual meeting of shareholders may validly transact shareholder business. *See* DGCL §211(a).

collectively take valid board actions. As mentioned above, the owners of a certain quantum of shares can usually compel a special meeting of shareholders. A *special meeting* is simply any shareholder meeting other than the annual meeting. Special shareholder meetings can also be called by the board or by a person or persons designated in the bylaws or Articles, such as the president. *See* DGCL §211(d) and MBCA §7.02(a)(1).

ii. Notice.   Unlike notice to the board, notice to the shareholders is regulated by the statutes. The statutes require between 10 and 60 days' notice of the date, time, and place of the annual meeting and require notice of a special meeting's purpose. *See* DGCL §222(b) and MBCA §§7.05(a), (c). In Delaware, for fundamental changes, the DGCL requires that notice be given at least 20 days in advance of the meeting. *See, e.g.*, DGCL §§251(c), 271(a).

In closely held corporations the shareholders might not change between the call of the meeting and the meeting itself. But suppose a shareholder has the temerity to sell his or her shares between the call and the meeting. Intuitively, the new shareholder should be able to vote the shares at the meeting. Suppose the sale occurs minutes before the meeting begins. In a closely held corporation such events might be easy enough to deal with. In a publicly held corporation, though, shares change hands every day and it would be impractical to keep track of transfers occurring close to the meeting.

Perhaps more important, if a transfer of shares takes place between the call and the meeting should notice to the transferring shareholder be imputed to the transferee shareholder? Should the transferring shareholder be under an obligation to inform the new shareholder of the impending meeting? If you have read Chapter 7, you remember the concept of a record date. The record date is an arbitrary date between the board's decision to undertake some action that requires a fixed list of shareholders (such as paying a dividend or holding a shareholder meeting) and the action itself. All shareholders of record on the record date, usually meaning shareholders at the close of business on the record date, are entitled to notice of the meeting and to vote the shares they hold on the record date at the meeting. Under the DGCL and the MBCA, the board may set one record date for determining the shareholders entitled to notice of a meeting and a later record date for determining the shareholders entitled to vote at the meeting. *See* DGCL §§213(a), 222(a) and MBCA §§1.40, 7.05(a), 7.07(e).

When the corporation's shareholders have divided into factions, management may want to aid one side or the other in the struggle. If a shareholder vote is looming, the board may be tempted to establish an early or late record date depending upon the board's assessment of whether the shareholder profile is shifting against or in favor of its desired outcome. The corporation's statutes prevent the board from acting too opportunistically in this regard by providing that the record date cannot be a past date.

All of this may seem both hypertechnical and hypointeresting. Nonetheless, complying with the requirements of the statutes, articles, bylaws, and board resolutions is undeniably the lawyer's task, and failure to observe all requirements can lead to trouble as the next case shows. If your attention to this case starts to flag, imagine you were McKesson's corporate counsel.

McKesson Corp. v. Derdiger

793 A.2d 385 (Del. Ch. 2002)

CHANDLER, CH.

BACKGROUND FACTS

McKesson [Corporation] is a Delaware corporation with its principal corporate office in San Francisco, California. Defendant [Howard] Derdiger is a stockholder of McKesson. On June 13, 2001, McKesson mailed copies of its proxy statement ("Proxy Statement") to its stockholders informing them of its Annual Meeting, scheduled for July 25, 2001. McKesson set the record date for stockholders eligible to vote at the Annual Meeting to be the close of business Friday, May 25, 2001, the day before the Memorial Day weekend. Due to the holiday, both exchanges trading McKesson stock, the New York Stock Exchange and the Pacific Stock Exchange, were closed from May 26 to May 28. Consequently, the parties agree that the identity of McKesson's record stockholders on May 25 remained identical until the Exchanges reopened on May 29.

On July 17, 2001, Derdiger's counsel delivered a letter to McKesson asserting that the record date failed to comply with the sixty-day requirement of §213(a). In addition, this letter requested that McKesson's Board reschedule the Annual Meeting and redistribute proxy materials to the stockholders who would be eligible to vote under the new record date. In response . . . , McKesson's counsel delivered a letter, dated July 23, 2001, to Derdiger's counsel, insisting that the May 25 record date complied with §213(a) and notifying Derdiger of the Company's intention to go forward with the Annual Meeting as scheduled. On July 24, 2001, the day before the Annual Meeting, Derdiger's counsel faxed a reply to McKesson's July 23 letter explaining his concern that the meeting, if held as scheduled, would be void for statutory non-compliance. As a result, any actions taken at the meeting would also be void, thereby exposing McKesson to potential "significant harm" in the future.[3] No response to defendant's July 24 letter was made and on July 25, 2001 McKesson held its Annual Meeting. Although McKesson's counsel asserts in his brief that the three management proposals were approved overwhelmingly and the three stockholder proposals were disapproved by wide margins, the parties have stipulated only that the inspector of elections certified "certain voting" results following the meeting.

In order to remove any uncertainty as to the legal validity of actions taken at the Annual Meeting on July 25, 2001, McKesson brought this action against Derdiger.[6] The Company seeks a declaratory judgment affirming both its compliance with §213(a) and the validity of all actions taken during the Annual Meeting. McKesson moved for summary judgment pursuant to Chancery Rule 56.

---

3. Compl., Ex. C (July 24, 2001 Letter from Derdiger's counsel to McKesson's counsel) (warning that . . . "someone could assert that seven board seats will need to be filled at next year's annual meeting. Also, the stockholders whose proposals are being submitted could assert claims in connection with the failure to legally submit their proposals").

6. Derdiger and his counsel are no strangers to litigation in this Court involving McKesson.

Derdiger, in turn, moved to dismiss McKesson's complaint for failure to state a claim upon which relief can be granted pursuant to Chancery Rule 12(b)(6). He also moved for summary judgment on his cross-claim, asking the Court to declare that the record date for McKesson's July 25, 2001 annual meeting did not comply with §213(a) and, accordingly, that the actions taken at the meeting are void and invalid.

ANALYSIS

A. Compliance with §213(a)

McKesson contends that it complied with §213(a) as there are precisely sixty days between May 25 and July 25. The Company cites *Aprahamian v. HBO & Co.*[8] in support of its contention that its choice of dates was consistent with the sixty-day maximum permitted under §213(a). In *Aprahamian*, the shareholder meeting at issue was scheduled for May 15, 1987 and the record date, as reported in the Opinion of the Court, was March 15, 1987. Consistent with the McKesson record and meeting dates, there were exactly sixty days *between the record* and meeting dates in *Aprahamian*.

Derdiger's counsel, however, points out that the clear language of §213(a) states that a record date "shall not be more than 60 . . . days *before*" the meeting date, not that there "shall not be more than 60 . . . days *between*" the record date and the meeting date. The defendant correctly sets forth the only way to determine whether the statutory imperative of §213(a) has been met. The statute looks at the number of days *before* the meeting date to determine a valid period of time within which a record date may be set. In this case, the meeting date was July 25, 2001. One day before July 25 is July 24. Two days before July 25 is July 23. Three days before July 25 is July 22. Continuing counting the number of days *before* the meeting date in this manner ends with May 26, 2001 as the sixtieth day *before* July 25, 2001. The statute commands that a record date "*shall not* be more than 60" days before the meeting date. McKesson's May 25, 2001 record date was sixty-one days before the Annual Meeting.

Derdiger also attacks McKesson's reliance on *Aprahamian* as support for the Company's method of calculating when a valid record date may be set under §213(a). The defendant asserts that McKesson's reading of *Aprahamian* is flawed due to a "typographical error" in the published version of the *Aprahamian* Court's decision. Derdiger's counsel found record evidence in the *Aprahamian* case indicating that the record date in HBO's notice of its annual shareholder meeting was actually *March 16, 1987* (not March 15 as the Court's published opinion erroneously recites), *i.e.*, exactly sixty days before HBO's May 15, 1987 annual meeting.[10] As a result, Derdiger argues that *Aprahamian* actually contradicts McKesson's position and supports his position that the May 25, 2001 record date did not correspond to the directive of §213(a). Alternatively, Derdiger contends that, even if the Court does not accept his argument regarding a typographical error in

---

8. 531 A.2d 1204 (Del. Ch. 1987).

10. *See, e.g.,* Def.'s Opening Br. at 6 ("The record date here fixed by the board for this annual meeting was *March 16.* . . . If that meeting is not convened . . . then under Section 213 arguably the record date of *March 16* will no longer be any good.") (emphasis added) (quoting *Aprahamian v. HBO & Co.*, Del. Ch., C.A. No. 8989, Hartnett, V.C. (May 11, 1987) (Tr. of Inj. Hr'g at 41)).

Aprahamian, that case cannot serve as binding precedent on an issue in which it is in apparent conflict with a statutory command.

McKesson insists that *Aprahamian* authorizes a new and expansive way of calculating the statutory sixty-day maximum allowed by the statute. In *Aprahamian,* on the eve of HBO's scheduled shareholder meeting, the management of HBO decided to postpone the meeting upon receiving information from their proxy solicitor that a group of insurgent shareholders might defeat the management's proposals. The plaintiff challenged that delay and this Court held that the postponement served no significant stockholder interest and directed that the annual meeting be convened as scheduled on May 15, 1987. The Court also directed the Company to immediately adjourn the May 15 meeting and shortly thereafter reconvene the meeting after giving notice to all the shareholders of the Court's decision. The explicit purpose of the Court's directives was to preserve HBO's established March 16, 1987 record date so that the identity of the shareholders originally entitled to vote, including those whose proxies had been garnered by the insurgents, would not change. The directives were necessary to preserve that record date because if HBO's "annual meeting does not convene by May 15, 1987, the proxies submitted by the stockholders may expire because of . . . §213 which provide[s] that a record date shall not be fixed for a date more than 60 days before the date of the annual meeting."[14] Although McKesson is correct that the *Aprahamian* Court apparently calculated the permissible sixty-day window of §213(a) in the manner the Company advocates, McKesson's erroneous belief resulted from that decision mistakenly referring to the record date as *March 15, 1987 (i.e., sixty-one* days before May 15, 1987).

Unlike McKesson, however, I am convinced that the *Aprahamian* Court calculated the sixty-day window in the same way as I explained above. That Court was neither employing a new method of counting the permissible sixty-day time period nor accepting sixty-one days as "close enough." The actual Order to adjourn and reconvene, as well as the notice of annual meeting of HBO stockholders, substantiates the *Aprahamian* Court's intention to calculate §213(a)'s sixty-day window as described herein. The *Aprahamian* Court's stated objective "to protect the record date" makes it clear that it intended to observe the sixty-day mandate of §213(a). Thus, the Order's only purpose for directing that the meeting be convened on May 15, albeit only long enough to adjourn, was to remain within the sixty-day statutory window, thereby preserving the *March 16* record date. Nothing in *Aprahamian* can be read, in my view, to support McKesson's position that either sixty days *between* the meeting and record date is statutorily acceptable or that sixty-one days is "close enough" to comply with §213(a).

The Legislature includes immutable time limits in statutes to serve particular purposes and such time limits are usually strictly enforced. An example of this can be seen in this Court's recent *Nelson v. Frank E. Best Inc.*[23] decision concerning the "Sunday rule." In that case, the Court held that even when the last day of the limitations period for making an appraisal demand pursuant to [DGCL] §262 falls on a Sunday, the statute calls for strict compliance. Recognizing the General Assembly's appreciation of the issue whether or not to exclude weekend days from

---

14. [*Aprahamian,* 531 A.2d] at 1206.
23. 768 A.2d 473 (Del. Ch. 2001).

limitation periods, the Court noted that the clear language of the statute is the most important factor upon which its interpretation hinges.[24]

No reason appears for treating the timing requirements of §213 less strictly than the timing requirements of §262. The Legislature's command in each instance is clear and unequivocal. Section 213(a) prescribes a maximum period of exactly sixty days that may separate the record date from a stockholder meeting date. Had the Legislature intended a more flexible interpretation of §213(a), it would have so provided with enabling language. The Court, therefore, is obliged to respect the statute's literal terms.

Sixty-one days separated the May 25, 2001 record date from McKesson's July 25, 2001 Annual Meeting. I conclude, therefore, that under §213(a) May 25, 2001 was not a valid record date for McKesson's Annual Meeting.

B. Consequences of Non-Compliance

McKesson contends that . . . equitable considerations should lead me nonetheless to declare that the actions taken at the July 25 Annual Meeting are valid. To this end, McKesson offers two related arguments.

First, according to McKesson, an order invalidating the actions taken at the Annual Meeting and requiring another meeting will impose a substantial and unnecessary burden on the Company. Because the group of shareholders on the May 25 record date was the same on May 28 (as a result of the legal holiday), McKesson posits that the results of the votes taken on July 25 would have been the same anyway. To convene another meeting, it contends, would thus be a costly, and useless, exercise.[25]

Second, McKesson insists that its conduct in these circumstances is not inconsistent with the policy reasons underlying the statute. The statute's purpose is to "permit and facilitate reasonable methods of notification" to stockholders eligible to vote in an upcoming shareholder meeting.[26] By establishing that a record date may not be set less than ten days before a shareholder meeting, the Legislature prevents a board from suddenly calling a shareholder meeting with a time horizon that would not permit proper notification of the company's shareholders. On the other hand, the ten-day minimum also "recogniz[es] the 'practical necessity of dispensing with notice to persons who attempt to become registered shareholders shortly before a

---

24. *Id.* at 475 (noting that in contrast to a provision excepting Sundays from the period of time permitted for sending a demand for appraisal under §262, there are many other instances where "the General Assembly has explicitly excluded final Sundays from the calculation of statutory deadlines").

25. McKesson also seems to suggest that this is not a stew of its own making in which it finds itself. It accuses Derdiger's counsel of delaying notification of the problem until eleven days before the date of the Annual Meeting. If McKesson had had more notice, it could have avoided this dispute by sending a notice to stockholders scheduling the meeting for July 24. The July 24 meeting, which would have been held solely to preserve the May 25 record date, would have been immediately adjourned and reconvened on July 25. *See* [DGCL] §222(c). . . . By waiting until July 17 to make his position known, Derdiger made it too late to send out a notice for a July 24 meeting. *See* [DGCL] §222(b) (written notice of any meeting shall be not less than 10 . . . days before the date of the meeting to each stockholder entitled to vote at such meeting).

Derdiger does not directly address this point, perhaps because McKesson did not formally advance it as an argument. Nevertheless, I need not address it, because it is based on speculation about what McKesson should or might have done in circumstances different from those that the parties have stipulated to in this proceeding, because the parties have not properly advanced it for decision by this Court, and because consideration of that argument would involve a balancing of equities that is not necessary to my final conclusion as to the consequences of McKesson's improperly set record date.

26. *Bryan v. Western Pac. R.R. Corp.*, 35 A.2d 909, 914 (Del. Ch. 1944); *Pabst Brewing Co. v. Jacobs*, 549 F. Supp. 1068, 1072 (D. Del. 1982) (same).

meeting.'"[27] The sixty-day maximum time period helps to assure that the list of stockholders eligible to vote at a shareholder meeting is not "stale" and represents those who still have a stake in the company. Therefore, by establishing a time period from ten to sixty days prior to a scheduled shareholder meeting during which §213(a) permits a board to set a corresponding record date, "the Legislature has balanced the interest of the corporation and its shareholders — that is, to allow the corporation sufficient time to determine the shareholders in order to give effective notice of corporate action and to assure that the shareholders who vote have an interest in the corporation."[28]

McKesson argues that since its May 25, 2001, record date was followed by non-trading holidays . . . , the composition of the Company's shareholder list did not change before May 26, the last day within the sixty-day time span. The shareholder list existing on May 25, therefore, did not become "stale" and McKesson's shareholders did not suffer harm as a result. Moreover, McKesson asserts that the "overwhelming" majorities that adopted the uncontroversial actions in question during the July 25 Annual Meeting still exist and would presumably cast the same votes. McKesson thus urges a "substantial compliance" or "no harm, no foul" approach to statutory interpretation when a corporate act does no violence to the fundamental statutory purpose. The most "equitable" outcome, McKesson concludes, is for the Court to recognize the underlying validity of the actions taken at the July 25 meeting, even if I find that the record date for the Annual Meeting was not in strict compliance with §213(a)'s sixty-day maximum.

It is tempting to accept McKesson's invitation to apply a "no harm, no foul" rule in the unusual circumstances of this case. That is particularly true when McKesson's Board acted in apparent good faith and in light of assertions by the Company of the uncontroversial nature of the issues voted on at the Annual Meeting, the overwhelming approval of management's proposals, and the likelihood of a similar result if those actions were declared void and another vote was required. Relying on equitable principles so as to modify an explicit statutory requirement, however, is a dangerous path for this Court to tread because of its "slippery slope" characteristics. It is true that our courts have, on occasion, invoked principles of equity and fairness to strike down corporate actions even when those actions technically satisfied every legal requirement. But McKesson has cited no authority for the reverse of that proposition — that equity properly may be invoked to rescue a corporate act or decision that violates a statutory command. In fact, this Court has been cautioned about the over use of its equitable powers.

The drafters of §213 sought to institute an unambiguous guideline for the scheduling of shareholder meetings. Thus, the Legislature adopted a bright-line rule, requiring that a board, in advance of a shareholder meeting, fix a record date which "shall not be more than 60 nor less than 10 days before the date of such meeting."[32] The language is clear and admits of no discretion to depart from its evident command.

[handwritten margin note: 2nd argument]

27. *Pabst Brewing,* 549 F. Supp. at 1072 (quoting *Bryan v. Western Pac. R.R. Corp.,* 35 A.2d 909, 914 (Del. Ch. 1944)).

28. *Id.*

32. The statute does contain a default provision, see [DGCL] §213(a), which applies in those instances in which "no record date has been fixed." If the board has fixed no record date, the default record date is at the close of business on the day next preceding the day on which notice of the meeting was given. In this case, since McKesson

If the Court were to accommodate McKesson's request to rewrite the statute "in this particular circumstance," it would expose the Court to accusations that it was engaged in judicial legislation. It would also open the door to similar claims, in which companies could attempt to rely on exceptional or "equitable" circumstances in order to cure an action that violates a clear statutory command. Injecting such legal uncertainty into an otherwise unambiguous statutory regime would neither advance the Legislature's intent nor the stability of the Delaware General Corporation Law. I cannot, therefore, hold that the actions taken at the Annual Meeting are valid based on the Company's "equitable" arguments.

There is one aspect of this case, however, that does permit me to hold that the actions taken at the Annual Meeting are valid. This is the fact that McKesson could, conceivably, have relied on a decision of this Court for the Company's stated belief that, by selecting a record date that had sixty days *between* it and the meeting date, it had complied with the requirements of §213(a). Although the extraordinary diligence of defendant's counsel has demonstrated that a typographical error could have been responsible for McKesson's erroneous belief, it is not reasonable to require that counsel seek out the trial transcript or other record material to determine whether the Court really meant what was contained in its published opinion. This is even the case when, as the defendant suggests, there was an obvious mistake in a judicial opinion.

If the defendant had been able to cite even one case pertaining to this issue directly contradicting *Aprahamian* that would have placed the plaintiff on notice (either constructively or actually) of the error in that case, then perhaps I would reach the contrary conclusion. In this Opinion, I clarify that the correct method for counting the maximum allowed sixty-day period for setting a record date for a shareholder meeting pursuant to §213(a) is to be conducted as described above. No company should ever be led astray in the future based on any misconception caused by this Court's *Aprahamian* Opinion. Due to the circumstances presented here (which by definition cannot occur again), and in light of the fact that there were no allegations as to any impropriety in connection with the Annual Meeting other than an improper record date, I hold that the actions taken at McKesson's July 25, 2001 Annual Meeting are valid.

Notes and Questions

1. Notes

a. McKesson Corporation's 2001 annual meeting was held on July 25, 2001. Chancellor Chandler's opinion was issued on January 10, 2002.

b. Mr. Derdiger was a shareholder of Access Health, Inc., which, in late September 1998, announced that it had negotiated to be acquired by HBO & Company in a transaction in which Access shareholders would receive HBO stock. Less than one month later, HBO & Company announced that it had negotiated to be acquired by McKesson Corporation in a transaction in which HBO shareholders

---

mailed notices of the meeting on June 13, Derdiger has argued (in the alternative) that if McKesson's flawed May 25 record date is treated as "no record date having been fixed," then under §213(a)'s default provision, the record date was actually June 12 (i.e., the day next preceding the day on which notice was given). In light of the conclusion I reach in this case, however, I do not need to reach the defendant's alternative argument on this issue.

would receive McKesson stock. These transactions were effected by January 12, 1999.

As Chancellor Chandler described it,

> Between April 28, 1999, and June 21, 1999, [McKesson] made a series of stunning announcements to the financial markets. These announcements indicated that its information technology subsidiary, formerly HBOC, had significantly overstated revenues, net income, earnings per share and other financial information for the three preceding financial years. [McKesson]'s stock price fell precipitously in reaction to this announcement. [McKesson] shareholders experienced paper losses of almost $34 per share, or just over fifty percent, on the day of the first announcement.

Derdiger v. Tallman, 773 A.2d 1005, 1008 (Del. Ch. 2000)

Many shareholders, including Mr. Derdiger, sued, seeking damages for fraud and breach of fiduciary duties.

c. The HBO & Company that was the defendant in *Aprahamian* is the same company that acquired Access Health and that, in turn, was acquired by McKesson. It is possible that the parties in this litigation had access to *Aprahamian* litigation documents that brought to light the typographical error.

d. Four management-sponsored items were on the annual meeting agenda. Electing three directors to three-year terms; approving an amendment to the certificate of incorporation to change the company's name from McKesson HBOC, Inc., to McKesson Corporation; ratifying the appointment of the independent auditors; and amending the compensation plan for the outside directors. The voting was closest on the proposal to amend the compensation plan for outside directors. That proposal passed by a vote of 192,692,929 votes in favor; 63,888,328 votes against; and 2,414,293 votes abstaining. In percentages, the proposal passed with slightly over 74 percent of the votes.

The three shareholder-proposed items were also on the agenda. One dealt with performance-based options, another with severance payments, and the third with the sale of the company. The voting was closest on a proposal regarding stock options. The proposal was defeated by a vote of 55,711,172 in favor; 139,667,310 against; and 13,224,895 abstaining. That is, the proposal received less than 27 percent of the votes cast.

2. Reality Check

a. Why was the record date impermissible?

b. If the record date was impermissible, why doesn't Chancellor Chandler order a new meeting?

c. Could McKesson have remedied the problem at some point between June 13 (the date it mailed notice to its shareholders) and the meeting? If so, how?

d. What equitable arguments did McKesson make and why did Chancellor Chandler reject them?

3. Suppose

a. Suppose the stock markets had been open on Memorial Day. Would the court's analysis or the result have been different?

b. For the McKesson Corporation 2002 annual meeting, the board set a record date of June 3, 2002; sent notice to shareholders on June 14, 2002; and held the meeting on July 31, 2002. Given the July 31 meeting, what are the earliest and latest possible record dates and notice dates under the DGCL?

c. If Chancellor Chandler had chosen to use the default rule in the DGCL for instances in which the board does not set a record date, what date would have been used? *See* footnote 32.

4. What Do You Think?

a. Is there any evidence that McKesson actually relied on the legal interpretation of *Aprahamian* that it asserts as precedent? If so, what is it? If not, should the court predicate its decision on such reliance?

b. Why might McKesson have set the record date as it did? How could this problem have happened? How could the problem have been avoided?

c. Why do you think Mr. Derdiger brought this lawsuit? What do you think he intended to accomplish?

iii. Quorum. The third element for a valid meeting is the presence of a quorum. A *quorum* is simply the minimum amount of voting power that must be present at a meeting for actions to be valid. The requirement of a quorum is to prevent a collective body from acting when so few members are present that the action may be thought to be unrepresentative of the whole body's intent. A quorum for shareholder meetings is defined by the percentage of *voting power* represented at the meeting, not by the percentage of *shareholders* present.

Under both the Delaware statute and the Model Act, the default rule is that a quorum for shareholder meetings is a majority of the voting power. That number may be raised or lowered under either statute. In Delaware, however, the quorum may not be lowered below one-third of the total voting power. *See* DGCL §216 and MBCA §7.25.

One strategic difference between a quorum for board meetings and a quorum for shareholder meetings is that a shareholder quorum once established is valid for the remainder of the meeting. This means that dissident shareholders cannot prevent unfavorable action by leaving the meeting and breaking the quorum. Strategically, they must decide in advance of the meeting whether adverse action is likely to be taken and decide whether to stay away in hopes that a quorum will not be present. It is typical practice for the chair of a shareholder meeting to declare the presence of a quorum as the very first item of business because, until such a declaration is made, shareholders can leave and possibly stymie any further action. *See* MBCA §7.25(b) (Delaware has a similar rule via case law).

iv. Sufficient Vote. The final requirement for valid shareholder action is a sufficient vote. The default rule in Delaware is that a matter is approved if it receives a majority of the votes present at the meeting. *See* DGCL §216(2). The MBCA default rule is slightly different: a matter is approved if it receives a *simple majority*. That is, if the "yes" votes are greater than the "no" votes regardless of how few votes are cast. *See* MBCA §7.25(c). Under the Delaware approach, an abstention has the effect of a "no" vote, while under the MBCA an abstention is a true abstention (i.e., a refraining from participation in the particular vote).

Here is an example of the two approaches. Assume a corporation has 1,000 shares outstanding, each of which has one vote per share. A shareholder meeting is properly called and noticed. The holders of 800 shares attend the meeting, meaning that a quorum (more than 500 shares) is present. A particular matter is put to a shareholder vote and the result is 375 yes, 370 no, and 55 abstain or not voted. Does the matter pass? It passes under the MBCA (because there were more "yes" votes than "no" votes) but fails under the DGCL (because fewer than half the 800 shares present voted yes). Indeed, under the MBCA the matter would have been adopted had the vote been 1 yes, 0 no, 799 abstain or not voted!

The DGCL, and the laws of most states (but not the MBCA), require a higher quantum of shareholder voting power for approval of fundamental changes such as amending the articles, mergers, dissolution, and selling all or substantially all of the corporation's assets, because such changes are, well, fundamental. *See, e.g.,* DGCL §§251(c), 271(a). The DGCL requires approval of such actions by an *absolute majority*, which means a majority of all the voting power, regardless of whether that power is present at the meeting. Thus, shares that are not present at the meeting are effectively "no" votes.

Finally, under both the DGCL and the MBCA, yet another definition of sufficient vote applies to electing and removing directors, because electing directors is seen as so central to healthy corporate operations. Directors are elected by a *plurality* of votes, meaning the candidates with the most votes are elected, regardless of how few votes are cast, as long as a quorum is present. *See* DGCL §216(3) and MBCA §7.28(a). The reason for this rule is to ensure that directors can be elected if a quorum exists. Directors do not run for particular slots but instead are elected at large.[2] The combination of the plurality rule and at-large qualities of director elections means that ties among candidates are not necessarily a hindrance to selecting a board. For example, assume a board of five directors and assume that the following candidates receive the following votes:

Candidate	Votes
A	350
B	350
C	300
D	200
E	200
F	150
G	150

In this instance *A, B, C, D,* and *E* are all elected, because they are the five candidates with the most votes. Sometimes, however, ties become important. Suppose the same board and candidates but a vote distribution like this:

Candidate	Votes
A	350
B	350
C	300
D	250
E	200
F	200
G	50

2. Remember, though, that some boards are classified, and in those circumstances directors run for election as representing a particular class or classes of stock.

Now, *A*, *B*, *C*, and *D* are elected but *E* and *F* are tied for the final slot. Case law supports the view that no one has been elected to the fifth slot, which means that the current incumbent remains in office because the statutes provide that a director remains in office until his or her successor has been elected. *See* DGCL §141(b) and MBCA §8.05(e). Such a director is called a *holdover*. If no incumbent is in the fifth slot then a vacancy exists, which can be filled by the newly elected board, in Delaware, and by either the newly elected board or the shareholders under the MBCA. *See* DGCL §223(a)(1) and MBCA §8.10(a).

In some corporations, both public and private, directors are elected by cumulative voting. This method is designed to allow a minority of shareholders to be certain of electing at least one director on a board. Although cumulative voting exists in some public corporations, it is primarily useful in the close corporation setting. For that reason, a more detailed discussion of cumulative voting is set out in the next chapter.

Putting It to Work

Problem 14-1

Adam, Beatrice, and Cameron are 3 of 15 shareholders owning a combined 20 percent of the common stock of a fast-food corporation, Town Burger, Inc. On May 25, Adam, Beatrice, and Cameron each send a written notice to the board of directors demanding that the corporation call a special meeting of shareholders for the purpose of removing Dennis as a director without cause. Adam, Beatrice, Cameron, and several other shareholders believe Dennis has been too inattentive to the corporation's business and therefore he should be removed.

The board, at its regularly scheduled meeting later that month, considered and denied the request. The board was fully informed and no director (except Dennis, who recused himself from participation and voting on the matter) acted other than in the genuine belief that denying the demand was in the best interest of Town Burger.

a. Did the board act validly under the MBCA? Under the DGCL?

Problem 14-2

Assume that, on the facts of the prior problem, the board called a special meeting for the purpose of voting on whether Dennis should be removed as a director without cause. The meeting was called on June 1st to be held in the Town Burger headquarters conference room on June 25th. Notice was sent to every shareholder on June 10th. The notice included the date, time, and place of the meeting and stated that the purpose would be to vote on whether Dennis should be removed without cause.

At the meeting, 8 of the 15 shareholders (including Adam, Beatrice, and Cameron) attended in person. Those 8 shareholders owned 840 of the 2,000 outstanding shares. The vote was 410 FOR removal, 390 AGAINST removal, and 40 ABSTAIN.

a. Was Dennis removed as a director under the MBCA? Under the DGCL?

* * *

v. The Shift to Simple Majority Vote.   In publicly held corporations, the nominating committee of the board recommends candidates for director positions. Current directors whose terms are expiring are typically re-nominated. The candidates nominated by the board will be elected easily. This is so for at least two reasons. First, the shares of most public corporations are sufficiently diffused that proponents of other candidates will not realistically be able to garner enough votes to defeat the board's candidates. Second, recall that directors are elected by a plurality. That corporate law rule means that any other vote than "for" would have no effect; it is only the number of "for" votes that matter. One shareholder owning a single share would elect the entire board simply by voting "FOR" for the board's nominees, even if every other shareholder voted "withhold" for every board candidate.

In some instances, however, dissident shareholders have enough resources to wage a *proxy fight*, which is an attempt to replace the current directors, or the board-nominated candidates, by fielding an alternative slate of board candidates and soliciting proxies from the shareholders. Proxy fights are expensive and are rarely undertaken except by a party interested in acquiring the entire corporation.

Beginning with the corporate scandals at the millennium, many mutual funds and pension funds, which typically are large shareholders in public companies, began to demonstrate their frustration with, and disapproval of, corporate managers by withholding their votes for directors. In response, the great majority of public companies amended their bylaws to provide for election of directors by simple majority.

As a matter of corporate law, the shift from the plurality standard to the simple majority standard is accomplished through a bylaw provision. A typical bylaw reads:

> [E]ach director shall be elected by the vote of the majority of the votes cast with respect to the director at any meeting for the election of directors at which a quorum is present. . . . For purposes of this Section, a majority of the votes cast means that the number of shares voted "for" a director must exceed the number of votes cast against that director.

Even with a simple majority vote standard, in the publicly held corporation it will be extraordinary for a board candidate to be defeated. Nonetheless, activist shareholders viewed the simple majority vote movement as an important victory for shareholder rights.

What happens when a board-nominated candidate does not receive a simple majority of votes? The result, of course, is not a vacancy but a holdover director. Under corporate law, failing to be re-elected is not the same as being removed. Further, many corporations limit removal of directors to removal for cause, which would not include failing to be re-elected, without more. This would result in a pyrrhic victory for the shareholders who successfully prevented the election of a director.

In light of the holdover director rule, corporations that adopt a simple majority vote bylaw also usually require that all directors, as a condition of being nominated by the board for another term, submit an irrevocable resignation that becomes effective if they do not receive a simple majority of votes. The resignation creates a vacancy that is then filled by the remaining board members. Under the MBCA, the vacancy can even be filled by the just-resigned director. *See* MBCA §10.22(a)(3). The same result could arguably be reached in Delaware, although the DGCL is not explicit. *See* DGCL §223(a). Of course, the directors must meet their duties of care and loyalty when selecting a person to fill any director vacancy.

Under both Delaware and the Model Act, bylaws may change the plurality default rule for electing directors and, if adopted by the shareholders, may not be changed by the board. Both statutes also permit a director resignation to be contingent on the result of a shareholder vote and permit such a contingent resignation to be irrevocable. *See* DGCL §§141(b), 216 and MBCA §§8.05, 8.07(b), and 10.22.

vi. The Importance of Being Present.   Presence is an important concept in quorum and sufficient vote contexts. A certain percentage of the shareholder voting power must be present to constitute a quorum and the validity of many shareholder votes is measured, in Delaware and other states, by the amount of shareholder voting power present. Under the DGCL the refreshingly intuitive rule is that shares are present when their owner is physically in attendance at the meeting. *See* DGCL §216. The MBCA speaks in terms of shares being "represented" at a meeting but provides that a shareholder may vote his or her shares in person. MBCA §7.21(a), 7.22(a).

Shares can be present in two other ways. The first is through a proxy. *See* DGCL §212(b), MBCA §7.22(a). A *proxy* is an agency relationship in which a shareholder appoints another person to attend a shareholders meeting on the shareholder's behalf and to vote the shareholder's shares. The word *proxy* itself is used to describe the relationship, the agent (who may also be called the *proxyholder*), or the writing (if any) in which the agency relationship is created and defined. The context should make clear which of these uses is intended. A proxy may be *limited*, in which the shareholder authorizes the agent to vote in a particular way, or *general*, in which the agent is authorized to use his or her discretion in voting. The common law, embodied in nearly every state in the principles expressed in the *Restatement (Third) of Agency*, governs proxies as a typical agency relationship.

The corporation's statutes, especially the MBCA, make a few changes to the common law rules. A proxy relationship may be created only by a writing or electronic transmission. *See* MBCA §7.22(b). The DGCL explicitly leaves the common law rules in place, although it gives safe harbors of the ways in which a proxy can be created. *See* DGCL §212(c). Both the MBCA and DGCL provide that a proxy is irrevocable if it explicitly states that intention and if it is coupled with an interest. *See* DGCL §212(e), MBCA §7.22(d). You may recall from Chapter 4 that the term "coupled with an interest" is a rather murky term of art in agency law. The MBCA gives some examples of an interest sufficient to support irrevocability, but the DGCL simply references the common law. *See* DGCL §212(e), MBCA §7.22(d). The MBCA provides that the principal's (i.e., shareholder's) death does not invalidate the proxy in the absence of actual knowledge by the corporation.

See MBCA §7.22(e); the DGCL is silent in this regard. Both statutes provide a default period for a proxy's validity. The MBCA provides 11 months and the DGCL provides 3 years. *See* DGCL §212(b), MBCA §7.22(c). Why did the drafters choose these rather odd time periods?

The second way shares can be present without their owner being physically at the meeting is through a virtual presence. Under the DGCL and MBCA, shares are present if their owner (or a proxyholder) may participate in the shareholder meeting through an electronic medium in which they may read or hear the proceedings in real-time and in which they have the opportunity to participate themselves. *See* DGCL §211(a)(2)b, MBCA §7.09. Certainly a conference telephone call meets the requirements and many kinds of computer linkages may, as well.

b. *Background and Context — The Annual Meeting of the Public Corporation*

As you might imagine, the logistics of holding a meeting of shareholders in a public company are frequently quite intricate and planning for such a meeting is very elaborate. This section describes a typical public company meeting.

Planning for the meeting usually begins a year or more in advance. Many public companies like to hold their annual meeting in a different location every year, sometimes to provide the opportunity for shareholders who live in disparate parts of the country to attend more easily, and sometimes to make attendance more difficult. The planners, who may be corporate employees or may be an independent firm retained to plan the meeting, must find and rent a venue that will accommodate the anticipated number of shareholders, which may range from a few dozen to several hundred. Because most public companies use a calendar fiscal year, that is, one that ends on December 31st, they schedule their annual meeting in the following spring. Probably 80 percent or more of public company annual meetings are held between February 15th and May 15th.

Once the date and place have been established, counsel can work backward to determine the range of dates within which notice must be sent and the range of consequently permissible record dates. Note that the corporation's bylaws (and, less frequently, the Articles) may contain provisions about the setting of the annual meeting or notice or record dates that, obviously, must be adhered to. The New York Stock Exchange suggests that corporations select a record date that is at least 30 days before the meeting date to ensure enough time for shareholders to receive and return their voting materials. Corporations usually plan to send notices to shareholders within a few days of the record date to minimize the number of notice recipients who have sold their shares.

Although the corporate statutes require only that directors be elected, at public company annual meetings at least one other item is typically included on the agenda: approval of the accounting firm that will serve as the company's independent auditor. The board of directors may have other items to bring before the shareholders, frequently approval of stock option plans for senior executives. *See, e.g., NYSE Listed Company Manual* §§303A.08, 312.03.

Further, shareholders may propose items for shareholder action. Many public corporations have an *advance notice bylaw* that requires a shareholder to give the board notice of his or her intention to move a proposal or nominate directors at the meeting. Such advance notice bylaws may require notice to the corporation's management months in advance of the meeting. Clearly the intent of such a bylaw is to thwart precipitous shareholder unrest and to provide management with information about shareholder dissent so that management can react. As a practical matter, a shareholder proposal first presented on the floor of the meeting would have little chance of passage because the vast majority of shares are present by proxy and the proxyholders either do not have the power to vote on unscheduled matters or, if they do have the power, tend to vote against such proposals.

The meeting itself may be a festive, welcoming celebration of the corporation and its achievements or a barebones, no nonsense, formality lasting fifteen minutes. Corporations that are financially successful tend to have the more elaborate meetings, while those corporations with dismal recent performance or callous management may prefer to sponsor more austere meetings. If the corporation manufactures consumer goods they may provide samples to shareholders who attend the meeting. Sometimes light refreshments, or even a real breakfast or lunch, is provided.

Only those who were record or beneficial shareholders on the record date and their proxyholders have a right to attend the annual meeting but in practice members of the press may be invited and others are usually permitted to attend. Often the chair of the board of directors or the company's chief executive officer will preside over the meeting. In any event, it is typical for such people to make presentations even if someone else presides. Usually all board members attend if possible, and at least some (frequently all) senior managers attend, as well. These people are seated on the stage and are available to answer questions from the audience, although in practice the presiding officer answers all questions. A lawyer is always seated next to the presiding officer to give immediate advice on the conduct of the meeting if necessary. That lawyer may be an employee of the corporation or someone from an independent law firm.

It may surprise you to learn that very few companies have explicit rules governing the conduct of the annual meeting. As you know, the DGCL simply requires a meeting and does not provide any conduct rules or guidelines. Likewise the articles are usually silent on the question. The bylaws sometimes name the person who is to preside over the meeting but, again, they do not usually contain any detailed provisions for running the meeting.

By now you may be assuming that *Robert's Rules of Order* is typically used as a guide. Nope. *Robert's* is designed for collective bodies that deliberate as well as approve actions. Because such a large proportion of shares are represented by limited proxies, no deliberation is possible. Further, as you recall, corporate law permits the shareholders to vote on only a few matters, and the consequences of those questions are often relatively circumscribed such that deliberation would be unproductive. Case law simply requires that annual meetings satisfy basic notions of "fairness." The MBCA provides that the bylaws or board shall appoint a chair of the meeting and that the chair may adopt "fair" rules for the conduct of the meeting. *See* MBCA §7.08(c).

Meetings usually begin with a declaration that a quorum is present. Often the next order of business is the opening and closing of the polls. Ushers hand out ballots to those record shareholders who wish to vote in person, though a minuscule percentage of shares is voted in this fashion. After those ballots are collected, the polls are closed and no more votes can be accepted. *See* MBCA §7.08(d). Then the presiding officer may introduce other senior people who may make presentations, or there may simply be a video presentation on the state of the company.

At some point, generally after the polls have been closed, the shareholders are given an opportunity to question management. The meeting may take anywhere from half an hour to two hours or so, at the end of which the presiding officer declares the meeting adjourned.

3. How Shareholders Take Action by Consent in Lieu of a Meeting

Just as directors may act without holding an actual meeting, so shareholders may act. The DGCL and MBCA permit consents to be obtained and submitted to the corporation electronically. *See* DGCL §§228(d), 232(c), MBCA §§1.40, 7.04(a), (b). Where the shareholders and the board are at odds, this shareholder power can become important because it permits the shareholders to amove the recalcitrant directors even where the board refuses to call a shareholder meeting.

Shareholders may take action even if they are not unanimous. Under the DGCL this power is the default rule. The MBCA permits non-unanimous shareholder action without a meeting only if granted in the articles of incorporation. *See* DGCL §228(a), MBCA §7.04(b). This power can be a useful tool in both the public and private company settings. If the consent action is proposed by the corporation's board, their resolution to seek consents is, in effect, the call. Where shareholders intend to act without board approval (most often attempting to act without the board's knowledge), the call is just the leaders of the shareholder group beginning to solicit consent.

If the board is soliciting consents it may send a request to every shareholder, which serves as notice that a consent solicitation is taking place. Insurgent shareholders, by contrast, usually do not solicit every shareholder but only those whom the leaders believe will be sympathetic to their cause. Under DGCL §228(e) and MBCA §7.04, however, if the consent solicitation is successful, the corporation must give "prompt" notice to all shareholders who would be entitled to vote that the shareholder action has been taken by consent.

Because no actual meeting takes place, the concepts of quorum and sufficient vote collapse into one. The proponents must obtain consents from shareholders holding an absolute majority of voting shares. For shareholder actions requiring a supermajority vote, the consents required are increased accordingly. *See* DGCL §228(a), MBCA §7.04. Many Delaware public corporations have bylaws that require shareholders to notify the board if they intend to take action by consent and to permit the board to set a record date if it chooses. Obviously, the intent of such a bylaw is to defeat the element of surprise. In corporations without such a bylaw, the record date for consent solicitations is the date the first consent is delivered to the corporation. *See* DGCL §213(b), MBCA §7.04.

Conceptually, a consent is unlike a proxy in that a consent is the equivalent of a vote, while a proxy is an authorization to someone else to vote in the future. Under both acts a consent can be revoked before sufficient consent are received by the corporation to take action. DGCL §228(c), MBCA §7.04(c). To prevent consent solicitations from taking an inordinate amount of time, and thus presenting the danger that some consenting shareholders have changed their minds, or are no longer shareholders, the MBCA provides that all valid consents must be delivered no later than 60 days after the date of the earliest dated delivered consent. *See* MBCA §7.04(c). The DGCL provides that all valid consents must be delivered within 60 days of the first consent's delivery. *See* DGCL §228(c).

4. Tabulating the Votes

The process of counting votes is purely mechanical in many senses but also presents situations when a lawyer's skills are vital. The outline of the basic process is the same regardless of whether the corporation is closely held or publicly held, but in the public corporation the process becomes more elaborate. This section is divided into two complementary questions. First, we look at who may vote. That is, which humans may cast votes in corporate elections. Second, we will look at the process of counting the votes with special emphasis on the process in the public corporation.

a. *Whose Vote Counts?*

One guiding principle of shareholder voting has been that elections must be concluded rapidly because uncertainty in determining the directors or whether a question put to the shareholders has been approved are extraordinarily detrimental to corporate welfare. Accordingly, the statutory requirements and presumptions have been adopted with the goal of swift resolution of corporate elections. In a similar policy choice, judicial review for corporate elections is available in summary form. *See* DGCL §225, MBCA §7.49.

The key statutory provision that effects this bright-line ethos for elections provides that only shareholders of record may cast votes.[3] *See* DGCL §212(a), 219(c) and MBCA §§7.07[4], 7.21(a). This provision heightens the importance of the record date shareholder list, which must be prepared rapidly after the record date and must be made available to shareholders until the meeting is adjourned. *See* DGCL §§212(a), 219(c), MBCA §7.20. Delaware allows corporation to use blockchain technology to keep stockholder records and to prepare the stockholder list. DGCL §224.

---

3. The MBCA contains a provision allowing the corporation to adopt, in advance, a policy of recognizing beneficial holders, but few companies take advantage of this method. *See* MBCA §7.23.

4. The MBCA contains one of the most curiously formalistic provisions in modern corporation law. It provides that, "Only shares are entitled to vote." *See* MBCA §7.21(a). Fortunately, we do not have to dwell on this provision in any detail as §§7.07 and 7.02(a) obliquely obviate the import of §7.21 by providing that "The bylaws may fix or provide the manner of fixing the record date . . . in order to determine the shareholders entitled to . . . vote. . . . If the bylaws do not fix or provide for fixing a record date, the board of directors of the corporation may fix a future date as the record date." MBCA §7.07(a).

The upshot is that the corporation must be able to trace a ballot or proxy to the record holder. If the shareholder of record is a single individual, his or her signed ballot or proxy is sufficient. The corporation need not verify that the person signing is actually the shareholder of record, unless the corporation has some information suggesting that the person is not the shareholder of record. The voting process can, however, quickly get more complicated when the name signed on the ballot or proxy is not that of the sole individual shareholder of record.

First, the shares might be held of record by more than one individual, such as a married couple, domestic partners, siblings, or simply joint owners. Second, the shares might be held of record by an entity such as another corporation, a partnership, or an LLC. In this setting the question becomes who can act for the record holder? Third, someone might assert the power to vote or give a proxy because the record holder is legally unable to do so. Examples are the trustee of a record shareholder (individual or entity) in bankruptcy, the executor or administrator of a deceased record shareholder, or the guardian of a minor or incompetent record shareholder. Note that this setting might be compounded where the record shareholder has co-executors or co-guardians. The DGCL has bright-line provisions covering these situations. *See* DGCL §217. The MBCA has adopted a similar provision but gives the corporation the power to accept or reject such votes or proxies in good faith. *See* MBCA §7.24.

These issues arise and may be quite important in closely held corporations, but the nature of shareholdings in public companies makes these problems chronic. First, the vast majority of public company shares are voted by proxy rather than in person. This is because public company shareholders are widely dispersed, because most have diversified investments and so have a small percentage of their wealth invested in one company, and their ownership percentage of a public company is ordinarily miniscule. Usually 98 or 99 percent of the shares voted at a public company's shareholder meeting are voted by proxy.[5]

Second, in public companies very few shareholders of record are also beneficial holders. This is the result of the way in which shares are traded in the public securities markets. Over a billion shares are traded every day and the great proportion of trades are *settled* (i.e., the seller gets the money and the buyer gets the shares) two business days after the day on which the trade was made. Most transactions involve a broker for the buyer and a broker for the seller and the official transaction is recorded as being between the two brokers rather than between the ultimate buyer and ultimate seller. Although in theory every trade could be settled separately, it would be impractical to do so. Instead, at the end of each trading day a central clearinghouse nets every brokerage firm's trades made with every other brokerage firm.

Transferring money between brokerage firms is easy, but transferring shares of stock is more difficult. If all shares were held of record by the beneficial holder,

---

5. Be careful to understand that this statement does not mean that 98 or 99 percent of the shares entitled to vote are represented at the meeting. In fact, unless a battle for control or some other controversial matter is being voted upon, upwards of 30 percent of the outstanding voting shares may not be represented. On occasion, the turnout is so low that corporate employees solicit large shareholders to ensure their presence to avoid the embarrassment of a lack of a quorum.

the selling shareholder would have to endorse the stock certificate (much as one endorses a check) deliver it to his or her brokerage firm, which would have to forward it to the corporation's *transfer agent* (i.e., the agent in charge of reissuing shares from sellers to buyers and noting such transfers on the shareholder list[6]), which would have to cancel the seller's certificate, reissue the shares in the name of the ultimate purchaser, and deliver that new certificate to the buyer's brokerage house so that it could be given to the new owner.

At the same time, the buyer's brokerage house would collect the purchase price from its customer and forward those funds to the seller's brokerage house to be delivered to the seller when the new share certificate was ready to be delivered to the buyer. All this would have to be completed by the third day after the trade. Even if this process could realistically be accomplished, it would be more than a tad Sisyphean because the next day more trades would take place, often involving the same ultimate buyers and sellers and stock in the same companies.

One way to simplify the system would be to have shareholders agree to allow their brokerage firms to be the record owner while the ultimate shareholder became a beneficial owner only. Then, the number of share transfers would be greatly reduced because the brokerage firm would aggregate the shares in each company its customers owned into one certificate per company. Each customer would simply receive a statement each month showing how many shares of each company he or she owned, the shares of which were being held of record by the brokerage house. In fact, this is partially a solution. Most individual beneficial shareholders do not receive stock certificates when they purchase shares. They simply become beneficial holders who have left their shares in *street name*, as this practice is called.[7] This solution would still be too cumbersome because nearly every stock certificate held by nearly every brokerage house would have to be reregistered every day to reflect the changes in the brokerage house's customers' accounts.

The real solution involved the creation of an entity, the Depository Trust Company (*DTC*), that acts simply as a custodian of shares. Each brokerage house has an account at DTC in which it deposits all the shares of all the corporations it holds for its customers. Thenceforth DTC simply debits and credits the account of each of its participating brokerage house customers (note that DTC does *not* have accounts for the brokerage houses' customers) with the net number of shares of each corporation owed or owing to other brokerage houses at the end of each trading day. The actual shares do not need to be transferred except when an ultimate beneficiary wishes to become a holder of record and so must obtain a share certificate. This *book entry system*, as it is known, has greatly reduced the administrative problems with trading in the public securities markets.

Now for the *coup de grâce*. It turns out that DTC is not the shareholder of record, either. To facilitate transfers when share certificates do need to be surrendered and reissued, DTC has established a partnership, *Cede & Co.*, to hold the shares. To sum up, most investors have accounts with brokerage houses, which in turn have accounts with DTC, which controls Cede & Co., which is the shareholder of record.

---

6. Most public companies retain a specialized subsidiary of a bank or trust company to act as transfer agent.
7. The "street" in question meaning Wall Street.

Now let's look at the consequence of this elaborate yet largely invisible system of share ownership for shareholder voting. If the beneficial owner is also the shareholder of record, he or she either can attend the shareholder meeting and vote in person (few public companies have made provision for their shareholders to vote in real time either online or by conference call) or the shareholder can vote by proxy.

As you remember, the vast majority of shares voted are voted by proxy. Public companies usually provide three methods for shareholders of record to grant a proxy. First is the traditional written proxy, which is usually a card sent by the management to each shareholder of record along with a letter asking the shareholder to fill out the card and date, sign, and return it to management (typically a committee of three trusted company employees acts as the proxyholders). Second, nearly all public companies provide a toll-free telephone number that the shareholder can call and, by using a menu of options and a unique PIN sent along with the proxy request, authorize a proxy. Finally, nearly all public companies provide a Web site at which the shareholder may also authorize a proxy, again using a unique PIN. As the proxies are received by the committee, they are submitted to the corporation and the committee of proxy holders thus votes the shares.

If the shares are held in street name the process is different. Because Cede & Co. is the record holder, the corporation holding the meeting (let's call it XYZ Corp.) must be able to trace all proxies to Cede & Co. After the record date for the XYZ Corp. shareholder meeting, Cede & Co. sends a general proxy to each brokerage house covering the number of XYZ Corp. shares that brokerage house owned on the record date. Each brokerage house then sends a request for instructions to each customer account that beneficially owns XYZ Corp. shares on the record date.[8] The customers' responses to that request are tallied and the brokerage house executes a limited proxy (usually written or via the Internet) instructing the XYZ Corp. proxy committee to vote.

Note that the brokerage house's proxy will doubtless instruct the XYZ Corp. proxy committee to vote some shares in favor and some shares against every matter presented at the meeting because its customers (the ultimate beneficial holders) will vote in different ways. On occasion, the beneficial holder wants to vote in person at the shareholder meeting. In such instances the beneficial holder must request the brokerage firm to execute a general proxy to the beneficial holder.

b. Who Counts the Votes?

In privately held corporations the votes are probably counted by senior managers or perhaps by the shareholder meeting's chair in front of the assembled shareholders. Proxies are not usually a serious problem because most shares are probably cast in person, and those that are cast by proxy typically involve only a simple written proxy from the shareholder of record to an agent. Even where the shareholders are bitterly divided, the process of counting the votes is still straightforward.

---

8. These requests for instruction look very much like the request for proxies that XYZ Corp. sends to its shareholders of record. Many ultimate beneficial holders assume that they are casting votes or giving a proxy when they return these requests for instructions but, as you now see, they are actually directing their brokerage firm to instruct the XYZ Corp. proxy committee to vote in a particular way.

By contrast, counting the votes for a public company shareholder meeting is much more complicated, even where none of the matters to be voted upon is contested. Fortunately, both statutory provisions and accepted practice in public corporations makes this process at least somewhat more orderly than it might otherwise be. First off, the DGCL and MBCA require public companies to appoint inspectors of election. These inspectors are charged with performing four tasks:

1. Determining the number of shares outstanding and the voting power each share possesses;
2. Determining how many shares are "present" or "represented" at the meeting;
3. Determining the validity of all proxies and ballots; and
4. Counting the vote.

See DGCL §231(b), MBCA §7.29(b).

Under the MBCA the inspectors also report the result of each matter submitted to the shareholders. Under the DGCL the inspectors do not take this step, presumably leaving the task of actually declaring the result to the chair of the meeting. *Compare* DGCL §231(b)(5) with MBCA §7.29(b)(5).

Complicating the inspectors' job are the following:

1. Many public companies have thousands of record holders and five to ten times as many beneficial holders.[9] The number of record holders varies widely. In general, companies with more institutional investors have fewer record holders than companies with more individual investors. For example, Walmart, Inc., has over 236,000 shareholders of record. By contrast, microsoft has about 101,000 shareholders of record and Amazon .com has only about 2,500 shareholders of record.
2. Probably 98 percent or more of the shares present will be present by proxy. The validity of a proxy is usually harder to ascertain than is the presence of a record shareholder.
3. Perhaps 80 percent of the outstanding shares are held in street name, which means that proxies for those shares are submitted through the multilevel system of Cede & Co., brokerage house, beneficial holder, which further complicates the job of ascertaining a proxy's validity.
4. Many brokerage houses submit multiple proxies, often on a daily basis, as the meeting date approaches, to reflect instructions from their customers. These multiple proxies may be cumulative (i.e., restating the votes from the prior proxy) or partial (i.e., simply reflecting the newly received instructions). Inspectors of elections must ascertain which type of proxy each brokerage house is submitting and must guard against the brokerage house inadvertently executing proxies for more shares than it is entitled to vote

---

9. Note that the number of outstanding *shares* doesn't really complicate the public company voting process, but the number of share*holders* certainly does. To see this more clearly, imagine a privately held company with only two stockholders. Each of them might own millions of shares, but the voting and counting process is simple because in the end there will only be two ballots and, at most, two proxies.

(a situation called a *broker overvote*). The DGCL and MBCA specifically permit the inspectors to go beyond the material submitted to them to resolve broker overvotes. *See* DGCL §231(d), MBCA §7.29(d).

Where a matter is contested, as in a takeover or other proxy fight setting, the pressures increase. Small wonder that the great majority of public companies retain a single independent firm to act as inspector of elections. That firm has experienced inspectors who not only know the process but, equally importantly, know the habits and practices of the various brokerage houses that will be submitting proxies.

In outline, the counting process is the same regardless of whether the election is routine or contested. Because of the paper-intensive nature of shareholder voting, much of the tabulation is done by hand. First the ballots and proxies are put in alphabetical order to match the shareholder list as of the record date. Ballots and proxies submitted by those whose name does not appear on the shareholder list are removed and the votes are not counted. Ballots and proxies that, on their face, are submitted by or on behalf of shareholders of record are counted if they are not overvotes. Ballots and proxies that represent overvotes or other problems are culled out and separately investigated in a process known as the "snake pit." Common problems in addition to overvotes are illegible signatures, variations between the signature and the record name, and multiple proxies or ballots purporting to vote the same shares.

In the last setting, where shares are "voted" by more than one proxy or ballot, the law of agency provides that the last act of the principal (i.e., the ultimate owner of the shares) controls over earlier acts. So, only the last-dated ballot or proxy is counted. Where multiple proxies are of even date, the last transmitted (determined by postmark or electronic transmission) controls. In the end, some of these problems cannot be resolved. In those settings the shares are effectively disenfranchised and the votes not counted because the inspectors cannot determine with sufficient certainty the intention of the ultimate owner.

B. SHAREHOLDERS' RIGHTS TO INFORMATION

1. Periodic and Transaction Reporting

Shareholders are provided information by their corporation, without the shareholders having to take any action, in two settings. *Transaction reporting* means information sent by the corporation with respect to a contemplated transaction, usually one the shareholders will vote upon. *Periodic reporting* is information provided at specific intervals, such as annually or quarterly, regardless of whether the corporation is anticipating a transaction. In Delaware and under the MBCA, shareholders need not be provided with any periodic reporting. However, each Delaware corporation must file an annual franchise tax report by March 1st which contains very basic information about the company but does not contain any report of the corporation's finances or operations. These reports are available online from the

Delaware secretary of state's web site. *See* DGCL §502. Delaware corporations need not provide shareholders with any transaction reporting but Delaware case law requires that the corporation provide shareholders with all material information before a shareholder vote. Corporate management must provide this information to all shareholders if the management is requesting that shareholders vote by proxy. However, if the management is not soliciting proxies, the information can be presented orally at the meeting prior to the shareholder vote and need not be sent to absent shareholders. Most other states probably have caselaw to similar effect.

Shareholders in public companies must receive *periodic reports* on the financial and operational condition of the company at least four times each year under the federal securities laws. Public corporations also make detailed public reports when they seek to raise more money from the public. This kind of *transaction reporting* is not required to be sent to existing shareholders but detailed information about the company and the securities to be sold is given to prospective purchasers. Both periodic and transaction reports are filed with the SEC and are available to the public on the commission's web site. Many public companies also make such reports available on their own web sites.

2. Inspection Right

a. Background and Context

Shareholders have another avenue for obtaining information about their corporation. They may examine certain corporate documents in certain circumstances. The following excerpt describes the origin and development of the shareholder inspection right in Delaware.

> It is well established that, as a matter of common law, a stockholder of a Delaware corporation possessed a qualified right to inspect or examine the stock ledger, as well as the books and records of the corporation. The stockholder's common law right of inspection may not be divested except by statutory enactment. At common law, the right of inspection was enforceable only through the issuance of a writ of mandamus from the Superior Court compelling the corporation to permit inspection by the stockholder. *State ex rel. Richardson v. Swift,* 30 A. 781, 781-82 (Del. Super. 1885) (*"Swift I"*), aff'd, *Swift v. State ex rel. Richardson,* 6 A. 856 (Del. Ct. Err. & App. 1886) (*"Swift II"*).
>
> For a writ of mandamus to issue, "[t]he right which it is sought to protect must [ ] be clearly established." *Swift II,* 6 A. at 861. The stockholder was therefore required to make specific factual averments in the petition to show clearly that he or she was entitled to the relief (inspection) sought.
>
> [T]he stockholder demanding inspection had to show that the inspection was for "proper purposes." Although hardly self-defining, a proper purpose was viewed under the common law as a purpose relating to the *interest* that the stockholder sought to protect by seeking inspection.
>
> In other words, the propriety of a demanding stockholder's purpose was measured by whether it related to the stockholder's interest *qua* stockholder, that is, a proper purpose in seeking inspection was viewed as a purpose germane to the petitioner's interest or status as a stockholder.
>
> In short, a stockholder's right to inspection is status-related. In this regard, inspection rights have been viewed as an incident to the stockholder's ownership of corporate property.

As an equitable owner of the corporation's assets, a stockholder possessed a right to reasonable information concerning the conduct of corporate management, as well as the condition of the corporation's business and affairs. As a matter of self-protection, the stockholder was entitled to know how his agents were conducting the affairs of the corporation of which he or she was a part owner.

In addition to the common law right of inspection, the right has been codified in some form in Delaware since the turn of the [twentieth] century. The original statutory enactment eliminated the formalistic pleading requirements of the extraordinary writ of mandamus by giving the stockholder a "positive right" to inspection of corporate books and records. Nevertheless, if the corporation could show that the petitioner sought inspection for an improper purpose, the court had the discretion to deny the stockholder access to the corporation's books and records.

With its enactment of Section 220 in 1967, the General Assembly sought to replace the formalized and burdensome mandamus procedure in the Superior Court with a summary procedure in the Court of Chancery by which a stockholder who has demonstrated a purpose reasonably related to his or her interest as such may gain swift access to the corporate books and records.

Shaw v. Agri-Mark, Inc., 663 A.2d 464, 466-468 (Del. 1995) (Walsh, J.)

b. The Current Setting

Under both the DGCL and the MBCA, shareholders have the right to examine some corporate documents. This right is called the shareholder *inspection right*. The shareholder bears nearly the entire cost of obtaining corporate information, while the corporation bears the cost of periodic and transaction reporting. For many shareholders inspection rights are largely of theoretic value for one of two reasons. First, the shareholder's stock might not be of sufficient value to justify spending the time and money to exercise the right of inspection. Second, even if the shareholder's stake is large enough to justify inspecting corporate records the shareholder's overall wealth might be diversified (spread over a number of unrelated stocks or other assets) so that any gain from inspecting a particular corporation's documents would not contribute a meaningful amount to the shareholder's total investment return. For some shareholders, whether economically rational actors or not, the inspection right may be a realistic avenue to obtain information the shareholder considers valuable.

The legal questions surrounding shareholder inspection rights fall into two categories. First, what information does a shareholder have a right to inspect simply by virtue of being a shareholder? Second, what information does a shareholder have a right to inspect if the shareholder makes an additional showing of some sort? The first category of questions is answered principally by reference to the statutes. The second category generates considerable litigation. Suffusing both categories is the question of whether a shareholder who may inspect a record may also copy it.

Both the DGCL and the MBCA provide shareholders at least some information simply by virtue of shareholder status. Any shareholder may inspect the list of record date shareholders before the shareholder meeting. This allows a shareholder to determine who else may vote and how many shares each other shareholder owns. Under the DGCL, any shareholder also has the right to inspect any voting trust agreements. The MBCA allows any shareholder to inspect (and copy) the basic constitutive documents (articles and bylaws), list of current officers and directors, the current annual report filed with the secretary of state, and other similar basic information simply by virtue of being a shareholder. *See* DGCL §§218(a), 219(a), MBCA §§7.20, 16.01(e), 16.02.

Other corporate information may be inspected or copied (and the record shareholder list and, in Delaware, a voting trust agreement, may be copied) only if the shareholder makes additional showings. Under both statutes the test is whether the shareholder has a "*proper purpose.*" The statutes put the burden of showing that the shareholder has no proper purpose on the corporation for demands to inspect a shareholder list and puts the burden to show a proper purpose on the shareholder for other demands. *See* DGCL §220(b), MBCA §16.02(c)(1). The DGCL defines a proper purpose as "a purpose reasonably related to such person's interest as a stockholder"; the MBCA does not define "proper purpose." DGCL §220(b).

The New Mexico Supreme Court has described the contours of "proper purpose":

> Shareholder access to corporate information should be limited to information reasonably related to the legitimate interests of the shareholder. A proper purpose is not harmful to the corporation or its shareholders. A proper purpose can be surmised where the shareholder's purpose in requesting the information bears some reasonable relationship to the interest that the shareholder wants to protect by seeking inspection. Generally, shareholders are entitled to full information as to the management of the corporation and the manner of expenditure of its funds, and to inspection in order to obtain information. A proper purpose can include a desire to place a monetary value on stock interests and to evaluate the conduct of officers and directors. Suitable subject matter for proper shareholder oversight also extends to efforts by the shareholder to determine the value of his stock and to determine the financial condition of the corporation. The propriety of such access is premised primarily on the rationale that a stockholder has the right to know corporate information that might affect his losses or gains, affecting the shareholder's ability to protect himself. In addition, such access allows for discovery and deterrence of abuses by corporate directors and officers.

Schein v. Northern Rio Arriba Elect. Coop., Inc., 932 P.2d 490, 493-494 (N.M. 1997) (Baca, J.)

Suppose a shareholder believes that corporate managers have caused the corporation to take actions that will harm the corporation. If the shareholder seeks to inspect and copy information to find grounds on which to sue the corporation and its managers, has the shareholder stated a "proper purpose"? Vice Chancellor Laster considered that question in the next case.

Louisiana Municipal Police Employees' Retirement System v. The Hershey Company
No. 7996-ML (Del. Ch. Mar. 18, 2014)*

LASTER, V.C.

So today's hearing is for the Court to consider the plaintiff's exceptions to a final report in Louisiana Municipal Police Employees Retirement System versus The Hershey Co.

---

* Transcript of Rulings of the Court from Oral Argument on Exceptions to the Master's Final Report.

The plaintiff takes exception to the Master's recommendation that the complaint be dismissed at the pleading stage because the plaintiff's request to obtain additional books and records under Section 220 fails to establish a credible basis from which the Court could infer possible mismanagement or wrongdoing at The Hershey Company.

The parties are Louisiana Municipal Police Employees' Retirement System, which everyone refers to affectionately as LAMPERS, which is a nonpartisan, nonprofit organization that provides pension benefits for the employees at municipal police departments in the State of Louisiana. Hershey, the defendant, is a Delaware corporation, with its principal offices in Hershey, Pennsylvania. It is the largest producer of chocolate in North America and a global leader in the chocolate and sugar confectionary industry, selling chocolate in approximately 70 countries worldwide.

The complaint seeks an order permitting LAMPERS to inspect and make copies of certain books and records set forth in its demand letter. Essentially, the complaint seeks more information.

Here, what I view as the key factual allegations of the complaint: Hershey controls 42 percent of the market for chocolate products in the United States and is a major player in the chocolate industry worldwide. Cocoa is the key ingredient used to manufacture chocolate. West African countries, including Ghana and the Ivory Coast, supply 70 percent of the world's cocoa. Hershey's major sourcing countries include Ghana and the Ivory Coast, as well as other West African nations.

Hershey is well aware of the pervasive use of child and forced labor in Ghana and the Ivory Coast. And I don't say that in a bad way. Part of what the allegations of the complaint show is that Hershey is engaged in steps to try to address these issues. But that said, it is established for purposes of this motion that Hershey is aware of the pervasive use of child and forced labor in Ghana and the Ivory Coast.

The laws of Ghana and the Ivory Coast forbid employers from forcing children to engage in dangerous activities such as carrying heavy loads, clearing land, things like that which require the use of sharp tools such as machetes, all things that are endemic to the production of cocoa. Those laws are routinely violated; hence, the use of child and forced labor is, indeed, pervasive.

In 2001 Hershey and other companies signed the Harkin-Engel Protocol, which established a goal of eliminating the worst forms of child labor in the cocoa sectors in Ghana and the Ivory Coast. There was a goal that by July 1, 2005, this consortium would develop and implement credible mutually acceptable voluntary industry-wide standards for public certification that cocoa beans and the derivative products have been grown and/or processed without any of the worst forms of child labor.

On March 31, 2011, the Payson Center for International Development at Tulane University released a report on the continued prevalence of child labor in the cocoa industry. This is 10 years after the protocol. Basically the Payson Report documents all the worst ills that one could imagine about this problem. Nearly 2 million children work illegally on cocoa farms. There's evidence of widespread violations of human trafficking laws. According to the Payson Report, Ghana and the Ivory Coast are common destinations for trafficked children. Again, this is all material for which the purpose of a motion to dismiss supports the inference of pervasive use of child and forced labor in Ghana and the Ivory Coast and Hershey's awareness of the issue.

Now, despite the effort starting in 2001 to come up with voluntary standards so that people could certify that their cocoa was used without the worst forms of child labor, there's still no certification process. There's an indication that one supplier, Cadbury's, has done some form of certification. Hershey's has not. On October 3rd, 2012, Hershey's announced that it would certify that its chocolate products were free of cocoa tainted with child labor and human trafficking violations by 2020.

As I discussed with counsel, I think from all this, it is quite reasonable to infer at the pleading stage — and counsel ultimately does not dispute — that right now Hershey's has to acknowledge that some of its cocoa is produced through child labor and as a result of individuals who were the victims of human trafficking.

Hershey's stockholders also have brought concerns about the use of child labor within Hershey's supply chain, as are other people who are drawing that inference. Despite these concerns, Hershey has declined to provide any details about its sources of cocoa or to disclose its suppliers or to provide information from which one can evaluate the nature of Hershey's involvement in the supply chain. As I discussed with counsel, however, one can infer at the pleading stage that it is reasonably tight because Hershey's extols the fact that it monitors its suppliers, that it has multi-part programs to ensure that its suppliers are doing the best they can to adhere to Hershey's code of conduct, which it requires suppliers to sign, and that Hershey's kicks out suppliers when it finds out about violations.

All those are really good things, don't get me wrong. But all those also support a reasonable inference at the pleading stage that Hershey's has deep involvement in and control over its supply chain. That is not a radical inference, given the market-leading status and dominant market share that Hershey's has and commands.

So these are the core facts as alleged in the complaint. The question is what inferences can you draw from them?

The conceivability standard [for Rule 12(b)(6) motions in Delaware], thus, asks whether there is "a possibility" that the allegations of the complaint could support relief.

Section 220 of the DGCL allows a stockholder to inspect a corporation's books and records for any proper purpose. It's well-established that investigation of mismanagement is a proper purpose. One can consult many Supreme Court decisions for that. The operative test as to what a stockholder has to show to establish a basis to inspect books and records to explore possible wrongdoing is *Seinfeld versus Verizon Communications. Seinfeld* said the following: "A stockholder is not required to prove by a preponderance of the evidence that waste and mismanagement are actually occurring. Stockholders need only show by a preponderance of the evidence a credible basis from which the Court of Chancery can infer that there is possible mismanagement that would warrant further investigation, a showing that may ultimately fall well short of demonstrating that anything wrong occurred. That threshold may be satisfied by a credible showing through documents, logic, testimony or otherwise that there are legitimate issues of wrongdoing."

The point is not whether you can infer wrongdoing. The point is whether you can infer possible wrongdoing.

So let's apply the actual test, whether there's a possibility of mismanagement and whether it's conceivable, based on the allegations of the complaint, that there is a possibility of mismanagement, because, recall, we're here on a motion to dismiss.

What that means, I think, is if there are two competing inferences from the allegations in the complaint at this stage, the plaintiff gets the inference. Moreover, the inference that the allegations have to support is not that there is actual wrongdoing, but that there is possible wrongdoing. The point of this lenient standard, I believe, is to drive Section 220 to a prompt merits hearing where the Court can actually make determinations about the sufficiency of the evidence and do the type of balancing that Hershey says is required by the credible basis standard.

In my view, the allegations in the complaint, read in the doubly plaintiff-friendly manner that is required in this procedural posture, support a reasonable inference of possible violations of law in which Hershey may be involved. And those possibilities are sufficient, in the words of our Supreme Court, "to warrant further investigation."

It may, indeed, prove that the documents that Hershey produces show that they are not involved in violations of law at all. That's part of the purpose of a Section 220 investigation, so that a lawyer like Mr. Barry and his client can get the information, evaluate it and say, "You know what. We had suspicions. We had reasonable suspicions, but we were wrong." That's one of the reasons you have Section 220.

So what is the credible basis for wrongdoing? As I've said, the allegations of the complaint support a reasonable inference that Hershey's products contain cocoa and cocoa-derived ingredients that were the result of child labor and human trafficking. There's also a reasonable inference, one possible inference, that the board knows some of its cocoa and cocoa-derived ingredients are sourced from farms that exploit child labor and use trafficked persons. The laws of Ghana prohibit exploitative child labor and human trafficking. The Children's Act prohibits the use of exploitive child labor, defining children as persons below the age of 18. The Human Trafficking Act prohibits the use of a trafficked person and also includes a duty to inform.

One possible inference from the complaint is that Hershey's cocoa sustainability efforts, which admittedly and necessarily put Hershey in contact with farmers in West Africa, results in Hershey knowing of instances involving the use of trafficked children on cocoa farms in Ghana that would have triggered the duty to inform. That is not the only possible inference, but it's one possible inference. And at this procedural stage, I have to credit it.

Hershey has not provided any information about its suppliers. One possible inference — not the only inference, but one possible inference is that Hershey's relationships with its suppliers could support a finding of the use of labor for an aiding and abetting claim. Not the only possible inference, but one possible inference.

The laws of the Ivory Coast similarly prohibit exploitative child labor and human trafficking. And courts in the United States, most notably in the recent *Doe v. Nestlé* decision recognized that it is possible for a U.S. corporation to be held liable for aiding and abetting violations of international law, such as the principle, hopefully universally acknowledged, against the use of child labor and human trafficking.

Now, as I've already said, Hershey's response has been to argue that plaintiff hasn't proved wrongdoing. That's not the test. Hershey's has also said that there's no evidence related directly to it, i.e., directly to Hershey's involvement. I think you can draw the inference from Hershey's inability to represent that it currently uses only certified cocoa and its undertaking to do so by 2020.

I think you can draw the inference of knowledge from Hershey's cocoa sustainability efforts, which include its eight "on-the-ground programs" through which Hershey has contact with farmers in West Africa and high-level visits, such as visits by Hershey's chairman.

You can draw the inference from a decision referenced in the complaint by Whole Foods to stop carrying Hershey's Scharffen Berger brand because of Hershey's inability to certify.

Again, what you don't need for 220 — and certainly not at the motion to dismiss stage — is a report that says Hershey itself has violated this applicable law. It's the possibility, which, as our Delaware Supreme Court said, falls well short of actual wrongdoing.

I'll have a trial. At the trial I'll actually be able to assess these documents, weigh competing inferences. I'm not telling you inspection is going to be granted. I'm just saying I can't dismiss it at this stage of the case.

Notes and Questions

1. Reality Check

a. Section 220 is designed to be an expedited process. The courts look with disfavor on attempts to drag out the process through motions to dismiss. Rather, they would prefer to deal with the corporation's objections in an expedited trial on the merits.

b. How does LAMPERS stand to benefit from the inspection it seeks?

c. How will Hershey benefit from allowing LAMPERS the inspection it seeks?

d. What is the standard for dismissal of a Section 220 action?

e. What is the *Seinfeld* standard for granting a demand for inspection?

f. What does LAMPERS have to show to defeat the motion?

g. Is there a question whether LAMPERS' motivation is a proper purpose?

2. Suppose

a. Suppose Hershey were incorporated under the MBCA. Would the analysis or result be different?

3. What Do You Think?

a. Do you think that, under the court's analysis, any stockholder who distrusts management can inspect and copy records relating to the company's business practices?

b. Do you think that shareholders should be allowed to inspect and copy corporate records that will reflect badly on the corporation?

The next case involves the question of a shareholder's right to inspect and copy information about the other shareholders rather than the corporation's books and records.

Hoepner v. Wachovia Corp.

2001 WL 34000145 (N.C. Sup. 2001)

Ben F. Tennille, Special Superior Court Judge for Complex Business Cases.

I.

On April 16, 2001, Wachovia Corporation ("Wachovia") and First Union Corporation ("First Union") announced that they had entered into a merger agreement, ("the First Union Merger Agreement") which will be submitted to the shareholders of Wachovia for approval at a shareholders meeting scheduled for August 3, 2001. Shareholders of record as of June 12, 2001will be entitled to vote on the proposed merger at that meeting.

On May 14, 2001, SunTrust Banks, Inc. ("SunTrust") made an unsolicited proposal for a merger between Wachovia and SunTrust.

On May 15, 2001, Mr. Hoepner, vice chairman of SunTrust and an owner of 280 shares of Wachovia common stock, submitted a letter to Wachovia demanding the right, pursuant to [MBCA §16.02] and the common law of North Carolina, to inspect and copy certain records and documents of Wachovia, namely a record of shareholders. His stated purpose for the demand was

> to enable [Mr. Hoepner] and SunTrust to communicate with other [Wachovia] stockholders with respect to matters relating to our mutual interests as stockholders of [Wachovia], including but not limited to the Solicitation. Solely in connection with the foregoing purposes, [Mr. Hoepner] intends to share the information requested above with SunTrust.

The solicitation referred to in Mr. Hoepner's letter is a proxy solicitation in opposition to Wachovia's solicitation of proxies from its shareholders to vote in favor of the First Union Merger Agreement.

On May 22, 2001, the Board of Directors of Wachovia rejected the SunTrust proposal.

On May 23, 2001, Wachovia refused Mr. Hoepner's request based on Mr. Hoepner's assertion that he intended to share the information with SunTrust, which, unlike Mr. Hoepner, had not established its status as a qualified shareholder. Wachovia does not question Mr. Hoepner's status as a qualified shareholder except for his stated intention to share the shareholder list with SunTrust. Wachovia contends that intention to share the information in a proxy fight disqualifies Mr. Hoepner because his demand is not made in good faith and for a proper purpose as required by [MBCA §16.02(c)(1)].

III.

A qualified shareholder has a statutory right to inspect and copy a "record of shareholders." [MBCA §16.02(b)(4)]; *see also Parsons v. Jefferson Pilot Corp.*, 426 S.E.2d 685, 689 (1993). Concurrent rights exist at common law. *See id.* ("[S]hare-holders of a corporation have a common law right to make a reasonable inspection of its books to assure themselves of efficient management."). Mr. Hoepner is admittedly a qualified shareholder under the statute and entitled to the shareholder list. Therefore, the primary question before the Court is whether Wachovia can prevent Mr. Hoepner from sharing the shareholder list with SunTrust, an unqualified shareholder, for use in the proxy fight between Wachovia and SunTrust. The issue is one of first impression in North Carolina.

Both the statutory scheme embodied in the North Carolina Business Corporation Act and the case law in North Carolina evidence a strong public policy of insuring fairness and equality between a corporation and its shareholders in a proxy solicitation. In *Parsons*, the North Carolina Supreme Court stated:

> We believe that the legislative intent embodied in [MBCA §16.02(b)(4)] is that shareholders be entitled to the information concerning the identity of shareholders which is possessed by the corporation in order that they may have the same opportunity as the corporation to communicate with the other shareholders.

Parsons v. Jefferson Pilot Corp., 428 S.E.2d 685, 690 (1993).

In its analysis the *Parsons* court cited *Sadler v. NCR Corp.*, 928 F.2d 48 (2d Cir. 1991), and *Cenergy Corp v. Bryson Oil & Gas P.L.C.*, 662 F. Supp. 114 (D. Nev. 1987) with approval. The *Cenergy* case was cited with approval in *Parsons* for the "view that requiring a corporation to divulge all of the shareholder information *in its possession* would completely effectuate the goal of fairness and equality between a corporation and its shareholders in proxy solicitation." *Parsons v. Jefferson Pilot Corp.*, 428 S.E.2d 685, 690 (1993). It is thus clear under North Carolina law that obtaining a shareholder list for the purposes of contacting the shareholders is a proper purpose.

In *Sadler*, the United States Court of Appeals for the Second Circuit directly addressed the issue of whether a qualifying shareholder could demand a shareholder list on behalf of a corporation involved in a proxy fight with the defendant. *Sadler v. NCR Corp.*, 928 F.2d 48 (2d Cir. 1991). In that case, AT&T, the unwelcome bidder, purposely engaged the Sadlers, the qualified shareholders, to make a demand on NCR, the target corporation, for the list of shareholders. The purpose of obtaining the list was so that AT&T could solicit the shareholders in its proxy fight. AT&T agreed to indemnify the Sadlers for any costs associated with the demand requirements and production of documents. NCR refused to provide the lists because of the agreement between AT&T and the Sadlers and because of AT&T's lack of qualified shareholder status. The Court of Appeals agreed with the lower court's statement that the Sadlers had a personal interest in seeing the tender offer succeed other than as nominees of AT&T and were therefore requesting the list for a proper purpose. Thus, the Court of Appeals stated that "the demanding stockholder is entitled to turn the list over to others involved in a proxy contest" absent any allegation of improper purpose or bad faith.

Courts in other jurisdictions have reached the same conclusion, holding that the shareholder is entitled to turn the list over to others involved in a proxy fight. *See, e.g.*, *Davey v. Unitil Corp.*, 585 A.2d 858, 861-63 (N.H. 1991) (ordering production to stockholder intending to give list to hostile offeror); *DeRosa v. Terry Steam Turbine Co.*, 214 A.2d 684, 688-89 (Conn. Sup. Ct. 1965) (ordering production of list to shareholder who intended to turn list over to third party); *Trans World Airlines, Inc. v. State*, 183 A.2d 174, 175-76 (Del. 1962) (holding that stockholder's agent's desire to defeat corporate claim against his principal was irrelevant to his right to list); *Hanrahan v. Puget Sound Power & Light Co.*, 126 N.E.2d 499, 591-92 (Mass. 1955) (ordering production of list to shareholders intending to provide list to others for a proxy fight).

In its response to summary judgment, Wachovia claims that the requirement of good faith precludes Mr. Hoepner from providing the shareholder lists to SunTrust. Wachovia's position is contrary to public policy. Given the strong policy arguments for providing shareholders an equal opportunity to communicate with other shareholders of the corporation, it would be improvident to impose upon the qualifying shareholder the burden of contacting the other shareholders on his own or with only the assistance of other qualifying shareholders. Such a burden would act as a significant barrier to a shareholder's ability to protect his interests and would fail to "completely effectuate the goal of fairness and equality between a corporation and its shareholders in [a] proxy solicitation." *Parsons v. Jefferson Pilot Corp.*, 428 S.E.2d 685, 690 (1993).

It should also be noted that section [MBCA §16.03] specifically states that a shareholder's agent "has the same inspection rights as the shareholder he represents."* [MBCA §16.03(a)]. Pointedly, [MBCA §16.03] does not limit the persons or entities that the shareholder may designate as agent nor does it state that the agent must also be a qualifying shareholder. Although it is not specifically claimed in the case at bar that SunTrust is acting as agent for Mr. Hoepner, the practical result of the permissible use of agents and the strong public policy favoring equal access to information indicates that sharing the lists with other interested parties for the purpose of a proxy fight is neither improper nor bad faith.

North Carolina General Statutes sections [MBCA §16.02] and [MBCA §7.20] are independent provisions. A shareholder may obtain the information specified under [MBCA §16.02] without regard to the existence of an upcoming shareholders meeting. Once a meeting is noticed, the shareholders' [inspection] rights under [MBCA §7.20] also become effective, but [the shareholders' rights to copy] are subject to the "good faith" and "proper purpose" limitations in [MBCA §16.02(c)]. Wachovia contends that [MBCA §16.02] does not impose upon it a continuing obligation to provide Mr. Hoepner with transfer sheets as those sheets come into Wachovia's possession. As previously indicated, there is a strong public policy favoring equal access to communication with shareholders. Although Wachovia is not required to create new documents to satisfy Mr. Hoepner's demands, inasmuch as holders of Wachovia shares change daily and Wachovia has constant access to that information, the Court believes that Mr. Hoepner is also entitled to daily transfer sheets pursuant to his request. Neither the statute nor does this Court require Wachovia to create or obtain any information it does not already possess. To the extent it has or obtains the records requested, it must provide those records to Mr. Hoepner to maintain the level playing field contemplated by the statute.

Mr. Hoepner's intention to share the list with SunTrust is neither an improper purpose, nor a violation of good faith, nor does it justify Wachovia's refusal to produce the lists. Mr. Hoepner has an interest independent of that of SunTrust and has met the qualifications under [MBCA §16.02]. Thus, Plaintiff's motion for summary judgment is granted.

Additionally, the Court grants Mr. Hoepner's request pursuant to [MBCA §16.04] that Wachovia bear the costs for the production of documents demanded, but denies other costs incurred by Plaintiff in pursuit of this litigation. The principal

---

* This language is a North Carolina variation on the MBCA language. ED

question raised by Wachovia, i.e., Mr. Hoepner's right to share the information with others for use in a proxy fight, was undecided under North Carolina law. In the future, a corporation withholding compliance with its statutory duties on the basis that the shareholder intended to share the information with others in a proxy solicitation would be subject to the imposition of costs as provided by the statute.

Notes and Questions

1. Reality Check

a. What information did Hoepner want from Wachovia? Why did he want it?

b. What information did the court find Hoepner was entitled to?

c. What role does "proper purpose" play in this case?

d. How does the court analyze the relation between Hoepner and SunTrust? Do you agree with the court's reasoning?

2. Suppose

a. Suppose Hoepner had requested and obtained other books and records information about the corporation instead of information about the shareholders. Could he share that information with SunTrust? Could he share that information with a major competitor of Wachovia?

3. What Do You Think?

a. How can sharing the list of shareholders with an entity that is making a hostile takeover bid be in the corporation's best interest?

b. Was SunTrust the agent for Hoepner under MBCA §16.03 or was Hoepner the agent for SunTrust? Does it make a difference who was the agent and who was the principal?

c. Why do both the MBCA and DGCL treat inspection of shareholder information differently from inspection of other books and records?

Putting It to Work

Problem 14-3

Sandy is a stockholder of record in Catty's Crafts Corp., a corporation that sells high-end interior design materials (e.g., expensive wall paint and wallpaper, door and window hardware, floor coverings, lighting fixtures). Catty's Crafts Corp. is a publicly traded corporation.

Sandy is concerned that corporate funds may have been mismanaged because Catty's Crafts Corp. reported annual earnings per share of $3.95, then, two weeks later, announced that the actual annual earnings per share were $3.05, and then, one week after that, reported that, upon further investigation, the actual earnings per share were $2.73. She also suspects, based on media reports, that some of the paint manufactured and sold by Catty's Crafts Corp. may contain dangerous amounts of lead.

Sandy submitted a written demand, under oath, to Catty's Crafts Corp., demanding to inspect and make copies of (a) the corporation's books and records relevant to determining the corporation's most recent annual earnings per share; (b) the corporation's books and records relevant to determining whether the corporation has in place an adequate system of monitoring its financial performance; (c) the corporation's books and records relevant to all materials used in all products manufactured or sold by the corporation; and (d) the list of stockholders entitled to notice of, and to vote at, the corporation's annual meeting of stockholders, which is to be held in one week.

a. Is Sandy entitled to the information she requests under the MBCA? Under the DGCL?

C. SHAREHOLDERS' POWER TO REDRESS HARM TO THE CORPORATION

1. The Current Setting

We now move to the third, and final, area of shareholder governance powers. It is different from the other areas in several important ways. First, much of the legal questions are actually civil procedure questions rather than business entities questions. The consequence of that difference is that this section will cover only a few of the legal issues. Second, the shareholders participate in the corporation's governance in a rather oblique way: they bring a lawsuit in which any remedy inures to the corporation itself rather than the shareholder. Perhaps the most important thing to take away from this section is the basic conception of this litigation. We start with that conception.

Imagine an ordinary situation in which a corporation has contracted with another party that breaches the contract. The board (or perhaps officers or other agents who have been authorized by the board) would decide how to react. Typically the corporation would make demand on the other party, perhaps engage in negotiations, and decide whether to bring suit against the breaching party. In this situation the shareholders clearly have no power to intervene in the corporation's decision about how to respond to the breach. The bedrock corporate law rule is that all corporate power is vested in the board, not the shareholders. *See* DGCL §141(a), MBCA §8.01(b).

Now suppose that the harm to the corporation was caused not by a breaching party to a contract but by the directors themselves. An example would be where the board caused the corporation to violate environmental laws that resulted in the corporation being fined. By now it may seem intuitive to you to conclude that the board might not be able to decide, consistent with their fiduciary duties, how to proceed in the best interest of the corporation. The directors are unlikely, to say the least, to cause the corporation to sue themselves! A similar example is where the senior officers, rather than the directors, caused the corporation to violate environmental laws. The board would be deciding whether to cause the corporation to sue people who are presumably close to the board members. Obviously the directors' judgment as to how to proceed in the corporation's best interest might be clouded.

It is in this situation—where the board's decision-making ability may be compromised—that the law of business entities allows the shareholders to file suit on the corporation's behalf to redress the harm. This type of litigation is called *derivative* because the shareholders' power to sue is derived from the corporation's power (putatively exercised by the board) to redress harm to itself. Thus the shareholder brings suit against the directors, officers, or other agents who are alleged to have harmed the corporation. Depending upon the jurisdiction, the corporation itself may be a nominal plaintiff, a nominal defendant, or neither. By far the most common theory of derivative actions is that the individual defendants have breached their fiduciary duties to the corporation and thus have harmed the corporation.

Because derivative litigation is an exception to the core idea that corporate affairs are strictly in the hands of the board, there are restrictions on shareholders' ability to file and maintain a derivative lawsuit. Potential plaintiffs obviously try to avoid these restrictions and so typically try to characterize their claims as individual rather than derivative. The line between individual and derivative litigation is sometimes murky and the case law is typically less than helpful. The Delaware Supreme Court has framed the test as follows:

> The derivative suit has been generally described as "one of the most interesting and ingenious of accountability mechanisms for large formal organizations."[10] It enables a stockholder to bring suit on behalf of the corporation for harm done to the corporation. Because a derivative suit is being brought on behalf of the corporation, the recovery, if any, must go to the corporation. A stockholder who is directly injured, however, does retain the right to bring an individual action for injuries affecting his or her legal rights as a stockholder. Such a claim is distinct from an injury caused to the corporation alone. In such individual suits, the recovery or other relief flows directly to the stockholders, not to the corporation.
>
> Determining whether an action is derivative or direct is sometimes difficult and has many legal consequences, some of which may have an expensive impact on the parties to the action. For example, if an action is derivative, . . . the recovery, if any, flows only to the corporation. The decision whether a suit is direct or derivative may be outcome-determinative. Therefore, it is necessary that a standard to distinguish such actions be clear, simple and consistently articulated and applied by our courts.
>
> [A] court should look to the nature of the wrong and to whom the relief should go. The stockholder's claimed direct injury must be independent of any alleged injury to the corporation. The stockholder must demonstrate that the duty breached was owed to the stockholder and that he or she can prevail without showing an injury to the corporation.

Tooley v. Donaldson, Lufkin, & Jenrette, Inc., 845 A.2d 1031, 1036, 1040 (Del. 2004) (Veasey, C.J.)

In brief, the distinctive aspects of derivative litigation include these:

1. To have standing, plaintiff must have been a shareholder at the time of the alleged harm to the corporation and at the time he or she files suit.
2. Nearly half the states (although neither Delaware nor the MBCA) permit defendants to require plaintiff to post security bonds if the plaintiff's shareholdings are minimal (typically less than 5% of the outstanding shares).

---

10. *Kramer v. Western Pacific Industries, Inc.,* 546 A.2d at 351 (quoting R. Clark, *Corporate Law* 639-40 (1986)).

3. The ordinary statutory presumption that all corporate powers should be in the board means that the board should decide whether the corporation will bring suit. From this presumption comes the procedural rule that a shareholder may not file a derivative action unless one of two procedural settings obtains. In one setting, the plaintiff must have requested (*demanded* is the word universally used) the board to initiate litigation, the board must have refused to do so, and that refusal must have been "wrongful." In the second setting, the plaintiff may file suit without making demand on the board if he or she can demonstrate that prior demand on the board would have been "futile" because the board could not have evaluated the demand fairly. FRCP 23.1 embodies this demand requirement and nearly all states have comparable procedural rules.

4. As with other representative litigation, such as class actions, the named plaintiff litigates on behalf of all shareholders and so cannot settle the litigation without court approval.

Our first case, *Beam v. Stewart*, takes up the question of when prior demand on the board would be futile, and therefore is excused.

Beam v. Stewart

833 A.2d 961 (Del. Ch. 2003)

CHANDLER, CH.

Monica A. Beam, a shareholder of Martha Stewart Living Omnimedia, Inc. ("MSO"), brings this derivative action against the defendants, all current directors and a former director of MSO, and against MSO as a nominal defendant. The defendants seek[ ] . . . to dismiss the amended complaint under Court of Chancery Rule 23.1 for failure to comply with the demand requirement and for failure adequately to plead demand excusal. . . .

Plaintiff Monica A. Beam is a shareholder of MSO and has been since August 2001. Derivative plaintiff and nominal defendant MSO is a Delaware corporation that operates in the publishing, television, merchandising, and internet industries marketing products bearing the "Martha Stewart" brand name.

Defendant Martha Stewart ("Stewart") is a director of the company and its founder, chairman, chief executive officer, and by far its majority shareholder. MSO's common stock is comprised of Class A and Class B shares. Class A shares are traded on the New York Stock Exchange and are entitled to cast one vote per share on matters voted upon by common stockholders. Class B shares are not publicly traded and are entitled to cast ten votes per share on all matters voted upon by common stockholders. Stewart owns or beneficially holds 100% of the B shares in conjunction with a sufficient number of A shares that she controls roughly 94.4% of the shareholder vote. Stewart, a former stockbroker, has in the past twenty years become a household icon, known for her advice and expertise on virtually all aspects of cooking, decorating, entertaining, and household affairs generally.

Defendant Sharon L. Patrick ("Patrick") is a director of MSO and its president and chief operating officer. The amended complaint reports that in 2001, MSO paid Patrick a salary of $700,000, a $280,000 bonus, and granted her options for 130,000 Class A shares. She also serves as the secretary of M. Stewart, Inc., which is described in the complaint as "one of Stewart's personal companies." Prior to Patrick's employment at MSO, she was a consultant to the magazine, *Martha Stewart Living*, and developed extensive experience in the media, entertainment, and consulting businesses. Patrick is also a longtime personal friend of Stewart.

Defendant Arthur C. Martinez ("Martinez") has been a director of MSO since January 2001. Martinez is the former chairman of the board of directors and chief executive officer of Sears Roebuck and Co. Martinez was also the chairman and chief executive officer of that company's retail arm, Sears Merchandise Group. Sears was a high-volume retailer of MSO products during Martinez's tenure there. He has served on the boards of Sears Roebuck and Co., Sears Merchandise Group, and Saks Fifth Avenue. In addition, Martinez now serves as a director of MSO, PepsiCo, Inc., Liz Claiborne, Inc., and International Flavors & Fragrances, Inc., and as the chairman of the Federal Reserve Bank of Chicago. A March 2001 article in *Directors & Boards* reported that Patrick and Stewart both consider Martinez to be "an old friend." Also, Martinez was recruited to serve on MSO's board by then-board member Charlotte Beers ("Beers"), another "longtime friend and confidante" of Stewart.

Defendant Darla D. Moore ("Moore") has been a director of MSO since September 2001, when Beers resigned and Moore replaced her. Moore's professional background includes a partnership at Rainwater, Inc., a private investment firm, a managing directorship with Chase Bank, and service as a trustee of Magellan Health Services, Inc. Moore, too, is reported to be a longtime friend of both Stewart and Beers, as evidenced by a 1996 *Fortune* magazine article highlighting the close friendship among the three women and by the amended complaint's report of Moore's attendance at a wedding reception in 1995, which was attended by both Stewart and Samuel Waksal and hosted by Stewart's lawyer, Allen Grubman.

Defendant Naomi O. Seligman ("Seligman") has been a director of MSO since 1999. She is a co-founder and senior partner of Cassius Advisors and a co-founder and former senior partner of Research Board, Inc. Seligman serves as a director of several public companies, including John Wiley & Sons ("JWS"), a publisher. The amended complaint relates a *Wall Street Journal* report that Seligman contacted the chief executive officer of JWS on behalf of Stewart to express concern over an unflattering biography of Stewart that was scheduled for publication by JWS.

Defendant Jeffery W. Ubben ("Ubben") has been a director of MSO since January 2002. He is the founder and managing partner of ValueAct Capital Partners, L.P. and a director of Insurance Auto Auctions, Inc. Ubben has formerly served as a managing partner and as a portfolio manager, working in the investment industry since at least 1987.

The amended complaint states that compensation paid to MSO's directors includes all of the following:

- $20,000 as an annual retainer;
- $1,000 for each meeting attended in person;

- $500 for each meeting attended telephonically; and
- $5,000 annually for serving as chairman of any committee.

Twenty-five percent of directors' fees are paid in shares of MSO's Class A common stock, with the remaining 75% payable either in Class A shares or cash at the choice of the director. In addition, MSO has a stock option plan for the directors.

The plaintiff seeks relief in relation to . . . the well-publicized matters surrounding Stewart's alleged improper trading of shares of ImClone Systems, Inc. ("Im-Clone") and her public statements in the wake of those allegations.

The market for MSO products is uniquely tied to the personal image and reputation of its founder, Stewart. MSO retains "an exclusive, worldwide, perpetual royalty-free license to use [Stewart's] name, likeness, image, voice and signature for its products and services." In its initial public offering prospectus, MSO recognized that impairment of Stewart's services to the company, including the tarnishing of her public reputation, would have a material adverse effect on its business. The prospectus distinguished Stewart's importance to MSO's business success from that of other executives of the company noting that, "Martha Stewart remains the personification of our brands as well as our senior executive and primary creative force." In fact, under the terms of her employment agreement, Stewart may be terminated for gross misconduct or felony conviction that results in harm to MSO's business or reputation but is permitted discretion over the management of her personal, financial, and legal affairs to the extent that Stewart's management of her own life does not compromise her ability to serve the company.

Stewart's alleged misadventures with ImClone arise in part out of a longstanding personal friendship with Samuel D. Waksal ("Waksal"). Waksal is the former chief executive officer of ImClone as well as a former suitor of Stewart's daughter. More pertinently, with respect to the allegations of the amended complaint, Waksal and Stewart have provided one another with reciprocal investment advice and assistance, and they share a stockbroker, Peter E. Bacanovic ("Bacanovic") of Merrill Lynch. Bacanovic, coincidentally, is a former employee of ImClone. Although the other investments recommended and facilitated by Waksal have thus far proven to be of no great news value, the ImClone investment — or more particularly Stewart's December 27, 2001, ImClone *divestment* — has been found to be somewhat more noteworthy. The speculative value of ImClone stock was tied quite directly to the likely success of its application for FDA approval to market the cancer treatment drug Erbitux. On December 26, Waksal received information that the FDA was rejecting the application to market Erbitux. The following day, December 27, he tried to sell his own shares and tipped his father and daughter to do the same. Stewart also sold her shares on December 27. That day she was traveling with another friend, Marianna Pasternak ("Pasternak"), when Stewart spoke with Bacanovic's assistant, Douglas Faneuil, and sold all of her ImClone shares. The next day, December 28, Pasternak's husband, Bart Pasternak, also sold 10,000 shares of ImClone. After the close of trading on December 28, ImClone publicly announced the rejection of its application to market Erbitux. The following day the trading price closed slightly more than 20% lower than the closing price on the date that Stewart had sold her shares. By mid-2002, this convergence of events had attracted the interest of the *New York Times* and other news agencies, federal prosecutors, and a committee of the United States House of Representatives. Stewart's publicized attempts to quell any suspicion were ineffective at best because they were undermined by additional information as it came to light and by the other parties' accounts of the events. Ultimately Stewart's prompt efforts to turn away unwanted media and investigative attention failed. Stewart eventually had to discontinue her regular guest appearances on CBS' *The Early Show* because of questioning during the show about her sale of ImClone shares. After barely two months of such adverse publicity, MSO's stock price had declined by slightly more than 65%. In August 2002, James Follo, MSO's chief financial officer, cited uncertainty stemming from the investigation of Stewart in response to questions about earnings prospects in the future.

Defendants have moved to dismiss the amended complaint under Court of Chancery Rule 23.1 for failure to make demand upon MSO's board of directors or adequately to plead why demand would be futile. Rule 23.1 . . . confers substantive rights that result in derivative complaints being subjected to more stringent pleading requirements. The plaintiff must state with particularity the efforts made to cause the company's board of directors to take action on the matters of concern to the plaintiff — to state how demand was made. If, as in this action, the plaintiff has failed to make a demand on the board, the plaintiff must state with particularity the reasons that demand should be excused.

Plaintiff concedes that demand was not made but asserts that demand would be futile because the board of directors is incapable of acting independently and disinterestedly in evaluating demand with respect to plaintiff's claims. Count I alleges that Stewart breached her fiduciary duties to MSO and its shareholders by selling (perhaps illegally) shares of ImClone in December of 2001 and by public statements she made regarding that sale. Because this claim does not challenge an action of the board of directors of MSO, the appropriate test for demand futility is that articulated in *Rales v. Blasband*. Particularly, the Court's task is to evaluate whether the particularized allegations "create a reasonable doubt that, as of the time the complaint [was] filed, the board of directors could have properly exercised its independent and disinterested business judgment in responding to a demand."[50] *Rales* requires that a majority of the board be able to consider and appropriately to respond to a demand "free of personal financial interest and improper extraneous influences."[51] Demand is excused as futile if the Court finds there is "a reasonable doubt that a majority of the Board would be disinterested or independent in making a decision on demand."[52]

The original complaint was filed on August 15, 2002. At that time the board members were defendants Stewart, Patrick, Martinez, Seligman, Moore, and Ubben. Thus, these six individuals constitute the board for purposes of evaluating demand futility. Demand is required if, in view of all the particularized allegations in the complaint and drawing all reasonable inferences in favor of the plaintiff, there is no reasonable doubt of the ability of a majority, here four of the six directors, to respond to [plaintiff's] demand appropriately.

---

50. *Rales* [*v. Blasband*], 634 A.2d. [927] at 934 [(Del. 1993)].
51. *Id.* at 935.
52. *Id.* at 930.

[Chancellor Chandler then applied the tests of independence and disinterestedness we saw in Chapter 12 to the defendant directors. The Chancellor found that Ms. Stewart was not disinterested and that Ms. Patrick was not independent. As to Mr. Martinez, Ms. Moore, and Ms. Seligman, the Chancellor found that the plaintiff had not sustained her burden of proof. The Chancellor did not discuss Mr. Ubben. The Chancellor then commented on the plaintiff's failure of proof:]

In sum, plaintiff offers various theories to suggest reasons that the outside directors might be inappropriately swayed by Stewart's wishes or interests, but fails to plead sufficient facts that could permit the Court reasonably to infer that one or more of the theories could be accurate. Evidence to support (or refute) any of the theories might have been uncovered by an examination of the corporate books and records, to which the plaintiff would have been entitled for this purpose.[64] Board minutes or voting records, for example, could reveal if the outside directors have in the past challenged Stewart's proposals, or not, voted in line with Stewart, or in opposition to her, and shown on which issues the outside directors have been more or less likely to go along with Stewart's wishes. Armed with such information, plaintiff (and this Court) would be in a much better position to evaluate whether there exists a reasonable doubt of the outside directors' resolve to act independently of Stewart. It appears, however, that plaintiff made no such investigation, instead relying largely, if not solely, on information from media reports to support the assertion that demand would be futile.

It is troubling to this Court that, notwithstanding repeated suggestions, encouragement, and downright admonitions over the years both by this Court and by the Delaware Supreme Court, litigants continue to bring derivative complaints pleading demand futility on the basis of precious little investigation beyond perusal of the morning newspapers. This failure properly to investigate whether a majority of directors fairly can evaluate demand may lead to either (or both) of two equally appalling results. If there is no reasonable doubt that the board could respond to demand in the proper fashion, failure to make demand and filing the derivative action results in a waste of the resources of the litigants, including the corporation in question, as well as those of this Court. If the facts to support reasonable doubt could have been ascertained through more careful pre-litigation investigation, the failure to discover and plead those facts still results in a waste of resources of the litigants and the Court and, in addition, ties the hands of this Court to protect the interests of shareholders where the board is unable or unwilling to do so. This results in the dismissal of what otherwise may have been meritorious claims, fails to provide relief to the company's shareholders, and further erodes public confidence in the legal protections afforded to investors.

It would be inappropriate to speculate on the merits of the underlying claims in any case, including this one, on a motion to dismiss under Rule 23.1. Therefore I have and express no opinion regarding the merits of Count I as may have been determined had it survived for trial. I would be remiss, though, if I failed to point out that with a bit more detail about the "relationships," "friendships," and "inter-connections" among Stewart and the other defendants or with some additional arguments as to why there may be a reasonable doubt of the directors'

---

64. [DGCL] §220; *Rales*, 634 A.2d at 934 n.10.

incentives when evaluating demand with respect to Count I, there may have been a reasonable doubt as to one or all of the outside directors disinterest, independence, or ability to consider and respond to demand free from improper extraneous influences. Nevertheless, on this pleading, no such doubt is raised. The defendants' motions to dismiss the amended complaint for failure adequately to plead demand futility are granted with respect to Count I.

Notes and Questions

1. Notes

a. In footnote 58 of the opinion Chancellor Chandler expanded a bit on the theory of the case against the directors other than Ms. Stewart.

> At oral argument, plaintiff's counsel suggested that the MSO board should have fired Stewart before the announcement of the federal indictment and of the SEC civil action. The failure to do so is purported to be a strong indication that the board as a whole is dominated and controlled by Stewart. This argument is unpersuasive for two reasons. First, the sole factual allegation upon which this inference is to be made is merely that Stewart was not removed from her positions as board chairman and chief executive officer before the indictment but has since been replaced. Even at oral argument plaintiff could not make factual allegations that would support an inference (1) that the board failed to consider what if any action might be taken in response to the negative media attention; (2) that the board failed to evaluate the risks and benefits of possible responses including those likely to result from taking no action; or (3) that the board's decision to wait before taking action was made on any basis other than the business judgment that to take action prematurely could unnecessarily worsen any harm to MSO and its shareholders that was already resulting from the negative publicity. The identification of which matters were or were not officially considered by the directors is precisely the sort of information that should be readily ascertainable by a shareholder through a books and records action authorized under [DGCL] §220. Second, the allegation is simply not made in the amended complaint and therefore cannot be considered by this Court for the purpose of demand futility analysis.

b. In the three years since the investigation of Ms. Stewart was made public in early 2002, MSO lost over $66 million. These losses stemmed primarily from the fact that (1) advertisers significantly reduced the advertising they purchased in MSO magazines; (2) MSO magazine circulation fell significantly; and (3) television stations and cable networks significantly reduced their purchases of the right to show MSO's television programs.

2. Reality Check

a. How did Ms. Stewart hurt the corporation, according to the complaint?
b. What standard applies when director-defendants challenge a derivative plaintiff's assertion that prior demand would have been futile? Who carries what kind of burden?

3. Suppose

a. Suppose Ms. Beam had made use of DGCL §220. Which corporate records should Ms. Beam have requested?

4. What Do You Think?

a. Why does FRCP 23.1 exist? Do you think such heightened procedural prerequisites should apply to derivative litigation? Do you think such prerequisites should apply to other kinds of litigation? If so, which?

b. Do you think Delaware places the burden appropriately in demand futility cases? If not, what changes would you make?

2. Background and Context

When a board of directors receives a shareholder demand to institute litigation, the directors may be compromised in terms of their ability to evaluate the demand fairly. This is certainly so when the demand indicates that the entire board should be defendants but may also be the case when only some of the board, or even none of the board are the targets of the proposed litigation. To enhance the likelihood of a fair decision on the shareholder demand, the board quite often delegates the task of evaluating the shareholder demand to a *special committee* of nonimplicated directors. Where all directors (or all but a small number) are putative defendants, the board sometimes expands the board and appoints new members for the express purpose of serving on the demand evaluation committee. Boards and special committees rarely find that acceding to the shareholder demand is in the best interest of the corporation. Rather, demand is almost always refused.

A similar dynamic applies where a derivative suit is filed on the theory that demand is excused because it would have been futile. That is, the board appoints directors who are not defendants as a special litigation committee. The committee may consist of, or be supplemented by, newly appointed directors. The litigation committee decides whether the litigation is in the best interest of the corporation. If, as is nearly always the case, the litigation committee finds that the litigation should be dismissed (or settled), a motion to that effect is made in the court in which the litigation is pending.

Where a shareholder's demand has been refused by the board, how should a court evaluate that refusal? This issue may be postured as a suit by the shareholder challenging the refusal or as a response by the board to a derivative suit filed despite demand refusal (on the theory that the board's refusal was wrongful). Likewise, where a derivative action is properly filed with no prior demand and the board or a special litigation committee determines that the derivative action is not in the best interests of the corporation and should be dismissed, the board or committee may file a motion seeking dismissal of the suit. In all these settings the constant question is what standard should the court use to evaluate the assertions? The final case in this chapter details an astonishingly wide range of judicial responses to that question.

In re DISH Network Deriv. Litig.

401 P.3d 1081 (Nev. 2017)

OPINION

By the Court, GIBBONS, J.:

Appellant Jacksonville Police and Fire Pension Fund (Jacksonville) brought suit, derivatively on behalf of DISH Network Corporation, challenging certain conduct of, among others, Charles W. Ergen, the chairman and chief executive officer of DISH. To investigate Jacksonville's claims, DISH's board of directors (the Board) created a Special Litigation Committee (the SLC), respondent in this matter. After the SLC concluded it was not in DISH's best interest to pursue Jacksonville's derivative claims, the district court deferred to the SLC's decision, dismissed the complaint, and awarded costs to the SLC.

In these consolidated appeals, we address the appropriate legal standard for a district court's consideration of an SLC's motion to defer to the SLC's recommendation that derivative claims should be dismissed because pursuing those claims would not be in the company's best interest. In doing so, we adopt the standard set forth in *Auerbach v. Bennett*, 47 N.Y.2d 619, 419 N.Y.S.2d 920, 393 N.E.2d 994 (1979), and conclude that the district court did not abuse its discretion in determining that the SLC was independent based upon its voting structure, which required an independent member's affirmative vote in order for any resolution of the SLC to have effect, and that the SLC conducted a good-faith and thorough investigation. We therefore affirm the district court's order granting the SLC's motion to defer and dismissing the complaint. With respect to costs, we affirm the district court's awards for electronic discovery costs and photocopying and scanning costs, but vacate the award for teleconference costs because we conclude that the district court lacked justifying documentation.

FACTS AND PROCEDURAL HISTORY

While we recognize that the underlying litigation and related proceedings involve extensive, complex, and contested facts, none of the issues before us concern the substantive merits of Jacksonville's claims or the SLC's determinations. Accordingly, we briefly summarize the events leading up to our review and focus on the facts most pertinent to the disposition of the instant consolidated appeals—i.e., the SLC's formation and investigation.

Background Summary

This case arises out of Ergen's purchases of secured debt of LightSquared L.P. and DISH's efforts to acquire LightSquared's assets after Ergen's purchases. Challenging this conduct, DISH stockholder Jacksonville brought claims for breach of loyalty and unjust enrichment against Ergen, and claims for breach of loyalty against DISH's Board and officers. LightSquared filed for Chapter 11 bankruptcy with approximately $1.7 billion face amount of secured debt outstanding. The secured debt is governed by a credit agreement, which lists DISH and Echostar Corporation, an entity controlled by Ergen, as disqualified companies such that neither can be an eligible assignee of the debt.

From April 2012 to April 2013, Ergen, through SP Special Opportunities, LLC (SPSO), another entity that he owns and controls, and using funds provided from his personal assets, purchased approximately $850 million of LightSquared's secured debt for a total purchase price of approximately $690 million. Ergen later informed DISH and Echostar of the opportunity to acquire LightSquared's assets through its bankruptcy. Ergen also disclosed to DISH's Board that he purchased LightSquared debt.

At a meeting held several days later and without the Ergens, the Board created the Special Transaction Committee (the STC) to determine whether DISH would pursue the LightSquared opportunity. On July 21, 2013, the STC recommended that DISH submit a bid, and the STC was dissolved that same day. Based on the STC's recommendation, on July 23, 2013, DISH submitted a $2.22 billion bid to acquire LightSquared's assets as part of a bankruptcy plan. However, on December 23, 2013, the Board authorized the termination of the bid.

Derivative Litigation

Before DISH terminated its bid, on August 9, 2013, Jacksonville instituted the instant derivative litigation. Originally, Jacksonville brought certain claims for breach of loyalty and unjust enrichment against Ergen and other directors and officers arising from, among other things, (1) Ergen's purchases, through SPSO, of LightSquared's secured debt; (2) the STC established by the Board to consider a bid for wireless spectrum and related assets of LightSquared; and (3) DISH's subsequent bid for the LightSquared assets. Jacksonville argued that Ergen's purchases of LightSquared's secured debt usurped corporate opportunities belonging to DISH, Ergen pressured DISH to make the bid in order to ensure that LightSquared could use the proceeds of DISH's bid to pay off Ergen's secured debt at substantial profit to Ergen, and Ergen interfered with the STC before it recommended the bid to the Board.

After DISH terminated its bid, Jacksonville filed its second amended complaint, adding as defendants the SLC members, among others, and further alleging the bid would have been beneficial to DISH and should not have been terminated. Thus, in addition to the events listed above, Jacksonville's claims stemmed from the withdrawal of DISH's bid and the establishment of the SLC.

The SLC's Formation and Investigation

On September 18, 2013, the Board created the SLC to investigate Jacksonville's claims and determine whether it was in the company's best interest to pursue the claims. The SLC initially consisted of long-standing board member Tom A. Ortolf and George R. Brokaw, who became a board member on October 7, 2013. In its status report to the court the following month, Jacksonville noted the flawed composition of the SLC, arguing Ortolf and Brokaw had close personal and professional ties to Ergen. On December 9, 2013, Charles M. Lillis, who became a board member on November 5, 2013, was added to the SLC. The resolutions appointing Lillis to the SLC made it so that the SLC could not act without Lillis's approval.

Ultimately, the SLC determined that it was not in DISH's best interest to pursue the litigation. As detailed in its report of over 300 pages, the SLC determined that the claims lacked merit, DISH could not prevail on the claims, and pursuit of the claims would be costly to DISH and undermine DISH's defenses asserted in other litigation. The SLC decided that the claims should be dismissed.

The SLC submitted its report to the district court on October 24, 2014. In the time leading up to the SLC's report, the district court considered multiple motions, status reports, and status conferences surrounding DISH's efforts to acquire LightSquared's assets, the events in LightSquared's bankruptcy and the adversary proceeding, and the derivative claims.

The SLC's Motion to Defer

After investigating for almost a year, the SLC moved the court to defer to the SLC's determination that the claims should be dismissed. After an initial hearing and reviewing the SLC's report and initial briefing on the motion to defer, the district court granted Jacksonville discovery pursuant to NRCP 56(f) regarding the SLC's independence and the thoroughness of the SLC's investigation. After discovery, the district court ordered supplemental briefing and oral argument. Ultimately, the district court granted the SLC's motion to defer, dismissing the case with prejudice, and Jacksonville timely appealed.

DISCUSSION

These consolidated appeals primarily concern the district court's granting the SLC's motion to defer to its decision to dismiss Jacksonville's derivative complaint. An SLC has the power to terminate a derivative complaint to the extent allowed by the state of incorporation. Although this court has yet to address this issue, two principal legal standards exist for considering an SLC's request to dismiss derivative claims. *See generally Zapata Corp. v. Maldonado*, 430 A.2d 779 (Del. 1981); *Auerbach v. Bennett*, 47 N.Y.2d 619, 419 N.Y.S.2d 920, 393 N.E.2d 994 (1979). Under both tests, the district court determines whether the SLC is independent and conducted a good-faith, thorough investigation. *Zapata*, 430 A.2d at 788; *Auerbach*, 419 N.Y.S.2d 920, 393 N.E.2d at 1001, 1002–03. The *Auerbach* test stops there—so long as the SLC is independent and employed reasonable procedures in its analysis, courts following this approach "may not second-guess [the SLC's] business judgment in deciding not to pursue the derivative litigation." *Hirsch v. Jones Intercable, Inc.*, 984 P.2d 629, 638 (Colo. 1999) (following *Auerbach*). The *Zapata* approach, on the other hand, adds a second step—if the court finds the SLC "was independent and showed reasonable bases for good faith findings and recommendations, the [c]ourt may proceed, in its discretion, to . . . determine, applying its own independent business judgment, whether the motion should be granted." *Zapata*, 430 A.2d at 789. Because Nevada's business judgment rule "prevents courts from 'substitut[ing] [their] own notions of what is or is not sound business judgment,'" *Wynn Resorts, Ltd. v. Eighth Judicial Dist. Court*, 133 Nev. ___, ___, 399 P.3d 334, 344 (2017) (alterations in original) (quoting *Sinclair Oil Corp. v.*

Levien, 280 A.2d 717, 720 (Del. 1971)), we conclude that *Auerbach* is the better approach. *See Lewis v. Anderson,* 615 F.2d 778, 783 (9th Cir. 1979) ("[T]he good faith exercise of business judgment by a special litigation committee of disinterested directors is immune to attack by shareholders or the courts."); *Miller v. Bargaheiser,* 70 Ohio App.3d 702, 591 N.E.2d 1339, 1342–43 (1990) (finding *Zapata's* "degree of scrutiny to be irreconcilable with the spirit of the business judgment rule").

Accordingly, and as a matter of first impression, we hold that courts should defer to the business judgment of an SLC that is empowered to determine whether pursuing a derivative suit is in the best interest of a company where the SLC is independent and conducts a good-faith, thorough investigation. *See Auerbach,* 419 N.Y.S.2d 920, 393 N.E.2d at 996 ("While the substantive aspects of a decision to terminate a shareholders' derivative action against defendant corporate directors made by a committee of disinterested directors appointed by the corporation's board of directors are beyond judicial inquiry under the business judgment doctrine, the court may inquire as to the disinterested independence of the members of that committee and as to the appropriateness and sufficiency of the investigative procedures chosen and pursued by the committee.") . . . . Additionally, we conclude that the application of this standard is a matter left to the sound discretion of the district court, and absent an abuse of that discretion, the district court's rulings will not be disturbed on appeal.

The District Court Did Not Abuse Its Discretion in Deferring to the SLC's Decision and Dismissing the Complaint

Jacksonville argues that the district court made numerous reversible errors in evaluating the independence and good faith of the SLC. We disagree.

Pursuant to *Auerbach,* 419 N.Y.S.2d 920, 393 N.E.2d at 996, and consistent with *Shoen v. SAC Holding Corp.,* 122 Nev. 621, 645, 137 P.3d 1171, 1187 (2006), and *In re AMERCO Derivative Litig.,* 127 Nev. 196, 222, 252 P.3d 681, 700 (2011), a shareholder must not be permitted to proceed with derivative litigation after an SLC requests dismissal, unless and until the district court determines at an evidentiary hearing that the SLC lacked independence or failed to conduct a thorough investigation in good faith. Here, the district court's hearing on the SLC's motion, which followed Jacksonville's discovery into the SLC's independence and good faith, was sufficient to constitute an evidentiary hearing because the district court and parties relied, at least in part, on deposition testimony. Based on the evidence before it, the district court ultimately found that the SLC was independent due to its voting structure, which required an affirmative vote by Lillis, an independent member, in order for any resolution of the SLC to have effect, and that the SLC conducted a good-faith and thorough investigation. While the SLC, as the party moving for dismissal, bears the burden of proof and is entitled to no presumption, the district court arrived at its conclusions without explicitly requiring Jacksonville to bear the burden of proof or presuming the SLC's independence and good faith. Accordingly, for the reasons discussed below, we conclude that the district court did not abuse its discretion in granting the SLC's motion and dismissing the complaint.

Independence

Jacksonville maintains that the district court erred by applying the test used in pre-suit demand futility cases, thereby presuming the SLC's independence and good-faith, placing the burden of proof on Jacksonville to overcome that presumption, and limiting its consideration of the SLC's independence to financial independence. We disagree.

The independence standard that applies to directors in the demand-futility context is equally applicable to determine whether an SLC is independent. In the demand-futility context, courts look "at 'whether the board that would be addressing the demand can impartially consider its merits without being influenced by improper considerations,' such that it could 'properly exercise [ ] its independent and disinterested business judgment in responding to a demand,'" *Shoen*, 122 Nev. at 639, 137 P.3d at 1183 (quoting *Rales v. Blasband*, 634 A.2d 927, 934 (Del. 1993)). Likewise, in considering whether an SLC properly exercised its independent business judgment in determining that litigation would not be in the company's best interest, courts should assess whether any improper influences prevented the SLC from impartially considering the merits of a derivative suit before recommending it be dismissed.

However, while a court may appropriately rely on cases in the pre-suit demand context for the independence inquiry, it should not presume an SLC to be independent nor require the derivative plaintiff to bear the burden of proof. *See Hasan v. CleveTrust Realty Inv'rs*, 729 F.2d 372, 376 (6th Cir. 1984) ("Neither the *Auerbach* approach nor the *Zapata* approach allows a reviewing court to extend to the members of a special litigation committee the presumption of good faith and disinterestedness. As the *Auerbach* court recognized, the policies of the business judgment rule do not protect from judicial scrutiny the complexion and procedures of a special litigation committee."); *Beam ex rel. Martha Stewart Living Omnimedia, Inc. v. Stewart*, 845 A.2d 1040, 1055 (Del. 2004) ("Unlike the demand-excusal context, where the board is presumed to be independent, the SLC has the burden of establishing its own independence by a yardstick that must be 'like Caesar's wife'—'above reproach.' Moreover, unlike the presuit demand context, the SLC analysis contemplates not only a shift in the burden of persuasion but also the availability of discovery into various issues, including independence.")). Thus, the formula for evaluating the independence of an SLC is still consistent with that which pertains in pre-suit demand cases, but the SLC is entitled to no presumption and bears the burden of proof.

Additionally, there is no exhaustive list of factors to be considered in evaluating independence. A lack of independence or disinterestedness may exist where the facts show "that the directors' execution of their duties is unduly influenced," or "that the majority is beholden to directors who would be liable or for other reasons is unable to consider a demand on its merits." *Shoen*, 122 Nev. at 639, 137 P.3d at 1183 (internal quotation marks and footnote omitted). "Additionally, director interestedness can be demonstrated through alleged facts indicating that 'a majority of the board members would be materially affected either to [their] benefit or detriment, by a decision of the board, in a manner not shared by the corporation and the stockholders.'" *AMERCO*, 127 Nev. at 219, 252 P.3d at 698. These same factors, among others, can and should be considered in assessing the independence of an SLC. Indeed, citing to cases evaluating the independence of directors in the demand-futility context and of SLC members, this court has "note[d] that, depending on the circumstances, allegations of close familial ties might suffice to show interestedness or partiality." *Shoen*, 122 Nev. at 639 n.56, 137 P.3d at 1183 n.56. Thus, the district court's independence inquiry is not limited to financial independence, and the relevant factors may be determined on a case-by-case basis.

In the instant case, the district court did not abuse its discretion when it relied on caselaw in the demand-futility context to support its conclusion that the SLC was independent. Although the SLC, as the party moving for dismissal, bore the burden of proof, the district court did not explicitly assign to Jacksonville the burden of proof nor did it explicitly apply a presumption in favor of the SLC. Rather, it acknowledged that the parties disputed whether a presumption applied and ultimately reached its conclusions "irrespective of which party bears the burden." Furthermore, the record on appeal suggests the district court *focused* its inquiry on the SLC members' financial independence, but does not clearly indicate the district court *limited* its inquiry to the same. As such, we conclude that Jacksonville's arguments regarding demand-futility standards and financial independence lack merit.

Jacksonville also argues that the district court erred by concluding the SLC was independent because two of the three members were not independent. We disagree.

When the SLC was established, it consisted of only two members—Ortolf and Brokaw, both of whom maintain close, personal relationships with Ergen and Ergen's family. For instance, emails between Ortolf and Cantey Ergen, Ergen's wife, sent days before the SLC report was finalized refer to "love and friendship" and their being "good friends," Ortolfs children have worked for DISH, Ergen's daughter refers to Ortolf as "Uncle Tom," and the Ortolfs have vacationed with the Ergens. In addition, Cantey Ergen is Brokaw's son's godmother, the Brokaws and Ergens have vacationed together, attended family dinners, and celebrated birthdays together, and two days after the SLC was formed, Cantey Ergen asked if she could sleep at the Brokaw's with a child and grandchild while visiting New York. While "business, social, and more remote family relationships are not disqualifying, without more," *AMERCO*, 127 Nev. at 232, 252 P.3d at 706 (PICKERING, J., concurring in part and dissenting in part), Ortolf and Brokaw's personal and professional ties with Ergen represent the type of improper influences that could inhibit the proper exercise of independent business judgment.

However, Jacksonville challenged the SLC's flawed composition based on Ortolf and Brokaw's personal and professional ties to Ergen and Ergen's family just weeks after the SLC was established. To address Jacksonville's concerns about the SLC's ability to act independently, Lillis was added to the SLC. Nonetheless, Jacksonville again raised the issue of independence in response to the SLC's motion to defer, and before ruling on the motion, the district court granted Jacksonville discovery into the SLC's independence and good faith. Ultimately, the district court found Lillis to be independent, and based on Lillis's independence *and* the SLC's voting structure, the district court determined that the SLC was independent too.

Unlike Ortolf and Brokaw's ties to the Ergens, the affiliations that Jacksonville challenges between Lillis and senior DISH executive Thomas A. Cullen are not substantial enough to undermine Lillis's independence. Jacksonville does not challenge the district court's finding that "[d]uring the relevant time period, Lillis had no financial or business connection to any defendant other than his service on the DISH Board." Rather, Jacksonville focuses on the facts that Lillis and Cullen have worked together in the past and see each other socially once or twice per year. Without more, these business and social affiliations are not disqualifying. *See AMERCO, 127 Nev. at 232, 252 P.3d at 706* (Pickering, J., concurring in part and dissenting in part). Therefore, we conclude that the district court did not abuse its discretion in concluding that Lillis was independent.

Once Lillis was added in response to Jacksonville's raising the issue of independence, the SLC could not act without Lillis's approval. The resolutions appointing Lillis to the SLC provided that "any and all actions or determinations of the [SLC] . . . must include the affirmative vote of Mr. Lillis and at least one (1) other committee member in order to constitute a valid and final action or determination of the SLC." Similar to cases involving two-person committees, Lillis's independence ensured the independence of the SLC as a whole because the SLC could not act without Lillis's affirmative vote. Therefore, despite Ortolf and Brokaw's relationships with the Ergens, we conclude that the district court did not abuse its discretion in concluding that the SLC was independent based on Lillis's independence and the SLC's voting structure.

Good-Faith and Thorough Investigation

Jacksonville next argues that the district court erred in determining the SLC conducted a good-faith, thorough investigation. We disagree.

In accordance with the business judgment rule, courts can "inquir[e] into the procedural indicia of whether the directors resorted in good faith to an informed decisionmaking process." *Wynn Resorts, Ltd. v. Eighth Judicial Dist. Court,* 133 Nev. ____, ____, 399 P.3d 334, 343 (2017). The inquiry into whether the SLC made its determination in good faith and on an informed basis "focuses on the process used by the SLC, rather than the substantive outcome of the process. Courts look to indicia of the SLC's investigatory thoroughness, such as what documents were reviewed and which witnesses interviewed." *Sarnacki v. Golden,* 778 F.3d 217, 224 (1st Cir. 2015).

> Proof, however, that the investigation has been so restricted in scope, so shallow in execution, or otherwise so *pro forma* or halfhearted as to constitute a pretext or sham, consistent with the principles underlying the application of the business judgment doctrine, would raise questions of good faith or conceivably fraud which would never be shielded by that doctrine.

Auerbach v. Bennett, 47 N.Y.2d 619, 419 N.Y.S.2d 920, 393 N.E.2d 994, 1003 (1979).

Here, the SLC's investigation, which was comprehensive by any objective measure, included the following: monitoring proceedings and reviewing documents in the LightSquared bankruptcy; conducting 21 interviews of 16 different people, including present respondents and former defendants, DISH senior executives, and regulatory and other technical experts; reviewing hundreds of thousands of pages of relevant documents; and holding more than 17 formal meetings in addition to multiple informal and telephonic meetings. The SLC requested legal advice on the issues raised by the matters under investigation throughout its investigation, and each member invested over 100 hours in the investigation. Accordingly, we conclude that Jacksonville's arguments regarding good faith and the SLC's investigation lack merit and, therefore, the district court did not abuse its discretion in determining that the SLC conducted a good-faith, thorough investigation.

CONCLUSION

Accordingly, for the reasons set forth above, we affirm the district court's order granting the SLC's motion to defer . . . .

[The opinion of Pickering, J., concurring in part and dissenting in part is omitted.]

Notes and Questions

1. Note

a. The MBCA requires dismissal if a majority of disinterested and independent (the MBCA uses the term "qualified", *see* MBCA §1.43(a)(2), (b), and (c)) board members or an SLC with a majority of disinterested and independent members determines "in good faith, after conducting a reasonable inquiry" that continuing the litigation is not in the best interest of the corporation. The burden of proof is on the plaintiff if a majority of the board were qualified directors at the time the determination to end the litigation was made. It is on the defendants otherwise. MBCA 7.44(d).

2. Reality Check

a. What is the procedural posture of this case?
b. What alternative tests does the court choose between?
c. Which alternative does the court choose, and why?

3. Suppose

a. Suppose that the court had adopted either the Delaware or the MBCA test. Would the analysis or result have been different?

4. What Do You Think?

a. Do you think that the Delaware rule, which, by making a demand a stockholder, concedes the board's independence, is a good one?
b. Is a universal demand rule a panacea for the troubles of derivative litigation?

5. You Draft It

a. Redraft MBCA §7.44 to embody the best rule for raising and evaluating challenges to a board.

D. FEDERAL SECURITIES REGULATION

The federal securities laws affect shareholder power in public companies in several ways. The dominant thrust of the securities laws is disclosure rather than substantive requirements. Nevertheless, at least one area of shareholder power, the solicitation of proxies by company management, has been heavily regulated under federal law since the 1930s. In this section we will briefly see four aspects of federal securities regulation of shareholder power.

First, we will look at federal rules that require public companies to place certain shareholder-proposed resolutions on the agenda for the annual shareholder meeting. Second, we will look at the federal rules governing proxies. Third, we will see that public companies have periodic disclosure requirements, which puts important information into the hands of shareholders. Finally, federal law requires certain shareholders to disclose information about their shareholdings and intentions.

1. Matters Requiring Shareholder Vote Under Federal Law

SEC Rule 14a-8 requires public companies to include a shareholder's proposal in its proxy materials sent to all shareholders if certain conditions are met. The rule is layperson friendly and is written in "plain English" in question-and-answer form. A person who has owned the lesser of 1 percent or $2,000 worth of voting stock for more than one year may submit one proposal each year. The proposal and any supporting statement may not exceed 500 words and must be submitted prior to the deadline, which must be stated in the prior year's proxy statement. The proponent must appear at the annual meeting to formally move the proposal.

A properly submitted proposal may be excluded by the company, but the company bears the burden of proving that the proposal is excludable. The company may exclude a proposal if it has been substantially included within the last five years and failed to garner 3 percent of the vote (if presented once), 6 percent (if twice), or 10 percent (if three times).

The grounds for excluding a new proposal fall into three broad categories. First are objections based essentially on state corporate law. Thus a company may exclude a proposal on the grounds that the proposal is impermissible under state corporate law (precatory motions are almost always permissible), the proposal relates to the election of directors or other matters already on the meeting agenda, or the proposal relates to specific amounts of dividends.

The second area for exclusion is, essentially, that passage would be a nullity. A corporation may exclude a proposal on the grounds that the corporation could not implement the proposal, the proposal has already been substantially implemented, or the proposal would be a violation of law including the proxy rules.

Third, proposals that are of minimal relevance to the corporation as a whole may be excluded. So, shareholder proposals may be excluded on the grounds that the proposal is to redress a personal grievance or the proposal relates to less than 5 percent of the company business and is not otherwise significantly related to the company's business.

The most contentious area, though, allows a corporation to exclude a shareholder proposal that "deals with a matter relating to the company's ordinary business operations." *See* Rule 14a-8(i)(7). The reason is that proposals that particularly rankle management are typically not excludable under any of the other categories. The SEC, which is the final arbiter of whether a shareholder proposal may be excluded, has vacillated between proshareholder and promanagement mindsets. Although the ultimate decision is intensely fact specific, in general, matters that concern day-to-day management issues are excludable and those that concern corporate policy may not be excluded. Often the policy proposals are matters of considerable, and controversial, public interest rather than narrowly related to the particular corporation.

2. Regulation of Proxy Solicitations

One criticism of public companies during the Great Depression of the 1930s was that corporate management controlled the outcome of corporate elections. This was because the incumbent board typically proposed a slate of directors (usually the incumbents) for nomination and election. The dispersed nature of public company shares made it unlikely that any significant alternative to the incumbents would be proposed. Congress, in 1934, punted the issue by declaring that no public company may solicit proxies from its shareholders in contravention of SEC rules. This left the SEC to invent the proxy rules, which are contained in Regulation 14A.

The SEC rules take a broad view of the definition of *proxy* and *solicitation*. *Proxy* means any collective shareholder action, and is not limited to shareholder meetings. *Solicitation* means any request to grant or revoke a proxy. Many kinds of communications between management and shareholders and communications among shareholders could thus be "solicitation" of "proxies." The SEC has exempted communications among shareholders that are not directed toward eventually obtaining a written proxy in connection with a shareholder vote.

Proxies must comply with rather precise SEC rules concerning form. The rules also require relatively comprehensive disclosure of material information regarding the corporation and its financial and operational performance and regarding the nominees for board positions. The company must file its proposed proxy statement with the SEC in advance of sending it to shareholders if the meeting agenda contains any contested matters or any nonroutine matters. In addition to the shareholder proposal rules set out above, the SEC has serious antifraud provisions to prevent false or misleading statements in proxy requests. The SEC also requires management to make certain shareholder information available to dissidents who intend to wage a proxy contest.

3. Reporting Requirements

Every public company must make periodic reports to its shareholders. The principal report is the annual report to shareholders, which is filed with the SEC on Form 10-K. This report is a comprehensive discussion of the company and the financial and operational results of the prior year. The 10-K also contains audited financial statements covering the prior year. Similar, but less comprehensive, reports are filed each quarter on Form 10-Q. These reports contain unaudited financial statements.

Finally, and perhaps most interestingly, public companies must file Form 8-K promptly after the occurrence of certain significant events. Many investors pay particular attention to 8-K filings. An 8-K must be filed when a company enters into or terminates a material contract not in the ordinary course of business, such as a merger agreement. Other areas requiring an 8-K filing include material, negative, financial developments; the resignation of a director or principal officer; and the amendment of the Articles or bylaws.

4. Ownership Reporting Requirements

The federal securities laws impose two basic kinds of reporting requirements for certain shareholders. First, any person or group, which is broadly defined, that acquires 5 percent of the voting stock of a public company must file a Schedule 13D. The schedule requires basic information about the stockholder, the source of the funds used to acquire the stock, and the purpose of the stockholding (e.g., investment or to effect a change in control). The purpose of the Schedule 13D requirement is to alert corporate management to potential hostile raiders and to alert other shareholders that a significant amount of stock has been accumulated under common control.

Second, Section 16(a) of the '34 Act requires all officers and directors, regardless of how little stock they hold, and all owners of 10 percent or more of the company's voting stock, to file Form 3. This describes the ownership status of any company stock held by the filer. Changes in ownership, whether purchases or sales, are reported on Form 4. Section 16(b) provides that the corporation may recover from anyone required to file under 16(a), any profit made or loss avoided on sales or purchases made within six months of each other. The provision is one of strict liability and the calculation of the six-month period can be tricky; corporate executives violate the provisions with some regularity.

E. TERMS OF ART IN THIS CHAPTER

Absolute majority	DTC	Proxy
Advance notice bylaw	General proxy	Quorum
Amove	Holdover	Settled
Annual meetings	Inspection right	Simple majority
Book entry system	Limited proxy	Special committee
Broker overvote	Notice	Special meeting
Call	Periodic reporting	Street name
Cede & Co.	Plurality	Transaction reporting
Demand excused	Precatory motion	Transfer agent
Demand refused	Proper purpose	
Derivative action		

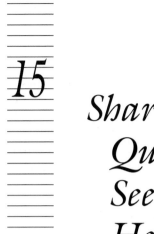

Shareholder Governance Questions Most Often Seen in the Privately Held Corporation

In this chapter we continue to explore the role of shareholders in corporate governance. The last chapter introduced you to the general corporate law principles of shareholder powers and used the publicly held corporation as the typical setting. Our focus here is on questions of shareholder participation that are typically encountered in nonpublic corporations. Many of these corporations, as you will see, are owned and operated by members of a single family, raising issues of family dynamics as well as corporate law.

We'll consider two main areas of shareholder governance in this chapter. First, we'll investigate the kinds of restrictions that can be imposed by the corporation and, ultimately, by the shareholders themselves, on corporate governance powers. Second, we'll look at the restrictions on shareholder governance powers that are imposed externally, that is, by courts and legislatures. In that section we'll see yet another aspect of fiduciary duties and look at the potential plight of minority shareholders in closely held corporations.

A. SELF-IMPOSED RESTRICTIONS ON SHAREHOLDER GOVERNANCE RIGHTS

Chapter 14 described the principal shareholder governance powers. These primarily concern the power to vote. In this portion of the chapter we take up five devices that planners may employ that affect shareholder governance powers in important ways.

1. Preemptive Rights: The Management Component

When we considered how money moves into a corporation and the concomitant economic rights given in return, we saw that a later issuance of shares could reduce the economic interests of the current shareholders if the newly issued shares were issued for less than their fair value. *See* Chapter 6. A similar dilution in management

675

power occurs when voting shares are issued even where the current shareholders' economic interests are protected. Consider this example:

> Each of the four shareholders of a corporation owns 250 shares of common stock.
>
> The fair value of the entire corporation is $1 million.
>
> The corporation needs another $1 million in permanent capital.
>
> As a consequence, the board (in reality, quite probably the four shareholders) resolves to issue 1,000 shares of common stock at $1,000 each to people who are not currently shareholders.

Economically, the current shareholders are probably not harmed. Each owned one-fourth of a corporation worth $1 million and thus had $250,000 in wealth. After the issuance of new shares, each of the original shareholders owns one-eighth of a corporation worth about $2 million[1] and thus retains his or her $250,000 of wealth.

But regardless of whether the original shareholders are helped or hurt economically by the new issuance, their voting interests have changed. True, each still has 250 votes (assuming one vote per share) but now, those 250 votes are only one-eighth of the total votes rather than one-fourth. If the newly issued shares will be held by a large number of unaffiliated shareholders, the original shareholders might retain, as a practical matter, their voting control. If the new shares are issued to a single shareholder, though, that shareholder has half the voting power, effectively relegating the original shareholders' voting power to that of minority shareholder status.

The voting power dilution from issuing shares can, obviously, be used strategically. In public companies, this danger is only theoretical because the shares are already so widely held and the newly issued shares are probably going to be equally widely distributed so no real harm to the current shareholders' voting power, which is functionally nonexistent, is done. In closely held corporations considerable harm can be done to existing shareholders.

As we described in Chapter 6, the courts, from an early date, found an equitable right in existing shareholders to purchase shares proposed to be issued so that their aliquot economic and managerial interests would be preserved. This right, called the *preemptive right*, permits each current shareholder to maintain his or her proportionate interest by purchasing the same percentage of to-be-issued shares on the same terms and conditions as proposed by the board of directors. Broadly speaking, preemptive rights were unavailable where the newly issued shares were to be issued for noncash consideration (on the theory that the corporation's need for the particular consideration was probably so important that cash was not a viable substitute); the newly issued shares were to be issued as part of the corporation's

---

1. This assumes that the additional money from the stock issuance increases the value of the company dollar for dollar. That assumption, although not unreasonable, is not always accurate. If the new money will allow the corporation to compete much more successfully than it did before, the value of the company might increase more than the money contributed. Thus, a company worth $1 million, that obtains an infusion of $1 million, might legitimately be worth $2.5 or $3 million. Conversely, if the additional money will not be sufficient for the company to prosper the corporation may lose value. This might be the case where management will misinvest the proceeds. So, the same company that was worth $1 million may, after the infusion of another $1 million, have a value of only $1.5 million. In fact, paradoxically, it is possible that the corporation might be worth even less than $1 million after the infusion of an additional $1 million!

initial plan of financing; or the newly issued shares were to be of a different class than those outstanding.

The corporation statutes in many states (although not Delaware) explicitly embody these exemptions. *See* MBCA §6.30(a)(3). Under the DGCL and MBCA, preemptive rights are opt-in. That is, a corporation's shareholders have no right to preempt subsequent issuances of stock unless the Articles so provide. *See* DGCL §102(b)(3), MBCA §6.30.

2. Supermajority Provisions

A very common technique for changing the default governing structure in a closely held corporation is to require a *supermajority* vote. A supermajority provision for board meetings may be placed in the Articles or bylaws. A supermajority provision for shareholder meetings must be in the Articles under the MBCA but may be in either the Certificate or the bylaws in Delaware. *See* DGCL §§102(b)(4), 141(b), 216, MBCA §§7.25, 7.27, 8.24.

At common law courts frequently held that a requirement of shareholder unanimity was unenforceable because it was contrary to public policy. The theory behind such results was that a primary difference between a corporation and a partnership was that shareholders' power should be proportional to their investment (i.e., to the shares they held) in contrast to the partnership model of treating partners as having equal management rights regardless of the disparity in their investments. Corporate drafters circumvented this case law by drafting supermajority provisions that, on their face, did not require unanimity but which, as a practical matter, did. For example, in a corporation with four 25 percent shareholders, a supermajority provision would require an 80 percent shareholder vote to effect certain shareholder actions. This provision would pass muster under the older common law rule. This approach to drafting supermajority provisions continues today in part because of uncertainty as to whether modern courts would strike down unanimity requirements.

Paradoxically, supermajority provisions in public companies serve to protect the incumbent management rather than the shareholders. In public companies the shareholders are typically widely dispersed without any effective control over management. Supermajority provisions, at the shareholder level, serve to increase the difficulty of an insurgent group of shareholders gaining influence over the corporation. Thus the company's directors are more securely in control of the corporation.

a. *Superquorum Provisions*

A related technique for giving minority shareholders more protection is to raise the quorum required for board meetings or shareholder meetings. *See* DGCL §§141(b) (director meetings), 216 (shareholder meetings), MBCA §§7.27 (shareholder meetings), 8.24(a) (director meetings). A superquorum requirement for board meetings may be placed in the Articles or the bylaws. Under the DGCL, shareholder superquorum requirements may also be in either the Certificate or bylaws but the MBCA permits such provisions in the Articles only. *See* DGCL §216, MBCA §7.27.

At least three pitfalls exist that may make superquorum provisions undesirable. First, the converse of the requirement that superquorum provisions need only be in the bylaws is that the bylaws may more easily be amended than the Articles and thus the provision more easily done away with. Second, a superquorum provision without supermajority provisions means that, if a quorum exists at a board or shareholder meeting, the minority could more easily be outvoted than if a super-majority provision existed. Thus the "protection" afforded by superquorum provisions may be illusory. Finally, superquorum provisions are rather blunt in their effect. That is, if a group of directors determines to stay away from a meeting to avoid a quorum, the corporation can take no action at all. If this situation becomes chronic, the corporation is in deadlock, which may result in dissolution or other dire remedies being imposed by a court. On the other hand, if the corporation has only a supermajority provision, the board may take action on a potentially wide range of vital but uncontroversial matters. So, as a matter of planning, supermajority voting provisions are usually preferable to superquorum provisions.

3. Cumulative Voting

Ordinarily, shareholders are entitled to cast one vote for every share they own for each matter presented for a shareholder vote. When electing directors, each director slot is considered a separate election, although the candidates run at large, so each shareholder may cast his or her shares for as many different candidates as there are slots. For example, when electing a board of three directors, the holder of 100 shares may cast (up to) 100 votes for three different people. This method is called *straight voting* or *statutory voting*. In the words of the MBCA, under straight voting, "each vote . . . may be voted for or against up to that number of candidates that is equal to the number of directors to be elected." MBCA §10.22(a)(1).

The plurality rule combined with the straight voting method means that the shareholder or coalition of shareholders that controls the most shares is able to elect all the directors. Where shares are widely dispersed or where other barriers to collective action exist the quantum of shares necessary to control the board may be no more than 20 percent or perhaps even less. In many settings such hegemony may be short-lived and competing shareholder factions are likely to arise, but in other settings the dominant shareholder group seems likely to remain so indefinitely. In the starkest situation of a corporation with two shareholders, a shareholder with slightly more than 50 percent of the shares can elect every member of the board — leaving the other shareholder, who owns nearly half the corporation, powerless.

The cumulative voting method was developed to redress this perceived inequity. Under *cumulative voting*, each shareholder may cast votes equal to the product of the number of shares owned multiplied by the number of director slots to be filled. The shareholder may cast those votes for one candidate or distribute the product among several candidates. Assume, again, a board of three directors and a shareholder owning 100 shares. That shareholder has 300 votes and may cast all 300 for one person or divide them as he or she sees fit. For example, the shareholder might cast 150 votes each for two candidates or 200 votes for one candidate and 100 for another. DGCL §214, MBCA §7.28(c).

So what? How does this help shareholders who control fewer shares than others? It means that as long as more than one director slot is being filled, some percentage of otherwise unrepresented shareholders can elect a candidate of its choice. How small or large a percentage is required to elect a candidate depends on how many director slots are to be filled. The more slots, the lower the percentage of shares needed to elect one candidate. The following chart shows the percentage required to elect one director:

Board Slots to Be Filled:	Shares Needed to Elect One Director:
2	>33%
3	>25%
4	>20%
5	>16%

In practice, cumulative voting issues often arise when it is impossible to obtain more shares. This is so because cumulative voting is primarily important in closely held corporations. By the time one set of shareholders is concerned with trying to elect a board candidate, the views of the shareholders have hardened and transfer of shares from one faction to another is unlikely. The question then becomes how many directors can be elected with a given number of shares? The following formula tells the answer:

Formula 1

To find the number of directors that can be elected with s shares:

$$D - \text{INT}\left(\frac{(S-s)\times(D+1)}{S}\right) = d$$

s = number of voting shares your faction controls
S = total number of voting shares
D = total number of director slots to be filled
d = the number of directors your faction can be certain of electing.

For those occasions when controlling more shares is possible, you can determine the number of shares necessary to elect a desired number of directors by using this formula:

Formula 2

$$\mathrm{INT}\left(\frac{S \times d}{D+1}\right) + 1 = s$$

s = number of voting shares your faction needs to elect "d" directors

Finally, and often critically, one must know how many *votes* to give one's candidate(s) to ensure election. The formula is:

Formula 3

To find the number of votes, *V*, necessary to cast for each candidate to ensure that candidate's election:

$$\mathrm{INT}\left(\frac{(S-s) \times D}{(D-d)+1}\right) + 1 = V$$

V = the number of votes that must be cast per candidate to ensure election of "d" directors.

Under the DGCL and the MBCA, cumulative voting is an opt-in provision meaning that straight voting applies unless the Articles provide for cumulative voting. You should be aware, though, that many states provide that cumulative voting is an opt-out provision (i.e., cumulative voting is the default rule) and a few states, such as California, require cumulative voting for electing directors.

The practical application of cumulative voting is often very nerve-wracking for lawyers. First, of course, its importance is greatest when shareholder factions are most at loggerheads, so your client will perceive that he or she has much at stake. Second, although the formulas are not difficult, clients and counsel have a way of miscalculating, which, of course, frequently leads to grief.[2] Third, under the MBCA, where cumulative voting exists, a shareholder must give notice of his or her intention to cumulate; thereafter all shareholders may vote cumulatively without notice. This is to prevent inattentive shareholder factions from being sandbagged by another faction that may garner extra seats by cumulating while the inattentive faction loses because it voted straight. Many states, however, do not include such a provision, thus making it possible to act strategically. Remember that the rule is that votes may be changed until the polls are declared closed and that once closed, the polls may not be reopened. *See* DGCL §231(c), MBCA §7.08(d).

Notes and Questions

1. Notes

a. Remember, your candidate(s) don't need to receive the highest number of votes. You want them to get only the minimum number necessary to be certain that they will be elected.

---

2. In part, these miscalculations are caused by the fact that many corporate resources print only Formula 2, which is often not germane to the parties. Compounding this source of confusion is that those other corporate resources also tend to print a misleading (though not actually incorrect) version of the formulas, which often contributes to miscalculations.

b. A related observation: Quite frequently you will have votes left over after casting the minimum necessary to ensure election of your candidate(s). Frequently these extra votes are simply distributed equally among the faction's candidates, which has the effect of wasting those extra votes. Rather, those extra votes should be cast for one additional candidate. It is sometimes possible to win a director slot to which your faction would not be "entitled" under cumulative voting by such an approach.

c. If you are reasonably certain that some shares controlled by opposing factions will not be voted at the meeting, you can reduce S in the formulas by the number of shares likely to be missing. Doing so will change the number of votes per candidate you must cast to ensure election and may suggest that you can win an additional board seat. Remember, though, that if you overestimate the number of shares that are absent, your faction may come to grief because you cast too few votes per candidate to elect all (or even to elect any) of your candidates.

d. Cumulative voting's effects can be blunted in three ways. First, a classified board can reduce (or increase) a particular faction's power to elect board members. Second, a staggered board increases the percentage of shares necessary to elect one more candidate because it reduces the number of slots to be elected at each annual meeting. At the most extreme, a shareholder faction that controls slightly more than 25 percent of the shares, and which can therefore elect one director on a three-person board, will have that power eviscerated if the board is staggered with three-year terms. In that setting only one director will be elected each year and, obviously, the shareholder faction that controls the most shares can elect all three directors, although it may take two years — three annual meetings — to achieve this result completely. Finally, reducing the size of the board has the same functional effect as staggering the board terms.

2. Suppose

a. Assume that a corporation with cumulative voting has 1,000 shares outstanding, seven directors are to be elected, and your faction controls 300 shares. How many candidates can your faction be certain of electing to the board?

b. Using the same assumptions, how many votes should you cast for each of your candidates to ensure all of them are elected? The answers are at the end of this Notes and Questions section.

3. What Do You Think?

a. Is cumulative voting an appropriate way to protect shareholders? Are all shareholders benefited by cumulative voting?

b. If you believe cumulative voting is beneficial, do you believe it should be mandatory for all corporations? If not, should it be mandatory for some corporations? If so, which ones?

c. Should a corporation with cumulative voting be allowed to blunt the consequences by classifying, staggering or reducing the size of its board? How would you enforce such restrictions?

4. Answers to "Suppose" Questions

a. Your faction can elect two directors. The calculation, using Formula 1, is,

$$D - INT\left(\frac{(S-s)\times(D+1)}{S}\right) = d$$

$$7 - INT\left(\frac{(1,000-300)\times(7+1)}{1,000}\right) = d$$

$$7 - INT\left(\frac{700\times8}{1,000}\right) = d$$

$$7 - INT\left(\frac{5,600}{1,000}\right) = d$$

$$7 - INT(5.6) = d$$

$$7 - 5 = d$$

$$2 = d$$

b. You should cast 817 votes for each of your two candidates. That answer is found using Formula 3:

$$INT\left(\frac{(S-s)\times D}{(D-d)+1}\right) + 1 = V$$

$$INT\left(\frac{(1,000-300)\times7}{(7-2)+1}\right) + 1 = V$$

$$INT\left(\frac{700\times7}{5+1}\right) + 1 = V$$

$$INT\left(\frac{4,900}{6}\right) + 1 = V$$

$$INT(816.67) + 1 = V$$

$$816 + 1 = V$$

$$817 = V$$

Note that your faction's 300 shares means you have 2,100 votes to cast (i.e., 300 × 7). If you simply give half your votes (1,050) to each candidate, each will certainly be elected. However, by using Formula 3 you know that 817 votes each will be sufficient to guarantee election. If you cast 817 votes per candidate you have 466 votes remaining (2,100 − 1,634), which you should cast for a third candidate. By doing so you might capture a third director slot if your opponents miscalculate or are sufficiently inattentive.

Putting It to Work

Problem 15-1

AlphaBytes, Inc. is a privately held software development company. The company is well established and is now generating significant money. AlphaBytes has 1,500 shares of common stock outstanding. The two founders are Alan and Brittany. Alan owns 800 shares and Brittany owns 500 shares. The remaining 200 shares are owned by about 20 AlphaBytes employees, who own between 1 and 45 shares each.

The board has been declaring the maximum legal dividend each month and your client, Brittany, believes that the reason for the dividends is that Alan is a notorious spendthrift who is in constant need of money. Brittany believes the corporation would be better off if it retained as much money as possible both to expand its operations (rather than funding expansion through expensive loans, as it is currently doing) and to generate a cushion of cash in case of a downturn in the company's fortunes. Although Alan and Brittany are long-time friends, their relationship has soured because of the difference of opinion regarding the dividends.

Brittany retains you to help her change the corporation's dividend policy. After reading AlphaBytes' articles of incorporation and bylaws you discover two interesting facts. First, the articles require that any dividends be approved by 60 percent of the board members. Second, the articles provide for cumulative voting for directors at the request of any shareholder, provided such request is submitted before the polls are closed. As far as you are aware, no shareholder has ever invoked this provision. AlphaBytes' articles provide for a seven-person board of directors with all directors elected annually. The seven incumbents include Alan, Brittany, and five of Alan's nominees.

The annual meeting of shareholders will be held in one week. Brittany wishes to continue to serve as a director and has identified a handful of friends whom she believes will be good directors and will be willing to vote against future dividends. You and Brittany believe that all 1,500 shares will be present at the meeting.

a. How many directors can Brittany elect if she controls only her own shares?

b. How many votes per candidate should Brittany cast to ensure her nominees are elected?

c. How many directors does Brittany need to elect to block any further dividends?

d. How many more shares does Brittany need to control to be sure of electing enough directors to block any further dividends?

e. If she succeeds in controlling enough shares to elect enough directors to block any further dividends, how many votes per candidate should Brittany cast to ensure her nominees are elected?

4. Agreements Regarding Shareholder Voting

Shareholders in nonpublic corporations frequently enter into agreements with one another about the way in which their shares will be voted. These agreements, obviously, modify the agreeing shareholders' governance powers and may affect the voting power of shareholders who are not parties to the agreement. Conceptually, these agreements should simply raise contract law, rather than corporate law, issues. Shareholders, as the owners of the corporation, classically have the right to take action solely in their own best interest and surely a voting agreement with other shareholders may be such an action. Nevertheless, the courts have long found certain shareholder voting agreements to be impermissible or subject to court-imposed restrictions. Likewise, the state legislatures have enacted statutes that cabin the power of shareholders to enter into and enforce voting agreements.

This section looks at the contours of shareholder voting agreements. We start with *voting trusts* and then look at *pooling agreements*. You ought to pay close attention to the definitions of these terms but also look behind the definitions to figure out why courts and legislatures have subjected certain kinds of agreements to heightened requirements. As we will see, the labels are largely conclusions applied to agreements that possess certain important characteristics.

a. *The Current Setting*

i. Voting Trusts. We start with a discussion of a classic corporate law technique affecting shareholder voting power: the voting trust. At common law voting trusts were viewed with great suspicion and usually were held to be unenforceable. In the early twentieth century, state legislatures began to pass statutes that permitted voting trusts, provided the trusts conformed to the requirements of the statutes. Read DGCL §218 and MBCA §7.30. Go ahead, read them.

Voting trusts are used in three basic situations. The intention is to give the economic rights of stock to one person or group and the management rights to another person or group. In close corporations voting trusts are often used as a device to smooth the transfer of wealth from one generation to the next. Take, as an example, a typical family-owned business corporation. The parents, who own all the stock, wish to pass the economic benefits to their children but do not wish to give the children the concomitant power to manage the corporation. By using a voting trust, the parents put the stock (or some of it) into the trust with themselves as the trustees and their children as the beneficiaries. During the life of the trust, the parents vote the shares, while the children are entitled to the dividends and other capital appreciation of the shares.

A second use of voting trusts is when a corporation enters bankruptcy, but the underlying economic business is viable. If the corporation is reorganized (rather than liquidated) the former creditors have often had their debt converted into stock.

The attitude of the former creditors may remain hostile to the business. After all, the creditors want their money. They don't want to own a business. In such a setting, these new, involuntary, shareholders may have an incentive to vote in ways that are not economically rational for the business as a whole. A voting trust, with the former creditors receiving the economic benefits, and the corporation's new management as trustees may solve the tension. Finally, a corporation that is in economic difficulty but not yet bankrupt may enter into a voting trust agreement as a condition of receiving a necessary loan.

The Delaware Supreme Court described the purpose of regulating voting trusts:

> First, . . . Section 218, from its original enactment in 1925, was designed to regulate agreements by "(o)ne or more stockholders." Not all trusts of corporate stock which, either expressly or by implication, give voting rights to a trustee are voting trusts. The Court of Chancery defined a voting trust in *Peyton v. William C. Peyton Corp.*, 194 A. 106, 111 (Del. Ch. 1937), *rev'd on other grounds*, 7 A.2d 737 (Del. 1939) in the following manner:
>
> > A voting trust as commonly understood is a device whereby two or more persons owning stock with voting powers, divorce the voting rights thereof from the ownership, retaining to all intents and purposes the latter in themselves and transferring the former to trustees in whom the voting rights of all the depositors in the trust are pooled.
>
> This definition has been adopted in several cases. Regulation of voting trusts is directed to a class of trusts created to unify voting. Thus, the voting trust statute was not intended to be all inclusive in the sense that it was designed to apply to every set of facts in which voting rights are transferred to trustees incident to or as part of the assignment of other stockholder rights. Rather, a voting trust is a stockholder pooling arrangement with the criteria that voting rights are separated out and irrevocably assigned for a definite period of time to voting trustees for control purposes while other attributes of ownership are retained by the depositing stockholders.
>
> Second, our case law makes it clear that the main purpose of a voting trust statute is "to avoid secret, uncontrolled combinations of stockholders formed to acquire control of the corporation to the possible detriment of non-participating shareholders." *Lehrman* [*v. Cohen*], 222 A.2d [800] at 807 [(Del. 1966)].
>
> Third, it is important to recognize there has been a significant change from the days of our original 1925 statute. Voting trusts were viewed with "disfavor" or "looked upon . . . with indulgence" by the courts. Other contractual arrangements interfering with stock ownership, such as irrevocable proxies, were viewed with suspicion. The desire for flexibility in modern society has altered such restrictive thinking. E. Folk, *The Delaware General Corporation Law*, Section 218 at 240-42 (1972). The trend of liberalization was markedly apparent in the 1967 changes to our own §218. Voting or other agreements and irrevocable proxies were given favorable treatment and restrictive judicial interpretations as to the absolute voiding of voting trusts for terms beyond the statutory limit were changed by statute. The trend was not to extend the voting trust restrictions beyond the class of trust being regulated and beyond the reasons for statutory regulation. That public policy cannot be ignored here.

Oceanic Exploration Co. v. Grynberg, 428 A.2d 1 (Del. 1981) (Quillen, J.)

Notes and Questions

1. Notes

a. The usual formulation of the common law definition of a voting trust is

(1) the voting rights of the stock are separated from the other attributes of ownership; (2) the voting rights granted are intended to be irrevocable for a definite period of time; and (3) the principal purpose of the grant of voting rights is to acquire voting control of the corporation.

Lehrman v. Cohen, 222 A.2d 800, 805 (Del. 1966) (quoting *Abercrombie v. Davies*, 130 A.2d 338 (Del. Ch. 1957))

b. Note that a common law voting trust that does not meet the requirements of the statute is void. In other words, the statute is the exclusive method of creating a valid voting trust.

c. The beneficiaries of a voting trust receive voting trust certificates that represent their ownership interest. These voting trust certificates are ordinarily transferable so beneficiaries can transfer their economic interest. When the trust expires, the beneficiary's transferee receives the shares.

2. Reality Check

a. What are the elements of a voting trust?

b. What are the elements of a valid voting trust under DGCL §218 and MBCA §7.30?

3. What Do You Think?

a. Do voting trusts have the potential to cause harm to corporations, shareholders, or third parties? If so, what dangers exist?

b. Do you believe the voting trusts statutes (DGCL §218 and MBCA §7.30) are traps for the unwary?

* * *

ii. Pooling Agreements.   As you see, if a court finds an agreement to be a "voting trust," the agreement must comport with the statutory requirements or it is unenforceable. What other voting agreements may shareholders enter into? One such agreement is a proxy (*see* Chapter 14). Where the shareholder grants a general proxy (i.e., giving the proxyholder discretion as to how to vote) and where the proxy is irrevocable, the agreement looks much like a common law voting trust. Yet courts almost always refrain from recharacterizing voting agreements that purport to be proxies as voting trusts. Thus even though irrevocable general proxies and voting trusts can effect similar ends, their validity will be judged under different criteria.

But shareholders may enter into other voting agreements that are neither common law voting trusts nor proxies. These agreements are typically lumped under the rubric *pooling agreements*.

The legislatures adopted provisions explicitly approving such agreements. The MBCA provides that agreements that determine how the shareholders *themselves* will vote *their own* shares are specifically enforceable. Axiomatically, those agreements are removed from the voting trust section. *See* MBCA §7.31. In a related provision, the MBCA also provides that being a party to a pooling agreement is an interest in shares that supports an irrevocable proxy. *See* MBCA §7.22(d)(5).

The cognate Delaware provision (DGCL §218(c)) is much more problematic. It validates written agreements that state how shares shall be voted, that state a procedure for determining how shares shall be voted, and that contain "agreements to agree" on how shares shall be voted. The statute is written in the passive voice, thus it is not explicit whether the agreement must require the shareholders to vote their own shares. It would seem, then, to encompass both some voting trusts and some proxies. As if the issue weren't muddled enough, DGCL §218(d) says that section 218 does not prohibit other shareholder agreements and irrevocable proxies, if they are "not otherwise illegal." What on Earth can this include?

Conceptually, if the statutes permit pooling agreements to be specifically enforced, how are those agreements functionally different from irrevocable proxies or voting trusts?

b. Background and Context

i. Vote Buying.   One other category of shareholder voting agreements continues to present sometimes difficult legal issues: agreements that may constitute "vote buying." Certainly a director who sells his or her vote has breached the duty of loyalty and possibly the duty of care, as well. But aren't shareholders entitled to vote their shares as they please? If so, shouldn't that logically include the power to sell their votes? Obviously a general proxy is simply a gratuitous form of transferring the power to vote. If shareholders may not sell their votes, what is the basis of this prohibition? Unless the shareholder owns a majority of the shares (and possibly where the shareholder owns a controlling, though not a majority, amount of the shares) no fiduciary duty runs to other shareholders.

The following excerpt discusses the rule against vote buying and the underlying policies for that rule. In this case, the company, Hewlett-Packard Co., was soliciting shareholder proxies in favor of the acquisition of Compaq Computer Corp. The acquisition was vehemently opposed by the descendents of the founders, Mr. Hewlett and Mr. Packard, who waged a bitter proxy campaign soliciting shareholders to vote against the merger. The final vote was very close and, on the day prior to the shareholder meeting, a shareholder switched its votes from "no" to "yes." That shareholder was an investment bank that had done work for Hewlett-Packard and hoped to do more work for the company.

> This Court has, on several earlier occasions, addressed so-called "vote-buying" allegations. In some instances the claims were successful and in others they were not. There does not, however, appear to be an obvious predisposition on the part of the Court one way or another toward vote-buying claims.[5]
>
> The appropriate standard for evaluating vote-buying claims is articulated in *Schreiber v. Carney*. *Schreiber* indicates that vote-buying is illegal *per se* if "the object or purpose is to defraud or in some way disenfranchise the other stockholders." *Schreiber* also notes, absent

5. In the seminal Delaware case on vote-buying, *Schreiber v. Carney*, the Court recounted the history of challenges to vote-buying agreements in Delaware jurisprudence. 447 A.2d 17, 23-26 (Del. Ch. 1982). The *Schreiber* Court noted that earlier cases "had summarily voided the challenged votes as being purchased and thus contrary to public policy and in fraud of the other stockholders." *Id*. at 23. Two principles were apparent from those cases. First, those cases held that vote-buying was illegal *per se* if that agreement was entered into for the purpose of either defrauding or disenfranchising other shareholders. Second, they indicated that vote-buying was illegal *per se* "as a matter of public policy, [because] each stockholder should be entitled to rely upon the independent judgment of his fellow stockholders." *Id*. at 24.

This second principle was based on the notion that there was a duty owed by all shareholders to each other. The rationale for that notion was that "while self-interest motivates a stockholder's vote, theoretically, it is also advancing the interests of other stockholders. Thus, any agreement entered into for personal gain, whereby a stockholder separates his voting right from his property right was considered a fraud upon this community of interests." *Id*. The *Schreiber* Court noted that the notion that vote-buying was illegal *per se* as a matter of public policy was " 'obsolete because it is both impractical and impossible of application to modern corporations . . . and [that] the courts have gradually abandoned it.' " *Id*. at 25 (quoting 5 Fletcher, *Cyclopedia Corporation* (Perm. Ed.) §2066). Furthermore, the Legislature has codified, at [DGCL] 218(c), the permissibility of creating voting agreements. As noted below, however, the principle that vote-buying is illegal *per se* if entered into for deleterious purposes survives.

these deleterious purposes, that "because vote-buying is so easily susceptible of abuse it must be viewed as a voidable transaction subject to a test for intrinsic fairness."[8] At first blush this proposition seems difficult to reconcile with the General Assembly's explicit validation of shareholder voting agreements in §218(c). Significantly, however, it was the management of the defendant corporation that was buying votes in favor of a corporate reorganization in *Schreiber*. Shareholders are free to do whatever they want with their votes, including selling them to the highest bidder. Management, on the other hand, may not use corporate assets to buy votes in a hotly contested proxy contest about an extraordinary transaction that would significantly transform the corporation, unless it can be demonstrated, as it was in *Schreiber*, that management's vote-buying activity does not have a deleterious effect on the corporate franchise.

I also disagree with HP's assertion that to establish the invalidity of a vote-buying agreement, a plaintiff must show that a majority of all outstanding shares was obligated to vote in favor of the transaction as a result of the vote-buying. Again, the focus of the Court's analysis should be on possible deleterious effects of a challenged vote-buying agreement on shareholders. Less than a majority of votes can be decisive in tipping the results of an election one way or another. If voiding the votes cast in accordance with a fraudulent vote-buying agreement with corporate management is sufficient to change the result of a vote, I am again of the opinion that the defrauded or disenfranchised shareholders should not be prevented from bringing a vote-buying claim.

Schreiber is instructive in demonstrating how a vote-buying agreement in which a board expends corporate assets to purchase votes in support of a board-favored transaction may be validly consummated. There, a vote-buying agreement was being contemplated in which corporate assets were to be loaned to a 35% shareholder on favorable terms as consideration for that shareholder's agreement to vote in favor of a management-endorsed merger. The company formed a special committee to consider the merger and also the advisability of entering into the vote-buying agreement. The special committee hired independent counsel and then determined that both the merger and the shareholder agreement would be in the best interests of the company and its shareholders. After arm's-length bargaining with the 35% shareholder, the parties arrived at agreeable terms for the loan and the special committee recommended the shareholder agreement to the full board. The board of directors unanimously approved the agreement as proposed and submitted the vote-buying proposal to the shareholders for a separate vote — in effect a vote on vote-buying in that particular setting. As a condition for passage of the vote-buying proposal, a majority of outstanding shares, as well as a majority of the shares neither participating in the agreement nor owned by directors and officers of the company, had to be voted in favor of the proposal. After distribution of a proxy statement that fully disclosed the terms of the agreement, the vote-buying proposal was easily approved by the shareholders.

The *Schreiber* Court noted all of these protective measures and ultimately held that "the subsequent ratification of the [shareholder agreement] by a majority of the independent stockholders, after a full disclosure of all germane facts with complete candor precludes any further judicial inquiry." I agree with the well-reasoned opinion by then–Vice Chancellor Hartnett in *Schreiber*. Absent measures protective of the shareholder franchise like those taken in *Schreiber*, this Court should closely scrutinize transactions in which a board uses corporate assets to procure a voting agreement. This is not to say that all of the protective measures taken in *Schreiber* must be present before the Court will validate vote-buying by management using company assets. Each case must be evaluated on its own merits to determine whether or not the legitimacy of the shareholder franchise has been undercut in an unacceptable way. It is certainly possible for management to enter into vote-buying arrangements with salutary purposes.

Hewlett v. Hewlett-Packard Co., 2002 WL 549137 (Del. Ch. April 8, 2002) (Chandler, Ch.)

---

8. [*Schreiber*] at 26; *see also In re IXC Communications, Inc. Shareholders Litig.*, 1999 WL 1009174 at *8 (Del. Ch.) ("Generally speaking, courts closely scrutinize vote-buying because a shareholder who divorces property interest from voting interest, fails to serve the 'community of interest' among all shareholders, since the 'bought' shareholder votes may not reflect rational, economic self-interest arguably common to all shareholders.").

Notes and Questions

1. Notes

a. The merger was narrowly approved by a majority of Hewlett-Packard Co. shareholders. The number of shares switched by the institutional shareholder would not have made a difference in the outcome.

2. Reality Check

a. What are the elements of vote buying?

b. Is vote buying always impermissible?

3. Suppose

a. Suppose Compaq, the other party to the merger, had paid Hewlett-Packard Co. shareholders to vote "yes" on the merger. Would that have constituted impermissible vote buying?

b. Suppose the younger Mr. Hewlett, the leader of the faction opposing the merger (and himself a board member of Hewlett-Packard Co. — at least, he was a director until the merger was approved) had paid Hewlett-Packard Co. shareholders to vote "no" on the merger. Would that have constituted impermissible vote buying?

4. What Do You Think?

a. Does the distinction between vote buying using the corporation's funds and vote buying using other funds make sense?

b. Do you think vote buying has the potential to harm the corporation, its shareholders or third parties?

c. Should the courts look at these transactions as vote selling rather than as vote buying? If they did, would that shift of emphasis suggest a different analysis of the transactions?

5. Other Shareholder Agreements Affecting Shareholder Governance Power

Two other types of agreements are worthy of some attention here. You should remember that the Articles of Incorporation may provide for explicit variation from the statutory norms we've set out at the beginning of this chapter. Also, you should remember that other kinds of governance provisions may affect shareholder power to govern. For instance, a capital structure with different classes of shares may have the effect, intended or not, of shifting or reducing certain shareholders' governance powers.

The first kind of shareholder agreement meriting examination is one that governs the conduct of the participating shareholders in their capacity as directors. A shareholder/director may find that acting in accordance with such an agreement may conflict with performing his or her fiduciary duties. For example, the shareholder agreement may commit the parties, as directors, to vote for certain individuals to serve as officers. When the board meets to choose officers, however, a director/shareholder may find that voting for the agreed-upon person is not in the corporation's best interest. Courts generally held that a director's fiduciary duties override any agreement that may require action inconsistent with those fiduciary duties. Exceptions to this rule were sometimes made when (1) all shareholders were parties to the agreement (on the rationale that the ultimate beneficiaries of the directors' fiduciary duties had agreed to limit those duties); (2) the shareholder agreement contained (expressly or by implication) a provision requiring adherence only where doing so would be in the best interest of the corporation; and (3) where the infringement on the directors' powers was said to be "slight." Many corporations' statutes now address this question directly. Under the MBCA, the board's power, and hence the directors' fiduciary duties, can be curtailed if allowed by the Articles of Incorporation and if certain other restrictions are met (see below). MBCA §§7.32(a)(3), (4).

Delaware takes a slightly different approach. The DGCL provides that "close corporations," as defined in the DGCL, may implement shareholder agreements that restrict board power. *See* DGCL §350. Close corporations under the DGCL are those that have 30 or fewer shareholders, have one or more restrictions on share transfer, are not registered with the SEC, and have explicitly elected to be governed under the DGCL's close corporation provision by placing such an election in the Certificate of Incorporation. *See* DGCL §342.

The second kind of shareholder agreement is more radical, in the literal sense, because it does more than restrict the ability of shareholder/directors to exercise fully their directorial fiduciary duties. The core, hence radical, change is that in such corporations it may no longer be fair to say that the business and affairs of the corporation are managed by or under the direction of the board. We will describe the legitimacy of these agreements only briefly because, for reasons we will see, they are seldom used.

In a Delaware close corporation the shareholders can control the business and affairs entirely and a minority of shareholders (or even a single shareholder) can be given the power to dissolve the corporation. *See* DGCL §§351, 355. Under the MBCA similar changes to the corporate power paradigm are permitted, and the MBCA is more explicit about the kinds of changes permitted. *See* MBCA §§7.32(a)(1)-(8).

Two theoretical problems arise with such agreements. First, they may result in the shareholders being characterized as co-owners of a business for profit. That, as you will see in Chapter 17, is the definition of a partnership and, under partnership law, all partners are individually liable for the partnership's debts. Certainly shareholders would wish to avoid the possibility that they might lose the limited liability that was doubtless one of the attractions of incorporating in the first place. Second, variation from the corporate paradigm is one element permitting a court to pierce the corporate veil and hold the shareholders personally liable. The MBCA cuts off these possibilities by stating that no partnership-like liability or veil-piercing liability may be imposed on shareholders simply because they have entered into an agreement permitted by the statute. *See* MBCA §7.32(f). The DGCL is more oblique on these questions but probably has the same effect. *See* DGCL §354.

These far-reaching shareholder agreements are seldom used in practice for two reasons. First, the statutes permitting them are of relatively recent vintage and so the contours of the permitted and prohibited agreements are not clear. Few lawyers and even fewer clients want to be the test case for a particular kind of agreement. Second, and more important, the pervasive validation of the limited liability company (*see* Chapter 18) since 1996 has given entity planners and their clients a surer way to divide entity power. The LLC statutes expressly anticipate that the default governance provisions can be varied in nearly any way by the operating agreement (which functions like the Articles of Incorporation). Thus there is usually little reason to resort to the kinds of radical shareholder agreements described in this subsection.

Notes and Questions

1. Notes

a. Some states have enacted a separate statute for close corporations. Planners can choose whether to incorporate a new venture under the close corporation statute or the general corporation statute. Other states, such as Delaware, have certain provisions that are applicable only to close corporations that have made an election to be governed under those close corporation provisions. *See* DGCL §§341-356. These close corporation statutes have not met with success, as discussed below.

6. The Problem of Deadlock

Deadlock, meaning an impasse among directors or among shareholders, is seldom a problem in publicly held corporations. From a shareholder perspective, the large number of shareholders makes the possibility of deadlock remote. At the director level, boards of directors of public companies typically act unanimously or at least with a strong consensus. Seldom do the boards of public companies take action by a bare majority vote. Where an action seems to be so controversial that unanimity is unlikely, boards tend to defer action until something close to a consensus can be reached. If such a consensus is not possible, boards in public companies generally decline to act rather than act by a sharply divided vote.

In closely held corporations, by contrast, the possibility of deadlock is often very real at both the shareholder and the board level. Note that supermajority provisions can produce deadlock even when the factions are of unequal strength. Thus a 25 percent shareholder can stymie corporate action if the Articles require, say, an 80 percent vote on certain actions, even though holders of 75 percent of the shares (which could be one shareholder) favor an action.

Sometimes deadlock is the unintended consequence of bad corporate planning. For example, a corporate planner may include a supermajority provision for all board actions, obviously raising the potential for deadlock. In reality, the clients may only have wanted to ensure that certain important corporate actions, such as issuing more stock, taking on a large debt, or merging with another company were approved by a supermajority. Thus the plan, as implemented, has a latent deadlock possibility. But often the possibility of deadlock is understood clearly and is accepted by the clients as an acceptable risk. One frequent setting for such a decision is where two parties want to form a corporation and each insists on absolutely equal division of managerial control.

Let's take a step back for a minute and ask what we mean by the "problem" of deadlock. One way in which deadlock may not be a serious problem is if the deadlock covers only one matter. For example, if the shareholders are deadlocked in the election of directors, the corporate statutes provide that the incumbent directors retain their offices. Thus unless the directors are deadlocked as well the corporation can continue to function. Another deadlock that may not affect the corporation centrally is the question of declaring dividends. Assuming the corporation could legally pay dividends, a board may be deadlocked in deciding whether (or deciding how much) to pay dividends. Again, the corporation as a going concern is not affected in its day-to-day operations, at least in the short term, by the failure of the board to decide whether to pay dividends.

Even where the deadlock extends to every corporate question, one might legitimately ask whether deadlock is a "problem." Presumably each faction understands the consequences of the corporation's inability to act. Each faction could surely decide the best course of action for itself and either continue the deadlock, capitulate to the other faction's preference, or seek a compromise. None of these three outcomes is inherently better or worse than the others, and so deadlock is only a "problem" to the extent we wish to view it as a suboptimal choice.

Further, every corporation statute provides for voluntary dissolution, which would permit the parties to end the business entity. Thus an additional solution to deadlock is to sell the corporation's assets (usually as a going concern rather than piecemeal) and divide the proceeds (net of creditor claims) among the shareholders in proportion to their shareholdings. Voluntary dissolution requires a board resolution and shareholder vote; if the deadlocked factions believe dissolution is the best solution, it is easily obtained. *See* DGCL §275, MBCA §14.02. Thus the parties can create their own exit from deadlock.

Is deadlock a societal problem? That is, does society have an interest in ending corporate deadlocks? One argument is that deadlock often means that assets are not being used as productively as possible, that society is usually worse off in such settings, and that society as a result has an interest in breaking deadlocks. In effect, this means that it is legitimate for the state (acting through the courts) to impose relief that ends deadlocks. Do you find this argument persuasive? Are there other arguments that bear on the question of society's interest in corporate deadlocks?

Corporate planners can provide at least three methods for ameliorating the possibility of deadlock. First, at the shareholder level, cumulative voting avoids deadlock if each faction can elect at least one director. Likewise a capital structure that provides for directors to be elected by different classes or series of stock can ensure that at least some directors can be elected as long as the separate classes or series are held by shareholders that are not at loggerheads. Second, the parties can agree to participate in dispute resolution mechanisms such as mediation or non-binding arbitration to explore the possibility of resolving the deadlock. Finally, under the MBCA, a shareholder agreement under §7.32 can include a provision that "transfers to one or more shareholders or other persons all or part of the authority to exercise the corporate powers or to manage the business and affairs of the corporation, including the resolution of any issue about which there exists a deadlock among directors or shareholders." MBCA §7.32(a)(6). *See also* DGCL §355, permitting comparable provisions in Delaware close corporations.

Putting It to Work

Problem 15-2

You represent both Adrian and Aliese, two large shareholders in a closely held corporation with a total of 13 shareholders. Adrian's and Aliese's combined shares are less than a majority. Both Adrian and Aliese agree about the way the corporation should be managed and usually vote the same way in shareholder votes. They know that if they could in some formal and long-term way "team up," they might be able to increase their power among the other shareholders.

a. What steps would you suggest to Adrian and Aliese to further their goals?

B. EXTERNAL RESTRICTIONS ON SHAREHOLDER GOVERNANCE RIGHTS

Up until now, this chapter has looked at various devices that planners can impose on a corporation that modify the default shareholder governance powers. Now we see similar devices that are imposed regardless of the planners' intentions. That is, these are restrictions on shareholder governance powers that are imposed by law. This area is one of the most curious in any business entities casebook. In this section we deal with yet another instance of fiduciary duties. Then we'll see that the state legislatures have provided additional shareholder rights and remedies. These topics are curious in that one might not think that additional fiduciary duties are necessary (reflect on the robust nature of the fiduciary duties in Chapters 11 and 12). Further, these additional fiduciary duties aren't very well defined by the courts. We'll also see that the way in which the legislatures have provided additional shareholder protections might not be the most logically cogent approach. As you read the rest of this chapter (and I hope you do read it) you might find it particularly helpful to think of the issues as a puzzle rather than as an explication of doctrine. One question that will probably be constant here is: Why does corporate law need the rules that are being imposed?

1. Shareholder Fiduciary Duties

a. *The Current Setting*

In prior chapters we worked though, in some detail, the fiduciary duties owed by directors to their corporations and shareholders. But in at least some of the cases we've considered in this course the courts have suggested that (some) shareholders are (sometimes) owed fiduciary duties by (some) other shareholders. In contrast to the fiduciary duties of directors, the fiduciary duties of shareholders are much more amorphous. At the most conceptual level, the idea of shareholder fiduciary duties seems nonsensical. The directors' function is to act on behalf of another (the corporation or its shareholders) so it may be natural to impose fiduciary duties on directors. Partners, who are both managers and owners, might also have fiduciary duties imposed on them as an intuitive matter. But shareholders are different because they are the owners, answerable to no one, and one of the purposes of a corporation is to decouple the owners' dependence on one another.

As you read this section, look for the origins of the shareholder fiduciary duties discussed in the cases. Think especially about *who* owes *what kind of duty* and *to whom*. Finally, think about whether imposing these duties makes sense as a matter of public policy.

The first case involves disputes among shareholders in closely held corporations.

Walta v. Gallegos Law Firm, P.C.

40 P.3d 449 (N.M. App. 2001)

BUSTAMANTE, J.

The Gallegos Law Firm, P.C. (GLF), is a New Mexico professional corporation engaged in the practice of law. Gallegos founded GLF in 1987 and has always served as the corporation's president. Walta joined GLF in January 1990. As of November 1994, GLF had five attorney-shareholders: Gallegos, Walta, Michael Condon, David Sandoval, and Glenn Theriot. At that time, Gallegos owned 4,000 shares (50%) of GLF's stock. Walta owned 2,000 shares (25%) of GLF's stock. The balance of the corporation's 8,000 issued and outstanding shares were held by Condon (1,000 shares), Sandoval (900 shares), and Theriot (100 shares).

While GLF enjoyed reasonable financial success, it experienced sporadic financial pressures during 1993 and 1994. This resulted in some dissension among its shareholders. As early as June 1992, Walta had spoken in opposition to GLF's acceptance of certain contingency fee cases. On a number of occasions, Walta told Gallegos that the manner in which GLF accepted contingency fee cases should be reformed. Walta thought GLF was becoming too indebted on its line of credit because of its contingency case load. Gallegos responded with annoyance at Walta's concerns because he believed his experience made him more qualified than Walta to evaluate such cases.

Walta felt Gallegos often singled her out as the source of his irritation. By 1993 GLF had become heavily involved in several contingent fee matters taken on by Gallegos that were taxing GLF's resources. Despite this, Gallegos had GLF spending heavily, including a corporate aircraft with added pilot and hangar expense. Expenses remained high and the bank lines of credit were heavily utilized. During an April 1993 shareholder meeting, Gallegos abruptly cut off Walta's efforts to discuss GLF's finances, saying:

> [H]e didn't need [her] to tell him how to do — how to manage a firm. That he had been practicing law for 35 years. He didn't need [her] input. He didn't need [her] to tell him how to take cases. . . .
>
> And then he said to [her,] "I am sick and tired of you nagging at me. You remind me of one of my ex-wives, and the same thing is going to happen to you that happened to her if you don't be quiet."

Later in 1993, Gallegos wanted Walta and Condon to sign a personal guarantee for GLF's burgeoning line of credit. When they disagreed with his demand, Gallegos discontinued their stock purchase rights.

In early November 1994, Gallegos invited Walta to lunch. Walta characterized this as an unusual event. He questioned Walta about her future plans, referenced Walta's growing practice, and specifically asked her whether she planned to leave GLF soon. Walta, surprised, said she had no plans to leave. Gallegos then repeated to Walta his "five year plan" to phase out of the practice of law and his desire to implement it. Gallegos indicated to Walta that he did not expect the GLF structure to change as he phased out of active practice.

A few days later on November 27, 1994, Gallegos circulated a memorandum to each of GLF's four other shareholders, including Walta, proposing that GLF purchase their stock, leaving Gallegos the sole shareholder. The memorandum was left on each shareholder's desk on the Sunday evening following Thanksgiving. As an alternative, Gallegos suggested Walta and the other three shareholders could purchase Gallegos' stock with Gallegos departing from the firm if any of the shareholders believed that the proposal was not reasonable and acceptable. The memorandum implied that Gallegos' desire to dissolve GLF was motivated by his wish to devote more time to his family and personal interests, and by a desire to change the manner in which he practiced law.

Walta testified that, immediately upon reading the memorandum, she believed the memorandum "fired" her, that it was directed at getting her out of GLF, and that her departure was a "done deal" over which she had no control. Walta concluded that Gallegos' proposals violated the GLF's by-laws, and she obtained legal advice concerning her rights. Walta kept all this to herself; she did not inform Gallegos that she objected to either proposal set forth in the memorandum until her last day at GLF, four months later on March 31, 1995. Walta testified that she did not talk to Gallegos about the memorandum because of the "angry tone" of the memorandum, and because she feared that Gallegos would retaliate against her for doing so.

The terms of the proposal included that "stock will be surrendered and valued in accordance with the corporate by-laws as of December 31, 1994 and your employment terminated at that time." The firm's by-laws distinguished between "vested" and "non-vested" stock when valuing a departing shareholder's stock surrendered to the corporation. Walta's 2,000 shares of GLF stock included both vested and non-vested stock. For non-vested stock, generally, the shareholder would be paid the equivalent of the purchase price of the stock or no less than "the exact cost of the stock to him or her." Walta and the other shareholders had paid $10 per share. Vested stock was not so easily valued.

Stock became "vested" only if a shareholder had at least three years of employment commencing from "the date that he or she first acquired shares in the corporation." A shareholder surrendering vested stock would receive "present book value . . . as of the effective date of termination." The by-laws defined "present book value" as follows:

> [T]he calculation of per share value resulting from total[ ]ing the assets of the corporation, subtracting the liabilities of the corporation, and dividing the net sum, if any, by the number of shares issued and outstanding. For this valuation, the corporate assets shall not include unbilled work in progress, but shall include collectible accounts receivable, including those billed for the month in which the shareholder's termination or disqualification is effective. Present book value shall be calculated as of the effective date of the shareholder's termination or disqualification.

If the computation of "present book value" yielded a negative value, or a value of less than $10 per share, the value of the vested stock would nevertheless be deemed to be the shareholder's acquisition price; $10 per share.

GLF's shareholders met on December 15, 1994. All five shareholders, including Walta, attended. At the conclusion of the meeting, Gallegos stated that he was open to extending the shareholders' transition until March 31, 1995; this was eventually done. On January 4, 1995, GLF's shareholders sent Gallegos a memorandum authored by Walta raising "[a] number of questions . . . as to the proposed buy-out," and suggesting a shareholders' meeting to discuss the buy-out. Gallegos responded on January 6, writing "The end of the transition period is firmly March 31, 1995." His memorandum further stated, "The operative date for stock evaluation is December 31, 1994. Payment for a departing shareholder's stock will be made on April 1, 1995 in full."

From December 15, 1994, until Walta's departure from GLF on March 31, 1995, Walta and Gallegos met on a number of occasions to discuss year-end firm finances with the firm's accountant, to discuss the transition of client files, to work on pending cases and other matters. Gallegos testified Walta did not ask him about the buy-out of her stock or the financial information for valuing the stock, and she did not venture an estimate of her own as to the value of the stock.

There was evidence that during this time GLF's working atmosphere was very strained. Gallegos communicated with Walta only on a "need to" basis, frequently in writing. Gallegos refused Walta access to GLF's monthly financial statements. Walta had to point out that Condon had access to them to get Gallegos to relent. Gallegos excluded Walta from GLF's presentations to prospective clients, although Condon and Sandoval continued to be included. Though GLF clearly promised to be busy in the months ahead, Gallegos offered Walta no contract work to assist her in her transition. When Walta attempted to purchase office furniture and books from GLF before she left, Gallegos refused, contrary to the offer in his November 27, 1994, memorandum. Walta was permitted to take only the furniture in her office, as was her right under the Shareholder's Agreement, and a few small items for which she paid book value. Walta testified she received no help from Gallegos in finding another job.

Due to her tenure, Walta felt that 1,000 shares of her stock was vested. Only Walta and Gallegos owned vested stock. Gallegos had represented in his November 27, 1994, letter that he would proceed under the by-laws in valuing the stock of departing shareholders under his proposed stock buy-out. However, on March 28, 1995, Walta received a copy of a letter from Gallegos to another shareholder, Theriot. As a new shareholder, Theriot was not vested and was not entitled to receive more than par value; ten dollars ($10) per share. Gallegos' letter to Theriot stated that under the "present book value" formula in the by-laws Gallegos had circulated, the stock had a "negative value" on December 31, 1994, and therefore, vested stock would only be valued at par, or $10 per share. Gallegos admitted to the jury that the letter was intended to deliver a message to Walta that she would only be paid $10 per share as well. Gallegos did not disclose that, in arriving at a "negative value" for GLF's stock, he had omitted certain accounts receivable from the calculation because he thought at that time they were not "collectible accounts receivables" within the definition of present book value in the by-laws.

To value Walta's vested stock, Gallegos testified he used a substitute for GLF's "collectible accounts receivable," and used December 31, 1994, as Walta's termination date. Gallegos testified he did not use actual "collectible accounts receivable" as stated in the by-laws' definition of "present book value" because GLF business practices did not and had never included preparation of a report that provided such information. GLF accounting was on a cash basis, rather than an accrual basis; accordingly no amount for accounts receivable was entered on the regularly produced balance sheets. Gallegos felt that whether or not an account receivable was, in the words of the by-laws "collectible," had to be a judgment call for management to make by manually examining each account and forming an estimate of future collectibility. Gallegos opined that it would have required considerable time and subjective judgment to collect information on accounts receivables and determine whether they were collectible.

Gallegos testified he valued Walta's stock using the same method used by the directors, including Walta, to value vested stock the only other time a shareholder with vested stock had left GLF. That shareholder, Michael Oja, resigned in February 1993. When valuing Oja's vested stock in April 1993, the directors used the dollar amount of accounts billed to clients for February 1993, the month of the shareholder's departure, as a substitute for "collectible accounts receivable." Although that procedure did not comply with the letter of the by-laws, all the directors, including Walta, had agreed to it. That method could result in an amount either more or less than the actual collectible accounts receivable; *e.g.*, billings from the first of the month could be paid and no longer "receivable" but would be included. Gallegos' method of calculation resulted in a stock value for both vested and non-vested stock of $20,000 — the amount Walta had paid for the stock.

At trial, experts for Gallegos, GLF, and Walta had the advantage of hindsight in totaling accounts actually collected after Walta left. Gallegos' expert concluded that as of December 31, 1994, the GLF had accounts receivable of $657,989, and that even under his conservative estimate, the value of Walta's vested shares as of December 31, 1994, was $41,275, not $20,000, as contended by Gallegos. The jury ultimately decided that all of Gallegos' stock was worth $62,550, the amount calculated by Gallegos' expert.

On March 31 Walta left a letter on Gallegos' desk informing him that "I believe my termination of employment with the firm is wrongful and without cause." Walta's letter also stated that she had retained an attorney "as my legal counsel" to whom she had delivered her GLF stock to "work out the surrender of the stock." She wrote: "You have indicated that the value which you will assign to my stock is $10 per share, the cost of the stock. I dispute your valuation, as well as your determination that December 31, 1994 is to be the date upon which the valuation is based."

Walta testified that between the time of Gallegos' stock buyout memorandum and her departure from GLF, it became apparent to her that Gallegos' actual intention in the stock buyout was to convert GLF to a corporation with a sole shareholder — Gene Gallegos, and to restructure the firm to remove only one attorney–Walta. Contrary to Gallegos' prior representations that going forward GLF would be comprised of only himself and a young associate, Walta discovered that before the end of 1994, Gallegos had offered shareholder Michael Condon continued full-time employment as a salaried associate with GLF after March 31, 1995. Condon accepted and was given a salary increase. Gallegos misrepresented to Walta that Condon was only working on contract. Walta also learned that shareholder David Sandoval had been offered continued full-time salaried employment, even though prior to the November 27, 1994, memorandum, Sandoval had already announced his resignation from GLF. Sandoval declined the offer. Walta also learned that Gallegos had offered shareholder Theriot contract employment indefinitely, without shareholder status. It was only Walta who was not asked to continue at GLF.

In sum, based primarily on her testimony, if believed by a jury, Walta's evidence and theory of the case was to the effect that Gallegos disliked her, was angry at her, was dictatorial in his management of GLF, and that the firm's buy-out of the four attorney-shareholders was accomplished solely to get rid of her.

In a June 6, 1995, letter, Walta's attorney valued her stock at $52,000, based on the valuation set for shareholder Oja in 1993, and the view that Walta's stock was 100% vested. Gallegos testified he disagreed with the amount claimed in the letter because her stock could not have been 100% vested.

In July 1996 Walta sued GLF and Gallegos for money damages, alleging six separate claims for relief, including breach of employment contract, breach of obligations owed to shareholders under the shareholder agreement, breach of fiduciary duties, retaliatory discharge, promissory estoppel, and intentional interference with contractual relationship.

The trial court directed a verdict against Walta on her retaliatory discharge and promissory estoppel claims. . . . The jury found in favor of GLF and Gallegos on Walta's breach of employment agreement and interference with contract claims. The jury found in favor of Walta, and against GLF, only on her claim for breach of the shareholder agreement, and in favor of Walta and against Gallegos alone for "breach [of] his fiduciary duties with respect to the Plaintiff's shareholder agreement and to Plaintiff Mary Walta." The jury awarded Walta compensatory damages in the amount of $62,550 against both GLF and Gallegos for the value of her stock. Though Walta requested punitive damages against both Defendants, the jury awarded them only against Gallegos individually, in the amount of $100,000.

The parties agree that some sort of fiduciary duty exists between them. They disagree as to its scope. Gallegos correctly asserts that the nature of the fiduciary duty owed between shareholders and directors of close corporations is a matter of first impression in New Mexico. We have a few cases involving small corporations in conflict, but they do not address this issue.

We start by examining the close corporation. In a widely cited opinion, the Massachusetts Supreme Judicial Court defined a close corporation as one "typified by: (1) a small number of stockholders; (2) no ready market for the corporate stock; and (3) substantial majority stockholder participation in the management, direction and operations of the corporation." *Donahue v. Rodd Electrotype Co.,* 367 Mass. 578, 328 N.E.2d 505, 511 (1975).

These characteristics of close corporations may sometimes be abused to allow majority shareholders to take advantage of minority shareholders. Minority shareholders are vulnerable to a variety of oppressive devices. These devices include refusing to declare dividends, draining of corporate earnings in the form of exorbitant salaries and bonuses paid to majority shareholders, denying minority shareholders corporate offices and employment, and selling corporate assets to majority shareholders at reduced prices. *Donahue,* 328 N.E.2d at 512-13.

To combat such tactics, courts have, over the years, recognized various versions of fiduciary duties that majority or controlling shareholders owe to minority shareholders. The general rule has been sufficiently developed by appellate opinions to establish that the fiduciary duty does not depend on shareholder control, but rather arises out of the nature of a closely held corporation. For example, some courts have explicitly recognized that the duty extends to minority shareholders in close corporations. As the *Donahue* court noted, "the minority may do equal damage through unscrupulous and improper sharp dealings, with an unsuspecting majority." *Donahue,* 328 N.E.2d at 515 n. 17.

Starting with its observation that "the close corporation bears striking resemblance to a partnership," *id.* at 512, the *Donahue* court's formulation stands today as the purest expression of the fiduciary duties owed by shareholders:

> Because of the fundamental resemblance of the close corporation to the partnership, the trust and confidence which are essential to this scale and manner of enterprise, and the inherent danger to minority interests in the close corporation, we hold that stockholders in the close corporation owe one another substantially the same fiduciary duty in the operation of the enterprise that partners owe to one another. In our previous decisions, we have defined the standard of duty owed by partners to one another as the "utmost good faith and loyalty." Stockholders in close corporations must discharge their management and stockholder responsibilities in conformity with this strict good faith standard. They may not act out of avarice, expediency or self-interest in derogation of their duty of loyalty to the other stockholders and to the corporation.

Id. at 515. (Footnotes and citations omitted.)

Since the *Donahue* decision, the Massachusetts court has refined its notion of fiduciary duty. Recognizing that self-interest is not necessarily synonymous with improper motivation, the court held that controlling groups should be allowed to demonstrate a legitimate business purpose for their actions. *See Wilkes v. Springside Nursing Home, Inc.,* 353 N.E.2d 657, 663 (Mass. 1976). Upon demonstration of such a purpose, the court then determines "the practicability of a less harmful alternative" to the minority interest. *Id.* This common sense approach alleviated the court's concern that "untempered application of the strict good faith standard" could unduly hamper corporate management. *Id.* at 663. This approach provides equilibrium to the majority's need to pursue legitimate business actions and the minority's vulnerability to oppression in a close corporation.

Though formulated somewhat differently, other courts have followed the *Donahue/Wilkes* lead. For example, the Mississippi Supreme Court characterized *Donahue* and other cases as decisions which "evince the evolving awareness by courts of the distinctive characteristics and needs of close corporations." *Fought v. Morris,* 543 So. 2d 167, 171 (Miss. 1989). The court in *Fought* stated that majority action must be "intrinsically fair" to minority interests and observed that the relationship between shareholders in close corporations was of trust and confidence — the same relationship which prevails in partnerships. *Id.* The Minnesota courts have similarly analogized close corporations to partnerships as a basis for the recognition of fiduciary duties owed between shareholders.

We agree with the reasoning and approach of these cases. While the analogy to partnership principles is incomplete because partners are provided more protection by statute from freeze-out tactics than corporate shareholders, it is still useful. The analogy recognizes the nature of close corporation organization and, because our partnership case law is reasonably well-developed, it provides a ready source of precedent helping to provide content to the concept of fiduciary duty. Thus, we hold that Gallegos owed Walta a fiduciary duty in his efforts to restructure GLF, including the purchase of her GLF stock. And, drawing on our partnership case law, we hold that breach of this fiduciary duty can be asserted as an individual claim separate from the remedies available under our statutory corporate law for oppressive conduct.

Of course, recognizing the fiduciary nature of a relationship does not give it content in any given context. As we noted in *McCauley* [*v. Tom McCauley & Son, Inc.,* 724 P.2d 232, 238 (N.M. App. 1986),] with regard to the concept of oppressive conduct, no specific catalog of elements is necessary or perhaps even appropriate. Too narrow a definition of an expansive term would be ossifying. We can, however, place this duty in the context of other standards of right conduct recognized by the law, and we can provide guidance for analogous cases where restructuring a close corporation includes termination of shareholder/employer and corporate purchase of shares.

First, it seems self-evident that a fiduciary duty is inconsistent with standards of conduct typically at play in arm's-length commercial or business transactions. As Chief Judge Cardozo noted: "Many forms of conduct permissible in a workaday world for those acting at arm's length, are forbidden to those bound by fiduciary ties. . . . Not honesty alone, but the punctilio of an honor the most sensitive, is then the standard of behavior." *Meinhard v. Salmon,* 164 N.E. 545, 546 (1928). The standard for a fiduciary, in this context, is thus higher than the duty of good faith and fair dealing imposed on all contractual relationships.

The duty between shareholders of a close corporation is similar to that owed by directors, officers, and shareholders to the corporation itself; that is, loyalty, good faith, inherent fairness, and the obligation not to profit at the expense of the corporation.

In adopting the Massachusetts approach, we are clearly aligning ourselves with the line of cases which impose a high duty of candor and good faith when majority shareholders are dealing with minority shareholders. *See, e.g., Orchard v. Covelli,* 590 F. Supp. 1548, 1556-57 (W.D. Penn. 1984) (recognizing an enhanced fiduciary duty for directors and officers when dealing with minority shareholders in a close corporation); *cf. Van Schaack Holdings, Ltd. v. Van Schaack,* 867 P.2d 892, 897 (Colo. 1994) (en banc) (adopting the "special facts" doctrine to impose an enhanced fiduciary duty to fully disclose material information bearing on the value of stock when purchased by the close corporation). While some commentators would label the approach we adopt as the "minority view," our review of the case law informs us that it is actually the prevalent view among those courts which have addressed the issue.

Having generally defined the rigor of the fiduciary duty, one must apply it to specific aspects of the legal relationship between shareholders in a close corporation. Issues are most likely to arise in connection with valuation of the stock, the related matter of disclosure of material facts relating to corporate officers, and adherence to contractual obligations between the shareholders.

The duty of full disclosure of material facts affecting the value of stock has been dealt with often by the courts. The majority of the cases impose a duty of full, voluntary disclosure. The requirement of full disclosure felicitously acts to equalize bargaining positions where valuation is typically difficult. The cases are clear that the duty requires disclosure beyond mere access to the books and records of the corporation. Our cases have consistently held that partners, as fiduciaries, are "required to fully disclose material facts and information relating to partnership affairs to the other partners, even if the other partners have not asked for the information." *Fate* [*v. Owens*, 27 P.3d 990 (N.M. App. 2001)].

In accordance with these authorities, we hold as a matter of New Mexico law that a majority shareholder, as well as an officer or director of a close corporation, when purchasing the stock of a minority shareholder, has a fiduciary obligation to disclose material facts affecting the value of the stock which are known to the purchasing shareholder, officer, or director by virtue of his position, but not known to the selling shareholder.

This case — as perhaps most cases of this kind will — includes a shareholder agreement. It is undisputed that Gallegos and GLF did not follow the letter of the shareholder agreement embodied in the GLF by-laws, either as to Walta's termination as an employee or the valuation of her shares in connection with the proposed buy-out. What is the nature of the fiduciary duty arising from shareholder agreements and when may noncompliance with such agreements be deemed a breach of the duty? This case is similar to *Fought v. Morris*. There, one of the shareholders wanted to sell his shares. Morris bought all of the departing shareholders' stock — contrary to the stock redemption agreement controlling such events between them. Thereafter, Morris "froze out" Fought and offered to buy his shares at an improperly reduced price which was calculated contrary to the formula set forth in their agreement. The Mississippi court held that breach of the shareholder agreement could also be a breach of the majority's fiduciary duty. The Court went on to hold that both the improper purchase and the improper value calculation were actionable breaches of Morris' fiduciary duty.

We adopt the *Fought* court's reasoning, noting, however, that not every noncompliance with a shareholder agreement is necessarily a breach of fiduciary duty — but in appropriate circumstances may be. As with most matters of judgment, whether a breach of fiduciary duty has occurred will normally be a question of fact for the jury.

We pause to note that the fiduciary duty we define here is a default standard applicable in the absence of a contrary agreement between shareholders. Shareholders are free to agree to different standards as long as the essence of right conduct is preserved.

In this case there was evidence to support a jury conclusion that Gallegos breached his fiduciary obligations owed to Walta. As majority shareholder of a close corporation, as well as an officer and director, Gallegos had a duty of openness to disclose material facts affecting the value of the stock in regard to the proposed buy-out. The shareholder agreement defined that duty in more detail. At the very least, that duty included compliance with the valuation formula set forth in the shareholder agreement, or a full and frank disclosure of any deviation from that formula and the reasons why.

The record supports a conclusion that Gallegos did neither. He purposely omitted a valuation for the collectible accounts receivables and did not disclose that fact to Walta. Then, when confronted by Walta, Gallegos continued to refuse to perform his obligations under the shareholder agreement. The jury found the corporation liable for breach of the shareholder agreement. That breach was a direct result of Gallegos' failure to respect Walta's rights as a minority shareholder, in the particular context of a buy-out, and, as the jury also found, to fulfill his obligations to her as a fiduciary. We conclude that both the law, as previously discussed, and the facts, as elicited at trial, support a jury verdict that Gallegos breached his fiduciary obligations in his dealing with Walta.

Finding no error in the trial court's submission of punitive damages to the jury, and finding substantial evidence to support the jury's verdict, we affirm.

Notes and Questions

1. Notes

a. One instrumental reason to impose fiduciary duties on shareholders has to do with shareholder litigation. In Chapter 14 we discussed shareholder derivative litigation and saw that it is disadvantageous to shareholder/plaintiffs who would much prefer to bring direct actions. By imposing fiduciary duties on shareholders that run directly to other shareholders, plaintiffs can bring direct actions, rather than having to sue derivatively.

2. Reality Check

a. Where did the court find the authority to impose fiduciary duties on shareholders?

b. What are the duties that shareholders owe one another?

c. How, precisely, did Mr. Gallegos breach his fiduciary duty *as a shareholder*?

3. Suppose

a. Suppose the court held that shareholders do not owe one another a fiduciary duty. Would the analysis or the result have been different?

4. What Do You Think?

a. Do you think shareholders should be subject to fiduciary duties to one another? If so, should those duties be imposed by courts or legislatures?

b. Should every shareholder owe fiduciary duties to every other shareholder? What about shareholders in publicly traded corporations?

c. Should minority shareholders owe fiduciary duties to majority shareholders? If so, does that constrain other protections that minority shareholders in close corporations frequently resort to?

d. Do you agree that a close corporation is like a partnership and that shareholders should, therefore, be treated like partners? Isn't it just as accurate to say that a partnership is like a close corporation and that partners should, therefore, be treated like shareholders?

e. Should shareholder fiduciary duties be different from director and officer fiduciary duties? If you believe they should be different, should they be more or less strict?

The Delaware courts have been surprisingly (and refreshingly?) brief about the question of shareholder fiduciary duties.

b. Background and Context

In *Allied Chemical & Dye Corp. v. Steel & Tube Co. of America*, 120 A. 486 (Del. Ch. 1923), a syndicate of speculators bought a majority of shares in the Steel & Tube Co. The board of directors, which was controlled by the syndicate, negotiated to sell all the corporation's assets to an unrelated corporation. The plaintiffs, Steel & Tube Co. minority shareholders, filed suit to enjoin the sale on the ground that the transaction was fraudulent because the price was inadequate. Chancellor Wolcott analyzed the claim for relief in this way:

> In reading this statute [the predecessor of DGCL §271] it will be observed that two things with respect to a sale are contemplated, viz. (a) an authorization of sale by the stockholders, and (b) a fixing of the terms and conditions by the directors.
>
> The majority [of stockholders] thus have the power in their hands to impose their will upon the minority in a matter of very vital concern to them. That the source of this power is found in a statute, supplies no reason for clothing it with a superior sanctity, or vesting it with the attributes of tyranny. When the power is sought to be used, therefore, it is competent for any one who conceives himself aggrieved thereby to invoke the processes of a court of equity for protection against its oppressive exercise. When examined by such a court, if it should appear that the power is used in such a way that it violates any of those fundamental principles which it is the special province of equity to assert and protect, its restraining processes will unhesitatingly issue.
>
> The requirements of the statute and of the certificate of incorporation all being satisfied, as they are in this case, it will be manifest that the only ground upon which [the complaining stockholder] can base his claim for relief is that of fraud. Notwithstanding that the right of the majority to sell all the assets is given by the statute, yet if the proposed sale is a fraud on the minority, it cannot stand.
>
> [I]t will be in order first to define the relations which equity will regard as subsisting between the controlling majority members of the corporation and the minority. That under certain circumstances these relations are of a fiduciary character is clear. The same considerations of fundamental justice which impose a fiduciary character upon the relationship of the directors to the stockholders will also impose, in a proper case, a like character upon the relationship which the majority of the stockholders bear to the minority. When, in the conduct of the corporate business, a majority of the voting power in the corporation join hands in imposing its policy upon all, it is beyond all reason and contrary, it seems to me, to the plainest dictates of what is just and right, to take any view other than that they are to be regarded as having placed upon themselves the same sort of fiduciary character which the law impresses upon the directors in their relation to all the stockholders. Ordinarily the directors speak for and determine the policy of the corporation. When the majority of stockholders do this, they are, for the moment, the corporation. Unless the majority in such case are to be regarded as owing a duty to the minority such as is owed by the directors to all, then the minority are in a situation that exposes them to the grossest frauds and subjects them to most outrageous wrongs.

Accordingly it has been held that if the majority stockholders so use their power to advantage themselves at the expense of the minority, their conduct in that regard will be denounced as fraudulent and the minority may obtain appropriate relief therefrom upon application to a court of equity. But the general language by which this rule is stated is not to be given its widest possible application. For it is not true that every personal advantage which the majority secures is to be regarded as vitiating in character. An examination of the cases to which special attention is directed by the complainants in this connection will disclose that the personal advantage accruing to the majority is in some way derived from, or intimately associated with, the corporate assets themselves.

After examining all the authorities cited on the briefs of both sides, I find that . . . the personal advantage which the alleged wrongdoers attempt to gather to themselves is in some way directly incident to the very property towards which they stand in the fiduciary relationship and which they seek to appropriate either in whole or in part to themselves, to the exclusion and injury of those whom they have at their mercy.

In the instant case there is no pretense that the personal advantage which the majority may derive from the sale consists in any wise in securing to themselves either the whole or any part of the corporate assets. So far as appears, they and the purchasers are complete strangers in interest. The complainants, however, contend that, though there is nothing in common between the interests of the purchaser and the majority favoring the sale, there is, nevertheless, such a personal advantage to be derived from the sale by the majority as in equity will vitiate the whole transaction.

My conclusion with respect to this branch of the case is, that the evidence before me fails to disclose such a peculiar and personal interest or advantage to be served by the sale as will, on the principles applicable to the conduct of one who acts in a fiduciary capacity, taint the proposed transaction with fraud, either actual or constructive. Whatever advantage is gained is purely incidental and collateral. This prospect of personal gain, though not thus to be condemned as fraudulent in character, may however be very properly regarded when, as will subsequently appear, the fairness and adequacy of the terms of sale are considered in connection with the present application.

The majority who are favoring the sale owe something more to the minority than to merely refrain from appropriating, either directly or indirectly, the corporate assets unto themselves. They owe the further duty of seeing to it that the assets shall be sold for a fair and adequate price. Any other kind of price would fail to meet the requirement of the statute that the terms and conditions of the sale should be such as are expedient and for the best interest of the corporation. Indeed, even if the statute contained no such requirement, equity would impose it. For if a trustee who has the right to sell the assets of his cestui que trust undertakes to do so, the duty is exacted of him that he demand and secure an adequate price. Even though the sale is of no affirmative advantage or profit to himself, yet, taking the negative aspect of the matter, if it injures the beneficiary by letting his equitable assets go for an unfair and inadequate price, the act of the trustee in making the sale will in equity be condemned as wrongful. I take it that authority need not be cited in support of this proposition.

This is the reason which underlies the rule, applicable here, that if the majority sell the assets they are required to obtain a fair and adequate price therefor and thus save from loss the minority who are helpless.

When the question is asked whether in a given case the price is adequate, it is readily seen that room is afforded for honest differences of opinion. When the price proposed to be accepted is so far below what is found to be a fair, one that it can be explained only on the theory of fraud, or a reckless indifference to the rights of others interested, it would seem that it should not be allowed to stand.

On final hearing, . . . it may be true that the view may be honestly entertained that at a fair price the assets would bring no more than the sum named in the contract. I have difficulty, however, in reaching such a conclusion on the present showing.

I now mention a feature of the case that contributes quite materially to that difficulty. The syndicate is in control of this corporation. It owns 57 percent of the common stock. It would not consider the proposition of buying into the corporation, unless it could secure a controlling interest. It got such an interest. I shall not reflect upon the gentlemen whom it elected as directors by characterizing them as mere tools to work the syndicate's will. At the same time, I shall not assume that capable and shrewd business men would deliberately purchase only on condition that their purchase would yield the control, and then, having secured the control, be so neglectful of their purposes as not to make sure of their realization. Until something more convincing appears, common sense demands that the proposed sale be regarded as the act of the syndicate.

Now what was the purpose of the syndicate? The affidavits are to the effect that the purpose and only purpose was to make a profit on the purchase of the [majority of the company] stock. If to make this profit it appeared advisable to put money into the plant and continue operations, that would be done; or if it appeared advisable to sell the stock, that would be done; or, if it appeared advisable to sell out the business, that would be done. "My purpose," says Mr. Williams, "was to follow whichever of these two (three) courses appeared to offer the greatest profit to the syndicate."

Now, while none of these things, either alone or in combination, will, as I have heretofore said, suffice to show such a personal interest as will raise a presumption of fraud, yet when the question of the fairness of price to the minority is under consideration they may be fairly taken into account, at least in disposing of the application for a preliminary injunction. These things will in no wise, in event of liquidation, give to the persons named any disproportionate advantage at the expense of the minority out of the assets of the corporation. But they are of such a nature as very reasonably suggests that in approaching the determination of the question of adequacy of price they might cause the interested persons to view the question not so much from the angle of stockholders interested primarily in securing the best possible price for assets, but from the angle of purchasers of stock interested primarily in securing a fair profit on a speculation. It is difficult to escape from the thought that the prospect of making about $2,000,000 within a year upon a layout of $1,500,000 with interest, is such an alluring one that those who are tempted by it are very apt to pass upon the interests of others who happen to be concerned in the transaction with less regard for their welfare than otherwise would be the case.

The preliminary injunction restraining the sale will issue as prayed. . . .

Allied Chemical & Dye Corp. v. Steel & Tube Co. of America, 120 A. 486 (Del. Ch. 1923) (Wolcott, Ch).

c. The Current Setting

Delaware cases have emphasized that a majority (or controlling) shareholder owes fiduciary duties, equivalent to those owed by directors, to minority shareholders when the majority shareholder causes the corporation to enter into a self-dealing transaction involving the disposition of the corporation's assets. That is, in such a setting the majority shareholder must show the entire fairness of the transaction. *See Sterling v. Mayflower Hotel Corp.*, 93 A.2d 107 (Del. 1952); *Singer v. Magnavox Co.*, 380 A.2d 969 (Del. 1977), *rev'd on other grounds*; *Weinberger v. UOP, Inc.*, 457 A.2d 701 (Del. 1983). The Delaware courts have declined to impose a *Wilkes*-like fiduciary duty outside of the self-dealing context.

> The protections afforded to minority stockholders in closely-held corporations under Delaware common law are no different than those in publicly-held corporations. While other jurisdictions have recognized special fiduciary duties among stockholders in closely-held corporations, the Delaware courts have not adopted a similar approach. Instead, utilizing general corporate law principles, they have mostly relied on entire fairness as a means of protecting minority stockholders.

Blaustein v. Lord Baltimore Capital Corp., 2013 WL 1810956, *14 (Del. Ch. Apr. 30, 2013).

2. Oppression and Unfairness by Shareholders

Now that you're as comfortable as you're going to be with the concept of shareholder fiduciary duties, we reach a sort of confluence of ideas. This confluence takes us back to the problem of deadlock. It moves to a new cause of action for minority shareholders, "oppression," and ends with the expansion of equitable remedies to be wielded in support of minority shareholder rights. As you read this material, try to keep the concepts of deadlock, dissolution, fiduciary duty, oppression, and expanded remedies separate. It seems easy (because each concept has a separate name) but you'll see that the concepts run together in a way that can be quite maddening.

a. From a New Remedy for Deadlock . . .

We asked above whether courts ought to break deadlocks. Because most deadlocks are the result of planning choices and every deadlock can be broken by compromise or capitulation, a good argument can be made that courts should not intervene when the harm is deadlock alone, without any allegation of statutory or fiduciary duty violation.

If courts do intervene to break deadlocks, what form of relief should the court enter? Presumably money damages will not end a deadlock, though it may compensate a party who has been financially injured by a deadlock. The court will have to enjoin one or both factions to do or refrain from doing something. The court could, in a proper case, order the corporation itself to take (or refrain from taking) some action if the corporation has been named as a party. Although at first blush these remedies seem to be simply examples of a court's classic power to do equity, remember that the claim for relief is deadlock — the factions' inability to agree on a course of action. If a court awards injunctive relief, on what basis will the judge decide who wins? Isn't the court doing nothing but imposing its own view of the corporation's best economic interest?

If the deadlock seems likely to be chronic, the court could appoint a neutral person to oversee the decision-making process to head off future deadlocks or to act as a tie-breaker. This solution, though, simply shifts the location of the decision from the court to a court-appointed person. Again, how will the outsider decide between two factions on any basis other than his or her own view of the corporation's best course of action?

In the mid-twentieth century courts frequently concluded that they could not break deadlocks by dissolving the corporation but that they did have the power to order the corporation's assets liquidated so that the proceeds would be distributable to the owners. As a practical matter, this liquidation brought about the corporation's dissolution. Strictly, courts almost uniformly held that they had no inherent power to dissolve a corporation because dissolution would be undoing something the legislature had affirmatively created.

State legislatures understood that court-ordered liquidation was substantially equivalent to dissolution. Many corporation statutes were then amended to grant courts the explicit power to dissolve a corporation because of deadlock. The MBCA grants courts the power to dissolve for deadlock, while the DGCL permits the Court of Chancery to liquidate, but not dissolve, a corporation. However Delaware courts have held that they have an inherent power to dissolve corporations in limited circumstances. *Carlson v. Hallinan*, 925 A2d 506 (Del. Ch. 2006). Note that where the *shareholders* are deadlocked, both the MBCA and DGCL permit relief to be awarded upon a showing simply that the shareholders are sufficiently deadlocked. Where the *directors* are deadlocked, both statutes require an additional showing of entitlement to equitable relief, such as the possibility of irreparable harm, before the court may intervene. Does the distinction between shareholder deadlock and director deadlock make any sense? *See* MBCA §§14.30(a)(2)(i), (iii), DGCL §§226(a), 291, 352(a). Thus dissolution became a new remedy for deadlock.

Shawe v. Elting
157 A.3d 152 (Del. 2017)

Seitz, Justice, for the Majority:

Philip Shawe and his mother, Shirley Shawe, have filed an interlocutory appeal from the Court of Chancery's August 13, 2015 opinion and July 18, 2016 order, and related orders, appointing a custodian under [DGCL] §226 to sell TransPerfect Global, Inc., a Delaware corporation. After a six-day trial filled with unprecedented evidence of a lengthy and seriously dysfunctional relationship between the owners, culminating in Philip Shawe's litigation misconduct, the Court of Chancery issued a 104-page opinion concluding that the warring factions were hopelessly deadlocked as stockholders and directors. The court carefully considered three alternatives to address the dysfunction and deadlock, and in the end decided that the circumstances of the case required the appointment of a custodian to sell the company.

On appeal, the Shawes do not challenge the Court of Chancery's many factual findings of serious dysfunction and deadlock. Instead, Philip Shawe claims for the first time on appeal that the court exceeded its statutory authority when it ordered the custodian to sell a solvent company. Alternatively, Shawe contends that less drastic measures were available to address the deadlock.

We disagree with the Shawes and affirm the Court of Chancery's judgment.

[S]hawe [has] attempted to raise statutory . . . arguments that were not considered by the Court of Chancery. Under this Court's long-standing rules and the important policy reasons guiding them, we do not consider arguments raised . . . for the first time on appeal. Our dissenting colleague has concluded, however, that even though the statutory argument was never considered by the Court of Chancery, it should be addressed for the first time on appeal. Thus, in response to the dissent, we explain why we disagree with its interpretation of the custodian statute.

I

TransPerfect Global, Inc. ("TPG") is a Delaware corporation that acts as a holding company for the main operating company, TransPerfect Translations International, Inc. ("TPI"), a New York corporation. Both entities will be referred to as the "Company." The Company provides translation, website localization, and litigation support services from 92 offices in 86 worldwide cities. It has over 3,500 full-time employees and maintains a network of over 10,000 translators, editors, and proofreaders in about 170 different languages. Elting and Shawe co-founded the Company and are co-chief executive officers and board members.

TPG has 100 shares of common stock issued and outstanding, divided fifty shares to Elting, forty-nine shares to Shawe, and one share to Shirley Shawe. In this Opinion, we refer to Philip Shawe as "Shawe," and Shirley Shawe by her full name. The one share allocated to Shirley Shawe allowed TPG to claim the benefits of being a majority women-owned business. We credit the Court of Chancery's finding, based on evidence introduced at trial, that Shawe "has treated his mother's share as his own property and himself as a 50% co-owner of the Company."[1] Elting and Shawe have been the only directors since the Company's reorganization in 2007.

To fully appreciate the personal nature of the long-running discord leading to the Court of Chancery's ruling, we go back to the Company's founding and the troubled romantic relationship between the founders. Elting and Shawe co-founded the business in 1992 while living together in a dormitory room attending New York University's business school. They were engaged in 1996, but Elting called the marriage off in 1997. As the Court of Chancery found, "Shawe did not take the break-up well, and would 'terrorize' her and say 'horrendous things' about her husband, Michael Burlant, whom she married in 1999." On two separate occasions, Shawe responded to the rejection by crawling under Elting's bed and refusing to leave.[3]

As the Company grew, the founders were not satisfied with their financial success, and brought their simmering personal discontent into the Company's business affairs. The Court of Chancery catalogued the serious clashes over the years between Shawe and Elting and their surrogates before, and remarkably, during the litigation:

- Shawe engaged in a secret campaign to spy on Elting and invade her privacy by intercepting her mail, monitoring her phone calls, accessing her emails (including thousands of privileged communications with her counsel), and entering her locked office without permission on numerous occasions as well as sending his so-called "paralegal" there at 4:47 a.m. on another occasion.
- Shawe co-opted the services of Company advisors . . . to assist him in advancing his personal agenda against Elting.
- Shawe unilaterally hired numerous employees to perform Shared Services functions (Accounting and Finance) and even to work in divisions Elting managed . . . without her knowledge or consent by creating "off book" arrangements and fabricating documents.

---

1. Elting demonstrated at trial that Shawe held a general proxy for Mrs. Shawe's one share, and consistently held himself out as the 50% owner of TPG.

3. When Elting ended their engagement, Shawe refused to leave the apartment and crawled under her bed and stayed there for at least half an hour. On another occasion, Elting was traveling alone in Buenos Aires looking for space to open a new office. She arrived at her hotel room to find that Shawe had showed up unannounced. When she asked him to leave, he crawled under her hotel bed and stayed there for about half an hour.

- Shawe sought to have Elting criminally prosecuted by referring to her as his ex-fiancée seventeen years after the fact when filing a "Domestic Incident Report" as a result of a seemingly minor altercation in her office.
- Shawe disparaged Elting and tried to marginalize her within the Company by gratuitously disseminating a memorandum . . . to employees in her own division accusing her of collusion and financial improprieties.
- Shawe disparaged Elting publicly by unilaterally issuing a press release in the Company's name containing false and misleading statements.

These were just some of the highlights of the facts found by the Court of Chancery after a lengthy trial. The court also made detailed findings about continuous acrimonious disputes over personal and business expenses, weekly if not daily temper tantrums, and "mutual hostaging" between the founders over proposed acquisitions, stockholder distributions, employee hiring, pay and bonuses, and office locations. The court also found that Shawe bullied Elting and those aligned with her, expressing his desire to "create constant pain" for Elting until she agreed with Shawe's plans. It was common for senior officers to be drawn into their disputes, who were then abused by threatened firings, substantial fines, inappropriate emails, and by withholding compensation and promotions.

Specific to the Company's operations, the Court of Chancery heard days of testimony leading to findings that:

- Elting refused to pay litigation counsel to defend significant ongoing patent infringement litigation.
- Shawe fired real estate professionals, public relations professionals, refused to execute leases, and interfered with the Company's payroll processes.
- Shawe refused to engage in an annual expense true up, and interfered with the annual review of the Company's financials and its audit process.
- Shawe falsified corporate records to avoid review by Elting.

II

While Shawe and Elting continued to harass each other, interfere with the business, and demoralize the employees, they filed four lawsuits against each other.[7] The conflict eventually distilled down to Elting's petition under [DGCL] §226 to declare a deadlock and appoint a custodian to sell TPG.

The court dedicated enormous resources to the dispute. It held twelve hearings, decided sixteen motions, and conducted a six-day trial. Before its final decision, the Court of Chancery took the measured step of appointing a custodian to serve as a mediator to assist Shawe and Elting to try and settle their disputes. The court also delayed its post-trial decision for two months to await the parties' ongoing efforts to

---

7. On May 8, 2014, Elting filed an action in New York seeking to remove Shawe as a TPI director. On May 15, 2014, she filed a verified petition for dissolution of Shawe & Elting LLC (Shawe and Elting's joint owned asset protection and distribution vehicle) in the Court of Chancery. On May 22, 2014, Shawe filed a verified complaint in the Court of Chancery individually and derivatively on behalf of TPG asserting claims against Elting for waste, breach of fiduciary duty, unjust enrichment, breach of contract, and indemnification. On May 23, 2014, Elting filed a petition in the Court of Chancery seeking the appointment of a custodian to sell the Company, and dissolution of TPG under the court's equitable powers. *Id*. at *18.

resolve the controversy. After the many attempts at settlement failed, the Court of Chancery issued its 104-page decision finding that "the evidence presented at trial warrants the appointment of a custodian to sell the Company to resolve the deadlocks between Shawe and Elting."

First, the Court of Chancery found that Elting had satisfied the requirements of §226(a)(1) to appoint a custodian for stockholder deadlock because the parties stipulated that they were divided and unable to elect successor directors. Next, the court held that Elting satisfied the three requirements of §226(a)(2) for appointment of a custodian due to director deadlock. As to the first requirement, the existence of deadlocks, the court reviewed in painstaking detail its many factual findings, now undisputed on appeal, supporting its conclusion that the distrust Shawe and Elting have for each other "strikes at the heart of the palpable dysfunction that exists in the governance of the Company." The Court of Chancery also held that the second requirement, the stockholders' inability to break the director deadlock, was satisfied by the parties' stipulation of deadlock.

Turning to the final requirement, harm to the business, the Court of Chancery considered the profitability of the Company, but also made the commonsense observation that the statute contemplates appointment of custodians for profitable corporations which, like distressed companies, can suffer or be threatened with irreparable injury. The court then catalogued some of the many examples of actual and threatened irreparable injury to the Company:

- Kevin Obarski (Senior Vice President of Sales) called the feud the "biggest business issue" the Company faces, and bemoaned that the "crazy arbitrary stuff" coming out of it was "the number 1 reason people leave to go to work at competitors."
- Michael Sank (Vice President of Corporate Development) agreed: "it's so obviously the biggest problem the company faces."
- Yu-Kai Ng (Chief Information Officer) identified as a Company goal . . . meeting the need to find a way for Shawe and Elting to work together "without negatively impacting everyone else."
- Mark Hagerty (Chief Technology Officer) testified that the conflict "hurts company morale" and "is detrimental to the company."
- Robert DeNoia (former Vice President of Human Resources) expressed his frustration with the "pervasive and continuous hostile environment where inappropriate behavior impacts the morale, health and well-being of myself and the staff."
- Roy Trujillo (Chief Operating Officer), in a letter drafted for submission to a special master appointed in the New York action, attributed the "mass exodus" in Accounting and Finance to "the ongoing disputes and stressful environment created by it." He further stated that "[e]mployees are resigning and leaving these departments at unprecedented rates," that "[t]he morale and retention issue will likely spread," and that "[t]he company's reputation is taking a beating, internally and externally."
- Kai Chu (an Accounting employee), attributed the "plummeting" morale and loss of employees in Accounting to the "diametrically opposed" orders that had been received from Shawe and Elting.

- Fiona Asmah (a Finance employee) testified that the disputes and conflicting directives have caused her and others to feel "caught in the middle," have created an "unhealthy work environment," and have "affected employee morale."

Shawe himself acknowledged "the potential for grievously harming" the Company by his continued feuding with Elting. The Court of Chancery also found that major clients who are free to use competitive services have expressed concerns about the dispute. Shawe and Elting have also been unable to agree on acquisitions which generally accounted for between 16.5-20% of the Company's annual revenue and 8-14% of its annual net profit. The Company has made no acquisitions since 2013.

When it came to the scope of the custodian's authority, the Court of Chancery considered three alternatives. First, the court could do nothing and "leave the parties to their own devices." The court rejected this option because the "management of the Company is one of complete and utter dysfunction that is causing the business to suffer and threatens it with irreparable harm notwithstanding its profitability to date." The Chancellor "found Elting's distrust of Shawe to be justified" and "Shawe's actions have cast a pall on the prospect that a third party would pay a fair price for her shares." The court thus decided against the "do nothing" option because "equity will not suffer a wrong without a remedy."

Second, the court considered whether to appoint a custodian to serve as a third director or act in some capacity to break the ties between the two factions. He rejected this option because:

> [I]t would enmesh an outsider and, by extension, the Court into matters of internal corporate governance for an extensive period of time. Shawe and Elting are both relatively young. Absent a separation, their tenure as directors and co-CEO's of the Company could continue for decades. It is not sensible for the Court to exercise essentially perpetual oversight over the internal affairs of the Company.

This left the Court of Chancery with a final option—"appoint a custodian to sell the Company so that Shawe and Elting can be separated and the enterprise can be protected from their dysfunctional relationship." The court recognized that the remedy was "unusual," and "should be implemented only as a last resort and with extreme caution." But after reviewing the statute and case law, the court determined that the Court of Chancery "has appointed custodians to resolve deadlocks involving profitable corporations and authorized them to conduct a sale of the corporation."

III

A

The statute, [DGCL] §226(a), provides that "[t]he Court of Chancery, upon application of any stockholder, may appoint 1 or more persons to be custodians, and, if the corporation is insolvent, to be receivers, of and for any corporation [ ]." As this prefatory language contemplates, custodians are appointed for solvent corporations, and receivers are appointed for insolvent corporations.

There are three pathways to appoint a custodian for a solvent corporation, two of which [DGCL §§226(a)(1) and (2)] are relevant to this case.

Shawe does not contest the Court of Chancery's ruling that a custodian may be appointed under §226(a)(1) due to the stockholder deadlock between Shawe and Elting, and their inability to elect successor directors. Nor could he. Shawe and Elting stipulated to the stockholder deadlock required by the statute.

The trial record amply supports the Court of Chancery's finding [under §226(a)(2)] that the deadlock and dysfunction between the founders is causing threatened and actual irreparable injury to the Company.

B

Having decided that the Court of Chancery properly exercised its discretion under §226 to appoint a custodian of the Company, we turn to Shawe's primary argument raised for the first time on appeal—that the custodian statute does not authorize the court to order the custodian to sell the Company over the stockholders' objection. Shawe also argues that instructing the custodian to sell the Company is an extreme remedy, and should not have been imposed without first attempting less-drastic remedies, such as using the custodian as a third director to break the ongoing deadlocks between the founders.

The argument is waived. Even if the argument was properly before us, we find that the arguments relied upon by the dissent for the first time on appeal lack merit.

Under the express language of the custodian statute [DGCL §226(b)], the Court of Chancery has the authority to "otherwise order" the custodian to "liquidate [the Company's] affairs and distribute its assets" rather than "continue the business of the corporation." In other words, the custodian's default duty is to continue the business of the corporation, but the Court of Chancery can displace the default duty by ordering that the company's affairs be liquidated.

Several sources confirm the Court of Chancery's broad authority under the statute, which includes ordering a sale. [T]he Court of Chancery has previously authorized a custodian to sell a company when faced with stockholder deadlock. This Court has also recognized the broad authority granted the Court of Chancery under the statute. Section 226(b) provides that the custodian shall have "all the powers and title of a receiver appointed under §291." Although we have cautioned that normally the custodian's authority "should be kept to a minimum" and "should be exercised only insofar as the goals of fairness and justice . . . require," we have also observed that the court's broad authority to set a receiver's duties under §291 leads to the same conclusion for a custodian's authority under §226(b):

> We interpret this section [226(b)] as setting forth the maximum statutory limits on the powers of the custodian. Section 291, to which §226(b) specifically refers, states: "the powers of the [receiver] shall be such and shall continue so long as the Court shall deem necessary." Thus, under §§226 and 291, the Court of Chancery may determine the duration of the appointment and the specific powers to be conferred upon the custodian.[38]

---

38. *Giuricich [v. Emtrol Corp., 449 A.2s 232 (Del. 1982)]*, at 240.

The dissent . . . appears to argue that a custodian is not empowered to exercise the powers of a receiver when the court "otherwise orders" that a deadlocked solvent company be sold. According to the dissent, . . . interpretive principles should be applied to require that the exception language be read to permit liquidation only in circumstances similar to §226(a)(3) (corporations that have abandoned their business) and §352(a)(3) (custodians for close corporations).

The problems with this interpretation of the statute are apparent. The dissent attempts to change the plain meaning of the statutory language by invoking rules of statutory interpretation. But if a statute is clear and unambiguous, "the plain meaning of the statutory language controls." This is because "[a]n unambiguous statute precludes the need for judicial interpretation."

Under a plain reading of §226(b), the custodian has the powers of a receiver under §291, and his duties are to continue the business unless the Court otherwise orders, and except under the special circumstances of abandoned businesses and close corporations. Rules of interpretation should not be invoked to contort the plain language of a statute in a manner inconsistent with its plain meaning.

Further, the dissent's interpretation also ignores the conjunctive words "and except." The statute cannot reasonably be read to express the three exceptions as a series of similar events. Instead, when the words "and except" are given meaning, the statute is reasonably read to list three distinct exceptions to the custodian's default duty to maintain the business—"except when the Court shall otherwise order;" and "except in cases arising under paragraph (a)(3) of this section;" or "§352(a)(2) of this title."

The dissent also points to §273, a section of the DGCL permitting dissolution of joint venture corporations when two 50% owner-stockholders are deadlocked. In many instances, that statute has been employed to break a deadlock through a sale of the corporation under the auspices of the Court of Chancery and a fiduciary appointed by it for that purpose. Contrary to what the dissent contends, it is by no means unprecedented for the Court of Chancery to have to address the fate of a solvent Delaware corporation by setting up a fair process to have it sold as a going concern, when that outcome is necessary to best protect its constituencies.

As the Chancellor observed, this case "was within a whisker" of §273. The only novelty here is that this case arises under §226, because the economic and functional reality of the deadlock does not fall precisely under §273. But, consistent with the flexible and efficient design of the DGCL, §226 allows the Court of Chancery to address this situation by using its power to deal with cases on a situational basis. Rather than read the key language "except when the Court shall otherwise order" as having no significance, we read it consistently with the overall design of the statute, and its intention to allow our Court of Chancery the discretion to deal sensibly with corporations that are unable to move forward with governance because their owners cannot take fundamental action to elect a new board. That the Chancellor looked for guidance to the remedies entered in cases under §273 . . . suggests that the court understood TPG's economic reality as identical to a 50-50 deadlock, and that the tools used to sensibly address those deadlocks would inform his discretion under §226.

It is also not convincing to characterize the method chosen by the Chancellor as somehow different for purposes of §226 because it involves a sale of the corporation's stock, rather than its underlying assets. Stockholders of Delaware corporations are only entitled to the rights that come with their stock, and those rights are subject to the Court of Chancery's power under statutes like §226. Many Delaware statutes, including those dealing with certain mergers, subject stockholders to giving up their shares over their objection.

When a stockholder buys stock in a Delaware corporation, it knows that our statute provides the Court of Chancery broad authority to address corporate deadlocks of various kinds, authority that may well affect fundamental ownership interests. Stockholders buy stock in Delaware corporations to gain from the underlying operations of the corporation. It is therefore inconsistent with the practical and efficient design of corporate law in the DGCL, to require asset sales and liquidations, simply to allow stockholders to hold their paper shares and receive a final, and likely lower, liquidating dividend. Nor is it the case that sales of corporate assets or of the entire corporation are somehow unusual when the corporation in managerial deadlock is profitable. The reality is that most of the cases in which the Court of Chancery has ordered a sale or its equivalent in the context of §273 dealt with profitable corporations. Those are the corporations that parties tend to fight over, especially in the Court of Chancery, because most insolvent corporation cases are handled by federal bankruptcy courts. Parties intractably deadlocked will rarely want what the dissent characterizes as a lesser remedy like asset sales and dissolution.

This case illustrates that reality well. Here, making a distinction between liquidation and sale has no real practical effect. TPG acts as a holding company for the main wholly-owned operating company, TPI, and other subsidiaries. If we accepted Shawe's interpretation of §226(b), after remand the Court of Chancery could exalt form over substance and order TPG's assets—TPI and other subsidiary companies—liquidated through a sale process, and the proceeds distributed to TPG and then its stockholders. Shawe concedes as much. Such meaningless corporate shuffling illustrates why a reasonable reading of the statute includes a custodian's authority to sell TPG instead of its parts. Neither Elting nor Shawe want an asset sale, and for good reason. Selling TPG as a going concern will protect TPG's employees from the ruinous consequences of an asset sale and provide the maximum return to the stockholders.

Shawe also faults the Court of Chancery for ordering a sale instead of experimenting with less-intrusive measures. We agree with Shawe that a sale is a remedy to be employed reluctantly and cautiously, after a consideration of other options. The Court of Chancery should always consider less drastic alternatives before authorizing the custodian to sell a solvent company. But the remedy to address the deadlock is ultimately within the Court of Chancery's discretion. The court did not abuse its discretion in this case.

First, the court attempted other less intrusive measures by appointing a custodian immediately after trial ended to serve "as a mediator to assist Elting and Shawe in negotiating a resolution of their disputes." Almost three months later, after the first attempt at mediation failed, the court gave the parties another month before issuing its post-trial opinion "to afford them additional time to seek to resolve their disputes through the auspices of the mediator." The Court of Chancery was also aware of repeated efforts to resolve the dispute in New York, including settlement discussions, a mediation, and multiple sessions with a court-appointed Special Master. The Court of Chancery gave the parties every opportunity to resolve their acrimonious dispute outside the courthouse.

Further, the court considered whether to appoint a custodian "to serve as a third director or some form of tie-breaking mechanism in the governance of the Company." But the court rejected this option . . . .

And, although Shawe characterizes the Chancellor's remedy as extremely intrusive, the appointment of a custodian to act as a constant monitor and tiebreaker—which is what would be required given the abundant record that Shawe and Elting cannot work together constructively—would itself be expensive, cumbersome, and very intrusive. Moreover, that approach would not facilitate, as the Chancellor's ruling does, the ability of the Company to capitalize on its business model in the efficient, flexible way that commerce demands. By preserving the Company as a whole in his remedy and allowing it to be owned and managed in the manner required to take advantage of evolving opportunities and to meet challenges effectively, the Chancellor's remedy also was well designed to protect the other constituencies of the Company—notably its employees—by positioning the company to succeed and thus to secure the jobs of its workforce.

The Chancellor was in the best position to assess the viability of options short of sale. Aware of the "extreme caution" that must be exercised before ordering a sale, he nonetheless determined that "the painfully obvious conclusion is that Shawe and Elting need to be separated from each other in the management of the Company. Their dysfunction must be excised to safeguard the Company." We will not second-guess that first-hand judgment on appeal.

V

The Court of Chancery's August 13, 2015 opinion and July 18, 2016 order, and the related orders, are affirmed.

VALIHURA, Justice, dissenting:

The Court of Chancery generally has broad discretion in fashioning certain equitable remedies. Although this might suggest that this Court should defer to the Chancellor who ordered one of the most extreme remedies possible—a sale of a financially successful corporation over the objections of one or more of its three stockholders—our review of the Court of Chancery's order requires construction of a statute, namely, [DGCL] §226 ("Section 226"). Embedded in this choice of remedy is the question of whether a court-appointed custodian has the power to force the sale of a stockholder's stock absent that stockholder's consent. My analysis of the statutory scheme suggests that the answer is "no." Accordingly, I respectfully DISSENT.[3]

---

3. Much of the Majority Opinion addresses the Court of Chancery's power to appoint a custodian—a proposition that is not seriously contested by anyone here. Rather, it is the Modified Auction's forced sale provisions that are chiefly at issue. As to that main issue, the Majority declines to formally address the key statutory arguments on the grounds of waiver. Instead, they offer several pages of pure *dicta* on the issue. I believe that the statutory arguments are fairly encompassed within Shawe's explicit argument below—that the Court of Chancery should not order a sale under Section 226. Clearly, Section 226 and its proper scope have been a central focus all along. Given that fact, I do not see how a statutory analysis credibly can be avoided.

Given that we are faced with a question as to the permissible limits of the Court of Chancery's power under Section 226, the flexibility typically afforded the Court of Chancery in fashioning equitable remedies must yield to the more specific principles underlying the relevant statutory provisions and common law interpreting these provisions. The first principle concerns the uncontested fact that, in the DGCL, stock is "personal property" and is generally subject to traditional property law policies favoring free alienation. Generally, where the possibility of defeasance of a stockholder's stock may occur over the stockholder's objection, those restraints on free transferability and alienation of stock are expressly set forth in the relevant statute. That fact strongly suggests that Section 226 should not be so broadly read as to allow for a forced sale or other divestiture of a stockholder's stock by mere implication. The second principle is the longstanding, uncontested common law principle that the involvement of the Court of Chancery and court-appointed custodians in a corporation's business and affairs should be kept to a minimum. This long-standing common law view is reflected in the fact that the parties here cannot point to a single case in the history of our Section 226 jurisprudence where a court has ordered a custodial sale of a company over a stockholder's objections. These specific policies should be the analytical focal point in construing Section 226 and the permissible limits of the trial court's power.

A holistic reading of the DGCL supports the view that divestiture of a stockholder's stock may occur over the stockholder's objection in a number of situations—but only when the relevant statute expressly so provides. Examples where a stockholder is forced to give up her shares have one thing in common—the relevant statutory provisions expressly contemplate that situation and provide fair notice that it may occur. Here, Section 226 contains no such express provision or notice of such potential forced divestiture. I know of no situations in the DGCL where a forced sale of stock can occur absent fair notice, and the Majority cites to none. The absence of authority grounded in the statute, the conceded absence of any similar cases under Section 226, and our common law's strong preference for the least intrusive remedies in cases involving court-appointed custodians suggest that the Chancellor went too far too fast in ordering the Modified Auction.

I

The Statutory Scheme Suggests that the Court of Chancery Lacked the Power to Order Stockholders to Sell Their Shares

Section 226(a) permits the Court of Chancery to appoint a custodian in the event of stockholder deadlock, director deadlock, or abandonment of the corporation.

In the case of shareholder deadlock, as here, "[t]he decision to appoint a custodian . . . is committed to the [c]ourt's discretion" and does not require a showing of irreparable injury to the corporation.

In the event of a court-ordered liquidation, the custodian takes custody of the assets of the *corporation*—not of the stockholder's stock (which is the stockholder's personal property).[12] Section 159 of the DGCL provides that "[t]he shares of stock in every corporation shall be deemed personal property and transferable as provided in Article 8 of [the Delaware UCC]."

Although the powers of the custodian under Section 226 are defined by reference to Section 291, as this Court has stated, Section 226 powers "are not as unlimited as the powers of a receiver appointed under the general equitable powers of the court, or under the forerunner to the present [Section] 226(a)(1)." Nor does Section 291 grant the receiver power over the personal property of the stockholders, although a receiver may sell the property of the corporation under certain circumstances.

Review of the relevant statutory scheme suggests that it is unlikely that the General Assembly intended to permit a stockholder's fundamental personal property rights to be abridged by mere implication. Where the DGCL does so permit restrictions on the stockholder's free transferability and alienation of her stock, including forced dispositions and transfers of stock ownership, it does so expressly. Examples include Section 251(c) (permitting approval of mergers by a majority of stockholders, such that dissenting stockholders are divested of their stock . . .); Section 273 (authorizing dissolution of a joint venture owned by two 50% stockholders); and Section 303(a) (involving actions that may be taken in bankruptcy proceedings that are deemed to be unanimous actions of the stockholders).

In contrast to each of the provisions above, Section 226 contains no language that suggests that a court-ordered custodian has the power to compel a forced disposition of a stockholder's personal property (stock).

Relatedly, [§202] of the DGCL [addresses] restrictions on transfers of stock and also [makes] clear that restrictions must be stated expressly and clearly.

This narrower construction of Section 226 is further supported by examining the special provisions for close corporations in Sections 352 and 353, which also embody concepts of notice and consent, as well as a statutory preference for less drastic, interim remedies to address deadlock situations.

Delaware law also provides for both statutory and equitable dissolution of Delaware corporations, either of which may cause the involuntary divestiture of stockholders' personal property interests.

Section 226(b) explicitly establishes the overarching requirement that "the authority of the custodian is to continue the business of the corporation and not to liquidate its affairs and distribute its assets." A dissolution under the circumstances here would be inconsistent with that express statutory requirement.[52] No one has

---

12. In a liquidation under Section 226(b), the corporation's property is sold. The stockholders continue to own shares, but the corporation is no longer a going concern, and its operating assets are replaced with cash. Liquidation is available by court order and when a corporation has abandoned its business, is insolvent, or needs to wind up its affairs—circumstances unquestionably not present here. Thus, I disagree with the Majority's statement that "in the context of this case, making a distinction between liquidation and sale has no real practical effect." The Majority further suggests that, after remand, the Court of Chancery could order TPG's assets liquidated through a sale process and distribute the proceeds to the stockholders. It further contends that "Shawe concedes as much." Shawe's statements cannot be fairly viewed as a concession that liquidation was an option here. No party during this appeal has even suggested that either a liquidation or a sale of assets is an option.

52. Moreover, the language in Section 226(b) creating three circumscribed "exceptions" to the general requirement that a custodian "continue the business of the corporation and not . . . liquidate its affairs and distribute its assets," cannot reasonably be read to authorize the forced sale of a solvent corporation to a third party over the objections of its stockholders. The exceptions in Section 226(b) allow for deviation from the general rule that the custodian must continue the business only "when the Court shall otherwise order and except in cases arising

seriously argued on appeal that a dissolution, an asset sale, or a liquidation is an option.[53] The Majority acknowledges that "[n]either Elting nor Shawe want an asset sale," which it says could result in "ruinous consequences[.]"

The Court of Chancery's decisions appointing a custodian and accepting the Custodian's recommendation with respect to the Modified Auction contain no textual analysis of the relevant statutory scheme. Instead, the Chancellor relied on two cases, which are distinguishable due to the presence of stockholder consent to the sales in both of those cases.

The question here is what are the limits, if any, of the court's power under Section 226? Our statutory scheme should be read harmoniously. Reading the statutory scheme harmoniously compels the conclusion that Section 226 does not permit the Court of Chancery to confer upon a custodian the power to sell a corporation over the objection of its shareholders. Thus, I believe that the Court of Chancery erred by ordering the Modified Auction.

II

The Common Law Rule of Judicial Restraint Regarding Custodial Powers Suggests a More Limited Remedy

Similarly, the policies of judicial restraint embedded in our common law underlying Section 226 suggest that the Modified Auction Order's forced sale provision goes too far. Historically, "the common law generally disdained judicial relief of any kind with respect to a solvent but deadlocked corporation." Though the

---

under paragraph (a)(3) of this section or §352(a)(2) of this title." [DGCL] §226(b). First, this "exception" language does not provide express notice of a possible defeasance of one's ownership interest in stock—unlike other statutes which explicitly contemplate defeasance, whether voluntary or involuntary, as a possibility. Nor does Section 226's reference to Section 291 provide sufficient notice of such a possible defeasance, since, among other things, Section 291 applies only to insolvent corporations. The Majority avoids this point altogether.

Second, the three exceptions necessarily modify the custodian's default obligation to continue the business of the corporation and not to liquidate its affairs or distribute its assets. The second and third exceptions simply provide for limited circumstances in which a custodian's default obligation does not apply—namely, where a corporation has abandoned its business (as in Section 226(a)(3)) or where a stockholder in a close corporation has the right, pursuant to the close corporation's certificate of incorporation, to dissolution of the close corporation (as in Section 352(a)(2)).

The first exception ("except when the Court shall otherwise order") logically should be read in the context of the second and third exceptions—both of which explicitly identify limited circumstances in which a custodian has no obligation to continue the business of the corporation. It is unreasonable, then, to read the first exception as empowering the Court of Chancery to fashion a remedy wholly incongruous with the two other exceptions. Therefore, the first exception, as the second and third, can only reasonably be read to allow only for a similar discontinuation of the business (*e.g.*, liquidation, distribution of assets, or dissolution).

In short, the exceptions in Section 226(b) do not authorize a forced sale of this solvent corporation to a third party over the objections of stockholders. Perhaps that is why the Majority endeavors mightily to equate the proposed forced auction of TransPerfect to one of the scenarios contemplated by the exceptions in Section 226(b) (which contemplate discontinuation of the business)—a liquidation, a dissolution, or a distribution of assets. The problem with that lies in the fact that a sale or auction of a thriving business is a far cry from a liquidation, dissolution, or distribution of assets. The remedy of a sale does not contemplate, as do liquidation, dissolution, and distribution of assets, the winding up of a corporation's business. Thus, to the limited extent that Section 226(b) empowers a custodian to undertake a liquidation, dissolution, or distribution of assets, that power does not, *a fortiori*, allow a custodian to auction the corporation over the objections of its stockholders.

53. The Majority's statement that I have suggested that "a lesser remedy like asset sales and dissolution" would be more acceptable remedies is perplexing and just plain wrong. Nowhere do I suggest that they are "lesser remedies" or that stockholders of solvent companies would prefer these remedies.

104. The Majority suggests that "less-intrusive measures" or "intermediate measures were attempted but failed." This is perplexing. A mediation and settlement efforts occurred, but no intermediate measures were "attempted and failed."

pre-1967 iteration of Section 226 vested in the Court of Chancery the discretion to appoint receivers of and for deadlocked corporations, the court was hesitant to interfere in the business of deadlocked but solvent companies.

[T]his Court has determined that "[t]he involvement of the Court of Chancery and its custodian in the corporation's business and affairs should be kept to a minimum and should be exercised only insofar as the goals of fairness and justice . . . require." Consistent with this sentiment, at least since the 1967 revisions, the parties have pointed to no case in which the Court of Chancery has exercised its power under Section 226 to order that a company be sold over stockholder objection.

Cases in which the Court of Chancery has appointed custodians for solvent corporations support a narrowly tailored, incremental approach to the custodian's power.

The case law applying Section 226 therefore supports the view that the sale of the Company, absent stockholder consent, is too drastic a measure, and that the trial court should consider implementation of remedies on an incremental basis.

III

In View of the Above, the Court of Chancery's Remedy Here Was, at a Minimum, Too Extreme and Was Not Authorized by the Statute

The Court of Chancery . . . appointed a custodian who had previously served as mediator to the parties. The court directed the custodian to "oversee a judicially ordered sale of the Company." The accompanying Order demonstrates that any stockholder not purchasing the Company may be required to sell his or her shares. The court also directed the custodian, "[i]n the interim," to "serve as a third director with the authority to vote on any matters on which Shawe and Elting cannot agree and which rise to the level that [the Custodian] deems to be significant to managing the Company's business and affairs."

In my view, the Court of Chancery failed to narrowly tailor the scope of the custodian's authority, which contemplates the possibility that each stockholder be a seller. The court could have appointed a third director, as provided for in the company's bylaws . . . . Although the Chancellor considered this option and appointed the custodian as an "interim" tiebreaker until the Modified Auction could be completed, he rejected this solution out of concern that the court would be involved in TransPerfect's affairs for too long. The Chancellor did not consider the possibility of appointing a custodian for a period of time or expanding the Board to include independent directors. If these less drastic remedies failed, the custodian could petition the court for more drastic relief . . . . But absent consent, however, I do not believe a forced sale is a statutorily authorized option.

IV

In conclusion, my construction of Section 226 takes account of property rights and due process protections because I believe these concepts are embedded in the relevant statutory framework. This is evident in Section 159's express statement that stock is personal property, and in the other provisions of our statutory framework that provide clear and express notice in situations where defeasance of that property right might occur. That is why, in reading our statutory scheme harmoniously, it is compelling *not to imply* the power of the Court to issue an order that can result in defeasance of these rights over the objections of the owners. This reading of Section 226 is consistent with the long-standing policy of strictly limiting the powers of court-appointed custodians.

Notes and Questions

1. Note

a. The Chancellor awarded over $7 million to Elting in sanctions because of Shawe's conduct connected with the litigation. The court found, among other things, that when litigation was imminent or ongoing, Shawe broke into Elting's office; remotely accessed her computer, accessing 19,000 of her emails, including 12,000 that were privileged communications between Elting and her lawyers; did not preserve his cell phone or laptop for discovery purposes (his cell phone was allegedly disposed of under highly bizarre and incredible circumstances); deleted 19,000 of his own emails (almost all of which were forensically recovered); and gave false interrogatory and deposition responses during discovery and false trial testimony. The Chancellor's findings and award were affirmed by the Delaware Supreme Court in an opinion filed the same day as the principal case. *Shawe v. Elting*, 157 A.2d 142 (Del. 2017).

b. In an omitted footnote of the opinion, the court noted that the parties retained 11 law firms between them to handle the litigation in the Court of Chancery.

2. Reality Check

a. What did the Chancellor see as his three options? Why did he pick the one he did? Do you think he chose the correct option? Do you think he had other options than the ones he identified? *See* the excerpt from *State ex re. Smith v. Evans*, near the end of this chapter.

b. Why does Justice Valihura dissent? On which issues does she agree with the majority?

c. What is the difference between a *receiver* and a *custodian*? *See* DGCL §§226 and 291.

3. Suppose

a. If this case had been decided under the MBCA, would the analysis or the result have been different?

4. What Do You Think?

a. Do you think a Delaware court has the power to order a custodian to liquidate the assets of a solvent corporation under DGCL §226? *Hint*: in every edition of this casebook prior to the decision in *Shawe*, the text stated that Delaware courts do not have this power.

b. Who is likely to buy TransPerfect?

c. Do you think a court should order the sale of a solvent corporation over the objections of all the shareholders? Should it do so over the objection of any shareholder?

b. ... to a New Cause of Action ...

Once legislatures became comfortable with the idea that courts should break at least some deadlocks by ordering that a corporation be dissolved, they began to think about whether other corporate dysfunctions could also be alleviated by dissolution. The results of that thinking are embedded in MBCA §14.30(a)(2), which you should read now.

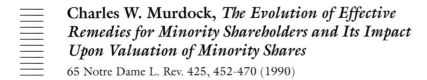

Charles W. Murdock, *The Evolution of Effective Remedies for Minority Shareholders and Its Impact Upon Valuation of Minority Shares*

65 Notre Dame L. Rev. 425, 452-470 (1990)

[I]t is worthwhile to examine the traditional four bases for involuntary judicial dissolution to evaluate them for their potential to afford relief. [See MBCA §14.30(a)(2)(i)-(iv).]

The provision that empirically seems to be the most fruitful avenue for minority shareholders to pursue, ... is one using a finding of oppression as the basis for liquidation. While the provision also speaks of illegal and fraudulent acts, the courts have consistently observed that, not only is oppression a concept separate and distinct from fraud and illegality, but also that it embraces conduct that would not be encompassed within those terms.

The Illinois Business Corporation Act of 1933 (the "1933 Act") is often viewed as the first modern corporation code and was the basis for the Model Business Corporation Act [1950]. Section 86(a)(3) of the 1933 Act was the basis for section 90(a)(2), later section 97(a)(2), and finally section 14.30(a)(2)(ii) of the various versions of the [MBCA], and introduced the concept of oppression as a basis for liquidation.

In interpreting the scope of "oppression" ..., no clear pattern developed until the 1960s. However, in 1957, the Illinois Supreme Court considered the concept of oppression and took a very broad view. In *Central Standard Life Insurance Co. v. Davis*, the court stated: "[W]e reject defendants' argument that the word [oppression] is substantially synonymous with "illegal and fraudulent." Misapplication of assets or mismanagement of funds are not, as we read the statute, indispensable ingredients of "oppressive" conduct."

The rhetoric providing a broad gloss in defining oppression bore fruit three years later when the court confronted another alleged case of oppression. The following factors combined to indicate oppression within the meaning of the statute: officers were hired and salary increases were given without director approval; loans were made to corporations in which the president had an interest without director approval; a subsidiary was organized without director approval; the matter of payment of dividends had not been presented to the board of directors; and the other family was excluded from all incidents of control and corporate participation. The court pointed out that it was "not necessary that fraud, illegality or even loss be shown to exhibit oppression"[209] and concluded that the cumulative effects of the aforementioned acts, and their indicated continuing nature, established oppression entitling the plaintiffs to liquidation. Although corporate dissolution was deemed to be a drastic remedy, "when oppression is positively shown, the oppressed are entitled to the protection of the law."[210]

[T]here followed a series of appellate court decisions decreeing dissolution based upon a broad reading of what constitutes oppressive conduct. Conduct which excludes a minority shareholder from participation in the enterprise or which can be characterized as heavy-handed or overbearing has sufficed to warrant dissolution. Misuse of corporate funds or assets has also led to a conclusion of oppression. Thus, where the defendant has taken excessive salaries or misused corporate assets, the courts have found oppressive conduct justifying dissolution. And, in a case in which an accounting was sought, the court indicated that the failure "to pay dividends to minority stockholders, due to large salaries drawn by officer-majority stockholders" could constitute oppressive conduct.[216]

Following, at least in part, the lead of Illinois, several other jurisdictions have adopted an expansive definition of oppression.

While the abstract formulations of what constitutes oppressive conduct appeared favorable to minority shareholders, such shareholders had difficulty in the 1970s obtaining relief in jurisdictions other than Illinois.

Finally, in 1979, a New Jersey court, in *Exadaktilos v. Cinnaminson Realty Co.*, . . . concluded that, "[w]hile the terminology employed by both the statute and case law certainly provides the court with the latitude necessary to deal with all the circumstances peculiar to any case brought to its attention, it fails to suggest any perspective from which to judge what is oppressive or unfair."[237] The *Exadaktilos* court . . . concluded that "[t]he special circumstances, arrangements and personal relationships that frequently underlie the formation of close corporations generate certain expectations among the shareholders concerning their respective roles in corporate affairs, including management and earnings."[238]

While the New Jersey court in *Exadaktilos* introduced the notion of expectations as a standard by which to measure whether the challenged conduct was oppressive, the reasonable expectations test reached full bloom in New York after the legislature, in 1979, provided for a buy-out of the minority shareholder as an alternative to dissolution when the minority alleged oppressive conduct by those in control.[242] [S]ince 1980 New York has played the dominant role by developing the reasonable expectations test to define oppressive conduct.

This approach stands in marked contrast . . . to the shareholder fiduciary duty rule — at least in those situations in which a court would, in effect, permit a

---

209. *Gidwitz v. Lanzit Corrugated Box Co*, 170 N.E.2d 131, 138 (Ill. 1960).
210. *Id.* at 138.
216. *Gray v. Hall*, 295 N.E.2d 506, 509 (Ill. App. 1973) (the court also indicated that withholding dividends to freeze-out a minority shareholder could be oppressive).
237. 400 A.2d 554, 560 (N.J. 1979).
238. *Id.* at 154, 400 A.2d at 561.
242. N.Y. Bus. Corp. Law §§1104-a, 1118 (McKinney 1986 & Supp. 1988).

"business purpose" defense to a claim of breach of fiduciary duty. For example, even *Wilkes* [*v. Springside Nursing Home, Inc.*, 353 N.E.2d 657, 663 (Mass. 1976)] recognized that conduct that appears to be a breach of duty can be justified by a business purpose. The difference in result may be rationalized by the difference in focus and the difference in remedy. In determining whether there has been a breach of fiduciary duty, the focus is upon wrongdoing by the person in control and the remedy is to invalidate the transaction, either by enjoining it or by awarding damages. In the reasonable expectations test, the focus is on the minority share-holder and the remedy is not to undo a corporate transaction but to permit or order another transaction — a buy-out of the minority shareholder. Thus, the crux is not identifying a traditional wrong but rather identifying the basis of the bargain — what were the explicit or implicit conditions pursuant to which the parties associated themselves together in the corporate form. This approach has become the touchstone for evaluating oppressive conduct in the 1980s.

[T]he New York Court of Appeals in *In re Kemp & Beatley, Inc.*,[283] . . . clarified that the concept of oppressive conduct, under the statute, is distinct from illegality or fraud and that the distinction has been resolved "by considering oppressive actions to refer to conduct that substantially defeats the 'reasonable expectations' held by minority shareholders in committing their capital to the particular enter-prise."[284] Accordingly, the court held that "utilizing a complaining shareholder's 'reasonable expectations' as a means of identifying and measuring conduct alleged to be oppressive is appropriate."[285] The court cautioned that expectations must be reasonable and objective.[286]

What the New York decisions make clear is that those in control of a corporation may no longer use the business judgment rule to shield from judicial scrutiny actions that are detrimental to minority shareholders. The courts have recognized the reality that compensation paid to those in control has a twofold function: to recompense services and to provide a return on investment. To deny a minority shareholder

---

283. 473 N.E.2d 1173 (N.Y. 1984).
284. *Id.* 1179. Before determining what reasonable expectations might be, the court stated:

It is widely understood that, in addition to supplying capital to a contemplated or ongoing enterprise and expecting a fair and equal return, parties comprising the ownership of a close corporation may expect to be actively involved in its management and operation.
. . .
His the shareholder in the close corporation] participation in that particular corporation is often his principal or sole source of income. As a matter of fact, providing employment for himself may have been the principal reason why he participated in organizing the corporation. He may or may not anticipate an ultimate profit from the sale of his interest, but he normally draws very little from the corporation as dividends. In his capacity as an officer or employee of the corporation, he looks to his salary for the principal return on his capital investment, because earnings of a close corporation, as is well known, are distributed in major part in salaries, bonuses and retirement benefits.

Id. 1178 (*quoting* F. O'Neal, *Close Corporations* 21-22 (2d ed. 1971)).

285. *Id.* at 1179.
286. The court stated:

Majority conduct should not be deemed oppressive simply because the petitioner's subjective hopes and desires in joining the venture are not fulfilled. Disappointment alone should not necessarily be equated with oppression.
Rather, oppression should be deemed to arise only when the majority conduct substantially defeats expectations that, objectively viewed, were both reasonable under the circumstances and were central to the petitioner's decision to join the venture.

Id.

employment when a job was part of his rationale in investing is oppressive, as is the failure to pay dividends to nonemployee shareholders when employed shareholders are receiving de facto dividends through salaries.

While a reasonable expectations test may appear as elusive to apply as oppression, it does provide a focus from which to evaluate a situation. That people often invest in a closely held corporation to provide a job is almost self-evident; if there is doubt, the proposition can be confirmed empirically by surveying representative businesses.

Notes and Questions

1. Reality Check

a. Why did legislatures create a cause of action for *oppression*?

b. What are the two approaches to defining oppression?

2. What Do You Think?

a. Should shareholders be able to recover for oppression? Isn't the claim for relief simply a claim for damages on the ground that one has been treated shabbily?

The preceding discussion of a cause of action for oppression and the varying definition of oppression may seem a bit removed from real life. The next case shows rather vividly the consequences of allowing relief for oppression and, even more centrally, the consequences of applying one definition of oppression rather than another.

Kiriakides v. Atlas Food Systems & Services, Inc.

541 S.E.2d 257 (S.C. 2001)

Toal, C.J.

FACTS

This is a case in which respondents, minority shareholders in a closely held family corporation, claim the majority shareholders have acted in a manner which is fraudulent, oppressive and unfairly prejudicial.[1] They seek a buyout of their shares under South Carolina's judicial dissolution statutes. A rather detailed recitation of the facts is necessary to an understanding of the plaintiffs' claims.

Respondents are 72-year-old John Kiriakides and his 74-year-old sister Louise Kiriakides. John and Louise are the minority shareholders in the family business, Atlas Food Systems & Services, Inc. (Atlas). Petitioners are their older brother, 88-year-old Alex Kiriakides, Jr., and the family business. . . .

Atlas is a food vending service which provides refreshments to factories and other businesses. The business began prior to World War II but slowed down while Alex was away during the war. After the war, Alex, John, and their father Alex, Sr., began working together to build the family business. Alex, Sr. died in 1949. Atlas

---

1. See S.C. Code Ann. §§33-14-300 & 33-14-310 (1990).

was incorporated in 1956. Currently, Alex is the majority stockholder, owning 57.68%; John owns 37.7%, and Louise owns 3%.

Throughout Atlas' history, Alex has been in charge of the financial and corporate affairs of the family business; he has had overall control and is Chairman of the Board of Directors. John is also on the three member Board. In 1986, John became President of Atlas, after years of running client relations and field operations. Two of Alex' children are also employed by Atlas, his son Alex III, and his daughter Mary Ann.[5] Alex III is (since John's departure as discussed below) President and is on the Board; Mary Ann is a CPA who performs accounting and financial functions. . . .[6]

For years, Atlas operated as a prototypical closely held family corporation. Troubles developed, however, in 1995, when a rift began between Alex and John. The initial dispute arose over property owned by John and Alex in Greenville. Alex convinced John to transfer his interest in the property to his son Alex III for a price less than it was worth. John signed the deed prepared by Alex believing he was conveying only a small portion of his interest in the property to Alex III. After discovering his entire interest had been transferred to Alex III, John became distrustful of Alex and began requesting documents and records concerning the family business. The relationship between the two became very strained. Several subsequent incidents served to heighten the tension.

[I]n mid-1996, a dispute arose over Atlas' contract to purchase a piece of commercial property. Notwithstanding the contract, John, Alex III and William Freitag (Senior Vice President of Finance and Administration) decided not to go through with the sale. Alex however, without consulting or advising John, elected to go through with the sale. When John learned of Alex' decision, he became extremely upset and allegedly advised Alex III he was quitting his job as President.[8] The next day, Alex III made plans with managers to continue operations in John's absence; John, however, went to the Atlas office in Greenville and visited Atlas offices in Columbia, Orangeburg and Charleston.

The following Monday, John went to work at Atlas doing "business as usual." He was told later that day . . . that management was planning John would no longer be President of Atlas. John circulated a memo indicating he intended to remain President; Alex III replied in a memo prepared with the aid of his father, refusing to allow John to continue as president of the company. The following day, Alex refused to allow John to stay on as president of Atlas, and designated Alex III as President. John was offered, but refused a position as a consultant.

In September 1996, Atlas offered to purchase John's interest in Atlas . . . for one million dollars, plus the cancellation of $800,000 obligations owed by John. John refused this offer, believing it too low.[10] John filed this suit in November 1996. . . . The complaint was subsequently amended, naming Louise as a plaintiff,

---

5. Neither John nor Louise have any children; Alex has four children: Alex III, Michael, Mary Ann and Cathryn.

6. Louise worked for several years in the counting room but has not worked for the company since the 1970's. She served as Secretary until 1988.

8. The referee found John subsequently made it clear he had no intentions of quitting.

10. In March, 1998, Atlas offered to buy the interests of John and Louise for four million dollars, less obligations of $825,000. John was advised by a tax attorney in 1995 that his stock in Atlas was worth about ten million dollars.

and adding claims for fraud under the judicial dissolution statute. The complaint sought an accounting, a buyout of John and Louise's shares, and damages for fraud.

After a five day hearing, the referee found Alex had engaged in fraud in numerous respects, and found Atlas had engaged in conduct which was fraudulent, oppressive and unfairly prejudicial toward John and Louise. The Court of Appeals affirmed in result.

LAW/ANALYSIS

a. Oppression Under S.C. Code Ann. §33-14-300

The referee found that, taken together, the majority's actions were "illegal, fraudulent, oppressive or unfairly prejudicial," . . . under S.C. Code Ann. §33-14-300(2)(ii) and §33-14-310(d)(4).[16]

The Court of Appeals affirmed the referee's holdings. In making this ruling, the Court of Appeals defined the statutory terms "oppressive" and "unfairly prejudicial" as follows:

(1) A visible departure from the standards of fair dealing and a violation of fair play on which every shareholder who entrusts his money to a company is entitled to rely; or
(2) A breach of the fiduciary duty of good faith and fair dealing; or
(3) Whether the reasonable expectations of the minority shareholders have been frustrated by the actions of the majority; or
(4) A lack of probity and fair dealing in the affairs of a company to the prejudice of some of its members; or
(5) A deprivation by majority shareholders of participation in management by minority shareholders.

Atlas contends the Court of Appeals' definitions of oppressive, unfairly prejudicial conduct are beyond the scope of our judicial dissolution statute. We agree. In our view, the Court of Appeals' broad view of oppression is contrary to the legislative intent and is an unwarranted expansion of section 33-14-300.

South Carolina's judicial dissolution statute was amended in 1963 in recognition of the growing trend toward protecting minority shareholders from abuses by those in the majority. Section §33-14-300(2)(ii) now permits a court to order dissolution if it is established by a shareholder that "the directors or those in control of the corporation have acted, are acting, or will act in a manner that is illegal, fraudulent, oppressive, or unfairly prejudicial either to the corporation or to any shareholder (whether in his capacity as a shareholder, director, or officer of the corporation)."[17] The official comment to section 33-14-300 provides:

16. Section 33-14-300(2)(ii) permits a court to order dissolution if it is established by a shareholder that "the directors or those in control of the corporation have acted, are acting, or will act in a manner that is illegal, fraudulent, oppressive, or unfairly prejudicial either to the corporation or to any shareholder (whether in his capacity as a shareholder, director, or officer of the corporation)."

17. Prior to 1963, dissolution could be based only upon illegal, fraudulent or oppressive conduct. In an attempt to afford minority shareholders greater protection, the legislature amended the statute in 1963 to include "unfairly prejudicial" conduct. *See* 1963 S.C. Acts 282 §89; S.C. Code §12-22.15(a)(4) (1970). The statute, as amended, "broadens the scope of actionable conduct by providing the frozen-out minority shareholder a right of action based on conduct by the majority shareholders which might not rise to the level of fraud." Joshua

> The application of these grounds for dissolution to specific circumstances obviously involves judicial discretion in the application of a general standard to concrete circumstances. The court should be cautious in the application of these grounds so as to limit them to genuine abuse rather than instances of acceptable tactics in a power struggle for control of a corporation.

Section 33-14-300 cmt. 2(b).

Although the terms "oppressive" and "unfairly prejudicial" are not defined in section 33-14-300, the comment to S.C. Code Ann. §33-18-400 (1990), which allows shareholders in a statutory close corporation to petition for relief on the grounds of oppressive, fraudulent, or unfairly prejudicial conduct provides:

> No attempt has been made to define oppression, fraud, or unfairly prejudicial conduct. These are elastic terms whose meaning varies with the circumstances presented in a particular case, and it is felt that existing case law provides sufficient guidelines for courts and litigants.[18]

Given the Legislature's deliberate exclusion of a set definition of oppressive and unfairly prejudicial conduct, we find the Court of Appeals' enunciation of rigid tests is contrary to the legislative intent.

Under the Court of Appeals' holding, a finding of fraudulent/oppressive conduct may be based upon any **one** of its alternative definitions. We do not believe the Legislature intended such a result. In particular, we do not believe the Legislature intended a court to judicially order a corporate dissolution **solely** upon the basis that a party's "reasonable expectations" have been frustrated by majority shareholders. To examine the "reasonable expectations" of minority shareholders would require the courts of this state to microscopically examine the dealings of closely held family corporations, the intentions of majority and minority stockholders in forming the corporation and thereafter, the history of family dealings, and the like. We do not believe the Legislature, in enacting section 33-14-300, intended such judicial interference in the business philosophies and day to day operating practices of family businesses.

Henderson, *Buyout Remedy for Oppressed Minority Shareholders*, 47 S.C. L. Rev. 195, 199 (Autumn 1995). . . . This trend arose due to the nationwide epidemic of unfair treatment of minority shareholders. *See* Harry J. Haynsworth, *The Effectiveness of Involuntary Dissolution Suits as a Remedy for Close Corporation Dissension*, 35 Clev. St. L. Rev. 25 (1986-87); F.H. O'Neal, *Oppression of Minority Stockholders: Protecting Minority Rights*, 35 Clev. St. L. Rev. 121 (1986-87). In the latter article, Prof. O'Neal observed:

> Unfair treatment of holders of minority interests in family companies and other closely held corporations by persons in control of those corporations is so widespread that it is a national business scandal.
> The amount of litigation growing out of minority shareholder oppression—actual, fancied or fabricated — has grown tremendously in recent years, and the flood of litigation shows no sign of abating.

Id. at 121, 403 S.E.2d 666.

18. The courts of this state have only peripherally addressed the meaning of "oppressive" or "unfairly prejudicial" conduct. In one of the earliest cases, *Towles v. S.C. Produce Assoc.*, 197 S.E. 305 (S.C. 1908), the Court found the failure to pay dividends for three years did not warrant dissolution under the statute since the lack of dividends had been in an attempt to rehabilitate a weak financial corporation. The *Towles* court noted, however, "this statute was intended to afford minority stockholders a method of relief against mismanagement of a corporation by majority stockholders, or the suspension of dividends for the purpose of freezing out minority stockholders, or depressing the market value of the stock of the corporation. . . ." 197 S.E. at 307. In *Segall v. Shore*, 236 S.E.2d 316 (S.C. 1977), the defendants had misappropriated over $1,000,000 of corporate profits in spite of an earlier opinion of this Court directing them to restore profits and account. The master found, and this Court upheld, that the defendants had acted oppressively and unfairly. In *Roper v. Dynamique Concepts, Inc.*, 447 S.E.2d 218 (S.C. App. 1994), the Court of Appeals held the issuance of additional shares of stock as a last ditch effort to raise capital for a financially troubled corporation was sufficient to overcome a claim of oppression, since the shares had been issued in good faith.

In adopting the "reasonable expectations" approach, the Court of Appeals cited the North Carolina case of *Meiselman v. Meiselman,* 307 S.E.2d 551 (N.C. 1983).[19] In *Meiselman,* a minority shareholder in a family-owned close corporation was "frozen out" of the family corporation in much the same fashion as John and Louise claim they have been frozen out of Atlas. The minority shareholder brought an action requesting a buyout of his interests under N.C.G.S. §55-125.1(a)(4), which permits a North Carolina court to liquidate assets when it is "**reasonably necessary for the protection of the rights or interests of the complaining shareholders.**" (Emphasis supplied.)

In holding the minority shareholder was entitled to relief, the *Meiselman* court noted that the trial court had focused on the conduct of the majority shareholder, using standards of "oppression," "overreaching," "unfair advantage," and the like. 307 S.E.2d at 567. The Court found this was error because the North Carolina statute in question required the trial court to focus on the plaintiff's "rights and interests" his "reasonable expectations" in the corporate defendants, and determine whether those rights or interests were in need of protection. *Id.*[20] The focus in *Meiselman,* based upon the language of the North Carolina statute, was upon the **interests** of the minority shareholder, as opposed to the **conduct** of the majority.

Unlike the North Carolina statute in *Meiselman,* section 33-14-300 does not place the focus upon the "rights or interests" of the complaining shareholder but, rather, specifically places the focus upon the **actions** of the majority, i.e., whether they "have acted, are acting, or will act in a manner that is illegal, fraudulent, oppressive, or unfairly prejudicial either to the corporation or to any shareholder." Given the language of our statute, a "reasonable expectations" approach is simply inconsistent with our statute.

We recognize that a number of leading authorities, such as Dean Haynsworth, advocate a "reasonable expectations" approach to oppressive conduct:

> The third definition of oppression, initially derived from English case law and long advocated by close corporation experts like Dean F. Hodge O'Neal, is **conduct which frustrates the reasonable expectations of the investors**. . . . It has gained widespread acceptance in recent years, particularly in cases involving close corporations where all the shareholders expect to be employed by the corporation and to be actively involved in its management and one of the shareholders is fired and then "frozen out" from any compensation or participation in management.

Harry J. Haynsworth, *Special Problems of Closely Held Corporations,* C688 ALI-ABA 1, 53 (1991) (emphasis supplied; internal citations omitted).

Although several jurisdictions have adopted "reasonable expectations" as a guide to the meaning of "oppression," it has been noted by one commentator that "no court has adopted the reasonable expectations test without the assistance of a statute." Ralph A. Peeples, *The Use and Misuse of the Business Judgment Rule in the*

---

19. *Meiselman* has been referred to as a "leading case" in adoption of this approach. See Dean F. Hodge O'Neal, *O'Neal's Close Corporations,* §9.30 at 144 (3d ed. 1991) (hereinafter O'Neal); . . . .

20. As in North Carolina, California also places the emphasis on the interests of the minority, as opposed to the actions of the majority. *See* Cal. Corp. Code §1800 (*cited* in O'Neal, *supra,* §9.29 at 131, n.8). *See also Matter of Kemp & Beatley, Inc.,* 473 N.E.2d 1173 (N.Y. 1984) (interpreting McKinney's Business Corporation Law §1104-a which allows court to liquidate assets if a) it is the only feasible means whereby the petitioners may reasonably expect to obtain a fair return on their investment or b) it is reasonably necessary to protect rights and interests of shareholders).

Close Corporation, 60 Notre Dame L. Rev. 456, 505 (1985).[22] One criticism of the "reasonable expectations" approach is that it "ignores the expectations of the parties other than the dissatisfied shareholder." *See Lerner v. Lerner Corp.,* 750 A.2d 709, 722 (Md. 2000). . . . One recent commentator has suggested that a pure "reasonable expectations" approach overprotects the minority's interests. Douglas K. Moll, *Shareholder Oppression in Close Corporations: The Unanswered Question of Perspective,* 53 Vand. L. Rev. 749, 826 (April 2000) (hereinafter Moll). Similarly, it has been suggested that the reasonable expectations approach is "based on false premises, invites fraud, and is an unnecessary invasion of the rights of the majority." J.C. Bruno, *Reasonable Expectations: A Primer on an Oppressive Standard,* 71 Mich. B.J. 434 (May 1992). *See also* Sandra K. Miller, *How Should U.K. and U.S. Minority Shareholder Remedies for Unfairly Prejudicial or Oppressive Conduct Be Reformed?,* 36 Am. Bus. L.J. 579, 632 (Summer 1999) (suggesting the "vague and uncertain reasonable expectation test undermines the institution of stare decisis and fails to foster judicial accountability").

We find adoption of the "reasonable expectations" standard is inconsistent with section 33-14-300, which places an emphasis not upon the minority's expectations but, rather, on the actions of the majority. We decline to adopt such an expansive approach to oppressive conduct in the absence of a legislative mandate. We find, consistent with the Legislature's comment to section 33-18-400, that the terms "oppressive" and "unfairly prejudicial" are elastic terms whose meaning varies with the circumstances presented in a particular case. As noted by one commentator:

> While business corporation statutes may attempt to provide certainty and clarity in the law to enhance the attractiveness of doing business, the definition of oppression has been left to judicial construction on a case-by-case basis. Such an approach has been suggested by the Model Close Corporation Supplement which expressly indicates that no attempt has been made to statutorily define oppression, fraud or prejudicial conduct, leaving these "elastic terms" to judicial interpretation. . . . The judicial construction of the definition of oppressive conduct is well-suited to the diversified, fact-specific disputes among shareholders of closely held corporations. However, the judicial development of a meaningful standard for defining oppressive conduct, apart from fraud or mismanagement, is a difficult task.

Sandra K. Miller, *Should the Definition of Oppressive Conduct by the Majority Shareholders Exclude a Consideration of Ethical Conduct and Business Purpose,* 97 Dick. L. Rev. 227, 229-230 (Winter 1993).

We find a case-by-case analysis, supplemented by various factors which may be indicative of oppressive behavior, to be the proper inquiry under S.C. Code §33-14-300.[25] Accordingly, the Court of Appeals' opinion is modified to the extent it adopted a "reasonable expectations" approach.

---

22. Peeples notes, "[t]he most unique feature of the reasonable expectations analysis is the lack of a bad faith requirement. At most, the plaintiff is required to show that he or she was not at fault, not that the defendant acted in bad faith." 60 Notre Dame L. Rev. at 504.

25. We agree with Professor Miller's suggestion that the best approach to the statutory definition of oppressive conduct may well be a case-by-case analysis, augmented by factors or typical patterns of majority conduct which tend to be indicative of oppression, such as exclusion from management, withholding of dividends, paying excessive salaries to majority shareholders, and analogous activities. Sandra K. Miller, *How Should U.K. and U.S. Minority Shareholder Remedies for Unfairly Prejudicial or Oppressive Conduct Be Reformed?,* 36 Am. Bus. L.J. 579, 585-586 (Summer 1999). In this regard, we note that we do not hold that a court may never consider the parties' reasonable expectations, or the other items enumerated by the Court of Appeals, as **factors** in assessing oppressive conduct; such factors, however, are not to be utilized as the sole test of oppression under South Carolina law.

b. Oppression under Circumstances of this Case

The question remains whether the conduct of Atlas toward John and Louise was "oppressive" and "unfairly prejudicial" under the factual circumstances presented. We find this case presents a classic example of a majority "freeze-out," and that the referee properly found Atlas had engaged in conduct which was fraudulent, oppressive and unfairly prejudicial.

The particular problems encountered by those in the close corporation setting was noted in *Meiselman,* 307 S.E.2d at 559 (citing J.A.C. Hetherington, *Special Characteristics, Problems, and Needs of the Close Corporation,* 1969 U. Ill. L. F. 1, 21):

> The right of the majority to control the enterprise achieves a meaning and has an impact in close corporations that it has in no other major form of business organization under our law. Only in the close corporation does the power to manage carry with it the de facto power to allocate the benefits of ownership arbitrarily among the shareholders and to discriminate against a minority whose investment is imprisoned in the enterprise. The essential basis of this power in the close corporation is the inability of those so excluded from the benefits of proprietorship to withdraw their investment at will.

This unequal balance of power often leads to a "squeeze out" or "freeze out"[26] of the minority by the majority shareholders. *See* F. Hodge O'Neal, *Oppression of Minority Shareholders: Protecting Minority Rights,* 35 Clev. St. L. Rev. 121, 125 (1986/1987); Anthony and Borass, *Betrayed, Belittled . . . But Triumphant: Claims of Shareholders in Closely Held Corporations,* 22 Wm. Mitchell L. Rev. 1173, 1175 (1996). In the close corporation, a shareholder

> [F]aces a potential danger the shareholder of a public corporation generally avoids — the possibility of harm to the fair value of the shareholder's investment. At its extreme, this harm manifests itself as the classic freeze out where the minority shareholder faces a trapped investment and an indefinite exclusion from participation in business returns. The position of the close corporation shareholder, therefore, is uniquely precarious.

Moll, 53 Vand. L. Rev. at 790-91.

Common freeze out techniques include the termination of a minority shareholder's employment, the refusal to declare dividends,[27] the removal of a minority shareholder from a position of management, and the siphoning off of corporate earnings through high compensation to the majority shareholder. Often, these tactics are used in combination.[28] Moll, 53 Vand. L. Rev. at 757-758. In a public

---

26. "Freeze out" is often used as a synonym for "squeeze out." The term squeeze out means the use by some of the owners or participants in a business enterprise of strategic position, inside information, or powers of control, or the utilization of some legal device or technique, to eliminate from the enterprise one or more of its owners or participants. 2 F. Hodge O'Neal & Robert B. Thompson, *O'Neal's Oppression of Minority Shareholders,* §1.01 at 1 (2d ed. 1999).

27. Majority freeze out schemes which withhold dividends "are designed to compel the minority to relinquish stock at inadequate prices. When the minority stockholder agrees to sell out at less than fair value, the majority has won." *Donahue v. Rodd Electrotype Co.,* 328 N.E.2d 505, 515 (Mass. 1975) (internal citations omitted). *See also* Robert B. Thompson, *The Shareholder's Cause of Action for Oppression,* 48 Bus. Law, 699, 703-4 (1993) (noting that in a classic "freeze out," the majority first denies the minority any return and then proposes to buy the shares at a very low price).

28. A host of factors is identified in 1 F. Hodge O'Neal and Robert B. Thompson, *O'Neal's Oppression of Minority Shareholders,* Chap. 3 (2d ed. 1999), including, but not limited to, dividend withholding, eliminating minority shareholders from directorate and excluding them from employment, siphoning off corporate earnings via high compensation, leases and loans favorable to majority shareholders, failure to enforce contracts for the benefit of the corporation, appropriation of corporate assets, contracts or credit for personal use, usurping corporate opportunities, transactions between a parent corporation and a subsidiary, withholding information from minority shareholders.

corporation, the minority shareholder can escape such abuses by selling his shares; there is no such market, however, for the stock of a close corporation. *Id.*[29] "The primary vulnerability of a minority shareholder is the specter of being 'locked in,' that is, having a perpetual investment in an entity without any expectation of ever receiving a return on that investment." Charles Murdock, *The Evolution of Effective Remedies for Minority Shareholders and Its Impact upon Valuation of Minority Shares*, 65 Notre Dame L. Rev. 425, 477 (1990).

The present case presents a classic situation of minority "freeze out." The referee considered the following factors: 1) Alex' unilateral action to deprive Louise of the benefits of ownership in her shares in Atlas, and subsequent reduction in her distributions based upon the reduced number of shares,[30] 2) Alex' conduct in depriving John and Louise of the 21% interest of [a related company's] stock, 3) the fact that there is no prospect of John and Louise receiving any financial benefit from their ownership of Atlas shares,[31] 4) the fact that Alex and his family continue to receive substantial benefit from their ownership in Atlas, 5) the fact that Atlas has substantial cash and liquid assets, very little debt and that, notwithstanding its ability to declare dividends, it has indicated it would not do so in the foreseeable future, 6) the fact that Alex, majority shareholder in total control of Atlas, is totally estranged from John and Louise, 7) Atlas' extremely low buyout offers to John and Louise, and 8) the fact that Atlas is not appropriate for a public stock offering at the present time.

These factors, when coupled with the referee's findings of fraud, present a textbook example of a "freeze out" situation. We find the referee properly concluded the totality of the circumstances demonstrated that the majority had acted "oppressively" and "unfairly prejudicially" to John and Louise.

CONCLUSION

Under South Carolina's judicial dissolution statute, the Court of Appeals erred in attempting to define oppressive and unfairly prejudicial conduct. Further, we reject the "reasonable expectations" approach adopted by the Court of Appeals. Under section 33-14-300, the proper focus is not on the reasonable expectations of the minority but, rather, on the conduct of the majority. Such an inquiry is to be performed on a case-by-case basis, with an inquiry of all the circumstances and an examination of the many factors hereinabove recited. We believe such an inquiry is in keeping with the Legislature's intention in enacting sections 33-14-300 and 33-14-310.

Under the factual circumstances presented here, we find the majority's conduct clearly constitutes oppressive and unfairly prejudicial conduct. . . .

---

29. Effectively, the minority shareholder's capital investment is "held hostage by those in control of the corporation because there is no marketplace in which the minority may sell their shares." Sandra L. Schlafge, *Comment, Pedro v. Pedro: Consequences for Closely Held Corporations and the At-Will Doctrine in Minnesota*, 76 Minn. L. Rev. 1071, 1076 (1992).

30. As detailed more fully in the Court of Appeals' opinion, Atlas made a 1990 distribution to Louise based upon her ownership of 271 shares of Atlas stock when the referee found Louise, in fact, owns 301 shares of stock.

31. The referee considered a number of factors in determining they would receive no financial benefit including salary, retirement benefits, John's lack of status as President, the fact that John would no longer receive loans from the company since he lost his employment, the loss of fringe benefits, the fact that John and Louise were paying their own attorney's fees, and the fact that a sale of Atlas was not contemplated. The referee then weighed these factors against the benefits still received by Alex and his family.

Notes and Questions

1. Notes

a. The South Carolina statute at issue in this case is similar to MBCA §14.30(a)(2)(ii).

2. Reality Check

a. On what grounds did the statutory provision permit relief?

b. How did the Supreme Court disagree with the Court of Appeals?

c. What definition of "oppression" does the Supreme Court use? Why does it select that definition? How many definitions have we seen now?

3. Suppose

a. If the South Carolina legislature had enacted language similar to that adopted by North Carolina, would the court's analysis have been the same?

b. If the South Carolina statute had been silent as to relief for oppression would the court have granted relief in this case? If so, on what theory?

c. Why was this litigation necessary? Isn't the result in this case simply the court's best judgment on an appellate record that must be very attenuated? Isn't the court just guessing who's been naughty and who's been nice?

4. What Do You Think?

a. I ask you again, should legislatures provide a claim for relief for oppression?

b. Which approach to protecting minority shareholders — that which focuses on the plaintiffs or that which focuses on the defendants — is more efficacious?

5. You Draft It

a. Draft a statute that permits relief for shareholder oppression. The following are representative statutes:

MBCA §14.30(a)(2)

§14.30. Grounds for Judicial Dissolution.
(a) The [name or describe court or courts] may dissolve a corporation:
    (2) in a proceeding by a shareholder if it is established that:
        (ii) the directors or those in control of the corporation have acted, are acting, or will act in a manner that is illegal, oppressive, or fraudulent.

SOUTH CAROLINA, S.C. CODE ANN. §33-14-300

The circuit courts may dissolve a corporation:
    (2) in a proceeding by a shareholder if it is established that:
        (ii) the directors or those in control of the corporation have acted, are acting, or will act in a manner that is illegal, fraudulent, oppressive, or unfairly prejudicial either to the corporation or to any shareholder (whether in his capacity as a shareholder, director, or officer of the corporation).

NORTH CAROLINA, NGCS §55-14-30

The superior court may dissolve a corporation:

(2) In a proceeding by a shareholder if it is established that . . . (ii) liquidation is reasonably necessary for the protection of the rights or interests of the complaining shareholder.

CALIFORNIA, CAL. CORP. CODE §1800

(b) The grounds for involuntary dissolution are that:

(4) Those in control of the corporation have been guilty of or have knowingly countenanced persistent and pervasive fraud, mismanagement or abuse of authority or persistent unfairness toward any shareholders or its property is being misapplied or wasted by its directors or officers.

NEW YORK, BUS. CORP. LAW §1104-a

(a) The holders of shares representing twenty percent or more of the votes of all outstanding shares of a corporation, . . . entitled to vote in an election of directors may present a petition of dissolution on one or more of the following grounds:

(1) The directors or those in control of the corporation have been guilty of illegal, fraudulent or oppressive actions toward the complaining shareholders;

(b) The court, in determining whether to proceed with involuntary dissolution pursuant to this section, shall take into account:

(1) Whether liquidation of the corporation is the only feasible means whereby the petitioners may reasonably expect to obtain a fair return on their investment; and

(2) Whether liquidation of the corporation is reasonably necessary for the protection of the rights and interests of any substantial number of shareholders or of the petitioners.

The Delaware courts have taken a dim view of minority shareholder oppression as a separate claim for relief. As you remember, Delaware also does not recognize an expansive fiduciary duty owed to minority shareholders. The Delaware Supreme Court spoke to the question of whether Delaware will create rules for the special protection of minority shareholders in close corporations:

> We wish to address one further matter which was raised at oral argument before this Court: Whether there should be any special, judicially-created rules to "protect" minority stockholders of closely-held Delaware corporations.[18]
>
> The case at bar points up the basic dilemma of minority stockholders in receiving fair value for their stock as to which there is no market and no market valuation. It is not difficult to be sympathetic, in the abstract, to a stockholder who finds himself or herself in that position. A stockholder who bargains for stock in a closely-held corporation and who pays for those shares . . . can make a business judgment whether to buy into such a minority position, and if so on what terms. One could bargain for definitive provisions of self-ordering permitted to a Delaware corporation through the certificate of incorporation or by-laws by reason of the provisions in [DGCL] §§102, 109, and 141(a). Moreover, in addition to such mechanisms,

---

18. *Compare* Robert B. Thompson, *The Shareholder's Cause of Action for Oppression*, 48 Bus. Law. 699 (1993) *and* F. Hodge *O'Neal and Robert B. Thompson, O'Neal's Close Corporations: Law and Practice*, §§8.07-8.09 (3d ed. 1987) (favoring court formulation of a special rule protecting the minority from oppression) *with* Frank H. Easterbrook and Daniel R. Fischel, *The Economic Structure of Corporate Law* 228-52 (1991) (noting that "courts have found the equal opportunity rule . . . impossible to administer," *id*. at 247).

a stockholder intending to buy into a minority position in a Delaware corporation may enter into definitive stockholder agreements, and such agreements may provide for elaborate earnings tests, buy-out provisions, voting trusts, or other voting agreements. *See, e.g.,* [DGCL] §218. . . .

The tools of good corporate practice are designed to give a purchasing minority stockholder the opportunity to bargain for protection before parting with consideration. It would do violence to normal corporate practice and our corporation law to fashion an ad hoc ruling which would result in a court-imposed stockholder buy-out for which the parties had not contracted.

In 1967, when the Delaware General Corporation Law was significantly revised, a new Subchapter XIV entitled "Close Corporations; Special Provisions," became a part of that law for the first time. While these provisions were patterned in theory after close corporation statutes in Florida and Maryland, "the Delaware provisions were unique and influenced the development of similar legislation in a number of other states. . . ." *See* Ernest L. Folk, III, Rodman Ward, Jr., and Edward P. Welch, 2 *Folk on the Delaware General Corporation Law* 404 (1988). Subchapter XIV is a narrowly constructed statute which applies only to a corporation which is designated as a "close corporation" in its certificate of incorporation, and which fulfills other requirements, including a limitation to 30 on the number of stockholders, that all classes of stock have to have at least one restriction on transfer, and that there be no "public offering." [DGCL] §342. Accordingly, subchapter XIV applies only to "close corporations," as defined in section 342. "Unless a corporation elects to become a close corporation under this subchapter in the manner prescribed in this subchapter, it shall be subject in all respects to this chapter, except this subchapter." [DGCL] §341. The corporation before the Court in this matter, is not a "close corporation." Therefore it is not governed by the provisions of Subchapter XIV.[19]

One cannot read into the situation presented in the case at bar any special relief for the minority stockholders in this closely-held, but not statutory "close corporation" because the provisions of Subchapter XIV relating to close corporations and other statutory schemes preempt the field in their respective areas. It would run counter to the spirit of the doctrine of independent legal significance, and would be inappropriate judicial legislation[22] for this Court to fashion a special judicially-created rule for minority investors when the entity does not fall within those statutes, or when there are no negotiated special provisions in the certificate of incorporation, by-laws, or stockholder agreements. The entire fairness test, correctly applied and articulated, is the proper judicial approach.

Nixon v. Blackwell, 626 A.2d 1366 (Del. 1993) (Veasey, C.J.).

19. [S]tatutory close corporations have not found particular favor with practitioners. Practitioners have for the most part viewed the complex statutory provisions underlying the purportedly simplified operational procedures for close corporations as legal quicksand of uncertain depth and have adopted the view that the objectives sought by the subchapter are achievable for their clients with considerably less uncertainty by cloaking a conventionally created corporation with the panoply of charter provisions, transfer restrictions, by-laws, stockholders' agreements, buy-sell arrangements, irrevocable proxies, voting trusts or other contractual mechanisms which were and remain the traditional method for accomplishing the goals sought by the close corporation provisions.

David A. Drexler, Lewis S. Black, Jr., and A. Gilchrist Sparks, III, *Delaware Corporation Law and Practice* §43.01 (1993).

We do not intend to imply that, if the Corporation had been a close corporation under Subchapter XIV, the result in this case would have been different.

22. *Providence & Worcester Co. v. Baker*, 378 A.2d at 124.

c. ... to More Remedies

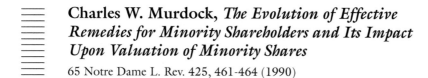

Charles W. Murdock, *The Evolution of Effective*
Remedies for Minority Shareholders and Its Impact
Upon Valuation of Minority Shares
65 Notre Dame L. Rev. 425, 461-464 (1990)

The concept of alternative remedies to dissolution is not new. In 1941, California broadened its grounds for involuntary dissolution by adding a provision that would permit liquidation when it was "reasonably necessary for the protection of the rights or interests of any substantial number of the shareholders, or of the complaining shareholders."[243] The legislature also enacted, in 1941, a provision providing for a buy-out of the complaining shareholder by the majority if the majority so elected. If the parties could not agree on price, the court would determine the fair cash value of the shares.

However, even though the courts were decrying dissolution as a drastic remedy, there was no rush by legislatures to provide alternative remedies, at least in the form of a buy-out option, until the 1970s. At least seven states enacted buy-out provisions in the 1970s and at least three additional states enacted such provisions in the 1980s. The statutory schemes range from simple to detailed and from a focus solely upon buy-outs to a multi-remedy approach. [See MBCA §14.34.]

Complementing these statutes are decisions in several jurisdictions in which the courts have recognized that the general equitable powers of a court suffice to order a remedy other than dissolution when the grounds for dissolution exist.

The focus of alternative relief typically has been upon buy-outs of minority shareholders. Accordingly, it cannot be gainsaid that minority shareholder buy-outs are firmly established throughout the states as alternative relief to dissolution when such shareholders have been subject to oppressive actions by those in control. The availability of alternative remedies, in turn, has had a substantial impact on the recognition of reasonable expectations as the basis for determining whether oppressive conduct exists.

The MBCA, in §14.34, provides that a defendant in an action for dissolution may irrevocably elect to purchase the plaintiff's shares for "fair value." The DGCL does not grant the Court of Chancery specific powers in this regard but, because the Court of Chancery has the full panoply of a traditional court of equity, the court could, conceivably, impose a wide range of remedies, including a forced or optional buy-out.

The courts of some states take great pride in listing the miscellaneous equitable powers they have found to remedy oppression. The following list is typical, I'm afraid.

---

243. 1941 Cal. Stat. 2057-58 (codified as amended at Cal. Corp. Code §1800(b)(5) (West 1977)).

We [identified] ten recognized alternatives to outright corporate dissolution when oppressive conduct has been proven:

> "(a) The entry of an order requiring dissolution of the corporation at a specified future date, to become effective only in the event that the stockholders fail to resolve their differences prior to that date.
>
> "(b) The appointment of a receiver, not for the purposes of dissolution, but to continue the operation of the corporation for the benefit of all of the stockholders, both majority and minority, until differences are resolved or 'oppressive' conduct ceases.
>
> "(c) The appointment of a 'special fiscal agent' to report to the court relating to the continued operation of the corporation, as a protection to its minority stockholders, and the retention of jurisdiction of the case by the court for that purpose.
>
> "(d) The retention of jurisdiction of the case by the court for the protection of the minority stockholders without appointment of a receiver or 'special fiscal agent.'
>
> "(e) The ordering of an accounting by the majority in control of the corporation for funds alleged to have been misappropriated.
>
> "(f) The issuance of an injunction to prohibit continuing acts of 'oppressive' conduct and which may include the reduction of salaries or bonus payments found to be unjustified or excessive.
>
> "(g) The ordering of affirmative relief by the required declaration of a dividend or a reduction and distribution of capital.
>
> "(h) The ordering of affirmative relief by the entry of an order requiring the corporation or a majority of its stockholders to purchase the stock of the minority stockholders at a price to be determined according to a specified formula or at a price determined by the court to be a fair and reasonable price.
>
> "(i) The ordering of affirmative relief by the entry of an order permitting minority stockholders to purchase additional stock under conditions specified by the court.
>
> "(j) An award of damages to minority stockholders as compensation for any injury suffered by them as the result of 'oppressive' conduct by the majority in control of the corporation."

Masinter [*v. WEBCO Co.*, 262 S.E.2d 433 (W. Va. 1980)], at 441-42, n. 12 (quoting *Baker v. Commercial Body Builders, Inc.*, 507 P.2d 387, 395-96 (Or. 1973) and citations omitted).

State ex rel. Smith v. Evans, 547 S.E.2d 278, 283-84 (W. Va. 2001)

Putting It to Work

Problem 15-3

The Garden of Olives, Inc. is a corporation that owns a nationwide chain of fast-casual restaurants. The business was founded over 50 years ago by Mary Kate and Ashley Olive and all the stock has remained in the family. Mary Kate was the original driving force behind the corporation and she owned 55 percent of the stock. Ashley was involved full time in the founding and operating of the business, but she never had the grand vision that her sister did and so was never as central to the corporation as Mary Kate. The stock is now owned by the third generation of Olive family members. Fifty-five percent of the stock is owned by Mary Kate's descendants and 45 percent by Ashley's descendants. As frequently happens, the two branches of the family do not get along. For the past three generations, the unwritten rule was that every Olive family member who desired to do so could work full time for the corporation in some capacity at a fair market wage for the job he or she was performing.

Within the last year, the restaurants' popularity has nosedived and the corporation is in significant financial difficulty. The corporation's board of directors, which consists of a majority of Mary Kate's descendants, has recently resolved to declare no further dividends because of the financial exigency. Although the Olive family members who work for the corporation are happy to be paid a fair wage, the corporation has been so successful that each family member's annual dividends greatly exceed his or her wage. Clearly the bulk of the economic benefit from owning stock in Garden of Olives, Inc. comes from the dividends rather than the wages.

Further, Justin, the board chair and CEO of the corporation (he is, of course, a descendant of Mary Kate) has terminated from employment every descendant of Ashley. His rationale is that the corporation is in financial difficulty, but in reality the corporation is very large, the number of Ashley descendants who work for the corporation is relatively small, and each earns no more than the fair market wage for his or her job. The money saved by eliminating every Ashley descendant's job is minimal compared to the corporation's overall financial state.

a. Is either the new dividend policy or the termination of the Ashley descendants "oppressive"?

Problem 15-4

Thanks to cumulative voting and the defection of a couple of small Mary Kate descendant shareholders, Ashley's descendants are able to elect half the board. It is clear that virtually every business decision requiring a board vote will be deadlocked. Further, the division of voting power seems likely to be evenly split for the foreseeable future. You have been retained by a small shareholder from the Ashley branch who wants to know what remedies are available either to end the deadlock or to punish the Mary Kate branch.

a. What advice can you give your client?

C. TERMS OF ART IN THIS CHAPTER

Cumulative voting	Preemptive right	Straight voting
Deadlock	Reasonable expectations	Supermajority
Oppression	test	Superquorum
Pooling agreements	Statutory voting	Voting trusts

Change of Control

In this chapter we take up a central dynamic in corporate life: the transfer of control. This aspect is cognate, in many ways, to our discussion of dividends and our discussion of restrictions on stock transfers in Chapter 7. You might remember that a business owner has two ways to realize the increase in the business's fortunes: (1) by taking a portion of the cash that passes through the business, whether denominated salary, profits, interest, or dividends; and (2) by selling some or all of the ownership interest. Here, the concern is with transfers that constitute a shift of a controlling interest. That interest usually, but not always, constitutes the entire ownership interest of the transferor.

We will consider several aspects of this topic. First, we will take a step back and ask why anyone would want to transfer or acquire control. The various motivations will drive your clients' business decisions so you should pay some attention to them. You might also want to re-read Chapter 3 on how economic decisions are made. Second, we will work through the mechanics of transferring control. Third, and relatedly, we will see factors that influence your clients' choice of the appropriate acquisition technique. Fourth, we will explore the process of acquiring control from beginning to end. That is, we will focus on the temporal aspects of negotiating, documenting, and effecting a change of control. Fifth will be a consideration of the corporate law issues that most often arise in change of control settings. This chapter bookends the corporate law topics with background and context sections. The first limns the history of mergers and acquisition activity in America. The second deals with hostile takeovers. Finally, we see the federal securities regulations applicable to changes of control.

A. BACKGROUND AND CONTEXT

As you saw in Chapter 2, one way businesses become large is by combining with others. The advantages are usually ones of vertical integration (i.e., combining with a supplier or a customer) or horizontal integration (i.e., combining with enterprises engaged in substantially the same business). Although changes in corporate control happen all the time, and for a variety of reasons, changes in control of large American corporations tend to occur in waves. The first such wave began in the late 1880s when large businesses typically desired to expand horizontally. They frequently saw such acquisitions as a way to eliminate competition and, thus, to move toward monopoly positions. The Sherman Antitrust Act of 1890 met with mixed success in preventing these combinations. The real impetus to end this wave of combinations, though, was a market crash in 1904. This made raising money more difficult and made the value of corporations, relative to one another, much more problematic.

The second period of intense combination among large corporations ran from the end of World War I until the market crash of 1929. This period saw more vertical combinations than horizontal ones, at least among consumer goods manufacturers and retailers. Banks and utility companies also combined in great numbers. In response to the crash, Congress passed the Glass-Steagall Act that effectively required banks that accepted money from the public ("commercial banks") to engage in less risky investments such as secured loans to businesses and mortgage loans to individuals. Banks that did not accept deposits from the public ("investment banks") were free to invest in more uncertain enterprises such as investing in stocks. These restrictions remained in place until 1999.

The Great Depression, which followed the 1929 crash, World War II, which followed on the heels of that depression, and the postwar recovery, effectively stifled large-scale corporate combinations. As the American economy expanded and its growth prospects seemed stable, companies again began to combine. Starting in the early 1960s, these "go-go years," as they are embarrassingly called, were largely informed by a powerful intellectual idea that had recently been rigorously developed. That idea was diversification. We saw in Chapter 3 that an investor who diversifies his or her wealth by owning a variety of unrelated assets has an expected return equal to the weighted average of the investments but at much less risk.

The economic elaboration of that theory took place in the 1950s and corporate leaders of the next decade put that theory into practice. Corporations could diversify as well as individual investors could. That is, a corporation could purchase control of other corporations in unrelated businesses. The corporation's (and hence its shareholders') expected return could increase if the acquired business had a higher expected return than the acquirer, but the overall risk was reduced. Hence, a vogue for *conglomeration* began. The hunt was on for corporations that were profitable and that could stand alone — that is, businesses that did not have to be integrated in operations or management with the acquiring business. At the top of these new conglomerates, senior managers monitored the corporation's various businesses and looked for new businesses to acquire. Each business operated separately, and its head was, in effect, the CEO. The passion for conglomeration was cooled by a combination of an economic recession in 1973 and the rise in popularity of mutual funds and pension funds. The recession dampened stock prices, which made conglomerate shares less useful to fund new acquisitions. With mutual funds, individual investors could diversify for themselves; they no longer needed to invest in a conglomerate. Pension funds performed similar diversification functions for investors who were also employees.

Within ten years of the 1973 recession, acquisition activity among large corporations returned with a vengeance. The 1980s were the quintessential years for corporate combinations in America. Again, much of the impetus was provided by economic theories. These theories had the effect of encouraging changes of control over the objection of the acquired company's management and board. These changes could be effected by a *hostile tender offer* in which the acquiring company offered shareholders of the target company a premium to the prevailing market price. Because the decision whether to accept the offer rested with each shareholder, the boards of target companies were unable to defeat a hostile tender offer directly. Nonetheless, directors of likely target companies did not take the advent of hostile tender offers lying down. We will see the corporate law responses to target directors' efforts to defeat tender offers. You might note that nearly all of modern corporate fiduciary duty law comes from the period between 1985 and 1995. The hostile tender offer era came to an end in 1990 when Michael Milken, who had been instrumental in assembling much of the capital with which hostile tender offers were financed, was indicted for violating the securities laws.

Between the mid-1990s and 2000, corporate combinations, at least in certain areas such as Internet technology and health care, were common. With the bursting of the dot-com bubble in early 2000, such activity was reduced considerably.

B. THE CURRENT SETTING

1. Motivations for Changing Control

Let's begin with the seller's motivation. Why would someone who owns a corporation transfer control? For many closely held small businesses, a major motivation is that the expected returns, including noneconomic returns, are no longer sufficiently large. This may be because the owners have become disenchanted with the noneconomic benefits of ownership or because the business's economic performance is insufficient. In effect, owning the entity that owns the business is no longer "worth it." If there is more than one owner, they may have a falling out that ultimately results in a sale of the business.

Another major motivation to transfer control is the age of the owners. The owners reach a point in their life cycles when they prefer to retire. A related motivation is where control rests in a family and the controlling family members wish to assure a smooth transition of control to the next generation.

Another motivation, especially for sophisticated owners, is that the underlying business has reached some size milestone such as sales, cash flow, or profits, that the owners established as the point at which they would transfer control. This may be because their own talents are particularly suited for building businesses rather than tending more mature businesses. It may also be that the owners have estimated the point at which the business's growth will slow, such that the expected annual increase in value will drop to a level the owners find unacceptable. Whatever the trigger, the owners established an *exit strategy* when they acquired ownership and that strategy now dictates that control change hands. Finally, control may change when the owners receive an offer they can't refuse. In economic terms, the owners have been offered a price at or above their *reservation price*, even if they hadn't planned on selling.

Why do acquirers want to acquire control of a particular corporation? One motivation is the flip side of senior family members wanting to pass control to the next generation. Those younger family members may have varying degrees of enthusiasm for acquiring control, but a desire to continue a family business is often a strong motivation.

A very common reason to acquire control of a corporation is that the acquirer already owns assets that connect in some way with the acquired corporation's assets. We talked a bit in Chapter 2 about economies of scale that can be achieved by vertical or horizontal integration. In other words, there may be operational benefits from controlling both sets of assets.

Although it is sometimes out of fashion, an acquirer may be motivated by a desire to diversify. That is, the acquirer already owns assets that are exposed to substantially different risks than the acquired corporation's assets. By combining both sets of assets under common control, the expected returns of each set should be relatively unaffected while the risk of owning both sets of assets is less than the risk of owning either asset separately.

Regardless of whether the acquirer's primary motivation is operational benefit or diversification, that motivation may be affected by the quality of the acquired corporation's management. Where the acquired corporation's management is strong, the acquirer's costs of operating the newly acquired assets may be lower than otherwise. On the other hand, where the acquired corporation's management is weak, the acquirer may find another financial benefit. The present management's skills may have depressed the value of the corporation's assets, thus leading to a lower sales price. Further, by replacing management, the acquirer can increase the acquired assets' economic value and, presumably, increase the price at which the acquirer could resell them later.

2. Techniques for Combining Entities

In all of the combination techniques that follow, we will talk about an exchange of something for consideration. In this context consideration takes one of three forms. First, of course, is money. Nuff sed. Second is stock of the acquiring entity. Third is debt of the acquiring entity. Sometimes these forms are combined and sometimes the acquired assets' owners have a choice between types of consideration. Note that if stock is the consideration, sufficient authorized but unissued shares must be available. The acquiring corporation may have to amend its articles to increase the number of authorized shares. This probably requires a shareholder vote. So careful planning for an acquisition suggests that you, as the acquiring corporation's lawyer, must ensure that sufficient authorized but unissued shares or treasury shares are available.

a. *Purchase of Assets*

Perhaps the most intuitive method of acquiring a business is simply to purchase its assets. This is, indeed, a common approach. The primary benefit is that the acquirer can purchase the assets without taking the liabilities. Remember, though, that the doctrine of successor liability might result in the liabilities of the selling entity (sometimes called the *target corporation*) following the assets even where the acquisition agreement specifically excludes liabilities. *See* Chapter 8.

As a matter of corporate law, acquiring assets simply requires the purchaser's board to adopt a resolution. The seller's board likewise can sell the assets via a board resolution *unless* the assets of a Delaware corporation to be sold are "all or substantially all" of the corporation's assets. In that case the DGCL requires that an absolute majority of the stockholders approve the transaction. *See* DGCL §271.

"All" is pretty easy, but what is "substantially all" and why is that standard included in §271?

Hollinger Inc. v. Hollinger International, Inc.

858 A.2d 342 (Del. Ch. 2004)

Strine, V.C.

Hollinger Inc. (or "Inc.") seeks a preliminary injunction preventing Hollinger International, Inc. (or "International") from selling the *Telegraph* Group Ltd. (England). . . . The key question addressed in this decision is whether Inc. and the other International stockholders must be provided with the opportunity to vote on the sale of the *Telegraph* Group because that sale involves "substantially all" the assets of International within the meaning of [DGCL] §271. The sale of the *Telegraph* followed a lengthy auction process whereby International and all of [its] operating assets were widely shopped to potential bidders. As a practical matter, Inc.'s vote would be the only one that matters because . . . it . . . controls 68% of the voting power. [Inc. cannot exercise control over International's management, however, because of an agreement reached to settle charges related to the misconduct of Inc.'s controlling shareholder.]

I. FACTUAL BACKGROUND

International regularly acquired and disposed of sizable publishing assets. [F]or example, International engaged in the following large transactions:

- The 1996 and 1997 sales of the company's Australian newspapers for more than $400 million.
- The 1998 acquisition of the *Post-Tribune* in Gary, Indiana, and the sale of approximately 80 community newspapers, for gross cash proceeds of approximately $310 million.
- The 1998 acquisitions of *The Financial Post* (now *The National Post*), the *Victoria Times Colonist,* and other Canadian newspapers for a total cost of more than $208 million.
- The 1999 sale of 78 community newspapers in the United States, for more than $500 million.
- The 2000 sale of other United States community newspapers for $215 million.

- The 2000 acquisition of newspapers in and around Chicago, for more than $230 million.
- The 2000 sale of the bulk of the company's Canadian newspaper holdings to CanWest for over $2 billion.

The last of the cited transactions is particularly notable for present purposes. As of the year 2000, the so-called "Canadian Newspaper Group"—most of its metropolitan and community newspapers were in Canada—accounted for over 50% of International's revenues and EBITDA.[6] The EBITDA measure is significant because it is a measure of free cash flow that is commonly used by investors in valuing newspaper companies.

International Operating Units After the CanWest Sale

The CanWest sale left International with the set of operating assets it now controls. These operating assets fall into four basic groups. . . . The Groups operate with great autonomy and there appear to be negligible, if any, synergies generated by their operation under common ownership.

THE JERUSALEM GROUP

The Jerusalem Group owns four newspapers that are all editions of the *Jerusalem Post,* which is the most widely read English-language newspaper published in the Middle East and is considered a high-quality, internationally well-regarded source of news about Israel. The Jerusalem Group makes only a very small contribution to International's revenues. In 2003, it had revenues . . . amounting to only around 1% of International's total revenues, and its EBITDA was nearly $3 million in the red.

THE CANADA GROUP

The Canada Group is the last of the Canadian publishing assets of International. It operates . . . 29 daily and community newspapers in British Columbia and Quebec . . . dozens of trade magazines, directories and websites . . . 17 community newspapers and shopping guides in Alberta. . . . The Canada Group is expected to generate over $80 million in revenues this year, a figure similar to last year.

THE CHICAGO GROUP

The Chicago Group is one of the two major operating asset groups that International controls. The Chicago Group owns more than 100 newspapers in the greater Chicago metropolitan area. Its most prominent newspaper is the *Chicago Sun-Times,* a daily tabloid newspaper that might be thought of as the "Second Newspaper in the Second City." That moniker would not be a slight, however, when viewed from a national or even international perspective.

Even though it ranks behind the *Chicago Tribune* in terms of overall circulation and readership, the *Sun-Times* has traditionally been and remains one of the top ten newspapers in the United States in terms of circulation and readership. Its sports coverage is considered to be excellent, its film critic Roger Ebert is nationally prominent, and its pages include the work of many well-regarded journalists. [T]he *Sun-Times* has generated very healthy EBITDA for International on a consistent basis during the recent past, producing $40 million in EBITDA in 2003, out of a total of nearly $80 million for the entire Chicago Group.

---

6. That is, earnings before interest, taxes, depreciation and amortization.

The Chicago Group also owns a valuable group of community newspapers that are published in the greater Chicago metropolitan area. These community papers have important economic value to the Chicago Group and to International. Their revenues and EBITDA, taken together, are roughly equal to that of the *Sun-Times*. In recent years, the Chicago Group as a whole has run neck-and-neck with the *Telegraph* Group in terms of generating EBITDA for International.

THE TELEGRAPH *GROUP*

The *Telegraph* Group includes the Internet site and various newspapers associated with the *Daily Telegraph,* including the *Sunday Telegraph,* as well as the magazines *The Spectator* and *Apollo.* The *Spectator* is the oldest continually published English-language magazine in the world and has an impressive reputation as a journal of opinion for the British intelligentsia, but it is not an economically significant asset. Rather, the *Telegraph* newspaper is the flagship of the *Telegraph* Group economically.

The *Telegraph* is a London-based newspaper but it is international in importance and readership, with a reputation of the kind that U.S. papers like the *New York Times,* the *Washington Post,* and the *Wall Street Journal* enjoy. It is a high-quality, broadsheet newspaper that is noted for its journalistic excellence, with a conservative, establishment-oriented bent. Its daily circulation of over 900,000 is the largest among English broadsheets but it trails the *London Sunday Times* in Sunday circulation by a sizable margin. Several London tabloids also outsell the *Telegraph* by very large margins. London may be the most competitive newspaper market in the world and that market continues to involve a vigorous struggle for market share that has existed since the early 1990s, when the *Times'* owner, Rupert Murdoch, initiated a price war. On balance, however, there is no question that the *Telegraph* Group is a profitable and valuable one. In the year 2003, it had over a half billion dollars in revenues and produced over $57 million in EBITDA.

II. LEGAL ANALYSIS

1. The Legal Standards to Measure Whether the *Telegraph* Group Comprises Substantially All of International's Assets

The origins of §271 did not rest primarily in a desire by the General Assembly to protect stockholders by affording them a vote on transactions previously not requiring their assent. Rather, §271's predecessors were enacted to address the common law rule that invalidated any attempt to sell all or substantially all of a corporation's assets without unanimous stockholder approval. According to leading commentators, the addition of the words "substantially all" was "intended merely to codify the interpretation generally accorded to the language of the pre-1967 statute that the word 'all' 'meant substantially all,' so that the statute could not be evaded by retaining a small amount of property not vital to the operation of the business."[44]

There are various metrics that can be used to determine how important particular assets are in the scheme of things. Should a court look to the percentage of the corporation's potential value as a sales target to measure the statute's application? Or measures of income-generating potential, such as contributions to

---

44. 1 R. Franklin Balotti & Jesse A. Finkelstein, *Delaware Law of Corporations & Business Organizations* §10.1, at 10-4 (3d ed. Supp. 2004) (quoting *Cottrell v. Pawcatuck Co.,* 128 A.2d 225 (Del. 1956)). . . .

revenues or operating income? To what extent should the flagship nature of certain assets be taken into account?

> The Supreme Court has long held that a determination of whether there is a sale of substantially all assets so as to trigger section 271 depends upon the particular qualitative and quantitative characteristics of the transaction at issue. Thus, the transaction must be viewed in terms of its overall effect on the corporation, and there is no necessary qualifying percentage.[51]

In other words,

> Our jurisprudence eschewed a definitional approach to §271 focusing on the interpretation of the words "substantially all," in favor of a contextual approach focusing upon whether a transaction involves the sale "of assets quantitatively vital to the operation of the corporation and is out of the ordinary and substantially affects the existence and purpose of the corporation." *Gimbel v. Signal Cos., Inc.,* 316 A.2d 599, 606 (Del. Ch. 1974), *aff'd,* 316 A.2d 619 (Del.). This interpretative choice necessarily involved a policy preference for doing equity in specific cases over the value of providing clear guidelines for transactional lawyers structuring transactions for the corporations they advise. *See* 1 David A. Drexler, et al., *Delaware Corporation Law And Practice* §37.03 (1999) ("[*Gimbel*] and its progeny represent a clear-cut rejection of the former conventional view that 'substantially all' in Section 271 meant only significantly more than one-half of the corporation's assets.").[52]

It would be less than candid to fail to acknowledge that the §271 case law provides less than ideal certainty about the application of the statute to particular circumstances. This may result from certain decisions that appear to deviate from the statutory language in a marked way and from others that have dilated perhaps longer than they should in evaluating asset sales that do not seem to come at all close to meeting the statutory trigger for a required stockholder vote. In the morass of particular percentages in the cases, however, remain the key principles articulated in *Gimbel,* which were firmly rooted in the statutory language of §271 and the statute's history. As has been noted, *Gimbel* set forth a quantitative and qualitative test designed to help determine whether a particular sale of assets involved substantially all the corporation's assets. That test has been adopted by our Supreme Court as a good metric for determining whether an asset sale triggers the vote requirement of §271.[55]

The test that *Gimbel* articulated — requiring a stockholder vote if the assets to be sold "are quantitatively vital to the operation of the corporation" and "substantially affect [] the existence and purpose of the corporation" — must therefore be read as an attempt to give practical life to the words "substantially all." It is for that reason that *Gimbel* emphasized that a vote would never be required for a transaction in the ordinary course of business and that the mere fact that an asset sale was out of the ordinary had little bearing on whether a vote was required.

2. Is the *Telegraph* Group Quantitatively Vital to the Operations of International?

The first question under the *Gimbel* test is whether the *Telegraph* Group is quantitatively vital to the operations of International. The short answer to that question is no, it is not quantitatively vital within the meaning of *Gimbel.*

---

51. *Winston v. Mandor,* 710 A.2d 835, 843 (Del. Ch. 1997) (footnotes omitted).
52. *In re General Motors Class H Shareholders Litig.,* 734 A.2d 611, 623 (Del. Ch. 1999).
55. *Oberly v. Kirby,* 592 A.2d 445, 464 (Del. 1991). . . .

Why?

Because it is clear that International will retain economic vitality even after a sale of the *Telegraph* because it is retaining other significant assets, one of which, the Chicago Group, has a strong record of past profitability and expectations of healthy profit growth.

Now, it is of course clear that the *Telegraph* Group is a major quantitative part of International's economic value and an important contributor to its profits. I am even prepared to decide this motion on the assumption that the *Telegraph* Group is the single most valuable asset that International possesses, even more valuable than the Chicago Group.

Let's consider the relative contribution to International's revenues of the *Telegraph* Group and the Chicago Group. When considering this and other factors the reader must bear in mind that the contribution of the Canada Group dropped steeply after the 2000 CanWest sale. Bearing that fact in mind, a look at the revenue picture at International since 2000 reveals the following:

	Revenue ($MM)							
Operating Unit	2000	%	2001	%	2002	%	Unaudited 2003	%
Telegraph Group	$562.1	26.8	486.4	42.4	481.5	47.9	519.5	49.0
Chicago Group	401.4	19.2	442.9	38.6	441.8	43.9	450.8	42.5
Canada Group	1,065.2	50.8	197.9	17.3	69.6	6.9	80.5	7.6
Jerusalem Group	67.3	3.2	19.1	1.7	13.2	1.3	10.4	1.0
Other	0.0	0.0	0.0	0.0	0.0	0.0	0.0	0.0
Total	2,096.0	100.0	1,146.3	100.0	1,006.2	100.0	1,061.2	100.0

Put simply, the *Telegraph* Group has accounted for less than half of International's revenues during the last three years and the Chicago Group's contribution has been in the same ballpark.

In book value terms, neither the *Telegraph* Group nor the Chicago Group approach 50% of International's asset value because the company's other operating groups and non-operating assets have value:

	Book Value of Assets ($MM)							
Operating Unit	2000	%	2001	%	2002	%	Unaudited 2003	%
Telegraph Group	$542.0	19.8	533.2	25.9	568.3	26.0	629.8	35.7
Chicago Group	613.7	22.4	595.9	29.0	557.9	25.5	537.9	30.5
Canada Group	551.6	20.2	448.7	21.8	214.0	9.8	262.0	14.9
Jerusalem Group	61.2	2.2	69.6	3.4	28.9	1.3	30.1	1.7
Other	968.8	35.4	410.5	19.9	819.1	37.4	302.8	17.2
Total	2,737.2	100.0	2,058.0	100.0	2,188.1	100.0	1,762.6	100.0

In terms of vitality, however, a more important measure is EBITDA contribution, as that factor focuses on the free cash flow that assets generate for the firm, a key component of economic value. As to that important factor, the Chicago Group is arguably more quantitatively nutritious to International than the *Telegraph* Group. Here is the picture considering all of International's operating groups:

EBITDA — All Operating Units ($MM)								
Operating Unit	2000	%	2001	%	2002	%	Unaudited 2003	%
Telegraph Group	$106.7	30.3	50.7	85.3	61.4	54.7	57.4	57.4
Chicago Group	59.8	17.0	47.6	80.1	72.1	64.2	79.5	79.4
Canada Group	190.5	54.1	(21.1)	(2.5)	(0.8)	(0.7)	(3.3)	(3.3)
Jerusalem Group	9.6	2.7	(1.5)	(2.5)	(2.8)	(2.5)	(5.3)	(5.3)
Other	(14.3)	(4.1)	(16.3)	(27.4)	(17.5)	(15.6)	(28.3)	(28.3)
Total	352.3	100.0	59.5	100.0	112.4	100.0	100.0	100.0

The picture that emerges is one of rough equality between the two Groups — with any edge tilting in the Chicago Group's direction. Importantly, the record evidence regarding the future of both Groups also suggests that their cash flow-generating potential and sale value are not greatly disparate.

The evidence therefore reveals that neither the *Telegraph* Group nor the Chicago Group is quantitatively vital in the sense used in the *Gimbel* test. International is not a human body and the *Telegraph* and the Chicago Group are not its heart and liver. International is a business. Neither one of the two groups is "vital" — i.e., "necessary to the continuation of [International's] life" or "necessary to [its] continued existence or effectiveness."[72] Rather, a sale of either Group leaves International as a profitable entity. . . .

3. Does the *Telegraph* Sale "Substantially Affect the Existence and Purpose of" International?

The relationship of the qualitative element of the *Gimbel* test to the quantitative element is more than a tad unclear. If the assets to be sold are not quantitatively vital to the corporation's life, it is not altogether apparent how they can "substantially affect the existence and purpose of" the corporation within the meaning of *Gimbel*, suggesting either that the two elements of the test are actually not distinct or that they are redundant. In other words, if quantitative vitality takes into account factors such as the cash-flow generating value of assets and not merely book value, then it necessarily captures qualitative considerations as well. Simply put, the supposedly bifurcated *Gimbel* test . . . simply involves a look at quantitative and qualitative considerations in order to come up with the answer to the single statutory question, which is whether a sale involves substantially all of a corporation's assets. Rather than endeavor to explore the relationship between these factors, however, I will just dive into my analysis of the qualitative importance of the *Telegraph* Group to International.

Inc.'s demand for a vote places great weight on the qualitative element of *Gimbel*. In its papers, Inc. stresses the journalistic superiority of the *Telegraph* over the *Sun-Times* and the social cachet the *Telegraph* has. If you own the *Telegraph*, Inc. notes, "you can have dinner with the Queen."[73] To sell one of the world's most highly regarded newspapers and leave International owning as its flagship the Second Paper in the Second City is to fundamentally, qualitatively transform International. Moreover, after the *Telegraph* sale, International's name will even ring hollow, as it will own only publications in the U.S., Canada, and Israel, and it will

---

72. American Heritage Dictionary 1924 (4th ed. 2000).
73. Healy Dep. at 206.

own only one paper of top-flight journalistic reputation, the *Jerusalem Post,* which has only a modest readership compared to the *Telegraph.*

The argument that Inc. makes in its papers misconceives the qualitative element of *Gimbel.* That element is not satisfied if the court merely believes that the economic assets being sold are aesthetically superior to those being retained; rather, the qualitative element of *Gimbel* focuses on economic quality and, at most, on whether the transaction leaves the stockholders with an investment that in economic terms is qualitatively different than the one that they now possess. Even with that focus, it must be remembered that the qualitative element is a gloss on the statutory language "substantially all" and not an attempt to identify qualitatively important transactions but ones that "strike at the heart of the corporate existence."

The *Telegraph* sale does not strike at International's heart or soul, if that corporation can be thought to have either one. During the course of its existence, International has frequently bought and sold a wide variety of publications. Thus, no investor in International would assume that any of its assets were sacrosanct. In the words of *Gimbel,* it "can be said that . . . acquisitions and dispositions [of independent branches of International's business] have become part of the [company's] ordinary course of business."[75]

Even more importantly, investors in public companies do not invest their money because they derive social status from owning shares in a corporation whose controlling manager can have dinner with the Queen. Whatever the social importance of the *Telegraph* in Great Britain, the economic value of that importance to International as an entity is what matters for the *Gimbel* test, not how cool it would be to be the *Telegraph's* publisher. The "trophy" nature of the *Telegraph* Group means that there are some buyers . . . who are willing to pay a higher price than expected cash flows suggest is prudent, in purely economic terms, in order to own the *Telegraph* and to enjoy the prestige and access to the intelligentsia, the literary and social elite, and high government officials that comes with that control.

Although stockholders would expect that International would capitalize on the fact that some potential buyers of the *Telegraph* would be willing to pay money to receive some of the non-economic benefits that came with control of that newspaper, it is not reasonable to assume that they invested with the expectation that International would retain the *Telegraph* Group even if it could receive a price that was attractive in light of the projected future cash flow of that Group. [T]he qualitative element of the *Gimbel* test addresses the rational economic expectations of reasonable investors, and not the aberrational sentiments of the peculiar (if not, more likely, the non-existent) persons who invest money to help fulfill the social ambitions of inside managers and to thereby enjoy (through the ownership of common stock) vicariously extraordinary lives themselves.

After the *Telegraph* Sale, International's stockholders will remain investors in a publication company with profitable operating assets, a well-regarded tabloid newspaper of good reputation and large circulation, a prestigious newspaper in Israel, and other valuable assets. While important, the sale of the *Telegraph* does not strike a blow to International's heart.

---

75. *Gimbel,* 316 A.2d at 608.

4. Summary of §271 Analysis

When considered quantitatively and qualitatively, the *Telegraph* sale does not amount to a sale of substantially all of International's assets. This conclusion is consistent with the bulk of our case law under §271. Although by no means wholly consistent, that case law has, by and large, refused to find that a disposition involved substantially all the assets of a corporation when the assets that would remain after the sale were, in themselves, substantial and profitable. In the cases when asset sales were deemed to involve substantially all of a corporation's assets, the record always revealed great doubt about the viability of the business that would remain, primarily because the remaining operating assets were not profitable. But, "if the portion of the business not sold constitutes a substantial, viable, ongoing component of the corporation, the sale is not subject to Section 271."[78] By any reasonable interpretation, the *Telegraph* sale does not involve substantially all of International's assets as substantial operating (and non-operating) assets will be retained, and International will remain a profitable publishing concern.[79]

Notes and Questions

1. Reality Check

a. Why does it matter whether the proposed sale by International is covered by DGCL §271?

b. Why was the phrase "substantially all" added to the statute?

c. How does Vice Chancellor Strine interpret that phrase?

d. What are the two parts of the Delaware test?

---

78. 1 R. Franklin Balotti & Jesse A. Finkelstein, *Delaware Law of Corporations & Business Organizations* §10.2, at 10-7 (3d ed. Supp. 2004).

79. As International points out, the MBCA now includes a safe harbor provision that is intended to provide a "greater measure of certainty than is provided by interpretations of the current case law." [MBCA] §12.02 cmt. 1 (2002). The safe harbor is an objective test involving two factors:

> If a corporation retains a business activity that represented at least 25 percent of total assets at the end of the most recently completed fiscal year, and 25 percent of either income from continuing operations before taxes or revenues from continuing operations for that fiscal year, in each case of the corporation and its subsidiaries on a consolidated basis, the corporation will conclusively be deemed to have retained a significant continuing business activity.

Id. §12.02(a).

Moreover, . . . the MBCA . . . usefully turn[s] the "substantially all" inquiry on its head by focusing, as *Gimbel* does in a more oblique way, on what remains after a sale. *See* [MBCA] §12.02 cmt. 1 (2002) (stockholder vote required if asset sale would "leave the corporation without a significant continuing business activity"). . . . The MBCA, in particular, recognizes that while the "significant continuing business activity" test differs verbally from the "substantially all" language employed in many state corporation statutes, adoption of the MBCA provision would not entail a substantive change from existing law, because "[i]n practice, . . . courts interpreting these statutes [using the phrase 'substantially all'] have commonly employed a test comparable to that embodied in 12.02(a)." [MBCA] §12.02 cmt. 1 (2002). The commentary specifically cites several Delaware judicial decisions as examples of cases employing such a test. *Id.* These approaches support the conclusion I reach.

Although not binding on me, these interpretive approaches provide a valuable perspective on §271 because they are rooted, as is *Gimbel,* in the intent behind the statute (and statutes like it in other jurisdictions). Indeed, taken together, a reading of §271 that: 1) required a stockholder vote for any sales contract to which a parent was a party that involved a sale by a wholly owned subsidiary that, in economic substance, amounted to a disposition of substantially all the parent's assets; combined with 2) a strict adherence to the words "substantially all" (à la the MBCA), could be viewed as the most faithful way to give life to the General Assembly's intended use of §271. That is, §271 would have substantive force but only with regard to transactions that genuinely involved substantially all of the corporation's assets.

2. Suppose

a. If International were incorporated in an MBCA state, would the analysis or result be different?

b. Suppose International had never sold an operating division before. Would the analysis or result be different?

3. What Do You Think?

a. Is the MBCA's approach really different from Delaware's?

b. Which of the two approaches is better?

c. How would you define "substantially all"?

d. Do you believe that the two parts of the Delaware test are really separate from one another?

e. Do you believe it makes sense to measure "substantially all" by the expectations of an economically rational investor?

4. You Draft It

a. Draft a statute that appropriately defines the transactions upon which shareholders should vote.

> Every corporation may at any meeting of its board of directors or governing body sell, lease or exchange all or substantially all of its property and assets, including its goodwill and its corporate franchises, upon such terms and conditions and for such consideration, which may consist in whole or in part of money or other property, including shares of stock in, and/or other securities of, any other corporation or corporations, as its board of directors or governing body deems expedient and for the best interests of the corporation, when and as authorized by a resolution adopted by the holders of a majority of the outstanding stock of the corporation entitled to vote thereon. . . .

DGCL §271(a)

> No approval of the shareholders is required, unless the articles of incorporation otherwise provide:
>
> > to sell, lease, exchange, or otherwise dispose of any or all of the corporation's assets in the usual and regular course of business;

MBCA 12.01(a)

> A sale, lease, exchange, or other disposition of assets, other than a disposition described in section 12.01, requires approval of the corporation's shareholders if the disposition would leave the corporation without a significant continuing business activity. A corporation will conclusively be deemed to have retained a significant continuing business activity if it retains a business activity that represented, for the corporation and its subsidiaries on a consolidated basis, at least (i) 25% of total assets at the end of the most recently completed fiscal year, and (ii) either 25% of either income from continuing operations before taxes or 25% of revenues from continuing operations, in each case for the most recently completed fiscal year.

MBCA §12.02(a)

Under the MBCA, but not the DGCL, if an asset sale requires shareholder approval, the shareholders who disapprove of the sale also have appraisal rights. This is the right to require the corporation to purchase the dissenting shareholder's shares for fair value. This right is described in more detail below.

Purchasing assets has several drawbacks, though, that may make other acquisition techniques preferable. One drawback is where transferring title to the assets requires a change in registration. Suppose, for example, that control of a package delivery service were to change. Such a company doubtless has many motor vehicles, title to each of which must be changed into the name of the purchaser. Another drawback is where some of the assets require third-party approval before they may be transferred. If the assets include real estate leases, for example, the leases may prohibit transfer or subleasing. Where such assets are few in number or are not critical to the business a sale of assets may be feasible. Often, though, these restrictions make an asset sale impracticable.

Putting It to Work

Problem 16-1

Zane Co. is a publicly traded software company. Zane has two divisions, Gaming and Social Media. The Gaming division is what made Zane Co. a household name and was, for years, the premier portion of Zane's business. In recent years, however, the Social Media division has eclipsed the Gaming division and is likely to continue to do so. Currently, the Gaming division represents 24 percent of Zane's assets, its revenues, and its profits. The Social Media division represents the remaining 76 percent.

Recently, a large cable channel company has expressed an interest in acquiring Zane's Gaming division. After arm's-length negotiation, the Zane Co. board adopted a resolution selling all of the assets and liabilities of the Gaming division to the cable channel for $500 million, which is likely to be its fair market value.

Some of Zane's shareholders (though not the members of the board of directors) think this disposition should have involved a shareholder vote.

a. What would you advise these shareholders under the MBCA?
b. What would you advise these shareholders under DGCL?

b. Purchase of Stock

If purchasing all the assets of the seller is unattractive, another technique is to purchase the target corporation's stock instead. A corporation acquired in this way becomes a *subsidiary* of the acquiring corporation. This has the virtue of transferring control of all of the seller's assets and liabilities at once without worrying about identifying each asset or having to reregister the title to some assets. Another advantage is that the liabilities of the acquired company and those of the acquiring corporation are kept separate. The only difference is that ownership of the acquired corporation has passed to the buyer.

An important aspect of acquiring control by purchasing stock is that target board action is not required. If the target board is in favor of the transaction, this quality is of no consequence. However, if the target board is, or seems likely to be, opposed to the transaction (perhaps because the target board will be replaced) then this quality is of great importance.

An additional benefit is that an acquirer that wishes to obtain control over the seller's assets but does not want to acquire the entire ownership interest of the assets may easily do so by buying stock. The acquirer negotiates to purchase more than 50 percent of the voting stock and thereby acquires control without entirely owning the assets.

From the acquirer's perspective, purchasing stock requires the same corporate action as purchasing assets. The board must pass a resolution and, if the consideration is purchaser's stock, must assure that sufficient authorized but unissued shares (or treasury shares) are available.

From the seller's perspective, selling stock might be easier than selling assets because shares are usually more easily transferred than assets. Further, a sale of stock does not trigger appraisal rights. From the standpoint of public policy, the decision to sell one's stock is an indirect way of "voting" on whether to sell all the corporation's assets. If a selling corporation shareholder does not believe the transfer to be advantageous, he or she can refuse to sell.

This power of a selling corporation's shareholder to retain his or her ownership interest is a bit illusory as we will see below. An acquirer can combine two techniques, purchasing stock and merging, to eliminate recalcitrant target corporation shareholders. The MBCA, though not the DGCL, provides a more streamlined version of acquiring all a selling corporation's stock by providing that all such stock is automatically converted into the consideration if the transaction is recommended by the target board and approved by a majority of the shareholders. *See* MBCA §§11.03, 11.04, 11.07.

c. Merger

Perhaps the most well-known acquisition device is a *merger*. In fact, many people loosely refer to any change of control transaction as a merger. Like a purchase of stock, a merger ensures that all assets and liabilities automatically pass to the acquirer. Like a purchase of assets, a merger requires a shareholder vote (and triggers appraisal rights) but does not leave the possibility of minority shareholders who refuse to give up their ownership interest. Conceptually, when two corporations merge, one disappears as a legal entity and its assets and liabilities automatically pass to the surviving corporation.

In general, the boards of both corporations (called the *constituent corporations*) must approve a *plan of merger*. This plan sets out the terms and conditions of the merger. Most important from our perspective, the plan must set out the effect of the merger on the capital structure of the constituent corporations. Usually the plan of merger provides that every share of the surviving corporation remains outstanding. Each share of the target corporation becomes the consideration (i.e., cash, debt, or shares of the surviving corporation). The plan of merger must also set out the Articles of Incorporation of the surviving corporation.

After both boards approve the plan of merger, they generally must recommend the transaction to their shareholders. An absolute majority of shares of each corporation must be voted in favor of the transaction. The corporations file articles of merger with the secretary of state and the merger becomes effective. *See* DGCL §§251, 259, MBCA §§11.02, 11.04, 11.06, 11.07.

When a merger becomes effective:

> all property owned by, and every contract right possessed by, each . . . corporation . . . that is a party to the merger, other than the survivor, are the property and contract rights of the survivor without transfer, reversion or impairment; [and] all debts, obligations and other liabilities of each . . . corporation . . . that is a party to the merger, other than the survivor, are debts, obligations or liabilities of the survivor;

MBCA §11.07(a)(3)-(4). *See also* DGCL §259.

Note that all shares are affected by the merger including those of target corporation shareholders who do not wish to receive the consideration. As we suggested above, a merger can be combined with a purchase of stock to eliminate recalcitrant target corporation shareholders. Here is how minority target shareholders are eliminated. An acquiring corporation purchases a majority of shares in the target. Then the acquirer causes the two corporations to merge, if necessary replacing the target corporation's board if those directors do not believe the merger to be in the best interest of the target corporation. The plan of merger provides that all target company shares will be converted into the consideration. The acquirer's ownership of a majority of target corporation shares guarantees that the plan will be approved by the target shareholders.

We turn now to two exceptions to the merger paradigm requiring both boards and both sets of shareholders to approve the merger. First, where the acquiring corporation already owns at least 90 percent of the target's stock, the statutes permit a merger upon only the resolution of the parent corporation's board of directors. Neither corporation's shareholders vote, although the target corporation shareholders have appraisal rights. *See* DGCL §253, MBCA §11.05. This is called a *short form merger*. Second, the acquiring corporation's shareholders do not vote and do not have appraisal rights, if the acquiring corporation will not be significantly changed by the merger. More precisely, if the acquiring corporation's Articles of Incorporation will remain essentially unchanged and if the stock to be issued in the merger will be less than 20 percent of the outstanding premerger shares, then the surviving corporation's shareholders do not vote and do not have appraisal rights. *See* DGCL §251(f), MBCA §11.04(h)(4).

The merger technique does have some drawbacks. First, the assets of the constituent corporations are not kept separate, which subjects all assets to the claims of both constituent corporations' creditors. Second, a merger requires the vote of the *acquiring* corporation's shareholders, unlike a purchase of assets or stock. A merger also triggers appraisal rights for the shareholders of both corporations.

d. Reverse Triangular Mergers

This is not an Olympic diving event. It's an acquisition technique. Acquiring corporations want to acquire targets with as few hurdles as possible. That means that acquiring corporation managers would prefer a transaction that

1. Does not require a vote of, and does not trigger appraisal rights for, the acquiring corporation's shareholders;
2. Allows the acquiring corporation to eliminate the ownership interests of recalcitrant target shareholders;

3. Keeps the assets of each corporation separate; and
4. Does not *require* target board approval.

None of the techniques we have seen up to now has all these qualities. A purchase of assets allows 1 and 2 but not 3 or 4. A purchase of stock allows 1, 3, and 4 but not 2. A merger permits 2 and 3 but not 1 or 4. A stock purchase followed by a merger allows 2 and 4 but not 1 or 3.[1] The solution has become known as a *reverse triangular merger*. This technique involves these steps:

a. The acquiring corporation forms a wholly owned subsidiary that issues all its stock to the acquiring corporation in return for what will be the acquisition consideration. That is, the only assets of the subsidiary are cash, acquiring corporation shares, or acquiring corporation debt.
b. The subsidiary purchases at least a majority of target corporation stock.
c. The subsidiary merges with the target and the *target* survives. Target shares not owned by the subsidiary[2] are converted into the consideration, thus eliminating the remaining target shareholders. Subsidiary shares are then converted into target shares. The acquiring corporation then owns all shares of the target corporation.

In this way the acquiring corporation has effected a corporation that has 1, 2, 3, and 4. This technique is called a *triangular* merger because three corporations are involved: acquiring, subsidiary, and target. It is a *reverse* merger because formally the target (i.e., the acquired company) is the survivor rather than the subsidiary. If this seems convoluted to you, get used to it. This is an extremely common technique.

Note, though, that if the acquiring company is publicly held and if the consideration is shares of acquiring company stock, the acquiring corporation's shareholders may be involved in the transaction after all. Stock exchange rules require the vote of an acquiring corporation's shareholders if the amount of shares to be issued in the transaction exceeds 20 percent of the pretransaction shares outstanding. Even if acquiring company shareholders vote, they do not have appraisal rights.

3. Choosing the Appropriate Acquisition Technique

Non-tax considerations typically revolve around minimizing the process required and minimizing disapproving shareholders' appraisal rights. In the public company setting, a shareholder vote is almost always favorable to the acquisition unless the consideration is widely perceived as inadequate. In the majority of instances, where the result of the shareholder vote is not in serious doubt, planners nonetheless consider the cost of sending notice, sending proxy materials, holding the meeting, and tabulating the vote in deciding whether some acquisition forms are preferable to others. Further, even where the result and cost of a shareholder vote are acceptable to the planners, the delay required to notice and hold a shareholder meeting, which

---

1. In this two-step method the target board's approval is usually legally required but, once control of the target has passed to the acquirer, this approval is a formality.
2. Target shares held by the subsidiary are simply cancelled.

is on the order of three weeks, at least, may militate against structuring the transaction in a way that requires the shareholders to vote.

Careful planners likewise calculate the likely number of shareholders who will seek appraisal rights and the likely cost of resolving those claims. Sometimes the transaction is made contingent upon no more than a certain number of shareholders exercising dissenters' rights.

In the abstract, tax considerations are the most important factor in choosing an acquisition technique. In any particular transaction, though, other considerations may outweigh the tax consequences. Because tax considerations are always important, we will elaborate on them here.

Particularly acute is the question of the tax consequences of the transaction on the target corporation (if it is to survive the transaction) and its shareholders. The core concept is *recognition*. That is, will the transaction be one that causes the target and its shareholders to report their gains (or losses)? If not, the transaction is said to be "tax free," although a better way to describe this is to say it is tax "deferred."

The animating idea is that Congress believes that a transaction in which a business's owners simply change the form of their ownership should not trigger taxation of gains or losses. Where a transaction exhibits two qualities, continuity of target shareholder ownership and continuity of target corporation business, whether conducted by the target or acquirer corporation, Congress believes that the target corporation and its shareholders should not recognize any gain or loss.

The most paradigmatic setting is a merger in which the consideration is surviving corporation stock. The target shareholders have gone from owning 100 percent of the target corporation to owning a proportionate interest of the surviving corporation, which owns the target corporation's assets. Target shareholders receive shares in the survivor corporation without paying any tax. In tax lingo, this is an *A reorg* because it falls within the Internal Revenue Code (IRC) §368(a)(1)(A).[3]

Building on this exclusion, Congress also exempted other transactions that seemed similar to a merger in that the target owners continue to own a proportionate share of an entity that controls the target corporation assets. A transaction in which the acquiring corporation purchases all target corporation stock in exchange for acquirer corporation voting stock has the same functional result as a merger. Congress exempted these transactions, which are called *B reorgs*.

A *C reorg* is just a bit more complex. A transaction will not result in recognition if the acquirer purchases all the target assets, again using acquirer stock for consideration, and the target corporation dissolves and distributes all its assets (i.e., acquirer stock) pro rata to its shareholders. The ultimate result is that the target shareholders own a proportionate interest in the acquirer corporation, which owns all target corporation assets. IRC §368(a)(1) has other exemptions from recognition but they don't concern us here.

Where the acquirer is using only cash or debt, the entire consideration is taxable. In many instances the target shareholders have such a low basis (essentially the price they paid for their target shares) and are united enough to pose a realistic threat of defeating the transaction so that a taxable transaction is out of the question. At other

---

3. The term *reorganization*, or *reorg*, is used in tax law to mean the types of transactions we're talking about in this chapter. The same term is also used in the non-tax setting to mean a corporate reorganization under the bankruptcy code. The context should make clear which of these two uses is meant.

times, the typical shareholder basis is high, relative to the consideration, or the shareholders are so widely dispersed (as in a public corporation) that they do not pose a credible threat to effecting the transaction. In those settings a taxable transaction is feasible.

Notes and Questions

1. Notes

a. The courts in a very few states may recharacterize a transaction, at the request of a shareholder, under the *de facto merger* doctrine. Thus a transaction structured as a sale of assets will be recharacterized as a merger, or a reverse triangular merger will be recharacterized as a merger between the target and the acquiring company rather than the acquiring company's subsidiary. The consequence of recharacterizing a transaction is to grant shareholders greater rights than the ostensible transaction provides. Typically this means providing appraisal rights and possibly a shareholder vote. The Delaware courts have rejected the de facto merger doctrine, on the policy ground that the legislature, in providing for alternative forms of transactions, intended to give planners choices that would be respected. This policy is referred to as the *equal dignity doctrine*, meaning that the Delaware courts regard the various statutory provisions for transactions as being of equal dignity with one another.

2. What Do You Think?

a. The ultimate result of all of the acquisition techniques is substantially the same: placing the target assets under the control of the acquiring corporation. Do you think corporate planners should be able to choose techniques that provide less shareholder protection?

b. Do you think corporate planners should be able to choose techniques that provide greater tax benefits?

c. If planners should, as a matter of public policy, be able to choose transaction forms that will be respected by the courts, are there ethical issues that should constrain transaction lawyers from selecting some forms over others?

4. The Acquisition Process

It will be helpful to give you an overview of the process by which control of one corporation passes to another. Because the vast majority of such transactions are negotiated between the corporations' managements, we will discuss that model here. The model in which target management opposes the change of control transaction is discussed below under the rubric *hostile takeovers*.

There are three watershed events in the acquisition process. As you might expect with legal matters, each of these watersheds is memorialized by a particular kind of document or documents. These documents are mainly contracts, although some are corporate documents such as board resolutions, plans of merger, and amendments to the Articles or bylaws. If you are curious as to what the documents actually say, the most convenient place to view exemplars is on the SEC's EDGAR database. These documents are typically filed as part of the disclosure obligations of public companies.

In the first period, the parties begin preliminary negotiations with one another. Often the personal chemistry between the principals will have great consequences for the success or failure of the proposed transaction. If the preliminary negotiations progress as far as agreement (however tentative it may be) on the price and form of consideration and, possibly, the form of the transaction, the parties may execute a *letter of intent.*

In contract categories, this is a contract with open terms. It is probably phrased as an agreement between the parties to negotiate with one another in good faith looking toward the acquisition of one entity by the other. It may contain confidentiality agreements and may or may not provide that, should negotiations end, one side will pay certain expenses (usually out-of-pocket expenses) of the other.

Although the parties will have investigated one another to some extent, once the letter of intent is executed, investigation begins in earnest. The purpose is to give comfort to one party that the other is bona fide. That is, that it owns what it claims to own, it owes what it claims to owe, that it can authorize the proposed transaction, and that, in general, the financial, operational, and regulatory qualities are as the corporation represents them to be. The target is always the object of scrutiny, but the acquirer may not undergo rigorous examination if the consideration is cash rather than acquirer stock or debt. This investigative process is known as *due diligence.*

If the due diligence reveals no insurmountable issues, the parties will execute a *definitive agreement.* This will probably run between 20 and 100 pages of often dense prose. Usually the definitive agreement addresses at least eight issues. First, the agreement identifies the *parties.* Second, it describes the *transaction* (e.g., is this a merger? Asset purchase? Stock purchase?). Third, the agreement specifies the *consideration* from each party. Sometimes this description is simple, sometimes complex. Fourth, the agreement describes the *closing*—that is, when, where, and how the consideration will pass. This aspect of the agreement often reads like the protocol for a Cold War exchange of spies.

The next four areas are the most delicate and most fervently negotiated. Each party makes *representations and warranties* about itself. Essentially, each party describes itself as a legal entity (e.g., a Delaware corporation in good standing) with a particular capital structure; describes the state of its finances (including potential liabilities to lenders and other creditors); and asserts that it can legally enter into the contemplated transaction.

Although in theory it may be possible to execute a definitive agreement and transfer the consideration at one time, as a practical matter there is a gap, which may be several months long, between the execution of the definitive agreement and the closing. It may seem to you that this gap period is anticlimactic. After all, the parties have bound themselves by presumably enforceable legal documents. The only thing that remains is to swap the consideration.

In reality, the gap period is one of particular uncertainty. A party may have a change of heart about the advisability of the transaction. This change of heart might, indeed, come from the entreaties of a third party—a *raider*—who attempts to convince the target corporation to agree to be acquired by the raider rather than the original acquiring corporation.

Relatedly, because the target management controls the target during the gap, the buyer faces a moral hazard in that the target may be operated opportunistically — thus reducing the value of the target when it changes hands. Moreover, approval of the transaction is frequently legally dependent on a vote of shareholders or on approval by a regulatory agency, neither of which can be guaranteed with certainty. Other predicates to closing require the parties themselves to take actions during the gap period, such as adopting resolutions or reducing assets to cash to pay the consideration. *Covenants* in the acquisition agreement address these concerns. At bottom, these are promises to assure that the target remains in status quo and that both parties use their best efforts to ensure that all predicate actions necessary to the closing are completed.

As we just noted, completing the transaction may become unpalatable to one side or the other. The *conditions* section of the definitive agreement spells out the conditions precedent to each party's obligation to close. If those conditions are not met, and if compliance is not waived, one party or both has the option to decline to close. These conditions closely track the representations and warranties and the covenants. In effect, each party, as a condition to being able to require the other party to close, must show that what it represented about itself was true when the agreement was signed *and* is true at the closing, as well. Further, the parties usually negotiate conditions that permit one or both parties to refuse to close if certain fundamental assumptions underlying the transaction have changed. These sorts of changes, referred to as *material adverse change* clauses, cover things like a major decline in the stock market or a major change in the economics of the target company's industry.

In the end, the transaction may not close for any number of reasons. Most starkly, one side may simply breach. Alternatively, the parties may mutually agree to end the deal. Definitive agreements usually contain a date by which the transaction must close or else either party may decline to continue. Another cause of the failure to close is that one or more conditions have not been met. A material adverse change may have occurred. Finally, the target board may find that it has a fiduciary duty not to close the transaction because closing would not be in the best interest of the corporation.

The *termination* section deals with the consequence of the failure of the transaction to close. One consequence might be that no rights or duties arise from the termination — a "no fault" setting. Another consequence is to require one party to make the other financially whole by reimbursing the other party's out-of-pocket costs. Another consequence might be to penalize the party responsible for termination. Usually the termination section provides that some provisions, such as a confidentiality agreement, continue after the closing.

5. Corporate Law Issues

a. Deal Protective Measures

A number of common provisions in the definitive agreement are the result of the parties' concern with the possibility that the transaction may not close. The acquirer, in particular, may have invested a great deal of money to put the deal together. If it doesn't close, the acquirer may not be able to recover those costs. If the target is publicly held, it may find itself the object of unwanted acquisition offers if the initial deal falls through. These offers may be at prices below the initial deal price. Despite the target board's opposition, the public shareholders may tender their shares to the new suitors and the unwanted acquisition will occur anyway.

Acquisition agreement clauses that are designed to ensure that the transaction closes are often called *deal protective measures.* Although in some ways these terms seem to be of ancillary interest, in fact, these terms present the most difficult issues of corporate law in change of control settings.

One deal protective measure was implied when we described the termination provisions above. A *break-up fee* is a termination provision that makes the target liable to the acquirer if the transaction fails to close. This provision helps to ensure that the transaction closes because the break-up fee is set high enough to dissuade the target from lightly changing its mind about the deal. Typically these break-up fees run up to 4 percent of the total value of the transaction, which easily can run into hundreds of millions of dollars for a major acquisition. A similar economic incentive is a *topping fee.* This provides for an additional payment to the acquirer if the transaction does not close and if, within a specified time such as two years, the target is acquired by another entity.

Another economic incentive is provided by *asset lock-up* clauses. These give the acquirer the option to purchase certain key target assets if the transaction does not close. This provision both increases the acquirer's certainty that it can gain control of the assets it most desires and helps to ensure that the original transaction will close because the asset lock-up discourages raiders from attempting to derail the deal.

Other deal protective measures are designed to cabin the parties' range of actions so as to heighten the likelihood that the transaction will close. A *no-shop* provision prevents the target board from actively seeking other potential acquirers. A *no-talk* clause prevents the target board from negotiating with, or providing nonpublic information to, any other party. No-talk clauses are often narrowed to permit target boards to share information if the third party makes, or is likely to make, a bona fide offer for the target. Sometimes the clause provides that the target must keep the acquirer informed about any such talks, provide to the acquirer any information also provided to the third party, or require the target to permit the acquirer to match any third-party offer.

None of these deal protective measures is objectionable under contract law, although some break-up fees might be questioned under liquidated damages doctrines. The corporate law issues revolve around whether the target board has met its fiduciary duties in agreeing to the measures. The Delaware Supreme Court described the underlying tensions in the next excerpt. Although the case involved a merger, the Court's description would apply equally to sales of assets under §271, which also require stockholder approval.

The Delaware corporation statute provides that the board's management decision to enter into and recommend a merger transaction can become final only when ownership action is taken by a vote of the stockholders. Thus, the Delaware corporation law expressly provides for a balance of power between boards and stockholders which makes merger transactions a shared enterprise and ownership decision. Consequently, a board of directors' decision to adopt defensive devices to protect a merger agreement may implicate the stockholders' right to effectively vote contrary to the initial recommendation of the board in favor of the transaction.

It is well established that conflicts of interest arise when a board of directors acts to prevent stockholders from effectively exercising their right to vote contrary to the will of the board. The "omnipresent specter" of such conflict may be present whenever a board adopts defensive devices to protect a merger agreement. The stockholders' ability to effectively reject a merger agreement is likely to bear an inversely proportionate relationship to the structural and economic devices that the board has approved to protect the transaction.

There are inherent conflicts between a board's interest in protecting a merger transaction it has approved, the stockholders' statutory right to make the final decision to either approve or not approve a merger, and the board's continuing responsibility to effectively exercise its fiduciary duties at all times after the merger agreement is executed. These competing considerations require a threshold determination that board-approved defensive devices protecting a merger transaction are within the limitations of its statutory authority and consistent with the directors' fiduciary duties.

Omnicare, Inc. v. NCS Healthcare, Inc., 818 A.2d 914, 930-931 (Del. 2003) (Holland, J.)

From a duty of loyalty approach, the target board, in agreeing to deal protective measures, might not believe that the transaction was in the best interest of the corporation. Even though in most transactions there is no self-dealing, the directors, which may include senior managers, may be concerned about retaining their positions after the transaction. They may have negotiated for such positions.

Turning to the duty of care, it is unlikely that target directors would not have all material information reasonably available when approving deal protective measures. Using the MBCA approach, director approval of deal protective measures would ordinarily be within "the care that a person in a like position would reasonably believe appropriate under similar circumstances." MBCA §8.30(b).

A more pointed duty of care problem arises when the board agrees to no-talk provisions. In the excerpt that follows, Asarco and Cyprus Amax had executed a definitive acquisition agreement with mutual no-talk provisions. Phelps Dodge wanted to enter into negotiations to purchase both Asarco and Cyprus Amax but the Cyprus Amax board desired to continue the original transaction. Phelps Dodge sought an injunction declaring the no-talk provision unenforceable. Chancellor Chandler described the duty of care problem that no-talk provisions present:

> Under our law, a board of directors must be informed of all material information reasonably available. The defendants properly argue that Cyprus Amax and Asarco are under no duty to negotiate [with Phelps]. . . . Nevertheless, even the decision not to negotiate, in my opinion, must be an informed one. A target can refuse to negotiate . . . , but it should be informed when making such refusal.
>
> No-talk provisions, thus, in my view, are troubling precisely because they prevent a board from meeting its duty to make an informed judgment with respect to even considering whether to negotiate with a third party.
>
> Now, here, despite the presence of publicly exchanged information, the no-talk provision has apparently prevented either Cyprus or Asarco from engaging in nonpublic dialogue with Phelps. Now, this should not be understood to suggest that Cyprus or Asarco were legally required to or even should have negotiated, privately or otherwise, with Phelps Dodge. It is

to say, rather, that they simply should not have completely foreclosed the opportunity to do so, as this is the legal equivalent of willful blindness, a blindness that may constitute a breach of a board's duty of care; that is, the duty to take care to be informed of all material information reasonably available.

Phelps Dodge Corp. v. Cyprus Amax Minerals Co., 1999 WL 1054255 (Del. Ch.) (Chandler, Ch.)

Note that the Delaware legislature, in reaction to some Delaware case law, has provided a deal protective measure in DGCL §146. The definitive agreement can provide that the transaction must be submitted to one or both sets of shareholders, even where a board determines during the gap period that the transaction is no longer in the corporation's best interest.

b. Sale of Control

We saw in the last chapter that courts impose heightened duties on controlling shareholders. The following excerpt discusses those duties in the specific setting in which a controlling shareholder desires to transfer control.

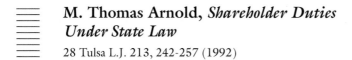

M. Thomas Arnold, *Shareholder Duties Under State Law*
28 Tulsa L.J. 213, 242-257 (1992)

SALE TO A LOOTER

A controlling shareholder is under a duty not to transfer control to another where the circumstances surrounding the proposed transfer are sufficient to put the shareholder on notice that the purchaser may loot the corporation. A controlling shareholder is under no duty to investigate a prospective purchaser of his or her shares absent circumstances that put him or her on notice that the purchaser intends or is likely to loot the corporate assets. Circumstances which may put the seller on notice of the purchaser's intent to defraud the corporation include . . . : (1) facts suggesting that the purchaser intends to finance the purchase or to secure the purchase price with corporate assets; (2) the knowledge that the corporation was the subject of looting in the past; (3) a request by the purchasers that assets of the corporation be converted into cash prior to the closing on the sale of shares and/or that the purchasers have access to its liquid assets immediately after closing; ([4]) the payment of an excessive price for the shares given the nature of the corporation's assets; ([5]) unfavorable credit reports on the purchaser or businesses controlled by the purchaser; and ([6]) prior frauds committed by the buyer on the seller. Evidence of facts that a reasonable investigation would reveal are not relevant to the question of whether the seller is on notice of facts suggesting that the buyer intends to or is likely to loot the corporation since no duty to investigate exists absent such notice. Generally more than one of these factors is present in the cases in which a seller of control is held to be on notice that the purchaser intends or is likely to loot the corporation.

Some scholars argue that a controlling shareholder should have a duty to investigate a prospective purchaser of his or her shares regardless of the absence of suspicious circumstances. Arguments supporting the imposition of such a duty include the possibility of substantial harm to the minority from a transfer of control, the fact that an investigation is unlikely to be very costly or difficult, and the fact that such investigations are already commonly done because sellers are concerned about the financial ability of the parties with whom they are negotiating. Thus, a strong argument can be made that the cost of imposing a duty on a seller of control to investigate the reputation and financial ability of a prospective purchaser of his or her control is outweighed by the potential harm such sales can cause to the minority.

On the other hand, some scholars question the wisdom of cases imposing liability for sale of control to a looter, arguing that it is difficult to detect potential looters, that looters acquire a reputation that prevents them from looting again, that most refusals to sell after a reasonable investigation are "false positives," and that the best way to deter looting is to punish looters very severely. These scholars conclude that a duty to investigate potential purchasers of control is costly and deters many beneficial transactions.

SALE AT A PREMIUM

Absent special circumstances, a controlling shareholder may sell his or her shares in a private sale at a premium price without any obligation to share the premium with other shareholders or to offer them an equal opportunity to participate in the sale of shares. A potential purchaser of controlling shares . . . will pay a premium for the opportunity to manage the firm's assets. Under current law this premium belongs to the seller of the controlling interest, is not a corporate asset, and need not be shared with other shareholders. In addition, the purchaser in a private sale of controlling shares has no duty to purchase all shares at the same price.

Arguably, allowing controlling shareholders to obtain a premium increases shareholder wealth by encouraging the sale of controlling shares to purchasers who will manage the corporate assets more efficiently. Under this view, a rule requiring a controlling shareholder to share the premium with other shareholders discourages the sale of controlling interests to such persons. On the other hand, even assuming that sale of control produces gains, the purchaser of a controlling interest might not share those gains with the minority shareholders, preferring instead to increase management perquisites while placing the shareholders on "starvation returns." Indeed, a potential purchaser of a controlling interest might be motivated by the belief that current management is inefficient in obtaining perks and may be willing to pay a premium for the opportunity to enjoy increased perks. Some scholars argue that the minority shareholders should share pro rata in any premium which a purchaser of a controlling interest is willing to pay, although the courts have consistently held that minority shareholders have no right to share in the premium.

Notes and Questions

1. Notes

a. Frequently a target corporation has a shareholder (or cohesive group of shareholders) that has enough stock to control the corporation but not a majority. In connection with the acquisition transaction, the acquirer may contract separately with that shareholder to obtain either the shares, an option to acquire the shares, or an irrevocable proxy to vote the shares in favor of the transaction. In such an instance the execution and enforceability of such a side agreement may be a condition to closing the transaction. This agreement with shareholders is also called a *lock-up* or a *shareholder lock-up*.

As you may intuit, these shareholder lock-up provisions both are deal protective measures, analyzed under contract law, and raise fiduciary duty issues for the controlling shareholders under a duty of loyalty.

b. It frequently happens that a merger is used by a controlling shareholder (often another corporation) to eliminate minority shareholders. As we saw from Chapter 15, controlling shareholders have a fiduciary duty to the minority at least when they use their control for their own benefit. In Delaware, and many other states, such a merger triggers the entire fairness standard, which requires the controlling shareholder to demonstrate its utmost good faith *and* the most scrupulous inherent fairness of the bargain.

Concomitantly, the subsidiary corporation's directors frequently face duty of loyalty issues because they may well have focused on their own continued employment or the controlling shareholder's best interest when they approved the merger terms.

2. What Do You Think?

a. Professor Arnold further discusses two different theoretical approaches to sale of control:

> The Equal Opportunity Theory
>
> A number of scholars argue that minority shareholders should have an equal opportunity to participate in any sale of a controlling interest in a corporation. They argue that an equal opportunity rule discourages sales of controlling interests where there is a risk of harm to the corporation through looting or mismanagement. Unless all shares are purchased, the controlling shareholder is a minority shareholder after the sale of control and therefore will be hesitant to sell to someone who will injure the value of the shares he or she retains. In addition, the sale of controlling shares in a corporation is analogized to a sale of corporate assets with a portion of the purchase price financed by the minority shareholders. Proponents of the theory urge that the sale of controlling shares is essentially a "corporate transaction" in which all shareholders should participate equally.
>
> A number of scholars challenge the equal opportunity theory on the grounds that it would deter many beneficial transactions. Some controlling shareholders will not want to become minority shareholders in the corporation; perhaps some purchasers will not want a substantial minority shareholder to remain after the purchase. Further, some purchasers will be unwilling or unable to buy all the corporate shares in order to avoid these problems. [A] leading proponent of the equal opportunity theory, argues that beneficial transactions generally will not be deterred since: (1) if the purchaser is optimistic about the possible gains from a change in management he or she will agree to buy all the shares; (2) if the controlling shareholder is optimistic about possible gains he or she will agree to retain some of his or her shares; and (3) if the minority shareholders are optimistic about possible gains they will waive their right to participate in the sale.

M. Thomas Arnold, *Shareholder Duties Under State Law*, 28 Tulsa L.J. 213 (1992)

Do you think the equal opportunity doctrine is preferable to the current approach?

c. Appraisal

The right of appraisal, often called dissenters' rights, is the right of a shareholder to surrender his or her shares to the corporation in return for fair value. This right attaches only when the corporation undertakes certain fundamental actions such as merging. The underlying philosophy of appraisal rights is that where a corporation has truly changed in important ways the disapproving shareholders should have the right to end their investment in the enterprise. The principal questions we will take up surrounding dissenters' rights are, which transactions trigger them? And what is "fair value"?

i. Which Transactions Trigger Appraisal Rights?   The MBCA, but not the DGCL, provides appraisal rights to shareholders of a corporation that sells substantially all its assets under §12.02. Both the DGCL and MBCA provide appraisal rights as the norm for the shareholders of the constituent corporations in any merger (and, under the MBCA, a forced share exchange). This norm is varied in two settings. First, where stockholders own publicly traded stock they could obtain substantially the same relief by selling as by seeking appraisal. So, such shareholders have no appraisal rights *if* the merger consideration (i.e., the shareholder's alternative to selling) is "traditional" consideration. In Delaware, this means stock in the survivor or stock in a nonconstituent company that is publicly traded. Under the MBCA, this means either publicly traded stock or cash. Note that stockholders of a public Delaware company *have* appraisal rights where the consideration is cash or debt and stockholders of an MBCA corporation *have* appraisal rights where the consideration is survivor stock that is not publicly traded.

Second, stockholders should not have appraisal rights if their corporation and their ownership interest in it will not be significantly different after the merger. The DGCL provides that stockholders of the parent corporation in a short form merger and stockholders not entitled to vote in a merger under DGCL §251(f) (stockholders' ownership interest will not be significantly diluted) do not have appraisal rights. Note that minority stockholders of the *subsidiary* in a short form merger *do* have appraisal rights. *See* DGCL §262(b).

The MBCA describes essentially the same rule more straightforwardly by providing that no appraisal rights attach to shares that will remain outstanding after a merger. The MBCA also provides that corporations may, in the Articles of Incorporation, opt out of appraisal rights. It also grants appraisal rights (despite any restrictions discussed above) to shareholders of corporations that merge with a controlling shareholder or with an entity controlled by one of its own senior executives. *See* MBCA §13.02.

ii. What Is "Fair Value"?   The next case discusses one of the most contentious issues concerning appraisal rights. Shareholders and corporations nearly always disagree about the fair value to which the shareholders are entitled. The following case discusses the statutory standard and its application. Note that the case also talks about two related but separate conceptual questions. First, where the target corporation had a controlling shareholder, should the fair value of the dissenting shareholders' shares be discounted (reduced) to reflect the fact that those shares have little management power? This is the *minority discount* question. Second, where the target corporation is not publicly traded, should dissenting shareholders' shares be discounted to reflect the fact that the shares are illiquid? This is the *marketability discount* question.

≡ **Matthew G. Norton Company v. Smyth**
≡ 51 P.3d 159 (Wash. App. 2002)

KENNEDY, J.

Matthew G. Norton Company (MGN) . . . held and managed a portfolio of commercial real estate, investments in certain private companies and venture capital funds, and a diversified portfolio of marketable stocks.

In early 1999, the Boards of Directors of MGN and Northwest Building Corporation (NWBC) proposed a corporate reorganization under which MGN would be merged into NWBC. . . . Each MGN shareholder would exchange his or her respective shares . . . for the same number of shares of NWBC stock. . . . The name of [NWBC] would then be changed to Matthew G. Norton Company.

MGN had 43 individual shareholders, all of them related in some way to Matthew G. Norton. None of the shareholders held a majority interest in MGN. The average ownership interest of all the shareholders of MGN was approximately 3 percent. Stephen G. Clapp, who is one of the respondents to this appeal, was the only shareholder of MGN to dissent to the proposal. He held 25,016 shares of stock in MGN, 3.1 percent of the outstanding shares. NWBC had only two shareholders, MGN and Theodore H. Smyth. . . . MGN owned 99.65 percent of the outstanding stock of NWBC. Smyth owned the remainder, which amounted to 142 shares. Smyth, who is the other respondent to this appeal, also dissented.

Matthew G. Norton Company hired the accounting firm of Arthur Andersen to conduct valuations of MGN and NWBC for purposes of determining "fair value" of the dissenters' shares . . . as of the date of the merger. Arthur Andersen employed a "net asset" valuation method, which, in the simplest of terms, [reflects] current market values of assets and liabilities as of the valuation date. All of this indicated a net asset value of $170.246 million for MGN and $99.446 million for NWBC.

[A]rthur Andersen noted that the shareholders are severely restricted in their ability to transfer or sell their shares. Arthur Andersen opined that it was appropriate to discount the net adjusted value of MGN by 35 percent and to discount the net adjusted value of NWBC by 40 percent. This discount had the stated purpose of reflecting the lack of marketability of each and every share in the company, and not the minority status of the shares of the dissenting shareholders.

Arthur Andersen concluded that as of March 31, 1999, the value of one share in MGN was $138 and that the value of one share of NWBC was $1,451. As is contemplated by [MBCA §13.24], Matthew G. Norton Company paid Mr. Clapp $3,509,146 (including accrued interest) for his shares in MGN, and paid Mr. Smyth $208,050 (including accrued interest) for the shares of NWBC. . . . Mssrs. Clapp and Smyth notified the Company that they were dissatisfied with these amounts. As permitted by [MBCA §13.26], Clapp demanded a total amount of $6,858,928 for his shares and Smyth demanded a total amount of $458,864. . . .

Matthew G. Norton Company, being unwilling to pay the dissenting shareholders any more money, filed its Petition for Determination of Fair Value of Shares of Dissenting Shareholder, pursuant to [MBCA §13.30]. In due course, Mssrs. Clapp and Smyth filed a motion for (partial) summary judgment, asking the court to rule that . . . the lack of marketability discount . . . is [not] available in a dissenter's rights valuation as a matter of law. The "fair value" of the shares of the dissenting shareholders has not yet been determined by the trial court.

At common law, unanimous shareholder approval was required in order to undertake major corporate actions. This made it possible for an arbitrary minority to establish a nuisance value for its shares by refusing to cooperate. To resolve this problem, state legislatures, such as Washington's, authorized corporate action by majority vote. To avoid unfair treatment of shareholders, legislatures granted dissenting shareholders the right to obtain "fair value" for their shares.

"Fair value" is defined for purposes of the dissenters' rights statute as "the value of the shares immediately before the effective date of the corporate action to which the dissenter objects, excluding any appreciation or depreciation in anticipation of the corporate action unless such exclusion would be inequitable." The term "value" is inherently ambiguous. It is clear, however, that our Legislature's use of the term "fair value" was not a slip of the pen — the Legislature did not intend to say "fair market value," instead. All of the states and the District of Columbia have dissenters' rights statutes. Forty-six states use the "fair value" standard or one of its iterations, exclusively. Only four states, California ("fair market value"), Louisiana ("fair cash value"), Ohio ("fair cash value") and Kansas ("value") use another term. The District of Columbia statute contains both "fair value" and "fair market value."

The statutory definition of "fair value" leaves to the parties, and ultimately the courts, the details by which fair value is to be determined, and leaves intact accumulated case law. . . . Proof of value may be made by any techniques or methods that are generally acceptable in the financial community. Official Comment to [MBCA §13.02], citing *Weinberger v. UOP, Inc.*, 457 A.2d 701 (Del. 1983). Determining fair value requires consideration of all relevant factors involving the value of a company, and may include elements of future value, excluding, however, the speculative elements of value that may arise from accomplishment or expectation of the transaction giving rise to the dissenters' rights. *Weinberger*, 457 A.2d at 713.

When Washington adopted its version of the Model Business Corporation Act in 1989, the Model Act was silent as to the propriety of discounts in determining "fair value." In 1999, the Model Act was amended to redefine "fair value" as follows:

> "Fair value" means the value of the corporation's shares determined:
> (i) immediately before the effectuation of the corporate action to which the shareholder objects;
> (ii) using customary and current valuation concepts and techniques generally employed for similar businesses in the context of the transaction requiring appraisal; and
> (iii) without discounting for lack of marketability or minority status[.]

Model Act §13.01(4) as amended effective April 15, 1999.

[A] number of courts had already rejected lack of marketability discounts before the Model Act was revised, and, for that matter, before Washington adopted its version of the Model Act. A number of states have rejected such discounts since the revisions to the Model Act, without benefit of amendments to their statutes. We conclude that the fact that our Legislature has not amended [the Washington Business Corporation Act] to conform to the most recent revisions to the Model Act does not preclude the courts of this state from disapproving such discounts as may be inappropriate in ascertaining "fair value."

As noted by the *Weinberger* court:

> The basic concept of value under [Delaware's dissenters' rights statute] is that the stockholder is entitled to be paid for that which has been taken from him, viz., his proportionate interest in a going concern. By value of the stockholder's proportionate interest in the corporate enterprise is meant the true or intrinsic value of his stock [that] has been taken by the merger.

Weinberger, 457 A.2d at 713. . . .

And in *Cavalier Oil Corp. v. Harnett*, 564 A.2d 1137, 1144-45 (Del. 1989), the court held that a minority shareholder in fair value cases is entitled to a proportionate interest in the corporation appraised as an entity and rejected application of a marketability discount, reasoning that such a discount is contrary to the requirement that the company be valued as a going concern.

In *Swope v. Siegel-Robert, Inc.*, 243 F.3d 486, 491-94 (8th Cir. 2001), the court reviewed decisions from Missouri, New Jersey, Delaware, Maine, South Dakota, Oregon and Kansas wherein the courts rejected lack of marketability discounts. . . . Based on the reasoning of those courts, the *Swope* court concluded:

> The marketability discount is incompatible with the purpose of the appraisal right, which provides dissenting shareholders with a forum for recapturing their complete investment in the corporation after they are unwillingly subjected to substantial corporate changes beyond their control. . . .
>
> . . .
>
> [T]he market for minority stock in a dissenting shareholders' appraisal proceeding, absent extraordinary circumstances, is not a relevant fact or circumstance to consider when determining fair value.

Swope, 243 F.3d at 493-94.

> " '[F]air value' in minority stock appraisals is not equivalent to 'fair market value.' Dissenting shareholders, by nature, do not replicate the willing and ready [sellers] of the open market. Rather, they are unwilling sellers with no bargaining power."

Swope, 243 F.3d at 492-93. . . .

As the *Swope* court also noted, the American Law Institute concludes that the proper interpretation of "fair value" is the proportionate share of the value of 100 percent of the equity in the company, without any discount for minority status, or, absent extraordinary circumstances, lack of marketability. *See Standards for Determining Fair Value*, Principles of Corporate Governance: Analysis and Recommendations (ALI) §7.22(a) and ALI §7.33 cmt. *e* (1994).

[T]hose courts that generally will not apply such a discount do not support a blanket rule that, "as a matter of law," a marketability discount should *never* be considered. *See Swope*, 243 F.3d at 494 . . . ; *Atlantic States Const., Inc. v. Beavers*, 314 S.E.2d 245 (Ga. App. 1984) . . . ; *Weigel Broadcasting Co. v. Smith*, 682 N.E.2d 745, 751 (Ill. App. 1996) . . . ; *Ford v. Courier-Journal Job Printing Co.*, 639 S.W.2d 553 (Ky. App. 1982) . . . ; *Advanced Communication Design, Inc. v. Follett*, 615 N.W.2d 285 (Minn. 2000) . . . ; *Lawson Mardon Wheaton, Inc. v. Smith*, 734

A.2d 738, 749 (N.J. 1999) . . . ; *Balsamides v. Protameen Chemicals, Inc.*, 734 A.2d 721 (N.J. 1999). . . .

[I]t is our task to establish guidelines for courts, litigants and appraisers in Washington that deal with our dissenters' rights statute. We conclude that the most logical starting place is to determine what it is that needs to be measured. As stated by the American Law Institute in its treatise on corporate governance:

> A focus on measurement technique is . . . meaningless absent agreement on what is to be measured. This is essentially a definitional problem, and it involves significant normative issues that cannot be resolved simply by reference to the "customary valuation concepts" then in use in the relevant market.
>
> . . .
>
> [Section] 7.22(a) focuses on what a buyer would pay for the firm as an entirety. . . . In focusing on the value of the firm, rather than the value of specific shares, §7.22(a) thus adopts the principle, long recognized by the Delaware courts, and more recently by the New York courts, that the appraisal remedy should award each shareholder a proportionate share of the firm's value. As a result, once an aggregate value for the firm is obtained, the court under §7.22(a) normally has only to prorate this value equally among all shares of the same class.

2 Principles of Corporate Governance §722 *Standards for Determining Fair Value.*

We agree. [O]ur Legislature did not adopt "fair market value" as the standard in granting dissenters' rights to shareholders for the "fair value" of their shares. The Arthur Andersen valuation reports for MGN and NWBC inappropriately equate "fair value" of the shares with "fair market value" — that being the very purpose for which lack of marketability discounts (as well as minority discounts) are applied, after all.

[T]o the extent that the trial court's order was intended to declare that, absent extraordinary circumstances, no such discount can be applied at the shareholder level, we affirm.

The parties have not had the opportunity to brief the extraordinary circumstances exception, and should be given opportunity to do so, following our remand, if either side believes any such circumstances to be applicable in this case.

Notes and Questions

1. Notes

a. Now that you've had more exposure to the idea of appraisal rights, you may wish to rethink your response to the question we posed earlier about whether corporate planners should be able to select a transaction form specifically to minimize shareholder rights.

b. The availability of appraisal rights is often more theoretical than real because the number of shareholders that perfect their appraisal rights is usually small, the costs of prosecuting an appraisal action is usually borne by each party, and attorneys' fees are not awardable against the corporation.

c. You should note that there is a significant strategic element in choosing to seek appraisal rights. First, to perfect the rights takes some diligence on the part of both the shareholder and the corporation. Second, once the shareholder has perfected appraisal rights, he or she has no power to discontinue the action. That is, unless the corporation agrees, the shareholder will get "fair value" rather than the merger consideration even if the court finds that "fair value" is less than the consideration, which is a not infrequent occurrence.

2. Reality Check

a. What was the dispute between the corporations and the dissenting shareholders?

b. How did the corporation determine its version of "fair value"?

c. How does Judge Kennedy resolve the disputes? Do you agree with the result?

3. What Do You Think?

a. Do you think that either the minority discount or the marketability discount should be routinely applied?

b. Should "fair value" be the standard? If not, what should be?

4. You Draft It

a. Draft an appraisal statute that describes the value to which a dissenting shareholder is entitled. The relevant DGCL and MBCA provisions follow.

> MBCA §13.01:
>
> (4) Fair value means the value of the corporation's shares determined:
> (i) immediately before the effectuation of the corporate action to which the shareholder objects;
> (ii) using customary and current valuation concepts and techniques generally employed for similar businesses in the context of the transaction requiring appraisal; and
> (iii) without discounting for lack of marketability or minority status. . . .

> DGCL §262(h):
>
> [T]he Court shall determine the fair value of the shares exclusive of any element of value arising from the accomplishment or expectation of the merger or consolidation, together with interest, if any, to be paid upon the amount determined to be the fair value. In determining such fair value, the Court shall take into account all relevant factors.

Putting It to Work

Problem 16-2

Seller Corp., a closely held company with three equal shareholders, and Buyer Corp., a publicly traded company, are in talks for Seller Corp. to be acquired by Buyer Corp. for $120 million in cash. The transaction will be structured as a merger with Buyer Corp. to be the surviving corporation. Seller Corp.'s shareholders, Xavier, Yanis, and Zelda, who are also its only directors, are in disagreement over whether to sell. Both Yanis and Zelda are ready to cash out, but Xavier believes that the purchase price of $120 million is grossly undervaluing their company. Nonetheless, Yanis and Zelda, as directors and then as shareholders, vote to approve the merger.

a. Assuming that Xavier votes against the merger, is he entitled to appraisal rights under the DGCL? Under the MBCA?

b. Suppose the transaction were structured as a sale by Seller Corp. of all its assets and liabilities to Buyer Corp. Again, assume that Xavier votes against the transaction. Is he entitled to appraisal rights under the DGCL? Under the MBCA?

c. If Xavier is entitled to appraisal rights, how would his shares be valued?

d. Do the shareholders of Buyer Corp. have any appraisal rights under the DGCL? Under the MBCA? Does your answer change depending on whether the transaction is structured as a merger or as a purchase of all of Seller Corp.'s assets and liabilities?

C. BACKGROUND AND CONTEXT — DEAL PROTECTIVE MEASURES, HOSTILE TAKEOVERS, AND DEFENSIVE MEASURES

As mentioned earlier, the 1980s saw an explosion of change of control activity among public companies, much of it despite the opposition of the target company's board of directors. Such a transaction is known as a *hostile takeover*. In a typical transaction, the acquiring company, or *raider*, approaches the target management to see whether a friendly transaction can be negotiated. Sometimes the target has executed a definitive agreement with another entity; the raider attempts to acquire the target out from under the other party.

If the raider is rebuffed, it may launch a *tender offer*. This is an offer to the target's shareholders to sell their shares to the raider at a premium to the current market price. Tender offers are highly regulated, but nearly all the regulation is contained in the federal securities laws rather than in state corporate laws.

The tender offer is nearly always made by a wholly owned subsidiary of the raider formed for the express purpose of acquiring the target. Usually the tender offer is conditioned on the raider's subsidiary being able to purchase more than 50 percent of target company shares. If the tender offer is successful, the raider promptly replaces the target's board and effects a reverse triangular merger. At the end of the process, the target is a wholly owned subsidiary of the raider.

Much of the law of directors' fiduciary duties in Delaware comes from these hostile takeovers. In this section we will look at four legal facets of these takeovers. First we will list some of the governance structures that corporations may adopt that deter unwanted changes of control. These structures can stand alone or they can be used in conjunction with deal protective measures if the target has agreed on a transaction with another party. Target boards may also take other actions to stave off a raider once a hostile raid has begun. Our second focus will be on the standards of review courts use in evaluating target board actions. Third, we will see that sometimes target boards are under an obligation to maximize shareholder value in the short term. Finally, we will see that many states have enacted antitakeover laws.

1. Corporate Structures That Deter Hostile Changes of Control

Many corporations want to ensure that any change of control transaction is approved by the board. Several corporate governance structures, sometimes called *shark repellents*, keep unwanted suitors from effecting a takeover. One technique is to require a supermajority shareholder vote for takeover transactions. This requirement must appear in the Articles of Incorporation. A second device is to stagger the board so that a raider must, in theory at least, wait for two annual meetings of target shareholders before being able to elect a majority of directors. In practice, if the raider has purchased a majority of shares, the target board often capitulates and resigns in favor of the raider's nominees. Under the DGCL, directors on a staggered board can only be removed for cause unless the Certificate of Incorporation provides otherwise. *See* DGCL §141(k). Where the board is not staggered or where the target is incorporated outside of Delaware, the Articles can be amended to provide that directors can only be removed for cause.

The corporation's Articles or bylaws can contain an *advance notice provision* that requires a shareholder to notify management several months in advance of a shareholders' meeting if the shareholder intends to nominate an alternative slate of directors or to propose an action for shareholder vote.

Under the DGCL the Articles can prohibit shareholders from acting by consent but cannot prohibit the shareholders from amending the bylaws. *See* DGCL §§109, 228. Under the MBCA the shareholders' power to act by consent cannot be taken away by the Articles. A similar provision is an Article provision prohibiting shareholders from calling a special meeting. Under the DGCL the default rule is that stockholders do not have the power to call a special meeting. *See* DGCL §211(d).

The final two shark repellents are more complex. The first involves putting a significant percentage of the company's stock in friendly hands. The second involves enduing the company's stock with latent rights designed to make a hostile takeover economically unfeasible.

Where a corporation wishes to provide pension benefits to its employees it can establish an employee stock ownership plan (*ESOP*). An ESOP is a separate entity from the corporation and is heavily regulated under federal law. Leaving the intricacies of ESOPs to other courses, suffice it to say here that the principal asset of an ESOP is frequently the employer corporation's stock. A typical ESOP may hold 10 or 15 percent of the corporation's stock, making it one of the largest stockholders. The idea is that the trustees of the ESOP and the current and retired employees, who are the ESOP beneficiaries, are likely to support incumbent management and will vote the ESOP shares as management recommends.

The final structural device to thwart raiders is the so-called *poison pill*, more formally known as a *shareholders' rights plan*. Corporate statutes permit corporations to issue options on their stock. A poison pill is implemented by authorizing the issuance of options (usually called "rights") on the target's stock. Shareholders receive one right for each share of stock and the rights are not separately tradable; all transfers of stock include the transfer of the associated right. The rights are not represented by separate certificates. The right gives the stockholder the option to buy a new series of preferred stock; the exercise price is set so that no economically rational shareholder would exercise the option.

The rights' potency in warding off raiders is hidden in the antidilution provisions. You may recall that an option usually contains language that adjusts the amount and price of the option if the corporation changes its capital structure. (*See* Chapter 7.) The poison pill's provisions allow the stockholder to purchase half-price stock if a raider acquires a particular percentage of shares, usually between 10 and 20 percent, and thereafter effects a merger, such as the typical merger to eliminate minority shareholders.

If the target will be the surviving company, as in a reverse triangular merger, the shareholders may purchase half-price stock in the target (a *flip in* provision). If another company will be the survivor the stockholders may buy half-price stock in the acquiring company (a *flip over* provision). The target board has the power to redeem the rights at a nominal price before the raider purchases more than the triggering percentage of stock. Thereafter, the rights are not redeemable.

The economic effect of a poison pill is to deter raiders from purchasing shares in a tender offer unless the target board redeems the rights. The target board thus becomes a central negotiator in the change of control transaction. The Delaware courts have upheld poison pills but courts in other states have on occasion held them to be invalid, usually on the ground that the rights are not really options (because they are not intended to be exercised) on the target's stock but simply are a structural device to entrench the target company's board.

2. Standard of Review of a Target Board's Actions

In addition to the structural safeguards described above and the deal protective measures included in most acquisition agreements, target corporations can take actions to ward off raiders *after* a raid has begun. The actions taken in the heat of battle, as it were, are frequently called *defensive measures*. As the great wave of hostile takeovers began in the 1980s, the Delaware courts found themselves dealing with case after case involving a legal challenge to a corporate structure, a deal protective measure, or a target board's defensive actions.

At the core of these cases was the raider's assertion that the target board breached its duty of loyalty by taking measures that secured the directors' positions rather than furthering the best interest of the corporation (i.e., accepting the raider's offer). The raider/plaintiffs argued that the entire fairness test ought to apply because the entire board was tainted by the duty of loyalty problem. Director/ defendants argued that the business judgment rule should apply because the conflict between the corporation's best interest and the directors' entrenchment was not sufficiently strong to warrant the entire fairness standard. The Delaware Supreme Court developed a test of *enhanced* or *intermediate* scrutiny for target corporation board actions in the face of an unwanted takeover attempt. This standard is often called the *Unocal* test, from the case that first articulated this standard, *Unocal Corp. v. Mesa Petroleum*, 493 A.2d 946 (Del. 1985). In theory it is more exacting than the business judgment rule and less stringent than entire fairness. Over the course of ten years, the Delaware courts elaborated the test and expanded the settings in which it is applied. At its most expansive, the *Unocal* test applies to any defensive measure adopted in response to an unwanted change of control transaction and also to any deal protective measure in an acquisition agreement, even where no third party has expressed interest in the target.

At its most elaborate, the *Unocal* test runs as follows. The defendant board must first demonstrate that has reasonably perceived a threat to corporate policy and effectiveness. It does so through good faith (in the generalized pre-*Stone v. Ritter* sense) and reasonable investigation. If the board shows a threat, it must then demonstrate that its response (i.e., the defensive measure in question) was reasonable in relation to the threat posed. This is sometimes called the proportionality prong of *Unocal*. To be reasonable in relation to the threat, a board action cannot be "draconian," meaning that it is neither coercive to the stockholders nor preclusive toward third parties. That is, the board's action must not force the stockholders to accept the board's preferred outcome, nor must it prevent a third party from a successful (though uninvited) change of control transaction. A board action is preclusive if it makes a change of control realistically unattainable (or mathematically impossible). If the board's action is neither coercive nor preclusive (and therefore not draconian), the board must demonstrate that its action is within the range of reason. That means, at its core, that the board must demonstrate that its action is a limited defensive response that corresponds in degree or magnitude to the perceived threat.

Although the *Unocal* test is extremely elaborate, the actual rigor seems to have varied. The first part of the test, reasonable perception of a threat to corporate policy and effectiveness, was effectively eviscerated. Boards can always show that they reasonably perceived a threat. The second part of the test, proportionality, seems to have wobbled between being quite deferential to target boards and quite antagonistic to them. When the courts have been deferential, the enhanced scrutiny seems not very different from the business judgment rule except that the burden of persuasion is on the board. When the courts have been antagonistic, the test seems relatively indistinguishable from entire fairness.

3. The Target Board's Obligation to Maximize Shareholder Value

As the Delaware courts focused on the question of the standard of review in takeover settings they also imposed a substantive obligation on target boards. That is, when certain predicates are met, a target board's actions must be designed to further a particular end. The next case discusses the rationale behind what has become known as *Revlon duties*. See *Revlon, Inc. v. MacAndrews & Forbes Holdings, Inc.*, 506 A.2d 173 (Del. 1986).

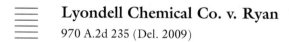 **Lyondell Chemical Co. v. Ryan**
970 A.2d 235 (Del. 2009)

BERGER, J.

We accepted this interlocutory appeal to consider a claim that directors failed to act in good faith in conducting the sale of their company. The Court of Chancery decided that "unexplained inaction" permits a reasonable inference that the directors may have consciously disregarded their fiduciary duties. The trial court expressed concern about the speed with which the transaction was consummated; the directors' failure to negotiate better terms; and their failure to seek potentially superior deals. But the record establishes that the directors were disinterested and independent; that they were generally aware of the company's value and its prospects; and that they considered the offer, under the time constraints imposed by the buyer, with the assistance of financial and legal advisors. At most, this record creates a triable issue of fact on the question of whether the directors exercised due care. There is no evidence, however, from which to infer that the directors knowingly ignored their responsibilities, thereby breaching their duty of loyalty. Accordingly, the directors are entitled to the entry of summary judgment.

FACTUAL AND PROCEDURAL BACKGROUND

Before the merger at issue, Lyondell Chemical Company ("Lyondell") was the third largest independent, publicly traded chemical company in North America. Dan Smith ("Smith") was Lyondell's Chairman and CEO. Lyondell's other ten directors were independent and many were, or had been, CEOs of other large, publicly traded companies. Basell AF ("Basell") is a privately held Luxembourg company owned by Leonard Blavatnik ("Blavatnik") through his ownership of Access Industries. Basell is in the business of polyolefin technology, production and marketing.

In April 2006, Blavatnik told Smith that Basell was interested in acquiring Lyondell. A few months later, Basell sent a letter to Lyondell's board offering $26.50-$28.50 per share. Lyondell determined that the price was inadequate and that it was not interested in selling. During the next year, Lyondell prospered and no potential acquirors expressed interest in the company. In May 2007, an Access affiliate filed a Schedule 13D with the Securities and Exchange Commission disclosing its right to acquire an 8.3% block of Lyondell stock owned by Occidental Petroleum Corporation. The Schedule 13D also disclosed Blavatnik's interest in possible transactions with Lyondell.

In response to the Schedule 13D, the Lyondell board immediately convened a special meeting. The board recognized that the 13D signaled to the market that the company was "in play,"[1] but the directors decided to take a "wait and see" approach.

On July 9, 2007, Blavatnik met with Smith to discuss an all-cash deal at $40 per share. Smith responded that $40 was too low, and Blavatnik raised his offer to $44-$45 per share. Smith told Blavatnik that he would present the proposal to the board, but that he thought the board would reject it. Smith advised Blavatnik to give Lyondell his best offer, since Lyondell really was not on the market. The meeting ended at that point, but Blavatnik asked Smith to call him later in the day. When Smith called, Blavatnik offered to pay $48 per share. Under Blavatnik's proposal, Basell would require no financing contingency, but Lyondell would have to agree to a $400 million break-up fee and sign a merger agreement by July 16, 2007.

Smith called a special meeting of the Lyondell board on July 10, 2007 to review and consider Basell's offer. The meeting lasted slightly less than one hour, during which time the board reviewed valuation material that had been prepared by Lyondell management for presentation at the regular board meeting, which was scheduled for the following day. The board also discussed the Basell offer, . . . and the likelihood that another party might be interested in Lyondell. The board

---

1. On the day that the 13D was made public, Lyondell's stock went from $33 to $37 per share.

instructed Smith to obtain a written offer from Basell and more details about Basell's financing.

Blavatnik agreed to the board's request, but also made an additional demand. Blavatnik asked Smith to find out whether the Lyondell board would provide a firm indication of interest in his proposal by the end of that day. The Lyondell board met on July 11, again for less than one hour, to consider the Basell proposal and how it compared to the benefits of remaining independent. The board decided that it was interested, authorized the retention of Deutsche Bank Securities, Inc. ("Deutsche Bank") as its financial advisor, and instructed Smith to negotiate with Blavatnik.

From July 12-July 15 the parties negotiated the terms of a Lyondell merger agreement; Basell conducted due diligence; Deutsche Bank prepared a "fairness" opinion; and Lyondell conducted its regularly scheduled board meeting. The Lyondell board discussed the Basell proposal again on July 12, and later instructed Smith to try to negotiate better terms. Specifically, the board wanted a higher price, a go-shop provision,[2] and a reduced break-up fee. As the trial court noted, Blavatnik was "incredulous." He had offered his best price, which was a substantial premium, and the deal had to be concluded on his schedule. As a sign of good faith, however, Blavatnik agreed to reduce the break-up fee from $400 million to $385 million.

On July 16, 2007, the board met to consider the Basell merger agreement. Lyondell's management, as well as its financial and legal advisers, presented reports analyzing the merits of the deal. The advisors explained that, notwithstanding the no-shop provision in the merger agreement, Lyondell would be able to consider any superior proposals that might be made because of the "fiduciary out" provision. In addition, Deutsche Bank reviewed valuation models derived from "bullish" and more conservative financial projections. Several of those valuations yielded a range that did not even reach $48 per share, and Deutsche Bank opined that the proposed merger price was fair. Indeed, the bank's managing director described the merger price as "an absolute home run." Deutsche Bank also identified other possible acquirors and explained why it believed no other entity would top Basell's offer. After considering the presentations, the Lyondell board voted to approve the merger and recommend it to the stockholders. At a special stockholders' meeting held on November 20, 2007, the merger was approved by more than 99% of the voted shares.

DISCUSSION

The class action complaint challenging this $13 billion cash merger alleges that the Lyondell directors breached their "fiduciary duties of care, loyalty and candor . . . and . . . put their personal interests ahead of the interests of the Lyondell shareholders." Specifically, the complaint alleges that: . . . 3) the process by which the merger was negotiated was flawed; [and] 4) the directors agreed to unreasonable deal protection provisions. . . .

The remaining claims are but two aspects of a single claim, under *Revlon v. MacAndrews & Forbes Holdings, Inc.*,[6] that the directors failed to obtain the best available price in selling the company. As the trial court correctly noted, *Revlon* did

---

2. A "go-shop" provision allows the seller to seek other buyers for a specified period after the agreement is signed.

6. 506 A.2d 173, 182 (Del. 1986).

not create any new fiduciary duties. It simply held that the "board must perform its fiduciary duties in the service of a specific objective: maximizing the sale price of the enterprise."[7] The trial court reviewed the record, and found that Ryan might be able to prevail at trial on a claim that the Lyondell directors breached their duty of care. But Lyondell's charter includes an exculpatory provision, pursuant to [DGCL] §102(b)(7), protecting the directors from personal liability for breaches of the duty of care. Thus, this case turns on whether any arguable shortcomings on the part of the Lyondell directors also implicate their duty of loyalty, a breach of which is not exculpated. Because the trial court determined that the board was independent and was not motivated by self-interest or ill will, the sole issue is whether the directors are entitled to summary judgment on the claim that they breached their duty of loyalty by failing to act in good faith.

This Court examined "good faith" in two recent decisions. In *In re Walt Disney Co. Deriv. Litig.*,[9] the Court discussed the range of conduct that might be characterized as bad faith, and concluded that bad faith encompasses not only an intent to harm but also intentional dereliction of duty:

> [A]t least three different categories of fiduciary behavior are candidates for the "bad faith" pejorative label. The first category involves so-called "subjective bad faith," that is, fiduciary conduct motivated by an actual intent to do harm. . . . [S]uch conduct constitutes classic, quintessential bad faith. . . .
>
> The second category of conduct, which is at the opposite end of the spectrum, involves lack of due care — that is, fiduciary action taken solely by reason of gross negligence and without any malevolent intent. . . . [W]e address the issue of whether gross negligence (including failure to inform one's self of available material facts), without more, can also constitute bad faith. The answer is clearly no.
>
> * * *
>
> That leaves the third category of fiduciary conduct, which falls in between the first two categories. . . . This third category is what the Chancellor's definition of bad faith — intentional dereliction of duty, a conscious disregard for one's responsibilities — is intended to capture. The question is whether such misconduct is properly treated as a non-exculpable, nonindemnifiable violation of the fiduciary duty to act in good faith. In our view, it must be. . . .[10]

The *Disney* decision expressly disavowed any attempt to provide a comprehensive or exclusive definition of "bad faith."

A few months later, in *Stone v. Ritter*,[11] this Court addressed the concept of bad faith in the context of an "oversight" claim. We adopted the standard articulated ten years earlier, in *In re Caremark Int'l Deriv. Litig.*:[12]

> [W]here a claim of directorial liability for corporate loss is predicated upon ignorance of liability creating activities within the corporation . . . only a sustained or systematic failure of the board to exercise oversight — such as an utter failure to attempt to assure a reasonable information and reporting system exists — will establish the lack of good faith that is a necessary condition to liability.

---

7. *Malpiede v. Townson*, 780 A.2d 1075, 1083 (Del. 2001).
9. 906 A.2d 27 (Del. 2006).
10. *Id.* at 64-66.
11. 911 A.2d 362 (Del. 2006).
12. 698 A.2d 959, 971 (Del. Ch. 1996).

The *Stone* Court explained that the *Caremark* standard is fully consistent with the *Disney* definition of bad faith. *Stone* also clarified any possible ambiguity about the directors' mental state, holding that "imposition of liability requires a showing that the directors knew that they were not discharging their fiduciary obligations."

The Court of Chancery recognized these legal principles, but it denied summary judgment in order to obtain a more complete record before deciding whether the directors had acted in bad faith. Under other circumstances, deferring a decision to expand the record would be appropriate. Here, however, the trial court reviewed the existing record under a mistaken view of the applicable law. Three factors contributed to that mistake. First, the trial court imposed *Revlon* duties on the Lyondell directors before they either had decided to sell, or before the sale had become inevitable. Second, the court read *Revlon* and its progeny as creating a set of requirements that must be satisfied during the sale process. Third, the trial court equated an arguably imperfect attempt to carry out *Revlon* duties with a knowing disregard of one's duties that constitutes bad faith.

The Court of Chancery identified several undisputed facts that would support the entry of judgment in favor of the Lyondell directors: the directors were "active, sophisticated, and generally aware of the value of the Company and the conditions of the markets in which the Company operated." They had reason to believe that no other bidders would emerge, given the price Basell had offered and the limited universe of companies that might be interested in acquiring Lyondell's unique assets. Smith negotiated the price up from $40 to $48 per share — a price that Deutsche Bank opined was fair. Finally, no other acquiror expressed interest during the four months between the merger announcement and the stockholder vote.

Other facts, however, led the trial court to "question the adequacy of the Board's knowledge and efforts. . . ." After the Schedule 13D was filed in May, the directors apparently took no action to prepare for a possible acquisition proposal. The merger was negotiated and finalized in less than one week, during which time the directors met for a total of only seven hours to consider the matter. The directors did not seriously press Blavatnik for a better price, nor did they conduct even a limited market check. Moreover, although the deal protections were not unusual or preclusive, the trial court was troubled by "the Board's decision to grant considerable protection to a deal that may not have been adequately vetted under *Revlon*."

The trial court found the directors' failure to act during the two months after the filing of the Basell Schedule 13D critical to its analysis of their good faith. The court pointedly referred to the directors' "two months of slothful indifference despite *knowing* that the Company was in play," and the fact that they "languidly awaited overtures from potential suitors. . . ." In the end, the trial court found that it was this "failing" that warranted denial of their motion for summary judgment:

> [T]he Opinion clearly questions whether the Defendants "engaged" in the sale process. . . . This is where the 13D filing in May 2007 and the subsequent two months of (apparent) Board inactivity become critical. . . . [T]he Directors made *no apparent effort* to arm themselves with *specific knowledge* about the present value of the Company in the May through July 2007 time period, despite *admittedly knowing* that the 13D filing . . . effectively put the Company "in play," and, therefore, presumably, also knowing that an offer for

the sale of the Company could occur at any time. It is these facts that raise the specter of "bad faith" in the present summary judgment record. . . .[22]

The problem with the trial court's analysis is that *Revlon* duties do not arise simply because a company is "in play." The duty to seek the best available price applies only when a company embarks on a transaction — on its own initiative or in response to an unsolicited offer — that will result in a change of control. Basell's Schedule 13D did put the Lyondell directors, and the market in general, on notice that Basell was interested in acquiring Lyondell. The directors responded by promptly holding a special meeting to consider whether Lyondell should take any action. The directors decided that they would neither put the company up for sale nor institute defensive measures to fend off a possible hostile offer. Instead, they decided to take a "wait and see" approach. That decision was an entirely appropriate exercise of the directors' business judgment. The time for action under *Revlon* did not begin until July 10, 2007, when the directors began negotiating the sale of Lyondell.

The Court of Chancery focused on the directors' two months of inaction, when it should have focused on the one week during which they considered Basell's offer. During that one week, the directors met several times; their CEO tried to negotiate better terms; they evaluated Lyondell's value, the price offered and the likelihood of obtaining a better price; and then the directors approved the merger. The trial court acknowledged that the directors' conduct during those seven days might not demonstrate anything more than lack of due care. But the court remained skeptical about the directors' good faith — at least on the present record. That lingering concern was based on the trial court's synthesis of the *Revlon* line of cases, which led it to the erroneous conclusion that directors must follow one of several courses of action to satisfy their *Revlon* duties.

There is only one *Revlon* duty — to "[get] the best price for the stockholders at a sale of the company."[26] No court can tell directors exactly how to accomplish that goal, because they will be facing a unique combination of circumstances, many of which will be outside their control. As we noted in *Barkan v. Amsted Industries, Inc.*, "there is no single blueprint that a board must follow to fulfill its duties."[27] That said, our courts have highlighted both the positive and negative aspects of various boards' conduct under *Revlon*. The trial court drew several principles from those cases: directors must "engage actively in the sale process," and they must confirm that they have obtained the best available price either by conducting an auction, by conducting a market check, or by demonstrating "an impeccable knowledge of the market."

The Lyondell directors did not conduct an auction or a market check, and they did not satisfy the trial court that they had the "impeccable" market knowledge that the court believed was necessary to excuse their failure to pursue one of the first two alternatives. As a result, the Court of Chancery was unable to conclude that the directors had met their burden under *Revlon*. In evaluating the totality of the circumstances, even on this limited record, we would be inclined to hold otherwise. But we would not question the trial court's decision to seek additional evidence if

22. *Ryan v. Lyondell Chemical Co.*, 2008 WL 4174038 at *2 (Del. Ch.).
26. *Revlon*, 506 A.2d at 182.
27. 567 A.2d 1279, 1286 (Del. 1989).

the issue were whether the directors had exercised due care. Where, as here, the issue is whether the directors failed to act in good faith, the analysis is very different, and the existing record mandates the entry of judgment in favor of the directors.

As discussed above, bad faith will be found if a "fiduciary intentionally fails to act in the face of a known duty to act, demonstrating a conscious disregard for his duties."[31] The trial court decided that the *Revlon* sale process must follow one of three courses, and that the Lyondell directors did not discharge that "known set of [*Revlon*] 'duties.'" But, as noted, there are no legally prescribed steps that directors must follow to satisfy their *Revlon* duties. Thus, the directors' failure to take any specific steps during the sale process could not have demonstrated a conscious disregard of their duties. More importantly, there is a vast difference between an inadequate or flawed effort to carry out fiduciary duties and a conscious disregard for those duties.

Directors' decisions must be reasonable, not perfect. "In the transactional context, [an] extreme set of facts [is] required to sustain a disloyalty claim premised on the notion that disinterested directors were intentionally disregarding their duties." The trial court denied summary judgment because the Lyondell directors' "unexplained inaction" prevented the court from determining that they had acted in good faith. But, if the directors failed to do all that they should have under the circumstances, they breached their duty of care. Only if they knowingly and completely failed to undertake their responsibilities would they breach their duty of loyalty. The trial court approached the record from the wrong perspective. Instead of questioning whether disinterested, independent directors did everything that they (arguably) should have done to obtain the best sale price, the inquiry should have been whether those directors utterly failed to attempt to obtain the best sale price.

Viewing the record in this manner leads to only one possible conclusion. The Lyondell directors met several times to consider Basell's premium offer. They were generally aware of the value of their company and they knew the chemical company market. The directors solicited and followed the advice of their financial and legal advisors. They attempted to negotiate a higher offer even though all the evidence indicates that Basell had offered a "blowout" price. Finally, they approved the merger agreement, because "it was simply too good not to pass along [to the stockholders] for their consideration." We assume, as we must on summary judgment, that the Lyondell directors did absolutely nothing to prepare for Basell's offer, and that they did not even consider conducting a market check before agreeing to the merger. Even so, this record clearly establishes that the Lyondell directors did not breach their duty of loyalty by failing to act in good faith. In concluding otherwise, the Court of Chancery reversibly erred.

CONCLUSION

Based on the foregoing, the decision of the Court of Chancery is reversed and this matter is remanded for entry of judgment in favor of the Lyondell directors.

---

31. *Disney* at 67.

Notes and Questions

1. Reality Check

a. What aspects of this case triggered the *Revlon* analysis?

b. When did the company become subject to *Revlon*?

c. What are the elements of *Revlon*?

d. Why did Justice Berger hold that the board did not violate its *Revlon* duties? Do you agree?

2. What Do You Think?

a. Does the *Revlon* standard make any sense, given that the court has the business judgment rule, the entire fairness test, and *Unocal* at its disposal?

4. Expanded Deference to Boards

At one time, the *Unocal* test was used in most M&A settings (except where there is a change of control that triggers *Revlon*). The Delaware Supreme Court has expanded the situations in which the business judgment rule applies. This, of course, has the effect of narrowing *Unocal*'s and *Revlon*'s importance without ostensibly lessening the enhanced scrutiny *Unocal* and *Revlon* supposedly require. This expansion seems to be part of a deliberate, but stealthy, shift by the Delaware judiciary to be more deferential to corporate boards in M&A transactions. The next two cases show the tenor of the courts' new approach. The first case, *Kahn*, involves a transaction in which a controlling stockholder of a subsidiary makes an offer to acquire all the subsidiary stock it does not already own. *Corwin*, the second case, considers the effect of an uncoerced, fully informed stockholder vote to be acquired (the acquirer in *Corwin* may or may not have controlled the target entity).

≡ ## Kahn v. M&F Worldwide Corp.

88 A.3d 635 (Del. 2014)

HOLLAND, Justice:

This is an appeal from a final judgment entered by the Court of Chancery in a proceeding that arises from a 2011 acquisition by MacAndrews & Forbes Holdings, Inc. ("M & F" or "MacAndrews & Forbes")—a 43% stockholder in M & F Worldwide Corp. ("MFW")—of the remaining common stock of MFW (the "Merger"). From the outset, M & F's proposal to take MFW private was made contingent upon two stockholder-protective procedural conditions. First, M & F required the Merger to be negotiated and approved by a special committee of independent MFW directors (the "Special Committee"). Second, M & F required that the Merger be approved by a majority of stockholders unaffiliated with M & F. The Merger closed in December 2011, after it was approved by a vote of 65.4% of MFW's minority stockholders.

The Appellants [MNF stockholders] initially sought to enjoin the transaction. They withdrew their request for injunctive relief after taking expedited discovery, including several depositions. The Appellants then sought post-closing relief against M & F, Ronald O. Perelman, and MFW's directors (including the members of the Special Committee) for breach of fiduciary duty. Again, the Appellants were provided with extensive discovery. The Defendants then moved for summary judgment, which the Court of Chancery granted.

Where a transaction involving self-dealing by a controlling stockholder is challenged, the applicable standard of judicial review is "entire fairness," with the defendants having the burden of persuasion. In other words, the defendants bear the ultimate burden of proving that the transaction with the controlling stockholder was entirely fair to the minority stockholders.

This appeal presents a question of first impression: what should be the standard of review for a merger between a controlling stockholder and its subsidiary, where the merger is conditioned *ab initio* upon the approval of **both** an independent, adequately-empowered Special Committee that fulfills its duty of care, and the uncoerced, informed vote of a majority of the minority stockholders. The question has never been put directly to this Court.

Almost two decades ago, in *Kahn v. Lynch* [*Commc'n Sys., Inc.*, 638 A.2d 1110 (Del. 1994)], we held that the approval by *either* a Special Committee *or* the majority of the noncontrolling stockholders of a merger with a buying controlling stockholder would shift the burden of proof under the entire fairness standard from the defendant to the plaintiff. *Lynch* did not involve a merger conditioned by the controlling stockholder on both procedural protections. That is the vital distinction between [that case] and this one. The question is what the legal consequence of that distinction should be in these circumstances.

We hold that business judgment is the standard of review that should govern mergers between a controlling stockholder and its corporate subsidiary, where the merger is conditioned *ab initio* upon both the approval of an independent, adequately-empowered Special Committee that fulfills its duty of care; and the uncoerced, informed vote of a majority of the minority stockholders. We so conclude for several reasons.

First, entire fairness is the highest standard of review in corporate law. It is applied in the controller merger context as a substitute for the dual statutory protections of disinterested board and stockholder approval, because both protections are potentially undermined by the influence of the controller. However, as this case establishes, that undermining influence does not exist in every controlled merger setting, regardless of the circumstances. The simultaneous deployment of the procedural protections employed here create a countervailing, offsetting influence of equal—if not greater—force. That is, where the controller irrevocably and publicly disables itself from using its control to dictate the outcome of the negotiations and the shareholder vote, the controlled merger then acquires the shareholder-protective characteristics of third-party, arm's-length mergers, which are reviewed under the business judgment standard.

Second, the dual procedural protection merger structure optimally protects the minority stockholders in controller buyouts. As the Court of Chancery explained:

> [W]hen these two protections are established up-front, a potent tool to extract good value for the minority is established. From inception, the controlling stockholder knows that it cannot bypass the special committee's ability to say no. And, the controlling stockholder knows it

cannot dangle a majority-of-the-minority vote before the special committee late in the process as a deal-closer rather than having to make a price move.

Third, and as the Court of Chancery reasoned, applying the business judgment standard to the dual protection merger structure:

> . . . is consistent with the central tradition of Delaware law, which defers to the informed decisions of impartial directors, especially when those decisions have been approved by the disinterested stockholders on full information and without coercion. Not only that, the adoption of this rule will be of benefit to minority stockholders because it will provide a strong incentive for controlling stockholders to accord minority investors the transactional structure that respected scholars believe will provide them the best protection, a structure where stockholders get the benefits of independent, empowered negotiating agents to **bargain for the best price and say no** if the agents believe the deal is not advisable for any proper reason, plus the critical ability to determine for themselves whether to accept any deal that their negotiating agents recommend to them. A transactional structure with both these protections is fundamentally different from one with only one protection.

Fourth, the underlying purposes of the dual protection merger structure utilized here and the entire fairness standard of review both converge and are fulfilled at the same critical point: **price.** Following *Weinberger v. UOP, Inc.* [457 A.2d 701 (Del. 1983)], this Court has consistently held that, although entire fairness review comprises the dual components of fair dealing and fair price, in a non-fraudulent transaction "price may be the preponderant consideration outweighing other features of the merger." The dual protection merger structure requires two price-related pretrial determinations: first, that a fair price was achieved by an empowered, independent committee that acted with care; and, second, that a fully-informed, uncoerced majority of the minority stockholders voted in favor of the price that was recommended by the independent committee.

To summarize our holding, in controller buyouts, the business judgment standard of review will be applied *if and only if:* (i) the controller conditions the procession of the transaction on the approval of both a Special Committee and a majority of the minority stockholders; (ii) the Special Committee is independent; (iii) the Special Committee is empowered to freely select its own advisors and to say no definitively; (iv) the Special Committee meets its duty of care in negotiating a fair price; (v) the vote of the minority is informed; and (vi) there is no coercion of the minority.

If a plaintiff that can plead a reasonably conceivable set of facts showing that any or all of those enumerated conditions did not exist, that complaint would state a claim for relief that would entitle the plaintiff to proceed and conduct discovery. If, after discovery, triable issues of fact remain about whether either or both of the dual procedural protections were established, or if established were effective, the case will proceed to a trial in which the court will conduct an entire fairness review.

This approach is consistent with *Weinberger, Lynch* and their progeny. A controller that employs and/or establishes only one of these dual procedural protections would continue to receive burden-shifting within the entire fairness standard of review framework. Stated differently, unless *both* procedural protections for the minority stockholders are established *prior to trial,* the ultimate judicial scrutiny of controller buyouts will continue to be the entire fairness standard of review.

[The court then concluded that the members of the Special Committee were independent, it was empowered, it exercised due care, and the stockholder vote was fully informed and uncoerced. Accordingly, the court affirmed the judgment for defendants.]

Corwin v. KKR Financial Holdings LLC

125 A.3d 304 (Del. 2015)

Strine, Chief Justice:

In a well-reasoned opinion, the Court of Chancery held that the business judgment rule is invoked as the appropriate standard of review for a post-closing damages action when a merger that is not subject to the entire fairness standard of review has been approved by a fully informed, uncoerced majority of the disinterested stockholders. For that and other reasons, the Court of Chancery dismissed the plaintiffs' complaint. In this decision, we find that the Chancellor was correct in finding that the voluntary judgment of the disinterested stockholders to approve the merger invoked the business judgment rule standard of review and that the plaintiffs' complaint should be dismissed. For sound policy reasons, Delaware corporate law has long been reluctant to second-guess the judgment of a disinterested stockholder majority that determines that a transaction with a party other than a controlling stockholder is in their best interests.

I. THE COURT OF CHANCERY PROPERLY HELD THAT THE COMPLAINT DID NOT PLEAD FACTS SUPPORTING AN INFERENCE THAT KKR WAS A CONTROLLING STOCKHOLDER OF FINANCIAL HOLDINGS

The plaintiffs filed a challenge in the Court of Chancery to a stock-for-stock merger between KKR & Co. L.P. ("KKR") and KKR Financial Holdings LLC ("Financial Holdings") in which KKR acquired each share of Financial Holdings's stock for 0.51 of a share of KKR stock, a 35% premium to the unaffected market price. Below, the plaintiffs' primary argument was that the transaction was presumptively subject to the entire fairness standard of review because Financial Holdings's primary business was financing KKR's leveraged buyout activities, and instead of having employees manage the company's day-to-day operations, Financial Holdings was managed by KKR Financial Advisors, an affiliate of KKR, under a contractual management agreement that could only be terminated by Financial Holdings if it paid a termination fee. As a result, the plaintiffs alleged that KKR was a controlling stockholder of Financial Holdings, which was an LLC, not a corporation.[3]

---

3. We wish to make a point. We are keenly aware that this case involves a merger between a limited partnership and a limited liability company, albeit both ones whose ownership interests trade on public exchanges. But, it appears that both before the Chancellor, and now before us on appeal, the parties have acted as if this case was no different from one between two corporations whose internal affairs are governed by the Delaware General Corporation Law and related case law. We have respected the parties' approach to arguing this complex case, but felt obliged to note that we recognize that this case involved alternative entities, and that in cases involving those entities, distinctive arguments often arise due to the greater contractual flexibility given to those entities under our statutory law.

The defendants filed a motion to dismiss, taking issue with that argument. In a thoughtful and thorough decision, the Chancellor found that the defendants were correct that the plaintiffs' complaint did not plead facts supporting an inference that KKR was Financial Holdings's controlling stockholder. Among other things, the Chancellor noted that KKR owned less than 1% of Financial Holdings's stock, had no right to appoint any directors, and had no contractual right to veto any board action. Although the Chancellor acknowledged the unusual existential circumstances the plaintiffs cited, he noted that those were known at all relevant times by investors, and that Financial Holdings had real assets its independent board controlled and had the option of pursuing any path its directors chose.

In addressing whether KKR was a controlling stockholder, the Chancellor was focused on the reality that in cases where a party that did not have majority control of the entity's voting stock was found to be a controlling stockholder, the Court of Chancery, consistent with the instructions of this Court, looked for a combination of potent voting power and management control such that the stockholder could be deemed to have effective control of the board without actually owning a majority of stock. Not finding that combination here, the Chancellor [held that KKR did not control Financial Holdings and therefore the entire fairness standard did not apply].

Although the plaintiffs reiterate their position on appeal, the Chancellor correctly applied the law and we see no reason to repeat his lucid analysis of this question.

II. THE COURT OF CHANCERY CORRECTLY HELD THAT THE FULLY INFORMED, UNCOERCED VOTE OF THE DISINTERESTED STOCKHOLDERS INVOKED THE BUSINESS JUDGMENT RULE STANDARD OF REVIEW

Because the Chancellor was correct in determining that the entire fairness standard did not apply to the merger, the Chancellor's analysis of the effect of the uncoerced, informed stockholder vote is outcome-determinative. . . .

As to this point, the Court of Chancery noted, and the defendants point out on appeal, that the plaintiffs did not contest the defendants' argument below that if the merger was not subject to the entire fairness standard, the business judgment standard of review was invoked because the merger was approved by a disinterested stockholder majority. The Chancellor agreed with that argument below, and adhered to precedent supporting the proposition that when a transaction not subject to the entire fairness standard is approved by a fully informed, uncoerced vote of the disinterested stockholders, the business judgment rule applies.

Furthermore, although the plaintiffs argue that adhering to the proposition that a fully informed, uncoerced stockholder vote invokes the business judgment rule would impair the operation of *Unocal [Corp. v. Mesa Petroleum Co.,* 493 A.2d 946 (Del. 1985)] and *Revlon [v. MacAndrews & Forbes Holdings, Inc.,* 506 A.2d 173 (Del. 1986)], or expose stockholders to unfair action by directors without protection, the plaintiffs ignore several factors. First, *Unocal* and *Revlon* are primarily designed to give stockholders and the Court of Chancery the tool of injunctive relief to address important M & A decisions in real time, before closing. They were not tools designed with post-closing money damages claims in mind, the standards they articulate do not match the gross negligence standard for director due care liability . . . and with the prevalence of exculpatory charter provisions, due care liability is rarely even available.

Second and most important, the doctrine applies only to fully informed, uncoerced stockholder votes, and if troubling facts regarding director behavior were not disclosed that would have been material to a voting stockholder, then the business judgment rule is not invoked. Here, however, all of the objective facts regarding the board's interests, KKR's interests, and the negotiation process, were fully disclosed.

Finally, when a transaction is not subject to the entire fairness standard, the long-standing policy of our law has been to avoid the uncertainties and costs of judicial second-guessing when the disinterested stockholders have had the free and informed chance to decide on the economic merits of a transaction for themselves. There are sound reasons for this policy. When the real parties in interest—the disinterested equity owners—can easily protect themselves at the ballot box by simply voting no, the utility of a litigation-intrusive standard of review promises more costs to stockholders in the form of litigation rents and inhibitions on risk-taking than it promises in terms of benefits to them. The reason for that is tied to the core rationale of the business judgment rule, which is that judges are poorly positioned to evaluate the wisdom of business decisions and there is little utility to having them second-guess the determination of impartial decision-makers with more information (in the case of directors) or an actual economic stake in the outcome (in the case of informed, disinterested stockholders). In circumstances, therefore, where the stockholders have had the voluntary choice to accept or reject a transaction, the business judgment rule standard of review is the presumptively correct one and best facilitates wealth creation through the corporate form.

For these reasons, therefore, we affirm the Court of Chancery's judgment on the basis of its well-reasoned decision.

Notes and Questions

1. Reality Check

a. After *Kahn* and *Corwin*, when would *Unocal* or *Revlon* be applied?

b. What are the conditions under which a target board's decision to be acquired will be subject to the business judgment rule?

2. What Do You Think?

a. Are the Delaware courts giving too much deference to target boards? When *Unocal* was applied with the greatest vigor did it entail too much judicial inquiry?

b. Do you think *Unocal* and *Revlon* were designed primarily for pre-closing litigation? No case before *Corwin* made that distinction explicit.

Putting It to Work
Problem 16-3

Pogs Central, Inc., is a privately owned company with about 20 shareholders, all of whom are related to the founder, Cory Matthews, who is also the board chair, CEO, and the largest shareholder (with 30 percent). Pogs Central is the third largest manufacturer of pogs, a very niche industry. Pogs is minimally profitable, primarily because Cory loves the game of pogs more than he loves making money. In July, completely out of the blue, one of the world's greatest pog players, the fabulously wealthy Topanga Lawrence, approached Cory and offered to buy Pogs Central. Cory, without the knowledge or approval of the four other board members, began to negotiate with Topanga and eventually they reached a deal to sell Pogs Central to Topanga for $10 million in cash. The deal includes a long-term employment contract for Cory at a very generous salary. In August, Cory presented the deal to the board, which discussed the matter for nearly an hour before unanimously approving the transaction and recommending that the stockholders adopt it. Neither Cory nor any other board member had done any analysis to determine what the present value of Pogs Central is or what a motivated buyer might be willing to pay for the company.

In September, just before the Pogs Central shareholder meeting to vote on the sale to Topanga, Slammers Company, the largest manufacturer of pogs, offered to buy Pogs Central for $10.1 million. Slammers is run by George Feeny and it is clear that if Slammers acquires Pogs Central Cory will be fired immediately. At a special Pogs Central board meeting, called to consider Slammers' offer, the board unanimously voted to reject the offer. At the Pogs Central shareholder meeting, the transaction with Topanga narrowly passed.

Some Pogs Central shareholders have now sued the board alleging that the board should have cancelled the transaction with Topanga and negotiated with Slammers.

    a. Was Pogs Central's board under *Revlon* duties? If so, when did they attach?
    b. If *Revlon* applied, did the board meet its obligations?

5. State Antitakeover Statutes

Many state legislatures, in response to pleas from local public companies, adopted statutes that were designed to preclude takeovers without target board approval. These statutes took various forms and raised constitutional issues, both because tender offers are pervasively regulated by federal securities laws and because every public company is engaged in interstate commerce. In *CTS v. Dynamics Corp. of America*, 481 U.S. 69 (1987), Justice Powell upheld one such statute, in Indiana, against both a Supremacy Clause argument and a Commerce Clause argument. In so doing the Court may have made the internal affairs doctrine (see Chapter 5) a constitutional requirement under the Commerce Clause.

After *CTS* many states, including Delaware, adopted what are known as *business combination acts*. See DGCL §203. In brief, these statutes prohibit certain control transactions, such as mergers or sales of all assets, between a corporation and an entity controlling more than a certain amount (15% in Delaware) of shares. Such a controlling entity is sometimes called an *interested person* in the statutes. These prohibitions end a few years (three in Delaware) after the interested person becomes such. The prohibitions also end if: (1) the board approves the transaction by which the entity became an interested person (e.g., the board approves of the acquirer's tender offer); (2) the board and a supermajority of shareholders (unaffiliated with the raider or the board) approve the control transaction after the interested person has become such; or (3) the transaction by which the interested person becomes such results in the interested person acquiring a large percentage (85% in Delaware) of the voting shares. The idea is that a raider that buys a substantial majority of stock in the initial tender offer should be able to exercise control immediately. The acquirer should also be able to proceed if the board has approved the initial control transaction. This is the case where the target has negotiated to be acquired or where the target board is capitulating to a raider, possibly because the raider has increased the consideration to a level the target board believes is advantageous to its shareholders. Acquisition agreements for Delaware corporations contain a waiver of DGCL §203's restrictions. Otherwise, a raider will either have to wait for a relatively long period of time to eliminate the minority shareholders or offer enough consideration to induce a substantial majority of minority shareholders to approve such a transaction. The MBCA does not contain a control share acquisition provision.

D. FEDERAL SECURITIES REGULATION

The federal securities laws loom large in change of control situations. They obviously are dominant when a corporation is the subject of a tender offer. But the federal securities laws also have an effect on many change of control transactions that do not involve tender offers. In this section we will see the federal securities issues that are most likely to be germane to negotiated acquisitions and then look briefly at the regulation of tender offers, including the restrictions on insider trading in tender offer contexts.

1. "Groups" Under Section 13(d)

We saw at the end of the last chapter that any person or group that owns more than 5 percent of the equity of a public company must file a Schedule 13D. One set of issues, that even experienced lawyers may overlook, is the definition of *group* and other related concepts under Section 13(d) of the '34 Act. Section 13(d)(1) requires any "person" to file after "*acquiring*" the "beneficial ownership" of any public company equity. Section 13(d)(3) says that if two or more people "act as a . . . group for the purpose of acquiring, holding, or disposing of" equity of a public company, such group shall be deemed a "person" for the purposes of Section 13(d). Thus any time more than one shareholder agrees to act in concert regarding ownership of securities, they are a group. The group needn't be planning any purchases or sales; it is enough that the group is acting in concert even to continue ownership.

The SEC deems a group to have "acquired" its shares at the moment the group is formed, even though no shares have changed hands. So, if more than one shareholder agree to act together regarding a public company's equity, they are a "group" and the group "acquired" all shares already owned by any of the group's members. *See* Rule 13d-5(b)(1). To bring these rules back to the change of control context, where an acquisition involves a public company, the acquirer, the target, the principal shareholders (if they are involved in the negotiations), and the officers and directors (assuming they own at least some shares) must be careful to realize whether they have formed a "group" at some point during the negotiations and, if so, whether the group has "acquired" more than 5 percent of the public company's equity. If so, a Schedule 13D must be filed promptly.

2. Going Private Transactions

Another area in which federal securities laws affect a change of control transaction is where the target corporation is publicly held, but the change of control transaction involves the repurchase of shares by the corporation such that the shares will no longer be publicly traded. Where this transaction is not regulated under the tender offer rules, it will be considered a *going private transaction* subject to Section 13(e). This sort of transaction is often undertaken by the corporation's managers who will remain shareholders after the going private transaction is complete. As an overview, a going private transaction requires the company to file a Schedule 13E-3, which contains detailed disclosure of the transaction, the company's owners after the transaction, and the source of funds used to eliminate the public shareholders' ownership. At bottom, the going private rules are meant to ensure that such transactions involve the same kinds of investor protection (e.g., full disclosure and sufficient time to make an informed decision) as would be provided in a tender offer.

3. Tender Offers

Perhaps the most pervasive and best-known federal securities rules in the change of control setting are the tender offer rules. These are promulgated under §§14(d) and 14(e) of the '34 Act. Speaking broadly, 14(d) prohibits any person from making a tender offer for more than 5 percent of a public company's equity without complying with SEC regulations. Section 14(e) prohibits any person from committing fraud in connection with a tender offer, in contravention of any SEC rules. Although both sections are rather detailed, the SEC has the power to promulgate additional rules and those rules have, effectively, superseded the statutory provisions in terms of providing the substantive regulation of tender offers.

Any sort of detailed look at the tender offer rules would take far too much time and space here, so what follows is a précis of the way the rules work. Perhaps the most surprising and, some would say, pernicious aspect of these regulations is that "tender offer" is not defined. The SEC's rationale has been that if it defined "tender offer," then people could easily structure transactions that skirt the regulations. This hasn't convinced many non-SEC lawyers. In any event, case law has provided a standard definition of *tender offer*. For over 25 years courts and commentators have looked to the eight-factor "*Wellman* test" enunciated by Judge Carter in a 1979 district court case, *Wellman v. Dickinson*.[4] These factors are: (1) active and widespread solicitation of public shareholders for the shares of an issuer; (2) solicitation made for a substantial percentage of the issuer's stock; (3) offer to purchase made at a premium over the prevailing market price; (4) terms of the offer are firm rather than negotiable; (5) offer contingent on the tender of a fixed number of shares, often subject to a fixed maximum number to be purchased; (6) offer open only a limited period of time; (7) offeree subjected to pressure to sell his stock; and (8) public announcements of a purchasing program that precedes or accompanies a rapid accumulation of stock.

The SEC rules prohibit the commencement of a tender offer without filing a Schedule TO. As you may imagine, the Schedule TO is a detailed disclosure document containing information about the bidder, its source of funds, the consideration for the tender offer, and the target company. The rules also define commencement as being the transmission to target shareholders of the means to tender their shares. So, a bidder can announce a tender offer without filing a Schedule TO so long as a filing is made before the actual method of tendering is provided to shareholders.

The target shareholders are protected in several ways by the SEC rules. The target company must either supply the bidder with its shareholder list or must transmit the bidder's tender offer material to its shareholders (at the bidder's cost). This is to ensure that target management cannot stymie the shareholders' choice by keeping information from them. The target management must publicly announce its position on the tender offer, although that position could be simply neutrality. To ensure that target shareholders are not stampeded into tendering, the tender offer rules provide that a tender offer must remain open for at least 20 business days (and an additional 10 business days if the consideration changes), shareholders may withdraw tendered shares at any time before the bidder purchases them. If the tender offer is for a limited amount of the target company shares, such as where the bidder only seeks 51 percent of the shares, intending to eliminate the remaining shareholders by merger, and more shares are tendered, the bidder cannot purchase the shares on a first-come-first-served basis but must prorate the purchases among all shareholders who tendered during the tender offer period. The SEC rules also require that tender offers be open to all target shareholders and that all tendering shareholders receive the highest price paid by the bidder to any shareholder.

The '34 Act and SEC rules prohibit fraud in connection with a tender offer. The most salient for our purposes are the prohibition against announcing a tender offer without the intention of "commencing" a tender offer within a reasonable time, making a false or misleading statement of material fact in connection with a tender offer, and buying or selling target or bidder shares while in possession of material nonpublic information. This last prohibition is the *insider trading* proscription for tender offers. Outside of the tender offer setting, a similar proscription on trading on the basis of material nonpublic information is implied under Rule 10b-5.

---

4. *Wellman v. Dickinson*, 475 F. Supp. 783 (S.D.N.Y. 1979).

E. TERMS OF ART IN THIS CHAPTER

Advance notice provision
Appraisal right
Asset lock-up
Break-up fee
Business combination acts
Conglomeration
Constituent corporations
Deal protective measures
Defensive measures
Definitive agreement
Dissenter's right
Due diligence
ESOP
Exit strategy

Fair value
Flip in
Flip over
Going private transaction
Group
Hostile tender offer
Insider trading
Interested person
Intermediate scrutiny
Letter of intent
Marketability discount
Material adverse change
Merger
Minority discount
No-shop
No-talk

Poison pill
Raider
Recognition
Reservation price
Reverse triangular merger
Revlon duties
Shareholder lock-up
Shareholders' rights plan
Shark repellents
Short form merger
Subsidiary
Target corporation
Tender offer
Topping fee
Unocal test

Part IV.

UNINCORPORATED ENTITIES

17

Partnerships

A. GENERAL PARTNERSHIPS

1. Background and Context

At its most essential, a partnership can be thought of as a business owned by more than one person. Partnerships first became commercially important in the late eighteenth and early nineteenth centuries when trading firms first became widespread. Recall that Ebenezer Scrooge and Jacob Marley were partners. Shortly after, courts and scholars began to deal with the legal consequences of common ownership of a business. Justice Joseph Story's *Commentaries on the Law of Partnership* (1841) had a major effect on the development of partnership principles. At bottom, the legal issues were ones of contract and agency. The co-owners (i.e., partners) could contract among themselves relatively freely. They could, for example, contract about how much money each would contribute, how the profits (or losses) would be divided, how the business was to be managed, and how the net assets were to be divided when one partner ceased to be a co-owner.

What the courts in England and America added to this was a system of presumptions; default rules to fill the areas in which the parties had neglected to agree. Courts created a presumption of symmetry, a presumption of equality, and a presumption that the contracts are personal such that another person could not be substituted for, or added to, the original owners. Thus, in the absence of an explicit agreement of the partners, losses would be divided in the same proportion as profits (symmetry). Each partner would have an equal right to manage the business; disputes among partners would be decided by a majority of partners, regardless of their ownership interests (equality). A partner's powers could not be transferred, and no one could become a partner without unanimous consent (personal contract).

As you see, the relation between partners was largely contractual. The relation between the partners and third parties involved agency. Obviously a business owner who contracted with, or committed a tort against, a third party would be bound under ordinary common law precepts. Courts applied agency law to allow third parties to recover against partners who had not themselves contracted or committed torts. In so doing, partners became agents of one another. In a co-owned business, then, each co-owner had the power to bind the other co-owners and, in turn, was bound by his or her co-owners' actions all as determined by agency law. This reciprocity made partners different from other principal/agent relationships such as employer/employee.

One of the most troublesome questions was deciding the consequence of a change in the co-owners of the business. In the starkest setting, a co-owner might die. A co-owner might also decide to stop being a co-owner, either because he or she wanted to retire or because the co-owner might want to continue in business alone or with others who were not currently co-owners. Finally, the co-owners might unanimously decide to allow a new person to be a co-owner. One corollary of the personal nature of a partnership was the rule that any partner had the absolute right to end the co-ownership, even though such ending might violate a contract with the other co-owners. As between the partners themselves, a default rule developed that when a partner ceased to be a co-owner, the partnership's assets would be liquidated and each partner paid his or her interest. Because liquidating a going concern typically resulted in a depressed sale price (because the assets were sold under compulsion to achieve a quick sale) partners often agreed in advance that the partnership's assets would not be liquidated when a partner ceased to be a co-owner. Rather, the remaining partners would continue the business and the partner who left would receive the value of his or her interest.

Regardless of the partners' agreement among themselves, agency law provided that a partner who ceased to be a co-owner nonetheless remained liable to third parties for existing obligations of the business. In symmetrical fashion, where all partners agreed to admit a new person as a co-owner, the new partner was only liable to third parties for subsequent business obligations. Thus a partner, as agent, could only bind those persons who were currently partners.

By the early twentieth century there was a strong movement to codify partnership law. This movement stemmed both from a more general turn-of-the-century impetus to codify the common law and from a particular sense that commercial areas, such as partnership law, should be uniform among jurisdictions to provide the predictability necessary for a national economy. Increasingly, partnerships conducted business in more than one state and partners were resident in several states. In 1902 the Conference of Commissioners on Uniform State Laws began a project to draft a uniform partnership act. After a dozen years of work, the original Uniform Partnership Act (UPA (1914)) was promulgated. The UPA (1914) was one of the most successful of the uniform acts, being adopted in every state except Louisiana (which, nonetheless, adopted most of the underlying principles of the act). Nonetheless, after 70 years, an ABA subcommittee recommended that the commissioners (now known as the National Conference of Commissioners on Uniform State Laws) draft a replacement act. That project resulted in a new Uniform Partnership Act, which went through several important amendments and finally emerged as the Uniform Partnership Act in 1997 (UPA (1997)). That act was revised in 2013. We will refer to the 2013 version as the "UPA." The vast majority of states have adopted the UPA (1997).

The description of partnership law so far has been phrased to suggest that partnership is really a shorthand term for a set of agreements, some actual and some implied, rather than an artificial "entity" itself (such as a corporation, a state, or a law school). In that sense, a partnership is simply a collection of the partners (the classic simile is that a partnership is like a friendship — a set of relationships but not a separate thing). But, as a consequence of the axioms from agency law that each partner can only bind the people who are currently co-owners (and not past or future co-owners), the partnership can be seen as an entity itself. Thus any change in the co-owners ended the entity. Where an additional person was added as a partner, the original partnership (an entity) was immediately succeeded by a second partnership. Where a partner ceased to be a co-owner, the original partnership ended (after a kind of twilight winding-up period) and the underlying economic business might be sold off piecemeal or sold as a going concern to a single person, another partnership (often consisting of the remaining original partners), or another entity such as a corporation. Under the Law Merchant, the legal principles applied throughout the Western world to commercial disputes, which was accepted in England from the sixteenth century, partnerships were thought of as entities separate from their partners. Thus there was frequently a tension between the common law conception of a partnership as an aggregate of individuals and the commercial law idea of a partnership as an entity.

The UPA (1914) melded both the aggregate and the entity theories of the partnership, often with unhappy results. The reason for this meld was that the original drafter, the great James Barr Ames, dean of the Harvard Law School, was a proponent of the entity approach. He died during the drafting process and his successor, William Draper Lewis, dean of the University of Pennsylvania Law School, continued the draft on the aggregate theory. You may be thinking that this is a typical academic dustup between two law professors arguing over how many angels can dance on the head of a dean. One of the most important changes the UPA (1997) made was to adopt the entity approach throughout. *See* UPA §201(a).

The use of the partnership as the dominant form for business entities ended around 1890 when the business corporation took its place. Nonetheless, many businesses were and are conducted as partnerships for several reasons. One reason is, as you will see in the next section, that a partnership can be formed inadvertently. That is, the parties might not realize they are forming a partnership. A related reason for partnerships is that some people deliberately choose the partnership form but do so without seeking legal advice as to the most advantageous business form. A third reason for doing business as a partnership is a lack of alternative forms. Until the 1970s, the learned professions (including law) were prohibited by state law from practicing as corporations. The reason for this limitation was rooted in protecting the public. Corporations have limited liability and it was widely believed that it would be unethical for a professional such as a lawyer or doctor to limit his or her liability for malpractice to a client or patient. Further, because partners have unlimited personal liability for the debts of the partnership, each partner in a professional partnership has a strong economic incentive to monitor the professional actions of the other partners. Thus one lawyer in a partnership has a distinct motivation to be sure that another partner has not missed a filing deadline or is not commingling firm funds with client funds; one doctor has a distinct motivation to be sure another doctor is not covering up medical negligence. This monitoring function would be diminished if one partner were not liable for the malpractice of another partner. From the late 1970s onward these restrictions were reduced or eliminated.

A fourth reason for choosing the partnership form is that, until the late 1990s, certain tax advantages could only be effectively obtained by partnerships. It is not unusual for new businesses to operate at a loss because start-up costs are high and revenues are low. Further, some businesses, such as drilling oil wells or making motion pictures, incur the vast majority of their (usually large) costs at the beginning and only later see any revenues. The Internal Revenue Code taxes partnerships as aggregates rather than entities. That is, the partnership itself does not pay tax; it merely files an informational return with the Internal Revenue Service. All profits or losses are reported by the partners. By contrast, a corporation is usually taxed as an entity; it reports income on its own return. Its shareholders only report income if and when the corporation distributes dividends. But losses cannot be distributed to shareholders. If a business incurs losses, its owners would ordinarily prefer to include those losses on their own income tax returns because the losses offset any income the owner has from other sources. Hence many businesses were organized as partnerships, at least until steady profits were anticipated. Since 1996 LLCs are usually taxed as partnerships. The LLC has several advantages over partnerships and is thus the form of choice for entities seeking partnership taxation. Nonetheless, many entities that were created as partnerships for tax purposes before 1996 still exist.

Notes and Questions

1. What Do You Think?

a. Do you think professional entities such as law firms and physician groups should be required to be formed as partnerships rather than as corporations or LLCs? Are there other ways to address the concerns for the public's protection than by restricting the form of the enterprise?

2. The Current Setting

The Uniform Partnership Act (UPA) in its current form was promulgated in 2013. It replaces a uniform act drafted in the early twentieth century (UPA (1914)). In most respects the UPA continues the substantive rules of the UPA (1914). In the cases that follow, citations to state codes have been replaced with citations to the UPA contained in square brackets.

a. Formation

We begin with the question of how a partnership is formed. This issue is not an abstraction. Whether a partnership has been formed greatly affects the parties' rights and liabilities.

Ziegler v. Dahl

691 N.W.2d 271 (N.D. 2005)

Sandstrom, J.

Michael Ziegler and Jack Kitsch appeal a summary judgment dismissing their claim that they were in a partnership with Steve Dahl, David Tronson, and James Legacie and are entitled to an accounting upon the winding up of the partnership. We affirm the district court's summary judgment.

I

Dahl, along with Tronson and Legacie, began marketing an ice fishing guide service on Devils Lake after the 1996-1997 ice fishing season. In the spring of 1997, Dahl conceived the name "Perch Patrol" for the guide service when he was asked by the local chamber of commerce to guide a camera crew from Midwest Outdoors Television. Dahl testified in his affidavit that each member of Perch Patrol agreed to be an independent contractor, each responsible for obtaining his own license and equipment. Dahl claimed they retained their own fees, but equally shared clients and marketing expenses.

Dahl asked Ziegler and Kitsch to help Perch Patrol guide ice fishermen on Devils Lake for the last part of the 1998-1999 ice fishing season. Ziegler testified in his affidavit that he considered Kitsch and himself employees of Perch Patrol for the remaining portion of the 1998-1999 season. They were paid for drilling holes in the ice, setting up shelters, and ensuring that the ice fishing clients were properly equipped. Neither Ziegler nor Kitsch had any client contact during that year.

Dahl presented Ziegler and Kitsch with a document titled "Perch Patrol Expansion" in the spring of 1999. The document contained sections called "Employee Proposal" and "Partnership Proposal." Under the "Employee Proposal," Ziegler and Kitsch would receive 50 percent of the number of clients over six per day, and Dahl, Tronson, and Legacie would provide all of the fishing equipment. Under the "Partnership Proposal," Ziegler and Kitsch would "be their own separate entity under the Perch Patrol" and both parties would be "responsible for providing their own gear including fish houses, heaters, vexilars, augers, chairs, bait lunches, ect [sic]." The partnership proposal also provided that both "parties shall share equally in both the costs and the efforts in these endeavors." The parties did not adopt either proposal.

The parties later agreed, but never reduced their agreement to writing, that Dahl, Tronson, and Legacie had the right to guide and receive fees from the first six clients, Ziegler and Kitsch had the next four, and Dahl, Tronson, and Legacie had clients 11, 12, 15, 16, 19, and 20. The agreement was later changed to split the fees received from each client after the first ten, and they agreed to divide equally among the five members the tips received by the guides.

On November 20, 1999, Ziegler and Kitsch each wrote a check payable to Dahl in the amount of $813.97. Ziegler and Kitsch claim the checks were an initial capital investment in a partnership, and Dahl claims they were for future marketing expenses. Dahl stated in his affidavit that he was responsible for all administrative activities for Perch Patrol, including establishing marketing agreements and plans with resorts, promoting the venture in promotional media, booking all reservations, distributing clients to guides, handling all funds, and planning each day's activities. All the parties attended at least some trade shows to promote the Perch Patrol guide service prior to the start of the 1999 ice fishing season.

On August 8, 2000, Dahl, Tronson, and Legacie informed Ziegler and Kitsch they could no longer guide with them. Dahl, Tronson, and Legacie continue to operate under the name Perch Patrol. . . .

The district court granted the motion for summary judgment dismissing Ziegler and Kitsch's claim that they were in a partnership, stating there was insufficient evidence to support a finding that a partnership was created.

III

definition of partnership →

A partnership is "an association of two or more persons to carry on as co-owners a business for profit. . . ." [UPA §102(11)]. The formation of a partnership in North Dakota is governed by [UPA §202]. . . .

A

Ziegler argues the district court erred as a matter of law by requiring intent as an element of a partnership.

'intent of the parties

One of the most important tests of whether a partnership exists between two persons is the intent of the parties. North Dakota adopted the [UPA] in 1995, adding the words "whether or not the persons intend to form a partnership" to the definition of a partnership. The drafters of the uniform law did not intend any substantive changes in the current law when they added the additional phrase to the definition of a partnership. Uniform Partnership Act §202, cmt. 1 (1997); *Byker v. Mannes,* 465 Mich. 637, 641 N.W.2d 210, 214 (2002).

> The addition of the phrase, "whether or not the persons intend to form a partnership," merely codifies the universal judicial construction of UPA [(1914)] Section 6(1) that a partnership is created by the association of persons whose intent is to carry on as co-owners a business for profit, regardless of their subjective intention to be "partners." Indeed, they may inadvertently create a partnership despite their expressed subjective intention not to do so. The new language alerts readers to this possibility.

The National Conference of Commissioners on Uniform State Laws amended the definition even though they were satisfied with the existing judicial construction of the definition of partnership. *Byker,* 641 N.W.2d at 214. "The commissioners emphasized that '[n]o substantive change in the law' was intended by the amendment." *Id.* This means the focus is not on whether individuals subjectively intended to form a partnership, but on whether the individuals intended to jointly carry on a business for profit. *Id.* at 211.

We have said participants in a business "must intend to be part of an association that includes *all* the essential elements of a partnership for that association to be a partnership." *Gangl v. Gangl,* 281 N.W.2d 574, 580 (N.D. 1979); *see also Tarnavsky v. Tarnavsky,* 147 F.3d 674 (8th Cir. 1998). The existence of this element focuses "on the intent of the participants to be a part of a relationship which includes the other essential elements of [a] partnership." *Id.* Intent does not need to "be vocalized either in writing or orally, if it can be derived from the actions of the parties." *Id.*

Dahl stated in his affidavit that neither he nor Tronson nor Legacie considered themselves, much less Ziegler or Kitsch, partners in Perch Patrol. Dahl said that he considered Perch Patrol to be an association of independent contractors and that Ziegler and Kitsch would be their own entities. The Perch Patrol expansion document given to Ziegler and Kitsch by Dahl did use the term partnership, but this proposal was never adopted. In Ziegler's affidavit, he said the parties did not accept the terms of the document, but contends the final agreement reflected the initial proposal. The terminology that parties give to their working arrangement is not determinative, "especially where the record indicates the parties did not intend to be a part of a relationship which included the other essential elements of a partnership." *Gangl*, 281 N.W.2d at 580. There was no evidence that Dahl or Tronson or Legacie intended to engage in activities that would form a partnership with Ziegler and Kitsch.

Other actions by the parties do not manifest an intent to form a relationship that constitutes a partnership. The parties did not file a partnership tax return, Dahl handled all of the administrative activities, each party provided his own equipment, and all of the major decisions were made without the input and direction of Ziegler and Kitsch. Ziegler and Kitsch argue the $813.97 checks written to Dahl were capital contributions showing their intent to buy into the partnership. Dahl, and even Ziegler in his affidavit, testified the checks were contributions toward meeting future partnership expenses. Because the parties never intended to engage in activities that would result in a partnership, the intent element is not satisfied.

B

1

Co-ownership is the second necessary element to prove the existence of a partnership. *Tarnavsky*, 147 F.3d at 677-78. Co-ownership includes the "sharing of profits and losses as well as the power of control in the management of the business." *Id*. Control is an indispensable component of the co-ownership analysis. *Gangl*, 281 N.W.2d at 580. If partners are co-owners of a business, they each have the power of ultimate control. An important qualification to that rule, however, is that a person does not need to control the business but only needs to have the right to exercise control in the management of the business.

Kitsch said in his affidavit that he participated in and made decisions regarding where to fish and that he provided other valuable knowledge and skill to Perch Patrol. He and Ziegler also claim Dahl contacted them daily to discuss business issues regarding Perch Patrol. Dahl said in his affidavit that no vote was ever taken on any issue relating to the operation and management of Perch Patrol and that he and Tronson and Legacie operated and managed all of the business functions. Dahl, in his affidavit, and Kitsch, in his deposition, said that Dahl was responsible for all of the administrative work for Perch Patrol. Ziegler and Kitsch stated in their depositions that they did what they were directed to do by Dahl, who told them which clients to guide and which ice, media, and trade shows to attend.

Ziegler and Kitsch failed to demonstrate that the discussions they had with Dahl were about the management and control of the business and that their discussions affected the activities of Perch Patrol. An example of Ziegler and Kitsch's lack of control in the management of the business was the decision by Dahl, Tronson, and

Legacie to cancel the rest of the guides in early March 2000 because of warmer temperatures and thawing ice. According to Dahl's affidavit, he contacted all the clients who had booked with Perch Patrol in March and canceled their reservations. He told Ziegler it was not an easy decision but he did not want to endanger the lives of clientele for a few more days of fishing. Dahl said in his affidavit that Ziegler responded, "if Perch Patrol formed a real partnership . . . and [Kitsch] and I were treated equally as you three, none of this would be an issue." Ziegler and Kitsch also argue their absence at breakfast meetings held by Dahl, Tronson, and Legacie to discuss business during the ice fishing season indicates they exercised their right of control by not attending the meetings. Their unwillingness to attend meetings demonstrates that they had the right to control where they ate breakfast, not that they had a right to exercise control in the management of the business. Viewing the evidence in the light most favorable to Ziegler and Kitsch, we see no competent evidence to support their assertion that they had a right to exercise control and management in Perch Patrol.

2

There must be a "community of interest in the profits of the business, and an agreement or right to share profits, and, generally, an obligation to share losses as well." The sharing of gross returns does not per se establish a partnership, because those returns could have been received in payment for "services as an independent contractor or of wages or other compensation to an employee." [UPA §202(b), (c)(3)(B)]; *Tarnavsky*, 147 F.3d at 678.

Under the working agreement, Dahl, Tronson, and Legacie were entitled to the first six clients and Ziegler and Kitsch were allocated the next four. Each party received the fees generated by guiding his own clients, and they did not pool or divide these fees. Ziegler and Kitsch could have gone the entire winter without receiving any client fees had there been no more than six clients per day, because each guide received money only for services he actually performed. Ziegler testified in his affidavit that Dahl periodically collected the fees generated each day and distributed the revenues after deducting shared expenses for telephone bills and office supplies, and that each person was responsible for one-fifth of these expenses. Income used to pay partnership expenses is not profit. A profit is the amount remaining after the expenses of the partnership are paid. After Dahl deducted expenses, the money went directly to the individuals who guided the clients and was not shared with any other member of Perch Patrol. This fee structure used by Perch Patrol correlates more closely with an independent contractor payment system than with profit sharing among partners.

C

The final element of a partnership is the necessity of a profit motive. *Tarnavsky*, 147 F.3d at 678. Dahl testified during his deposition that his intent was to make a profit guiding, and there is no dispute that Perch Patrol was operated to generate client fees.

IV

We conclude the district court did not err in ordering summary judgment, because Ziegler and Kitsch failed to show that the first two elements were present in their working agreement. Because we conclude a partnership did not exist, Ziegler and Kitsch's argument that the district court erred in not compelling Dahl to disclose Perch Patrol's client list is moot. We therefore affirm the summary judgment.

Notes and Questions

1. Notes

a. As you see from this case, partnerships may be formed inadvertently. That is, a "partnership" is not a specific intent entity.

b. In addition to UPA §202(a), §202(c) lists several presumptions to be used in determining whether a partnership has been formed.

2. Reality Check

a. What elements are necessary to form a partnership? Are those elements statutory or common law?

b. Which elements does the court find are missing here? Do you agree?

3. Suppose

a. If Ziegler and Kitsch had routinely attended the breakfast meetings, would that make it more or less likely that they were partners in Perch Patrol?

4. What Do You Think?

a. Do you think that the "partnership proposal" makes it more likely or less likely that the parties intended to form a partnership?

b. Do you think that the question whether a partnership was formed should turn on whether the various parties chose to attend breakfast meetings? More generally, if a person could exercise control of a business but chooses to let others control, does he or she have the requisite control to be considered a co-owner?

c. Do you agree with the court's analysis of the import of the parties' division of Perch Patrol's profits?

d. How much weight do you think the courts should give to the parties' testimony regarding their intent? Do you think a party's answer to the question "did you intend to form a partnership?" is helpful? If not, how would you rephrase the question?

In re KeyTronics

744 N.W.2d 425 (Neb. 2008)

McCormack, J.

NATURE OF CASE

The issue in this case is whether a business partnership was formed between Don King and Scott Willson and, if so, what business activities were part of that partnership. The Uniform Partnership Act at §[202(a)], states that "the association of two or more persons to carry on as co-owners a business for profit forms a partnership, whether or not the persons intend to form a partnership." Willson brought an action for the winding up and an accounting, alleging formation of a partnership, and King counterclaimed for wrongfully withholding property, denying the partnership. The district court found that King and Willson had "pooled resources, money and labor," but found no partnership existed because there was no "specific agreement." Alternatively, the court found that because King did not commit his preexisting business to any specifically formed partnership, the scope of the partnership did not encompass any activity-garnering profits. Willson appealed the district court's order. We reverse, and remand for further proceedings.

BACKGROUND

King and Willson first met sometime in 1999 when Willson, an electronics technician and computer programmer, was working at a computer store. King was doing business at that time under the name of "Washco," as a sole proprietorship, and King contracted with the store for a computer repair. Washco sold and installed carwash systems and accessories. It also serviced existing carwash systems and the systems it sold. Washco later became Wash Systems, Incorporated.

One of the products King offered to his customers was the "QuikPay" system. QuikPay is a cashless vending system for carwashes. Customers use a memory chip key that can be placed on their key chain and used with a controller at the carwash. Either a cash value can be placed on the key, or an account can be established through which carwash usage recorded on the key is billed monthly.

Washco purchased QuikPay systems for resale from Datakey Electronics Inc. (Datakey). Datakey's main line of business was the manufacture and sale of keys with reprogrammable memory and their corresponding "Keyceptacles" for a variety of applications. The QuikPay carwash system was only one such application, and it was becoming unprofitable for Datakey.

Part of the reason that the QuikPay system was unprofitable was that the keys for QuikPay could only be obtained from an attendant. If the key was set up for cash, when the credit ran out, the key could only be recharged through an attendant. Glen Jennings, president of Datakey, explained that since most carwashes are unattended, this reliance on the presence of the carwash owner or employee was limiting the product's market. The system needed some "peripherals" to make it self-service. Datakey had decided, however, not to dedicate its limited engineering resources to the design or manufacture of such "peripherals." It was looking into the possibility of working with an outside source as the original equipment manufacturer of such items.

As QuikPay's largest distributor, King was aware that QuikPay's limitations made the product unattractive to many of his customers. King was also having other problems with the system. In the spring of 2002, Willson was working at a new company as a computer programmer. King contacted Willson privately to see if Willson could develop a combined "key dispenser" and "revalue station" for the QuikPay system that would make the system self-service. King also asked Willson if he would design and install an interface between the QuikPay system and the carwash of one of King's customers. King explained that although most carwashes already contained a third-party interface that would easily connect with the QuikPay system, a few did not. Without such an interface, King was unable to sell QuikPay to these customers. Designing such an interface was beyond King's technical expertise.

There is little evidence in the record as to what sort of business arrangement was made with regard to Willson's services in designing the interface. King states only that compensation "was never discussed," and, in fact, Willson was never paid for his work. It is undisputed that Willson individually designed and installed at least four specific customer interfaces that allowed King to sell the QuikPay system to those customers.

As to the development of the key dispenser-revalue station, King testified there was an oral agreement among himself, Willson, and Scott Gardeen. Gardeen was an employee of Datakey who was an original designer of QuikPay and was King's main contact with Datakey. According to King, they agreed they would form a corporation whenever Willson developed the key dispenser-revalue station. Gardeen also recalled discussing their business as a future corporation because they were concerned about personal liability issues inherent to partnerships. Willson, on the other hand, had no memory of specifically discussing the formalities of their business relationship. He was sure that they had agreed they would all "be a part of it" and that they "each had a piece of the pie."

The three parties met in Des Moines, Iowa, in the spring of 2002 to discuss the venture in which they would design and build the key dispenser-revalue station and sell it to Datakey. It was agreed that Willson would write the software and do the firmware, hardware, and any other electrical or software work; Gardeen would contribute his knowledge of the system and his contact with Datakey; and King would contribute financial resources and his experience and contacts as QuikPay's largest distributor.

Together, Willson, King, and Gardeen came up with the name "Secure Data Systems" for their business. They discussed the fact that the entity's initials, "SDS," were also the initials of their first names, Scott, Don, and Scott. By the summer, Willson had built a hand-held revalue station for a meeting with Jennings. Jennings indicated that if a final, marketable key dispenser-revalue station were developed, Datakey would be interested in a business relationship with Secure Data Systems.

In the meantime, King was becoming increasingly frustrated with maintenance of the QuikPay system for his customers. In September 2002, King sent a letter to Gardeen complaining about various issues with the system. The main complaint was that controllers were not operating properly. Although Datakey provided King with replacement controllers, King had to drive long distances to his customers' sites to manually implement the replacement or make other repairs he had not anticipated. In the letter, King stated:

> I can not [sic] continue to expose my self [sic] to the expense of keeping this stuff running. Besides the expense I don't have the time. I don't see that I have any other choice but to back away from selling additional clients. At least until the current problems are stable or we have a new controller. I don't feel like I can honestly charge or pass expense's [sic] on to my customer when this product continues [to] have problems.

King then proposed:

> Because of [Willson's] future interests, I believe he would be more motivated to address issues with the current controller than a programmer with no interest in the system. [Willson] has mentioned that programming cost can exceed one hundred dollars an hour. If . . . Willson were to work on the current system I believe he should be compensated for his work.

I would have to discuss it with . . . Willson, but I don't believe he would demand those kind[s] of fees.

King suggested that Datakey allow Willson access to its proprietary software.

King continued to involve Willson in dealing with other technical issues relating to King's QuikPay customers. Willson explained: "[T]here w[ere] a lot of problems with the QuikPay units. Sometimes they would put the wrong version of firmware on there or they wouldn't program for them at all and the units just wouldn't function properly." It became King's regular practice to copy Willson into his e-mail correspondence with Datakey concerning QuikPay system maintenance. According to Willson, King and Willson communicated regularly about both the development of the key dispenser-revalue station and QuikPay maintenance. Willson testified that he did not demand or receive payment for these services, but believed they were part of his contribution to the partnership.

Around October 2002, Datakey decided to discontinue its QuikPay line. Its minimal sales of QuikPay were outweighed by Datakey's costs in addressing support issues for the product. To each of its customers, Datakey sent one controller for every two they had ever purchased, and informed them that Datakey would no longer be supporting their product.

Datakey referred all of its customers to King at Washco for continued support of the system. Datakey's customer base consisted of approximately 20 or 30 customers with a total of at least 200 QuikPay controllers in use. It is unclear how many QuikPay customers King had had prior to this time. Datakey also gave to King, without charge, all of the parts and equipment relating to QuikPay that Datakey had in stock. This inventory had an original procurement cost of approximately $200,000. Datakey had already given King and Willson access to its software source codes. Jennings explained, "[W]e were happy to have somebody who would give [QuikPay customers] best-efforts supports [sic], because obsoleting a product can reflect poorly on our name." In addition, Datakey hoped to be able to continue selling its keys and Keyceptacles to QuikPay customers, if those systems were kept "alive" by King.

Willson testified that from the moment King acquired Datakey's customers and inventory, Willson was very involved in making this acquisition a success. Willson testified that King immediately asked him to put together a list of things that they needed from Datakey to make all the inventory work. The record contains an e-mail from Willson to King with this list. In the e-mail, Willson also offered to accompany King to Minneapolis, Minnesota, to Datakey's headquarters if necessary and Willson stressed that they would need as much information as possible from Datakey "in order to make this a successful venture."

Willson explained that he was in charge of assembly and repairs of the QuikPay inventory once they received it. The inventory was shipped in pieces, and many of the old input/output, or I/O, boards had to be updated with the newest version of the QuikPay program so that the QuikPay units would function properly. Willson stated that his direct and indirect involvement in customer service for the QuikPay line also increased at this time.

Willson stated he was in frequent communication with King regarding the QuikPay acquisition from Datakey and the development of their new customer base. Willson said he discussed with King in detail what would be appropriate pricing for

QuikPay repairs and equipment. The record contains evidence of an e-mail from King to Willson with the QuikPay pricing schedule. According to Willson, he and King discussed ways to minimize costs of the QuikPay units. For example, Willson stated that they jointly made the decision to discontinue about half of the QuikPay box styles previously available to customers so that they could cut down on Secure Data Systems' costs. Willson also stated that they discussed creating a new brochure to promote the QuikPay line to customers. "[B]etween helping customers and modifying boards and getting the units put together and tested so that [King] could sell those," Willson stated that when he had time, he also continued to work on developing the key dispenser-revalue station.

King testified that by the beginning of 2003, he had deliberately separated his QuikPay sales, maintenance, and its future development from his Washco carwash business and had moved all QuikPay business to Secure Data Systems. Around the same time, Willson developed a Web site for Secure Data Systems with e-mail accounts for King and Willson.

King continued to operate Washco as he had previously, selling and maintaining the non-QuikPay carwash systems and accessories. There is no allegation that Willson was ever involved in non-QuikPay Washco ventures.

King and Willson had difficulties with some of the inventory acquired from Datakey. The record contains a draft letter that King e-mailed to Willson, in which King expressed his frustration to Gardeen, who, as mentioned, was King's main liaison with Datakey. Apparently in reference to himself and Willson, King repeatedly referred in the letter to "we" and "us." King stated that he would rather be writing a letter to Jennings thanking him for "the faith that he extended to us that we have the ability to make the QuikPay system work." But, the system had been "pieced mealed [sic]" to "us" and remained incomplete. King made several complaints and described some of the future challenges his acquisition would present:

> Regarding the [computer] software, because of licensing agreements, you told us that we had [to] go out and buy [a specific computer application]. We did and as you know it did not work. Now you are telling us that we are going to have to go out and buy [another computer application]. . . .
>
> . . .
>
> You suggested that we get on with development of a new controller and write all new software. When the parts run out, end users will simply have to purchase new controllers and software. Development of a new controller and software will differently happen. . . .
>
> With the exception of the data back up problem in the [computer] software, the controller and firmware with the latest updates appear to be stable. On the other hand we have no idea what is going to surface down the road.

King reminded Gardeen that there were customers with substantial commitment to Datakey's key and that they "deserve better." King asked Datakey for more assistance and reiterated that "we are looking forward to a long and successful association with Datakey."

Jennings explained that when King took over the QuikPay system, Datakey had sent King compact discs with the source files and other information Datakey thought would be needed to support the system, but King was still having trouble getting things to run. Both Jennings and Gardeen testified that it was apparent that Willson was the person working with King to get the QuikPay equipment working. And there was substantial correspondence between Datakey and Willson regarding the QuikPay system. Eventually, Jennings sent an e-mail to Willson, copied to King, explaining that rather than trying to figure out which file might still be missing from the compact discs sent to them, Datakey would simply rebuild the system on a computer and lend that computer to Willson as a reference tool. This was, in fact, done.

When Jennings was asked whether he knew who the owners of Secure Data Systems were, he answered that he "understood that . . . King and . . . Willson were involved in Secure Data Systems." Upon further questioning, Jennings testified, however, that it was "never clarified" whether both King and Willson owned Secure Data Systems or whether one worked for the other.

In May 2003, King and Willson went together to an international carwash convention in Las Vegas, Nevada. King suggested to Willson that he make up Secure Data Systems business cards for King and Willson. The cards presented Willson as "System Designer & Engineer" and King as "Sales." The cards described Secure Data Systems as carrying the "QuikPay Product Line." According to King, "you just simply don't go to a convention like that without a card telling people who you are." In an e-mail sent by Willson to King at the end of April, Willson asked King not to print up too many cards yet because the next month he was planning on having a second telephone line installed "specifically for Secure Data Systems so customers will have limited access to me as well," and he wished to add that number to his card.

After the Las Vegas trip, King and Willson had an argument about the Secure Data Systems Web site because Willson had made reference to a trademark name and logo on the site and King was concerned about legal liability. Willson stated that he became upset because of the way he felt he was being treated by King during the argument. After the argument, Willson sent an e-mail to King stating, "[R]egarding Secure Data Systems and our partnership, I have decided to take your suggestion and leave you in complete control and give you complete ownership." Both King and Willson testified, however, that they soon reconciled after this disagreement. They then continued with their relationship as before, apparently without King's ever objecting to Willson's characterization of their business relationship as a partnership, and himself as a co-owner.

By the spring of 2003, Willson explained that his work for Secure Data Systems consisted primarily of dealing with QuikPay maintenance and repair issues, although he continued to try to finish the key dispenser-revalue station whenever he had time. Willson made changes in the QuikPay software to fix some "annoy answers" and other problems that customers wanted fixed. Willson then placed the software "patch" on the Secure Data Systems' Web site for downloading by Secure Data Systems' customers. There were also firmware upgrades that had been designed by Datakey that had to be implemented. On one occasion, Willson had to recover data and repair a unit that had been struck by lightning.

Another maintenance job that Willson did was to continue to modify I/O boards. Willson explained that the "older style [of I/O boards] were burning out due to a transistor, a component of the board not being set up right." This particular modification had been designed by Datakey, and Willson only implemented it. By September, Secure Data Systems had hired another company to do the I/O board modifications because, as Willson explained, the boards took about 45 minutes each and there came to be too many of them.

Willson testified that King would call him regularly with any number of QuikPay maintenance problems. According to Willson, King was usually the direct contact with QuikPay customers. Willson would correct the issues during the evening and early morning hours and put the repair information onto the Secure Data Systems' Web site for King to look at the next morning. Willson stated that he also worked directly with QuikPay customers on occasion.

As early as June 2003, Willson had asked King to clarify what King thought Willson's priorities should be concerning his contribution to Secure Data Systems. King had asked Willson to deal with a customer complaint as to the failure of QuikPay's managing software to automatically record cash keys for accounting. In an e-mail to King, Willson explained that he would rewrite a portion of the software, but that these QuikPay maintenance issues were taking time away from developing the key dispenser-revalue station:

> We need to get the vending machine completed, but I get mixed signals from you alot [sic] as to what you want to do. (ie. [sic] Vending machine, expresskey patch and now this). I realize that they are all important and need to be add[re]ssed and taken care of, but we need to stop moving back and forth, finish one and move on to the next as we talked about before. Drop me a line and let me know what you think we need to be focusing on.

King replied:

> I don't intend to send mixed messages. I feel our priorities ha[ve] always been and should remain on the Revalue Station. We should follow up with a new controller, software and hand held read/writer. . . .
>
>   This issue with this customer in Columbus[, Nebraska,] is not the first time we have heard this complaint. It is however the first time we have had a customer complain this strongly about it. Issues like this and the complaints that brought about the software patch, etc., arise routinely in the course of the day to day activities of doing business. We can not [sic] ignore these issues. We have to deal with them in a manner that allows us to stay focused and still do the best we can to deal with the complaints. It may mean that we can only address a giv[en] issue with a band aid [sic] or on a temporary basis. If it [is] something that we can not [sic] provide we then have no other choice but to advise the customer as such. If it is something that is going to take a lot of time then we need to value the importance while keeping our priorities in mind.
>
>   I am going to continue to call you when these things come up. Again it is not by intention to change priorities. We need to discuss these issue[s], if we can do anything, the importance and how we want to handle what ever [sic] comes along.

The record contains 17 repair tickets dating from March to November 2003, totaling $4,150.77 in repairs done by Willson on QuikPay systems for various customers. King admits that either directly or indirectly, customers were billed off of these tickets that King obtained through the Secure Data Systems' Web site. Another bill is found in the record sent by King to a client for $600.26 in controller repairs, which King told the client had been done by "Scott." At trial, Willson estimated that he had put at least 2,000 hours into QuikPay sales and maintenance and in developing the key dispenser-revalue station.

In correspondence with clients, King often referred to Willson as the person doing technical work for QuikPay. Willson also sent e-mails communicating directly with QuikPay clients on various issues. In an e-mail dated August 12, 2003, Willson describes himself as the software and hardware designer with Secure Data Systems and he refers to King as his "partner." The record contains correspondence between

King and Willson discussing Secure Data Systems' purchases for QuikPay maintenance and development. In an e-mail from November 2003, King forwarded to Willson the price list for what he had been quoting customers for QuikPay repairs.

In October 2003, King sent an e-mail to a potential customer in which King referred to Willson as "the other half of Secure Data Systems." This potential customer had an old version of QuikPay, and King was trying to sell the owner updates that Willson, who "does all the programming" had made to the software and firmware. These updates, King explained, coupled with the necessary hardware updates, would resolve the owner's current complaints with his QuikPay system. King referred the customer to the Secure Data Systems' Web site for Willson's instructions as to how the owner should send his database in for updating.

Willson incurred out-of-pocket expenses in 2002, but those were apparently reimbursed by King. Willson stated that because these out-of-pocket expenses were relatively small, King had instructed him to make a list of those expenses so that King could claim them on his taxes and Willson would not have to worry about filing a special form. Willson was not aware that he was supposed to file a partnership tax form, and he never did so.

Again, in the first half of 2003, Willson testified that he incurred out-of-pocket expenses, and he stated that he did not always seek reimbursement for those expenses from King. It is undisputed that later that year, King gave Willson a credit card number and verification code so he could charge Secure Data Systems' business to the card. It is unclear whether Willson believed the card was an official Secure Data Systems' card. It was, in fact, King's personal credit card that he had designated for Secure Data Systems' business. Willson used the card to purchase parts that he needed in working on QuikPay maintenance and in development of the key dispenser-revalue station. There is no evidence that Willson was required to get King's prior approval before incurring Secure Data Systems' related expenses.

When Willson was asked why he invested his time and expertise into QuikPay without any remuneration, he explained, "That was my contribution to the company. I mean that was my piece." Willson claimed that King periodically kept Willson informed about how much money was in the bank that had accrued in profits derived from QuikPay sales and maintenance. Willson alleged that sometime in 2003, he and King discussed distributing some of the profits through draws or bonuses at the end of the year.

Still, Willson "started getting uneasy." Willson explained that he "wasn't feeling comfortable continuing to repair controllers [and] create a vending machine when the only reassurance I had was, don't worry, I'm not going to leave you hanging." Willson contacted a law firm to draw up papers to formalize the partnership. These papers were never drafted. According to Willson, when he told King he was looking into creating a written agreement for their relationship, King "assured [him] that he was having his attorneys look at it," and King asked for his and his wife's Social Security numbers. Willson's wife testified at trial that she remembered when King asked for their Social Security numbers.

At the same time that Willson was seeking more formal guarantees of his partnership interest, King was expressing his impatience with the fact that Willson had not yet produced a key dispenser-revalue station. Willson's wife explained that shortly before the meeting, King had come over to their house to pick up something that Willson had worked on for QuikPay over the lunch hour and that King had complained about Willson's "dedication." She explained:

> I was very upset because at that time I wanted [Willson] to take our son to preschool and he couldn't go because he had to finish whatever it was [King] had him working on, something with the QuikPay. And I asked [King] how could you question his—you know, he's doing all—everything you ask him to do. He does everything that needs to be done. I didn't know of any incomplete things. Every time he had a chance, he was talking to [King] or getting things done that needed to be done with QuikPay.
>
> He never told [King] no. He didn't ask for any money, and I didn't understand how [King] could question [Willson's] dedication.

King and Willson had a meeting with their wives to discuss their respective concerns. Apparently, their respective unease was at least temporarily resolved. Willson's wife described the meeting as follows:

> And they were mainly focused on where they were going, the revalue station was their key. That's what they wanted to do. And [King] kept staying [sic], well, we have to make our customers happy. We have to get the QuikPay working. If that doesn't work, then you know the revalue station is—you know, he said we had to make our customers happy. And so he was telling [Willson] this as we were sitting at [a restaurant], and I thought the meeting went well. We had talked again about officers or I don't know how the business works. I was just trusting that [Willson] would let me know.

On cross-examination, Willson's wife clarified that when King was discussing keeping customers happy, he was referring to the existing QuikPay system and not the key dispenser-revalue station Willson was trying to develop. Willson similarly testified that at the meeting, they discussed "officers or something like that. For a corporation, I don't really understand all how that works, but at that time I felt at ease."

During this general time period, King discovered that the name "Secure Data Systems" had already been taken for incorporation and this was discussed with Willson. The name "KeyTronics" was suggested by Willson's wife. In December 2003, Willson developed a new Web site for "KeyTronics." Willson then moved over the "service tracker" program and other information from the previous Secure Data Systems' Web site to the new Web site for "KeyTronics."

The record contains an e-mail dated December 13, 2003, in which King tells Willson that he had to cancel the "Secure Data [credit] Card" in order to get the name on the card changed to "KeyTronics." Willson sent King a list of his understanding of what the current objectives were for "KeyTronics." This list included completing projects relating to the development of the key dispenser-revalue station as well as certain goals relating to sales, inventory, and repairs for the existing QuikPay system. Willson testified that he was still optimistic about getting a key vending machine finished but that his relationship with King was deteriorating. Willson testified that "[w]e were arguing more, and nothing was getting done as far as paperwork."

King and Willson had another meeting around the end of December and agreed to end their relationship and any joint QuikPay or key dispenser-revalue station activities. Approximately 2 weeks after this meeting, King called Willson and offered to compensate him for the time he had spent in maintaining or repairing QuikPay. Willson refused and brought this action instead.

The record indicates King currently conducts QuikPay business under "KeyTronics, Inc." which is registered in King's name alone. Its sole line of business is the QuikPay system. King pays two independent contractors to assist him in installation, troubleshooting, and repairs.

King generally denied at trial any partnership relationship with Willson. King minimized Willson's assistance with regular QuikPay business and pointed out that Willson was never able to produce a marketable key dispenser-revalue station. King conceded that Willson had repaired 40 individual QuikPay controllers. He also noted that Willson had looked into some "glitches" in QuikPay's software package and had worked on an "LCD design" to go with the QuikPay controller. King indicated that Willson had worked on some I/O boards. Still, King could not believe that Willson had invested 2,000 hours in QuikPay or the key dispenser-revalue station, explaining, "[Willson] played softball, went out and helped his dad two nights a week, took Japanese lessons. I truly don't know where you would come up with those kind of hours, the activity that he was doing."

King denied any agreement to share profits and equally denied any agreement to compensate Willson as an employee or independent contractor. King presented no explanation as to why, without any promise of remuneration, Willson contributed to King's QuikPay profits. King simply stated that the QuikPay business was solely his. He was distributing and maintaining QuikPay before he met Willson, and he asserted that the acquisition of Datakey customers and inventory did not significantly alter his business.

King did not recall asking for either Willson's or Willson's wife's Social Security number. He did vaguely admit to, at some point, telling Willson or his wife that he had spoken with an attorney about incorporating. King generally denied consulting with Willson about pricing for QuikPay or otherwise sharing in control of the QuikPay business. King emphasized that any work Willson did, which, again, he considered minimal, was always at King's request.

In its order, the district court, as the trier of fact, concluded: "[T]he evidence indicates that Willson and King pooled resources, money and labor." But, "the parties never entered into any specific agreement which would establish a partnership." Even if a partnership had been established, however, the court concluded that there would be no profits from the joint venture because "nothing in the evidence reflects that [King] ever committed his existing business and its related assets to the development efforts for the key system."

ANALYSIS

This case is governed by the Uniform Partnership Act. Section [202(a)] of the Act defines that a partnership is formed by "the association of two or more persons to carry on as co-owners a business for profit" and explains that this is true "whether or not the persons intend to form a partnership."

Obviously, the relationship between King and Willson is "of two or more persons." In addition, whether the business of QuikPay maintenance, or even the development of the never-produced key dispenser-revalue station, qualifies as a business "for profit" is not in issue. It is not essential that the business for which the association was formed ever actually be carried on, let alone that it earn a profit. Rather, a business qualifies under the "business for profit" element of [UPA

§202(a)] so long as the parties intended to carry on a business with the expectation of profits.

Still, Willson admits he is not pursuing an action for an accounting of a partnership that would be limited to the development of a key dispenser-revalue station. That product was never produced and did not independently garner any profits to account for. We are instead asked to determine whether King and Willson were partners in an enterprise that involved both the development of the key dispenser-revalue station and the sales and maintenance of the regular QuikPay line. If so, Willson claims that King must account to Willson for any profits relating to all QuikPay business.

The elements disputed by the parties are whether there was an "association" formed for QuikPay business, and whether such association, if created, was as "co-owners." The existence of a partnership is a question of fact under the evidence.

ASSOCIATION

We first consider whether King and Willson formed an association. King correctly points out that inherent to the term "association" is the idea that the relationship between the "two or more persons" be intentional. King argues that no partnership was formed because he never intended to form a partnership relationship with Willson. "In the domain of private law the term association necessarily involves the idea that the association is voluntary."[17] It is perhaps for this reason that the district court found it significant that King and Willson "never entered into any specific agreement which would establish a partnership."

But, as [UPA §202(a)] explicitly states, the intent necessary to form an association does not refer to the intent to form a partnership per se. There is no requirement that the parties have a "specific agreement" in order to form a partnership. People do not become partners when they attain co-ownership of a business for profit through an involuntary act. But, if the parties' voluntary actions form a relationship in which they carry on as co-owners of a business for profit, then "they may inadvertently create a partnership despite their expressed subjective intention not to do so."[19] Intent, in such cases, is still of prime concern, but it will be ascertained objectively, rather than subjectively, from all the evidence and circumstances.

Because of this, King's focus on his intent to form a corporation, as opposed to a partnership, does more to prove an intent to form the requisite association than to disprove it. It is, in fact, not unusual for courts to find a partnership relationship between parties that were operating with the intent to form a corporation and to specifically avoid a partnership relationship. Even where a corporation has successfully been formed, courts have found a partnership relationship between the shareholders when the corporation is a mere agency for convenience in carrying out the joint venture or partnership.

In considering the parties' intent to form an association, it is generally considered relevant how the parties characterize their relationship or how they have previously referred to one another. The joint use of a business name is evidence of an

17. [UPA (1914)] §6, comment 1(1).
19. [UPA] §202(a), comment 1 at 93.

association. This is especially true when the business name is composed of the parties' names or initials.

It is undisputed that King and Willson discussed the fact that Secure Data Systems had the initials of Scott, Don, and Scott. Granted, at its inception, Secure Data Systems was an association among three parties focused on the limited task of creating a key dispenser-revalue station. But, despite King's claim that the acquisition of all of Datakey's QuikPay inventory and customer base was insignificant, after this occurred, King removed any QuikPay operations from his Washco business. He instead began to conduct all QuikPay business exclusively through Secure Data Systems. Willson was clearly associated with King in that venture.

At that point, in e-mail correspondence with Datakey in regard to various complaints with the QuikPay system, King no longer referred to himself in the first person singular, but instead in first person plural, as "us" or "we." Business cards were created for King and Willson describing their respective positions in Secure Data Systems. King and Willson went as joint representatives of Secure Data Systems to a Las Vegas carwash convention. King and Willson worked together both in servicing the QuikPay line, assembling and repairing Datakey's old inventory, and developing the key dispenser-revalue station. Various e-mails to customers and to Datakey evidence their joint efforts in this regard. To King and to others, Willson referred to himself and King as partners. Specifically in regard to ventures involving the regular QuikPay system, King referred to Willson as "the other half of Secure Data Systems." We believe the evidence is clear that King and Willson formally associated to develop a key dispenser-revalue station and that further, this association expanded in scope to encompass all QuikPay operations.

CO-OWNERSHIP

Still, King asserts that any reference he made to Willson as the "other half of Secure Data Systems" was an insignificant figure of speech. Most importantly, according to King, there was no partnership because Willson never had co-ownership of the QuikPay business. King claims that he started selling and maintaining QuikPay by himself and asserts that he maintained full control of that business line. According to King, Willson simply did what King asked him to—apparently for free.

Being "co-owners" of a business for profit does not refer to the co-ownership of property,[27] but to the co-ownership of the business intended to garner profits. It is co-ownership that distinguishes partnerships from other commercial relationships such as creditor and debtor, employer and employee, franchisor and franchisee, and landlord and tenant. Co-ownership generally addresses whether the parties share the benefits, risks, and management of the enterprise such that (1) they subjectively view themselves as members of the business rather than as outsiders contracting with it and (2) they are in a better position than others dealing with the firm to monitor and obtain information about the business.

The objective indicia of co-ownership are commonly considered to be: (1) profit sharing, (2) control sharing, (3) loss sharing, (4) contribution, and (5) co-ownership of property. The five indicia of co-ownership are only that; they are not all

[handwritten margin note: objective indicia]

27. See [UPA §202(c)].

necessary to establish a partnership relationship, and no single indicium of co-ownership is either necessary or sufficient to prove co-ownership.

The district court found that King and Willson had "pooled resources, money and labor." This is significant evidence of contribution. The record demonstrates that Willson contributed his time and expertise not only to the business of developing the key dispenser-revalue station, but also to the continued operations of the regular QuikPay product line. And even if Willson had not more directly contributed to regular QuikPay business, we again note that the business of QuikPay and the business of developing a peripheral product that would ensure QuikPay's continued viability in the marketplace were inextricably commingled. This was especially true with regard to Willson's contribution when King emphasized that Willson had to help keep the QuikPay system running because, otherwise, the development of the key dispenser-revalue station would lose its customer base and become irrelevant.

The continuing investment of one's labor without pay is generally considered a strong indicator of co-ownership. It is evidence that, as Willson testified he explicitly understood, the party is not an outsider contracting with the business. Valid consideration for an ownership interest in a partnership may take the form of either property, capital, labor, or skill, and the law does not exalt one type of contribution over another.

In this case, Willson contributed his time and expertise without any compensation for approximately 1 year. Conservatively, Willson estimated his contribution as totaling over 2,000 hours. King did not present evidence of how many hours he had spent in the QuikPay venture. But more importantly, we conclude on our review of the record that without Willson's technical assistance, King would have been unable to continue QuikPay's viability after Datakey abandoned the product. That King could have dealt with certain issues by hiring contractors or employees is irrelevant. He chose not to do so—presumably because the promise of the key dispenser-revalue station made a partnership relationship more worthwhile—and saved himself the expense of paying for this labor.

We also find that despite King's protestations to the contrary, the evidence shows that King and Willson shared control over QuikPay business. We note that control is "elusive because of the many gradations of control and because partners often delegate decision-making power." Still, Willson testified that he and King consulted with each other over what appropriate pricing would be as they picked up Datakey's equipment and customers. This is evidenced by an e-mail of the price list that King sent to Willson. Under King's theory of the case, the e-mail would have been completely unnecessary, because according to King, Willson contributed very little and had no direct contact with customers or their billing.

Willson testified that he and King made joint decisions to cut certain costs. Willson set up the invoice system they used to bill QuikPay customers, and there is no indication that such a system was anything other than that of Willson's independent initiative and design. Willson made technical decisions on how best to assemble, repair, or maintain various aspects of the QuikPay system. The June 2003 e-mail written by King illustrates King's understanding that he and Willson would jointly address QuikPay customer issues as they arose and jointly evaluate Secure Data Systems' priorities as they went along.

Willson also testified that he had an agreement with King to share profits, although King denies this. Of the five indicia of co-ownership, profit sharing is possibly the most important, and the presence of profit sharing is singled out in [UPA §202(c)(3)] as creating a rebuttable presumption of a partnership. However, what is essential to a partnership is not that profits actually be distributed, but, instead, that there be an interest in the profits. Willson's testimony that they agreed to share in the profits of the business is, in light of all the evidence, simply more credible than King's statement that compensation "was never discussed." And even King vaguely admits that they had an understanding to share profits of the key dispenser-revalue station, if that were developed. It seems reasonable to assume that this same understanding would apply to Willson as his participation and the scope of the venture expanded to encompass all QuikPay business.

We do not find any evidence that King and Willson had an agreement for loss sharing. But we find this of little import, since purported partners, expecting profits, often do not have any explicit understanding regarding loss sharing. Likewise, although King and Willson admittedly do not own any joint property, in an informal relationship, the parties may intend co-ownership of property but fail to attend to the formalities of title. Moreover, in this case, it is unclear that there is much QuikPay "property" at all. Certainly, as King's counterclaim alleged, Willson has possession of some QuikPay equipment. To the extent that a bank account is property, we note that although Willson had delegated financial matters to King and was not a signatory to the bank account where Secure Data Systems' revenues were deposited, Willson testified that King did keep him abreast of the financial status of that account. Willson believed he had an ownership interest in the funds in that account.

We conclude that the objective, as well as subjective, indicia are sufficient to prove co-ownership of the business of selling, maintaining, and developing Quik-Pay. Having already concluded that there was an association for the same, we conclude that Willson proved that he and King had formed a partnership for the business of selling, maintaining, and developing QuikPay.

CONCLUSION

Because Willson has proved a partnership relationship with King, he is entitled to a winding up and an accounting in accordance with the Act. The district court erred in concluding otherwise. Accordingly, we reverse the decision and remand the cause for further proceedings.

Notes and Questions

1. Notes

a. Secure Data Systems later changed its name to KeyTronics.

2. Reality Check

a. Does the *KeyTronics* court use the same standard as the *Ziegler* court to determine whether a partnership has been formed?

b. What inference does the court draw from the fact that the parties intended to form a corporation in the future? Do you agree with that inference?

c. What significance does the court place on the fact that the parties named their venture Secure Data Systems? Do you agree that the name is relevant to whether the parties formed a partnership?

3. Suppose

a. Suppose Gardeen sued Willson and King seeking a declaratory judgment that he was a partner. How would the court analyze that claim and what result would it reach?

b. Suppose the *KeyTronics* court decided the *Ziegler* case. Would the court's analysis or the result have been the same?

c. Suppose the *Ziegler* court decided the *KeyTronics* case. Would the court's analysis or the result have been the same?

d. Imagine King paid Willson for his services by the job. Imagine he was paid a flat amount each month. Imagine he was paid a percentage of the gross revenues. Imagine he was paid a percentage of profits. Would any of these situations have changed the court's analysis or the result?

4. What Do You Think?

a. Why is the result different in *Ziegler* and *KeyTronics*?

b. Are both *Ziegler* and *KeyTronics* correctly decided? Are both wrong?

c. Do you think King and Willson had the same understanding of their business relationship? If not, whose understanding should control and why? Can there be a partnership without a common understanding?

The UPA standard is straightforward: "[T]he association of two or more persons to carry on as co-owners a business for profit forms a partnership, whether or not the persons intend to form a partnership." UPA §202(a). Some state courts have added additional requirements to the core definition. In addition to such required elements, the UPA provides a series of presumptions to be applied in certain fact settings. First, joint ownership of property does not, without more, establish a partnership. Second, the sharing of gross returns does not, without more, establish a partnership. Third, receiving profits creates the presumption that the receiver is a partner in a partnership unless the profits are payment for such things as principal or interest on a debt, compensation as an employee, or rent. *See* UPA §202(c). The comments to the UPA elaborate:

> [U]nder this act "co-ownership" is a key concept. Ownership involves the power of ultimate control (albeit a power that can be substantially diminished by agreement) and a right to share in the profits of the co-owned business. To state that partners are co-owners of a business is to state that: (i) they share in the profits (if any) of the enterprise; and (ii) *ab initio* at least, they collectively have the power of ultimate control.

> UPA §202, cmt.

Under UPA §102(1), " 'Business' includes every trade, occupation, and profession."

In *Ziegler* and *KeyTronics*, whether a partnership existed determined the rights of the "partners" between themselves.

Putting It to Work

Problem 17-1

Satisfaction, an amazing Rolling Stones tribute band, has recently released their garage debut album to startling success. Because of this, they sign up Ian Faith as their manager to help them tour and make it big. Ian Faith is an experienced and highly successful band manager and is also quite wealthy. He receives a percentage of the band's gross revenues and has full control over all the band's bookings and business affairs, but has no input into any artistic decisions nor into when or where the band will record or go on tour.

On the way to a sold-out bar show, a roadie employed full time by Satisfaction, and driving Satisfaction's tour bus, hits a pedestrian in a cross walk. The tour bus speeds off. However, the injured pedestrian is able to snap a license plate photo and proceeds to pursue a tort claim against Satisfaction.

a. Is Ian a partner in Satisfaction?

Once a partnership is formed, questions often arise as to whether another person has been admitted as a partner. Because one of the central tenets of partnership law is that the relations among the partners are personal, the default rule is that no one can be admitted as an additional partner (i.e., no one may become a co-owner) without unanimous consent of the existing partners. *See* UPA §402(b)(3). Of course, the partners may unanimously agree in advance that new partners may be admitted by less than unanimous action or by action of a subgroup of partners. The converse setting is governed by a similar rule: when a partner ceases to be a co-owner of a business for profit, that person is no longer a partner. That situation is treated under section *f* below.

b. Financing and Partners' Ownership Interests

i. Partner Contributions. Some courts insist that each partner contribute something to form a partnership. The UPA, however, simply defines a partnership as *co-ownership*. A person can acquire an ownership interest without making any contribution, and in the real world it does occasionally happen that a person is made a partner (i.e., given an ownership interest in a business that is co-owned with others) gratuitously. More typically, that interest is in return for past contributions to the business or in the expectation of future contributions. This will become plainer when we look at the ways in which a person may contribute to a business.

The most intuitive contribution is, of course, money. Another kind of contribution is property that the business will find useful or necessary. A lease on favorable terms or in a favorable location may, for example, be a valuable contribution to a partnership and may justify, as an economic matter, an ownership interest to the person contributing the lease. Other property, such as vehicles or inventory, may be useful though not uniquely valuable. Finally, intangible property such as intellectual property, whether protected by copyright or patent or not, may be contributed to a business in return for an ownership interest.

In addition to money and other property, a person may contribute services such as working in the business's operations or providing professional services such as legal or accounting services in return for an ownership interest. Further, a person may contribute an agreement to provide services in return for an ownership interest in the business. When a person is given a partnership interest for "no contribution," often the reason is to recognize the person's past contribution to the partnership. For example, a partnership in which an employee makes a sustained or particularly valuable contribution (such as a law firm in which an associate performs well for a decade or more) may reward the employee with an ownership interest for which the person has made no contribution. There may in fact be no contribution in the sense of consideration (because the employee was remunerated through a salary for his or her past efforts) and the ownership interest may come with no explicit agreement to contribute additional services (although such additional contribution would surely be an expectation). Nonetheless, an economist might characterize the business as one in which the employee received an ownership interest in exchange for past service and the agreement to provide future services.

Another typical setting involving services is where one partner provides all, or almost all, the money and property for a new business and another partner provides the knowledge and skill, through providing services, to the partnership. A new restaurant is a paradigm of this setting. A talented but impecunious chef may find financial backers (possibly well-heeled patrons of the restaurant where the chef is currently employed) and open a new restaurant. The chef will contribute nothing but an agreement to provide future services while the other partners will provide all the necessary cash.

Not only may some partners put in cash, others property, others services, and still others nothing, but the division of the partners' ownership interests may be completely unrelated to the relative value of their contributions. This quality is fundamentally different from the corporate law norm. Remember, in corporate law shareholders who purchase identical shares contemporaneously must pay the same amount per share (even though they may pay in different kinds of consideration such as cash, property, or services). This aspect of partnership law is described in section *d* below.

ii. Partnership Property.   Because a partnership is now definitely an entity separate from its partners, partnership property belongs to the partnership rather than to the partners collectively. *See* UPA §§203, 501. In practice, the question frequently arises whether a particular piece of property (which may well be intangible) was contributed to, or purchased by, the partnership from a partner (often in return for the partner's ownership interest) or whether the property was simply being used by the partnership with the consent of its owner, the partner.

This question is important when the partnership is insolvent and creditors seek to seize whatever partnership assets exist. The question also is important when the partnership is successful and one partner claims that key property is personal, not partnership, property. After Kurt Cobain, frontman of the band Nirvana, died, his widow was engaged in litigation with the two other members of Nirvana. Much of the dispute rested upon whether Mr. Cobain owned all of Nirvana (making the other members employees) or at least owned nearly all of the songs that the band performed. Mr. Cobain's widow took the view that Nirvana belonged to

Mr. Cobain, while the other members believed a partnership had been formed and that the partnership owned all the assets. While resolution of this question is frequently important, the legal standard is relatively simple: UPA §203 defines partnership property as "[p]roperty acquired by a partnership. . . ." The ultimate question is the intent of the parties. *See* UPA §204.

UPA §204 provides rules and presumptions for determining whether property is partnership property. Two of the most important presumptions are (1) that property acquired with partnership assets is partnership property, regardless of how the property is titled, and (2) that property acquired in the name of a partner (or partners) and without using partnership assets is not partnership property, even though it is used in the partnership's business. UPA §204(c), (d). In keeping with the ethos that every partner is equal unless otherwise agreed, every partner has an equal right to possess and use partnership property for partnership purposes but not otherwise. UPA §401(i).

iii. Partners' Interest in the Partnership. Rather strangely, the UPA does not contain a defined term that comprises a partner's entire interest in the partnership. The More You Know! However, the Comment suggests that a partner's interest in the partnership consists of governance and information rights, and economic rights. UPA §102, cmt. A partner's economic rights consist of the right to receive distributions but not the right to compel a distribution. UPA §§401(a), 405. That right is the only transferable right a partner has. UPA §§102(23), 503. UPA §401 also contains other economic aspects of being a partner, but those rights are not transferable. A partner's transferable interest can also be involuntarily seized by a judgment creditor of the partner. This seizure is called a *charging order* and works like a lien. It may be foreclosed upon and sold at a judicial sale. UPA §504.

A partner has equal rights with every other partner to manage the partnership and can use partnership property, but only for partnership purposes. UPA §401(h), (i). A partner also has the right to inspect the partnership books and records, the right to request other partnership information, and the right to receive material information even without asking. A partner has a concomitant obligation to provide to the partnership any material information the partner possesses. UPA §408. Other rights are scattered throughout the UPA.

Note that, although a partner can transfer his or her right to receive distributions, the transferee does not become a partner through the transfer and the partner retains his or her other partnership attributes. UPA §§402, 503(f). As well, a transferee of a right to distribution has none of the governance or informational rights of a partner. UPA §503(a)(3).

iv. Allocations and Distributions to Partners. The economic rights of a corporation's owners are determined by the percentage of outstanding shares he or she owns. By contrast, partners' economic interests are, in the first instance, a matter of agreement among them, need not be equal, and may change over time. *See* UPA §105(a). The next case shows some of the problems that can arise from this quality of partnership law. The partnership here was a limited liability partnership, but the UPA principles are applicable.

Overland v. Scheper Kim & Harris LLP

2013 WL 4027455 (Cal. App. Aug. 6, 2013)

BOREN, P.J.

A former partner in a four-partner law firm argues that upon dissociating he was entitled to a payout of 25 percent of the firm's value pursuant to [UPA §701]. We find that the trial court did not err by determining plaintiff's share in the partnership to be 4 percent. We also find that the trial court did not abuse its discretion by awarding plaintiff less in attorney fees than he requested.

FACTUAL AND PROCEDURAL BACKGROUND

Facts

The following factual summary is taken from the trial court's statement of decision. Appellant and respondent both adopt the trial court's recitation of facts in their appellate briefs.

Overland Borenstein Scheper & Kim LLP (OBSK) was a limited liability law partnership that formed on March 15, 2004. The partners were Mark Overland, Mark Borenstein, David Scheper, and Diann Kim. Each was a general (or, "equity") partner of OBSK.

OBSK never had a written partnership agreement or a comprehensive oral partnership agreement. The partners made decisions by consensus, with each partner having an equal say.

OBSK did not require capital contributions by the partners and did not accumulate working capital from year to year. Fees and other revenue were used to pay expenses, salaries, and a fixed draw to the partners. The firm's only property was the equipment, furniture, and supplies necessary for its operations.

None of the partners thought about partnership capital, equity, ownership shares, or any aspect of their shares of the partnership assets. The predominate asset of the partnership was profit. Profits were distributed to each partner at the end of every calendar year. Some of the partnership's cash was retained for expected expenses and obligations, but most was distributed to the partners by December 31. In the last months of each year, partners agreed between themselves on their respective share of profits. To determine profit distributions, the partners made a consensus determination of merit, giving heavy weight to each partner's financial contribution to the firm.

Because this system for determining profit shares was merit-based, the actual profit shares differed from year to year and varied considerably among OBSK partners. Only in the partnership's first year did the partners receive roughly equal shares. Through the years, Overland received the following share of partnership profits: 2004, 25.5 percent; 2005, 16.807 percent; 2006, 18.31 percent; 2007, 12.1 percent; 2008, 8.3 percent; 2009, 4.0 percent.

In May 2009, Borenstein, one of the founding partners, resigned from OBSK and became a Los Angeles Superior Court judge. At that point, the partners had no agreement as to whether a general partner would receive compensation upon leaving the firm. Borenstein did not make any specific request for compensation, did not ask his partners to purchase his interest in the firm, and did not seek any payment in connection with his dissociation. The remaining partners ultimately agreed that Borenstein would receive deferred compensation but not any additional compensation from 2009 profits. They did not set policy by so deciding, specify any terms that would apply to other partners, or determine that the partnership would never pay any amount to a departing partner in the future.

Scheper Kim & Overland LLP (SKO) was a limited liability law partnership that formed when Borenstein dissociated from OBSK. SKO operated in the same manner as OBSK. It never had a written partnership agreement nor a comprehensive oral partnership agreement. The partners made decisions by consensus. SKO did not require capital contributions or accumulate working capital; revenues were used to pay expenses, salaries, and a fixed draw to the partners, and profits were distributed to the partners at the end of the year. At the end of 2009, the partners used the same merit-based system for dividing profits as was used by OBSK, resulting in the following profit shares: Scheper 68.0 percent; Kim 28.0 percent, and Overland 4.0 percent. In September of 2009, SKO took on a new partner, Marc Harris, who had the same rights and duties as a general partner as Scheper, Kim, and Overland, but who did not receive a portion of the 2009 profits.

On February 16, 2010, Overland notified the SKO partners that he would dissociate from the firm, and he requested a buyout of his partnership interest. Kim responded to Overland's request by stating that she had consulted a partnership lawyer, Joel McIntyre, who said that it was not likely a buyout would be due because the firm's assets were far outweighed by its liabilities. McIntyre later testified at the trial in this matter, and stated that he did not recall having any discussion with Kim about Overland or the firm's finances, and did not recall giving Kim any advice of the kind she described.

Overland dissociated from SKO effective April 30, 2010. The parties stipulated that, as of that date, SKO's equity was $2,825,000. At the time he left, Overland owed the firm $21,084 for insurance premiums that had been paid on his behalf.

The partnership name became Scheper Kim & Harris LLP (SKH) after Overland left the firm. On August 27, 2010, SKH formally responded through its attorneys to Overland's request for a buyout of his partnership interest. SKH refused to pay Overland any amount, stating that the SKO partners had agreed that a dissociating partner would receive no payment for his or her interest. The partnership demanded that Overland pay $21,084 to the firm for unpaid insurance premiums.

In the final months of 2010, Scheper, Kim, and Harris made their compensation decisions for the year. They distributed the firm's profits among themselves and did not award any profits to Overland above the draw he received during the first four months of 2010.

The Trial and Decision

Trial lasted over five days, beginning on April 16, 2012. In May 2012, the trial court issued a tentative decision and statement of decision, to which both parties lodged objections. On May 31, 2012, the trial court overruled all objections and declared the statement of decision final.

The trial court's statement of decision was exceedingly thorough. The trial court analyzed the relevant provisions of California's Uniform Partnership Act . . . , and concluded that Overland was entitled to receive a portion of SKO's equity equal to his share of the firm's profits as of the date of his dissociation. The court found that the consistent agreement and practice of the partnership was to determine the partners' respective profit shares by a consensus determination of merit, giving heavy weight to their financial contributions, and that the most reliable and just measure of Overland's share was the one determined shortly before his April 2010 dissociation—the 2009 year-end share of 4 percent. This share translated to a buyout amount of $113,000 (4.0 percent of the firm equity of $2,825,000), less $21,084 for unpaid insurance premiums, for a total of $91,916.

Additionally, the trial court awarded attorney fees and expert expenses to Overland. The court noted that Kim falsely told Overland that the firm had no assets. Further, the court found Kim's testimony that the partnership lawyer, McIntyre, had told her Overland would not be owed a buyout, "entirely unbelievable." In finding that an award of fees and expenses was appropriate, the court wrote: "It appears that SKH has been determined to completely deny payment to Overland and has been in continual search of a factual and legal basis for doing so. SKH has argued that Overland has taken extreme and unjustified positions during this litigation; the Court has largely agreed and has ruled accordingly. But SKH set the tone of the litigation with its unjustified and ever-shifting denials of Overland's request for a buyout at any price." Overland requested attorney fees, expert fees, and costs in the amount of $488,521.45. Finding that much of those expenses were unrecoverable, the trial court awarded a total of $97,145.71 in fees and costs.

Judgment was entered on September 13, 2012. Overland timely appealed.

DISCUSSION

Overland appeals from the judgment on several grounds. He argues that, under the UPA, the trial court was required to award him 25 percent of the partnership value upon his dissociation.

I. THE TRIAL COURT'S VALUE DETERMINATION WAS PROPER

The terms of a partnership are controlled first by the partnership agreement. If a partnership does not have an agreement, or if the agreement is silent on certain matters, then the UPA governs. [UPA §105(a), (b)].

The trial court here found that the partnership did not have an agreement as to "whether" Overland was "entitled to compensation for his interest." Since there was no such agreement on this issue, the relevant UPA provision applied. Pursuant to section [701(a)], a partnership is to cause a "dissociated partner's interest in the partnership to be purchased for a buyout price determined pursuant to subdivision (b)." Thus, the partnership had an obligation to purchase Overland's interest.

The parties stipulated that the value of the partnership was $2,825,000 on the date of Overland's dissociation. Overland argues that he should have been awarded 25 percent of that amount, because [of UPA §401(a)]. This section could possibly apply, however, only if there was no agreement as to what Overland's share was. [UPA §105(a)]

We agree with SKH that the trial court made the factual determination that the parties *agreed* on what Overland's share was.

The trial court supported its decision that Overland was entitled to a buyout price equivalent to 4 percent of the firm equity as follows: "Overland contends that his buyout price under [UPA §701(b)] should be based upon a share of SKO's profits that is equal to his other partners. . . . There is no factual support for this position, and it is contrary to the clear intention of the partners. Except for the first year of operation, the OBSK and SKO partnerships never distributed their profits in equal shares. The partners always determined their profit shares by a consensus determination of merit, giving heavy weight to the partners' financial contributions to the firm. This resulted in vastly different profit shares. Adopting Overland's equal share approach would be directly contrary to the consistent agreement and practices of the partnership. . . . [¶] The partners of OBSK and SKO never distributed their profits in equal shares, and imposing that approach in this case would be entirely inconsistent with the partners' agreement and intent. . . . Using the firm's actual profit share is particularly appropriate in this case, because the distributable assets of SKO (like OBSK) were based on profits from the firm's collections and not from property, capital accounts or other assets contributed by the partners."

The trial court correctly recognized that a partnership agreement can be written, oral, or implied. [UPA §102(12)] Substantial evidence supported the conclusion that by oral and implied agreement each partner had an individual, unique share of profits largely dependent on his or her financial contribution to the firm. Awarding Overland 25 percent of the partnership value, as he sought, would have been contrary to this agreement.

Having found that Overland had a unique share, the trial court analyzed the evidence to determine what that share was. Substantial evidence supported the trial court's conclusion that Overland's share was 4 percent. The court had a number of different percentage shares to choose from in making its decision. For example, in 2007, Overland received 12.1 percent of partnership profits, in 2008 he received 8.3 percent, and in 2009, 4.0 percent. The court did not err by selecting the 2009 share of 4 percent, given that it was determined only several months before Overland's dissociation. As noted by the trial court, because the firm's distributable assets were composed almost entirely of profits, not capital accounts or assets contributed by the partners, the 2009 profit share was a particularly appropriate measure to use.

DISPOSITION

The matter is remanded to the trial court for modification of the judgment to reflect a prejudgment interest rate of 10 percent. In all other respects, the judgment is affirmed. The parties shall bear their own costs on appeal.

Notes and Questions

1. Notes

a. This case was decided under a prior version of the UPA. The citations in brackets are to the current UPA. There are no substantive differences between the prior and current versions of the UPA that are relevant to this opinion, though there are some language differences.

2. Reality Check

a. If the parties had made no agreement regarding distributions, what solution would the UPA provide? Did the court consider the UPA default rule? Should it have done so?

The UPA default rule for allocating distributions and losses is quite an important one because so many partnerships are formed inadvertently with no explicit agreement for sharing distributions or losses. "Each partner is entitled to an equal share of the partnership distributions and is chargeable with a share of the partnership losses in proportion to the partner's share of the distributions." UPA §401(b). Three aspects of this rule are worthy of particular note. First, in keeping with the personal nature of partnership law, each partner is equal, regardless of the amount of money contributed. That is, if one partner puts up 60 percent of the money and the other partner puts up 40 percent, each is entitled to receive 50 percent of the distributions (unless they agree otherwise).

Second, notice that the language describing losses is a bit curious: a partner is allocated losses "in proportion to the partner's share of the distributions." The effect of the UPA rule is that if the partners make no agreement as to distributions or losses, both are allocated per capita. If the partners explicitly agree about dividing distributions but not losses, the losses mirror the distributions. The reason why the rule is stated this way is because partners, particularly those who begin business without legal advice, frequently agree upon an allocation of distributions but are silent about losses because they do not anticipate losing money! Of course, the partners may agree to allocate losses and may do so in a proportion different from the allocation of distributions. This sort of agreement is quite frequent. For example, one partner may be particularly necessary for the venture to succeed because of that partner's background, knowledge, or contacts. This partner may be unwilling to participate unless he or she receives a larger share of the distributions and a smaller share of the losses.

The final point worth noting is that "entitled to an equal share" is not the same as being entitled to receive money. Whether to distribute profits to the partners is a business decision to be decided in the ordinary course of the partnership's operation. UPA §405(b). Note, though, that for federal income tax purposes, a partner who is allocated a profit must report that profit as income on his or her tax return. This raises the distinct possibility that a partner will recognize income for the year from the partnership but will not have received any cash distribution with which to pay the taxes on that profit.

What if a partner works for the partnership? The default rule is that a partner is not entitled to remuneration for working for the partnership, except when the partnership is being dissolved. *See* UPA §401(j). The reason for this rule is that the partners, as owners, are remunerated by the distributions, and each expends efforts in the partnership on behalf of all. It frequently is the case, however, that the partners will agree that one or more partners should receive remuneration in the form of salary for efforts on behalf of the partnership. An example is the situation in which a chef opens a restaurant with capital supplied by other partners. The chef will likely contribute little or no cash but will likely be the only partner employed in the restaurant. The partners may well agree that the chef should receive a wage in addition to a share of the distributions.

Putting It to Work

Problem 17-2

Satisfaction is ready to take the music industry by storm and the band anticipates nothing but continued and substantial financial and artistic success. They agree to allocate their profits as follows:

Nick, the lead singer, will take 40 percent of profits.
Leif, the guitarist and keyboardist, will take 25 percent of profits.
Lonnie, the guitarist and saxophonist, will take 25 percent of profits.
Charles, the drummer, will take 10 percent of profits.

After having to pay out of pocket for a new tour bus after the unfortunate run-in with a pedestrian, the band was counting on their sophomore album being wildly successful. Unfortunately, it is not, and the band is faced with a predicament they did not see coming: they suffer a $200,000 loss.

a. How will these losses be apportioned among the members of the band?

c. Personal Liability

One of the key consequences of the partnership form is that the partners have unlimited personal liability for the debts of the partnership. UPA §306(a). Every other business entity covered in this course provides limited liability for at least some participants. In the inadvertent partnership setting, the spectre of unlimited personal liability can be devastating. The UPA provides that a partnership creditor cannot levy on the assets of the partners until the assets of the partnership are exhausted and the creditor obtains a judgment against the partner. *See* UPA §307. Typically a partnership creditor will bring suit against both the partnership and its partners in one lawsuit so that, if successful, the plaintiff can levy on the partnership assets first and then seek satisfaction against the partners without having to return to court for an additional judgment.

The UPA provides that partners are jointly and severally liable for all partnership obligations. UPA §306(a). This means that a judgment creditor entitled to proceed against the partners may seek payment from some partners but not others. This will happen when one or more partners have substantial assets that are easily seized. If a partner pays more than the partner's share of partnership debts, measured by the proportion of losses each partner is to bear, he or she may recover contribution from other partners when the partnership is dissolved. *See* UPA §806(c).

An exception to personal liability is made in the case of new partners and dissociated partners. Under the UPA, a newly admitted partner is not personally liable for preexisting partnership debts but, in practice, such partners may be required to assume those liabilities as a condition to being made a partner. *See* UPA

§306(b). Conversely, a <u>dissociated partner remains personally</u> liable for partnership obligations incurred <u>before dissociation</u> and, in limited circumstances, may be liable for partnership obligations incurred after dissociation. *See* UPA §703(b). A dissociated partner remains liable for partnership obligations incurred <u>within two years</u> after dissociation to persons who <u>reasonably believed</u> at the time of the obligation that the dissociated partner was a partner and who is not deemed to have had notice that the partner was dissociated. UPA §703(b). A dissociating partner or the partnership can file a statement of dissociation, which cuts off postdissociation liability. UPA §704.

Putting It to Work

Problem 17-3

Satisfaction, an amazing Rolling Stones tribute band, has recently released their garage debut album to startling success. Because of this, they sign up Ian Faith as their manager to help them tour and make it big. Ian Faith is an experienced and highly successful band manager and is also quite wealthy. <u>He receives a percentage</u> of the band's <u>gross revenues</u> and has <u>full control over</u> all the band's bookings and business affairs, but has <u>no input</u> into any artistic decisions nor into when or where the band will record or go on tour.

On the way to a sold-out bar show, a roadie employed full time by Satisfaction, and driving Satisfaction's tour bus, hits a pedestrian in a cross walk. The tour bus speeds off. However, the injured pedestrian is able to snap a license plate photo and proceeds to pursue a tort claim against Satisfaction.

a. Does it matter whether Ian signs up with the band before or after the accident?

[handwritten: 1.) Is Iano A Partner   2.) 306   3.) But 306 B]

[handwritten: 1.) when does the partner become a Partner   2.) when does the obligation occur]

d. *Management*

The UPA default rule is that every partner has an equal right to participate in the management of the partnership. *See* UPA §401(f). This management right includes a concomitant right to receive information from the partnership and other partners and a corresponding duty to render information to other partners. *See* UPA §§408(b), (c). In keeping with the partnership norm that all partners are equal, the default rule is that matters in the "ordinary course of business" are decided by a majority of partners (regardless of their relative contributions or shares in the profits or losses) but that other matters, including amending the partnership agreement, require unanimity. *See* UPA §401(k). Where the partners are evenly divided on an issue, courts generally hold that a change from the status quo operation of the partnership has not been approved by a "majority."

"Each partner is an agent of the partnership for the purpose of its business." UPA §301(1). Clearly, then, every partner has actual authority to take actions that further the partnership's business. Every partner also has actual authority to do anything outside the partnership's business that all of the partners authorize. Can the partnership ever be bound by a partner's actions that are outside the partnership's business *and* have not been authorized by the partners? As you read this case you should review Restatement (Third) of Agency §7.07(2).

≡ **Barrett v. Jones, Funderburg, Sessums, Peterson &**
≡ **Lee, LLC**

27 So.3d 363 (Miss. 2010)

CHANDLER, Justice, for the Court

¶ 1. The Circuit Court of Lafayette County imposed sanctions against all members of the Scruggs Katrina Group (SKG), a joint venture, along with Don Barrett and Richard Scruggs individually, based upon the misconduct of Richard F. Scruggs, who pleaded guilty to conspiracy to bribe the trial judge in the underlying lawsuit over attorneys' fees. The SKG co-venturers, including the Scruggs Law Firm, P.A. (the Scruggs Firm); Nutt & McAllister, PLLC (the Nutt Firm); the Barrett Law Office, P.A. (the Barrett Firm); and the Lovelace Law Firm (the Lovelace Firm), along with Don Barrett and Richard Scruggs individually, were defendants in a fee-dispute lawsuit filed by a former co-venturer, the law firm of Jones, Funderburg, Sessums, Peterson & Lee, LLC (the Jones Firm). The trial court sanctioned the defendants by striking their answer, striking their motion to compel arbitration, entering a default against all defendants, and ordering the defendants to pay the plaintiffs' reasonable attorneys fees and costs incurred since July 17, 2007.

¶ 2. In these interlocutory appeals, the Barrett Law Office, P.A. (the Barrett Firm); Don Barrett, individually; and the Lovelace Law Firm (the Lovelace Firm) (hereinafter, collectively, "the appellants") argue that: (1) the imputation of Richard Scruggs's bad-faith misconduct to the appellants exceeded the circuit court's inherent power to sanction; [and] (2) the court erred by sanctioning the appellants because Richard Scruggs had acted outside the ordinary course of business of the joint venture. . . .

¶ 3. We find that the trial court had the discretionary authority to impose sanctions against SKG based upon the acts of a single partner that occurred in the ordinary course of business of SKG. However, we conclude that the trial court erred by finding that Richard Scruggs's misconduct occurred in the ordinary course of SKG business. Therefore, we reverse the order of sanctions against the appellants. The trial court already has determined that, but for the sanctions, this case is subject to mandatory arbitration. Therefore, we remand this case for the entry of an order compelling arbitration.

FACTS AND PROCEDURAL HISTORY

A. Preliminary Proceedings

¶ 4. On March 28, 2007, the Jones Firm filed an amended complaint, alleging that the parties had executed the SKG joint venture agreement in November 2005. The joint venture agreement provided that the Scruggs Firm's role was that of lead counsel, the Barrett Firm's role was that of witness development, the Nutt Firm's role was that of funding and client relations, the Jones Firm's role was that of briefing, and the Lovelace Firm's role was that of expert retention and adjuster retention. The agreement provided for the removal of a member of the joint venture by a supermajority vote, consisting of affirmative votes by four of the co-venturers. The Nutt Firm was to provide one million dollars per year in capital contributions, with any further necessary contributions to be paid pro rata by the other co-venturers. The proceeds of the joint venture were to be distributed . . . in the following order:

> (1) Reimburse Nutt/McAlister for all expenses paid, (2) Refund all capital contributions, (3) Payment of 35% of net fee to Nutt/McAlister for financing the litigation and for their professional efforts, (4) the remaining 65% of the net fees will be divided among the remaining venturers taking into consideration all factors including Rule 1.5 of the Model Rules of Professional Conduct, and contribution to the success of the litigation.

The joint-venture agreement further provided that "any dispute arising under or relating to the terms of this agreement shall be resolved by mandatory binding arbitration. . . . "

¶ 5. In the amended complaint, the Jones Firm alleged that SKG's settlement with State Farm Insurance Company had yielded $26,500,000 in attorneys' fees. The Jones Firm claimed that, despite its performance of the bulk of SKG's most difficult discovery and trial work, Richard Scruggs and Don Barrett had conspired to set the Jones Firm's fee allocation at one million dollars, an unacceptably low percentage. Further, the Jones Firm alleged, upon its refusal of the unfair fee allocation, the other four members of SKG voted to remove it from the joint venture and tendered a check for three percent of the net fees, which the Jones Firm refused. Based upon this conduct, the Jones Firm asserted claims against the co-venturers, and Richard Scruggs and Don Barrett individually, for breach of contract, tortious bad-faith breach of contract, breach of fiduciary duties, usurpation, conversion, intentional interference with prospective business advantage, fraud, constructive trust, conspiracy, and unconscionability. The Jones Firm requested a declaratory judgment that it is entitled to twenty percent of all past and future attorneys' fees collected by SKG. The Jones Firm also requested punitive damages, pre-judgment interest, post-judgment interest, costs, expenses, and reasonable attorneys' fees. The Jones Firm also claimed that the defendants had waived any right to arbitration by repeatedly refusing requests to arbitrate.

¶ 6. The defendants answered and filed a motion to stay the proceedings and compel arbitration. They asserted that all of the Jones Firm's claims arose under the joint-venture agreement, and thus were subject to the agreement's provision for mandatory binding arbitration of any disputes arising under or related to the agreement. After a series of filings concerning the arbitration issue, a hearing occurred before Judge Henry Lackey on July 17, 2007.

¶ 7. However, on November 29, 2007, Judge Lackey entered an order of recusal, and on December 5, 2007, this Court appointed Judge William F. Coleman to preside over the case. On December 7, 2007, the Jones Firm moved for sanctions against the defendants based upon the November 28, 2007, six-count federal indictment of Richard Scruggs and his law partners, David Zachary Scruggs (Zach Scruggs) and Sidney Backstrom, along with Timothy Balducci of the law firm Patterson and Balducci, PLLC, and Steven Patterson, a non-attorney member of Patterson and Balducci, PLLC. The indictment charged Scruggs and the other named codefendants, inter alia, with a conspiracy to attempt to influence Judge Lackey to grant the motion to compel arbitration by offering to pay Judge Lackey $40,000 in exchange for a favorable order.

¶ 8. In summary, the indictment charged the following. Between March 15 and March 28, 2007, Richard Scruggs, Zach Scruggs, Balducci, and Patterson met at the offices of the Scruggs Firm to discuss how to influence the outcome of the case. On March 28, 2007, Balducci met with Judge Lackey and made an overture. However, Judge Lackey became a cooperating witness for the Federal Bureau of Investigation, and he began assisting their investigation in an undercover capacity. On May 4, 2004, Backstrom transmitted a proposed order to Balducci, who in turn transmitted it to Judge Lackey. On September 21, 2007, Balducci and Judge Lackey agreed that Balducci would pay Judge Lackey $40,000 in cash on behalf of Scruggs and the Scruggs Law Firm in exchange for a favorable order. On September 27, 2007, Balducci delivered $20,000 in cash to Judge Lackey. On October 18, 2007, Balducci delivered the order to Richard Scruggs and received from Richard Scruggs a $40,000 check and false documentation that cloaked the bribery reimbursement as fees for jury-selection work and preparation of jury instructions in another case. The same day, Balducci delivered $10,000 to Judge Lackey. On November 1, 2007, Balducci delivered another $10,000 to Judge Lackey. The same day, Balducci and Richard Scruggs discussed making a third $10,000 payment to Judge Lackey; on November 5, 2007, Balducci took hand delivery of the $10,000 check and associated false documentation.

B. The Trial Court's Rulings

¶ 10. Judge Coleman entered three orders on the pending motions, two of which are the subject of these consolidated appeals. The first order held that the parties were bound to mandatory arbitration of the fee dispute; the second order held that the court was empowered to sanction the defendants by striking the motion to compel arbitration and entering a default judgment; the third order imposed that sanction and the other requested sanctions.

¶ 13. At the April 15-16, 2008, hearing on the motion for sanctions, it was established that in the United States District Court for the Northern District of Mississippi, Richard Scruggs, Backstrom, Balducci, and Patterson all had pleaded guilty to conspiracy to commit bribery of an elected state official, that Zach Scruggs had pleaded guilty to misprision of a felony, and that all were awaiting sentencing. No members of the other defendant law firms had been charged in the bribery investigation.

¶ 18. In a bench ruling, Judge Coleman found that in March 2007, Balducci had met with members of the Scruggs Firm and had agreed to influence Judge Lackey for a favorable decision in the Jones case. Judge Coleman further found that this attempt to influence developed into a conspiracy among Richard Scruggs, Zach Scruggs, Backstrom, Balducci, and Patterson to bribe Judge Lackey, which was carried out. However, Judge Coleman found that "there is little, if any, evidence that the other defendants participated or were aware of the bribe or part of the conspiracy."

¶ 21. [O]n August 14, 2008, this Court, sitting en banc, granted the petition for an interlocutory appeal and stayed all proceedings in the trial court. On August 25, 2008, the Jones Firm and the Scruggs Firm filed a "Joint Motion to Partially Lift Stay and to Dismiss Certain Parties to Appeal," and stated that the Jones Firm had settled with the Nutt Firm, Richard Scruggs, and the Scruggs Firm. This Court granted the joint motion. Accordingly, the remaining appellants are the Barrett Firm, Don Barrett, and the Lovelace Firm.

DISCUSSION

I. WHETHER THE IMPOSITION OF SANCTIONS AGAINST THE APPELLANTS EXCEEDED THE TRIAL COURT'S INHERENT POWERS.

¶ 24. At issue is the trial court's finding "that as to the conduct on the part of one or more of the defendants in this matter, the actions for one, if shown to have occurred in the furtherance of the purpose of the joint venture, are the actions for all, and the [c]ourt may order sanctions accordingly." The appellants argue that, absent a finding of bad faith personal to the party to be sanctioned, a court lacks the inherent power impose a sanction on that party. In other words, the appellants argue, a court may not use vicarious liability to sanction an innocent party through the imputation of bad faith to that party.

¶ 26. The appellants contend that a court's inherent power to sanction arises upon a showing that the party to be sanctioned acted in bad faith, and that bad faith cannot be imputed to another party through the doctrine of vicarious liability. The Jones Firm counters that there was evidence before the trial court that the appellants had constructive notice of the criminal acts, because the $40,000 in bribe money was reimbursed from joint-venture funds; thus, there was evidence that they acted in bad faith. Nonetheless, the trial court rejected this evidence, concluding that there was "little, if any" evidence the appellants had knowledge of the bribery conspiracy, and the court ordered sanctions based upon the vicarious liability of joint venturers. We find that the trial court's refusal to attribute knowledge of the bribery conspiracy to the appellants was not manifestly erroneous; therefore, the finding was within the court's discretion. For that reason, this Court proceeds to review the trial court's decision to award sanctions based upon vicarious liability.

¶ 31. A joint venture is a single-purpose partnership. As a joint venture, SKG was governed by Mississippi's partnership law, the Uniform Partnership Act . . . . Under the Act, a joint venture is liable for any penalty incurred as the result of a wrongful act or omission, or other actionable conduct, of a joint venturer acting in the ordinary course of business of the joint venture. [UPA §305]. In the absence of an agreement with the claimant or as otherwise provided by law, all co-venturers are jointly and severally liable for joint-venture obligations. [UPA §306(a)]. A litigant may sue a joint venture "in the name of the partnership" or ["a partner may be joined in an action against the partnership or named in a separate action."] [UPA §307(a), [UPA §307(b)]. However, a judgment against a partnership may not be satisfied from a partner's assets unless there is also a judgment against the individual partner. [UPA §307(c)].

¶ 32. We find that the trial court's treatment of this lawsuit as one against SKG or SKG assets was not an abuse of discretion. The lawsuit was an attempt by the Jones Firm to obtain what it asserted to be its rightful share of joint-venture profits under the joint-venture agreement. Rather than suing SKG, the Jones Firm chose to sue the co-venturers, a litigation strategy encouraged by [UPA §307(c)], and two individuals who were not co-venturers. Given the facts that: (1) under [UPA §307(c)], a partnership creditor must sue an individual partner in order to obtain a judgment against the individual partner's assets; (2) accordingly, the trial court found that this suit was against SKG or SKG assets brought in the name of SKG's partners; (3) partners are jointly and severally liable for partnership obligations; and (4) under [UPA §305], a partnership may be liable for "any penalty" incurred as a result of the wrongful act or actionable conduct by a partner in the ordinary course of partnership business; thus, this Court finds that the trial court possessed the discretion to sanction SKG, but only upon a finding that Richard Scruggs's misconduct was within the ordinary course of business of SKG. We proceed to review the trial court's implicit finding that the misconduct occurred within SKG's ordinary course of business.

II. WHETHER RICHARD SCRUGGS'S WRONGFUL ACTS WERE IN THE ORDINARY COURSE OF BUSINESS OF THE JOINT VENTURE.

¶ 33. Under [UPA §305], a partnership is liable for "loss or injury caused to a person, or for a penalty incurred, as a result of a wrongful act or omission, or other actionable conduct, of a partner acting in the ordinary course of business of the partnership or with [the actual or apparent] authority of the partnership." [UPA §301(1)] provides that:

> Each partner is an agent of the partnership for the purpose of its business. An act of a partner, including the execution of an instrument in the partnership name, for apparently carrying on in the ordinary course the partnership business or business of the kind carried on by the partnership binds the partnership, unless the partner had no authority to act for the partnership in the particular matter and the person with whom the partner was dealing knew or had received a notification that the partner lacked authority.

It is undisputed that Richard Scruggs's misconduct was not actually authorized by SKG, and there is no assertion that he acted with apparent authority under [UPA §301(1)]. Therefore, we confine the discussion to vicarious liability under [UPA §305], under which a partnership is liable for "any penalty" incurred by a partner's misconduct committed in the ordinary course of business of the partnership. This Court is guided by several cases in which a trial court exercised its discretion to decide whether to hold an innocent partner liable for damages or judicial sanctions based upon another partner's misconduct.

¶ 34. The Jones Firm cites *Duggins v. Guardianship of Washington*, 632 So.2d 420 (Miss. 1993). In *Duggins,* an attorney, Duggins, associated another attorney, Barfield, to represent a guardianship in a medical-malpractice suit. The two attorneys agreed that they would divide the fees equally. Duggins's role was to compile medical records and medical bills and maintain contact with the client; Barfield was to draft and file the complaint, arrange for expert witnesses, and attempt to negotiate with the defendant's insurer. However, Barfield made material misrepresentations to Duggins and the client and misappropriated settlement funds, for which he eventually was disbarred and convicted of a felony. A chancellor determined that Barfield and Duggins were liable to the guardianship in tort and for breach of contract, and that Duggins was vicariously liable for Barfield's misconduct because it was committed in the scope of the partnership. In addition to compensatory damages, the chancellor ordered Barfield and Duggins to pay punitive damages and attorney's fees. On appeal, Duggins contended that, like the client, he was but an innocent victim of the nefarious Barfield and, thus, he could not be held vicariously liable for Barfield's misconduct.

¶ 35. This Court affirmed. We first determined that the legal relationship between Duggins and Barfield constituted a joint venture governed by the Uniform Partnership Act. We then examined the Uniform Partnership Act's provisions governing a partnership's liability to third parties. The court examined . . . the prior version of [UPA §301(c)], and . . . the prior version of [UPA §305]. The Court found that Barfield's misconduct was imputable to Duggins under the Uniform Partnership Act because the misconduct was "well within" the scope of the joint venture's business. The Court found that "Barfield's actions were committed while in the furtherance of the partnership and was certainly within the partnership business. The handling of client funds is clearly within the realm of an attorney's representation of a guardianship in a legal action." Thus, the Court determined that Duggins was vicariously liable for Barfield's actions. The Court further found Duggins vicariously liable for punitive damages, stating:

> If the partner acted within the course and scope of actual or apparent authority, then even liability for fraudulent wrongs can be imputed to the partnership. The other partners, though innocent without knowledge of the act or omission, can be vicariously liable. . . . [Prior cases] found punitive damages appropriate against an innocent partner for actions done by another partner while engaged in work within the scope of the partnership.

Id. at 429-30 (citations omitted).

¶ 36. However, in affirming the damages assessed against Duggins, this Court did not solely rely upon partnership principles, but also upon the chancellor's finding that Duggins was guilty of omissions that had contributed to the guardianship's loss of assets. We noted that the guardianship had relied on Duggins, as well as Barfield, to pursue its interests, and the chancellor recognized that "there were sufficient 'red flags' which should have caused Duggins to realize that something was amiss." Therefore, we stated, in addition to Barfield's misdeeds, "Duggins' negligence and inaction in investigating Barfield's suspicious conduct allowed the guardianship to be stripped of all its assets."

¶ 37. The appellants cite *Idom v. Weeks & Russell*, 99 So. 761 (1924). In *Idom,* the sheriff of the town of Ackerman rallied the citizenry after two burglaries and a sighting of suspicious characters. Weeks and Russell were partners who owned and operated a drug store, and Russell, without Weeks's knowledge or authorization, decided to lie in wait overnight at the store with a gun in case burglars tried to break in. Tragically, Russell shot and killed Idom, an innocent person who was checking on the store.

¶ 38. In a suit by Idom's widow against Russell and Weeks, this Court held that, while Russell was liable for the killing, his partner, Weeks, was not liable because Russell had not acted in furtherance of partnership business. The Court reviewed the rules pertaining to a partner's liability for the acts of another partner. The Court stated that whether a partner is so liable is governed by the law pertaining to principal and agent, such that:

> If the act or tort of the partner be committed while he is engaged in the partnership business, and is in furtherance of the interest of the partnership, then the partnership and all partners are liable. . . . If a tort be committed by one partner while engaged in a transaction within the scope of the partnership business, and such tort be committed in furtherance of the interests

of the partnership, it will be liable. But it will not be liable for a tort committed by one partner in a transaction outside of the partnership business, where he acts from his own private malice or ill will, unless the act which constituted the tort was authorized by the members of the partnership, or subsequently ratified by them; the act itself having been done in their behalf and interest.

Id. at 763 (citations omitted). The Court defined "course of business" as "what is usually done in the management of trade or business."

¶ 39. The Court determined that Russell's act of lying in wait for burglars at the partnership's drug store emanated from his own private malice or ill will and was not within the scope of the partnership's business. There was testimony that, after the shooting, Russell told the sheriff that he was in the store for the purpose of trying to capture the burglars; he mentioned no intent to protect the partnership's property. From this, the Court concluded that "[a]ccording to this statement of Russell his dominant purpose was not for the preservation of the partnership property but rather to try and capture the burglars." The Court found that the scope of the partnership business did not contemplate that one partner, when the place of business is closed for the night, should conceal himself inside the store for the purpose of capturing burglars.

¶ 42. We turn to the facts at hand. The SKG joint-venture agreement specified that the joint venture's purpose was to "bring a number of lawsuits on behalf of individuals and businesses who were wrongfully denied insurance coverage for property damage arising out of Hurricane Katrina." SKG earned $26.5 million in profits from the Katrina litigation. When a fee dispute arose, SKG ousted the Jones Firm, resulting in its suit against SKG's remaining co-venturers for a share of the joint-venture profits. When the Jones Firm sued, the remaining co-venturers hired attorneys and filed a motion to compel arbitration pursuant to the joint-venture agreement's arbitration clause. As with other SKG expenses, the Nutt Firm advanced the defense fees, and the testimony of Lovelace and of Barrett, by stipulation, indicates that some co-venturers/codefendants made the strategic decision on behalf of all the co-venturers/codefendants to file a motion to compel arbitration. Subsequently, Richard Scruggs pleaded guilty to a conspiracy to bribe the trial judge to enter an order granting the motion to compel arbitration. Members of the other co-venturer law firms testified that they lacked any knowledge of the conspiracy and did not authorize or ratify it.

¶ 43. The record aptly demonstrates that the scope of SKG's business did not contemplate an attempted bribery of the trial judge. This unauthorized criminal act constituted extraordinary behavior outside the ordinary course of SKG business and amounted to an act of "private malice or ill will" equivalent to the conduct in *Idom*. There was no evidence that Scruggs intended, by this act, to benefit SKG; in fact, the Nutt Firm, having been allotted thirty-five percent of the net fee by the joint-venture agreement, could not have lost its share of the net fee at a trial over the division of the remaining sixty-five percent. Because the misconduct of Richard Scruggs was outside the ordinary course of SKG business, the trial court abused its discretion in finding otherwise. Moreover, unlike in *Duggins*, there was no evidence of "red flags" that should have alerted the Barrett Firm, Don Barrett, or the Lovelace Firm to Scruggs's activities. Because there was no basis for sanctioning the appellants, we reverse the order imposing sanctions upon them.

[handwritten margin note: Bribing judge not part of ordinary course of business]

CONCLUSION

¶ 44. The trial court erred by sanctioning the appellants because Richard Scruggs's wrongful acts did not occur in the ordinary course of SKG business. Because the trial court already has ruled that, but for the sanctions, this case is subject to mandatory arbitration, we reverse the order of sanctions and remand this case for the entry of an order compelling arbitration.

¶ 45. **REVERSED AND REMANDED.**

WALLER, C.J., GRAVES, P.J., RANDOLPH and LAMAR, JJ., concur. CARLSON, P.J., dissents with separate written opinion joined in part by PIERCE, J.

CARLSON, Presiding Justice, dissenting.

¶ 46. I agree with the majority inasmuch as "the trial court possessed the discretion to sanction SKG, but only upon a finding that Richard Scruggs's misconduct was within the ordinary course of business of SKG." However, as to issue two, concerning whether Scruggs was acting in the ordinary course of business, I must disagree with the majority's conclusion that Scruggs was not acting in furtherance of SKG.

¶ 47. Vicarious liability falls under the auspices of [UPA §305(a)] . . . :

I do not interpret this statute as implying that the other partners need have knowledge (actual or constructive) of the wrongful or actionable conduct to be held liable—so long as the wrongdoer has acted in the ordinary course of business of the partnership. I believe *Duggins v. Guardianship of Washington Through Huntley,* 632 So.2d 420 (Miss. 1993), is in accord with this premise, because this Court clearly stated therein: "[O]ther partners, though innocent without knowledge of the act or omission, can be vicariously liable." Unlike the majority, I do not interpret the holding in *Duggins* as having also relied on the fact that Duggins should have known of his partner's malfeasance due to the presence of "red flags." The majority interprets *Duggins* as follows:

> [I]n affirming the damages assessed against Duggins, this Court did not solely rely upon partnership principles, but also upon the chancellor's finding that Duggins was guilty of omissions that contributed to the guardianship's loss of assets. We noted that the guardianship had relied on Duggins, as well as Barfield, to pursue its interests, and the chancellor recognized that "there were sufficient 'red flags' which should have caused Duggins to realize that something was amiss." Therefore, we stated in addition to Barfield's misdeeds, "Duggins' negligence and inaction in investigating Barfield's suspicious conduct allowed the guardianship to be stripped of all its assets."

(Maj. Op. at ¶ 37) (quoting *Duggins,* 632 So.2d at 429) (internal citations omitted). I submit that what the majority quotes as the holding in *Duggins* is merely dicta, and that the holding of the case is not premised on Duggins's negligence. A plain reading of the statute does not lend itself to an interpretation that actual or constructive knowledge of the wrongful conduct is required for liability to attach.

¶ 48. That having been said, even if this Court is prepared to hold in today's case that an innocent partner can be held liable for the acts of another only if the circumstances are such that "there were sufficient red flags," then I wish to point out that the $40,000 used in the bribery scam was paid out by SKG to Richard Scruggs under the pretense that Richard Scruggs owed $40,000 to Timothy Balducci for voir dire services in the *Lisanby* case, a Katrina case which had never been tried. I am persuaded by the Jones Firm's argument that this fabricated invoice for a case that had never been tried was sufficient notice to SKG, its associated firms, and the respective partners of those firms that something was amiss.

¶ 49. Moreover, Richard Scruggs did not act on his own behalf in concocting this bribery scheme but on behalf of all the remaining associated firms in SKG. The testimony by Judge Lackey indicated that the *quid pro quo* in this scheme was to be an exchange of $40,000 for a ruling from Judge Lackey in favor of SKG's motion to compel arbitration. This ruling would have been favorable as to all the SKG defendants—not Scruggs alone. This bribery attempt, albeit a fraud upon the court, was committed in furtherance of the interests of all the SKG firms. Had this bribery attempt succeeded with an unscrupulous judge, then presumably SKG stood also to reap the benefit of a favorable ruling in arbitration proceedings against the Jones Firm—retaining all of the disputed profits that perhaps rightly belonged to the Jones Firm and lining all of the pockets of the SKG firms and their respective partners. Surely, if this were the scenario and the bribe had been successful, this Court would not then say the arbitration ruling should stand. In fact, I submit that this Court would unhesitatingly agree that such a judgment must be set aside. Why then are we saying a trial judge abused his discretion in striking an answer and motion—a motion that was accompanied by an attempted fraud upon the court?

¶ 50. The majority relies on the holding in *Idom v. Weeks & Russell*, 99 So. 761 (1924), wherein the Court held that Weeks was not liable for his partner Russell's act of lying in wait within the drug store for burglars and subsequently shooting an innocent passerby. . . .The *Idom* holding was premised on the fact that Russell's lying in wait and disposing of burglars was outside of the scope of the partnership agreement between Weeks and Russell to own and operate a drug store. According to *Idom,* the shooting constituted an act of "private malice or ill will" on the part of Russell.

¶ 51. The majority likens Scruggs's conduct to that depicted in *Idom* because it was an "unauthorized criminal act" outside of SKG's ordinary course of business that amounted to "private malice or ill will." The majority neglects to see the mutual benefits in the form of retained profits that would have been bestowed upon the Scruggs firm and the Barrett and Lovelace firms alike had the bribery attempt not been brought to light by an honorable whistle-blower in Judge Lackey. I submit that had Russell been engaging in dispensing medication to a patron without a prescription, albeit a criminal act, then this Court in *Idom* would have held that there was partnership liability, since Russell's criminal act would have had a mutual benefit to the partnership in the form of increased revenue. Scruggs's conduct was to protect all the coffers of SKG—not just his own. After all, the ordinary course of business for lawyers on the most basic level is that lawyers are in the business of winning—arguing for and receiving favorable rulings from trial judges. Such was the intention of Scruggs in the course of his self-confessed criminal act—the $40,000 was to secure a favorable ruling to compel arbitration—a ruling from which each and every SKG firm stood to benefit.

¶ 52. Accordingly, with the utmost respect for my esteemed colleagues in the majority, I must respectfully dissent, because I would not find an abuse of discretion on the part of the trial judge in imputing Scruggs's criminal conduct to the remaining SKG defendants. I believe that sanctions were properly imposed in today's case, and I would thus affirm the trial court, *in toto*.

Notes and Questions

1. Notes

a. This case was decided under a prior version of the UPA. The citations in brackets are to the current UPA. There are no substantive differences between the prior and current versions of the UPA that are relevant to this opinion.

b. The Mississippi Supreme Court, in line with the practice of some other courts, lists the appellant first in the caption. In this case, the Jones Funderburg law firm is the plaintiff.

c. UPA §301(1) reads in part, "Each partner is an agent of the partnership for the purpose of its business. An act of a partner, . . . , for apparently carrying on the ordinary course the partnership business *or business of the kind carried on by the partnership* binds the partnership. . . ." (emphasis added). The italicized portion of the act broadens the power of a partner to bind the partnership beyond that granted under Agency law. Section 301(2) reads, "An act of a partner which is not apparently for carrying on in the ordinary course the partnership's business or business of the kind carried on by the partnership binds the partnership only if the act was authorized by all the other partners." Under the UPA, then, a partnership is liable for an action in furtherance of what a paradigmatic partnership of this kind would do, even where this particular partnership explicitly does not do that thing.

d. As *Barrett* makes clear, UPA §305 imposes liability on the partnership for a partner's "wrongful act or omission, or other actionable conduct" if the partner was acting either with actual or apparent authority or "in the ordinary course of business of the partnership. . . ." The Comment asserts that the phrase "ordinary course" in §305 includes wrongful acts, but only where those acts, if done rightly, would be in the ordinary course of the partnership's business. Note that UPA §305 imposes liability more narrowly than UPA §301. Why are the statutes different in their scope?

2. Reality Check

a. Why does Justice Carlson dissent? Do you agree with the majority or dissent?

b. What sanctions did the trial court impose? Do you agree that they were appropriate?

3. What Do You Think?

a. The court discusses two cases, *Duggins* and *Idom*. Are the facts in this case more like *Duggins* or more like *Idom*?

b. Do you think *Duggins* and *Idom* were correctly decided?

c. Do you think that the defendants should be vicariously liable for punitive damages?

d. Could, and should, the law firms have agreed in advance as to how the remaining 65 percent of the attorney's fees awarded would be distributed? If they had done so, wouldn't this litigation have been avoided?

The partnership may file a statement of authority with the secretary of state that grants or limits a partner's authority. *See* UPA §303. If the statement grants authority to a partner, a third party may bind the partnership for an action in accordance with the grant, even though the third party did not know of the statement on file. But, if the statement limits the authority of a partner, a third party is bound only if the third party had actual knowledge of the limitation or if the action involved the transfer of real estate. In the real estate setting, purchasers and sellers will normally undertake a title search and the UPA provides that a third party is deemed to know of (i.e., will be estopped to deny) a limitation on authority in a filed statement. Such statements of authority are often useful to third parties who anticipate entering into significant transactions with a partnership and who want added assurance that the partners with whom they deal are authorized to take actions on behalf of the partnership.

e. Fiduciary Duties

Partners have long been held to be fiduciaries for one another and the partnership itself. The UPA (1914) contained the following statement of partners' duties:

> Every partner must account to the partnership for any benefit, and hold as trustee for it any profits derived by him [or her] without the consent of the other partners from any transaction connected with the formation, conduct, or liquidation of the partnership or from any use by him [or her] of its property.

> UPA (1914) §21(1)

Perhaps the most controversial part of the UPA revision in the 1990s concerned a change in partners' fiduciary duties. The pertinent UPA sections are 409 and 105(c) and (d). The next case is an icon: *the* classic statement of partner fiduciary duties.

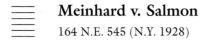

Meinhard v. Salmon

164 N.E. 545 (N.Y. 1928)

CARDOZO, C.J.

On April 10, 1902, Louisa M. Gerry leased to the defendant Walter J. Salmon the premises known as the Hotel Bristol at the northwest corner of Forty-Second street and Fifth avenue in the city of New York. The lease was for a term of 20 years, commencing May 1, 1902, and ending April 30, 1922. The lessee undertook to change the hotel building for use as shops and offices at a cost of $200,000. Alterations and additions were to be accretions to the land.

Salmon, while in course of treaty with the lessor as to the execution of the lease, was in course of treaty with Meinhard, the plaintiff, for the necessary funds. The result was a joint venture with terms embodied in a writing. Meinhard was to pay to Salmon half of the moneys requisite to reconstruct, alter, manage, and operate the property. Salmon was to pay to Meinhard 40 per cent. of the net profits for the first five years of the lease and 50 per cent. for the years thereafter. If there were losses, each party was to bear them equally. Salmon, however, was to have sole power to "manage, lease, underlet and operate" the building. There were to be certain pre-emptive rights for each in the contingency of death.

They were coadventurers, subject to fiduciary duties akin to those of partners. As to this we are all agreed. The heavier weight of duty rested, however, upon Salmon. He was a coadventurer with Meinhard, but he was manager as well. During the early years of the enterprise, the building, reconstructed, was operated at a loss. If the relation had then ended, Meinhard as well as Salmon would have carried a heavy burden. Later the profits became large with the result that for each of the investors there came a rich return. For each the venture had its phases of fair weather and of foul. The two were in it jointly, for better or for worse.

When the lease was near its end, Elbridge T. Gerry had become the owner of the reversion. He owned much other property in the neighborhood, one lot adjoining the Bristol building on Fifth avenue and four lots on Forty-Second street. He had a plan to lease the entire tract for a long term to some one who would destroy the buildings then existing and put up another in their place. In the latter part of 1921, he submitted such a project to several capitalists and dealers. He was unable to carry it through with any of them. Then, in January, 1922, with less than four months of the lease to run, he approached the defendant Salmon. The result was a new lease to the Midpoint Realty Company, which is owned and controlled by Salmon, a lease covering the whole tract, and involving a huge outlay. The term is to be 20 years, but successive covenants for renewal will extend it to a maximum of 80 years at the will of either party. The existing buildings may remain unchanged for seven years. They are then to be torn down, and a new building to cost $3,000,000 is to be placed upon the site. The rental, which under the Bristol lease was only $55,000, is to be from $350,000 to $475,000 for the properties so combined. Salmon personally guaranteed the performance by the lessee of the covenants of the new lease until such time as the new building had been completed and fully paid for.

The lease between Gerry and the Midpoint Realty Company was signed and delivered on January 25, 1922. Salmon had not told Meinhard anything about it. Whatever his motive may have been, he had kept the negotiations to himself. Meinhard was not informed even of the bare existence of a project. The first that he knew of it was in February, when the lease was an accomplished fact. He then made demand on the defendants that the lease be held in trust as an asset of the venture, making offer upon the trial to share the personal obligations incidental to the guaranty. The demand was followed by refusal, and later by this suit. A referee gave judgment for the plaintiff. . . . The case is now here on an appeal by the defendants.

Joint adventurers, like copartners, owe to one another, while the enterprise continues, the duty of the finest loyalty. Many forms of conduct permissible in a workaday world for those acting at arm's length, are forbidden to those bound by fiduciary ties. A trustee is held to something stricter than the morals of the market place. Not honesty alone, but the punctilio of an honor the most sensitive, is then the standard of behavior. As to this there has developed a tradition that is unbending and inveterate. Uncompromising rigidity has been the attitude of courts of equity when petitioned to undermine the rule of undivided loyalty by the "disintegrating erosion" of particular exceptions. *Wendt v. Fischer*, 154 N.E. 303. Only thus has the level of conduct for fiduciaries been kept at a level higher than that trodden by the crowd. It will not consciously be lowered by any judgment of this court.

[handwritten margin note: the famous quote]

The owner of the reversion, Mr. Gerry, had vainly striven to find a tenant who would favor his ambitious scheme of demolition and construction. Baffled in the search, he turned to the defendant Salmon in possession of the Bristol, the keystone of the project. He figured to himself beyond a doubt that the man in possession would prove a likely customer. To the eye of an observer, Salmon held the lease as owner in his own right, for himself and no one else. In fact he held it as a fiduciary, for himself and another, sharers in a common venture. If this fact had been proclaimed, if the lease by its terms had run in favor of a partnership, Mr. Gerry, we may fairly assume, would have laid before the partners, and not merely before one of them, his plan of reconstruction. The pre-emptive privilege, or, better, the pre-emptive opportunity, that was thus an incident of the enterprise, Salmon appropriated to himself in secrecy and silence. He might have warned Meinhard that the plan had been submitted, and that either would be free to compete for the award. If he had done this, we do not need to say whether he would have been under a duty, if successful in the competition, to hold the lease so acquired for the benefit of a venture then about to end, and thus prolong by indirection its responsibilities and duties. The trouble about his conduct is that he excluded his coadventurer from any chance to compete, from any chance to enjoy the opportunity for benefit that had come to him alone by virtue of his agency. This chance, if nothing more, he was under a duty to concede. The price of its denial is an extension of the trust at the option and for the benefit of the one whom he excluded.

No answer is it to say that the chance would have been of little value even if seasonably offered. Such a calculus of probabilities is beyond the science of the chancery. Salmon, the real estate operator, might have been preferred to Meinhard, the woolen merchant. On the other hand, Meinhard might have offered better terms, or reinforced his offer by alliance with the wealth of others. Perhaps he might even have persuaded the lessor to renew the Bristol lease alone, postponing for a time, in return for higher rentals, the improvement of adjoining lots. We know that even under the lease as made the time for the enlargement of the building was delayed for seven years. All these opportunities were cut away from him through another's intervention. He knew that Salmon was the manager. As the time drew near for the expiration of the lease, he would naturally assume from silence, if from nothing else, that the lessor was willing to extend it for a term of years, or at least to let it stand as a lease from year to year. Not impossibly the lessor would have done so, whatever his protestations of unwillingness, if Salmon had not given assent to a project more attractive. At all events, notice of termination, even if not necessary, might seem, not unreasonably, to be something to be looked for, if the business was over and another tenant was to enter. In the absence of such notice, the matter of an extension was one that would naturally be attended to by the manager of the enterprise, and not neglected altogether. At least, there was nothing in the situation to give warning to any one that while the lease was still in being, there had come to the manager an offer of extension which he had locked within his breast to be utilized by himself alone. The very fact that Salmon was in control with exclusive powers of direction charged him the more obviously with the duty of disclosure, since only through disclosure could opportunity be equalized. If he might cut off renewal by a purchase for his own benefit when four months were to pass before the lease would have an end, he might do so with equal right while there remained as many years. He might steal a march on his comrade under cover of the darkness, and then hold the captured ground. Loyalty and comradeship are not so easily abjured.

We have no thought to hold that Salmon was guilty of a conscious purpose to defraud. Very likely he assumed in all good faith that with the approaching end of the venture he might ignore his coadventurer and take the extension for himself. He had given to the enterprise time and labor as well as money. He had made it a success. Meinhard, who had given money, but neither time nor labor, had already been richly paid. There might seem to be something grasping in his insistence upon more. Such recriminations are not unusual when coadventurers fall out. They are not without their force if conduct is to be judged by the common standards of competitors. That is not to say that they have pertinency here. Salmon had put himself in a position in which thought of self was to be renounced, however hard the abnegation. He was much more than a coadventurer. He was a managing coadventurer. For him and for those like him the rule of undivided loyalty is relentless and supreme. A different question would be here if there were lacking any nexus of relation between the business conducted by the manager and the opportunity brought to him as an incident of management. For this problem, as for most, there are distinctions of degree. If Salmon had received from Gerry a proposition to lease a building at a location far removed, he might have held for himself the privilege thus acquired, or so we shall assume. Here the subject-matter of the new lease was an extension and enlargement of the subject-matter of the old one. A managing coadventurer appropriating the benefit of such a lease without warning to his partner might fairly expect to be reproached with conduct that was underhand, or lacking, to say the least, in reasonable candor, if the partner were to surprise him in the act of signing the new instrument. Conduct subject to that reproach does not receive from equity a healing benediction.

ANDREWS, J. (dissenting):

It may be stated generally that a partner may not for his own benefit secretly take a renewal of a firm lease to himself. Yet under very exceptional circumstances this may not be wholly true.

Where the trustee, or the partner or the tenant in common, takes no new lease but buys the reversion in good faith a somewhat different question arises. Here is no direct appropriation of the expectancy of renewal. Here is no offshoot of the original lease. The issue, then, is whether actual fraud, dishonesty, or unfairness is present in the transaction. If so, the purchaser may well be held as a trustee.

Some time before 1922 Mr. Elbridge T. Gerry became the owner of the reversion. He was already the owner of an adjoining lot on Fifth avenue and of four lots adjoining on Forty-Second Street, in all 11,587 square feet, covered by five separate buildings. Obviously, all this property together was more valuable than the sum of the value of the separate parcels. Some plan to develop the property as a whole seems to have occurred to Mr. Gerry. He arranged that all leases on his five lots should expire on the same day as the Bristol Hotel lease. Then in 1921 he negotiated with various persons and corporations seeking to obtain a desirable tenant who would put up a building to cover the entire tract, for this was the policy he had adopted. These negotiations lasted for some months. They failed. About January 1, 1922, Mr. Gerry's agent approached Mr. Salmon and began to negotiate with him for the lease of the entire tract. Upon this he insisted as he did upon the erection of a new and expensive building covering the whole. He would not consent to the renewal of the Bristol lease on any terms. This effort resulted in a lease to the Midpoint Realty Company, a corporation entirely owned and controlled by Mr. Salmon. For our purposes the paper may be treated as if the agreement was made with Mr. Salmon himself.

In many respects, besides the increase in the land demised, the new lease differs from the old. Instead of an annual rent of $55,000 it is now from $350,000 to $475,000. Instead of a fixed term of twenty years it may now be, at the lessee's option, eighty. Instead of alterations in an existing structure costing about $200,000 a new building is contemplated costing $3,000,000. Of this sum $1,500,000 is to be advanced by the lessor to the lessee, "but not to its successors or assigns," and is to be repaid in installments. Again no assignment or sale of the lease may be made without the consent of the lessor.

This lease is valuable. In making it Mr. Gerry acted in good faith without any collusion with Mr. Salmon and with no purpose to deprive Mr. Meinhard of any equities he might have. But as to the negotiations leading to it or as to the execution of the lease itself Mr. Meinhard knew nothing. Mr. Salmon acted for himself to acquire the lease for his own benefit.

I assume that where parties engage in a joint enterprise each owes to the other the duty of the utmost good faith in all that relates to their common venture. Within its scope they stand in a fiduciary relationship. I assume prima facie that even as between joint adventurers one may not secretly obtain a renewal of the lease of property actually used in the joint adventure where the possibility of renewal is expressly or impliedly involved in the enterprise. I assume also that Mr. Meinhard had an equitable interest in the Bristol Hotel lease. Further, that an expectancy of renewal inhered in that lease. Two questions then arise. Under his contract did he share in that expectancy? And if so, did that expectancy mature into a graft of the original lease? To both questions my answer is "No."

The one complaint made is that Mr. Salmon obtained the new lease without informing Mr. Meinhard of his intention. Nothing else. There is no claim of actual fraud. No claim of misrepresentation to any one. Here was no movable property to be acquired by a new tenant at a sacrifice to its owners. No good will, largely dependent on location, built up by the joint efforts of two men. Here was a refusal of the landlord to renew the Bristol lease on any terms; a proposal made by him, not sought by Mr. Salmon, and a choice by him and by the original lessor of the person with whom they wished to deal shown by the covenants against assignment or under-letting, and by their ignorance of the arrangement with Mr. Meinhard.

What then was the scope of the adventure into which the two men entered? It is to be remembered that before their contract was signed Mr. Salmon had obtained the lease of the Bristol property. Very likely the matter had been earlier discussed between them. The $5,000 advance by Mr. Meinhard indicates that fact. But it has been held that the written contract defines their rights and duties. Having the lease, Mr. Salmon assigns no interest in it to Mr. Meinhard. He is to manage the property. It is for him to decide what alterations shall be made and to fix the rents. But for 20 years from May 1, 1902, Salmon is to make all advances from his own funds and Meinhard is to pay him personally on demand one-half of all expenses incurred and all losses sustained "during the full term of said lease," and during the same period Salmon is to pay him a part of the net profits. There was no joint capital provided.

It seems to me that the venture so inaugurated had in view a limited object and was to end at a limited time. There was no intent to expand it into a far greater undertaking lasting for many years. The design was to exploit a particular lease. Doubtless in it Mr. Meinhard had an equitable interest, but in it alone. This interest terminated when the joint adventure terminated. There was no intent that for the benefit of both any advantage should be taken of the chance of renewal — that the adventure should be continued beyond that date. Mr. Salmon has done all he promised to do in return for Mr. Meinhard's undertaking when he distributed profits up to May 1, 1922. Suppose this lease, nonassignable without the consent of the lessor, had contained a renewal option. Could Mr. Meinhard have exercised it? Could he have insisted that Mr. Salmon do so? Had Mr. Salmon done so could he insist that the agreement to share losses still existed, or could Mr. Meinhard have claimed that the joint adventure was still to continue for 20 or 80 years? I do not think so. The adventure by its express terms ended on May 1, 1922. The contract by its language and by its whole import excluded the idea that the tenant's expectancy was to subsist for the benefit of the plaintiff. On that date whatever there was left of value in the lease reverted to Mr. Salmon, as it would had the lease been for thirty years instead of twenty. Any equity which Mr. Meinhard possessed was in the particular lease itself, not in any possibility of renewal. There was nothing unfair in Mr. Salmon's conduct.

I might go further were it necessary. Under the circumstances here presented, had the lease run to both the parties, I doubt whether the taking by one of a renewal without the knowledge of the other would cause interference by a court of equity.

So far I have treated the new lease as if it were a renewal of the old. As already indicated, I do not take that view. Such a renewal could not be obtained. Any expectancy that it might be had vanished. What Mr. Salmon obtained was not a graft springing from the Bristol lease, but something distinct and different — as distinct as if for a building across Fifth avenue. I think also that in the absence of some fraudulent or unfair act the secret purchase of the reversion even by one partner is rightful. Substantially this is such a purchase. Because of the mere label of a transaction we do not place it on one side of the line or the other. Here is involved the possession of a large and most valuable unit of property for 80 years, the destruction of all existing structures and the erection of a new and expensive building covering the whole. No fraud, no deceit, no calculated secrecy is found. Simply that the arrangement was made without the knowledge of Mr. Meinhard. I think this not enough.

Pound, Crane, and Lehman, JJ., concur with Cardozo, C.J., for modification of the judgment appealed from and affirmance as modified.

Andrews, J., dissents in an opinion in which Kellogg and O'Brien, JJ., concur.

Judgment modified, etc.

Notes and Questions

1. Notes

a. Louisa M. Gerry acquired the fee in 1891. At the time, it was subject to an 1860 lease to William H. Webb, who had constructed the Hotel Bristol. Mrs. Gerry died in 1920, and the property passed to her widower, Elbridge T. Gerry, then in his late 80s. *See City of New York v. Gerry*, 165 N.Y.S. 659 (Sup. Ct. 1917).

b. A description of some of the tenants in the building and of Mr. Salmon's actions as landlord may be found in *Waldorf-Astoria Segar Co. v. Salomon*, 95 N.Y.S. 1053 (App. Div. 1905); *Moses v. Salomon*, 135 N.Y.S. 408 (App. Div. 1912); and *New York v. Gerry*, 165 N.Y.S. 659 (Sup. Ct. 1917).

c. As the judges point out, the lease was commercially successful. For a year-by-year breakdown of revenues, expenses, and net profits on the lease, see *Appeal of Salmon*, 3 B.T.A. 723, 724 (Bd. Tx. App. 1926). Part of the reason for the success was an increased demand for office space in what is now midtown Manhattan:

> For many years prior to 1910, the retail business section in New York City had centered around Sixth Avenue and Twenty-third Street [about one mile south of the Hotel Bristol. ED.]. The establishment of manufacturing industries in that section made it undesirable for retail businesses; they first located at Twenty-third Street and Broadway and moved up first to Thirty-fourth Street between Broadway and Fifth Avenue and spread north to Fifth Avenue up to Forty-second Street, and certain of the specialty shops moved up between Forty-second Street and Forty-eighth Street.
>
> All of these factors centered the attention of the real estate interests in New York City upon the locality of Forty-second Street and Fifth Avenue. Tenants on that street, in the vicinity of Fifth Avenue, were offered good bonuses for their leases. There were many deals pending in 1913 and 1914, and long-term leases on desirable properties were in great demand.
>
> *Appeal of Salmon*, 3 B.T.A. 723, 724 (Bd. Tx. App. 1926)

The total rent went from about $148,000 in 1910 to $194,000 in 1914 and the profits for those years went from $36,000 to $65,000.

A further reason for the profitability of the lease was that rents skyrocketed with the end of World War I. For example, in 1918, the last year of the war, rents were $237,000 and profits were $73,000. Two years later, rents were $317,000 and profits were $140,000. *See Appeal of Meinhard*, 3 B.T.A. 612 (Bd. Tx. App. 1926).

d. Apparently this litigation delayed the razing of the Bristol building. As soon as the decision of the Court of Appeals was final, the parties began the new project. Salmon elected to have Meinhard participate as a joint venturer rather than as a shareholder of Midpoint Realty. The new building, known as 500 Fifth Avenue, was designed by Shreve, Lamb & Harrison, which was then involved in designing the Empire State Building. The building was completed in 1930 and the delay cost the parties dearly. The Great Depression following the October 1929 stock market crash made the building unprofitable to operate. The construction of the building had been financed by $7,000,000 of bonds secured by the lease from Gerry. A $1,000 bond (a typical denomination for a bond like this) was trading as low as $110 in September 1932. By the end of World War II, the lessee was $1,500,000 behind in interest on the bonds and $400,000 behind in its rent. Meinhard died in 1931 and his interest was purchased by Salmon. Salmon died in the 1950s, his son died in 1986, and the building was then sold for $124,000,000.

e. The UPA (1914) was in effect in New York at the time of this case, although neither judge found the statute to be directly applicable. Section 21(1) provided, "Every partner must account to the partnership for any benefit, and hold as trustee for it any profits derived by him [or her] without the consent of the other partners from any transaction connected with the formation, conduct, or liquidation of the partnership or from any use by him [or her] of its property."

f. Information about the building's current use may be found at www.500fifthavenue.com.

2. Reality Check

a. Do you agree with Chief Judge Cardozo that Meinhard "would naturally assume from silence, if from nothing else," that Mr. Gerry would extend the lease? Before the lease expired, did Meinhard ever inquire from Salmon or Gerry whether the lease was going to be renewed?

b. Chief Judge Cardozo writes, "A different question would be here if there were lacking any nexus of relation between the business conducted by the manager and the opportunity brought to him as an incident of management." How strong a "nexus of relation" must there be between the current lease and the new venture to impose fiduciary duties? Chief Judge Cardozo writes, "If Salmon had received from Gerry a proposition to lease a building at a location far removed, he might have held for himself the privilege thus acquired, or so we shall assume." This observation seems to conflate two qualities. The more salient is geographical. How far away from Fifth and 42nd must the new venture be before Salmon is free to accept without Meinhard? The second quality is the identity of the offeror. If the adjoining properties were owned by someone other than Gerry could Salmon have proposed to Gerry and the other property owner to construct a building on both parcels without including Meinhard?

In this regard, consider the following facts:

In August 1901, eight months before the lease from Mrs. Gerry to Salmon, Salmon purchased the property at 19 W. 42nd Street, virtually next door to the Hotel Bristol. See *Stevens v. Salomon*, 79 N.Y.S. 136 (N.Y. Sup. Ct. 1902).

In 1903 Salmon purchased the property on the northwest corner of Sixth and 42nd Street, one block away from the Bristol. *See City of New York v. De Peyster*, 105 N.Y.S. 612 (App. Div. 1907).

In 1919 Salmon leased an apartment building called the Nevada at the corner of Broadway and 69th, about one and one-half miles from the Hotel Bristol. In 1925 Salmon purchased the land under the Nevada. *See Kentucky Farm & Cattle Co. v. C.I.R.*, 30 T.C. 1355 (1958).

By 1927 Salmon owned the land at 11 W. 42nd Street, directly next door to the Gerry property and had constructed a building on that land, called Salmon Tower, which was designed by the same architects that built the new building on the corner.

Salmon Tower was used as the headquarters of Salmon's real estate holdings. *See Levy v. C.I.R.*, T.C.-Memo. 1960-22.

By 1928 Salmon also owned the Bryant Park building at 55 W. 42nd Street, at the opposite end of the block from the Hotel Bristol. *See Levy v. C.I.R.*, T.C.-Memo. 1960-22.

c. Does it make a difference that Salmon was an experienced real estate developer in New York, while Meinhard, "was in the woolen business and was entering upon his first venture in real estate"? *See Meinhard v. Salmon*, 229 N.Y.S. 345 (App. Div. 1928).

d. Does the way in which the parties describe their relationship determine the scope of the venture? The intermediate appellate court described a 1908 disagreement between the parties that resulted in a minor modification of the agreement:

> In correspondence that passed between the parties at the time, the defendant Salmon agreed, in consideration for such compensation, "to devote such time and attention as may be necessary for furthering our *joint interests* in the building," and in this same communication, dated February 8, 1908, the defendant stated that "this agreement shall bind both of us for the remainder of our *ownership of the lease* of the said premises." This letter also provided that, except as modified, the original agreement should continue in force.
>
> *Meinhard v. Salmon*, 229 N.Y.S. 345, 348 (App. Div. 1928)

e. Does it matter that the industry practice, apparently a practice followed by Salmon, was and is to have each piece of property owned by a separate entity (typically a corporation)? This facilitates transfer (because only the stock of the owning corporation need be transferred rather than title to the real estate) and keeps each property's liabilities relegated to the assets of that property. It also allows each property to be separately financed and permits a developer such as Salmon to have different additional investors in each property. Thus an investor who participates with a developer in property *A* would not necessarily expect to participate with the same developer in property *B*.

3. Suppose

a. Suppose the court had used UPA (1914) section 21? Would the analysis or result have been different?

b. If this case arose today and a court applied UPA §409, would the result be clearer?

c. What if this case were decided under contract principles? Would the implied covenant of good faith and fair dealing help Salmon? Meinhard? *See* UPA §409(d).

d. Suppose Meinhard based his claim on agency law rather than partnership law? *See Restatement (Third) of Agency* §§8.01, 8.02, 8.04, 8.10, 8.11. Cf. §8.06.

One of the most controversial aspects of the UPA is its treatment of fiduciary duties. More particularly, many commentators believe the UPA gives too much power to partners to limit or effectively eliminate fiduciary duties. This is the result of UPA §§105(a)–(c), and 409. Under §105(a) and (b), the UPA is a fallback set of rules to fill gaps left by the parties in their partnership agreement. Section 409 imposes specific duties, fiduciary and otherwise, on partners, which some observers believe are too narrow. Section 105(c) allows the parties to further narrow those duties.

The next case illustrates the question of the power of partners to define the duties they will owe. Note that the entity involved is a limited partnership (described in a later section of this chapter) rather than a general partnership. However, the relevant statutes are applicable to both limited partnerships and general partnerships and it is fairly clear that the court would reach the same conclusion on the same reasoning if the entity had been a general partnership.

≣   **Clancy v. King**
≣   954 A.2d 1092 (Md. 2008)

HARRELL, J.

On 26 February 1992, Thomas L. Clancy, Jr., perhaps best known as the author of many popular "techno-thriller" novels, and Wanda King, his wife at the time, entered into an agreement (the "JRLP Partnership Agreement"), under Maryland law, forming the Jack Ryan Limited Partnership (JRLP). The purpose, as later amended, of JRLP is to "engage in activities relating to the writing, publishing and sale of books or in any other lawful activity. . . ." Clancy and King [are the only partners of] JRLP. Section 5.5 of the 33 page JRLP Partnership Agreement states in pertinent part:

> A. The General Partners or their Affiliated Persons may act as general or managing partners for other partnerships engaged in businesses similar to that conducted by the Partnership. Nothing herein shall limit the General Partners or their Affiliated Persons from engaging in any such business activities, or any other activities which may be competitive with the Partnership or the [JRLP-owned] Property, and the General Partners or their Affiliated Persons shall not incur any obligation, fiduciary or otherwise, to disclose or offer any interest in such activities to any party hereto and shall not be deemed to have a conflict of interest because of such activities. . . .
>
> E. The General Partners shall be under a fiduciary duty to conduct the affairs of the Partnership in the best interests of the Partnership, including the safekeeping and use of all Partnership funds and assets and the use thereof for the benefit of the Partnership. The General Partners shall at all times act in good faith and exercise due diligence in all activities relating to the conduct of the business of the Partnership.

Section 5.7 of the JRLP Partnership Agreement provides that:

> Neither the Partnership nor any Partner shall have any rights or obligations, by virtue of this Agreement, in or to any independent ventures of any nature or description, or the income or profits derived therefrom, in which a Partner may engage, including, without limitation, the ownership, operation, management, syndication and development of other businesses, even if in competition with the Partnership's trade or business.

JRLP, in furtherance of its purpose, contracted with S & R Literary, Inc., in a 23 March 1993 letter agreement, forming a joint venture known as "Tom Clancy's Op-Center" (Op-Center). S & R Literary is controlled by its President, Dr. Steve R. Pieczenik. The original purpose of the Joint Venture Agreement was to develop a proposal for a television series.[3] Proceeds from the efforts undertaken pursuant to

---

3. The television miniseries aired on NBC; however, the network declined to continue the series thereafter. The scope of the Op-Center franchise was expanded to paperback books. . . .

the Op-Center joint venture were to be split evenly between JRLP and S & R Literary. The Op-Center Joint Venture Agreement pertinently states:

> 2. All decisions with respect to the development, use and exploitation of the proposal shall be made by mutual agreement between Steve R. Pieczenik and Tom Clancy; provided, however, that if, after discussion, no agreement is reached, the decision of Tom Clancy should prevail.

The signature page of the Joint Venture Agreement appears as follows:

> If the foregoing is in accordance with your understanding, please indicate your agreement by signing and returning copies hereof to us.
>
> Very truly yours,
> JACK RYAN LIMITED PARTNERSHIP By [Mr. Clancy]
>
> AGREED TO AND ACCEPTED:
>   S. & R. LITERARY, INC. By [Dr. Pieczenik]
>
> AGREED TO (insofar as I am concerned):
>   [Mr. Clancy]
>   [Dr. Pieczenik]

To develop the paperback book series, Pieczenik assembled a team including . . . Jeff Rovin, an author-for-hire. According to the testimony, Clancy had very little to do with the development of the series. Although he "glanced at a few" of the books, Clancy did not read, cover-to-cover or in any meaningful part, any of the books in the series. Apparently his chief contribution to the effort was the aura lent to the enterprise by the association of his name and reputation.

The Op-Center paperback books proved to be successful. Every book appeared on the New York Times Paperback Bestseller list. As of July 2003, the Op-Center book series generated over $28 million in domestic and foreign profits, after deducting writers' fees, commissions, and other expenses.

In 1996, in the midst of the Op-Center series of books, Clancy and King, as husband and wife, separated. Their divorce was finalized by the Circuit Court for Calvert County on 6 January 1999. Leading up to the divorce, Clancy and King entered into a Marital Property Agreement. Although the Marital Property Agreement did not alter the respective ownership interests of Clancy and King in JRLP, it designated Clancy as Managing Partner of JRLP. The Marital Property Agreement also contained a provision by which a party breaching the agreement would have to pay the non-breaching party's resultant costs.

After a total of 10 books were published in the Op-Center series, and Books 11 and 12 slated for publication, Clancy set the stage for the possible removal of his name from the Op-Center series. JRLP and S & R Literary agreed, in a jointly signed letter dated 23 October 2001, that Clancy's name would be used in connection with Books 13 and 14 in the series. The letter agreement provided further that, after the publication of Book 14, JRLP could withdraw permission to use Clancy's name in connection with future books in the series.[8]

---

8. If JRLP exercised its option to withdraw Clancy's name, the profit sharing arrangement under the Op-Center Joint Venture Agreement would be altered. Instead of a 50-50 split, 75% of the profits from the series would belong to S & R Literary. Thus, JRLP's share would be reduced to 25% of the profits.

King filed a Complaint in the Circuit Court for Calvert County on 3 July 2003 alleging that Clancy breached his fiduciary duty to her and JRLP by, *inter alia*, stating that he intended to prevent the use of his name in connection with later books in the Op-Center series. She sought injunctive relief to prohibit Clancy, as Managing Partner of JRLP, from taking action detrimental to the Op-Center series, an order placing her in the role of Managing Partner of JRLP, and recovery of attorneys' fees and expenses.

It was not until 19 January 2004 that Clancy "pulled the trigger" on his announced intent to withdraw his name prospectively from the Op-Center series. Through counsel in a 19 January 2004 letter, he expressed his refusal to permit the Op-Center joint venture to use his name in connection with the series beyond Book 14. Specifically, the letter stated:

> Although [Clancy], individually, permitted the joint venture to use the name "Tom Clancy" in the series title in connection with Op-Center paperback books 1 through 14, he has withdrawn permission to the joint venture for further and future use of his name in the titles to the Op-Center paperback book series beyond book 14. Please accept this letter as confirmation of the fact that [Clancy] will not permit the joint venture to use his name in the title to the Op-Center paperback book series beyond book 14.

On 20 January 2004, Clancy filed in the case initiated by King a Counterclaim for Declaratory Relief. Clancy sought a declaration holding:

> (1) That beyond rights granted by [him] to the Joint Venture to use the "Tom Clancy" name in the publication of Books 1 through 14 of the Op-Center paperback book series, the Joint Venture does not possess the right to use the name "Tom Clancy" in the Op-Center series title;
>
> (2) That the Joint Venture does not have the right to use the name "Tom Clancy" in the series title for hardback book publications;
>
> (3) That all decisions with respect to the development, use and exploitation of the Op-Center concept are at the unfettered discretion of [Clancy], individually;
>
> (4) That [Clancy] may withhold or withdraw any license to use his name in Joint Venture business endeavors for any reason, including for purely personal competitive reasons;
>
> (5) That JRLP does not possess the right to use the name "Tom Clancy";
>
> (6) That Wanda King does not possess the right to use the name "Tom Clancy"; [and]
>
> (7) That [Clancy] does not owe a duty, as managing partner or otherwise, to JRLP such as would require him to permit the use of his name in JRLP's business ventures, including through its participation in the Joint Venture.

The Circuit Court bifurcated the trial. The object of the first portion of the trial was to determine whether Clancy breached his fiduciary duty to JRLP and King. The second part of the trial was to determine, if necessary, equitable relief and damages due to King. On 5 August 2005, the Circuit Court concluded that Clancy breached his duty to JRLP and the Op-Center joint venture. The court ordered that King be appointed as managing partner of JRLP as it related to the Op-Center series, which included "collaborating and negotiating with Dr. Pieczenik, on behalf of the joint venture, publishing, royalty and other contracts for the management of the Op-Center brand." A later order awarded King attorneys' fees and expenses in the amount of $518,431.71.

Clancy noted a timely appeal to the Court of Special Appeals. The intermediate appellate court affirmed, in an unreported opinion, the Circuit Court's judgment.

Issue 1

We granted Clancy's Petition for Writ of Certiorari, to consider . . . : Whether the lower courts erred in failing to recognize that principles of contract preempt fiduciary duties where the contract is unambiguous and the parties have made their intentions clear?

DISCUSSION

Clancy concedes that, contract law aside,[13] his pertinent actions, which animated King's suit, would violate the fiduciary duty he owed to JRLP. Thus, for proper analysis of the controversy presented for our review involving the interpretation of the JRLP Partnership Agreement and the Op-Center Joint Venture Agreement, we need not dwell unduly on common law or statutory fiduciary duties.

105(d)(3)
Specif. to duties that don't violate

Section [105(a) of the UPA] notes that "relations among the partners and between the partners and the partnership are governed by the partnership agreement." [UPA §]105(d)(3) permits partnerships to "identify specific types or categories of activities that do not violate the duty of loyalty."[15] * King concedes that a partner's fiduciary duties may be modified by partnership agreement.

Thus, the first step in the proper analysis of the questions presented by the instant case is to examine the contracts governing the operation of JRLP and the Op-Center Joint Venture.

There are essentially two contracts of concern in the present case. The first, the JRLP Partnership Agreement, clearly and unambiguously limits the duty of loyalty ordinarily owed by Clancy to JRLP and King. [The court quotes sections 5.5A and 5.7 of the JRLP Partnership Agreement set out above.]

In short, these provisions trumped the usual duty not to compete with the . . . partnership and, to a large extent, the duty not to usurp partnership opportunities.[18]

Thus, Clancy was under no obligation to allow JRLP to participate in the Op-Center Joint Venture. Clancy was free to retain all profits and management of the Op-Center Joint Venture for himself as an individual.[19]

As to the second contract of special relevance in the present case, the Op-Center Joint Venture Agreement, states: [The court quotes section 2 set out above.]

In other words, "Tom Clancy" has final authority over "[a]ll decisions" regarding the "development, use, and exploitation" of the Op-Center project. The Joint Venture Agreement is between two parties, JRLP and S & R Literary, but also was

---

13. A limited partnership is essentially a creature of contract or a series of contracts. *See* [UPA §]103(a) ("[R]elations among the partners and between the partners and the partnership are governed by the partnership agreement."); [ULPA (1976)] §403 ("Except as provided in this title *or in the partnership agreement,* a general partner of a limited partnership has the rights and powers and is subject to the restrictions and liabilities of a partner in a partnership." (emphasis added)). . . .

15. [UPA §]105 is applicable to limited partnerships, as well as general partnerships. [ULPA (1976)] §108. [*NOTE that the language here is based on a prior version of the UPA. ED.]

18. Cases from other jurisdictions firmly establish that fiduciaries and those to whom they owe such duties, by contract, may permit actions that otherwise would be flagrant violations of common law and statutory fiduciary duties.

19. This is evidenced further by the variety of other ventures with which Clancy is involved and in which JRLP has no interest, such as the *Tom Clancy's Splinter Cell* books and video game line and *Tom Clancy's Net Force*. King was aware of these other ventures at the time that she signed the JRLP Partnership Agreement. King, at least at the time of her divorce from Clancy, maintained a 40% interest and served as a director of a competing venture, Jack Ryan Enterprises, Ltd.

signed by Clancy and Pieczenik individually. The face of the contract makes clear the dual capacities of the various signatories.

The contract is in the form of a letter from JRLP to S & R Literary. Thus, where the contract refers to "you," it refers to S & R Literary. By contrast, when the contract uses the third person plural "we" or "ours," the contract refers to JRLP. The use of the name "Tom Clancy" in paragraph two means "Tom Clancy individually." Finally, the signature page clearly contemplates that Clancy signed the contract both as General Partner of JRLP and as an individual. [The court quotes the signature page set out above.]

There would be no reason for Clancy's and Pieczenik's signatures to appear twice on the signature page unless they also were signing in their individual capacities. The Circuit Court and the Court of Special Appeals correctly recognized that Clancy reserved for himself, individually, in the Op-Center Joint Venture Agreement, management and control of the Op-Center venture.

If traditional common law and statutory fiduciary duty principles were paramount to the analysis and outcome of the present case in the posture in which it reaches us, portions of this contract clearly would be improper self-dealing and a usurpation of a partnership opportunity. Clancy reserved control of the project to himself, not the entity to which he owed fiduciary duties. Instead, the JRLP Partnership Agreement clearly contemplates that Clancy may compete with JRLP. In fact, Clancy, under the JRLP Partnership Agreement, may contract to control individually the entire management and profits of the Op-Center Joint Venture. There is no reason, therefore, that he could not contract for less of an interest in the Op-Center activities for himself individually. In essence, Clancy agreed to retain full and final management authority for himself individually, while assigning the profits and ownership of the venture to JRLP. Thus, the terms of the Op-Center Joint Venture contract were permitted by the terms of the JRLP Partnership Agreement.

A fiduciary, under appropriate circumstances, may acquire and enforce legal rights against the firm for which he or she serves as a fiduciary. Thus, a fiduciary may enforce validly obtained legal rights against his or her firm, even if that transaction results in a profit for the fiduciary at the firm's expense. In the present case, Clancy contracted in both the JRLP Partnership Agreement and the Op-Center Joint Venture Agreement regarding an intellectual property right, namely, control over the use and exploitation of "Tom Clancy's Op-Center." He now seeks to enforce that contracted-for-right. . . . The rationale for reserving such a right is obvious. Clancy is a commercially successful and highly-franchised artist. It is perfectly legitimate and rational for such an artist to seek to retain creative control over a project which bears his or her name, regardless of the degree of artistic contribution he or she actually contributes to the endeavor.[24]

The fact that Clancy validly reserved the right to control the use and exploitation of the Op-Center project does not end the inquiry. According to the terms of the JRLP Partnership Agreement and contract law generally, Clancy must exercise his discretion in good faith. Section 5.5E of the JRLP Partnership Agreement states

---

24. Because Clancy is an artist who by contract retained creative control over a project which bears his name, we are hard-pressed to conceive of a contractual situation which more implicates the necessity for personal satisfaction in the contract. It is for this reason that the subjective "good faith" standard applies to Clancy's actions, instead of the objective "reasonable person" standard.

that "[Clancy and King] shall at all times act *in good faith* and exercise due diligence in all activities relating to the conduct of the business of the Partnership."

Even if the contract did not contain this general good faith term, Maryland contract law implies such an obligation. *See* [UPA §]105(c)(6) (noting that the partnership agreement may not "[e]liminate the obligation of good faith and fair dealing"); *id.* §409(d) ("A partner shall discharge the duties to the partnership and other partners under this title or under the partnership agreement and exercise any rights consistently with the obligation of good faith and fair dealing."). . . .

The requirements of good faith in contract law are similar to the good faith doctrine in partnership law. In matters of personal discretion in contract, the party with the discretion is limited to exercising that discretion in good faith.

If a significant motive for Clancy exercising his contractual right to withdraw his name from the Op-Center series was to decrease the profitability of the series, thereby denying his JRLP partner and ex-wife revenue, because he desired to spite or punish King for or as a consequence of their divorce, it reasonably could be maintained that he acted in bad faith towards both the Op-Center Joint Venture and JRLP. One certainly breaches the promise of good faith owed in contract and as fiduciary in a partnership by working actively to decrease directly the profits of the business venture.[27] Thus, Clancy may not act to impair the value of the Op-Center franchise out of personal spite toward his business partner, King. Such motivation would constitute bad faith.

In the present case, the trial court made only a finding that Clancy did not act in the best interests of JRLP.[28] As noted above, Clancy only needed to act in good faith

---

27. Jerry Seinfeld, perhaps an unlikely legal illustrator, once epitomized the duty of good faith in contract. In an episode of his television show, Jerry's character purchased a jacket at a men's clothing shop. The terms of the contract permitted Jerry to return the item for refund at his discretion. When Jerry attempted to return the jacket after an unrelated personal quarrel with the salesman, the following discussion took place.

> **Jerry:** Excuse me, I'd like to return this jacket.
> **Clerk:** Certainly. May I ask why?
> **Jerry:** For spite.
> **Clerk:** Spite?
> **Jerry:** That's right. I don't care for the salesman that sold it to me.
> **Clerk:** I don't think you can return an item for spite.
> **Jerry:** What do you mean?
> **Clerk:** Well, if there was some problem with the garment. If it were unsatisfactory in some way, then
> we could do it for you, but I'm afraid spite doesn't fit into any of our conditions for a refund.
> **Jerry:** That's ridiculous, I want to return it. What's the difference what the reason is?
> **Clerk:** Let me speak with the manager . . . excuse me . . . Bob!
> (walks over to the manager and whispers)
> **Bob:** What seems to be the problem?
> **Jerry:** Well, I want to return this jacket and she asked me why and I said for spite and now she won't
> take it back.
> **Bob:** That's true. You can't return an item based purely on spite.
> **Jerry:** Well, so fine then . . . then I don't want it and then that's why I'm returning it.
> **Bob:** Well you already said spite so. . . .
> **Jerry:** But I changed my mind.
> **Bob:** No, you said spite. Too late.

Seinfeld: The Wig Master (NBC original television broadcast 4 April 1996).

In attempting to exercise his contractual discretion out of "spite," Jerry breached his duty to act in good faith towards the other party to the contract. Jerry would have been authorized to return the jacket if, in his good faith opinion, it did not fit or was not an attractive jacket. He may not return the jacket, however, for the sole purpose of denying to the other party the value of the contract. Jerry's post hoc rationalization that he was returning the jacket because he did not "want it" was rejected properly by Bob as not credible.

28. Specifically the trial court found:

toward his business partners, even if such actions actually were adverse to the interests of JRLP. As there is potentially competing evidence in the record as to whether Clancy acted in good faith and/or bad faith, the judgment below shall be reversed and the case remanded for further proceedings not inconsistent with this opinion.

[handwritten: remanded based on good faith / bad faith determ]

Notes and Questions

1. Notes

a. Mr. Clancy was a well-known and successful author. His first book was *The Hunt for Red October*. Other hits include *Patriot Games, Clear and Present Danger*, and *The Sum of All Fears*. Jack Ryan is the name of the protagonist in each of those novels.

2. Reality Check

a. Why did Mr. Clancy and Ms. King form JRLP?

b. Why did Mr. Clancy and Dr. Pieczenik form the Op-Center Joint Venture?

c. According to Ms. King, how did Mr. Clancy's actions damage JRLP? Does Mr. Clancy disagree?

d. What legal theories did Ms. King and Mr. Clancy assert against each other?

e. Where did the court look first to decide this dispute?

f. How did the court choose between contract law and fiduciary duty law?

3. Suppose

a. Suppose this case were decided under the *Meinhard* standard. Would the court's reasoning or the result be different?

b. Suppose *Meinhard v. Salmon* were decided under the *Clancy* reasoning. Would the court's reasoning or the result be different?

4. What Do You Think?

a. As noted above in footnote *, the Maryland version of UPA §105(d)(3)(B) allows a partnership agreement to "identify specific types or categories of activities that do not violate the duty of loyalty"; while the UPA language reads, if not manifestly unreasonable to "identify specific types or categories of activities that do

---

While there is evidence that Mr. Clancy wants to end the Op-Center series because sales are going down and it is hurting his literary reputation, there is proof to the contrary that the books in the "Clancy" brand are going down in sales no more than the general decline in book sales. Penguin Group USA cannot be too concerned with the expansion of the "Clancy" brand because they just agreed to add two (2) books to a new branded series: Splinter Cell, a computer game. Therefore, this Court is not persuaded that the Op-Center series is damaging Mr. Clancy in any way because there is evidence to show that the sales of the other series of books not authored by Mr. Clancy are declining as well. Further, the evidence that Mr. Clancy does not want Mrs. King to benefit in any way from the Op-Center series further supports the contention that he was not acting in the best interests of JRLP in requesting his name be withdrawn from the series and that there should not be any further publications with his name. It is this Court's opinion that Mr. Clancy breaches his fiduciary duty not only to JRLP and his partner, Mrs. King, but also to the joint venture formed for the development of the Op-Center series.

Although the trial court discussed some of the evidence indicating as much, it made no discernable, reviewable finding that Clancy made the decision to withdraw his name in bad faith.

not violate the duty of loyalty." If the Maryland statute tracked the UPA exactly, would the court's reasoning or the result have been different?

b. Should the UPA narrow the fiduciary duties among partners? Should it allow the partners to tailor the scope of those duties? Do you believe the UPA does these things? *See* UPA §§409(a), (b), (c), (e), 105(c)(5), (6). *Compare* UPA (1914) §21(1) which states:

> Every partner must account to the partnership for any benefit, and hold as trustee for it any profits derived by him [or her] without the consent of the other partners from any transaction connected with the formation, conduct, or liquidation of the partnership or from any use by him [or her] of its property.

c. Do you think the standard of appropriate behavior should depend on the business context? Do some businesses have different (or higher or lower) customs than others? Note that at about the same time as the *Meinhard v. Salmon* litigation was commenced Salmon was embroiled in a lawsuit concerning the property at the northwest corner of Sixth and Forty-Second Street, one block west of the property involved in *Meinhard v. Salmon*. Much of the other litigation turned on Salmon's strategic ownership of a strip of land 20 feet long and *1 inch wide. See Finch v. Unity Fee Co., Inc.*, 208 N.Y.S. 369 (App. Div. 1925). Do you suppose the Court of Appeals was aware of *Finch* and, if so, should it have informed its view of the equities in *Meinhard v. Salmon*?

d. Do you believe Mr. Clancy violated his fiduciary duties under the UPA? Did he violate his fiduciary duties under Maryland's version of the UPA? Do you believe Mr. Clancy violated the duty of good faith and fair dealing imposed under the UPA?

5. You Draft It

a. Draft a UPA provision that either imposes appropriate, non-waivable duties on partners or imposes appropriate default duties on partners and permits the partners to modify or eliminate some or all of those duties, as appropriate. The relevant UPA (1914), UPA, and Maryland UPA provisions are set out below:

> **Partner Accountable as a Fiduciary.**
> (1) Every partner must account to the partnership for any benefit, and hold as trustee for it any profits derived by him without the consent of the other partners from any transaction connected with the formation, conduct, or liquidation of the partnership or from any use by him of its property.
>
> **UPA (1914) §21(1)**

> **Standards of Conduct for Partners.**
> (a) A partner owes to the partnership and the other partners the duties of loyalty and care stated in subsections (b) and (c).
> (b) The fiduciary duty of loyalty of a partner includes the duties:
>> (1) to account to the partnership and hold as trustee for it any property, profit, or benefit derived by the partner:
>>> (A) in the conduct or winding up of the partnership's business;
>>> (B) from a use by the partner of the partnership's property; or
>>> (C) from the appropriation of a partnership opportunity;
>> (2) to refrain from dealing with the partnership in the conduct or winding up of the partnership business as or on behalf of a person having an interest adverse to the partnership; and

(3) to refrain from competing with the partnership in the conduct of the partnership's business before the dissolution of the partnership.

(c) The duty of care of a partner in the conduct or winding up of the partnership business is to refrain from engaging in grossly negligent or reckless conduct, willful or intentional misconduct, or a knowing violation of law.

(d) A partner shall discharge the duties and obligations under this [act] or under the partnership agreement and exercise any rights consistently with the contractual obligation of good faith and fair dealing.

(e) A partner does not violate a duty or obligation under this [act] or under the partnership agreement solely because the partner's conduct furthers the partner's own interest.

UPA §409

PARTNERSHIP AGREEMENT; SCOPE, FUNCTION, AND LIMITATIONS.

(a) Except as otherwise provided in subsections (c) and (d), the partnership agreement governs:

(1) relations among the partners as partners and between the partners and the partnership;

(2) the business of the partnership and the conduct of that business; and

(3) the means and conditions for amending the partnership agreement.

(b) To the extent the partnership agreement does not provide for a matter described in subsection (a), this [act] governs the matter.

(c) A partnership agreement may not:

. . .

(5) alter or eliminate the duty of loyalty or the duty of care, except as otherwise provided in subsection (d);

(6) eliminate the contractual obligation of good faith and fair dealing under Section 409(d), but the partnership agreement may prescribe the standards, if not manifestly unreasonable, by which the performance of the obligation is to be measured;

. . .

(8) relieve or exonerate a person from liability for conduct involving bad faith, willful or intentional misconduct, or knowing violation of law;

. . .

(d) Subject to subsection (c)(8), without limiting other terms that may be included in a partnership agreement, the following rules apply:

. . .

(3) If not manifestly unreasonable, the partnership agreement may:

(A) alter or eliminate the aspects of the duty of loyalty stated in Section 409(b);

(B) identify specific types or categories of activities that do not violate the duty of loyalty;

(C) alter the duty of care, but may not authorize conduct involving bad faith, willful or intentional misconduct, or knowing violation of law; and

(D) alter or eliminate any other fiduciary duty.

(e) The court shall decide as a matter of law whether a term of a partnership agreement is manifestly unreasonable under subsection (c)(6) or (d)(3). The court:

(1) shall make its determination as of the time the challenged term became part of the partnership agreement and by considering only circumstances existing at that time; and

(2) may invalidate the term only if, in light of the purposes and business of the partnership, it is readily apparent that:

(A) the objective of the term is unreasonable; or

(B) the term is an unreasonable means to achieve the term's objective.

UPA §105

Effect of Partnership Agreement; Nonwaivable Provisions

(a) Except as otherwise provided in subsection (b) of this section, relations among the partners and between the partners and the partnership are governed by the partnership agreement. To the extent the partnership agreement does not otherwise provide, this title governs relations among the partners and between the partners and the partnership.

(b) The partnership agreement may not:

. . .

(3) Eliminate the duty of loyalty under §404(b) . . . , but:

(i) The partnership agreement may identify specific types or categories of activities that do not violate the duty of loyalty; however, the partnership agreement may not be amended to expand or add any specific types or categories of activities that do not violate the duty of loyalty without the consent of all partners after full disclosure of all material facts; or

(ii) All of the partners or a number or percentage of not less than a majority of disinterested partners specified in the partnership agreement may authorize or ratify, after full disclosure of all material facts, a specific act or transaction that otherwise would violate the duty of loyalty;

(4) Unreasonably reduce the duty of care under §404(c) . . . ;

(5) Eliminate the obligation of good faith and fair dealing under §404(d), but the partnership agreement may prescribe the standards by which the performance of the obligation is to be measured, if the standards are not manifestly unreasonable;

(6) Vary the power to dissociate as a partner under §9A-602(a) of this title, except to require the notice under §9A-601(1) of this title to be in writing;

(7) Vary the right of a court to expel a partner in the events specified in §9A-601(5) of this title;

(8) Vary the requirement to wind up the partnership business in cases specified in §9A-801(4), (5), or (6) of this title;

(9) Vary the law applicable to a limited liability partnership under §9A-106 of this subtitle; or

(10) Restrict rights of third parties under this title.

Maryland version of UPA §105.

Putting It to Work

Problem 17-4

Having learned their legal lesson, the four band members of Satisfaction retain the services of an attorney to draft a partnership agreement. The following sentence was included in their agreement:

All partners are under a fiduciary duty to manage all partnership funds and assets to the benefit of the band. No other fiduciary duties apply, in whole or in part, to any band member.

After touring the Midwest with the band, Nick authors four new solo songs and performs those songs without the other members' knowledge in various Midwest venues. Much to the shock and dismay of the other band members, Nick achieves a flash of success, and the three remaining members ask you to sue him for breach of fiduciary duty.

a. Are Nick's actions a breach of the partnership agreement?

b. If the partnership agreement were silent on the question of fiduciary duties, would Nick's actions violate the UPA?

f. Dissociation

When a partner ceases to be co-owner the partner is said to be *dissociated*.[1] We will consider two main questions. First, when is a partner dissociated? In other words, when is a partner no longer a co-owner? *See* UPA §601. Second, what are the consequences of dissociation? *See* UPA §603.

A partner is dissociated in five settings. First, a partner is dissociated upon the happening of an agreed-upon event, such as repayment of a loan from the partner or the passage of time. Second, a partner is dissociated upon becoming a debtor in bankruptcy. This causes dissociation because partners are individually liable for the partnership's debts and if a partner is bankrupt, the partnership's creditors are hindered.

Third, a partner may be expelled. This power of expulsion is limited because partners have equal management rights and a power to expel would generally be considered antithetical to that equality of partners. The partners can unanimously agree in advance to vary the default rule against expulsion. Further, the partners can unanimously expel a partner where it is unlawful to continue the business with that partner or where a partner that is a corporation has dissolved. Finally, the partners can unanimously expel a partner who has transferred *all* of his or her transferable interest in the partnership. A court may also order a partner's expulsion on equitable grounds because the partner "has engaged or is engaging in wrongful conduct that has affected adversely and materially, or will affect adversely and materially, the partnership's business," or the partner "has committed willfully or persistently, or is committing willfully or persistently, a material breach of the partnership agreement or a duty or obligation under Section 409," or where the partner "has engaged or is engaging in conduct relating to the partnership's business which makes it not reasonably practicable to carry on the business with the person as a partner." This last ground is also cause for the court to dissolve the partnership. *See* UPA §801(4)(c).

Fourth, a partner's death causes dissociation. This is so because of the personal nature of the partnership relationship. The *partner* is no longer a co-owner, although the partner's estate and then the partner's heirs succeed to the partner's transferable interest. The final method for dissociation is, as death is, rooted in the personal nature of the partnership relationship. Any partner may become dissociated simply by express will. Note that this power *cannot* be contracted away by agreement. Even if the partners agree that they will not dissociate, any partner may do so by express will. UPA §§103(c)(9), 601(1), 602(a).

What happens when a partner is dissociated? Unless dissociation causes dissolution of the partnership (*see* section *g* below), the dissociated partner's interest is bought out by the partnership. The price is based upon a hypothetical value of the dissociating partner's account as if the partnership had dissolved on the date of dissociation and the assets sold for the greater of (1) liquidation value or (2) value as a going concern without the dissociated partner. UPA §701(b). The UPA's comments elaborate:

> The rules in this section are merely default rules. The partners may, in the partnership agreement, fix the method or formula for determining the buyout price and all of the other

---

1. Those of you who have studied psychology may think that the UPA's drafters' choice of the term *dissociation* is especially ironic.

terms and conditions of the buyout right. Indeed, the very right to a buyout itself may be modified, although a provision providing for a complete forfeiture would probably not be enforceable. *See* Section 119.

The terms "fair market value" or "fair value" were not used because they are often considered terms of art having a special meaning depending on the context, such as in tax or corporate law. Liquidation value is not intended to mean distress sale value. Under general principles of valuation, the hypothetical selling price in either case should be the price that a willing and informed buyer would pay a willing and informed seller, with neither being under any compulsion to deal. The notion of a minority discount in determining the buyout price is negated by valuing the business as a going concern. Other discounts, such as for a lack of marketability or the loss of a key partner, may be appropriate, however.

Since the buyout price is based on the value of the business at the time of dissociation, the partnership must pay interest on the amount due from the date of dissociation until payment to compensate the dissociating partner for the use of his interest in the firm.

UPA §701, cmt.

This price is reduced by any amount the dissociating partner owes the partnership even if payment on that obligation is not presently due.

This rule has the effect of accelerating payment of amounts not yet due from the former partner to the partnership, including a long-term loan by the partnership to the former partner. Where appropriate, the amounts not yet due should be discounted to present value. A dissociating partner, on the other hand, is not entitled to an add-on for amounts owing to him by the partnership. Thus, a departing partner who has made a long-term loan to the partnership must wait for repayment, unless the terms of the loan agreement provide for acceleration upon dissociation.

UPA §701, cmt.

The buyout price is also reduced by any damages the partnership suffers if dissociation is wrongful. *See* UPA §§701(c), 602(c).

Dissociation by an individual partner is wrongful only if it breaches an express agreement or if, prior to the end of a term partnership, the partner dissociates by express will, by becoming a debtor in bankruptcy, or by expulsion by a court order. A wrongfully dissociating partner is liable for damages for wrongful dissociation (and may be additionally liable for other damages such as breaching the partnership agreement) and cannot participate in the winding up of the partnership if it is dissolved. UPA §§602(b), 802.

Moreover, a dissociating partner's rights and duties toward the partnership change upon dissociation, regardless of whether the partner is dissociating rightfully or wrongfully. The dissociating partner's right to participate in the management of the partnership ends unless the partnership itself is being dissolved. Also, although the partner's duty of care and loyalty continue as to events prior to dissociation, the partner is under no further fiduciary obligation and, most pertinently, can enter into competition with the partnership.

g. Dissolution

It is imperative to keep in mind the distinction between the end of the partnership as a legal entity and the end of the business as a going concern. Typically the business of the partnership will continue even when the partnership itself ceases. In that case the business is transferred to another entity (i.e., another partnership or a corporation, LLC, or individual) and continues to do business. On occasion, though, the business will cease and the assets will be sold off piecemeal. The partnership may continue in a different business or it may end.

Under the UPA, a partnership *dissolves* (i.e., ceases to exist) in six instances. First, and most obviously, is where it becomes unlawful to continue all or substantially all of the partnership's business. *See* UPA §801(4)(A). Second, the partnership dissolves if all the partners agree (UPA §801(2)(B)). Third, if the partnership was formed for a particular length of time or for a particular undertaking (sometimes called a *term partnership*), dissolution occurs upon the expiration of that time or the completion of the undertaking (UPA §801(2)(C)). Fourth, if a partner in a term partnership ceases to be a partner for certain reasons (essentially death, bankruptcy, or wrongfully withdrawing from the partnership) half the remaining partners may opt to dissolve the partnership. UPA §801(2)(A).

Fifth, courts have equitable power to dissolve a partnership on several grounds. The court may dissolve if "the economic purpose of the partnership is likely to be unreasonably frustrated" UPA §801(4)(B) or where "it is not otherwise reasonably practicable to carry on the partnership business in conformity with the partnership agreement" UPA §801(4)(D). Turning from the partnership and its business to a problematic partner, the court may dissolve where it is "not reasonably practicable to carry on the business in partnership with that partner." UPA §801(4)(C). Note that the court also has the power, in that instance, to remove the problematic partner (i.e., dissociate that partner) rather than dissolve the entire partnership. *See* UPA §601(5)(C). The court also has the equitable power to dissolve the partnership at the behest of a transferee of a partner's interest. UPA §801(5).

Finally, the UPA gives each partner in a partnership at will (i.e., a partnership that is not a term partnership, *see* UPA §102(13)), the absolute right to compel the partnership's dissolution at any time. UPA §801(1). This preserves the partnership ethos that, absent an agreement otherwise, a partnership is a voluntary association of two or more people and hence may be ended when one of those people is no longer associated with the others. This power is of particular strategic importance because it gives each partner the ability to raise the possibility that the partnership's business may be sold off against the wishes of the other partners. As with most other default rules, this power can be varied or eliminated by agreement.

A dissolved partnership must wind up its business by marshalling its assets and paying off its debts (including debts owed to partners). UPA §802(a), (b)(1). If there is money remaining after all debts are paid, the default rule is that the partnership then repays any partner who has made a contribution to the partnership that has not yet been repaid. If there are funds remaining after that, the partners receive a distribution in proportion to their agreement (in equal shares if they have not otherwise agreed). UPA §§806(b) and 401(a). If there are insufficient funds to pay the partnership's debts, the partners must contribute in proportion to their agreement to contribute to losses. UPA §§806(c), 401(a). If any partners fail to make such a contribution, the other partners must make up the shortfall, with a right to seek reimbursement from the defaulting partners. UPA §806(c), (d). If distributions are made in the winding up process, they must be in money, and not in property. UPA §(f).

Putting It to Work

Problem 17-5

Leif is fed up with Satisfaction in general and Nick in particular. He has retained your services to get him out of the band. Even though they are currently on tour for the next four months, Leif believes he and the other band members of Satisfaction have creative differences that run too deep to repair and that Nick is particularly dysfunctional. Nick has taken to showing up late for performances and frequently skips rehearsals. Because of this, Leif asks you to help him leave the band, but still retain his share of the money the tour has yet to earn. He also does not want the band to continue making its planned third album without him.

    a. What do you suggest for Leif?

B. OTHER PARTNERSHIP FORMS

1. Joint Ventures

Up until now we have been concerned with what are sometimes called *general partnerships* to distinguish them from the entities we are about to discuss. In ordinary lawyer parlance, "partnership" and "general partnership" are synonymous. Four other entities are related to general partnerships and merit mention, at least briefly, here. First, a *joint venture* has both a business connotation and a more legal denotation. Business people (and lawyers as well) often refer to a joint venture as a narrowly focused business opportunity undertaken by a handful (quite often only two) established businesses. These preexisting businesses might be in unrelated fields or might even be competitors. The reason for their cooperation may be that a particular undertaking may be too expensive or too risky for one to take alone. Or, it may be that one of the participants has a contractual right to develop an opportunity (such as the right to certain intellectual property or the right to develop natural resources in a particular geographical area) but lacks the expertise to do so. In this popular description, a joint venture refers to the business opportunity itself rather than the entity through which the opportunity is developed. Even where the participants form a jointly owned corporation or LLC that undertakes the new business, that business may be called a joint venture.

    A (slightly) more precise legal description of a joint venture is a partnership (i.e., two or more people co-owning a business for profit) formed for a limited time or for a limited purpose. In this sense, a joint venture is a kind of term partnership. The difference between a joint venture and a term partnership is, then, essentially one of degree with a joint venture being formed for a shorter time or more sharply defined purpose than a term partnership. Frequently, as well, a term partnership is distinguished from a joint venture by the number of partners. As the number grows much beyond three or four, courts are more likely to find that the entity is a term partnership rather than a joint venture.

    So what? Once we have successfully identified an entity as being a joint venture and not a term partnership what difference does that make? Typically there are two kinds of differences. First, courts tend to give a narrower construction to the scope of the enterprise if they declare it to be a joint venture. This means that the participants' fiduciary duties are more circumscribed than if a term partnership were involved. This difference, as you may intuit, is largely circular: courts see a narrower purpose and declare it to be a joint venture; because it is a joint venture, the court will view its purpose or duration as being relatively narrow. Obviously courts do not need a separate term — joint venture — to make that kind of distinction. The second difference the characterization "joint venture" makes is a bit more substantive. Some courts find that a joint venture is not subject to all the strictures of the UPA. Which UPA rules do not apply to joint ventures? It depends upon which rules are in contention between the parties in the litigation. Mostly the courts find joint ventures make a difference when one party argues that a UPA default rule applies in its favor and where the court finds that applying such a rule would not be equitable. Declaring an entity to be a joint venture and, therefore, not subject to all of the UPA's scheme, allows the court to impose a result it finds fairer than the UPA rule in the particular instance. Note that the UPA states that it applies to joint ventures that meet the basic statutory definition of a partnership. *See* UPA §202, cmt. 2.

In the end, then, a joint venture is a somewhat chimerical entity. Labeling a business a joint venture may simply be a description or may be a way to ameliorate a strict application of the UPA.

2. Limited Partnerships

a. Background and Context

As you may recall from Chapter 2, before the mid-nineteenth century, states generally did not adopt corporations acts as we know them. Rather, each corporation had to obtain a charter from the state legislature. These were often expensive to obtain, and success in obtaining a charter frequently depended upon the entrepreneurs' having (or acquiring) sufficient political support in the state legislature. But in 1822, New York became the first state to enact a limited partnership act, which served some of the same purposes as incorporation. A limited partnership is a general partnership in which additional owners, called *limited partners,* invest money in return for interests that are different from those of the general partners. First, the limited partners' interests were freely transferable. Second, the limited partners had no management rights. Indeed, they were prohibited from taking part in the management of the business. They were strictly *silent partners.* Third, in recognition that the limited partners had no say in how their money was used or how the business was run, their liability was limited to the amount of their investment.

The underlying economic problem that limited partnerships (and corporations) solved was how to finance businesses that required more capital than a typical small business or trading firm. With the rise of factories in the early nineteenth century, the number of such businesses increased greatly. Raising sufficient capital in a general partnership was problematic because money was needed from a large number of individuals. Giving each a say in the partnership quickly became unwieldy, yet investors were reluctant to place all their assets at risk (as each general partner must do) in return for little or no management authority. The limited partnership allowed money to be raised from a small group of general partners, who would manage the enterprise, and from a much larger group of limited partners. An additional advantage was that a limited partnership could be formed simply by filing with the appropriate governmental authorities (usually a county clerk) rather than going to the expense of obtaining a charter from the legislature.

The Uniform Limited Partnership Act was first adopted in 1916. It was modernized a bit in 1976 and 1985 and was completely rethought in 2001. From the beginnings of limited partnerships until ULPA (1976), one of the most often-litigated questions was whether a limited partner had exercised sufficient control in the business so that he or she should be treated as a general partner and, hence, subjected to unlimited personal liability for partnership debts. The case law until 1976 was relatively strict that nearly any management activity by a limited partner (with the exception of voting to remove a general partner, which was a common right vested in the limited partners) was sufficient to subject the limited partner to personal liability. The 1976 and 1985 amendments broadened significantly, and controversially, the management powers of limited partners, while at the same time narrowing the instances in which limited partners would be held personally liable. A second trend in limited partnership law was the quest to find ways to insulate the general partner from liability. This was most frequently accomplished by having the general partner be a corporation, often with no other business purpose than to serve as the general partner. The corporation/general partner was, of course, controlled by the individuals who would otherwise have been the general partner. Thus, for all practical purposes, an entity was created in which all participants had limited liability. The advent of the limited liability limited partnership (see below) has made this status more secure.

Until the mid-1990s, limited partnerships were frequently used for enterprises that were expected to generate losses. Their use in this setting was because limited partnerships were taxed as partnerships, which allowed losses, to be passed through to the partners, unlike a corporation's losses, which must be carried over from year to year. After 1996 the LLC could serve the same functions as a limited partnership — limited liability for all participants and pass-through taxation — and so quickly supplanted the limited partnership as the entity of choice for new ventures.

b. The Current Setting

A limited partnership is similar to a general partnership but with one or more additional investors called limited partners. Unlike a general partnership, a limited partnership cannot be formed inadvertently but must be created through a simple filing with the secretary of state, much like a corporation is formed. Each limited partnership must have one or more general partners who function just as general partners in a general partnership do. The limited partners have curtailed governance powers and are not agents of the partnership. Their liability is limited to the amount of their investment and, ordinarily, their interests are freely transferable.

Today, the limited partnership is used primarily in two settings. First, it is used in a few very sophisticated commercial settings in which the participants find that mandatory corporate or LLC provisions require or prohibit agreements that the parties desire. An example is a venture capital firm that seeks to raise a large amount of money to invest in start-up enterprises. Such firms typically do not raise all the capital at once, but rather do so as each investment opportunity is found. One potential hazard of such an entity is the possibility that some investors will refuse or be unable to contribute additional funds. This will hamper the ability of the venture capital fund to make necessary investments, and so the venture capital firm's managers wish to ensure that the other investors have sufficient motivation to contribute when necessary. While, of course, such a provision can be created by contract, a more effective *in terrorem* method would be to make the investors' ownership interest *assessable* so that a failure to contribute on demand results in a forfeiture of the investor's entire ownership interest. Partnerships are a more reliable vehicle in which to provide for assessable interests than are corporations or LLCs, both of which have a presumption against assessability. It may also be easier, as a practical matter, to make those interests nontransferable in a limited partnership than in a corporation or LLC, which eliminates the possibility that recalcitrant investors will attempt to shirk their obligation to contribute more money by transferring their interest to someone else.

Second, limited partnerships are used as an estate-planning device. For example, parents establish a limited partnership to which the family business is contributed in return for all the ownership interest. The parents serve as general partners and are allocated 1 percent of the ownership interest. The parents serve as the limited partners, as well, at first and, over time, give portions of their limited partnership interests to their children. The limited partnership interests have strict restrictions on transfer (typically transfer is allowed only to other family members) and only the bare minimum of statutorily required governance interest. Because of the restrictions on transfer and the lack of management power, the value of each limited partnership interest should legitimately be discounted, often by as much as 30 or 40 percent, below the value of a similar economic interest without such restrictions. For example, suppose a family business is worth $1,000,000. Assume further that the business is owned by a family limited partnership as we have just described and that the general partnership interest is entitled to 1 percent while the limited partnership interest is divided into 99 portions, each entitled to 1 percent of the equity. If the parents give a 1 percent limited partnership interest to a child, the value of that gift is not $10,000 (i.e., 1% of $1,000,000) but probably closer to $6,000 to $7,000 because the child has no governance or management rights and cannot transfer the interest outside the family. In this way, the parents can effect an orderly transfer of family wealth to future generations (obviously the gifts can be made to grandchildren as easily as to children) while retaining complete control (which may or may not be a good thing from society's viewpoint but is almost always a good thing from a parent's viewpoint) and at a lower tax cost (because taxes are assessed based upon the legitimately discounted value of the interests transferred). While the Internal Revenue Service closely scrutinizes such family limited partnerships (because the tax savings reduce the public fisc), they have been largely upheld by the courts.

3. Limited Liability Partnerships and Limited Liability Limited Partnerships

Stop! Don't we have enough business entities, what with partnerships, limited partnerships, corporations, and LLCs, not to mention sole proprietorships? Well, for your information, we don't have enough business entities. We have to talk about two more, and that doesn't include such things as Massachusetts business trusts and joint stock companies, which are so arcane they're ignored altogether in this book.

The principal drawback of partnerships and limited partnerships, at least from the general partners' perspective, is unlimited personal liability for entity debts. The remaining two entities furnish limited liability to participants who otherwise would be personally liable. Limited liability partnerships (LLPs — NOT to be confused with LLCs) are general partnerships that have made an election to be treated as LLPs and that file a form with the secretary of state. *See* UPA §901. The effect of becoming an LLP is to shield all partners from personal liability for all partnership debts. Partners remain liable for their own actions as partners. For example, a lawyer who is a partner in a law firm LLP remains liable to clients for his or her own malpractice. The partnership itself also remains liable for such malpractice. If, however, the assets of the malpracticing partner and the assets of the partnership are insufficient to cover the partnership's debts, the effect of the LLP election is to shield the other partners from liability for the shortfall. *See* UPA §306(c). The same liability shield is provided to general partners in a limited partnership that elects to become a limited liability limited partnership (LLLP); the limited partners, of course, already have limited liability.

The impetus to create LLPs and LLLPs came before LLCs were widely available. Since 1996, LLCs have supplanted LLPs and LLLPs. Nonetheless, LLPs and LLLPs remain niche entities that serve a particular, though narrow, purpose.

C. FEDERAL SECURITIES REGULATION

If a partnership interest is a security then the federal registration requirements (and various exemptions) and the antifraud provisions of Rule 10b-5 all apply. Further, the periodic reporting requirements for public companies and the federal regulation of proxy solicitations may also apply if a partnership is a security. None of the federal statutes specifically names partnership interests, which may suggest that Congress did not intend them to be securities because partnerships were certainly well-known business entities when Congress was adopting the Securities Act of 1933 and the Securities Exchange Act of 1934. No Supreme Court case has decided the question. The Supreme Court would almost certainly apply the test from *SEC v. W.J. Howey Co.*, 328 U.S. 293 (1946). Under the cases interpreting *Howey*, the court must decide whether there was (1) an investment of money, (2) in a common enterprise in which the investor was led to expect profits, (3) primarily from the efforts of the promoter or a third party. In analyzing partnerships, the key element will be the "efforts of the promoter or a third party."

The principal case analyzing general partnerships under the securities laws is *Williamson v. Tucker*, 645 F.2d 404 (5th Cir.), *cert. denied*, 454 U.S. 897 (1981), in which the court held that a partnership interest is a security under *Howey* only if the investor can establish one of three elements:

1. That the agreement among the parties leaves so little management power in the investor's hands that the investor is analogous to a limited partner; or
2. The investor is so inexperienced and unknowledgeable in business affairs that he or she cannot intelligently exercise his or her managerial powers; or
3. The investor is so dependent upon some unique entrepreneurial or managerial talent of the promoter that the investor cannot replace the promoter or otherwise meaningfully exercise his or her managerial powers.

Very few cases have held that interests in a general partnership are securities. On the other hand, the *Williamson* court's first factor suggests that it considered limited partnership interests to be included in the definition of "security." In general, courts have held limited partnerships to be subject to the securities laws. One question that remains open is whether, with the expansion of limited partner power under the 1976, 1985, and especially under the 2001 revisions of the Uniform Limited Partnership Act, courts will hold that limited partners have sufficient management power that they should be considered analogously to general partners and thus denied the protection of the securities laws. This rationale seems especially likely where the limited partners are sophisticated commercial entities or investors rather than in the family limited partnership setting.

D. TERMS OF ART IN THIS CHAPTER

At-will partnership	General partnerships	Silent partners
Charging order	*Howey* test	Term partnership
Dissociated	Joint venture	*Williamson* test
Dissociation	Limited partnership	
Dissolution	Partnership	

18

Limited Liability Companies

A. BACKGROUND AND CONTEXT

The final business entity we will consider is the limited liability company (LLC). It is probably the most popular choice for newly formed businesses. The reason is that it combines limited liability for the firm's owners and managers with pass-through taxation. Corporations also provide limited liability but are taxed as separate entities, leading to a double taxation of corporate profits, once at the corporate level and again when the corporation pays dividends to its shareholders. Partnerships provide pass-through taxation (i.e., profits are not taxed at the partnership level; profits and losses are reported directly by each partner) but, classically, do not provide limited liability. While Subchapter S corporations, limited partnerships with a corporate general partner, limited liability partnerships, and limited liability limited partnerships can all approximate the advantages of LLCs, none is as flexible and all are more cumbersome than the LLC. Chapter 19 will treat in greater detail the question of choosing the appropriate form for doing business.

The following excerpt explains why the LLC was developed. Professor Hamill sees three threads in the story. In her view, the motivation for developing the LLC began with the disparate tax treatment of corporations and partnerships. Second, certain kinds of businesses perceived a need in the 1970s for an entity that combined complete limited liability and pass-through tax treatment. Finally, lawyers representing those and other businesses brought their drafting and lobbying skills to bear in convincing the states and the IRS to permit the LLC.

Susan Pace Hamill, *The Origins Behind the Limited Liability Company**
59 Ohio St. L.J. 1459 (1998)

The explanation behind the LLC's birth boils down to innovative professionals creating solutions when the current legal system fails to meet client needs. The

---

* The material in this excerpt has been rearranged from the original. *ED.*

particular client whose needs sparked the invention of the LLC was an independent oil explorer experiencing increased opportunities in international oil and gas exploration during the turbulent 1970s, when the major producers struggled with problems related to the Middle Eastern oil supply.

[T]he LLC's . . . roots can be traced to the first modern income tax, enacted within months of Congress' ratification of the Sixteenth Amendment in 1913. . . . Corporations, as well as unincorporated organizations deemed associations, would bear an entity level tax just like individuals while partnerships would bear no tax, creating flow-through taxation to the partners. Congress viewed the corporation as an appropriate target for an income tax due to its formal creation by and recognition as a separate entity by state issued charters. The ordinary general partnership, viewed as an inappropriate target for the tax, involved no state law filing and constituted a mere aggregate of the partners, each facing personal liability exposure with management and dissolution powers over the partnership.

The increasing level of dependence on foreign oil throughout the last half of the twentieth century, followed by the abrupt and severe reduction of that supply by the early 1970s, forced the major oil producers and other participants in the oil industry to seek crude oil from alternative sources. This need for oil outside traditional Middle Eastern sources created a market for greater numbers of independent oil producers than had ever existed in prior years. In order to secure the necessary capital to conduct drilling operations, many of these independent producers sold [limited] partnership interests to investors. . . .

In the mid-1970s, a few entrepreneurial-minded attorneys and accountants representing a U.S. independent oil and gas company invented the LLC, [and] successfully persuaded the Wyoming legislature in 1977 to enact the first LLC statute. . . . Armed with the enacted LLC legislation, the Hamilton Brothers Oil Company . . . filed a request with the IRS . . . asking for a favorable partnership classification ruling. The IRS, reluctant to allow a domestic entity with corporate limited liability partnership classification, predictably stalled the ruling process. After a great deal of correspondence between Hamilton Brothers Oil Company's representatives and the IRS, an additional request for a ruling filed by the Wyoming Secretary of State and supported by the Governor, as well as another correspondence involving the Commissioner of the IRS and Wyoming Senators, the IRS finally issued a favorable private letter ruling to Hamilton Brothers Oil Company regarding its Wyoming LLC [in] 1980, more than three years after the initial request.

Florida enacted an LLC statute in 1982, presumably to lure capital into the state. . . . [T]he IRS . . . stated that it would study the effect limited liability should have on entity classification. That study took over five years and predictably, while its tax status remained in limbo, further growth in LLC legislation and businesses using LLCs stopped; no other states enacted statutes and few businesses (less than one hundred) chose to become LLCs. As long as its ability to be taxed as a partnership remained questionable, the LLC stood no chance of expanding throughout the country.

[In] 1988, the IRS issued Revenue Ruling 88-76, a public interpretation of the law all taxpayers can rely upon, permitting the Wyoming LLC to secure partnership classification despite the presence of limited liability. Although a clear watershed in the LLC's development, the Wyoming Revenue Ruling's requirements, rendering interests in an LLC very difficult to transfer and the LLC itself highly dissolvable, limited the practical use of LLCs to small, closely held businesses and joint ventures.

After the IRS's landmark decision to recognize the LLC's right to be taxed under the partnership provisions, the states slowly and cautiously started to enact legislation allowing for the formation of LLCs. It took until 1990 — the year Colorado and Kansas both passed LLC statutes — for any states to step forward and recognize the creation of LLCs in light of the IRS's revenue ruling.

The Tax Reform Act of 1986, in addition to destroying the market for [limited] partnership syndications, materially increased the tax burden imposed on corporations. . . . Business ventures expecting significant taxable income, which also wished to obtain direct statutory limited liability without facing the restrictions inherent in a Subchapter S election, had, for the first time, strong reasons to support the LLC. On behalf of many clients conducting business in ventures recognizing substantial taxable income, the second group of LLC proponents pushed for more flexibility on the partnership classification front and encouraged the states to enact statutes.

From 1992 through 1996, LLC legislation swept across the country. By the end of 1994, [o]nly three remaining states were without LLC legislation, and by the close of 1996, they had passed statutes establishing the LLC in all U.S. jurisdictions. In an incredible stampede that took less than twenty years, most of it occurring from 1990 through 1996, LLCs traveled from an obscure unknown business form in 1977 to a well-recognized alternative for doing business.

[In] 1995, the IRS announced a proposal to eliminate the partnership classification rules by allowing certain unincorporated businesses, including domestic LLCs, to elect partnership or corporate taxation, and the rise of the LLC contributed greatly to this development. The public overwhelmingly favored the proposal. [In] 1996, the final regulations, dubbed the "Check-the-Box" regulations, permanently eliminated all partnership classification considerations for LLCs and all other domestic unincorporated entities. All persons filing under an LLC statute automatically receive partnership taxation. The elimination of all partnership classification issues allows those using LLCs the freedom to craft the dissolution, transferability and management provisions to satisfy business goals alone.

Notes and Questions

1. Reality Check

a. What were the tax and non-tax motivations that led to the development of the LLC?

b. Why did states become eager to enact LLC statutes in the early 1990s?

c. What advantages do LLCs have over other entities?

2. What Do You Think?

a. Much of the debate surrounding LLCs has centered on whether business entities that offer limited liability should also receive pass-through tax treatment. Do you think the two concepts should be related? Why have these two concepts been linked?

b. In another part of her article, Professor Hamill suggests that the success of the LLC form has led to other new entities such as the LLP and LLLP and that this fragmentation is confusing and unnecessary. Do you agree? Do you think business firms need so many entity choices? If change is needed, what change should be imposed? Who should impose such changes? The states? The federal government? The bar?

B. THE CURRENT SETTING

1. Introduction

The limited liability company (LLC) is an entity that has important elements of both corporations and partnerships. The formation requirements are similar to those of corporations, involving a public filing of a brief document. The LLC also provides limited liability both for owners and managers, as in a corporation. On the other hand, the default governance provisions of LLCs give management rights to all owners, in similar fashion to a partnership. As with partnership statutes, LLC statutes anticipate that the parties will typically supplement or supplant the default provisions with a written agreement. Many, if not most, operating agreements create a management structure similar to that of a corporation, giving the owners circumscribed management powers and giving control to managers who need not be owners. LLCs are treated like partnerships under the Internal Revenue Code, although the parties could elect to be taxed as a corporation (under the so-called check the box provision of the Code) instead.

The philosophy of one of the most important LLC statutes, that of Delaware, is discussed in the following excerpt.

POLICY OF THE DELAWARE ACT

The basic approach of the Delaware Act is to provide members with broad discretion in drafting the Agreement and to furnish default provisions when the members' agreement is silent. The Act is replete with fundamental provisions made subject to modification in the Agreement (*e.g.* "unless otherwise provided in a limited liability company agreement . . .").

For example, members are free to contract among themselves concerning management of the LLC, including who is to manage the LLC, the establishment of classes of members, voting, procedures for holding meetings of members, or considering matters without a meeting.

Although business planners may find comfort in working with the Act in structuring transactions and relationships, it is a somewhat awkward document for this Court to construe and apply. . . . To understand the overall structure and thrust of the Act, one must wade through provisions that are prolix, sometimes oddly organized, and do not always flow evenly.

FREEDOM OF CONTRACT

Section 18-1101(b) of the Act provides that "it is the policy of [the Act] to give the maximum effect to the principle of freedom of contract and to the enforceability of limited liability company agreements." Accordingly, the following observation relating to limited partnerships applies as well to limited liability companies:

> The Act's basic approach is to permit partners to have the broadest possible discretion in drafting their partnership agreements and to furnish answers only in situations where the partners have not expressly made provisions in their partnership agreement. Truly, the partnership agreement is the cornerstone of a Delaware limited partnership, and effectively constitutes the entire agreement among the partners with respect to the admission of partners to, and the creation, operation and termination of, the limited partnership. Once partners exercise their contractual freedom in their partnership agreement, the partners have a great deal of certainty that their partnership agreement will be enforced in accordance with its terms.

Martin I. Lubaroff & Paul Altman, *Delaware Limited Partnerships* §1.2 (1999) (footnote omitted)

> In general, the commentators observe that only where the agreement is inconsistent with mandatory statutory provisions will the members' agreement be invalidated. Such statutory provisions are likely to be those intended to protect third parties, not necessarily the contracting members. . . .

Elf Atochem North America v. Jaffari, 727 A.2d 286 (Del. 1999) (Veasey, C.J.)

The tone of the above excerpts may imply that LLCs both are unlike other business entities and are founded on a public policy of aggressive freedom of contract for the owners and managers. Sentiments like these are quite frequent among legal commenters. But the reality is that both assertions are more nuanced. Vice Chancellor Laster puts these claims about the nature of LLCs in some perspective.

> It is frequently observed that LLCs "are creatures of contract,"[1] which they primarily are.[2] The Delaware Limited Liability Company Act (the "LLC Act") provides that "[i]t is the policy of this chapter to give maximum effect to the principle of freedom of contract and to the enforceability of limited liability company agreements." [Del. LLC Act] §18-110(b).

---

1. *TravelCenters of Am., LLC v. Brog*, 2008 WL 1746987, at *1 (Del. Ch. Apr. 3, 2008). . . .

2. The adverb "primarily" recognizes the critical but sometimes overlooked non-contractual dimensions of the entity. *See In re Seneca Invs. LLC*, 970 A.2d 259, 261 (Del. Ch. 2008) ("An LLC is primarily a creature of contract . . . .").

[T]he purely contractarian view discounts core attributes of the LLC that only the sovereign can authorize, such as its separate legal existence, potentially perpetual life, and limited liability for its members. *See* [Del. LLC Act] §§18-201, 18-303. To my mind, when a sovereign makes available an entity with attributes that contracting parties cannot grant themselves by agreement, the entity is not purely contractual. Because the entity has taken advantage of benefits that the sovereign has provided, the sovereign retains an interest in that entity . . . . Put more directly, an LLC agreement is not an exclusively private contract among its members precisely because the LLC has powers that only the State of Delaware can confer. Those powers affect the rights of third parties, who at a minimum must take into account the LLC's separate legal existence and its members' limited liability shield.

In re Carlisle Etcetera LLC, 114 A.3d 592, 605-06 (Del. Ch. 2015); *see Feeley v. NHAOCG, LLC*, 62 A.3d 649, 659-63 (Del. Ch. 2012); *Auriga Capital Corp. v. Gatz Props., LLC*, 40 A.3d 839, 849-56 (Del. Ch. 2012) (STRINE, C.), *aff'd*, 59 A.3d 1206 (Del. 2012). *See generally* Daniel S. Kleinberger, *Two Decades of "Alternative Entities": From Tax Rationalization Through Alphabet Soup To Contract As Deity*, 14 Fordham J. Corp. & Fin. L. 445, 460-71 (2009) (identifying historical, jurisprudential, and policy reasons why LLCs should not be regarded as purely contractual entities); Sandra K. Miller, *The Best of Both Worlds: Default Fiduciary Duties and Contractual Freedom in Alternative Business Entities*, 39 J. Corp. L. 295, 315-24 (2014) (reviewing empirical studies and presenting data about alternative entity agreements that undermine premises of purely contractarian approach). Whatever one's personal thoughts might have been on the matter, "the General Assembly in 2013 adopted an amendment to the LLC Act inconsistent with the purely contractarian view" of LLCs. *Carlisle*, 114 A.3d at 605 (citing H.B. 126, 147th Gen. Assemb. (Del. 2013) (amending [Del. LLC Act] §18-1104 to provide that "In any case not provided for in this chapter, the rules of law and equity, including the rules of law and equity relating to fiduciary duties and the law merchant, shall govern")); *see* Miller, *supra*, at 314 (noting that the debate over the purely contractual status of LLCs "was resolved by legislation that was signed into law on June 30, 2013).

Because of this freedom, "the parties have broad discretion to use an LLC agreement to define the character of the company and the rights and obligations of its members." *Kuroda* [*v. SPJS Hldgs., LLC*, 971 A.2d 872 (Del. Ch. 2009)], at 880. One "attraction of the LLC form of entity is the statutory freedom granted to members to shape, by contract, their own approach to common business 'relationship' problems." *Haley v. Talcott*, 864 A.2d 86, 88 (Del. Ch. 2004) (STRINE, V.C.). "Virtually any management structure may be implemented through the company's governing instrument." Robert L. Symonds, Jr. & Matthew J. O'Toole, *Delaware Limited Liability Companies* §9.01[B], at 9-9 (2015).

Using the contractual freedom that the LLC Act bestows, the drafters of an LLC agreement can create an LLC with bespoke governance features or design an LLC that mimics the governance features of another familiar type of entity. The choices that the drafters make have consequences. If the drafters have embraced the statutory default rule of a member-managed governance arrangement, which has strong functional and historical ties to the general partnership (albeit with limited liability for the members), then the parties should expect a court to draw on analogies to partnership law.[3] If the drafters have opted for a single managing member with other generally passive, non-managing members, a structure closely resembling and often used as an alternative to a limited partnership, then the parties should expect a court to draw on analogies to limited partnership law.[4] If the drafters have opted for a manager-managed entity, created a board of directors, and adopted other corporate features, then the parties to the agreement should expect a court to draw on analogies to corporate law.[5] Depending on the terms of the agreement, analogies to other legal relationships may also be informative.

It is important not to embrace analogies to other entities or legal structures too broadly or without close analysis, because "the flexibility inherent in the limited liability company form complicates the task of fixing such labels or making such comparisons." Symonds & O'Toole, *supra*, §1.04[C][1], at 1-17. The drafters of an LLC agreement may have adopted partnership-like features for particular aspects of their relationship and corporate features for others.

---

3. *See* [Del. LLC Act] §18-402 (establishing the default rule that management of an LLC is "vested in its members in proportion to the then current . . . interest of members in the profits of the limited liability company owned by all of the members," with the decision of members owning a majority of such profit interest controlling); *Kelly v. Blum*, 2010 WL 629850, at *11 n.73 (Del. Ch. Feb. 24, 2010) (identifying parallel between member-managed LLC and partnership). As in a general partnership, the LLC Act's "default framework generally contemplates a unity of membership and management control." Symonds & O'Toole, *supra*, §9.01[A][1], at 9-5.

4. *See Kelly*, 2010 WL 629850, at *11 n.73. The field of limited partnership law is particularly fertile, because the LLC Act was "modeled on the popular Delaware LP Act" and "its architecture and much of its wording is almost identical to that of the Delaware LP Act." *Elf Atochem N. Am., Inc. v. Jaffari*, 727 A.2d 286, 290 (Del. 1999). When a manager-managed entity has passive members, those members are often "treated much like a limited partner under the LP Act." *Id.*

5. *See Kelly*, 2010 WL 629850, at *11 n.73 (suggesting corporate analogy for manager-managed LLC where operating agreement created board of managers similar to that of corporation); Symonds & O'Toole, *supra*, §9.01 [B], at 9-9 ("A limited liability company may be structured on the basis of a corporate model . . ."); *see, e.g., Fla. R & D Fund Inv'rs, LLC v. Fla. BOCA/Deerfield R & D Inv'rs, LLC*, 2013 WL 4734834, at *2, *7 (Del. Ch. Aug. 30, 2013) (addressing LLC agreement that created a board of directors to manage the entity); *Kahn v. Portnoy*, 2008 WL 5197164, at *4 (Del. Ch. Dec. 11, 2008) (interpreting LLC agreement which created board of directors to manage the entity and which provided that the " 'authority, powers, functions and duties (including fiduciary duties)' of the board of directors will be identical to those of a board of directors of a business corporation organized under the Delaware General Corporation Law . . . unless otherwise specifically provided for in the LLC Agreement"); *Seneca Invs.*, 970 A.2d at 261 (interpreting LLC agreement which provided that, subject to certain exceptions, "the Company will be governed in all respects as if it were a corporation organized under and governed by the Delaware General Corporation Law . . . and the rights of its Stockholders will be governed by the DGCL"); *see also Matthew v. Laudamiel*, 2012 WL 2580572, at *1 (Del. Ch. June 29, 2012) (interpreting LLC agreement that created board of managers to oversee business and affairs of entity); *VGS, Inc. v. Castiel*, 2003 WL 723285, at *2 (Del. Ch. Feb. 28, 2003) (same).

The analogy may break down in other areas as well, such as in terms of the extent to which the interests and the rights they carry are fully alienable. *Compare* [DGCL] §202 (establishing default rule of alienability with transferee obtaining stockholder status), *with* [Del. LLC Act] §18-702 (establishing default rule of assignability with assignee having "no right to participate in the management of the business and affairs of a limited liability company except as provided in a limited liability company agreement" or until admitted as a member).

Obeid v. Hogan, 2016 WL 3356851 at *5-*7 (Del. Ch. Jun. 10, 2016) (Laster, V.C.).

Some states, such as Delaware and New York, created their LLC statute essentially by modifying their limited partnership acts (which are typically based on the Revised Uniform Limited Partnership Act). Other states created their LLC statute by amalgamating their limited partnership act with their corporations statute. The Uniform Limited Liability Company Act has been adopted in several states but is not (at least not yet) accepted nationally. Nonetheless, there is much more substantive uniformity among the states than the variety of LLC statutes would suggest. Virtually every LLC statute has common elements such as: (1) a minimal filing requirement to create an LLC; (2) default management and capital structures giving each owner voting rights and rights to distributions; (3) free transferability of an owner's financial interest but not his or her management interest; and (4) a specific grant of power to the participants to vary most of the default rules by written agreement.

2. Formation

a. *Statutory Requirements*

To create an LLC, every state requires the promoters to file a brief document with the secretary of state. This document is usually called the articles (or certificate) of organization or the articles (or certificate) of formation. The articles require the promoters to state the name of the LLC, which must indicate that the entity is an LLC. The articles also frequently require a statement of the LLC's purpose. The purpose can include any lawful business, except those expressly prohibited or subject to other governmental regulation, such as banking and insurance. The LLC statute of most states uses the term "purpose" rather than "business" to permit LLCs to engage in nonprofit or philanthropic enterprises. Many large philanthropic groups are structures as LLCs, in part so that they are not constrained by tax and other regulations on tax-exempt organizations. The Chan-Zuckerberg Initiative (started by the founder of Facebook), the Emerson Collective (started by the widow of the founder of Apple), the Omidyar Network (started by a founder of eBay), and Google.org are all LLCs.

Because the LLC is an artificial entity, the statutes require the articles to name a resident agent and office for service of process. The articles in some states must specify whether the LLC will be managed by the owners (usually called "members") or by managers (who need not be members) and, in either case, the articles must state the names of the people who will manage the LLC initially. The statutes usually specify that the LLC comes into existence upon the filing of the articles.

b. *Promoter Liability and Defective Formation*

A promoter who incurs personal liability prior to the formation of an LLC should not be relieved of that liability simply because the LLC comes into existence later. Nonetheless a promoter and another party should be able to agree in advance to a novation when the LLC is formed and accepts a liability or should be able to agree that the promoter will remain primarily or secondarily liable after the LLC is formed and accepts a liability. The underlying policy seems analogous to that of promoters of corporations. *See* Chapter 5 for a more detailed discussion of promoter liability.

On occasion, a promoter will contract with another party on behalf of the LLC even though the LLC has not yet come into existence. Where both parties know that the LLC has not been formed should the agreement be treated as an agreement that binds the promoter? Should it be treated as an agreement that the promoter will use best efforts to form the LLC and cause the LLC to accept an offer from the other party? Should the answer turn on the parties' intention? What if their intentions differ from each other? What if their intention is not clear? Are there larger interests that should override the parties' intention?

What about the setting where the promoter knows that the LLC has not been formed but the other party does not know? Should the promoter be personally liable on the agreement? Where both parties believe, erroneously, that the LLC has been formed, the de facto entity doctrine and the estoppel doctrine might govern by analogy to the defective incorporation settings. Few states have a provision in their LLC statute analogous to §2.04 of the MBCA, which covers defective incorporation. *See* Chapter 5 for a more detailed discussion of defective incorporation.

P.D.2000, L.L.C. v. First Financial Planners, Inc.

998 S.W.2d 108 (Mo. Ct. App. 1999)

ROBERT E. CRIST, Senior Judge.

The relevant facts are that Ray Sulka, a resident of California, developed information systems and implemented computer technology advancements for individuals and companies in various industries. He was also a financial planner, who in February 1996 became a registered agent of defendant, First Financial Planners, Inc. (hereinafter FFP), a Missouri corporation founded and controlled by Roy Henry. In June 1996, Sulka and Henry entered into an agreement for Sulka to evaluate FFP's computer needs and to structure a plan for technological improvements. Sulka fully performed under this agreement and submitted a report to Henry.

On July 21, 1996, Sulka and Henry executed a second agreement on behalf of their respective corporations, P.D.2000, L.L.C. (hereinafter P.D.2000) and FFP. Henry signed as president of FFP and Sulka signed as president of P.D.2000. The agreement was titled "INDEPENDENT CONTRACTOR AGREEMENT" and provided for P.D.2000 to develop a security system and a financial planning system for FFP as well as an intranet communication structure for FFP branch offices and certain clients (hereinafter the contract). The contract provided that P.D.2000 would receive $25,000.00 per month for services performed and P.D.2000 would pay all expenses incurred in performing the contract out of that amount.

The contract stated that FFP "acknowledges that [P.D.2000] was in the process of forming an LLC in the state of Nevada."

Sulka began performing services for FFP immediately after entering into the contract in July 1996. FFP made two payments under the contract, making the checks payable to "Sulka West." On September 26, 1996, FFP terminated the contract with P.D.2000 without paying the termination fee.

On October 7, 1996, the articles of incorporation for P.D.2000 were filed with Nevada. On that same date, P.D.2000 executed a formal ratification of Sulka's pre-incorporation activities.

P.D.2000 then brought the present action against FFP for breach of contract and sought the termination fee pursuant to the contract. At trial, FFP's defense was that P.D.2000 did not have the capacity to enforce the contract. The jury found in favor of P.D.2000 and assessed damages at $300,000.00. The trial court entered judgment in accordance with the verdict in the amount of $359,744.80, which consisted of damages plus court costs and prejudgment interest.

In its sole point on appeal, FFP contends the trial court erred in denying its motions for directed verdict and for judgment notwithstanding the verdict, because P.D.2000 lacked the capacity to contract or to enforce the contract. It argues that the *Restatement (Second) of Agency* section 88 (1958) precludes an action on a pre-organization agreement by a subsequently formed entity, i.e. P.D.2000, when the other party to the contract, i.e. FFP, has withdrawn from the contract prior to its ratification.

Bader Automotive & Industrial Supply Co. Inc., v. Green, 533 S.W.2d 695 (Mo. App. 1976), is on point. In that case, in 1971, plaintiff, Richard Bader and defendant, Glynn Green, entered into an employment agreement containing a covenant not to compete. *Id.* at 696-697. At the time the agreement was executed, Bader had not incorporated his business and signed the agreement in his own name. *Id.* at 697. Green worked as an employee selling auto body supplies for Bader until 1973 and received his income on checks issued by the corporation during that time. *Id.* at 697-698. Green attempted to avoid the terms of the agreement, particularly the covenant not to compete, by claiming that the corporation could not ratify a contract that had been executed before the date of incorporation. *Id.* at 699. This court responded, "It is a well settled principle that '[w]here one contracts with a body assuming to act as a corporation or by a name distinctly implying a corporate existence, both parties in a suit upon the contract are usually estopped from denying such corporate existence.'" *Id.* (quoting *Schneider v. Best Truck Lines, Inc.*, 472 S.W.2d 655, 659 (Mo. App. 1971)).

Here, after it was incorporated, P.D.2000 ratified the contract between Henry and Sulka. The fact that the contract was signed by Sulka, who was the organizer of the corporation was sufficient to bind the corporation. *See Bader*, 533 S.W.2d at 699. Thus, although the contract was executed by the parties prior to P.D.2000's formal corporate birth, it became the contract between FFP and P.D.2000 after formation of the corporation and upon its adoption by the corporation. *See id.*

FFP relies on *Davane, Inc. v. Mongreig*, 550 N.E.2d 55 (Ill. App. 1990), for the proposition that if a party enters into a contract with an agent, who is unauthorized because its principal does not exist at the time of contracting, that party may withdraw from the contract.

Davane, however, is distinguishable from the case before us. Here, unlike the defendants in *Davane*, FFP had full knowledge of the corporate status of P.D.2000 at the time of contracting. FFP was aware that P.D.2000 was not incorporated and the contract specifically stated that P.D.2000 was in the process of incorporating in Nevada. FFP also knew that Sulka was the agent of P.D.2000 when he signed the contract and that he would be the person to perform services under the contract. In addition, similar to the employment situation in *Bader*, P.D.2000 had partly performed under the contract when FFP repudiated it. Sulka began working pursuant to the contract immediately after its execution and was issued two paychecks by FFP. He moved to St. Louis and signed a one-year lease for an apartment. He took the requisite steps to incorporate in Nevada. In contrast, in *Davane*, when the defendants withdrew, the contract was executory in nature because title to the property had not been transferred. Thus, we find the *Davane* decision is not controlling.

Given the facts of this case, FFP is estopped to deny the existence of P.D.2000. The trial court did not err in refusing to grant FFP's motions for directed verdict and for judgment notwithstanding the verdict.

The judgment of the trial court is affirmed.

James A. Pudlowski, P.J. and Clifford H. Ahrens, J.: Concur.

Notes and Questions

1. Reality Check

a. What two facts were central to the court's holding?

b. The court notes that the contract said that "[P.D.2000] was in the process of forming an LLC in the state of Nevada." Is that accurate?

2. Suppose

a. Suppose both parties believed the LLC had been formed. What if only Henry believed the LLC had been formed? Finally, suppose only Sulka believed the LLC had been formed. Would the result in each of these settings be different from the result in the opinion?

b. Would the result have been different if Sulka had not partially performed? Why?

c. Imagine that Sulka's partial performance had been damaging to Henry. Could Henry recover from Sulka personally or would Henry have been limited to recovering only from the LLC?

d. Suppose the LLC had been formed and had adopted the contract shortly before Henry terminated the contract. Would the result or analysis be different?

e. Could Sulka personally have enforced the contract if the LLC had never been formed?

3. What Do You Think?

a. The court chose between two rules. One rule estops a party who knowingly contracts with a nonexistent entity from terminating the contract. The other rule prohibits enforcement of a contract with a nonexistent entity where the other party has terminated the agreement prior to the entity's creation. How did the court choose between the two rules? Do you think it made the right choice?

4. You Draft It

a. Draft a contract clause that makes it clear that FFP is bound immediately upon executing the contract.

b. Draft a contract clause that makes it clear that FFP is only bound if an LLC is formed and ratifies the contract.

c. Operating Agreements

An LLC's operating agreement is the detailed agreement among all the members and sometimes all the managers. It deals with such matters as the names of the members and their respective economic interests; the managers (if any) and how power will be allocated between members and managers and, among the managers, whether there will be particular officers with delegated duties. An LLC's operating agreement is analogous to a partnership agreement. Sometimes the LLC itself is a party to the agreement. The operating agreement must be distinguished from other agreements that some members or managers may have with one another. These agreements, while they may have important consequences for the operation of the LLC, are not binding on LLC participants who are not parties. Therefore, these nonunanimous agreements are like shareholder agreements in the corporate setting. Only the articles of organization and the operating agreement officially control the LLC.

3. Financing

a. Capital Contributions

An LLC's members are free to decide among themselves how much money will be contributed in total and how much of that total each member will contribute. The members need not contribute equal amounts. The LLC statutes also provide that any form of consideration can be accepted by the LLC. This means that cash, tangible and intangible property, promissory notes, services rendered, and agreements to render services in the future can all be valid consideration.

b. Allocations and Distributions to Members

Allocation and distribution are two different, though related, concepts. Allocation refers to assigning the LLC's profits and losses among its members. Distribution refers to the transfer of LLC property (usually cash) to members. A distribution may reflect a share of members' profits or an advance to the members of anticipated profits, or it may reflect a repurchase of some or all of a member's interest. Because the promoters of LLCs usually elect to have the LLCs taxed as partnerships, which pass through to the owners both profits and losses, the members must decide how to allocate losses as well as profits among themselves. Frequently losses are allocated differently than profits because of differing motivations among the participants. For example, a member who also intends to be the primary manager of an LLC may agree with the other members that he or she will receive more of the profits and less of the losses than the other members in recognition of the efforts he or she will expend in running the business. LLC statutes typically provide as a default rule that profits shall be allocated in proportion to each member's contribution and that losses shall be allocated in proportion to each member's share of the profits.

Allocation is principally important only to the LLC's members. By contrast, distribution is also important to the LLC's creditors because property distributed to members is obviously unavailable to satisfy creditors' claims. For this reason, and also because property in the hands of members becomes difficult or impossible to retrieve for the creditors' benefit, LLC statutes restrict an LLC's power to make distributions. Most states use the "equity insolvency" test, which prohibits distributions if, afterward, the LLC will be unable to pay its debts as they become due. Most states also combine that test with some version of the "bankruptcy insolvency" test under which the LLC is prohibited from making a distribution if afterward its assets are less than its liabilities. A good faith analysis of the LLC's financial position and the effect a distribution will have on that position should insulate the LLC decision makers from liability under these statutes.

Members have no statutory right to compel a distribution. The operating agreement sometimes sets out a rule such as one that requires the LLC to distribute the maximum amount permissible under the statute. Another common rule requires the LLC to distribute cash sufficient to cover members' tax liability on the profits allocated to them. Alternatively, the operating agreement frequently leaves the question of distributions to the discretion of the managers. Both the drafter of the operating agreement (typically a lawyer) and the persons who control the LLC (whether members or managers) must be careful when deciding on a distribution policy for the LLC. Not only must the LLC comply with the statutory restrictions on paying distributions, but the tax consequences of distributions to the members must be taken into account as well. If the LLC will show a loss for the year (as is typical of many businesses in their early years), the loss is allocated to the members in accordance with the operating agreement or default rule. In the normal setting, these losses are advantageous to the members because they reduce each member's taxable income. However, where the LLC losses are so large that they are greater than the member's taxable income from every other source, the best the taxpayer can do is carry over his or her losses to the next tax year. In other words, the taxpayer cannot take full advantage of the LLC's losses because the Internal Revenue Code does not permit taxpayers to receive "negative income tax."

If the LLC generates a profit for the year, the analysis becomes more complicated. As with losses, profits are allocated to the members in accordance with the operating agreement or default rules. But remember that *allocation* is different from *distribution*. The allocation of profits increases the member's taxable income, but without a distribution there is no increase in the member's bank account. The danger is that the member will have an increased tax liability but no extra cash to meet that liability. Obviously the effect of an allocation without a distribution will vary from member to member. Some members may have substantial wealth outside the LLC and will easily be able to pay the tax liability on the LLC's profit allocation. Other members, though, may not have significant wealth beyond their LLC interest, and meeting the tax liability on their allocation of profits will be a great hardship.

The solution from the members' personal tax standpoint is for the LLC to distribute the maximum amount permissible under the statute each year. However, many business entities have a chronic need for capital both during their early years and often later as well. A struggling entity may not be able to borrow additional capital at all or may not be able to borrow at interest rates it considers fair. Attracting additional investors may be unacceptable to the current investors because of the dilution of their ownership and management interests. Obtaining additional capital from the present investors may be unpalatable for the same reason; some investors may not want the resulting dilution of their interests. Further, some current investors may simply be unable to invest additional money. For these reasons, a business entity's best source of capital is often simply the money its business generates in excess of the money needed for its direct expenses. Thus it may not always be possible for the LLC's operators to distribute cash, even though the members will be disadvantaged by a profit allocation without a corresponding distribution. Both those who are planning an LLC's structure and those charged with running an LLC must be aware of these tax and finance dynamics, the members' differing distribution preferences, and the capital needs and financing options of the LLC.

If a distribution is declared, the LLC statutes provide as a default rule that members have no right to receive LLC property rather than cash.[1] The converse of this default rule is not true, however. A member can be forced to accept property instead of cash as a distribution if all members are receiving the same proportion of the distribution in property. A distribution of property can be a distinct disadvantage for members where the property is difficult to value or where there is no ready market for the property. The LLC and the members will have different incentives for valuing the property and, regardless of valuation, where no ready market for the property exists, disposal is at best protracted and may be decidedly cumbersome.

4. Members' Interest

a. Financial

A member's financial interest consists of the right to receive an allocation of the profits and losses, in accordance with the operating agreement or the statute, and the right to receive assets (after creditors have been paid) upon the dissolution of the LLC. In most LLCs the operating agreement contains the parties' agreement for distributing assets on dissolution. Often these agreements provide that assets will

---

1. It may seem unlikely that a member would prefer property (which could be a machine the LLC uses in its business or raw or partially finished materials, or items in inventory) to cash, but a distribution of property and one of cash can have different tax consequences for the member. The transfer of property from the LLC to a member is not usually a taxable event, while the transfer of money usually is.

be distributed in accordance with the members' share of the profits. Sometimes the operating agreement provides that assets shall be used for the partial or complete return of members' initial contribution and only then will they be distributed in accordance with the profit allocation. Where the operating agreement is silent about distributing assets on dissolution, the statutory default rule applies. The statutes in the various states contain a variety of default rules in this regard, and no single system can be said to be typical. In general, the default systems mirror the variations that are typically found in operating agreements.

Every LLC statute provides that the members and managers shall not be personally liable for the LLC's debts. This provision is one of the key advantages of the LLC form over partnerships. Members are, of course, liable to the LLC and its creditors to pay their agreed-upon contribution and some operating agreements provide that members may be required to contribute additional money in the future. As you will remember from Chapter 8 above, equitable principles of corporate law suggest that in some circumstances the business form should be disregarded and liability should be imposed on the entity's owners. This is usually called "piercing the corporate veil" and is based in common law rather than in statute. In the LLC setting, though, a few states (including, for example, California) have statutes specifically imposing personal liability on LLC members "under principles of common law of this state that are similar to those applicable to business corporations and shareholders in this state." In states without such a statutory provision, courts tend to impose similar results on the same policy grounds used in deciding whether to pierce the corporate veil. Many states have recognized that LLCs may be managed more informally than corporations and provide by statute that failure to observe certain formalities is not a ground for disregarding the LLC as an entity. The next case shows that the analogy to corporate veil piercing may be more difficult than first appears.

Puleo v. Topel

856 N.E.2d 1152 (Ill. App. 2006)

Presiding Justice QUINN delivered the opinion of the court:

Plaintiffs Philip Puleo, Malex Corporation, Amy Derksen, Chani Derus, Robert Filiczkowski, YSPEX, Inc., Jacob Lesgold, Van Ratsavongsay, and Bryan Weiss appeal the order of the circuit court dismissing their claims against defendant Michael Topel (Topel). On appeal, plaintiffs contend that the circuit court erred by finding that Topel could not be held personally liable for obligations incurred on behalf of defendant Thinktank, LLC (Thinktank), after the company was involuntary dissolved.

The record shows that effective May 30, 2002, Thinktank, a limited liability company (LLC) primarily involved in web design and web marketing, was involuntarily dissolved by the Illinois Secretary of State. The dissolution was due to Thinktank's failure to file its 2001 annual report as required by the Illinois Limited Liability Company Act (the Act).

Thereafter, on December 2, 2002, plaintiffs, independent contractors hired by Topel, filed a complaint against Topel and Thinktank in which they alleged breach of contract, unjust enrichment, and claims under the account stated theory. Those claims stemmed from plaintiffs' contention that Topel, who plaintiffs alleged was the sole manager and owner of Thinktank, knew or should have known of Thinktank's involuntary dissolution, but nonetheless continued to conduct business as Thinktank from May 30, 2002, through the end of August 2002. They further contended that on or about August 30, 2002, Topel informed Thinktank employees and independent contractors, including plaintiffs, that the company was ceasing operations and that their services were no longer needed. Thinktank then failed to pay plaintiffs for work they had performed.

[T]he circuit [court] granted plaintiffs' motion for judgment on the pleadings against Thinktank . . . [and] entered a final order dismissing all of plaintiffs' claims against Topel with prejudice.

Plaintiffs now appeal that order.

In this court, plaintiffs contend that the circuit court erred in dismissing their claims against Topel. In making that argument, plaintiffs acknowledge that the issue as to whether a member or manager of an LLC may be held personally liable for obligations incurred by an involuntarily dissolved LLC appears to be one of first impression under the Act. That said, plaintiffs assert that it has long been the law in Illinois that an officer or director of a dissolved corporation has no authority to exercise corporate powers and, thus is personally liable for any debts he incurs on behalf of the corporation after its dissolution. Plaintiffs reason that Topel, as managing member of Thinktank, similarly should be held liable for debts the company incurred after its dissolution.

We first look to the provisions of the Act as they provided the trial court its basis for its ruling. When reviewing a statute, the cardinal rule is to ascertain and give effect to the intent of the legislature. The plain meaning of the language in the statute provides the best indication of legislative intent. Where the statutory language is clear, the court must give it effect without resorting to other aids for construction. Further, when a statute is amended, it is presumed that the legislature meant to change the law as it formerly existed.

As stated, the circuit court relied on section[ ]10-10 of the Act in making its ruling. Section 10-10 provides:

> (a) Except as otherwise provided in subsection (d) of this Section, the debts, obligations, and liabilities of a limited liability company, whether arising in contract, tort, or otherwise, are solely the debts, obligations, and liabilities of the company. A member or manager is not personally liable for a debt, obligation, or liability of the company solely by reason of being or acting as a member or manager.
> (b) (Blank).
> (c) The failure of a limited liability company to observe the usual company formalities or requirements relating to the exercise of its company powers or management of its business is not a ground for imposing personal liability on the members or managers for liabilities of the company.
> (d) All or specified members of a limited liability company are liable in their capacity as members for all or specified debts, obligations, or liabilities of the company if:
>> (1) a provision to that effect is contained in the articles of organization; and
>> (2) a member so liable has consented in writing to the adoption of the provision or to be bound by the provision.

Section 10-10 clearly indicates that a member or manager of an LLC is not personally liable for debts the company incurs unless each of the provisions in subsection (d) is met. In this case, plaintiffs cannot establish either of the provisions in subsection (d). They have not provided this court with Thinktank's articles of organization, much less a provision establishing Topel's personal liability, nor have they provided this court with Topel's written adoption of such a provision. As such, under the express language of the Act, plaintiffs cannot establish Topel's personal liability for debts that Thinktank incurred after its dissolution.

As plaintiffs contend, similar to the Business Corporation Act (BCA), the Act explicitly provides that an LLC continues after dissolution only for the purpose of winding up its business. However, as plaintiffs concede in their brief, the Act does not contain a provision similar to section 3.20 of the Business Corporation Act, which provides:

> "All persons who assume to exercise corporate powers without authority so to do shall be jointly and severally liable for all debts and liabilities incurred or arising as a result thereof".

> **Prior to its amendment, section 10-10 provided:**

> (a) A member of a limited liability company shall be personally liable for any act, debt, obligation, or liability of the limited liability company or another member or manager to the extent that a shareholder of an Illinois business corporation is liable in analogous circumstances under Illinois law.
> (b) A manager of a limited liability company shall be personally liable for any act, debt, obligation, or liability of the limited liability company or another manager or member to the extent that a director of an Illinois business corporation is liable in analogous circumstances under Illinois law.

In 1998, however, the legislature amended section 10-10 and in doing so removed the above language which explicitly provided that a member or manager of an LLC could be held personally liable for his or her own actions or for the actions of the LLC to the same extent as a shareholder or director of a corporation could be held personally liable. As we have not found any legislative commentary regarding that amendment, we presume that by removing the noted statutory language, the legislature meant to shield a member or manager of an LLC from personal liability.

Nonetheless, plaintiffs ask this court to disregard the 1998 amendment and to imply a provision into the Act similar to section 3.20 of the Business Corporation Act. We cannot do so.

In the case at bar, we . . . decline plaintiffs' request to ignore the statutory language. When the legislature amended section 10-10, it clearly removed the provision that allowed a member or manager of an LLC to be held personally liable in the same manner as provided in section 3.20 of the Business Corporation Act. Thus, the Act does not provide for a member or manager's personal liability to a third party for an LLC's debts and liabilities, and no rule of construction authorizes this court to declare that the legislature did not mean what the plain language of the statute imports.

We, therefore, find that the circuit court did not err in concluding that the Act did not permit it to find Topel personally liable to plaintiffs for Thinktank's debts and liabilities. We agree with plaintiff that the circuit court's ruling does not provide an equitable result. However, the circuit court, like this court, was bound by the statutory language.

Accordingly, we affirm the judgment of the circuit court of Cook County.

Notes and Questions

1. Reality Check

a. What is the theory the plaintiffs use to try to hold Mr. Puleo personally liable?
b. Why did the court reject the plaintiffs' arguments?

2. Suppose

a. Imagine that Illinois had never adopted a statute addressing personal liability for LLC members or managers. Would the court's analysis or the result be different?
b. Imagine that Illinois enacted section 10-10 in its original version and never amended it. Would the court's analysis or the result be different?
c. Imagine that Illinois initially enacted section 10-10 in its current version (i.e., never adopted the original language) and never amended it. Would the court's analysis or the result be different?

3. What Do You Think?

a. Do you think that original section 10-10 or the amended section 10-10 is the better statute? Do you think there is a better approach?
b. Do you agree with the inference the court drew from the legislature's amendment of the LLC liability statute? Are there other inferences that could be drawn from the amendment?
c. Do you think LLC statutes should explicitly import "piercing the veil" concepts from corporate law? Suppose the state supreme court radically changes the law of piercing the corporate veil after the LLC statute is adopted? Should a trial court automatically apply the new piercing law to LLCs?
d. Do you think corporation statutes should codify piercing principles?
e. Do you think corporation statutes should reference LLC piercing principles?

4. You Draft It

a. Draft a statute that reflects the appropriate rule regarding the personal liability of LLC members and managers. The text of the original version of Illinois section 10-10, and the amended version of Illinois section 10-10 are set out below.

Illinois 805 ILCS 180/10-10 (original version):

> (a) A member of a limited liability company shall be personally liable for any act, debt, obligation, or liability of the limited liability company or another member or manager to the extent that a shareholder of an Illinois business corporation is liable in analogous circumstances under Illinois law.
>
> (b) A manager of a limited liability company shall be personally liable for any act, debt, obligation, or liability of the limited liability company or another manager or member to the extent that a director of an Illinois business corporation is liable in analogous circumstances under Illinois law.

Illinois 805 ILCS 180/10-10 (amended version):

(a) Except as otherwise provided in subsection (d) of this Section, the debts, obligations, and liabilities of a limited liability company, whether arising in contract, tort, or otherwise, are solely the debts, obligations, and liabilities of the company. A member or manager is not personally liable for a debt, obligation, or liability of the company solely by reason of being or acting as a member or manager.

(b) (Blank).

(c) The failure of a limited liability company to observe the usual company formalities or requirements relating to the exercise of its company powers or management of its business is not a ground for imposing personal liability on the members or managers for liabilities of the company.

(d) All or specified members of a limited liability company are liable in their capacity as members for all or specified debts, obligations, or liabilities of the company if:

(1) a provision to that effect is contained in the articles of organization; and

(2) a member so liable has consented in writing to the adoption of the provision or to be bound by the provision.

Putting It to Work

Problem 18-1

Randall and Shannon Black come to you after a dispute arose between them and P&S Pools, LLC, whom the Blacks hired to dig a new pool in their back yard. The operator of P&S Pools, Paul Peterson, submitted a proposal in February to the Blacks titled "P&S Pools Proposal 14-443 Per Paul Peterson." The proposal was subsequently accepted by the Blacks and construction started immediately. The Blacks received a bill for the work in May directing payment to be made to "P&S Pools."

In July, the Blacks learned that the new pool Paul had constructed was found to leak when too many floaties were in the pool. Randall and Shannon want the pool repaired for free, and Paul refused.

The LLC statute in this jurisdiction states:

"Unless the Operating Agreement otherwise provides, a limited liability company is managed by its Members."

"A Member, Manager, or other agent of a limited liability company is not, merely on account of this status, personally liable for the acts, debts, liabilities, or obligations of the limited liability company."

"The case law of this State that sets forth the conditions and circumstances under which the corporate veil of a corporation may be pierced applies to limited liability companies."

The only Members of P&S Pools, LLC, are Paul Peterson and his wife, Sara. The LLC has no written operating agreement. Paul works full time at the pool construction business and makes all decisions concerning the business. Sara works part time keeping the business's accounts. Paul and Sara have never held a formal meeting of the LLC's Members. The LLC has no insurance and few assets; all the construction equipment used in the business is rented for each new job. The LLC has a bank account that is separate from Paul and Sara's personal bank account and Sara is careful not to commingle funds.

,Look to agency stuff as well tort stuff

a. Are Paul or Sara liable to the Blacks under a veil-piercing theory? *other ways to get at this*

b. If they are liable, does that discourage or encourage LLC formation?

c. Do you think that the LLC should or should not be pierced on these facts?

b. *Managerial*

Most LLC statutes provide as a default rule that the LLC will be managed by the members. Many of the statutes provide that members' managerial power will be exercised in proportion to each member's contribution. In other words, in an LLC where *A* contributes $60,000, *B* contributes $35,000, and *C* contributes $5,000, the parties' voting power would be *A* 60 percent, *B* 35 percent, and *C* 5 percent. In other states, the members' managerial power is per capita. In the example just given, the parties' voting power would be *A* one-third, *B* one-third, and *C* one-third, even though their contributions were unequal. In every state the default management scheme can be varied by the operating agreement and many if not most operating agreements make at least some change from the default rule. Typical management structures and issues are discussed in more detail below.

c. *Additional Members, Transferability, and Dissociation*

After an LLC has been formed, additional members may be admitted. In many LLCs, the operating agreement permits additional members to be admitted either by the managers or by a majority or supermajority of the members.

Most LLC statutes distinguish between a transfer of a member's economic interest and a transfer of that member's management interest. A member's economic interest is freely transferable, but the transferee does not become a member unless specifically admitted under the operating agreement, which typically requires the approval of a majority of other members. As with a corporation or limited partnership, good reasons often exist for the parties to prohibit or limit the transferability of an owner's interest. Even where both economic and management interests are transferable, the transferring member remains liable for additional contributions, if any, under the operating agreement. A creditor of a member can usually obtain a charging order, which acts as a lien on the member's economic interest. This charging order is analogous to a charging order on a partner's interest and can be foreclosed in the same manner.

Dissociation is the term used by LLC statutes to mean that a member is no longer a member. Most LLC statutes permit a member to dissociate at will, subject to a restriction in the operating agreement. LLC statutes also generally provide that a member is dissociated upon the transference of all of his or her economic interest or upon the occurrence of certain events, largely tracking those that cause dissociation of a limited partner. These events include the death or bankruptcy of a member. A dissociated member is usually not entitled under the statute to any payment from the LLC, but some operating agreements provide for the return of some or all of a member's contribution upon dissociation.

A member who transfers his or her economic interest or dissociates by selling his or her interest back to the LLC may face the problem of later determining exactly what interests were transferred, the value of those interests, and what rights and obligations the member retains. The following case illustrates some of these issues.

Five Star Concrete, L.L.C. v. Klink, Inc.

693 N.E.2d 583 (Ind. Ct. App. 1998)

STATON, J.

We affirm in part, reverse in part and remand.

On June 14, 1994, Klink, Inc. ("Klink") and four other corporations, all engaged in supplying ready-mix concrete, formed Five Star, a limited liability company ("LLC"), in order to furnish concrete to large construction projects. Klink contributed $38,500.00, 12.5% of the initial total capitalization, and was issued 12.5 ownership units.

In a letter dated October 13, 1995, Klink formally notified Five Star of its intent to withdraw from membership effective October 10, 1995. The remaining members decided to purchase Klink's ownership units and to continue the business. To accomplish this end, Five Star members met on October 23, 1995 and agreed that Klink would receive $61,047.22 for the value of its "units."

After Five Star's fiscal year ended December 31, 1995, Klink was allocated $31,889.02 of income, representing its share of the LLC's profits for the approximate ten-month period of 1995 when Klink was a member. The allocation did not result in a monetary distribution to Klink. Instead, the allocation was made only for the purpose of properly determining Klink's tax liability. After receiving notification of the allocation, Klink filed a complaint against Five Star claiming that it was entitled to a distribution of cash in the sum of $31,889.02. Klink moved for summary judgment on its claim, and Five Star responded with its own motion for summary judgment, asserting that Klink had already been paid for its entire interest. Following a hearing, the trial court granted Klink's motion, finding that Klink had a legal right to receive a distribution of $31,889.02. The court also denied Five Star's cross-motion. Five Star appeals both rulings.

I. DISTRIBUTION OF $31,889.02

Here, there is no dispute that the allocation, Klink's portion of Five Star's income, was proper. Five Star was being taxed as a "pass-through" entity, and the allocation was required by tax law as well as by the Operating Agreement. However, Klink insists that when there is an allocation to a dissociating member there is a corresponding obligation to make a cash distribution of income equal to the allocation. We do not agree.

Nowhere does the Indiana Business Flexibility Act (the "Act") provide that allocation of income to members for income tax purposes creates an automatic legal right to receive a distribution in the amount of that income, even when a member is withdrawing from the LLC. Indeed, there are times that such a distribution would be unlawful. See Ind. Code §23-18-5-6.[4]

---

4. A distribution may not be made if after giving effect to the distribution: (1) the limited liability company would not be able to pay its debts as the debts become due in the usual course of business; or (2) the limited liability company's total assets would be less than the sum of its total liabilities plus, unless the operating agreement permits otherwise, the amount that would be needed if the affairs of the limited liability company were to be wound up at the time of the distribution to satisfy any preferential rights that are superior to the rights of members receiving the distribution. IC 23-18-5-6 (1993).

The Operating Agreement is also silent regarding the timing and amount of distributions; thus, under the Act, these decisions are to be made by the majority of the members. The evidence construed in favor of Five Star shows that Five Star made a distribution to all members in July of 1995; Klink's share was approximately $12,500.00. However, neither this distribution nor any other was made based upon the amount of income allocated to a member. Further, since that date no distributions were made to any members.

We conclude that the allocation of profits for tax reporting purposes did not provide Klink with a legal right under either the Act or the Operating Agreement to receive a distribution in the same amount. Summary judgment in favor of Klink was improvidently granted.

It does not follow, however, that Klink's interest in Five Star's profits for the ten-month period of 1995 should be ignored. Here, the member's share of Five Star's profits and losses is part of the total economic interest transferred in the buy-sell agreement. However, in this case, we cannot value that interest as a matter of law. This brings us to Five Star's next argument.

II. DIVESTMENT OF ECONOMIC INTEREST

The minutes of the October 23, 1995, meeting memorializing the Five Star members' buy-sell agreement states that Klink would receive $61,047.22 for the value of its "units." Five Star contends that it is entitled to summary judgment because, when Klink sold its "units" to Five Star for $61,047.22, Klink divested itself of its entire economic interest, including its right to profits. Klink counters that the use of the term "units" proves that it sold less than all its interests for that amount.

Pursuant to the Operating Agreement, "unit" refers to "an interest in the Company representing a contribution to capital." This supports Klink's argument that it sold less than all of its economic rights in Five Star when it accepted the $61,047.22. However, as Five Star points out, under the same Operating Agreement, the members' interests are represented by the units held by each member. Thus, each unit generally entitled the members to one vote and to a proportionate share of the LLC's net income, gains, losses, deductions and credits. "Units," as used in the minutes, could reasonably denote either all or only part of Klink's economic interests in Five Star.

The designated evidence supports an inference that the parties entered into the contract with materially different meanings attached to the word "unit." The trial court recognized the factual dispute and properly denied Five Star's motion for summary judgment.

III. VALUATION METHOD

Five Star maintains that the valuation method chosen by the parties demonstrates that Klink actually received the fair market value of its entire interest. We analyze this as a separate argument.

Here, the parties determined fair market value by examining Five Star's September 30, 1995, balance sheet. Liabilities of $104,495.42 were subtracted from assets valued at $592,873.16, leaving $488,377.74. That amount was then multiplied by 12.5%, Klink's percentage of ownership, resulting in the agreed sum of $61,047.22.

Five Star claims that, . . . by using this valuation method, Klink received the amount upon which its complaint is based.

Valuing the interest of a member is a "complex task," more of a business matter than a legal one. . . . There is no best method for valuation and much depends on the nature of the business. . . . We do not agree with Five Star that resolution of this matter is appropriately decided as a matter of law. Five Star is not entitled to summary judgment on this ground.[5]

Affirmed in part, reversed in part and remanded.

GARRARD and RUCKER, JJ., concur.

Notes and Questions

1. Note

a. Under most LLC statutes at the time this case was decided, a member who had the power to dissociate ("withdraw" is a synonym used in the opinion) could cause the LLC to dissolve unless the other members elected to continue the business, as the remaining members of Five Star did in this instance.

2. Reality Check

a. What did Klink believe it transferred to the LLC when it sold its "units"? What did Five Star believe it received when it bought Klink's "units"?

b. On remand, how will the trial court decide what was transferred? How will it value that transfer?

3. Suppose

a. If the operating agreement clearly defined "unit" as a member's entire economic interest would Klink or Five Star have a better argument for relief?

b. Suppose Klink had sold its units in October 1995 to Alpha, a third party, for the same price, $61,047.22? If Five Star had computed its profits only for the entire calendar year of 1995, how should the profits be allocated between Klink and Alpha?

c. Assume some profits are allocated to Alpha, but no distribution is made. Can Alpha seek money from Klink to cover its tax liability? If some profits are allocated to Klink, can it seek money from Alpha? What if there are losses instead?

d. If a distribution is made shortly after the sale to Alpha, is Alpha entitled to all the distribution? None? If Five Star dissolved soon after, and had enough net assets to repay the members' original contribution, would Klink or Alpha be entitled to Klink's original $38,500 contribution?

5. Upon remand, the buy-out provision in the Operating Agreement may become relevant. It provides that, if Five Star elects to purchase the interest of a "Former Member" and no pre-determined purchase price of a "unit" had been established within a two-year period: [t]he fair market value shall be determined by a certified public accountant selected by the selling Member and a certified public accountant selected by the Company or purchasing Member, although all Members may select the same accountant. If the two accountants cannot agree as to the fair market value, the value shall be determined by a majority vote of said accountants and a third certified public accountant selected by said accountants.

4. What Do You Think?

a. Apparently Klink representatives attended the October 23, 1995, meeting at which Klink's units were valued and agreed with the valuation. Do you think Klink should be estopped from seeking further compensation?

b. Do you think the ambiguity in the term *unit* was foreseeable? If so, which party should have the ambiguity resolved in its favor? Why? If the ambiguity was foreseeable, how could the parties' lawyers have prevented the ambiguity before it resulted in this dispute?

c. Five Star began business in June 1994. The opinion does not state whether distributions were made in 1994, nor whether the LLC had profits or losses for that year. In 1995, though, Klink received a $12,500 distribution and $61,047.22 for the sale of its units for a total of $73,547.22. Its allocation of the 1995 profit was $31,889.02, which suggests a maximum federal tax liability of about $11,000. Do you think that, as a matter of fairness, Klink has been amply compensated for its investment?

d. In footnote 5, the court quotes the operating agreement language for valuing a Member's interest. Do you think the procedure is a workable one?

5. You Draft It

a. Draft a clause for the buy-sell agreement that supports Klink's position.

b. Draft a clause for the buy-sell agreement that supports Five Star's position.

Putting It to Work

Problem 18-2

Skaterzzz is an LLC that manufactures roller skate wheels for roller derby professionals. Its written operating agreement provides:

> 7.1 Transfer of Interest. A Member may transfer all or any portion of its Interest to any Person at any time.

> 7.2 Admission of New Members. No Person shall be admitted as a Member of Skaterzzz after the date of this LLC Agreement without the written consent of all Members and delivery to Skaterzzz of a written acknowledgment (in form and substance satisfactory to the Members) of the rights and obligations of this LLC Agreement and an agreement to be bound hereunder.

Skaterzzz has three Members, Moe (50% interest), Larry (30%), and Curly (20%). The operating agreement provides that voting power is proportional to ownership interest. Larry and Curly have become dissatisfied with the direction of the business that Moe is taking. Larry is inclined to challenge Moe, but Curly simply wants out of the business. Larry agrees to purchase Curly's ownership interest in the LLC. Moe admits that §7.1 permits Larry to acquire Curly's economic interest in the LLC, but argues that Curly's voting rights can only be transferred by compliance with §7.2. Of course, Moe refuses to consent to any transfer under §7.2.

a. Can Larry purchase Curly's managerial as well as economic rights in the LLC under §7.1, or must the transfer of the managerial rights comply with §7.2? *See Achian Inc. v. Leemon Family LLC*, 2011 WL 3518270 (Del. Ch.).

5. Management

a. Statutory Default Rules

As noted above, in the distinct majority of states member-managed LLCs are the default rule. Most states require any variation from this rule to be stated in the articles of organization, but some states permit variations to be stated in the operating agreement. A majority vote is required for action to be approved (although, of course, the members may validly change that rule to require a supermajority or even unanimous vote on some or all issues). Although a few states require member meetings and have corporatelike provisions for call, notice, and quorum, most statutes are silent, leaving the question of when and how member meetings are to be conducted entirely in the hands of the members themselves.

Being a "member" may, by itself, be construed to create a kind of apparent authority or position of power, allowing a member to bind an LLC. This power may potentially allow a member to bind the LLC for acts outside the LLC's business or acts that were specifically forbidden by the LLC's other members, if a third party reasonably believes the member is authorized to act for the LLC. Some LLC statutes contain a specific default grant or denial of authority to members, qua members, but other acts are silent, relying on agency law principles. Most statutes permit limitations on a member's or all members' authority to be stated in the articles filed with the secretary of state, but such restrictions are probably not binding on third parties who are unaware of them.

b. Manager-Managed Structures

As an alternative to the default rule of member-managed LLCs, many operating agreements provide for management by managers. As noted above, managers need not be members, although in the closely held entity setting they often are members. In theory, the operating agreement could allocate power among members and managers in an infinite variety of ways. In practice, though, most LLC operating agreements that effect a manager-managed structure create a division of power that replicates that of a corporation. Under this scheme the members vote once each year for the election of managers. Members usually have the right to remove managers during their term even without cause. Often members are required to vote on proposals for extraordinary transactions involving the LLC, such as mergers or dissolution.

In a manager-managed LLC, the operating agreement could provide for a hierarchy of managers; some managers being in charge of others. Mostly, though, operating agreements reflect a corporate model in which the managers are analogous to the board of directors. In that setting the managers are co-equal. They probably have the power to appoint persons to be agents of the LLC, much as corporate officers and employees are agents of a corporation. Most LLC statutes provide a default rule that managers have the same authority to bind the LLC as members in a member-managed LLC do. That is, each manager has the power to bind the LLC to any action that is apparently for carrying on in the usual way the business of the LLC. This power is, of course, in addition to any actual authority the manager possesses.

The operating agreement will suffice to divide power between members and managers. However, because the default LLC rule is typically for a member-managed entity, apparent authority or estoppel concepts may allow third parties to bind LLCs for unauthorized actions by members in manager-managed LLCs. Most LLC statutes require the articles of organization to state whether the LLC will be member or manager managed, and every statute permits the articles of organization to contain statements that limit the authority of members or managers or particular individuals. Such disclosure is probably not sufficient to preclude third parties without actual knowledge of the provisions from asserting apparent authority or estoppel arguments. A special rule sometimes applies in transferring LLC real estate. A few statutes provide that grants or limitations of authority contained in the articles of organization are sufficient to bind third parties, even without actual notice, as to the authority of members or managers to effect a real estate transfer.

6. Fiduciary Duties

What fiduciary duties exist in LLCs has proven to be one of the most important, and controversial, questions. What duties do managers owe to the LLC and members? What duties do members owe one another, and do those duties differ depending upon whether the LLC is member-managed or manager-managed? The statutes are not definitive (and often, not terribly helpful) on these questions, and in many states the statutes are completely silent. At the beginning of this chapter, we observed that many commentators believe that two qualities distinguish LLCs from other entities such as corporations and partnerships: LLCs are a new form of entity, not a hybrid of old forms, and LLC rules are determined by the parties themselves without mandatory provisions imposed by law. But, as we also saw, neither of those assertions is as strong as some commentators claim. From a policy standpoint, then, fiduciary duties in LLCs present a central tension that must be resolved on public policy rather than strictly law-based grounds. On the one hand, the sui generis nature of LLCs and the freedom of contract ethos suggest that any duties should be strictly the product of the parties' intent as expressed in the operating agreement or in the articles. On the other hand, those who operate LLCs, whether managers or members, are expressly aggregating other people's money with the understanding that the LLC will then be operated in the interests of the members. That operation and understanding implies some obligation on those who operate LLCs to do so faithfully and diligently. Put another way, courts and legislatures must decide (1) what fiduciary duties, if any, exist by default in an LLC and (2) to what extent, if any, can those duties be varied or eliminated.

The following case is one of the first to grapple with this tension. The LLC in this case was member-managed.

McConnell v. Hunt Sports Enterprises

725 N.E.2d 1193 (Ohio Ct. App. 1999)

TYACK, J.

On June 17, 1997, John H. McConnell and Wolfe Enterprises, Inc. filed a complaint for declaratory judgment . . . against Hunt Sports Enterprises, Hunt Sports Enterprises, L.L.C., Hunt Sports Group, L.L.C. ("Hunt Sports Group") and Columbus Hockey Limited ("CHL"). CHL was a limited liability company formed under R.C. Chapter 1705. A brief background of the events leading up to the formation of CHL and the subsequent discord among certain of its members follows.

In 1996, the National Hockey League ("NHL") determined it would be accepting applications for new hockey franchises. In April 1996, Gregory S. Lashutka, the mayor of Columbus, received a phone call from an NHL representative inquiring as to Columbus's interest in a hockey team. As a result, Mayor Lashutka asked certain community leaders who had been involved in exploring professional sports in Columbus to pursue the possibility of applying for an NHL hockey franchise. Two of these persons were Ronald A. Pizzuti and McConnell.

Pizzuti began efforts to recruit investors in a possible franchise. The deadline for applying for an NHL expansion franchise was November 1, 1996. On October 31, 1996, CHL was formed when its articles of organization were filed with the secretary of state pursuant to R.C. 1705.04. The members of CHL were McConnell, Wolfe Enterprises, Inc., Hunt Sports Group, Pizzuti Sports Limited, [Ameritech,] and Buckeye Hockey, L.L.C. CHL was subject to an operating agreement that set forth the terms between the members. Pursuant to section 2.1 of CHL's operating agreement, the general character of the business of CHL was to invest in and operate a franchise in the NHL.

On or about November 1, 1996, an application was filed with the NHL on behalf of the city of Columbus. In the application, the ownership group was identified as CHL. . . . Also included within the application package was Columbus's plan for an arena to house the hockey games. There was no facility at the time, and the proposal was to build a facility that would be financed, in large part, by a three-year countywide one-half percent sales tax. The sales tax issue would be on the May 1997 ballot.

On May 6, 1997, the sales tax issue failed. The day after, . . . Dimon McPherson, chairman and chief executive officer of Nationwide Insurance Enterprise ("Nationwide"), met with [Lamar] Hunt, and they discussed the possibility of building the arena despite the failure of the sales tax issue. Hunt was interested, and Nationwide began working on an arena plan. On or about May 9, 1997, the mayor spoke with [NHL Commissioner Gary] Bettman and let him know that alternate plans would be pursued, and Mr. Bettman gave Columbus until June 4, 1997, to come up with a plan.

By May 28, 1997, Nationwide had come up with a plan to finance an arena privately and on such date, Hunt Sports Group did not accept Nationwide's lease proposal. On May 29, 1997, Nationwide representatives again met with representatives of Hunt Sports Group. Again, Hunt Sports Group indicated that the lease proposal was unacceptable. . . . The June 4, 1997, NHL deadline was discussed.

Hunt Sports Group stated that it would continue to evaluate the proposal, and it wanted the weekend to do so. Nationwide informed appellant that it needed an answer by close of business Friday, May 30.

On May 30, 1997, McPherson called McConnell and requested that they meet and discuss "where [they] were on the arena." McConnell testified that the conversation was "totally out of the blue. [McPherson] said that Nationwide was going to finance and build an arena, and that he had offered the Hunt group the opportunity to pick up the lease and bring a franchise in." McPherson told McConnell about appellant's rejection of the lease proposal and discussed the NHL's June 4 deadline. McConnell stated that if Hunt would not step up and lease the arena and, therefore, get the franchise, McConnell would. Hunt Sports Group did not contact Nationwide on May 30, 1997.

Hunt Sports Group told Nationwide that it still found the terms of the lease to be unacceptable. On June 3 or June 4, McConnell, in a conversation with the NHL, orally agreed to apply for a hockey franchise for Columbus. On June 4 . . . Hunt informed McPherson that he was still interested in pursuing an agreement with Nationwide.

On June 4, 1997, the NHL franchise expansion committee met. The expansion committee recommended Columbus to the NHL board of governors as one of four cities to be granted a franchise.

On June 5, 1997, the NHL sent Hunt a letter requesting that he let them know by Monday, June 9, 1997, whether he was going forward with his franchise application. Hunt responded that CHL intended to pursue the franchise application. Hunt indicated that the application was contingent upon entering into an appropriate lease for a hockey facility.

On June 9, 1997, a meeting took place at Pizzuti's office. The NHL required that the ownership group be identified and that such ownership group sign a lease term sheet by June 9, 1997. Brian Ellis, president and chief operating officer of Nationwide, presented the lease term sheet. . . .

Hunt indicated the lease was unacceptable. Ameritech and Buckeye Hockey, L.L.C. indicated that if Hunt found it unacceptable then they too found it unacceptable. Pizzuti and Wolfe agreed to participate along with McConnell. McConnell then signed the term sheet as the owner of the franchise. Christie [a McConnell family representative] faxed the signed lease term sheet to Bettman that day along with a cover letter and a description of the ownership group. Such ownership group was identified as: John H. McConnell, majority owner, Pizzuti Sports, L.L.C., John F. Wolfe and "[u]p to seven (7) other members."

On June 17, 1997. . . , the complaint in the case at bar was filed. On or about June 25, 1997, the NHL board of governors awarded Columbus a franchise with McConnell's group as owner.[2] Hunt Sports Group, Buckeye Hockey, L.L.C. and Ameritech have no ownership interest in the hockey franchise.

[C]ount one of the first amended complaint sought a declaration that section 3.3 of CHL's operating agreement allowed members to compete against CHL to obtain an NHL franchise.

---

2. The ownership group is now formally known as COLHOC Limited Partnership ("COLHOC"). Portions of the record indicate COLHOC was formed before the June 9, 1997, meeting. JMAC, Inc. [the investment entity for the McConnell family] is the majority owner, and JMAC. Hockey L.L.C. is the general partner of COLHOC.

Section 3.3 of the operating agreement states:

> Members May Compete. Members shall not in any way be prohibited from or restricted in engaging or owning an interest in any other business venture of any nature, including any venture which might be competitive with the business of the Company.

Appellant [Hunt Sports Group] emphasizes the word "other" in the above language and states, in essence, that it means any business venture that is different from the business of the company. Appellant points out that under section 2.1 of the operating agreement, the general character of the business is "to invest in and operate a franchise in the National Hockey League." Hence, appellant contends that members may only engage in or own an interest in a venture that is not in the business of investing in and operating a franchise with the NHL.

Appellant's interpretation of section 3.3 goes beyond the plain language of the agreement and adds words or meanings not stated in the provision. Section 3.3, for example, does not state "[m]embers shall not be prohibited from or restricted in engaging or owning an interest in any other business venture that is different from the business of the company." Rather, section 3.3 states: "any other business venture *of any nature*." (Emphasis added.) It then adds to this statement: "including any venture which might be competitive with the business of the Company." The words "any nature" could not be broader, and the inclusion of the words "any venture which might be competitive with the business of the Company" makes it clear that members were not prohibited from engaging in a venture that was competitive with CHL's investing in and operating an NHL franchise. Contrary to appellant's contention, the word "other" simply means a business venture other than CHL. The word "other" does not limit the type of business venture in which members may engage.

Hence, section 3.3 did not prohibit appellees from engaging in activities that may have been competitive with CHL, including appellees' participation in COL-HOC. Accordingly, summary judgment in favor of appellees was appropriate, and appellees were entitled to a declaration that section 3.3 of the operating agreement permitted appellees to request and obtain an NHL hockey franchise to the exclusion of CHL.

[A]ppellant contends the trial court erred in excluding evidence that would have shown appellees breached fiduciary duties. For the reasons that follow, we find the trial court did not err in excluding certain evidence.

Before we can review the propriety of the directed verdict in this case, the law on fiduciary duty and interference with a prospective business relationship must be addressed. The term "fiduciary relationship" has been defined as a relationship in which special confidence and trust is reposed in the integrity and fidelity of another, and there is a resulting position of superiority or influence acquired by virtue of this special trust. In the case at bar, a limited liability company is involved which, like a partnership, involves a fiduciary relationship. Normally, the presence of such a relationship would preclude direct competition between members of the company. However, here we have an operating agreement that by its very terms allows members to compete with the business of the company. Hence, the question we are presented with is whether an operating agreement of a limited liability company may, in essence, limit or define the scope of the fiduciary duties imposed upon its members. We answer this question in the affirmative.

A fiduciary has been defined as a person having a duty, created by his or her undertaking, to act primarily for the benefit of another in matters connected with such undertaking. A claim of breach of fiduciary duty is basically a claim for negligence that involves a higher standard of care. In order to recover, one must show the existence of a duty on the part of the alleged wrongdoer not to subject such person to the injury complained of, a failure to observe such duty, and an injury proximately resulting therefrom. These principles support our conclusion that a contract may define the scope of fiduciary duties between parties to the contract.

Here, the injury complained of by appellant was, essentially, appellees competing with CHL and obtaining the NHL franchise. The operating agreement constitutes the undertaking of the parties herein. In becoming members of CHL, appellant and appellees agreed to abide by the terms of the operating agreement, and such agreement specifically allowed competition with the company by its members. As such, the duties created pursuant to such undertaking did not include a duty not to compete. Therefore, there was no duty on the part of appellees to refrain from subjecting appellant to the injury complained of herein.

"Operating agreement" is defined in R.C. 1705.01(J) as all of the valid written or oral agreements of the members as to the affairs of a limited liability company and the conduct of its business. R.C. 1705.03(C) sets forth various activities limited liability companies may engage in and indicates such are subject to the company's articles of organization or operating agreement. Indeed, many of the statutory provisions in R.C. Chapter 1705 governing limited liability companies indicate they are, in various ways, subject to and/or dependent upon related provisions in an operating agreement. . . . Here, the operating agreement states in its opening paragraph that it evidences the mutual agreement of the members in consideration of their contributions and promises to each other. Such agreement specifically allowed its members to compete with the company.

Given the above, we conclude as a matter of law that it was not a breach of fiduciary duty for appellees to form COLHOC and obtain an NHL franchise to the exclusion of CHL. In so concluding, we are not stating that no act related to such obtainment could be considered a breach of fiduciary duty. In general terms, members of limited liability companies owe one another the duty of utmost trust and loyalty. However, such general duty in this case must be considered in the context of members' ability, pursuant to operating agreement, to compete with the company.

Judgment affirmed in part and reversed in part.

BOWMAN, J., concurs.

PEGGY L. BRYANT, J., concurring in part and dissenting in part.

Notes and Questions

1. Reality Check

a. What was the main disagreement between the Hunt faction and the McConnell faction?

b. Was the court's result based more upon contract law or fiduciary duty law?

2. Suppose

a. If Hunt had not objected to the lease terms and if McConnell had obtained the franchise for COLHOC anyway, would the court's analysis and result have been the same?

b. Suppose the operating agreement had been silent about the members' duties toward one another? Would the analysis or result have differed?

c. Assume the operating agreement explicitly said that the members owed each other no fiduciary duties. Would the court have enforced that provision?

d. Assume the operating agreement explicitly said that the members owed each other the same fiduciary duties as partners in a general partnership? How would the court have analyzed this dispute?

3. What Do You Think?

a. Do you think the Hunt group or the McConnell group acted in a more inappropriate way? Both groups? Neither group?

b. Do you think this case is analogous to *Meinhard v. Salmon* in that a key issue is the scope of the enterprise? What are the differences between the two cases?

c. Do you think states should impose no fiduciary duties on LLC members as a default rule? If states should impose fiduciary duties on LLC members, how should those duties be defined? Do you think members should be able to contract out of some or all of such default duties?

The Delaware experience with default fiduciary duties in LLCs is illuminating both because of Delaware's importance in business entities laws and because of the rather public nature of the struggle to establish the appropriate rule. Then-Chancellor Strine summarized the situation as follows:

> The Delaware LLC Act does not plainly state that the traditional fiduciary duties of loyalty and care apply by default as to managers or members of a limited liability company. In that respect, of course, the LLC Act is not different than the DGCL, which does not do that either.
>
> The LLC Act is more explicit than the DGCL in making the equitable overlay mandatory. Specifically, §18-1104 of the LLC Act provides that "[i]n any case not provided for in this chapter, *the rules of law and equity*, including the law merchant, *shall govern*." (emphasis added). In this way, the LLC Act provides for a construct similar to that which is used in the corporate context. But unlike in the corporate context, the rules of equity apply in the LLC context *by statutory mandate*, creating an even stronger justification for application of fiduciary duties grounded in equity to managers of LLCs to the extent that such duties have not been altered or eliminated under the relevant LLC agreement.[34]

34. Section 18-1101(c) of the LLC Act provides: "*To the extent that, at law or in equity, a member or manager or other person has duties (including fiduciary duties)* to a limited liability company or to another member or manager or to another person that is a party to or is otherwise bound by a[n] [LLC] agreement, *the member's or manager's or other person's duties may be expanded or restricted or eliminated by provisions in the [LLC] agreement;* provided, that the [LLC] agreement may not eliminate the implied covenant of good faith and fair dealing." (emphasis added). Although §18-1101(c) allows parties to an LLC agreement to contract out of owing fiduciary duties to one another, the fact that these duties can be contractually avoided suggests that they exist by default in the first place. When read together, the most logical reading of §18-1104 and §18-1101(c) that results is that if, *i.e.,* "to the extent that," equity would traditionally make a manager or member a fiduciary owing fiduciary duties, then that manager or member *is* a fiduciary, subject to the express right of the parties to contract out of those duties. By contrast, if a member or manager would not be considered a fiduciary owing circumstantially-relevant duties under traditional equitable principles, then the member or manager is immune from fiduciary liability, not because of the statute, but because equity itself would not consider the member or manager to have case-relevant fiduciary duties. The "to the

It seems obvious that, under traditional principles of equity, a manager of an LLC would qualify as a fiduciary of that LLC and its members. Thus, because the LLC Act provides for principles of equity to apply, because LLC managers are clearly fiduciaries, and because fiduciaries owe the fiduciary duties of loyalty and care, the LLC Act starts with the default that managers of LLCs owe enforceable fiduciary duties.

This reading of the LLC Act is confirmed by the Act's own history. Before 2004, §18-1101(c) of the LLC Act provided that fiduciary duties, to the extent they existed, could only be "expanded or restricted" by the LLC agreement. Following our Supreme Court's holding in *Gotham Partners,*[41] . . . the General Assembly amended . . . [§18-1101(c)] to permit the "eliminat[ion]" of default fiduciary duties in an LLC agreement. [W]hy would the General Assembly amend the LLC Act to provide for the elimination of "something" if there were no "something" to eliminate in the first place? The fact that the legislature enacted these liability-limiting measures against the backdrop of case law holding that default fiduciary duties did apply in the LLC context, and seemed to have accepted the central thrust of those decisions to be correct, provides further weight to the position that default fiduciary duties do apply in the LLC context to the extent they are not contractually altered.

Thus, our cases have to date come to the following place based on the statute. The statute incorporates equitable principles. Those principles view the manager of an LLC as a fiduciary and subject the manager as a default principle to the core fiduciary duties of loyalty and care. But, the statute allows the parties to an LLC agreement to entirely supplant those default principles or to modify them in part.

Reasonable minds can debate whether it would be wise for the General Assembly to create a business entity in which the managers owe the investors no duties at all except as set forth in the statute and the governing agreement. Perhaps it would be, perhaps it would not. That is a policy judgment for the General Assembly. What seems certain is that the General Assembly, and the organs of the Bar who propose alteration of the statutes to them, know how to draft a clear statute to that effect and have yet to do so. The current LLC Act is quite different and promises investors that equity will provide the important default protections it always has, absent a contractual choice to tailor or eliminate that protection. Changing that promise is a job for the General Assembly, not this court.

Auriga Capital Corp. v. Gatz Properties, 40 A.3d 839, 849-52, 856 (Del. Ch. 2012) *aff'd* 59 A.3d 1206 (Del. 2012) (Strine, C.)

The Supreme Court of Delaware affirmed the result but chastised Vice Chancellor Strine for his speculations, finding,

[T]he merits of the issue whether the LLC statute does — or does not — impose default fiduciary duties is one about which reasonable minds could differ. Indeed, reasonable minds arguably could conclude that the statute [§18-1101(c)] — which begins with the phrase, "[t]*o the extent that,* at law or in equity, a member or manager or other person has duties (including fiduciary duties)" — is consciously ambiguous. That possibility suggests that the "organs of the Bar" (to use the trial court's phrase) may be well advised to consider urging the General Assembly to resolve any statutory ambiguity on this issue.

Gatz Properties LLC v. Auriga Capital Corp., 59 A.3d 1206, 1219 (Del. 2012)

The Delaware General Assembly wasted no time in responding to the courts' suggestion and amending the statue. Section 18-1104 now reads

In any case not provided for in this chapter, the rules of law and equity, including *the rules of law and equity relating to fiduciary duties* and the law merchant, shall govern. (added language italicized).

---

extent that" language makes clear that the statute does not itself impose some broader scope of fiduciary coverage than traditional principles of equity.

41. *Gotham Partners, L.P. v. Hallwood Realty Partners, L.P.,* 817 A.2d 160 (Del. 2002).

The legislative history states only that the amendment was intended "to confirm that in some circumstances fiduciary duties not explicitly provided for in the limited liability company agreement apply. For example, a manager of a manager-managed limited liability company would ordinarily have fiduciary duties even in the absence of a provision in the limited liability company agreement establishing such duties. Section 18-1101(c) continues to provide that such duties may be expanded, restricted or eliminated by the limited liability company agreement."

The nature and extent of fiduciary duties, if any, in an LLC is of course a necessary predicate to considering whether a member or manager has breached any duties. These issues are frequently litigated in the Delaware courts and Vice Chancellor Glasscock has synthesized the Delaware approach:

> Under the Delaware Limited Liability Company Act ("LLC Act") our Courts have implied fiduciary duties to managers of an LLC, unless contractually waived. This approach has been embodied in the LLC Act itself.[224] In other words, the intention of the parties to the agreement that fiduciary duties apply to managers is implied where that agreement does not provide otherwise. The LLC Act is explicitly contractarian, however, and permits the elimination of some, or all, fiduciary duties for members, managers or others through a provision in an LLC agreement, "provided, that the limited liability company agreement may not eliminate the implied contractual covenant of good faith and fair dealing."[225] Similarly, in the context of construing LLC agreements, this Court has recognized that "[a]lthough fiduciary duties may be disclaimed, agreements' drafters must do so clearly, and should not be incentivized to obfuscate or surprise investors by ambiguously stripping away the protections investors would ordinarily receive."[226] Thus, this Court has consistently found that removal of a manager's default fiduciary duties from an LLC agreement must be clear and unambiguous.

CelestialRX Investments, LLC v. Krivulka, 2017 WL 416990, at *16 (Del. Ch. Jan. 31, 2017) (Glasscock, V.C.).

Notes and Questions

1. Reality Check

a. You may find it helpful to your thinking to read the current version of the relevant Delaware LLC sections, which are set out in the You Draft It section below.

b. Did the Delaware LLC statute originally provide that fiduciary duties could be eliminated by the operating agreement? Does it provide for that possibility now?

c. What is the source or sources of fiduciary duties in Delaware LLCs?

d. What does the Delaware LLC statute currently provide in terms of default fiduciary duties and the power of the parties to modify or eliminate them?

e. Is it clear whether default fiduciary duties in Delaware LLCs apply to Managers in manager-managed LLCs? To Members in manager-managed LLCs? To Members in member-managed LLCs?

---

224. *See* H.B. 126, 147th Gen. Assemb. (Del. 2013) (amending [Del. LLC Act] §18-1104 to provide the following: "In any case not provided for in this chapter, the rules of law and equity, including the rules of law and equity relating to fiduciary duties and the law merchant, shall govern.").

225. [Del. LLC Act] §18-1101(c).

226. *Ross Holding & Mgmt. Co. v. Advance Realty Grp., LLC*, 2014 WL 4374261, at *15 (Del. Ch. Sept. 4, 2014).

2. Suppose

a. Assume that the LLC in *McConnell* was governed by the Delaware LLC statute. Would the court's analysis or the result have been different?

3. What Do You Think?

a. Why do you suppose Delaware, the most sophisticated state in terms of business entities law, had so much difficulty determining whether LLCs should have fiduciary duties by default?

b. Do you think that Chancellor Strine or the Supreme Court was correct?

c. Do you think Delaware has arrived at the correct rule for default fiduciary duties in LLCs? What rule would you advocate?

d. Do you think the General Assembly's amendment to §18-1104 accomplishes what the legislature intended? Is the language as clear as it should be?

4. You Draft It

a. Redraft the statutes so that it is clear that neither Members nor Managers have default fiduciary duties.

b. Redraft the statutes so that it is clear that Managers, but not Members, have default fiduciary duties.

c. Redraft the statutes so that it is clear that Members in member-managed LLCs and Managers in manager-managed LLCs have default fiduciary duties but that Members in manager-managed LLCs do not.

The statutes read,

> It is the policy of this chapter to give the maximum effect to the principle of freedom of contract and to the enforceability of limited liability company agreements.

6 Del. C. §18-1101(b)

> To the extent that, at law or in equity, a member or manager or other person has duties (including fiduciary duties) to a limited liability company or to another member or manager or to another person that is a party to or is otherwise bound by a limited liability company agreement, the member's or manager's or other person's duties may be expanded or restricted or eliminated by provisions in the limited liability company agreement; provided, that the limited liability company agreement may not eliminate the implied contractual covenant of good faith and fair dealing.

6 Del. C. §18-1101(c)

> In any case not provided for in this chapter, the rules of law and equity, including the rules of law and equity relating to fiduciary duties and the law merchant, shall govern.

6 Del. C. §18-1104

Putting It to Work

Problem 18-3

Skaterzzz (from Problem 18-2) needed to expand its manufacturing capability and was looking around for additional warehouse space to buy and convert to a new manufacturing plant. Shemp, Moe's nephew, owned a suitable warehouse and offered it to Skaterzzz. Moe, on behalf of Skaterzzz, entered into a written contract with Shemp to purchase the warehouse at a price about 15 percent above the fair market value.

a. If the operating agreement is silent as to fiduciary duties, has Moe breached his duties to Skaterzzz? Does your answer depend upon where Skaterzzz is formed? Assume that Skaterzzz is a Delaware LLC. Then assume that Skaterzzz is an Ohio LLC.

7. Dissolution

duty of loyalty

Dissolution means the end of the LLC as an entity. As with the dissolution of any other business entity, you must be careful to distinguish between the dissolution of the entity and the cessation of the business it operates. Generally, even when a business entity dissolves, its business continues and is sold or transferred as a going concern to another owner. In outline, when an LLC dissolves, it ceases to operate its business, its assets are disposed of (if the business is not transferred as a going concern, its assets may be sold off piecemeal), usually for cash, and the proceeds are applied to creditors' claims. If cash remains after the creditors have been satisfied, the members share it according to the statutory default rule or the operating agreement. If, as is much more typical, the LLC has insufficient money to satisfy the creditors, the entity usually files for bankruptcy, and the creditors divide the assets according to the federal bankruptcy laws, but cannot seek additional assets from the members.

Typically, LLC statutes provide for dissolution in three settings. The first is where all the members vote to dissolve. This provision might be invoked where the business is not as successful as the members had anticipated or where the parties have had a significant falling out with one another. The second setting is dissolution in accordance with the operating agreement. A common provision in the operating agreement is to require dissolution whenever approved by a majority (or often a supermajority) of members.

Some LLCs permit a single member or a minority of members to force the LLC's dissolution. This agreement is likely to occur in very small LLCs where each member is active and where each member's contribution is considered so important that the character of the LLC would be destroyed if the member left. Other operating agreements may specify that the LLC dissolves upon the expiration of a certain time period or upon the achievement of a particular event such as completing the business project for which the LLC was formed. Again, this is relatively unusual but not completely unknown. It is safe to say that most operating agreements today either provide that the LLC shall have perpetual existence (subject to the members' vote to dissolve) or are silent.

Third, LLC statutes provide that a court may order dissolution. As with dissolution of corporations, this power is equitable, which means that a petitioning party must not only show that the statutory requirements for dissolution are met but that justice would be best served by dissolution. The statutes usually provide for dissolution in three situations. An LLC's creditor may petition for dissolution. In effect, this action seeks to stop the LLC from continuing to do business. Second, any member (or in some states members holding at least 10% of the ownership interests) may petition for dissolution on the ground of illegality, waste, or oppression. Finally, such member or members may petition for dissolution on the ground that it is "not reasonably practicable" to continue the LLC. The reasons why it may no longer be reasonably practicable to carry on the business of the LLC tend to fall into three categories: (1) the relatively unusual setting in which the business becomes regulated or prohibited; (2) one or more of the members may have taken such actions that, while not constituting illegality, waste, or oppression, nonetheless make it impracticable to continue the business; and (3) the relationship between the parties may simply have deteriorated to the point where it is no longer reasonably practicable to carry on the LLC's business. In this final instance, dissolution is something in the nature of a "no fault" remedy.

Typically the persons charged with operating the LLC (whether members or managers) are charged with winding up the entity. If the parties are in substantial disagreement either over who may wind up the LLC or how the winding up should proceed, they may petition the court, which may either make rulings in the matter or, more frequently, appoint a receiver to oversee the winding up. Once the assets of the LLC have been reduced to cash, the statutes all require that creditor claims be satisfied in full before any cash is paid to the members. Members who are also LLC creditors are treated as creditors for this purpose, at least in the absence of unfairness. When the assets of the LLC are sufficient to satisfy the creditors in full and additional assets remain, the LLC statutes contain default rules for distributing the money to members. The statutes in most states provide that money be distributed first to satisfy distributions declared but not already paid. Second, money is distributed pro rata until each member's initial contribution is repaid. Finally, money is distributed pro rata in accordance with the LLC's profit allocation rule. In all states the operating agreement may vary the default rule but may not, of course, change the requirement that, in dissolution, creditors be satisfied in full before assets are distributed to members. A typical operating agreement variation is to provide that assets will be distributed strictly in accordance with the members' profit allocation, ignoring their capital contributions.

If there is insufficient cash to satisfy the creditors in full, a common occurrence, the members' limited liability means that the creditors bear the loss. As you might imagine, where the amount is sufficiently large, creditors will attempt to hold the members personally liable on one of three grounds. First is outright fraud, second is disregarding the entity (i.e., piercing the veil as in the *Puleo* case above), and third is failing to follow the statutory requirements for dissolution.

New Horizons Supply Coop. v. Haack
590 N.W.2d 282 (Wis. Ct. App. 1999)

Deininger, J.

BACKGROUND

On May 30, 1995, Haack signed a "CARDTROL AGREEMENT" whereby the "Patron" agreed "to be responsible for payment of all fuel purchased with" the "Cardtrol Card" issued under the agreement by a predecessor to New Horizons.

"Kickapoo Valley Freight, LLC" is shown as the "Patron" in the first paragraph of the form agreement, and it is signed by "Allison Haack," with no designation indicating whether her signature was given individually or in a representative capacity on behalf of Kickapoo Valley.

An employee of New Horizons testified at trial that in September 1997, when the Kickapoo Valley account was in arrears, she contacted Robert Koch about the bill. Koch referred her to his sister, Haack, who apparently took care of paying the bills for the company. When contacted, Haack told the New Horizons employee that she would start paying $100 per month on the account. When no payment was received in October, Haack was contacted again, and she then informed New Horizons that Kickapoo Valley had dissolved, "that she was . . . a partner, that Robert had moved out of state, and that she planned to assume responsibility and would again start to make a hundred dollars per month beginning in October." The employee also testified that during the October telephone conversation, Haack told her she had the assets of the business: a truck, which was secured by the bank; and some accounts receivable "that they were trying to collect." When contacted in November, Haack again promised a payment, but in December, Haack told the New Horizons employee "not to call her at work anymore."

When attempts to contact Haack at her home phone number proved unsuccessful, New Horizons commenced this action to collect the account balance, $1,009.99, from Haack "DBA KICKAPOO VALLEY FREIGHT." Haack testified that Kickapoo Valley had been organized as a limited liability company, but she did not introduce articles of organization or an operating agreement into evidence.[3] Haack did offer as exhibits a Wisconsin Department of Revenue registration certificate, as well as some correspondence from the department, showing the enterprise identified as "Kickapoo Valley Freight LLC." Haack stated her defense to New Horizons' claim was that the account was in the business name, that she was not personally liable for debts of the limited liability company, and that she had not personally guaranteed the obligation.[4]

According to Haack, her brother, Robert Koch, had suffered a nervous breakdown and left the state; the truck was sold, with all proceeds going to the bank who held the lien on it; and there were "no additional assets," but that she was "left with quite a lot of debt that I had signed for." She acknowledged that she told New Horizons that she "would try to take care" of the account "several times" after the business ceased operations. Finally, Haack testified that she had not filed articles of dissolution or notified creditors of the termination of the business when it ceased operations in the fall of 1997.

In response to questions from the court regarding her investment in the company, and the limits of her liability and that of Mr. Koch, Haack answered that both of them had "lost" their investments in the company. She also testified that the company was taxed as a partnership, and that she had with her copies of a sale agreement whereby "the assets" of the company were sold and the proceeds were

---

3. Haack testified that a Mount Horeb attorney had drafted and filed the necessary papers to establish Kickapoo Valley as a limited liability company, but that she did not receive copies of those documents. She also testified that she had drafted the operating agreement herself, but that she did not bring a copy of the operating agreement to court with her.

4. New Horizons' witness conceded on cross-examination that "I don't have a personal guarantee other than the signature on your agreement for purchases."

given to the bank in order to release the lien on the truck. None of those documents were introduced as exhibits, however, and they are not a part of the record. Haack later testified that the assets that were sold consisted of a "truck, a pallet jack and the customer list." She did not testify as to the disposition of any cash or accounts receivable remaining at the time the business was dissolved.

[W]e conclude that entry of judgment against Haack on the New Horizons' claim was proper because she failed to establish that she took appropriate steps to shield herself from liability for the company's debts following its dissolution and the distribution of its assets.

[A] fact-finder could have inferred from Haack's testimony and from her exhibits showing that the Department of Revenue apparently recognized Kickapoo Valley as a "LLC," that Haack and her brother had properly formed a limited liability company.

The record is devoid, however, of any evidence showing that appropriate steps were taken upon the dissolution of the company to shield its members from liability for the entity's obligations. [T]he order for distributing the company's assets following dissolution is fixed by statute, and the company's creditors enjoy first priority, see §183.0905, STATS. A dissolved limited liability company may "dispose of known claims against it" by filing articles of dissolution, and then providing written notice to its known creditors containing information regarding the filing of claims. See §183.0907, STATS. The testimony at trial indicates that Haack knew of New Horizons' claim at the time Kickapoo Valley was dissolved. It is also clear from the record that articles of dissolution for Kickapoo Valley Freight LLC were not filed, nor was the cooperative formally notified of a claim filing procedure or deadline.

Section 183.0909, Stats., provides in relevant part as follows:

> A claim not barred under §§183.0907 or 183.0908 may be enforced under this section against any of the following: . . .
> (2) If the dissolved limited liability company's assets have been distributed in liquidation, a member of the limited liability company to the extent of the member's proportionate share of the claim or to the extent of the assets of the limited liability company distributed to the member in liquidation, whichever is less, but a member's total liability for all claims under this section may not exceed the total value of assets distributed to the member in liquidation.

It appears from the record that certain of Kickapoo Valley's assets were sold, and that the proceeds from that sale were remitted to the bank which held a lien on the company's truck. There is nothing in the record, however, showing the disposition of other company assets, such as cash and accounts receivable. New Horizons' witness testified that, in October 1997, Haack had claimed to be attempting to collect the accounts of the dissolved company and hoped to pay the instant debt from those proceeds. We do not know the value of the accounts receivable in question, however, or the amounts of any other company debts to which the proceeds of the accounts may have been applied, because Haack presented no testimony on the issue.

In this regard, we agree with the trial court's comments regarding the lack of evidence in the record to show that Kickapoo Valley's affairs were properly wound up following its dissolution occasioned by Robert Koch's dissociation from the enterprise. Although Kickapoo Valley Freight LLC may have been properly formed and operated as an entity separate and distinct from its owners, Haack did not establish that she distributed the entity's assets in accordance with §183.0905, STATS., following Kickapoo's dissolution. Her failure to employ the procedures outlined in §§183.0906 and .0907, STATS., left her vulnerable to New Horizons' claim under §183.0909(2), STATS., absent proof that the value of any assets of the dissolved company she received were exceeded by the cooperative's claim.

Thus, although Haack correctly contends that the judgment cannot be sustained on the ground relied upon by the trial court, we "nevertheless . . . look to facts in the record 'in favor of respondent which [seem] to be insurmountable.'" *See State v. Alles*, 316 N.W.2d 378, 388-89 (1982) (citation omitted).

By the Court. — Judgment affirmed.

Notes and Questions

1. Note

a. The provision in the Wisconsin statute for shielding members from personal liability in dissolution by giving notice of dissolution to known creditors is a common one.

2. Reality Check

a. What assets did Kickapoo Valley possess? What became of them?

3. Suppose

a. Suppose Haack only received $500 in distributions from the LLC. How much could New Horizons Supply Cooperative have recovered?

4. What Do You Think?

a. While an LLC is operating as a going concern, its members have limited liability (subject to piercing, of course). When the LLC dissolves, though, members have limited liability only if they follow the notice procedure, as demonstrated in this case. Do you think the distinction between the two settings is justified? Why?

b. Because state statutes provide a method of imposing personal liability in dissolution settings where the entity does not notify known creditors (as in this case), do you think creditors of a dissolving LLC should be able to make piercing the veil arguments as well or do you think the statutory method should be exclusive?

c. Most states have a provision like the Wisconsin statute that limits members' personal liability where the dissolving LLC does not notify known creditors to the lesser of the creditor's claim or the amount distributed to the member. Do you think this statutory limit makes sense, especially given that personal liability under the piercing the veil theory is not limited?

C. FEDERAL SECURITIES REGULATION

If an ownership interest in an LLC is a security, then LLCs and their legal counsel must be concerned with the federal registration requirements (and various exemptions), the periodic reporting requirements for public companies, the federal regulation of proxy solicitations, and the antifraud provisions of SEC Rule 10b-5, among other legal issues. None of these problems applies, however, if LLC interests are not "securities." None of the federal statutes specifically names interests in LLCs as securities and no Supreme Court case has decided the question. The Supreme Court would almost certainly apply the test from *SEC v. W.J. Howey Co.*, 328 U.S. 293 (1946). Under the cases interpreting *Howey*, the court must decide whether there was (1) an investment of money, (2) in a common enterprise in which the investor was led to expect profits, (3) primarily from the efforts of the promoter or a third party. In analyzing LLCs under this test the key element will be the "efforts of the promoter or a third party." The *Howey* analysis for LLCs should be similar to that for general partnerships because the management structure of an LLC can vary, as it can in a partnership, from entities in which all members participate equally to entities in which all management power is delegated to a nonmember manager.

The principal case analyzing general partnerships under the securities laws is *Williamson v. Tucker*, 645 F.2d 404 (5th Cir.), *cert. denied*, 454 U.S. 897 (1981), in which the court held that a partnership interest is a security under *Howey* only if the investor can establish one of three elements:

1. That the agreement among the parties leaves so little management power in the investor's hands that the investor is analogous to a limited partner; or
2. The investor is so inexperienced and unknowledgeable in business affairs that he or she cannot intelligently exercise his or her managerial powers; or
3. The investor is so dependent upon some unique entrepreneurial or managerial talent of the promoter that the investor cannot replace the promoter or otherwise meaningfully exercise his or her managerial powers.

The few lower-court cases that have considered the question have applied the *Williamson* test to LLCs. In *Keith v. Black Diamond Advisors, Inc.*, 48 F. Supp. 2d 326 (S.D.N.Y. 1999), the court found that the investment in the LLC was not a security because the operating agreement provided for member management. In *SEC v. Parkersburg Wireless LLC*, 991 F. Supp. 6 (D.D.C. 1997), the court found that the investment in the LLC was a security because the investors could not, as a practical matter, exercise any significant management control.

D. TERMS OF ART IN THIS CHAPTER

Allocation	Limited liability company	Member
Dissolution	Manager	Member managed
Distribution	Manager managed	Operating agreement

Part V.
CHOICE OF FORM

19

Choice of Entity

This chapter covers a very practical question: What kind of entity should own a particular business? Too many practitioners have a very easy answer: an LLC. The problem is not that the answer is wrong, but that it isn't *always* right. The answer also is insidious because the disadvantageous consequences of choosing the wrong entity may not become apparent for years. For that reason lawyers believe that they can get away with making unthinking choices about the business entities that are appropriate for their clients' businesses.

There is another perennial answer to the choice of entity question: whatever the client wants. This answer is always "right" in that, except for illegality, a lawyer should effect the client's desires even when not in the client's best interest. Clients occasionally have eccentric views of the type of entity they desire for their businesses. When the client insists upon an inappropriate entity choice, you must make certain that the client understands the possible consequences of his or her choice. This is best done with a letter that spells out the scope of your engagement, the counsel you have given your client as to the appropriate form, and the fact that the client insists upon a different form.

Our approach in this chapter is straightforward. We will begin with the most salient considerations in choosing the appropriate business form. Then, we will explore a method for choosing the appropriate business form. Finally, we'll look at the "problem" of the plethora of entity forms.

I have been keeping something from you for several hundred pages now, and it's time you knew the truth. A corporation can be taxed in one of two ways for purposes of federal income tax. The shareholders of a corporation that has 100 or fewer shareholders and has one class of stock can unanimously elect to be taxed under Subchapter S of the Internal Revenue Code. Ingeniously, these entities are called "S corporations." Generally speaking, entities cannot be shareholders of S corporations. Further, shares of S corporation stock may differ as to voting rights but must be identical in other respects. Corporations whose shareholders have not elected, or could not elect, Subchapter S treatment are taxed under IRC Subchapter C. Throughout this chapter you may assume that a corporation is a C corporation unless otherwise stated.

A C corporation is taxed as a separate entity, just as individuals are, though there are differing rules for corporations and individuals. This means that income of a business owned by a corporation is taxed twice, once at the corporate level and again when the income is distributed to shareholders as dividends. Depending upon the relative rates of taxation, this *double taxation* characteristic can be extremely problematic or essentially a nuisance. By contrast, S corporations are not taxed separately. Rather, profits and losses are allocated directly to the shareholders who include those profits or losses on their own income tax returns. As we will see, this *pass-through taxation* is essentially similar to the way partnerships and most LLCs are taxed.

A. VARIABLE CHARACTERISTICS IMPORTANT IN CHOOSING AN ENTITY

It may not be obvious, but the criteria one uses in selecting an entity form are a function of the differences between the entities. If a particular characteristic is identical across every entity, it can't be a criterion for choosing between them. Thus the focus here is on characteristics that differ among the entities and that might make a practical difference to clients.

In this section we identify and organize the differences among business entities that may be important in deciding which entity is most appropriate for a particular new business. Many discussions of choice of entity issues divide these differences into tax issues and non-tax issues, but we will use a different thematic approach that recognizes that the important characteristics may concern the relationship between investors as well as the tax consequences of contemplated actions for the entity and for its investors.

We will start by looking at the differences most relevant to the initial organization of the entity. Many clients and their lawyers begin and end with these considerations without taking a longer view. Then we will look at the differences in operating the enterprise. We further divide these into financial operation and managerial operation. Finally, we look at the differences germane to transferring ownership interests in the entity.

1. Organizational Differences

The differences between entities in initial organization are few. When the entity's organization is more broadly conceived as encompassing the entity's financing, both at start-up and over time, then the differences are more important. Creating an entity and drafting the initial operative documents and side agreements takes about the same amount of lawyer and client time and money.

One of the major differences among forms has to do with the entity's capitalization. In general, any kind of entity can give the parties the mix of economic and managerial rights they desire. However, where the parties anticipate that within a few years they will solicit equity capital from more than about 20 others who will not be active in day-to-day management, then there are differences among the entities.

The only realistic ownership interest for such investors is stock in a corporation. Further, in many instances the parties' desire for differing managerial or financial rights may rule out an S corporation.

The other major difference among forms is that S corporations have restrictions on the number and kind of owners. These restrictions do not apply to the other forms.

2. Operational Differences

a. Financial

Business entities differ from one another in their financial operation in three ways. First, when planning the financial rights each investor will get, you may remember that shares of the same class or series of stock must be identical. So, all investors holding the same kind of shares will receive the same per-share right to dividends. Also, you may remember that shareholders purchasing stock contemporaneously must pay the same price per share. In effect, the economic rights a shareholder receives are proportional to his or her investment relative to that of other investors. While these rules ensure equal treatment of shareholders (proportionate to their shareholdings), they inhibit the planner's ability to tailor financial rights to each investor. By contrast, partnerships and LLCs need not make the investors' economic rights proportionate to their relative investment.[1]

The second financial difference is that the profits and losses of C corporations are recognized only by the entity, not by its shareholders. The profits and losses of S corporations, partnerships, and LLCs are allocated to their owners, pursuant to the owners' agreement. C corporation shareholders, then, do not recognize income until the corporation pays dividends, which gives the owners at least some control over the timing of their income. Owners of the other entities do not have such control over the timing of their income.

Finally, the entities vary as to the tax consequences of distribution of property or money from the entity to its owners. Remember, allocation means assigning profits or losses to owners; it is not synonymous with the distribution of assets to owners. Distributions by partnerships, S corporations, and LLCs, are generally not taxed because the owners have already paid tax when the profits were allocated to them. Dividends by C corporations are taxed as ordinary income to the shareholders. Further, a C corporation cannot allocate or "distribute" its losses to its shareholders. This means that shareholders of a C corporation that experiences losses cannot take advantage of those losses through reducing their own income, as partnership, S corporation, and LLC owners can.

---

1. You may remember that at the end of Chapter 17 we discussed partnership forms more exotic than the general and limited partnerships. Specifically, we adverted to the existence of limited liability partnerships (LLPs) and limited liability limited partnerships (LLLPs). Both forms are taxed as partnerships as LLCs are. Both also provide limited liability for all participants much like that afforded to LLC members and managers and to corporate shareholders. Be aware that the differences in limited liability provisions vary among the states. Also, some states treat LLCs as entities for state income tax purposes but not LLPs or LLLPs. Thus depending upon state law, LLPs and LLLPs are essentially equivalent to LLCs or may be different in important ways. Because, in general, LLPs and LLLPs are equivalent to LLCs, we will not mention them again.

b. Managerial

The differences in this area are not so much bright-line ones as practical differences in the default provisions. Generally, any kind of plan for allocating management power can be effected in any of the entities, although with varying degrees of ease and efficacy.

The division of managerial power between the entities must be very clear to you by now. In corporations, all power is in the board subject to an annual referendum of the shareholders. In partnerships, every partner has equal management power. In LLCs the default rule is the partnership model (although some states provide that default power is proportional to the capital contributed rather than per capita among the members). As with the financial operation of the entity, disparate treatment of the parties, especially treatment that is not proportional to the amount invested, is easier to accomplish in noncorporate entities.

The entities also vary in the default power of an owner to bind the enterprise in the absence of actual authority. Shareholders have no power to bind the corporation but every partner is an agent of the partnership and can bind the partnership even beyond the partnership's business if the action is consistent with the kind of business in which the partnership is engaged. *See* UPA §301. LLC members have the same presumptive power to bind the entity as partners do, but that presumption may be more easily overcome in the LLC setting because (a) there's no equivalent of section 301 expansion of authority beyond the actual business conducted by the entity, and (b) many LLCs are manager managed so a third party's expectations should be different as to members than as to partners.

Perhaps the most salient difference between the entities is in the personal liability of owners. General partners are jointly and severally liable for the entity's debts.[2] Limited liability exists in varying degrees in the other entities. Shareholders are not liable for the corporation's debts in the absence of piercing the corporate veil settings. Limited partners are similarly not liable for a limited partnership's debts. Members' limited liability is the same as that of shareholders or limited partners, but the settings in which the entity will be pierced are more uncertain. Some state statutes explicitly provide that corporate piercing doctrine be applied to LLCs. Other statutes are silent and little case law exists at present. We looked at this issue in Chapter 18.

Many planners view limited liability in start-up businesses as an illusory quality because creditors (either lenders of capital or trade creditors) will typically require the principals to agree to personal liability as a condition of extending credit. Nonetheless, where the enterprise is likely to face tort claims rather than contract claims, limited liability is a genuine distinction between the forms.

3. Differences Regarding Transferred Ownership Interest

Here again the primary non-tax differences between the forms are not typically mandatory provisions but rather default rules that can be altered more or less

---

2. Where the partners are not individuals but rather limited liability entities, there may be no human who is personally liable. Still, the principle is the same.

satisfactorily. The tax consequences of transfer are significantly different among the forms, however, and cannot be completely eliminated.

Stock is freely alienable unless the Articles of Incorporation provide otherwise. The transferee has complete ownership of the shares and the transferor retains none. Further, the shareholders themselves may have contracted to restrict the transferability of shares. Remember, however, that an agreement that separates the economic interest from the managerial interest may be invalid if the result is a voting trust that does not comply with the statute.

A companion issue to transferability is that of *guaranteed exit*. That is, do owners have a right to relinquish their ownership interest at will and receive money from the entity? Stock can be made redeemable, but at least some stock must not be redeemable or callable. Again, the parties may contract to purchase an owner's interest in certain settings but in the absence of such agreements a shareholder has no guaranteed exit.

Only the economic portion of a partnership or LLC interest is freely transferable. The management portion remains with the original partner or member. Further, even though a partner has transferred all his or her economic interest, he or she remains personally liable for the partnership's liabilities. The transferee does not become a partner or member but merely has certain economic rights in the entity. In both the partnership and LLC setting, the parties can agree that an owner's full interest may be transferred and may also provide that such new owner automatically becomes a partner or member. Especially in the partnership context, however, such provisions would be unusual because of the intertwined nature of partners' interests. As to exit, the default partnership (and under some LLC statutes) rule is that a partner or member may dissociate at any time and receive the value of his or her ownership interest in cash, unless the dissociation was wrongful. That is, partners and possibly members have guaranteed exit. This rule is frequently but not always negated by agreement among the parties.

The differing tax consequences of ownership transfer among the entities make this area particularly important. The tax consequences of stock are easy. Such transfer has no effect on the corporation or other stockholders. The transferor recognizes gain or loss and the transferee's basis is the fair value of the stock at the time of transfer. Dividends are recognized as income by the stock's owner on the record date; this bright-line rule makes it easy to know whether the transferor or transferee receives the gain. If the entity is an S corporation, the buyer and seller prorate the year's profits and losses.

Partnership and LLC transfers raise much more complex issues. The entity and thus the other owners are affected as well as the buyer and seller. To give you just an outline of the difficulties, imagine a partnership or LLC with four equal owners. The entity has one asset, which was purchased for (i.e., the entity's basis is) $100,000. Several years later the asset's value is $1.1 million. One owner transfers his or her entire financial interest for fair value to a new owner for $275,000. The transferor has a capital gain of $250,000 (i.e., $275,000 consideration less $25,000 basis). If the entity now sells the asset for $1.1 million, each partner has income of $250,000 (one-fourth of the $1 million gain). This is unfair to the new owner who just paid $275,000 for an asset (the ownership interest) worth $275,000. The new owner's basis should be $275,000 rather than $25,000. This is called an "inside basis" problem and the Internal Revenue Code permits the partnership to solve the problem by letting the new owner (but not the continuing owners) increase ("step up") his or her basis to $275,000. Thus on the sale the three original owners have income of $250,000 and the new owner has no income. If the entity is anticipating many transfers of ownership interests, keeping track of the owners' differing bases quickly becomes a nightmare. As a practical matter, then, a partnership or LLC is infeasible for entities in which there are likely to be many changes of ownership.

B. HOW TO CHOOSE THE APPROPRIATE ENTITY

Having surfaced the important differences among the various business entities, we now come to choosing the most appropriate entity for a particular business, recognizing that no entity may be perfect. What follows is one protocol for achieving the goal. Among the information you will want to obtain from your clients, the questions that bear on the choice of entity can be divided into those that require or eliminate certain forms and those that only militate toward or away from certain forms. As you gather this information you might want to press your clients particularly hard about their answers to ensure they understand the consequences of their preferences. You should be aware that state and local regulations might change this protocol. For example, some states treat all LLCs as entities for income tax purposes rather than following the federal default rule of pass-through taxation. Another common variation among states is in the kind of limitations on liability that partners in LLPs enjoy. Thus you must be particularly attentive to the vagaries of the jurisdiction in which you practice.

Client choices that require or eliminate certain forms:

Will the owners be restricted to 100 or fewer individuals (or certain trusts)?

If not, an S corporation is unavailable.

Is it important to control the timing of income receipt and recognition for the owners? Relatedly, is income anticipated with such certainty and magnitude that the timing question is genuinely important?

If so, a C corporation or LLC electing to be taxed under Subchapter C is required.

Is it important for the owners to recognize losses? Relatedly, are losses anticipated with such certainty and at such a magnitude that the question of recognizing losses is genuinely important?

If so, an S corporation, partnership or LLC is required.

Is the possibility of uninsurable tort liability such that the owners must be protected from personal liability?

If so, a partnership is unavailable.

Do the owners anticipate that there will be multiple transfers of ownership interests?

If so, a corporation or LLC electing to be taxed under Subchapter C are the only realistic entities.

Client choices that militate toward or away from certain forms:

Do the owners anticipate raising capital from many owners?

If so, a C corporation or LLC electing to be taxed under Subchapter C is more appropriate.

Do the owners anticipate that their financial rights will not be proportional to their investment or managerial interests?

If so, a partnership or LLC is more appropriate.

Will management of the entity be permanently allocated with little or no owner power to change that management?

If so, a limited partnership or LLC is more appropriate.

Will management of the entity be allocated with some (e.g., annual) owner power to change that management?

If so, a corporation or LLC is more appropriate.

Will management of the entity be shared among the owners?

If so, a partnership or LLC is more appropriate.

Will the owners have the power to bind the entity?

If so, a partnership or LLC is more appropriate. If not, a corporation is more appropriate.

Is free transferability of economic and managerial ownership important?

If so, a corporation is more appropriate.

Do the owners want to ensure they may exit the business?

If so, a general partnership or LLC is more appropriate.

Putting It to Work

Problem 19-1

Adrenaline-junkie triplets Sara, Sandy, and SierraDel are interested in forming a new business venture where yoga enthusiasts can take their practice to the next level by meditating while skydiving. While yoga enthusiasts are generally healthier than people in the general population, the combination of yoga and skydiving is riskier than skydiving because the participants may become so focused that they forget to pull the ripcord. The sisters have found that no insurance company will insure their new business.

The triplets come to you to advise them on which type of entity to form and are eager to get started. However, they bring you the following bits of information that may influence your legal advice:

a. SierraDel, independently wealthy through savvy stock investments, is willing to put up all the capital but does not want to receive an income. Too much personal income for the year would negatively affect her for tax purposes. She will be content to sell her share of the enterprise down the road when the business has become wildly successful.

b. Sara, not wealthy in the least, is certified as both a yoga instructor and a skydiving instructor and is the obvious choice to run the day-to-day business. She will need to receive money from the business from the beginning to keep her life comfortable.

c. Sandy has planned the business model with one airplane and one instructor but she anticipates an intense market for this innovative extreme sport. She believes that the business will need to expand in three years and hopes to gain publicity as soon as they get the business up and running. Even better, Sandy hopes to attract venture capitalists as investors in the next year or two, with the goal of taking the company public in five years.

d. The sisters have a ne'er-do-well brother whom their parents have insisted the sisters "take care of." In an effort to keep their parents from strong-arming them into bringing their brother into the business venture, they would like to have strong restrictions on transfers of ownership.

What kind of business entity would you suggest the triplets form? How do the sisters' concerns influence your decision?

C. FIXING THE PROBLEM

OK, *what* problem? The "problem" of too many, and too indistinct, entities. As you know, until the mid-1990s corporations, general partnerships, and limited partnerships were the only significant entity choices. More important, the differences between the entities were not amenable to significant amelioration. With the spread of the LLC and, to a lesser extent the LLP and LLLP, and with the increased power of planners to vary entity default rules, the current system evolved.

But the current system need not persist. In recent years academics and thoughtful practitioners have focused on the question whether the current system is desirable and, if not, how it might be changed. Below are observations from two of the most thoughtful commentators. The first article describes the landscape of entities and suggests reform.

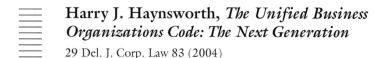

Harry J. Haynsworth, *The Unified Business Organizations Code: The Next Generation*
29 Del. J. Corp. Law 83 (2004)

In 1990 only two states had statutes authorizing LLCs. By the end of 1996, all fifty states and the District of Columbia had LLC statutes. In 2002, forty percent of all new businesses in the United States were formed as LLCs and in at least twenty-eight states more LLCs than corporations were formed. In the period between 2000 and 2002, the number of new businesses formed as corporations declined from fifty-nine percent in 2000 to forty-eight percent in 2002.

The increase in the number of business forms is bewildering to practicing lawyers, judges, law professors, and legislators. Almost every year, a new type of entity or a major revision to an existing business organization statute is promulgated or enacted. Frequently, the cause of the statutory modifications have been precipitated by changes in federal tax law. LLC legislation in the 1990s is an example. In 1996 the IRS approved the so-called check-the-box regulations which eliminated many of the prior requirements necessary for partnership taxation. This change was followed by [a] nationwide flurry of LLC statutory amendments.

The differences between the various state business organization statutes are significant and the problems resulting from these differences are growing. In many respects, Delaware is ahead of most states in trying to maintain reasonable consistency between the statutory provisions that govern each type of organizational format. When a change is made in one business entity statute, the practice in Delaware is to enact parallel statutory language in all the other business entity statutes that have similar provisions. This is not an easy task because the various statutory provisions are currently in four separate titles of the Delaware Code.

The Model Business Corporation Act (MBCA), which also includes special supplements for close corporations and professional corporations, has been amended extensively in the past twenty years to take into account developments in corporate law. Approximately twenty-four states have adopted all or substantially all of the MBCA. Most of the Model Act states have not, however, adopted all the various amendments to the Model Act approved by the ABA Committee on Corporate Laws. Twenty-nine states adopted the 1964 version of the Model Nonprofit Corporation Act but only two states have adopted the 1987 Revised Model Nonprofit Corporation Act.

The National Conference of Commissioners on Uniform State Laws, which has traditionally drafted uniform acts governing unincorporated organizations, has promulgated new versions of the Uniform Partnership Act and the Uniform Limited Partnership Act and has approved two new uniform unincorporated organizations acts in the past decade. The Revised Uniform Partnership Act . . . was approved in 1997. It has been adopted in thirty states including Delaware . . . but the remaining states still have the 1914 version of the Uniform Partnership Act. The Uniform Limited Partnership Act . . . was extensively revised and reapproved in 2001. Most states, however, still have the 1985 version of the ULPA. The two new uniform acts governing unincorporated organizations are the Uniform Limited Liability Company Act (1996), adopted in eight states, and the Uniform Unincorporated Nonprofit Association Act (1996), adopted in ten states.

Not only has the enactment of the recently promulgated uniform unincorporated organization acts been spotty, but these acts also contain material differences in wording for similar provisions. Some of the states that have enacted them have made significant non-uniform amendments, many of which may have unintended adverse consequences that can create traps for the unwary.

The lack of uniformity in style, format and substance is particularly acute with respect to limited liability company legislation. In many cases, amendments that fundamentally change the basic rights of the LLC members have been enacted at the insistence of a small group of lawyers. Several states, for example, have amended their statutes at the request of estate planning lawyers to provide that a member cannot sell or dispose of his or her interest unless the operating agreement otherwise provides. This will supposedly reduce the valuation of ownership interests with resulting favorable tax consequences for inter-family transfers of LLC ownership interests. The Uniform Limited Liability Company Act, however, which uses the Uniform Partnership Act as its model, provides that a member can dispose of his or her economic interest (but not the governance rights) unless otherwise agreed in the operating agreement. In states that have adopted the no-exit default rule, a serious trap for the unwary lawyer who might assume that because LLC statutes are based on a partnership model the partnership exit rights, or something similar, can exist. The lock-in created by this change in the default exit rule can lead to the same problems that have faced minority shareholders in closely held corporations who have no market for their shares. Most corporate codes, however, now contain involuntary dissolution provisions and buy-out rights that provide reasonable remedies from arbitrary and oppressive action by the minority shareholders. Members of LLCs in states that have the no-exit default rule may not, however, have these same exit rights, unless the lawyer representing the members is astute enough to draft them in the operating agreement.

My suggestion for reform is to create a unified business organizations code. The idea of a unified business organizations code is not new. The perplexing question has always been what such a code would look like. At one extreme are hub-and-spoke proposals that would attempt to eliminate all the non-essential differences between the various organizational forms leaving a single formulation for each major element, for example, the fiduciary duties of equity owners. The end result would presumably be a business organizations code having a large core that applied to all the various forms and separate rather short chapters for each of the different forms that continue to exist. Another type of hub-and-spoke proposal seeks to harmonize and compile all of the common basically administrative provisions in the various organizational statutes such as definitions, filing of documents, and other formalities of formation, permissible names, purposes and powers, required records and inspection rights, registered agents and registered offices, service of process, indemnification, registration of foreign entities and the administrative powers of the Secretary of State in one article of the unified code and then have separate articles for each of the organizational forms. These articles would be basically the same as before consolidation into a single code, except for the omission of definitions and other provisions that would be moved to the general provisions article. The basic difference between these two hub-and-spoke proposals is in the amount and scope of material that is in the hub.

Other proposals for a unified code have focused on eliminating some of the existing forms. These proposals generally advocate retaining the traditional corporate code designed for large, publicly held corporations, and a separate code for small or closely held businesses with limited liability for the equity owners, broad contractual flexibility for matters relating to the owners rights inter se, and pass-through tax consequences.

The plethora of new business entity forms in recent years has spawned renewed interest in this approach.

A legitimate question that might be asked is: if all existing businesses can continue to operate under the statutes governing them before the new consolidated code was adopted, what positive purpose does the new code serve? The most logical response is that the new code will govern all new businesses established after it is enacted, and if it truly meets their needs, most, if not all, of the existing businesses will, over a period of time, convert to the new form or forms. This conversion process, however, could take innumerable years.

A counter argument is that a great deal of convergence of the various forms has already taken place and the consolidation code will speed up a process that is well underway. Therefore, the conversion and transition issues may not be that difficult to resolve. The proponents of this line of reasoning will point to the many cases where courts have applied partnership fiduciary duty principles to close corporations on the basis that they are really partnerships in a corporate form. Many state corporate codes also specifically authorize shareholder management agreements that can allow shareholders in a close corporation to eliminate the board of directors and have a management system similar to a partnership. Moreover, many partnership and limited liability company acts increasingly contain provisions formerly found only in corporate codes.

The convergence that has taken place, however, is not necessarily a good thing. For example, the attempt to apply partnership fiduciary duties to close corporations has not been universally praised as a positive development. More importantly, convergence does not necessarily lead to consolidation. In short, convergence may occur while leaving all the various business forms intact.

A more telling argument against eliminating one or more of the existing organizational forms is the fact that the business organization marketplace provides empirical evidence of the demand for each of the existing forms. The number of limited partnerships, for instance, continues to increase despite the growing popularity of limited liability companies. Moreover, corporations, including close corporations, continue to be formed at a somewhat reduced but nevertheless brisk rate.

Another argument against undertaking a business organizations code with the objective of elimination of some of the existing organizational formats is the role federal tax policy has played in the development of the various types of business organizations. The rapid development of limited liability companies after . . . authorizing limited liability companies to be taxed as partnerships is only the most recent example.

Finally, statutes and regulations other than tax law also impact on the choice of business form decision. Some states prohibit certain types of businesses from operating in a particular form. In Oklahoma, for example, it is not permissible for a liquor store to operate as an LLC. Moreover, regulations of professional firms in many states may make one type of organizational format either more or less desirable than other possible forms. There are many other state and federal statutes that can have major impact on which organization form best fits the needs of a particular business. The elimination of one or more forms could have the unintended consequence of causing significant adverse regulatory problems for existing businesses that have been organized in a format that complies with (or successfully avoids) these regulations.

Notes and Questions

1. Reality Check

a. Why is entity reform necessary?
b. What are the arguments against entity reform?
c. What is Dean Haynsworth's vision for reform?

2. Suppose

a. Suppose entity rationalization became a reality. Would this book be 400 pages shorter? Would this course have two fewer credits?

3. What Do You Think?

a. Why have so many different business entities developed?
b. Do you think entity reform is necessary or desirable?
c. Is Dean Haynsworth's vision realistic?

≡ **Richard A. Booth,** *Form and Function in*
≡ *Business Organizations*
≡ 58 Bus. Law. 1433 (2003)

Lawyers and academics who deal with the law of business organizations on a regular basis tend to minimize the differences between partnerships, corporations, and other forms of business organization. It is possible — perhaps even quite easy — to set up a corporation that works like a partnership or a partnership that works like a corporation. Some of us even question whether the law matters in this realm other than in connection with taxes — and now it may not matter much there. The question that naturally arises is why not get rid of this ever expanding alphabet soup of corporations, partnerships, limited partnerships, limited liability companies (LLCs), . . . and replace it with a unified system? In other words, is it not time for entity rationalization?

The standard response is that not every lawyer specializes in the law of business organizations. Indeed, not everyone who sets up a business organization is a lawyer. In other words, there are certain efficiencies inherent in off-the-rack forms of organization. Standard form firms reduce transaction costs and therefore make it cheaper and easier to form a business. Standard form firms mean that it is not necessary to reinvent the wheel every time one forms a business organization.

This answer — which might well be the first to occur to most lawyers — is strikingly parochial. It assumes that law is for lawyers in that it focuses on the convenience of those who design business organizations. But what about those who work with or within the structure of a corporation or partnership? How are they affected by the difference in structures? Does it matter to a junior partner or a lower level officer in a corporation that he or she is working in a partnership or corporation? And what about investors, suppliers, and customers? Does it matter to them whether they deal with a corporation or partnership?

It seems clear that there are fundamental differences between forms. Viewed from within, a corporation is a hierarchy with the chief executive officer (CEO) at the top of the pyramid. It is essentially a vertical form of organization. A partnership, on the other hand, is basically a horizontal form of organization. Of course, most businesses are somewhat mixed. Division heads within a corporation may have considerable freedom. And a managing partner may have considerable authority. It seems clear, however, that those within an organization may have a strong preference for one form or the other, and that one form or the other may be better for certain lines of business. For example, banks, investment banks, and brokerage firms were once invariably partnerships. Now they are primarily corporations, but many are still essentially partner-owned as a result of massive stock option plans. Law firms are still primarily partnerships. . . . Accounting firms have become more like corporations. And medical practices have become even more like corporations with the advent of health maintenance organizations. There are also examples of migration in the other direction. [T]he heavy use of stock options as compensation in technology firms, together with the relatively small percentage of shares typically offered to the public, is . . . reminiscent of a partnership. These examples all suggest that choice of form may affect the culture of a firm, and indeed that choosing the wrong form or mixing and matching elements may be harmful.

Why do people choose the business forms that they do? And why do they modify some default rules but not others? Presumably, one would want to know the answer before tinkering too much with existing forms as they have evolved over the years. To be sure, I assume here that entity rationalization means simplification to some degree and not just codification. I do not necessarily assume that the goal of entity rationalization is a single form of organization. My point is that even if entity rationalization only involves the designation of certain features of the law or procedures that will be common to all forms of organization, we need to be sure that those features are not linked in some special way to other form-specific features. On the other hand, if entity rationalization means that businesspeople will have more choice (generally a good thing), we need to think about what we should do (if anything) to steer them away from choices that, like certain drugs, may not interact well with each other.

WHY PEOPLE FORM FIRMS

Before attempting to answer this question, one must deal with a still more fundamental question. Who cares? Why does it matter? Is it not enough simply to observe that people do form firms, whatever the reason may be? The answer is that if individuals form firms for a variety of reasons, it may be appropriate to have a variety of forms. Moreover, we should not limit our focus to formation. An equally important question is why do people join firms? Some forms of organization may be more attractive to recruits than others.

I have identified at least five general reasons: (i) delegation and specialization, (ii) diversification, (iii) separation and legitimacy, (iv) managing competition, and (v) discipline and incentives. There may be more.

Delegation and Specialization

People often retain agents because they do not have the time or expertise to conduct their own business. In other words, it may be cheaper to hire someone to do some tasks than it is to do them yourself, whether in terms of out-of-pocket expenses or in terms of opportunity costs. And if you need someone to perform a particular task repeatedly, it may be cheaper still to hire one or more employees.

But why would an employee take a job in such a pyramid scheme in which the employer keeps the profits? One answer is that a firm may be able to generate more business opportunities than could a self-employed individual. Moreover, the firm may have other resources or tools that the employee needs in order to do the work — tools that the employee could not afford to acquire individually.

Diversification

[P]articipants in a firm may also benefit from diversification in a variety of ways. A firm may be able to generate a more regular stream of business opportunities than could an individual. Also, the firm may be able to smooth out the income stream for individuals. Similarly, by joining a firm, one may be able to call on others to fill in if one is too busy or even simply to manage one's schedule and get in a round of golf. A firm may also provide a form of insurance by absorbing the costs of accidents through vicarious liability.

Separation and Legitimacy

In some cases, people form a firm simply to separate business from self. Of course, one of the primary motivations here is limited liability and the insulation of assets from unrelated liabilities. But limited liability aside, forming a corporation (for example) may give the business more legitimacy than doing business under one's own name as a sole proprietor. It suggests to the world that the business is something more than (and different from) the individual who owns it. And indeed this separation of business from participants is what allows a corporation to raise equity capital from outside investors.

A related, but somewhat more substantial reason for forming a firm is that when two or more people have joined together to conduct a business, it suggests that the business may be better thought out and therefore more trustworthy than a business that has been started by a single individual who may have idiosyncratic ideas. Similarly, it may be easier to attract others to join a firm than it is to retain the services of an independent contractor or free-lance agent to provide some needed input. Or association with a firm may add value to an agent's contribution. My basic point here is that there is a tendency to view firms primarily in terms of internal control structure. But external appearance may also matter. To sum up, people sometimes form firms simply to gain status for the enterprise or to define status to the world.

Managing Competition

In some cases, people form firms to reduce competition. In other words, two or more competitors might form a partnership in order to split the available profits, while saving the costs of competing (such as advertising). Of course, by eliminating competition, a firm may also be able to raise prices or restrict output. Although this may be illegal under the antitrust laws for very large businesses, it is fairly clear that it is an important reason for some smaller businesses. Whatever one might think of such tactics, and whether or not such agreements are ultimately enforceable, it is quite clear that non-competition is a motive. In any event, it is far easier to achieve the same result by forming a firm. . . .

Although it is clear that businesspeople might form a firm to reduce competition, it is also possible that forming a firm may increase competition. In some cases, consumers are more likely to seek out a department store or supermarket than a boutique or specialty shop. Of course, the opposite is true as well. The point is that a firm with a wider array of products and services may sometimes be more attractive to consumers. Or the firm may serve to concentrate talent in such a way that it produces a better product. For example, a law firm (or a law faculty for that matter) may produce better services or written product because the various members are able to have their work reviewed, checked, or commented on by others.

Discipline and Incentives

One final motivation for forming a firm (or joining one) is that association with a group may generate additional motivation, perhaps particularly for people who are not self-starters. In other words, it may be that people form or join firms to force themselves to work harder or to impose discipline that may be difficult to self-impose.

To sum up, there are several distinct reasons why people form firms. Curiously, most of those reasons seem to turn more on the relationship of active participants to each other or on the relationship of the firm to various third parties (including creditors), than on the relationship between participants and investors. Of course, investors are interested in how well managers work with each other, but not too interested. A diversified investor cares little about the fortunes of individual companies. It may be, therefore, that we lawyers, judges, and academics have given short shrift to how well the rules work for those who toil day to day in the trenches of partnerships and corporations. Moreover, the recent spate of corporate scandals strongly suggests we should focus more on internal controls than we have in the past, particularly in connection with firms that do not have a large, involved shareholder. External monitors may not be nearly as important as we have made them out to be.

Does Form Follow Function?

The fact that there seem to be several discrete reasons for forming firms suggests the possibility that there may be a need for several discrete firm forms or — assuming complete freedom of contract — that several distinct forms are likely to evolve.

In summary, . . . if one were to eliminate the arguably artificial incentives of limited liability and differing tax treatment from the mix of reasons for choosing a particular form, there would still be good reasons for choosing one form over another.

It almost goes without saying that managers and investors may have a distinct preference for one form over another. Indeed, most people would likely say that organization law is primarily about the relationship between investors and managers. But suppliers and customers may also care about organizational form. In other words, it also seems quite possible that third parties may have a preference for dealing with a particular kind of firm.

It is difficult to believe that an entrepreneur does not think about how choice of entity will help the business succeed. Indeed, many say that venture capital firms prefer to deal with corporations. Although there are several technical reasons offered for this preference (such as worries about unrelated business income for nonprofit investors), most have been debunked. In the end, however, it may be that investors are simply worried that there may be too many surprises lurking in the customized structure of alternative forms such as LLCs. Thus, it may be that one function of the corporate form is to provide a more or less standardized package of rights (or at least parameters) that can be more easily and reliably understood by potential investors and other third parties. As it turns out, this is nothing new. The stock exchanges have always imposed listing standards, presumably for similar reasons. And recent events notwithstanding, one of the essential functions of generally accepted accounting principles (GAAP) is to foster comparability across companies. Although one might question the need for standardization, it seems clear that in a world of innumerable investment opportunities, a firm can compete better for capital if it is more easily understood by potential investors. In other words, it costs less for investors to invest in a familiar form of organization. That is not to say that a new control feature of some sort might not be attractive and indeed afford the firm an edge from time to time. But that does not mean that it makes sense to reinvent the wheel with every deal. Boilerplate has its value.

There is probably less bureaucracy in a partnership and more choice of who will handle your business. Indeed, it is clear in a partnership that each partner has the authority to bind the firm. With a corporation, on the other hand, there is an ultimate authority and it is fairly clear that all of the assets of the business are pledged in connection with each transaction undertaken. As I have argued elsewhere, the ultimate rationale for limited liability is that it facilitates bargaining with creditors. In the absence of limited liability, entrepreneurs would be presumed to risk all of their wealth in connection with each and every venture. With limited liability, an entrepreneur must agree to assume any risk beyond her investment in the venture. In other words, creditors are forced to negotiate for additional security.

IMPLICATIONS FOR ENTITY RATIONALIZATION

The fact that form follows function and the fact that certain features of organization law tend to be found together, living in symbiosis as it were, suggest that firm form matters. But the fact that discrete forms exist and persist does not necessarily imply that we should maintain rigid or even prototypical firm forms. And it certainly does not imply that we should return to the days of mandatory rules and the traditional corporate norm. After all, businesspeople and business lawyers might easily negotiate their way to the proper combinations even in the absence of a statute. Perhaps it would be more efficient for the law to provide a menu of provisions from which the parties may choose, though it is unclear whether such a creature would be a statute or law in any traditional sense.

On the other hand, if organization law is essentially contractual, then why do we need it at all? Although it may be somewhat extreme to suggest the repeal of organization law altogether, it is not self-evident that we should bother to rationalize the system. It is not clear that these contracts are any more important than others. For example, franchising is an important form of business organization, but there is no general franchise law designed to relieve the parties of the need to specify the terms. For some reason, the law leaves franchising almost entirely to negotiation, albeit a rather one-sided negotiation. Then again there are many forms of contractual arrangements that are the subject of fairly elaborate efforts to set down some standard terms, for example, the Uniform Commercial Code (UCC) and the *Restatement of Agency*. It bears noting that neither of these emanated in the first instance from a governmental authority. Both were the work of the American Law Institute (ALI), and the UCC was a joint effort with the National Conference of Commissioners on Uniform State Laws (NCCUSL). Similarly, most jurisdictions have standard forms for very common contracts, such as retaining a real estate broker or conveying residential real estate. So it may be that rationalization will come not from above but from convention. Or it may be that the first authoritative source of law tends to remain authoritative. Why does the law come from so many different sources and take so many different forms? What belongs in a statute and what should be left to contract? Organization law itself comes from multiple sources: state law, federal law, the American Bar Association (ABA), NCCUSL, the ALI, the various stock exchanges, and maybe even the Financial Accounting Standards Board (FASB). Undoubtedly, we should think hard about why a particular rule comes from a particular authority before we undertake to rationalize the system.

The ultimate question, however, is why do we have organization law at all? The easy answer is that it is cheap and convenient. But that is not a good enough answer. If it were, then no one would object to the notion that it is essentially a contract that may be varied at will. There are at least two ways in which organization law differs from a simple standard form contract.

First, organization law provides a set of default rules for individuals who fail to plan. This may be a good enough reason to worry about getting it right. Indeed, the common law of partnerships and later corporations, from which modern statutory law evolved, was (by definition) all about controversies, that is, sorting out the rights of various business constituencies. Statutes arose slowly and section by section as various common controversies were settled by legislative fiat. It is important to remember also that failure to plan may be intentional. Business people often fail to plan because they sense that they are unlikely to reach an agreement with each other or because it is just too expensive to specify each detail. Thus, choosing a form is about choosing the preferred set of default rules. In addition, organization law may also be about reserving power to change these complex contracts without renegotiation among parties, whether by changing the law, or effectively agreeing to have the courts supply the missing terms through such vague concepts as fiduciary duty. The courts have traditionally been very reluctant to reform contracts except in the context of mutual mistake, and even then it is more likely that the contract will be voided. To be sure, contract law generally implies a duty of good faith. RUPA now explicitly incorporates a duty of good faith among partners. And corporation case law has recognized a duty of good faith. But the duty of good faith has seldom made a difference even though it has been repeatedly cited by bondholders.

Second, organization law provides a catalyst of sorts that makes it easier to reach an agreement in a complex multilateral setting. There are at the very least three parties to most businesses: participants, investors, and third parties, including creditors as well as suppliers and customers. All of these groups must negotiate somehow over both control and financial return. Needless to say, such a negotiation can be exceedingly complex and, like a game of rock-paper-scissors, may not — indeed probably will not — have a single stable solution. In the absence of well-crafted default rules, it may often be impossible to reach an agreement at all. In other words, prepackaged firms may be designed to solve complex bargaining problems involving multiple constituencies.

As I noted earlier, the best explanation for limited liability is that it facilitates bargaining between investors and creditors. Others have argued recently that partnership law may perform a similar function by setting default rules where the most deals are likely to end up anyway. For example, it has been argued that the default rule that partners are entitled to equal financial return may have evolved because those who are willing to agree to such a deal are more likely in the end to make deals and form firms (and ultimately succeed in making money). Thus, those who agree to equal shares will prosper, and those who insist on a greater share or are willing to accept a lesser share will evolve away. It has also been argued that partnerships are much more popular in the UK because they are somewhat more difficult to dissolve.

Although the foregoing arguments suggest that organization law matters, they do not really speak to the question of whether it is important to rationalize or unify the extant system. The jury is still out on this question. Clearly rationalization would have some benefits, but it would also have some costs. Perhaps the most obvious benefit is statutory simplification. It is far from clear, however, that this can be achieved.

A more concrete benefit may come from the identification and elimination of conflicting statutory provisions. For example, corporation law specifies the consequences of defective incorporation — joint and several liability for knowing participants. But presumably a non-corporation is also a partnership by default, the consequences of which are very different. In many situations, it is not at all clear which of these two provisions should apply. Presumably, a unified statute would eliminate such problems.

A subtler benefit arises from the fact that the law may sometimes confuse organizational rules with rules designed to regulate certain businesses that gravitate to a given form. For example, personal liability for partners may be more a function of attitudes toward professional malpractice than of partnership law. Clearly, such concerns weighed heavily in the evolution of the LLP. Similarly, limited liability for shareholders may be more a function of team production than of corporation law. Entity rationalization may help clarify these rules. For example, withdrawing such crutches as the prohibition on practicing law in the corporate form will force regulators to say what they mean.

On the other hand, some issues that appear to be matters of professional ethics, or otherwise outside the realm of organization law, may in fact properly be part of organization law. For example, the enforceability of non-competition agreements has been viewed as a matter of professional rules in some cases, simple contract in other cases, and fiduciary duty in still other cases. If in fact controlling competition is a proper reason for forming a firm, it may be that non-competition agreements should be viewed as part of organization law. Clearly, corporation law views competition as within its purview. But partnership law is essentially silent on the subject.

This raises the more general question of what should be included in organization law and what should not. For example, some states have recently added provisions relating to divisive reorganizations. Perhaps we should also consider statutory provisions relating to poison pills, tracking stock, or the terms of compensatory stock options. Such additions to statutory law, are not clearly necessary. These devices have arisen without benefit of legislative clergy. Still, most states have fairly elaborate provisions outlining the most common terms of preferred stock, even though with a few exceptions these provisions must be reiterated with specificity in the articles of incorporation in order to be enforceable. Is it really necessary that they be in the statute? Indeed, the rights of various ownership units in partnerships are often far more complex than those of preferred stock. Yet partnership law is almost totally silent about the ways in which financial rights may be varied.

One of the distinct risks of entity rationalization — at least under a menu approach that permits relatively free mixing and matching of terms — is that businesspeople will overplan and choose terms that do not work well together. The default rules for a particular organization may be internally coordinated in ways that are difficult to sort out. Mixing and matching rules from different organizations may be dangerous. The challenge is to determine which elements are safely modified and which are not. Too much freedom of contract, or making it too easy to mix and match terms, may also confuse the courts about which rules go together. Both phenomena are illustrated by the Massachusetts experience.

In *Donahue v. Rodd Electrotype Co.*, the court ruled that in a closely held corporation shareholders owe each other duties similar to those that partners owe each other because they are effectively locked in by the lack of a liquid market through which they might be able to exit (cash out). The result was that a minority shareholder was able to force the corporation to repurchase her shares because the majority shareholder had sold a block of his own shares back to the corporation. Although this rule seems sensible enough given the facts of the case, it quickly led to a series of unintended consequences. In a sense, it gave the minority shareholder exit rights similar to those in a partnership without considering the concomitant right to force dissolution of the firm.

The unintended consequences were quick to follow. In *Wilkes v. Springside Nursing Home*, the plaintiff minority shareholder argued in effect that he could not be fired from his positions as director, officer, and salaried employee, a position that is clearly consistent with the status of partner. In *Smith v. Atlantic Properties*, the four shareholders retained veto power over fundamental business decisions and fell into deadlock (and tax troubles) as a result of their inability to choose between dividends and reinvestment. In *Merola v. Exergen Corp.*, the plaintiff claimed that he had become a partner as a result of buying stock and hence could not be fired. And the question remains open whether the shareholder-to-shareholder duties created in *Donahue* mean that a minority shareholder can sue directly (rather than derivatively) when a controlling shareholder uses his power to the disadvantage of the minority. In short, Massachusetts bought into a multistep rejiggering of its corporation law prompted, at least in part, by shareholder opportunism in the wake of new found rights. And majority shareholders found that they did not have the power (or wealth) they may have thought they had.

On the other hand, Delaware and Maryland have more or less resisted the temptation to develop a special body of case law for close corporations. Indeed, it is well settled in Delaware that shareholders have no duty to each other. But it is also well settled that a controlling shareholder may not use that control to exact a benefit to the detriment and exclusion of the remaining shareholders. In any event, Delaware and Maryland have seen relatively little close corporation litigation. Moreover, it may well be that failure to appreciate the subtle interconnections between default rules may explain why the close corporation election has proved to be unpopular.

CONCLUSION

Business organization law matters. The fact that one can bargain around the law does not mean that most people do so. Indeed, it may be that the law is vital to getting any negotiation going. Bargaining happens in the shadow of the law. Thus, there is every reason to try to get the default rules right and to take great care in making sure that the rules are right in relation to each other. To the extent that entity rationalization eliminates unintentional conflicts between forms, it is a good thing. But simplification for its own sake is risky business.

Notes and Questions

1. Notes

a. We dealt with the Massachusetts rule announced in *Donahue* and *Wilkes* in Chapter 15 when we looked at the fiduciary duties of shareholders.

2. Reality Check

a. What is Professor Booth's assessment of entity rationalization?

b. How should entity rationalization be brought about, according to Professor Booth?

c. How is Professor Booth's vision of entity rationalization different from that of Dean Haynsworth?

3. What Do You Think?

a. Do you think that entity reform is necessary or desirable?

b. Do you think entity reform is more likely to come about from intentional efforts or from practical evolution?

D. TERMS OF ART IN THIS CHAPTER

C corporation	Enterprise rationalization	Pass-through taxation
Double taxation	Guaranteed exit	S corporation

Glossary

Absolute majority A majority of all the voting power, regardless of whether that power is present at the meeting; thus, absent votes are no votes. Chapter 14.

Accounting statements Independent accountants review the accounting records of their clients and prepare standardized reports, *accounting statements*, based on that review. Chapter 3.

Accredited investors A term of art that refers to rich people who invest in corporations. Chapter 6.

Actual authority A principal is bound to third parties by anything the agent does that is in accordance with the principal's "manifestation" to the agent. Chapter 4.

Adjustment and anchoring In many situations, people make estimates by starting from an initial value that is adjusted to yield the final answer. Adjustments are typically insufficient. That is, different starting points yield different estimates, which are biased toward the initial values. We call this phenomenon *anchoring*. Chapter 3.

Advance notice bylaw A clause that requires a shareholder to give the board notice of his or her intention to move a proposal or nominate directors at a meeting. Chapter 14 and Chapter 16.

Adverse selection Principals choosing suboptimal agents, or agents choosing suboptimal principals. Chapter 4.

Affiliated corporations Corporations under common control, whether parent-subsidiary or sibling corporations. Chapter 8.

Affirmative covenants Things that a borrowing corporation agrees to do or refrains from doing in order to make a loan less risky, such as maintaining certain financial ratios or agreeing to make all payments of other loans in a timely fashion. Chapter 6.

Agency costs The total of the expenditures made in ameliorating the moral hazard plus the residual loss resulting from moral hazard and risk differences between agent and principal. Chapter 4.

Agent In economics, one who uses some degree of judgment in performing a service for a principal's benefit. In law, one who agrees to act on behalf of another and subject to the other's control. Chapter 4.

All purpose clause A clause in the articles of incorporation that grants the corporation the power to pursue any lawful business. Chapter 10.

Allocation Assigning a partnership's or LLC's profits and losses among its members. Chapter 17 and Chapter 18.

Amotion The power of the shareholders to remove directors during their term. Chapter 9 and Chapter 14.

Angels Rich individuals who provide venture capital. Chapter 6.

Annual meeting Shareholder meeting that occurs once a year during which shareholders elect directors and engage in other valid shareholder action. Chapter 14.

Antidilution provision A provision that prevents a shareholder's ownership interest from being reduced by change in capital structure. Chapter 7.

Apparent authority An agent's power to bind the principal stemming from a third party's belief, traceable to the principal's manifestation, that the agent is authorized to act for the principal. Chapter 4.

Appraisal right A right, available in certain fundamental corporate changes, to require the corporation to purchase a dissenting shareholder's shares for fair value. Chapter 16.

Asset lock-up These clauses give the acquirer the option to purchase certain key target assets if the transaction does not close. Chapter 16.

At-will partnership A partnership that continues and exists indefinitely. Chapter 17.

Availability Situations in which people assess the frequency or probability of an event by the ease with which instances or occurrences can be brought to mind. Chapter 3.

Bacon Money.

Balance sheet An accounting statement that divides things you own on a particular date into assets and liabilities. It further divides both assets and liabilities into those that are liquid and those that are illiquid. Chapter 3.

Barristers British lawyers who have the exclusive right to appear in court on behalf of clients and derive their title from having been admitted to the bar. Chapter 1.

Beans Money.

Berle and Means type of corporation In corporate law scholarship, the paradigm of the large, publicly held corporation that is run by senior managers. Chapter 2.

Blank stock (or blank check provision) Stock authorized in the Articles of Incorporation as noncommon stock, the terms of which have not been determined. The characteristics of the stock are set by the board of directors. Chapter 6.

Board of directors The group of people that manages the business and affairs of every corporation and exercises all corporate power. Chapter 9.

Bonding An assurance, such as an insurance policy or a financial penalty clause in an agency agreement, that assures principals that agents will not shirk or behave opportunistically. Chapter 4.

Bonds Debt securities issued by a corporation that are typically secured by the corporation's assets. Chapter 6.

Book entry system System whereby an entity, the Depository Trust Company, credits or debits a brokerage house's account with the net number of shares of each corporation owed or owing to other brokerage houses at the end of each trading day. Shares are not actually transferred. Chapter 14.

Brass Money.

Bread Money.

Break-up fee A termination provision that makes the target liable to the acquirer if the transaction fails to close. Chapter 16.

Break-up value The value of a business comprising assets that would be worth more if operated separately. Chapter 3.

Broker overvote When a brokerage house inadvertently executes proxies (on behalf of shareholders) for more shares than it is entitled to vote. Chapter 14.

Bucks Money.

Business A business engages in sustained activities intended to generate more wealth than they use. Chapter 2.

Business combination acts Statutes that prohibit certain control transactions, such as mergers or sales of all assets, between a corporation and an entity controlling more than a certain amount (15% in Delaware) of shares. Chapter 16.

Butter Money.

Buy-sell agreement A restriction on the transfer of shares in which both sides are required to effect a transaction. Chapter 7.

C corporation A corporation that is taxed as a separate entity, meaning the corporation's income is taxed twice, once at the corporate level and again when distributed to shareholders as dividends. Chapter 19.

Call The decision to hold a meeting at a particular time and place, and often, for a particular reason. Chapter 9 and Chapter 14.

Call option A real option that permits a business to do something. A financial option that connotes the standard right sold by a person other than the corporation to purchase securities of the corporation from that person. Chapter 6.

Callable Stock that the corporation has the power to require the shareholder to return for a predetermined price. Chapter 6.

Capital For no-par value shares, capital is some portion of the consideration paid for those shares. For par value shares, capital is, at minimum, the par value of the shares. Chapter 7.

Capital expense An expense for an asset that is expected to last longer than one year. Chapter 3.

Capital formation The method by which a corporation gets money into the corporation. Chapter 6.

Capital gain The gain that an equity holder realizes when he or she sells equity in a corporation. Chapter 6.

Capital structure A corporation's choice of how much debt and equity it should have. It also refers to how much common stock and noncommon stock a corporation should issue. Chapter 6.

Caremark **claim** When the plaintiff alleges a failure to establish and monitor information systems within the corporation. Chapter 12.

Cede & Co. A partner of DTC that holds the actual shares of stock to facilitate transfer when necessary; the shareholder of record for shares traded under the book entry system. Chapter 14.

Charging order A court order seizing a partner's transferable interest for the benefit of a judgment creditor of that partner; similar to a lien. Chapter 17.

Charter limitation A provision in the articles of incorporation that caps or eliminates monetary liability of directors for breach of their duty of care. Chapter 12.

Clams Money.

Class of stock Common stock or preferred stock. Chapter 6.

Classified board A board in which the power to elect at least one director is vested in, or denied to, at least one class or series of stock. Chapter 9.

Close (or closely held) corporations A corporation owned by few shareholders, or even by one person. Chapter 6.

Collar A loan with a minimum and maximum variable rate. Chapter 6.

Commercial paper market Loans to corporations that are good credit risks and need to borrow large amounts of money on a regular cycle. Chapter 6.

Common stock Shares that have (1) one vote per share on any matter submitted to the shareholders, (2) the right to its proportionate amount of any dividend, and (3) the right to its proportionate amount of the corporation's assets upon dissolution. Chapter 6.

Conflict of interest An incentive for a director or officer to act other than in the best interest of the corporation. Chapter 11.

Conglomeration A corporation's strategy of purchasing unrelated business that can stand alone. Chapter 16.

Constituent corporations Corporations that are parties to a merger. Chapter 16.

Continuity of enterprise exception An exception to the rule that a corporation is not liable for liabilites of a corporation from which it has purchased all assets. The transferee corporation is liable if the transferor's business itself is continued as a going concern even when there is no continuation of ownership between the transferor and transferee corporations. Chapter 8.

Convergence In corporate law scholarship, the theory that the forces of global competition will lead nations to adopt a single efficient form of corporate governance. Chapter 2.

Convertible Stock that may be exchanged for other securities of the corporation. Chapter 6.

Coping Efforts to manage specific demands (and conflicts between them) that are appraised as taxing or exceeding a person's resources. Chapter 3.

Corporate lawyer as conciliator A lawyer who is called upon to help resolve a conflict between the client and another, often regarding a potential transaction. Chapter 1.

Corporate lawyer as counselor A lawyer who gives advice to the client. Chapter 1.

Corporate lawyer as facilitator A lawyer who negotiates the substantive elements of a transaction such as price, quantity, and other essential points; ensures that the transaction complies with applicable regulations; or drafts writings that both accurately capture the agreed-upon terms and legally effect the anticipated transaction. Chapter 1.

Corporate lawyer as guardian A lawyer who protects the client and the public against some contemplated actions by persons acting on the client's behalf. Chapter 1.

Corporate opportunity A business opportunity presented to an officer or director that is so closely associated with the corporation's current business activities that the officer or director may not accept the opportunity for himself or herself in place of the corporation. Chapter 11.

Corporate social responsibility The corporate law theory that requires corporate managers and directors to take into account the needs not only of shareholders but of workers, consumers, and communities when making business decisions. Chapter 10.

Corporate survival statute Statutes designed to protect shareholders and corporate creditors when a solvent corporation dissolves. The statute permitting a soon-to-be dissolved corporation to notify its known creditors and to give notice to the public of the impending dissolution and thereby cut off future liability. Chapter 8.

Corporation by estoppel An equitable defense to individual liability predicated on defective incorporation. A third party can be estopped from denying the existence of the corporation when it reasonably believes it is dealing only with an existing corporation. Chapter 5.

Counterparty risk The possibility that the other side of a transaction will not perform, either because of unwillingness or inability. Chapter 3.

Coupled with an interest A form of agency relationship that is irrevocable because of the agent's heightened interest in the subject of the agency relationship. Chapter 4.

Credit rating agencies Agencies that rank corporations by their perceived credit worthiness. Chapter 13.

Crowdfunding A method of raising capital by collecting small amounts of money from a large number of investors, typically through solicitation on a social media platform. Chapter 6.

Cumulative Preferred stock as to which the dividends, if not declared and paid, accumulate. The corporation is prohibited from paying dividends on other stock until the accumulated dividends have been paid in full. Chapter 6.

Cumulative voting A method of voting for directors in which each shareholder has the number of votes equal to the number of shares owned multiplied by the number of director slots to be filled. The shareholder may cast those votes for one candidate or distribute them among several candidates. Chapter 15.

Currency risk The possibility that exchange rates may change during the course of a transaction resulting in more or less home currency than was anticipated. Chapter 3.

DCF *See* Discounted cash flow. Chapter 3.

De facto An equitable defense to individual liability predicated on defective incorporation. A de facto corporation exists when an individual makes a good faith but ineffective attempt to incorporate. Chapter 5.

De jure A corporation that has substantially complied with all mandatory provisions that are intended to be conditions precedent to incorporation. Chapter 5.

Deadlock An impasse among directors or among shareholders. Chapter 15.

Deal protective measures Acquisition agreement clauses that are designed to ensure that a transaction closes. Chapter 16.

Debentures Debt securities issued by a corporation that are typically unsecured. Chapter 6.

Debt A temporary investment in a corporation that entails mandatory periodic interest payments and a return of the investment. A loan. Chapter 6.

Declared A dividend is declared when the board of directors authorizes the corporation to pay it. Chapter 7.

Default *See* Counterparty risk. Chapter 3.

Defeased A loan that the corporation repays out of a trust in which sufficient assets have been set aside to repay the loan in full. Chapter 6.

Defective incorporation The situation in which obligations are incurred in the name of a corporation that has not yet been formed. The corporation's promoter may be individually liable for such obligations. Chapter 5.

Defensive measures Actions taken by a target corporation's board to defeat raiders after a raid has begun. Chapter 16.

Definitive agreement The written acquisition contract between corporations. Chapter 16.

Delist A stock exchange's action that prohibits further trading in a particular company's securities. Chapter 7.

Demand excused Shareholder-plaintiff may file a derivative suit without making demand on the board if he or she can demonstrate that prior demand would have been "futile" because the board could not have evaluated the demand fairly. Chapter 14.

Demand refused A board's refusal to grant a shareholder's demand that the corporation redress harm caused to it. If the refusal was wrongful, the shareholder can file a derivative suit. Chapter 14.

Derivative action A lawsuit filed by shareholders on behalf of the corporation to redress harm to the corporation that the board will not redress. Chapter 14.

Diluted A reduction in a shareholder's ownership interest caused by the issuance of more shares. Chapter 6.

Disclosed principal A principal whose identity is known to a third party. Chapter 4.

Discount rate The rate used to calculate the present value of future money. The discount rate is an interest rate in reverse. Chapter 3.

Discounted cash flow A method of valuing an asset that will generate money in the future. It involves projecting net cash flows for a determined period, setting a terminal value of the asset at the end of the projected period, and then discounting those values at a set rate to determine the net present value. Chapter 3.

Discounting to present value The process of determining how much money one needs to invest today to receive a given amount at a certain time in the future. Chapter 3.

Dissenter's right The right of a dissenting shareholder to sell his or her shares to the corporation for fair value when the corporation engages in certain fundamental changes such as a merger or sale of all assets. Chapter 16.

Dissociated When a partner ceases to be a co-owner of a partnership. Chapter 17.

Dissociation The process by which a partner ceases to be a co-owner of a partnership, and his or her interest is bought out by the partnership. Chapter 17.

Dissolution The process by which a partnership or an LLC ceases to exist. All assets are disposed of, all creditors are paid, and the partners or members receive distributions of the any remainder. Chapter 17 and Chapter 18.

Distribution The transfer of partnership or LLC property (usually cash) to partners or members. Chapter 17 and Chapter 18.

Diversification Investing in assets that respond differently to particular risks. Diversification can reduce overall risk while preserving the assets' expected return. Chapter 3.

Dividend A distribution of the increased value (or part of it) of a corporation to its shareholders. Chapter 7.

Domestic corporation A corporation incorporated within the state. Chapter 5.

Double taxation Income earned by a corporation is taxed twice. Once when earned by the corporation and again when distributed to shareholders as a dividend. Chapter 19.

Dough-ray-mi Money.

DTC Depository Trust Company; an entity that acts as a custodian of shares and credits or debits the accounts of brokerage houses. Chapter 14.

Ducats Money.

Due diligence The acquiring corporation's investigation of a corporation to be acquired. Chapter 16.

Duty of care The fiduciary duty of a director to act on an informed basis or with the care that a person in a like position would reasonably believe appropriate under similar circumstances. Chapter 11.

Duty of loyalty The fiduciary duty of a director to take and approve only those actions the director believes to be in the corporation's best interest. Chapter 11.

Economic realities test An inquiry used by the IRS and courts to recharacterize debt as equity, when an unrelated third party would not have been willing to make a loan of similar size on similar terms to the corporation. Chapter 6.

Employee An agent whose principal controls or has the right to control the manner and means of the agent's performance of work. Chapter 4.

Enterprise liability A doctrine that allows a creditor to seek repayment not only from the debtor corporation but from related entities, as well. Chapter 8.

Enterprise rationalization A proposal that the multiple forms of entities be replaced by a unified system with one entity form complemented by a menu of options and choices. Chapter 19.

Entire fairness The standard of review of a directors' action in which the burden is on the defendants to demonstrate their utmost good faith and the most scrupulous inherent fairness of the bargain. It has two components: fair dealing and fair price. Chapter 12.

Equitable subordination A doctrine that protects creditors of a bankrupt corporation. The bankruptcy court may subordinate (i.e., give a lower preference to) debt that the court deems to resemble a shareholder's ownership interest more that a debt. Chapter 6 and Chapter 8.

Equity Ownership interest in a corporation. Chapter 6.

ESOP Employee stock ownership plan, which provides pension benefits to a corporation's employees through a trust that holds the corporation's stock. Also, a method of deterring hostile takeovers. Chapter 16.

Estoppel A theory under which a principal is liable for an agent's action, even if neither authorized nor apparently authorized, if third parties have changed their position in reliance upon their belief that the action was authorized and the principal caused (intentionally or carelessly) the belief, or if the principal, knowing of the belief, did nothing to notify the third parties of the facts. Chapter 4.

Event of default A significant or sustained violation of negative covenants by a debtor corporation. Chapter 6.

Exchange Act (or the '34 Act) One of two principal acts of Congress in the area of federal securities regulation. Chapter 6.

Exit strategy A motivation for changing control of a corporation that is triggered by some previously determined plan. Chapter 16.

Expected return The expected return of an investment is the sum of the value of each possible outcome multiplied by each outcome's likelihood. Chapter 3.

Fair value The value a dissenting shareholder is entitled to for his or her shares. Chapter 16.

Family capitalism Firms in which the entrepreneur and his or her close associates (and their families) who built the enterprise continue to hold the majority of stock, maintain a close personal relationship with their managers, and retain a major say in top management decisions. Chapter 2.

Financial capitalism Firms in which the financial institutions providing the corporation's capital are represented on the firm's board. The corporation's managers share top management decisions, particularly those involving the raising and spending of large sums of capital, with the representatives of the financial institutions. Chapter 2.

Flip in A provision, related to a poison pill, that allows shareholders to purchase half-price stock in the target if it will be the surviving entity in a merger. Chapter 16.

Flip over A provision, related to a poison pill, that allows shareholders to purchase half-price stock in the acquiring company if it will be the surviving entity in a merger. Chapter 16.

Floating interest rate A loan with an interest rate that varies over the life of the loan, possibly with a minimum or maximum rate. Chapter 6.

Foreign corporation A corporation that has been incorporated in another U.S. state. Chapter 5.

Foreign investment risk When investing assets in another country, the possibility that the other country might change its rules regarding foreign investment. Chapter 3.

Form S-1 A form required by the SEC to register a corporation's securities for sale to the public. Chapter 6.

Fraudulent conveyance A doctrine designed to protect a corporation's creditors. If a corporate debtor transfers assets for less than fair value at a time when it was insolvent and for the purpose of harming its other creditors, those other creditors can trace the transferred assets into the hands of the transferees. Chapter 8.

Frogskins Money.

GAAP Generally Accepted Accounting Principles. The rules that tell accountants how to present the results of an audit. Chapter 3.

General partnerships Synonym for partnership used to distinguish an entity from other partnership forms such as limited partnerships. Chapter 17.

General proxy A proxy in which the agent is authorized to use his or her discretion in voting. Chapter 14.

Go public To sell securities of a corporation to the public for the first time. Chapter 6.

Going concern value The value of an asset operated as a discrete business. Chapter 3.

Going private transaction A transaction such as a merger or tender offer by which a public corporation becomes a private one. Chapter 16.

Greenmail The premium price that a corporation pays to to an obstreperous shareholder to reacquire the shareholder's shares. Chapter 7.

Group More than one shareholder agreeing to act in concert regarding ownership of publicly traded securities. Chapter 16.

Guaranteed exit An agreement by which a shareholder has a right to require the corporation to repurchase the shareholder's interest. Chapter 19.

Happy cabbage Money.

Hay Money.

Heuristics Short-cuts that people routinely employ in deciding how much information to get, how to analyze information, and how to make decisions. Chapter 3.

Holdover A director who has continued in office after the expiration of his or her term because no successor has been elected. Chapter 9 and Chapter 14.

Horizontal integration A combination of businesses engaged in the same enterprise. Chapter 2.

Hostile tender offer An offer to shareholders at a premium price for at least a majority of the shares, which offer is opposed by the corporation's board. Chapter 16.

Howey **test** Test to determine whether an investment is an investment contract and therefore a security. The elements are (1) an investment of money, (2) in a common enterprise, (3) in which the investor was led to expect profits (4) primarily from the efforts of the promoter or a third party. Chapter 17.

Ice Money.

Indemnification An agreement to pay a director's (or agent's) expenses incurred in defending a third party's claim against the defendant. Chapter 12.

Indenture A document that sets out the terms of the loan and is executed by the borrowing company and an investment bank, acting as trustee for the ultimate lenders. Chapter 6.

Inflation risk The possibility that inflation will be different than anticipated thus increasing or decreasing the value of money to be received in the future. Chapter 3.

In-house lawyer A lawyer who works as an employee *of* the client rather than as an employee of a law firm that is hired *by* the client. Chapter 1.

Initial public offering (IPO) The sale of a corporation's securities to the general public for the first time. Chapter 6.

Insider trading Buying or selling publicly traded securities while in possession of material nonpublic information. Chapter 7.

Insolvency test A test to determine whether a corporation has lawfully declared a dividend. The elements are whether, after the dividend, the corporation's assets will exceed its liabilities and whether the corporation can pay its debts as they come due. Chapter 7.

Inspection right A shareholder's right to examine certain corporation documents in certain circumstances. Chapter 14.

Interested person An entity controlling a certain percentage of a target corporation's shares. Chapter 16.

Intermediate scrutiny Standard of review in Delaware that applies to a board's defensive actions during a hostile takeover; in between the business judgment rule and the entire fairness standard. Chapter 16.

Internal affairs The relations inter se of the corporation, its shareholders, directors, officers, and agents. The internal affairs doctrine is a choice of law rule that provides that a corporation's interal affairs are governed by the law of the state of incorporation. Chapter 5.

Intrastate exemption An exemption from the registration requirements of the federal securities laws for securities that are offered and issued only to the residents of the state in which the issuing corporation is incorporated and doing business. Chapter 6.

Investment contract An investment of money in a common enterprise in which the investor has an expectation of profit to come solely from the efforts of others. Chapter 6.

Issued Shares that a corporation has exchanged for consideration. Chapter 6.

Joint venture A partnership formed for a limited time or for a limited purpose. Chapter 17.

Kale Money.

Legal capital test A test to determine whether a corporation may declare dividends. Dividends can be paid only if the corporation's legal capital is unimpaired. Chapter 7.

Letter of intent An agreement between the parties to negotiate with one another in good faith looking toward the acquisition of one entity by the other. Chapter 16.

Lettuce Money.

Limited liability company An entity that combines limited liability for the firm's owners and managers with pass-through taxation. Chapter 18.

Limited partnership A partnership with one or more general partners, who manage but have unlimited liability, and one or more limited partners, who do not manage but have limited liability. Chapter 17.

Limited proxy A proxy in which the shareholder authorizes the agent to vote in a particular way. Chapter 14.

Liquidity The relative ease with which an asset can be transferred. Chapter 3 and Chapter 6.

Lolly Money.

Long green Money.

Manager A person, either member or nonmember, selected to run an LLC. Managers have actual authority to bind the LLC and have fiduciary duties. Chapter 18.

Manager managed An LLC managed by managers rather than members. Chapter 18.

Managerial capitalism Firms in which ownership is widely scattered, salaried managers dominate top as well as lower and middle management, and in which those managers determine long-term policy as well as manage short-term operating activities. Chapter 2.

Marketability discount Discount applied to the value of a dissenting shareholder's shares in a close corporation to reflect the lack of marketability. Chapter 16.

Material A principal component of securities regulation. Information is material is there is a substantial likelihood that a reasonable investor would consider it important in deciding how to act. Chapter 7.

Material adverse change Clause that permits a party to refuse to close a transaction if certain fundamental assumptions underlying the transactions have changed. Chapter 16.

Member A person with an ownership interest in the LLC. Chapter 18.

Member managed An LLC managed by its members rather than by managers. Chapter 18.

Mere continuation exception A successor liability doctrine in which the key element is whether there is a common identity of the officers, directors, and stockholders among the selling and purchasing corporations. Chapter 8.

Merger A transaction in which the assets and liabilities of one corporation are transferred by operation of law to another corporation and the first corporation ceases existence. Chapter 16.

Middle manager Supervises managers below and reports to managers above. Chapter 2.

Minority discount The discount applied to the value of a dissenting shareholder's shares, when the corporation has a majority shareholder, to reflect the lack of managerial power. Chapter 16.

Monitor A method used to decrease the costs of the agency relationship. It can include watching the agent work, measuring the agent's efforts, or contractual limitations on the agent's discretion. Chapter 4.

Moolah Money.

Moral hazard The risk that a party with discretion to act will choose an action that decreases the expected value of the transaction to the other party in a way that the other party cannot effectively prohibit. Chapter 4.

Negative covenants Agreements between a debtor corporation and a lender that prohibit the debtor from taking certain actions that may disadvantage the lender. Chapter 6.

Net cash flow The cash generated by an asset net of the cash used to acquire or maintain the asset. Chapter 3.

Net present value The cost of an asset minus its present value. Chapter 3.

Nexus of contract A theory that views the corporation as an aggregate of various inputs acting together to produce goods or services. Chapter 10.

No-shop A clause in an acquisition agreement that prevents the target board from actively seeking other potential acquirers. Chapter 16.

No-talk A clause in an acquisition agreement that prevents the target board from negotiating with, or providing non-public information to, a party other than the acquirer. Chapter 16.

Notice The requirement that the board or shareholders must become aware that a meeting has been called. The time and content requirements of the notice are different for board and shareholder meetings. Chapter 9 and Chapter 14.

Officer An officer is a person who holds a corporate position to which particular kinds of duties or powers are attached. The term includes a president, vice president, secretary, principal financial officer, principal accounting officer, or any person routinely performing corresponding functions. Chapter 9.

Oil of palm Money.

Oof Money.

Operating agreement The detailed LLC governance agreement among all the members, and sometimes all the managers, that sets forth the names of the members and their respective economic interests, the managers (if any) and how power will be allocated between members and managers and among the managers, and whether there will be particular officers with delegated duties; analogous to a partnership agreement. Chapter 18.

Operating expenses Expenses for assets that are expected to be used up in within one year. Chapter 3.

Oppression A cause of action by minority shareholders. Under one approach, oppression is conduct that substantially defeats the minority shareholders' reasonable expectations. Under a second approach, oppression is inequitable conduct by the majority. Chapter 15.

Option The power but not the obligation to do something, or a power granted by a corporation to a particular person to purchase securities. Chapter 3 and Chapter 6.

Option writer The seller of a standardized right to purchase securities from, or sell securities to, the writer. Chapter 6.

Ordinary income Income from such sources as wages, dividends, or interest income that is taxed at a higher rate than capital gains. Chapter 6.

Outstanding Authorized and issued shares that remain in the hands of some entity other than the corporation itself. Chapter 6.

Overissue Shares issued in excess of the number of shares authorized in the articles of incorporation. Chapter 6.

Par value An arbitrary value, usually nominal, for a class or series shares, which is stated in the articles of incorporation. Shares may not be issued for less than par value. Chapter 6.

Participating Preferred stock that receives dividends along with the common stock after it has received its preferential dividend. Chapter 6.

Participation theory of liability A theory under which a corporate officer is personally liable for a tort committed by the corporation when the officer is sufficiently involved in the commission to the tort. Chapter 8.

Partnership The association of two or more persons to carry on as co-owners a business for profit. Chapter 17.

Pass-through taxation Tax treatment of an entity, such as a partnership or LLC, in which income and losses realized by the entity are allocated to the entity's owners. Thus the entity itself does not pay income tax. Chapter 19.

Peanuts Money.

Periodic reporting The requirement that a public company provide certain information to its shareholders annually and quarterly. Chapter 14.

Pewter Money.

Piercing the corporate veil An equitable doctrine that holds a corporation's shareholders liable for the corporation's debts if the corporation is unable to pay. Chapter 8.

Plurality The largest percentage of votes cast, even if less than a majority. Chapter 14.

Poison pill An anti-takeover device by which the target shareholders have the right to purchase half-price stock in a raider if the raider acquires a particular percentage of shares, usually between 10 percent and 20 percent, and thereafter effects a merger. Chapter 16.

Pooling agreements An agreement among shareholders that states how shareholders themselves will vote their own shares; these agreements are not subject to voting trust statutes. Chapter 15.

Potatoes Money.

Precatory motion Motion at a shareholders meeting that would constitute only a recommendation to the board. Chapter 14.

Preemptive right The equitable right of shareholders to purchase shares proposed to be issued so that their respective economic and managerial interests will be preserved. Chapter 15.

Preferred stock A class of stock that has a priority or preference over other stock (common stock) in either the payment of dividends, the distribution of assets on dissolution, or both. Chapter 6.

Price The actual consideration for a particular investment. Price may be determined by active negotiation between the parties or it may be determined by reference to a market. Cf. Value. Chapter 3.

Principal The person or entity (1) for whom an agent has agreed to act and (2) who has the right to control the agent. Chapter 4.

Private benefits The goods or services that an agent has obtained opportunistically through the agency relationship and for which the agent bears only a part (or none) of the cost. Chapter 4.

Private placement exemption An exemption from the federal registration requirements given to securities sold by a corporation in transactions not involving a public offering. Chapter 6.

Product line exception A successor liability doctrine in which the key is whether the successor corporation produces essentially the same products as the transferor corporation. Chapter 8.

Progressive corporate law The school of corporate law scholarship that espouses the view that the corporation should be viewed as a community comprising shareholders, creditors, directors, managers, employees, and possibly customers. Corporate law scholars seek to impose on the corporation a responsibility not to society in general, but to those groups that make up the corporate community. Chapter 10.

Promoters The persons who organize a new corporation. Chapter 5.

Proper purpose A shareholder, when exercising certain inspection rights, must establish that the purpose for inspection is reasonably related to such person's interest as a shareholder. Chapter 14.

Proxy An agency relationship in which a shareholder appoints another person to attend a shareholders meeting on the shareholder's behalf and to vote the shareholder's shares. Chapter 14.

Pseudo-domestic corporation A corporation that has its headquarters and principal place of business in state *A*, but is incorporated in state *B*, is, as to state *B*, a pseudo-domestic corporation. As to state *A*, it is a pseudo-foreign corporation.

Put option A real option that permits the owner to cease an activity. A standardized right sold by someone (the option writer) other than the corporation to sell securities of the corporation to the writer. Chapter 3 and Chapter 6.

Quorum The minimum amount, typically a majority, of voting power that must be present at a meeting for actions to be valid. Chapter 9 and Chapter 14.

Raider An entity that seeks to obtain control of another entity against the wishes of the other entity's management. Chapter 16.

Ratcheting The risk that a principal will increase an agent's work without increasing the agent's recompense. Chapter 4.

Ratification A doctrine under which a principal is liable for an agent's actions, when no actual or apparent authority exists. Ratification occurs when the principal manifests assent to the agent's actions, thus electing to treat the action as authorized. Chapter 4.

Rational self-interest The paradigm of human behavior in classical economics. It posits that people, in economic settings, act logically to acquire as much for themselves as possible. Chapter 3.

Real options A business's relations with others, viewed as options. Real options are distinguished from financial options and hedges. *See* Option. Chapter 3.

Reasonable expectations test A test for shareholder oppression. It focuses on the minority shareholders's reasonable expectations in committing their capital to the particular enterprise. If conduct by the majority substantially defeats those expectations, the minority have been oppressed. Chapter 15.

Recognition An event such as a sale that requires a taxpayer to report gain or loss. Chapter 16.

Record date The date on which the shareholders entitled to receive a dividend or to vote at a meeting are fixed. Chapter 7.

Redemption The right of the corporation, contained in the articles of incorporation, to repurchase shares of a particular class or series. Chapter 6.

Registration statement The statement required to be filed with the SEC before a corporation may offer securities to the public. Chapter 6.

Regular meeting A periodic (e.g., monthly) meeting of a board of directors. Chapter 9.

Regulation D An SEC regulation that exempts certain stock sales by a corporation from registration requirements. Chapter 6.

Regulatory risk The possibility that a government might impose unanticipated regulations. Chapter 3.

Reinvestment risk The possibility that a lender will not be able to reinvest the loan principal at equally favorable terms when the principal is repaid. Chapter 6.

Renounce An agent's unilateral ending of the agency relationship. Chapter 4.

Representativeness A heuristic in which the likelihood of *A* being related to *B* is determined by how closely *A* resembles *B*. Chapter 3.

Reputational intermediaries A person or entity that vouches for one entity's merits to another entity. Chapter 13.

Reservation price The lowest price at which a seller would sell an asset or the highest price at which a buyer would buy an asset. Chapter 16.

Respondeat superior The doctrine by which a principal is liable for an employee's tort committed within the scope of employment. *See* Vicarious liability. Chapter 4.

Restitution The doctrine by which a principal is liable to third parties when (1) the principal is unjustly enriched by the agent's actions and (2) those actions are not within the agent's actual or apparent authority. Chapter 4.

Restrictions on transfer Limitations on a shareholder's power to sell, give, bequeath, or retain ownership of shares. Chapter 7.

Retired Reacquired shares that are not held as treasury shares. Chapter 7.

Reverse stock split An amalgamation of shares at a fixed ratio into fewer shares. Chapter 7.

Reverse triangular merger A merger of an acquiring corporation subsidiary with and into the target corporation. Chapter 16.

***Revlon* duties** The directors' duty, imposed by *Revlon, Inc. v. MacAndrews & Forbes Holdings, Inc.*, 506 A.2d 173 (Del. 1985), to act reasonably to seek the transaction offering the highest value reasonably obtainable in the sale of corporate control. Chapter 16.

Revoke The principal's unilateral termination of the agency relationship. Chapter 4.

Rhino Money.

Risk The possibility that something different than expected will happen. Chapter 3.

Roses Money.

Round lot The typical trading unit of 100 shares. Chapter 7.

S corporation A corporation that has elected to be taxed under Subchapter S of the Internal Revenue Code. S corporations are not taxed separately. Profits and losses are allocated directly to the shareholders who include those profits or losses on their own tax returns. Chapter 19.

Salvage value The value of a nonoperating asset derived from the value of its components. Chapter 3.

Sarbanes-Oxley Act of 2002 A federal act that constrains public corporation board power first, by requiring that the corporation have an audit committee of independent directors who retain and oversee the corporation's independent accounting firm; and second, by requiring senior officers to certify the corporation's financial statements and to certify that the corporation has a *Caremark* system of effective internal controls. Chapter 13.

Scienter The element of Rule 10b-5 liablity that requires a defendant to have intended to deceive. Chapter 7.

Scope of employment An employee acts within the scope of employment when performing work assigned by the employer or engaging in a course of conduct subject to the employer's control. Chapter 4.

Scrap value *See* Salvage value. Chapter 3.

Scratch Money.

Secondary trading market Markets such as the New York Stock Exchange or NASDAQ that permit securities to be traded among participants who are not issuing corporations. Chapter 6.

Securities The standardized rights granted by a corporation in return for money investments. Stock, bonds, and debentures are typical securities. Chapter 6.

Securities Act (or the '33 Act) One of two major federal acts that regulate the public issuance and trading of securities. Chapter 6.

Securities analyst Securities analysts investigate a particular industry and its businesses and write analytical assessments of both the industry and the businesses that compete. These analyses are used by brokerage houses to recommend stock to their clients. Chapter 13.

Securities and Exchange Commission (SEC) An independent federal agency that has regulates publicly held companies and stock exchanges. Chapter 6.

Self-dealing Self-dealing occurs when a director or officer enters into a contract with the corporation, usually to buy something from, or sell something to, the corporation. Chapter 11.

Series of stock A subset of a class of stock. Chapter 6.

Settled When a securities trade becomes complete, meaning the seller gets the money and the buyer gets the shares. Chapter 14.

Share A unit of ownership in a corporation. Chapter 6.

Shareholder The owner of stock. Chapter 6.

Shareholder lock-up A side agreement between an acquirer and a target's controlling shareholder by which the shareholder agrees to sell its shares, or agrees to give a proxy, to the acquirer. Chapter 16.

Shareholder primacy The idea that, because shareholders own the corporation, directors and officers are required to act in the shareholders' interest. Chapter 10.

Shareholders' rights plan Formal term for a poison pill. Chapter 16.

Shark repellents Corporate governance structures that keep unwanted suitors from effecting a takeover. Chapter 16.

Shirking A moral hazard faced by principals, in which the agent chooses to perform less well than the parties anticipated. Chapter 4.

Short form merger Where the acquiring corporation owns at least 90 percent of the target's stock, the statutes permit a merger upon only the resolution of the acquiring corporation's board of directors. Chapter 16.

Shrapnel Money.

Signaling Tactics used by both principals and agents to convince others that they will perform well in an agency relationship. Signaling may include such actions as providing references or obtaining educational degrees. Chapter 4.

Silent partners Partners who do not take part in the management of the business. Chapter 17.

Simoleons Money.

Simple majority A majority of votes cast. Votes not present and votes present but not voting are not included in calculating the denominator. Chapter 14.

Sinking fund Money segregated by a borrowing corporation to ensure that it can make loan payments when due. Chapter 6.

Skrilla Money.

Soap Money.

Solicitors British lawyers who have not been admitted to the bar and could not be heard in court. They undertake all other legal work, however, including what today would be called corporate work. Chapter 1.

Special committee A committee of non-implicated directors assigned to evaluate a shareholder's demand for litigation against other directors. Chapter 14.

Special litigation committee A committee of nondefendant directors assigned to investigate the allegations against the defendant directors who are being sued for breach of fiduciary duties. The committee also recommends whether pursuing those allegations is in the best interest of the corporation. Chapter 12.

Special meeting A board meeting other than a regular meeting. A shareholder meeting other than the annual meeting. Chapter 9 and Chapter 14.

Special purpose clause A clause in the article of incorporation that states the single purpose for which the corporation was formed. Chapter 10.

Spinach   Money.

Spondulicks   Money.

Staggered terms   A corporate governance device in which the directors are divided into two or three classes, with each class holding terms of two or three years, so that only one class of directors is elected each year. Chapter 9.

Statement of cash flows   A financial statement that presents the net cash used in three areas over a period of time. Chapter 3.

Statement of income   A financial statement that presents revenues and expenses over a period of time. Chapter 3.

Statutory voting   *See* Straight voting. Chapter 15.

Stock   Collective ownership interests in the corporation, used interchangeably with shares. Chapter 6.

Stock right   Rights given to the holders of stock, such as the right to vote or receive dividends. Chapter 6.

Stock split   The division of outstanding shares into more shares, such that the ownership interests are not affected. Chapter 7.

Stockholder   Someone who owns shares of stock. Chapter 6.

Straight voting   A system of shareholder voting for directors. A shareholder may cast one vote for every share he or she owns for each director slot. Thus each shareholder may cast votes equaling the number of his or her shares for as many different candidates as there are slots. Also called Statutory voting. Chapter 15.

Street name   Shares of stock as to which the record holder has no ownership interest but holds the stock on behalf of a brokerage house that also has no ownership interest but that, in turn, holds the stock for a customer, which is the beneficial owner. Chapter 14.

Subordinated   Debt that has a lower priority for repayment than other debt. Chapter 6.

Subscription agreements   Contracts to purchase shares, usually in a corporation that has not yet been formed. Chapter 6.

Subsidiary   A corporation that has the majority of its voting stock owned by another corporation. Chapter 16.

Successor liability   A doctrine that holds a corporation liable for the debts of a second corporation that sold all its assets to the first corporation. Chapter 8.

Sugar   Money.

Supermajority   A provision in the articles of incorporation or bylaws that requires a greater than majority vote at either the board or the shareholder level. Chapter 15.

Superquorum   A provision in the articles of incorporation or bylaws that increases the quorum requirements above the default statutory rule, for board meetings or shareholder meetings. Chapter 15.

Surplus   A corporation's net assets less its capital. Chapter 7.

Syndicate   A group of investors that makes a joint investment to a corporation, either by making a loan or by underwriting the corporation's public offering. Chapter 6.

Synergy value   The value of operating an asset in conjunction with other assets the investor already owns. This conjoined operation might produce more profits than operating the assets separately. Chapter 3.

Target corporation   The corporation that is purchased in a change of control transaction. Chapter 16.

Team production   An economic endeavor in which multiple actors are required and in which the results are not easily attributable to the efforts of particular actors. Chapter 4.

Tender offer   An offer to the target's shareholders to sell their shares to the raider at a premium to the current market price. Chapter 16.

Term partnership   A partnership formed for a particular length of time or for a particular undertaking. Chapter 17.

Terminal price   The likely sales price of an asset at the end of its holding period. Chapter 3.

Time value of money   The increased value of a unit of money in the present over the value of the same unit of money in the future. Chapter 3.

Topping fee   A contract clause that requires additional payment to the acquirer if an acquisition transaction does not close and if, within a specified time such as two years, the target is acquired by another entity. Chapter 16.

Traditional logic of property   The idea that a corporation should be run for the benefit of shareholders because they own the corporation and hence, indirectly, the corporation's property. Chapter 10.

Transaction reporting The requirement that a public company provide certain information to its shareholders with respect to a contemplated financial transaction. Chapter 14.

Transfer agent A corporation's agent in charge of reissuing shares from sellers to buyers and noting such transfers on the shareholder list. Chapter 14.

Treasury stock Shares that have been reacquired by the issuing corporation but that have not been retired. Chapter 7.

Ultra vires A doctrine that limits corporate action to the ends and means stated in the articles of incorporation or corporation statute and validly approved by the corporation. Chapter 10.

Underwriter An investment banker that facilitates the public offering of a corporation's securities by buying securities from the issuer and reselling them to the investing public. Chapter 6.

Undisclosed principal A principal is undisclosed where a third party has no knowledge that the agent is acting on behalf of any principal. Chapter 4.

Unidentified principal A principal is unidentified when a third party knows that the agent is acting on behalf of a principal, but does not know the principal's identity. Chapter 4.

Units Stock and warrants sold as a package. Chapter 6.

Unocal test A standard of review that applies to a target board's defensive actions during a hostile takeover. It is intermediate in strictness between the business judgment rule and the entire fairness standard. It takes it name from *Unocal Corp. v. Mesa Petroleum Co.*, 493 A.2d 946 (Del. 1985). Chapter 16.

Utility The economic and noneconomic worth of an asset to its owner. Chapter 3.

Value The economic worth of an investment to an owner. The wealth an asset will likely produce for its owner. Chapter 3.

Venture capital Money invested in non-public corporations by entities unconnected with the corporation with a view to preparing the corporation to go public. Chapter 6.

Vertical integration A combination of a business with its suppliers or customers. Chapter 2.

Vest The ability of an option holder to exercise the option. Chapter 6.

Vicarious liability A doctrine under which a principal is liable for an agent's torts. *See* Respondeat superior. Chapter 4.

Voidable preferences Corporate property transferred to certain corporate insiders within one year prior to the corporation's bankruptcy if the transfer was for an antecedent debt, had the effect of giving the insiders more than they would have received in bankruptcy, and was made while the corporation was insolvent. Voidable preferences may be recovered for the benefit of the corporation's creditors. Chapter 8.

Voting trusts Stock as to which (1) the voting rights are separated from the other attributes of ownership; (2) the voting rights granted are intended to be irrevocable for a definite period of time; and (3) the principal purpose of the grant of voting rights is to affect voting control of the corporation. Chapter 15.

Warrant A long-term option (i.e., over one year) to purchase securities. Chapter 6.

Waste An exchange of corporate assets for consideration so disproportionately small as to lie beyond the range at which any reasonable person might be willing to trade. Chapter 10 and Chapter 12.

Williamson test Test to determine whether a partnership interest is an investment contract and hence is a security. The test is whether (1) the agreement among the parties leaves so little management power in the investor's hands that the investor is analogous to a limited partner; or (2) the investor is so inexperienced and unknowledgeable in business affairs that he or she cannot intelligently exercise his or her managerial powers; or (3) the investor is so dependent upon some unique entrepreneurial or managerial talent of the promoter that the investor cannot replace the promoter or otherwise meaningfully exercise his or her managerial powers. *See Williamson v. Tucker*, 645 F.2d 404 (5th Cir. 1981). Chapter 17.

Working capital Cash needed to run a business on a day-to-day basis. Chapter 6.

Table of Cases

Italics indicate principal cases.

Index